Lecture Notes in Computer Science 8528

Commenced Publication in 1973
Founding and Former Series Editors:
Gerhard Goos, Juris Hartmanis, and Jan van Leeuwen

P.L. Patrick Rau (Ed.)

Cross-Cultural Design

6th International Conference, CCD 2014
Held as Part of HCI International 2014
Heraklion, Crete, Greece, June 22-27, 2014
Proceedings

Springer

Volume Editor

P.L. Patrick Rau
Tsinghua University
Department of Industrial Engineering
100084 Beijing, China
E-mail: rpl@mail.tsinghua.edu.cn

ISSN 0302-9743 e-ISSN 1611-3349
ISBN 978-3-319-07307-1 e-ISBN 978-3-319-07308-8
DOI 10.1007/978-3-319-07308-8
Springer Cham Heidelberg New York Dordrecht London

Library of Congress Control Number: 2014939123

LNCS Sublibrary: SL 3 – Information Systems and Application, incl. Internet/Web and HCI

Typesetting: Camera-ready by author, data conversion by Scientific Publishing Services, Chennai, India

Printed on acid-free paper

Springer is part of Springer Science+Business Media (www.springer.com)

Foreword

The 16th International Conference on Human–Computer Interaction, HCI International 2014, was held in Heraklion, Crete, Greece, during June 22–27, 2014, incorporating 14 conferences/thematic areas:

Thematic areas:

- Human–Computer Interaction
- Human Interface and the Management of Information

Affiliated conferences:

- 11th International Conference on Engineering Psychology and Cognitive Ergonomics
- 8th International Conference on Universal Access in Human–Computer Interaction
- 6th International Conference on Virtual, Augmented and Mixed Reality
- 6th International Conference on Cross-Cultural Design
- 6th International Conference on Social Computing and Social Media
- 8th International Conference on Augmented Cognition
- 5th International Conference on Digital Human Modeling and Applications in Health, Safety, Ergonomics and Risk Management
- Third International Conference on Design, User Experience and Usability
- Second International Conference on Distributed, Ambient and Pervasive Interactions
- Second International Conference on Human Aspects of Information Security, Privacy and Trust
- First International Conference on HCI in Business
- First International Conference on Learning and Collaboration Technologies

A total of 4,766 individuals from academia, research institutes, industry, and governmental agencies from 78 countries submitted contributions, and 1,476 papers and 225 posters were included in the proceedings. These papers address the latest research and development efforts and highlight the human aspects of design and use of computing systems. The papers thoroughly cover the entire field of human–computer interaction, addressing major advances in knowledge and effective use of computers in a variety of application areas.

This volume, edited by P.L. Patrick Rau, contains papers focusing on the thematic area of Cross-Cultural Design, addressing the following major topics:

- Cross-cultural product and service design
- Cross-cultural issues in interaction
- Social aspects and implications of cross-cultural design

- Cross-cultural issues in e-commerce, marketing and branding
- Cross-cultural design for knowledge sharing and learning
- Cross-cultural design for the smart city

The remaining volumes of the HCI International 2014 proceedings are:

- Volume 1, LNCS 8510, Human–Computer Interaction: HCI Theories, Methods and Tools (Part I), edited by Masaaki Kurosu
- Volume 2, LNCS 8511, Human–Computer Interaction: Advanced Interaction Modalities and Techniques (Part II), edited by Masaaki Kurosu
- Volume 3, LNCS 8512, Human–Computer Interaction: Applications and Services (Part III), edited by Masaaki Kurosu
- Volume 4, LNCS 8513, Universal Access in Human–Computer Interaction: Design and Development Methods for Universal Access (Part I), edited by Constantine Stephanidis and Margherita Antona
- Volume 5, LNCS 8514, Universal Access in Human–Computer Interaction: Universal Access to Information and Knowledge (Part II), edited by Constantine Stephanidis and Margherita Antona
- Volume 6, LNCS 8515, Universal Access in Human–Computer Interaction: Aging and Assistive Environments (Part III), edited by Constantine Stephanidis and Margherita Antona
- Volume 7, LNCS 8516, Universal Access in Human–Computer Interaction: Design for All and Accessibility Practice (Part IV), edited by Constantine Stephanidis and Margherita Antona
- Volume 8, LNCS 8517, Design, User Experience, and Usability: Theories, Methods and Tools for Designing the User Experience (Part I), edited by Aaron Marcus
- Volume 9, LNCS 8518, Design, User Experience, and Usability: User Experience Design for Diverse Interaction Platforms and Environments (Part II), edited by Aaron Marcus
- Volume 10, LNCS 8519, Design, User Experience, and Usability: User Experience Design for Everyday Life Applications and Services (Part III), edited by Aaron Marcus
- Volume 11, LNCS 8520, Design, User Experience, and Usability: User Experience Design Practice (Part IV), edited by Aaron Marcus
- Volume 12, LNCS 8521, Human Interface and the Management of Information: Information and Knowledge Design and Evaluation (Part I), edited by Sakae Yamamoto
- Volume 13, LNCS 8522, Human Interface and the Management of Information: Information and Knowledge in Applications and Services (Part II), edited by Sakae Yamamoto
- Volume 14, LNCS 8523, Learning and Collaboration Technologies: Designing and Developing Novel Learning Experiences (Part I), edited by Panayiotis Zaphiris and Andri Ioannou
- Volume 15, LNCS 8524, Learning and Collaboration Technologies: Technology-rich Environments for Learning and Collaboration (Part II), edited by Panayiotis Zaphiris and Andri Ioannou

- Volume 16, LNCS 8525, Virtual, Augmented and Mixed Reality: Designing and Developing Virtual and Augmented Environments (Part I), edited by Randall Shumaker and Stephanie Lackey
- Volume 17, LNCS 8526, Virtual, Augmented and Mixed Reality: Applications of Virtual and Augmented Reality (Part II), edited by Randall Shumaker and Stephanie Lackey
- Volume 18, LNCS 8527, HCI in Business, edited by Fiona Fui-Hoon Nah
- Volume 20, LNCS 8529, Digital Human Modeling and Applications in Health, Safety, Ergonomics and Risk Management, edited by Vincent G. Duffy
- Volume 21, LNCS 8530, Distributed, Ambient, and Pervasive Interactions, edited by Norbert Streitz and Panos Markopoulos
- Volume 22, LNCS 8531, Social Computing and Social Media, edited by Gabriele Meiselwitz
- Volume 23, LNAI 8532, Engineering Psychology and Cognitive Ergonomics, edited by Don Harris
- Volume 24, LNCS 8533, Human Aspects of Information Security, Privacy and Trust, edited by Theo Tryfonas and Ioannis Askoxylakis
- Volume 25, LNAI 8534, Foundations of Augmented Cognition, edited by Dylan D. Schmorrow and Cali M. Fidopiastis
- Volume 26, CCIS 434, HCI International 2014 Posters Proceedings (Part I), edited by Constantine Stephanidis
- Volume 27, CCIS 435, HCI International 2014 Posters Proceedings (Part II), edited by Constantine Stephanidis

I would like to thank the Program Chairs and the members of the Program Boards of all affiliated conferences and thematic areas, listed below, for their contribution to the highest scientific quality and the overall success of the HCI International 2014 Conference.

This conference could not have been possible without the continuous support and advice of the founding chair and conference scientific advisor, Prof. Gavriel Salvendy, as well as the dedicated work and outstanding efforts of the communications chair and editor of *HCI International News*, Dr. Abbas Moallem.

I would also like to thank for their contribution towards the smooth organization of the HCI International 2014 Conference the members of the Human–Computer Interaction Laboratory of ICS-FORTH, and in particular George Paparoulis, Maria Pitsoulaki, Maria Bouhli, and George Kapnas.

April 2014

Constantine Stephanidis
General Chair, HCI International 2014

Organization

Human–Computer Interaction

Program Chair: Masaaki Kurosu, Japan

Jose Abdelnour-Nocera, UK
Sebastiano Bagnara, Italy
Simone Barbosa, Brazil
Adriana Betiol, Brazil
Simone Borsci, UK
Henry Duh, Australia
Xiaowen Fang, USA
Vicki Hanson, UK
Wonil Hwang, Korea
Minna Isomursu, Finland
Yong Gu Ji, Korea
Anirudha Joshi, India
Esther Jun, USA
Kyungdoh Kim, Korea
Heidi Krömker, Germany
Chen Ling, USA
Chang S. Nam, USA
Naoko Okuizumi, Japan
Philippe Palanque, France
Ling Rothrock, USA
Naoki Sakakibara, Japan
Dominique Scapin, France
Guangfeng Song, USA
Sanjay Tripathi, India
Chui Yin Wong, Malaysia
Toshiki Yamaoka, Japan
Kazuhiko Yamazaki, Japan
Ryoji Yoshitake, Japan

Human Interface and the Management of Information

Program Chair: Sakae Yamamoto, Japan

Alan Chan, Hong Kong
Denis A. Coelho, Portugal
Linda Elliott, USA
Shin'ichi Fukuzumi, Japan
Michitaka Hirose, Japan
Makoto Itoh, Japan
Yen-Yu Kang, Taiwan
Koji Kimita, Japan
Daiji Kobayashi, Japan
Hiroyuki Miki, Japan
Shogo Nishida, Japan
Robert Proctor, USA
Youngho Rhee, Korea
Ryosuke Saga, Japan
Katsunori Shimohara, Japan
Kim-Phuong Vu, USA
Tomio Watanabe, Japan

Engineering Psychology and Cognitive Ergonomics

Program Chair: Don Harris, UK

Guy Andre Boy, USA
Shan Fu, P.R. China
Hung-Sying Jing, Taiwan
Wen-Chin Li, Taiwan
Mark Neerincx, The Netherlands
Jan Noyes, UK
Paul Salmon, Australia
Axel Schulte, Germany
Siraj Shaikh, UK
Sarah Sharples, UK
Anthony Smoker, UK
Neville Stanton, UK
Alex Stedmon, UK
Andrew Thatcher, South Africa

Universal Access in Human–Computer Interaction

Program Chairs: Constantine Stephanidis, Greece, and Margherita Antona, Greece

Julio Abascal, Spain
Gisela Susanne Bahr, USA
João Barroso, Portugal
Margrit Betke, USA
Anthony Brooks, Denmark
Christian Bühler, Germany
Stefan Carmien, Spain
Hua Dong, P.R. China
Carlos Duarte, Portugal
Pier Luigi Emiliani, Italy
Qin Gao, P.R. China
Andrina Granić, Croatia
Andreas Holzinger, Austria
Josette Jones, USA
Simeon Keates, UK
Georgios Kouroupetroglou, Greece
Patrick Langdon, UK
Barbara Leporini, Italy
Eugene Loos, The Netherlands
Ana Isabel Paraguay, Brazil
Helen Petrie, UK
Michael Pieper, Germany
Enrico Pontelli, USA
Jaime Sanchez, Chile
Alberto Sanna, Italy
Anthony Savidis, Greece
Christian Stary, Austria
Hirotada Ueda, Japan
Gerhard Weber, Germany
Harald Weber, Germany

Virtual, Augmented and Mixed Reality

Program Chairs: Randall Shumaker, USA, and Stephanie Lackey, USA

Roland Blach, Germany
Sheryl Brahnam, USA
Juan Cendan, USA
Jessie Chen, USA
Panagiotis D. Kaklis, UK
Hirokazu Kato, Japan
Denis Laurendeau, Canada
Fotis Liarokapis, UK
Michael Macedonia, USA
Gordon Mair, UK

Jose San Martin, Spain
Tabitha Peck, USA
Christian Sandor, Australia
Christopher Stapleton, USA
Gregory Welch, USA

Cross-Cultural Design

Program Chair: P.L. Patrick Rau, P.R. China

Yee-Yin Choong, USA
Paul Fu, USA
Zhiyong Fu, P.R. China
Pin-Chao Liao, P.R. China
Dyi-Yih Michael Lin, Taiwan
Rungtai Lin, Taiwan
Ta-Ping (Robert) Lu, Taiwan
Liang Ma, P.R. China
Alexander Mädche, Germany
Sheau-Farn Max Liang, Taiwan
Katsuhiko Ogawa, Japan
Tom Plocher, USA
Huatong Sun, USA
Emil Tso, P.R. China
Hsiu-Ping Yueh, Taiwan
Liang (Leon) Zeng, USA
Jia Zhou, P.R. China

Online Communities and Social Media

Program Chair: Gabriele Meiselwitz, USA

Leonelo Almeida, Brazil
Chee Siang Ang, UK
Aneesha Bakharia, Australia
Ania Bobrowicz, UK
James Braman, USA
Farzin Deravi, UK
Carsten Kleiner, Germany
Niki Lambropoulos, Greece
Soo Ling Lim, UK
Anthony Norcio, USA
Portia Pusey, USA
Panote Siriaraya, UK
Stefan Stieglitz, Germany
Giovanni Vincenti, USA
Yuanqiong (Kathy) Wang, USA
June Wei, USA
Brian Wentz, USA

Augmented Cognition

Program Chairs: Dylan D. Schmorrow, USA, and Cali M. Fidopiastis, USA

Ahmed Abdelkhalek, USA
Robert Atkinson, USA
Monique Beaudoin, USA
John Blitch, USA
Alenka Brown, USA
Rosario Cannavò, Italy
Joseph Cohn, USA
Andrew J. Cowell, USA
Martha Crosby, USA
Wai-Tat Fu, USA

Digital Human Modeling and Applications in Health, Safety, Ergonomics and Risk Management

Program Chair: Vincent G. Duffy, USA

Design, User Experience, and Usability

Program Chair: Aaron Marcus, USA

Distributed, Ambient and Pervasive Interactions

Program Chairs: Norbert Streitz, Germany, and Panos Markopoulos, The Netherlands

Juan Carlos Augusto, UK
Jose Bravo, Spain
Adrian Cheok, UK
Boris de Ruyter, The Netherlands
Anind Dey, USA
Dimitris Grammenos, Greece
Nuno Guimaraes, Portugal
Achilles Kameas, Greece
Javed Vassilis Khan, The Netherlands
Shin'ichi Konomi, Japan
Carsten Magerkurth, Switzerland
Ingrid Mulder, The Netherlands
Anton Nijholt, The Netherlands
Fabio Paternó, Italy
Carsten Röcker, Germany
Teresa Romao, Portugal
Albert Ali Salah, Turkey
Manfred Tscheligi, Austria
Reiner Wichert, Germany
Woontack Woo, Korea
Xenophon Zabulis, Greece

Human Aspects of Information Security, Privacy and Trust

Program Chairs: Theo Tryfonas, UK, and Ioannis Askoxylakis, Greece

Claudio Agostino Ardagna, Italy
Zinaida Benenson, Germany
Daniele Catteddu, Italy
Raoul Chiesa, Italy
Bryan Cline, USA
Sadie Creese, UK
Jorge Cuellar, Germany
Marc Dacier, USA
Dieter Gollmann, Germany
Kirstie Hawkey, Canada
Jaap-Henk Hoepman, The Netherlands
Cagatay Karabat, Turkey
Angelos Keromytis, USA
Ayako Komatsu, Japan
Ronald Leenes, The Netherlands
Javier Lopez, Spain
Steve Marsh, Canada
Gregorio Martinez, Spain
Emilio Mordini, Italy
Yuko Murayama, Japan
Masakatsu Nishigaki, Japan
Aljosa Pasic, Spain
Milan Petković, The Netherlands
Joachim Posegga, Germany
Jean-Jacques Quisquater, Belgium
Damien Sauveron, France
George Spanoudakis, UK
Kerry-Lynn Thomson, South Africa
Julien Touzeau, France
Theo Tryfonas, UK
João Vilela, Portugal
Claire Vishik, UK
Melanie Volkamer, Germany

HCI in Business

Program Chair: Fiona Fui-Hoon Nah, USA

Andreas Auinger, Austria
Michel Avital, Denmark
Traci Carte, USA
Hock Chuan Chan, Singapore
Constantinos Coursaris, USA
Soussan Djamasbi, USA
Brenda Eschenbrenner, USA
Nobuyuki Fukawa, USA
Khaled Hassanein, Canada
Milena Head, Canada
Susanna (Shuk Ying) Ho, Australia
Jack Zhenhui Jiang, Singapore
Jinwoo Kim, Korea
Zoonky Lee, Korea
Honglei Li, UK
Nicholas Lockwood, USA
Eleanor T. Loiacono, USA
Mei Lu, USA
Scott McCoy, USA
Brian Mennecke, USA
Robin Poston, USA
Lingyun Qiu, P.R. China
Rene Riedl, Austria
Matti Rossi, Finland
April Savoy, USA
Shu Schiller, USA
Hong Sheng, USA
Choon Ling Sia, Hong Kong
Chee-Wee Tan, Denmark
Chuan Hoo Tan, Hong Kong
Noam Tractinsky, Israel
Horst Treiblmaier, Austria
Virpi Tuunainen, Finland
Dezhi Wu, USA
I-Chin Wu, Taiwan

Learning and Collaboration Technologies

Program Chairs: Panayiotis Zaphiris, Cyprus, and Andri Ioannou, Cyprus

Ruthi Aladjem, Israel
Abdulaziz Aldaej, UK
John M. Carroll, USA
Maka Eradze, Estonia
Mikhail Fominykh, Norway
Denis Gillet, Switzerland
Mustafa Murat Inceoglu, Turkey
Pernilla Josefsson, Sweden
Marie Joubert, UK
Sauli Kiviranta, Finland
Tomaž Klobučar, Slovenia
Elena Kyza, Cyprus
Maarten de Laat, The Netherlands
David Lamas, Estonia
Edmund Laugasson, Estonia
Ana Loureiro, Portugal
Katherine Maillet, France
Nadia Pantidi, UK
Antigoni Parmaxi, Cyprus
Borzoo Pourabdollahian, Italy
Janet C. Read, UK
Christophe Reffay, France
Nicos Souleles, Cyprus
Ana Luísa Torres, Portugal
Stefan Trausan-Matu, Romania
Aimilia Tzanavari, Cyprus
Johnny Yuen, Hong Kong
Carmen Zahn, Switzerland

External Reviewers

Ilia Adami, Greece
Iosif Klironomos, Greece
Maria Korozi, Greece
Vassilis Kouroumalis, Greece
Asterios Leonidis, Greece
George Margetis, Greece
Stavroula Ntoa, Greece
Nikolaos Partarakis, Greece

HCI International 2015

The 15th International Conference on Human–Computer Interaction, HCI International 2015, will be held jointly with the affiliated conferences in Los Angeles, CA, USA, in the Westin Bonaventure Hotel, August 2–7, 2015. It will cover a broad spectrum of themes related to HCI, including theoretical issues, methods, tools, processes, and case studies in HCI design, as well as novel interaction techniques, interfaces, and applications. The proceedings will be published by Springer. More information will be available on the conference website: http://www.hcii2015.org/

General Chair
Professor Constantine Stephanidis
University of Crete and ICS-FORTH
Heraklion, Crete, Greece
Email: cs@ics.forth.gr

Table of Contents

Cross-Cultural Product and Service Design

Cross-Cultural Issues in Interaction

Social Aspects and Implications of Cross-Cultural Design

Cross-Cultural Issues in E-commerce, Marketing and Branding

Cross-Cultural Design for Knowledge Sharing and Learning

Cross-Cultural Design for the Smart City

Cross-Cultural Design for Creativity

Cross-Cultural Product and Service Design

A Reflective Study in Metaphorical Products Design from the Mapping of Relational Similarity Perspective

Kung-Ling Chang

Dept. of Crafts & Design, National Taiwan University of Arts, Taipei, 220, Taiwan
kling@ntua.edu.tw

Abstract. Cultural materials always have new applications in products design, a designer as an agent that "specifies the cultural properties of a design object ". Metaphors design needs to propose a few observations to transform the ideas into an external form and make on the creative cultural products design. There is a relation between Cultural materials (sources) and products (targets), the designer needs to grasp the main points of discriminating the methods which transfers materials into a product by metaphors. Several categories of metaphors exist, including simile, metaphor, allegory, metonymy and analogy. Three categories out of five categories are most useful metaphors in practice, including simile, metaphor and metonymy, whereas the abstract ideas of metaphors were not easily understood by many beginners, students would rather design easily such as "displacement" and "simile", that caused me to established an operable practice model for beginners. Comprehend the model of an integrated design process in order to enhance the application of cultural materials through design practice and education, the model can be a valuable reference for case study, design practice and reorientation in metaphors of products design.

Keywords: Creative Cultural Products, Metaphor Design.

1 Introduction

A cultural product is related to a cultural material by metaphors with transformation. If a product related to the metaphorical design, it will capture the capacity in the relation between materials (sources) and products (targets), it is a principal point to discriminate which products is the metaphorical design or not. In this regard, the techniques of products design with "Displacement" is easily to memorize and the prefer one for users, but there are lacks of relations between sources and targets. "Feature Transformation" is another technique which transformed the features of external form into a product and it was given another practical applications. "Feature Transformation" is also easily to memorize, but the likeability isn't good in proportion to the memory; the other technique is "Figurative Expression" which is not only easily to memorize but also good in likeability (Chang, 2012). How a material was transformed into a product, the relational-matches is the subject of metaphors. In regard to the transformation, "Figurative Expression" is superior to "Displacement" in significance.

P.L.P. Rau (Ed.): CCD/HCII 2014, LNCS 8528, pp. 3–13, 2014.

This research based on the references and case studies in metaphors to figure out the viewpoints, the efforts was advanced to the study model of metaphors, to focus on discriminate the categories of metaphors as the efforts.

2 Literature Review

2.1 Displacement and Metaphor

Replacing the external form of the product with another iconic figure without any related is considered to be the "Displacement", the external form of materials (sources) as a replacement for products (targets); There is a relational matter to transform an icon, symbol or an insinuation into a product design with figurative language is considered to be the "Metaphor" (Lin, 2008). Therefore, the quote from sources is related to targets or not, that is difference in terms of discrimination for Displacement and Metaphor.

Table 1. Comparison Sheet : The abstract of Displacement and Metaphor

	Subject matter
Displacement	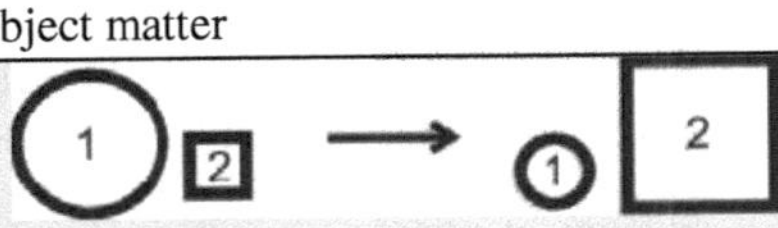 source: (Lin, 2008) • Transferring the subject to the other and quoting out of context.
	• Replacing the external form of the product with another iconic figure without any related.
Metaphor	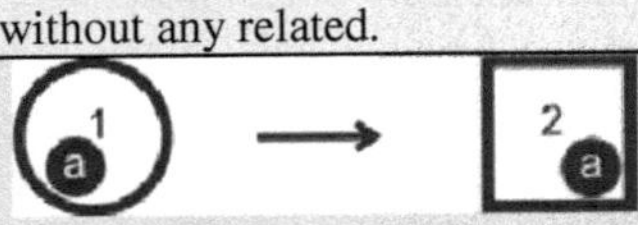 source: (Lin, 2008) • There is an inner meaning in the source that is similar to the target.
	• Design with figurative language to transform an icon or symbol into a product design.

2.2 The Concept of Metaphor

Figurative Language is given the interpretation in non-literal meaning. When the semantic interpretation that is ineffective in a literal manner, we utilize the technique of Figurative Language to impart the effect to a target. Figurative Language begin to take effect through utilize the Figurative Language, it can interpret unfamiliar and abstract matters with intimate, concrete and obvious. The effect inspired the language much more significative, expressive and vibrant (Wang, 2011).

There are over twenty categories of Figurative Language exist (Wang, 2011). Many scholars such as Zeng (2012) and XIE (2013) had referred to that the simile, metaphor, allegory, metonymy and analogy are frequently used. In the field of the generalized categories of Metaphors in design, Professor Wang (2011) had referred to the most useful metaphors are including simile, metaphor and metonymy.

2.3 The Chief Categories of Metaphors

1. **Simile.** The target comprises a form generation which employ the form of a source, its appearance, and its property as a new mode. In other words, the new creations resemble the source in formal features.
2. **Metaphor.** The appearance of the target comprises a form generation which employ the features and property of a source in a mild and indirect way. In other words, the relationship between new creations and the source is implied.
3. **Metonymy.** Exchanging the appearance and property of a source for a target, the target possesses some parts from the source to interpret its own property. The appearance and property of source is an emblem of the new creations.

2.4 The Relations between Sources and Targets

Three Types of the Similarities. Metaphorical product design is a synthesis of the source and the target. We will find the pleasure in metaphor when we figure out the information that the designer's thought on the product. There is a mapping process of transformation learning when we comprehend the new things by familiar things. According to Gentner's (1988) structure-mapping theory, the similarities between the sources and targets that includes Mere Appearance Similarity, Relational Similarity and Literal Similarity. Professor Wang (2011) summarized about the similarities : A relationship between the source and target which called "Literal Similarity" are matched with appearance similarity and relational similarity. A relationship which called "Surface Similarity" or "Mere Appearance Similarity" are matched with features, but unconcerned with logical relation. A relationship which called "Analogy" are matched with relational similarity, but without any feature. "Analogy" and "Surface Similarity" jointly referred to as metaphor.

Relational Similarity

Composing Schema Mapping. The similarity in structural mapping is a representation of components. Compare target with source, to spread out the consist of components in target and source for viewing. For the purpose of acquiring a properly effect of structural mapping, designers could be in the finding of structural properties of a source, and base on the properties to find a properly target to match the expression of the source. Designers will explained a product's components by analogy with that of a source's components.

Behavioral Mapping. The action presents a relationship based on the operation, for developing meanings of sources targeted at products, and contributes to our understanding of the implication preferences of the products. Wang (2011) took "Excalibur" (Toilet brush) as an example which was designed by Philippe Starck, the "Excalibur" and Toilet brush are well-known, but their relationship are unfamiliar. When King Arthur was getting out the sword from the stone that is analogous to the toilet brush will be getting out from the set. There is a relational similarity about limbs movements, the similarity allow the designer make a breakthrough on the mere appearance similarity problem. Action of closestool wash with "Excalibur" will changing the somber mood into an unusual holy-hearted mood by the technique of Metaphor.

Innate Character Mapping. There is lots of cases could be studied which are about the innate character mapping, it's easily to grasp the innate characters with this kind of sources, designers who transform the sources into the targets will grasp the main characters between, the source's character which is matched with a target and have a properly meaning in value added. Take an example in "barn" and "money box" to explain as follow : A barn owen the innate characters in storing crops, A money box owen the innate characters in storing coins. If the money box was designed with an appearance of barn, the source(barn) and the target(money box) have the same act of keeping something in a place while it is not being used. The money box inherited the value from the barn.

Table 2. Comparison Sheet: Three types of mapping

	Relational Similarity		**Instances**
Types of Mapping	Innate Character Mapping	Storage	**Money Box** The money box inherited the value from the barn.
	Behavioral Mapping	Limbs Movements (Rotate)	**Corkscrew** When a user using this corkscrew who will be associated with the dancing of a dancer.
		Limbs Movements (Take out)	**Excalibur** When a user is getting out the toilet brush from the set that is analogous to King Arthur was getting out the sword from the stone.
	Composing Schema Mapping		**Excalibur**/ Toilet brush **Sword** / Brush; **Stone** / Set

3 Methodology

This research based on the references and case studies in metaphors to figure out the model for beginners. Comprehend the model of an integrated design process in order to enhance the application of cultural materials through design practice and education. The model can be a valuable reference for case study and reorientation in metaphors of products design.

The discrimination model (Figure 1) was designed by process in four steps : ❶Questions about Relational-Matches, ❷According to the answers of step1 to discriminate the initial similarities, ❸to take the similarities one step ahead by inspection. ❹To categorize the outcome of step3 into a metaphor category.

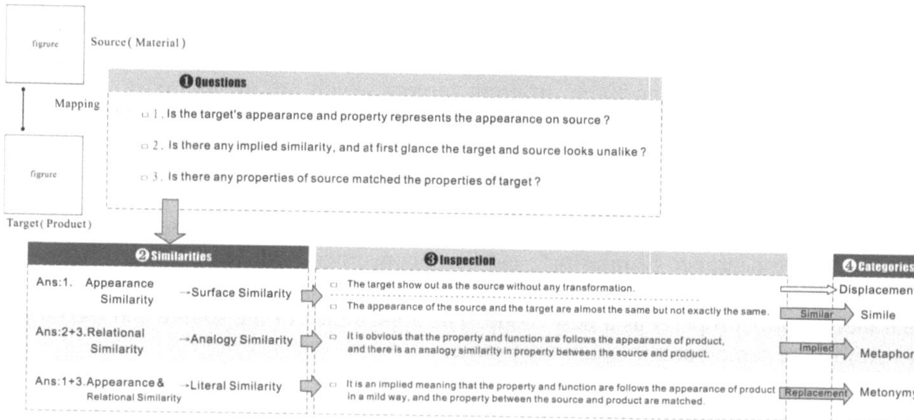

Fig. 1. The discrimination model of Metaphorical products. (Source: Chang, 2013)

4 Design for the Products of Roof Truss by Metaphors

The practice of this task choose the "Chinese Roof Truss" to be a source with a range of products. The source is a traditional wooden truss that belong to the Lin An-Tai old homestead. This old house was built in 1783~1785 and extended in 1822~1823(Wang, 2006).

There is a removal event of the Lin An-Tai old homestead in 1978, the urban planning was given precedence over the preservation of the Lin An-Tai Old House. In order to relocation preservation, the bricks, rocks and all the members of wooden structure were took apart and marked. The Lin An-Tai old house was rebuild in 1987. There was an interval of nine years between the removal and the rebuild.

Fig. 2. The panorama view of the Lin An-Tai old homestead before the removal

Fig. 3. The old house was in a removal proceeding

Fig. 4. Nowadays, the relocation preservation of the Lin An-Tai old homestead

There were three targets of products which were designed with the same source. However, the three targets of products were set in different logical relation. These results serve as the reference material for the requirement comparison among the simile, metaphor and metonymy. Therefore, principles of the standards for the tasks were as follow:

1. In order to augment the differential effects in the practice, the source and the target must be set in different category domain.
2. In order to compare the three different targets which are all related to the same source, the three targets must be as the different kind of products.

4.1 The Development Process of Simile Design

The characteristic of "Simile design" of the mapping between a source and a target belongs to "Appearance Similarity", and be unconcerned with "Relational-Matches". The target comprises a form generation which employ the form of a source, its appearance, and its property as a new mode. The appearance of the source and the target are almost the same but not exactly the same.

Table 3. Design for the product by simile

<table>
<tr><td colspan="5">Design for the product of roof truss by simile</td></tr>
<tr><td rowspan="2">Source
↑
Relations
↓
Target</td><td></td><td rowspan="2">Similarities</td><td colspan="2">Appearance Similarity</td></tr>
<tr><td></td><td>Mapping</td><td>There is unconcerned with any "Relational-Matches"</td></tr>
<tr><td>Explanation</td><td colspan="4">The roof truss transforms into the structures of the clothes hanger, the members of truss provide for functioning well on the hanger, its interval between the members of truss brings convenience for items of accessories to hangs on.
Designer : Kung-Ling, Chang</td></tr>
</table>

4.2 The Development Process of Metaphor Design

The characteristic of "Metaphor Design" of the relation between a source and a target is implied. The appearance of the target comprises a form generation which employ the features and property of a source in a mild and indirect way. The characteristic of "Metaphor Design" involves in part-ownership in analogy.

The source and the target aren't within the similar category. However, the implied meaning is established in the added value by matches of the source and the target (between-category similarity).

4.3 The Development Process of Metonymy Design

The characteristic of "metonymy design" of the mapping between a source and a target which called "Literal Similarity" are matched with appearance similarity and relational similarity.

Table 4. Design for the product by metaphor

Design for the product of roof truss by metaphor				
Source ↑ Relations ↓ **Target**		Similarities	Relational Similarity	
			Mapping	**Beams/** removal proceeding **Toothpicks/** removal proceeding
Explanation	• Taking out the toothpicks is analogous to the beams will be getting out from the roof. It seems to be designed by simile on external form of a house. But, there is a meaning when the user was taking out the toothpicks from the can that is analogous to the beams will be getting out from the roof. There is a relational similarity about limbs movements, the similarity allow the designer make a breakthrough on the mere appearance similarity problem. Designer : Kung-Ling, Chang			

"Metonymy Design" emphasize an existing relationship between a source and a target. "Metonymy Design" exchanging the appearance and property of a source for a target. "Replacing" is a technique of expression within the radius of their relationship, the target possesses some parts from the source to interpret its own property.

Table 5. Design for the product by metonymy

Design for the product of roof truss by metonymy				
Source ↑ Relations ↓ **Target**		Similarities	Appearance Similarity &Relational Similarity	
	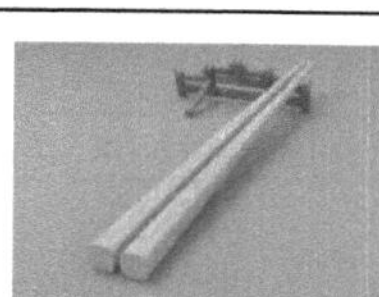		Mapping	**Truss/** load-bearing **Rack/** load-bearing
Explanation	The chopsticks rack was designed as a wooden truss. Putting the chopsticks on the rack is analogous to putting the beams on the truss. Users will have an association with building a house. Designer : Kung-Ling, Chang			

5 Results and Discussion

5.1 Simile Product Design Reviews: Clothes Hanger

According to the "Questions" on step❶ in the discrimination model(figure1), the clothes hanger is answer to the description of Option-1:

O-1: Is the target's appearance and property represents the appearance on source ?

It's sure on "Option-1", the hanger's appearance and property represents the appearance on roof truss. The members of truss provide for functioning well on the hanger, its interval between the members of truss brings convenience for items of accessories to hangs on. Organizing the categories is based on the choosing of individual steps, the classification in this model belongs to "Simile".

5.2 Metaphor Product Design Reviews: Toothpicks Can

According to the "Questions" on step❶ in the discrimination model(figure1), the toothpicks-can are answers to the descriptions of Option-2 and Option-3:

O-2: Is there any implied similarity, and at first glance the target and source looks unlike ?

It's sure on "Option-2". Compared with simile design, the can's appearance is designed in a mild way. There is an implication for users on the hole of gable.

O-3: Is there any properties of source matched the properties of target ?

There is a meaning when the user was taking out the toothpicks from the can that is analogous to the beams will be getting out from the roof. Organizing the categories, the classification in this model belongs to "Metaphor".

5.3 Metonymy Product Design Reviews: Chopsticks Rack

According to the "Questions" on step❶ in the discrimination model (figure1), the chopsticks rack are answers to the descriptions of Option-1 and Option-3:

O-3: Is the target's appearance and property represents the appearance on source ?

It's sure on "Option-1", the rack's appearance and property represents the appearance on roof truss.

O-3: Is there any properties of source matched the properties of target ?

In the field of behavioral mapping, the beams and the chopsticks are matched by their properties. Putting the chopsticks on the rack is analogous to putting the beams on the truss. Organizing the categories, the classification in this model belongs to "Metonymy".

5.4 A Metaphorical Method for Cultural Product Design Model

Metaphor and Metonymy are both involves in relational similarity. As a technique of expression, Metaphor is manipulated with "Behavioral Mapping", Metonymy is manipulated with "Innate Character Mapping", and therefore concerned with the scenarios in the removal event of the Lin An-Tai old homestead. Keep moving forward to give the explanations with the models that were showed in Figure 6&7, the model gave an opportunity to rethink the metaphorical product design from the mapping of relational similarity perspective, this model(Figure 5) is a metaphorical method for cultural product design that base on the mapping of relational similarity, it will provide an operation mode in design practice for designers.

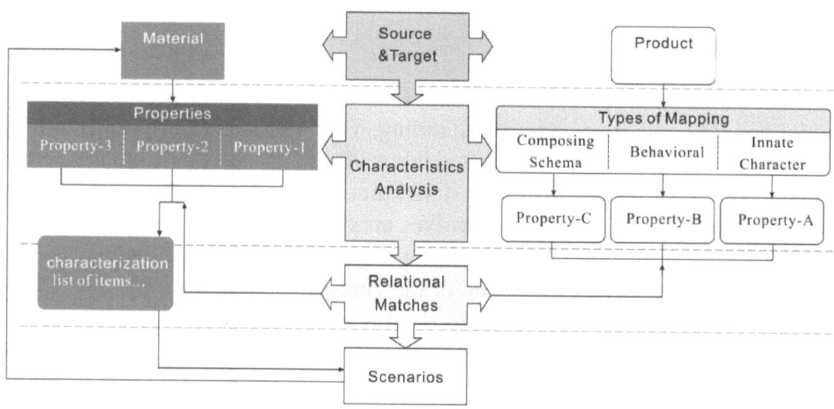

Fig. 5. A cultural product design model with a metaphorical method

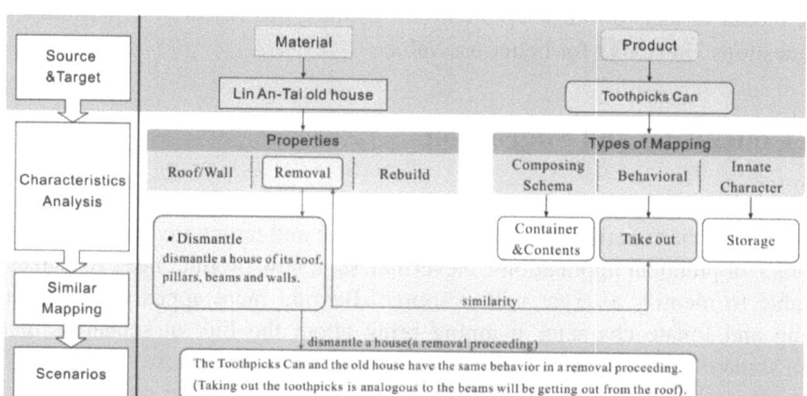

Fig. 6. Rethinking of metaphor product design from the mapping of relational similarity perspective

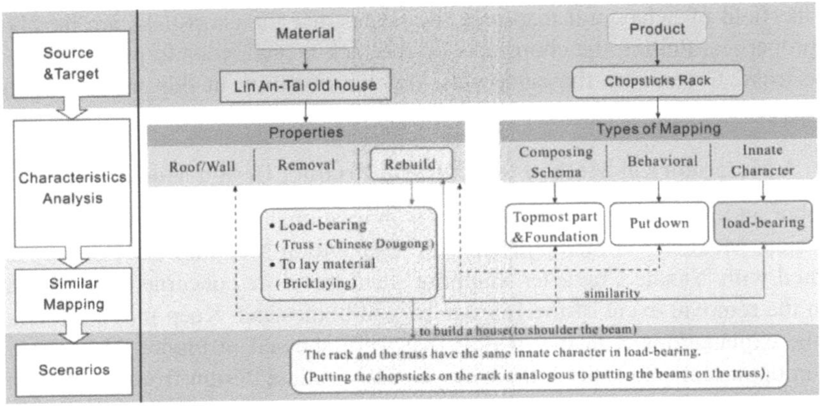

Fig. 7. Rethinking of metonymy products design from the mapping of relational similarity perspective

5.5 Discussion

The discrimination model presents a process, based on metaphor theory, for developing guidelines for categories and understanding. This model is clearly unfit to hold all categories of metaphors. However, it is deals with the essentials of understanding in metaphors. Therefore, the results of the discrimination is in proportion to a chief category of metaphors. A result possibly involves another categories of metaphors.

The classification of toothpicks can in the discrimination model belong to "Metaphor", but this work involves in portion of the characteristic in analogy. The characteristic of analogy is ignored in the model.

Giving an investigation into the discrimination model for "Allegory", the results will belong to "Metaphor". "Allegory" is a kind of implied meaning that is similar to "Metaphor", it is thus evident that the discrimination model is capable of widely used in metaphors, even though the characteristic of analogy and allegory is ignored. Taking the model further to follow up the investigations, this research will attempt to add the "Questions" in step❶ for better use value.

6 Conclusion and Suggestion

A new product employs the new function of practical application that is not to be compared with the function of a source. The source and target are quite different from each other in practical applications. Nevertheless, a new product need to makes users more able to identify a target with a source. Beyond mere appearances, behavioral mapping and Innate character mapping bring about the link in scenarios that may awaken some of user's special feelings, consonance and memories.

This research established an operable model to transform the main aspects into a comprehensible process, the model can be a valuable reference for case study, for designers be good at using symbols and using implications in products design.

Up to now, Relational Similarity is the topic for discussions, but the Composing Schema Mapping is still not going to have a discussion. Composing Schema Mapping is a manipulation which about the similarity and the analogy of features, composing an integral whole product. Composing Schema Mapping will be a subject in design practices of my works. Composing Schema Mapping should be a technique to transform the cultural materials into a new form with contemporary techniques and materials, that creates new images and new tectonics, especially in architecture or space design. If this works can be well done, the cultural materials will not only be a figure which be put on products or be placed in architecture.

References

1. Chang, K.-L.: The Technique of Expression in Creative Cultural Products. In: 2012 Conference on Crafts Creation, Cultural & Creativity Design, p. 233 (2012)
2. Chang, K.-L.: A Reflective in Metaphors of Creative Cultural Products Design. In: 2013 Conference on Crafts Creation, Cultural & Creativity Design, p. 108 (2013)
3. Tsen, J.: A study on Ambient Media from Structure-mapping Theory Perspective. Journal of Design 17(2), 73–96 (2012)
4. Lin, M.-H., Huang, C.-C.: The Logic of The Figurative Expressions and Cognition in Design Practices. Journal of Design 7(2), 2–7 (2002)
5. Lin, M.-H., Fang, Y.-M., Cheng, S.-H.: The Intention, Depth and Technique of Expression in Humor Product Design. Journal of Design 13(3), 71 (2008)
6. Hsieh, H.C., Lee, C.F.: A Pedagogical Study of Local Culture as a Subject for Design Creation Education. Taiwan Journal of Arts 9(92), 120 (2013)
7. Wang, C.-Y.: After the removal of the Lin An-Tai old homestead, Cases Study of Historic Buildings belong to Relocation Preservation in Taiwan, p. 23. Chung Yuan Christian University, Taiwan (2006) (unpublished dissertation)
8. Wang, H.-H.: Design by Metaphors, Taipei (2011)

Other URLs of Interest:
National Repository of Cultural Heritage,
http://newnrch.digital.ntu.edu.tw/prototype/index.php

Introduction Strategies of Service-Oriented Product System Design for the Transformation and Upgrading of Small and Medium Manufacturers in China

Jiajia Chen[1,2]

[1] School of Social and Behavioral Sciences, Nanjing University
163 Xianlin Avenue, Xixia District, Nanjign 210023, China
[2] School of Industrial Design, Nanjing University of Arts
15 Huju North Rd., Gulou District, Nanjing 210013, China
chachachen@126.com

Abstract. With the global market competition intensified, Chinese manufacturers, especially SMEs now are facing the enormous challenges in sustainable development. Learning from other countries in the practical experiences of service design and industrial design, service-oriented product system design can be a solution. This will not only allow SMEs to accumulate their design powers, but also will enhance their competitive advantage. In this paper, firstly, the author analyzed and summarized the reasons for service design's coming-into-being in China through literature research. Secondly, based on the results of in-depth interview and fieldwork of a number of SMEs done by the author, several aspects such as design development status, service design awareness & demands, potential conditions of establishing product service system have been discussed. Finally, the author provided actionable introduction strategies for small and medium manufacturers to transform and upgrade their business model from "manufacture-based" to "design innovation-led".

Keywords: transformation and upgrading, service-oriented product system design, small and medium manufacturers, design strategy.

1 Introduction

From industrial society to post-industrial society, most developed countries have achieved great social and economic development based on services. China is definitely not an exception. After entering the new millennium, China has been seeking new modes of economic development. Design innovation has been heatedly discussed as a driving force of economic development in China over ten years. It is not until January of 2014 that design innovation has been officially incorporated into the policy of the economic restructuring. And design service, as Premier Li Keqiang has pointed out, 'has the high knowledge and added value, at the same time, the low consumption and pollution of our resources. It should be integrated deeply into related industries. And it is the core content of our economic restructuring, which will help us to improve the quality of products, meet different needs of our people, create a catalyst for change in industries, expand the employment and promote industrial upgrading.'(www.gov.cn, 2014).According to the existing studies on service design in China, there are mainly

P.L.P. Rau (Ed.): CCD/HCII 2014, LNCS 8528, pp. 14–23, 2014.

three reasons for its coming-into-being. The first reason is the transition from 'function economy' to 'service economy', which, as Daniel Bell has mentioned in his book 'the coming of post-industrial society', is the main form of economy in post-industrial society. Due to the historic reasons and present situation of uneven regional development, there are mixed economy forms in China. In developed regions such as the Pearl River Delta and the Yangtze River Delta, there is a clear transition from function economy to service economy. While in undeveloped regions such as central and western areas in China, function economy is still the main form. In the former, industrial design has been successfully introduced and applied into local industries for over 20 years, but service design is still a new concept. Fortunately, through frequent communications with foreign design experts and numbers of design festivals, service design has abstracted some attention in local industries, mostly are big sized companies and enterprises. In the latter, industrial design has just been introduced to the local industries, only few companies and enterprises have benefited from it. So the prospect of service design's development in China is not optimistic in this stage. The second reason is the most pressing needs in the voice of sustainable development for China. Some owners of manufactures commence to use design as a trigger to change the tradition definition of products and its whole lifecycle. But design, in their point of views, is just another tool which can be tried to make quick money. In fact, they do not care whether it is industrial design or service design that can contribute to their economic interests; all in all, they still base their business on producing physical products. Services, for them, are help to sell products, but should be within an acceptable cost. In this case, it seems that the application of service design concepts to China's local industries cannot fulfill its born vocation of encouraging sustainability at this time. It still has a long way to go.The third reason can be seen in research in practical application of service design. It poses case studies that how service design helps to encourage new form of business model and social innovation with cultural purpose in several developed Asian counties and areas such as Japan, South Korea and Taiwan. In these researches, for the sake of reaching an agreement on the understanding of design values, cultural influences have to be taken into consideration. In most cases, traditional culture has been re-introduced by design and services, which seems to come back to life and can be transformed into economic and social innovations. What's more, local culture has formed a new kind of industry, which is called culture and creative industry. Even though, many scholars cast doubts on the development of this new form of industry. As many so-called cultural and creative industry parks have been introduced and built up in big cities in China such as Beijing and Shanghai for almost 15 years ago. And a number of design experts with global reputation at home and abroad have been invited to open their offices or branches in these parks with the financial support from the local governments. Till now, it has not proclaimed any achievement on regional or city development. What we can often see in these parks are customized and small-production designed brands, which cannot definitely bring most manufacturers through their troubles. To make matters worse, a certain quantity of cultural and creative industry parks have been occupied by restaurants and clubs for entertainment. Design, itself has been pushed into the corner and acts as a tool for beautification. Not to mention service design! Service design is also facing an embarrassing situation: has it helped to create GDP? Yes, but very little. Has it helped to create new business models to help small or medium business? Yes, theoretically. But not for sure when it comes into practical worlds. Has it done good to the local culture? Yes, and there seems to have more spaces to expand its influences. The rise of small brands from cultural and creative parks can afford expensive experience for small and medium manufacturers in China when they make up their minds to make a change. In this case, service design should move hand in hand with local cultures. On the whole, as the main form of China's economy is moving from function economy to service economy, manufacturing still makes important contribution to China's GDP. And more than 98% of manufactures are small and medium manufacturers (SEMs). Most of them have the awareness of design no more than making a beautiful logo. Some of them start to accept industrial design as one of powerful tool to change their products. Few of them have the knowledge of service design as we can see from the following paragraph in the third part. As a result, industrial design and service design cannot be introduced to them one by one as most western countries have done before. Together with other means of design, they should be introduced to SEMs in China in a package, which is service-oriented product system design.

2 Service-Oriented Product System Design

China has a long history in seeing the world, acting and thinking in a systemic way. Different from western philosophy, Chinese seldom discuss the universe with a dualism method. Instead, Chinese are accustomed to solve the problem in whole. As we all know, industrial design provides solutions to solve problems for mass production. And it is the way to create material objects. The transition from industrial society to post-industrial society requires SEMs to transform and update from OEM to ODM, even OBM. So in the process of transition, market competition will gradually shift from product competition, even brand competition to service competition. The common views of SMEs such as 'product is the source of profit', 'service is aimed at selling more products 'should be developed into 'service is the main source of profit'. And the mission of industrial design should extend from shaping physical appearances of products to combine tangible products and intangible services in the total solution. Besides, service-oriented product system design should include service models which can lead to new business models, products, interaction and other necessary means of design. And service models including different services should be presented through different physical evidences such as websites, products, APP that can be experienced by the users. Most important of all, services should be regarded as the key factor to the success of the whole system. And they can help to realize the ultimate goal of design: solve problems for people in their daily life and at the same time, meet their needs in multi-levels.

3 Results of In-Depth Interview on Service Design

All the interview samples have been chosen randomly in the data base of SMEs in the national economic and information technology commission. As we can see from figure 1, there are 10 SMEs in the Pearl River Delta Region, 8 SMEs in the Yangze River Delta Region, 5 SMEs in Beijing-Tianjing-Tangshan Delta Region and 4 SMEs in the middle or west regions.

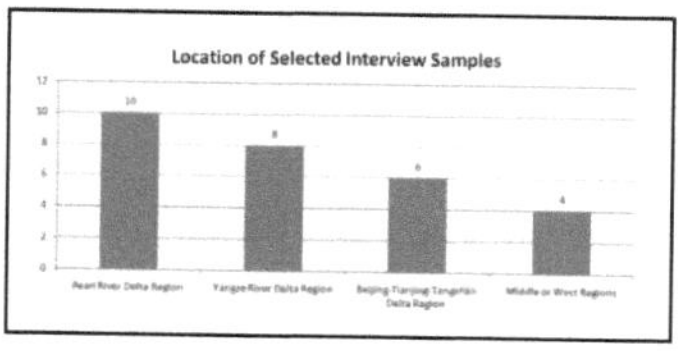

Fig. 1. Location of Selected Interview Samples

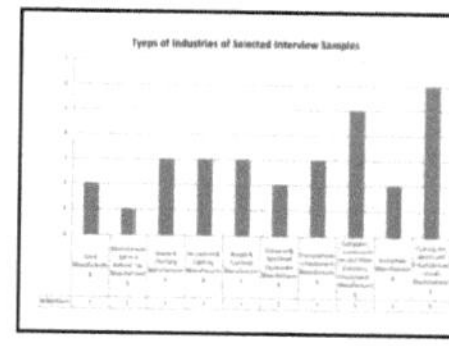

Fig. 2. Types of Industries of Selected Interview Samples

Based on 30 depth interviews with SMEs in China done by the author, the followings are the main results.

3.1 Time to Know about Design, Industrial Design and Service Design

As shown in figure 3 and figure 4, we can see clearly that after 2000, most of interviewees know about industrial design and have an idea of what design can bring to them. But there is still few interviewees do not have the recognition of industrial design. From the interview, there are mainly two reasons: firstly, there is no need for industrial design as one of interviewees from food manufacturing has said. Secondly, industrial design has been mistaken for mechanic design as one of interviewees from textile and clothing manufacturing has proved. Also one interviewee from middle and west regions is not aware of what is industrial design even if he shows to the author the changes that he is going to make for his products.

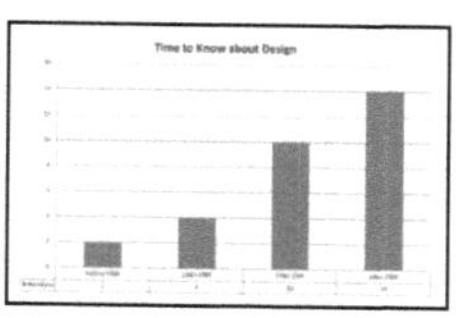

Fig. 3. Time to Know about Design

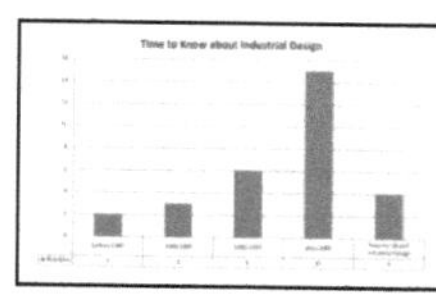

Fig. 4. Time to Know about Industrial Design

As we can see from figure 5, most SMEs do not know about service design. Among the few interviewees who claim to have an idea of service design, only 3 of them have a clear definition of service design, while others can only tell the differences between products and services. But fortunately, from the interview, the author finds out that around half of interviewees are managing to develop in a systemic way.

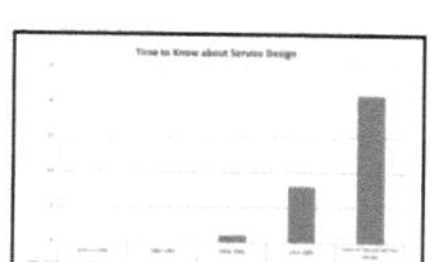

Fig. 5. Time to Know about Service Design

3.2 Design Development Status

The figure 6 shows that 50% of interviewees are purely OEM type. Only 10% of interviewees are purely ODM type. Around 36% of interviewees are mixed type, which indicates the trend from OEM to ODM or OBM. This arouse the hope of successfully introduce service design to SMEs.

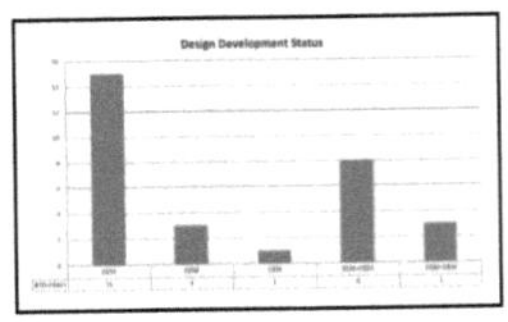

Fig. 6. Design Development Status

3.3 Role and Types of Design of Assisting in Expanding Market

It can be included from figure 7 that design has an effect on assisting in expanding market for most interviewees.

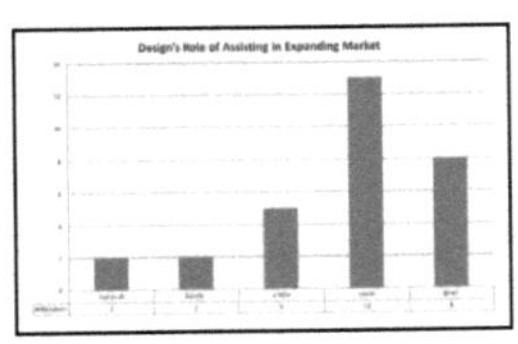

Fig. 7. Design's Role of Assisting in Expanding Market

As is shown by figure 8, we can see that package design is the most in need by interviewees. The next is VI system design followed by web design. Product design and exhibition design shares the equal importance to most of interviewees. Service design, defined by most interviewees in common sense such as after-sales services, is needed by half of interviewees. Other type of design such as textile design is needed by only a few numbers of interviewees.

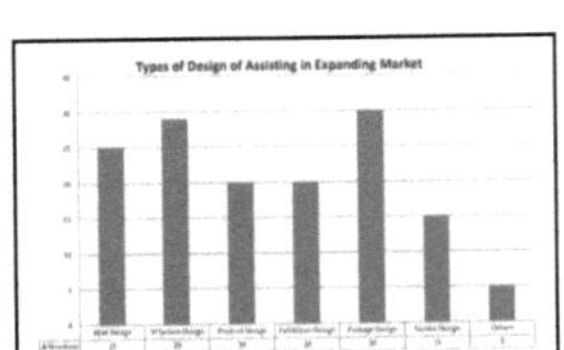

Fig. 8. Types of Design of Assisting in Expanding Market

3.4 Importance of Design in Product Development

As shown in figure 9, more than half of the interviewees think design is important in their product developments. According to the interviewees, design can help them to 'think widely and freely', 'create small changes to products but in a profitable way', and in most cases design can 'beat competitors because design can make products more attractive'. And we find out from several interviewees that design can bring something unpredictable to product development. One interviewee from OBM SME told us that design completely help the factory transform from a manufacturer to a local organizer. Their case is quite special because they give up almost half of the manufacture, rent the space to other smaller manufactures and provide management help such as quality control for them.

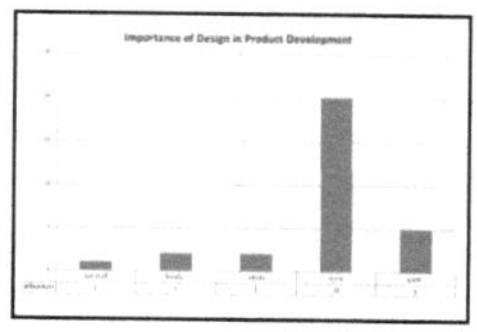

Fig. 9. Importance of Design in Product Development

3.5 Present Designer Status

Figure 10 shows the present designer status of interviewed SMEs. We can see that more than half of interviewees have the in-house design capability. And the rest choose to look for outside design cooperation, which are schools, independent designers and design companies.

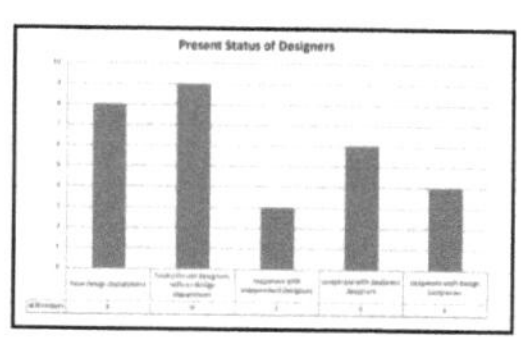

Fig. 10. Present Designer Status

3.6 Demands in Service Design

In the last part of interview, the author gave a presentation on service design to each interviewee. After the interviewee finally understand the meaning of service design. The author asked them their opinion on whether it is needed to introduce service design to their enterprises. According to figure 11, half of the interviewees cannot decide at that moment. But almost half of the interviewees have specific needs on service design.

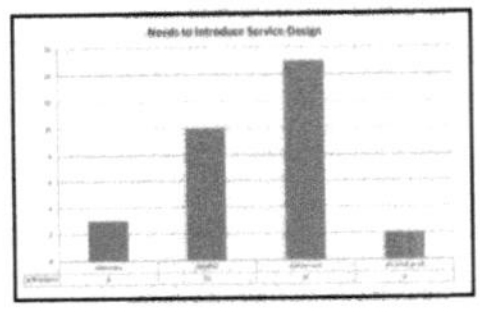

Fig. 11. Needs to Introduce Service Design

3.7 Potential of Establishing Service-Oriented Product System

Although most interviewees think it is not easy to establish service-oriented product system in their business, they do have the wish to have a try if given suitable circumstances.

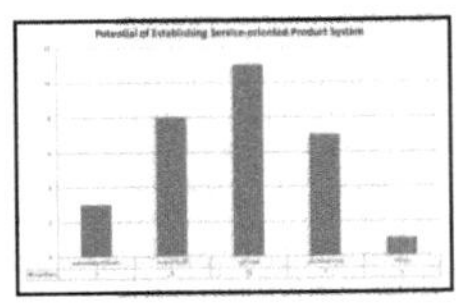

Fig. 12. Potential of Establishing Service-oriented Product System

3.8 Conclusion of the Depth Interview

From the interview, the author found out the advantage and disadvantages of introducing service design to SMEs. One advantage is that manufacturing in Pearl River Delta, Yangtze River Delta, Beijing-Tianjin-Tangshan Delta have a huge number of SMEs. These SMEs are developing from OEM to ODM or OBM and they have considerable needs in different types of design. Another advantage is that there is also potential to introduce service design to SMEs in these regions. Electronics, digital products, furniture, household utensils and medical equipments can be updated with a longer lifecycle and with new innovations that led by flexible services. The final advantage is that in these regions, there are numbers of professional design companies and design schools, which can be the important human resource for introducing service design.But there are also disadvantages. One is the lack of the understanding of service design. Service design, as the new born design thinking in China in recent years, has just begun to be accepted by professional designers. Head of SMEs need to be educated to understand this design thinking and should be educated to overcome the gap of different perceptions of design and business. The other disadvantage comes from SMEs themselves. They can neither build up a more comparatively complete R&D department nor restrain designers with talents as most large enterprises do. Not to mention service designer is completely new types of design profession in China now. But in the coming future, no more than 5 years, the whole situation will have a great change.

4 Introduction Strategies of Service-Oriented Product System Design

4.1 Government Level

Due to China's special social pattern, the introduction of service-oriented product system design should firstly be advocated by the government at all levels. Not only the supporting measures should be made and carried out, but also the government should share information database in public social media among similar manufacturers. In addition, the government units such as economic and information commissions in different regions should offer specialized consultancy to help SMEs to solve their problems. Furthermore, exhibitions to display and present service-oriented product system design should be held to extend the influence and get SMEs be educated. In the end, the government offer financial help to SMEs for their attempt to make a change.At the same time, the government should continue to standardize the design market. The system of professional qualifications authentication on designers should be build up. Then the price for design can be regulated. So the long existing vicious circle between SMEs and designers at all levels can be ended.

4.2 Academic Level

Design schools should act as the pioneer to research and practice service-oriented product system design. To begin with the identification of the content of service-oriented product system design for SMEs is important. Design schools compared with design companies, have disadvantages in the design service price and fast reaction to the project. But design schools have great advantages in systemic research and design for innovations. They can cooperation with related areas such as business schools and information technology schools on product planning, user analysis and so on.Next, for the sake of long-time cooperation with SMEs, design schools can start the work in single, easy projects, such as logo design and package design. Then if the SME is satisfied with the previous work, they can move on a single product design project. After at least two or three years' successful experience, SMEs can set up confidence on design and their cooperation's with design schools. In the end, they can grow up together with a full range of design: service-oriented product system design. This win-win relationship of both sides will break the choke point that design school is lack of practical experiences in manufacture, at the same time; SMEs can be educated of service-oriented product system design.In the third place, design schools should offer low-cost training program for SMEs on service-oriented product system design. In-house designers can work with students from design schools on a real project provided by the SMEs. It can be held in workshops, research studios or even a competition! Academic experts can go to SMEs for teaching. Design students with educated knowledge of service-oriented product system design can go for an internship in SMEs.

4.3 SMEs Level

All in all, SMEs should change themselves. They have to force themselves to transform from product sellers to service providers. They have to set up a long term research on the development of their enterprises. In this case, they have to research on users with inner or outer resources. They have to research on new product development other than copying from others. They have to stop to have a think on their future developments. Based on the knowledge of service-oriented product system design, they can plan their future development. They can set up milestones step by step. And they should overcome the difficulties of raising capitals by seeking support from local governments and cooperate with design schools. Finally, SMEs can have a try on other ways into the market such as e-business. E-business is more than setting up a website and just sells things. E-business is the quickest way to get to know the final users and understand what they need. Starting with the users' needs, SMEs can improve the services. Then the improved services can be expressed by products, websites, APPs and so on.

5 Conclusions

From products to services, competition in the market of the 21st century has been moved from product and brand competition to service competition. The changes in concepts have helped China transferred from an industrial society to a new stage of development. At this stage, the economic structure changes from the commodity-producing economy to a service-based economy. This is bound to be a re-definition of traditional industrial design. Along with the fusion of service design, now industrial design will change into a service-oriented product system design, which is believed to be one of the future trends. Manufacture is an important part of China's economic development, representing China in the world's core competitiveness. With the global market competition intensified, Chinese manufacturers, especially SMEs now are facing the enormous challenges in sustainable development. On the one hand, the world economy slows down, market demands shrink, wages of the labors rise, the prices for the raw material rise, RMB appreciation turns worse… all of these facts result in the further compression of profit margins of SMEs. On the other hand, SMEs in China share almost the same business model, and their design innovation ability is weak, therefore, the upgrading and transformation of s SMEs are imminent.Although service design as a new concept has been discussed a lot by Chinese scholars, it still has not been integrated into manufacture industry of China. Service design in China should be targeted at achieving commercial innovation instead of social innovation first. The latter has been introduced by the first group of Chinese scholars who has studied abroad. Due to its sensitive nature and ineffective performance in local industries, social innovation has been misunderstood by Chinese government and excluded from mainstream design fields in the past few years. By applying the main idea and methods of service design and product design, service-oriented product system design can be an effective way to provide integrated design solutions for commercial innovation. Applying service-oriented product system design to SMEs will not only allow those manufacturers to accumulate their design powers, but also will enhance their competitive advantage.

References

1. Chao, W., Xiao, H.: Design Changes and Growth: Sustainable Design Strategies of Enterprises. In: Tsinghua International Design Management Conference (2009)
2. Bell, D.: The Advent of Post-industrial Society: An Exploration of Social Forecasting. Xinhua Publishing House (1997)
3. Shengnan, X.: Internet-based Service Design Research. Business Review 5, 51–52 (2009)
4. Sakao, T., Lindahl, M.: Introduction to Product/Service-System Design. Springer (2009)
5. Miaosen, G., Manzini, E., Casalegno, F.: Collaboration Services Based on Mobile Communication Scenario and its Design Content. Packaging Engineering 22, 37–39 (2010)
6. Shijian, L., Shangshang, Z.: Service Design. Machinery Industry Press (2011)
7. Stickdorn, M., Schneider, J.: This is Service Design Thinking: Basices, Tools, Cases. Wiley (2012)
8. Hemin, D.: Research on the Methods of Product Service System Design. Modern Manufacturing Engineering 8, 42–46 (2013)
9. Keqiang, L.: Speaking at Executive Meetings of the State Council (2014), `http://www.gov.cn`

The Research of Regional Culture Characteristics of Tourism Commodities Based on Cross-Cultural Experience

Jianxin Cheng, Le Xi, Junnan Ye, and Wangqun Xiao

School of Art, Design and Media, East China University of Science and Technology
M. Box 286, No.130, Meilong Road, Xuhui District, Shanghai 200237, China
cjx.master@gmail.com, xilutar@sina.com,
yejunnan971108@qq.com,
xiaoyao-1916@163.com

Abstract. The booming of modern tourism contributes to an increasing enhancement of the worldwide innovation level of tourist commodities, as well as the continuous expanding scope and scale of output to the world. In a time when tourism activities are increasingly internationalizing and globalizing, the connection between tourism commodities and cross-cultural tourists are getting closer and closer, and the tourism experience economy that advocates cross-cultural experience has received widespread attention. The development of tourism experience economy is of great significance to the protection and development of regional culture, the realization of the sustainable development of tourism and the promotion of the internationalization of the tourism industry in China. With the popularity of the application of modern information technology, the information transmission and cognition between tourists and tourism commodities have become more and more direct and convenient. When facing cross-cultural tourists, the cognition and cultural connotations of tourism commodities are also increasingly challenged. How tourism commodities are perceived and accepted by cross-cultural users and how we better meet the needs of cross-cultural users in product experience, regional cultural characteristics, and design are hotspots in the study of experience economy. Based on the study of regional cultural characteristics, this paper proposes the application system of the regional cultural design and research of "Archaeology - Interpretation - Innovation" to utilize the systematic design thinking framework to enhance the regional cultural connotations and characteristics of tourism commodities. It also studies how to effectively convey the experience of these cultural connotations and characteristics to the cross-cultural users. Meanwhile, with China Luoyang Peony Festival as an example, through in-depth studies of history, culture and art in Luoyang, this paper extracts the characteristics with local features and values from the rich regional culture and combines the Eastern and Western thoughts' semantic cognition of regional cultural symbols to study the effects of these characteristics on the design of tourism commodities and the experience of cross-culture. By establishing an analytical framework, this paper carries out a comparative study of these unique regional cultural characteristics. Through a design case of the tourism commodity, it also demonstrates the

P.L.P. Rau (Ed.): CCD/HCII 2014, LNCS 8528, pp. 24–34, 2014.

design and application methods of these cultural characteristics so that a certain degree of enhancement and promotion can be brought to the innovative design approach of tourism commodities and that some reference can be provided for the study of the experience of tourism commodities. Finally, this paper provides proposals for the direction of future research of regional cultural design and application system of "Archaeology - Interpretation - Innovation".

Keywords: Cross-cultural Experience, Tourism Commodity, Regional Culture, Product Design.

1 Introduction

The combination of regional culture and tourism creates a huge consumer market. As an important medium to build the regional image and convey the regional culture, tourism commodities play an important role in this consumer market (Zhong, 2005) . The proportion of tourism commodities in the tourism industry also marks the development level of cultural industry in the tourism region. Being different from local specialties, tourism commodities possess characteristics of high cultural connotations, distinctive regional features and outstanding memorial values and collection values. It also covers extensive categories, such as daily necessities, handicrafts, accessories and ornaments (Zhong,2005). As an important part of the local tourism industry, tourism commodities have gained more and more attention and concern. Essentially, tourism is a kind of regional cultural experience(Wang,2005). In this process, as a carrier, culture is inextricably linked to the region. Especially in the face of tourism experience of cross-cultural tourists, as the core value of tourism commodities, how regional features are effectively communicated and perceived has been a major concern in our previous studies.

As designers and developers of tourism commodities, when facing the complex features of the regional culture, we should not only keenly discover the needs of the market, but also dig out the connotations of the regional culture and apply them to the design processes in an effective manner. The tourism commodities with unique regional cultural features have important implications for the development and dissemination of tourist culture (Zhong,2005). This paper focuses on the peony culture in Luoyang, China, introduces the main features of the regional culture in Luoyang and the distinctive characteristics of the peony culture in Luoyang, explores the excavation and application methods of the regional culture characteristics, puts forward a regional cultural design and application system of " Archaeology - Interpretation - Innovation", and discusses how to combine Eastern and Western cognitive thinking together to interpret such distinctive regional cultural features. This study attempts to establish a systematic and effective product design process to reflect the regional cultural features on tourism commodities through innovative means and to communicate them to the cross-cultural tourists in an effective manner. The results can be used to help designers to have a deeper understanding of the regional cultural features, reshape the regional cultural image of tourism commodities, and get market recognition and feedback.

2 Research Background

This study explores the design and development of tourism commodities in Luoyang. Luoyang is a typical regional culture and a representative one in China, and peony culture occupies an important position in Luoyang culture. They are of great significance to the cross-cultural cognition and experience of the regional cultural features of tourism commodities.

Located in western Henan, China, Luoyang is one of "the four holy cities" (Jerusalem, Mecca, Luoyang and Athens) in the world(Wang,Han,Wan,2013). It is not only the oriental starting point of Silk Road, but also a world cultural city named by the United Nations(Ni,2012). China's name is derived from the ancient city Luoyang(Ni,2012). Since Xia Dynasty, the first dynasty in Chinese history, there have been thirteen dynasties who established their capitals in Luoyang. Therefore, as the capital, Luoyang has a history of 1500 years, making it renowned for "the Imperial City of One Thousand Years"(Ni,2012). The Luoyang-centered Heluo culture is the source and core of Chinese civilization. "The River Maps and Luo Book" also originated from here and Confucianism, Buddhism, Taoism, Metaphysics and Neo-Confucianism all started from here(Wang,Han,Wan,2013). Heluo region is considered to be the birthplace of Chinese culture and "the River Maps and Luo Book" is regarded as the onset of Chinese characters(Wang,Han,Wan,2013). Heluo culture shows the characteristics of China's orthodox culture. The climate in ancient Heluo region has four distinct seasons and fertile land(Ni,2012). It is located right in the center of Mainland China and has been China's political, economical and cultural center since the pre-Qin period. It is named "the center of China"(Shao,2008).

Peony is China's national flower and peony is renowned for Luoyang, " the Imperial City of One Thousand Years and the City of Peony"(Ni,2012). As an old saying goes, "Luoyang peony is the finest under heaven"(Shao,2008). Luoyang peony has large buds and gorgeous colors as well as national beauty and heavenly fragrance(Shao,2008). Since ancient times, Luoyang peony has been endowed with the meanings of wealth, good fortune, and prosperity and represents the style of the Chinese nation as a great country. Peony settled down in Luoyang since the Sui Dynasty(Shao,2008). Due to the appropriate land, its flowers are colorful and beautiful, topping all the other flowers in the world. Luoyang was the capital of the Tang Dynasty and the development of peony culture in Tang Dynasty laid a solid foundation for the development of China's peony and the flourishing of peony culture(Shao,2008). The famous Luoyang Peony Festival is held in April every year. During that month, the entire Luoyang city is surrounded by the booming peony flowers. Guests from every corner of the world come here to admire the beauty of the peony flowers. According to the latest statistics released by the Luoyang Municipal Tourism Bureau, the 31th Luoyang Peony Festival in 2013 has attracted 18,699,500 tourists with a total tourism revenue of 11.22 billion RMB(Luoyang Municipal Tourism Bureau,2013). Among these tourists, the number of foreign ones was 172,500 and the tourism earned 41.8115 million USD; The tourist areas (spots) have been visited by 15,894,600 tourists. The average occupancy rate of the urban star-rated hotels was 85% (Calculated by the Municipal Tourism Development Commission and released by Statistics Bureau of Luoyang City). It can be seen that, in terms of regional cultural influence, Luoyang Peony Festival is very unique. At the same time, Luoyang is also one of the most famous tourist cities in China. Among the 300 copies of the questionnaire conducted by us, Longmen Grottoes (World Cultural Heritage), White Horse Temple, Guanyu's Mausoleum and Tian Zi Jia Liu all are the representative tourism images of Luoyang (Table 1).

Table 1. Statistical analysis of recognitions of tourism images in Luoyang

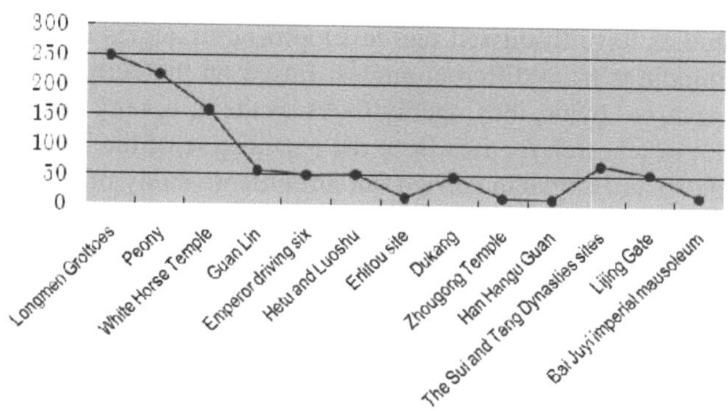

Table 2. Statistical analysis of recognitions of tourism commodities in Luoyang

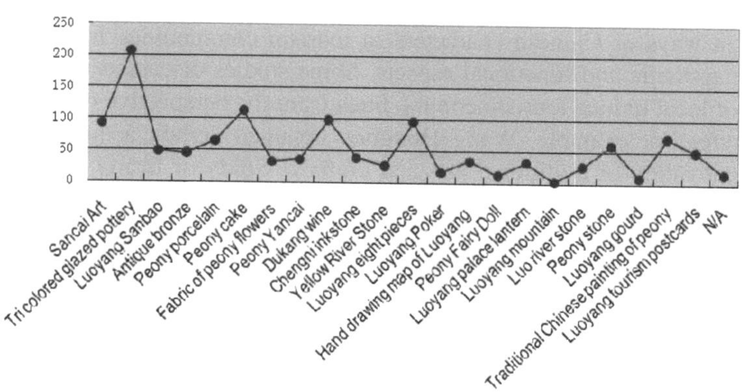

The tourism commodities in Luoyang market are also mainly characterized by Heluo culture and peony culture. Among the 300 copies of the questionnaire conducted by us, Tang Sancai, Peony Porcelain, the peony cake, the Eight Pieces and Dukang Wine are best-known (Table 2). It also indirectly confirms that peony culture elements holds a high proportion in the tourism commodities in Luoyang. But it can also be found that what dominate the tourism commodity market are mainly traditional crafts and local products and that a small number of cultural and creative commodities do not form the market influence. In another statistics carried out by us, three prominent issues exist in the tourism commodities in Luoyang, which are the homogenization of tourism commodities, the failure to better reveal the local characteristics of Luoyang, and low cultural values, respectively. The designing, packaging and marketing ways of the tourism commodities in the market are still relatively traditional and original, and they do not have too much attraction in the eyes of cross-cultural tourists. How to enhance the cultural connotations and regional cultural features of tourism commodities to satisfy the culture communication and cognition in the cultural experience is the starting point of this study.

3 Literature Review

The previous studies have discussed the development strategies and design methods of tourism commodities from different angles. Based on the current related literature collected and organized by us, they mainly focus on the following directions:

There are a lot of research focuses from the perspective of the local traditional culture. For example, Tan Fangyuan carried out an in-depth study of the connotations of "the blessing" in Chinese culture in Design of Tourism Commodities in Chinese "Blessing" Culture, and proposed the application methods in the design. In Inheritance and Application of Regional Culture in the Packaging Design of Featured Commodities in Dongguan, Zhang Li mentioned the importance of a tight bond between the traditional culture and contemporary design elements. In his paper The Application of Chinese Characters in the Design of Tourism Commodities, Wang Yadong started from Chinese characters, a symbol of the traditional Chinese culture, analyzed the six methods that built the Chinese characters, summarized the application principles of Chinese characters in the design of tourism commodities, and explored the combination ways of Chinese characters in tourism commodities from the cultural, emotional, aesthetic and functional aspects. Some studies discussed the development strategies of local unique tourism commodities from the perspective of the local traditional culture. For example, Wang Hongbao obtained certain achievements in the study of innovation of traditional arts and crafts in Study of Brand Enhancement of Tourism Commodities on the Basis of Regional Culture - A Case Study of Yan-Zhao Culture. In Application of "Intangible Cultural Heritage" Resources of Western Hubei in the Design of Tourism Souvenirs, Qian Yu and Peng Hong applied the characteristic connotations of "Intangible Cultural Heritage" resources of western Hubei to the local tourism souvenirs and fully interpreted the design process from the imagery to the "materialization". In Discussions of Several Problems about the Olympic Souvenirs, with the 2008 Beijing Olympic Games as an example, Li Chuanzhi and Ma Jinfu gave a comprehensive summary and elaboration of the development and business strategies of tourism souvenirs. In Studies on Intercultural Communication of Graphic Design in the International Context, Hu Rong made a thorough study of cross-cultural cognitive differences in the international context, and applied the research results in the design case. Gao Taiping carried out an in-depth study of the connotations and features of the regional culture in Luoyang from the perspective of Chinese philosophical thinking in A Discussion of Development Ideas about Key Tourist Resources in Luoyang.

In short, the regional culture is a central theme in current studies. However, some common shortcomings and deficiencies exist in these studies: firstly, these studies lack enough breadth and fail to give a comprehensive understanding of the regional culture. Most studies are based on a local cultural phenomenon and a complete research system has not been formed. The lack of complete and systematic research methods also make it difficult to extend the research results to other areas. Secondly, these studies put more emphasis on the refining of local culture and the cross-cultural cognitive differences are rarely mentioned. In the face of cross-cultural users, the effectiveness of the design is hard to be reflected.

4 Research Methods

In this study, we put forward a regional cultural design and application system of "Archaeology-Interpretation-Innovation" so that a systematic design thinking framework can be used to enhance the regional cultural connotations and features of tourism commodities and that the experience of these cultural connotations and features can be effectively communicated to the cross-cultural users. This framework has three levels, which are Cultural Archaeology, Semantic Interpretation and Design Innovation, respectively. These levels are interrelated and constitute a system (Figure 1). They made a combination of excavation and study of native culture, philosophical interpretations and cross-cultural semantic interpretations of Eastern and Western thinking, and the innovations on cultural connotations and experience of products based on modern design thinking.

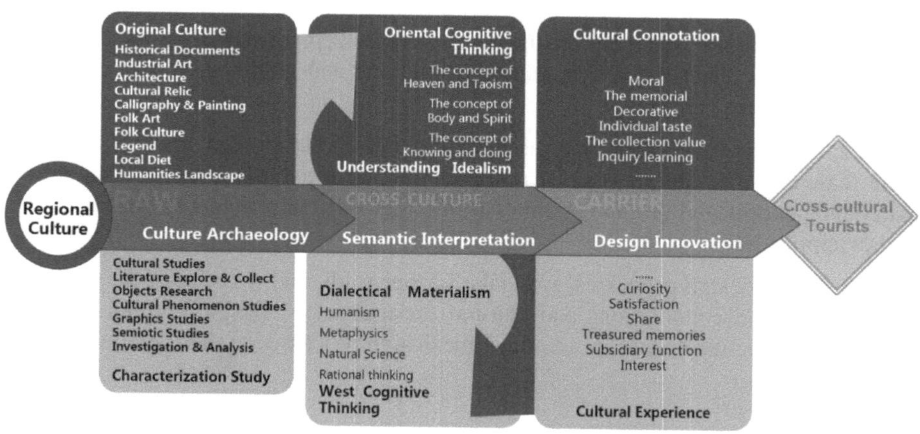

Fig. 1. The regional cultural design and application system of "Archaeology - Interpretation - Innovation"

Level 1: Cultural Archaeology. The cultural archaeology mentioned in this study refers to the excavations of the original cultures in the design sense, and the collection, sorting and analysis of the original cultures like historical literature, traditional arts and crafts, architecture and cultural relics. We use research methods like cultural studies, artifacts research, semiotics of cultural phenomena studies, and graphics research to explore and conclude the regional cultural features.

Level 2: Semantic Interpretation. Semantic interpretations presented in this study means that the Eastern and Western philosophy is used to carry out cross-cultural semantic interpretation on the regional cultural features. We strive to use the main ideas in the Oriental classical philosophy to analyze the profound connotations of the regional culture and compare them to the Western philosophy so that they can be effectively communicated to the cross-cultural objects. According to the characteristics of the cultural experience of cross-cultural tourists, the emotional elements are refined to accumulate reliable material basis for the subsequent design.

Level 3: Design Innovation. Based on the related design material and basis refined in the phase of Semantic Interpretation, a design innovation is performed on the cultural connotations and cultural experience of tourism commodities. In terms of the cultural connotations of these products, the tourism commodities' characteristics like moral, memorial, decoration and individuation are highlighted, which are all full of cultural connotations; in terms of the cultural experience of these products, the experience characteristics like adventure, satisfaction, memory and fun are emphasized. Through design innovations, the regional cultural features of tourism commodities can better serve the needs of cross-cultural experience, thereby enhancing the attractiveness and competitiveness of these products.

Based on the regional cultural design and application system of "Archaeology-Interpretation-Innovation", our study is divided into three stages:

Stage 1: We carry out extensive collection, screening and sorting of the background information of the regional culture in Luoyang, list the typical cultural features in Luoyang, sequence the recognitions of these features, and select the most representative regional cultural features. On the basis of these representative cultural features, we extensively collect the design materials, patterns and graphic symbols associated with these features.

Stage 2: We perform cross-cultural semantic interpretation and transformation of these features, select internationally accepted tourism souvenirs, transform the design materials, patterns and graphic symbols of the regional cultural features with modern design approaches.

Stage 3: In the design processes, we make further study and revision of the characteristics of cultural connotations and cultural experience. At the same time, in accordance with the actual situation, we adjust the design processes of these products a bit.

5 Results

Based on the regional cultural features of tourism commodities, we conduct a survey of the regional culture in Luoyang. Among the 300 copies of the questionnaire retrieved, as famous tourist markers, Longmen Grottoes, Peony and White Horse Temple rank top three. In the questionnaire survey about the cultural symbols in Luoyang, among a total of 29 typical cultural symbols in Luoyang, Peony Flower City, Heluo culture and Luoyang Peony Festival rank top three (Table 3). It can be seen from the survey that peony culture plays an important role in the regional culture in Luoyang and is an iconic symbol of Luoyang City.

Table 3. The results of the survey of typical symbols in Louyang

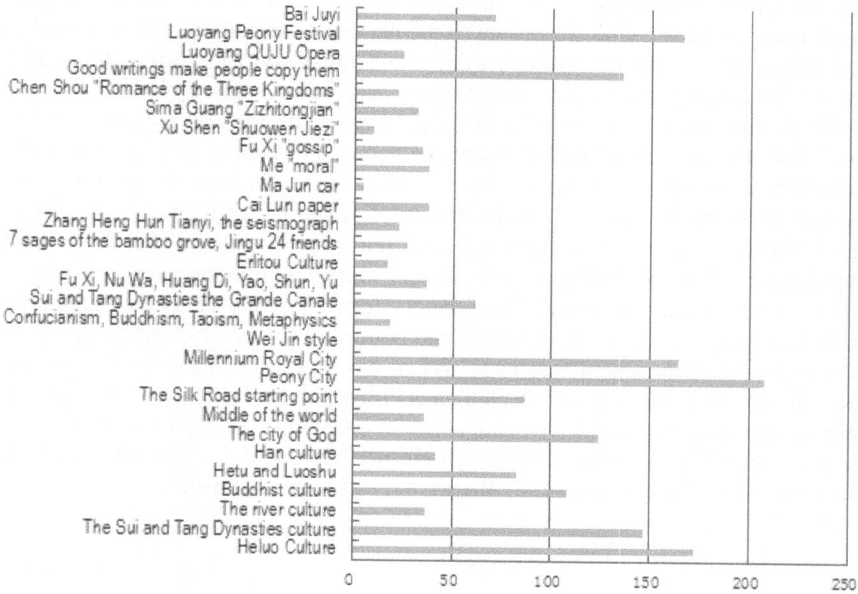

In the following studies, we list the typical peony varieties in Luoyang and conduct a cognitive survey. The results are shown in Table 4 in descending order.

Table 4. The results of the cognitive survey of peony varieties in Luoyang

			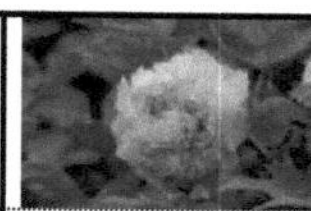	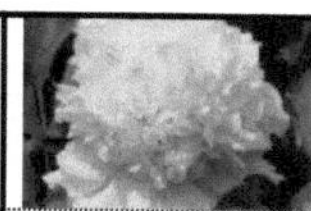
Luoyang Red	Black peony	Qiao sisters	Green Peony	Yao Huang
AVG. 0.533	AVG. 0.413	AVG. 0.287	AVG. 0.287	AVG. 0.250
	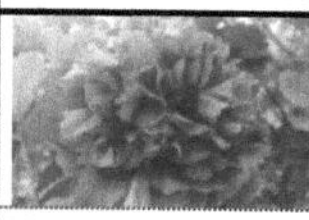			
Luoyang Fairy	The champion Red	Drunk Yang Fei	Wei violet	Purple blue
AVG. 0.213	AVG. 0.210	AVG. 0.177	AVG. 0.160	AVG. 0.133
			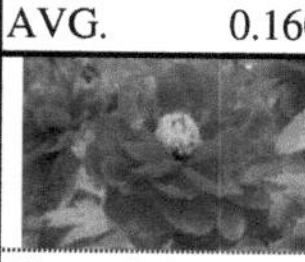	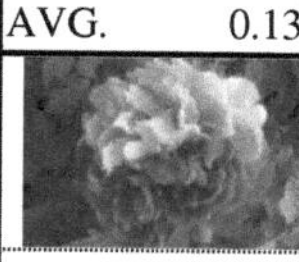
White jade	Hu Hong	snow white tower	Fire refining elixir	Coral algae
AVG. 0.083	AVG. 0.077	AVG. 0.073	AVG. 0.050	AVG. 0.050
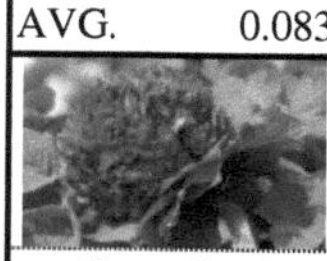		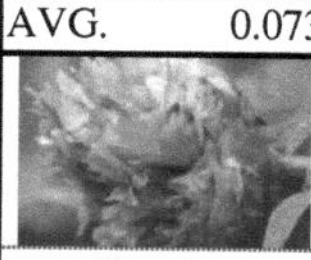		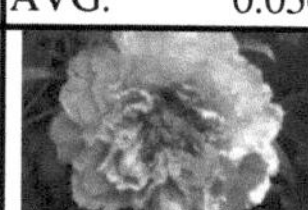
Case of red	Yellow peony	Shearing	Jin Pao red	Meat lotus
AVG. 0.033	AVG. 0.030	AVG. 0.023	AVG. 0.020	AVG. 0.013

Later, we list and compare the cross-cultural cognitive elements of peony, and divide the peony culture into eight disciplines based on the Eastern and Western cognitive layers (Figure 2). Meanwhile, according to the nature of the carrier of these morals, we collect and select appropriate carriers from international tourism commodities. In this study, we select two product cases: fridge magnets and Luoyang soup bowl.

In the product design phase, we add the graphic creativity to these products based on the characteristics of cultural elements of peony and further improve the cultural connotations and experience connotations of these products from the perspectives of shape and decoration (Figure 3). In the design of peony fridge magnets, we adopt the imagery form of red peony in Luoyang, and put an emphasis on the gorgeous and plump features of peony in the graphic design, meaning abundance and blessings; in the design of Luoyang soup bowl, the imagery form of peony is also adopted. Peony elements are integrated into the design of the bottom of the bowl. A aesthetic imagery feature of peony is its aroma fragrance. When the users eat all the food in the bowl and see the peony at the bottom which means "fragrance at the bottom", it encourages people not to waste food and advocate a frugal and non-extravagant attitude. At the same time, in Chinese pronunciation, "fragrance" is equal to "good fortune". The plump huge peony flower also symbolizes good fortune and prosperity.

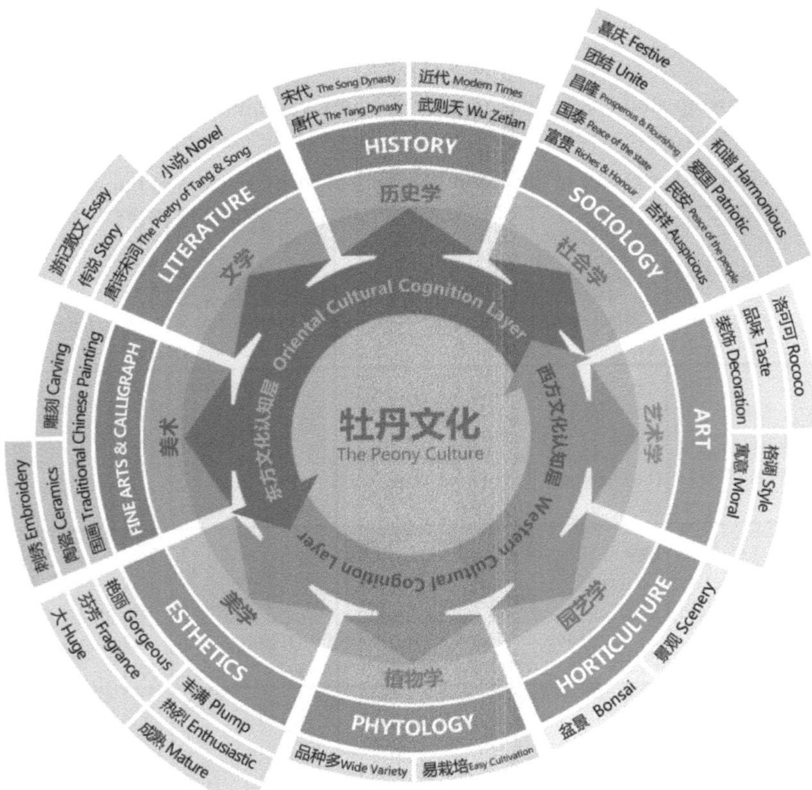

Fig. 2. Peony culture - Cross-cultural cognitive layer

Fig. 3. Product design case based on the regional culture features in Luoyang

6 Conclusions and Discussions

The excavation researches for regional cultural features continue. Among them, the excavation, interpretation and innovation methods of the regional cultural features can help us specify the research ideas and methods of the regional cultural features and carry out more reasonable and in-depth excavation, transformation and interpretation of the regional culture, thereby achieving the desired innovative application. Judging from the current research situation, there are still some issues to be further improved and developed. Firstly, A feedback survey system for cross-cultural users is needed. A remote access system should be established to collect data so as to evaluate the product experience of cross-cultural users. We will continue to develop relevant quantitative analysis system in the future studies. Secondly, it is also needed to further improve the quantitative evaluation system of the cognitive elements of the regional cultural features. In terms of the cognitive elements extracted from the regional cultural features, how to classify and quantify them still remains an issue that requires further study.

References

1. Dan, W., Jianxin, H., Ruli, W.: The Millennium Imperial Capital - Luoyang, pp. 8–12. Peking University Press, Beijing (2013)
2. Xiying, N.: Luoyang, pp. 6–10. CNPIEC, Guangzhou (2012)
3. Rulin, S.: View of Luoyang from the Silk Road Starting Point, pp. 9–11. Kun Lun Press, Beijing (2008)
4. Zhiping, Z.: Study on Tourism Commodities, pp. 21–27. China Tourism Press, Beijing (2005)
5. Mingran, Y.: "Walking" Art - Cultural and Creative Design of Tourist Souvenirs. New Materials and Decoration 7, 187–189 (2013)
6. Yucheng, W.: Culture of Tourism, pp. 16–24. China Tourism Press, Beijing (2005)
7. Xiaomin, G.: Study on the Use of Semantic Interpretation of Culture in the Design of Tourism Commodities. Guangzhou: Guangdong Construction Vocational Technology Institute (2012)
8. Fangyuan, Q.: Research on China Fu Culture in Tourism Commodities Design. Jiangnan University (2010)
9. Congfeng, Y.: Research on Formation of Regional Cultural Characteristics of Tourist Souvenirs. Jiangnan University (2004)
10. Li, Z.: Inheritance and Application of Dongguan Regional Culture Characteristics in the Packaging Design. Quality of Goods - Academic Observation 7, 109–110 (2012)
11. Yadong, W.: Application of Chinese Characters in Design of Tourist Souvenirs. Capital Normal University (2011)
12. Hongbao, W.: Study on the Promotion of Tourism Commodity Brand based on Regional Culture - Take Yan Zhao Culture as an Example. Industry and Technology Forum 10, 67–68 (2008)
13. Yu, Q., Hong, P.: Application Research on West Hubei "Intangible Cultural Heritage" Resource in the Souvenir Design. Art. 100(8), 211–213 (2012)
14. Chunzhi, L., Jinfu, M.: Discussion on some Problems of Olympic Tourism Souvenirs. Journal of Capital Institute of Physical Education 3(20), 27–29 (2008)
15. Rong, H.: Cross-cultural Communication Studies on Graphic Design in International Context. Hunan Normal University (2009)
16. Taiping, G.: Discussion on the Development of Tourism Resources in Luoyang 7, 66–68 (2011)

Towards the Development of an Inter-cultural Scale to Measure Trust in Automation

Shih-Yi Chien[1], Zhaleh Semnani-Azad[2], Michael Lewis[1], and Katia Sycara[3]

[1] School of Information Sciences, University of Pittsburgh, Pittsburgh, PA, 15260 USA
[2] Department of Psychology, University of Waterloo, Waterloo, Ontario, N2L3G1 Canada
[3] Robotics Institute, Carnegie Mellon University, Pittsburgh, PA 15213 USA
shc56@pitt.edu, ml@sis.pitt.edu,
zsemnani@uwaterloo.ca, katia@cs.cmu.edu

Abstract. Trust is conceived as an attitude leading to intentions resulting in user actions involving automation. It is generally believed that trust is dynamic and that a user's prior experience with automation affects future behavior indirectly through causing changes in trust. Additionally, individual differences and cultural factors have been frequently cited as the contributors to influencing trust beliefs about using and monitoring automation. The presented research focuses on modeling human's trust when interacting with automated systems across cultures. The initial trust assessment instrument, comprising 110 items along with 2 perceptions (general vs. specific use of automation), has been empirically validated. Detailed results comparing items and dimensionality with our new pooled measure will be presented.

Keywords: Trust, Automation, Culture, Technology Adoption, Human Computer Interaction (HCI), Human Factors.

1 Introduction

Human interaction with automation is a complex process. Humans may fail to use automation when it is advantageous (disuse), fail to monitor it properly when in use (misuse), or accept its recommendations and actions when inappropriate [1]. Trust (in automation) has most often been studied indirectly through its purported influence on behavior often without any direct cognitive measure. Studies have shown [2–4] that trust towards automation affects reliance (i.e., people tend to rely on automation they trust and not use automation they do not trust) and can be consistently measured.

While the reliability of the automation has a major influence on the operator's decision to trust and use automation, internal (e.g., personality) and external (e.g., cultural norms) factors can also significantly influence the level of trust [5]. Different contexts within trust have lead to definitions of trust as an attitude, an intention, or a behavior [6–8]. A widely accepted definition of trust is lacking, however, it is generally agreed the trust is best conceptualized as a multidimensional psychological attitude involving beliefs and expectations about the trustee's trustworthiness derived from experience and interactions with the trustee [9].

P.L.P. Rau (Ed.): CCD/HCII 2014, LNCS 8528, pp. 35–46, 2014.

In both the interpersonal trust literature and automation trust literature [10], trust has been said to have both cognitive and affective features. In the interpersonal literature, trust is also seen involving affective processes, since trust development requires seeing others as personally motivated by care and concern to protect the trustor's interests [11]. In the automation literature, cognitive (rather than affective) processes may play a dominant role in the determination of trustworthiness, i.e., the extent to which automation is expected to do the task that it was designed to do [12]. In the trust in automation literature, it has been argued that trust is best conceptualized as an attitude [13] and a relatively well accepted definition of trust is: "*an attitude which includes the belief that the collaborator will perform as expected, and can, within the limits of the designer's intentions, be relied on to achieve the design goals*" [14]. The conceptualization of trust as an attitude having both cognitive and relational aspects is especially relevant to our research on how culture may modulate trust construal and dimensions of trustworthiness. It has been hypothesized, and supported by various studies, that *individual differences* [5], [13], [15], [16] and *culture* [17] affect the trust behavior of people with respect to automation. For example, it has been shown [18] via replication of Hofstede's [19] cultural dimensions for a very large-scale sample of pilots, that even in such a highly specialized and regulated profession, national culture still exerts a meaningful influence on attitude and behavior over and above the occupational context. In fact, there would be no need for an intervening variable such as trust if outside factors did not exert a substantial influence over trust decisions.

While models of trust, Lee and See [13], invariably acknowledge the multiplicity of these influences. However, the majority of research on trust in automation has focused on the relation between automation reliability and operator usage often without measuring the intervening variable, trust. The utility of introducing an intervening variable between automation performance and operator usage lies in the ability to make more precise or accurate predictions with the intervening variable than without it. This requires that trust in automation be influenced by factors in addition to automation reliability/performance. There are two general limitations to the current literature. First, most of the work on cultural influences on trust has been done in the context of interpersonal trust [20], [21]. Second, most of the very limited work studying culture and trust in automation has been abstract and suggestive, without empirical validation. With respect to trust in automation across cultures, two of the very few studies [22], [23] examined the effects of culture-sensitive interactions on the willingness of adopting an information technology. However, the studies focused mainly on online behaviors and failed to contribute a uni-dimensional instrument to examine the wide variety of contexts in applying automated systems. Despite the plethora of research in trust and culture in inter-personal relations, there is a dearth of studies investigating the effect of culture on trust in automation. To address these issues, the overall objective of our research is to develop a fundamental understanding of general principles and factors pertaining to trust in automation, and how trust mediates reliance on automation across cultures.

2 Instrument Development

Attempts to measure trust in automation such as Muir's questionnaire [12] or the many questionnaires created for individual studies have not (in general) benefited from the same rigor in development and validation that has characterized measures of interpersonal trust. The Empirically Derived (ED) scale developed by Jian et al. [24] is a notable exception that has been subjected to a validation study [25] and used elsewhere [26]. Madsen and Gregor's Human-Computer Trust (HCT) instrument [8] demonstrated construct validity and high reliability within their validation sample and has subsequently been used to assess trust in automation in air traffic control simulations [27]. The SHAPE Automation Trust Index (SATI) [28] is the most pragmatically oriented of these formally developed measures, with items refined for usability and construct validity in focus groups of air traffic controllers. All three scales have benefited from empirical study and systematic development yet each has its flaws. ED addresses trust in automation in the abstract without reference to an actual system. The HCT stopped short of confirmatory factor analysis leaving its true dimensionality uncertain. The SATI neglected psychometric tests of construct and content validity.

The initial steps involve developing an instrument capable of reliably assessing trust in automation. Developing this begins with the pool of items from the ED, HCT, and SATI and augmented items from 5 existing studies intended to increase the reliability of the discovered dimensions. The initial instrument comprises 110 items falling into a variety of constructs, as shown in Appendix A.

2.1 Pilot Test – General vs. Specific Automation

Despite the variety of automated systems (e.g., smartphone apps vs. industrial robots), the trusting beliefs would be influenced significantly regarding the purpose of the automation. To develop an instrument capable of reliably assessing trust in automation, the initial step began with identifying the purpose of the aforementioned items to general or specific uses of automation. 45 participants were recruited from the University of Pittsburgh community for categorizing the characteristics of the selected items. The participants first read the following description:

> "Please respond to the following statements about your trust in automation. By automation, we mean any technology or service that you have used before, including apps, devices, functions, or systems. Based on your experience, use the following scale to rate the extent to which you agree(5) or disagree(1) with the statements below. Note, no wrong responses to any of the statements, the most critical is to record your own true opinion on each item. *If you think the provided instruction is not sufficient to answer the question, please rate insufficient information.*"

The instrument was measured using a 5-point Likert scale (from strongly disagree to strongly agree), however, an item may be rated as insufficient if the participants believed the item/question has to refer to a targeted system. Once an item was rated as insufficient more than once, the item was categorized as specific use. Additionally, after reviewing the general items, 7 items with high neutral rates (more than 1/3 of the participants) were also classified as specific purpose. Among the 110 items, 70 items fell into the general cluster, whereas 40 items were in the specific group.

2.2 Scale Refinement

An initial test has been conducted to refine our trust instrument. A pool of questions, consisting of 110 items along with 2 perceptions (general vs. specific use of automation) was adopted. A total of 65 paid participants was recruited on Amazon Mechanical Turk (MTurk). The instrument was measured using a 5-point Likert scale, asking respondents to detail their trust beliefs in automated systems. The instrument comprised two parts, general and specific uses of automation. Automated navigation devices (e.g., GPS) were introduced as the specific automation (table 1); in the general automation, instead of pointing out targeted systems, the participants can name any experienced automated tools.

Table 1. Descriptions of general and specific automation

General automation	By "Automation" we mean any technology or service that takes actions automatically and that you have used, including apps, devices, functions, or systems.
Specific automation	By "Automation" we focus mainly on GPS Navigation System including all types of navigation devices that you have used, such as an automotive navigation system (e.g., Garmin) or Smartphone navigation apps (e.g., Google map).

Data gathered in the test was used to refine our scale by rewording or identifying problematic items. Exploratory factor analysis (EFA) was used to determine the dimensionality of the data and loading of items in order to refine the instrument. A principal components factor analysis with varimax rotation was performed to examine the number of factors produced. A five-factor model was returned that explained 52.4% of the variance in general automation (details not shown here due to space constraints); whereas 70.2% of the variance of the specific automation was represented by a five-factor model (Appendix B). The internal consistency and reliability were examined (table 2, 3). If the resulting Cronbach's alpha is lower than 0.7, the factor will be eliminated (as factor 4 in table 3). Through the aforementioned analysis, 59 items (40 general and 19 specific automation) that met the validity and reliability criteria were retrieved to refine the instrument. The finding factors greatly involved in three clusters: performance expectancy, process transparency, and purpose influence. Performance expectancy is defined as an individual's belief that applying an automation will help the individual to enhance job performance; process transparency involves the encountered difficulties based on the perceived transparency of an automaton (i.e., how an automation functions); purpose influence relates to a person's knowledge of what the automation is supposed to do (i.e., initial trust or faith in automation).

Table 2. Reliability Statistics in General Automation

General Auto	Cronbach's Alpha	Cronbach's Alpha Based on Standardized Items	Num of Items
Factor 1	.922	.922	13
Factor 2	.867	.871	6
Factor 3	.892	.890	9
Factor 4	.863	.870	7
Factor 5	.718	.732	5

Table 3. Reliability Statistics in Specific Automation

Specific Auto	Cronbach's Alpha	Cronbach's Alpha Based on Standardized Items	Num of Items
Factor 1	.943	.944	10
Factor 2	.836	.835	3
Factor 3	.818	.821	3
Factor 4	.626	.628	2
Factor 5	.760	.797	3

3 Conclusion

Trust has been frequently cited as a contributor to decisions about using and monitoring automation [13]. In this paper, we report initial steps toward developing an instrument capable of reliably assessing trust in automation across cultures.We began with the pool of 53 items from the ED, HCT, and SATI and augmented them with new items intended to increase the reliability of discovering dimensions. A total of 110 items (70 general and 40 specific) were empirically validate via MTurk. Through the validity and reliability tests, 59 items (40 general and 19 specific) were selected.

To further examine the external validity of the instrument, another round of data collection will be conducted to cross-validate the instrument. We will additionally collect data on Hofstede's [19] cultural dimensions to provide a fuller picture of cultural differences and their relation to the trust scale being developed. We expect the research will have a significant impact on the design, implementation and evaluation of automation to make it more trustworthy in general and in aiding the appropriate trust calibration for optimized reliance across cultures.

Acknowledgements. This research has been sponsored by AFOSR FA9550-13-1-0129.

References

1. Lyons, J.B., Stokes, C.K.: Human-Human Reliance in the Context of Automation. Human Factors The Journal of the Human Factors and Ergonomics Society (2012)
2. Lee, J., Moray, N.: Trust, control strategies and allocation of function in human-machine systems. Ergonomics 35(10), 1243–1270 (1992)

3. Muir, B., Moray, N.: Trust in automation. Part II. Experimental studies of trust and human intervention in a process control simulation. Ergonomics (1996)
4. Lewandowsky, S., Mundy, M., Tan, G.P.: The dynamics of trust: comparing humans to automation. Journal of Experimental Psychology. Applied (2000)
5. Masalonis, A.J., Parasuraman, R.: Effects of training operators on situation-specific automation reliability 2, 1595–1599 (2003)
6. Mayer, R.C., Davis, J.H., Schoorman, F.D.: An Integrative Model of Organizational Trust. Academy of Management Review (1995)
7. Moray, N., Inagaki, T., Itoh, M.: Adaptive Automation, Trust, and Self-Confidence in Fault Management of Time-Critical Tasks. Experimental Psychology: Applieed (2000)
8. Madsen, M., Gregor, S.: Measuring human-computer trust. In: 11th Australasian Conference on Information Systems, vol. 53, pp. 6–8 (2000)
9. Jones, G.R., George, J.M.: The Experience and Evolution of Trust: Implications for Cooperation and Teamwork. The Academy of Management Review (1998)
10. Adams, B., Webb, R.: Trust in small military teams. In: 7th International Command and Control Technology Symposium (2002)
11. Lewis, J., Weigert, A.: Trust as a social reality. Social Forces (1985)
12. Muir, B.: Trust in automation: Part I. Theoretical issues in the study of trust and human intervention in automated systems. Ergonomics 37(11), 1905–1922 (1994)
13. Lee, J., See, K.: Trust in automation: designing for appropriate reliance. Human Factors 46(1), 50–80 (2004)
14. Moray, N., Inagaki, T.: Laboratory studies of trust between humans and machines in automated systems. Transactions of the Institute of Measurement and Control (1999)
15. Singh, I.L., Molloy, R., Parasuraman, R.: Individual differences in monitoring failures of automation. Journal of General Psychology 120(3), 357–373 (1993)
16. Merritt, S., Ilgen, D.: Not All Trust Is Created Equal: Dispositional and History-Based Trust in Human-Automation Interactions. Human Factors: The Journal of the Human Factors and Ergonomics Society 50(2), 194–210 (2008)
17. Karvonen, K.: Designing trust for a universal audience: A multicultural study on the formation of trust in the internet in the nordic countries. In: HCI (2001)
18. Merritt: Culture in the Cockpit: Do Hofstede's Dimensions Replicate? Journal of Cross-Cultural Psychology 31(3), 283–301 (2000)
19. Hofstede: Cultures And Organizations - Software of the Mind. Development (1991)
20. Gunia, B.C., Brett, J.M., Nandkeolyar, A.K., Kamdar, D.: Paying a price: culture, trust, and negotiation consequences. The Journal of Applied Psychology (2011)
21. Fulmer, C.A., Gelfand, M.J.: Dynamic Trust Processes: Trust Dissolution and Restoration, pp. 1–32 (2010)
22. Kim, D.: Cognition-Based Versus Affect-Based Trust Determinants in E-Commerce: Cross-Cultural Comparison Study. In: ICIS, pp. 741–753 (2005)
23. Lee, I., Choi, B., Kim, J., Hong, S.: Culture-technology fit: effects of cultural characteristics on the post-adoption beliefs of mobile internet users. International Journal of Electronic 11(4), 11–51 (2007)
24. Jian, J., Bisantz, A., Drury, C.: Foundations for an empirically determined scale of trust in automated systems. International Journal of Cognitive (2000)
25. Spain, R.D., Bustamante, E.A., Bliss, J.P.: Towards an Empirically Developed Scale for System Trust: Take Two. Proceedings of the Human Factors and Ergonomics Society Annual Meeting 52(19), 1335–1339 (2008)

26. Master, R., Jiang, X., Khasawneh, M.T., Bowling, S.R., Grimes, L., Gramopadhye, A.K., Melloy, B.J.: Measurement of trust over time in hybrid inspection systems. Human Factors and Ergonomics in Manufacturing 15(2), 177–196 (2005)
27. Luz, M.: Validation of a Trust survey on example of MTCD in real time simulation with Irish controllers (2009)
28. Organisation, E., The, F.O.R., Of, S., Navigation, A.I.R., Air, E., Management, T.: Guidelines for Trust in Future ATM Systems: Measures Guidelines for Trust in Future ATM Systems: Measures Guidelines for Trust in Future ATM Systems: Measures (2003)
29. Im, I., Hong, S., Kang, M.S.: An international comparison of technology adoption. Information & Management 48(1), 1–8 (2011)
30. Venkatesh, V., Morris, M., Davis, G., Davis, F.: User acceptance of information technology: Toward a unified view. MIS Quarterly 27(3), 425–478 (2003)
31. Hwang, Y., Lee, K.C.: Investigating the moderating role of uncertainty avoidance cultural values on multidimensional online trust. Information & Management (2012)
32. Srite, M., Karahanna, E.: The role of espoused national cultural values in technology acceptance. MIS Quarterly 30(3), 679–704 (2006)
33. Limayem, M., Khalifa, M., Frini, A.: What makes consumers buy from Internet? A longitudinal study of online shopping. Systems, Man and Cybernetics (2000)
34. Mcknight, D., Carter, M.: Trust in a specific technology: An investigation of its components and measures. ACM Transactions on Management Information Systems (2011)
35. Halpert, A., Horvath, A., Preston, F., Somerville, K., Semnani-azad, Z.: Technological Adoptiveness Scale (TAS): Internal Properties and Construct Validity (2008)

Appendix A. Initial trust instruments: root constructs and definitions

International Comparison of Technology Adoption	Constructs	Definitions*
ICTA (International Comparison of Technology Adoption [29]) compared the use intention of information technologies across different cultural contexts. The UTAUT instrument [30] was selected to examine the cultural effects. The survey comprised 14 items within 5 factors, in which 11 items/4 factors were chosen for our test. *All the definitions are cited from [30].	Performance expectancy	"An individual believes that using the system will help him or her to attain gains in job performance."
	Effort expectancy	"The degree of ease associated with the use of the system."
	Social influence	"The degree to which an individual perceives that important others believe she should use the new system."
	Facilitating conditions	"The degree to which an individual believes that an organizational and technical infrastructure exists to support use of the system."
Culture-Technology Fit	**Constructs**	**Definitions***
CTF (Culture-Technology Fit [23]) investigates the trustworthy relationship between cultural contexts and post-adoption beliefs in the use of the mobile Internet. CTF includes 30 items/10 factors (3 items for each). The cultural profiles (uncertainty avoidance and individualism) were selected for our test. *All the definitions are cited from [23].	Uncertainty Avoidance	"The extent to which the members of a culture feel threatened by uncertain or unknown situations."
	Individualism	"Individualism represents a preference for a loosely knit social framework in which people are expected to take care of themselves and to look after their own interests."
Online Trust Beliefs	**Constructs**	**Definitions**
OTB (Online Trust Beliefs [31]) examined the moderating role of uncertainty avoidance in online trust beliefs between subjective norms and the integrity & ability dimensions. OTB adopted 16 items within 6 factors from	Uncertainty Avoidance	"Uncertainty avoidance is the level of risk accepted by the individual. This dimension examines the extent to which one feels threatened by ambiguous

[32] and [33], in which 12 items/5 constructs were selected for inclusion in our test.		situations [32]."
	Subjective Norms	"Social factors that are likely to influence the online shopping intentions/behavior [33]."
	Benevolence	"The belief that the trusted party, while hoping to make a profit, wants to do good to the customer [31]."
	Integrity	"A trusted party adheres to accepted rules of conduct, such as honesty and keeping promises [31]."
	Intention	The behavioral intent of a buyer to precede the act of purchasing [31].
Trust in Specific Technology	**Constructs**	**Definitions***
TIST (Trust in Specific Technology [34]) examines different kinds of trust across contexts and technologies, from specific (e.g., Excel or spreadsheet products) to general uses in automated tools. The scale comprises 26 items within 7 factors, in which 19 items/6 constructs are adapted to our test. *All the definitions are cited from [34].	Specific Technology - Reliability	"The belief that the specific technology will consistently operate properly."
	Specific Technology - Functionality	"The belief that the specific technology has the capability, functionality, or features to do for one what one needs to be done."
	Situational Normality - Technology	"One feels comfortable when one uses the general type of technology of which a specific technology may be an instance."
	Structural Assurance - Technology	"One believes structural conditions like guarantees, contracts, support, or other safeguards exist in the general type of technology that make success likely."
	Faith in General Technology	"One assumes technologies are usually consistent, reliable, functional, and provide the help needed."
	Trusting Stance - General Technology	"One presumes that one will achieve better outcomes by assuming the technology can be relied on."

Empirically Derived	**Constructs**	**Definitions**
ED (Empirically Derived [24]) incorporates a three-phased experiment, comprised a word elicitation study, a questionnaire study, and a paired comparison study, was performed to empirically develop a scale to measure trust between people and automated systems. 12 items, falling into two factors (trust & distrust), are incorporated in the instrument. All the items are selected to our test.	Trust	The *trust* factor comprises 7 main items: confidence, security, integrity, dependability, reliability, trust, and familiarity.
	Distrust	The *distrust* factor comprises 5 main items: deceptiveness, underhandedness, suspiciousness, wariness, and harm.
Human-Computer Trust	**Constructs**	**Definitions***
HCT (Human-Computer Trust [8]) scale is designed to examine trust in intelligence systems (taxi dispatch system was used in their study). HCT instrument comprises 25 items (5 constructs, each with 5 items to reflect the concept). All the items are adapted to our test. *All the definitions are cited from [8].	Perceived Reliability	"Reliability of the system, in the usual sense of repeated, consistent functioning."
	Perceived Technical Competence	"A system is perceived to perform tasks accurately and correctly based on the information that is input."
	Perceived Understandability	"A human supervisor or observer can form a mental model and predict future system behavior."
	Faith	"A user has faith in the future ability of the system to perform even in situations in which it is untried."
	Personal Attachment	"A user finds using a system agreeable and it suits her taste."
SHAPE Trust Index	**Constructs**	**Definitions***
SATI (SHAPE Automation Trust Index [28]) measures human trust of automated systems in controlling air traffic management tasks. The scale measures controller's trust twice, pre	Reliability	"The extent to which you can rely on the machine to consistently support the tasks."

and post-adoption use, in order to obtain human feedback and sensitively examine the fluctuation in trust. The first part comprises 4 questions and the second part consists of 8 sections. 16 items within 7 constructs, are chosen for inclusion in the test. *All the definitions are cited from [28].	Accuracy	"Accuracy of machine in supporting successful completion of tasks."
	Understanding	"The extent to which the machines' decision on when and how to intervene and support the task requires assessment, knowledge, and understanding of the task."
	Faith	"The extent to which you believe that the machine will be able to intervene and support the tasks in other system states in the future."
	Liking	"The extent to which you can anticipate and expect the machine to support the tasks."
	Familiarity	"The extent to which you have confidence in the machines' decision on when and how to intervene and support the task."
	Robustness	"The extent to which you can count on the machine to provide the appropriate support to the tasks."
Technological Adoptiveness Scale	**Constructs**	**Definitions**
TAS (Technological Adoptiveness Scale [35]) is a 12 item measure that examines a person's relative openness to adopting and using new technology. 9 items were chosen for inclusion in our test.	General Technology - Adoptiveness	The attitude of openness in adopting any technology that has been released recently and is unfamiliar to a user.

Appendix B. EFA (exploratory factor analysis) results: specific use of automation (21 items/5 factors). The model of specific items with a threshold value 0.4, in order to eliminate the noise. Note. (r): recode values.

Rotated Component Matrix[a]					
	Component				
	1	2	3	4	5
I can rely on automation to ensure my performance.	.830				
Automation improves my performance.	.750				
It is easy to follow what automation does.	.725				
Automation makes use of all the knowledge and information available to produce its solution to the problem.	.708				
The advice automation produces is as good as that which a highly competent person could produce.	.696				
Automation correctly uses the information I provided.	.680				
I am confident in automation.	.646				
Automation always provides the advice I require to make my decision.	.627				
Using automation increases my productivity.	.606				
Using automation enables me to accomplish tasks more quickly.	.542				
Automation has sound knowledge about the type of problem for which it is intended.		**.726**			
Automation is friendly to use.		**.702**			
Automation uses appropriate methods to reach decisions.		**.618**			
Automation may result in unpredictable situations. (r)			.838		
Automation does not fail me.			.783		
I believe automation could be faulted. (r)			.761		
I understand how automation works.				.827	
I am wary of automation. (r)				.611	
I am suspicious of automation's intent. (r)					**.842**
Automation is deceptive. (r)					**.758**
Automation behaves in an underhanded manner. (r)					**.750**

The Research on the Logistics Service Design Based on the Theory of Brand Image: A Case for FEELER

Qing Ge[1], Yin Wang[2], and Nan Zhou[1]

[1] Hangzhou Vacational & Technical College, Zhejiang 310018, P.R. China
geqing2014@126.com, zhier_3000@163.com
[2] Zhejiang Sci-Tech University, Zhejiang 310018, P.R. China
wangyin1973@126.com

Abstract. The problems in the domestic logistics industry currently require logistics equipment suppliers to help customers to do the service designwhich is an effective means to enhance corporate brand image on based of the brand image theory by the case of service design through the whole process of logistics equipment manufacturers: FEELER.

Keywords: Logistics industry, Service design, Brand image.

1 Introduction

The modern logistics industry is an important service industry to promote economic globalization. Logistics is consisted by six links: object transportation, distribution, warehousing, packaging, handling, distribution processing and related logistics information,which integrates of the basic function of transportation, storage, loading and unloading, handling, packaging, distribution processing, distribution, information processing etc..And it's a controlling system from raw materials, manufactured goods, to finished goods and information. However, there are three main problems in Chinese logistics industry:

- The enterprise and the customer only pay attention to the quality and selection of a single device, but not make the system reach optimization.
- The enterprise and the customer still keep the price as the primary factors in selecting logistics equipment, but ignore the study on internal quality and safety index.
- The enterprise and the customer ignored the effect of the function of the equipment with the blindness in system planning, design, causing inconvenience to use or waste of resources.

These problems require logistics equipment suppliers not only to provide the hardware for the customer, but also to help customers to do some service work, such as customer service, demand forecasting, order processing, distribution, inventory control, transportation, warehouse management, factory and warehouse layout and location, transportation and handling, procurement, packaging, collecting information

P.L.P. Rau (Ed.): CCD/HCII 2014, LNCS 8528, pp. 47–58, 2014.

and so on. The logistics equipment suppliers will more effectively convey the corporate brand image, enhance the brand value, to attract high-quality customers through them. And we will study the logistics equipment service design based on the theory of brand image by the brand case: FEELER.

2 Analysis of the Brand Image Theory

2.1 Brand Image Theory Is the Basis of User Experience

The brand originated is the identity function. After the brand symbol theory, brand cognitive theory and brand relationship theory, Professor Livy proposed that brand was a cluster existed in human mind image or concept. It's the sum of knowledge or attitude about brand and more depended on the mind of consumers in the explanation than the product itself. There was a transfer of sovereignty from producers to consumers in Professor Livy's research. Then America scholar Kevin Ryan Keller also expressed the same idea:" Brand was the reflection from consumers. Because the differences reflected were the result of consumer understanding of the brand. If no these differences, product with brand name was still the general product in essence.

A company may provide the stimulus through its marketing plans or other behaviours from its brand, but something still in the consumers' minds. So the brand was a sense of presence rooted in the reality, but reflected the personal habits. Obviously the brand is the consumer awareness of the product. Brand ultimately depends on the consumers' understanding of the product characteristics related with the subjective factors such as consumer tastes or personality. There are some complex mental activity, for example, paying close attention to a brand, distinguishing, thinking and understanding a brand, in the process of consumer brand awareness. Although a existence of objective features in a product is important, the consumers only recognize and accept the characteristics they feel.

Therefore, the brand is not only a kind of visual recognition, but also a consumer's psychological activity in essence. So a brand relationship model is formed from the brand recognition to the brand image as fig.1. Figure 1 shows the whole brand relationship process from enterprise to consumer. The brand recognition is used by enterprises for brand communication in which the consumers get the brand experience and brand association and eventually forming the brand image. But there are some noises along with this process, including objective factors of external social environment and subjective factors of consumer. These factors ultimately influence the enterprise brand image. If the objective social environmental factors can not be changed, all we can do is change the consumer's own subjective factors by reducing noise to a minimum.

The consumer's subjective factors can be attributed to the existence of "mental model" based on cognitive psychology. That means people's general ideas (views) are often produced by "Leaping inference" for they just make the specific matter to simple concept instead of the details in facts. This "mental model" caused the "cognition divisions" which is often due to a poor user experience between enterprises and consumers and made the brand recognition of enterprise a uncorrect and invalid brand image in consumers' minds, thus affecting the enterprise's brand value promotion. Therefore we must enhance brand user experience to reduce the "cognitive differences" so that to establish a brand image conforming to the standard of the enterprise.

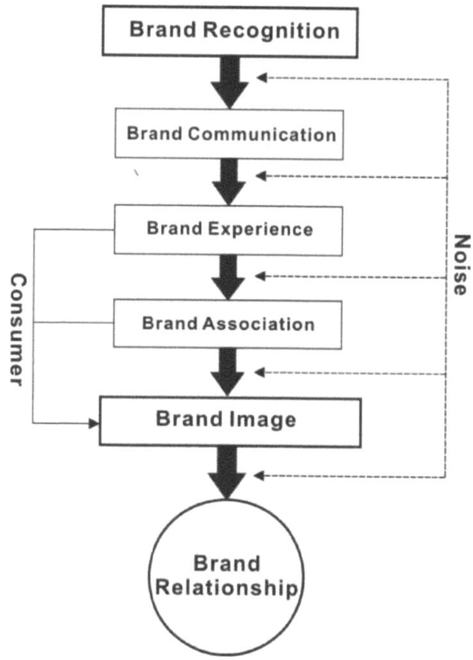

Fig. 1. Brand relationship model

2.2 Service Design Is an Effective Way to Enhance the User Experience

User experience generally refers to people's cognitive impression and feedback of product, system or service which they used or desire to use. And it's the all feelings including emotions, beliefs, preferences, cognitive impression, reaction of physiology and psychology, behavior and achievement etc. before or after using a product or system. Service design can effectively plan or organize people, infrastructure, communication , materials and supplies and make people be with them on people-centered concept to improve the user experience and service quality.

So it is an effective way to narrow our "cognition divisions" between brand identity and brand image. This will greatly help to enhance the user experience and the value of brand. Next, we will carry on the service design research based on the brand of logistics equipment suppliers FEELER as an example.

3 Analysis of the Brand FEELER

We take the customer brand experience as the object of study to do a investigation with sampling in FEELER customer group by depth interviews, field observation and so on. Then the brand image is decomposed into eight brand elements: the brand name, the brand logo, the brand slogan, the brand personality, the brand emotion, the number of users,the products appearance and the ideal price based on the results of the investigation. After that, we conduct psychological evaluation of customer brand experience based on eight elements and establish the service design system in pre-sale, sale and after sale including logistics planning, equipment R&D and sales, based on which we provide a set of handling service design as Fig.2.

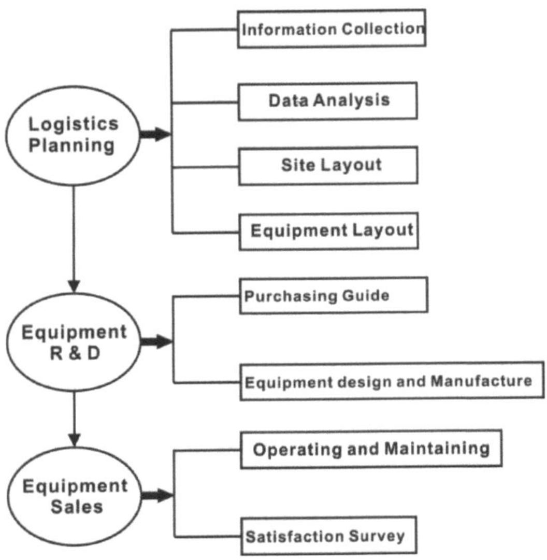

Fig. 2. The whole process of the service design by logistics equipment manufacturers FEELER

3.1 Logistics Planning

Information Collection. The purpose of information collection is to collect a comprehensive understanding of the project. There are outline of the project, project status, project objectives and project requirements.Outline of the project is mainly the overall presentation of the project, including the background of this project; new projects or renovation project; land use; the sponsor and project time requirements. The project Status is the present business and logistics situation description, including the business scope, business type, warehouse, process, existing problems and so on. The project objectives is to meet the needs of business development, so the planning must be clear requirements to support sales. This is the most basic requirement of the distribution center planning and design.The calculation method to support sales: Sales = inventory * inventory turnover * single box value. The project needs is the customer's request which mainly manifests in six aspects: the planning objectives; business; warehouse area; the relevant requirements of logistics equipment and facilities; office area ; other requirements.

Data Analysis (EIQ Analysis). The technological process of EIQ analysis as shown below.

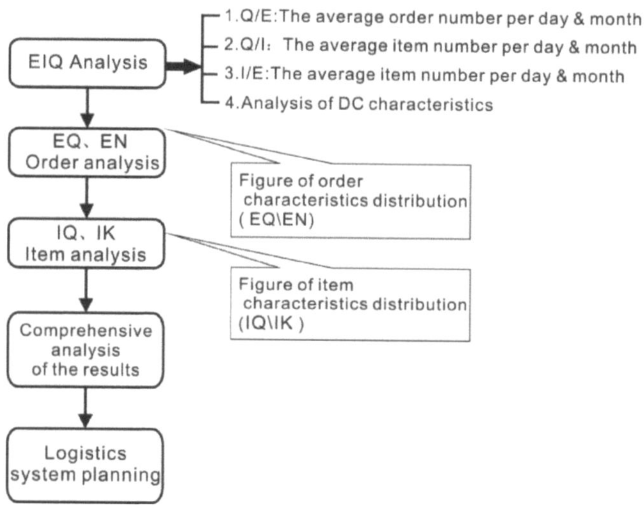

Fig. 3. The technological process of EIQ analysis

EIQ analysis is to master the important customers' demand characteristics. E—Order Entry, I—Item, Q—Quantity. We can use the three key elements of logistics E, I, Q to shipping characteristics, study the needs characteristics of distribution center, provide planning basis for distribution center.

Analysis of EIQ project includes: analysis of EN - item number analysis per order (N for Japanese "Nnai (species)"'s initials); analysis of EQ - quantity analysis per order; analysis of IQ - quantity analysis for each single product; analysis of IK - ordering number for each single product(K for Japanese "Kasanatsut (repeat)"'s initials).

EIQ analysis contents as shown below:

knowing the quantity of customer orders and order mode(the whole bracket, box or single) and providing the data of customers' products and sales area.

Determining the item demand characteristics and picking method. IQ analysis and IK analysis, by which we can understand the distribution of each kind of products, is a reference of product storage, picking, classification and provides product sales trends.

Calculation of inventory and related operating space requirements. Total IQ shipped average number * the number of items=the overall demand; total IQ shipped average number * the number of items * the number of inventory days=the stock total demand; the average EQ * the number of orders= the distribution vehicle demand or space of platform region.

Assessment of resource requirements. We can calculate the quantity of equipment and manpower demand to picking whole bracket, box or single piece according to shipments and standard working hours.

The storage planning and management. We can design the warehouse from the EIQ data analysis to obtain the most economical benefit on the operation efficiency and space utilization rate for products storage.

Offering the data of operation efficiency. We can compare the efficiency in the each stage of logistics operation and find the problems in the logistics system to avoid that the external environment changed, but the managers still felt good with the EIQ analysis. So EIQ can be used as a tool for analysis and diagnosis of the logistics center and is a magic weapon of logistics procedure optimization.

Providing sales or shipments forecast data. Historical EIQ data not only can be used to a sales forecasting as an important reference, but also predict future logistics flow and make us do operation plan better to improve the inventory turnover rate, work efficiency and reduce the lead time to distribute.

An important reason for the selection of logistics equipment. We can determine the equipment category or the degree of automation in logistics center to avoid the financial resources waste by the analysis of the EIQ data.

Site Layout. Sit layout refers to the distribution of internal office, sorting center, special warehouse, goods storage area, the platform, operation site in in the sorting center, and the arranged position of each function area . This work needs four aspects: the operation process, the needs of proposal, data analysis, GSP.

There are six site layout steps. The first step is that the logistics technology, processes and systems should be chosen. The logistics headquarters will determine the single plane graph with construction headquarters after demonstration by board of directors according to the business scale and the strategic objectives of the group proposal. The second step is to determine the in storage area and out storage area. The delivery cart cannot block the passage of the park and the receipt and storage spaces should be considered. The third step is to determine the first floor office area and the specific location of the warehouse. The first floor, such as cold storage warehouse, and office should be preferably designed. And the cold storage warehouse is in relatively independent region in order to facilitate the management. The receipt and acceptance management office should meet the requirements of 50 square meters. The office area not need to enter the warehouse operation should be isolated from the warehouse (glass isolation). The fourth Step is to determine the equipment layout. The fifth Step is to determine the storage area layout. The sixth step is to determine the warehouse management office and special warehouse on the other floors. The Special warehouse mainly is the gifts library, return library or unqualified Library. The warehouse management office is also the operating sites, so as close as possible to the elevator. The gifts library should be designed in a reasonable size. The return library and unqualified library should be adjacent.

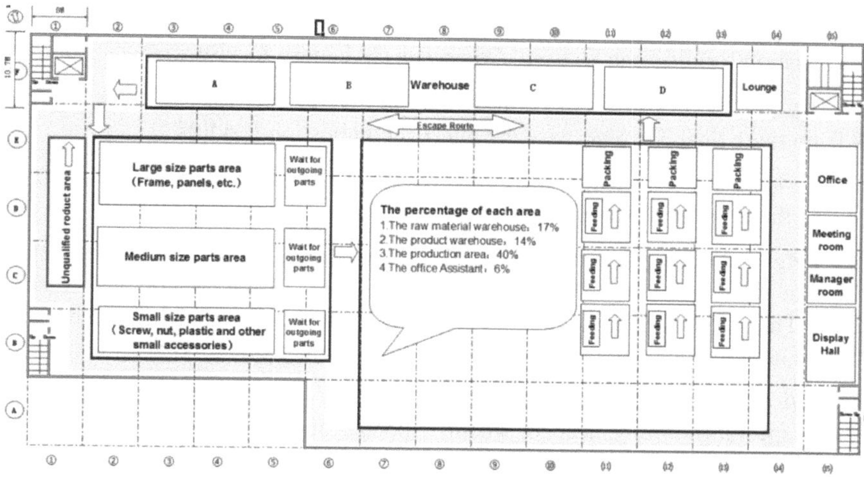

Fig. 4. A layout diagram for FEELER's customers

Equipment Layout. There are six principles of logistics equipment layout: ensuring the delivery line not to blocked channel and flow smoothly; ensuring the delivery line to occupy less area of the warehouse; a conveyor line can be multi-used to streamline the delivery line number in the premise of unification, efficiency; avoiding the transmission line to interference; conveying line must be maximum load to satisfy the operation requirement; transmission line operation should meet the principle of delivery goods, personnel safety and construction safety.

3.2 Equipment R & D

Purchasing Guide. Purchasing Guide is mainly to help customers to do a series of products procurement, equipment operation and maintenance training based on customer logistics planning.

Because forklift is the most widely used handling equipment in a distribution center, we use forklift which is a kind of mainly equipment manufactured by FEELER as an example to illustrate the the factors of purchasing forklift as fig.5.

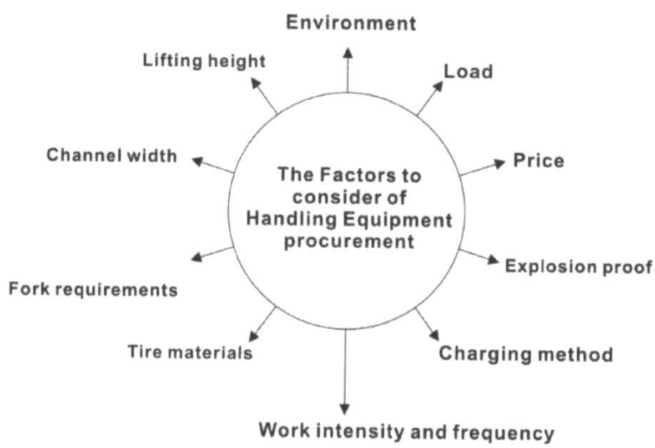

Fig. 5. The factors of purchasing forklift

Environment. If we are in outdoor work or distribution center of harsh environment, the combustion forklifts can be used, Otherwise the battery forklift.

Load. The weight of goods determines the load. Generally, load of battery forklift truck is no more than 3T, otherwise the internal combustion forklifts.

Channel width. The balance forklift requires the most wide channel for its fastest speed and the electric powered reach truck needs less.

Lifting height. The applications of pallet forklift, stacker, reach forklift, balance forklift are different selected generally according to lifting height and transport distance. The pallet forklift usually be used for plane carrying; the balance forklift usually be used below lifting height of 6M; otherwise the reach forklift.

Fork requirements. We should to determine whether the side shift fork be needed whether a special fixture be needed, whether special fork length be needed.

Tire. A different kind of tyre, general rubber tire or polyurethane tire, is chosen according to the ground and cleaning requirements. The rubber tire's coefficient of friction is big, but easy to leave the tire marks; polyurethane tire does not leave the tire marks, but easy to slip in the smooth hard ground.

Explosion proof requirements. Whether the explosion-proof is required according to the operation.

Charging requirements. Some forklift's charging voltage is 220V, some 380V. The vehicle charging or battery charging should be consided. The concentrated charging or distributed to several regional charging should be considered when the forklift number of distribution center is large.

Work intensity and frequency. Battery forklift is equipped with battery usually according to the 8 hour operation. If the work intensity, as two or three class manufacturing, the spare battery must be needed.

Price. Generally a battery forklift is more expensive than a internal combustion forklift and a VNA forklift is more expensive than a reach forklift which more expensive than balance weight forklift.

We can carry on the equipment design and manufacture based on the above factors.

Equipment Design and Manufacture. Next we can develop and design the corresponding logistics equipment based on the study above. For example, small tonnage balance electric forklift trucks for the small indoor warehouse loading and handling, ordinary 3~10 tons balance weight internal combustion forklift for the general outdoor logistics sites, such as wharf, the open space of a factory, the square, etc., more than 10 tons of large tonnage forklift for the site, mining area, forest, etc..

There are the old logistics equipment by FEELER(Fig.6) and the new we designed below.(Fig. 7)

Fig. 6. The old logistics equipment by FEELER

Fig. 7. The re-designed logistics equipment by us

Equipment Operation and Maintenance Training. Next we need to maintain the equipment operation training to the customers. The pictures below is part of the forklift operation and maintenance training instructions of FEELER (Fig.8.).

Fig. 8. The forklift operation and maintenance training instructions of FEELER

Customer Satisfaction Survey. Finally, we need to conduct a customer satisfaction survey. The table below is parts of the customer satisfaction survey by FEELER.

4 Summary

The paper put forward the service design is an effective means to enhance corporate brand image on based of the brand image theory and verified the correctness and effectiveness of the proposal by the case of service design through the whole process of logistics equipment manufacturers: FEELER. And this will help us to further research on brand, service design and user experience in future work.

Table 1. Forklift satisfaction questionnaire

Forklift	The total number: —	The number of Brand1 : —	Performance satisfaction	□5 □4 □3 □2 □1
			Stable quality satisfaction	□5 □4 □3 □2 □1
			Price satisfaction	□5 □4 □3 □2 □1
			After-sale service satisfaction	□5 □4 □3 □2 □1
		The number of Brand2 : —	Performance satisfaction	□5 □4 □3 □2 □1
			Stable quality satisfaction	□5 □4 □3 □2 □1
			Price satisfaction	□5 □4 □3 □2 □1
			After-sale service satisfaction	□5 □4 □3 □2 □1
		The number of Brand3 : —	Performance satisfaction	□5 □4 □3 □2 □1
			Stable quality satisfaction	□5 □4 □3 □2 □1
			Price satisfaction	□5 □4 □3 □2 □1
			After-sale service satisfaction	□5 □4 □3 □2 □1

Table 1. *(continued)*

	Planning amount to purchase in 2013 ___	The main brand and purchase amount intention	Brand1: ____ Quantity:____
			Brand2: ____ Quantity:____
			Brand3: ____ Quantity:____
	The main reason to purchase in 2013 ___	**1. Company business scale increasing** ___% in total amount to purchase.	
		2. Replacing ___% in total amount to purchase ; The average time of use out of forklift___years ;	
		3. New technology needs ___% in total amount to purchase ; The main new technology_________	
		4. Other reasons_____________	
	The procurement plan in 2014 ___	expected to increase this year______%	

References

1. Jian, Qiang, Zhu: The recognition of the brand image and communication. Xia Men UP, Xia Men (2010)
2. Knapp, D.E.: The Brand Mindset. Enterprise management publishing house, Beijing (2008)
3. Aaker, D. A.: Building Strong Brand. China Machine Press, Beijing (2012)
4. Thomas, L.: Design Thinking: Integrating Innovation, Customer Experience, and Brand Value. Electronic Industry Press, Beijing (2012)
5. Robert, D.: Service Design Patterns:Fundamental Design Solutions for SOAP/WSDL and RESTful Web Services. China Machine Press, Beijing (2013)

Comparing Chinese and German's Emotional Reaction to Perfume

Mengyu Guo, Zhe Chen, Hui Li, Pei-Luen Patrick Rau*, Long Zeng, Xiangheng Wang, Nico Wendler, and Lahcen Feddol

Institute of Human Factors and Ergonomics,
Department of Industrial Engineering, Tsinghua University, Beijing, P.R.C.
rpl@tsinghua.edu.cn

Abstract. In this study of comparing Chinese and German's emotional reaction to perfume, three kinds of measurements including Self-report, Facial Action Coding System (FACS), Skin Conductance are used for measuring participants' emotions to 6 types of perfume with the objectives of: 1) validating the measurements of emotion to perfume, 2) describing the relationship between perfume and emotion and 3) comparing the cultural difference between Chinese and German regarding their emotions to perfume. The experiment results indicate that the three types of measurements are all effective to describe emotions to perfume and some interesting findings about the emotional reaction to perfume are noticed using the three measurements together. The cultural differences between Chinese and German are found in two aspects: 1) Chinese tend to more like perfume of Green tea and 2) Chinese tend to show no emotional response on face even if they have stronger feelings inside.

Keywords: Cultural difference, emotional reaction, perfume, emotion measurements.

1 Introduction

People have such experience that when a pleasant perfume comes they feel joyful and relaxed. Past research has shown that Lavender Fragrance have some positive effect on people's relaxation [1].

The relationship between emotion and odor is an interesting topic for researchers of user experience. Olfaction starts when scent goes to the nasal cavities and makes some stimuli to receptor neurons [2]. Two kinds of receptor cells, the signaling cells and the axons, have been found [3]. The signals received by the signaling cells are sent to the axons, where scent is processed [2].

Moreover, skin will react to odor. First, smell goes to nose and sensory cells, then the limbic system, i.e., the place of emotions. After that, brain reacts to the pleasantness or unpleasantness of odors. Emotional reaction finally results in body reaction to the emotions, which have influence on people's decision about buying a soap or shower gel [4].

---

* Corresponding author.

P.L.P. Rau (Ed.): CCD/HCII 2014, LNCS 8528, pp. 59–67, 2014.

1.1 Necessity and Importance

As is known that gesture, facial expression and color have different meanings in different cultures, especially in Chinese and German cultures [5]. How about odor? Are there any differences on the emotional reaction to various odors among different cultures? The answer to this question is important to both perfume companies and catering industry because fragrance (sense of smell) is a primary driver in consumer choice. If the differences do exist, it is necessary to find out what they are. This study aims to help perfume companies to find a better way to provide consumers in different culture with odor-related products.

1.2 Goals

The first goal of the study is to validate a measurement system composed of self-report, FACS and Skin Conductance. The second goal is to address a question about rela-tionships between specific emotions evoked verbally by odors and physiological changes. Do odors that could evoke verbally specific emotions (e.g. joy, anger, fear, surprise, disgust or sadness) also cause specific patterns of peripheral response? The third goal is to find a cultural influence on emotional reaction to odor.

2 Literature Review

Literatures suggest that there is an interaction be-tween odor and emotion. Physiologically, it makes sense that the different structures within the Limbic System would response together to some degree [6]. Research also suggests that the startle reflex might act as a psycho physiological indicator of the emotional valence of foreground stimulation [7]. Both odorant stimuli are rated as equal intense by the subjects, and heart rate and electrodermal activity are not influenced differentially by the two odors [8].

Arousal and pleasantness have been considered as the main dimensions of affective responses to environment. Pleasantness is the degree of favorable feelings a subject can feel under given circumstances, while arousal is the degree of excitement a subject feels.

While smelling an odor, there are some other changes on skin, like temperature, conductance, and skin blood flow. The main reaction of skin is the appearance of sweat. Known as a lie detector, the measurement of the skin conductance is a way to find out whether someone is lying or not. This also has connections to person's feelings. Lying makes people feel uncomfortable and then leads to the appearance of sweat.

2.1 Cultural Differences between Chinese and German

There are some cultural differences between Chinese and German from other perspectives. From Hofstede's model, comparisons between German and Chinese are made. The IDV scores are considerably higher in Germany (67) than in China (20), meaning that the German society is more like individualism and the Chinese society is more like collectivism [9]. This probably suggests that Chinese have more tolerance to bad odors than German [10].

2.2 Measurements of Emotion

There are many kinds of measurements in emotion researches: the self-report of subjective experience, observer ratings, facial measures, brain-based measures, vocal measures [11].

Self-report and Observer Ratings. Self-report measures emotion by asking participants to rate their feelings on a single emotional construct. Self-report measurement can be easily constructed and easily understood by participants with low re-source. A SAM self-report is commonly used. In this study, participants smell perfumes and evaluate them on the arousal and pleasantness dimensions, using a scale developed by Bradley, who developed a picture-oriented instrument called the self-assessment manikin (SAM) to assess directly the pleasantness and arousal (and also dominance) associated with an object or event.

The pleasantness dimension ranges from smiling to frowning and the arousal dimension ranges from excited to relax.

Participants will also select one word from emotion list (fear, anger, sadness, surprise, neutral, joy or disgust) as the best descriptor to their reaction to the odor.

Facial Measures. Several facial measurements are found. The most important one is the Electrodermal Activity (EDA), which is very similar to the lie detector: the skin conductance.

In a reaction to emotion, there is sweat on skin. Sweat is a good conductor to the skin conductance, which can be visualized through a low voltage. It starts about 0.5 to 4 seconds after a stimulus and quickly goes back to the original level.

To obtain a good result, attention has to be paid to some requirements. Hand is a good place for testing skin conductance and the electrodes need to be placed on the non-dominant hand. The participant should feel relaxed and have a normal breathe rate. One test should at least last for 30 seconds.

Facial Action Coding System. Facial Action Coding System (FACS) is a system to taxonomies human facial expressions, originally developed by Paul Ekman in 1976 [11]. It is a common standard to systematically categorize the physical expression of emotions, and it has been proven useful to psychologists and animators.

The use of FACS has been proposed for the analysis of depression [12], and the measurement of pain in patients unable to express themselves verbally [13].

FACS is designed to be self-instructional. A variant of FACS has been developed to analyze facial expressions in chimpanzees [14].

There are five steps to do a facial analysis, including face image acquisition, ore-processing procedure, feature extraction, classification, post-processing. Vide-otaping is usually used for FACS.

3 Research Methodology

3.1 Hypothesis

- Hypothesis 1: Results from three types of emotional measurements can reflect the emotional reaction to perfume.
- Hypothesis 2: Perfume has some effect on emotions for both Chinese and German participants.
- Hypothesis 3: Cultures have an influence on emotional reaction of German and Chinese to odors.

3.2 Participants

Since main objective of the study is to test the measurement of emotional reaction to perfume, only 12 participants are invited, 6 Chinese and 6 Germans. All participants come from similar background (all are engineering students).

Table 1. Demographic information

	Chinese	German
Female	3	3
Average age	22	23.5
Use perfume in daily life	2	2
Use perfume before experiment	4	2
Have a good experience with odor	6	5
Have a bad experience with odor	3	3
Agree people from different culture have different preference to perfume	6	5

3.3 Tasks

Six kinds of perfume are used in the experiment: flower perfume, which are sweet Osmanthus and Violet, fruit perfume, which are Lemon and Apple, and plant perfume, which are Green Tea and Lavender.

3.4 Procedure

The study uses three kinds of measurements: self-reports of subjective experience, FACS, Skin conductance to measure the emotions of different odors. For each participant, the three measurements will be put into effect at the same time. And the perfume will be given to the participant separately according to random order. Skin conductance is recorded when participant sniff the perfume and video record is taken at the same time. After all participants finish sniffing one perfume, we ask them to fill the self-report form. The self-report form composes of four parts, including level of pleasantness, excitement, and suitable for man, and best descriptor to current emotion.

3.5 Data Analysis

Correlation analysis is used for address the relation-ship between emotion and odor. Video is analyzed for FACS analysis. Statistical test will test if there is any difference between German and Chinese in self-rating. Skin reaction results are recorded and for drawing figures to showing cultural differences.

4 Results and Analysis

4.1 Self-report

It is required that participants assess pleasant, exited, and suitable for male using number from 1 to 9 after smelling perfume. 9 means participants are strongly pleasant, strongly exited or most suitable for male.

The difference between Chinese and German is obvious to perfume green tea and lavender given the absolute value difference. Chinese think the lavender's odor is more pleasant than the green tea, but the German have an opposite opinion. For the question 'whether suitable for male use', Chinese give a much lower point than German. But except for this, the difference between the two groups is not obvious.

Table 2. Rating about "pleasant"

	Chinese	German
Sweet Osmanthus	6.6	6.6
Violet	5.8	6.4
Lemon	3.8	4.4
Apple	6	6.6
Green Tea	5.2	7.4
Lavender	6.2	4.8

The difference about "pleasant" between Chinese and German is not obvious to perfume sweet osmanthus, violet, lemon and apple. But for perfume green tea Chinese choose a much lower point and lavender a much higher one. ANOVA test is used to analyze the significance level of the difference between the two groups. From the ANOVA test, the only significant difference between Chinese and German participants is pleasantness to Green Tea. Considering the low number of participants in the ex-periment, attention should be paid to draw a conclusion based on this result.

Table 3. Rating about "excited"

	Chinese	German
Sweet Osmanthus	3.2	4.2
Violet	5.2	4.4
Lemon	4.4	4.6
Apple	3.6	3.2
Green Tea	6	5.8
Lavender	5.4	5.8

With respect to "exited", there are some differences from "pleasant", Chinese give a relative high point to sweet osmanthus and lower point to violet. However, foe the rest perfume, Chinese and German almost give the same assessment.

For whether the perfume is suitable for male or female, the difference is not as obvious as "pleas-ant". For the perfume lavender, Chinese give a point 3.6, which means it's more suitable for female, but German think it is more masculine and give a point 5.6. But there are some perfume which they get a consistent result, like lemon and violet.

Table 4. Rating about "suitable for male"

	Chinese	German
Sweet Osmanthus	3.4	2.6
Violet	3.2	3.6
Lemon	4.8	4.6
Apple	3.2	2.8
Green Tea	4.4	4
Lavender	3.6	5.6

Neither the level of "exited" and "suitable for male" show a statistical difference between German and Chinese.

The personal feeling descriptor about the same perfume is much different between the two groups. There is also something consistent, Sweet Osman-thus for example. There are four persons who used the word "pleasure" in German group, and three in Chinese group. There is some information about the culture related difference. Green tea and lavender for example, for the former perfume German use more optimistic word relatively to Chinese, but for the latter one, Chinese give more positive assessment.

However, because using the adjective to describe the perfume is usually affected by the knowledge of philology and odor experience, more analyses are needed.

On perfume sweet osmanthus and apple there are same number of people who choose it as the one like best. But no Chinese choose lemon and no German choose violet and green tea.

About the "one hate most", two groups have much difference on perfume lavender, little difference on violet and apple. Chinese people like apple's odor than lavender, but opposite for German.

There is not much difference between two groups on the background about odor. About the questions "Whether used perfume before experiment", "Whether have good mood experience with odor" and "Whether agree people from different country have different answer about perfume", there is some difference between two groups, but the different level is very low. Answers' differences on all three questions are only 20%, i.e. 1 person.

In short, for the reaction to perfume there is no obvious difference between German and Chinese. This is not much consistent with our expectations. This may due to the globalized market, which makes people all over the world can use the same product, especially the perfume or other odor related product.

4.2 FACS

The objective of the video analysis is to analyze the participants' emotions, based on the participants' facial expressions.

According to the analysis of the videos, Germans express themselves more easily, and every time they smell an odor there is a positive expression on the face (relaxed or smile), while Chinese don't express any emotions through facial expression.

4.3 Skin Conductance

The values are recorded with 32 Hz, which means 32 values per second. For each second, 32 values were written down. For each second an Average value for this second (Av.) and the deviation within this second among the participants' mean value (Dev.) are generated.

For each participant, rank the perfumes according to their skin conductance from 1 to 6 (1 strongest re-action, 6 weakest reactions). The most intensely emotional reaction is ranked in Table 5.

Table 5. Rank of most intensely reaction in SC

	Chinese	German
1	Sweet Osmanthus	Violet
2	Violet	Sweet Osmanthus
3	Apple	Green Tea
4	Lavender	Lavender
5	Green Tea	Lemon
6	Lemon	Apple

The result indicates that Chinese react more intensively to each odor group (flower +93%, green +49%, fruit +119%).

5 Conclusion and Discussion

Based on the self-report, it seems like that Chinese's favorite odor is Green tea, and German's is Lemon. Excerpt these two odors, both Chinese and German prefer the odor of apple as their favorite. A possible explanation to this result is that different eating habits of two groups lead to the different preference of odor. Chinese drink more green tea in their daily life, and to most Chinese people, they are familiar with the odor of green tea. But to German people, most of them have never taste the green tea.

The video-taping result tells us that Germans ex-press emotion more with face than Chinese. It is well know that Chinese have the personality characteristic of cautiousness. So it is probably that Chinese are more willing to hide their emotions from other people. But the result of skin conductance indicates that actually Chinese participants response much stronger than German participants. So different cultural groups response in different ways to odors, while Germans express more with face, and Chinese ex-press more with body.

From the results, there is no other correlation relationship between favorite smell and body reaction besides some possible relationship between pleasantness and skin conductance. The possible explanation to this is that the sample size is too small to find some significant relationships.

The study has some suggestions to the designer of odor-related products, especially the designer in the international enterprises. First of all, for the widely used products, such as shampoo, soap, it is better to prefer odor of green tea for Chinese customer instead of Lemon. Since many foreign companies usually have same product design as in their own countries, many of these kinds of products like the odor of lemon. Second, it is better to design an odor based on local people's eating habit. Third, if a designer wants to know how Chinese's emotional reaction to the odors, they'd better choose skin conductance as the measurement, and if their target customers are German, they may use video-taping measurement. Anyway, self-report measurement would be a com-plementary alternative. And last, if designer want to know some significant relationship between emotions and odor, a larger size of participants should be invited.

References

1. Field, T., Diego, M., Hernandez-Reif, M., Cisneros, W., Feijo, L., Vera, Y., Gil, K., Grina, D., Claire He, Q.: Lavender Fragrance Cleansing Gel Effects on Relaxation. International Journal of Neuroscience 115(2), 207–222 (2005)
2. Travis, J.: Making sense of scents. Science News 155(15), 236–238 (1999)
3. Axel, R.: The molecular logic of smell. Special Editions 16(3), 68–75 (2006)
4. Milotic, D.: The impact of fragrance on consumer choice. Journal of Consumer Behaviour 3(2), 179–191 (2003)
5. Weber, E.U., Hsee, C.K., Sokolowska, J.: What folklore tells us about risk and risk taking: Cross-cultural comparisons of American, German, and Chinese proverbs. Organizational Behavior and Human Decision Processes 75, 170–186 (1998)

6. Zald, D., Pardo, J.: Emotion, olfaction, and the human amygdala: amygdala activation during aversive olfactory stimulation. Proceedings of the National Academy of Sciences of the United States of America 94(8), 4119 (1997)
7. Miltner, W., Matjak, M., Braun, C., Diekmann, H., Brody, S.: Emotional qualities of odors and their influence on the startle reflex in humans. Psychophysiology 31(1), 107–110 (1994)
8. Hofstede, G.H.: Culture's consequences: International differences in work-related values. Sage Publications, Inc. (1984)
9. Kanzler, S.: Knowledge sharing in heterogeneous collaborations - a longitudinal investigation of a cross-cultural research collaboration in nanoscience. Journal of Business Chemistry (2010)
10. Larsen, R., Fredrickson, B.: 3 Measurement Issues in Emotion Research. Well-being: The Foundations of Hedonic Psychology 40 (2003)
11. Ekman, P., Friesen, W.: Facial action coding system: A technique for the meas-urement of facial movement. Consulting Psychologists Press, Palo Alto (1978)
12. Reed, L., Sayette, M., Cohn, J.: Impact of depression on response to comedy: A dynamic facial coding analysis. Journal of Abnormal Psychology 116(4), 804 (2007)
13. Lints-Martindale, A., Hadjistavropoulos, T., Barber, B., Gibson, S.: A psycho-physical investigation of the Facial Action Coding System as an index of pain variability among older adults with and without Alzheimer's disease. Pain Medicine 8(8), 678–689 (2007)
14. Parr, L., Waller, B., Vick, S., Bard, K.: Classifying chimpanzee facial expressions using muscle action. Emotion (Washington, DC) 7(1), 172 (2007)

Designing "Fashion" into Uniform for Taipei City Public Cleaner Team

Chiui Hsu, An-Feng Zhang, and Robert Chen

Graduate School of Creative Industry Design, National Taiwan University of Arts
Ban Ciao City, Taipei 22058, Taiwan
hsu.chiui@msa.hinet.net, 25154579@qq.com, Rchen1@dmu.sc.uk

Abstract. There are nearly 7,000 street cleaners in Taipei city and their uniform is part of the city color; however, what they wear everyday for work is neither highly impressive nor fully functional. This workwear re-designing project is developed by adopting design thinking as a premise for the improvement of the uniform of Taipei's cleaner team to enhance the overall image and to improve the street cleaners' work efficiency and safety. The project requires involving multiple perspectives and conducting analyses of tremendous amount of data collected through discussions with the citizens from Adaptive City with topics ranging from sustainable environment and public issues to core social values. By integrating design thinking into this project, various perspectives can be introduced while more and more core design values can be verified. In a hope to make design an idea publically recognized and a value widely accepted as well as to highlight everyday aesthetics and quality city life, the study will create comfortable workwear with emblematic color combinations, adopting proper promoting strategies, applying innovative procedures, and eventually refreshing certain specific occupational image.

Keywords: Design thinking, Adaptive City, core design values, Taipei City Public Cleaner Team, innovative procedures.

1 Introduction

As a leading cultural city that offers frequent large-scale exhibitions and commercial activities, Taipei is often the first choice in traveling destination for foreign guests and tourists. With abundant foreign travelers, "a neat city appearance" is often the impression implanted in the minds of the numerous travelers traveling in and out of this city. The maintenance of city appearance and the reason why urban streets and alleys can uphold their cleanness is mainly due to the front line cleaning personnel of the city, who are dedicated diligently to their posts and work hard to maintain a clean environment. In Taipei City, more than 7,000 cleaner team members shuttle between the urban lanes and alleys day and night, while these unsung heroes work hard quietly, their professional work image has yet to be respected by many. Changing the uniform and equipment of the city's cleaner team will indirectly change the impression that a city projects; thinking and implementing the enhancement of the professionals' specialized

P.L.P. Rau (Ed.): CCD/HCII 2014, LNCS 8528, pp. 68–79, 2014.

equipment is an urban action to transform the living environment of Taipei. Considering and implementing design thinking as a premise to seriously improve the overall image of the cleaners and cleaning work of the Taipei City Public Cleaner Team is a positive force in fashion design, with a hope to further enhance city branding of Taipei City through the transformation of costume design.

Yellow is the main color of the Taipei City Public Cleaner Team's original uniform, trolleys, and the body of the garbage truck. The color of the clothing is dark and dull; despite the fact that there were brighter yellow polo shirts between 2007 and 2011, the cleaner team has become invisible in the city considering how Taipei City is flooded with the color yellow (taxis, school buses, and reflective signs etc.) [1] . Furthermore, heavy and bulky cleaning equipment as well as cold and bland cleaning tanks has imperceptibly made the phrases "voiceless, petty, rustic equipment, lack of aesthetics" equivalence of the cleaner team. With an analysis of environmental color, this study intends to explore the core issues of what the cleaner team needs at work through design thinking and from the viewpoint of user needs; with an integration of fashion design and through the image enhancement of the cleaner team uniform design, a modern look for the environment and Taipei City's Cleaner Team will be created.

2 Literature Review

To carry out this study, it is necessary to understand how job uniforms present professional images at work. What are the important needs and what are the functions, safety or technical indicators required? Therefore, literature review includes literatures relevant to the topic, examples of international applications, and practical needs for the design of domestic cleaning personnel's uniforms. Since ancient times, dress codes and provisions are created due to different levels of social status, implying coercion, restriction, and unification as well as a sense of taming through power. Modern workplace also has unified format based on common practice, for example uniforms for cooks, bank tellers, flight attendants, pilots, or business workplace. The uniform itself requires good quality and color; not only can it convey organization image externally, creating benign interaction with external environment, but also internally express a unified spirit of promise and identification. Its function and effectiveness is basically divided into external and internal (Chunmei Chen, 2000). In other words, a person identifies with the various messages delivered by the uniform about the group and activity; it also reflects the spirit of the workers and professionals. For example, when companies require employees to wear uniform to work, once the employees put on the uniform, they immediately realize they are on duty, in their working positions or environment. As social critic Fussell[4]vividly stated in his work Uniforms with deep moral revealing the social language of uniforms; from external and internal point of views, it has the following substantial symbolic meanings: (1) disciplined, integrated, and equal; (2) teamwork and image; (3) shared disgrace and honor, mutually identifying with each other; (4) being in line with the spirit of professional services. Obviously, uniform demonstrates psychological and material need, both in internally and externally. Color, style, and material/texture are the three main elements of costume design. The composition of clothing includes colors, materials, function, structure and aesthetic form (Cheng Lee, An Introduction to Clothing, 2007)[1]; since job uniforms are the clothing for work, the importance of material and function is self-evident, increasing efficiency, cohesion, and protection of job safety. However, different jobs and posts have dissimilar functional requirement for clothing styles. The main concern for the functional design of the style is that the structure of cutting should meet the requirement of the work and environment; it should reflect the features of the job and to accommodate body movements and human factors. Among the many factors, the design shall not go astray from functionality; if the style of the uniform becomes irrelevant to the specific functionality of a certain content, regardless how innovative and outstanding the style is, it may become worthless.

In addition to the above design principles, "A Study of Official Uniform in Taiwan Street Cleaners" (Yuting Tsai, 2008, page 9)[5]points out that government administrative units and systems have their specific image and organizational regulations and requirements which are different from the group uniforms in general private corporation systems; the former has a stronger emphasis on the presentation of government symbols and have certain restrictions on design flexibility and budget. Therefore, as this study focuses on the cleaner team members of Taipei City's Department of Environmental Protection, government budget must be taken into considerations to better meet the requirements of the cleaner team members.

2.1 International Examples

Analyzing the information on official cleaner team websites from foreign countries, the cleaner team uniforms from western countries such as Paris in France, Berlin in Germany, Russia, Copenhagen in Denmark, Barcelona, and London in UK adopt three or more vibrant and eye-catching color combinations. The uniforms have particular emphasis on the use of high-tech standard and safety function materials; the reflective stripe design also complies with the European regulation on safety function. While meeting needs of human nature, the uniforms convey a sense of fashion, bestowing the wearer a professional and confident image as being safe, comfortable, and energetic in their work. Of course, the professional image and appealing appearance presented by the styles of job uniforms will not be homogenous; the overall consideration combines various factors such as color, fabric, function, style, and environment. Uniform design, whether it is the pattern structure or outline detail, affects the aesthetics. Cleaner team uniform reflects not only the beauty of the wearer, but also the beauty of the industry, the environment, and the professional services, causing a high level of impact on the public's perception and self-identification of the workers and professionals.

2.2 Improving the Design Specifications and Requirements of Domestic Cleaner Team Uniform

The design of cleaner team uniform involves factors and constraints from numerous aspects and is in fact a perfection of the innovative design of system engineering. Hence, a better and deeper understanding of the need of the work and the industry will result in a more thoughtful and humane design in the functionality of the clothing. Empirical data from the Taipei City Department of Environmental Protection indicates that cleaners have clearly expressed that the basic requests for the janitorial workwear are comfort, elasticity, and durability. Over the past years, nevertheless, money has been spent on altering the style while the material remains non-sweat absorbent and airtight. Failings such as winter coats being unable to keep warm and leaking raincoats are not improved. The biggest issue in the past is budget constrain, being unable to satisfy the need in material quality for all design items. Related design specifications and requirements that need to be improved are summarized as follows in Table1.

Table 1. Cleaner team uniform enhancement design need

item / Content	**cleaner workwear**	**Work hat**	**Reflective work vest**	**Reflective conical hat**	**Raincoat**
Direction of design	Comfortable, breathable, safe, visually pleasing, and discernable.	Matches the overall design of the work-wear.	Matches the overall design of the work-wear.	The style matches the overall design of the work-wear.	Interweave water-proof reflective cloth and mesh through high frequency provide breathability efficacy.
Design element	Light and compact/with a visual effect of "high efficiency of environment relief"	Matches the overall design of the work-wear.	Matches the overall design of the work-wear/with high visibility of alertness.	Local elements	high visibility of alertness.
Design material	Eco-friendly, recycle, reuse. Alteration of material.	Comply with the material and production standards of European regulation EN471-Class2.	Comply with the material, water-proof, and breathability standards of European regulation EN471-Class2.	Comply with the material, water-proof, and breathability standards of European regulation EN471-Class2.	Enhance durability – water-proof and breathability.
Design colors	Expect low key for the overall color tone; safety concern for the colors.	New adjustments; expect further low key.	Look forward to adjustment.	Look forward to adjustment.	Look forward to adjustment.

Source: Taipei City Department of Environmental Protection(2013)

2.3 Practical Problems and Needs for Cleaner Team Uniform

In terms of empirical experience, cleaners from different categories and nature of work are invited to actually try on the clothes, pants, coats and hats for summer and winter to understand their reaction in the areas of comfort, breathability, stretch and elasticity, washing effect, the position and depth design of the pockets, and straight pants with wide cut to reach a better understanding of the actual issues in wearing and use. The clothing problems and needs from the fitting stage and initial communication and interview with the cleaners since 2012 are organized in Table 2.

Table 2. Practical questions in the cleaner team uniform enhancement design

Safety	Comfort	Function	Material	Image
Move toward safe colors	Poor comfort.	Poor breathability.	Web design material easily gets hooked to other things at work.	Maintain professional image.
Reflective stripes need to meet European regulation	Poor elasticity.	Poor performance in sweat-absorption	Color of the reflective stripe vest fades after cleansing.	Willing to wear tidy uniforms.
Safety level setting for the washing fastness of the reflective stripes.	Heavy clothes; difficult for movements.	Water leaks easily into the cuffs of the raincoat.	Decrease the quantity of workwear offered; increase the material quality of the workwear.	Enhance the environmental quality of the city.
Safe workwear	Unfitting pocket position	Poor friction for the pants	Use of eco-friendly materials	Visually pleasing image

Summarizing the information and data in Tables 1 to 3, the study concludes that safety and comfort are most important in terms of the needs in workwear uniforms. The requirement of the materials mostly include elasticity, moisture wicking, breathability, ability of staying warm, stain proof, and washing fastness; the material must be improved and the focus should be on quality, not quantity. Of course, the overall image must be professional, visually appealing, and being acceptable by the general public. Based on the composition and function of the uniforms as well as the content of improvement requirement, the research information is organized into three main categories including material, appearance, and design as shown in Table 3.

Table 3. Content of the composition and functional requirements of cleaner uniform

Items	Content
Material (function)	1. Comfort / fabric elasticity / breathability / increase the proportion of cotton, cotton 55% and recycled polyester 45% / eco-friendly material 2. Safety technology indicators / color fastness / levels of reflection / certified / washing fastness and durable functional fabric / improvement in technical indicators change in fabric weaving method 3. windproof / warm / water pressure resistant material / wind coats need to be waterproof / coats must be water pressure resistant (2,500 ~ 3,000 mm)
Appearance (cutting)	1. Production method and details of the cuff / pocket size must meet practical needs. 2. Cutting must be suitable for work while being stylish and fashionable. 3. Emphasize tailoring design, quality, comfort, and aesthetics.
Design (direction)	1 Color and image / dyeing requirements / color differential value (Δ E is lower than 2.0) 2. The design must consider functions in wearing and material, tying in wit style and aesthetic features. 3. Reflective stripes, distinguishing colors, safety, and visual image. 4. Workwear for winter or rainy days must be easy to wear and use; must also be stylish with appealing design.

3 Methodology

Based on the above literature and examining through the perspectives of mankind and humanity, design thinking is integrated into the design strategy development for the cleaners' clothing, focusing on the color, material, appearance, and sense of design. Considering the needs of workers as the starting point of fashion design, an in-depth analysis is carried out regarding the cleaner team members' way of work and a discussion is conducted about the clothing needs in different categories of professional cleaners' working environment. The design thinking of the clothing is further discussed, searching for the workers' core need at work and to analyze the environment relationship through the process of exploring the requirement regulation of uniform design and through step by step contemplation of the issues. Through extensive discussion, actual problems are discovered and uniform design needs as well as problems that need to be improved are further understood through inductive analysis by inviting experts and scholars for consultation and related institutions for workshops and seminars. Finally, uniform design strategy that meets the need of human nature and directions as well as methods for improvement can thus be proposed. The implementation sequence is developed based on natural and cultural environment, color and environmental analysis, experience observing, cleaner team work, theme setting, elements, design, graphics, proofing, testing with cleaners participation, and future design plan.

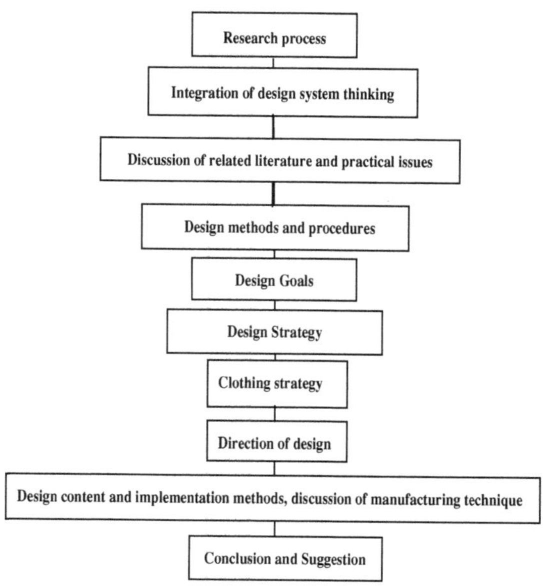

For the Research process from Integration of design system thinking to discussion of related literature and practical issues that includes the analysis of international cases Information collection and integration of workwear design specifications and requirements, then development of design methods and procedures which are observation of experience、design the survey of interdisciplinary experts、workshops and seminars with related institutions. Next on is design goals comply with material improvement, professional image, and acceptance of the general public.

For the design strategy of Color, material and system engineering start from Natural and cultural environment analysis, furthermore experience and observe the work of the cleaner team. Further clothing strategy and direction of design particular emphasis with safe、certified、comfortable、washing fastness and durability、visual image、ppealing appearance and easy to use and wear. The final step of design content and implementation methods, discussion of manufacturing technique are design and implementation, pattern make production, testing and correction, sample production, testing with cleaner involvement and future design and planning.

4 Results and Discussion

4.1 Design Strategy

User-centered core thinking is implemented through design thinking and the perspective of use based on human needs is adopted from the very beginning; through examining the role of material in the work of the cleaner team, systematic design method, steps, and design strategy can thus be induced by discussing the need. Cleaners have responded that while the style has changed each year, the material has not improved; they hope the design this year can satisfy their long existing simple and consistent needs: safe, comfortable, enhancement of moisture wicking function, and significant improvement in the material. The research design goals of this study, therefore, are material improvement, professional image, and acceptance of the general public. Design strategies include color strategy, material strategy, and systems engineering strategy.

Since the current clothing for the cleaners is fairly colorful, it has a lower effect of recognition among the workers and professionals from various fields of work. However, bright colors not only serve an alerting function, they are also used to unify the overall direction of design, design content and method, and investigation of manufacture technique; it can also enhance professional images to become recognizable. Therefore, this study starts with "color and environment"from the very beginning, exploring the safety of "human" at work, exclusive recognition color, professional image, and stylish appearance. For example in Taiwan, postman wears green, police wears blue, and fireman wears orange, showing that recognizable images of colors have a great impact on the image and recognition of workers and professionals. As a result, in order to study the professional image represented by cleaner team members and the hues of workers and professionals in the colors, one must start with the workwear colors to observe the details of human, human in work, as well as human and environment. The color theme is decided by considering various issues including image pictures of the workers/professionals, hues of the workers/professionals, analysis of the workwear colors, workers/professionals and the environment, a comparison of the cleaner uniform's old and new color combination. A polling is thus held to choose between monochrome or two-tone to create the color theme. Two sets of color themes are generated while one will eventually be chosen to be the final dye color for the proofing.

Color Strategy. The color strategy emphasizes safety at work, professional image, and an exclusive color recognition system.

1. To change the current equipment colors of the cleaner team and to propose a new color strategy enabling cleaners to become sparkling embellishments of Taipei to create a fresh and professional image.
2. Seven sets of color combinations are proposed in the workshops based on the principles of high saturation, environment connection, and prevention of similarity with other professions. Two directions of color combination are thus selected as Group A and Group B to match the characteristics of the fabric[Figure1-3]. A meeting is held to determine the final set of color.

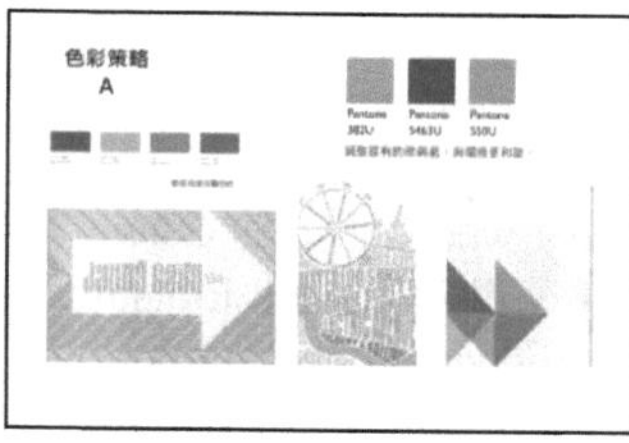

Fig. 1.

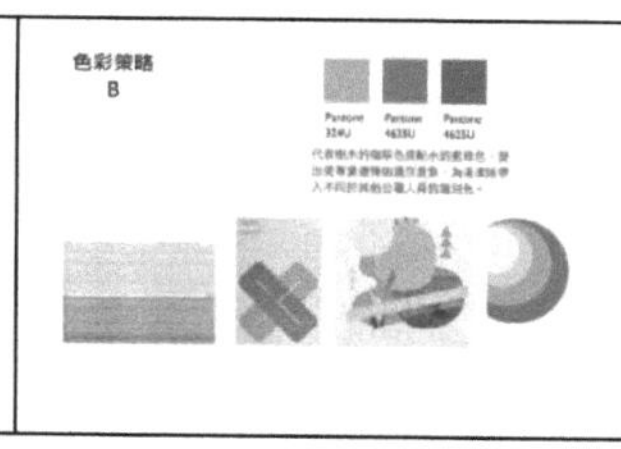

Fig. 2.

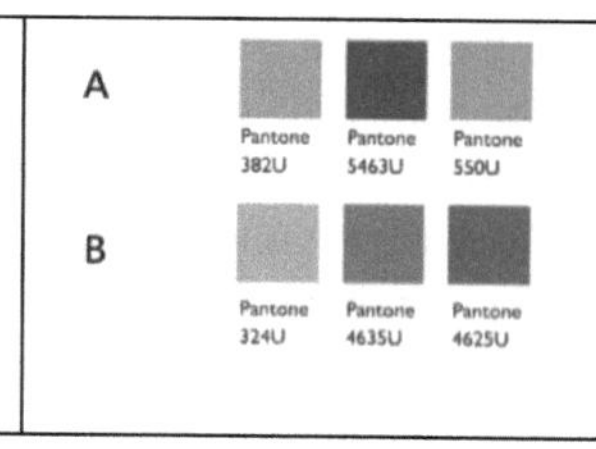

Fig. 3.

Group B is the ultimate selection for color combination and proportion to be used for the dye color and design for the final proofing.

Material Strategy. Next, material strategy, which is choosing eco-friendly, quality, and optimized material and exploring material technique standards and manufacturing technique: considering the role that the material will play in the life of clothing, tactile quality created by the material, possibility of manufacture; the choice of various materials will determine design features and precision, carrying out the purposes of optimization and detailing. In terms of material use such as function, eco-friendliness, specifications, ingredients, or post processing, there will be various technical standards of the needs due to different styles and items.

System Strategy. Systematic design must start from innovative design process: improvement of new product design, improvement of craftsmanship, improvement and functions, materials and organizational improvement, color adjustment, and improvement of working methods. Issues that must be taken seriously not only include color consideration (safety), changing of the material, design and improve perspectives, but also changing of the contract method as well as taking into account the conflict between quality and funding.

Design Strategy. The main focuses of the design strategies include improvement of the material, quality over quantity, and professional image; the main features are eco-friendly,comfortable, safety, and uniqueness; the directions of design include safe, certified, comfortable, wash fastness and durable, visual image, appealing appearance, easy to use and wear. Since the budget for belts is too low and users do not necessarily need it, sleeve covers design that team members often use are thus proposed. A poll is conducted regarding the consideration of quality and quantity and the cleaners' final resolution is to reduce the number of items in order to use quality fabric. The costume design for the cleaners is mainly based on practicality, safety, and comfortable material. Increase of the material durability level brings greater convenience for the cleaner team members at work while extending the length of use. The selected materials are characterized by moisture absorption and wicking which would not become clammy under blazing sun; it conforms to European EN471 safety standard while the overall luminance area of the clothing is increased.

Simplicity is the main focus for the raincoat design and related details include reducing seam lines, two piece clothing, and water proof pockets on the pants. On the other hand, stretch denim will be used for the pants and the problem of shallow pockets will be resolved. The design of the conical hat is planned to be integrated with the work hat; the material will be improved and detachable cloth will be attached to the rear for sun-blocking while the vest will adopt zipper design for easy wearing. It is crucial to design suitable pattern make; a good pattern make and look will influence job safety, efficiency, comfort and aesthetics, it will further have an impact on appearance and fashion image design. Through systematic design thinking, overall professional image building, improvement in clothing function and fashion aesthetics, and a unique sense of professionalism will be generated, in addition to comfort and safety, when cleaners put on their uniforms.

Uniform Design Result for Taipei Cleaners

Table 4. Result of cleaner uniform enhancement design in this study

content / item	ues of practical need for cleaner uniform	Result of cleaner uniform enhancement design	Material and function standard/indicators
Tops	Material needs to be better, breathable and easy to dry is ideal, better in keeping warm, monochrome-based, low-key for a professional presentation, great moisture wicking function, improvement in material quality, material improvement is missing in each year's alteration of style.	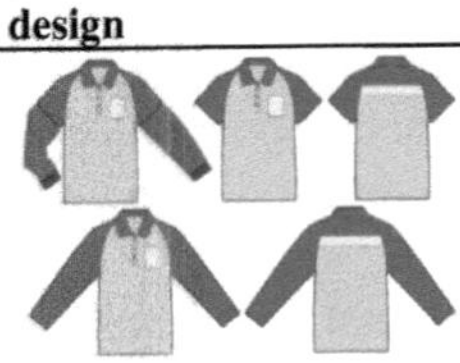	Tops-aquatimo + polyester, Pants-cotton 75%/ T23%/OP2% Moisture absorption, quick-drying, breathable, cool, antibacterial

Table 4. (*continued*)

Pants	Non-elastic material creates inconvenience for movements. The material should be light, be able to keep warm, and easy to clean. The location of the pockets provides low functionality.	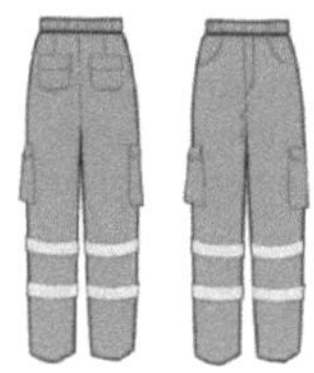	Summer： 93%nylon/7%OP, 210g/y+ European standard reflective stripe Witer: 90%nylon 10% spandex, 216G/M2+ European standard reflective stripe
			Anti-UV, moisture absorption, quick drying, durable, and elasticity.
Coat	Cannot shield against wind, collar get stained easily and is hard to clean, need to be better in keeping warm, the color is too ugly.		Coat + fleece vest 100% polyester, 110g/m2
			Water repellency, windproof, Anti-UV, breathable, quick drying, and light weight.
Wind jacket	The material is waterproof and windproof; can be used as a raincoat if the rain is not too heavy, need to be warm, tend to be heavy in weight.		100% polyester, 110g/m2
			Water repellency, windproof, anti-UV, breathable, quick drying, light in weight.
Raincoat	one-piece is suggested which makes it easier to put on and take off when it is warm sweeping, breathable material is crucial, waterproof tapes fall off extremely easily, prevent water seepage, high-frequency sealing should be used.		Raincoat-water pressure 3000mm, poly-500x94/200Dx200D
			Windproof, waterproof, breathable, durable.
Reflective vest	Bad pattern make, Velcro or front-opening are better, adjust the vests to fit better	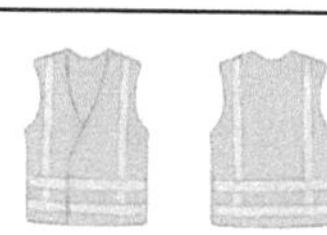	100%polyester, 150g/y
			breathable, lightweight, non-absorbent, high visibility, Level EN471-2
Work hat	Breathable is crucial, the brim of conical hats can be bigger and wider, girth/size of head need to be adjustable.		100%nylon,155g/m2, 5000mm+5000g/m2
			Waterproof, breathable
Gloves	None		92% aquatimo, 8%OP
			Elastic, anti-UV, breathable

Table 4. (*continued*)

Additional notes for clothing	The emphasis should be on quality, not quantity; the clothing should be durable and practical; material selected should be non-shrinking; allowing team members to have suitable sizes.	1. Insulation feature meets the standard of FTTS-FA-010 TYPE A infrared textiles. 2. Moisture absorption, wicking, and quick-drying features meet the standard of FTTS-FA-004. 3. Cool feeling features qualifies for FTTS-FA-019 Instant 4. Cool feeling textile standard (heat flow ≧ 0.14) 5. Wet and dry friction: level 4 6. Water repellency meets the standard of FTTS-FA-011 7. Water repellency textiles standard (Level 80). 8. Anti-UV features matches FTTS-FA-008 9. UV textile standard (level C) 10. Raincoat - pressure 3000mm, poly 500x94 / 200Dx200D **Improvement of material; focus on quality, not quantity; professional image.**
In terms of proofing, the priority can be given to the actual color and material, proving an authentic experience for the judges, team members, and the general public.		

The most important segment in design enhancement is the improvement of the janitorial uniforms' material perception. Unlike designs in the past which have a tendency of being restricted by budget concern, the proposed design puts a stronger emphasis on functionality and comfort. The environment and four seasons of Taiwan are characterized by hot and steamy summers and cold and damp winters, which are greatly different from Western countries. In terms of design, clothing details include detachable sleeves, sun-blocking equipment, the combination of wind jacket and coat, and removable inner-layer fleece vests. The tailoring takes into consideration mid-age body shape and the average size of the cleaners with matching overall color scheme Large quantity of cheap outfit was purchased in the past; this study hopes that the current funding can be used for texture quality improvement, comfort, and convenience, lowering the replacement rate. The study hopes to resolve the problems in clothing material, being unable to absorb sweat and keep warm, as well as worksite danger resulting from non-fitting and unsuitable clothing. Cleaner team members have long criticized how Taipei citizens seem to ignore their existence, through design enhancement, the public's perspective of seeing Taipei City Public Cleaner Team as social minority is expected to change.

5 Conclusion and Suggestion

Through material technique indicators and discussion of manufacturing technique, this study hopes to contribute to creating the connection between design and industry. The study has conducted several practical wearing experiences to explore the actual needs, also creating innovative stylish feeling generated by the need from empirical design. In the process, testing experience specifically enhanced the interaction and communication between the government and the general public. Cleaner team is like a city business card, becoming an image of city branding; fresh and energetic, the new image of the uniform will improve the look of the cityscape, increasing work efficiency, winning and creating stronger sense of self-identification of the cleaners in the workplace.

In the past, the budget for each cleaner was NT$3,600, which was for ten items of equipment including summer tops and pants, coats, wind jacket. This situation of having numerous items of low quality has long been criticized by the cleaner team. In this design project, from the discussion of materials and manufacturing technique, initial patterns make design **to** sample production as well as testing and revision, not only cleaners are arranged to participate in the actual testing experience, the general public are also invited to try out the clothing and join the experience. Most people agree and identity with the color scheme, green hills and blue waters, emerald blue lakes, and earth tone colors are preferred combinations of the general public. However, some people suggested that the main color light turquoise get stained easily. Considering the fact that the cleaner team spend long hours outdoor with trash and dirt, the clothing material must be cleaned easily while demonstrating water fastness and durability. Regarding this problem, the percentage of blue in light turquoise will be raised while increasing the evaluation technical indicators. The overall costume design has gained great acceptance and identification among the cleaner team. Finally, everyone reached a resolution to choose quality over quantity: reduce the number of items and use the best, more durable, and safer quality material. This will not only present and deliver a professional image of the workers and professionals as well as a sense of fashion aesthetics, but the durability, comfort, and popularity of the great design and quality will reduce unnecessary waste of resources in changing the workwear every year. This study suggests fulfilling the expectation of apparel change for all members in the future. In terms of purchase strategy, two-year budget can be adopted to gather enough fund to purchase great quality and design, this is also the most expected positive impact in the integration of design thinking into government policy.

References

1. Lee, C.: An Introduction to Clothing. China Textile Press (2007)
2. Chunmei: Taiwan uniform design and practice groups to explore (1994-1999). Produced the next century Textiles and Clothing education and re search and development. In: Proceedings of the International Symposium, Taipei, pp. 175–199. School of Fu Jen Catholic University, Institute of live lihood fabric (2000)
3. Ashin Translate. Paul Fussell, Uniforms Rye, Field Publishing (2004), http://www.books.com.tw/exep/prod/booksfile.php?item=0010272347
4. Tsai, Y.: A Study of Official Uniform in Taiwan Street Cleaners for example, p. 9. Shuter Design Institute of Applied Science and Technology (2008)
5. Source: Taipei City Department of Environmental Protection (2011)
6. Taipei City Cleaner uniform enhancement design team (2012)

Research on the Extraction and Visualization of Automobile Brand Form Gene Based on Multi-roles' Expectation Image

Weifeng Hu [1,2,*], Xiangyang Xin[1], and Binbin Li[1]

[1] School of Design, Jiangnan University, Wuxi, China
[2]State Key Laboratory of Advanced Design and Manufacture for Automobile Body, Hunan University, Changsha, China
hwf1979@163.com

Abstract. The extraction and visualization of automobile brand form gene based on multi-roles' expectation image was studied from the brand form feature and brand semantic feature two aspects. Using the protocol analysis, interview method and sketch analysis, the automobile brand form genes were extracted from users, automobile form designers and enterprise related personnel. Then the automobile brand form genes were visualized and quantitative described through the Bezier splines, mood board and semantic differential method. Finally, taking the Kia automobile as an example, the method was proved to be rational and feasible.

Keywords: Automobile styling, Brand Form Gene, multi-roles' Expectation Image, Visualization.

1 Introduction

With the market competition and anabatic technological homogeneity, brand has already been separated from the "trademark" function that is for product differentiation and become a powerful weapon of enterprise competition. As the bridge between enterprise and consumer, product is the important express of enterprise brand image, which accurately reflect the meaning of brand. As to some famous transnational corporations, their product form could maintain good brand recognition in spite of the frequent change of product. Thus, these products could enjoy market supremacy. Though many Chinese enterprises have been aware of the importance of brand, they generally focused on brand awareness, but not the build of product brand image. As a result, their products, especially automobile, lack distinct brand identity and enough competitive power in market [1,2].

Product brand form gene has gradually become an important research area in the study of product design and enterprise brand image. In the world, some researches obtained the brand form genes and studied their continuity based on Shape Grammar,

* Corresponding author.

P.L.P. Rau (Ed.): CCD/HCII 2014, LNCS 8528, pp. 80–88, 2014.

Product Semantics, cognitive psychology, Visual decomposition and so on. Interiorly, some researchers studied the extraction and visualization of brand form gene, heredity and variation, evolutionary trend and so on. However, some questions were arose in these researches as following: (1) lack the researches about the relationship between product brand form gene and relative roles such as consumer, relevant personnel of enterprises, designer and so on. That is mean we can not express the correlation between product brand gene and people's emotion, aesthetic and value. (2) Most of the current researches are focused on visual character and have no enough attention on brand image based on semantics. Besides, we can not efficiently visualization of product brand form gene. Therefore, this study put forward a method of extraction and visualization of automobile brand form gene based on multi-role's exception image.

2 Product Brand Form Gene

Gene is the nucleic acid fragment containing specific genetic function. Through gene recombination and mutation, organisms continuously evolution and then obtain the stronger ability to adapt to the external environment. The similar idea of evolution is also existed in product form design. Product form gene constantly interacts with design scenario or product environment, which result in the evolution of product to proper form. The repeated application of "basic form" during the process of form evolution was the same as genetic and these basic forms are considered as vocabulary of design elements. The expression of genetic characteristics of vocabulary of design elements is product form gene. Brand form genes are ones closely related with product brand. They are defined as the expression of minimum knowledge granularity of unique characteristics about brand impression. Brand form gene constantly changed along with time and product variation. The brand image is gradually formed through continuously emphasized and repeated of some product brand form genes in different time and on different product form [3,4,5]. For example, automobile form includes lamp, grille, side profile and so on. The continuously strengthened and repeated application of shield grille and round asymmetric vehicle logo in different time and on different automobile form result in the formation of unique brand image of Alfa Romeo (Fig. 1) [6].

Fig. 1. Brand form gene of Alfa Romeo automobile

Brand form feature is defined as the form feature that correlated with brand and it is the visible entities of brand form gene. Automobile brand form feature is the assemblage of many specific Automobile form characteristics that accumulated for a long time in Automobile enterprise. These characteristics include the unique form elements about brand and their evolution process. The extraction of Automobile brand form feature is the collation and mining of enterprise brand and the process of systematically cognitive enterprise brand. Automobile brand form feature can be separated into brand form feature dots, brand form feature lines, brand form feature surfaces. As to the expression of form, though dots are important, they are not plenitudinous. Though surfaces can express all contents of form, they are too complex to express. Lines are origin from dots and can compose surfaces, thus brand form feature lines are proper objects to study brand form feature [7].

The transfer of product brand image is not only through product form, but also through the semantic description and emotional cognition. Semantic has rich connotation and a large amount of information. If they are extracted from different conditions, the information are much more broad. Some semantic features are used to describe the connotation of the brand and highlight the characteristics of the brand. They are defined as semantic features. Automobile brand semantic feature is the Automobile enterprises' core values, the unique brand concept and feature and sublimation of enterprise culture. In this study, brand semantic feature is expressed by semantic vocabulary.

As the product brand cognitive method, brand semantic features and brand from features are correlated. Through the combination of automobile brand form and semantic features, their extraction and expression is very important to automobile brand form management and can provide brand form standard for automobile form innovation and differential design. Finally their extraction and expression is useful to establish automobile form brand spectrum management system.

3 Extraction of Brand Form Gene

3.1 Extraction of Automobile Brand Form Feature

Extraction of automobile brand form feature can provide original data for automobile brand management system establishment. The analysis and refine of brand form feature for main products belong to the same brand is the expression process through standard graphic for brand form elements. Due to the differences of cognition of different roles for product brand features, it's necessary to extract the product brand form feature based on multi-role.

Designers focus on professional analysis of automobile form design. They extract automobile brand form feature based on their expertise including cognitive experiment, protocol analysis [8] and so on. During the experiment, designers are required to report their analysis and thinking process according to the characteristics and requirements of the problem when they are designing the automobile form. The researchers will record and videotape these oral reports and then detailedly analyze them to obtain the information on designers' cognitive activity.

The related roles in enterprise mainly include enterprise managers and salesman. They have different understanding and describing on enterprise culture, brand concept and product positioning. The extraction of brand form feature of these people should use interview and sketch analysis method.

The preference and view of consumers on product form directly determine the competition ability of product in market. Therefore, the extraction and expression of product brand form gene must pay full attention to consumers. The extraction of automobile brand form feature based on consumers is mainly through questionnaire survey.

3.2 Extraction of Automobile Brand Semantic Feature

Form semantic feature is always expressed through language description [9]. In this study, the extraction of automobile brand semantic feature from the following aspects: linguistics, user, enterprise and designer (Fig. 2).

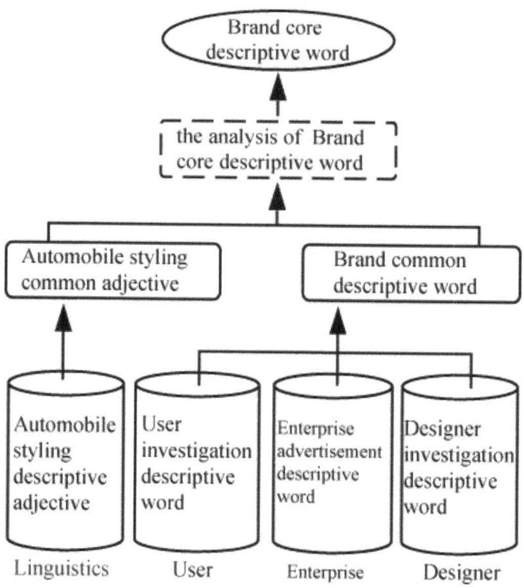

Fig. 2. Process of extracting product brand semantic feature

Linguistics: The adjective words are obtained through literature survey based on Osgood' Semantic Differential Method. The etymology is generally required wide enough to ensure comprehensively sample in the domain semantic space. Then through a series of filter mechanisms, those redundancy and repeated adjectives information in semantic space are cut and filtered. Finally, through the survey of enterprise related people, designers and consumers, the proper adjectives to describe Automobile form are obtained.

User: the practical and open questionnaire survey that carried on typical user will guide them describe the knowledge and experience about product brand, evaluation and recommendations on product form, the use experience and so on. Then through a series of frequency statistics, the brand semantic description vocabularies are obtained.

Enterprise: Through the interview of enterprise managers, salesman and so on, the understanding and experience of enterprise on brand semantic feature are obtained. In addition, the advertising languages of product should also be studied to obtain the relative brand semantic feature.

Designer: A number of designers with more than five years of automobile design experience are selected to carry out experts' interview and focus group discussion. Then through a series of statistic analysis, the brand semantic vocabularies based on designer are obtained.

4 Visualization of Brand Form Gene

Visual information and language information plays similar important role in identifying and remember product form. Combine these information and make consumer having stable memory form of product brand gene will greatly improve the cognitive efficiency of automobile brand form. Therefore, it's necessary to visualization of brand form gene.

4.1 Visualization of Brand Form Feature

In this study the visualization of brand form feature is carried out through the geometrical description of form feature lines. Because the automobile brand form feature lines are always free curves, the geometrical description can be summarized into several continuous segments l and their positions and attribute relationships. For example, automobile profile (E1E2E3) can be expressed as:

$$E_1E_2E_3=\{l(1,2), l(2,3),\ldots, l(n,1)\} \tag{1}$$

The segment l can be expressed by the anchor point p and control point c of this curve. As following:

$$l(i,j) = (p_i, p_i, c_{i,j}) \tag{2}$$

Because of most automobile form feature lines are smooth, so the form feature lines could be fitted through the Bezier Splines' construction and transformed into feature lines genotypes composed of the feature points' coordinates. The expression of Bezier Splines as following:

$$B(t) = (1-t)^2P_0 + 2t(1-t)P_1 + t^2P_2\ ,\ t\epsilon[0,1] \tag{3}$$

Taking the side profile (E1, E2, E3) as an example, the gene elements of form feature lines are divided into two sorts: anchor point (marked with P_i, i=1, 2…n) and control point (marked with C_i, i=1, 2…n). The side profile genotypes are expressed through the combination of two gene elements (Fig. 3).

4.2 Visualization of Brand Semantic Feature

The visualization of brand semantic feature focuses on the scenario visualization of vocabulary and the establishment of semantic space.

The brand semantic adjectives are reflected on a psychological scale through Osgood semantic differential method. Then the brand semantic space is established and it is accurately location. Figure 4 shows the 7 points scale of brand semantic adjective "simple-complex". The adjective is divided into seven grades and the each grade is value assignment.

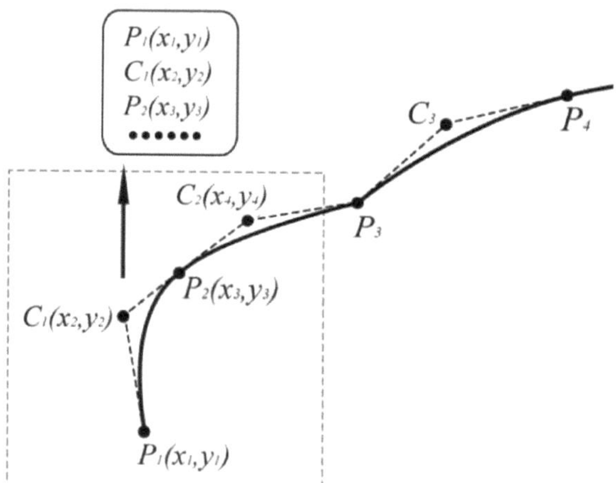

Fig. 3. Side profile (E1, E2, E3) and its expression of Bezier Splines

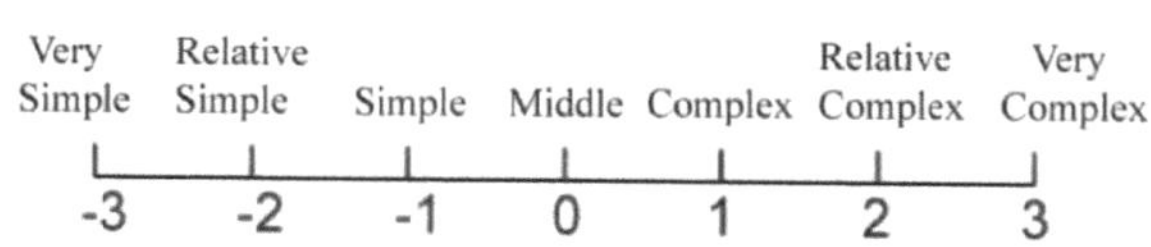

Fig. 4. 7 points scale of brand semantic adjective "simple-complex"

Semantic expression refers to the language description of objects in specific condition and environment. Out of scenario, the rich of semantics will result in the fuzzy and uncertain of describing objects. The establishment of proper scenario will guide the process of design. The Mood Board is usually used to establish the scenario. In this study, as a tool of semantic feature visualization, the Mood Board is adopted to establish the brand visual scenario space.

5 Case Study

Taking Kia as an example, the brand form genes were extracted and visualized in this study.

5.1 Extraction of Kia Brand Form Feature

During the extraction of Kia feature lines, the expert samples were used to reduce the sample volume and obtain more effective data. In this study, seven designers who have more than five years experience in industrial design and participated in at least one actual automobile design project were selected to extract and analyze the features of four main automobiles of Kia (K2, K5, K7 and Sportage-R).

The First Phase: The automobiles were expressed through sketches which should be accurate and the number was not limited.

The Second Phase: Designers began to carry out the concept design according to the demand of Kia automobile. These concept designs were expressed through sketches that should be clearly enough to reflect the design concept. The main descriptions of design concept should be noted and explained on the sketches.

The Last Phase: Designers were demanded to extract the brand form feature lines according to the sketches draw in the above two phases (Fig. 5)

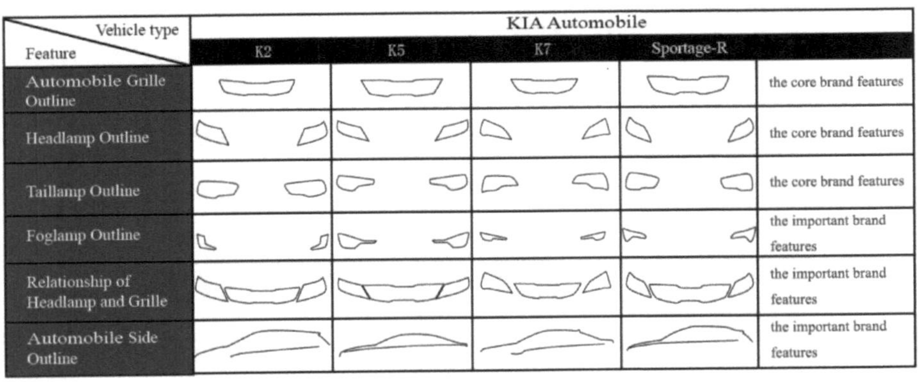

Fig. 5. Extraction of some brand form feature lines of Kia automobile

Because designers have deep understanding on automobile form, the feature lines extracted by them would be highly summarized and accurate. Then the data loss would be small during the automobile form transform. However, due to the lack of deep understanding of automobile brand and market location, these feature lines extracted by designers were one-sided. Thus, enterprise related people and consumers all should participate in the extraction. In this study, 15 staff (managers and salesman) from Kia and 30 users were selected to participate in this experiment through interview and sketch analysis method. The content of interview include: (1) the brand image of Kia; (2) the brand planning and location of Kia. The content of sketch analysis include: (1) find the most marked and continuous form features on the sketches; (2) find the form elements that could reflect the brand form feature of Kia; (2) summarize the change trend of Kia automobile form.

Based on the above experiments' results, the brand form features of Kia automobile could be summarized as follows: the whole vehicle body is smooth, slightly hale and full of change; the " tiger growl" form of grille; the grille and headlamp shape are matched that reflect the meaning of bird fly.

Through analysis the core brand features of Kia automobile were separated into: (1) the "tiger growl" feature of grille; (2) the sharp feature of headlamp and taillamp. The important brand features include: (1) the overall body feature is smooth, slightly hale and full of change; (2) the grille and headlamp shape are matched that reflect the meaning of bird fly; (3) the "water ladle" form of foglamp (Fig. 5).

5.2 Extraction of Kia Automobile Brand Semantic Feature

Linguistics: Thirty objectives generally used to descript Automobile form extracted by State Key Laboratory of Advanced Design and Manufacture for automobile Body in Hunan university were selected as the semantic pool[10].

User: The surveys were carried out on thirty users of Kia automobile to obtain their description of brand semantic feature of Kia automobile. These descriptions were further recognized and recorded as electronic document and the descript objects were noted to help the following statistics.

Enterprise: According to the interview results of enterprise managers and salesman, the analysis of review of Kia automobile and TV advertising language, the Kia brand descript adjectives were extracted.

Designer: Through the interview of seven experts, the Kia brand was described. Then the word frequency statistics and cluster analysis were carried out to obtain the key semantic adjectives on Kia brand.

After the above extraction work, the three levels of Kia brand semantic features and their corresponding adjectives are summarized as following:

Key adjectives (2): cool, athletic

Brand adjectives (3): generous, hale, fluency;

Common adjectives (18): strict-loose, stable-movement, rational-perceptual, rough-exquisite, straight-curved, concrete-abstract, simple-luxury, unified- opposite, hard-soft, commercial-leisure, conservative-faddish, porcelain-impolite, elegant- luxuriant, complex-simple, friendly- aggressive, decent-delicate, harmonious- contradictory, biting-gentle.

Using design Mood Board, the semantic adjectives was transformed into the visualized tool aiding brand design management. In the core semantic Mood Board, the key semantic words and the synonyms were correlated, the concept of adjectives were explained, and the related pictures were insert to form semantic situations space. In addition, the corresponding brand form features of semantic features were also list and described in order to assist the following form design and brand management.The situations expression of common adjectives is actually a scaling relation of form image in automobile form design practice. Therefore, in the construction of the semantic Mood Board, the addition of psychological scale of semantic adjectives more accurately aided designers locate the brand form semantic space.

6 Conclusion

In the present study, the concept of product brand form gene was introduced and the extraction and visualization of automobile brand form gene based on multi-roles' expectation image were developed. In the case of Kia automobile, the method was proved to be feasible and reasonable, which would help designers more accurately locating the brand form semantic space.

Acknowledgements. This work was financially supported by the National Social Science Fund (12BG055), the open research fund program of the state key laboratory of advanced design and manufacturing for vehicle body (31115018), Ministry of Education in China project of humanities and social sciences (11YJCZH063) and the Fundamental Research Funds for the Central Universities (JUSRP11246).

References

1. Yang, Y., Lei, T., Pan, Y.: Product identity, a new method in user-centered design acitivty. China Mechanical Engineering 17, 1105–1109 (2006) (in Chinese)
2. McCormack, J.P., Cagan, J.: Speaking the Buick language: capturing, understanding,and exploring brand identity with shape grammars. Design Studies 25, 1–29 (2004)
3. Yang, Y., Zhang, Y.: Research on Personalized Form Design Based on Product Brand Characteristics Family. China Mechanical Engineering 20, 460–466 (2009) (in Chinese)
4. Zhang, W., Zhao, J.: Study on Audi Brand Form Gene. Packaging Engineering 28, 84–86 (2007) (in Chinese)
5. Sun, S., Bao, E., Pan, Y.: Component feature model for product layout design. Journal of Computer-Aided Design & Computer Graphics 11, 28–32 (1999) (in Chinese)
6. Zhao, D., He, R.: Brand Styling and Feature Research of Alfa Romeo. Art & Design 219, 72–74 (2011) (in Chinese)
7. Hu, W., Zhao, J., Zhao, D.: Study on Styling Image of Vehicle Based on Form Feature Lines. China Mechanical Engineering 20, 496–500 (2009) (in Chinese)
8. Van Someren, M.W.: The Think Aloud Method: A Practical Guide to Modeling Cognitive Processes. The Academic Press, London (1994) (in Chinese)
9. Tan, H., Zhao, J., Zhao, D.: Construction and Application of the Quantitative Model of Automobile Form Features. Journal of Hunan University (Natural Sciences) 36, 27–31 (2009) (in Chinese)
10. Zhu, Y.: Semantic Study on Automobile Form and Design Process Configuration. Hunan University, ChangSha (2009)

EEG-Based Measurement of Emotion Induced by Mode, Rhythm, and MV of Chinese Pop Music

Mao Mao[1] and Pei-Luen Patrick Rau[2]

[1] Department of Psychology, University of Cambridge, Cambridge CB2 3EB, United Kingdom
mm992@cam.ac.uk

[2] Department of Industrial Engineering, Tsinghua University, Beijing 100084, P.R. China
rpl@tsinghua.edu.cn

Abstract. This present study aims to gain insights of how listeners feel about Chinese pop music and music video (MV) by examining music-induced emotion through subjective, physiological and regional brain activation measurement. This study focused on how the following aspects influence emotion: a) mode (major, minor, pentatonic), b) rhythm (firm vs. flowing), c) MV (narrative, live performance, parody). The results suggest that Chinese traditional pentatonic mode elicits sublime feelings, corresponding to lower HRV and less frontal-parietal beta power difference. Emotion elicited by major/minor mode is predictable according to discovered mode-emotion pattern from previous studies. As for the effect of MV on emotion, previous studies concerning emotion induced by narrative and live performance MV can be extended to Chinese pop MV. Extreme positive emotion and corresponded beta power spectrum are distinctive emotion cues for parody MVs. We also noted that firm rhythm in Chinese pop music is associated with high arousal level, while flowing rhythm may induce sublime feelings. This study indicates that musical features (audio) and music video styles (visual) in Chinese pop music can elicit different emotions. Emotion measures such as psychological ratings, HRV and EEG power spectral analysis should be comprehensively considered when interpreting listeners' emotion.

Keywords: Chinese pop music, emotion, music video, EEG, measurement.

1 Introduction

Past and recent studies, with psychological and neurological evidences, show that musical features (e.g., mode, rhythm, tempo, melody, harmony) as well as music-related visual stimuli (e.g., video, performance) can elicit different felt emotions (emotion induced by music). Mode, also termed scale, is an ordered series of single pitches up or down stepwise [1]. Mode plays a crucial role in expressing musical emotion and inducing emotion among listeners. Researchers focusing on Western music have made an agreement on mode that it distinguishes between positive and

P.L.P. Rau (Ed.): CCD/HCII 2014, LNCS 8528, pp. 89–100, 2014.

negative musical excerpts [2]. Pentatonic mode, as one of the traditional Chinese musical styles existing in ancient Chinese music and folk songs, is becoming increasingly popular in pop music. Different from major and minor modes (also termed heptatonic mode) that are widely used in western classical music, pentatonic mode is defined as "a musical mode with five notes per octave". Clinically, pentatonic music is mostly used in music therapy to approach a concordant status [3, 4]. The relation between major/minor mode and felt emotion has been explored in a myriad of studies, and the basic connection between major/minor mode and human emotion is widely accepted in both academia and music field. On the contrary, few studies ever paid attention to how pentatonic mode in pop music induces emotion, thus left the question why Chinese pop music with traditional Chinese musical features became a hit unanswered. This unique characteristic of Chinese pop music is worth studying not only because of the large potential market share and loyalty, but also because of their value in interpreting the popularity of Chinese pop music with traditional elements.

Rhythm, the primary element of all music [5], is defined as a serial figure based on an arrangement of discrete time intervals [6]. Gabrielsson made a relatively comprehensive understanding of rhythmic experience, indicating that emotion is one of the major effects of rhythm in human perception and cognition [7]. Unlike mode, the effects of rhythm on listeners' felt emotion in Western music are generally accepted among researchers and musicians. Moreover, rhythmic aspects are the major determinants of physiological response to music [2]. Chinese pop music inherits many modern, imported rhythmic styles like R&B, ballads, pop and rock. However, it is unclear that how rhythm inherited from worldwide popular music is felt in Chinese pop music.

Assisting the thriving popularity of Chinese pop music, MV (music video) is initially used as the promotion of music sale. MV can induce strong emotional response in a short period, and it incorporates various art forms (e.g., video, movie, advertisement) to attract audience. As videocassette recorders and karaoke equipment became common to spread cultural products widely, MV in Chinese pop music made its original form as demonstration tapes (with singers in addition to back-up music and on-screen lyrics) played in karaoke bars (KTV) [8]. Later, films, soap operas, as well as concerts and performances have been added into music videos to attract consumers. In 2000, Malaysian Chinese artist Fish Leong's music video "Courage" was rated as the most popular KTV. One of the major contributions to her success is the proper use of narrative stories in MVs. Another global success—Gangnam style from the rapper PSY—combines western rhythm and the intriguing "horse riding move" perfectly together, making it the most "viral" MV around the world. When interpreting this, psychological researchers found that activated emotional responses induced by music helps to improve users' sharing willingness of pieces like Gangnam Style [9]. While a wealth of studies concerning world popular MV have been exploring the effect of MV type (e.g., MV with films, live performance) on listeners' emotion, most of the results related to Chinese pop MV are descriptive and qualitative. Additionally, questions involving emotion still remain: How different types of MV influence human emotion? Can human emotion be measured and quantified for better understanding?

Music is always perceived as the expression of emotions (perceived emotion); and it induces listeners' felt emotion and emotional activations of central and peripheral physiological and psychological systems [10]. Numerous studies have provided insights into the psychological, physiological and neural basis of emotion induced by music. Researchers figured out four major groups of factors influencing emotion: musical elements (e.g., rhythm, tempo, pitch, mode and harmony), individual factors (e.g., musical expertise, personality traits, motivation), performance and outer environment. Most existing studies have been around western classical music, while music from other cultures, especially pop music, has been left fairly untouched. In addition, except for some widely agreed features (e.g., tempo, rhythm), the majority of research concerning this issue presents obvious inconsistency, and most manipulation of this area is still exploratory [5].

In the present study, we focus on three music-related features, namely mode, rhythm and MV and their impacts on emotion in a scope of Chinese pop music. We adopt a multimodal emotion measurement including self-report, EEG and physiological aspects to examine emotion. Our findings would suggest implications for musical service design. The rest of the paper is organized as follows: first, we define the scope of musical features related to human emotion; second, we present the first study that explore how musical features influence human emotion; third, we introduce another study focused on MV and emotion; fourth, results of the two studies is discussed.

2 Theoretical Foundation

2.1 Musical Features and Emotion

There are a myriad of studies aiming at exploring how major/minor mode evokes emotion. Major mode may be associated with emotions that are happy, graceful, serene, while minor mode may sound dreamy, dignified, tension, disgust or anger [6]. While prior studies have identified basic emotional expression pattern of major and minor mode, the question whether pentatonic mode induces specific emotion is unknown. Hence, we introduce pentatonic mode into this study, in order to figure out the relationship between mode and its induced emotion. However, mode is not a necessary condition for felt emotion, and the basic major-happy and minor-sad pattern could be overruled with other musical features like tempo [6].

The connection between rhythm and perceptual process has been discussed psychologically and musically for a long time. In Juslin's studies on specific mechanisms that mediate emotion in musical events, rhythm plays an important role in cueing music-induced emotion [10, 11]. Researchers found that music with strong pulse and tempo may help to 'drive' the pulse [10]. This is because the external rhythm of music influences some internal body rhythm of people (e.g., heart rate, respiration), so that the inner rhythm adjusts toward and finally coincides with the musical rhythm [11]. Scholars tended to divide the motion of rhythm into firm (the rhythm proceeds in a averaged and stable pattern with full chord or drumbeats on every beat) and flowing (the rhythm is in a more smooth and flowing motion such as syncopating rhythm and pickup bars), in order to explore the relationship between rhythm and emotion evoked. Hevner claimed that firm rhythm was associated with adjectives of emotion such as dignified and vigorous, while flowing rhythm represented the feelings of happy, playful and sprightly [12]. Gomez and Danuser (2007) explored physiological aspects of emotion and rhythm, claiming that rhythmic factors were the major determinants of physiological responses to music, and firm rhythm with accentuated and staccato beats were most strongly correlated with these emotional responses (e.g., higher skin conductance) [2].

It is noteworthy that music selection in previous studies was not homogenous, and it is not proper to merely apply existing findings in Western classical music into Chinese pop music. Hence, this study aims at verifying the effect of mode and rhythm on felt emotion of Chinese pop music, and the interaction effects of the two features. The findings will thus provide concrete implications for musical services in the market of Chinese pop music.

2.2 Music Video (MV) and Emotion

In the realm of art and business, music is always accompanied by visual contents such as film, MTV (Music Television), advertisement, game and live performance, etc., and is becoming a separate genre of pop music industry. With the help of various film techniques such as lighting, visual effects and editing, music video is capable to evoke strong feelings in a short period of time. A large body of literature on music video exists in film and advertising research, and the conclusive result is that including visual information into musical stimuli enhances the emotional experience and positive evaluation of music [13]. Additionally, different types of MV have been studied. Hall et al. found that young people prefer MVs that emphasize storyline and visual imagery that aids in interpreting the lyrics. Geringer et al. [14] compared the emotion induced by *Beethoven's Symphony No. 6 in F major* accompanied by live symphony performance and film excerpt of the Disney movie *'Fantasia'* respectively, concluding that users in the film group presented higher emotional ratings on the music, while users in the symphony performance group had lower emotional ratings but higher cognitive performance. This finding was in line with the idea of Elaboration Likelihood Model (ELM), which was raised in 1999 by Petty and Wegner [15]: MV can enhance the likelihood of central route processing if the participant is motivated to understand the conveyed information. However, animated and narrative videos increase emotional responses and positive ratings.

Emotion has been emphasized in studies of music videos. It is found that the relation between emotion and virality is about more than just valence, and emotional arousal drives social transmission [9]. Based on corresponding research in advertisement and film, this present study aims to examine how the three types of Chinese pop MV: narrative, live performance and parody influence human emotion.

3 Study 1: Music and Emotion

3.1 Methodology

Participants. Twelve healthy students (7 males; 21-24 years old; mean age=23.1) at both undergraduate and graduate levels were recruited in a Chinese university. All participants were right-handed, free of past and present neurological or psychiatric conditions. We did not choose left-handed individuals because they may differ in hemispheric specialization for emotion [16]. Written informed consent was obtained from each participant before the formal experiment.

Experimental Design and Stimuli. We performed within-subject design in this study, in which two independent variables were included: mode (major, minor, and pentatonic) and rhythm (firm vs. flowing). Additionally, six music excerpts were selected from the top charts of Chinese pop music in recent thirty years. Musical stimuli were determined according to six treatments comprised by the independent variables: major-firm (*Red Sun* from Hacken Lee Hak Han); major-flowing (*Is It True* from Julie Su); minor-firm (*If This Is Not Love* from Jacky Cheung); minor-flowing (*Shan Zha Shu* from Shilei Chang); pentatonic-firm (*Pu Sa Man* performed by Huan Liu); and pentatonic-flowing (*Hong Yan* from E Er Gu Na). Excerpts of 60s in length were edited to begin from the prelude and were vocal-free in order to eliminate the effect of human voice and lyrics. All excerpts featured a full ensemble instrumental performance and a mode-rhythm combination. Musical stimuli were presented with a Philips Acoustics (Mode No. MMS177/15) through a laptop, and synchronized with the physiological and EEG data collection. An expert group n=3, knowing musicology well and having more than 3 years singing or instrument playing experiment) was invited to evaluate the belonged level of mode and rhythm of proposed stimuli. This procedure acted as the manipulation check of independent variables, in order to make sure that each music excerpt represented the exact treatment.

Procedure. Participants came to the lab, provided information about the experiment and tasks, and completed an online pre-experiment survey about demographic information, physical health and music training experience. At the same time, another experimenter helped the participant to wear measurement devices in certain order: Emotiv EPOC headset (See Fig.1-b), BVP sensor. Prior to the formal experiment we recorded a 20-sec data to test whether the devices worked well, and whether the volume of music was at a comfortable level. When the formal experiment began, each excerpt was preceded by a 30-sec interval to collect baseline records, and followed by a proper interval during which participants completed a questionnaire about the emotion they experienced when listening. The order of six excerpts was randomized to eliminate the effect of last music. After each excerpt the participants were asked to finish a questionnaire assessing their emotional status with the music.

3.2 Measurement and Data Acquisition

Psychological Ratings. Dimensional emotion was assessed by adapted SAM (Self-Assessment Manikin) self-reported scale. This graph-based scale contained two items (arousal, valence) and each item was rated on a 9-point Likert scale (1-strongly, 9-not at all). It was particularly constructed to measure the two main dimensions of emotion. We adapted the GEMS-25 self-reported emotion scales developed by Zentner [17] to measure users' discrete expressions of emotion with 25 items. The 25 items were grouped into 9 sub-types of emotion, which were further averaged into three major types of emotion: sublimity, vitality, and unease. This scale was rated with a 5-point Likert scale (1-not at all, 5-strongly). The internal consistency for sublimity was $\alpha = 0.815$, and for vitality was $\alpha = 0.963$. The emotion "unease" was eliminated because of low inner consistency.

HRV was measured in terms of SDNN (Standard Deviation of NN intervals) with BVP sensor of BioNeuro Infiniti Multimedia Biofeedback software. The sensor was placed on one finger segment of the palmar side of thumb with an elastic band. The acquired SDNN data was made further standardization with the last 10-sec baseline recording.

EEG has high time resolution, making it the proper measurement of the dynamic of human emotion during music. In this study, the EEG signal was collected with saline sensors from six scalp locations: left and right affront lobe (AF3, AF4), left and right mid frontal (F3 and F4) and parietal (FC5, FC6) lobes (See Fig.1-a). These sites represent the left and right hemispheres, anterior and posterior regions of the brain, and were demonstrated to be most activated and effective in reflecting human emotion in brain activities [16]. The Emotiv EPOC neuroheadset was used to record participants' brain activity continuously during each excerpt. There are 14 channels in Emotiv EPOC (AF3, F7, F3, FC5, T7, P7, O1, O2, P8, T8, FC6, F4, F8, AF4) according to the international 10-20 system and a two-dimensional spiral controller. Two electrodes (CMS/DRL) located just behind the ears are used as references. The sample rate of Emotiv is 128Hz; and the broadband of it is 0.2-45 Hz. The digital data is notch filtered between 50 and 60 Hz; and the resolution of the A/D transformation is 16 bits.

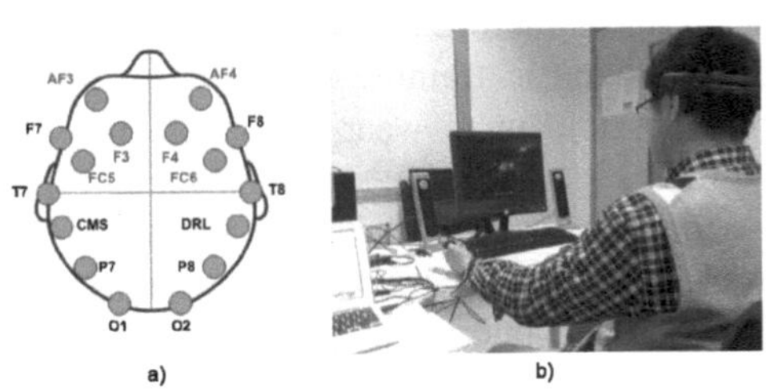

Fig. 1. Multimodal emotion measurement: a) Emotiv EPOC electrode positioning; b) apparatus

Human emotion was assessed by power spectral analysis, which was commonly used to characterize the perturbations in the oscillatory dynamics of on-going EEG [18]. Users' brain activity corresponding to emotion was further represented by power spectral moments [18, 19]. EEG signal was first pre-processed with band pass filtering to keep frequencies in the range of 0.5-40Hz, as it is essential to eliminate EEG recordings with artifact present (due to eye blinks, eye movement, and other motor movements). Then the cleaned EEG data was transformed with FFT (Fast Fourier Transform) with a 0.5-sec non-overlapping window to five frequency bands: Delta (0.5-4Hz), Theta (4-7Hz), Alpha (8-12Hz), Beta (13-30Hz), Gamma (30-40Hz). The power spectral moment for each channel was then computed according to the formulation proposed by Khushaba et al. [18]. Necessary normalization of high-order spectral moment (e.g., second moment in Khushaba's work) based on low-order moments (e.g., zero moment) was conducted to produce more stable results against noise [20]. Finally, we standardized the power spectral moment for each stimulus with the last 10-sec baseline recording so as to diminish the effect of individual difference.

3.3 Results and Discussions

We performed repeated measures MANOVA with Mode and Rhythm as within-subjects factors to compare subjective emotion ratings from GEMS-25, EEG recordings and HRV data after necessary normalization. Valence and arousal were analyzed with Kruskal Wallis Test. The relation between emotion and EEG ratings were depicted by Pearson correlation analysis with significant level of 0.01.

Mode. Participants' emotion induced by major mode was significantly more positive (χ^2 = 5.986, p=0.05), and of higher arousal level (χ^2 = 7.951, p=0.019) than that induced by minor mode. Accordingly, a pairwise comparison on the mean ratings of vitality revealed a significant difference between the ratings of major and minor pieces ($F_{1,11}$=6.994, p=0.023), replicating previous results with western classical music as stimuli [21]. The findings indicate that major mode is more likely to activate people and evoke feelings of vitality, happiness and excitement. Identical to previous studies concerning Western musical features and valence-arousal pattern of emotion, major scale is associated with positive, high-level arousal emotion (vitality), while minor scale is associated with relatively negative and medium/low arousal level emotion.

Participants' psychological, physiological, and EEG data was of significant difference between Chinese pentatonic and major/minor mode. The pairwise comparison of MANOVA revealed that participants listening to pentatonic mode experienced significantly higher level of sublimity than that induced by minor mode ($F_{1,11}$=7.357, p=0.020) and major mode. This effect of pentatonic vs. heptatonic scale was also reflected in HRV results ($F_{2,22}$=5.644, p=0.011, partial η^2 = 0.361): SDNN during pentatonic mode was significantly lower than that of minor mode, and there were no significant difference between SDNN of major and that of minor mode. In a further investigation of connection between emotion and EEG activation, Pearson correlation between subjective ratings and EEG frequency bands showed that beta power over parietal regions decreased linearly with increasing ratings of sublimity (r=-.332, p=.004). In addition, we put the two sub-dimensions of 'unease'—tension and sadness—separately into the statistical model, finding that beta power over all ROIs (left, right, frontal and parietal) was significantly positively correlated to tension ratings

(p<.01). Results revealed that emotion induced by pentatonic scale was associated with sublimity, lower HRV and lower beta power over parietal regions, which indicated low activation during the stimuli. HRV and parietal beta brain activity could also be used as cues for understanding musically cultural difference, namely, sublimity.

Rhythm. When contrasting the effect of rhythm, a significant difference of felt arousal between music with firm and flowing rhythm was observed ($F_{1,11}$=8.412, p=.004). No significant difference of valence was found. As for music-specific emotions, participants felt significantly higher level of sublimity when listening to flowing rhythm than firm rhythm ($F_{2,22}$=6.559, p=.026). The ratings of vitality did not present any significant effect. The findings showed that the effect of rhythm is mostly reflected in the dimension of arousal and sublimity. No significant interaction effect of mode and rhythm was observed on participants' emotion status. As for EEG data, correlation analysis showed that gamma power on the right hemisphere (r=.312, p=.008), and gamma power on the parietal regions (r=.288, p=.014) was positively correlated with arousal (See Fig.2). Hence, firm rhythm in pure music elicits higher level of arousal, while flowing rhythm induces sublimity. These results clearly demonstrate that the discovered music-emotion patterns of firm/flowing rhythm can predict Chinese pop music listeners' felt emotion.

4 Study 2: Music Video (MV) and Emotion

4.1 Methodology

Participants. We recruited 30 right-handed students (aged 21-28, mean age 23.4, 16 males) for study 2. We selected participants who had no formal musical training (besides typical school education) and had never learnt to play a musical instrument or vocal performance by an online screening questionnaire. The questionnaire consisted of three questions concerning basic musical theory and only those who answered less than two questions correctly would be considered. Additionally, we only selected participants who were familiar with over 60% music that would be used in this study. A question in the screening questionnaire asked participants to recite at least one sentence of lyrics of the song. All participants reported no history of hearing or neurological disease.

Experimental Design and Stimuli. We performed within-subject design in study 2. The MV stimuli comprised six excerpts of MV among the Chinese KTV top charts, and they are of different duration between three to five minutes that contained reasonable parts. The six MV excerpts reflected different MV (narrative, live performance, and parody) and rhythm (firm vs. flowing): narrative-firm (*Nuan Nuan* by Fish Leong); narrative-flowing (*Ye Zi* by A Sang); live-firm (*Kung Pao Chicken* by David Tao); live-flowing (*Ting Hai* by Jacky Cheung); parody-firm (*The Most Dazzling Folk Style* by Phoenix Legend); parody-flowing (*The Meteor Rain* by a TVB parody group). These stimuli were pre-assessed by the same group of musical experts (n=3) to make sure that all excerpts met their category of MV and rhythm. MV excerpts were presented with a LG display (19', Mode No. LGE1908ST) and a Philips Acoustics (Mode No. MMS177/15) connected with a laptop. The procedure of experiment was similar to that in study 1. As for the GEMS-25, since the internal reliability of all the three dimensions (e.g., sublimity, vitality, unease) was above 0.6 ($\alpha_{\text{sublimity}}$=.859, α_{vitality}=.914, α_{unease}=.694), they were all accepted as dependent variables indicating emotion.

4.2 Results and Discussions

Narrative MV. No significant effect of MV on arousal was examined, and the average ratings of arousal of all MV excerpts were nearly of medium level. When listening to narrative MV, listeners' felt sublimity was significantly stronger than that during live and parody MV ($F_{2,56}$=32.073, p<.01); further pairwise comparison showed that felt sublimity during live performance was significantly stronger than that during parody MV (p<.01). In addition, the mean ratings of unease as participants' watching narrative MV were significantly stronger than that under live performance and parody MV (χ^2=25.674, p<0.01), corresponding to the fact that the emotional plots in narrative MVs evoked the similar emotion. Furthermore, EEG results showed that gamma power over the whole ROI (AF3, AF4, F3, F4, FC5, FC6) was higher during narrative MV: the main effect of MV was significant ($F_{2,28}$=3.468, p=.040) in the repeated measures MANOVA with factors MV (narrative, live performance, parody), Rhythm (firm vs. flowing) and Hemisphere (left vs. right). Hence, our results confirm that emotion induced by narrative MV was more extreme than emotion elicited by live performance MV: more approaching positive valence, more sublime and more related to unease. These findings are consistent with the proposition of Geringer, Cassidy and Byo [14], in which video with narrative plots helps to enhance the intensity of emotion. Another interpretation of this observation may be referred to Goldberg's study, in which video stimuli with narrative plots could suppress the trend of losing interests when enjoying music [22]. The EEG spectral analysis of MV also supports the above findings: the significantly greater gamma power during narrative MV was consistent with the findings of Müller et al. that emotion processing enhance gamma power in frontal scalp areas [23].

Live Performance MV. Participants' ratings of vitality induced by live performance MV was significantly higher than that induced by parody MV (marginal) and narrative MV ($F_{2,56}$=22.111, p<.01), and the mean ratings of vitality during narrative MV was the least among the three types of MV. Live performance MV was also associated with the lowest gamma power (See Fig.2).

Parody MV. Positive emotion evoked by parody MV was significantly higher than that evoked by narrative and live performance MV (χ^2=17.996, p<.01). The analyses corresponded to the observation that more listeners laughed during parody MV and more reported happiness and amusement while watching this type of MV. MV significantly affects beta power in the repeated measures MANOVA with factors MV (narrative, live performance, parody), Rhythm (firm vs. flowing) and Region (frontal vs. parietal) ($F_{2,44}$=3.887, p=.028). Specifically, beta power during parody MV was significantly higher than that induced by live performance MV (p=.015) (See Fig.2).

Among the three types of MV, parody MV was found to elicit emotions that were different from traditional types as narrative and live performance MV. First of all, the highly amusing contents drive people laugh, and this was reflected by both field observation and significantly higher subjective ratings of positive valence than narrative and live performance MV. This finding is in line with the Congruence-Associationist Model (C-A Model) that was proposed by Cohen in 2005 [24]. That is, emotion induced by music and the original emotion contained in video is approaching congruence. Specifically, music with central valence together with positive valenced video elicit positive self-reported emotion among subjects, music with positive valence along with positive valenced video may induce stronger feelings of happiness and excitement [13]. Second, subjects' ratings on sublimity and vitality were almost not affected by rhythm in the context of parody MV. We may infer that video possibly contribute more than rhythm in enhancing listeners' emotion. Third, our study confirmed above findings by assessing brain activities. Beta power over the frontal-parietal areas was significantly higher in parody MV, indicating that beta power is predictive and sensible to MV-induced emotions. Specifically, both beta power over parietal regions and right hemisphere decreased linearly with positive emotions. This was in line with Koelstra's findings that the increase of beta power on the left-mid areas and decrease of beta power on the right-frontal areas was associated with positive emotions induced by music videos [25]. Taken together, these studies illustrate that positive emotion and high level of arousal are strongly associated with parody MVs; and how beta power asymmetry could be used to identify emotion elicited by different types of MV. This may also extend to the theories explaining why parody MVs are virally spread [9] through a comprehensive perspective of emotion.

Rhythm Effects in the Context of MV. In the context of MV, rhythm affected valence, arousal, vitality and unease significantly (p<.01 for each). More specifically, emotion induced by firm rhythm was significantly more positive (less unease) than flowing ones, were of higher level of arousal, vitality than MV with flowing rhythm.

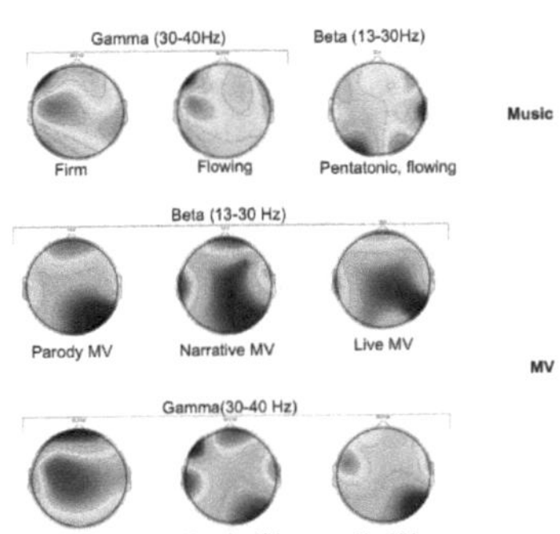

Fig. 2. EEG Map of Beta and Gamma power in MV

5 Conclusion

This study investigated the impact of mode, rhythm and MV on emotion elicited by Chinese pop music. It supports that different mode (major, minor, pentatonic), rhythm (firm vs. flowing) and MV (narrative, live performance, and parody) influence listeners' emotion, and previous theoretical findings concerning Western classic music could be partly used in understanding emotional status related to Chinese pop music (e.g., major/minor mode, rhythm). In addition, this study also explores emotion induced by specific musical features in Chinese pop music like pentatonic mode and parody MV, finding that Chinese traditional pentatonic mode elicits emotion different from heptatonic mode, and emotion induced by parody MV is distinctive compared with narrative and live performance MV.

EEG power band beta, gamma and theta, and HRV jointly predict emotional cues when people are listening to music or watching music videos. The overall power spectrum, asymmetrical activation, as well as the difference of power bands between frontal and parietal areas should be comprehensively considered when explaining how certain music or music video influence human emotion. The findings also suggest that multimodal emotion measurement can be used to guide information retrieval techniques in interpreting, predicting human emotion with acceptable accuracy.

Acknowledgements. This study was funded by a National Science Foundation China grant 71188001. Thank Yubo Zhang for his support and insight.

References

1. Chew, E.: Towards a mathematical model of tonality (2000)
2. Gomez, P., Danuser, B.: Relationships between musical structure and psychophysiological measures of emotion. Emotion 7, 377–387 (2007)
3. Accordino, R., Comer, R., Heller, W.B.: Searching for music's potential: A critical examination of research on music therapy with individuals with autism. Res. Autism Spectr. Disord. 1, 101–115 (2007)
4. Perlovsky, L.: Musical emotions: Functions, origins, evolution. Phys. Life Rev. 7, 2–27 (2010)
5. Hodges, D.A.: Handbook of music psychology. IMR press San Antonio (1996)
6. Hallam, S., Cross, I., Thaut, M.: Oxford Handbook of Music Psychology. Oxford University Press (2008)
7. Krumhansl, C.L.: Rhythm and pitch in music cognition. Psychol. Bull. 126, 159 (2000)
8. Gold, T.B.: Go with your feelings: Hong Kong and Taiwan popular culture in Greater China. China Q. 136, 907–925 (1993)
9. Berger, J., Milkman, K.L.: What makes online content viral? J. Mark. Res. 49, 192–205 (2012)
10. Juslin, P.N., Vastfjall, D.: Emotional responses to music: The need to consider underlying mechanisms. Behav. Brain Sci. 31, 559–575 (2008)
11. Juslin, P.N.: Music and emotion: Seven questions, seven answers. Music Mind Essays Honour John Slob., 113–135 (2011)

12. Hevner, K.: Experimental studies of the elements of expression in music. Am. J. Psychol. 48, 246–268 (1936)
13. Boltz, M.G., Ebendorf, B., Field, B.: Audiovisual interactions: The impact of visual information on music perception and memory. Music Percept. 27, 43–59 (2009)
14. Geringer, J.M., Cassidy, J.W., Byo, J.L.: Nonmusic majors' cognitive and affective responses to performance and programmatic music videos. J. Res. Music Educ. 45, 221–233 (1997)
15. Petty, R.E., Wegener, D.T.: The elaboration likelihood model: Current status and controversies (1999)
16. Schmidt, L.A., Trainor, L.J.: Frontal brain electrical activity (EEG) distinguishes valence and intensity of musical emotions. Cogn. Emot. 15, 487–500 (2001)
17. Zentner, M., Grandjean, D., Scherer, K.R.: Emotions evoked by the sound of music: characterization, classification, and measurement. Emotion 8, 494 (2008)
18. Khushaba, R.N., Greenacre, L., Kodagoda, S., Louviere, J., Burke, S., Dissanayake, G.: Choice modeling and the brain: A study on the Electroencephalogram (EEG) of preferences. Expert Syst. Appl. 39, 12378–12388 (2012)
19. Saltzberg, B., Burton Jr, W.D., Barlow, J.S., Burch, N.R.: Moments of the power spectral density estimated from samples of the autocorrelation function (A robust procedure for monitoring changes in the statistical properties of lengthy non-stationary time series such as the EEG). Electroencephalogr. Clin. Neurophysiol. 61, 89–93 (1985)
20. Flusser, J., Zitova, B., Suk, T.: Moments and moment invariants in pattern recognition. Wiley (2009)
21. Hevner, K.: The affective character of the major and minor modes in music. Am. J. Psychol. 47, 103–118 (1935)
22. Goldberg, M.E., Chattopadhyay, A., Gorn, G.J., Rosenblatt, J.: Music, music videos, and wear out. Psychol. Mark. 10, 1–13 (1993)
23. Müller, M.M., Keil, A., Gruber, T., Elbert, T.: Processing of affective pictures modulates right-hemispheric gamma band EEG activity. Clin. Neurophysiol. 110, 1913–1920 (1999)
24. Cohen, A.J.: How music influences the interpretation of film and video: Approaches from experimental psychology. Sel. Rep. Ethnomusicol. Perspect. Syst. Musicol. 12, 15–36 (2005)
25. Koelstra, S., Yazdani, A., Soleymani, M., Mühl, C., Lee, J.-S., Nijholt, A., Pun, T., Ebrahimi, T., Patras, I.: Single Trial Classification of EEG and Peripheral Physiological Signals for Recognition of Emotions Induced by Music Videos Brain Informatics. Presented at the, Berlin/Heidelberg (2010)

The Research on the Value Experience in the Brand Culture of SuShan and the Design of Product System Service

Jie Wei, Chenmiao Liu, and Jing Wang

School of Design, JiangNan University, 1800 Li hu Avenue, Wuxi, 214122, China
wejoy@126.com, 727867698@qq.com, 18751560373@163.com

Abstract. Chinese fan transformed from a practical object to art piece after integrated with traditional calligraphy and painting. Later with calligraphy and painting as a vehicle, it penetrated into all aspects of the traditional Confucianism-oriented Chinese culture, to establish the distinctive fan culture. Suzhou fan is an important branch of Chinese fan culture with various kinds, whose techniques pursue being premium, refined and elegant. It is enriched with the essence of the culture of South Yangtze River, with long history. With the development throughout history, Suzhou fans have experienced dramatic changes in areas including management model, skills, material and functions and values---- practical value is being marginalized; only the cultural experience within Suzhou fans is being sought and explored. The fast development of traditional brands requires scientific and effective means of service design to guide design to win customers, strengthening the competition of enterprises. This article will discuss the value experience of Suzhou fan brand culture from all kinds of aspects including positioning and categorization, revolution of craftsmanship, models and styles, brand experience model, promotion and sales; under the changes of materials, events, emotion and law, to create a systematic service design of the product for customers. This article will take systematic service design research methodology, analyze from social, cultural, economic and sustainable development aspects and treat service as a platform, Suzhou fans as a tool, starting from stories, by using customer participation creatively, to come up with the ways and contents provided by service. In this way, consumers can integrate themselves into the history and culture of Suzhou fan, from the perspective of value experience and economic development to further seek the cultural theme inside consumers' mind, creating the brand image emphasizing on experience. Based on the status quo, we will state clearly the problems of the inheritance and development of Suzhou fans. We carried on questionnaires and data investigation; in which the questionnaire items include: popularity, memory, likability, reputation, brand connection, overall brand equity; to offer suggestions on sustainable development and brand value improvement from sensorial experience, emotional experience, thinking experience and behavioral experience, etc,. This subject is aimed at not only playing the role of the uniqueness of Suzhou fan, but also under this premise to integrate Suzhou fan with innovative craftsmanship and new technologies, to develop and design Suzhou fan for different market segments; to design the service system proposal that

P.L.P. Rau (Ed.): CCD/HCII 2014, LNCS 8528, pp. 101–110, 2014.

can be used, satisfied, highly effective and can satisfy special social psychology; to improve the sense of values of Suzhou fan brands, promote the regional economic image, develop industrial advantages, brand advantages, market advantages and regional advantages, realizing the effective integration of industrial cluster and regional brands.

Keywords: Suzhou Fans, Brand Culture; Value Experience; systematic Product service design.

1 Suzhou Fans

The history of Chinese fans is very long. In the beginning, it was used to cool off; later it is changed to show etiquette and appreciation, representing the strong ethnic characteristics. Many kinds of traditional artistic patterns with long history are all integrated into the fans, such as Chinese painting art, calligraphy, poems, carving art, etc,. Suzhou fan has become an important branch of hand fan culture, with 600 years history. The main categories include four kinds: folding fans, sandalwood fan, round silk fan and paper fan. Suzhou fan is famous for its delicacy, known as the "elegant fan of Suzhou", is a bright pearl of Suzhou handicraft, listed on China Intangible cultural heritage in 2006.

2 Suzhou Fan Brand Culture and Connotation?

Suzhou is an ancient city with 2000 years. The reasons of the long lasting of Suzhou fan culture are: good human environment, profound cultural heritage, distinctive social environment and the poetic and literary lifestyle. All these provided external environment and nutritious space [1] for the prosperity and development of Suzhou fan culture and brands. In Ming Dynasty, many talented and successful figures gathered in Suzhou. Moreover, in Ming Dynasty, the intellectuals of Suzhou promoted the thoughts on craft and the craftsmanship techniques and the communication between craftsmen and scholar-officials. In particular, this has formed the delicate and elegant characterized "Suzhou styled" crafting, showing attention on all aspects of aesthetics. In craft, it pursues the artistic theme of "made by nature" style, focusing on the South Yangtze River regional characteristics, taking natural materials such as bamboo, sandalwood and silk etc,. to be the raw material. Under this background, Suzhou folding fan became the popular" refined object held in sleeves". When one holds a folding fan with calligraphy and paintings on it, and starts to play with it, he will be holding the refined and cultured temperament naturally.

3 The Status Quo of Suzhou Fans

There had been twists and turns in the development of Suzhou fans. Due to the tragic history of late Qing Dynasty, the economy of South Jiangsu Province transferred, which exerted some impact on the development of Suzhou fan; during the

Chinese-Japanese war, the livelihood of people had been destructed to such an extent that the production and sales of Suzhou folding fans declined day by day; the invasion of Japanese fan culture into China was also one of the contributors to the setback of sandalwood fans; after the new China(People's Republic of China)was established, due to the high proportion of handicraft industry in national economy , during the economic recovery period, Suzhou as the prosperous place of handicrafts, proposed the policies of protecting, developing and enhancing the handicraft industry to actively help handcrafters to recover and develop production, and help them to overcome all kinds of difficulties in human labor, finance, production and management. Related authorities visited artists and organized them to be back to the industry from all channels to save the handicraft skills that were endangered. In 2006, the Suzhou fan-making skill was listed in the first batch of China Intangible cultural heritage. The enforcement of intangible cultural heritage protection policies better promoted the inheritance and protection of the skill of making fans, which leads to the emphasis laid back again on the Suzhou fan-making skill, making the fan-making craftsmen to feel their great importance in industrial art.

As far as Suzhou fan has been developing till today, although it went through dramatic social changes, Suzhou is still a place beneficial to the growth of handicraft industry. Along with the changes of economy, customs and life, the skills of Suzhou fans have gone through dramatic transitions. The ecological change of Suzhou handicraft states that: the development of handicraft is not constant, only the Suzhou fan handicraft that adapts to the ecological environment can walk the long way.

4 The Wide-Spread of Suzhou Fan Brand Culture Requires the Up-to-Date Design Method

Suzhou fan culture used to be prevailing for hundreds of years in history. With the social and environmental changes, especially under the current fever of collection, based on certain economic conditions, the materially rich industrial society has accelerated the replacement of fans by new technologies for its cooling functions. Only the cultural experience in the Suzhou fan is still being sought and explored. Cultural recourses possess certain dynamic features. If you only emphasize on the past advantages, there can be no effective integrated development on the unique cultural resource of Suzhou fans. [2]However, if these features can be well-applied, we can utilize our existing cultural resource to develop cultural industry. This article will discuss the value experience of Suzhou fan brand culture from all kinds of aspects including positioning and categorization, revolution of craftsmanship, models and styles, brand experience models, promotion and sales; under the changes of materials, events, emotion and law, to create a product service system design for customers. With the great importance attached and protection policies implemented on intangible cultural heritage by the country, here we will offer some guidance advice on the development of Suzhou fans.

5 Group Segments, Demand Analysis / Research to Position the Comments of Customers

Design questionnaire / marketing research

1. What's your age?
   20-35 35-45 45-60 60-80
2. What's your occupation?
   Student Company staff Senior executive Civil Servant
3. What's your gender?
   Male Female
4. Do you know Suzhou fan?
   Don't know Know a little bit Know very much Being studying on It
5. The impression on Suzhou fan. Do you like it?
   Don't like it. Reject it Like it. Like it very much
6. Would you search any history introduction on this field?
   No. Sometimes will. Yes. Often study on it.
7. What's your impression on Suzhou? Would you like South Yangtze River styled special objects because your preference on Suzhou?
   No Maybe Yes Often
8. Do you like the culture of South Yangtze River? Would you come to travel?
   Dislike It's all right Like Like it very much
9. Is there obvious difference between Suzhou fan and other fan art like Sichuan fan and Beijing fan?
   Not obvious Don't pay attention to that Know a bit Big difference
10. If you choose Suzhou fan, how would you use it?
    To fan the wind and cool oneself Composing poem and paint Stage performance Home decoration
11. Would you go and buy in a specialty shop?
    No Yes.
12. If you buy, what is your purchasing channel?
    Tourist attraction Specialty shop Local grocery store Online
13. If you buy Suzhou fan, which part do you focus more on?
    Framework of fan Fan Decoration on the fan Fan bag

14. Which of the framework material of Suzhou fan below do you like most?
Hawksbill sea turtle Bamboo Incienso wood Ebony
New technological Synthetics

15. Would you use it yourself or give it as a gift to friends and families?
Use myself Give as a gift
16. What's the feeling of the expected Suzhou fan that you would buy?
Elegant Cultured Magnificent Gentle and delicate
17. Do you think traditional Suzhou fan is necessary to add technical innovation?
Yes Not sure No
18. Would you improve your status and image by using Suzhou fan?
Yes. No.
19. Have you bought this kind of book?
Haven't seen Have seen, but didn't buy Bought Often buy
20. Have you seen the specialty store in your hometown?
No. Yes
21. After you buy, would you introduce it to your friends and families?
Yes Depends/Maybe No

Conclusion: Today, there are four kinds of people who like holding fans including performers of Pingshu(storytellers), Xiangsheng(crosstalk) artist(artist who play comedic performance by the format of dialogue) , some people who have certain cultural taste and social status when they play chess and drink tea, and some scholars and calligraphers and painters who mimic ancient scholars like Tang Yin and Zhu Da. Most people like and accept the South Yangtze River culture which can induce them to like special objects which obtain the culture of this region.

6 The Value Experience Model of Suzhou Fan Brand Culture

In the past, the focus of design is the hard design elements including product shape, function and materials. Today, as user experience, user participation, user psychology and other soft design elements are upgraded from being attached to hard design elements to the same status of the hard one [3], people are emphasizing on the consumer satisfaction rate. With the design concept of using the soft to rule the hard, it broadens the knowledge system and operation depth.

Experience: Bernd H. Schmitt from Columbia University pointed out in *Experience Marketing* art that experience is the individual feeling of an individual's response to some stimulation, which is caused by direct observation or participation in events, the result of the interaction between the events happened and individual mental status [4]

Brand Experience: Brand experience value includes sensorial experience value, emotional experience value, social experience value [5], knowledge experience value Sensorial experience value is the sensorial experience gained from branded product by sense of visual, listening and touching and aesthetic value; emotional experience value is some emotion or emotional state given by the brand to the consumer, in which emotional state includes happiness and the level of arousal; social experience value is what consumers feel about their self-realization, sense of social achievement and social acceptance from the branded product; knowledge experience value originates from the knowledge and horizon broadened and improvement of intelligence brought by the branded product. Getting in touch with the brand can make oneself to think more.

The value experience of the brand of Suzhou fan:

1. Sensorial experience value is the sensorial and aesthetic value obtainment of the appearance, function and performance of Suzhou fan. High sensorial value experience depends on the property of the product, while sensorial experience value obtained depends on good visual sense, touch sense and so on, which will also improve the comments given by consumers to the quality of the branded product. The feature of Suzhou fan design is like how you feel when you hold the framework of the fan---- the tenacity of the bamboo is very strong, Hawksbill sea turtle is hard, sandalwood is soft; the xuan paper or white silk of the fan; the smell of the sandalwood can calm people; the beauty of the painting and calligraphy of the fan; the detachment and naturalness of the painting and calligraphy can give people different sensorial feelings to satisfy different groups of people with delicate craft, moisturized color, smooth lines, comfortable touch and tranquil inner mind. On the other hand, the research on sensorial preference is beneficial to the growing of Suzhou fan industry.2. Well-designed Suzhou fan has certain aesthetic value and emotional experience can stimulate the emotional value of people and resonate them to further transform consumers from the acceptance of the brand and brand preference to higher leveled brand loyalty. The reason why consumers can be loyal to certain branded fan is because the culture of the brand meets the cultural need of consumers. The material used by Suzhou fan is characterized natural material in the South Yangtze River region, which can arouse people to crave for the beautiful scenery of South Yangtze River. The themes of the painting and calligraphy on the fan varies from stories to animals to plants to scenery to display and decoration, giving different emotional experience and connection. The shape of the fans including hexagon, Chinese flowering crabapple, round shape on the round fan can offer different emotional experience. The Suzhou fan compared to other fan culture has more apparent features, focusing on the culture in South Yangtze River, and further seeking the emotion inside to inspire some emotion, or happiness or

warmth, or reminiscence to better strengthen the impression of Suzhou fan brand.3. The social experience of Suzhou fan brand experience, the sense of achievement and social acceptance when using Suzhou fan, is the feeling that by using this brand, the user can feel he's well-respected by the society. Today, under the requirement of promoting traditional culture and protecting intangible cultural heritage, the whole society is attaching great importance on traditional culture, all kinds of folk culture is emerging again. Suzhou fan brand has a long history, which is positive and can represent positive culture with certain social taste. In terms of the satisfaction of using the fan to change one's identity, consumers can also experience the safeguard of social interest in the consumption. Suzhou fan brand has the function of protecting complete social interest, moral value, political value and ecological value. 4. The knowledge experience of Suzhou fan is the information value and knowledge gained from the brand. We can say that Suzhou fan culture is the essence of South Yangtze River culture. In particular, the creation of paintings and calligraphy, the making of framework of the fan and bamboo carving, all of which are involving in the culture in Suzhou region. To some degree, Suzhou fan is a reflection of Suzhou culture.

When being used, it can enable people to know the history and culture in a certain period, and the hobby of scholars, have access to more knowledge and broaden the view.

Suzhou fan needs more attention and the enhancement of added value---- the reason why brand can bring added value is because the brand can bring added value to the customer, which is the additional value this brand can give to the customer compared to its rival. The researchers who study based on the brand equity of the customers all support to analyze the customer need to improve brand equity. The process of consumer's every purchase and use is an experience process of the brand. When the experience process ends, whether consumers can the expected experience value can have impact on the comment of the brand. Below, we will start from the perpective of customers to conduct theoretical analysis to design the effective path which fits with the long term development of Suzhou fan brand.

7 The Service System Study on Suzhou Fan Brand

Promotion Channel

1. Upgrade the Suzhou fan brand image, boost the consumption behavior value including functional, occasional, social, emotional value and cognitive effect, covering all kinds of experience. In terms of the design of Suzhou fan culture experience, the experience ways that gets the contact with consumers should be diversified, including advertisement, PR, communications in the original region, cultural experience, packaging promotion, channel promotion, retail terminal promotion and so on. Diversified communication channel can bring cultural experience from all aspects.

2. Exhibition of Suzhou fan. "The painting and calligraphy on the fan" is centering on painting and calligraphy. The fan is working for the painting and calligraphy which in turn use the fan to play the role of its own artistic charm. Exhibition can attract scholars, painters, calligraphers to gather together, establishing the public relation with celebrities can upgrade the Suzhou fan brand to a new level.
3. Collect the maintenance knowledge into one booklet and organize related knowledge into one book to send to customers as gifts.
4. Utilize advertisement to improve the added value of the product..Under the guidance of providing service to the consumers and satisfying them, by making beautiful advertisement to deliver brand concept and good feelings to consumers, improving consumer satisfaction, it can form consumer's stable preference on the brand, further leading the consumers to keep buying this product.

In terms of management:

1. Build and manage customer data base.By building and managing relative complete customer data base, companies can deeply understand the expectation, attitude and behavior of customers, in order to better serve customers and add the value of customers. The customer data base contains the information of : customer's age, occupation, income, preference; the expectation and preference and behavior of customers; how consumers purchase, etc,.
2. Establish association. Organize studying or knowledge collection and inner-industrial discussion.
3. Enhance the related legal and institutional building and create a good environment of cultural industrial development

In terms of brand concept:

1. Shape and build well-known brand and wellknown factories, enhancing the symbolizing meaning of the product. Throughout time, well-known brands can bring high added value, consumers also prefer branded products and are satisfied with them.
2. To present the symbolizing meaning of the product. For example, the reason why people tend to paymore for well known brand is because the value of well-known brand contains the confidence and promise of the brand. It's not the using value of the brand that people enjoy, but the self-dignity and honor given symbolized by the brand.
3. Suzhou fan new design should expand towards brands. The cognition of consumers on brand design first comes from the knowledge of its product function. If it can satisfy consumers physically and mentally, this kind of satisfaction is related with its own information. Consumers have high appreciation on the product. When they have strong credibility, they will transfer the credibility on abstract brands, and highly appreciates the brand, to form good brand image.

In terms of design:

1. Excellent package can be beneficial to the product to be sent as a gift. From the ancient times till now, fans are often treated as the gifts given between the emperor and officials, gifts given between nations, and as gifts given between friends and families. China is well known as a country of etiquette, which maintains the long lasting culture of "present"("礼"which has the same pronunciation of the first character of etiquette in Chinese). By using good packaging design can also improve the added value of the product.
2. The culture of South Yangtze River is integrated with the product. The design should try to integrate with the cultural scenery of South Yangtze River to improve brand impression.
3. Duplicate and create beauty at the same time. Not only should they search and seek the atmosphere which is to restore the feelings, taste and mental state of the ancient, but also analyze needs to innovate. In terms of innovation, one should also learn from the ancients to integrate all kinds of styles. Emphasizing on the combination of the expression of traditional culture and modern cultural innovation industry, requires people to create new aesthetical inclination and life concept. "Taking advantage of the ancient to apply in today's life fulfills modern aesthetic ways." Is an important principle of developing cultural resource.
4. Categorize according to proper price for different groups of people. The research and analysis states that currently the main uses of Suzhou fans roughly include communication between people, keeping healthy, collection, and practical use. For different consumers, they have different culture, aesthetical interest and economic conditions. If you cannot keep track on the changing of consumers, the economic benefit will decline.
5. The decoration of fans focuses on the meaning, fan bags and fan pendant. The fan decoration of fan is an important link of sensorial experience. The design of fan decoration can be a part of improving sensorial experience.
6. Utilize craft design to improve added value. By modifying and designing of processing craftsmanship and applying new material, improving the working accuracy of both inside and outside of the product, it can reach the aim of improving product quality and product level to increase added value of the product.
7. To inject cultural and connotation to the product, improve cultural added values of the product. Cultural consumption is an important trend of modern marketing consumption. Such high end cultural behavior is a kind of spiritual pursuit. Therefore, the design can attach some culture on the product and lead the consumers to enjoy the cultural knowledge, transform commodity consumption to cultural consumption, satisfying consumers mentally to improve the satisfaction rate and realize high added value.
8. Utilize emotional design to improve added value. In design of Suzhou fan, one should inject emotion to it to enhance emotional appeal to touch consumers, improving added value. Despite the material satisfaction, when a product can offer pleasure, it automatically improve the consumer satisfaction and become high value added product.

In terms of marketing:

1. Can be used as stage and performance tools, establishing long term promotion partnership.
2. Sell in well known tourist sites in South Yangtze River
3. Establish well-known factories, fan shops or specialty stores.
4. Inline marketing

8 Conclusion

Chinese culture has thousands of years of evolution, forming unique core value and cultural system, with rich cultural experience and emotional value [7]. This kind of cultural genes are deeply hidden in everyone's genes. If the good culture of Chinese people and service can integrate into its own cultural elements, and effectively form appealing emotional experience and cultural brand, it can lead Made in China to become prominent cultural product and enormous priceless value. These objects not only can get rid of low cost competition, but can also export the spirit treasure and excellent core value hidden in Chinese culture to encourage Chinese people.

References

1. Li, W.: The study on modern development of traditional handicraft of Suzhou fan (May 2012)
2. Weijun, Y., Xiaofei, R.: The dimensional composition and thoughts within Chinese cultural resources (June 2009)
3. Binbin, L.: Psychology of design. China light Industry Press (February 2013)
4. [USA] Schmitt, B.H.: Experience Marketing (2001)
5. Qigeng, L., Mingyang, Y.: The process mechanism of Brand experience value's impact on brand equity. Journal of Systems and Management (June 2011)
6. Chonghong, L.: The discussion on the impact of design on consumer's recognition of brands. Journal of Chienkuo Technology University (June 2006)
7. Guodong, Z.: Starting from the cultural experience of brand-—the impact of low cost competition and corresponding strategy. Sales and Management (August 2010)

A Service Design Research on New Information Technology of Fruit Brand Experience and Innovation

Liang Yin[1], Bin Bin Li[2], and Shengli Lu[3]

[1] Design Campus, Politecnico di Milano, Milano 20159, Italy
[2] School of Design, Jiang nan University, Wuxi 214122, China
[3] Wuxi PeachWell IOT Technology Co. Ltd Wuxi 214122, China
yl401402@hotmail.com, lbbwx@vip.sina.com, lu_sunny@139.com

Abstract. This article focus on studying brand experience under the background of IOT through data selecting and analysis , try to make a service design plan according to the design-driven branding innovation. We take a local fruit brand as study object named "Taozhiyuan" , not only focus on logo or package but try to establish a co-design platform which all the stakeholders and take part in . This platform is based on the system supported by the Wuxi PeachWell IOT Technology Co. Ltd .

We exploit our own toolkit for brand experience under the help of anti-counterfeit and packaging technology of sponsor. Then we try to establish the cultural identity and value features of "Taozhiyuan" based to brand identity and package design, according to this we will develop the innovative approach and new method under the idea of design-driven brand innovation.

According to the Schmitts theory of five-element-pattern brand experience, we carry out design- -intervention and make service design plan about branding innovation system including: information technology platform own by ourselves, platform for user data collection, analysis system for user data , operating a platform for user service system, according to this , we want to approach branding innovation and improvement in the end.

Keywords: New information technology, Fruit brand, Brand Experience, Brand innovation, Product service design.

1 Experience Theory Based User Information Collective Platform for Taozhiyuan Yangshan Juicy Peach

In this topic, we study the experience evaluation of the hang packag of PeachWill Brand Yangshan Peach (the original package A). To enhance its brand image, we designs new packages(the new package B, the new package C) to facilitate our empirical research. And we did association analysis on the data and factors got from the psychological evaluation of user experience by designing experience evaluation chart (Yangshan Peach semantic analysis chart). In view of the above, the empirical research is conducted in order to improve Wuxi's local fruit brand

P.L.P. Rau (Ed.): CCD/HCII 2014, LNCS 8528, pp. 111–117, 2014.

In this topic, we chose the hand package with anti-counterfeiting trace technology of Peachwill as our target of Yangshan Peach's brand package experience evaluation, which is Package A for short. And based on brand experience theory, our research group of the design school designed package B&C for Peachwill Brand to compare psychological evaluation of the original package and the new designs.

A) Original B) New C) New

Fig. 1. Package Design Proposals for Yangshan Peach Brand

The semantic analysis scale of Yangshan peach package design, our evaluation tool, consists of 20 adjectives (Test Variables). Our evaluation objects are original package A (referred as package A below), redesigned package B (referred as package B below), and redesigned package C (referred as package C below). And we get the result from Customer Satisfaction Index, referred as CSI below.

We mainly discuss the common point, different point, maximum and minimum value of three packages' CSI. In appliance with Schmitt's brand experience theory, we collect adjectives about sensory experience, affective experience, behavioral experience, intellectual experience and relative experience of Yangshan peach package experience. After pre-experiment, finally we made the testing questionnaire.

In our questionnaire interview, we mainly collect various people's CSI about Yangshan peach package experience and do association analysis and factor analysis between customer feature and their CSI.

We hope that the result analysis of our empirical research will lead the improvement of Yangshan peaches' package service design.

2 User Participatory Based Experience Information Respond Platform for Taozhiyuan Yangshan Juicy Peach

According to Figure 2:

Package A's CSI ranges from 2.42 to 3.63. The element with the highest consumer evaluation is "protective" of behavior experience with CSI (3.63), while collectable element gets the lowest CSI evaluation with 2.42. To package A, the elements with highest CSI are unique (3.31), warm-colored (3.45), and protective (3.63). However elements with lowest CSI are high-class (2.75), good-quality (2.82), spiritual (2.84), and collectable (2.42), which belong to the affective experience and intellectual experience.

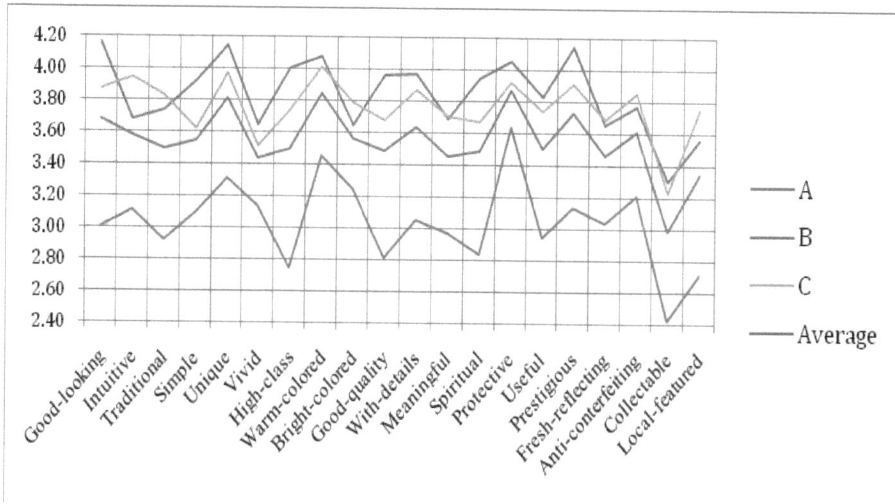

Fig. 2. Experience Analysis of Brand Package A、 B、 C

Package B gets CSI score from 3.31 to 4.15 with consumer's positive evaluation in all aspects, among which, the lowest CSI appears in collectable of intellectual with 3.31 score. And package B's unique and prestigious elements of affective experience get the highest average CSI of 4.15.

Package C achieves CSI of 3.23 to 4.02. Its highest CSI score is 4.02 of warm-colored element of sensory experience, while the lowest CSI score is 3.23 of collectable element of intellectual experience.

From average CSI curves, we can tell that the CSI arranges from 2.99 to 3.87. The highest score exists in the "protective" element of behavioral experience with CSI score 3.87 for the reason that the three packages uses patented suspension technology of hang package. User's collectable evaluation of intellectual experience has the highest average CSI of 2.99, suggesting that as a high-class gift package, all the three packages of Yangshan peach need improvement in intellectual experience.

Comparing the curves of package A、 B、 C, packages A's CSI in lower than package B & C'in every evaluation aspect. In 13 aspects out of 20, package B achieves higher CSI than package C. So users experiences best about package B. So the overall experience rank is B better than C, and better than A (B>C>A).

In summary, the suspension design of package A, B, C enhances customer experience in protection. To package A, consumers accept its simple red- white appearance in sensory experience. However it still has improvement space for users' affective and intellectual experience. The peach flower element of package B & C positively enhance consumers' brand experience. But as high-class package, package B &C have to bring customers better intellectual experience, especially in collectable.

Comparing simplicity and details, customers more like simplicity, rather than a lot of details. In other words, it's the more details, the better. Package design with certain details and simplicity at the same time would achieve customer brand experience promotion.

3 Information Technology Based Service Design for Taozhiyuan Yangshan Juicy Peach

The high-tech company mainly producing high-end juicy peaches Wuxi Taozhiyuan Internet Technology Co. Ltd is the base for case study and empirical research. Chose as object of our brand package design, the sling-style and anti-counterfeiting package and the Internet support platform are two competitive features of the brand package of Taozhiyuan Yangshan Juicy Peach, which have both value in sustainable system design and service design. Because Taozhiyuan represents the high-end brand package design. At the same time, its Internet support platform meet the development trend of contemporary agriculture. The sling-style and anti-counterfeiting package adopted two key designs: the sling-style that the juicy peach is slanged up so that it is effectively protected from collision and extrusion during transportation; the disposable lock-up that only by breaking that can the consumer take out the juicy peach, which guarantees non-repetitive usage of the package.

With the package, the company established three platforms based on Internet and cloud computing technology:

- the tracing system which allows every juicy peach be traced ;
- the perceptive delivery system, which creates better consumer experience by realizing perceptiveness during the whole process including purchase、pick-up、delivery、check-out and inquiry;
- the after-sale service platform, which collects consumer evaluation, regulate cooperator behavior in order to control quality, deal with online consumer complain in time and offer better inquiry.

IT-based service design for Taozhiyuan Yangshan Juicy Peach realized design-driving brand leverage by optimizing its fruit-brand satisfaction and reputation.

3.1 High-End Brand package for Taozhiyuan Juicy Peach

Among all kinds of fruit, peach is considered as the most mysterious one. In china, the well-beings, wishes, exorcising, birthday, wedding, thanksgiving and other social activities are all related to peach. So peach is one of top choice for presents since time immemorial. As one of the best present, "the premium one" achieved highest profit among all kinds of high-end juicy peach of Taozhiyuan in 2012.

3.2 Introduction of the Pick-Up Electronic Code of High-End Brand Package

The pick-up electronic code, part of the perceptive delivery platform of Taozhiyuan, is mainly designed to make juicy peach more appropriate as presents by virtualization. Usage process as follows:

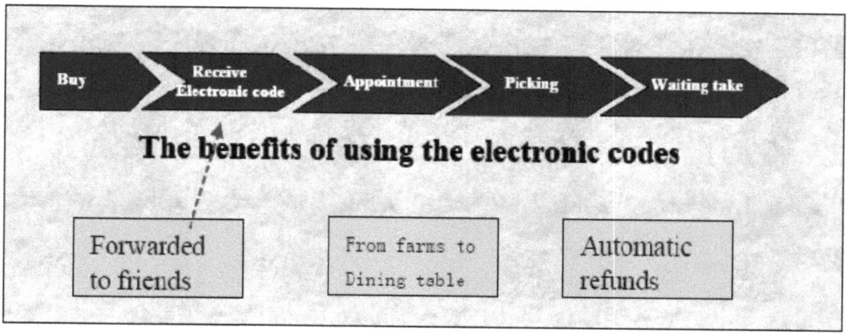

Fig. 3. Flowchart of Taozhiyuan Pick-up Electronic Code

Through pre-order, consumers not only get access to authentic juicy peach, but also first-hand fresh fruits delivered by "sweet from field to home" delivery model with discount on price. Two to three days after preorder, consumers can receive the fresh peach with a pick-up sheet with an ID number. Once it be promoted publicly, market share will increase, especially among high-end consumers and will form positive scale effect.

Taozhiyuan high-end brand package conveys the qualified, tasty, pure and authentic sensitive and knowledgeable experience of their product. On the other hand, it offers warm, thoughtful, convenient and instant service as emotional and behavioral experience to their users through the pick-up electronic code of its Internet support platform

4 Network-and-Internet Based Service Design

As information technology develops in a high speed at this age of experience economy, sophisticated service system is the guarantee of brand development. Donald. A. Norman suggested, "The only way to solve the complexity of service is to regard it as a system and design all the experience as a whole. If we design each part separately, it will finally turn out that each separated part can hardly work together."1 In our opinion, the tangible product and intangible service that integrates the fruit brand and tourism resources in Wuxi, combines local culture and the brand image of Yangshan juicy peach, establishes online information service platform and develops MT-related application to form online and offline experience model will create memorable experience. And we have 3 suggestions as follows:

4.1 Establish Fruit Brand Information Service Platform In Feature of Wuxi Local Culture

There is close relationship between the geographic feature and its cultural tourism or local product such as Wuxi Yangshan Juicy Peach, Shandong Fuji Apple, Xinjiang Hetian Dates and Ningxia Wolfberry.

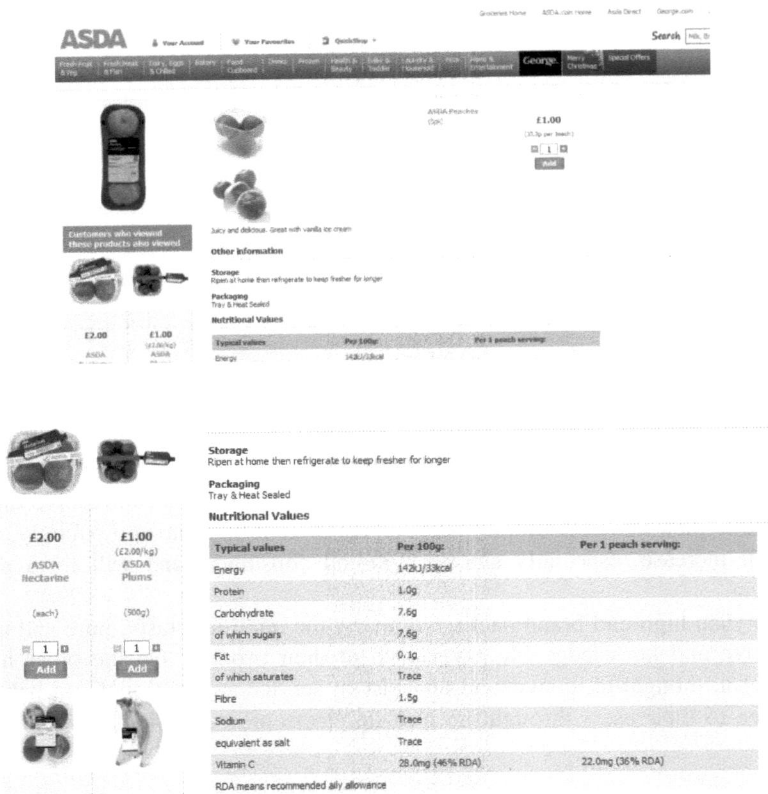

Fig. 4. Website of British Supermarket

Therefore, the geographic area is the label of a product. And the distinguished geographic and cultural feature will enhance the impressiveness of a product. Bearing the rich culture of Wu, the Wu style and spirits cultivates various local-featured agricultural products including Yangshan Juicy Peach. So to encourage a better understanding in Wuxi and its fruit brands, we should promote the fruit brands with Wuxi culture and express with its fruit brands by integrating all the fruit brands in Wuxi, referring to some styles of foreign supermarket websites, and establishing information service platform.

4.2 MT-Related Application as Assistance

The development of mobile Internet makes it possible to anyone to get access to anything they need anytime and anywhere. To embed the promotion of Wuxi fruit brand into people's mobile live, we need to develop an application in feature of Wuxi local culture and in association with its information service platform, which integrates the tourism resources and fruit brand information in Wuxi. Through application service such as introduction of local characteristics, navigation, information update and activity notifications, it will increase both first-time and returning tourists to Wuxi and realize the sustainable development of tourism and mordent agricultural products in Wuxi.

4.3 Brand Promotion with Panoramic and Whole-Coursed Experience

Appealing to consumer need in close-to nature life experience, the existing experience activities, such as farm stay, fruit picking and plant adoption enriches fruit brand promotion in Wuxi. However, existing experiences are comparatively limited. So we can start up the local-featured fruit brand experience for the visitors at their first step in Wuxi by expanding brand promotion from one location to an entire city and enhance their impression in Wuxi fruit brand by making brand experience into a continuing activity.

In conclusion, under the background of experience economy, we should shift fruit brand promotion from product to user experience, establish brand image with local culture, push the species boundary of fruit brand and increase fruit brand value in a untied, open and orderly-competitive modern market system.

References

1. Deng, W.J., Yeh, M.L., Sung, M.L.: A customer satisfaction index model for international tourist hotels: Integrating consumption emotions into the American Customer Satisfaction Index. International Journal of Hospitality Management 35, 133–140 (2013)
2. Schimitt, B.: Experiential Marketing:How to get customers to sense feel think act relate to your company and brand, p. 271. The Fress Press, New York (1999)
3. Brakus, J.J., Schmitt, B.H., Zarantonello, L.: Brand experience: What is it? How is it measured? Does it affect loyalty? Journal of Marketing 73(3), 52–67 (2009)
4. Meroni, A.: Designing foe Social Innovation: the project Feeding Milano Energy for Change (2010), http://www.ltds.ufrj.br/inovabr/apresentacoes/meroni.pdf
5. Norman, D.A.: Living with Complexity. The MIT Press, London (2010)

The Research of Product Design Evaluation Method Based on Brand Intention Recognition

Mei Yu Zhou, Chaoxiang Yang, and Jue Wu

East China University of Science and Technology, Shanghai, China
zhoutc_2003@163.com, darcy_yang@foxmail.com, jojowujue@126.com

Abstract. Traditional designers generally make subjective evaluation and decision-making based on their perceptual experiences, while the speed of current products replacement are becoming faster and the design objects are becoming more complex. The rapid development of information technology requires product design evaluation scientific and systematic. Only relying on intuition, subjective evaluation and decision-making cannot meet the demands of the times. So, to find a systematic and scientific product design evaluation approach is the objective requirement of the promotion enterprise's brand value and the reality of user satisfaction of product requirements. This paper attempts to apply the theory of Kansei Engineering to establish a set of practical evaluation for product design. On the basis of the user experience of brand and its products, collected perceptual evaluation data through questionnaires for factor analysis methods, using the combination of product design principles to determine the product objectives and model of design evaluation to establish a brand value of the product design evaluation methods. Based on Kansei Engineering, brand building and product perceptual evaluation of image space and evaluation standard. On the basis of user perceptual evaluation to determine the criteria weight coefficients of correlation, and then on product design target for the design of accurate positioning, forming a system of brand value enhancement oriented product design evaluation system.

Keywords: Kansei Engineering, Image, Design Evaluation, OLED Lamps.

1 Introduction

With the advent of new technologies, products based on these new technology are increasing. However, the lack of similar products as a reference, new technology products will faced with many uncertainties when entering the market, how do consumers think of new technology products, how about their degree of recognition, satisfaction? whether the products Meets their expectations of new products or not, etc.? This paper attempts to apply the theory of sensibility Engineering to OLED lighting products design development, evaluate it, to judge contact between lighting products and emotional needs of consumers.

Sensibility engineering is a design techniques proposed by Japanese scholars in the 1970s, It change consumers' emotion to the product design elements[1], It is divided

P.L.P. Rau (Ed.): CCD/HCII 2014, LNCS 8528, pp. 118–128, 2014.

into forward, reverse and forward and reverse combination these three types of sensibility Engineering. the reverse sensibility engineering is part of the designer support systems, It's mainly used to evaluate the Design of designers emotionally, to help designers grasp the characteristics of products, understand the relationship between products and consumer's sensibility, To determine whether the designer's design concept meet consumer expectations or not[2]. According to the research objectives we proposed research process shown in Figure 1:

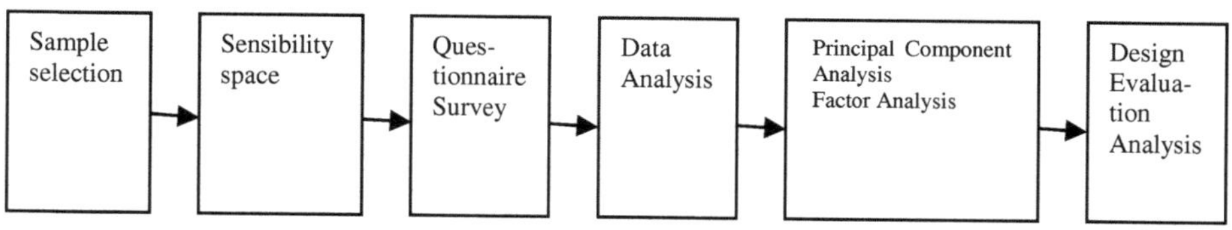

Fig. 1. Research process

The main contents of this study:

First, we use 45 OLED lamps design as samples, On the basis of full discussion, people involved in the design of lighting identified three lighting design as our study objects. And select program 1, program 2 and program 3 renderings as the evaluation object.

Secondly, in order to determine the respondent's feel and preferences of the three programs, we select 120 emotional adjectives about lamps from books, newspapers, magazines, advertising and other media, finalized 10 pairs of sensibility space[3]. Expressed as{V1,V2,V3,V4,V5,V6,V7,V8,V9,V10}={ Expensive - cheap, personality - public safety - the dangerous freedom - detention, figurative - abstract, innovation - imitation, fine - rough, exaggerated - restrained and elegant - tacky, soft - fortitude }.

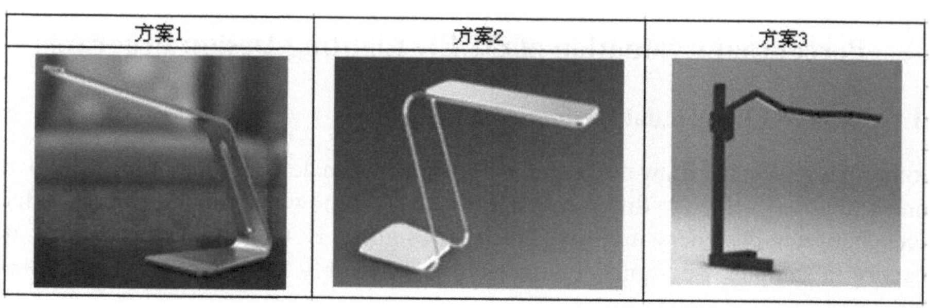

Fig. 2. Three evaluation object finalized

Again, According to the above emotional vocabulary and design samples, design questionnaire survey by the semantics difference method. according to respondents own sense ,they were asked to select vocabulary by understanding and personal preference, Each pair of Kansei vocabulary with five levels to distinguish the degree of preference.

Additionally, selected survey object. Mainly divided into two categories: designers and ordinary consumers, As the population in different areas concern different angles and details, In order to analyze easily, The selected survey object's Category, code and the number of investigations are as shown in Table 1.

Table 1. Survey information and the corresponding code table

Variable name	Category	Code	Number of people	Percentage%
designer	designer	Pd	15	100%
Sex	Male	P1	30	60%
	Female	P2	20	40%
Educational background	Master and above	P3	33	66%
	Undergraduate and below	P4	17	34%
Monthly income	5000￥below	P5	27	54%
	5000-10000￥	P6	23	46%

Finally, the data analysis. use semantic differences and factor analysis, measure out the average data of observed values based on emotional vocabulary, While by gender, age, education and income status, as measured by factors such as predictive value, find out the association; If the consumer emotional preferences and lamps correspondence on statistical data, It can be speculated that the lamps sample correlation with consumers emotional preferences.

2 Perceptual Evaluation of OLED Lighting Design Programs

2.1 Sample 1 Perceptual Evaluation and Analysis

From table 2, We can draw designers and male and female consumers in the [innovation - imitation] value are difference at 1.8 and 1.95, show emotional evaluate differences between designers and consumers, Designers is not completely reflect its imagery in sample 1. designers and consumer's Monthly income 5000￥ and 5000-10000￥below in the [innovation - imitation] value are difference at 1.87 and 1.81, show emotional evaluate differences between designers and those consumers, Designers is not completely reflect its imagery in sample 1 too Designers and consumers who are undergraduate and below in the [innovation - imitation] value are difference at 2.17, show huge emotional evaluate differences between designers and those consumers in sample 1.

Table 2. OLED lighting sample 1 perceptual evaluation data analysis table

Emotional vocabulary	P_d	P_1		P_2		P_d	P_3		P_4		P_d	P_5		P_6	
	average value	average value	Differ with Pd	average value	Differ with Pd	average value	average value	Differ with Pd	average value	Differ with Pd	average value	average value	Differ with Pd	average value	与P_d差异
V_1	-0.59	-0.29	0.30▲	-0.69	0.1▲	-0.59	-0.5	0.09▲	-0.21	0.38	-0.59	-0.21	0.38	-0.5	0.09▲
V_2	-0.66	-0.96	0.03▲	-0.54	0.12▲	-0.66	-0.81	0.15▲	-0.86	0.20▲	-0.66	-0.1	0.56	-0.73	0.07▲
V_3	-0.59	-1.07	0.48	-0.85	0.26▲	-0.59	-1.12	0.53	-0.79	0.20▲	-0.59	-1.07	0.48	-0.96	0.37
V_4	-0.28	-0.85	0.57	-0.69	0.41	-0.28	-1.04	0.76	-0.36	0.08▲	-0.28	-0.93	0.65	-0.73	0.45
V_5	0.07	0.48	0.41	-0.15	0.08▲	0.07	0.38	0.31▲	0.07	0	0.07	0.5	0.43	0.15	0.08▲
V_6	1.1	-0.7	1.8★	-0.85	1.95★	1.1	-0.77	1.87★	-0.71	1.81★	1.1	-1.07	2.17★	-0.58	1.68★
V_7	-0.83	-0.93	0.1▲	-0.77	0.06▲	-0.83	-0.88	0.05▲	-0.86	0.03▲	-0.83	-0.71	0.12▲	-0.96	0.13▲
V_8	0.14	-0.04	0.1▲	0.08	0.06▲	0.14	0.15	0.01▲	-0.29	0.43	0.14	-0.14	0.28▲	0.08	0.22▲
V_9	-0.9	-1.19	0.39	-0.77	0.13▲	-0.9	-1.08	0.18▲	-1	0.1▲	-0.9	-1.43	0.53	-0.85	0.05▲
V_{10}	0.21	-0.33	0.54	-0.15	0.36	0.21	-0.38	0.59	-0.07	0.28▲	0.21	-0.36	0.57	-0.23	0.44

Note: If the designers and consumers are basically the same, then use ▲ ; On the contrary, there are significant differences as designers and con sumers in the evaluation of emotional awareness, use ★.

Table 3. OLED lighting sample 2 perceptual evaluation data analysis table

Emotional vocabulary	P_d	P_1		P_2		P_d	P_3		P_4		P_d	P_5		P_6	
	average value	average value	Differ with Pd	average value	Differ with Pd	average value	average value	Differ with Pd	average value	Differ with Pd	average value	average value	Differ with Pd	average value	Differ with Pd
V_1	-0.38	-0.04	0.34	0	0.38	-0.38	-0.12	0.26 ▲	0.14	0.24 ▲	-0.38	-0.07	0.31 ▲	0	0.38
V_2	-0.38	-0.52	0.14 ▲	-0.69	0.31 ▲	-0.38	-0.58	0.20 ▲	-0.57	0.19 ▲	-0.38	-0.57	0.19 ▲	-0.58	0.20 ▲
V_3	-0.28	-0.7	0.42	-1.08	0.8	-0.28	-0.73	0.45	-1	0.72	-0.28	-0.36	0.08 ▲	-1.08	0.8
V_4	-0.59	-0.85	0.26 ▲	0	0.59	-0.59	-0.77	0.18 ▲	-0.21	0.38	-0.59	-0.64	0.05 ▲	-0.54	0.05 ▲
V_5	0.52	-0.41	0.93	-0.15	0.67	0.52	-0.69	1.21 ★	0.14	0.38	0.52	-0.29	0.23 ▲	-0.35	0.17 ▲
V_6	-0.66	-0.67	0.01 ▲	-0.23	0.43	-0.66	-0.54	0.12 ▲	-0.5	0.16 ▲	-0.66	-0.43	0.23 ▲	-0.58	0.08 ▲
V_7	-1.14	-0.81	0.33	-0.85	0.29 ▲	-1.14	-0.73	0.41	-1	0.14 ▲	-1.14	-0.79	0.35	-0.85	0.29 ▲
V_8	-0.17	-0.26	0.09 ▲	-0.15	0.02 ▲	-0.17	0.04	0.21 ▲	-0.71	0.54	-0.17	-0.29	0.12 ▲	-0.19	0.02 ▲
V_9	-0.48	-0.96	0.48	-0.46	0.02 ▲	-0.48	-0.81	0.33	-0.79	0.31 ▲	-0.48	-0.86	0.38	-0.77	0.29 ▲
V_{10}	-1.1	-0.89	0.21 ▲	-0.77	0.33	-1.1	-0.85	0.25 ▲	-0.86	0.24 ▲	-1.1	-0.71	0.39	-0.92	0.18 ▲

Table 4. OLED lighting sample 3 perceptual evaluation data analysis tab

Emotional vocabulary	P_d	P_1		P_2		P_d	P_3		P_4		P_d	P_5		P_6	
	average value	average value	Differ with Pd	average value	Differ with Pd	average value	average value	Differ with Pd	average value	average value	average value	average value	Differ with Pd	average value	Differ with Pd
V_1	-0.52	-0.89	0.37	-0.62	0.10▲	-0.52	-0.85	0.33	-0.71	0.19▲	-0.52	-0.71	0.19▲	-0.85	0.33
V_2	-1.14	-1.33	0.19▲	-1.31	0.17▲	-1.14	-1.54	0.4	-0.93	0.21▲	-1.14	-1.36	0.22▲	-1.31	0.17▲
V_3	-0.24	-0.59	0.35	0.15	0.09▲	-0.24	-0.5	0.26▲	-0.07	0.17▲	-0.24	-0.36	0.12▲	-0.35	0.11▲
V_4	-0.03	-1.15	1.12★	-1.15	1.12★	-0.03	-1.27	1.24★	-0.93	0.9	-0.03	-1.07	1.04	-1.19	1.16★
V_5	-0.21	0.26	0.47	-0.08	0.14▲	-0.21	0.35	0.56	-0.21	0.00▲	-0.21	0.07	0.28▲	0.19	0.4
V_6	-0.52	-1.11	0.59	-1.62	1.10★	-0.52	-1.46	0.94	-0.93	0.41	-0.52	-1.21	0.69	-1.31	0.79
V_7	-0.1	-0.81	0.71	-1.15	1.05	-0.1	-1	0.9	-0.79	0.69	-0.1	-1	0.9	-0.88	0.78
V_8	-0.93	-1	0.07▲	-1.08	0.15▲	-0.93	-1.12	0.19▲	-0.86	0.07▲	-0.93	-1.14	0.21▲	-0.96	0.03▲
V_9	-0.17	-1.11	0.94	-0.69	0.52	-0.17	-1	0.83	-0.93	0.76	-0.17	-1.21	1.04	-0.85	0.68
V_{10}	0.28	0.3	0.02▲	0.15	0.13▲	0.28	-0.27	0.55	-0.21	0.07▲	0.28	-0.36	0.64	-0.19	0.47

Table 5. Initial variable

	V_1	V_2	V_3	V_4	V_5	V_6	V_7	V_8	V_9	V_{10}
V_1	1.000	0.955	-0.618	0.575	-0.222	0.848	0.295	0.713	0.330	0.329
V_2	0.955	1.000	-0.707	0.629	-0.327	0.931	0.396	0.839	0.358	0.284
V_3	-0.618	-0.707	1.000	-0.589	0.155	-0.741	0.100	-0.916	0.188	-0.094
V_4	0.575	0.629	0-.589	1.000	-0.519	0.712	0.252	0.740	0.328	0.564
V_5	-0.222	-0.327	0.155	-0.519	1.000	-0.312	-0.657	0-.290	-0.629	-0.267
V_6	0.848	0.931	-0.751	0.712	-0.312	1.000	0.415	0.875	0.340	0.462
V_7	0.295	0.396	0.100	0.252	-0.657	0.415	1.000	0.138	0.828	0.480
V_8	0.713	0.839	-0.916	0.740	-0.290	0.875	0.138	1.000	0.043	0.237
V_9	0.330	0.358	0.188	0.328	-0.629	0.340	0.828	0.043	1.000	0.526
V_{10}	0.329	0.284	-0.094	0.564	-0.267	0.462	0.480	0.237	0.526	1.000

2.2 Sample 2 Perceptual Evaluation Data Analysis

From table 3, We can analyze the difference of designers and male consumers in[Personality - public], [freedom - detention], [innovation - imitation], [exaggerated - introverted], [soft - fortitude] are within 0.32, Designer's emotional cognitive and emotional vocabulary is basically the same with male consumers ; the difference of designers and female consumers in[Personality - public], [rough - Fine], [exaggerated - introverted], [elegant - tacky]are qithin 0.32, Designer's emotional cognitive and emotional vocabulary is basically the same with female consumers. the difference of designers and consumers whose monthly income are below 5000￥ in[Figurative - abstract]is within 1.21, there were significant differences in designer and such consumers, Designer's grasp of [Figurative - abstract] is not accurate. The difference of designers and master and above in[Personality - public], [freedom - detention], [figurative - abstract], [innovation - imitation], [fine - rough], [exaggerated - introverted], [elegant - the tacky], [soft - fortitude]are within 0.32, Designer's emotional cognitive and emotional vocabulary is basically the same with master and above.

2.3 Sample 3 Perceptual Evaluation Data Analysis

From table 3, We can analyze the difference of designers and male consumers in[Freedom - imprisonment] are within 1.12, Designer's emotional cognitive and emotional vocabulary has big difference with male consumers ; the difference of designers and female consumers in[Freedom - detention], [innovation - imitation] are 1.12 and 1.10, Designer's emotional cognitive and emotional vocabulary has big difference with female consumers ; the difference of designers and consumers whose monthly income are below 5000￥ in[Freedom - imprisonment]is within 1.24, Designer's emotional cognitive and emotional vocabulary has big difference with these consumers ; Designer's grasp of [Freedom - imprisonment] is not accurate. The difference of designers and master and above in[Freedom - imprisonment]are within 1.16, Designer's emotional cognitive and emotional vocabulary has big difference with these consumers. designer's grasp of [Freedom - imprisonment] is not accurate.

Through the above research, we find out the differences between the various groups of consumers' and designers in cognitive perceptual evaluation of each sample OLED lighting product. This article will be followed by further integration of OLED lighting products analysis which is not easy to master[4]. In the next study, we will analysis relevance of each single sample its evaluation of Cognitive and appearance, which focuses on the individual consumer groups, whose emotional evaluation is not easy to grasp for designer.

3 Relevance Analysis

This paper using principal component for factor analysis, assuming that the variable is a linear combination of pure factor. According to the principle that factor eigenvalues greater than 1 is needed to determine which components should be retained. The first component's variance percentage explained is maximum in the total variance, the next component of the variance explained decrement. their cumulative contribution rate shows percentage of common factor contained. If the cumulative contribution rate is high, indicating that the factor model's part can explained the original variables [5]. This paper extracted three main factors from the original array, 86.283% of the total variance. Factor analysis on Sensibility data draw Correlation matrix(Table 6)and Factor Scree plot(figure 3).

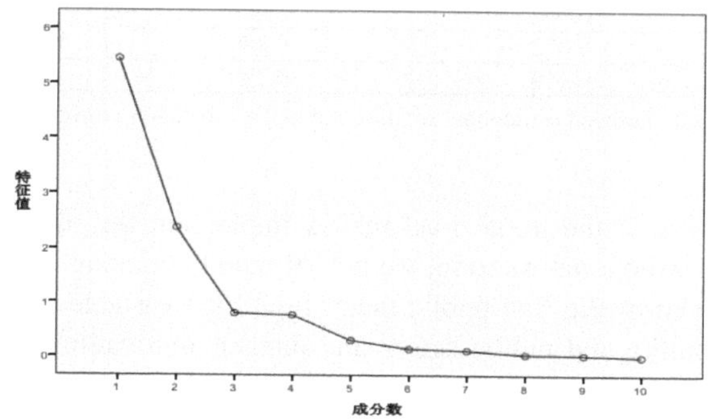

Fig. 3. Scree plot

From figure 3, we can see that the eigenvalues is higher before factor no.3, Connected into a steep curve, after factor no.6 there has been a certain change, after this the eigenvalues is low, this shows that the three factors we extracted are appropriate. After the correlation coefficient matrix orthogonal rotation, we get the following orthogonal factor loadings table, arranged by the different sizes of factor loadings, we get factor loading table as table 7 below.

Table 6. The initial component loading matrix

	component		
	1	2	3
V_1	0.855	-0.179	-0.069
V_2	0.926	-0.173	-0.182
V_3	-0.707	0.624	0.060
V_4	0.821	-0.020	0.272
V_5	-0.528	-0.544	0.354
V_6	0.950	-0.153	0.033
V_7	0.508	0.761	-0.192
V_8	0.862	-0.432	-0.049
V_9	0.480	0.811	-0.071
V_{10}	0.528	0.426	0.712

Note: Main component a. has been extracted three component.

Table 7. Component loading matrix after varimax orthogonal rotated

	成份		
	1	2	3
V_1	0.834	0.234	0.138
V_2	0.906	0.315	0.058
V_3	-0.924	0.194	0.030
V_4	0.685	0.213	0.485
V_5	-0.228	-0.805	0.003
V_6	0.889	0.254	0.266
V_7	0.085	0.909	0.204
V_8	0.962	0.023	0.082
V_9	0.022	0.889	0.320
V_{10}	0.159	0.279	0.930

Note: By using Kaiser standardized orthogonal rotation method a. Rotation convergenced after five iterations [6].

As shown in Table 7, the initial load matrix implement the of the maximum variance components orthogonal rotation, we get "Rotated component matrix" as shown in table 8, and we know the first public factor high load variables are Expensive and inexpensive, personality and public safety and danger, innovation and imitation, exaggeration and introverted, freedom and imprisonment, according to its semantic, they are summed up as style factor. The second public factor high load variables are concrete and abstract, fine and coarse, elegant and tacky, summed up as quality factor. The third public factor high load variables are Soft and fortitude, summed up as value factor, As shown in Table 9.

Table 8. Common factor data Sheet

Common factor	Emotional semantic space	Higher load factor	Eigenvalues	Variance contribution rate	Cumulative contribution rate
factor 1（Style factor）	V_1	0.834	4.640	46.402%	46.402%
	V_2	0.906			
	V_3	-0.924			
	V_4	0.889			
	V_5	0.962			
	V_6	0.685			
factor 2（Quality factor）	V_7	-0.805	2.643	26.429%	72.830%
	V_8	0.909			
	V_9	0.889			
factor 3（Value factor）	V_{10}	0.930	1.345	13.452	13.452%

Figure 4 is a three-dimensional map consisting of three common factors, It can be seen that the high load indicator on the first component is the style factor, the high load indicator on the second component is the quality factor, the high load indicator on the third component is the value factor.

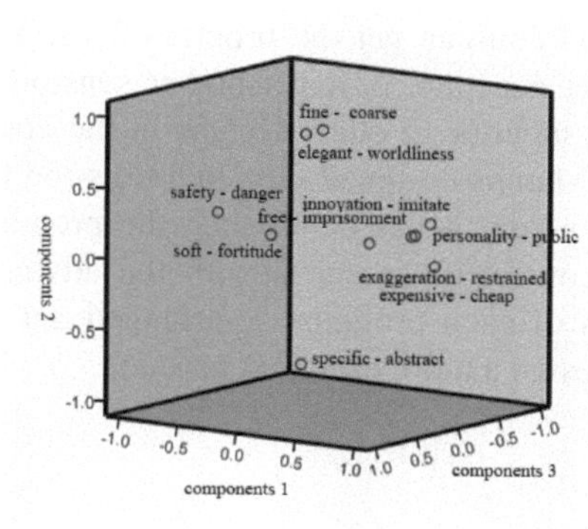

Fig. 4. Three-dimensional component chart in a rotating space

Table 9. component score coefficient table

	component		
	1	2	3
V_1	0.183	0.038	-0.055
V_2	0.210	0.103	-0.180
V_3	-0.250	0.131	0.108
V_4	0.093	-0.083	0.353
V_5	-0.023	-0.407	0.308
V_6	0.177	0.003	0.070
V_7	-0.049	0.398	-0.096
V_8	0.233	-0.058	-0.064
V_9	-0.082	0.351	0.047
V_{10}	-0.113	-0.175	0.896

Note: Extraction Methods: Kaiser standardized orthogonal rotation method.

As shown in figure 4 and Table 9,10, In the OLED lighting design elements emotional vocabulary imagery evaluation analysis, style factor,quality factor,value factor separately explained the overall variance 46.40%、26.43%、13.45%。style factor is common factor of V1、V2、V3、V4、V5、V6, from the factor score coefficient matrix, we can get that V2、V3、V5 can deside style factor ; quality factor is common factor of V7、V8、V9, we can get that V7、V8、V9 can deside quality factor ; value factor is common factor of V10, we can get that V10 can deside value factor ; Therefore, when we begin to design, we should pay more attention to the factors which affect common factor the most, so as to grasp the direction and positioning of design more accurately.

Table 10. Consumer's perceptual evaluation point analysis and comparison chart

	V_1	V_2	V_3	V_4	V_5	V_6	V_7	V_8	V_9	V_{10}
program1	-0.4	-0.83	-1.00	-0.8	0.28	-0.75	-0.88	0.00	-1.05	-0.28
program2	-0.03	-0.58	-0.83	-0.58	- 0.33	-0.53	-0.83	-0.23	-0.8	-0.85
program3	-0.8	-1.33	-0.35	-1.15	0.15	-1.28	-0.93	-1.03	-0.98	-0.25

As shown in Table 10, You can get the program 3 LED lamps designed sample have very good Consumer acceptance, it get higher sensibility evaluation too, This OLED lighting design is superior to other designs in the consumer's sensibility imagery. the program 1 LED lamps designed sample have good Consumer acceptance, it get good sensibility evaluation, it has better than the program 1 in the consumer's sensibility imagery. Of course, if we can absorb the advantages of each program, remove the shortcomings of each program, re-arranged and re-combination the design, we will be able to design a more excellent product.

4 Conclusion

Based on The sensibility engineering, this article propose a set of relatively complete user-oriented product design evaluation methods and procedures, to sum up, it mainly addresses the following three issues. First, this study is based on OLED lighting products design under the new technology, combining The sensibility engineering methods and product design, and tried to blend the emotional needs of the user into OLED lighting style, design quality and design values, expexting the OLED lighting product design orientation is consistent with user expectations. Secondly, based on careful analysis of the emotional needs of users on OLED lighting, we use semantic differential method in survey, And analyze the collected sensibility data, contrast perceptual cognitive differences of product design between consumers and designers, in order to evaluate if the product's positioning of designers accord to user, to achieve product design evaluation and optimization, trying to meet new technology product design evaluation's systematic, objective requirements.

References

1. Bai, X.: Industrial design process and research of evaluation system of the new product development. Sichuan University (2006)
2. Nagamachi, M.: Kansei Engineering: a New Ergonomic Consumer-oriented Technology for Product Development. International Journal of Industrial Ergonomic 15(1), 3–11 (1995)
3. Jiao, G.: Design and research of agricultural vehicle based on Kansei Engineering. Journal of Shandong University (2010)
4. Nagamachi, M.: Kansei engineering as a powerful consumer-oriented technology for product development. Applied Ergonomics (32), 289–294 (2002)
5. He, Y.: The differences research based on the consumers of electronic lock products and perceptual cognition of form of designers. East China University of Science and Technology (March 2010)
6. Yi, L., Wang, L.: Availability modeling and evaluation based on opinion mining of product. Development Research and Design Technology 1000-3428, 16-0270-05 (2012)

Cross-Cultural Issues in Interaction

Development of a Scale to Assess the Linguistic and Phonological Difficulty of Passwords*

Jennifer Romano Bergstrom[1], Stefan A. Frisch[2], David Charles Hawkins[1], Joy Hackenbracht[1], Kristen K. Greene[3], Mary F. Theofanos[3], and Brian Griepentrog[1]

[1] Fors Marsh Group, Arlington, VA, USA
{jbergstrom,dhawkins,jhackenbracht,bg}@forsmarshgroup.com
[2] University of South Florida, Tampa, FL, USA
sfrisch@usf.edu
[3] National Institute of Standards and Technology, Gaithersburg, MD, USA
{kristen.greene,mary.theofanos}@nist.gov

Abstract. Institutions often require or recommend that their employees use secure, system-generated passwords. It is not clear how well linguistic and phonological language properties map onto complex, randomly-generated passwords. Passwords containing a mix of letters, numbers, and other symbol characters may or may not be similar to common patterns in spoken or written English. The Linguistic Phonological Difficulty (LPD) scoring rubric was created by considering the extent to which a string of characters in a password resembles ordinary spoken or written language patterns. LPD is a score calculated through a six-rule process that considers these spoken and written patterns of English as well as memory load. These rules can be applied to any password. Our research explores mapping linguistic and phonological language properties onto complex randomly generated passwords to assess behavioral performance.

Keywords: passwords, memorability, linguistics, phonology.

1 Introduction

The username-password authentication system is used to protect information from unwanted or illegal use and inspection [1]. Generally organizational password policies require criteria such as minimum number of characters, inclusion of symbols, capital letters and numbers to increase the complexity and security of passwords. However, there is typically an interaction between password complexity, memorability and security [2]. Specifically, people are more likely to remember passwords when they are required to generate items instead of just read them [3] and when deep information processing and elaboration are necessary [4]. Deeper processing increases recall because more connections are made between elements in a password, thus providing more neural pathways to aid in recollection. Additionally, users tend to generate

---

* The rights of this work are transferred to the extent transferable according to title 17 U.S.C. 105.

P.L.P. Rau (Ed.): CCD/HCII 2014, LNCS 8528, pp. 131–139, 2014.

passwords that are easy to remember, such as biographical data (e.g., birth date, names of significant others, favorite items), and these passwords can be guessed or broken by other individuals or computer programs. Increasingly, organizations are suggesting the use of system-generated passwords to avoid such issues with user generated passwords.

Many existing password-generation software programs have options available for constructing pronounceable random passwords (e.g., non-word consonant-vowel-consonant groups) [5], but it is unclear whether such programs use algorithms based on the linguistic and phonological properties of natural language (in our case, English). While it seems obvious that leveraging the natural properties of a given language should aid users in better remembering passphrases—indeed, there are numerous studies on passphrase memorability [6, 7]—it is less clear how linguistics and phonological language properties map onto complex, randomly-generated passwords.

Our research explores this potential mapping by examining randomly-generated passwords as linguistic units. In this paper, we attempt to quantify the linguistic and phonological complexity of 10 randomly generated passwords [8] to measure how password complexity impacts behavioral performance. We aimed to answer the following questions:

1. Is there a positive relationship between linguistic and phonological complexity and password entry errors, such that as linguistic and phonological complexity increases, errors increase?
2. Is there a positive relationship between linguistic and phonological complexity and the average time it takes to enter a password, such that as linguistic and phonological complexity increases, entry time increases?
3. Is there a positive relationship between linguistic and phonological complexity and self-reported password difficulty, such that as linguistic and phonological complexity increases, perceived difficulty increases?

2 Linguistic Phonological Difficulty

We quantified the complexity of 10 experimental passwords [8] by creating linguistic phonological difficulty (LPD) scores. The LPD scoring rubric was created by considering the extent to which a string of characters in a password resembles ordinary spoken or written language patterns. The over-arching rationale is that any password character string that has the structure of an English sentence or pronounceable unit would benefit from connections to familiar long-term memory chunks [9].

Passwords containing a mix of letters, numbers, and other symbol characters may or may not be similar to common patterns in spoken or written English. For example, punctuation generally comes at the ends of written phrases or sentences and never at the beginning of a sentence. Even in spoken English, final boundaries are marked with lengthening and pitch change [10]. Thus, we might expect a password to be easier to process if it has symbols that break the password into smaller chunks in the same manner as punctuation breaks up a sentence. Similarly, in written English, capitalization is used at the beginning of sentences, the beginning of some words, or throughout an acronym or abbreviation. Thus, we might expect a password with chunks that have initial capitalization or capital letters throughout (e.g., Pfd, SQEF) to be easier to process than a chunk with mixed capitalization (e.g., pFd, sqeF).

Less obvious patterns of language use can also be violated in randomly generated passwords. Letters and digits usually appear in separate chunks (e.g., an address like 4401 Crater Lake Road, Tampa, FL, 33624), and so we might expect passwords with a mixing of letters and numbers to be more difficult. Further, most random strings such as d3bn can only be remembered by remembering each unit; however some arrangements can create pronounceable chunks even if they are nonsensical (e.g., b8er as "baiter").

LPD is a score calculated through a six-rule process that considers these spoken and written patterns of English as well as memory load. These rules can be applied to any password. The six-rule coding process is as follows, and the LPD score is the sum of the point score of each of the rules.

> Rule 1: Parse by symbol. If the string begins with a symbol, then put phrase boundaries before each symbol, and score 1 point for un-sentence-like parsing difficulty. Otherwise, put phrase boundaries after each symbol and score 0 points for difficulty. (Symbol start)
>
> Rule 2: Score for memory load difficulty based on the number of phrases – 1-2 phrases = 0 points, 3 phrases = 1 points, 4 phrases = 3 points, 5 phrases = 5 points, 6 phrases = 7 points, such that for each additional phrase = 2 points. (Number of chunks)
>
> Rule 3: Score for memory load difficulty based on the size of each phrase – For each phrase of 1-3 characters = 0 points, 4-5 characters = 1 point, 6-7 characters = 2 points, 8-9 characters = 3 points, 10-11 characters = 4 points, 12-13 characters = 5 points. (Number of characters)
>
> Rule 4: Score 1 additional difficulty point for each letter string (i.e., two or more letters in a row) within a phrase with un-sentence-like capitalization (e.g., a capital letter anywhere in the string other than the initial position). NOTE: A string with all capital letters = 0. (possible points: 1 or 0 per string – there may be more points if there is more than one string within a password). (Unsentence like capitalization)
>
> Rule 5: Score 1 additional difficulty point for each phrase with mixed character strings (e.g., 8f1) as opposed to segregated letter strings (e.g., 81f or f81) for strings of 3 or more characters. (Mixed character string)
>
> Rule 6: Subtract 1 difficulty point for each phrase with a pronounceable character sequence (e.g., kef is a pronounceable syllable, kfe is not; this also can be applied to a small set of number and letter mixes, for example 8t1 is 'eighty one'). (Pronounceability chunking)

The 10 experimental passwords assessed in this study and their LPD scores are displayed in Table 1. The decriptive characteristics (i.e., how often the rules occurred across all 10 passwords) are displayed in Table 2. The passwords were those used in [8].

Table 1. The 10 experimental passwords and LPD scores

Password	Rule 1	Rule 2	Rule 3	Rule 4	Rule 5	Rule 6	LPD Score
5c2'Qe	0	0	1	0	1	0	2
m#o)fp^2aRf207	0	3	2	1	0	-1	5
m3)61fHw	0	0	1	1	0	0	2
d51)u4;X3wrf	0	1	2	0	1	0	4
p4d46*3TxY	0	0	3	1	1	0	5
q80<U/C2mv	0	1	2	0	1	0	4
6n04%Ei'Hm3V	0	1	2	0	2	-1	4
4i_55fQ$2Mnh30	0	1	3	1	0	0	5
3.bH1o	0	0	1	1	1	0	3
a7t?C2	0	0	1	0	1	0	2

Table 2. Descriptive characteristics of LPD of the 10 experimental passwords

Variable	*Mean*	*SD*	Min	Max
Rule 1-Symbol Start	0	0	0	0
Rule 2-No. of chunks	0.7	0.90	0	3
Rule 3-No. of characters	1.8	0.75	1	3
Rule 4-Unsentence like capital	0.5	0.50	0	1
Rule 5-Mixed char. string	0.8	0.60	0	2
Rule 6-Sounds like	-0.2	0.40	-1	0
LPD Score	**3.6**	**1.20**	**2**	**5**

2.1 LPD Coding: Inter-rater Agreement

Before LPD scores were calculated for the 10 experimental passwords (shown in Table 1), we conducted training in which two coders (with Human Factors and Industrial/Organizational Psychology backgrounds), blind to the purpose of the study, were taught how to rate LPD. One of the main researchers trained the two coders by reviewing the rules and using examples that were similar in nature to the experimental passwords to demonstrate the coding. The two coders then worked on passwords independently and then the three (researcher and coders) reviewed the independent coding and discussed discrepancies. The coders engaged in this frame of reference training on three practice sets (8, 11, and 11 passwords, respectively) until consensus was reached on the scoring rules. After the frame of reference training, the coders received a final set of 78 passwords and coded them independently. They coded the individual rules and summed them for the total LPD score. An agreement for each rule was calculated by dividing the number of agreed upon scores by the total number of passwords. Inter-rater agreement for the each of the six LPD scoring criteria was at or above 95%. Seven passwords were scored differently on no more than two rules – the coders and the researcher discussed the discrepancies, and the coders came to a consensus. There was one disagreement on number of characters, four on unsentence-like capitalization, and three for pronounceability chunking. The pronounceability chunk is more subjective than the other rules; researchers expected for some scoring variability to exist in this rule. The discrepancy for number of characters can be attributed to a simple error, but the number of errors in unsentence-like capitalization could suggest that some ambiguity remained on what qualified as a letter string. Despite these discrepancies, the high degree of inter-rater agreement suggests that it is possible for two independent coders to be trained in the LPD scoring criteria and reach consensus for LPD on a large set of randomly generated passwords. Finally, the two coders independently rated the 10 passwords used in this study. They agreed on all but one rule for one password (6n04%Ei'Hm3V); they discussed the discrepancy ("Hm" can be considered a pronounceable syllable; as if one was pondering) and came to a consensus on the score.

3 Applying the LPD Scale

In order to test the efficacy of the LPD scale we used the performance data (times, errors, and self-reported difficulty ratings) reported in [8], a password typing entry and memorization study performed on smartphones and tablets. In [8], participants were asked to enter a randomly generated password 10 times, on the entry screen. The passwords are shown in Table 1.

The errors were operationalized as the total number of times the password was entered incorrectly during this entry phase. For entry time, we computed an index of the average time (in seconds) participants spent entering each password during this particular phase. Participants in [8] completed a difficulty-rating questionnaire in which they rated the perceived difficulty of each password on a 5-point Likert scale (1=Very Difficult; 5=Very Easy). To ease in interpreting effects consistent with the error and entry time data, the difficulty ratings were reverse scored, such that 5=*Very Difficult* and 1=*Very Easy*.

3.1 Smartphone

Table 3 displays the descriptive statistics for the smartphone performance data used to test the LPD scale. To examine the relationship between LPD and each of the performance outcomes, we first estimated the zero-order correlations between LPD and performance, in terms of the number of errors, average entry time, and self-reported difficulty. As shown in Table 4, as LPD increased so did the number of entry errors ($r = .28$), the longer the average entry time ($r = .60$), and the greater the perceived difficulty ($r = .55$).

Table 3. Smartphone Performance data

Variable	*Mean*	*SD*	Min	Max
Entry Errors	2.2	3.03	0	10
Mean Entry Time	15.26	8.87	3.38	80.73
Difficulty Rating	3.09	1.31	1	5

Because number of errors and mean entry time positively correlated with participants' age and gender (*r*s > .23 and > .08, respectively) and negatively correlated with password order (*r*s > -.07), we ran a series of linear regressions to test the relationship between LPD and each of the performance outcomes controlling for age, gender, and order. To account for the repeated measures aspect of the design, we adjusted for dependence when estimating standard errors. The results are the same as reported in Table 4.

Table 4. The correlation of LPD with performance outcomes for Study 1. $^{***}p < .001$

	LPD Score	Entry Errors	Mean Entry Time	Difficulty Rating
LPD Score	1			
Entry Errors	$.28^{***}$	1		
Mean Entry Time	$.60^{***}$	$.39^{***}$	1	
Difficulty Rating	$.55^{***}$	$.35^{***}$	$.46^{***}$	1

Next, instead of focusing on the overall LPD score, we examined the relationship between the individual LPD rules and each of the performance outcomes. All rules were entered as simultaneous predictors in a linear regression, with the exception of Rule 1 (Symbol Start) which was excluded because it had zero variance among the ten passwords. The standardized β coefficients for the individual LPD rules are shown in Table 5. These results suggest that the number of characters per chunk (Rule 3), relative to the other LPD rules, appears to be most related to the number of entry errors, mean entry time, and perceived difficulty (βs = .24, .42, .50, respectively).

Table 5. Standardized β coefficients regressing LPD onto performance outcomes in Study 1. $^{*}p < .05$, $^{**}p < .01$, $^{***}p < .001$

	Entry Errors	Mean Entry Time	Difficulty Rating
Rule 2-No. of chunks	.01	$.24^{***}$	-.00
Rule 3-No. of characters	$.24^{***}$	$.42^{***}$	$.50^{***}$
Rule 4-Unsentence like capital	$-.12^{***}$	$-.21^{***}$	$-.26^{***}$
Rule 5-Mixed char. string	$-.16^{*}$	$-.20^{***}$	$-.33^{***}$
Rule 6-Sounds like	$-.19^{**}$	$-.31^{***}$	$-.39^{***}$

3.2 Tablet

Table 6 displays the descriptive statistics for the performance data for tablet.

Table 6. Descriptive statistics for performance data for Tablet

Variable	*Mean*	*SD*	Min	Max
Entry Errors	1.21	2.46	0	10
Mean Entry Time	14.81	12.62	3.33	154.01
Difficulty Rating	3.06	1.28	1	5

Our analyses were the same as in smartphone. Again, we estimated zero-order correlations between LPD and each of the performance outcomes. As shown in Table 7, the results were the same as in smartphone. Specifically, as LPD increased, so did the number of entry errors (r = .14), the longer the average entry time (r = .42), and the greater the perceived difficulty (r = .52).

Table 7. The correlation of LPD with performance outcomes for Study 2. $^{***}p < .001$

	LPD Score	Entry Errors	Mean Entry Time	Difficulty Rating
LPD Score	1			
Entry Errors	.14***	1		
Mean Entry Time	.42***	.32***	1	
Difficulty Rating	.52***	.28***	.40***	1

Second, we again estimated a series of linear regressions to test the relationship between LPD and each of the performance outcomes controlling for age, gender, and order. To account for the repeated measures aspect of the design, we adjusted for dependence when estimating standard errors. The results are the same as reported in Table 7.

Table 8. Standardized β coefficients from a regression of the LPD onto performance outcomes in Study 2. $^{*}p < .05$, $^{**}p < .01$, $^{***}p < .001$

	Entry Errors	Mean Entry Time	Difficulty Rating
Rule 2-No. of chunks	-.03	.07	-.03
Rule 3-No. of characters	.11**	.33***	.48***
Rule 4-Unsentence like capital	-.09	-.18***	-.27***
Rule 5-Mixed char. string	-.13	-.16***	-.33***
Rule 6-Sounds like	-.20**	-.29***	-.41***

Last, we examined the relationship between the individual LPD rules and each of the performance outcomes. The standardized β coefficients for the individual LPD rules are shown in Table 8. These results suggest that the number of characters per chunk (Rule 3), relative to the other LPD rules, appears to be most related to mean entry time and perceived difficulty (βs = .33, .48, respectively).

4 Conclusion

Organizational password policies often require criteria such as minimum number of characters, inclusion of symbols, capital letters and numbers to increase the complexity and security of passwords. The effectiveness of passwords is diminished by the fact that as passwords become more complex, they are harder to remember [2]. Complex passwords can be given to users; however it is more difficult for people to remember passwords that they do not create themselves [3]. We developed a scale for quantifying the linguistic and phonological complexity of randomly generated passwords. We tested the scale to examine the extent to which it predicted task completion time, error rates, and perceived difficulty from previously collected data [8]. Given the parsing of passwords into chunks by special characters (non-letter and non-digit), Rule 3 (number of characters per chunk) appeared to contribute the most to perceived difficulty, number of errors, and average entry time. While this rule was the most predictive, it may be possible to simplify the LPD scale by reducing the set of remaining rules. Nonetheless applying measures of linguistic and phonological difficulty to complex system generated passwords seems a promising avenue of future research.

One caveat to this work is that exploiting spoken or written language patterns is necessarily language specific. For example, Spanish questions and exclamations use punctuation before and after the sentence, unlike English. Similarly, the set of characters that create a possible word string in English (e.g., strab) may not be possible in another language (e.g., strab is not a possible word in Spanish).

Future research is needed with a larger number and variety of passwords. As shown in Table 1, there was minimal variance in the current 10 passwords on some measures, which makes it difficult to confidently assess the effects of the individual rules. The most predictive rule, Rule 3, was also one of the rules with the greatest range. The list of passwords in the present study did not explore extreme violations of the other rules in use of symbols, number of chunks, use of capitalization, or mixing of character strings. Future work should examine these elements and the impact on performance and the importance of LPD above and beyond traditional measures of complexity, such as number of characters/screens [8]. In addition, the point scores for the LPD rules implicitly weight the rules (e.g. Rule 2 adds two points per phrase while Rule 3 adds one points per character within a phrase). The different linguistic and phonological aspects of the rules may indeed have different weights that must be empirically determined.

Acknowledgements. This work was funded by the Comprehensive National Cyber-security Initiative (CNCI). The authors gratefully acknowledge Dr. Yee-Yin Choong for her thoughtful review and feedback and Ashley Barbee for assistance in coding.

References

1. Zviran, M., Haga, W.J.: Password Security: An Empirical Study. Journal of Management Information Systems 15(4), 161–184 (1999)
2. Keith, M., Shao, B., Steinbart, P.J.: The Usability of Passphrases for Authentication: An Empirical Field Study. International Journal of Human-Computer Studies 65, 17–28 (2007)
3. Vu, K.L., Proctor, R.W., Bhargav-Spantzel, A., Tai, B., Cook, J., Schultz, E.E.: Improving Password Security and Memorability to Protect Personal and Organizational Information. International Journal of Human-Computer Studies 65, 744–757 (2007)
4. Craik, F.I.M., Lockhart, R.S.: Levels of Processing: A Framework for Memory Re-search. Journal of Verbal Learning and Verbal Behavior 11, 671–684 (1971)
5. Gasser, M.: A Random Word Generator for Pronounceable Passwords. Mitre Corporation Report MTR-3006 (1975)
6. Bonneau, J.: Linguistic Properties of Multi-Word Passphrases. In: USEC Workshop on Useable Security, Kralendijk, Bonaire, Netherlands (2012)
7. Bonneau, J.: The Science of Guessing: Analyzing an Anonymized Corpus of 70 Million Passwords. In: IEEE Symposium on Security and Privacy (2012)
8. Greene, K.K., Gallagher, M.A., Stanton, B.C., Lee, P.Y.I.: Can't Type That! P@$$w0rd Entry on Mobile Devices. In: Proceedings of the Human Computer Interaction International Conference, Crete, Greece (2014)
9. Gobet, F., Lane, P.C.R., Croker, S., Cheng, P.C.-H., Jones, G., Oliver, I., Pine, J.M.: Chunking Mechanisms in Human Learning. Trends in Cognitive Science 5, 236–243 (2001)
10. Pierrehumbert, J.B.: The Phonetics and Phonology of English Intonation. Unpublished Ph.D. dissertation. MIT (1980)

An Examination of Typographic Standards and Their Relevance to Contemporary User-Centred Web and Application Design

Ian Christopher Dyer

Alibaba Hangzhou, China
chris@alibaba-inc.com

Abstract. The implementation of the various modes of typography on the Internet and device applications is now a relatively straightforward task, following a technological renaissance that began around 5 years ago that increased the importance of typography in web and application-based design.

Graphic designers had long desired to move beyond the early restrictions caused by the limited numbers of fonts that browsers could handle and display (and the even more restricted overlap between Windows and OSX operating systems). This desire fuelled an innovation boom that led to the wide array of font replacement and deployment technologies available today.

The new challenge for graphic designers is device fragmentation: keeping designs consistently readable across a variety of screen resolutions, screen types and devices. Yet, pure research on how users perceive, interact with and process the fundamental units of information transmission – words – remains limited. Extant studies are mostly confined to early (and outdated) papers in the 1980s and 1990s, investigations on the efficacy of e-ink, or other tenuously-related areas of human-computer interaction.

The presentation and comprehension of words and information is therefore restricted to niche areas of study for academic researchers and vehicles of aesthetic expression for graphic designers, with almost no communication between either group. This has led to a comprehensive lack of industry-standard best practices for typography, which is surprising considering the current focus of human factor-related disciplines in user-centered design.

This paper aims to collate and examine the history of typography, existing research, readability on electronic devices and current typographic trends, and lay down a roadmap for future research.

Keywords: Typography, HCI, Reading comprehension, Readability, Usability, Web design, Application design.

1 Introduction

With the establishment of the Internet as a ubiquitous communication and information delivery system utilised by users across private, public, academic, business, and government networks [1], rigid and well-considered standards have emerged across a

P.L.P. Rau (Ed.): CCD/HCII 2014, LNCS 8528, pp. 140–149, 2014.

broad range of technologies employed by Internet systems, processes, software and devices.

An example of such a technology is XML (Extensible Markup Language). XML was designed as a platform-agnostic solution to create a single portable, hierarchical data format comprehensible by both machines and humans. The properties of XML are defined in the XML 1.0 specification produced by the W3C which standardizes parameters like valid characters, encoding detection, escaping, comments, international use, well-formedness and error-handling [2].

Such detailed standards are entirely absent for the use of typography on the Internet, device interfaces and applications. The features of current tools used to create human-readable content on the internet (e.g. Adobe Illustrator, Adobe Photoshop, CSS3 and others) have only recently reached something approaching parity with each other. Furthermore, those systems themselves have only recently begun to offer the kind of basic functionality that dedicated typesetting tools have provided for many years [3].

With the mass-fragmentation of not only devices types, but also widely-varying device use scenarios well under way, practical research-derived typographical standards and best practices for fundamental use cases is long overdue.

2 Background

2.1 The History of Type

In the early days of personal computing, typography was a primitive, unconsidered and utilitarian aspect of information consumption. These limitations were partly due to hardware constraints (e.g. small, monochrome VDUs with low resolutions) and partly due to the fact that implementing type lay within the domain of software engineers that had little to no experience presenting information in readable ways.

The importance of type began to accelerate with increases in desktop computer power, screen sizes, resolution and graphics processing, all of which coincided with the mass-migration of graphic print designers who switched their careers over to website design in the early 2000s. Whilst this enhanced the presence of typography as an art form, there were still very few pure typography specialists or guidelines of use.

Today, industry still lacks specialist typesetters for all but very niche requirements. That there is no longer a seat for someone whose specialty is setting type—page makeup now typically being the province of the graphic designer and pasteup artist—only complicates the problem. [3] Ellen Lupton, curator of contemporary design at Cooper-Hewitt, National Design Museum in New York City notes: "Despite heroic efforts to create a critical discourse for design, our field remains ruled, largely, by convention and intuition." [4]

This is evident throughout industry – graphic designers often rely on received wisdom, folk lore, design trends or purely aesthetics when utilising typography in their work. Oft-repeated mantras like '…serif font for headers, sans-serif font for body' [8] originated at a time when low-resolution monitors predominated and serif fonts appeared blocky and difficult to read at these resolutions (Fig. 1).

The advent of high ppi (pixels per inch) displays on both mobile and desktop screens has long rendered this kind of rule redundant, yet these stylistic atavisms persist in the absence of any other up-to-date guidelines.

2.2 Technical Advances

Implementing the vast number of fonts and typefaces available in the mid-2000s for use on websites was a technical challenge. When graphic designers needed to use fonts that the browser could not display (e.g. for header text using the company's typeface), they would typically rely on the use of raster images, which created a number of collateral SEO and usability issues.

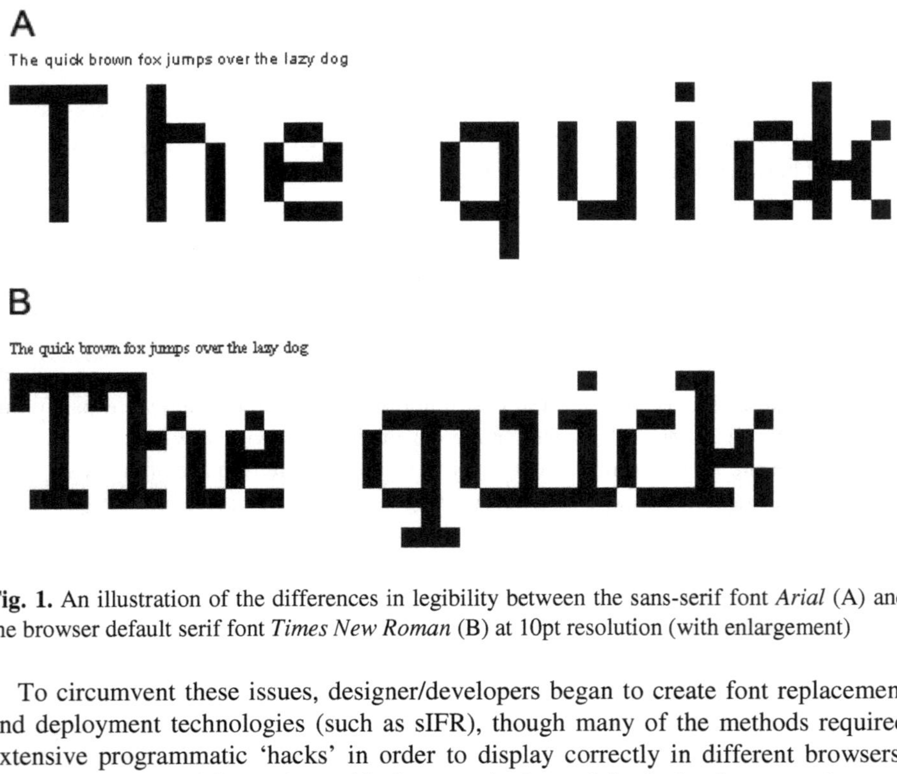

Fig. 1. An illustration of the differences in legibility between the sans-serif font *Arial* (A) and the browser default serif font *Times New Roman* (B) at 10pt resolution (with enlargement)

To circumvent these issues, designer/developers began to create font replacement and deployment technologies (such as sIFR), though many of the methods required extensive programmatic 'hacks' in order to display correctly in different browsers. The groundswell of frustration with these methods, and the lack of typography support in general, pushed the W3C to evolve the CSS web standard specifications to be on a par with desktop publishing programs.

2.3 Present Day

While still not fully implemented today, CSS3 now features much greater text support [5, 6]. Properties such as the @font-face rule allow direct embedding of almost any font [7], and fundamental text controls like overflows, word-wrapping and even

Photoshop-like effects such as drop shadow are now supported by most current browser versions [8].

Recently, the design and technology industries have redirected their efforts away from the graphically rich, difficult-to-scale and distracting interfaces that characterized digital design in the 2000s, and moved significantly in the direction of cleaner, unobstructed designs that place the user's access to clearly-presented content unambiguously at the center of importance.

3 Product Design

3.1 Complications

The expansion of browser capabilities and the proliferation of typefaces is clearly a major step forward for designers, allowing much greater freedom for creative expression in a much more usable way. However, a corollary also exists here: there are still no research-derived typography-specific standards in existence that will enable the consistent delivery of content which is easy for the user to read and process as efficiently as possible.

Creating such standards is further complicated by device fragmentation. The mosaic of different device types now available (contributed significantly to, but not exclusively by, the customizable open-source Android mobile operating system) has arguably exacerbated the problem by orders of magnitude (Fig. 2) [10, 11]. A custom typeface that is quite readable on a large desktop PC may be much more difficult to read on a small smartphone.

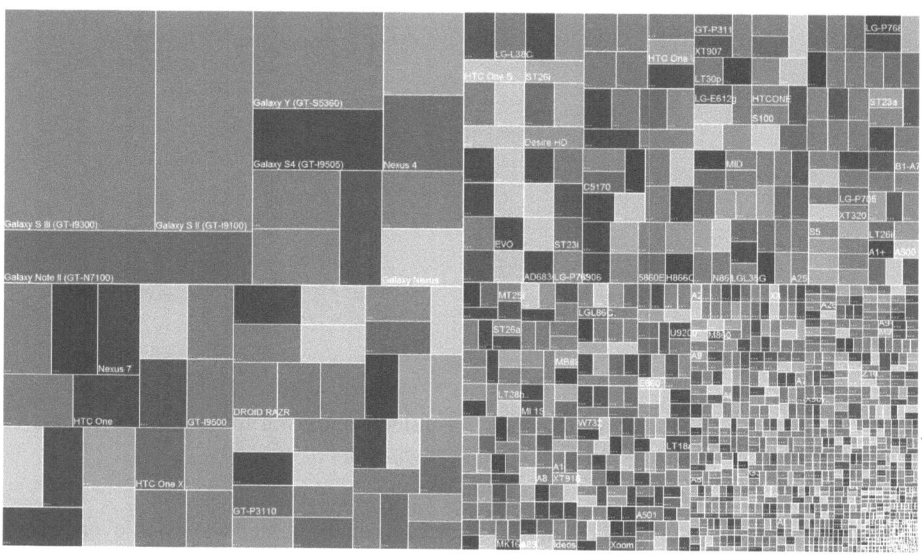

Fig. 2. Visualisation showing the number of Android devices that downloaded Open Signal's Wi-Fi/cellular network app

The new paradigm of responsive design is making some headway towards alleviating these kinds of issues of scale and readability. As discussed earlier with font replacement technologies, responsive design is a solution still in its infancy, and has yet to overcome many of the challenges of nascent technology (i.e. inconsistent application; low penetration; high technical overheads, etc.)

3.2 Processes

During the product design processes (Fig. 3) (A), the design phase normally starts from high considerations at the beginning of the project (the devices used), through the screen types on those devices, to the design of the app or website itself, down to the content and finally the typography, and perhaps (not in all cases) a consideration of the environment.

From the user's perspective (B), the considerations are almost reversed. Information is usually consumed on a device that is already owned by the user, or one that they are very familiar with (such as a workstation), so this is a very low concern. Most of their time is actually spent navigating the product or consuming the information within it, so the presentation of that content is of a very high concern.

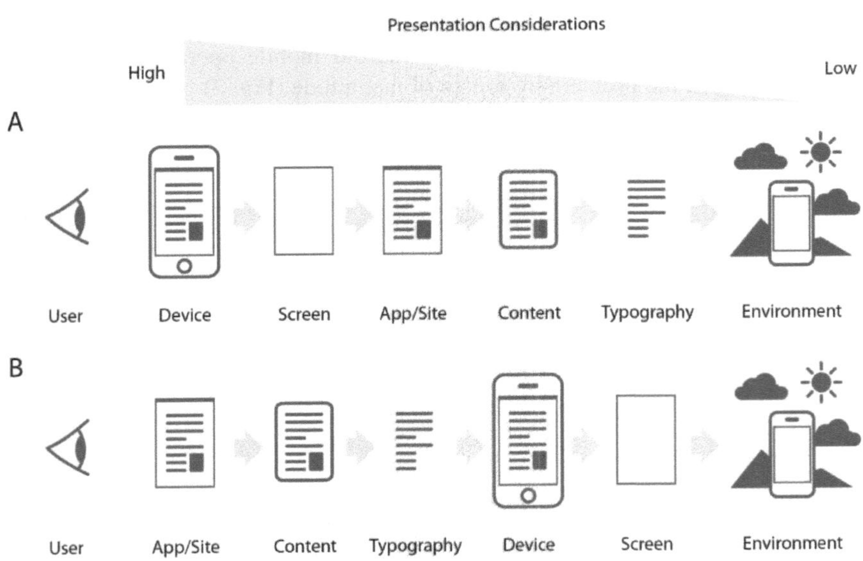

Fig. 3. Generalized illustration of the relative consideration given to information design. A: From the product design perspective; B: From the user perspective.

Product designers are considering the user in a much greater way than ever before, as evidenced by the growing fields of user research, information architects and interaction designers, though much more emphasis is needed on the mechanisms of information consumption in the product design pipeline.

4 Current Trends

With very little in the way of comprehensive research to use as a benchmark, a qualitative look at the current typographical trends can be employed to try and gain some understanding of how typography is being used, and what research (if any) has led in that direction.

Large companies have dedicated research and development teams, so in order to try and make some inference on their design methods, the products of four big technology companies (Microsoft, Apple, Google and Sony) were examined.

Microsoft, Apple, Sony and – to a lesser extent – Google (Android) share strong similarities in their treatment of typography. A cursory glance at their products reveals a general congruence of typographical form (fig.3).

Microsoft spent a huge amount of time and resources dedicated to their new design language (formerly known as 'Metro', now known as 'Windows 8 user interface' [12]) which has formed the design basis of most of their new products.

The focus for this new design language is 'content before chrome' [13]. That is to say, the information the user is interested in takes precedence, superseding the former over-reliance on rich graphical elements that tended to distract the user's attention away from the content [14]. Windows 8 UI was announced as follows:

"Metro is our design language. We call it metro because it's modern and clean. It's fast and in motion. It's about content and typography. And it's entirely authentic." [15]

Windows 8 UI leans heavily on the use of typography as wayfinders and navigation elements. The flagship font (designed in-house) is called 'Segoe UI' and comes in 5 weights:

- Segoe UI Light (200)
- Segoe UI Semilight (300)
- Segoe UI Regular (400)
- Segoe UI Semibold (600)
- Segoe UI Bold (700)

The 'Semilight' and 'Light' weights are used for most text [16], and this gives a very distinctive, slender yet modern feel to Microsoft's products and is highly readable.

Apple's iOS7 human interface guidelines follow a similar path to Microsoft; not only in their design philosophy, but also by focusing much more on typography and the clarity of text at all scales [17]. Apple's employment of the slender 'Helvetica Neue Thin' font across many areas of iOS 7, bears some strong similarities to Microsoft's Windows 8 UI typography strategy.

Sony also uses a slender font for many of its UI features on the Playstation 4, whilst Google's Android uses a slightly heavier bespoke font called Roboto and only calls into use the thin weight in rare cases.

Without knowing the details of these companies' internal research results, it is impossible to assert whether this apparent congruence of form is due to the research teams converging on the same design solutions, or whether the design teams are simply 'aping' each other's work under a design zeitgeist.

If the former is true, it provides a tantalizing hint that research can reveal fundamental typographic design rules that will allow the creation of consistently readable content structures.

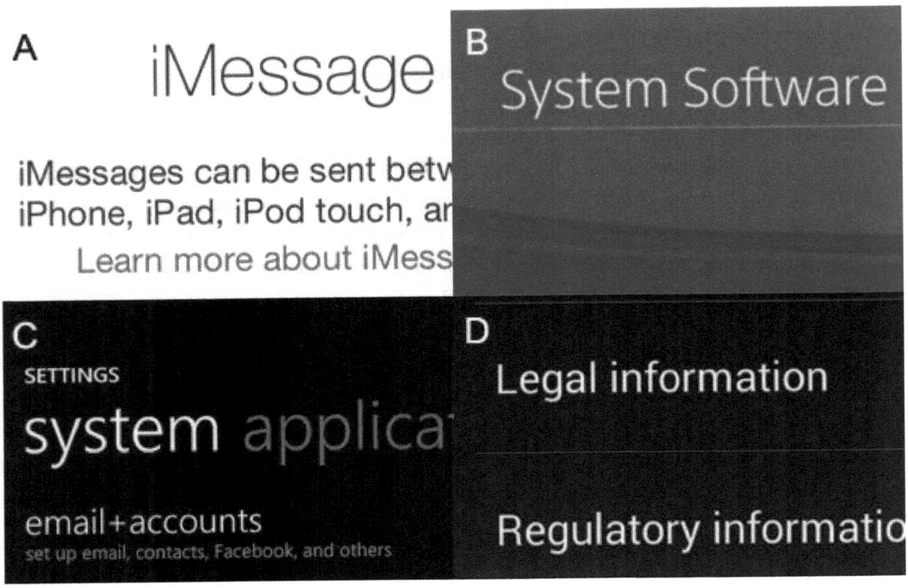

Fig. 4. Screenshots illustrating typography used in the operating systems of four different companies. A: Apple iOS7 (iMessage screen); B: Sony Playstation 4 (software update screen); C: Microsoft Windows Phone 8 (settings screen); D: Google Android (settings screen).

5 Suggested Approach

In order to create a research project based around the relative legibility of fonts, the interplay of user, device, content (typography) and environment needs to be considered.

An in-depth analysis of user perception and information processing lay outside the scope of this paper. However, a list of the basic elements affecting a user's ability to consume comprehend information are presented (fig. 4).

These elements can be further broken down into some of the more important variables that can affect the speed at which information is perceived and processed (fig. 5).

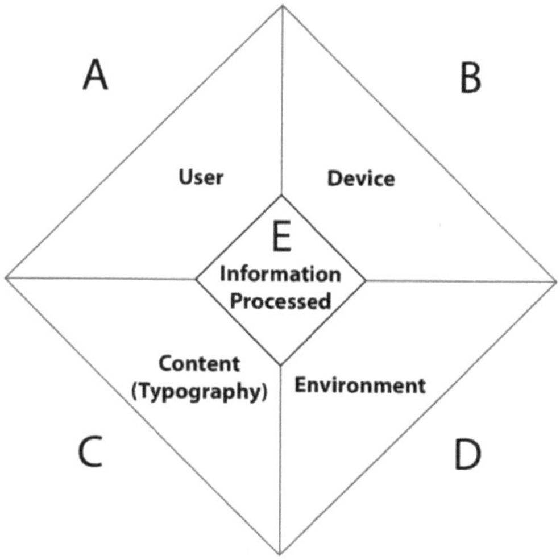

Fig. 5. Factors affecting user experience with regards to consumption of information. A: The user. B: The device. C: Content (typography). D: Environment. All factors culminate with E: the information processed.

Table 1. A breakdown of some of the primary factors affecting user consumption of information. The key variables asserted are highlighted.

	A: User	B: Device	C: Content (typography)	D: Environment
Variables	**Literacy**	**Screen size**	**Size**	**Ambient light**
	Distance to screen	**Screen brightness**	**Color**	**Ambient sound**
	Fatigue level	Screen type	**Typeface**	**Location**
	Visual acuity	Screen resolution	**Weight**	Temperature
	Task	Form factor	**Words per line**	
			Casing	
			Leading	
			Tracking	
			Kerning	
			Margin	
			Padding	
			Context	

As can be seen, there are handful of variables used when presenting typographical content. The parameters of these variables are mostly discrete, i.e. they are set using integers (except perhaps for color), which is useful when performing analysis.

Selecting which of the hundreds of thousands of available typefaces to use for testing (incorporating all of the different varieties, such as slab serif, sans serif, italicised, etc.) poses a huge challenge. Samples of typefaces should be carefully selected from each variety; all comprising a representative spread fonts that users may commonly encounter on the Internet and through device use.

6 Conclusion

From this cursory investigation into typography past and present, it should be clear that the way users interact with, and process words on, different devices in different use scenarios does not currently receive the attention given to other areas of research.

Significant amounts of research time is devoted to eye tracking/gaze interaction studies, and conclusions drawn from them are primarily based on information architecture, navigation structures, advertising efficacy, reading, searching, item location, design, etc.

The limited number of existing typography studies show that is a complicated, multi-faceted field of design with a large number of variables that are sensitive to other conditions.

Recent enhancements in technologies like CSS3 represent a significant maturation of the design and development industries, and have opened up fertile ground for a rigorous analysis-based development of typography and content consumption.

Future studies should strongly focus on real-world device use scenarios, and aim to provide a basic typographical toolkit with which to arm the graphic designer when creating content for human consumption.

References

1. Wikipedia article on the Internet, `http://en.wikipedia.org/wiki/Internet`
2. Wikipedia article on XML, `https://en.wikipedia.org/wiki/XML`
3. Felici, J.: The Complete Manual of Typography, 2nd edn., Peachpit, California, pp. 17–18 (2012)
4. Lupton, E.: `http://elupton.com/2009/10/science-of-typography/#more-113`
5. W3C CSS3 introduction, `http://www.w3schools.com/css/css3_text_effects.asp`
6. W3C CSS3 Text working draft, `http://www.w3.org/TR/css3-text/`
7. W3C CSS3 @font-face, `http://www.w3schools.com/css/css3_fonts.asp`
8. Mills, C.: Practical CSS3: Develop and Design, Peachpit, California, p. 87 (2013) ISBN-10: 0-321-82372-9, ISBN-13: 978-0-321-82372-4
9. Peck, W.: Great Web Typography, ch. 1, p. 7. Wiley Publishing Inc. (2003)
10. Open Signal Android Fragmentation Report (2013), `http://opensignal.com/reports/fragmentation-2013/`
11. Android OS, `http://www.android.com/meet-android/`
12. Windows Dev Center, `http://msdn.microsoft.com/en-us/windows/apps/hh779072`

13. Microsoft UK Developers,
http://www.microsoft.com/en-gb/developers/articles/content-before-chrome-and-on-demand-ui
14. Modern Design at Microsoft,
http://www.microsoft.com/en-us/news/stories/design/
15. Microsoft Research – Microsoft's new design language,
http://research.microsoft.com/apps/video/default.aspx?id=170075
16. Windows Dev Center,
http://msdn.microsoft.com/en-us/library/windows/apps/hh700394.aspx
17. Apple's iOS7 Human Interface Guidelines,
https://developer.apple.com/library/ios/documentation/userexperience/conceptual/mobilehig/

How Does User's Access to Object Make HCI Smooth in Recipe Guidance?

Atsushi Hashimoto*, Jin Inoue, Takuya Funatomi, and Michihiko Minoh

Kyoto University, Kyoto, sakyo-ku, Yoshida Honmachi 606-8501, Japan
ahasimoto@mm.media.kyoto-u.ac.jp
http://mm.media.kyoto-u.ac.jp

Abstract. This paper aims firstly to provide a flexible framework for developing recipe guiding system that displays information step-by-step along to events recognized in user's activity, and secondly to introduce an example of our implementation on the proposed framework. Those who are working on a task requiring high concentration can be easily distracted by the interactive systems that require any kind of explicit manipulations. In such situation, recognizing events in the task is helpful as an alternative of the manipulations. The framework allows a system designer to incorporate his/her own recognizer to the guiding system. Based on this framework, we implemented a system working with user's grabbing and releasing objects. A grabbed object tells the user's intention of what is about to do next, and releasing the object indicates its completion. In the experiments using the WOZ method, we confirmed that these actions worked well as switches for the interface. We also summarize some of our efforts for automating the system.

1 Introduction

We are what we eat. This phrase applies not only to the body, but also to the mind. Daily food habits are deeply related to both our physical and mental health. A pleasant meal is one of the most important elements in our quality of life.

In proportion to its importance, food preparation is a difficult task. People desire to have a delicious dish, a variety of tastes, and achieve a good nutritional balance simultaneously. The requirements of such a dish become more important when you participate in a potluck party, or if you have a family member with health issues. For such purposes, recipes are helpful. A good recipe book will ensure a delicious dish, the variation, and the balanced intake; however, we cannot help but arrange the recipe according to our familiar tastes by ignoring important information, such as amount of seasoning, heat level, and so on. It results poor variations and a biased nutrition.

This happens because we normally refer to a recipe before starting cooking, but not during the cooking. It is inconvenient to look for the information from

* Corresponding author.

P.L.P. Rau (Ed.): CCD/HCII 2014, LNCS 8528, pp. 150–161, 2014.

a long recipe text continuously, while keeping an eye on a knife edge for safety, and on a hot pan for proper timing. In such a situation, the information should be provided step by step *without distracting the users*. It is also necessary that the system is usable for any family member because home kitchen is normally shared with a family. Hence the interface should be *intuitive for any kind of people*. In this sense, the interface must have a high level of smoothness on the interaction.

In this paper, we introduce a frame work for automatic recipe guiding system in Section 2, and show our approach based on user's grabbing and releasing objects in Section 3 and 4.

2 Framework of the Recipe Guiding System

The traditional style of recipe is often ignored while cooking. This happens because many recipe shares a common part of processes. The experienced users can bring such a part without recipe guidance. When considering a non-distractive interface for these users, it is a natural way to understand what is going on in the kitchen automatically, and provides appropriate information continuously.

For the purpose of describing the possible situations while cooking a dish, we propose a recipe format of Hand Work Markup Language (HWML)[1]. HWML targets to provide a machine readable format of recipe. In order to clarify the generality of HWML, we first model a human cooking activity in 2.1, and then explain the important elements of HWML in 2.2.

We also provide a platform of recipe guiding system CHIFFON[2] in 2.3. This system provides a research platform of the guiding system along to HWML.

2.1 Modeling Human Cooking Activity

A recipe gives information for achieving the goal of making a dish, as a form of cooking steps. Each step corresponds to a sub-goal, and has a direction (often via text and images). The direction gives users an intension to execute the directed task. These relationship fits naturally into the idea of Norman's seven stages of action [1].

A typical traditional recipe is shown in Fig. 1. Many recipe sites seem to adopt this style of format, but the exact format is not opened. One example of open format is RecipeML [2]. RecipeML has two main component of <ingredient> and <direction>. A <ingredient> element describes foods with their amount in a machine readable format. In the contrast to the structured <ingredient> tag, the <direction> element is just a sequence of <step> elements. Each <step> element contains a direction written in a natural language, and is not machine readable.

[1] Its definition by RELAX NG schema and examples are available on `http://mm.media.kyoto-u.ac.jp/members/a_hasimoto/hwml`

[2] CHIFFON stands for the system guiding CHeff's Ideas For Food preparatiON in the spirit of guiding a recipe like chiffon cake, which cannot be well taught by traditional recipes. The detail of CHIFFON is also referable at `http://mm.media.kyoto-u.ac.jp/members/a_hasimoto/chiffon`

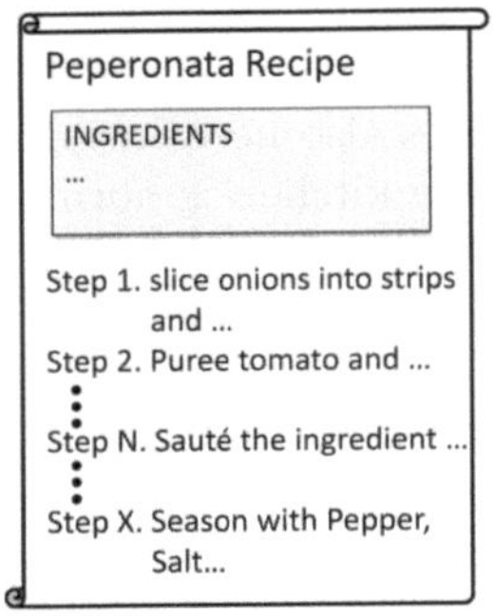

Fig. 1. General style of recipe

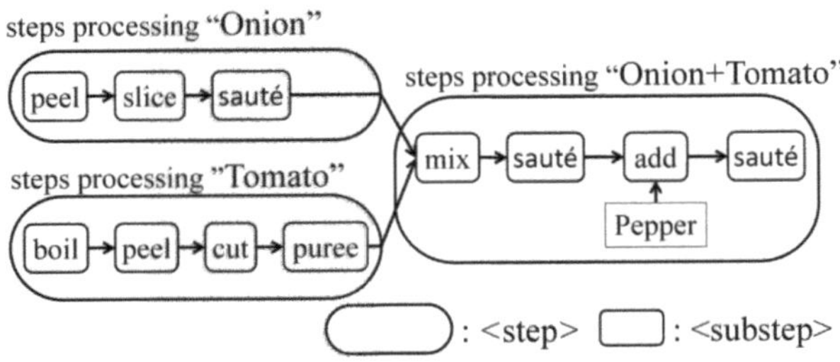

Fig. 2. Graphical recipe representation

In a real activity of cooking, the order of step is replaceable. For example, the cook can start the cooking with any ingredient. For representing the partial order of steps, Hamada [3] proposed a graphical recipe (Fig. 2). In the graph, when two nodes are not lineal relatives, the order relation is not defined between them, and you can execute whichever in first. This gives the partial order.

The above graph representation describes what the cook does for making a dish; however it is not satisfactory to represent what is going on in the kitchen. Some steps create a child process of cooking, in which the state of foods changes without any direct operation by the cook. Therefore, we need a food-centered viewpoint to describe such processes of cooking. A typical process is heating. A cook will start another step after putting foods into the hot pan. While doing the other step in parallel, the cook must care about the foods in the pan. When the foods are cooked enough, the cook must turn the stove off.

This kind of cooking progress is not taken into consideration by the graph representation of recipe. We model this type of progress as a communication between parent process and child process. Recent smart electronic appliances are able to complete their process without user's help. Such a child processes is asynchronous. The parent process just direct to start the process.

On the other hand, most of child processes require user's help. In such cases, the child process requests the parent process to check the state of foods, via a synchronous communication. The user stops the current operation of the main process at his/her own discretion, and works on the child process at his/her own discretion if necessary.

2.2 Recipe Format for Guiding Recipe

The same way as RecipeML, HWML also consists of two main components of <materials> and <directions>. The important difference appears in <directions>. A <step> element of HWML has an attribute @*parent*, which specifies the step executed before the element. This enables to describe the partial order relationship of steps shown in Fig. 2.

It is important for a guiding system how finely a direction in a recipe is described. A fine description increase the number of cooking steps. In this sense, the fineness of directions defines the unit of a step In the concept of our guiding system, we roughly decided the strategy as follows. For the beginner cooks, the direction should be enough simple to translate the intention given by the direction to motion sequence [1]. On the other hand, such simple directions may annoy the experienced cooks. In order to be useful for both users, we prepare the simple directions, but keep it ignorable.

This is realized by multimedia contents of the recipe. When the direction includes the information characterizing the taste of recipe, it should be provided with voice announce in order to attract user's attention. A typical example is amount of seasoning. Otherwise, the direction is provided text and static images, which will be displayed on the monitor silently. The user will ignore such information when he/she can bring the cooking forward without the system. Sometimes, the simple direction is still not understandable for the beginner cooks because of unfamiliar ingredients and unfamiliar cooking terms. For such cases, HWML allows attaching a video clip to the direction. The movie clip directly carries down how to execute the step directly to such users.

In order to clarify the problem of the partial order relations and the fineness, we arranged a lower element of <step>, namely, <substep> elements. This is also shown in Fig. 2. The partial order relations are described by the attribute of <step>, and the fine directions are described in the <substep> elements which are children of the <step> elements.

The request of communication from a child process is represented by < notification> element. The message in this element is supposed to pop up over the direction of main process with a sound. The main process is stopped at the user's judgment, and the child process is further processed by the user. The <notification> elements can also be used as an egg-timer with message. Any intelligent cooking utensils and electric appliances can use <notification> to notify information to the users.

2.3 CHIFFON: The Framework for Recipe Guiding System

In addition to HWML, we also prepared a framework of CHIFFON for developing the systems working with HWML. CHIFFON has the three modules of *viewer*, *navigator* and *recognizer* (Fig. 3). The viewer works on a web browser (Fig. 4), and communicates with the other two modules via HTTP protocol with data described in JSON format.

This framework is highly flexible in the sense that the navigation algorithm and the recognizer can be replaced to arbitrary one, as long as communicating with viewer along the protocol. It is open for research purpose and the researchers can implement their own algorithm of navigation to try their dynamic scheduling algorithm such as [3, 4], and try their recognizer for an automatic guiding system.

Any recognition targets can be described and utilized in a recipe written in HWML. For that, HWML has two tags of <event> and <trigger>. An <event> element identifies the recognition target, which is any event in the cooking.

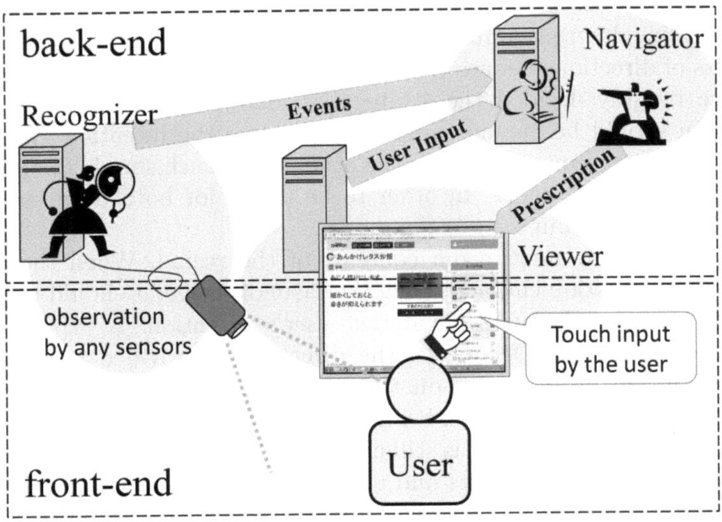

Fig. 3. The framework of CHIFFON modules

A <trigger> element refers <event> elements, and is written as a child of a <substep> or <notification> element. The parent <substep>(or <notification>) element is displayed when the referred event has occurred.

A designer of the recognizer can control the viewer by putting <event> and <trigger> elements in the recipe, and define the strategy to display <substep> and <notification> in the navigation. The navigation algorithm checks occurrence of the events via communication with the recognizer. When any event indicated in a <trigger> element occurs, the navigator sends a prescription to the viewer to show the corresponding element of <substep> or <notification>.

3 Feasibility Study for a Recipe Guiding System Based on User's Access to Object

3.1 Predicting the Next Step from User's Access to Object

Using CHIFFON framework, we developed a recipe guiding system for a feasibility study of a non-distractive interface based on the events of grabbing and releasing objects. We call these events "*access to objects*." The users naturally access objects even in the busy situations of cooking. It is also an important property that, in human-to-human interaction, the grabbed object is often a focus of interest. It is natural to ask "how should I use this?" when holding an object. The object in hand represents what he intends to do next. The access to objects is expected to serve as a non-distractive and intuitive trigger to provide the information.

Here, what we have to keep in mind is that the user may grab an object just to put it aside at every moment in cooking. In such cases, the object does

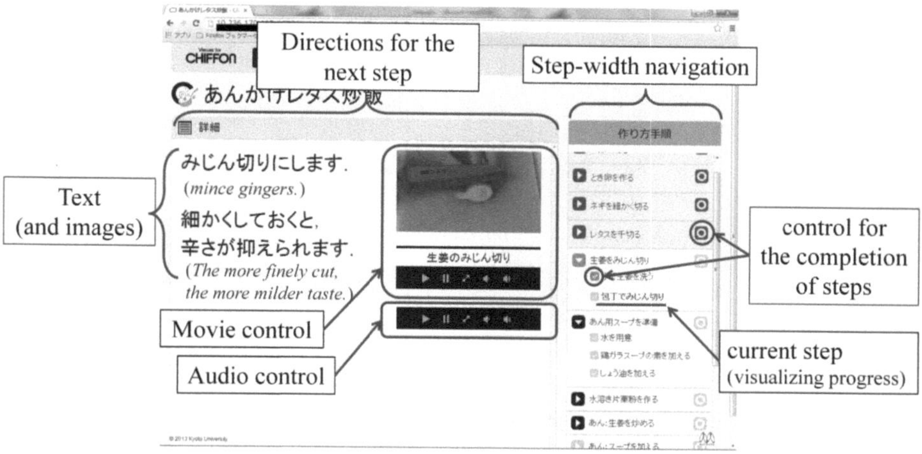

Fig. 4. Example of displayed directions for the step in execution

not related to the next step. Therefore, the problem is to distinguish which objects are related to the next step, and which are not. We need to pass over the unrelated object based on contextual information. For this purpose, we tracked the progress of cooking on the graph, and narrow down the candidates of the next step. The progress tracking was realized by only accesses to objects.

3.2 Experimental Evaluation on the Real Cooking

In order to evaluate the possibility of the proposed interface, we organized the experiments as follows. First, we prepared a recipe written in HWML with events of *object-grabbing* and *object-releasing* to each substep.

The recognizer is implemented as an interface shown in Fig. 5, which recognizes above two events by the Wizard of OZ (WOZ) method. Each switch corresponds to an object appearing in any of triggers. When the switch is down by the wizard, an event of *object-grabbing* is sent to the navigator, and *object-releasing* when up. The other experimental settings are described below.

Recipe. We performed the experiments with a recipe of "lettuce fried rice with starchy sauce." The number of steps in its graphical representation is 30.

Subjects. Two subjects made the dish with our system. Both subjects have cooked a dish more than four times per week on average at least over two years. Before starting cooking, ten minutes were given to the subjects for making a rough plan to cook it in the subject's favorite way.

Kitchen environment. The subjects cooked the dish in the kitchen in our laboratory, which has an archive system to analyze their activity (Fig. 6).

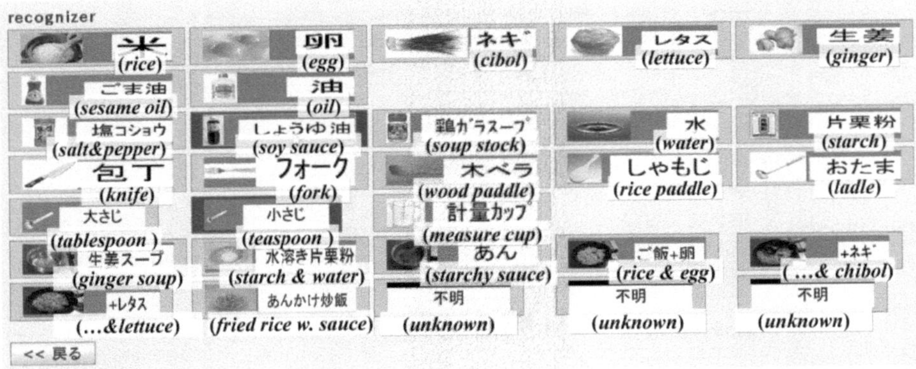

Fig. 5. Interface for the wizard in the WOZ method

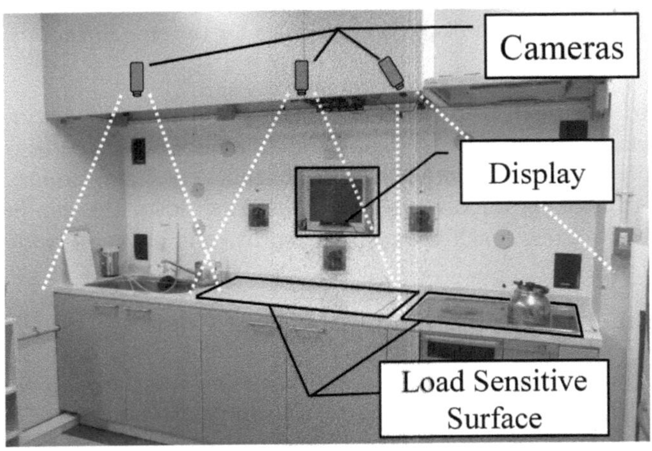

Fig. 6. Kitchen environment with the archive system in our laboratory

The accuracy of the displayed steps by the proposed system is shown in Table 1. Despite the large number of failed displays, the errors were corrected manually only two times by both subjects. This means that most of failed displays were not referred by the subjects.

4 Toward the Automated Guiding System

To automate the system proposed in Section 3.2, the recognizer by WOZ must be replaced to a combination of detecting access to objects, and recognizing the accessed objects. In this section, we introduce our efforts to automate these two tasks.

Table 1. Accuracy of displayed steps

	Subject A	Subject B
# of right steps displayed	161	128
# of false steps displayed	46	63
Accuracy	77.8%	67.0%
Error correction by Subject	2	2

4.1 Detecting Access to Objects

There are several approaches to detect the motion of grabbing and releasing objects. The one is to attach tags or markers to the objects [5–7]. This approach is not suitable for our purpose because food is included in the targets of detection. The tags and markers must be editable, and be attached to items at every food shopping. Even if the tags are attached to food containers, the user has to notify each combination of container and food to the system in advance. The maintenance cost is clearly too high to be used every day, especially for a home application.

Another approach is image processing [8, 9]; however a kitchen is a difficult environment for image processing. Many metallic surfaces appear on the cook-top, and water makes also unwished effects to the observed images. There is also another problem of occlusion. An observation from the ceiling cannot avoid the occlusion by human body, but one from the wall may also be occluded by tall objects on cook-top. The occlusion delays and even disables the detection of access to objects. This is undesired to provide timely information.

To deal with this problem, we developed a method using both camera and load sensitive surface (Fig. 8), which was originally proposed by Schmidt et al. [10] and have been already brought into a kitchen by Chi et al. [11].

The load sensitive surface consists of four load sensors under the table top. The load sensors can timely detect the change in the total weight of objects loaded onto the surface. It is not affected by the occlusion in images. A displacement of objects generates change in load values observed by the sensors. The position of displaced object is estimated from the ratio of load variation at four sensors, which indicates the location of center of gravity (COG); however this traditional approach works only when one object is moved at once. When two or more objects displaced at once, it is not clear from the load values which objects are accessed and where they are.

We overcame this problem by the location of objects estimated by image processing. There are many methods to track object's location [12, 13]. Some of those methods can estimate object's location in a certain accuracy even under the occlusion.

We proposed a method which timely detects the access to objects, even when several objects are accessed at once [14]. The location of COG yielded by displacing two objects is predictable when the weight and location is known for each object. We generate some hypotheses of the combination of displaced objects whenever any variation of load is detected. The hypotheses are evaluated by the location of objects, which is given by image processing. When the locations are

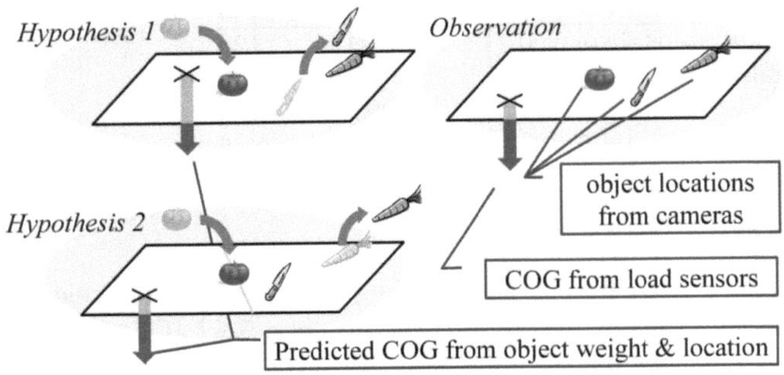

Fig. 7. Detecting access to objects by camera and load sensing surface

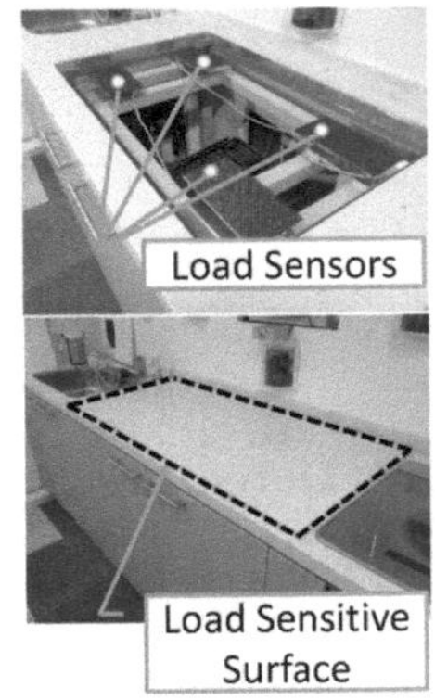

Fig. 8. Load sensitive table embedded on cook-top

known, the ratio of load variation can be expected for each hypothesis (Fig. 7). We choose the most probable hypothesis based on how similar the expected ratio and the observed one are. For the detail of the method and experimental results, please refer our previous report [14].

We embedded the load sensors on the cook-top in our kitchen (Fig. 8), but the above method is not evaluated yet in this environment with the system in Section 3.2. This is one of our future works.

4.2 Recognizing Objects on the Cook-Top

In order to use the access to objects for the input to the interface, it is necessary to know what kind of object was accessed. This is known as the problem of object recognition. There is a large amount of techniques to recognize objects [15]. Those methods are generally very effective to manufactured product, such as cooking utensils, fabricated food, and their packages.

The main problem occurs with fresh foods. A fresh food has only poor visual characteristics of color, shape and texture. Their color is dominated by only several pigments. Hence, many categories of food share exactly the same color. The shape is depends on growing condition as much as its species.

Textures are more helpful than color and shape, and there are several research using this feature for the recognition task [16–18]. These studies suppose the applications in supermarket and grocery stores. In such a situation, a high quality image of food is expected as an input to the recognition system, where the high quality means an optimal pose of food, and enough resolution to obtain the texture. Because human has a high adaptivity, the user will learn the best pose and position to hold the foods.

In contrast to those applications, the high quality images are not promised in our application. The resolution will be limited in order to observe whole cook-top by only several cameras, and the food is observed only as a small region.

The pose of foods is also not optimal. Hence, it is difficult to achieve satisfactory accuracy for the use in the interface.

For enhancing the accuracy, our research group proposed two methods of food recognition [19, 20], which maximized the merits of observing whole cooking processes.

In [19], Yamakata used a graph constraint to recognize food. She tracked food mixed in the cooking, and obtained a tracking result in the same form of the graphical recipe. This graph is compared with the recipe graph, and the most likely matching result is adopted as the recognition result.

We focused the chance of destructive inspection in cooking [20], namely cutting process. When foods are cut, it yields the signals of sound and load. The signals are expected to reflect how hard the object is, and how the structure in inside of food is. By integrating these signals with visual information, we obtained 79.0% of accuracy to recognize 23 classes of foods.

5 Discussion

In this paper, we developed the system guiding the recipe for cooking. Developing an HCI system in home kitchen offers us various challenging issues: highly free activity by users, flexible scenario of the recipe, foods which cannot be tagged, and, most importantly, the compatibility for daily use. We consider that realizing the proposed interface contributes to many other applications of making things.

For example, the word "recipe" is not used only in cooking context. Any kind of instructions to make things are often called "recipe." One active area is object assembling. Many interfaces for assembling task are proposed in the field of augmented reality [21–23]. In the assembling task, various objects are accessed by the worker, and our system will also work in assembling context.

It should also be noted that the proposed system should collaborate with various research fields. First, it is costly to prepare the graphical recipe with triggers manually. Ideally, it should be obtained by natural language processing automatically, or at least, it should be learned by some observations by experienced users.

The nutritional information should be visualized and recorded, just as the system by Chi et al. [11]. The information may be shared with hospitals for making nutritional instructions. It may also contribute to the field of prevention medicine, but the privacy should be saved simultaneously.

6 Conclusion

Those who are working on a task requiring high concentration, such as food preparation, can be easily distracted by the interactive systems that require any kind of explicit manipulations. When providing information in such situation without any distraction, recognition techniques to detect any events in cooking and a good strategy for displaying the guidance are the critical components of interface. For the purpose of enhancing such studies, we developed a format of recipe and a framework for recognition and navigation, respectively named HWML and CHIFFON.

Using the CHIFFON framework and HWML, we tested an interactive system based on the access to objects. Foods and utensils are accessed naturally while preparing food, and are informative to predict the next step automatically. In the experiments, this interaction model worked well with only two manual inputs against 30 steps of the recipe from both two subjects. We confirmed that the access to objects contributes to realize a smooth human-computer interaction.

We also developed several basic techniques for realizing the proposed system without the WOZ method. The system should detect the access to objects automatically and timely. We introduced the method by combination of camera and load sensors for this task. Food recognition is another problem because its appearance includes only poor features to be distinguished. For this problem, we showed a method using a cutting process. It yields several signals which reflects foods' physical properties. Owing to the signals, we achieved 79.0% of accuracy against 23 food categories.

We also brought several visions of the proposed systems and further researches. Some of them are already studied actively by the different research groups. The proposed systems should be matured enough for collaborating with such studies.

Acknowledgment. This work was supported by JSPS KAKENHI Grant Number 24240030.

References

1. Norman, D.A.: The design of everyday things. Basic Books (2002)
2. FormatData: The Recipe Markup Landuage (RecipeML) (2006), `http://www.formatdata.com/recipeml/`
3. Hamada, R., Okabe, J., Ide, I., Sakai, S., Tanaka, H.: Cooking navi: assistant for daily cooking in kitchen. In: Proc. of the 13th ACM International Conf. on Multimedia, pp. 371–374 (2005)
4. Matsushima, Y., Funabiki, N., Zhang, Y., Nakanishi, T., Watanabe, K.: Extensions of cooking guidance function on android tablet for homemade cooking assistance system. In: IEEE 2nd Global Conf. on Consumer Electronics, pp. 397–401 (2013)
5. Nakauchi, Y., Fukuda, T., Noguchi, K., Matsubara, T.: Time sequence data mining for cooking support robot. In: Proc. of International Symposium on Computational Intelligence in Robotics and Automation, pp. 481–486 (2005)
6. Siltanen, S., Hakkarainen, M., Korkalo, O., Salonen, T., Saaski, J., Woodward, C., Kannetis, T., Perakakis, M., Potamianos, A.: Multimodal user interface for augmented assembly. In: IEEE 9th Workshop on Multimedia Signal Processing, MMSP 2007, pp. 78–81. IEEE (2007)
7. Ueda, M., Funatomi, T., Hashimoto, A., Watanabe, T., Minoh, M.: Developing a real-time system for measuring the consumption of seasoning. In: IEEE International Symposium on Multimedia, pp. 393–398. IEEE (2011)
8. Prasad, V.S.N., Kellokumpu, V., Davis, L.S.: Ballistic hand movements. In: Perales, F.J., Fisher, R.B. (eds.) AMDO 2006. LNCS, vol. 4069, pp. 153–164. Springer, Heidelberg (2006)

9. Hashimoto, A., Mori, N., Funatomi, T., Mukunoki, M., Kakusho, K., Minoh, M.: Tracking food materials with changing their appearance in food preparing. In: IEEE International Symposium on Multimedia, pp. 248–253 (2010)
10. Schmidt, A., Strohbach, M., Van Laerhoven, K., Friday, A., Gellersen, H.: Context acquisition based on load sensing. In: Borriello, G., Holmquist, L.E. (eds.) UbiComp 2002. LNCS, vol. 2498, pp. 333–350. Springer, Heidelberg (2002)
11. Chi, P.-Y.(P.), Chen, J.-H., Chu, H.-H., Lo, J.-L.: Enabling calorie-aware cooking in a smart kitchen. In: Oinas-Kukkonen, H., Hasle, P., Harjumaa, M., Segerståhl, K., Øhrstrøm, P. (eds.) PERSUASIVE 2008. LNCS, vol. 5033, pp. 116–127. Springer, Heidelberg (2008)
12. Yilmaz, A., Javed, O., Shah, M.: Object tracking: A survey. ACM Computing Surveys 38(4), 1–45 (2006)
13. Grabner, H., Matas, J., Van Gool, L., Cattin, P.: Tracking the invisible: Learning where the object might be. In: IEEE Conf. on Computer Vision and Pattern Recognition, pp. 1285–1292 (2010)
14. Yasuoka, R., Hashimoto, A., Funatomi, T., Minoh, M.: Detecting start and end times of object-handlings on a table by fusion of camera and load sensors. In: Proc. of the 5th International Workshop on Multimedia for Cooking and Eating Activities, pp. 51–56 (2013)
15. Jafri, R., Ali, S.A., Arabnia, H.R., Fatima, S.: Computer vision-based object recognition for the visually impaired in an indoors environment: a survey. The Visual Computer, 1–26 (2013)
16. Bolle, R.M., Connell, J., Haas, N., Mohan, R., Taubin, G.: Veggievision: A produce recognition system. In: Proc. of IEEE Workshop on Applications of Computer Vision, pp. 244–251 (1996)
17. Faria, F.A., dos Santos, J.A., Rocha, A., Torres, R.S.: Automatic classifier fusion for produce recognition. In: Proc. of the 25th Conf. on Graphics, Patterns and Images, pp. 252–259 (2012)
18. Arivazhagan, S., Shebiah, R.N., Nidhyanandhan, S., Ganesan, L.: Fruit recognition using color and texture features. Journal of Emerging Trends in Computing and Information Sciences 1(2), 90–94 (2010)
19. Yamakata, Y., Kakusho, K., Minoh, M.: Object recognition based on object's identity for cooking recognition task. In: 2010 IEEE International Symposium on Multimedia, pp. 278–283. IEEE (2010)
20. Hashimoto, A., Inoue, J., Nakamura, K., Funatomi, T., Ueda, M., Yamakata, Y., Minoh, M.: Recognizing ingredients at cutting process by integrating multimodal features. In: Proc. of the ACM Multimedia 2012 Workshop on Multimedia for Cooking and Eating Activities, pp. 13–18 (2012)
21. Zauner, J., Haller, M., Brandl, A., Hartmann, W.: Authoring of a mixed reality assembly instructor for hierarchical structures. In: ACM International Symp. on Mixed and Augmented Reality, vol. 1, pp. 237–246 (2003)
22. Yuan, M.L., Ong, S.K., Nee, A.Y.C.: Assembly guidance in augmented reality environments using a virtual interactive tool. In: Innovation in Manufacturing Systems and Technology (2005)
23. Tang, A., Owen, C., Biocca, F., Mou, W.: Comparative effectiveness of augmented reality in object assembly. In: Proc. of the SIGCHI Conf. on Human Factors in Computing Systems, pp. 73–80 (2003)

Evaluating the Effects of Cultural Preferences on Website Use

Hsiu Ching Laura Hsieh

Department of Creative Design,
National Yunlin University of Science and Technology,
123 Section 3, University Rd., Douliou, Yunlin, Taiwan 64002
laurarun@gmail.com

Abstract. Cultural diversity makes it impossible for designers developing web design depending on instinctive knowledge or personal experiences. Therefore, there is a need to investigate the requirements and preferences of target-culture users. Based on the results of local website auditing in the author's previous research [6], there are significantly different preferences for web interface design between Taiwanese and Australian cultures. Further, it is questioned that, if the cultural preferences are incorporated in the web, the effects of web communication can be improved. Thus, the aim of this paper is to evaluate the effects of cultural preferences on website use. The methodologies in this research would be introduced in the following. First, two cultures are selected. Second, hypotheses are constructed. Third, four experimental websites are constructed. Fourth, the usability test is established. Based on the results of the usability test, the findings would be presented to help web developers and enable designers to become aware of the possibilities of effective communications with a specific culture.

Keywords: cultural preferences, usability, interface design.

1 Introduction

The world has become a global marketplace. Globalization affects computer-based communications, and this is particularly obvious in web design applications, which can be accessed globally. Under the context of globalization, Hofstede [3] suggested that web developers could accommodate diverse cultural markets by applying localization as an alternative strategy to developing the global market. Therefore, there is a need to investigate the requirements and preferences of target-culture users. Based on the results of local website auditing in the previous research of Hsieh, Chen, and Hong [6], there are significantly different preferences for web interface design between Taiwanese and Australian cultures. Furthermore, it is questioned whether those cultural differences could be applied to improve web usability. Therefore, this research is to evaluate the effects of cultural preferences on website use.

P.L.P. Rau (Ed.): CCD/HCII 2014, LNCS 8528, pp. 162–173, 2014.

2 Literature Review

2.1 Culture and Cultural Theories

Referring to Hofstede [4] definition of culture, in which personal patterns of thinking, feeling and behaviors were accumulated in the lifetime from the childhood and the ways of feeling, thinking, and mental programming would vary the received social environments. From the investigation of IBM employees in 53 countries from 1978 to 1983, Hofstede defined the patterns of differences and similarities among the responses of employees and proposed five dimensions for the culture theory, introduced as the follows.

Long-Term Orientation vs. Short-Term Orientation. Long-term orientation presented a critical part in Asian countries influenced by Confucianism that people from such countries strongly believed in the necessity of an unequal relationship for the stability of a society. The harmony between family and society was clearly defined in the hierarchical relationship, and virtuous behaviors were identified by hard work and perseverance. On the contrary, cultures with short-term orientation revealed opposite attributes [4] [7].

Individualism vs. Collectivism. Individualism in culture implied loose ties with which all inclined to care about themselves or their nuclear family and usually tended to independence from others. A collectivist culture tended to valuing more group welfare than individual one and group relationship in which the major factor was loyalty. Individualistic countries, on the other hand, valued the individual accomplishments while collectivistic countries stressed on the benefits of working in a group [4] [7].

Power Distance, referring to the extent of less powerful members in a society expecting and accepting unequal power distribution. Countries with higher power distance cultures presented the features of hierarchical structures in the organizations, with stricter relationships between superiors and the subordinates than in countries with low power distance. Low power distance cultures revealed the characteristics of more equal relationships between superiors and the subordinates and the more stable structure of an organization [4] [7].

Masculinity vs. Femininity, referring to gender roles in a culture. Countries with strong masculine cultures tended to focusing on challenge, social recognition, and the pursuit of welfare. On the contrary, countries with less defined masculine cultures tended to collapsing gender distinction, overlapping gender roles, and emphasizing security, care of others, and the environment [4] [7].

Uncertainty Avoidance, referring to the extent of people expecting to avoid uncertain conditions. People with low uncertainty avoidance cultures were more comfortable with uncertain situations, while the ones from cultures with higher uncertainty avoidance tended to preferring rules and rejecting changes because of the anxiety resulted from uncertainty [4] [7].

2.2 Culture and Web Usability

Using the word "culturability" which combined two words of "usability" and "culture", Barber and Badre [1] constructed a cultural marker approach as a kind of systematic usability method to examine hundreds of websites and defined cultural markers, such as colors, fonts, icons, metaphors, geography, sounds, motions, flags, language, preferences for text and graphics, directionality of written language, help features, and navigation tools, in order to facilitate the user's performance. By interviewing target culture people about their experiences, Sun [13] examined the effects of cultural markers (cultural preferences) on web usability and concluded that people preferred interactive interface with cultural markers from their own cultures as the web usability could be strengthened by cultural markers. Based on Baber and Badre's cultural marker approach, Smith et al. [11] figured out the culturally preferred design elements in Taiwanese and Indian cultures and defined such design elements as cultural attractors, which were the interface design attributes of the websites, reflecting their denotations matching the expectations of the local culture. Cultural design preferences could directly map into culturally appropriate design elements for a website, but were usually inclined to the stereotype. When the cultural design preferences were successfully applied to a website, they could markedly increase the usability of websites and thus address the needs of the target culture audience. As Sun mentioned, exhaustive studies could be reduced when a company realized the type of cultural markers being used for a particular culture.

2.3 Web Characteristics for Effective Communication

According to Smart et al. [10] , it was essential to identify several vital categories (i.e., typography, site structure and cognitive design, medium use, message content, appeal, accessibility) of web design characteristics for helping the designers convey desired meaning and the users more easily obtain the intended meaning. Based on the objective and requirement of this research, the key components of web for effective communications are illustrated as below.

1)Visual Presentation, including images, photos, symbols, icons and graphics. The attributes of visual representation can efficiently transmit a message to the viewer in an attracting manner. Russo and Boor [9] stated that images, similar to words, were the visual language of a culture, but could not always be translated. The images, symbols and icons recognized in the culture might have no meaning or even contrary signification in another culture. **2)Navigation**, referred to different kinds of navigational tools, menu formats, links, and search capabilities. Without precise assistance in attaining information, the users may get lost in a website. Marcus and Gould [7] declared the influences of culture on the navigation in web design. Audiences from cultures with a high uncertainty dimension tending to a navigation structure intended to prevent them from getting lost, while cultures with a low uncertainty dimension inclined to less control of navigation. **3)Links.** In the other works, Sun [13] investigated the users from America, Germany, China and Brazil with regard to their design preferences and found the existence of different preferences. It was discovered that the German audience preferred to the links in the navigation bar, which could be set up in alphabetical order; but, such preference was not favored by Chinese and Brazilian users. Based on the above literature review, preferences for links differ across cultures. **4)Layout**, the display structure directing scanning information and reflecting the orderly flow of tasks. When the layout is properly designed, it is easier for the viewer accessing to information and comprehending the information within a contextual and structural model so as to facilitate the communication between the user and the system [13]. According to Barber and Badre [1], users from different cultural backgrounds presented different preferences for orientation and layout structure in web pages. **5)Multimedia**, referring to sounds, animation, moving text and streaming video. When the multimedia is properly utilized, the user's experiences can be enriched. Integrating multimedia into web interface design can be a very powerful means for transmitting information beyond that of text, visual representations, still images and pictures; it may also prove to be an effective means to mislead and distract the audience [2].

3 Methodologies

The methodologies in this research are introduced in this section. First, two cultures are selected. Second, hypotheses are constructed. Third, four experimental websites are constructed. Fourth, the usability test is established.

3.1 Two Cultures Are Selected

The cultural categories used in this study are based on national culture and operationalized with websites from Taiwan and Australia that possess different cultural attributes, based on Hofstede's country cultural dimensions [4] presented in Table 1.

Table 1. Hofstede's country cultural dimensions [4]

Cultural dimension	Power Distance		Individualism & Collectivism		Masculinity & Femininity		Uncertain Avoidance		Long term & short term time orientation	
	Rank	Score	Rank	Score	Rank	Score	Rank	Score	Rank	Score
Australia	41	36	2	90	16	61	37	51	15	31
Taiwan	29/30	58	44	17	32/33	45	26	69	3	87

3.2 Hypotheses

In the author's previous research [6], where local website auditing was constructed, it is found that there are significantly different preferences for web interface design between Taiwanese and Australian cultures(Table 2 and Table 3). The further related hypotheses are proposed - if the websites are embedded with culturally preferred elements and incorporated with their cultural dimensions, they can be more effective in communications. To testify the related hypotheses, a web experiment is constructed. In the website experiment, the culturally preferred design elements are embedded in websites and the communication effectiveness (usability) would be evaluated from four aspects including learnability, efficiency, minimal errors, and satisfaction. The details of the hypotheses are shown as below.

1. If the Nantou government website is embedded with culturally preferred design elements that reflect Taiwanese culture, it can be more effective in the communication for Taiwanese users
2. If the Geelong government website is embedded with culturally preferred design elements that reflect Australian culture, it can be more effective in the communication for Australian users.

Table 2. Significant Taiwanese culturally preferred attributes

Variables	Components
Visual representation	Iconic symbols Images of leader Photo of accomplishment Images of group Cute style illustration
Navigation	Accessibility icon
Links	Popup a new window Dynamic button
Layout	Three-column Horizontal menu on top
Multimedia	Stream video Flash animation Moving picture Moving text Opening

Table 3. Significant Australian culturally preferred attributes

Variables	Components
Visual representation	Images of daily life Banner within color shape
Navigation	Search Accessibility on text
Links	Mouse over-underlined Stay in the same window
Layout	Two-column Flexible width design Info. guide on bottom

3.3 Four Experimental Websites being Constructed

Websites of the government genre are chosen. The Nantou county government website is selected as one of the templates to develop the website. This is because the Nantou county government website represents typical Taiwanese cultural features based on Hofsted's cultural model[4]. The Geelong city council website is selected as the other template to develop the website. This is because the Geelong city council website represents typical Australian cultural features based on Hofsted's cultural model[4].The content of the selected websites (the Geelong council and the Nantou county government) are applied to create Taiwanese style and Australian style for each city. Four experimental websites are constructed and introduced as below.

- Chinese version of the Nantou website is embedded with Taiwanese culturally preferred attributes.
- English version of the Geelong website is embedded with Taiwanese culturally preferred attributes.
- Chinese version of the Nantou website is embedded with Australian culturally preferred attributes.
- English version of the Geelong website is embedded with Australian culturally preferred attributes.

3.4 Evaluation Criteria for Usability Test

Based on Nielsen [8], four evaluation criteria are interpreted as the following. 1) Efficiency can be the assessment of the time needed for carrying out a task. The process of more rapidly executing a task implies the greater efficiency. 2) Learnability points out the easiness to learn the system. 3) Minimal errors indicate the evaluation criteria of errors being defined as users making as few errors as possible when using the system. 4) Satisfaction refers to the extent of the users preferring the system.

4 Construction of Web Experiment and Usability Test

4.1 Participants and Experiment Procedure

Fifteen Australian participants were recruited in this experiment, and these participants were native English speakers, averagely aged 30 years old, stayed in Taiwan less than 3 months, taught English, and were born and brought up in Australia. Taiwanese participants were native Chinese speakers, the PhD and Master students from National Yunlin University of Science and Technology, and aged 30 years old averagely. Each participant was invited to Laboratory DA405 in National Yunlin University of Science and Technology to participate in the web experiment. The Taiwanese participants were asked to carry out the tasks assigned on the two versions of the Nantou websites, and the Australian participants were asked to carry out the tasks assigned on the two versions of the Geelong websites according to the instruction and task assigned. When the participants executed the tasks, they interacted and navigated with the websites, during which the time and clicks for carrying out each task were captured and recorded. Finally, the usability questionnaires were used for their responses, subjective opinions, and satisfaction from the participants.

4.2 Task Assigned

Using Spool et al.'s method [12], the questions were designed so that the answer comprised a single fact and only one correct answer. Four sets of tasks were constructed for each website. The tasks were equivalent for Chinese version of the Nantou website which was embedded with Taiwanese culturally preferred attributes and English version of the Geelong government website which was embedded with Taiwanese culturally preferred attributes; and, the tasks were equivalent for Chinese version of the Nantou website which was embedded with Australian culturally preferred attributes and English version of the Geelong website which was embedded with Australian culturally preferred attributes. Taiwanese participants needed to locate requested pages on both styles of the Nantou website, and Australian participants needed to locate requested pages on both styles of the Geelong website.

Table 4. Tasks assigned for the Chinese version Nantou website

Evaluation criteria	Web components	Task assigned for the Nantou web embedded with Taiwanese culturally preferred attributes	Task assigned the Nantou web embedded with Australian culturally preferred attributes
Efficiency	Links	Taiwanese culturally preferred attributes：open a new window	Australian culturally preferred attributes：stay in the same window
		Task assigned: What is the number one product in Top Ten Souvenirs in Nantou?	Task assigned: How many tourism factories are there in Nantou?
Learnability	Layout	Taiwanese culturally preferred attributes：three columns	Australian culturally preferred attributes：two columns
		Task assigned: What is the e-mail address of the government?	Task assigned: What is the contact telephone number of the government?
errors	Multimedia	Taiwanese culturally preferred attributes：flash animation	
		Task assigned: What activities are taken place in Nantou in 2014?	

Table 5. Tasks assigned for the English version Geelong website

Evaluation criteria	Web components	tTask assigned for the Geelong web embedded with Taiwanese culturally preferred attributes	Task assigned for tthe Geelong web embedded with Australian culturally preferred attributes
Efficiency	Links	Taiwanese culturally preferred attributes：open a new window	Australian culturally preferred attributes：stay in the same window
		Task assigned: Pretend you are a visitor and need to find the tourism service number. What is it?	Task assigned: If you're a visitor, could you find the tourism service number on visiting page?
Learnability	Layout	Taiwanese culturally preferred attributes：three columns	Australian culturally preferred attributes：two columns
		Task assigned: Could you find the email of Geelong government?	Task assigned: Could you find the contact number for Geelong's government?
errors	Multimedia	Taiwanese culturally preferred attributes：flash animation	
		Task assigned: What activities will be held in 2014 in Geelong?	

Task Design for Efficiency: the operation tasks of different links between two cultures (opening a new window as preferred in Taiwanese websites, while opening at the same page was preferred in Australian ones) were observed the effects on efficiency. For example, an icon for "Nantou Souvenirs" was shown on the front page of

Chinese Version in Nantou websites, and a new window would be opened after clicking on the icon. The text button, on the other hand, was shown on the front page of Australian websites, and the window was opened at the same page for the link.

Task Design for Learnability: The web design for the two cultures (three columns were preferred in Taiwanese websites, while double columns were preferred in Australian ones) and the two versions helped understand the effects of cultures on learnability, and the evaluation was recorded with the task timing.

Task Design for Error: Embedding media elements into Taiwanese websites with culturally preferred attributes, the participants of the two cultures were observed the effects on usability, which was recorded by the number of clicks with a mouse.

Questionnaire Design for Satisfaction: the use's responses to the real perception needed to be observed with other setting questions. The subjective satisfaction was recorded the subjective perception of the user with Likert's 7-point scale.

5 Results

Table 6. Taiwanese's response between website reflecting Taiwanese culture and website reflecting Australian culture

Evaluation criteria	Nantou prototype reflecting Taiwanese culture	Nantou prototype reflecting Australian culture
Efficiency (sec)	10.6	18
Learnability (sec)	18.9	24.5
Errors (clicks)	5.5	--
Satisfaction (mean of questionnaire)	5.6	5.1

Table 7. Australian users' response between prototype reflecting Taiwanese culture and website reflecting Australian culture

Evaluation criteria	Geelong prototype reflecting Taiwanese culture	Geelong prototype reflecting Australian culture
Efficiency (sec)	43	40
Learnability (sec)	29.7	28.1
Errors (clicks)	6.1	--
Satisfaction (mean of questionnaire)	5.1	4.6

5.1 Efficiency

Table 8 shows the efficiency results of Taiwanese users between two styles of the Nantou websites, where Taiwanese participants spend averagely 10.6 sec on websites embedded with Taiwanese culturally preferred elements, while it takes averagely 18 sec for the ones embedded with Australian culturally preferred elements.

Table 8. Paired T-test of the efficiency of Taiwanese users between two styles of the Nantou websites

Evaluation criteria	Mean	SD	SEM	t	f	Sig (two tailed)
Efficiency (TW-AU)	10.6/18	14.0368	3.6243	2.044	14	.060

Table 9 shows the efficiency results of Australian users between two styles of the Geelong websites, where Australian participants spend averagely 43 sec on the websites embedded with Taiwanese culturally preferred elements, while it takes averagely 40 sec for the ones embedded with Australian culturally preferred elements.

Table 9. Paired T-test of the efficiency of Australian users between two styles of the Geelong websites

Evaluation criteria	Mean	SD	SEM	t	f	Sig (two tailed)
Efficiency (TW-AU)	43/40	33.0424	8.5315	.352	14	.730

5.2 Learnability

Table 10 shows the learnability results of Taiwanese users between two styles of the Nantou websites, where Taiwanese participants spend averagely 18.9 sec on the websites embedded with Taiwanese culturally preferred elements, while it takes averagely 24.5 sec for the ones embedded with Australian culturally preferred elements.

Table 10. Paired T-test of the learnability of Taiwanese users between two styles of the Nantou websites

Evaluation criteria	Mean	SD	SEM	t	f	Sig (two tailed)
Learnability (TW-AU)	18.9/24.5	26.3083	6.7928	-.816	14	.428

Table 11 shows the learnability results of Australian users between two styles of the Geelong websites, where Australian participants spend averagely 29.7 sec on the websites embedded with Taiwanese culturally preferred elements, while it takes averagely 28.1 sec for the ones embedded with Australian culturally preferred elements.

Table 11. Paired T-test of the learnability of Australian users between two styles of the Geelong websites

Evaluation criteria	Mean	SD	SEM	t	f	Sig (two tailed)
Learnability(TW-AU)	29.7/28.1	29.70 45	7.6697	.2 14	14	.834

5.3 Errors (Clicks)

In regard to the test of error, where multimedia elements are embedded to the websites with Taiwanese culturally preferred elements, Taiwanese participants take averagely 5.5 clicks and Australian participants take averagely 6.1 clicks, Table 6 & 7. The T-test results of multimedia do not appear the significant standard, but Taiwanese participants reveal less clicks than Australian ones do.

5.4 Satisfaction (Mean of Questionnaire)

The following table shows the subjective satisfaction of Taiwanese participants with websites embedded with Taiwanese culturally preferred elements and Australian culturally preferred elements. From the table, Visual Representation achieves the significant difference (p<0.05). Although other items do not appear remarkable differences, Navigation, Visual Representation, and Overall Satisfaction reveal better satisfaction on embedded Taiwanese culturally preferred elements, while Links and Layout show better satisfaction on embedded Australian culturally preferred elements.

Table 12. Paired T-test of satisfaction of Taiwanese users between two styles of the Nantou websites

		Mean	SD	SEM	t	Degree of freedom	Sig (two tailed)
Links	(TW-AU)	5.1/5.7	1.995	.515	-1.035	14	.318
Layout	(TW-AU)	5.4/5.6	1.781	.460	-.435	14	.670
Navigation	(TW-AU)	5.7/5.2	2.100	.542	.984	14	.342
Visual representation	(TW-AU)	6.1/4.6	2.031	.524	2.797	14	.014
Overall satisfaction	(TW-AU)	5.6/5.1	1.727	.446	1.047	14	.313

The following figure shows the subjective satisfaction of Australian participants between websites embedded with Taiwanese culturally preferred elements and Australian culturally preferred elements. From the table, Links and Visual Representation achieves the significant difference (p<0.05). Although other items do not appear remarkable differences, Links and Layout reveal better satisfaction on embedded Australian culturally preferred elements, while Navigation, Visual Representation, and Overall Satisfaction show better satisfaction on embedded Taiwanese culturally preferred elements.

Table 13. Paired T-test of satisfaction Australian users between two styles of the Geelong websites

		Mean	SD	SEM	t	Dgree of freedom	Sig (two tailed)
Links	(TW-AU)	4.2/5.9	2.187	.565	-3.070	14	.008
Layout	(TW-AU)	4.5/5.5	2.187	.565	-1.653	14	.121
Navigation	(TW-AU)	5.3/4.7	2.613	.675	.889	14	.389
Visual representation	(TW-AU)	5.6/4.1	1.642	.424	3.460	14	.004
Overall satisfaction	(TW-AU)	5.1/4.6	1.995	.515	1.035	14	.318

6 Discussion and Conclusion

Related to the results of efficiency test (Table 8 and Table9), Taiwanese participants take 10.6 seconds on the Nantou website reflecting Taiwanese style, but 18seconds on the Nantou website reflecting Australian style. On the contrary, Australian users take 40 seconds on the Geelong website reflecting Australian style, whilst 43 seconds on the Geelong website reflecting Taiwanese style. With regard to learnability test (Table10 and Table11), Taiwanese users take a shorter time on the Nantou website incorporating with Taiwanese cultural preferences than on the Nantou site reflecting Australian style. Australian users, on the other hand, perform better in the Geelong website incorporating with Australian culturally preferences than in the Geelong site reflecting Taiwanese style.

Regarding to errors test (Table 6 and Table7), Taiwanese users take less clicks (5.5 times) on the Nantou website reflecting Taiwanese culture, comparing with Australian users using 6.1 clicks for the Geelong website reflecting Taiwanese culture. The results reveal that Taiwanese users perform better in the website embedded with Taiwanese cultural preferences. With regard to Satisfaction test (Table 6, Table7, Table12, and Table13), Taiwanese users are more satisfied with Taiwanese style web, based on the results of the overall satisfaction questionnaires, particularly satisfied with the visual representation of Taiwanese style. But Taiwanese users are highly satisfied with staying at the same window that is not expected as the hypothesis. Australian users are also satisfied with Taiwanese style visual representation that is not consistent with the hypothesis, either. The possible assumption for the above condition is that cultures keep on evolving; particularly, the young generation in the Internet era is influenced by other culture easily. Generally, the results are aligned with the hypothesis that if the Nantou website is embedded with culturally preferred design elements reflecting Taiwanese culture, it can be more effective in the communication for Taiwanese users. Also, If the website is embedded with culturally preferred design elements reflecting Australian culture, it can be more effective in the communication for Australian users. This research has the potential to help web developers and designers develop a web interface design that is culturally appropriate.

Acknowledgement. The author gratefully acknowledge the support for this research provided by Taiwan National Science Council under grants no. NSC 102-2410-H-224-035-.

References

1. Barber, W., Bardre, A.: Culturability: The Merging of Culture and Usability. In: Proceedings of the 4th Conference on Human Factors and Usability (1998), `http://zing.ncsl.nist.gov/hfweb/att4/proceedings/barber`
2. Brinck, T., Gergle, D., Wood, S.D.: Designing Web sites that work: usability for the Web. Morgan Kaufmann Publishers, San Francisco (2002)
3. Hofstede, N.: Global Issues, local Concerns. Technical Communication, 145–148 (Second Quarter 1999)

4. Hofstede, G.: Cultures and Organizations: Software of the Mind. McGraw-Hill, New York (2005)
5. Hsieh, H.C., Holland, R., Young, M.: A Theoretical Model for Cross-Cultural Web Design. In: Kurosu, M. (ed.) HCD 2009. LNCS, vol. 5619, pp. 712–721. Springer, Heidelberg (2009)
6. Hsieh, H.C.L., Chen, C.-H., Hong, S.D.: Incorporating Culture in Website Design: A Comparison of Taiwanese and Australian Website Characteristics. In: Rau, P.L.P. (ed.) CCD/HCII 2013, Part II. LNCS, vol. 8024, pp. 393–403. Springer, Heidelberg (2013)
7. Marcus, A., Gould, E.W.: Cultural Dimensions and Global Web User-Interface Design. Interactions, 33–46 (July/August 2000)
8. Nielson, J.: Usability Engineering. Academic Press, San Francisco (1993)
9. Russo, P., Boor, S.: How fluent is your interface? Designing for international users. Human Factors and Computer Systems. In: Proceedings of 4th Conference on Human Factors in Computing Systems, pp. 342–347. Addison-Wesley, Boston (1993)
10. Smart, K.L., Rice, J.C., Wood, L.E.: Meeting the Needs of Users: Toward a Semiotics of the Web. IEEE Technology & Teamwork, 593–605 (2000)
11. Smith, A., Dunckley, L., French, T., Minocha, S., Chang, Y.: A process model for developing usable cross-cultural websites. Interacting with Computers 16(1), 63–91 (2004)
12. Spool, J.M., Scanlon, S., Schroeder, W., Snyder, C., De Angelo, T.: Web Site Usability: A Designer's Guide. Morgan Kaufman Publishers Inc. (1999)
13. Sun, H.: Building a culturally-competent corporate web site: an exploratory study of cultural markers in multilingual web design. In: Proceedings of the 19th Annual International Conference on Computer Documentation, pp. 95–102 (2001)

A Study of Kinect-Based Smart TV Control Mode

He Li, Jing Qiu, and Long Gao

School of Mechatronics Engineering,
University of Electronic Science and Technology of China
2010082020004@std.uestc.edu.cn, qiujing_2000@hotmail.com,
764819527@qq.com

Abstract. TV plays a more and more important role in daily life. And it will be a protagonist in our home. However, the progress of smart TV control mode did not catch up with the development of smart TV's software and hardware. In this paper, a survey was conducted to confirm the way of future smart TV control mode. According to the results of the survey, an experiment was executed in order to investigate design parameters of the new smart TV control mode. Therefore, the precautions on design the smart TV control mode was proposed.

Keywords: Kinect; Gesture Control; Smart TV Control Mode.

1 Introduction

As a common household device in daily life, TV is becoming more and more important. It is an obbligato entertainment terminal for home as well. However, the traditional TV can only receive real-time and specific programs provided by Medias. Though this kind of TV can be simple and convenient, it cannot satisfy the people's requirements of diversity and intelligent (Liu, 2011; Dahl, 2008). Accompanied with the requirements, smart TV is appeared as a part of smart home (Bjorkskog, 2007). Compared with traditional TV, smart TV also contains the functions such as web search, game etc. A study was conducted to investigate the relationships between smart TV advertisement and consumer's behavior in USA. The results indicated that smart TV is necessary as an important element to enrich the current media plan (YuMe Company, 2013).

Recently, a few types of the smart TV have been commercially marketed, e.g. Google smart TV, Samsung smart TV, Haier smart TV. Since 2006, the number of applying for patents in the field of smart TV is about 1200[Wang, 2012].However, the studies on smart TV control mode do not catch up with the development of hardware and software. Fu Yong and his fellows applied the technique of Gyroscope and Acceleration Sensor, proposed and realized a new concept of smart TV controller (Fu et al., 2012). However, this method is still based on the concept of traditional TV control mode. The disadvantages of the traditional TV control mode (Chang et al., 2012):

Along with the increasing of household electronic devices, there are more and more controllers in our homes. The operators can be confused because of the controllers;

P.L.P. Rau (Ed.): CCD/HCII 2014, LNCS 8528, pp. 174–183, 2014.

- The way, that controls traditional TV by pressing the buttons, cannot meet the operator's requirements of natural and intelligent for human-computer interaction;
- Along with the increasing of controlling functions, the traditional TV controller turns to be clumsy;
- Traditional TV controllers cannot meet the requirements on functions and applications of smart TV.

Hence, the society urgently needs a new TV control mode. The new control mode will be human-centered and can make the interaction between human and machine more fluent what's more it can enrich the user's experience (Sun et al.,2012). Cox. D et al. also proposed a concept that transfers the method of game control to TV [Cox et al., 2012].

In 2010, Microsoft published the Kinect that as a new game device. As a revolutionary human-computer interaction device, the Kinect can cause a revolution in human computer interaction (Sun, 2012; Chen, 2013). A Kinect sensor has three cameras. Two of cameras generate the deep images; the remaining generates the color image. Meanwhile, a Kinect sensor has a microphone array composed with 4 microphones. Hence, it can realize the functions, e.g. motion capture, speech input, image recognition, speech recognition (Chen, 2013).This visual sensing unit can real-time track and record the space position of 20 joints of the body in the rate of 30 frames per second using a space Cartesian (Zhang, 2012).

In recent years, studies on the application of human-interaction based on Kinect gradually increased. Chen has been studied the gesture recognition, proposed the technology path of application, and used it to teaching practice (Chen,2013). Wang et al. proposed an application of Kinect and created a three-dimensional animated character based on the bone points (Wang et al., 2012). Chang and his fellows proposed the technical framework for a new Kinect-based control mode, and proved the feasibility of Kinect-based smart TV control mode (Chang et al., 2012).

In the current study, the aim is to figure out the smart TV control mode's development tendency. Meanwhile, the key issue is to propose a better control mode for smart TV in terms of technical parameters.

2 Methods

2.1 Experiment Design

Intending to confirm the new smart TV control mode, a survey about TV control mode was conducted by means of questionnaire. The questionnaire consisted of two parts:

- Background information, e.g. name, gender, age, home address, live time.
- TV control mode information: 42 questionnaires of present and future TV control modes were proposed.

In order to achieve our purpose mentioned above, some results will be presented as follows:

- For the question "Your vision for the future TV control mode", the result shows that almost a half of interviewees preferred body control to be new smart TV control mode.
- For the question "In the circumstance of no TV remote controller, which body action do you want to use to control the TV?",50% of interviewees supported hand control to be new smart TV control mode.
- For the question "In the circumstance of no TV remote controller, which hand action do you want to control the TV", 88.2% of interviewees preferred to use wave for controlling a new smart TV.

Based on the results of the survey, an experiment was executed to define technical parameters for a hand-wave control mode. The detailed purposes are as follows:

- to define an envelope space that all participants' motions confined in it;
- to define an average instantaneous velocity of wave that was used to control the smart TV;
- to evaluate usability of the proposed smart TV control mode.

In this experiment, a background questionnaire was developed to collect participants' habits and perspectives on watching TV, e.g. TV condition, participants' attitude to tradition TV control mode, and TV remote controller. The method of Wizard of Oz was used in the experiment (Mäkelä et al., 2001) (S. Carbiniet al. 2006), so that the participants could wave naturally their hands. During the experiment, a tester controlled actually TV as participants waved their hands to 'control'. The ways for TV controlling were as follows: wave right for next channel; wave left for front channel; wave up for sound increase; wave down for sound decrease; drawing the corresponding arabic numerals for specific channel; and drawing a circle for return (Fig. 1).

During the experiment, two situations for TV controlling were considered: sitting posture and standing posture. For each posture, 28 times for hand wave were designed: 5 wave left, 5 wave right, 5 wave up, 5 wave down, 4 arabic numerals, and 4 circles.

A questionnaire was developed to collect participants' perspectives of the new smart TV control mode. Five questions were included in this questionnaire:

- 'Your satisfaction towards this TV control mode',
- 'Do you think it is difficult to control this TV by this way for you', for this two questions five options were set, as for very satisfied, satisfied, ordinary, no, never. 'Do you think this TV control mode effective'
- 'Do you think the TV control mode is easy to learn'
- 'The control actions reasonable?'

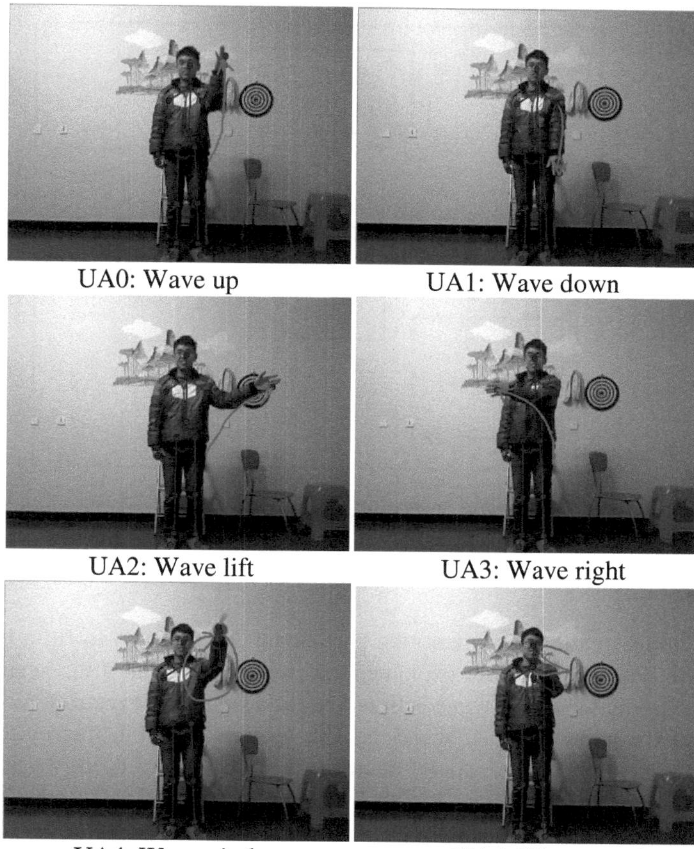

UA0: Wave up UA1: Wave down

UA2: Wave lift UA3: Wave right

UA4: Wave circle UA5: Wave number

Fig. 1. The ways for TV controlling

2.2 Participants

During the experiment, 21 volunteers (11 males, 10 females) were recruited from our university. Their ages ranged from 19 to 24, with an average age of 22±1.33. 21 volunteers come from 10 provinces of China, and 90.48% of volunteers lived in their hometown more than 10 years.

2.3 Experiment Material and Equipment

During the experiment， a 32-inch Changhong TV was placed in front of a test room. A Kinect was placed on TV. A computer was connected the Kinect to record participants' 'controlling' hand movements. Furthermore, a chair for participants was putting front of the TV. The distance between them is 3m. A remote TV controller was used to control TV (Fig. 2).

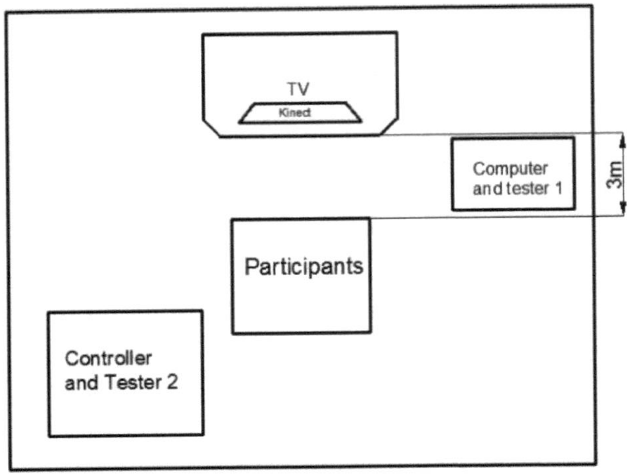

Fig. 2. The Experiment Room

2.4 Procedure

At the beginning of the experiment, the participants were asked to fill a background questionnaire. Participants were explained exactly how to control the smart TV front of them by waving hand. All wave actions for each posture were tested randomly one by one. Then the participants sit ahead the TV. A tester issued instructions for control commands, e.g. next channel, sound decrease, return. According to the instructions, Participants wave their hands to 'control' the TV. Meanwhile, the other tester controlled the TV by remote controller beyond participants' views. After that, the participants were required to control the TV by stand posture. At the end of the experiment, a questionnaire was delivered to participants to collect their attitude toward the new proposed smart TV control mode. The whole process takes about twenty minutes.

2.5 Data Collection and Analysis

Kinect can generate a space Cartesian refers itself, X-axis in the horizontal direction, Y-axis in a vertical direction, Z-axis in a front and rear direction, the original point is in the center of Kinect (Fig. 3). Hence, Kinect was used to collect the experiment data, including the real-time position of 20 joints all over the body and the moving speed of the wrist.

Wrist was tracked for determine envelope space. In order to analyze the wrist movement data generated by Kinect, valid control motions were defined. For example, the starting point of control motion for wave up was defined to be the start of the valid control motion, and the highest point defined to be the end of the valid control motion. Then, the frames corresponding with the valid control motion were selected from the video produced by Kinect during the experiment. Hence, the value of

X-Coordinates, Y-Coordinates, Z-Coordinates of wrist was selected. The maximum and the minimum values could be determined. Therefore, an envelope space could be determined, in which all valid control motions were confined.

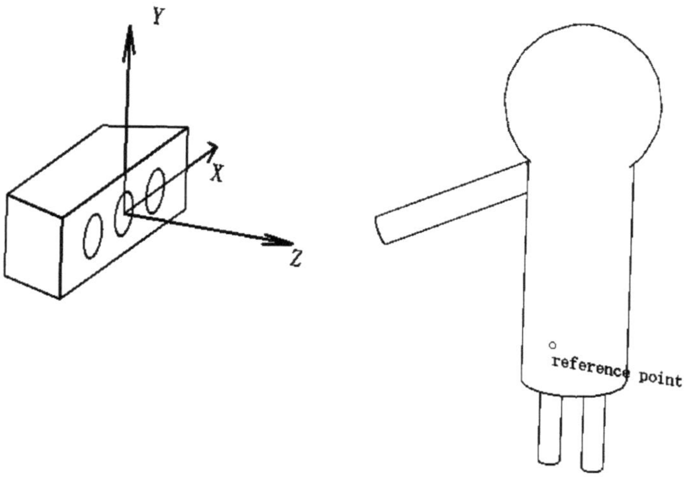

Fig. 3. Cartesian of Kinect

Furthermore, hip center was selected as reference point in standing posture; shoulder center was selected as reference point in sitting posture. Thus, not only the envelope space but the distance between envelope space and human body can be calculated (Fig. 4).

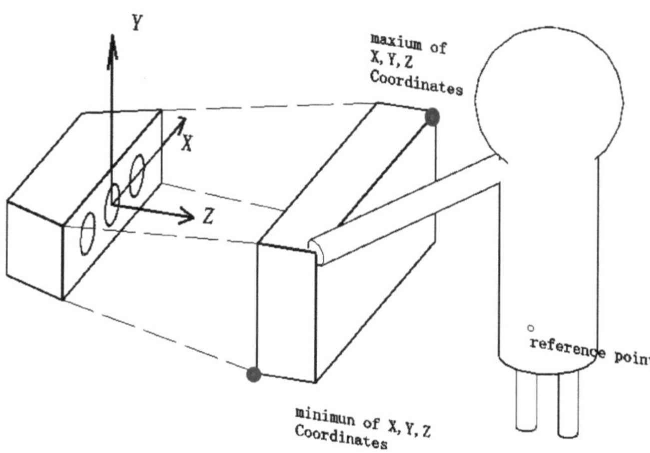

Fig. 4. Envelope Space in Standing Posture

The distance between two frames was calculated using Function (1).

$$d=\sqrt{(x_1 - x_0)^2+(y_1 - y_0)^2+(z_1 - z_0)^2} \tag{1}$$

Kinect can track and record the space position of 20 joints of the body in the rate of 30 frames per second, so the time between two frames can be calculated by Function (2).

$$t=\frac{1s}{30} = 0.033s \tag{2}$$

Hence the speed between two frames can be calculated by Function (3).

$$v=\frac{d}{0.033s} \tag{3}$$

According to calculating the average speed of several frames which composing a valid control motion, a valid control motion's average speed was found.

2.6 Results

This experiment, 21 volunteers' 588 motions was collected and analyzed. Table 1 shows the space envelope of standing for both sexes. Male's range of actions is larger than female's. The space envelope of sitting posture for both sexes was presented in Table 2. The similar results as standing posture can be observed from Table 2. Male's range of actions is larger than female's in sitting posture.

Table 1. Standing space envelope for Male and Female

	Max.(m)	**Min.(m)**	**Range(m)**	**Reference point(m)**
			(Male/Female)	
X (m)	1.9285/0.2673	1.2165/-0.5980	0.7120/0.8654	-0.0431/-0.1675
Y(m)	3.0707/0.8273	2.1838/0.0119	0.8869/0.8155	0.0149/0.1815
Z(m)	2.5992/2.1917	2.5092/1.7164	0.0899/0.4752	2.3004/2.1021

Hence, Male's range of actions is larger than female's for both sitting and standing postures. This reason may owe the difference in gender or males are more powerful than female. Meanwhile, standing posture's range of actions is larger than sitting posture, for the reason that participants be more active when they stood.

Furthermore, the average speed of all motions is 1.2957m/s. And the maximum speed of all motions is 4.4998m/s. It was found that males' speed is faster than females'. The reason may be difference in gender. And males were more active than female.

Table 2. Sitting space envelope for Male and Female

Axis	Max.(m)	Min.(m)	Range(m)	Reference point(m)
	(Male/Female)			
X	0.8666/0.2675	0.4496/-0.4941	0.4170/0.7616	0.0043/-0.1762
Y	2.4767/0.3629	2.2014/-0.3813	0.2753/0.7443	0.3024/0.1318
Z	1.8601/2.1836	1.4653/1.8280	0.3948/0.3557	2.0890/2.2181

For the five questions of acceptability for our proposed mode, Fig.5 illustrates the results of perspectives of the participants. According to Fig.3, 81% of them show their satisfactions toward the new control mode. 76% of them hold that it is easy to operate. All of them reported it was easy to learn. 95% of them reported the actions to control TV was reasonable.

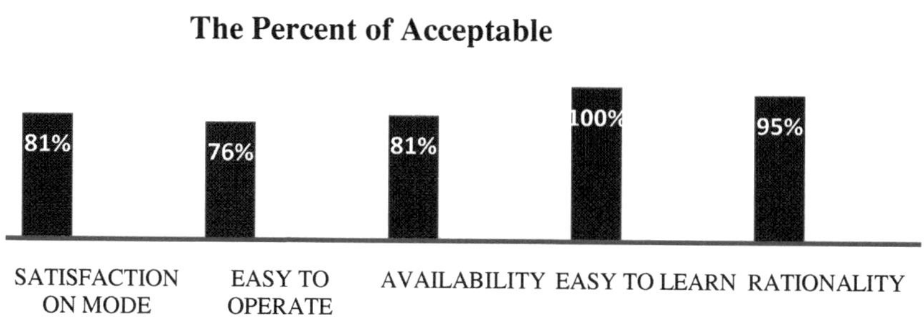

Fig. 5. Acceptability for proposed mode

3 Discussion

According the experiment, we put forward the new smart TV control mode design ideas:

- For instructions: during the stage of creating the smart TV instructions, it should pay more attention to the forms of instructions based on our results. Such as, the range of instructions should within the space. A large space or long distance may cause discomfort for the users, and make them be tired easily. A small space or short distance may result in a situation of uncertain;
- For instruction's speed: it should be noticed of definition of the speed of instructions. A fast speed would increase the burden on the users. Meanwhile, a low speed may cause some uncertain situations;
- For guidance to control: A guide should be designed for operators to control TV. For example, an instruction should be displayed in a special place of the scream during controlling TV. To release operators' burden in remember control motions;

- For feedback: The mechanism of feedback allows the operators to confirm their operations which he/she is going to give out, hence TV can executive orders more exactly.

4 Conclusion

By means of questionnaire, a new gesture-based smart TV control mode was proposed. Furthermore an experiment was conducted to draw design ideas and design parameters of Kinect-based Smart TV control mode. According to the results of availability evaluation, the new control mode is available and satisfied. Kinect as an advanced and full-featured mutual device, owing to the functions like motion capture and joint tracking, provides a platform for this new smart TV control mode. This study has significance toward the appearance of new smart TV control mode.

In the future, we emphasize more functions for smart TV. Meanwhile, we should emphasize the way that human-computer interaction, which more intelligent and convenient.

Acknowledgement. This study was supported by the Natural Science Foundation of China(71201017)and the National Higher-education Institution General Research and Develop-ment Funding (ZYGX2012J101).

References

1. Liu, G.H.: Research and implementation for television program search system of interactive TV., Dissertation. Fudan University, Shanghai (2011)
2. Dahl, Y.: Modeling human-computer interaction in smart spaces: existing and emerging techniques. In: Asai, K. (ed.), Human Computer Interaction: New Developments (2008), `http://www.intechopen.com/books/human_computer_interaction_new_developments/modeling_human-computer_interaction_in_smart_spaces__existing_and_emerging_techniques`
3. Björkskog, C.: Human computer interaction in smart homes. Seminar on Human-Computer Issues in Ubiquitous Computing , Department of computer Science, University of Helsinki (2007), `https://www.hiit.fi/u/oulasvir/58307110/smarthomes.pdf`
4. YuMe Company: Understanding the smart TV user (January 20, 2013) `http://www.yume.com` (retrieved)
5. Wang, X.: The interactive technology on Smart TV patents. IC Application 10, 14–15 (2012)
6. Fu, Y., Ping, T.T., Zhou, M.Y.: Design and implementation of new human-computer interaction space of flat panel TV's remote controller. TV Technology 36, 27–29 (2012)
7. Chang, Z.W., Huang, J.F., Han, C.X.: Somatosensory control technology on TV. Radio and TV Information 03, 89–90 (2012)

8. Sun, M.H.: Research and Implementation of 3D recognition technology on television system based on human-computer interaction. Dissertation. Qing Dao: Ocean University of China (2012)
9. Cox, D., Wolford, J., Beardsley, D.: An evolution of game controllers and tablets as controllers for interactive TV applications. In: Proceedings of 14th ACM International Conference on Multimodal Interaction (ICMI 2012), pp. 181–188. ACM, New York (2012)
10. Chen, J.: Kinect-based gesture recognition technology and its application in teaching, Dissertation, pp. 1–6. Shanghai Jiaotong University, Shang Hai (2013)
11. Wang, X.: Ma Qiang, Wang Wanliang. KINECT driven 3D character animation using semantic framework. In: Proceedings of IEEE CCIS2012, Hangzhou, China (2012)
12. Zhang, D.: Discussion on Kinect applications. Logistics Engineering and Management, Sixth 34, 39–41 (2012)
13. Mäkelä, K.: Esa-Pekka Salonen, Markku Turunen, Jaakko Hakulinen, Roope Raisamo.: Conducting a Wizard of Oz Experiment on a Ubiquitous Computer System Doorman. In: Proceedings of the International Workshop on Information Presentation and Natural Multimodal Dialogue (2001)
14. http://www.doc88.com/p-3611626504250.html
15. Carbini, S., Delphin-Poulat, L., Perron, L., Viallet, J.E.: From a wizard of oz experiment to a real time speech and gesture multimodal interface. In: Signal Process (2006), http://zbmath.org/?q=an:05623216
16. Shin, D.-H., Hwang, Y., Choo, H.: Smart TV: are they really smart in interacting with people? Understanding the interactivity of Korean Smart TV. Behaviour& Information Technology, pp.156–172 (2013)
17. Lee, S.-H., Sohn, M.-K., Kim, D.-J., Kim, B., Kim, H.: Smart TV interaction system using face and hand gesture recognition. In: IEEE International Conference on Consumer Electronics (ICCE), Shenzhen (2013)
18. Lee, W.-P., CheKaoli, Huang, J.-Y.: A smart TV system with body-gesture control, tag-based rating and context-aware recommendation. Knowledge-Based Systems 56, 167–178 (2013)
19. Junyi, X., Alfredo, S.R.: A real-time respiratory motion monitoring system using KINECT: proof of concept. Medical Physics 36, 2682 (2012)
20. Choppin, S., Wheat, J.: The potential of the Microsoft Kinect in sports analysis and biomechanics. Sports Technology 6, 78–85 (2013)
21. Kozono, K., Aoki, M., Ono, M., Kamikawa, Y., Arimura, H., Toyofuku, F.: SU-E-I-92: Accuracy Evaluation of Depth Data in Microsoft Kinect. Medical Physics 39, 3646 (2012)

Explore Elder Users' Reading Behaviors with Online Newspaper

Weijane Lin[1], Hui-Chun Lin[2], and Hsiu-Ping Yueh[2]

[1] Department of Library and Information Science, National Taiwan University
[2] Department of Bio-Industry Communication and Development, National Taiwan University
No. 1. Sec. 4., Roosevelt Rd., Daan Dist., Taipei 10617, Taiwan, R.O.C.
vjlin@ntu.edu.tw

Abstract. This study aimed to explore elder users' reading behavior with online newspaper. The average age of twelve elder users is 68.67 years old. They were required to find news in the UDN online newspaper on the touch screen and enlarge or shrink the news pages to the appropriate size. The results showed that elder users didn't know how to flip the pages to read other news, and they spent more time looking for the zoom in and zoom out icons comparatively. They sometimes misunderstood the meanings of other function icons. Our findings suggest that it could put instructions on the UDN online newspaper interface to show how to use the function icons, helping elder users reading news and enlarge or shrink pages easily. The function of zoom in and zoom out could replace with using two fingers to pinch the pages, just like using touchpad or smart phone. In addition, the function icons position should be consistent, elder user will not be confused when they enter into the detailed news.

Keywords: Elder users, Touch screen, Online Newspaper.

1 Introduction

According to the report of international labor force in 2004 by Executive Yuan in Taiwan, by the definition of the elders as population who aged over 65 years old, Taiwan has become an aging society since 1993, and the elder proportion increased rapidly. In the end of June 2013, the elderly people population is about 2.64 million, 11.5% of the total population. The rate suggested a significantly higher aging speed compared to other developing countries around the world (Ministry of the Interior, 2013). On the other hand, along with the technological and societal development, elderly people were gradually accustomed to and trained to use IT products in their daily life activities such as entertaining, socializing, and learning. Their needs have also gained attention economically from the governmental and industrial sectors. While most elderly people facing functional degradation, these problems make them challenging to use technology products (Greenberg, 2012; Lee, Chen, & Hewitt, 2011). The obstacles of using technology could be resulted from internal and external factors. Psychological factors are also common barriers that make elderly people did not want to learn and use computer information technology (Lee, Chen, & Hewitt, 2011).

P.L.P. Rau (Ed.): CCD/HCII 2014, LNCS 8528, pp. 184–192, 2014.

Recently, the technology of touch screen has been widely used in many IT equipments, such as ATM machines, MRT, train ticketing system, ibon, FamiPort, Taipei bicycle rental system. The direct manipulating interface of touch screen provided an intuitive connection between people and machines, which also allowed good hand-eye coordination that can quickly interact without having practice. However, size of the touch screen could be problematic for elderly people considering theier physical conditions such as muscle fatigue (Taveira, & Choi, 2009).

Reading is one of the common activities of elderly people to obtain daily life information and news. Newspaper with high accessibility in specific supported elder people's needs to remained connected to the society (Chiou, 2009). UDN as the major newspaper publishers in Taiwan offered the original printed newspapers in digital forms for users to read daily news online. Many public libraries adopted this sytem to provide users with digital newspaper reading services. For instance, Taipei City library displays UDN online newspapers with large touch screen, and has gained remarkable appraisal from the elderly users. Motivated by the aforementioned phenomenon, this study intends to explore the elder users' experiences with the UDN online newspaper. The usability of the product is assessed by user experiments and interviews to provide further suggestion for the interface and interaction design of UDN online newspaper.

1.1 Elderly People and Technology Product Designs

Factors such as physical limitations, the access to technologies, cost, and the passive attitude of using technologies could hinder users' acceptance toward technology use (Pedell, Beh, Mozuna, & Duong, 2013). Aging problems caused physical limitations, including action recession, cognitive degeneration, poor hearing and visual decline (Doyle, 2010). Elderly people took more time to explore and recognize information, and they could not recognize what appears on the screen simultaneously (Asano, Saito, Sato, Wang, Gao, & Rau, 2007). Degradation of cognition and memory capacity made elderly people cannot learn new things quickly (Zajicek, 2001). In terms of access to technology and cost, elderly people also face financial problems as well as learning opportunities, also the motives to use technology remain low since rare benefit can be expected by the elder users (Pedell etc., 2013).

Ng, Tao and Or (2013) noted that elderly people aging problem will lead to action and cognitive decline, resulting in poor performance of operational tasks, they discussed about elderly people using the touch screen, trackball and mouse as input devices. Their findings suggested that the touch screen could help elderly people overcome physical limits caused by aging, the performance time of using touch screen became shorter and more efficient, and it reduced the error rate. But the study also pointed out that the touch screen cannot entirely solve the usability problem since the manipulation of touch screen actually produced more body movements that made elderly people feel fatigue.

Previous studies in technology use suggested that the elder and younger users possessed different needs and behaviors (Charness, 2008). In a complex and long-term research data analysis, elderly people showed intra-individual, occasion-to-occasion, they behave differently in tasks because of personal differences and internal ability (Hultsch, MacDonald, & Dixon, 2002). Individual differences of elderly people will also affect the willingness of using products. While the reading devices and products for elder users have not gained enough concern (Tsai, Ro, Chang, & Lee, 2011), for the important daily activity of reading newspaper, it is worthy of further exploration empirically.

1.2 Elderly People and Touch Screen Research

Researchers who studied problems and errors of elderly people by using a handheld touch device that they divided problems and errors into two parts: user point of view and machine design. User problems and errors include lack of experience, poor vision, hand muscle weakness, search strategies incorrect and previous experience lead to obstacles and conflicts. Machine errors include unclear icons, the font was too small, the screen sensitivity was too high or too low, the display mode were different to users' expectations and product feedback to the user was inappropriate (Bradley, Langdon & Clarkson, 2011).

Tsai, Ro, Chang, and Lee (2011) used small touch screens for elder users to read e-book. Their findings suggested that the page presentation would affect reading performance of the elderly. As the elderly people slid the pages with fingers, the page presentation of e-book on the touch screen used flip page would be better than scroll-bar page, and more intuitive for elderly people. Werner , Werner, and Oberzaucher (2012) compared experienced and inexperience computer elder users when using tablet PCs, and found that elderly people had computer experience performed better than elderly people without computer experience, but the elderly people without computer experience could use thumb and index finger to enlarged the screen intuitively. In the studies of larger touch screens, Jin, Plocher and Kiff (2007) required elderly people manipulated tasks on a 17-inch touch screen. Their study found that the larger the keys the shorter the reaction time, and elder's performance accuracy was also higher. Lepicard and Vigouroux's (2010) study also supported that elderly people used both hands to manipulate touch screen produced more errors.

The above literatures show that the elderly people who were unfamiliar with the operation of touch screens, tablet PC and smart phones, would push the icons too light or too heavy, and aroused the incorrect functions. Font size, icon size, and key size would affect the operation fluency of elderly people. And the elderly people would manipulate the touch interfaces with references to their life experiences, which suggested that the more intuitive the manipulation the more convenient for them.

2 Methods

2.1 Materials

As mentioned above, UDN online newspaper was selected as the experimental material for this study (see Figure 1). It renewed at 6:00 AM every day, and we selected UDN Daily News of October 24, 2013 as the main material for reading tasks.

A 23-inch large touch screen was selected for elderly reading and designed the tasks for searching news, adjust the page size, and reading news content.

Fig. 1. The full news page of UDN online newspaper

2.2 Participants

The participants in this study are the elderly people who were 65 years and older. Twelve participants were recruited, 6 males and 6 females, their average age was 68.67 years old. Their education level are all above senior high school, and they all have fair eyesight with glasses and no problems with the movement. All of the elderly users have not used UDN online newspaper system before.

2.3 Procedures and Tasks

In this study elderly users were required to complete the tasks by using touch screen to read UDN online newspaper. The reading tasks include finding and reading the assigned article in the newspaper without any assistance.

Task 1: Please find the assigned news article.
Task 2: Please find the zoom-in icon and enlarge the news page.
Task 3: Please find the zoom out icon and shrink the news page.
Task 4: Adjust the page to appropriate size that you can read the news comfortably.
Task 5: Please read the news article completely.

After performing the tasks and reading the news completely, the elderly users were required to answer a question about the topic of the news, the question was "what ingredient would be harmful to human health in the cooking oil that government must to check it out at once?" All of the elderly users were give the correct answer "Gossypol" to the question. In addition, we also interviewed the elderly users for using UDN online newspaper on the touch screen, and record the opinions of them.

3 Results

Table 1 shows the average completion time and frequency of errors. In task 1 elderly users spent average 85.42 seconds finding the assigned news article, and they spent average 44.17 seconds dragging the detailed news page to the specific news of the task. The frequency of errors is 0.67. In task 2, elderly users spent average 53.5 seconds finding the zoom out icon and successfully enlarge the news. The frequency of errors is 1.06. In task 3 the mean task completion time was 18.69 seconds, most elderly users knew the plus and minus icon were the symbols of enlarge or shrink the pages, but there was an elderly users push the print icon and flip icon. In task 4 elderly users had to adjust the news page to appropriate size that they could read the news comfortably. Every users required different font size, some users maximized the News page for reading. Some users responded the news text page was too large that they couldn't slightly shrink the page, and the screen was too small when they push the minus icon. It was inconvenient in use. In task 5 elderly users spent average 111.58 seconds reading the news.

Table 2 shows the first reading performance of elderly users. The results indicated that elderly users made more mistakes in task 2, the errors included pinch the page with two fingers to enlarge the news, push the flip icon, push the original size icon, push the most suitable height icon. Five elderly users were unable to successfully push the zoom in and out in icons because they didn't understand the meaning of plus or minus symbols which could enlarge and shrink the news pages. And in the task 3 and task 4, only one elderly user push the incorrect icon.

Table 1. The average completion time and frequency of errors of reading tasks

Tasks	Average completion time (seconds)	frequency of errors
Task 1: Please find the assigned news article		0.67
• Find news headline		
• Drag the news pages to detailed news content	85.42 44.17	
Task 2: Please find the zoom in icon and enlarge the news page.	68.25	1.08
Task 3: Please find the zoom out icon and shrink the news page.	28.25	0.17
Task 4: Adjust the page to appropriate size that you can read the news comfortably.	45.83	0.08
Task 5: Please read the news completely.	111.58	0

Table 2. The first reading behavior of elderly users

Tasks	The first reading behavior		Number of People	Percentage
Task 1: Please find the assigned news article	Correct	Push the flip icons	10	83%
	Error	Slide the page with two fingers and enlarge A1	2	17%
Task 2: Please find the zoom in icon and enlarge the news page.	Correct	Push the plus icon	7	60%
	Error	Pinch the page with two fingers to enlarge the news	1	8%
		Push the flip icon	1	8%
		Push the original size icon	1	8%
		Push the most suitable height	1	8%
		Just slide the page	1	8%
Task 3: Please find the zoom out icon and shrink the news page.	Correct	Push the minus icon	11	92%
	Error	Push the flip icon	1	8%
Task 4: Adjust the page to appropriate size that you can read the news comfortably.	Correct	Push the plus icon or the minus icon	11	92%
	Error	Push the original size	1	8%

More than half of the elderly users could find the zoom out and zoom in icons, the plus and minus symbols were similar to computer operation for zooming in the web pages. In addition, there are a small number of elderly users did not understand the meaning of plus and minus symbols because they seldom used computers in their daily lives.

Elderly users appreciated using UDN online newspaper system for reading because it could solve the problems of traditional newspaper. The font size could zoom in and zoom out according to their need, and their hands didn't get ink. On the other hand, touch screen was regarded as more intuitive than mouse, and it was easy to tap and pinch on the touch screen for reading. However some users said that they didn't want to read the online newspaper because it didn't meet the reading habits and needs in daily lives such as cutting coupons, newspaper clipping, highlighting sentences.

4 Conclusion and Future Work

Elderly people didn't know how to search and select other news in the UDN online newspaper system, they stayed at the front page without entering into the detailed news. We suggested that putting instructions on the interface to help elderly users flip pages for searching more news, and how to drag pages to the news they want. And when elderly users touch the specific news, the next page will go to the news directly instead of dragging the news pages, it can also help elderly users accelerate the speed of searching news and reading fluency. The result was similar to that in Fisk et al. study, which suggest that technology products with instructions on how to use the system would make it easy to use and operate by elderly people(Fisk et al., 2004). While Craik (1986) also noted that the performance of elderly people rely mainly on the support of environments, if they recall on their own will produce errors, therefore, the design principles must contain environment support and instructions for users.

In the detailed news pages, some elderly users couldn't zoom in and zoom out the page smoothly. They didn't know the meanings of function icons such as original size, the most suitable height, the most suitable width, and magnifier icon with plus and minus symbols on it. Some elderly users had the experiences of using smart phone and touch pad, they used to pinch the screen with two fingers to enlarge the page, and change the pages with the flip gesture. They considered that the functions of zoom in and zoom out news pages could use the gesture similar to the gesture of smart phone and touch pad. The result was similar to Bradley et al. study, which noted that user problems and errors include lack of experience, search strategies incorrect and previous experience lead to obstacles and conflicts. Machine errors include unclear icons, the display mode were different to users' expectations (Bradley et al., 2011).We suggest that putting instructions beside the function icons, so that the elderly users can use the icons easily and adjust the news page to appropriate size. Change mode of the zoom in and zoom out to the mode of smart phone or other touch devices.

Furthermore, elderly users couldn't detect the function icons when they entered into detailed news page. Since the function icons are at the bottom of the page in full news pages, in the detailed news page the function icons are at the top of the page, elderly users need to find the function icons such as flip page again. In addition, some new function icons are not appear in the full news page such as the original size, the most suitable height, the most suitable width, and print, elderly users may have to learn the meanings of these new icons. The result is similar to Al-Razgan et al. study, which suggested that the smart phones main navigation instructions must appear in the "every page", extremely important functions were not disappear absolutely, common and important icons could put at the top of the screen to prevent elderly people pressing the wrong buttons (Al-Razgan et al., 2012).

We suggest that the function icons should be put at the same position in the full news pages and detailed news pages, so that elderly users won't be confused and reduce the speed of searching the function icons. Finally, more rigorous and sophisticated ways to collect experimental data would be conducted in the further investigation.

References

1. Asano, Y., Saito, H., Sato, H., Wang, L., Gao, Q., Rau, P.-L.P.: Tips for designing mobile phone web pages for the elderly. In: Jacko, J.A. (ed.) HCI 2007. LNCS, vol. 4550, pp. 675–680. Springer, Heidelberg (2007)
2. Al-Razgan, M.S., Al-Khalifa, H.S., Al-Shahrani, M.D., AlAjmi, H.H.: Touch-Based Mobile Phone Interface Guidelines and Design Recommendations for Elderly People: A Survey of the Literature. In: Huang, T., Zeng, Z., Li, C., Leung, C.S. (eds.) ICONIP 2012, Part IV. LNCS, vol. 7666, pp. 568–574. Springer, Heidelberg (2012)
3. Bradley, M., Langdon, P., Clarkson, P.J.: Older User Errors in Handheld Touchscreen Devices: To What Extent Is Prediction Possible? In: Stephanidis, C. (ed.) Universal Access in HCI, Part II, HCII 2011. LNCS, vol. 6766, pp. 131–139. Springer, Heidelberg (2011)
4. Craik, F.I.M.: A functional account of age differences in memory. In: Klix, F., Hagendorf, H. (eds.) Human Memory and Cognitive Capabilities: Mechanisms and Performances, pp. 409–422. Elsevier Science Publishers, North-Holland, Amsterdam (1986)
5. Charness, N.: Aging and human performance. Human Factors: The Journal of the Human Factors and Ergonomics Society 50(3), 548–555 (2008)
6. Chiou, T.-J.: An investigation of the reading habits and the reading needs of public libraries of the elderly in Taiwan. The Quarterly Publication of National Taiwan Library 5(3), 11–30 (2009)
7. Doyle, J., Skrba, Z., McDonnell, R., Arent, B.: Designing a touch screen communication device to support social interaction amongst older adults. Paper presented at the Proceedings of the 24th BCS Interaction Specialist Group Conference, Dundee, United Kingdom (2010)
8. Fisk, A.D., Rogers, W.A., Charness, N., Czaja, S.J., Sharit, J.: Designing for older adults: principles and creative human factors approaches, 2nd edn., pp. 29–248. CRC Press, U.S.A. (2004)
9. Greenberg, S.: A profile of older Americans. Administration on Aging. US Department of Health Human Services, Washington, DC (2012)
10. Hultsch, D.F., MacDonald, S.W.S., Dixon, R.A.: Variability in reaction time performance of younger and older adults. Journal of Gerontology: Psychological Sciences 57B, P101–P115 (2002)
11. Jin, Z.X., Plocher, T., Kiff, L.: Touch Screen User Interfaces for Older Adults: Button Size and Spacing. In: Stephanidis, C. (ed.) HCI 2007. LNCS, vol. 4554, pp. 933–941. Springer, Heidelberg (2007)
12. Lee, B., Chen, Y., Hewitt, L.: Age differences in constraints encountered by seniors in their use of computers and the internet. Computers in Human Behavior 27(3), 1231–1237 (2011)
13. Lepicard, G., Vigouroux, N.: Touch Screen User Interfaces for Older Subjects. In: Miesenberger, K., Klaus, J., Zagler, W., Karshmer, A. (eds.) ICCHP 2010, Part II. LNCS, vol. 6180, pp. 592–599. Springer, Heidelberg (2010)

14. Ministry of the Interior, http://www.moi.gov.tw/stat/news_content.aspx?sn=8057
15. Ng, H.-C., Tao, D., Or, C.: Age Differences in Computer Input Device Use: A Comparison of Touchscreen, Trackball, and Mouse. In: Rocha, Á., Correia, A.M., Wilson, T., Stroetmann, K.A. (eds.) Advances in Information Systems and Technologies. AISC, vol. 206, pp. 1015–1024. Springer, Heidelberg (2013)
16. Pedell, S., Beh, J., Mozuna, K., Duong, S.: Engaging older adults in activity group settings playing games on touch tablets. Paper presented at the Proceedings of the 25th Australian Computer-Human Interaction Conference: Augmentation, Application, Innovation, Collaboration, Adelaide, Australia (2013)
17. Taveira, A.D., Choi, S.D.: Review study of computer input devices and older users. International Journal of Human-Computer Interaction 25(5), 455–474 (2009)
18. Tsai, W.-C., Ro, Y.-L., Chang, Y.-T., Lee, C.-F.: The effects of font size and page presentation method of E-book reading on small screens for older adults. In: Stephanidis, C. (ed.) Universal Access in HCI, Part III, HCII 2011. LNCS, vol. 6767, pp. 94–101. Springer, Heidelberg (2011)
19. Werner, F., Werner, K., Oberzaucher, J.: Tablets for Seniors – An Evaluation of a Current Model (iPad). In: Wichert, R., Eberhardt, B. (eds.) Ambient Assisted Living. ATSC, vol. 2, pp. 177–184. Springer, Heidelberg (2012)
20. Zajicek, M.: Interface design for older adults. In: Proceedings of the 2001 EC/NSF Workshop on Universal Accessibility of Ubiquitous Computing: Providing for the Elderly. Alcácer do Sal, Portugal (2001)

An Approach of Indoor Exercise: Kinect-Based Video Game for Elderly People

Zhe Liu[1], Chen Liao[1], and Pilsung Choe[2]

[1] Department of Industrial Engineering, Tsinghua University, Beijing, China
liuzhehelen@163.com, mrliao89@gmail.com
[2] School of Business Administration, Northeastern University, Shenyang, China
pschoe@gmail.com

Abstract. Exercising is essential for elderly people to maintain their health in a good condition. However, elderly people usually have a tendency to stay at home due to their physical limitations or limited weather conditions in which they are willing to go outside for exercise. In addition, elderly people are easily injured with heavy exercise equipment, which also makes them reluctant to exercise. In this study, we followed the process of "user-centered design" in developing an indoor exercising video game using the Kinect system to overcome aforementioned problems. We first investigated user requirements based on interviews with real users and then developed a Kinect-based game for elderly people. We lastly evaluated the usability of the game; the results show that the Kinect-based indoor exercising game can be effectively used for better exercise, entertainment, and communication.

Keywords: Kinect, elderly people, indoor exercise, augmented reality, user-centered design.

1 Introduction

Because an adequate volume of physical activities everyday helps individuals keep healthy, physical exercise could be crucial to people's health, especially to those who are older than 65. However, it's really challenging to maintain a tight exercise schedule for them [1]. Elderly people are often unwilling to go outside considering their limited physical conditions. In China, the situation of severe air pollution becomes another reason. Although elderly people hold a positive attitude toward exercise, they can hardly find any motivation for sports, and the fear of injury could be another hindrance [2]. Thus, there is a potential demand of designing an interface to take indoor exercise for elderly people who are either unwilling or not able to go outside.

The key procedure of designing such an exercising interface is to find motivation factors for elderly people [3]. Previous studies [4, 5] showed that games are effective in motivating exercise and increasing exercising time. We used the user-centered design approach to innovate an interactive sports game for elderly people to encourage their exercises at home and meanwhile provide them with great entertainment. Their body movements in front of the Kinect sensor are tracked and projected to a TV

P.L.P. Rau (Ed.): CCD/HCII 2014, LNCS 8528, pp. 193–200, 2014.

screen where they can see themselves in the game background. The Kinect-based video game, both easy and interesting to play, is considered to be very helpful in motivating elderly people to exercise at home as well as enriching their daily lives.

This article firstly introduces an analysis of interviews we conducted with elderly people. We collected their opinions and preferences for both outdoor and indoor exercise to generate a list of requirements which is used in the later design of the game. Shortcomings of current indoor sports equipment are summarized with a brief introduction of the Kinect-based game in Section 3. A detailed illustration of the design of the Kinect-based video game is then presented. Some improvements based on a usability test are suggested. Discussion and conclusions are summarized in the last section.

2 User Requirement Gathering: Interviews

To study user behaviors of outdoor activities and demands for indoor exercise, we conducted a series of interviews with 10 senior citizens in March 2013. 4 males and 6 females, in the ages of 65 to 80, participated to answer a list of 22 questions about their current exercise situations and concerns they had when doing sports. All subjects were recruited and interviewed in a local park in Beijing, China.

During the interviews, we mainly investigated their hobbies, frequency, duration, and volume of exercises, influence of air pollution, attitude toward indoor exercise, and type of indoor exercise they prefer. Since peer motivation can be quite significant in doing sports, we also surveyed their relationship with children and other citizens around the same age. Additional concerns about exercise they had were also included in generating a list of requirements we need to consider in designing the game.

As identified, most subjects enjoy having exercises before breakfast in the morning or after lunch in the afternoon because the exercises do not only provide them with a way to keep fit, but also an opportunity to meet some friends and chat. As for the type of exercises, they often prefer easy and light exercises, such as taking a walk around or practicing Tai Chi in a park, because they fear to be hurt by heavy exercises and equipment that they cannot handle. Eight subjects reported themselves doing exercises for half to one hour every day while the others exercised about twice a week with less than one hour each time. All subjects complained that the serious air pollution had great impact to their exercise schedule, causing them either to decrease the frequency, duration, or the volume of outdoor exercises. When indoor exercise was mentioned, they worried about whether the atmosphere at home is suitable, since they may focus on housework and forget about exercises if they stay at home. They further added a requirement to meet old friends even though they could not go outside.

Results from the interview shed light on the demand of a new application for indoor exercise. All subjects showed interests in the idea we put forward about a video game for exercises at home and were willing to have a try. They expected to have a gaming device of good usability, great entertainment, high safety, and social connectivity at an affordable price. A list of user requirements for the indoor sports game is summarized as below.

- The game should have adequate volume of exercises to be effective, but the duration of each game round should be limited to avoid overtiredness.
- The game should be easy to start with and self-explainable. It should be easy for elderly people to understand.
- The game should have voice messages or controls considering the low-vision of elderly people.
- The game should provide different scenes for different game tasks. Different tasks should enable users to exercise different body parts, especially their legs.
- The game should encourage users to maintain a healthy schedule by doing exercises every day. But if users do not have a big progress, the punishment should not be too big.
- The game would be better if social connectivity is provided between neighborhoods, or users could share their scoreboards with each other.

3 Improvement of Existing Indoor Exercise Equipment

There are globally 841 million people who are more than 60 years old in the world today [6]. Solving exercise problems for them will give a way for them to keep fit and enjoy daily life. Currently, besides some drugs are argued to have effectiveness in keeping people fit, rare products are found to be especially designed for elderly people. However, we proposed that with the help of some well-designed devices and exercises, elderly people could be guided and encouraged to exercise safely, correctly and persistently. And most important, they could get all this done just at their own home.

3.1 Shortcomings of Existing Equipment

Current indoor exercise devices, such as the stepper, ergometer, and treadmill, do not limit their targeted users as elderly people. Thus when these devices are trimmed into an environment for elderly people, they could have several inherent drawbacks as follows.

- First, these devices basically consist of mechanical parts, and are leveled up by adding loads through fictions or masses. However, the mechanical parts of these devices or the loads may hurt them accidentally, as elderly people may have limited control abilities of body movements.
- Second, since these devices focus only on exercise itself without offering any kinds of entertainment or rewards, users could hardly find any motivation to have long-term exercise. Thus, it's hard for elderly people to cultivate a regular exercise behavior.
- Third, these devices are mainly designed for an individual user. However, people may feel lonely when they practice only themselves. Most people may have fun if they could exercise with their close friends.

3.2 Improvement Using the Kinect System

The Kinect is a world-leading sensor that has enabled a series of applications in video games. Its unique advantages over traditional indoor exercise devices could be summarized as below

- The Kinect enables elderly people to interact with game system by recognizing their natural gestures and body movements through a camera and IR sensors without a traditional hand-held controller [7] or complex operation commands, which contributes to the learning easiness for elderly people.
- Besides color map data, the Kinect could also provide depth map data and skeleton position data. By interpreting the 3D information, user's image can be easily captured, recognized and extracted from the background, which can be used in creating an augmented reality environment. Substituting the background also provides a privacy protection for the user.
- The Kinect can be connected to a PC via an USB port [7]. Because it has an SDK for application developers, more marvelous features could be developed and realized on the PC.

As a result, the Kinect has been chosen to realize most of the functions elderly people preferred, with its strong abilities in recognizing people's natural gestures and skeletons, as well as providing a user-friendly and extensible interface for elderly people. Users need no more objective game controllers. In addition, voice commands are supported, which makes Kinect the perfect choice to fit into an indoor environment in front of a TV. The prototype game is revised and improved from a set of sample codes in the Kinect for Windows Developer Toolkit, with changes to improve the game experience.

4 Prototype Design and Development

4.1 Apparatus

As shown in Fig.1, the Kinect-based prototype consists of four parts: a player, a Kinect sensor, a PC, and a display screen. The Kinect and the display screen are connected to the PC where the prototype software is running. Real-time data of image, depth, and skeleton position is obtained from the Kinect sensor and processed by the PC software. The player just needs to stand three to four meters away from the Kinect sensor in order that his or her whole body can be captured. Few seconds after the game software is started, the player skeleton will be tracked and on screen there will be a hand image to represent the mouse in a normal PC environment. The player is able to move one of his or her hands to "click" on any buttons to configure game difficulties, duration, or background music – just move the hand image onto the button and hold it for a few seconds. This set of gestures is inherited from the Kinect system library and proved to be quite natural to users. Later if a commercial game is released, an Xbox can substitute the PC and the display screen can be any displays such as a TV or a projector.

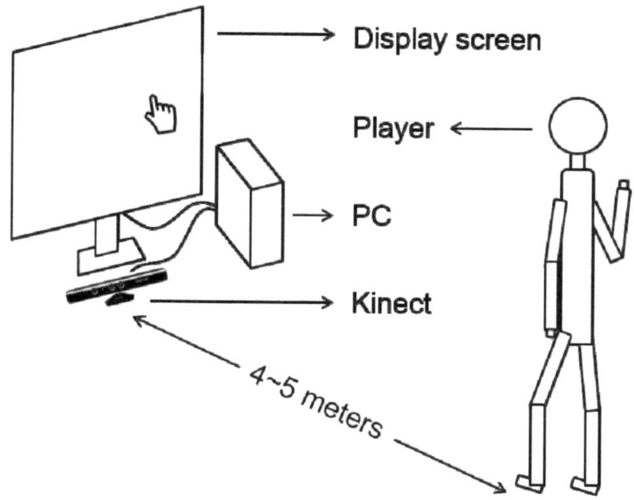

Fig. 1. Prototype apparatus

4.2 Game Design

This game has special designs for elderly people to provide exercise and fun, as well as a chance for users and their friends playing together.

Before the game starts, players could configure game intensity and duration so that it fits their individual condition. During the game, to better provide an exercise environment and protect the privacy of all players, the system plays background music and cuts the player out of his home environment, setting him on a green grass or a playground where he prefers. Then he is challenged to get as many points as possible in a given period of time (2 minutes), by hitting twice of bubbles that keep falling down from the sky. Because hitting falling objects to gain points is a common sense, it is easy for elderly people who have limited game experience to notice and understand. To increase fun during the game, bubbles are engraved with different points, both positive and negative, but covered with a question mark when first falling down. When the player hits the bubble with his or her body for the first time, the question mark disappears and the real point is shown. The player is then challenged to react soundly in order to avoid negative points and to get more positive points. Bonus points are awarded depending on different body parts the player uses to hit the bubbles. Each time the player hits the bubble, there will be appropriate a text message and ringtone to give direct feedback. The time left and score gained are shown at the corner of the screen as a motivation source. Voice commands are also supported to either pause, stop or restart the game.

Moreover, social influence is deliberately designed so that multi-player game mode generates more motivation on an individual and all players could share their best scores with friends through an online score board after the game. By setting suitable background and music to create an atmosphere for exercise and establishing a platform for players sharing their scores and view rankings, elderly people are encouraged to exercise at home for a while every day.

5 Prototype Evaluation: An Experiment

In order to check whether our design has met elderly people's demand and evaluate its usability, a prototype game was developed and evaluated by 6 elderly people (2 males and 4 females, aged from 55 to 80) in June 2013. All subjects were randomly contacted in a local park in Beijing, China.

The evaluation experiment consisted of three steps: a brief introduction to the game, one-minute game trial, and a follow-up interview to collect their comments. One experimenter firstly introduced the game, and then the subject could have a try and ask any questions. After that, the player should play the prototype game for one minute, then answered a list of open-ended questions and gave any suggestions to the game design. The game duration was set to one minute in consideration that we had one subject of 80 years old and other configurations (intensity and background music) were set the same to waive any deviations and random factors to the evaluation experiment.

Usability issues and suggestions from the subjects are summarized in the following form according to the usability dimensions (effective, efficient, engaging, easy to learn, and error tolerate) [8].

Table 1. Usability issues and suggestions from the evaluation experiment

Usability dimensions	Usability issues	Suggestions	Count
Effective	No choice on exercise intensity and duration.	Provide choices on exercise intensity and duration. (already implemented, but not available in the experiment)	3
	The sound of hitting different bubbles is the same. It's hard to distinguish.	Select different ringtones music for different bubbles.	2
Efficient	The player may need to "press" several times to start the game.	Add "quick start" mode in the menu.	1
	Setting web connections with friends is too complex.	Simplify the procedure and add appropriate voice commands	4
Engaging	Selection of background images is quite limited.	Add more options for background images.	5
	Selection of background music is quite limited.	Add more options for background music.	5
	It's boring just to hit the bubbles all the time.	Add more types of exercises and design new and difficult game levels.	2

Table 1. *(continued)*

Easy to learn	There are no teaching videos or tutorials at the first time of playing.	Add a teaching video to introduce the game	3
Error tolerant	There is no warning if the player stands too close to the Kinect sensor.	Provide a text or an audio message if the player stands too close or is untracked	1
	The negative point for "bomb" bubbles is too big.	Reduce the negative point from -100 to -50.	2

6 Discussion and Conclusions

Compared with current indoor exercise devices, the Kinect-based video game is better for elderly people in the following three aspects.

First, the video game exposes its player to less danger. Because elderly people have limited control abilities, traditional indoor exercise devices may accidentally hurt users. However, using Kinect as a sensing device, players are free to interact with the display with their body as the controller. No more physical controllers are needed.

Second, the video game offers more entertainment and thus motivations. Unlike traditional devices that focus only on heavy exercises, this game has successfully created an augmented reality environment in which players may feel relaxed and attracted by the background image and music. The mechanism of getting points and awards by exercising has helped players to increase exercise volume unconsciously. To win, as a strong motivation, also helps to maintain a long-term exercise habit for elderly people.

Third, via the online platform of the video game, players can still have fun together with their friends, just like when they exercise together outside. Current devices all work individually and keep elderly people away from their peers, which may exert a negative influence to their social life. However, the online platform offers players an access to share their scores and comments on their friends. This has not only increased entertainment of the game, but also added peer competition into the motivation, thus having a positive effect on prompting elderly people to exercise.

Although all subjects showed their great interests in the game and evaluated it highly successful, feedbacks from the evaluation experiment pointed out the directions we need to consider to further improve our game design. The game should have more deliberate designs to have levels of different difficulties and game tasks. Messages in the game should have more clear instructions than only information. And feedback should be distinguishable and consistent with what shown on the display. We are also challenged to balance between the functionality and simplicity: at one hand, we need to provide kinds of exercises that could help exercise different body parts; at the other hand, we need to keep it simple stupid in order it is easy to learn and understandable for elderly people.

To summarize it up, in this study we have carried out a "user-centered design" for the elderly people in developing a Kinect-based indoor exercise video game. User requirements collected from an interview of 10 elderly people for indoor exercise were studied and a prototype video game based on the Kinect sensor has been designed and developed to satisfy these demands. An evaluation experiment was conducted on 6 elderly people and further improvement suggestions were given. Compared with existing indoor exercise devices, this video game has better safety, entertainment, motivation, and social connectivity in promoting elderly people's long-term indoor exercise.

References

1. World Health Organization. Global Recommendations on Physical Activity for Health (2010), http://whqlibdoc.who.int/publications/2010/9789241599979_eng.pdf
2. Dishman, R.K.: Motivating older adults to exercise. Southern Medical Journal 87(5), S79 (1994)
3. Vallerand, R.J., Losier, G.F.: An integrative analysis of intrinsic and extrinsic motivation in sport. Journal of Applied Sport Psychology 11(1), 142–169 (1999)
4. Betker, A.L., Szturm, T., Moussavi, Z.K., Nett, C.: Video game–based exercises for balance rehabilitation: a single-subject design. Archives of Physical Medicine and Rehabilitation 87(8), 1141–1149 (2006)
5. Betker, A.L., Desai, A., Nett, C., Kapadia, N., Szturm, T.: Game-based exercises for dynamic short-sitting balance rehabilitation of people with chronic spinal cord and traumatic brain injuries. Physical Therapy 87(10), 1389–1398 (2007)
6. United Nations: World Population Prospects-The 2012 Revision (2013)
7. González-Ortega, D., Díaz-Pernas, F.J., Martínez-Zarzuela, M., Antón-Rodríguez, M.: A Kinect-based system for cognitive rehabilitation exercises monitoring. Computer Methods and Programs in Biomedicine (2013)
8. Quesenbery, W.: The five dimensions of usability. Content and Complexity: Information Design in Technical Communication, 75–93 (2003)

Interaction Design of a Semi-automatic Video Face Annotation System

Cailiang Liu, Tao Xiong, Chenguang Zhang, and Zhibing Wang

Hulu LLC 10/F, Building B, ChuangXin Plaza, Tsinghua Science Park, Beijing 100084, P.R. China
{cailiang.liu,tao.xiong,chenguang.zhang,zhibing.wang}@hulu.com

Abstract. In this paper, we propose an intelligent system that allows people to annotate face tracks of video content. To reduce the workload, we adopt two strategies in the system: 1) visually similar face tracks could be grouped together to reduce human reaction time; 2) face models could be learned to automatically recognize celebrity identities, leaving annotator only simple judgement tasks. With more precise face models, the recognized results require much less time for confirmation. Altogether, these strategies significantly reduce the workload of human annotation/confirmation. Experiments on a very large video repository prove the efficiency and effectiveness of the proposed system.

Keywords: User Interfaces, Video Content Analysis, Video Advertisement, Face Track Annotation.

1 Introduction

Internet is becoming an important distribution channel for multimedia content. More and more people choose to watch video content via internet, not only because of its rich content, but also because of its free and low cost. Many companies also foresee this big opportunity, i.e., by displaying advertisements to the population to stimulate consumption, they can help product companies profit more, shape and promote their public figure. With limited impression views by the populations, advertising companies have to maximize the click through rate per impression to help product companies profit more. That is, display the advertisement to the most potential buyers. Generally, there are two ways to achieve this: 1) understand users preferences from their online behavior history and display advertisements related to user preference; 2) associate advertisements to related multimedia content. The first way can be regarded as mining stable and long-term preferences. In addition, the second way can be regarded as mining short-term or instant preferences. It could be very useful especially for trailer or commenting videos. Users watching such videos commonly because they concern about the recent development of the story or they want to discuss about the story with the online community. They often like goods (hats, watch, clothes, cars etc) related to celebrities in the video.

P.L.P. Rau (Ed.): CCD/HCII 2014, LNCS 8528, pp. 201–210, 2014.

The commercial value of the first way has been mined a lot while the value of the second way is largely underdeveloped. Video content analysis technologies can help find out concept or objects in video. But the researches for the problem is still in early stage [1, 2]. Automatic extraction of general objects or concept is still intractable. Besides advertisement, video content analysis could also help user navigate and locate video content in finer level. As shown in Figure 1, video content analysis results could also be used to integrate and summarize information from all over the internet.

Fortunately, after near 10 years' development, the extraction of some specific concepts becomes mature and usable, such as face, pedistrian and trademark detection [3–5]. These concepts are relevant to our motivation. Considering that people are the most frequent subjects in TV episodes or movies, in this paper, we focus on the face recognition problem, which is far more difficult and challenging than just face detection[6, 7]. More specifically, we choose to tackle the problem in a semi-automatic way, by designing an interactive and intelligent annotation system.

Fig. 1. Face match features on website. Users can see celebrity information by hoving mouse on faces.

There has been user interfaces for face or object annotations [8–12]. However, the existing user interfaces[13, 11] could not tackle our problem: 1) they aim at static faces while we focus on video face track as a basic unit. The face images are more challenging, including occlusion, large variance and severe blur; 2) they lack of a face model for each person, which can automatically annotate faces leveraging existing labels; 3) they lack of user interfaces that group visually similar faces to reduce user workload.

To address the above issues, we propose a semi-automatic video face annotation system. The system is composed of three parts: 1) backend services that extract and process face tracks; 2) annotation user interface; 3) confirmation user interface. For each video, as shown in Figure 2, there are 3 steps for users to label the faces: 1) randomly choose some faces and cluster visually similar faces for user annotation; 2) with these bootstrap information, the system builds face models for each labeled person and automatically tag the rest faces; 3) the visually similar tagged faces are clustered together for confirmation. The higher recognition accuracy, the shorter time it will take users to confirm. Summarizing all above, the contributions of the paper are two folded: 1) we propose a semi-automatic way to assist celebrity face annotation for videos; 2) we adopt two strategies to design user interfaces to improve the efficiency of the annotation process.

1.1 Related Work

Designing user interfaces for object annotation and pattern recognition has been a long history [14, 10, 8, 15, 16, 12, 13, 11]. In traditional image annotation system, user interfaces are often introduced to label positive and negative examples with respect to some concepts [13, 11]. Because of the difficulties in concept modelling, it requires heavy annotation workload to build an accurate model. Cui et al., Tian et al. [13, 11] propose a system to reduce annotation workload via efficient clustering. Zhang et al. [15] propose a bayesian framework that calculate a name list to reduce annotation time. Later, Zhang et al. [16] propose a framework to calculate the name list for annotating multiple photos at a time. However, it requires people browse the whole album to select the photo set. Suh et al. [17] propose a cluster-based annotation strategy. Different from other work, it also introduces clothes features and event information to improve accuracy.

All the previous work [15, 16, 13, 11] focus on automatic personal album management. However, we are motivated to mine celebrities in TV episodes or movies. In TV episodes or movies, there are diverse face images, e.g., faces with many poses and facial expressions, faces with motion blur or occlusions. This leads to many difficulties in building face models. Fortunately, there are regular celebrities, each celebrity with enough face examples to build accurate models. Moreover, in our scenario, it requires 100% accuracy to annotate celebrities. So manual confirmation should be involved. Since there are many similar story segments in TV episodes or movies, as shown in Figure 3, introducing clustering-based annotation could improve the efficiency of the system.

1.2 Our Method

With the requirements summerized above, we propose a semi-automatic annotation system to address the problem. The system intelligently combines state-of-art face recognition technologies and efficient user interfaces. For the system overview, please see Figure 2. There are mainly three parts:

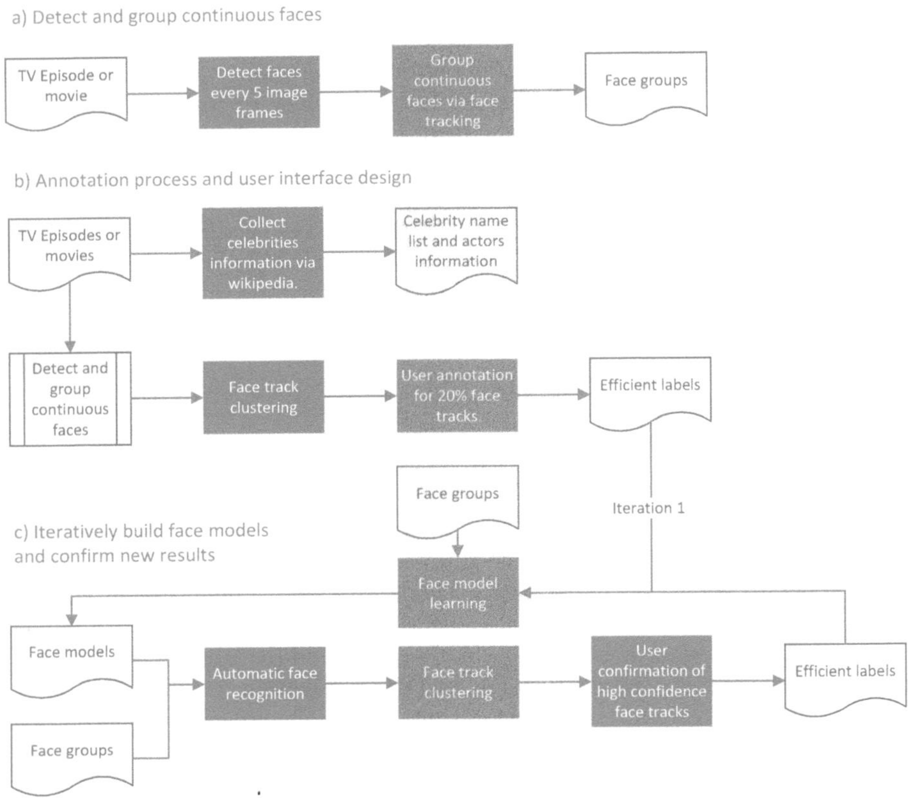

Fig. 2. Overview of the system architect. a) system detects faces and group continuous faces into face groups/tracks for each TV episode/movie; b) system prepares celebrity information for each TV series and select 20% face track clusters as diverse as possible for initial labels; c) initial user labels are fed to system to learn face models and the automatically recognized results are left for user confirmation.

Fig. 3. Similar face tracks of a TV episode. The figure shows track images of the same person from 6 shots. Each cell shows 4 images and the start time of a face track.

- For each video, the system first detects faces for every 5 frames. Then, the system runs a face tracker to group time continuous faces into face tracks.
- When a series of TV episodes come, the system crawls celebrities information and name list via web. This information will be used in annotation pages. Since the system requires a number of face labels to build accurate models, in the bootsrap stage, 20% of the face tracks are selected for user annotation. The selected face tracks should be as diverse as posssible to cover as many poses as possible.
- With enough labels, the system builds KNN-based face models [18] for each celebrity. Then the system automatically recognize the rest face tracks. To ensure that the recognition is 100% accurate, users are required to confirm the recognized results. To improve the efficiency of the confirmation step, the recognized face tracks are also grouped into clusters. Because visually similar faces take much less time for confirmation. In addition, the system allows users to confirm just the face tracks with high confidence. New confirmed labels are fed back to iteratively improve face models.

The paper is composed of five sections. Sectoin 1 introduces background and related work of video face annotation. For the details about how we design the user interfaces and how we combines the state-of-art face recognition technology and user interfaces, please see Section 2. Section 3 describes the automatic recognition algorithm in detail. Experiments proved the efficiency of our system and user interface design. For the details of experimental results, please see Section 4. Section 5 concludes the efficiency of the system and user interface design.

2 Interactive Annotation

We propose user interfaces to assist people annotation and reduce the annotation workload. We design a web portal for annotation tasks. There are three pages in the web portal: a selection page for TV series selection, an annotation page for initial celebrity labels and a confirmation page to confirm automatic recognition results.

The TV series selection page allows people choose which TV serire to annotate. Please see Figure 4 for the detail of the page. The number in the upper-right corner of every TV series indicates the number of videos to annotate. In the web page, users can search TV series via the search box in the navigation bar. Users can also filter TV series by selecting unfinished shows or top shows on the left navigation area. By clilcking the dashboard link, users can view the statistical data.

2.1 Annotation Page

Figure 5 shows the page for face tracks annotation. On the left, there is a candidate list of celebrities of the TV series. On the right side, a cluster of face tracks is shown. The rough number of face tracks per cluster is 40. The first,

Fig. 4. Series selection page

middle and last faces of a face track are shown to help people verify that it is a complete track. (There may be some errors during motion faces tracking.) To help people identify celebrities, there is also a face image with larger scene context. Possible identities are given in the candidate list. To reduce annotation time, annotators can select multiple face tracks before determining the identity for these face tracks together.

Fig. 5. Clustering-based annotation/confirmation page

2.2 Confirmation Page

The confirmation page is used to help people select the correct recognition results, because we require that all the celebrity information shown to user should be 100% correct. It is similar to the annotation page, as shown in Figure 5. On the left panel, there is a celebrity list. For each celebrity, there are a face image, the number of tracks that assigned to him/her and the number of tracks that are confirmed. To reduce workload of user confirmation, users can simply mark the annotation results as 'Error'. Similarly, in the face track area, three face images are shown to represent each face track. In addition, a face image with larger context information is also shown to help identify the celebrity. This helps a lot when the face image is dark.

Because only one click is required for confirmation, the confirmation time is much shorter than annotation time. It is straightforward that it will take less confirmation time when the recognizer is more accurate. For more details of the experiments, please see Section 4. Because there are many similar face tracks and story scenes in a TV episode, grouping these similar face tracks could reduce the reaction time from people. Therefore, we also cluster similar face tracks in confirmation step. Rather than marking each face track right or wrong one by one, it will take less time to select a group of similar face tracks and then confirm it right or wrong.

The recognizer generates a confidence score for each recognition result. Generally, the confidence score is lower for the low quality face tracks or the face tracks that are unknown. The confirmation page automatically rank confident face tracks in the first pages. Users can simply leave the face tracks with low confidence score and continue to the next iteration of automatic recognition and confirmation. With new confirmed face images, the face models become more accurate. The unconfident face tracks could be correctly recognized with better face models. These strategies improves the efficiency of the system.

3 Algorithms

In the backend system, as shown in Figure 2, we detect faces for every 5 image frames using a multi-view face detector[19]. Then continuous faces are grouped together via a klt face tracking algorithm [20]. A face group or a face track is a basic unit for processing and annotation.

To cluster face tracks, various clustering algorithms could be used, such as kmeans[21], top-down hierarchical clustering[22], agglomerative clustering[23] and so on. We select agglomerative clustering because we can cut at any level to control both the number of face tracks to roughly 40 and the variance of the cluster. Different from single face clustering, each pair of face track are two faces series. Faces series distance should be defined to cluster face tracks. We define the face track distance as the minimal 4-4 faces distance. The median of distances within 16 4-4 face distances is used as final track distance.

To measure face-face distances, the local binary pattern (LBP) face features are used [7]. LBP features measure difference between adjacent pixels. For each pair of pixels, there are only two possible values - higher or lower. Therefore, LBP features are robust to illumination changes. At every pixel location, pixel differences make up an 8-bit code. In a fixed region (eye, nose and so on), we count the number of all kinds of LBP code. This makes up a distribution of codes.

Besides the robustness to light changes, the distribution also reflects texture properties of facial components.

With new labeled face tracks, the backend system automatically updates face models for every celebrities. Because there are many celebrities, KNN-based models are better choices rather than SVM-based models. It is efficient and requires no training. In recent years, Wright et al.[18] propose a KNN-based classification method using sparse representation. It significantly outperforms other methods. Inspired by the method[18], we also decompose every face as linear combinations of its nearest neighbors. Together with label information, the linear coefficients are used to vote for identity label. The sparsity concentration index (SCI) is used as confidence value for prediction. For every 5-face subset with inner dissimilarities greater than some value, we use the median voting as a recognition candidate. Finally, we take the highest 5-face voting as the track recognition result. This alleviates the wrong-match problem that a face of person A is very similar to a face of person B in feature space.

4 Experiments

To evaluate the effectiveness and efficiency of the proposed system, we measure the time used for the annotation tasks. We hire 8 persons to annotate video face tracks. At first, these people are not experts for face annotation. They are not familiar with the celebrities in the TV series. Initially, they are required to annotate only after they finish watching each TV episode. In our video repository, there are totally 186 TV series, 4860 videos. The typical length of a TV episode is about 40 minutes. And each TV episode has about 1294 face tracks averagely.

In the experiments, we measure the annotation time per video (all tracks), annotation time per track, confirmation time per video and confirmation time

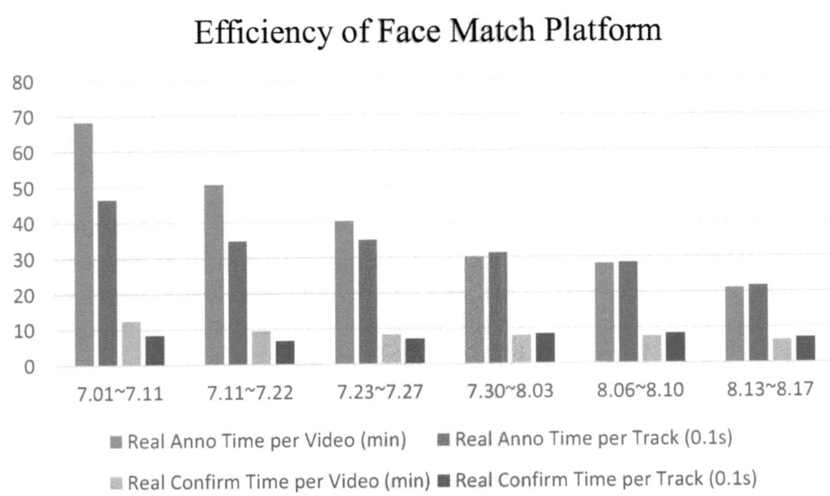

Fig. 6. Efficiency of face match platform

per track. The system measures user performance at 6 different period, as shown in Figure 6. During these periods, 140 videos are annotated and confirmed per person. As time goes on, users get familiar with celebrities in TV series. With more and more celebrity labels, face models become more precise iteratively. As expected, the average time for annotation tasks per person descreas continuously, as shown in Figure 6. Please also notice that, the confirmation time is significantly smaller than annotation time. It proves the effectiveness of the strategy that we continuously utilize existing celebrity labels and leave the simpler confirmation tasks for users.

5 Conclusions and Future Work

Video content analysis is very important for online video websites. Besides advertisement targeting, it also allows internet users to navigate and locate content more easily. In this paper, we propose an intelligent annotation system that allows users to annotate faces for video content. Because celebrities are the most frequent and important subjects in TV episodes. To reduce users workload, we adopt two simple strategies in interaction design: 1) visually similar face tracks could be annotated together to reduce user reaction time; 2) with large amount of existing celebrity labels, precise face models could be learned to help annotate. Experiments proves that the two strategies significantly reduce the user annotation time.

In future, more intelligent algorithms could be proposed to learned preciser models. More face features could be added to backend system to produce more robust and consistent clusters. These are expected to reduce annotation time further. In some TV series, there could be new celebrities unknown to system. Algorithms that automatically discover new celebrities could also be introduced.

References

1. Rui, Y., Huang, T.S., Ortega, M., Mehrotra, S.: Relevance feedback: a power tool for interactive content-based image retrieval. IEEE Transactions on Circuits and Systems for Video Technology 8(5), 644–655 (1998)
2. Marques, O., Furht, B.: Content Based Image and Video Retrieval, vol. 21. Springer (2002)
3. Viola, P., Jones, M.J.: Robust real-time face detection. International Journal of Computer Vision 57(2), 137–154 (2004)
4. Dalal, N., Triggs, B.: Histograms of oriented gradients for human detection. In: IEEE Computer Society Conference on Computer Vision and Pattern Recognition, CVPR 2005, vol. 1, pp. 886–893. IEEE (2005)
5. Hesson, A., Androutsos, D.: Logo and trademark detection in images using color wavelet co-occurrence histograms. In: IEEE International Conference on Acoustics, Speech and Signal Processing, ICASSP 2008, pp. 1233–1236. IEEE (2008)
6. He, X., Yan, S., Hu, Y., Niyogi, P., Zhang, H.J.: Face recognition using laplacianfaces. IEEE Transactions on Pattern Analysis and Machine Intelligence 27(3), 328–340 (2005)

7. Ahonen, T., Hadid, A., Pietikainen, M.: Face description with local binary patterns: Application to face recognition. IEEE Transactions on Pattern Analysis and Machine Intelligence 28(12), 2037–2041 (2006)
8. Nakazato, M., Manola, L., Huang, T.S.: ImageGrouper: Search, annotate and organize images by groups. In: Chang, S.-K., Chen, Z., Lee, S.-Y. (eds.) VISUAL 2002. LNCS, vol. 2314, pp. 129–142. Springer, Heidelberg (2002)
9. Wilhelm, A., Takhteyev, Y., Sarvas, R., Van House, N., Davis, M.: Photo annotation on a camera phone. In: CHI 2004 Extended Abstracts on Human Factors in Computing Systems, pp. 1403–1406. ACM (2004)
10. Grudin, J., Bargeron, D.: Multimedia annotation: an unsuccessful tool becomes a successful framework. Communication and Collaboration Support Systems. TH a. TIEK Okada. Ohmsha (2005)
11. Tian, Y., Liu, W., Xiao, R., Wen, F., Tang, X.: A face annotation framework with partial clustering and interactive labeling. In: IEEE Conference on Computer Vision and Pattern Recognition, CVPR 2007, pp. 1–8. IEEE (2007)
12. Ames, M., Naaman, M.: Why we tag: motivations for annotation in mobile and online media. In: Proceedings of the SIGCHI Conference on Human Factors in Computing Systems, pp. 971–980. ACM (2007)
13. Cui, J., Wen, F., Xiao, R., Tian, Y., Tang, X.: Easyalbum: an interactive photo annotation system based on face clustering and re-ranking. In: Proceedings of the SIGCHI Conference on Human Factors in Computing Systems, pp. 367–376. ACM (2007)
14. Kuchinsky, A., Pering, C., Creech, M.L., Freeze, D., Serra, B., Gwizdka, J.: Fotofile: a consumer multimedia organization and retrieval system. In: Proceedings of the SIGCHI Conference on Human Factors in Computing Systems: The CHI is the Limit, pp. 496–503. ACM (1999)
15. Zhang, L., Chen, L., Li, M., Zhang, H.: Automated annotation of human faces in family albums. In: Proceedings of the Eleventh ACM International Conference on Multimedia, pp. 355–358. ACM (2003)
16. Zhang, L., Hu, Y., Li, M., Ma, W., Zhang, H.: Efficient propagation for face annotation in family albums. In: Proceedings of the 12th Annual ACM International Conference on Multimedia, pp. 716–723. ACM (2004)
17. Suh, B., Bederson, B.B.: Semi-automatic photo annotation strategies using event based clustering and clothing based person recognition. Interacting with Computers 19(4), 524–544 (2007)
18. Wright, J., Yang, A.Y., Ganesh, A., Sastry, S.S., Ma, Y.: Robust face recognition via sparse representation. IEEE Transactions on Pattern Analysis and Machine Intelligence 31(2), 210–227 (2009)
19. Huang, C., Ai, H., Li, Y., Lao, S.: High-performance rotation invariant multiview face detection. IEEE Transactions on Pattern Analysis and Machine Intelligence 29(4), 671–686 (2007)
20. Gejguš, P., Šperka, M.: Face tracking in color video sequences. In: Proceedings of the 19th Spring Conference on Computer Graphics, pp. 245–249. ACM (2003)
21. Hartigan, J.A., Wong, M.A.: Algorithm as 136: A k-means clustering algorithm. Applied Statistics, 100–108 (1979)
22. Johnson, S.C.: Hierarchical clustering schemes. Psychometrika 32(3), 241–254 (1967)
23. Defays, D.: An efficient algorithm for a complete link method. The Computer Journal 20(4), 364–366 (1977)

Thumbs Up to Gesture Controls? A Cross-Cultural Study on Spontaneous Gestures

Alison Meier[1], Kelly Goto[1], and Michael Wörmann[2]

[1] gotomedia & UX Fellows, 2169 Folsom St. m-302, San Francisco, CA 94110, USA
{alison,kelly}@gotomedia.com
[2] Facit Digital & UX Fellows, Neuhauser Strasse 17, D-80331 Munich, Germany
m.woermann@facit-digital.com

Abstract. As a growing number of three-dimensional motion and gesture-controlled consumer electronics come to market, there are new challenges for user experience design for globally merchandized devices, because gestures naturally vary between regions and cultures. The UX Fellows network undertook a study to learn how people from different countries would gesture to control consumer electronics. Eighteen agencies interviewed 360 people from 18 countries around the world to see how people would spontaneously gesture to achieve specific TV commands. Results from each country were aggregated and compared to determine which countries used the same gestures and which used different ones.

Keywords: gesture, motion, culture, international, consumer electronics.

1 Introduction

Commercial products that respond to three-dimensional gestures are becoming accessible in the market, first in video game consoles like Xbox Kinect, then in smartphones like the Samsung Galaxy S4, and now in computers via the Leap Motion device. Despite the commercial availability of devices controlled by gestures and even their low price point, no common gesture language exists. As technology becomes increasingly capable of understanding that we are signaling with our hands, the practicality of communicating in this manner relies on the design of easy to use gesture languages.

Gestures are usually defined as interactions where hands move in the air in a way that replaces a more traditional mouse and pointer or touchscreen interaction. Some gestures function as pointing gestures, where the hand or finger simply replaces the pointer as used in a mouse. These are called pointing gestures. This study examines a different kind of gesture, what we call semantic gestures, where the hand (or hand and arm) performs series of movements that are recognized by the device. We define a gesture language as a set of semantic gestures.

The goals of a gesture language are twofold: first, the machine must be able to recognize and interpret distinct gestures. Second, the gestures must incur minimal burden

P.L.P. Rau (Ed.): CCD/HCII 2014, LNCS 8528, pp. 211–217, 2014.

on the user by being both easy to use and easy to remember [1]. "Easy to use" includes the need for gestures to require minimal physical exertion as well as be socially acceptable [2].

A previous study [3] found that user-defined gestures—in which individuals choose their own gestures for each action—are easier to remember than pre-defined gestures. Yet user-defined gesture languages would lead to infinitely fragmented languages, in which users would have to be willing to and capable of creating their own set of gestures for each device. An alternative to user-defined gestures is "user-elicited" gestures, in which "sets are generated by a representative group of users in a study…and are then carefully compiled and selected to form an 'agreed upon' gesture set that is still recognizable by the system" [3, 4].

As a user-elicited gesture language should be defined by a "representative group of users," the global nature of consumer electronics markets indicates that the representative group should consider cross-cultural expectations regarding gestures. Although some previous work [5] acknowledges cultural differences in gestures, no previous study has attempted to understand the specific instances of cultural disagreement over three-dimensional gestures. A past study [6] of touchscreen gestures found high agreement across cultures for direct manipulation gestures and low agreement for symbolic gestures. Three-dimensional gestures are inherently more symbolic than touchscreen gestures, so presumably the disagreement would increase as well.

2 The Study

UX Fellows, a network of user experience research agencies around the world, undertook a study to understand how people from around the world would interact with consumer electronics using gestures, in particular the television. Participants were asked to imagine they could control a TV using semantic gestures and to demonstrate how they would perform a series of commands.

Participants then rated how difficult they found it to determine each gesture. Eighteen agencies (each representing a different country) participated in the study. Each conducted identical sessions with 20 participants in its home country for a total of 360 participants around the world. The following countries were represented:

1. Argentina (AR)
2. Australia (AU)
3. Belgium (BE)
4. Canada (CA)
5. China (CN)
6. Germany (DE)
7. Finland (FI)
8. France (FR)
9. India (IN)
10. Italy (IT)
11. South Korea (KR)
12. Mexico (MX)
13. Netherlands (NL)
14. Russia (RU)
15. Spain (ES)
16. Turkey (TR)
17. United Kingdom (UK)
18. USA (US)

2.1 Recruiting Methodology

Each agency recruited participants in its home country using the same criteria. The criteria included the following:

- Regular use of an HD flat screen TV (manufactured within the past 6 years)
- Regular use of at least three consumer electronics devices or services such as a Blu-Ray player, video on demand, home theater system, or gaming consoles
- Regular use of a touchscreen device such as a smartphone, tablet, or MP3 player
- No past use of gesture-controlled devices such as Xbox Kinect or a gesture-enabled TV
- Electronics-savvy consumers (a high interest in electronics and on top of the latest technologies)
- Likely to buy consumer electronics from major international brands (no national, retailer, or "no name" brands)

Pre-tests indicated that usage of touchscreen devices influenced gestures selected, so UX Fellows opted to bias toward touchscreen users rather than away from them, as more and more people are being exposed to touchscreens over time.

Participant ranged from ages 16 to 65, with a mean age of 32. Forty-nine percent of the participants were female.

2.2 Session Methodology

Sessions were conducted on an individual basis with one participant at a time with a moderator. Each session lasted about 15 minutes.

Care was taken to set up the session environment in a consistent manner by each agency. Participants were placed in front of a turned-off flat screen TV. A moderator sat to the side of the TV, while participants sat on a couch or comfortable chair.

As a warm-up exercise, participants were asked to demonstrate everyday gestures used in real life (rather than with electronics) such as "I can't hear you," "call me," and "very tasty." Then the participant was asked to rate how easy it was to think of a gesture (1 = easy to 5 = difficult). After the warm-up, participants were asked to demonstrate how they would gesture to the switched off TV to complete a series of commands. For example, the moderator would ask, "How would you switch on the TV?" and the participant would demonstrate a gesture and then explain why they selected that gesture. They were asked to rate the how easy it was to think of the gesture the same as with everyday gestures.

They were told in advance that their gestures did not need to be a cohesive set (for example, volume up did not need to be the inverse of volume down). The moderator was careful not to use gestures while speaking, to avoid biasing the responses. The session was captured by video recording.

3 Results

Results of each country's sessions were aggregated and then compared to the other countries. The TV tasks were grouped in three categories—high consistency, medium consistency, and low consistency—based on the number of countries that reported the majority of participants using the same gesture for the same command. On average, TV task gestures had a higher average mean difficulty (2.1) compared to everyday gestures (1.6) (1 = easy to 5 = difficult).

3.1 Everyday Gestures

There was high consistency between most everyday gestures. Gestures that were identical across most countries include "be quiet," "call me," and "write an email." Signaling numbers 2, 4, and 5 were nearly identical between countries, though there were differences when demonstrating the number 3: a few countries used the thumb and first 2 fingers, while most used the first 3 fingers.

A few gestures were similar for the majority of countries except for a couple of countries. For example, "come closer" was different in East Asian countries than most countries. Chinese participants gestured "I don't know" by waving the hand with the palm facing forward, while participants from other countries shrugged shoulders.

Most countries used a thumb pointed up to gesture "OK," although a significant minority had the index finger meet the thumb in a circle with the other fingers spread. "Very tasty" and "I can't hear you" varied greatly between countries.

Everyday gestures were generally easy to think of and had an average mean difficulty of 1.6. The most difficult everyday gesture to think of was "write an email" with a mean difficulty of 3.0. Despite this difficulty, almost all countries used the same gesture to demonstrate this concept.

3.2 TV Tasks: High Consistency Gestures

Some gestures had a high degree of consistency between countries with all or all but a few countries using the same gesture (see Table 1). Most of these gestures represented basic commands, such as changing the volume, fast-forwarding or rewinding, or pausing video-on-demand (VOD). Participants rated these gestures as generally easy to think of, with rating averages from 1.5 to 2.0.

Table 1. Gestures with a high degree of consistency between countries

Command	Most Frequent Gesture	Mean Difficulty	Countries with divergent gestures
Volume up	Lift hand or index finger	1.8	0
Volume down	Downward movement of hand, palm down	1.5	0
Pause current program	Fingers spread palm forward	2.0	1 (NL)

Table 1. *(continued)*

Pause VOD	Fingers spread palm forward	1.5	1 (NL)
Confirm on-screen dialog (OK)	Thumb up	1.9	3 (CN, IT, KR)
Fast forward VOD	Arm wave right to left	1.9	3 (AU, NL, UK)
Rewind VOD	Arm wave left to right	1.7	3 (AU, NL, UK)

3.3 TV Tasks: Medium Consistency Gestures

Another group of gestures were consistent for about half or 2/3 of the countries (see Table 2). Gestures that had a medium level of consistency between countries included slightly more complex commands such as volume up and down, muting sound, and cancel. The mean difficulty of these gestures increased slightly to an average range of 1.6 to 2.3. In this category, a number of participants used gestures borrowed from touchscreen interactions, such as swiping to navigate a menu. The direction that they swiped (left to right or right to left) varied between countries.

Table 2. Gestures with a medium degree of consistency between countries

Command	Most Frequent Gesture	Mean Difficulty	Countries with divergent gestures
Channel up	Hand swipe right to left	1.8	5 (AU, CA, ES, KR, US)
Stop VOD	Fingers spread palm forward	2.1	5 (CN, FI, KR, NL, RU)
Channel down	Hand swipe left to right	1.6	6 (AU, CA, ES, KR, UK, US)
Mute volume	Index finger to lips	2.0	7 (AU, BE, CN, FI, MX, RU, UK)
Backward navigation in menu	Hand swipe left to right	2.3	8 (AR, AU, BE, CA, ES, MX, RU, US)
Deny on-screen dialog (cancel)	Thumb down	1.8	9 (AR, AU, BE, CN, IT, KR, MX, RU, TR)
Skip chapter VOD	Draw a bow from left to right	2.2	9 (BE, CN, ES, FI, FR, IN, MX, NL, UK)

3.4 TV Tasks: Low Consistency Gestures

The final cluster of gestures had very low agreement between countries, with only few countries agreeing on a gesture. Difficulty averages also increased, ranging from 2.0 to 3.2. These gestures were primarily complex interactions with minimal real-world counterparts, such as share current program and context for current program. On the other hand, extremely basic commands such as switching on and off the device also fell in this category.

Table 3. Gestures with a low degree of consistency between countries

Command	Most Frequent Gesture	Mean Difficulty	Countries with divergent gestures
Switch on device	Fist with thumb pressing down (like remote control)	2.0	10 (BE, CA, CN, DE, FI, FR, IT, KR TR, US)
Previous chapter VOD	Draw bow from right to left in air	2.0	10 (BE, CN, ES, FI, FR, IN, MX, NL, UK, US)
Switch off device	Clap hands	2.9	10 (AR, CA, ES, IN, IT, KR, MX, NL, RU, TR)
Restart VOD	Palm facing TV	2.0	11 (AR, AU, BE, DE, ES, KR, MX, NL, RU, UK, US)
Share current program	Spread both hands upward to both sides	3.2	12 (AR, CN, FI, FR, IN, KR, MX, NL, RU, TR, UK, US)
Electronic program guide	Both arms at chest swung out wide	2.8	13 (AU, BE, CN, FI, IN, IT, KR, MX, NL, RU, TR, UK, US)
Context info for current program	Spread hands	2.8	14 (AR, AU, BE, CN, DE, ES, FI, FR, IN, KR, RU, TR, UK, US)
Home page	Arm in circular motion	2.9	14 (AR, AU, BE, CA, DE, ES, FI, IN, IT, MX, NL, TR, UK, US)

3.5 TV Tasks: Lack of Clustering among Regions

We found it notable that there was often little consistency between neighboring countries, even when the countries could be considered culturally similar. For example, Canada and the United States disagreed on gestures over a quarter of the time. The Netherlands and Germany disagreed over half the time (participants from the Netherlands frequently used gestures that were different from the global majority.)

On the other hand, some gestures were identical in countries that are in very different regions and have minimal cultural similarity. For example, participants from Australia, China, and Mexico all used the same gesture to indicate mute volume (moving hand from right top to left bottom). This gesture was different from the majority gesture.

3.6 Desirability of Gestures to Control Consumer Electronics

In open-ended discussion following demonstrating gestures, participants generally reported interest in controlling their electronics with gestures, in particular the "coolness factor" of using a new technology and not being tied to a remote control.

Participants did express concerns about using gestures, however—in particular needing to learn a gesture "language," the accuracy with which the machine recognizes the gestures, interference from other people in the room or unintentional gesturing, and being comfortable while watching TV.

3.7 Study Limitations

Many countries are not represented in this study, including entire regions such as Africa. In addition, each agency conducted the research in the city in which it is located, so many regions within each country are not included. For example, the United States agency conducted the research in San Francisco, California, which may not be representative for the country as a whole. Ideally, future versions of this study will include more countries and larger samples within each country.

In addition, participants in each country often used different gestures. Results were considered based on the majority usage. In many cases, a gesture may have been used by a minority of participants in the country that may be worth noting, especially if it was used by participants in other countries, either in a minority or majority capacity.

4 Conclusion

Findings support the possibility of creating a global gesture language for most basic TV interactions. With the exception of turning the TV on and off, most typical TV interactions could be completed with semantic gestures that people in most countries find natural.

For complex tasks, it is possible to use different gestures on a country-by-country basis, but because we did not observe regional clusters, this could lead to a highly fragmented gesture language that varies greatly from location to location.

As technology continues to advance and devices become even more capable of accurately recognizing semantic gestures, the success of gesture interactions will depend on the gestures themselves. Creating a gesture language for complex tasks for a global market that is easy to remember, socially acceptable, and easy to perform will be a significant challenge for designers and developers.

Acknowledgments. Thank you to all of the UX Fellows agencies who participated in this study and contributed to analyzing and reporting the results. Full results as well as a video of participants performing some of the gestures can be found at http://www.uxfellows.com/gesture.php.

References

1. Oh, U., Findlater, L.: The challenges and potential of end-user gesture customization. In: Proc. CHI 2013, pp. 1129–1138 (2013)
2. Ashbrook, D., Starner, T.: MAGIC: a motion gesture design tool. In: Proc. CHI 2010, pp. 2159–2168 (2010)
3. Nacenta, M., Kamber, Y., Qiang, Y., Kristensson, P.: Memorability of pre-designed and user-defined gesture sets. In: Proc. CHI 2013, pp. 1099–1108 (2013)
4. Wobbrock, J., Morris, M., Wilson, A.: User-defined gestures for surface computing. In: Proc. CHI 2009, pp. 1083–1092 (2009)
5. Vatavu, R.: User-defined gestures for free-hand TV control. In: Proc. of the 10th European Conference on Interactive Tv and Video, pp. 45–48 (2012)
6. Mauney, D., Howarth, J., Wirtanen, A., Capra, M.: Cultural similarities and differences in user-defined gestures for touchscreen user interfaces. In: Ext. Abstracts CHI 2010, pp. 4015–4020 (2010)

A Low-Cost Approach to Face Behavior for Mental Work

Jing Qiu[1], Jun Lu[1], Youyuan Pan[1], and Rolf Helbig[2]

[1] School of Mechatronics Engineering, University of Electronic Science and Technology of China, Chengdu, Sichuan, P.R. China
qiujing@uestc.edu.cn
[2] Retired Deputy Director of Institute of Ergonomics, Darmstadt University of Technology, Darmstadt, Hessen, Germany

Abstract. Human behavior displays human mental activities and observable directly in work environment.Hence, a method based on face behavior not directly related to task execution in work is proposed to assess the workload in mental work situations. In the current study, the relationships between face behavior and mental workload for simulated mental tasks were investigated. Ten subjects were recruited and asks to perform various levels of a mental task. The Effect of task on face behavior was found.The results showed that face behavior can be used as an indicator for workload assessment.

Keywords: Face Behavior, Mental Workload, Workload Assessment.

1 Introduction

The measurement of workload is a key issue in ergonomics research. To date, workload measures in mental work can be: physiological measures, e.g., heart rate variability (HRV),blood pressure(BP),and electroencephalogram (EEG), subjective questionnaires, e.g., NASA-TLX and SWAT, performance or errors during task execution,and gross motor activity (hand movement and eye movement etc.). As many researchers indicate that each approach has limitations (O'Donnell and Eggemeier, 1986; Wierwille and Eggemeier, 1993; Meshkati et al., 1995; Farmer and Brownson, 2003; Cain, 2007), e.g. continuity of questionnaires, measurability of physiological measures due to individual differences (Schmidtke, 2002; Nachreiner, 2002). Based on the performance and error for workload measurement, the performance of both primary and secondary tasks has been analysed. The performance of primary and secondary tasks is dependent on the strategy of task performance. O'Donnell and Eggemeier (1986) pointed out that underload may enhance performance and overload may result in a floor effect. Task-performing body behaviour only reflects the input to and the output from the person, rather than the entirety of internal activities in the brain. Moreover, the effect of the workload on an operator in a mental work setting is generally interpreted by the integration of all of the measurements used.

P.L.P. Rau (Ed.): CCD/HCII 2014, LNCS 8528, pp. 218–227, 2014.

With gradually increasing automation in the human-machine system, the role of an operator has been moved to supervisory controller from manual worker (Sheridan, 1987). Hence, motor actions of the operator are being gradually decreasing and may only be episodic, while sensory-perceptual and mental activities are increasing (Bedny and Karwowski, 2006). Thus, it can be difficult to observe task-performing body behaviors in such work settings due to their infrequent occurrence. Hence, the total activity (both mental and external activities) of the operator would not be entirely revealed if only their sensory-motor actions were analysed. Currently, the analysis of actions directly involved in the test tasks, such as eye movements and gross motor actions, have been widely and comprehensively accepted for workload assessment. Non-task-performing and nonverbal body behavior (e.g. face behavior)occur to accompany and support task-performing body behavior. Although human-machine interaction is different from human-human communication, nonverbal behavior can be elicited by machines during human-machine interaction in the close-loop human-machine system, which is similar to human-human communication (King, 1997). Hence, the same behavior in terms of rates for tasks and types can occur as in human-human communication, where facial expression is the most innate (Argyle, 1998, cited from King, 1997). Furthermore, as Feyer (2007) concluded that both task-performing and non-task performing body behaviours (activities) makes an influence on the interactions and human performance. Also, observable body behaviour can reflect mental processes (Keijzer, 2005).

To date, face behavior, as one part of body behavior, has not gained much interest in workload assessment in mental work settings. The studies of King (1996, 1997) are relative early for the effect of cognitive activity on facial expression. King (1997) made a survey of facial expression in human-computer systems. The results showed that rates of facial expressions were higher for computer-based tasks. Based on his study, King (1996) argued that facial expressions were related to cognitive activities based his study. In the model of Guhe et al. (2006), mouth openness is a parameter for the predictor of mental workload. Recently, a study by Stone and Wei (2011) indicated that facial expression can be a effective index of workload for arithmetic tasks. They used FACS (Facial Action Coding System) approach by Ekman and Friesen (1978) to code face behavior. However, this face coding approach needs a well-trained coder and is very time-consuming. Meanwhile, the relationships between the facial muscle activity and workload were investigated in previous studies. The results of these studies indicated that the specific facial muscle activity are correlated to mental status (Veldhuizen et al., 2003; Capa et al., 2008). They showed indirectly the correlation between face behavior and workload in the mental settings.

Therefore, the purpose of this study was to investigate that face behavior, which can be directly observed and measured used a low-cost Kinect sensor during mental work, can be regarded as a effective, continuous, and un-intrusive method for making workload measurements. The major assumption used in this study was that behaviour can be used to represent mental processes given some context. A novel method based on human behavior not directly related to task performance, is proposed to assess the workload in mental work settings. In this study, we examined the links between non-task-related body behaviors (face behavior and head posture), while occurred while human executed simulated tasks for mental work settings.

2 Method

2.1 Subjects

10 male subjects (mean age: 22.8 years, SD of age: 1.3 years) were recruited to participant the experiment. They were students from our university. All subjects were right-handed. All of them reported that they had experience with the Final Defense game and other various computer games. Meanwhile, they reported that they had no mental or physical health problems or diseases.

2.2 Experimental Design

To simulate mental work environments, some key issues should be taken into account:

- Ease to Learn: the selected task should be easy to learn with regard to the individual learning abilities;
- Non-boredom: the selected task should be engaging for subjects in order to avoid boredom;
- Natural body behavior: the selected task should last enough time to make subjects displaying natural body behavior.

Thus, a person shooter game (Final Defense) was selected in the current study (Figure 1). The subjects' objective was to identify all incoming enemy assault from sea landing and prevent them to protect the beach. Hence, the game can simulate various stages of information processing (information acquisition, information analysis, decision selection, and action implementation). The difficulty of the task was varied by modifying the number of enemy assault. There were five levels of task difficulties.

Fig. 1. A snapshot of the task

2.3 Experimental Equipment and Material

The test system consisted of 19-inch LCD display,a standard work table with 70cm tall, a vertically adjustable and rotational chair with a backrest. Four Panasonic camcorders were used to capture subjects' entire body. There were two Kinect sensors were used to capture body behavior, one for face behavior and the other for upper body behavior. Meanwhile, 14-channels electroencephalography (EEG) measure system was applied to capture electrical brain activities with a wireless EEG headset. The locations of F8,F4,Cz,C3,Fz,F3,F7,C4,P7,P3,P8,Oz,Pz and P4 were recorded according to the international 10-20 system (Jasper,1958). Figure 2 shows a snapshot of the test system from one camera recording. The locations of two Kinect sensors are illustrated in Figure 2 as well.

Fig. 2. A Snapshot of the Lab Structure

2.4 Procedure

The test began with explanation of the tasks and the experimental procedure to a subject. Each subject was asked to fill with a biographical questionnaire. The subject should then find his/her comfortable seated working position in front of a display. After that, the subject practiced the tasks with different difficulties one by one. The order of the tasks was randomly assigned to the subjects. Then,all tasks were continually performed by the subjects.

2.5 Data Collection and Analysis

As mentioned earlier, a Kinect sensor is very low-cost compared with other commercial tools for face behavior analysis. The Kinect sensor can track the head pose and face behavior. A right-handed coordinate system is used to quantize tracking results[1] in the Kinect. The origin of the coordinate system is located at

[1] `http://msdn.microsoft.com/en-us/library/jj130970.aspx`

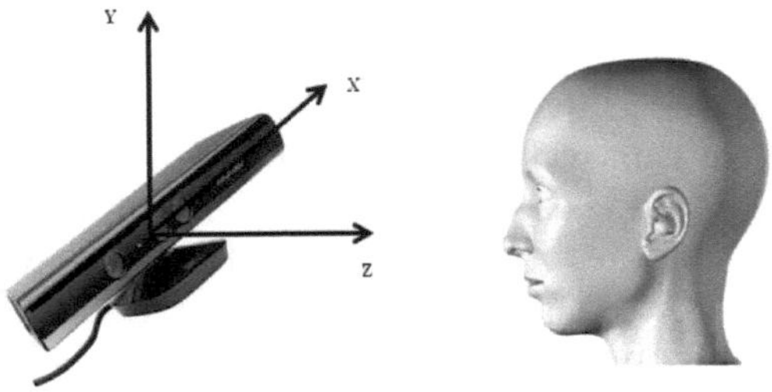

Fig. 3. Kinect Coordinate System

the Kinects optical center. Z axis is pointing towards a user and Y axis is pointing up, as Figure 3 shows. The X, Y, and Z position(rotation and translation) of the users head are captured as well based on the Kinect coordinate system. 87 two dimensions and 13 additional points on the face can be tracked. A Kinect sensor can also provide a subset defined in the Candide3 model[2], which are weights of six Animation Units (AUs)(Figure 4). The means and SDs of AUs of each task levels were used for statistical analysis.

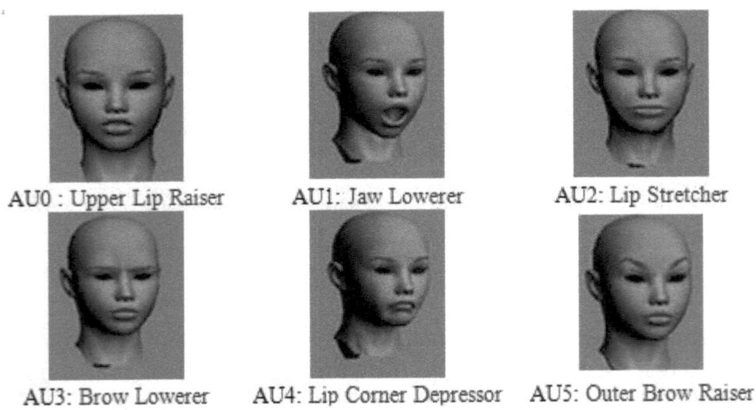

Fig. 4. Definition of AUs in Kinect

The values of power spectral density (PSD) for the EEG signals were calculated with Welch method in Matlab. The mean of PSD at θ, α, and β frequency bands were used for statistical analysis.

[2] `http://www.icg.isy.liu.se/candide/`

In the current study, the statistical analysis was performed using SPSS Version 21 with the significance level set at 10%. The Generalized Estimating Equations (GEE) was used to analyze the effects of tasks on Face behavior. The GEE method, proposed by Liang and Zeger (1986), is a procedure to extend generalized linear models and analyze repeated measurements and correlated data (Hanley, 2003; Hardin, 2001). We used QICC (the corrected quasi-likelihood under an independence model criterion) for the goodness-of-fit test. Pair-wise comparisons between the tasks were analyzed using the Bonferroni adjustment method.

3 Results

The EEG α frequency band were significantly affected by task difficulty levels ($\chi_4^2 = 63.737$, $p = 0.000$). Meanwhile,the significant task effect on β frequency band was found ($\chi_4^2 = 39.476$, $p = 0.000$). From Figure 5, it can be observed that means of PSD in α and β frequency bands is obviously lower in lowest level than in other levels. These results are consistent with the results in other studies (Stone and Wei, 2011).

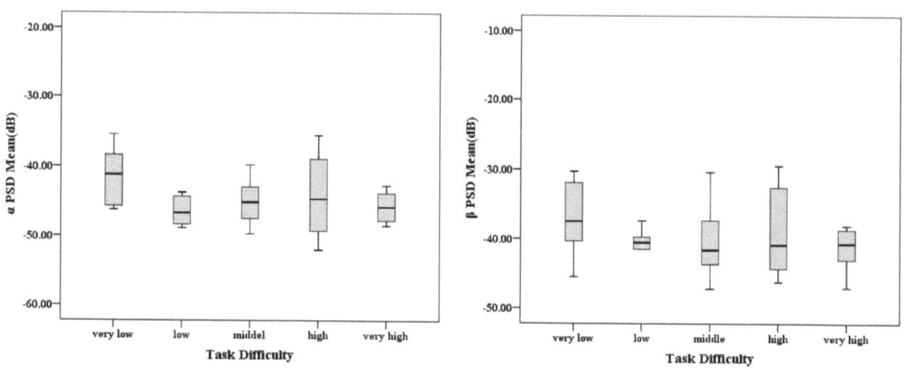

Fig. 5. Means of α and β frequency bands over Task Difficulty Levels

An significant task effect on changes of head rotation in the z axis was found ($\chi_4^2 = 29.827$, $p = 0.000$). The task effect on head translation in the z axis was found to be slightly significant ($\chi_4^2 = 8.519$, $p = 0.74$)(Figure 6). The subjects kept their heads straighter and closer to the display under higher task difficulty levels, which is coincident with our other study (Qiu and Helbig, 2012). Meanwhile, the tasks impacted significantly on SD of head rotation ($\chi_4^2 = 29.827$, $p = 0.000$).

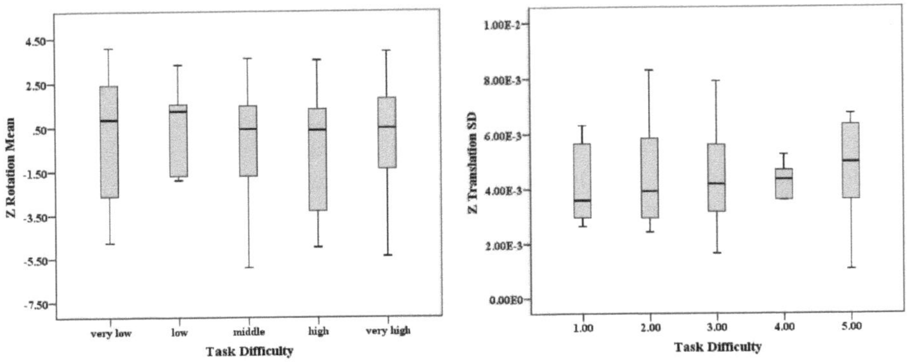

Fig. 6. Head Pose over Task Difficulty Levels(left:mean of z Rotation, right: SD of z Translation)

The effect of the task difficulty levels on the AU2 was significant ($\chi_4^2 = 29.516$, $p = 0.000$),as Figure 6 shows. The results of the pair-wise comparisons showed that value of AU2 during the first level task was significantly larger than those during fourth and fifth level tasks. The subjects showed less the lip stretcher Action under low task levels. The AU3 was affected slight significantly by the task difficult levels ($\chi_4^2 = 10.578$, $p = 0.032$, Figure 7). From Figure 7, it can be observed that the subjects displayed the brow lower action under the high task levels. An significant impact of task difficulty levels on the AU4 was found as well ($\chi_4^2 = 11.022$, $p = 0.026$,). Therefore, the subjects presented more the lip corner depressor action under the high task levels, as Figure 5 illustrates.

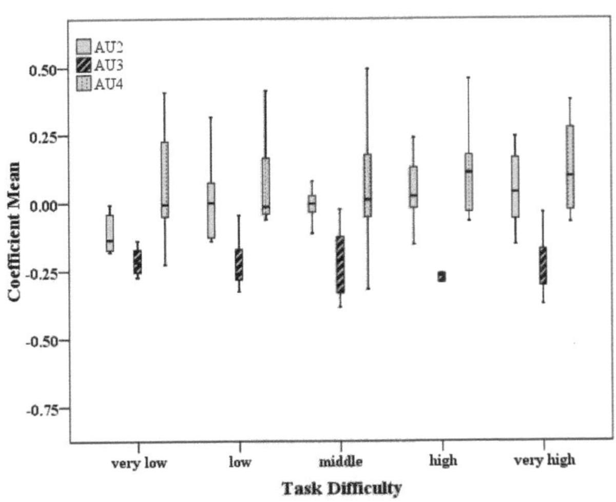

Fig. 7. Means of AUs over Task Difficulty Levels

The effect of the tasks on the SD of the AU2 was significant ($\chi_4^2 = 41.674$, $p = 0.000$).The SD of the AU2 in the most difficult task was significantly greater than that of the other tasks (Figure 8). Meanwhile, the SD of the AU3 was affected significantly by the task difficulties ($\chi_4^2 = 10.087$, $p = 0.039$). Also, the task difficulties make an significant effect on the SD of the AU5 ($\chi_4^2 = 12.818$, $p = 0.012$).

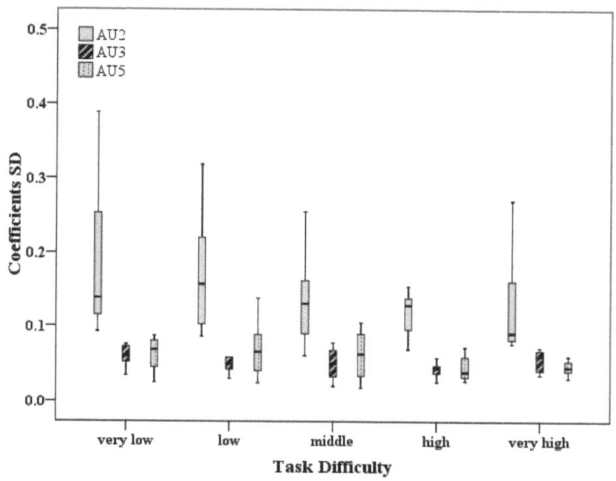

Fig. 8. SDs of AUs over Task Difficulty Levels

4 Discussion

A summary of previous literature of mental workload indicated that the present methods of workload measurement meet a few challenges. Therefore, directly and contiguously observable non-task-performing behaviors could be as novel and alternative workload measures under mental work sittings.In the present study, the relationships between task difficulties and face behavior were studies during simulated mental tasks.

The significant influences of the tasks on the face behavior was found as Stone and Wei (2011). With regard to the mean of AU2, the subjects' lips were stretcher under high task demand. The significant task effect on the SD of AU2 indicated that the subjects made their lips stretch for more times. Meanwhile, the subjects displayed their browns lower under the high task demand. Also, the brows of the subjects were lower with high occurrence. The results of AU4 showed that the subjects depressed theirs lip corners for longer time under the high task demand. Furthermore, the subjects' outer brows raised more occurrences under the high task demand.

The results of the present study shows that the differences in face behavior were barely discernible for midrange workload levels. One possible explanation might be that non-task-performing behavior is nonlinearly correlated with workload as Bedny et al. (2000) indicated. To develop and validate a method for measuring workload through body behavior analysis, further research is required. Other body behaviors (e.g., body posture and movement) can be analysed as part of the workload assessment. Body behavior should be studied in its entirety to measure workload.

5 Conclusion

In this study, the relationships between face behavior and task demand were investigated using the Kinect-base face tracking method. The results showed that the subjects display more depressed face behavior(lip stretcher, brow lowerer and lip corner depressor) during higher workloads.In addition, they kept their heads closer to the display under a higher workload. Based on these findings of the current study, face behavior may be used as an indicator of the workload in mental work settings. It is recommended that different levels of the same type of mental task be used in further research to develop a supplementary method for workload assessment based on face behavior.

Acknowledgement. This study was supported by the Natural Science Foundation of China(71201017) and the National Higher-education Institution General Research and Development Funding (ZYGX2012J101).

References

[Argyle, 1998]Argyle, M.: Bodily Communication C, 2nd edn. Methuen & Co. Ltd., London (1998)

[Bedny and Karwowski, 2006]Bedny, G., Karwowski, W.: A Systemic-Structural Theory of Activity: Applications to Human Performance and Work Design. CRC Press, Florida (2006)

[Cain,2007]Cain, B.: A Review of the Mental Workload Literature. Technical Reports, RTO-TR-HFM-121-Part-II, Defence Research and Development Toronto, Canada (2007)

[Capa et al., 2008]Capa, R.L., Audiffren, M., Ragot, S.: The interactive effect of achievement motivation and task difficulty on mental effort. Internaltional Journal of Psychophysilogy 70, 144–150 (2008)

[Ekman and Friesen, 1978]Ekman, P., Friesen, W.V.: Facial action coding system. Consulting Psychologists Press, Palo Alto (1978)

[Famer and Brownson, 2003]Famer, E., Brownson, A.: Review of workload measurement, analysis and interpretation methods. European Organisation for the Safety of Air Navigation 33 (2003)

[Feyer, 2007]Feyen, R.G.: Bridging the Gap: Exploring interactions between digital human models and cognitive models. In: Duffy, V.G. (ed.) Digital Human Modeling, HCII 2007. LNCS, vol. 4561, pp. 382–391. Springer, Heidelberg (2007)

[Guhe, 2005]Guhe, M., Liao, W.-H., Zhu, Z.-W., Ji, Q., Gray, W., Schoelles, M.: Non-Intrusive Measurement of Workload in Real-Time. In: Proceedings of the 49th Annual Meeting of the Human Factors and Ergonomics Society, Orlando, Florida (2005)

[Hanley, 2003]Hanley, J., Negassa, A.D., Forrester, J.: Statstical analysis of correlated data using generalized estimating equations: An orientation. American Journal of Epidemiology 157, 364–375 (2003)

[Hardin, 2001]Hardin, J.W., Hilber, J.M.: Generalized estimating equations. Chapman & Hall CRC, Boca Raton (2001)

[Jasper, 1985]Jasper, H.: The 10-20 electrode system of the International Federation. Electroencephalography and Clinical Neurophysiology 10, 371–375 (1985)

[Keijzer, 2005]Keijzer, F.: Theoretical behaviorism meets embodied cognition: twotheoretical analyses of behavior. Philosophical Psychology 18, 123–143 (2005)

[King, 1996]King, W.: Reflections of Thought: Cognitive Facial Expressions in the Human Interface. In: Proceedings of the 5th IEEE International Workshop on Robotand Human Communication, Tsukuba, Japan, November 11-14 (1997)

[King, 1997]King, W.: Human - Computer Dyads? A Survey of Nonverbal Behavior in Human-Computer Systems. In: Proceedings of Workshop on Perceptural User Interfaces (PUI 1997), Banff, Cananda, Los Alamitos, CA, October 19-21 (1997)

[Liang and Zeger, 1986]Liang, K.-Y., Zeger, S.L.: Longitudinal data analysis using generalized linear models. Biometrika 73, 13–22 (1986)

[Meshkati et al., 1995]Meshkati, N., Hancock, P.A., Rahimi, M., Dawes, S.M.: Techniques in mental workload assessment. In: Wilson, J., Corlett, E. (eds.) Evaluation of Human Work: A Practical Ergonomics Methodology, pp. 749–782. Taylor and Francis Ltd., Bristol (1995)

[Nachreiner, 2002]Nachreiner, F.: über einige akutuelle Probleme bei der Erfassung, Messung und Beurteilung psychischer Belastung und Beanspruchung. Zeitschrift für Arbeitzwissenschaft 56, 10–21 (2002)

[O'Donnell and Eggemeier, 1986]O'Donnell, R., Eggemeier, F.T.: Workload assessment methodology. In: Boff, K., Kaufman, L., Thomas, J., Boff, K., Kaufman, L., Thomas, J. (eds.) Handbook of Perception and Human Performance, pp. 41–49. Wiley, New York (1986)

[Qiu and Helbig, 2012]Qiu, J., Helbig, R.: Body Posture as an Indicator of Workload in Mental Work. Human Factors: The Journal of the Human Factors and Ergonomics Society I54, 626–635 (2012)

[Schmidtke, 2002]Schmidtke, H.: Von sinn und unsinn der messung psychischer belastung und beanspruchung. Zeitschrift für Arbeitswissenschaft 56, 4–9 (2002)

[Sheridan, 1987]Sheridan, T.: Supervisory control. In: Salvendy, G. (ed.) Handbook of Human Factors, pp. 1243–1268. John Wiley and Sons, New York (1987)

[Stone and Wei, 2011]Stone, R.T., Wei, C.-S.: Exploring the Linkage between Facial Expression and Mental Workload for Arithmetic Tasks. In: Proceedings of 55th Annual Meeting of the Human Factors and Ergonomics Society, Las Vegas, USA, September 19-23 (2011)

[Veldhuizen et al., 2003]Veldhuizen, I.J.T., Gaillard, T., De Vries, A.W.K.J.: The influence of mental fatigue on facial EMG activity during a simulated workday. Biological Psychology 63, 59–78 (2003)

[Wierwille and Eggemeier, 1993]Wierwille, W.W., Eggemeier, F.T.: Recommendations for mental workload measurement in a test and evaluation environment. Human Factors 35, 263–285 (1993)

The Great Authentication Fatigue – And How to Overcome It*

M. Angela Sasse[1], Michelle Steves[2], Kat Krol[1], and Dana Chisnell[3]

[1] University College London, Department of Computer Science, London, UK
{a.sasse,k.krol}@cs.ucl.ac.uk
[2] U.S. Dept. of Commerce, National Institute of Standards and Technology, MD, USA
michelle.steves@nist.gov
[3] UsabilityWorks, Boston, MA, USA
dana@usabilityworks.com

Abstract. We conducted a two-part study to understand the impact of authentication on employees' behaviour and productivity in a US governmental organisation. We asked 23 participants to keep a diary of all their authentication events within a 24-hour period, and subsequently interviewed them about their experience with authentication. We found that the authentication tasks employees have to perform not only carry significant workload, but that the way in which authentication disrupts primary tasks reduces productivity and creates frustration. Our participants reported a range of coping strategies, including use of tools and re-organising their work to avoid security. Avoidance meant they logged in less frequently, stopped using certain devices and services. They also reported not pursing innovative ideas because of "the battle with security" that would be required. Our case study paints a picture of chronic 'authentication fatigue' resulting from current policies and mechanisms, and the negative impact on staff productivity and morale. We propose that organisations need to urgently re-think how they authenticate users in a pervasive technology requirement, and advocate a paradigm shift from explicit to implicit authentication.

Keywords: Authentication, usable security, productivity, workload, diary study.

1 Introduction

1.1 Usable Security (NOT)

Nearly 20 years ago, Zurko and Simon (1996) argued for 'user-centred security' because "mechanisms and models that are confusing to the user will be misused" [p. 32]. Two papers in 1999 demonstrated specific examples of this, and laid the

P.L.P. Rau (Ed.): CCD/HCII 2014, LNCS 8528, pp. 228–239, 2014.

foundation for the discipline now known as 'usable security': in "Users Are Not the Enemy" Adams & Sasse (1999) reported why users do not follow password policies, and in "Why Johnny Can't Encrypt" Whitten & Tygar (1999) showed why even motivated non-technical users trying to encrypt fail. Since then, there have been hundreds of usable security research papers, and authentication has attracted the most attention – several dozen 'more usable' authentication mechanisms have been produced. So has there been any change in practice – has authentication become more usable? A study by Inglesant & Sasse (2010) in a corporate environment led the authors to conclude with a resounding 'no': despite the introduction of single sign-on (SSO) mechanisms, users still had more passwords than they could manage, and they struggled with the complexity and frequent expiry. Both corporate policies and advice given to consumers keep asking users for more: longer, more complex passwords, which should be changed frequently. This advice is outdated and does not hold in the face of scientific examination (Herley, 2009; 2014).

To round out previous research performed in the private and commercial sectors, we situated the study documented here in the public sector. We sought answers to the following questions: *How does authentication fit into employees' daily activities?* and *How do staff manage and perceive the costs of authentication and the cumulative impacts, balanced against their perception of the need for security?* While the detailed results can be found in Steves at al. (2014), in this paper, we summarise the key insights on how users deal with the authentication burden that many find unmanageable. Combining our results with insights from other recent studies, we diagnose a case of chronic authentication fatigue. Has the time finally come for organisations to acknowledge that the burden of authentication has reached a level that is untenable? When users struggle to manage, they may inadvertently put their own and their organisation's security at risk levels that are unacceptable; therefore, we argue that a fundamental re-think of authentication is required to safeguard individual and organisational productivity and security.

1.2 Why 'Usable Security' Mechanisms Don't Work

The ISO standard defines usability as "the extent to which a product can be used by specified users to achieve specified goals with effectiveness, efficiency, and satisfaction in a specified context of use." (ISO 9241-11) But security mechanisms are currently developed and implemented without reference to any of these three constraints. In particular, security designers and practitioners fail to consider that users encounter authentication in the context of a goal – checking email, paying a bill, etc. The primary goal is what drives users' behaviour, and the task they carry out to achieve has a certain workload (physical and mental effort); associated with it. The security mechanism presents a secondary task – a hurdle the user has to overcome in order to complete the primary task, and achieve their goal. The workload associated with the security task is often disproportionate to the importance or length of the primary task. Brostoff & Sasse (2000) found users were not willing to spend one minute authenticating if they were planning to only spend a couple of minutes using a system. Security experts generally do not consider user effort (Herley, 2014) or that different primary tasks or physical or social contexts mean you may need a different mechanism.

1.3 Understanding Authentication in Context

The study presented in this paper was supported by the National Institute of Standards and Technology (NIST) to characterise authentication in modern organisations, and understand the short- and possibly long-term consequences on their behaviour. We asked 23 US government employees to keep an authentication diary for a day, and used the diary entries to ground a subsequent hour-long interview, in which we asked participants to recount the context of the authentication event and how it affected their work. We also probed participants' experiences with authentication more generally, and what they did to cope with the burden. On average, participants authenticated 23 times on that day and the failure rate was around 10%. The main frustrations they reported were (1) the need to re-authenticate (e.g., after a time-out), (2) managing a large number of credentials for different systems, (3) the workload associated with changing passwords, which expire at differing intervals, (4) logging in to infrequently used systems and (5) struggling with RSA[1] tokens. Participants reported a number of coping strategies, which can be divided into *management* or *avoidance*.

In the next section, we briefly review previous authentication and diary studies and their findings. Then we discuss the design of our study and present its results. We then focus on the main problems our participants encountered and how they tried to deal with them. We conclude by giving recommendations for what needs to change in the thinking about authentication and suggest avenues for further research.

2 Background

In the recent years, there have been several studies seeking to understand the authentication effort in a real life context. Florêncio & Herley (2007) looked at the number of passwords and the scale of password reuse through a browser toolbar. They found that on average, users entered 8.1 different passwords per day and had 25 accounts requiring passwords. Two shortcomings arise from the study of authentication events via only one browser: (i) a browser may be used by more than one person; and (ii) users may authenticate with other applications outside of the browser or on multiple devices. Hayashi & Hong (2011) asked participants to fill out an authentication diary for two weeks. They found that for 60% of accounts, participants did not use any memory aids. They preferred to re-use an existing password rather than create a new one and write it down. On contrary, in an organisational context as studied by Inglesant & Sasse (2010), 9 out of 15 participants admitted writing passwords down, especially after having changed it or if they only used it infrequently. In their study, 32 employees in two organisations kept an authentication diary for a week and were later interviewed discussing each password and its context of use. They found that

[1] The reference to any commercial products in this document is not intended to imply recommendation or endorsement by National Institute of Standards and Technology, nor is it intended to imply that the products are necessarily the best available for the purpose.

password policies focused on password strength, enforced frequent change and were not designed using principles from the field of Human-Computer Interaction (HCI).

3 Study Description

Our study collected two types of data; (1) quantitative data was drawn from self-reports through an authentication diary and (2) qualitative data gathered through an hour-long interview after completion of the diary.

Participants. Participants were recruited via a call for volunteers throughout the organisation using e-mail. Of the 25 participants who responded, 23 (14 male and 9 female) provided their authentication diary data at the time requested and we were able to interview 22 of them. Age of participants was: 50+ (11), 40s (3), 30s (5) and 20s (3). All participants were knowledge workers, 13 were researchers with computer science related education or job. Three were researchers without a background in computer science (but in physics, cognitive science etc.). Two were IT systems administrators. The remaining two participants were administrative support staff.

Study Set-Up. In the first part of the study, participants were asked to keep an authentication **diary** for the duration of 24 hours, all of them on the same day. In the briefing session before the commencement of the study, we provided participants with sheets for logging of their authentication events. We interviewed each participant within a month of the diary day. The diary data served as a point of departure for the **interview** which explored the participant's individual perspective on authentication.

4 Diary Results

Authentication Events and Errors. In total, participants recorded 528 authentication events during the 24-hour collection period. On average, they authenticated 23 times during that day (min. = 4, max = 40). Out of the total of 528 events, there were problems in the case of 48 (9.1%). The most frequent reason for authentication problems were mistyped (24 occurrences, 50%) and wrong passwords (7, 14.6%).

Memory Aids. Of the 528 events reported in the study, 168 (31.8%) involved using some memory aid. The memory aids can be divided into three groups. (I) Participants have the passwords stored for them. Within this group, (i) there are cases where the password is entered for the user: when stored in the client (e.g., in the browser, 13 occurrences) or in a password manager (2); and (ii) there are cases where the password has to be entered by the user but is stored either on paper (11) or in a file (4). (II) There are passwords that users create to be memorable; for example, when a portion of the password stays the same as the previous one (1) or the password is based on a memorable phrase (1). (III) Password entry is replaced with a biometric fingerprint scan (4).

5 Interview Results

5.1 Workload Perception

We observed a discrepancy between the perceived and actual number of authentication events. In the briefing meetings before data collection, some participants requested more diary forms as they were expecting to authenticate more often than what the standard set of forms could hold. After the diary day in the interviews, participants were asked what the biggest surprise about their experience was and several stated that they actually authenticated fewer times than they had expected beforehand. This might be an indication that they perceive authentication as a burden and a nuisance. Clifford Nass, from Stanford, an expert on multi-tasking and task switching told us: *"I suspect that unlike multitasking, in which the task switching is voluntary and hence people have an incentive to downplay the costs, authentication is not voluntary, thereby making people aware of the cognitive cost."* (Personal communication, 2012). Other research confirms that task-switching has a 'ripple effect' on focus, concentration and efficacy – not only on the next task, but any task for the next 20 to 30 minutes (e.g., Monsell, 2003). The frustration over the disruptive effect of authentication could be due to *Zeigarnik effect* – humans are more likely to remember tasks that were interrupted and left unfinished. The lack of closure that stems from an interrupted and unfinished primary task promotes some continued task-related cognitive effort which might impact the secondary task of recalling a password (Schiffman & Greist-Bousquet, 1992). In the interviews, P3 complained about the disruptive effect of using RSA tokens: *"So actually taking the time away from the computer, I walk to get my bag. Someone else stops me in the hallway. I have a conversation with them. Then soon I go back and I remember to login, but I'm like, "Oh." The strong idea I had in my head of a message that I wanted to send might have become a little more fuzzy, the idea of what I was doing. "Why did I open that other new tab and not go to the..." So there's the little things. I feel like those little things really, when you have an idea of what you want to do next and then you have to deviate from that, I think at least for my brain it throws you off a little bit."*

5.2 Specific Problems

We conducted a thematic analysis of the interview transcripts and identified several aspects of authentication employees struggled with.

Frequent Re-authentication. Participants reported struggling with re-authentication after a time-out. The computers in the organisation are set to lock after 15 minutes of inactivity (to limit the window of opportunity for an attacker to exploit an unlocked machine while the employee is away). P21 emphasised this causes stress: *"You end up having to almost set a timer in your head to go back to the computer and type something within every 10 minutes or so. And some minor studies of productivity I've been involved with indicate that it's better to be focused on a task as opposed to have lots of interruptions throughout the day."*

Multiple Passwords, Their Length and Complexity. Participants reported struggling with password creation due to different requirements for each system. They found it hard to come up with strong passwords at frequent intervals.

Infrequently Used Passwords. Participants reported having problems recalling passwords they use rarely: *"You have to think if you are going to be the responsible person, then you have to think of different passwords for everything and it is very frustrating. So when it gets to those infrequently used passwords, then I get really irritated." (P11)* P17 stressed: *"Once again security has gotten in my way and it takes me extra time because now I got to look that one up because I don't use that one often enough."*

Password Expiry. Another obstacle to keeping one's passwords synchronised across applications is that some passwords expire at different intervals – this was certainly the case for many of the organisation's applications. To address this issue, many participants who synchronised passwords to some degree also used the complementary strategy of updating all their passwords at once.

Interruption of Workflow. A number of participants emphasised the disruptive effect authentication has on their work, they felt it had a negative effect on their productivity: *"And it gets in the way. It definitely takes way more time out of my day, both just time having to deal with this and then the break in the flow of work."* (P19)

Problems with Tokens. Some participants reported struggling with the usability of tokens. They found the RSA token hard to use because (i) the display showing the six-digit code was too small and (ii) the change of number every 60 seconds was making the reading and entering of digits a cumbersome task. At the organisation, RSA tokens are necessary for accessing the VPN (Virtual Private Network) from outside the campus. To authenticate, the user has to enter their username, PIN (Personal Identification Number) and the code given by the token, then their username and password. The problem is that the system needs a few second to process the credentials at both stages and if the code expires before this is completed, the user has to start the authentication process again. P12 also found their token was out-of-sync and sometimes it can take them up to three attempts to log in.

Also using PIV cards[2] has posed some challenges. This type of card is normally inserted to the computer to authenticate using a PIN. However, the card is also used to open doors, and P19 reported often leaving the card in the computer, exiting the room and then being locked out: *"So I would forget this every single time. And I've been locked out of the building. I've been locked out of the floor. I've been reprimanded for leaving this in the computer. And there's nothing I could have done other than somehow setting reminders every two minutes to don't forget this."* (P19)

---

[2] At the time of the study, all employees at the organisation had a Personal Identity Verification (PIV) smartcard with an associated 6-8 digit PIN. However, a relatively small number used it on a regular basis, in part because they do not have the requisite card reader and middleware or operating system. Even employees who use smartcard authentication almost exclusively must still manage their agency domain password, which expires every 90 days.

Lack of Integration. Four employees reported using a biometric fingerprint reader for some logins. Biometrics are considered to be "usable by default" because they do not require recalling a password or carrying a token (Fairhurst et al., 2003). However, there were physical usability problems for one of the participants, who needed to use moisturiser to make the prints readable: *"This is worse, because it works by a biometric, and my finger doesn't read very well. I have to smear it with moisturizer, and then I forget what the actual password is. When it really just won't read my finger, I can't unlock it and I can't remember."* (P2) And in this organisation, the underlying infrastructure and policies had not been adjusted – the underlying password – which users avoid by using the fingerprint reader – expires every 90 days. When this happens, the user has to find their current password (usually written on a piece of paper kept in the drawer), change the old password, write the new one down, and enrol their fingerprint. This illustrates how the usability of authentication cannot be assured by simply replacing the 'front-end' but keeping the underlying policies and technology infrastructure the same.

6 Employees' Coping Strategies

Our participants reported a number of strategies for coping with unmanageable authentication workload. The coping strategies fell into two groups: participants either tried to manage and be in control of their authentication effort, or avoid authenticating altogether. The two ways to cope are best summarised by P17: *"Yes, I'm trying not to log in that often. And also, if I am logged in, I'll keep going in. Hitting 'check mail' just to make sure it doesn't time me out."*

6.1 Management : Trying to Stay Efficient

Centralising. Most participants attempted to reduce their authentication effort by employing password managers or synchronising passwords across multiple systems: *"centralizing it and creating the strongest password for centrally possible has been my tactic. Try to get it all in one bucket."* (P3) Most had no awareness of the potential risks of doing so, others were aware but felt they had no choice – it was this, or constantly floundering when a password was needed. The other strategy was employing a password manager (such as LastPass) and storing all their passwords in it.

Batching and Proactive Authentication. Another common coping strategy for managing authentication was batching of primary tasks: employees reported that they try to group several tasks that required access to the same system together, so they only needed to login once. Thus, the secondary security cart is driving the primary task horse, and this has implications for organisational productivity, since it delays completion of tasks. Participants also reported planning ahead and 'authenticating in advance' if they expected a message or file they needed for their work, so they could access it without being delayed by authentication.

6.2 Avoidance: Not Using Devices or Services

Giving up on devices. A number of participants reported that they cope with authentication by limiting the number of devices they authenticate to; P19 stated: *"If I had a laptop I would have to log in twice, once when you turn it on because the hard drive's encrypted, and then again to actually get into Windows or the operating system. [...] So I never wanted an agency laptop for that reason. I don't want to have to log in more times than I need to. That goes to the whole password security policy that we have here, is everything that leaves the agency has to be encrypted."* Those participants who refused to have an agency laptop were now incommunicado during business trips, meaning colleagues had to wait several days for response required to complete their own work.

Preventing Log-Out. Others reduced the frequency of authentication by avoiding re-authentication, they kept the screen active by moving their mouse or joked about installing "mouse jiggler" software.

Logging in Less Frequently. Participants also reported that they would turn around their email faster if it were not for the authentication burden. They reported that they particularly reduced the frequency with which they logged in remotely (e.g., from home), because this required additional security steps.

6.3 Learning about Workload

Our participants developed the coping strategies to consolidate the effort associated with security, and minimise disruption of the primary tasks. To understand the workload they faced, we conducted an analytical assessment of the workload certain authentication events would pose using the GOMS-KLM modelling technique (Card, Moran, & Newell, 1980). GOMS (Goals, Operators, Methods and Selection rules) and KLM (Keystroke-level Modelling) decompose the interaction between a human and a computer to basic physical and cognitive actions – such as recalling a password (GOMS) or clicking a button (KLM). Once a given task has been decomposed into steps, standard times a practiced user needs to complete each step can be assigned. A GOMS-KLM analysis is traditionally done as a paper-and-pencil analysis, but can be carried out automatically using CogTool (2014).

We used both methods and calculated how long authentication tasks would take our participants. Authentication with the username and policy-compliant password takes 10 seconds. Using LastPass reduces this time to around 4 seconds. This number may not look like a huge saving, but using LastPass posed significantly less of a disruption to the primary task – which means the cost associated with re-starting the primary task was significantly lower.

A few participants said they preferred to keep a piece of paper with the password written on, even if it took several minutes to locate, rather than try to recall their password. This shows a fundamental truth from the field of HCI – users prefer extra physical to extra cognitive effort. In the specific case of authentication, authentication is a hurdle dropped in the path of task completion. If the authentication task requires cognitive resources, it can interfere with the cognitive effort of the primary task. Our participants reported having authenticated, only to find they could not recall what they wanted to do – and needing significant time to backtrack in the task and resume work. Our GOMS-KLM shows the password manager minimises disruption caused by password recall and entry.

7 The Cumulative Burden of Authentication

So authentication takes time, is a burden, disrupts primary tasks and reduces productivity. Among our participants, there was measurable authentication effect and the experience shaped their perception of, and attitudes to, security. Inspired by several participants' telling us they were 'tired' with some aspects of authentication, we call this effect 'authentication fatigue'.

7.1 Implications for Organisations

A previous study (Inglesant & Sasse, 2010) found that staff re-organised their work to minimise authentication effort. In the study presented here, we collected further examples of long-term consequences: some participants reported they had returned devices, others stopped to taking it when travelling for work.

Several participants said they had reduced the amount of additional work they did outside of regular office hours because of the authentication burden. Staff avoided logging in or did so less frequently from home or when travelling: "*Things get put off until when it's, 'OK, I have a block of time. It's worth it for me to get the token, to log in and to sit there and do like an hour's worth of work or half an hour or something like that." […] But if it's for like fleeting little, 'Oh, I have this great idea' or 'I want to send this e-mail' or something, then I'm more likely to put it off until I have that sort of block of time where a log-in is worth it. […] especially if it's something that wasn't actually due. It's after hours. You've already put in your nine hours or however many hours you're doing and then you think of something at home, it definitely is less likely that you're going to get online to actually do that thing that you're thinking of. You're just going to wait until the next day.*" (P11) So colleagues and customers need to wait for information or assistance, which in turn holds up their work, and that great idea might have been forgotten by the next time our participant logged in.

The security policies that frustrated our participants are arguably not keeping up with technology development and modern ways of working. The authentication burden escalated for employees who used touch screen devices, where entry of credentials took longer and failed more often. The consequences of authentication can embarrass staff in front of customers and peers: "*I'd have 150 people waiting for a presentation. I'm waiting for 15 minutes for that sucker to boot up, so I can actually use it. Then, because I'm not admin and I can't change any setting on that box, when the screensaver kicks in, then I've got to log in all over again and reinitialize everything and start my presentation all over again and figure out where I was in the*

120 slides that I use and make my way there. All the time the audience is right? That's a combination of security and other miscellaneous things. But, like I said, it gets in the way. You're trying to do something, which should be straightforward, but you can't." (P17) It is not surprising that employees try to avoid such problems or create workarounds, that while within existing policy, may inadvertently undermine security.

8 Recommendations

8.1 Consolidating Authentication: SSO

The organisation in which our participants worked had SSO, but as in Inglesant & Sasse (2010), most participants reported that they had credentials for a system on which it had not been implemented. Participants said they would prefer one complex and longer password rather than many passwords with different requirements as they do right now. P11 shared with us his dream to only have one password: *"I guarantee for me I would sit down and practice that thing and practice that thing and practice that thing until it's automatized and I wouldn't forget it and I would be totally happy to enter a 20-digit password if I could use the same one and not have to go through this hullabaloo of calling and resetting."*

SSO could also solve the problem that participants in our study sometimes did not know which password to use to access which system. But it seems that, in practice, organisations find it difficult to consolidate all credentials behind a single gateway.

Federated identity (a solution where users can use credentials from one provider to log into a multitude of services) offers another potential way of reducing the number of authentication credentials individuals have to manage. But from a security perspective, many organisations will be unwilling to outsource authentication of their own staff. Furthermore, a recent study found that users can be confused and alarmed when being re-directed to an external identity provider (Brostoff et al., 2013).

8.2 "Technology Should Be Smarter Than This!"

Compared to the speed with which new devices are being developed, the masses of data we generate when we use them, and the explosion of apps and services which track our every move, the security policies and mechanisms we interact with seem frozen in time. When computer passwords were first introduced in the 60s, they were a badge that gave members of a technical elite access to a rare and expensive piece of equipment – so you had only one password, it was short, didn't expire, and nobody minded if you used the name of your dog or favourite Star Trek character. 50 years later, security clings to the same mechanism even though we now interact with a much larger number of devices and services, and more complex credentials.

In an age where commercial companies are able to use the masses of data we produce to identify and profile us with what many think is a frightening degree of accuracy (e.g., Nikiforakis et al., 2013), it is bizarre that users' activity is constantly disrupted by systems insisting that we prove who we are. In an age where there is so much emphasis on interactions being seamless and sleek and delivering users the best possible experience, users are still bothered with authentication which causes frustration and affects their productivity. The aim of the usable security community should be to learn from both the identifying capabilities of commercial companies and the sleek interaction tips from the user experience (UX) design community.

8.3 Shifting from Implicit to Explicit Authentication

As cloud computing is becoming more and more powerful, even long and seemingly strong passwords need less time to be cracked. In this situation, companies push for 2-factor authentication to achieve better security. It is predominantly tokens, smart-cards or mobile phones that are used to create the second factor. Although the solution may appear plausible, it is rather error-prone and creates additional work for the user. They have to remember to have the token with them and it can pose usability challenges as we have seen in our study. In other contexts of use, for example the case of mobile phone-based 2-factor authentication, one has to remember to have the phone with them and wait for the credential to arrive. But what if the phone is out of battery or there is no reception? This highlights a few of the shortcomings of the state-of-the-art 2-factor authentication. Because of this, we call for a paradigm shift from explicit to implicit authentication.

0-Effort, 1-Step, 2-Factor Authentication. P18 mentioned in the interview: *"Well, I think that if I just logged in, then it should be able to understand that I just logged in and not ask me for the password again. [...] You shouldn't have to do extra work to authenticate. Because yeah, it can just pick up what you do."* and this best summarises the shape we believe authentication should take in the future. Computers could authenticate users based on what they do as part of their work. A good way of doing this is through the use of biometrics and in particular behavioural biometrics such as typing rhythm or voice. It has been suggested in the past (Thorpe et al., 2005) that users could be authenticated based on their thoughts. What sounded like a far-fetched idea a decade ago, appears to be a plausible alternative today due to the emergence of brain-computer interfaces such as the Emotiv EPOC (Emotiv, 2014) headset. Introduced to enhance the UX, the Emotiv headset was meant to provide a faster input method for games. The idea behind this EEG-based technology is to steer games by the player's thoughts and facial expressions. The fact that the headset is relatively low-cost and increasingly more popular could make it possible for the user to think their password or any other credential rather than having to enter it explicitly.

Shi et al. (2011) explored the possibility of implicit authentication through observations of user behaviour (location and patterns of messaging, browsing etc.). Roy Maxion's work on keystroke dynamics shows that users can be recognised by the way the type with high levels of accuracy (Killourhy & Maxion, 2009). Also in the age of touch screens and gesture-based interaction, systems could authenticate users based on the way in which they gesture or interact with touch-screens as part of their primary task. In this way, we could achieve 0-effort, 1-step, 2-factor authentication.

References

1. Adams, A., Sasse, M.A.: Users are not the enemy. Communications of the ACM 42(12), 40–46 (1999)
2. Brostoff, S., Jennett, C., Malheiros, M., Sasse, M.A.: Federated identity to access e-government services: Are citizens ready for this? In: 2013 Workshop on Digital Identity Management, pp. 97–108. ACM (2013)
3. Brostoff, S., Sasse, M.A.: Are Passfaces™ more usable than passwords? A field trial investigation. In: People and Computers XIV—Usability or Else!, pp. 405–424. Springer London (2000)
4. Card, S.K., Moran, T.P., Newell, A.: The keystroke-level model for user performance time with interactive systems. Communications of the ACM 23(7), 396–410 (1980)
5. CogTool (2014), `http://cogtool.hcii.cs.cmu.edu/`
6. Emotiv (2014), `http://www.emotiv.com/`
7. Fairhurst, M.C., Guest, R.M., Deravi, F., George, J.: Using biometrics as an enabling technology in balancing universality and selectivity for management of information access. In: Carbonell, N., Stephanidis, C. (eds.) UI4ALL 2002. LNCS, vol. 2615, pp. 249–259. Springer, Heidelberg (2003)
8. Florêncio, D., Herley, C.: A large-scale study of web password habits. In: 16th International Conference on World Wide Web, pp. 657–666. ACM (2007)
9. Hayashi, E., Hong, J.: A diary study of password usage in daily life. In: SIGCHI Conference on Human Factors in Computing Systems, pp. 2627–2630. ACM (2011)
10. Herley, C.: So long, and no thanks for the externalities: The rational rejection of security advice by users. In: Workshop on New Security Paradigms, pp. 133–144. ACM (2009)
11. Herley, C.: More is Not The Answer. IEEE Security & Privacy 12(1), 14–19 (2014)
12. Inglesant, P.G., Sasse, M.A.: The true cost of unusable password policies: Password use in the wild. In: SIGCHI Conference on Human Factors in Computing Systems, pp. 383–392. ACM (2010)
13. ISO 9241-11. Ergonomic requirements for office work with visual display terminals (VDTs)-Part 11-Guidance on usability. Intern. Organisation for Standardisation (1998)
14. Killourhy, K.S., Maxion, R.A.: Comparing anomaly-detection algorithms for keystroke dynamics. In: 2009 Dependable Systems & Networks, pp. 125–134. IEEE (2009)
15. Monsell, S.: Task switching. Trends in Cognitive Sciences 7(3), 134–140 (2003)
16. Nikiforakis, N., Kapravelos, A., Joosen, W., Kruegel, C., Piessens, F., Vigna, G.: Cookieless monster: Exploring the ecosystem of web-based device fingerprinting. In: IEEE Symposium on Security and Privacy (2013)
17. Schiffman, N., Greist-Bousquet, S.: The effect of task interruption and closure on perceived duration. Bulletin of the Psychonomic Society 30(1), 9–11 (1992)
18. Shi, E., Niu, Y., Jakobsson, M., Chow, R.: Implicit authentication through learning user behavior. In: Burmester, M., Tsudik, G., Magliveras, S., Ilić, I. (eds.) ISC 2010. LNCS, vol. 6531, pp. 99–113. Springer, Heidelberg (2011)
19. Steves, M., Chisnell, D., Sasse, A., Krol, K., Theofanos, M., Wald, H.: Report: Authentication Diary Study. NISTIR 7983 (2014), `http://dx.doi.org/10.6028/NIST.IR.7983`
20. Thorpe, J., van Oorschot, P.C., Somayaji, A.: Pass-thoughts: Authenticating with our minds. In: 2005 Workshop on New Security Paradigms, pp. 45–56. ACM (2005)
21. Whitten, A., Tygar, J.D.: Why Johnny can't encrypt: A usability evaluation of PGP 5.0. In: 8th USENIX Security Symposium, vol. 99. McGraw-Hill (1999)
22. Zurko, M.E., Simon, R.T.: User-centered security. In: 1996 Workshop on New Security Paradigms, pp. 27–33. ACM (1996)

Clear, Unambiguous Password Policies: An Oxymoron?*

Michelle Steves[1], Kevin Killourhy[2], and Mary F. Theofanos[1]

[1] National Institute of Standards and Technology, Gaithersburg, Maryland, United States
[2] Formerly of the National Institute of Standards and Technology, Gaithersburg, Maryland, United States
{michelle.steves,mary.theofanos}@nist.gov

Abstract. Password policies – documents which regulate how users must create and manage their passwords – can have complex and unforeseen consequences on organizational security. Since these policies attempt to govern user behavior, users must be clear as to what is expected of them for a policy to be effective. While a culprit of misinterpretation, policy ambiguity also prevents researchers from comparing and contrasting policy statements. To tackle ambiguity, we developed a formal language for stating what behavior is and is not allowed when creating, managing, and changing passwords. This formal language lends itself to policy analysis and visualization. A corpus of 41 password policies was translated into the formal language and analyzed. Having these clear, unambiguous policy statements enables us to explore password policies in much greater detail, discuss the relative merits of different statements, compare and contrast policies, and begin to examine the interplay between usability and security in password policies.

Keywords: Usable security, password policy, formal language, Extended Backus-Naur Form.

1 Introduction

As part of the Research and Development thrust of the United States' Comprehensive National Cyber-Security Initiative, we undertook an exploration of the relationship between usability and security in password policies. In this domain, as in many areas of computer security, we find a mixture of security concerns and usability concerns. Adams and Sasse [1] observed that when users feel that password rules are preventing them from accomplishing their work, they will work around them. For instance, if files cannot be easily shared among account owners, users will share an account, violating the password policy restriction on sharing. Usability issues related to security policies affect security-related behaviors and by extension, security outcomes.

Password policies are documents that specify how passwords must be created, stored, changed, and managed. Depending on the security concerns of the policy writer, these documents regulate everything from length and lifetime, to when and

P.L.P. Rau (Ed.): CCD/HCII 2014, LNCS 8528, pp. 240–251, 2014.

how a user can transmit passwords. For example, the SANS Institute [16] has shared a template password policy for use by policy writers. The template requires that user-account passwords be changed every six months, and it offers guidance on what constitutes a strong password (e.g., "at least fifteen alphanumeric characters"). The template requires that users not reveal their password, not check "remember password" boxes in applications, and not store passwords in written form.

These policy statements are created with security concerns in mind. The restriction on users storing their password in writing is meant to protect the password, but it requires user "buy in" if that protection is to exist. Consequently, the role of the user cannot be discounted when developing a policy. Since some security requirements are all but unenforceable, security depends on a policy that can effectively explain what is expected of a user. Unfortunately, security concerns that prompt statements in a password policy are rarely understood by users. Typical policy requirements include a password with an 8 character minimum length (or 15 in the example above), comprised of mixed-case letters, numbers, and special characters, and which does not contain dictionary words or personal information. Cheswick [3] has called these "eye of newt" policy statements in part because they sound like a magic formula to a user.

A typical user is likely governed by multiple policies both at work and at home (e.g., to access corporate email servers, personal financial information, and e-commerce sites). Ambiguities in these policies, discrepancies among them, and the sheer number of different policies may cause confusion. As a result of this cognitive burden, users may choose weak passwords, write them down, or violate policies in other ways. As policy violation becomes an accepted matter of course, the security goals of the policy are not met. Consequently, overall security may be weakened.

2 Problem and Approach

In a preliminary survey of password policies, we discovered an unexpected problem both for our research effort and for users: ambiguity. We were surprised at the frequency with which there was disagreement over what a policy statement meant. If we had difficulty agreeing, would users who are expected to follow these policies also have different interpretations? An example of the difficulty can be seen by examining a statement in the password policy of one Federal agency:

Passwords contain a combination of letters, numbers, and at least one special character.

Different people have interpreted this statement to mean each of the following:

1. Users must create passwords with at least one letter, at least one number, and at least one special character (i.e., defining a combination to mean one or more of each).
2. Users must create passwords with at least one special character (i.e., defining a combination to mean zero or more of each, except special characters since at least one is explicitly required).
3. Users must create passwords with at least two letters, two numbers, and one special character (i.e., because letters and numbers are both plural).

All interpretations are reasonable and as a result a reader cannot be sure whether his or her interpretation is correct.

Ambiguity is both a usability issue and a security issue. Users faced with such a policy cannot know which passwords are in compliance and which are not. Users who take the time to create a memorable, strong password only to have it rejected as non-compliant, are unlikely to try as hard the second time. Researchers cannot accurately assess security when there is disagreement over the security properties. For instance, each of the three interpretations corresponds to a password space of different size; the strength of the password depends on the size of this space.

3 Background

Our effort exists within 30 years of research into password usability and password policies. Research studies have periodically tried to characterize the passwords that people choose [4], [6], [11], [14], and [20] to name a few. These works usually rely on a list of passwords obtained by a system-administrator, observed through a toolbar, or revealed through a security compromise. They provide empirically grounded insight into the actual passwords that people choose. While these studies do not consider password policies directly, they are related to our research on policy since users' password choices are governed in part by policy requirements.

Some researchers have attempted to examine the connection between password policy and user behavior already. Mannan and Oorschot [13] surveyed users of online banks regarding their understanding of bank's security requirements. They found a disconnect between bank guidelines and user practice. For instance, bank password-change recommendations were on the order of a few months, yet the majority of users do not change their passwords within a year. Furnell [8] surveyed 10 popular websites, examining the password-creation guidelines, the enforcement of password-composition restrictions, and the reset policy. Inglesant and Sasse [9] surveyed 32 staff members at a research university and a financial-services organization about their password usage. They found that password policies which ignore human factors may result in unexpectedly poor security (e.g., shared and written-down passwords).

Many authors have observed the increasing burden of password management on users. Summers and Bosworth [19] argue for user guidance and enforcement to prevent users from choosing easily guessable passwords. Spafford [18] argued that the best practices shared by many modern password policies are actually artifacts based on out-of-date risk assessments. For instance, he traces requirements that passwords be changed monthly to the computing power of Department of Defense machines in the 1970s. He advocates updating these out-of-date best practices to modern, sound practices based on individual risk assessments. Farrell [5] introspectively determined that he used over 61 passwords, 15 of which were committed to memory. He argues that policy writers must acknowledge the increasing burden of password management on their users.

Some research has attempted to make writing security policies easier. A visualization of access-control policies is presented in [21]. An extensive list of guidelines for anyone architecting a system for writing security and privacy policies is provided in [10].

Some research has focused specifically on writing password policies. A language for expressing a password-policy scenario in a formal language is presented in [17]. Using simulation, a measure of system harm resulting from the given scenario can be estimated. An ontological framework for reasoning about the security and usability costs of different policy decisions is presented in [15]. These works show the potential for password policies written in formal language. That effort partners well with the aim of our current work to bridge the gap between ambiguous, informal policy statements and clear, explicit, formal policy statements.

Perhaps the closest research efforts were those documented in [2] and [7]. Bonneau and Preibusch [2] surveyed the empirical password policies of 150 websites. By creating accounts and systematically changing the password, they were able to infer the enforced lengths and complexity requirements. Florêncio and Herley [7] surveyed length and complexity requirements for 75 websites according to their password policies. Their primary finding was that length and complexity requirements are not explained by the size of the assets protected but by the dependence on advertising dollars. In other words, sites that depend on users for revenue have weaker, more accommodating policies.

While our research overlaps that of [2] and [7], the focus of our work differs in important ways. Foremost, our interest in capturing the diversity and ambiguities in password policies reflects a different research goal. Our investigation moves beyond length and complexity requirements and into the numerous other requirements and guidance that password policies provide.

4 Creating a Taxonomy of Policy Statements

We created the taxonomy by first analyzing a corpus of collected password policies. Then, we developed the grammar whereby the regulations of the password policies could be expressed as explicit expectations on user behavior when creating, changing, storing, or communicating passwords. Next, we used this grammar to translate the 41 password policies into a formal, well-defined language. Finally, we explore how policies, once represented in this language, lend themselves to comparison, visualization, and further analysis. Each of these steps in our method is described in the following sections.

4.1 Collecting a Policy Corpus

We employed two methods for collecting password policies for study. We collected workplace policies by searching Federal Government websites. We collected personal-site policies by searching popular websites. The two approaches enabled us to collect 41 policies: 22 concerning workplace passwords, and 19 concerning personal-site passwords.

In an effort to collect workplace policies, we visited each of the Federal Departments and Agencies listed at www.usa.gov (August 2010). On each site, we attempted to find the password policy. To qualify, the policy document itself had to be obtained. Policies were also checked to ensure that they applied to employees of the organization (rather than outside users of a service provided by the organization). Policies judged to govern workplace behavior concerning passwords were added to the corpus. From the sites visited, we obtained 22 policies.

To collect a comparatively sized set of policies from sites that users might visit for personal use, we began with the corpus of online password policies assembled in [7]. This paper explains the collection methodology in detail, and importantly, one aim was a representative collection. In [7], 77 policies were examined and links to 56 of them were provided. We visited all 56 links. If a link was broken or we could not find a minimal set of policy rules, we excluded the policy from our corpus by necessity. For a policy to be included in our corpus it must have, at a minimum, a requirement or recommendation about password length or a statement about which character sets are acceptable. Following this procedure, we added 15 policies to our corpus. Because our corpus contained a paucity of financial-service policies, and because we felt that such policies would be important in our corpus (as they are policies from personal-use sites that are likely to have detailed security concerns), we visited the top business and financial services websites, ranked by US traffic, according to www.alexa.com (in August 2010). We employed the same strategy to find a password policy governing users of these sites as above. Following this procedure, we added four policies, for a total of 19 personal-use policies and 41 policies overall.

4.2 Developing a Taxonomic Grammar

While reading and becoming familiar with the regulations and guidelines of the policies in the corpus, we made several attempts at organizing the policies and policy statements into rules. Our final product was a formal language in which policies were represented as a set of statements formed from a subset of English. However, in the process of arriving at this approach, we attempted two other approaches: feature vectors (an n-dimensional vector of features to represent a policy) and qualitative coding.

Our first attempt at organizing password policies was to encode them as feature vectors. Earlier research, such as that by Florêncio and Herley [7], effectively encoded password length, composition requirements, and lifetime in this manner. However, because our interest was in capturing other aspects of policy behavior (e.g., what word and letter combinations are forbidden, and whether users can use password vaults), this approach quickly became unwieldy.

Our second attempt at organizing policy statements was to analyze password policies in the style of a social scientist trying to organize research data. Using a software package for qualitative data analysis, a researcher tagged sentences and sections in a password policy with a topic code. For instance, a line insisting that strong passwords have a minimum of 15 characters would be coded "Length," and a line stating that passwords must be alphanumeric would be coded "Character Content." We identified 9 top-level codes, in this way: Length, Lifetime, Lockout, Storage, Use, Character

Set, Character Content, Content Features, and Forgotten. The plan was to subdivide each of these into different kinds of statements within each topic area. This approach also became unwieldy, as the distinction between topic areas was subject for debate.

These failed attempts contributed to our final, more successful, approach to studying password policies. Rather than trying to divide the password policy into topic areas, as in the previous approach, we simply translated each policy statement into clear language that explicitly states what is expected of the user. For instance, "strong passwords are at least 15 characters and alphanumeric" became two statements: (1) "users must create passwords that are at least 15 characters long" and (2) "users must create passwords where every character is a letter or a number." Note that the user is the subject of the sentence, making it clear that the policy applies to the user (compare "passwords must be stored as cryptographic hashes" which is probably, but not explicitly, regulating the behavior of a system administrator, not a user).

After rewriting several policies, we discovered that some sentences were being reused. Reviewing what we had written, we observed that other sentences were saying the same thing but in different ways. By restricting ourselves to a grammar in which a policy statement could only be expressed in one way – and two different statements imposed two different requirements, even if only subtly – the idea of a formal grammar for expressing password policies arose.

The actual grammar of the formal language was specified using an extension of the Backus-Naur Form (EBNF). The language and the procedure for translating a policy into the language is described in [11], as well as, both the EBNF syntax and a description of the semantics.

4.3 Translating Policies to the Formal Language

Translation involved two steps. First, sentences, bullets, or policy statements that were within scope were identified. Then, each statement was translated to one or more statements in the formal language. Each of these steps is described in much greater detail in [11], but the procedure is fairly straightforward. The translated policy documents were checked with a language parser to ensure that the syntax of each statement was correct. In the end, all 41 policies in the corpus were translated into the formal language.

4.4 Analysis and Visualization

The translated policy documents enable analysis and visualization that would not be possible with the raw documents. Specifically, since the formal grammar has the property that semantically equivalent statements are syntactically equal, we can analyze statement prevalence and frequency. Further, since the language has a hierarchical characteristic whereby similar statements start the same way, a tree-like visualization of password policies becomes possible.

Policy Summary Statistics. Some summary statistics provide a clear picture of the diversity of password policies. The 41 policies yielded 449 statements in total.

The policy with the fewest statements had only one: *Users must create passwords with length greater than or equal to 6 characters.* The policy with the most statements had 38. The median number of statements per policy was 9.

Of the 449 total statements, there were 153 unique statements, meaning that there is overlap across policies. The statement which appeared in the most policies was *Users must create passwords with length greater than or equal to 8 characters.* This statement appeared in 23 policies (56%). The next most prevalent statement appears in only 15 policies (37%): *Users must not communicate passwords to anyone.* Regarding the infrequent statements, 71 of the 153 statements (46%) appeared in only one policy. Additionally, of the 41 policies, no two policies shared the exact same set of statements.

Visualization with Policy Trees. One powerful advantage of the taxonomy of password statements is a visualization based on the parse tree. Figure 1 shows an example of such a visualization. Each statement can be broken up into phrases based on which grammar rule matched the words. For instance, the policy statement "*Users / must // create passwords / with length / greater than or equal to / 8 characters*" has vertical bars delimiting the phrases. The double vertical bar indicates a blank phrase (contrasting with the phrase "*not*" which can appear instead of the blank).

We can visualize each policy statement as a series of line segments, one per phrase, which radiate out from a central point. If two policies start with the same phrases, they follow the same path. When the two policies use different phrases, the paths diverge. Since a policy is a collection of statements, we can view it as a tree.

Figure 1 shows a tree with 153 paths from the center of the circle to the outside, each corresponding to a different one of the 153 unique statements in the corpus. The darker paths correspond to policy statements made by the (now obsolete) National Institute of Standards and Technology (NIST) password policy. The lighter paths correspond to statements that are in other policies and not NIST's. The arcs around the outside of the figure reflect that different slices (or wedges) of the circle correspond to different prefix phrases. The median number of phrases is 6 in a policy, with a minimum of 4 ("Users | must | not | communicate passwords | except in an emergency") and a maximum of 7 ("Users | must || create passwords || in the set of | strings with | at least 2 unique characters"). Note that, by convention, since all policies start with the phrase "Users," we do not count it when counting the number of phrases in a statement.

We believe the visualizations provide a useful indication of policy complexity and structure. Policies with more statements produce denser trees. We also find these visualizations to be useful in comparing policies by placing trees for two policies side-by-side. Since policy statements correspond to the same path relative to the side-by-side centers, it is possible to spot paths that are shared and paths that are not. It is also possible to compare regions of coverage (e.g., which policies have many strict "must" regulations and which policies have more suggestive "should" guidelines).

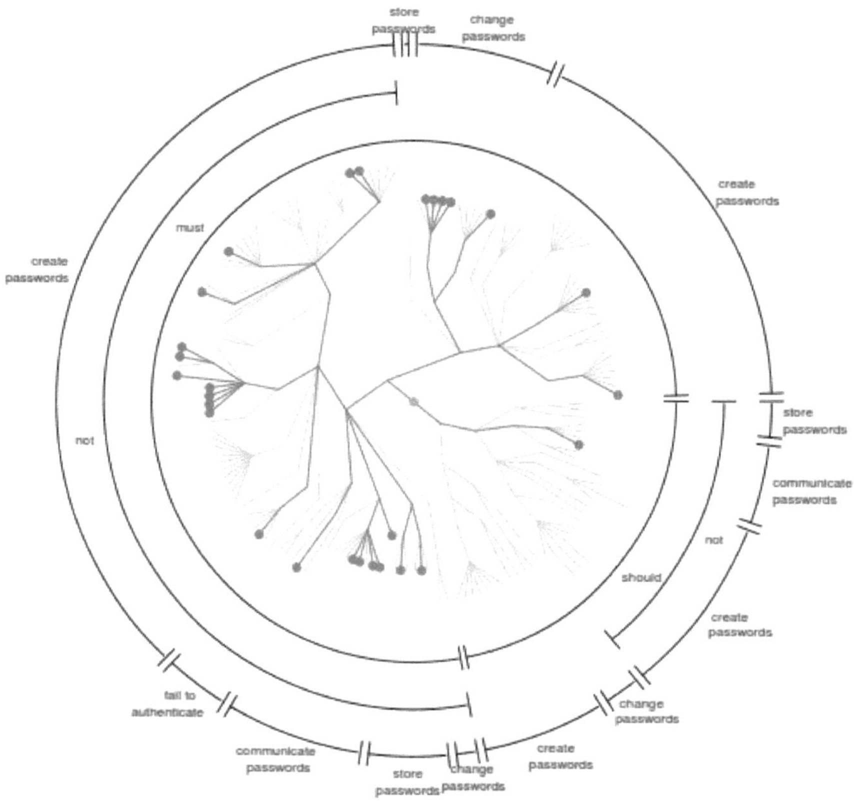

Fig. 1. Password policy tree-like visualization

5 Explorations

To highlight the potential of this taxonomy of password-policy statements, we conducted several exploratory investigations. First, we compared policies that have a known relationship to see how that relationship is reflected in the visualization. Second, we compared the workplace policies to the personal-site policies to see whether workplace policies are stricter (as would be expected based on earlier results by Flor^encio and Herley [7]).

5.1 Comparing Policies: NIST, the Census Bureau, DOC and the Marines

The password-policy visualizations make it easy to explore and compare different password policies. Figure 2 shows four policies in a 2 × 2 tiling. The policies on the top row are from NIST and the Census Bureau. The policies on the bottom line are from the Department of Commerce (DoC) and the Marine Corps Enterprise Network (MCEN). Note that NIST and the Census Bureau are both organizations within the Department of Commerce.

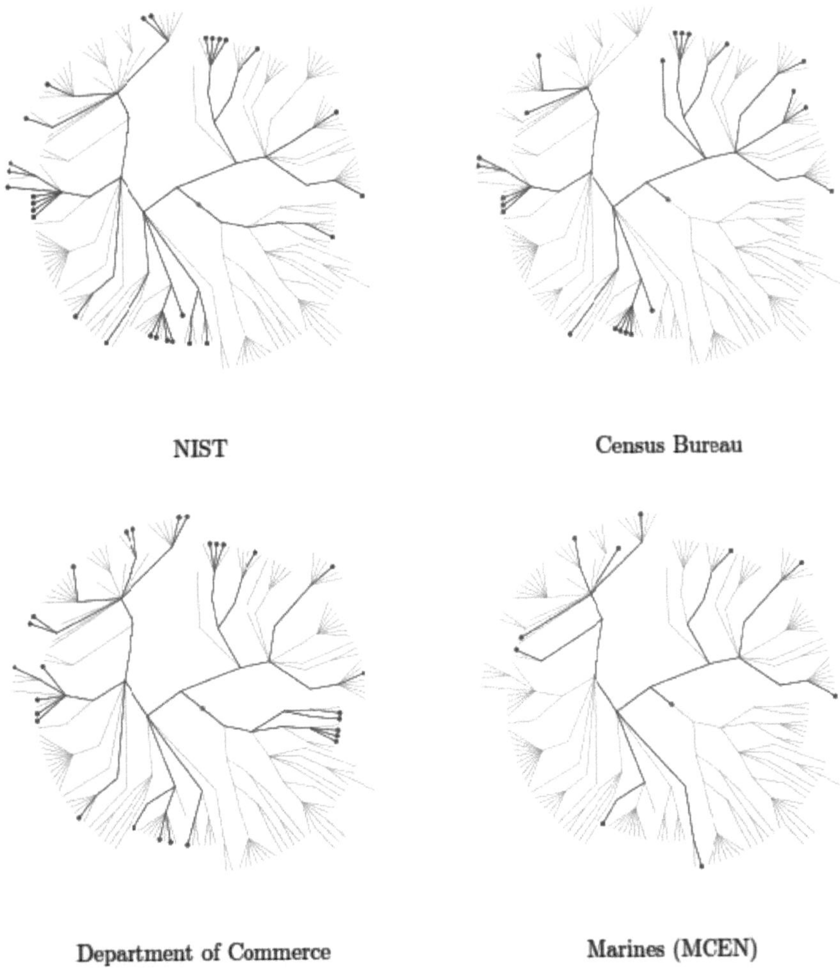

Fig. 2. Panels comparing four different workplace password policies

Given their department-level connection, one might expect to see similarities between the NIST and Census policies. Indeed, we observe similarities, and also some differences. For instance, between 12 o'clock and 1 o'clock are a set of restrictions on when passwords must be immediately changed. Specifically, the prefix is "Users must change passwords immediately if" and there are five different completions, corresponding to the path's split into a five-tined fork. Neither NIST nor Census includes the first completion: sent unencrypted (i.e., a requirement that passwords be changed immediately if sent in clear text). Both NIST and Census include the next three completions: found non-compliant, directed by management, and compromised. NIST also includes the final completion while Census does not: shared. NIST's policy allows passwords to be communicated to others in an emergency, but this statement tries to ensure that shared passwords are changed as soon as possible.

The similarities between the two policies suggest a common source. The two policies share many of the same statements with the password policy for the Department of Commerce, shown in the lower left of Figure 2. The DoC policy shares the three regulations on immediate password change: found non-compliant, directed by management, and compromised. However, there are some discrepancies between the department-level policy and those of the organizations in the department. For instance, in the 3 o'clock position, both NIST and Census have the same path while DoC has a slightly different one (i.e., NIST and Census have a path that angles downward in the last phrase while DoC has a path that angles slightly upward. This corresponds to an 8 character minimum for NIST and Census and a 12 character minimum for DoC.

In contrast to the NIST, Census, and DoC policies which have dozens of statements, the Marine (MCEN) password policy in the lower right is less densely populated. It is comprised of only 10 statements. This policy says nothing about the conditions under which passwords must be immediately changed. Also, in the 6 o'clock position, the MCEN policy has a rule that is in none of the other three: Users must not change passwords before 7 days. The MCEN policy is one of a few that set a limit on how often a user can change his or her password (presumably to prevent them from returning too quickly to an old password). This exploration of the common and the unusual across policies promotes discussion of what statements should be in a policy.

We also found it interesting that, despite their differences, the NIST, Census, and DoC policies look similar, especially when compared with a policy from unrelated organizations in the Federal government.

5.2 Comparing Policy Groups: Workplace and Personal-Site

In addition to comparisons of individual policies, we can compare sets of policies by comparing the statements which appear in each set. For instance, one might want to compare workplace and personal-site policies to see whether workplace policies tend to contain more statements containing requirements. Florêncio and Herley [7] found that sites which draw ad-revenue have more lenient policies, and sites which do not need to entice their users to join (i.e., workplaces) are stricter.

A statistical analysis of the number of statements in each policy reveals that the median for workplace policies was 10 statements, and the median for personal-site policies was 7. Moving beyond summary statistics, it is possible to visually contrast the workplace policy tree and the personal-site policy tree. The workplace tree is comprised of the union of all the workplace statements, and the personal-site tree is comprised of the personal-site statements (not shown due to space limitations).

Partitioning of policies into workplace and personal-site is only one possible partitioning of many. Since the personal-site policies are comprised of sites ranging from banks to sports news, we expect that a subdivision of the personal-site policies would be informative. One might imagine that banks and other financial services companies would have more restrictive policies as security is more of a concern. The formal-language representation and visualization lends itself to such partitioning, exploration, and analysis.

6 Summary and Future Work

This work arose from a need to deal with ambiguities in current password policies. These ambiguities not only prevent researchers from comparing and contrasting policy statements, they can also cause users to misinterpret what is expected of them. To tackle ambiguity, we developed a formal language for stating what behavior is and is not allowed when creating, managing, and changing passwords. This formal language lends itself to policy analysis and visualization.

We have used this language to begin to explore the diversity and complexity of password policies by examining a corpus of password policies. Having clear, unambiguous policy statements enables us to study password policy statement properties. What quantifiable security benefits are provided by a statement or set of statements? What usability issues are introduced? These usability issues can also be quantified and studied empirically in order to understand the security and usability interplay.

In addition to the study of policy statement properties, the formal language enables us to examine how users interpret individual policy statements and develop a mapping of the formal policy statements to plain language statements that remains unambiguous, minimizes misinterpretation, and enhances understanding by users.

References

1. Adams, A., Sasse, M.A.: Users are not the enemy. Communcations of the ACM 42(12), 41–46 (1999)
2. Bonneau, J., Preibusch, S.: The password thicket: Technical and market failures in human authentication on the web. In: 9th Workshop on the Economics of Information Security (WEIS 2010), Cambridge, MA, June 7-8 (2010), `http://weis2010.econinfosec.org/papers/session3/weis2010_bonneau.pdf` (accessed January 2014)
3. Cheswick, B.: Rethinking passwords, Baltimore, MD. Presentation at the Solaris Security Summit (2014), `http://www.cheswick.com/ches/talks/baltimore.pdf` (accessed January 2014)
4. Dell'Amico, M., Michiardi, P., Roudier, Y.: Password strength: An empirical analysis. In: Proceedings of 29th IEEE Conference on Computer Communication (INFOCOM 2010), Mar 14-19, pp. 1–9. IEEE Press, San Diego (2010)
5. Farrell, S.: Password policy purgatory. IEEE Internet Computing 12(5), 84–87 (2008)
6. Florêncio, D., Herley, C.: A large-scale study of web password habits. In: Proceedings of the 16th International World Wide Web Conference (WWW 2007), Banff, Alberta, May 8-12, pp. 657–666 (2007)
7. Florêncio, D., Herley, C.: Where do security policies come from? In. In: Proceedings of the 6th Symposium on Usable Privacy and Security (SOUPS 2010), Redmond, WA, July 14-16. ACM Press, New York (2010)
8. Furnell, S.: An assessment of website password practices. Computers & Security 26, 445–451 (2007)

9. Philip, G.: Inglesant and M. Angela Sasse. The true cost of unusable password policies: Password use in the wild. In: Proceedings of the 28th International Conference on Human Factors in Computer Systems, Atlanta, GA, April 10-15, pp. 383–392. ACM Press, New York (2010)
10. Johnson, M., Karat, J., Karat, K.-M., Grueneberg, K.: Optimizing a policy authoring framework for security and privacy policies. In: Proceedings of the 6th Symposium on Usable Privacy and Security (SOUPS 2010), Redmond, WA, July 14-16, ACM Press, New York (2010)
11. Killourhy, K., Choong, Y.-Y., Theofanos, M.: Taxonomic rules for password policies: translating the informal to the formal language. National Institute of Standards and Technology, Gaithersburg, Maryland, NISTIR 7970 (December 2013)
12. Klein, D.V.: Foiling the cracker; a survey of, and improvements to unix password security. In: Proceedings of the 2nd USENIX Security Symposium, Portland, OR, August 27-28, pp. 5–14. USENIX (1990)
13. Mannan, M., Oorschot, P.C.V.: Security and usability: The gap in real-world online banking. In: Proceedings of the New Security Paradigms Workshop (NSPW 2007), North Conway, NH, September 18-21, pp. 1–14. ACM Press, New York (2007)
14. Morris, R., Thompson, K.: Password security: A case history. Communications of the ACM 22(11), 594–597 (1979)
15. Parkin, S.E., van Moorsel, A., Coles, R.: An information security ontology incorporating human-behavioural implications. In: Proceedings of the 2nd International Conference on Security of Information and Networks (SIN 2009), Famagusta, North Cyprus, October 6-10, pp. 46–55. ACM Press, New York (2009)
16. SANS Institute. SANS password policy (2006), `http://www.sans.org/security-resources/policies/Password_Policy.pdf` (accessed January 2014)
17. Shay, R.J.K., Bhargav-Spantzel, A., Bertino, E.: Password policy simulation and analysis. In: Proceedings of the ACM Workshop on Digital Identity Management, Fairfax, VA, pp. 1–10. ACM Press, New York (November 2, 2007)
18. Spafford, G.: Security myths and passwords (2006), `http://www.cerias.purdue.edu/site/blog/post/password-change-myths/` (accessed January 2014)
19. Wayne, C.: Summers and Edward Bosworth. Password policy: The good, the bad, and the ugly. In: Proceedings of the Winter International Symposium on Information and Communication Technologies, Cancun, Mexico, January 5-8, pp. 1–6. Trinity College, Dublin (2004)
20. Wu, T.: A real-world analysis of Kerberos password security. In: Proceedings of the ISOC Symposium on Network and Distributed System Security (NDSS 1999), San Diego, CA. Internet Society (1999)
21. Xu, W., Shehab, M., Ahn, G.-J.: Visualization based policy analysis: Case study in SELinux. In: Proceedings of the 13th ACM Symposium on Access Control Models and Technologies (SACMAT 2008), Estes Park, Colorado, June 11–13, pp. 165–174 (2008)

ARITH Product Evaluation System

A User-Centered Study on Web Products Evaluation

Eric Yang and Zhong Wang

Alibaba.com Inc., Hangzhou, P.R. China
mihuprivate@gmail.com

Abstract. Practical web evaluation theories lack reliability and practicality in terms of information quality, usability, user experience, market value and other factors. As a result, our team attempted to create a user-centered indicator system named ARITH to measure key user goals by integrating existing theories and methodologies with data on millions of users. This system is a strategic system that allows products analysis from various business angles. It functions as a supplement to existing product evaluation methods.

Keywords: Website assessment, user data, interaction design.

1 Introduction

Since the 1980s, a series of researches have been published focusing on product quality evaluation. From the earliest information quality evaluations [1-3] to those in recent years which revolve around the quality of user experience [4,5], both academia and large Internet companies are researching this field in order to achieve the key goal of the Internet - to attract more users for commercial gain. Furthermore, compared with subjective evaluation methods based on users or experts, evaluation with web metrics are more objective and easily obtained as they are more reliable and practical. Therefore, web metrics have become a mainstream facet of product evaluation.

These studies have already reached a certain level of maturity. But in terms of practical application, a number of issues must still be re-solved:

1. The comprehensiveness of evaluation dimensions. On the one hand, single assessment systems like WebQual [6] and Google Heart [7] of-ten only focus on certain levels, like business, technology or user experience. This makes it difficult to obtain a complete picture of the product's quality. On the other hand, when selecting data dimensions, different teams have different preferences. Business strategists, technology teams and design teams set goals and interpret data from their respective positions. As a result, the teams are unable to reach consensus on the objectivity of the results.
2. The reasonableness of evaluation indicators. Most indicators were standardized and defined after going through methods like Delphi - they are relatively scattered and lack trustworthiness. And it's hard to prove whether they are appropriate for different product evaluation types.

P.L.P. Rau (Ed.): CCD/HCII 2014, LNCS 8528, pp. 252–261, 2014.

3. Evaluation process usability. In order to remove the issue of noise during the evaluation process, the industry has attempted to drive research by combining multiple measurements (such as the fuzzy comprehensive method, user motivation method) and using analytics tools like Google Analytics, Adobe Omniture, Webtrends and Webtrekk. But these methods and tools all present operational costs and technical barriers.
4. Evaluation result guidance. Results-oriented evaluation is the main-stream product evaluation theory. By using the AHP/FMEA analytics method or large-scale user measurement, one can often only reach a horizontal comparison of good and bad. But how product design teams should, on the basis of these results, investigate product defects for improvement, is currently rarely mentioned and very difficult to accomplish for evaluation systems.

In response to these issues, we attempted to put forward an index system to evaluate key goals of web user behavior from the user's perspective, and map the product for analysis from different business dimensions. So we promote a strategic product evaluation system: ARITH.

As a result of these issues, ARITH proposes a new evaluation method: Set targets based on actual goals for the product. By utilizing large-scale user groups which are capable of reflecting user behavior, attitudes, experience, technology and other metrics, one can characterize the interaction between the user and the product in terms of each dimension. Thereby one can establish a reasonable system of indicators and measurement methods. Ultimately, one can use the evaluation results to analyze and guide future iterations and optimization of the product at the business, design and technical level.

The theoretical framework for the ARITH method is already complete. We have begun using it in several projects, and are in the process of systematizing the method. In the next stage we hope to test and improve the method in large-scale projects.

2 Conceptual Framework

2.1 The User Perspective

Obvious differences exist between a product's business units, design units and technology units in terms of what constitutes a good or bad product. Furthermore, research suggests that quality is influenced by different factors for different types of websites. As a result, applying the same quality evaluation standards to all websites is unfeasible. Because users are third-party and end-users of the product, their behavior is the most objective reflection of a website's quality [8].

User's behavior and attitudes are diverse and complicated. It is necessary to explore the product-customer relationship in order to discover which customers correctly reflect whether a product's quality. Combining the theory of customer lifetime values with studies that re-search user-product conversion cycles [1], as well as studies that explore the relationship of time and user experience [9], ARITH has devised a five stage model to explain user-product relationships and user behavior and attitudes. The five stages are: 1. Usability, 2. Usefulness, 3. Ease of Use, 4. Desirability, 5. Loyalty. Undergoing this series of trans-formational stages, it is assumed that users will become loyal customers of a product, brand or service.

2.2 Establishing Evaluation Dimensions

After introducing the above five stage model to explain user-product relationships and user behavior and attitudes, it is now essential to explore typical user behavior and attitudes which represent these 5 stages. Objective behavior and the motivations behind such actions can guarantee a much more real representation of the data, and can better reflect users' overall evaluation of a product.

Stage 1: In the 'usability' stage, the interaction time between users and products is limited to the first point of contact. During this stage, users often have an attitude of 'testing' out a product for the first time. A user using a product to complete a task is a typical representation of this stage.

Stage 2: During the 'usefulness' stage, more and more users come into contact with the product. Furthermore, when users begin to believe that the product can satisfy their needs on a particular website, the user-product relationship fully completes its cycle from the 'Usability' stage to the 'Usefulness' stage. When this occurs, the acceptance of larger user bases will be reflected in this stage.

Stage 3: During the 'Ease of Use' stage, user-product contact time becomes longer and longer. This illustrates that the user not only believes that the product can, on a standard level, help them to achieve their goals. On another level this also suggests that a particular user believes that the product is more useful and simple to use than other products. Therefore how often a user uses our products will be mainly reflected in the retention rate of certain user groups.

Stage 4: When a user discovers a certain product's usefulness, they may often want to visit the product's individual website in order to try out and use that product. This is known as the 'Desirability' stage. This big transition often depends on the rate of the user's subjective inter-est. The higher a user's level of interest is, the more that particular user will be willing to use a certain product.

After going through these four stages of transformation, a user will experience a product's quality, service and other factors which can help a user to produce and form feelings, preferences, and loyalty for a product. This can then stimulate a user to continue to use a certain product over a long period of time. This behavior is typical of the final stage of the cycle, the 'Loyalty' stage. Users in this stage of the cycle will have a subjective degree of awareness for a certain product, and in some cases, the brand of the product too.

So far, using user perspectives as a starting point, a graphic representation of ARITH's five dimensions of product evaluation (Adoption, Retention, Identification, Task Success, and Happiness) can be seen below:

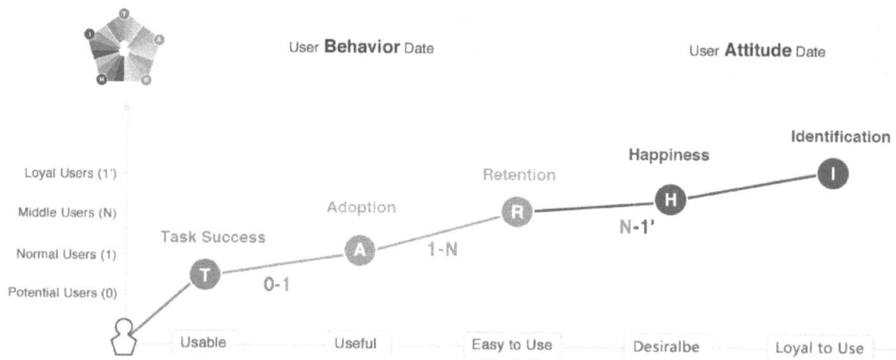

Fig. 1. Explanation of ARITH Evaluation Dimensions

2.3 User Behavior & Attitudes and Evaluating Dimension Mapping

To gain a more comprehensive knowledge and understanding of the behavior and attitude of users and their perspectives towards business, user experience, technology and so on; we classify common web data into standards, along with quantitative and qualitative indexes, business performance indexes, objective system indexes which affect user experience (for example web page response speed), and user indexes (geographical location, quality of equipment used etc.). Then define single indexes according to algorithmic structure and significance.

There is a detailed definition of ARITH's Five dimensions (Table 1) in order to guide evaluators in being able to better map the data of the corresponding dimensions. When measuring each index, selecting a big result index (M) to measure the quality of the dimension and select multiple segmentation indexes (m_n) as an aid to determine whether the result index reflecting the dimension quality is credible or not. This also acts as a key factor in helping product developers search out the background performance of the result indicators.

It is worth mentioning that there is no strict standards and definitions of results indexes or sub-division indexes. Instead, ARITH provided the basic foundations and common indexes of dimension subdivisions for reference. During ARITH's practical application, the evaluator can judge these indicators on the basis of their own expertise and through a large amount of practical application add some common indicators to ARITH's reference definition.

2.4 Evaluation Results Analysis

Interpretation of the product evaluation is a process of mapping the product's performance onto its elements. Similar to a health checkup, the ARITH system measures all indexes related to health. This analysis will start with the biggest indexes and include an association analysis between single dimensions and multi-dimensions.

Table 1. Detailed Definition of ARITH's Five Dimensions

Basic Dimension Definition	Result Indicator(M)	Sub-divided Indicator(m_n)
Task Success: To understand product usability through observing how users complete their target tasks and meet their target goals.	**Task Success:** Refers to a particular user group successfully completing a particular task. Refers to both single users' task completion rates and multiple users' task completion rates' accumulation effect.	**Cost of Task Success:** Refers to the effort spent by a user to accomplish a specific task. Usually measured from two aspects: Time and operation action.
		In the Middle of Task Success (Failure): Refers to the user (especially users who have unfinished tasks) in the process of completing the task. Measured by user's degree of involvement and the possibility of errors.
Adoption: Measures the behavior of new customers to record the degree of how each new customer adopts each product. Used to understand the conversion rate of prospective customers to regular customers.	**Growth of for Unique Visitors for New Products**	**Users Acceptance Rate:** Tracks the degree of activity of first time users of a product or feature. E.g. The depth of activity; length of time using the product (feature) etc.
		Cost of Website Acceptance: Refers to the input-output cost ratio for the website to attract new users. Usually measured through users' original channel (both paid for and free) and the channel cost.
Retention: Measures the behavior of repeat customers to gauge the product's ability to obtain customers. The dimension will measure the differing circumstances of ordinary customers and repeat customers.	**User Retention Rate for Products:** Refers to the changing of the number of repeat users. Including changes of users who return for product objectives and returning users who leave again.	**Retaining Effect:** Refers to the depth of use, frequency of use and contribution to the website of returning users.

Table 1. (*continued*)

Happiness: This dimension will measure products based on users' emotional experiences of the product. This will mainly include subjective feelings such as a consumer's mood and their sensory levels, etc.	**Users Satisfaction of Product:** Refers to the feedback given by a user detailing their satisfaction levels. Comparing the perceived performance of a certain product against their expectations.	**Visual Perception:** Refers to the user's aesthetic standards and feedback on whether or not the product's visual aspects attract the user's attention.
		Ease of Use of Features: The user's feel for the operation and use of a product or feature.
		The Clarity of Information Structure: Feedback of the information transmitted by the product e.g. Content distribution and content structure etc.
		Richness (quality) of Information: Feedback on the product's ability to transmit information that can substantially help the user complete their task(s).
		Clarity of Copy: Feedback of how clear and easily understood the information and copy of a product is.
		Performance: Feedback on the product's reaction speed and validity, etc.
Identification: This dimension aims to understand and measure user's customer loyalty through their knowledge and understanding of certain products and brands.	**Awareness:** After a user is exposed to or uses a product, they will gradually become aware of that particular product or brand.	**Familiarity:** How fully the users understand the product.
		Differentiation: Refers to the difference between how the user perceives the product and how the website wants to convey it.
		Consistency: Refers to the consistency between how the user perceives the product and how the website wants to convey it.

A single dimension analysis helps the evaluator to narrow the scope of the problem, as well as to screen the different levels of the product, including the commercial level, functional layer and emotional layer. For example, the Task Success dimension usually reflects the product's functional state.

Multidimensional association analysis is an essential linchpin. We should avoid misreading or overlooking a single dimension. For example, take correlation analysis of the 3 dimensions T, A, R. In the situation that T is high while A is low and R is low, it may be the case that the product demands itself may not be very strong in the user community. If T is high while A is low and R is high, this may mean that product may have problems in terms of the growth of new user traffic to the website.

In addition, the relationship between the problems exposed by the indexes and the corresponding problems between business, technology and design is in a vacuum environment. When analyzing actual results one must consider all considers of noise and disturbance. For example, for large e-commerce sites like Alibaba, the quality of the product information itself has a great influence on user behavior and attitudes. This causes the index performance to also have a certain degree of influence. Although millions of pieces of large sample size user data can cushion the impact, it still presents a factor to be considered when tracing back to the original problem.

In conclusion, regarding the explanation of detailed indexes, industry and academic circles have many data analysis theories and methods. We will not repeat them here.

3 Implementation

ARITH attempts to utilize a simple process to complete a set of indexes. By illustrating a product or feature's objectives, ARITH establishes a set of individual objectives and evaluation dimensions, thus establishing set index monitoring methods. Evaluators can convert the results of the analysis into the final optimization and relay it back to the business unit.

3.1 Project Implementation Process

The rapid iteration characteristic of the Internet allows ARITH to be used during the beginning, middle and end of the product development process. During the middle and later stages of product development, our team has already attempted to apply this method. The following is a summary of some the process application methods.

Verify Requirements and Confirm Monitoring Objectives. There is wide range of products, each with their own individual characteristics. In order to accurately position the monitoring target we need to extensively gather opinions, monitor the products, and get a comprehensive definition and analysis on the plans to monitor products. This is a stage of conflict between departments, so the following points must be taken into consideration:

Each different team member within the organization may have differing understandings and views. During this process it is necessary to collect different views towards the project, along with the final consensus of all core members.

Large-scale projects may be implemented on a phased basis. At different stages or special stages, the local goals may different from the overall objectives. Focus on achieving the goal of the current stage and monitor any changes to the overall goals.

Establishing Dimensions - Determining Indexes - Monitoring Implementation. After the required goals are determined, it is necessary to consider which dimensions can reflect this requirement monitoring goal (including direct and indirect aspects) and which dimensions correspond to which sub-indexes. For example, for products in the introduction stage, monitoring should focus on whether or not the customer can functionally use the product, new customer adoption rate (functionality); overall user satisfaction etc. Evaluators must then determine in terms of user success rate dimensions, which actions will represent when a target has been achieved.

After sub-dimension indicators are confirmed, one must consider what the source of data is: What is based on real-time analysis, what is quantitative, what is qualitative, how can it be obtained, etc. During this process, establishing dimensions and collecting data are key. One must pay attention to the following factors:

1. The process of converting project objectives involves data on the product's dimensions. Final decisions on the establishment of dimensions should be made on the basis of objectives, access to data and resources.
2. Data collection is best planned during the design process. During the project development process, plan for some special identifiers to perfect data collection.
3. Collecting and analyzing data during later stages may cause a few issues. During formal implementation it is possible to check if there is any replacement data, if there is not then it is possible to use related data to verify.

Analysis Optimization. The ARITH method provides two levels of analysis: Single dimensional analysis and multidimensional association analysis (Please refer to ARITH definition).

During the process, analysis and optimization should be combined in order to avoid analysis for the sake of analysis. One must pay attention to the following points:

1. Analyzing methods and dimensions is a very diverse process and not just restricted to analysis of the above two layers.
2. If a project implements monitoring analysis at different stages, try to keep the data before and after definition consistent with that of the data collection channel. The definition and channel may present differences for similar projects, so they can only serve as a reference point for consideration. They cannot be directly compared.
3. During the analysis, it is recommended that the opinions and ideas of the team members (especially members with a professional background) conducting the analysis should be taken into consideration, ensuring the effectiveness of the analysis.
4. Optimization should be implemented in the actual project with periodic reviews.

3.2 Systematic Trial

The original intention of the ARITH method is to implement the ARITH model into the long term data monitoring analysis of websites, to act as a data processing system and one of the application displays embedded into the data platform (See figure 2).

In terms of systemization, before the process is in the exploration stage, it is important to pay attention to the following points:

1. Systemization of the process emphasizes universality and in turn sacrifices some of its uniqueness. It is not possible for any system to be a perfect fit for all projects. In order to maintain the premises of universality, if one encounters any special circumstances, one must implement data processing or other methods to re-collect the data.
2. Throughout the systemization process, one must select appropriate ARITH dimensions that will be adaptive to the specific product. For example, the most suitable definition of a project for monitoring forms will be the dimensions of T, A, R and H.
3. The ARITH Method is only one model of a system. During the system design process, more possibilities should be taken into consideration.

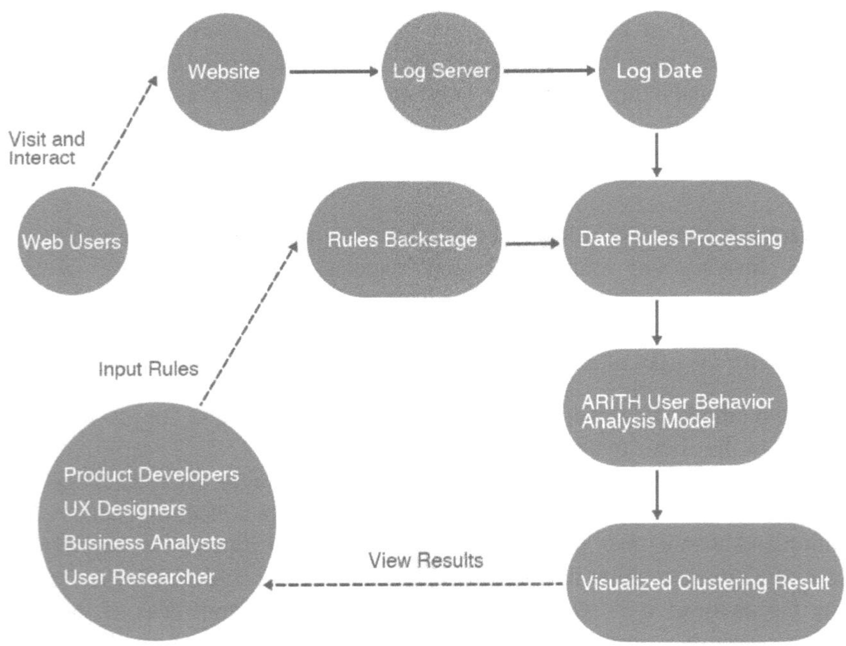

Fig. 2. Systematized Data Platform

4 Conclusion

The ARITH evaluation system is constructed from a user's perspective to provide comprehensive and objective evaluations of the five dimensions. It's a simple and feasible evaluation process and its results offer guidance on design. It is a powerful supplement to existing evaluation theories and methodologies. In the future more projects will need to be put into practice to verify the reasonability and feasibility of the ARITH method. For products if offers diverse perspectives and explanations. For business strategists it offers a method for making decisions.

The ARITH evaluation system is of course not the only evaluation model provided by Alibaba. Different departments are concerned with different scenarios and will propose diversified evaluation models, each serving a different scenario. For example, the PC department and the mobile department are both focused on different methods and are concerned with different aspects. We are excited for more evaluation methods to emerge. This will enrich product evaluation systems to provide a more comprehensive monitoring service.

Acknowledgements. We would like to thank our colleagues Smith Kyle Shannon, Marcus Gavin James, and Lijuan Cao for their professional translations and the Alibaba International User Experience Design team for their dedicated support to this paper.

References

1. Chiou, W.-C., Lin, C.-C., Perng, C.: A strategic framework for website evaluation based on a review of the literature from 1995–2006. Information & Management 47, 282–290 (2010)
2. Aladwania, A.M., Palvia, P.C.: Developing and validating an instrument for measuring user-perceived web quality. Information & Management 39, 467–476 (2002)
3. Moustakis, V.S., Litos, C., Dalivigas, A., Tsironis, L.: Website quality assesment criteria. In: Ninth International Conference on Information Quality, pp. 59–73 (2004)
4. Yang, Z., Caib, S., Zhouc, Z., Zhou, N.: Development and validation of an instrument to measure user perceived service quality of information presenting Web portals. Information & Management 42, 575–589 (2005)
5. Yu, J., Xiao-lin, L., Xue-Song, L.: Quality of Experience Assessment Model and KQI Weight Calculation Method. Computer Engineering 39(2) (2013); 金瀹,李校林,李雪松,用户体验质量评估模型及KQI权重计算方法,计算机工程,第39卷,第2期 (2013年)
6. Loiacono, E.T., Watson, R.T., Goodhue, D.L.: WebQual: a measure of Website quality. 2002 Marketing Educators'Conference: Marketing Theory and Applications 13 (2002)
7. Rodden, K., Hutchinson, H., Fu, X.: Measuring the User Experience on a Large Scale: User-Centered Metrics for Web Applications. In: Proceedings of CHI (2010)
8. Wells, J.D., Valacich, J.S., Hess, J.S.: What signal are you sending? How website quality influences perceptions of product quality and purchase intentions. MIS Quarterly 35, 373–396 (2011)
9. Karapanos, E.: User experience over time. Modeling Users' Experiences with Interactive Systems, 57–83 (2013)

First-Time User Experience with Smart Phone New Gesture Control Features

Jia Zhou, Jie Zhang, Bingjun Xie, Ning Liu, Ming Jiang, Huilin Wang, and Qiqing Gan

Department of Industrial Engineering, Chongqing University, 400044, China
{Zhoujia07,carolzhhang,alwansmiths,liuningcqu, foggyjiang,azerrman}@gmail.com, couthsilver@hotmail.com

Abstract. This study aims to investigate experience of users who use new gesture control features of smart phones and tablets for the first time. To achieve this goal, two laboratory-controlled experiments were conducted. The first experiment focused on new finger gesture features (i.e., pinch), and the second experiment focused on new hand gesture features (i.e., turn over to mute, tap to top, direct call, palm swipe to capture, and palm touch to mute). A total of 19 younger adults and older adults participated in two experiments. They used both new gesture control features and traditional features (e.g., touch) to complete tasks. Their errors and subjective feedback were recorded. Results revealed the relative advantages and disadvantages of new gesture control features over traditional features. Based on the results, design suggestions were provided.

Keywords: Finger gestures, Hand gestures, Smart phones, User experience.

1 Introduction

With rapid development of interaction technologies and mobile infrastructure, smart phones and tablets are integrating more and more features. Under this circumstance, many people prefer to buy a smart phones/tablets with more features rather than another one with fewer features at the same price.

Traditional features (e.g. pinch zooming) are so widely used that they become the necessity of smart phones and tablets, and new features (e.g., hand gestures, fingerprint detecting features, gaze features) are revealed to wow users during the launching of a new smart phone/tablet.

However, little is known about users' first-time experience with new features. Some users are not aware of certain features. Suppose they are aware of certain features and they briefly try to use these features. They may still refuse to use them again if their first-time experience using new features is bad, then they would turn to other choices. First-time user experience is so important that it may influence people's purchase intention, continuous use of smart phones and tablets, and their brand loyalty.

This study aims to investigate first-time user experience with new features of smart phones and tablets. Specifically, younger adults and older adults would use finger gesture features and hand gesture features for the first time in two

P.L.P. Rau (Ed.): CCD/HCII 2014, LNCS 8528, pp. 262–271, 2014.

laboratory-controlled experiments. The results would not only reveal usability problems, but also help practitioners improve intuitiveness of new features.

2 Related Work

The direct input on smart phones and tablets could help solve older adults' problems with feature phones (e.g. hierarchical menu and multi-tap). However, older adults' mental models with feature phones are not applicable to smart phones and tablets anymore, and the lack of computer experience hinders them from developing correct mental models [1]. Thus, older adults still encountered difficulties with smart phones and tablets. This is reflected in their errors during pointing tasks [2] and text input tasks [1]. In our previous study [3], we investigated older adults' use of pinch zooming and reported quantitative results derived from the survey. We would report qualitative results of errors associated with pinch zooming in the first experiment.

Compared with older adults, younger adults had different needs of smart phone features. Young adults generally used more features and were more willing to accept new features than older adults, but younger adults did not use features consistently and they even quickly abandoned many features [4]. Younger adults' quick judgment with new features is of reference value for practitioners, so this study also investigated younger adults' use of new features in the second experiment.

3 Methodology

Two laboratory-controlled experiments were conducted. The first experiment examined new finger features for certain older adults: pinch and touch. The second experiment examined new hand features for certain younger adults and certain older adults: turn over to mute, tap to top, direct call, palm swipe to capture, and palm touch to mute.

3.1 Finger Gesture Experiment

There were 12 older adults (Mean age=66.4; SD=5.6; Range=59-77) participated in this experiment. They were mainly retired faculty recruited from the Senior College of Tsinghua University. They were well educated and had 13-year experience with desktop computers, but they had little experience with smart phones and tablets.

Participants used both pinch and touch in zooming tasks to view photos, PDF documents, map, and web pages. They used smart phones and tablets, including Apple iPod Touch (3.5″, iOS), Dell Streak (5″, Android), Samsung Galaxy Tab (7″, Android), and Apple iPad (9.7″, iOS), and they used four applications on each device including the photo album (the default application in iOS/Android), the document reader (the default application in iOS, and Office Suite in Android), Google map (the default application in iOS/Android), and the web browser (Internet Explorer in Android, and Safari in iOS). Each application supported pinch zooming or touching buttons labeled with "+"/"-".

Participants first signed consent forms and filled in the questionnaire about demographic information and experience with computers and mobile phones. Then, they watched the demonstration from the instructor. Next, they completed the following four tasks:

- Task 1: Brow the album which contains six photos. Zoom in to view the predefined digit on each photo and write it down.
- Task 2: Read the three-page PDF document. Zoom in each page to read the predefined contact and write down answers to the cloze test.
- Task 3: View the map and get walking directions. Zoom in the map to view the predefined route and write down walking directions to the destination.
- Task 4: Browse web pages. Zoom in to read text on predefined web pages and write down answers to the cloze test.

Afterward, they filled in the questionnaire about their attitude toward the experience and had a brief interview. This study was conducted in a standard usability-testing laboratory. Two camcorders were set up to record this experiment: one on the top of the display and the other one on the upper right.

3.2 Hand Gesture Experiment

There were five younger adults (three at age 21 and two at age 20; four males, one female) and two older adults (one at age 68 and the other at age 69; two females) participated in this experiment. People who had never used hand gestures used in the experiment were eligible for this study. Recruiting flyers were distributed in Chongqing University. Younger participants were undergraduate students and older participants were typical older adults who did exercise on campus.

Within-subjects design was used. Each participant used both new hand gesture features and traditional features to complete tasks on Samsung Galaxy S III (4.8″, Android). There are two reasons for choosing this device. First, Samsung is one of the brands that dominate smart phone market, and it is keen on adding innovative gesture-control features. Second, 4.8″ is still one of mainstream sizes for smart phones.

The procedure of this study is similar to the first experiment except the following differences: participants' innovativeness was measured through the questionnaire which had five items adapted from [5]; there was one additional instructor who interviewed participants after each task; there was no demonstration. Instead, the instructor introduced each feature and showed the physical manual and the interactive manual in the phone setting if necessary; this experiment was recorded through five cameras around the ceiling of the laboratory through Guard 4000. Participants completed four tasks:

- Task 1: Mute incoming call ringtones through three methods: touch & drag the reject button, turning over, and palm touch (shown in Figure 1).
- Task 2: Make a phone call through two methods: touch the call button and direct call (i.e., lift the phone to the ear [6]).

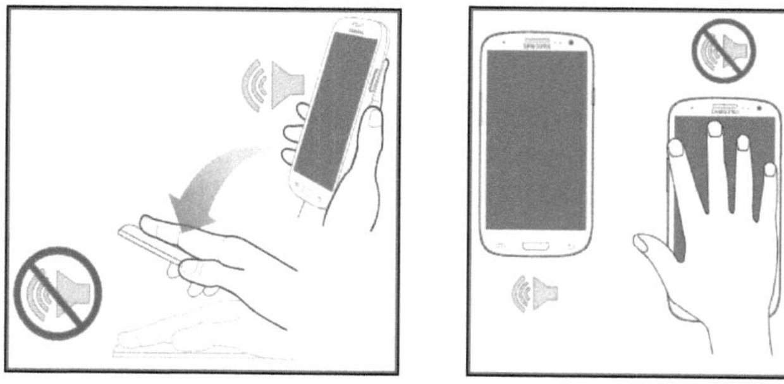

Fig. 1. Turning over to mute (left) and palm touch to mute (right). (Source: Samsung Galaxy S III User Manual, p. 23 and p. 25)

- Task 3: Go to the top of the contact list through two methods: touch & drag and tap to top (shown in Figure 2).
- Task 4: Capture a screen shot through two methods: press the home button & the power button simultaneously and palm swipe (shown in Figure 2).

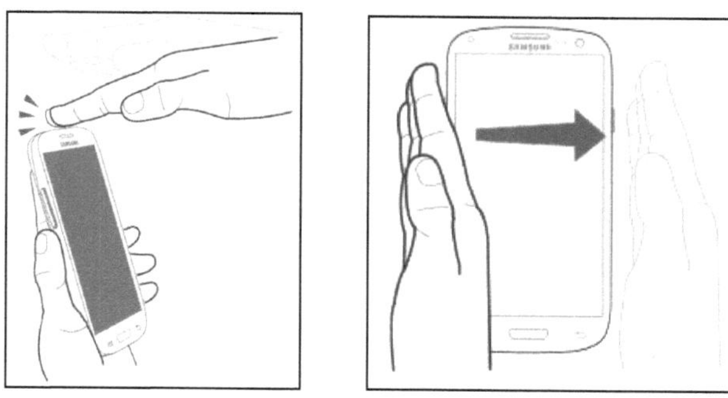

Fig. 2. Tap to top (left) and palm swipe for screen shots (right). (Source: Samsung Galaxy S III User Manual, p.24 and p. 25)

After using each feature, participants filled in the questionnaire with the following seven questions. The first six questions measured perceived ease of use, which were adapted from Post Study System Usability Questionnaire (PSSUQ) [7]. Q7 is the overall question to measure intention to use the feature [8]. The questionnaire was first translated into Chinese and then back translated into English. The wording was slightly adopted and five-point Likert scale was used.

- Q1: Overall, I am satisfied with how easy it is to use this feature.
- Q2: It was simple to use this feature.
- Q3: I was able to complete the tasks and scenarios quickly using this feature.
- Q4: I felt comfortable using this feature.
- Q5: It was easy to learn to use this feature.
- Q6: I believe I could become productive quickly using this feature.
- Q7: I intend to use this feature in the future.

4 Results and Discussion

Data were collected through questionnaire, interview, and videos. We first went through all the videos to develop a framework of errors. Then, we analyzed video through Noldus Observer XT 8.0 (shown in Figure 3). The results included the number of errors, outcomes of each error (i.e., work out independently, ask for help, and give up), and task completion time.

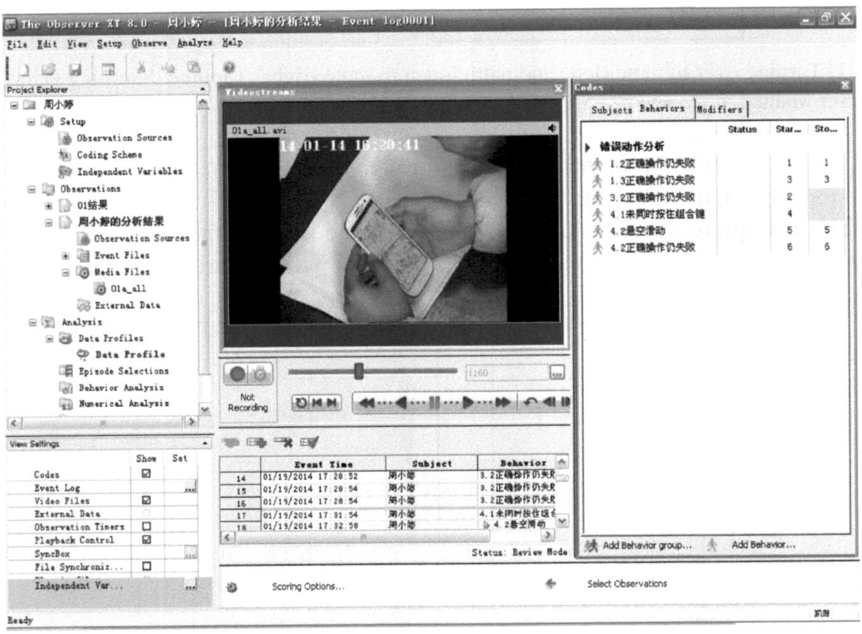

Fig. 3. The interface of data analysis using Noldus Observer XT 8.0

4.1 Finger Gesture Features

Pinch zooming is one of the most popular features of smart phones. Although it is intuitive and easy to learn, older adults may still make a lot of errors during their first-time usage.

As shown in Figure 4, participants who used pinch zooming accidently touched unrelated buttons (e.g., Home Button). They understood physical buttons relatively well, but they seemed to have difficulty in distinguishing on-screen buttons and dim buttons (e.g., Return Button and Setting Button). When participants accidently touched on-screen/dim buttons, they would complain that devices were too sensitive.

Another two frequently happened errors were zooming in and zooming out a photo too much. Participants tended to repeatedly pinch but failed to realize that the photo did not actually change. This is because there was no explicit hint showing that a photo was already at its largest/smallest size, and participants had to tell the differences in the photo before and after zooming. However, their attention was easily distracted by animations of zooming, and they seemed to perceive that animations of zooming indicated the differences in the photo, which in turn implied that the photo did not reach its smallest/largest size.

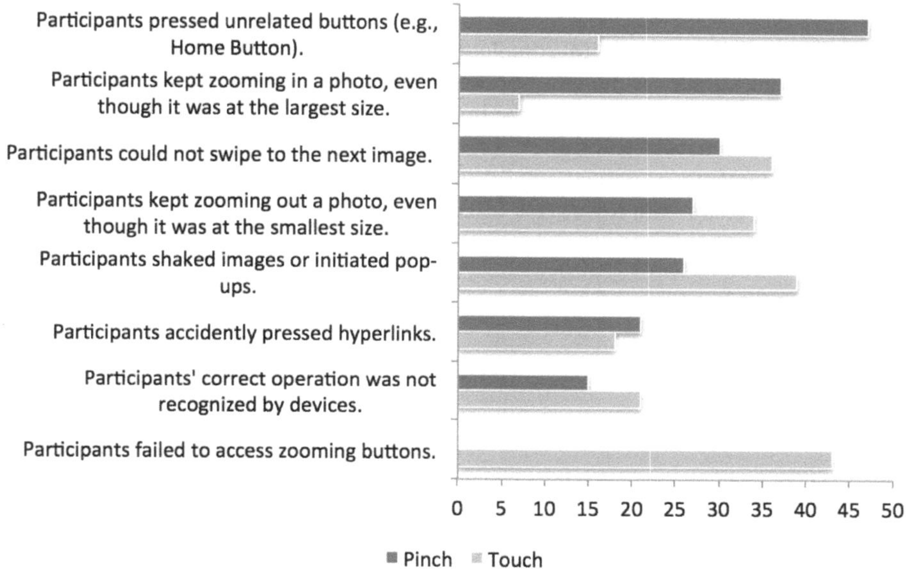

Fig. 4. Top six errors of pinch and touch in zooming tasks

Apart from this, participants had difficulties with swiping. Some participants did not zoom out the enlarged photo but directly swiped. They usually moved the photo around and got disoriented in the partial view within the enlarged photo. What made the disorientation even worse were the small movements of photos and pop-ups caused by participants' unstable hands.

Different from pinch, which does not require a specific input area, touch has the specific input area: zooming buttons. The smaller input area of touch reduces the possibility of pressing unrelated buttons. Despite of this advantage, touching a smaller input area also sets higher requirement for motor ability and thus resulted in more errors caused by unstable hands.

Regardless of touch or pinch, the third most frequent error was that certain participants could not swiped to the next page. The above-mentioned reasons for errors associated with pinch are also applicable to touch, and there is one more reason: pinch enables zooming based on any desired point of an image, while touch uses the central point of an image as the default base for zooming. This implies that participants who touched zooming buttons generally needed more movement of the image to view details.

Touch also caused a new problem: zooming buttons are usually hidden, and participants first needed to touch/drag the screen to access zooming buttons. Even if zooming buttons are accessed, they will quickly disappear again. This repeated process of accessing hidden zooming buttons was prone to errors, so it became the most frequently happened error associated with touch.

4.2 Hand Gesture Features

Participants took 58 minutes to complete this experiment on average. They made seven errors per minute. Although they were encouraged to independently figure out ways to overcome errors, they asked the instructor for help 15 times.

The number of success and failure for each trail was recorded, and task effectiveness was the percentage of successful trails out of all trails. As shown in Figure 5, gesture features resulted in lower task effectiveness than traditional features in task 3 (tap to top) and task 4 (screen shots).

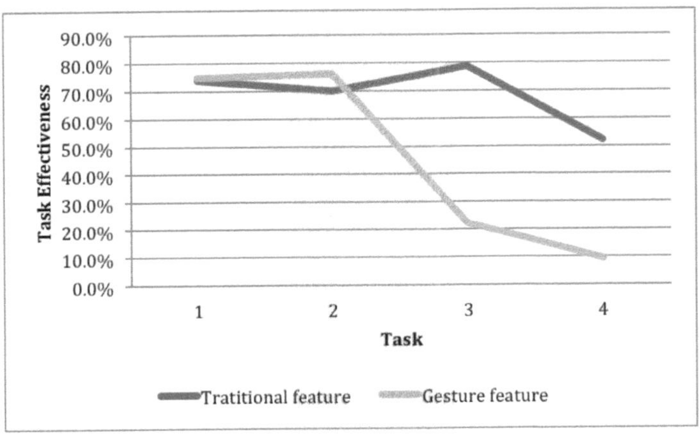

Fig. 5. Task effectiveness of tradtional features and gesture features

Consistent with results about task effectiveness, gesture features also resulted in more errors and longer task completion time in task 3 and task 4 (shown in Figure 6). In task 3, one error took up 78.9% of errors associated with the tap to top feature: participants' correct operation was not recognized. They tapped on the top of the phone twice, but the phone did not respond. Four participants made this error, and in the interview, three of them indicated that they may not use the tap to top feature in future but would stick to the traditional feature.

In task 4, one error took up 61.9% of errors associated with palm swipe: participants' palm did not touch the display during swiping. However, participants should not be blamed because both the physical manual and the interactive manual did not indicate the need to touch the display. Six participants made this error, but all of them indicated that they would like to use the palm swipe feature in the future. Another error took up 27.9% of errors associated with palm swipe: participants' entire palm covered the display.

In task 1 and task 2, errors were fewer than but similar to those in task 3 and task 4. Again, participants' correct operation was not recognized (turning over to mute: five times; palm touch to mute: 11 times; direct call: two times) and participants' palm did not touch the display (palm touch to mute: 25 times). Major errors associated with traditional features included touching unrelated buttons (six times) and combined operation of the home button and the power button (17 times).

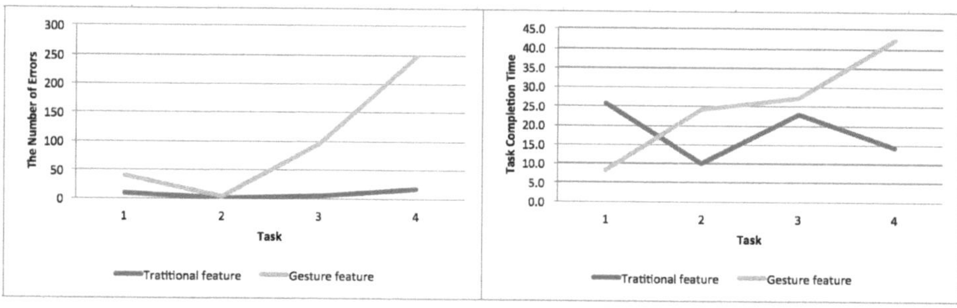

Fig. 6. The number of errors and task completion time

Despite of the above-mentioned errors, participants were generally positive towards both traditional features and gesture features of smart phones (shown in Figure 7). Their rating on intention to use features and perceived ease of use was not always consistent with their performance. Particularly, participants perceived the palm swipe feature easier to use and had higher usage intention compared with simultaneously pressing the home button and the power button.

To further unveil participants' real feeling behind the tendency of giving high ratings, the results of interview were analyzed. The most popular gesture features for participants were palm swipe for screen shots, followed by turning over to mute and palm touch to mute. Although they made errors when they used these gesture features, they preferred gesture features to traditional features in task 1 and task 4 as long as they learned how to use them. In contrast, they preferred traditional features to gesture features in task 2 and task 3. They indicated that the differences between traditional features and gesture features were not obvious and they would stick to their habit.

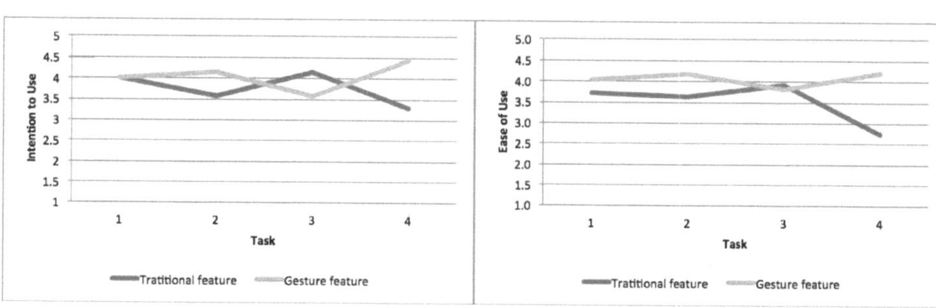

Fig. 7. Intention to use features and ease of using features

We also compared younger participants and older participants. Older participants' performance was slightly better than younger participants, and they had slightly more positive attitude towards new features. One possible reason is that two older participants' innovativeness (2.80 on the five-point Likert scale) was higher than that of younger participants (1.68).

5 Conclusion

This study investigated first-time user experience with new gesture control features in two experiments. The first experiment focused on new finger features for certain older adults and the second experiment focused on new hand features for certain younger adults and certain older adults. To examine the advantages/disadvantages of these gesture features, they were compared to traditional features. Based on the results, four main findings were derived:

First, older participants who used pinch zooming for the first time were prone to errors associated with touching unrelated buttons, in particular, on-screen buttons and dim buttons. Besides, they kept zooming in/out a photo even though it already reached its largest/smallest size. Practitioners may provide explicit feedback of the largest/smallest size of an image in a way that does not distract older adults' attention.

Second, participants who used palm gestures (i.e., palm swipe for screen shots and palm touch to mute) for the first time were prone to errors associated with floating swipe and entire palm touch. Manuals should specify the inappropriate distance from palm to the display and the inappropriate size of touch area.

Third, participants who used other three hand gestures (i.e., tap to top, turn over to mute, direct call) were prone to errors that participants' correct operation was not recognized. This error could easily result in the lost of users. Practitioners should take the variety of gestures into account to make the devices responsive and provide immediate feedback for wrong gestures.

Fourth, participants perceived their operation was correct as long as they followed instructions in the manuals. Instructions in physical and interactive manuals should provide detailed instruction to ensure initial success.

References

1. Zhou, J., Rau, P.L.P., Salvendy, G.: Older adults' text entry on smart phones and tablets: investigating effects of display size and input method on acceptance and performance. International Journal of Human-Computer Interaction (in press)
2. Hwangbo, H., Yoon, S.H., Jin, B.S., Han, Y.S., Ji, Y.G.: A study of pointing performance of elderly users on smartphones. International Journal of Human-Computer Interaction 29(9), 604–618 (2012)
3. Zhou, J., Rau, P.L.P., Salvendy, G.: A Qualitative Study of Older Adults' Acceptance of New Functions on Smart Phones and Tablets. In: Rau, P.L.P. (ed.) HCII 2013 and CCD 2013, Part I. LNCS, vol. 8023, pp. 525–534. Springer, Heidelberg (2013)
4. Zhou, J., Rau, P.L.P., Salvendy, G.: Age-related difference in the use of mobile phones. Universal Access in the Information Society, doi:10.1007/s10209-013-0324-1

5. Goldsmith, R.E., Hofacker, C.F.: Measuring consumer innovativeness. Journal of the Academy of Marketing Science 19(3), 209–221 (1991)
6. Samsung Galaxy S III User Manual, `http://www.samsung.com/us/support`
7. Lewis, J.R.: Psychometric evaluation of the PSSUQ using data from five years of usability studies. International Journal of Human-Computer Interaction 14(3-4), 463–488 (2002)
8. Zhou, J., Rau, P.L.P., Salvendy, G.: Older Adults' use of smart phones: An investigation of the factors influencing the acceptance of new functions. Behaviour & Information Technology, doi:10.1080/0144929X.2013.780637

Social Aspects and Implications of Cross-Cultural Design

Designing "Friendly" into Public Park for Taipei City

Li-Yu Chen[1,*], Ying-Ming Su[2], and Annie Chen[3]

[1] Department of Interior Design, Chung Yuan Christian University, Chung Li, Taiwan
chenly@cycu.edu.tw
[2] Department of Architecture, National Taipei University of Technology, Taipei, Taiwan
ymsu@ntut.edu.tw
[3] Graduate School of Commercial Design, Chung Yuan Christian University, Chung Li, Taiwan
annie928@ms22.hinet.net

Abstract. Taipei City has officially been selected the 2016 World Design Capital (WDC) this year, campaigning under the slogan "Adaptive City: Design in Motion". A successful design capital should demonstrate the different design thinking of the city. This study aimed to provide the value-added creation of friendly thinking through engineering techniques that emphasize the safety of public parks, thus forming the content of the creative design of Taipei City to develop characteristics that improve the city. First, this study investigated the functions and composition of public parks and the meaning of friendly design. The user-tool system model was applied to analyzed children playground in order to obtain the item of playground design need. Finally the friendly design guidelines for playgrounds are proposed according to entrance, perimeter containment, route, zones, equipment, signage, and surface materials.

Keywords: User Friendly, Playground, Park, Universal Design, User Center Design.

1 Introduction

Taipei City has officially been selected the 2016 World Design Capital (WDC) this year, campaigning under the slogan "Adaptive City: Design in Motion". A successful design capital should demonstrate the following through design thinking: (1) transform the design thinking from use to user to the perceptual field that creates the city; (2) transform the design thinking from function to feeling to the authenticity provided by the city; 3) transform the design thinking from high-tech to high-touch to the qualia that designs the city. In terms of the development of design, Taiwan demonstrated the core value of "the ultimate goal of incorporating design technology into arts and humanities". Therefore, modern designers need to blend the design thinking of emotional technology and humanized design to create humanized products and service environment with qualia [1].

Therefore, how to show care for product users from the humanized needs of users has become an important issue in current product design. In recent years, human

* Corresponding author.

P.L.P. Rau (Ed.): CCD/HCII 2014, LNCS 8528, pp. 275–286, 2014.

factors ergonomics has emphasized the "user-centered design" principle, which has gradually been valued by the public. The user-centered design principle refers to "a philosophy that emphasizes the usability and understandability of products according to the user's needs and interests". In other words, only the user-centered design principle can detect the overall problem between user-product-function and user-tool-environment. This finding is consistent with the "used by the great majority of people" advocated by "universal design".

While becoming a design capital, investigating how to enhance the humanized design of the open space in the city, in particular the friendly design of public parks, has become an important issue for obtaining a quality life through good park environment. This study specifically selected playgrounds in public parks to analyze environmental design from the perspective of user-centered design by transforming the needs of the technical aspect of universal design into the needs of the perceptual aspect of users, thus resulting in the expression aspect. The establishment of this model is completed from the user friendly design thinking of the effect aspect. User-centered thinking was used for design analysis, using friendly design to examine the overall structure and establish a public park friendly design model, thereby facilitating the authenticity and creating the perceptual field of the city.

2 User Friendly Design

User-friendly is a kind of design thinking which puts user as the main character , and user to be considered the center role during the design process from problem analysis, solving with techniques , achieving the goals. The process is also the solution of "user-accessible" furthermore is the basic of "universal design". Thus user-friendly-design can be thought as a process started with exploring the need of user, identifying the interface of user accessibility, outputting the solution as universal design.

It is imperative that the more people we design for, the more criteria should be fulfilled .By recognizing that design can play either an enabling or disabling role, it becomes possible to develop strategies that address the challenge of designing for the whole population. The Inclusive Design Cube, an outcome of the EPSRC-funded i~design research programmed, extends the pyramid into three capability dimensions to more fully represent the whole population and it proposes three related design approaches, which combined can address the needs of the whole population[2]. (Fig.1).

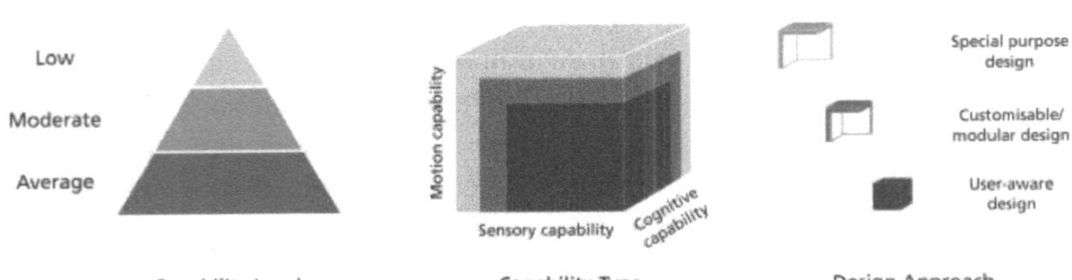

Fig. 1. The Inclusive Design Cube. (Source: John Clarkson, P., Coleman, R., History of Inclusive Design in the UK, Applied Ergonomics (2013) in press)

2.1 User Centered Design

“User-centered design” (UCD) is a broad term to describe design processes in which end-users influence how a design takes shape. It is both a broad philosophy and variety of methods [3].

“user-centered design” originated by Donald Norman in the 1980s, he suggested four basic suggestions on how a design should be:

- Make it easy to determine what actions are possible at any moment.
- Make things visible, including the conceptual model of the system, the alternative actions, and the results of actions.
- Make it easy to evaluate the current state of the system.
- Follow natural mappings between intentions and the required actions; between actions and the resulting effect; and between the information that is visible and the interpretation of the system state [4].

2.2 Accessible Design

Accessible design means designing products such that both individuals with and without disabilities can use them. This includes people with vision, hearing, mobility, cognitive and other impairments, as well as anyone who might be experiencing a temporary disability due to an illness or accident. Accessible design also accounts for the elderly population, which is generally characterized by a gradual loss of ability of some sort. Accessible design also ensures effective implementation of technology in a variety of environments or conditions that would cause individuals who are not normally impaired to be temporally impaired [5].

Accessibility is the degree to which a product, device, service, or environment is available to as many people as possible. Accessibility can be viewed as the "ability to access" and benefit from some system or entity. The concept often focuses on people with disabilities or special needs and their right of access, enabling the use of assistive technology.

2.3 Universal Design

Universal Design involves designing products and spaces so that they can be used by the widest range of people possible. Universal Design goes further by recognizing that there is a wide spectrum of human abilities. Everyone, even the most able-bodied person, passes through childhood, periods of temporary illness, injury and old age. By designing for this human diversity, we can create things that will be easier for all people to use. The term Universal Design was coined by Ronald L. Mace. In 1997, Ron Mace collaborated with a group of architects, product designers, engineers and environmental designers to develop the Seven Principles of Universal Design. The seven principles of Universal Design are: Equitable Use, Flexibility in Use, Simple and Intuitive Use, Perceptible Information, Tolerance for Error, Low Physical Effort, Size and Space for Approach and Use [6].

3 Public Parks in Taipei city

3.1 Definition of Public Parks

Public parks are a green environment that provides the public with outdoor cultivation, appreciation, entertainment, recreation, and exercising. Since public parks are located in populated areas, they are closely associated with the daily lives of people. Public parks usually have a specific scope, entrance, area, and facilities for recreation, entertainment, and exercising. The quantity, area, and green ratio of public parks have become an important index for demonstrating urban development and quality of life of people. People's motives to visit natural areas and the various activities they carry out reflect the demands people place on natural areas, and the needs they expect to be fulfilled. [7].

When establishing a holistic care living environment, the user needs and safety of people with reduced mobility, senior citizens, women, and children need to be considered in public parks planning. The friendly design concept is applied to public parks and related facilities so that everyone can make use of public parks safely and conveniently, thus expanding the humanized care of design to various aspects. Therefore, the environmental friendly issue of public parks in Taipei was observed to establish friendly design evaluation items from the age appropriateness, entrance, understandability of instructions, diversity of activity behavior, richness of entertainment functions, to environmental safety and health.

3.2 Public Parks in Taipei City

Taipei city urban planning consists of 1,068 parks, green fields, squares, and children's playgrounds with a total area of 1,984 hectares. As of the end of 2012, 838 areas have been completed with an area of approximately 1,367 hectares. Each citizen has up to an average of 5.113 m2 of parks and green fields based on the population of 2,673,226 of Taipei City [8].

The scope and functions of public parks in Taipei City are divided into natural parks, comprehensive parks, neighborhood parks, and riverside parks. Among which, the environment of natural parks have complete natural resources. The priority of natural parks is to preserve natural resources, setting up only basic facilities such as trails, chairs and benches, and interpretive signs to preserve animal and plant resources. Comprehensive parks are larger and mainly targets all citizens of the city; therefore, this type of parks offer the most variety of facilities such as activity centers, sports fields, and swimming pools and others to satisfy the recreational needs of tourists. Neighborhood parks are smaller and located in the alleys of communities; its main design purpose is to satisfy the needs of local residents. Riverside parks simplify and greening riversides with large areas in accordance with river improvement projects to establish various sports fields, ice rinks, and bicycle trails, etc.

The basic composition of public parks includes entrance, route, user zones, buildings, facilities, and signs. Neighborhood parks have trails, trash can, recreational facilities, playground equipment, decorative facilities, and signs, etc. In addition to the aforementioned facilities, large-scale community parks have washing facilities, restrooms, and sports facilities, etc. Metropolitan parks should have administrative offices, public payphones, and warning signs in addition to the aforementioned.

3.3 Playground in Public Parks

The development of public playgrounds in Taiwan can be divided into four stages according to the main materials used for playgrounds and the development of children's entertainment environment: cement and concrete products, iron and steel products, wooden products, and plastic products. Children's playgrounds in Taiwan originated from the 1960s. Due to the high durability towards the use of cement and concrete products during that period, parks were filled with facilities made from cement. In the 1970s, due to the massive use of iron and steel materials, steel pipes became the basic component for making playground equipment. Therefore, facilities are styled using the characteristics of steel pipes' susceptibility for processing to crop and bend steel pipes by welding screw locking to complete the assembly. This gives facilities more variety of changes and more flexibility compared to that of cement and concrete products. From the 1980s to 1990s, the demand for imported logs and square-shaped wood was the reason why outdoor and indoor playgrounds during that time were mostly made from imported timber and hardwood by locking screws. Therefore, that period was also known as the wilderness playground period. The playground equipment such as slides (except for chutes), swings, climbing frames, and horizontal hanging ladders during that time were mostly made from wooden materials. Due to the development of plastics technology from the 1990s to the past 20 years, contemporary fiberglass reinforced plastics (FRP) and polyvinylchloride (PVC) were used for the mass production of playground equipment in numerous parks due to their durability and colorfulness [9]. Prefabricated materials were used to assemble a variety of playground equipment (Fig.2). Mass production benefits the quality of standardized products while destroying the uniqueness of playground designs.

Fig. 2. The four stage of playground development in Taiwan

Children's playgrounds are mainly composed of the following: billboards (instruction signs), fences, entrance, route, playground equipment, and pavements. Playground equipment can be divided, according to movements, into the following:

balancing, climbing, sliding, swinging, and rotating facilities. The most commonly seen are balance beams, climbing and upper body equipment, horizontal (overhead) ladders, sliding poles, slides, seesaws, spring rockers, and swings, etc.

4 Current Issues of Public Playground

4.1 Accessible or Inclusive

Accessible is defined as: "easy to approach, reach, enter, speak with or use." The synonyms include words such as: available, reachable, attainable, operative, open, unrestricted. Inclusive is defined as: "all encompassing, all embracing" or "covering everything or everyone." The listed synonyms are: broad, comprehensive, all together, global, sweeping, whole. When we use them to describe playgrounds, we should be describing two different types of environments and conditions [10].

An accessible playground is one where everyone can go around by foot or using a mobility device. An accessible playground should fulfill the following requirements: no barriers at the entrance or along pathways, use ramps to lead up to upper decks, a wheelchair user can access the play equipment.

An inclusive playground is one that has an aim to make it not only accessible, but to encourage and enable children to engage with one another. A playground needs to be accessible, but that an accessible playground is not always inclusive.

An inclusive playground addresses the needs of all people including those who have disabilities. An inclusive playground accommodates everyone and challenges them at their own developmental level. An inclusive playground should fulfill the following requirements: play activity is accessible and usable for all, Include different types of play, have a mix of physical, sensory, and social activities.

4.2 Playground Issues Existing in Taiwan

There are some problems existing in parks of Taiwan which are: playground sites not being obvious, wrong choice of play equipment, lack of playground instruction, unsafe entrance, lack of security fence, insufficient use zone, unsafe surface material [11-12] .These issues can be analyzed with S-A-F-E system, abbreviation from (S)safety of play activity, (A)accessible of playground, (F)fair of use, (E)easy for user(Fig.3).

- Safety

The "safety" issues includes: Fall height of play equipment, entrapment hazards of play equipment, safety use zone, impact absorbing safety surface, playground fence.

- Accessible

The "accessible" issues including: entrance of park, map of playground, the route from park entrance to playground, entrance of playground, path between play equipment and accessible of play equipment.

- Fair of use

The "fair of use" issues includes: variety kinds of play activity, age appropriate play area, play need of disability child, reasonable quantity of toilet.

- Easy for user

The "easy for user" issues includes: instruction for use, easy usability, scale of play equipment, scale of play space, ancillary facilities of playground (toilet, sink, Water dispenser)

Fig. 3. S-A-F-E issues of playground

5 Human System Design Module

Much of the research organization and design philosophy follows a user-tool system design model presented by Kreifeldt (1974) and reproduced in Fig4. Fig.4 details the various influences and interactions in a user-tool system and in particular emphasizes the three-fold objects of the design: man, tool (product), task; the two interfaces: the user-tool interface (manipulation), and the tool-task interface (engagement), and a number of interactions in the system [13].

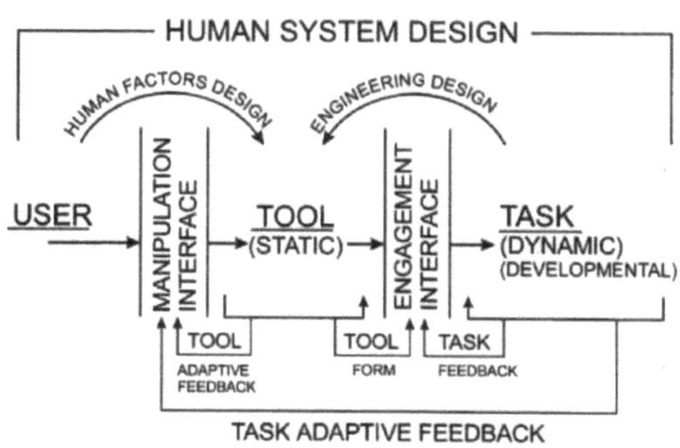

Fig. 4. User-tool system design. (source: R. Lin, J.G. Kreifeldt / International Journal of Industrial Ergonomics 27 (2001) 259-269)

The purpose of the product design is to satisfy the user by product and accomplish a task by tools (work). The user-tool (manipulation) interface combine user and tool through human factors design, and the tool-task (engagement) interface combine tool and task through engineering design. Manipulation interface is the focus consideration in human factors and also user-friendly consideration. The engagement interface is the focus consideration in engineering design and technology consideration.

Chen & Lin (2006) analyzed playground design by using User Tool System Module, " playground user" was applied in human factor design and "task of play" was applied in engineering design in order to get the "playground design" outcome.This research find out: the assessment of "user" including: sex, age, ergonomic, Physiological function, psychological function, favorite, special need. the assessment of "playground" including : fun, operation, ecology, production, aesthetic, humanity. The assessment of "task" including: Physical Activity, sociology, language, psychological development, environment sensitive, proper reaction. The assessment of "manipulation interface" including: play process, circulation, activity, approach, expansion, default uses. The assessment of "engagement interface" including: expression, operation, connection, safety, maintain [14].

6 User-Friendly Design Guidelines for Public Playground

Most of playgrounds are consisted of entrance, perimeter containment, path, signage, equipment, use zone and its surface material, after checking these parts through user-tool system module some guidelines obtained to planning a friendlier playground.

6.1 Entrance

Connecting the inside and outside of playground, Entrance play a role to orient people to the playground. The entrance area to the playground space should familiarize children with play space layout, features, and activities before they arrive in the play space.

- Orientation - The orientation effects of landscaping can be used here to good effect.
- Acclimatize - This space should allow people to acclimatize to the environment.
- Visual care -There should be a low level of visual, and a clear line of sight from the entry way into the play space in order to let parent can care their child by visual.
- Flat level & ramp-There should be a flat ground level or ramp in entrance area for young children and wheelchair users.

6.2 Perimeter Containment

Perimeter boundary around the play space should be created by using walls, fences, landscape. A gate at the entry is to ensure the ones play safe. The gates need to be designed so that it can't open by a child, but should be operated by an adult.

- Boundary define - Consider designs that make the fence be a clearly boundary.
- Safety protect- Consider play activity protection for children safety.

- Visual penetrate- allow parents or caregivers to keep track of children as they move throughout the playground environment.
- Identifiable openings - Have a few clearly identifiable openings. The location and direction of the orientation path will help identify these openings.

6.3 Path

An orientation path that surrounds the play area allows users to survey the different activities without engaging in them.

- Observation- lets a child to decide whether to participate or not.
- Accessible- route is defined as a pathway which designed to provide access for individuals with disabilities, including those who use wheelchairs or mobility devices, with a minimum clear width distance of 1500 mm and a maximum slope of 1:20 [15].
- Identification- Delineate where the path ends and the play area begins by providing a visual or tactile cue.
- Consistent –use same colors or textures to keep the path be consistent.

6.4 Zoning

Area zoning will allow fewer opportunities for accidents to occur, and will also encourage children to use the playground in a suitable way.

- Age appropriate- playgrounds intended to serve children of all ages, the layout of pathways and the play area should show the distinct areas for the different age groups.
- Buffer-The areas should be separated by a buffer zone, which could be an area with shrubs or benches for parent or caregiver.
- Safety-This separation and buffer zone will reduce the chance of injury from older, more active children running through areas filled with younger children with generally slower movement and reaction times.

6.5 Equipment

When selecting playground equipment, it is important to know the age range of the children who will be using the playground. Children at different ages and stages of development have different needs and abilities.

- Accessible-providing play equipment that is accessible to children with disabilities and encourages integration within the playground.
- Age appropriate-Playgrounds should be designed to stimulate children and encourage them to develop new skills, but should be in scale with their sizes, abilities, and developmental levels.

- Encourage development-Play components should be chosen carefully to engage multiple senses, develop skills and encourage social interaction.
- Fare of use-Play components are to be linked to an accessible route through the playground. One of each type of play component is to be accessible.

Some playground equipment may causing high dangerous injury, are not recommended for use on public playgrounds, including: Trampolines, Swinging gates, Giant strides, Climbing ropes that are not secured at both ends, Heavy metal swings, Multiple occupancy swings, Rope swings [16].

6.6 Signage

Signs and Labels around playground equipment are used to provide safety information. Some signs are for information, some are for warning, and some are for user education. The signs and labels typically contain theses information as follows [17]:

1. Information signs: (1) Manufacturer's Identification (2) Age appropriateness (3) Supervision recommendation (4) Ideal surfacing depth markers (Recommended)
2. Warning signs: (1) Removal of helmets, drawstrings, or accessories around the neck (2) Hot play surfaces (3) Hard Surfaces
3. User education: (1) Rules (Recommended)(2) General Information (Recommended)(3) Street Signs (Recommended)

- Safety-Signage with a plan view of the area and a site map defining individual site features and activities should be provided for larger play spaces.
- Age appropriate- use diagrams instead of words will let information more clear for children.
- Easy for user-Signs should be brief and to the point. Multi-language or diagram in signs can be more effective.

6.7 Surface Material

Playground surface is the material that lies directly beneath and around playground equipment. There are two categories of surfacing material: unitary and loose. Unitary Surfacing Material is a manufactured material used for protective surfacing in the use zone that may be rubber tiles, mats, that forms a unitary shock absorbing surface. Loose-Fill Surfacing Material is material used for protective surfacing in the use zone that consists of loose particles (i.e. engineered wood fiber and rubber mulch). Tiles made of rubber composite are widely used as a protective surfacing against head injury in playgrounds since they have good climate resistance and low maintenance costs [17].

- Safety-Both of the two kinds of materials are suitable for protect child's safety
- Accessible- accessible surfacing should be firm, stable and slip resistant enough to be accessible by individuals using mobility aids or wheelchairs. if Loose-Fill Surfacing Material is used for protective surfacing ,special panel could be used for the path for wheelchair user.

- Aesthetic- a user friendly playground its surfaces should designed with aesthetic thinking to please the user.

7 Conclusion

Friendly design is both a user-center concept and concept to satisfy the most of peoples. After analyze the playground through user-tool system design model, design guidelines was proposed through design demands about safety, fair, easy, universal. The study found: a friendly playground design should consider comprehensively various factors such as the environment safety, approach accessible, play quality, and aesthetics, which will enhance the city adaptivity from a friendly park playground design thinking.

References

1. Lin, R.T.: Design 2266 In Taiwan product design year book2013-2014. Sungood Publications, Taipei (2013) (in Chinese)
2. John Clarkson, P., Coleman, R.: History of Inclusive Design in the UK, Applied Ergonomics (2013), http://dx.doi.org/10.1016/j.apergo.2013.03.002
3. Abras, C., Maloney-Krichmar, D., Preece, J.: User-Centered Design. In: Berkshire Encyclopedia of Human-Computer Interaction: When Science Fiction Becomes Science Fact, vol. 2, pp. 763–768 (2004)
4. Norman, D.: The design of everyday things, p. 188. Doubleday, New York (1988)
5. Definition of Accessible Design (n.d.): http://www.ittatc.org/technical/litreview/d.php (retrieved December 25, 2013)
6. Universal Design Definition and Principles. (n.d.): Center for Universal Design, College of Design, North Carolina State University, http://www.design.ncsu.edu/cud/about_ud/udprinciples.htm (retrieved December 25, 2013)
7. Chiesura, A.: The role of urban parks for the sustainable city. Landscape and Urban Planning 68(1), 129–138 (2004)
8. Taipei city planning and parks, green spaces, playground, square reservations. Parks and Street Lights Office, Public Works Department, Taipei City Government (May 30, 2013), http://pkl.taipei.gov.tw/ct.asp?xItem=1000849&CtNode=46922&mp=106011 (retrieved December 25, 2013)
9. Chen, L.Y.: The safety management of children playground, p. 39. Lio-ho Publications, Taipei (2009) (in Chinese)
10. Kaplan, M.: Accessible vs Inclusive (2003), http://www.pgpnewscenter.com/columnist/mara-kaplan/accessible-vs-inclusive (retrieved November 25, 2013)
11. Ting, H.C., Sun, T.Y., Chang, L.T.: An Study on Early Childhood Pre-service Teachers' Perception of Kindergarten's Outdoor Playground Safety. Chia Nan Annual Bulletin: Humanity (34), 665–675 (2008) (in Chinese)
12. Chen, C.L.: The risk management of play equipment in park. Journal of Children Sport Play (1), 60–68 (2005) (in Chinese)

13. Lin, R.T., Kreifeldt, J.G.: Ergonomics in Wearable Computer Design. International Journal of Industrial Design 27, 259–269 (2001)
14. Chen, L.Y., Lin, R.T.: The Human System Module Applied in Playground Design. In: Proceeding of EST 2006 (2006)
15. City of Toronto, Accessibility Design Guidelines, p. 25 (2004)
16. U.S. Consumer Product Safety Commission, Public playground safety handbook, Maryland, p. 7 (2010)
17. Signs and labels in The Play and Playground Encyclopedia (n.d.): `http://www.pgpedia.com/s/signs-and-labels#footnote1j6bcq61` (retrieved November 25, 2013)
18. Huang, T.J., Chang, L.T.: Design and evaluation of shock-absorbing rubber tile for playground safety. Materials & Design 30(9), 3819–3823 (2009)

Design for Social Interaction in Public Spaces

Jun Hu, Joep Frens, Mathias Funk, Feng Wang, and Yu Zhang

Department of Industrial Design, Eindhoven University of Technology Den Dolech 2, 5612AZ Eindhoven, The Netherlands
j.hu@tue.nl

Abstract. The merge of the Web of People and the Internet of Things leads to a shift from technology-push product or system oriented design to data-driven service centric design. The growth and development of social computing have dramatically increased the complexity but also offer new opportunities and solutions in the societal context. We look into the challenges in designing for social interaction in public spaces, in particular in cities and professional environments. With several examples in designing interactive public installations, we present the design techniques and practices used in these examples, as well as the evaluation methods that have been found to be useful in evaluating the user experience such as social connectedness and inclusion.

1 Introduction

In the era of social networking and computing, the merge of the Web of People and the Internet of Things leads to a shift from technology-push product or system oriented design to data-driven service centric design. Products have become the terminals of the services and systems have become the platforms to deliver the services. Social computing started in late 1990's and early 2000's serving as platforms not only for sharing online content and conversation, but also for processing the content of social interaction and feeding back into systems [1], driven by a flattened and bottom-up social structure. The growth and development of social computing have dramatically increased the complexity, on other hand, bring up new solutions against the complexity, towards social innovation, by harvesting the collective intelligence from the Web of People, including the designers, the users and the organizations, and the collective intelligence from the Internet of Things, in order to realize greater value from the interaction among people and things, which in turn, inventing innovative and hopefully also sustainable ways of living.

In this paper we will look into the challenges brought up by social computing, in designing for social interaction in public spaces, in particular in cities and professional environments. Currently the cities are coming to life in the digital world. How this digital city becomes meaningful to us remains to be seen but the first signs point towards visual solutions that augment the buildings, bridges, statues etc [2]. The augmented layer can be used as decoration, but also as public media where the social interactivity can take pace. One of the ways to approach these challenges is for example interactive public installations. The current development in digital public installations

P.L.P. Rau (Ed.): CCD/HCII 2014, LNCS 8528, pp. 287–298, 2014.

involves a significant amount of new carriers in not only material, but also in technology, resulting new dynamic and interactive forms that require the artists and designers to construct their work from a system view and with a good understanding of human-system interaction. It is no longer about carving stones and casting bronze; it is time to sculpture the interactive experience with the public participation [3, 4].

With several design cases of interactive public installations, we will not only present the design techniques and practices of these examples, but also try to present our attempts in evaluating the experience of interacting with the installations, such as the feeling of social connectedness and inclusion.

2 Design Cases

2.1 Moon Rising from Sea

This installation is designed for the city of Taicang, China. The installation is roughly 10 by 10 meters on its base and 8 meters high. On top of the base are constructions that give the impressions of a large sail, and the moon rising from the waves. On the surface of the sail are reliefs of Taicang's sea culture. Images, animations and videos can be projected onto the inner surface of sail in the evenings (Fig. 1). One of the concepts to utilize this platform is to allow the public to contribute their photos from social media, for an interactive photo show, to induce the feeling of social connectedness [5-7], and to reinstate the historical values of Taicang as port to the world.

Fig. 1. Moon rising from sea

2.2 Leave Your Mark

With the installation "Leave your mark", people can "draw" and leave their mark behind on the public space, to express themselves (Fig. 2). The concept involves projection mapping to digitally augment buildings. A person walks by, grabs a piece of "chalk" and starts drawing or writing on it, leaving their mark. In some locations the installation will be provided with a camera. The feed of this camera will be projected onto the installation at another location. If a person walks by this second location, she could possibly see someone, a complete stranger, leaving the mark on the first installation. The goal is to increase feelings of inclusion and connectedness of the citizens of the city to each other and to the public space they are in [5].

Fig. 2. Leave your mark

2.3 CONNECT

Nowadays professional social connections are mostly maintained in the digital world using e-mail or social media. The use of these media is less personal and therefore less confrontational. CONNECT is a tool which a participant shows her attending by presenting a designed badge from an event to a wall and shares her professional connections in the digital social networks to other participants (Fig. 3). By means of this information, it triggers conversations among the participants [8]. Sensors are used to detect the badges and projection mapping techniques are used to leave portraits and to create lines representing connections from social media.

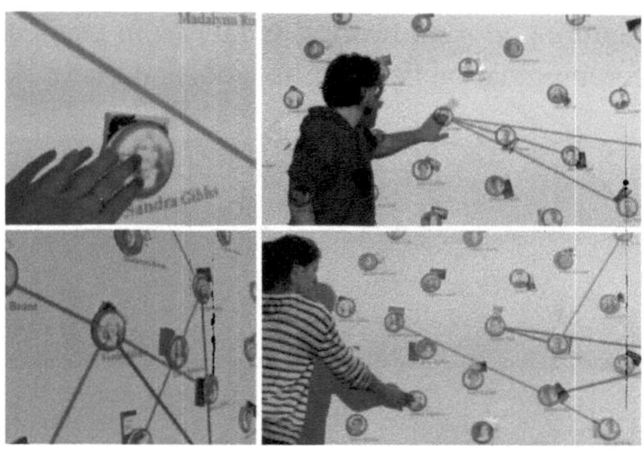

Fig. 3. CONNECT

2.4 Flink

FLink is a service that motivates people in a public shared and flexible work space to have more social interaction. It is a combination of physical objects (tokens and the Meeting Point), and a Mix & Match service (Fig. 4). The token is part of the check-in system at the entrance. The Meeting Point is the (eye height) physical object located next to the coffee machine. By fitting the token to the Meeting Point with its "Mix" side, photos of the other flexible workers with complementary expertise will show up in the cells of the Meeting Point. By fitting with the "Match" side, the token will show matching expertise of the others [9]. Sensors are used to detect the tokens and their sides, and back projection is used to display matching or mixing profiles.

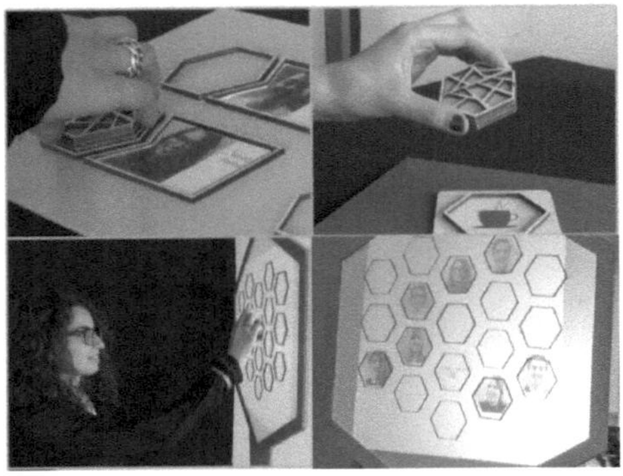

Fig. 4. Flink

2.5 Blobulous

Blobulous allows participants to interact through projected avatars, which react to their movement and body signals (Fig. 5). Blobulous uses a large public display to show abstract avatars, blobs of dots, one for each participant and moving around slowly. The movement is connected to the participant's movement. The participant's heart rate is mapped to the color of her avatar. The mapped colors range from blue (cold, low engagement) to red (warm, high engagement) [7, 10]. Wireless heart rate sensors are used to capture and send heart rate data from users and a Zigbee network is created to handle communication between sensors and the projected avatars.

Fig. 5. Blobulous

2.6 Oeco

Oeco (Office ecosystem) links the individual work space to a common room by sharing the pictures on social media in an artistic manner (Fig. 6). These pictures are represented by dandelions. A user can be immersed in his work; other people can see the crawling dandelion from outside the working cell and it is better not to disturb. The florets of the dandelions follow the user when coming to the common room.

When people meet, their dandelions blows up and come together, opens into shared pictures among them, to trigger their memories and conversations [11]. These dandelions are displayed within a screen, or projected into the walls or furniture when floating away or towards theses screens using projection mapping techniques.

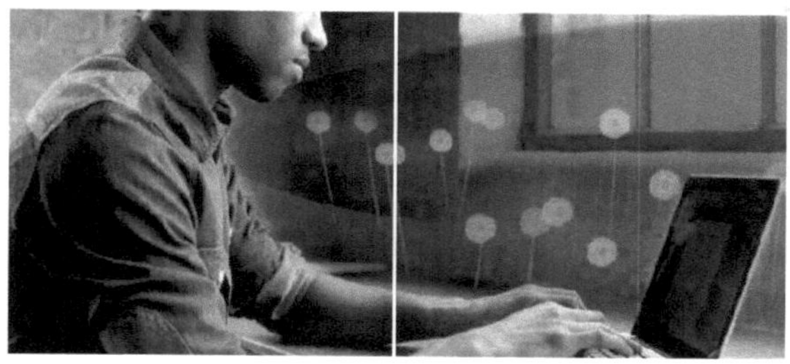

Fig. 6. Oeco

2.7 Strijp-T-ogether

Strip T is an old industrial area rebuilt to accommodate and foster creative industries. However there is hardly any social interaction among people from different companies. Strijp-T-ogether is designed to stimulate the social interaction. It consists of a mobile platform and a projection in the main entrance hall (Fig. 7). The photo of a space is used on the mobile as the background and an addition can be made by drawing or adding other graphical objects. These additions will be projected into the space and will also be shown on the mobile of the others as background. People can then react on each other's drawings and additions to trigger social interaction [12].

Fig. 7. Strijp-T-ogether

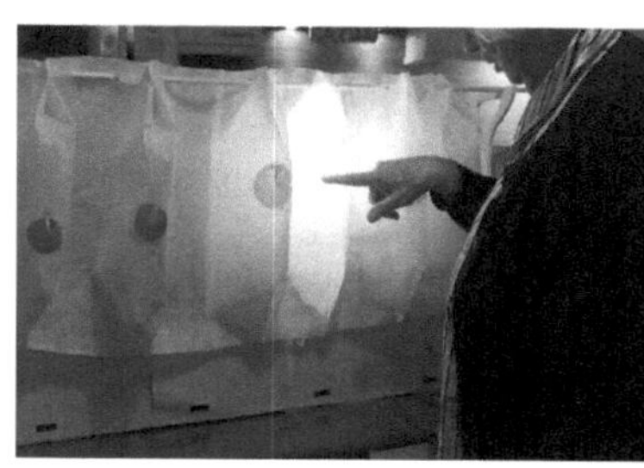

Fig. 8. Delightia

2.8 Delightia

Next to providing social experience, public installations may also have a specific purpose for a target user group. Inspired by the lighting, music and reminiscence theapies, this design is to use light and sound to help the elderly to get rid of dull and passive feelings at an elderly care center (Fig. 8). By interacting with the installation, the dementia elderly perceive the stimuli that resemble their memories of natural lighting and the sound of water drops with calm background sound of a brook [13]. Interacting together or observing the others interacting may trigger conversations among the elderly themselves or between the elderly and the caregivers.

3 Techniques and Practices

In the design process of above mentioned projects, many design techniques were found to be useful. These techniques are summarized in the following, but it is not our attention to make an exhaustive list of useful design techniques for designing social interaction in public spaces. Rather, we share our experience and observations in applying these techniques in a real-life context with intercultural design teams.

3.1 Inspired by Cultures

The projects "Moon rising from sea", "Leave your mark", CONNECT, Flink and Oeco are direct or indirect results of the international workshops "Interactive Patina of Culture" (IPoC), in Taicang, China, by Eindhoven University of Technology and Jiangnan University in 2013 [14]. The concept of IPoC is in the space between cultural studies, experience design and human-computer interaction. In interaction design we know that culture matters [15, 16]. "Patina" conveys the understanding that time and use of artifacts will result in ageing, in becoming closer to the person and cultural identity of the user, also known as "graceful ageing". It is however not limited to the designed artifacts: design practice and the designer will – over time – work in, with, and for a cultural context. The assignment of the workshop was to design a series of interactive public installations and the concept of IPoC acted as a mechanism to bring qualities of the two cultures together.

3.2 Inspired by Traditional Dynamic Arts

Dynamic art forms and interactive public installations have much in common: both have a time core to drive the dynamics; both have to manage inside a public space and the space has to be carefully structured for functions and interactions; both have to accommodate active or passive participants with different roles and goals. Traditional dynamic arts have much to offer and it is time to explore how the elements and techniques could contribute to interaction design. During the IPoC workshops, one of the efforts was paid to apply performance techniques and elements from dynamic art forms in the design process and to investigate how the installation would blossom when approached from a performance art perspective that essentially includes the users as well as a broader physical or social context [17, 18].

3.3 Sensitizing Workshops

Designing in inter-cultural teams is a challenge, not only to align the content-wise aspects of the design task at hand, but more so the way of working together. Every design process has phases that go smoothly, but also phases that need focus, perseverance and determination. While this can be already hard for design teams that share a cultural background, intercultural communication complicates this issue. Professional intercultural design cannot be taught or learned in a short amount time. Explicit interest in socio-cultural aspects of design is needed so that mixed design teams can fluently work together. Establishing a common ground for understanding and reducing potential friction simply by bringing team members closer together will help.

One approach, called "sensitizing workshops", is to facilitate a low-threshold design activity that combines several related (technical) aspects of a more serious design task to be executed later on with an exploration of senses. The reason is two-fold: (1) techniques, technology and materials to be used later on can be tried in an explicitly low-risk setting, and (2) exploration of senses uses the human body and how we feel and naturally act as a "natural" common ground for discussion and collaborative design. The combination is a short workshop that involves the design team on many levels, but also anchors their shared experiences in a positive common achievement.

During the IPoC workshops, this technique was introduced early on and resulted in significantly more momentum and better results during the first phases, which led to conceptually deeper results in the end, improved the overall confidence of team members and established a natural flow of activities as all team members understood their strengths and weaknesses better which allowed them to make better decisions.

3.4 Cardboard Modelling

Installations in public spaces are three dimensional, or if we take time into account because of the dynamic nature of interaction, four dimensional. Cardboard modelling, especially when integrated with advanced mechanical and electronic techniques and components, is a powerful tool for tangible or rich interaction [19, 20]. In the IPoC workshops, this was the key technique used for exploring and demonstrating design space and the concepts. Fig. 9 shows the cardboard models of earlier concept of "Moon rising from sea" (left) and "Leave your mark" (right).

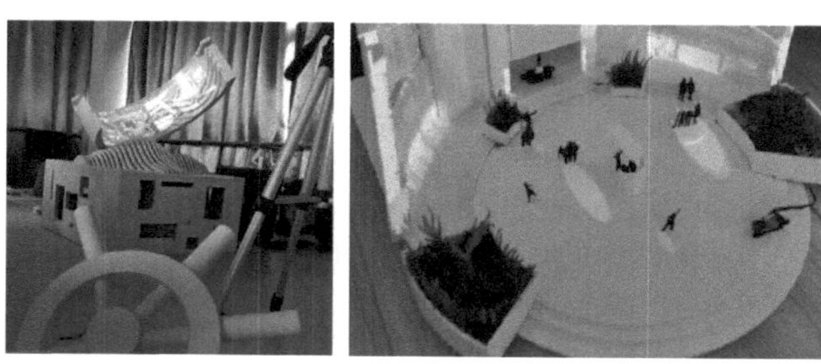

Fig. 9. Cardboard modelling

3.5 Acting Out

When designing for social interaction in public spaces, the interactive nature of the design requires conceptualizing, visualizing and communicating the dynamics of the interaction. The integration of industrial design processes and software design processes is often necessary [15, 21]. The acting-out design approach [22] utilizes the designers body to simulate the elements and the behavior of the design, providing and communicating the insights at earlier stages of a design process when a prototype is not yet available. It may also provide a good bridge that helps to make the transition from a general concept to an engineering level smoother. This approach is used in the the IPoC workshops in projects such as Flink, CONNECT and StrijP-T-ogether.

3.6 Video Prototyping

High-fidelity prototyping of installations in a large scale or for a big or busy public space is often costly and challenging, if not impossible. Video prototyping allows the designers to create simulation of the installation and the interaction using simple materials and equipment [23]. Interface elements can be created using paper, cardboards, pens, acetates and other materials, allowing for experiencing the interaction by viewing the video simulation at earlier stages of the design with minimal requirements of resources and materials. This technique was used in the conceptual phase of both Strijp-T-ogether and Oeco.

A combination of video prototyping and acting out can be also used in context with the help of portable projectors: prepared video prototypes are projected onto artifacts and objects in the real-life context using projection-mapping techniques. This serves as documentation for evaluation, but also as input for further design iterations.

4 User Experience Evaluation

Here it is not to extensively review the literature how user experience shall be evaluated in public spaces. Instead, we present the methods that were used for evaluation in the projects mentioned earlier and that were found to be handy for designers.

4.1 Qualitative Methods

Mood Boards. They are often used at the conceptual phase to generate ideas and concepts that is after certain styles or the overall "feel" that the designers are trying to achieve. But in the project Delightia it is also found to be useful to reflect the user's emotion and attitude towards certain concepts or products, especially when the users find it difficult to express themselves [13]. In the evaluation of Delightia, participants in the evaluation were asked to make choices from a restricted selection of images for certain aspects, which gave a good insight of how they felt about the design.

Interviews with Experiential Prototypes. Interactive installations for public spaces have to be experienced in the actual space for the users to understand the design and to give valuable input or feedback. In the project Flink, prototypes from the iterations were placed in the targeting environment and controlled in a manner of Wizard of OZ. Users in the environment are interviewed after they have experienced the design for their input for next iteration of the design [9]. In the project Delightia, it would be impossible for the elderly with dementia to image the design without a prototype in place, although it was easily understood by the caregivers. Interviewing the elderly without actually experiencing the prototype would have been an effort in vain [13].

Co-reflection. In the project Strijp-T-ogether, co-reflection was used as a qualitative and constructive approach on evaluating whether the installation triggers social interaction [12]. Co-reflection can be defined as a "collaborative critical thinking process involving cognitive and affective interactions between individuals who explore their experiences to reach new intersubjective understandings" [24]. "Co-reflection sessions can be developed in three parts: exploration on the current situation, ideation through a discovery process and confrontation between users and designers. Each part builds upon the next" [25].

Observations in Context. It is important to observe in the context when design for public spaces in order to understand the situations and to get a good grasp of the problems to be solved or the opportunities to be identified. Observations can be done by not only the designers themselves, but also the users [12], the experts [13] and other stakeholders [9, 12] by giving them explicit tasks and instructions. Observing in context has demonstrated its effectives not only to get the input for the ideas and concepts, but also in evaluating whether the design has achieved its goal – but in the latter case, a prototype would be necessary.

4.2 Quantitative Measures

Connectedness. Social Connectedness Scale Revised (SCS_R) questionnaire [26] was chosen to evaluate the level of social connectedness of participants in the projects "leave your mark", Blobulous and Strijp-T-ogether. SCS-R is based on an earlier version of Social Connectedness Scale [27]. SCS-R consists of 20 items (10 positive and 10 negative). The negatively worded items are reverse scored and summed with the positively worded items to create a scale score with a possible range from 20 to 120. Then, the mean score with a possible range from 1 to 6 is calculated by dividing the total scale score by 20 (or 20 scale items). A higher score on the SCS-R indicates a stronger feeling of social connectedness.

Social Inclusion. The Inclusion of community in self scale [28] is a simple yet effective pictorial measure consisting of six pairs of circles. Each pair of same-sized circles overlaps slightly more than the preceding pair (Fig. 10). Each circle on the left of the pair represents the participant, while the circle on the right represents the community. Connectedness to the community at large is assessed by the participant marking the pair of circles that best describe her relationship with the community. It is found to be useful in projects "Leaving your mark" and "Strijp-T-ogether".

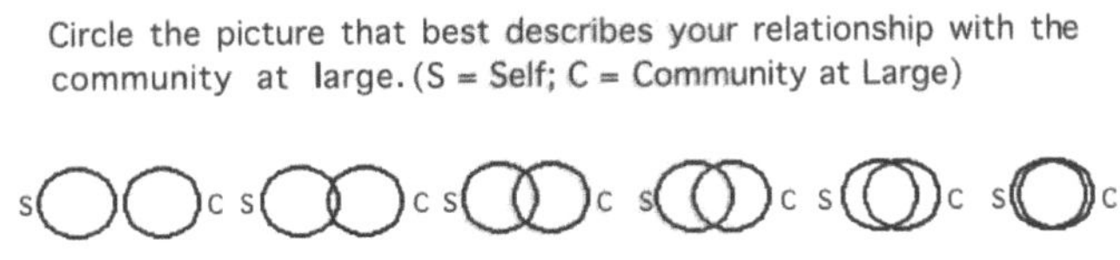

Fig. 10. Inclusion of community in self scale [28]

Attractiveness. AttrakDiff [29] is an instrument for measuring the attractiveness of interactive products. With the help of pairs of opposite adjectives, users can indicate their perception of the product. These adjective-pairs make a collation of the evaluation dimensions possible (Fig. 11, right). The following product dimensions are evaluated: Pragmatic Quality, Hedonic Quality - Stimulation, Hedonic Quality - Identity and Attractiveness. Hedonic and pragmatic qualities are independent of one another, and contribute equally to the rating of attractiveness and they are mapped into a visual output (Fig. 11, left). This method has been used to measure the attractiveness of Blobulus [10] and Oeco [11].

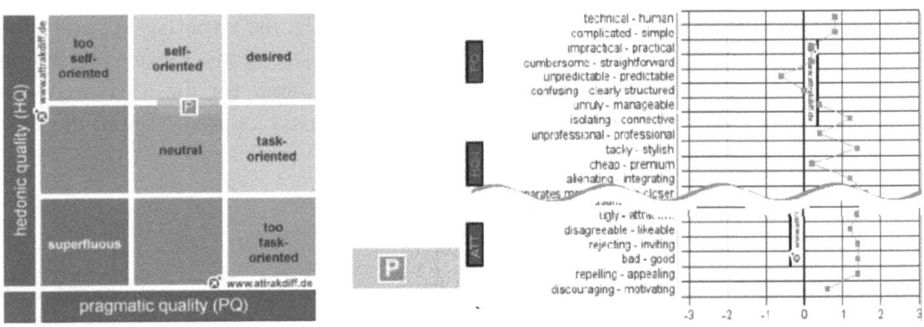

Fig. 11. AttrakDiff

Communication. Many public installations might have a goal to facilitate the social communication (for example in our design cases, "Moon rising from sea", "Leave your mark", CONNECT, Flink and Strijp-T-ogether). It is important to understand the emotional benefits and costs of such an installation. The Affective Benefits and Costs of Communication Technologies (ABCCT) [30, 31] could come in handy. It provides the measurements that are valuable to know for public installations, such as Emotional expressiveness, engagement and playfulness, opportunity for social support and threat to privacy.

5 Concluding Remarks

We presented eight design cases of interactive installations for social interaction in public spaces. The targeted spaces and user groups, design concepts and implementing technologies vary, aiming at different social experiences. However the design techniques and the user experience evaluation methods overlap and many of these techniques and methods have been found to be useful. The effort in designing for social interaction in public spaces is to be continued – we consider it to be an interesting and promising area in design research on social computing, especially in the era of the merge of the Web of People and the Internet of Things that leads to a shift from technology-push product or system oriented design to data-driven service centric design.

Acknowledgement. We would like to thank Yasemin Arslan, Sophie Brenny, Tove Elfferich, Joes Janmaat, Jing Gu and Duy Le for their active and valuable contributions in the design cases presented in this paper. We also thank the Sino-Dutch Design Center for Social and Cultural Computing for their support for the IPoC workshops.

References

1. Erickson, T.: Social Computing. In: The Encyclopedia of Human-Computer Interaction, 2nd edn. (2013)
2. Bartneck, C., Hu, J., Salem, B., Cristescu, R., Rauterberg, M.: Applying Virtual and Augmented Reality in Cultural Computing. IJVR 7, 11–18 (2008)
3. Hu, J., Wang, F., Funk, M., Frens, J., Zhang, Y., van Boheemen, T., et al.: Paticipatory Public Media Arts for Social Creativity. Presented at the Culture and Computing 2013, Kyoto, Japan (2013)
4. Wang, F., Hu, J., Rauterberg, M.: New Carriers, Media and Forms of Public Digital Arts. In: Culture and Computing, pp. 83–93 (2012)
5. Brenny, S., Hu, J.: Social Connectedness and Inclusion by Digital Augmentation in Public Spaces. In: 8th International Conference on Design and Semantics of Form and Movement (DeSForM 2013), Wuxi, China, pp. 108–118 (2013)
6. Le, D., Funk, M., Hu, J.: Blobulous: Computers As Social Actors. In: Experiencing Interactivity in Public Spaces (EIPS), CHI 2013, Paris, pp. 62–66 (2013)
7. Funk, M., Le, D., Hu, J.: Feel Connected with Social Actors in Public Spaces. In: Workshop on Computers As Social Actors, co-located with 13th International Conference on Intelligent Virtual Agents (IVA 2013), pp. 21–33 (2013)
8. Elfferich, T.: Design for Social Interaction in Public Spaces. Department of Industrial Design, Eindhoven University of Technology, Report M11 (2013)
9. Arslan, Y.: Flink!, Department of Industrial Design, Eindhoven University of Technology, Report M11 (2013)
10. Hu, J., Le, D., Funk, M., Wang, F., Rauterberg, M.: Attractiveness of an Interactive Public Art Installation. In: Streitz, N., Stephanidis, C. (eds.) DAPI 2013. LNCS, vol. 8028, pp. 430–438. Springer, Heidelberg (2013)
11. Gu, J.: Oeco. Office Ecosystem, Department of Industrial Design, Eindhoven University of Technology, Report M11 (2013)
12. Janmaat, J.: How to stimulate soicial interaction within a working area. Department of Industrial Design, Eindhoven University of Technology, Report B32 (2013)
13. Gu, J., Zhang, Y., Hu, J.: Lighting and Sound Installation for Elderly with Dementia. In: International Conference on Culture and Computing, Kyoto, Japan, pp. 169–170 (2013)

14. Frens, J., Funk, M., Hu, J., Zhang, S., Kang, K., Wang, F.: Exploring the Concept of Interactive Patina of Culture. In: 8th International Conference on Design and Semantics of Form and Movement (DeSForM 2013), Wuxi, China, pp. 211–214 (2013)
15. Hu, J.: Design of a distributed architecture for enriching media experience in home theaters (2006)
16. Hu, J., Bartneck, C., Salem, B., Rauterberg, M.: ALICE's adventures in cultural computing. International Journal of Arts and Technology 1, 102–118 (2008)
17. Zhang, Y., Gu, J., Hu, J., Frens, J., Funk, M., Kang, K., et al.: Learning from Traditional Dynamic Arts: Elements for Interaction Design. In: International Conference on Culture and Computing, Kyoto, Japan, pp. 165–166 (2013)
18. Zhang, Y., Frens, J., Funk, M., Hu, J., Rauterberg, M.: Scripting Interactive Art Installations in Public Spaces. In: 16th International Conference on Human-Computer Interaction, Creta Maris, Heraklion, Crete, Greece (2014)
19. Frens, J.: Cardboard modeling studio: a designerly exploration tool for rich and embodied interaction. In: Proceedings of the Fifth International Conference on Tangible, Embedded, and Embodied Interaction, pp. 365–368 (2011)
20. Frens, J., Djajadiningrat, J., Overbeeke, C.: Form, interaction and function, an exploratorium for interactive products. In: Proc. of Asian Design Conference (2003)
21. Hu, J., Feijs, L.M.: An Adaptive Architecture for Presenting Interactive Media Onto Distributed Interfaces. In: Applied Informatics, pp. 899–904 (2003)
22. Hu, J., Ross, P., Feijs, L., Qian, Y.: UML in Action: Integrating Formal Methods in Industrial Design Education. In: Hui, K.-c., Pan, Z., Chung, R.C.-k., Wang, C.C.L., Jin, X., Göbel, S., Li, E.C.-L. (eds.) EDUTAINMENT 2007. LNCS, vol. 4469, pp. 489–498. Springer, Heidelberg (2007)
23. Bojic, M., Goulati, A., Szostak, D., Markopoulos, P.: On the effect of visual refinement upon user feedback in the context of video prototyping. In: Proceedings of the 29th ACM International Conference on Design of Communication, pp. 115–118 (2011)
24. Yukawa, J.: Co-reflection in online learning: Collaborative critical thinking as narrative. International Journal of Computer-Supported Collaborative Learning 1, 203–228 (2006)
25. Tomico, O., Frens, J.W., Overbeeke, C.: Co-reflection: user involvement for highly dynamic design processes. In: CHI 2009 Extended Abstracts on Human Factors in Computing Systems, pp. 2695–2698 (2009)
26. Lee, R.M., Draper, M., Lee, S.: Social connectedness, dysfunctional interpersonal behaviors, and psychological distress: Testing a mediator model. Journal of Counseling Psychology 48, 310 (2001)
27. Lee, R.M., Robbins, S.B.: Measuring belongingness: The Social Connectedness and the Social Assurance scales. Journal of Counseling Psychology 42, 232 (1995)
28. Mashek, D., Cannaday, L.W., Tangney, J.P.: Inclusion of community in self scale: A single: item pictorial measure of community connectedness. Journal of Community Psychology 35, 257–275 (2007)
29. User Interface Design GmbH, AttrakDiff Tool to measure the perceived attractiveness of interactive products based on hedonic and pragmatic quality, ed (2012), `http://www.attrakdiff.de/en/Home/`
30. Yarosh, S., Markopoulos, P.: Design of an instrument for the evaluation of communication technologies with children. In: Proceedings of the 9th International Conference on Interaction Design and Children, pp. 266–269 (2010)
31. Yarosh, S., Markopoulos, P., Abowd, G.D.: Towards a Questionnaire for Measuring Affective Benefits and Costs of Communication Technologies. In: CSCW 2014, Baltimore, Maryland, USA (2014)

Smart Asia: A New Platform for Collective Intelligence

Christopher Grant Kirwan

Reignwood Innovation Technology Center, Beijing 100022, China
mustafa.kirwan@gmail.com

Abstract. Asia today is experiencing unprecedented urban growth and development, fast becoming the world's leading consumer of the planet's natural resources, and is now at the tipping point of becoming unsustainable. North America and Europe have finally begun to slow this negative trend through the use of sustainable practices and social innovation models supported by advanced technologies. It is critical for Asia to follow suit by developing environmentally safe solutions for growth, following the best practices from countries around the world. To be successful, this will require willing collaboration by public and private organizations, sharing information on demographics, health, food, water, weather, transportation, and other key urban indices. By developing a virtual framework combining an open-source operating system and collaborative interface we term Collective Intelligence, the goal is to build a Smart Asia platform capable of providing a holistic solution to meet both human quality of life needs and the sustainability of the natural environment.

Keywords: Collective Intelligence, Leapfrog, Operating Systems, Urban Interface, Smart Asia.

1 Introduction

1.1 Context

The threat of imminent disaster to our planet manifest in recent environmental disasters or another global economic meltdown may be the catalyst for world leaders to reach across geo-political and cultural boundaries to create new innovative partnerships and networks and a shared set of values. To achieve Smart Asia as a platform to solve challenges to both human quality of life and the sustainability of the natural environment, an integrated solution utilizing a combination of strategic planning, creative financing, innovative marketing, and appropriate technologies will need to be adopted. In our effort to create a Smart Asia, government, business, academia and the public at large must willingly work together to find equitable ways to share economic opportunities, create new partnerships, and exploit new technologies rather than allowing the interests of powerful corporations or individuals to limit their potential to provide collective benefits to society. In addition, all nations must move away from the present fossil-fuel based economy toward a new era of bio-organic and artificial intelligence as the basis of a developing a sustainable planet. This new Smart Asia

P.L.P. Rau (Ed.): CCD/HCII 2014, LNCS 8528, pp. 299–308, 2014.

platform must also address how we are working and communicating across boundaries of culture, language and professional/technical disciplines. A Collective Intelligence no longer constrained by the divisions and boundaries of nations, governmental policies and technology IP or imposed security restrictions, must be a bridge between diverse industries, fields of knowledge, and cultural backgrounds to facilitate this critically needed information sharing and decision-making process. The goal will be to serve not only our leading urban centers but also rural communities that must remain viable to maintain social, economic and environmental balance and growth at local, regional and global scales.

Asia now has the potential to develop a network of information-sharing and processing, Collective Intelligence, drawing on the vast economic strength, human capital, natural resources and technological capability of the region. If harnessed correctly, this pan-Asia network, including both developing and developed markets, would provide the supply and demand for innovative solutions to the massive growth, industrialization and urbanization occurring in real-time throughout Asia. This network would include China, India, Japan, South Korea and the ASEAN block (Association of South Asian States) amounting to a total population of 4.3 billion or 60% of the world population and more than 200 cities with populations of one million or greater. ASEAN alone accounts for 600 million people in its 10 member states, with more people than the EU. As a model of Collective Intelligence and potentially the foundation of the Smart Asia platform, ASEAN has proposed the creation of the 'ASEAN Community' and 'ASEAN Connectivity Master Plan' to be implemented by 2015.

However, to achieve this level of connectivity there are major challenges ahead with individual government systems and economic standards within ASEAN countries differing greatly, making it difficult for the union to act as a single unit. Another key factor in the ability for Collective Intelligence to succeed is the future cooperation between Asian governments and the critical role the world's second and third leading economies, China and Japan, will play in building a mutually sustainable master plan for regional growth, peace and collective prosperity. Seeing an opportunity to move forward proactively, China unveiled a new foreign policy in 2013 designed to strengthen ties with neighboring countries. While Japan, a long-standing ASEAN strategic partner and South Korea have both pledged to support the ASEAN Connectivity plan, providing financing and advanced technology. These positive diplomatic, economic and technological indicators are critically needed steps toward building the foundation of Collective Intelligence and a Smart Asia platform.

1.2 Considerations for Developing a Smart Asia Platform

One of the greatest challenges facing Asia, and most of the world, is the disparity between urban and rural areas caused by this century's unprecedented urban migration and the explosion of the megalopolis. According to China National Bureau of Statistics (NBS), in 2012 the urban population outnumbered the rural population in China. A key aspect of the Smart Asia platform is to provide solutions for development in both urban and rural communities, overcoming differences in regional social, economic, and geographic conditions by deploying cost effective solutions that allow all populations to connect to the energy grid and telecommunication infrastructure, and to create and operate businesses regardless of physical location and socio-economic status. In a functioning Smart Asia platform, users will be enabled to freely exchange information, move and operate independently, creating new, shared resources and develop more sustainable communities in both urban and rural contexts – with a combination of China, Japan, India and South Korea, all with advanced technology and trained workforce, working together to lead the new Smart Asia development.

1.3 Smart Asia Operating System – Hybrid Top-Down / Bottom-Up

The key to creating Collective Intelligence is the utilization of new models for deploying a broad spectrum of information collection, processing and management. This operating system must be simultaneously top-down and bottom-up. For such a hybrid operating system to properly function and evolve, a Master Operating System must be developed to accommodate both existing proprietary technologies and open-source hardware and software. The resulting OS must be a holistic solution, incorporating a collaborative approach, cross-disciplinary teams, open source technologies, and a global telecommunications network with the goal of creating a functioning Smart Asia platform linking both urban and rural populations throughout participating countries in Asia.

1.4 Smart Asia Interface – Big Data / Filters / Visualization / Interaction

Creating a Smart Asia interface will involve: 1) Collecting large amounts of information (Big Data) from both human and environmental sources, 2) using new software capable of uncovering, filtering and visualizing key patterns and data, and, 3) creating user-friendly interface to interact effectively with end-users in real time. The participation of millions of people interacting within virtual systems will provide critically-important information on patterns of consumption as well as a wide range of other data representing environmental, financial, technological and societal trends.

2 Principles of Collective Intelligence and Smart Asia

The following set of guiding principles seek to define the characteristics of a Collective Intelligence system and the varying ways it could be applied to creating a Smart Asia platform:

- **Virtual Framework – Cross-Border Cooperation**
  The greatest challenge to achieving Collective Intelligence and a Smart Asia is the current geo-political disputes between countries throughout Asia. Disagreements over borders and governmental policies are to be expected since national boundaries and socio-economic preferences usually stem from long-standing historical conditions. However our proposed virtual framework could help to

overcome these limitations by creating a new level of information sharing and networking that is not constrained by the current realities and historical factors. The 'ASEAN Connectivity Master Plan' is a good example of the potential of such cross-border cooperation.

- **Broad-Scale Interface – Distribution within Urban and Rural Contexts**
  A key challenge is the need to create a semblance of balance and equity in the physical, social and economic development of urban and rural environments. The recent urban migrations and projected concentrations of growth are indicators of the massive changes taking place in real time, revealing the imbalances that most of the world's developing countries are facing, particularly in Asia. China, a prime example with a projected 350 million new people migrating to urban centers by 2025, must protect and support its agricultural communities in order to ensure that food sources and raw materials will adequately provide for the entire population.

- **Real-time Data – Environmental Balance and Sustainability**
  The many natural disasters being experienced around the globe make it mandatory that a collaborative effort be made to monitor the causes of global warming and its effect on human, plant and animal populations. Developing the capability to track changes in real-time through deploying a network of sensors linked to data filtering and visualization applications will permit us to understand and respond to both long-term environmental change and short-term effects due to natural and man-made factors.

- **Citizen Interaction – Social Engagement**
  The capacity today to connect all segments of our populations through mobile phones and other internet devices, and to collect and apply a multitude of behavioral data will allow both public and private sectors (governments, NGO's, companies) to access critical data to better serve the needs of the end user. At the same time, end users will be able to contribute and participate directly as part of the *Collective Intelligence* interface by self-publishing real-time information and providing valuable performance feedback.

- **Adaptive Technologies – Appropriate Solutions to Specific Contexts**
  A major goal for Smart Asia will be the identification and adaptation of appropriate technological solutions that will aid in meeting the needs of specific populations rather than allowing domination of large enterprises, which often do not act in the best interest of the public. To provide solutions in this critical matter, organizations with recognized expertise and credibility such as universities, research institutes and NGO's would be engaged to evaluate the most appropriate technologies to meet the requirements of specific local contexts as well as to train people for management and operation of selected technological systems, hardware and software.

- **Open Source Framework – Information Sharing and Collaboration**
  The Internet has provided us with an amazingly accessible medium for the open exchange of information and open source code and we must capitalize on it to the fullest extent. Governments and corporations must aggressively adopt and support new models for information sharing, otherwise the ability for co-development will be limited and typically end up under the control of specialized groups and companies. For sensitive cross-border collaboration to become a reality, all public and private participants must also strive to meet clear standards of transparency and reliability.

- **Artificial Intelligence – Big Data / Data Visualization / Data Analysis**
  Advanced computational capability now makes possible the collection and analysis of huge data sets and dramatic new visualizations (mapping) of such key data. This new art/science will provide both organizations and the general public with a more intuitive understanding of broad trends and patterns and the ability to analyze and make decisions using real-time information on a myriad of social, economic and environmental factors. Additionally, artificial intelligence will allow the filtering and processing of the massive streams of data more efficient.

3 Case Studies

Smart Asia requires technology solutions that embody the principles of Collective Intelligence suggested in this paper and to adopt social innovation models that better engage and serve the relevant stakeholders. Additionally, Smart Asia requires sustainable approaches addressing the greater socio-economic and environmental opportunities and challenges. The following three case studies attempt to illustrate a more holistic view of how technology can serve as both Operating System and Interface, responding to the immediate context specifics, targeted user requirements and providing a broader platform for connectivity.

3.1 Case Study: Telecommunications – RUBI Smart Phone

Empowering Agricultural Communities in Southeast Asia. Without adequate communication technology solutions, farming communities throughout Southeast Asia do not have access to the Internet and are not able to stay informed on critical market data to better manage their businesses. The RUBI smart phone is designed to allow farmers who typically do not use computers or have access to more sophisticated technology to conduct business in an easy and targeted way. By developing a communication device that has limited but very useful functions, RUBI enables local farmers the ability to conduct transactions including trading and making payments to distributors that link their products to urban centers. Conversely, RUBI allows migrant workers in cities to pay remittance to their family members in rural communities.

Currently being developed by a group of committed technology providers and designers in Asia as a consortium working across geo-political boundaries, RUBI is an example of a solution that seeks to connect both urban and rural communities and resources by providing a leapfrog solution especially where more advanced technology hardware and software is not required and is not readily understood or absorbed by rural populations. Additionally, RUBI is an example of a bottom up rather than top down approach since it addresses the real needs of the end user by providing an appropriate technology solution giving rural inhabitants a necessary tool to make their lives more sustainable. For Asian governments and particularly the Chinese government this is a key issue. The necessity to keep local agricultural communities viable will require new technologies that allow farmers and other small rural businesses to connect to the larger market network without the need to travel or to invest in expensive equipment. At the same time, solutions are required that do not involve extensive training and are intuitive for the end users. RUBI has an additional function that can allow small groups to share an individual unit as did rural communities when the telephone was first introduced, and a single TV set functioned as a community centerpiece when they first became available. This shared resource also strengthens community bonds and reinforces local collective activity.

3.2 Case Study: Renewable Energy – Biomass Gasification

A Cooperative Model for Sustainable Economic Development. Empire Asia Energy Group, a private investment company based in Bangkok, Thailand, in partnership with the Earth Group & Green Planet Association has developed a comprehensive scheme to provide electricity to rural areas throughout regions in Asia that are located off the grid, as well as serving as a platform to stimulate rapid rural economic development. The proposed model combines the establishment of Biomass Gasification power plants to produce clean electricity on a 7-24 basis to be distributed via local medium voltage lines and using local biomass for a constant supply of fuel. The local biomass is generated by easily grown specialized tree varieties adapted to each region including the Leucaena tree, that can be processed into wood chips, which also provide value added benefits to the environment, improving soil, protecting from erosion, producing animal feed as well as employing thousands of direct and indirect workers. Each 1-MW power plant requires a total of 800 acres of Leucaena cultivation that earns revenue from both supplying the fuel and from producing and selling animal feed. The easily replicable 1-MW packaged "very small power plants" (VSPPs) can be quickly set up at any location in the countryside where power is needed. The power can be delivered to the national grid and or sold to local industries and companies under a highly desirable "distributive energy approach," and while capitalizing on new attractive government incentives for using clean energy especially in remote locations.

The biomass generated by the Leucaena has no real competition in the renewable energy field (solar, wind, ethanol, etc.) in terms of both its low capital and operating costs (lowest cost per continuous KwH of any competitive system) and by virtue of its 7-24 overall reliability (greater than 90% availability) and its ability to attract maximum benefits from government and international agency programs, including receiving carbon credit from the power generation operation and from the associated Leucaena plantation. This Cooperative Empowerment plan, based on the Biomass Gasification business model, allows local cooperatives to partner for resources and financial management, providing sustainable options for farmers to generate new sources of revenue, increase the generation of clean energy and to become more self-sufficient, accelerating economic development and quality of life for the entire community.

3.3 Case Study: Infrastructure – Aerotropolis

Clustering Synergy Functions and Linking Global Networks. Today, a new regional economic catalyst and globally linked model has been developing around airports and along transportation corridors radiating from them, forming a new urban typology termed the *Aerotropolis*. Analogous in shape to the traditional metropolis made up of a central city and its rings of commuter-heavy suburbs, the Aerotropolis consists of an airport city and outlying corridors and clusters of aviation related real estate development. A number of these clusters in Asia including Kuala Lumpur International Airport and South Korea's Songdo International Business District have become globally significant airport edge-cities, examples of planned urban mega-development; a combination giant airports, planned cities, logistics and business hubs.

As a prime example, the Kuala Lumpur International Airport (KUA) in Malaysia's capital is currently expanding as an Aerotropolis and has been a key driver of KL's economic development. The project is currently being developed as a destination for international business and conferences and a global supply chain hub comprising cargo warehousing and logistic facilities. At the same time, the real estate development plan has been designed to balance this self-sustaining multifunctional airport with creating an environmental friendly district including office campus, hotels and entertainment, integrated with parks and gardens and a large green buffer zone. KUA remains the only airport in the world with the Green Globe GG certification. Originally the airport was developed to serve the Malaysia Multimedia Super Corridor (MSC) providing the basis for industrial, commercial, educational and residential development. Companies located within the MSC are globally connected with direct access to supply chain processes, R&D, just-in-time manufacturing, storage and distribution.

By clustering operations and developing synergistic functions supported through a combination of telecommunications, transportation and new technologies infrastructure, Aerotropolis models promote efficiency and integration of resources, stimulate regional economies and link international networks. The biggest challenge facing the Aerotropolis model is the current reliance on fossil fuel and the massive environmental impact question. The planning and design of such large-scale frameworks require much more attention to the integration and balance of man-made and natural systems. However, well-planned Aerotropolis models incorporate multiple synergistic functions and thus create better-optimized systems for logistics reducing the overall carbon footprint. At the same time, the opportunity to imbed new sensor technologies to monitor the natural environment will allow a better integration and management of these resources. Smart Asia is absolutely needed to insure these resources are managed properly.

4 Conclusion

Smart Asia will require sustainable strategies that adapt to local environments, finding solutions that fit the needs of the end user while leveraging the resources of collectives and larger networks. Each of the documented case studies represent solutions at differing scales from personal, to community, to city and has linkages beyond their immediate context and geographic boundaries. Each solution integrates multiple functions, optimizes resources and utilizes communication technologies to support a holistic platform connecting entities within a broader system. Simultaneously, each solution demonstrates building at an appropriate level of engagement and considers both top-down and bottom-up approaches. Each of these examples also reinforce *The Third Industrial Revolution* concept, described by author Jeremy Rifkin, that presents the case that self sufficiency and localized solutions are now more viable due to the ability of technology and networks to link people, communities and larger systems together. This newfound freedom is just at the beginning stage; *Leap Frog* technologies will enable emerging economies to develop cost effective solutions by avoiding unnecessary and inefficient development while allowing end users to shape the required functions through the use of open source applications designed to meet their real needs and adapt to context specific requirements.

Importantly, it is necessary to recognize that self-sufficiency also requires integration and connectivity beyond the immediate situational context. In system theory and in the life of organisms, open systems have a lesser tendency toward entropy than closed systems where new material and resources do not enter into and inform the process. Open systems have the capacity to adapt and transform by interacting with outside conditions; in this case, the capability to share across borders and organizational boundaries that will be critical to the sustainability of the Collective Intelligent operating systems.

Supporting the Smart Asia platform is the formation of a cross-university, cross-discipline, collaborative research program by a core team including Tsinghua University (China), Seoul National University (South Korea) and Chiba University (Japan) and linked to an international network of academic and world organizations. Already in the third year of this joint research initiative under the theme Urban Media, the collaboration explores theory, methodologies and applications for the ways new media shapes and influences the operation of cities. This year's focus has expanded to initiate the dialogue of what constitutes Smart Asia, a broader platform for applying what knowledge has been gained to-date and catalyst for the subject of this paper. A key objective of the Smart Asia collaboration is to link research with real projects in Asia. Research teams will identify specific opportunities for collaboration with industry to jointly conduct test projects, determine the effectiveness of the new technologies, demo applications, secure governmental approvals, attract capital investment and generate public interest. This effort will represent a more comprehensive approach by developing an in-depth understanding of user needs and requirements for projects and technologies to be successful in a wide variety of specific contexts.

A much broader effort, through increased government support, private sector investment and academic research will be needed to successfully develop a system of Collective Intelligence and to establish the proposed Smart Asia platform. This process is now in the beginning stage and shows great promise; however to continue its momentum, creative approaches, new partnerships and most importantly, trust must be established between participants to meet the pressing social, economic, energy and environmental challenges facing Asia and other rapidly-developing regions. This paper is an effort to stimulate the required collaboration and connectivity by establishing a set of guiding principles and presenting examples of how Smart Asia and Collective Intelligence may be realized through a combination of government policies, real projects, academic research and cross-disciplinary exchange. It is also a medium to share these concepts with individuals and organizations that will be able to further develop Smart Asia.

Acknowledgements. I am pleased to recognize contributions to this paper made by the following colleagues:

- Academic Research & Collaboration – Professor Fu Zhiyong, School of Art & Design and co-founder of Design Beijing Lab, Tsinghua University, Beijing, China.
- Business & Technology Applications – Colin Liu, Senior Vice President, Director of International Business Division, The Reignwood Group, Beijing, China.
- Case Studies – Edward S. Grant, VP Development, Empire Asia Group, Bangkok, Thailand.
- Editorial Support – Ernest E. Kirwan, AIA, retired architect / planner and faculty member, Harvard Graduate School of Design, Cambridge, Massachusetts, USA.

References

1. Flood, R.L., Carson, E.R.: Dealing with Complexity: An Introduction to the Theory and Application of Systems Science. Springer (1993)
2. Marcus, F., Forlano, L., Satchell, C., Gibb, M.: Chapter 13 Urban Media: New Complexities, New Possibilities—A Manifesto. In: From Social Butterfly to Engaged Citizen: Urban Informatics, Social Media, Ubiquitous Computing, and Mobile Technology to Support Citizen Engagement, MIT Press, Cambridge (2012)
3. Kasarda, J.D. (ed.): Global Airport Cities. Insight Media – Sovereign House, Twickenham (2010)
4. Kasarda, J.D., Lindsay, G. (eds.): Aerotropolis, Farrar, Straus and Giroux, New York (2011)
5. Rifkin, J.: The Third Industrial Revolution. Palgrave MacMillan, New York (2011)
6. Solana, J.: Europe's Smart Asian Pivot (2013), `http://www.project-syndicate.org/commentary/the-eu-s-startegic-advantages-in-asia-by-javier-solana`
7. Asian Voices: A New Era for ASEAN?

8. http://www3.nhk.or.jp/nhkworld/english/tv/asianvoices/archives201312020600.html
9. Master Plan on ASEAN Connectivity (2011), http://www.asean.org/resources/publications/asean-publications/item/master-plan-on-asean-connectivity-2
10. Master Plan on ASEAN Connectivity Implementation, Project by Japan-ASEAN Integration Fund (JAIF)., http://www.asean.emb-japan.go.jp/news12_06.html
11. Mission of the Republic of Korea to ASEAN / ASEAN Connectivity, http://asean.mofa.go.kr/english/as/asean/policy/policy/index.jsp
12. Myanmar's moment: Unique opportunities, major challenges. McKinsey Global Institute (2013)

Designing "Female Prospect" into Public Space for Taipei City

Yi-Tsu Peng[1], Yu-Di Huang[1], Jun-Liang Chen[1], and Chuck Chen[2]

[1] Graduate School of Creative Industry Design, National Taiwan University of Arts, Taiwan
{yitsupeng,freeimage5361}@gmail.com, artistted@hotmail.com
[2] C.Y. LEE & Partners Architects, Taiwan
chuck@mail.cylee.com

Abstract. With the global trend and the active participation and promotion by organizations and individuals from all fields who care about female issues, there has been a considerable degree of progress on substantive issues concerning female and public space in Taiwan over the recent 20 years. This is a gradual and interlocking process, especially in our capital of Taipei. In this dissertation the process of this evolvement will be clearly stated by the timeline-based recording approach. Comparisons will be made with respect to the modification of national policy in response to relevant social issues and events, and the specific presentation of its implementation in today's public space with future prospects.

Keywords: male, Public Space, Public Space Design, Universal Design.

1 Introduction

The use of public space is an important part of people's daily lives, and the urban public space is also an important field for activities promoting social connotations [1]. The consideration of public space from a female perspective has been the subject of global concern in the recent half century. Feminist geographer Linda McDowell (1999/2006) once indicated that the importance of public space is that it is the most significant part of the composition of 'public' diversity. Therefore, the goal for policy makers and urban planners is definitely to make the public space equally friendly and accessible for the public with various demands. Foreign feminist law scholars have also shown various cases of law amendments due to recognition of female roles under constant social development [2]. Based on such belief, this study was involved in the field of female and space ever since the middle of 1990s not long after the initial awareness of female roles in Taiwan, and research papers were composed with respect to the female's demand for community parks in public space. Since then there have been a lot of concern and responses from all fields in Taiwan with respect to female subjects. Therefore, in this study the timeline-based review and examination with respect to the subject of female and space will be carried out. With Taipei as the research object, subjects and actions of females in public space and the subsequent

P.L.P. Rau (Ed.): CCD/HCII 2014, LNCS 8528, pp. 309–320, 2014.

feedback and results will be reviewed and summarized in order to understand the improvement of female's demand for public space over these 20 years. In addition, the new demand subjects resulted from the progress of time will also be observed in order to collate the direction of subsequent effort in the future.

The subject of this research is to investigate public space in Taipei from a female perspective. The public space is defined as a public area open to general public. It is a social space that is generally open and accessible to people [3]. The public space includes outside spaces such as roads, squares, parks, beaches, etc., and/or government buildings which include indoors spaces such as libraries and transfer stations. Females in this study will include the 18-year-old (or older) adult female defined by the Constitution of ROC, and the growing young ladies in high schools or elementary schools with physical and psychological state of femininity.

The content of research in this dissertation is about the summarization of archives and data of public space subjects from female perspective recorded in timeline format. The author hopes to systematically summarize all efforts and results of local people dedicated to the cross-era subject of female use of public space in the recent 20 years from relevant literatures and records. In addition, the demands of female users for public space will be summarized from literatures, and comparison will be made to the improvement results at current stage. Field observations will be carried out with respect to the females' behaviors of using the public space in Taipei City nowadays in order to understand the improvement of overall environment in response to females' demands. Meanwhile, investigations of emerging subjects from all aspects resulted from the use of public space due to time evolution will be further emphasized.

2 Deductive Process of Female's Expectation on Public Space

The subject of female and public space in Taiwan first drew attention back in the early 90s, and since then it has gone through decades of growth and evolution. Thanks to the efforts and dedications of predecessors for all these years, today we get to enjoy a public environment which is comfortable for females. First of all, it was the founding of Awakening Foundation as shown in Figure 1.

In 1982, a group of female friends caring about gender equality founded the "Awakening Magazine" in order to achieve the ideals of awakening female self-consciousness, fighting for female rights, and promoting gender equality. In 1987, funds were raised to found the "Awakening Foundation" for the purposes of further development of social resources and unification of female power. Awakening Foundation is a organization advocating various reforms based on gender equality, which has contributed to the passing of numerous bills [4]. This can be regarded as the beginning of focus on women related subjects in Taiwan. Based on timeline recording approach, it describe all subjects, evolution, and development related to female and public space in Taiwan as shown in Table 1.

Fig. 1. Founding of the Awakening Foundation

Table 1. The main issues of female and public space

	The main issues of female and public space
1987	▪ "Awakening Foundation" is established.
1993	▪ "Women Association on Community Development in Taipei" is established and abbreviated as WACD.
1994	▪ "Fembooks publishing house & bookstore" is established.
1995	▪ The United Nations forth world woman conference is hold. ▪ "Gender workshop" is established by Taipei government. ▪ "Center for the study of sexualities" is established by National Chiao Tung University.
1996	▪ The "Occupying the men's room" event. ▪ The "Refuse to pay the money for using the ladies' room" event. ▪ Construction and Planning Agency Ministry of The Interior is modified the "Architectural Technological Rule architectural facility chapter" to adjust the male and female public toilet proportion.
1998	▪ The Public Space and Women's Safety conference is hold.
1999	▪ Taipei Rapid Transit Corporation (Taipei Metro) is setting the women's waiting area during the night. ▪ "Taipei Women's Center" is established.
2001	▪ Taipei Metro is setting "The counter-pinhole photographs surreptitiously" in the ladies' room and the nursing room.
2002	▪ "Taipei Women's Policy White Paper".
2003	▪ Two professors of Taiwan represented: Women's safety is beginning from the space design.
2009	▪ Taipei City Council passes the rule of "Taipei Public Space Nursing Self-regulations". ▪ No Gender Restroom event is occurred in sever campuses of Taipei.
2010	▪ Taiwan Railways Administration is setting the women's waiting area during the night in all stations. ▪ "The proportion of the male and female public toilet can't be lower than 1:3" in the Building Ordinance is finished the Third Reading procedure in the Legislative Yuan of Republic of China.
2011	▪ "Gender Friendly Restroom".
2012	▪ Taipei Metro is setting The Four Relieve Measures.
2013	▪ Taipei Metro's innovational service for the disadvantaged customers is getting the recognition of the global public translate field.

3 Designing "Female Prospect" into Public Space

3.1 The Demand of Public Space

From the aforementioned timeline-based statement and the summarized results of events related to subjects of female and public space developed in Taiwan over the recent 20 years, different dimensions of female's demand for public space can be generalized. Foreign scholars have investigated people's demands for public space and divided them into several categories such as safety, attractive appearance, psychological comfort, symbolic ownership, activity base situational establishment, and usage policy [5]. The author has also summarized females' demands for public space into several categories (such as safety, spatiality, basic facility, beauty and atmosphere, and a sense of belonging) in previous publications for further research, and specific research results have been obtained [6]. Therefore, in this dissertation we will also start from these key points of design to observe public space today from a female perspective and to carry out in-depth field investigation.

3.2 Universal Design

Universal Design was first proposed by American architect Michael Bednar. It was not until 1989 did American designer Ronald L. Mace begin to use the term "Universal Design" frequently, which basically means products, environments, and communications that can be used by everyone [7]. At the Center for Universal Design (CUD) at North Carolina State University, a group of architects, product designers, engineers, and environmental design researchers established seven principles of UD to provide guidance in the design of products and environments [8]. See Table 2.

Table 2. Principles and design reference criteria of Universal Design

Universal Design	
Principle	Design reference criteria
Equitable Use	• Provide all users with same or equivalent methods • Avoid user discrimination • Provide all users with same privacy or safety measures
Flexibility Use	• Provide options for application methods • Adjustability in coordination with user' s pace
Simple and Intuitive Use	• Eliminate unnecessary complexity • In compliance with user' s expectation and intuition
Perceptible Information	• Enhance the legibility of important information • Provide sensory disabled with diversified equipment operating techniques
Tolerance for Error	• Arrange the sequence of devices in order to reduce the danger or error, and provide warnings and safety protective devices
Low Physical Effort	• Allow user to maintain natural pose • Use reasonable operating force • Reduce repeated actions
Size and Space for Approach & use	• Sufficient and appropriate spaces and devices with easy access • Provide a clear line of sight for important device

3.3 The Correlation between the Concept of Universal Design and Female Demand for Public Space

The correlations of environmental application of Universal Design concepts, especially for the demands for public space, can be summarized as shown below:

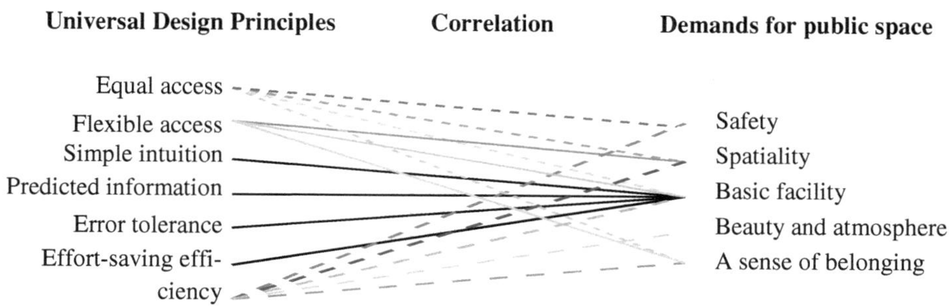

The color lines represent the parts closely related to female's use of public space, which are:

- - - Safety at night - - -Equality of respect — Activity participation – – Interconnected space facilities
- - - Public space allocation — Friendly space – – Avoid dangerous space – –Healthy, clean, and natural
- - - Female facility — Flexible facilities – – Special space requirements – – Space dependence

As for the examination of aforementioned universal design principles corresponding to the females' demand for public space, further case study will be carried out in the following Chapter 4.

4 Case Study

The case study of public space in Taipei City is as shown below. As indicated by relevant literatures, the scope of public space can be divided into several categories including outside public space (such as public parks, mountain forests, and beaches), indoor public space (such as airports, train stations, subway stations), and road system (such as sidewalks, bicycle paths, and road dividers). The most representative among them will be selected as the objects for observation and analysis. The current status of females' use of public space in Taipei City will be explained by actual examples from the perspective of overall design.

In addition, from the perspective of user demands for public space, in this study we will start from several major categories including safety, spatiality, basic facility, beauty and atmosphere, and a sense of belonging in order to observe public space from a female perspective and to carry out in-depth field investigation. Various types of public spaces in Taipei City have been selected for case analysis.

4.1 Outside Public Space — Take Daan Forest Park as an Example

Also known as "The lung of Taipei", Daan Forest Park is located in the centry area of Taipei City with Jianguo South Road on the east side, Xinshen South Road on the west side, Heping East Road on the south side, and Xinyi Road on the north side. With a total area of 25.9293 hectares, it is one of the famous unban parks in Taiwan.

1. Safety

– The peripheral of the park is based on penetrating fence or no-fence design allowing safer activities for female and disadvantaged groups and a more comfortable and spacious overall atmosphere.
– Night lighting in the park has been emphasized by widespread light sources in order to avoid blind spots. Therefore, there are a lot of female users in the park participating in activities or accompanying children during night time while feeling safe about doing so.

2. Spatiality

– There is a huge hinterland in Daan Forest Park, which can be divided into various regions by the trails corresponding to various types of activities, yet there is no physical partition among them. The advantage of this design is to allow people with different demands to participate in activities in their respective areas while being able to visually take care of each other. This is a thoughtful design for women who usually play the role of caregivers.

3. Basic facility

– There are a total of six public restrooms located in different activity areas. This provides great convenience to females, especially those who assume the role of caregivers for children, elderly or disabled.
– Basic suppliers have been provided in these public restrooms in the park in order to improve the overall quality and enhance the comfort level of female users.

4. Beauty and atmosphere

– The park is segmented from the roads by trees. Formosan sweet gums were planted in the center of sidewalk in order to block out the noise and pollution of the external roads.
– People standing on the bandstand on top of the slope will have a clear view of all landscapes in the park. This outdoor space based on the integration of natural greenness and cultural lives are often used for all kinds of music events and arts performances thus adding to the cultural atmosphere of this

park. Sitting on the lawn, listening to the music concert, and enjoying the relaxing and pleasant time - this is female users' favorite atmosphere.

- The ecological pond located in the northwest side of the park is based on natural scenery with diversified plants bred along the shore. The artificial island in the pond has become a favorite habitat for a variety of birds. Walking along the water shore and observing the natural ecology can be indeed a spiritual feast for sentimental women.

- There are double seats installed in all aforementioned areas. For female users who emphasize interpersonal emotional exchange, these are perfect areas for sharing each other's lives.

5. A sense of belonging

- Increasing number of activities (such as annual flower exhibition) introduced to the park will lead to enhanced sense of belonging of users - especially for female participants such as volunteering mothers.

4.2 Inside Public Space— Take Taipei Train Station and All MRT Stations in Taipei as the Example

Taipei Train Station was built in 1891, which was 122 years ago. After several restructurings, the current station building was inaugurated in 1989. The construction of Taipei MRT started from the "Taipei Metropolitan Mass Rapid Transit System Plan" in 1986. The first operational line, Wenshan Line (known as Mucha Line at that time) was open for traffic in March 1996. After years of construction, the entire system currently has become the transportation backbone of Taipei metropolitan area.

1. Safety

- Women waiting area at night" on the platform has been set up in all Taiwan Railway Stations throughout Taiwan and all MRT stations in order to make female passengers feel safe while taking public transportation at night[9].
- The mechanism of "anti-pinhole camera" has been implemented in restrooms and breastfeeding rooms in Taipei MRT for enhancing the safety.
- Various measures such as "Safe Waiting at Night", "Safe Restroom Access", "Safe Ride", "Safe Departure from Station" have been implemented in Taipei MRT in order to better protect the safety of women.

2. Spatiality

- The breastfeeding rooms have been built to provide breastfeeding fem ales with an interference-free environment for breastfeeding[10].
- With the enforcement of regulation on the ratio of men's room and women's room (which shall be at least 1:3) in public venues[11], females no longer have to wait in long lines for

using the restroom except some early stages (such as Tamsui Line) before the aforementioned regulation was promulgated. Competent authority should provide responsive measures to solve this issue, such as expanding the space of women's room or re-arrange the ratio of spaces of men's room and women's room.

3. Basic facility

- Women no longer have to pay for the access to public toilet in Taiwan Railway Station, and there are more women's rooms than before, indicating more emphasis on the respect for females.
- The establishment of "Gender-friendly restroom" with the facilities of safety handrails, safety backrest, children toilet, child safety seat etc. has provided great convenience to females with kids or elders.

4. Beauty and atmosphere

- As for the building of MRT station, the beauty and atmosphere have both been greatly improved, especially for the Xinyi Line which was just completed earlier this year, and the renovation of food court on the second floor of Taiwan Railway Station.

5. A sense of belonging

- With the installation of breastfeeding room, the increased number of women's rooms, and no more charge for women's room, women no longer feels like they are invisible secondary citizens. Instead, a sense of belonging has grown in their minds.

4.3 Public Road System — Take the Ring-Type Bicycle Path System in Taipei and U-Bike as the Example

After years of organization, the ring-shape bicycle path system in Taipei City has connected numerous sporadic recreational sites along the riverside greenbelt around the city and formed the recreational network of the outer ring of Taipei Metropolitan area, which starts from the Mucha Zoo in the downstream of Jingmei River in the south and then extended to the Tamsui MRT station in Tamsui River Ba sin in the north. This route along the river shore is mostly at a certain distance away from downtown, such that there is a huge hinterland and a lot of greenness along both sides of the path.

U-Bike is the most popular public program among Taipei citizens, which is set to be the alternative transportation means along urban transit system. It can also be regarded as an alternative shuttle bus.

During the interviews conducted by the author, these two facilities related to road public space are particularly welcome and recognized by female users, mainly due to the dual significance in sports and in environmental protection/energy saving/carbon reduction.

1. Safety

As indicated by the experience of interviewees in using U-Bike, the quality control has been rather solid in terms of brake system, lighting, overall structure, and maintenance. The only things missing are the night time lighting and chain locking mechanism for the bike rental of this ring-type bicycle path system.

2. Spatiality

Both ring-type bicycle path system and U-Bike cover a rather broad range of paths. There are U-Bike rental stations near important MRT stations covering the entire downtown of Taipei, while the ring-type bicycle path system is based on the ring-type system planning along the peripheral of Taipei City.

3. Basic facility

- There are facilities of tire inflation, drinking water dispenser, and restrooms in all rental stations along the ring-type bicycle path system.
- There are sufficient numbers of portable toilets installed in multiple spots along the ring-type bicycle path system providing great convenience to female users who have higher demands for restrooms.

4. Beauty and atmosphere

- The public spaces surrounding the bicycle ways have been healthier and cleaner, the atmosphere highly regarded by female users has been improved. Female interviewees feel rather pleasant by either wandering in the riverside ring-type bicycle path system or enjoying the urban exploration alone.
- The bicycle path system and U-Bike in Taipei have been highly praised by female interviewees because they have not only relieved the load of public transportation, but also reduced air pollution and enhanced the quality of life.

5. A sense of belonging

- As the kind of sport which is not too intense and capable of maintaining physical and mental health and fitness, bike riding has been well-received by females. A lot of women have found their confidence and the sense of belonging in this field.
- Overall, from the females' perspectives of safety, spatiality, basic facility, beauty and atmosphere, and a sense of belonging, the public space in Taipei City has been greatly improved over the recent 20 years and become more and more in line with females' demand.

5 Result and Discussion

As indicated by the results of aforementioned case analysis, after being examined by universal design principles in coordination with the demand for public space, multiple specific achievements have been shown by the public space in Taipei City based on females' expectations, which have been summarized in Table 3.

Table 3. Achievements of the "Female Prospect" into Public Space for Taipei City

		Space Demands	Achievements of the "Female Prospect" into Public Space for Taipei City
Universal Design Principle	Equitable Use	Safety	• The park is based on penetrating fence or no-fence design allowing safer activities for female and disadvantaged groups. • "Women waiting area at night" on the platform has been set up in all Taiwan Railway Stations and MRT stations to make female feel safe while taking public transportation at night. • The mechanism of "anti-pinhole camera" has been implemented in restrooms and breastfeeding rooms in Taipei MRT for enhancing the safety. • Various measures such as "Safe Waiting at Night", "Safe Restroom Access", "Safe Ride", and "Safe Departure from Station" have been implemented in Taipei MRT in order to better protect the safety of women.
		Spatiality	• With the enforcement of regulation on the ratio of men's room and women's room (which shall be at least 1:3) in public venues, females no longer have to wait in long lines for using the restroom.
		Basic Facility	• In recent years basic suppliers such as toilet paper have been provided in these public restrooms in the park in order to improve the overall quality and enhance the comfort level of female users.
		A sense of belonging	• You no longer have to pay for the access to public women's room in Taiwan Railway Station, and there are more women's rooms than before, indicating more emphasis on the respect for females. • The purpose of the campus uni-sex toilet movement in 2009 was to pursue gender equality and to provide a space dedicated for non-heterosexuals.
	Flexibility Use	Spatiality	• The establishment of "Gender-friendly restroom" with the facilities of safety handrails, safety backrest, children toilet, child safety seat, and baby diaper platform has provided great convenience to females with children or elders.
		Basic Facility	• There are sufficient numbers of portable toilets installed in multiple spots along the ring-type bicycle path system providing great convenience to female users who have higher demands for restrooms.
		A sense of belonging	• Increasing number of activities introduced to the park will lead to enhanced sense of belonging of users - especially for female participants such as volunteering mothers.

Table 3. (*continued*)

	Size and Space for Approach and Use	Safety	• Night lighting in the park has been emphasized by widespread light sources in order to avoid blind spots.
		Spatiality	• The breastfeeding rooms have been built to provide breastfeeding females with an interference-free environment for breastfeeding.
		Basic Facility	• The bicycle path system and U-bike in Taipei City have connected the sporadic public spaces and formed a belt-like recreational network in order to relieve the load of public transportation and enhance the quality of life.
		Beauty and Atmosphere	• The public spaces surrounding the roads have been healthier and cleaner, and the beauty and atmosphere highly regarded by female users have been improved.
		A sense of belonging	• The breastfeeding rooms built in public venues in Taipei City have enhanced the sense of belonging among females.

By comparing Table 3 above with the overall public space design in Taipei City today, it appears that significant progress has been made in all aspects (safety, spatiality, basic facility, beauty and atmosphere, and a sense of belonging) after active efforts devoted by people from all fields and years of gradually accumulated growth. Among all demands for public space, safety is the one most emphasized by females, whose active pursuit has led to the achievement in this aspect today. Therefore, in terms of including females' expectation into the design of public space in Taipei City, in addition to the design itself, the most important thing is the change of laws and regulations and people's view on women's rights and interests in order to accomplish the mission of making public space to better meet the requirements of female users.

It has also been found during field observation and interviews that there is insufficient number of women's rooms in some old public facilities (such as MRT Lines built in earlier stages) which is not in compliance with the principle of proportionality; the platform of opinion box is too high for most female users; and the indicative systems for general public (such as the motion line system and indicating signs in the underground level of Taipei Main Station) are too complicated. These are all areas which can be further improved in the future.

6 Conclusion

With women's organizations and people from all fields caring about women's subjects paying significant attentions from various aspects to the role of public space user played by female in Taiwan over recent 20 years, the entire society and government policy have been urged to face the issue of substantive gender equality, and to convert the passive attitude into active attitude in order to implement such concept to the use of various public spaces and facility improvement. The best example is the first Municipality, Taipei City, which is currently equipped with comfortable public spaces for female users. However, this is the result of 20 years of hard work. As for the Xinyi

Line of Taipei MRT which was just opened for traffic this November (2013), we carried out onsite investigation on the overall planning of the largest public space in Taipei City – Daan Forest Park Station, which can represent the latest results of public space project constructed by our government. In this MRT station we can find not only the high-quality overall design from all aspects (visual, auditory, and all other senses) based on integration of inner and outer park environments, but also complete services meeting the qualitative and quantitative demands of female users with respect to public space. For example, there are 10 fully-equipped spacious and bright women's rooms with breastfeeding rooms nearby. There are dedicated intercoms installed outside the door for users to notify the station personnel in order to remotely open the locked door. In addition to the complete and safe equipment, there is also security mechanism as the secondary protection such that there should be no worries for breastfeeding women. The author also noticed that there is a large-area "friendly space" created between men's room and women's room equipped with adult toilet (including safety armrest and backrest) for the disabled, children toilet, and baby seat on the inside, and baby diaper platform and hand washing/drying station on the outside. This is a comfortable and spacious space dedicated for people on wheelchairs, parents and kids, elderly, and disabled. We believe that, in addition to the continuous focus on extended female subjects and the improvement on public space environment and equipment, the attention to the right to life of disadvantaged groups in public space will become the next public space subject to be actively emphasized by the general public and our government. We have already started working on this social responsibility and mission.

References

1. Grundström, K.: Gender and use of public space, Housing Development and Management–HDM. Lund University (2005)
2. Pruit, L.R.: Gender, Geography. Berkeley Journal of Gender, Law & Justice 23(2) (2013)
3. Wikipedia: Public Space (2011), `http://en.wikipedia.org/wiki/Public_space`
4. Awakening Foundation: About Awakening (2009), `http://www.awakening.org.tw/chhtml/`
5. Hester, R.T.: Planning Neighborhood Space with People, pp. 57–75. Van Nostrand Reinhold, New York (1984)
6. Peng, Y.T.: The demand of neighborhood park for women in Taichung city. Tunghai University (1995)
7. College of Design: The Center for Universal Design, North Caloraindo University (2008)
8. Burgstahler, S.: Universal Design: Process, Principles, and Applications, University of Washington (2012)
9. Reporter: Taiwan Railways is promoted the, Waiting Zone for Female Passengers at Night, TVBS News (2009)
10. Taipei news: Nursing in public space, The Liberty Times (2009)
11. Building Law of Republic of China: chapter 97 revision (2010)

Social Sustainability in Design: The Window as an Interface for Social Interaction

Gaia Scagnetti and Federico Casalegno

Mobile Experience Lab, 20 Ames Street, E15-320, Cambridge, MA 02139, USA
gaia.scagnetti@gmail.com, casalegno@mit.edu

Abstract. The way people organize the space of their house is strongly related to their local culture. In the process of designing a *sustainable* home not only is fundamental to make architectural choices toward an environmental and economical sustainability but it is also imperative to pay attention to the process of integration in the local cultural environment. This paper presents the results of an ethnographic research that informs and understands the implementation of a *Sustainable Connected Home* prototype. The paper demonstrates how the local context and the social sustainability discourse could provide impetus to technological innovation for sustainable design. It also provides a framework for future discussions on the definition of social sustainability in the context of design interventions.

Keywords: Architectural design, design research, innovation, case study/studies, social sustainability, qualitative research.

1 Introduction

Design plays a fundamental role in addressing the sustainable development, especially when it comes to the house. In the process of designing a *sustainable* home not only is fundamental to make architectural choices toward environmental and economical sustainability but it is imperative also to pay attention to the process of integration in the local cultural environment: this means equally to use local resources, to respect and learn from the native traditions and benefit from local expertise and to treasure the everyday practices that embody the local culture. In Csikszentmihalyi words: 'Thus the importance of the home depends not only on survival needs (to bring up infants, to sleep and eat in comfort), on the particular economy (hunting pastoral, farming or industrial), or on the climate; it also depends on value, tradition, and literary and religious associations that cannot be predicted from determining conditions' (Csikszentmihalyi and Halton 1981).

As the Design Agenda for Sustainability has stated, it is necessary to 'sustain promising social and technological innovations and to re-orient existing drivers of change towards sustainability' (Manzini 2009); this means to combine the technological development toward a more sustainable society with a reflective research on the social dimension of sustainability; even though the research on environmental sustainability has been carried on for more than 20 years, the social dimension of sustainability has

P.L.P. Rau (Ed.): CCD/HCII 2014, LNCS 8528, pp. 321–330, 2014.

been acknowledged only recently and still needs to be questioned and discuss in order to support and foster the development toward a sustainable society.

This paper presents the results of an ethnographic research conducted in Trentino (Italy) in summer 2008 with the purpose of mapping the cultural context where a Sustainable Connected Home[1] prototype would be implemented in 2010. In our initial hypothesis, the Sustainable Connected Home is a home that 'is not only built with sustainable materials and that uses green energy, but also takes full advantage of all the digital world has to offer to create a building that can respond to its environment and to the needs of its inhabitants more intelligently. It employs the latest in what we know about artificial intelligence, as well as advanced robotics, to improve the quality of life for those who live in the home. And, going even further, it is a home that by its very existence and the way it works optimizes human behavior and thus promotes social sustainability' (Mitchell and Casalegno 2008). The Sustainable Connected Home has four main design objectives:

- Sustainable architecture; implementation of a vivid and specialized architecture that embodies particular sustainable principles, integrated into the landscape in an efficient and elegant way.
- Smart energy system; use of natural sources of energy for the energy supply of the home such as solar panels, rainwater retention, biomass and windmills.
- Information and communication technologies; integration of information and communication technologies to create a responsive system between users, architecture and energy systems.
- Social sustainability; integration of the individual home with the community with a focus on the social aspects of sustainable living and the local economy

Even though there is almost a consensus about the meaning of environmental and economic sustainability on the contrary the definition, indicators and strategies to address *social* sustainability remain still under discussion. In particular the discourse on sustainability in the context of design is particularly crucial and opens valuable possibilities for in-depth inquiry.

This paper elaborates on the definition of social sustainability, by presenting a qualitative research results aimed to inform a design project that present technological solution for sustainable design and it attempts to provide a framework for future discussions of the social sustainability definition in the context of design interventions.

2 Social Sustainability

Social sustainability has been defined as the third pillar of the tree bottom line of sustainability together with Economic and Environmental spheres (Elkington 1998;

[1] A project made within the *Green Homes Alliance*, between the Mobile Experience Lab, Design Laboratory, at the Massachusetts Institute of Technology, and the Fondazione Bruno Kessler, Italy. The concrete aim of the alliance is the advance research in sustainable architecture and renewable energy. Within the Alliance, we aim to build in 2010 a full scale prototype of a Connected Sustainable Home.

Barron and Gauntlett 2002). 'Social sustainability occurs when the formal and informal processes, systems, structures and relationships actively support the capacity of current and future generations to create healthy and livable communities. Socially sustainable communities are equitable, diverse, connected and democratic and provide a good quality of life' (McKenzie 2004).

Even if the concept is gaining more and more attention since the Bruntland Report (Future 1987) and it has been recognized as a fundamental task for sustainable development, there is still no consensus about its definition and measurements (Colantonio and Lane 2007; Lilley 2009; Littig and Griessler 2005; G.V.R.D. 2004).

Social sustainability has been described in terms of meeting basic needs, overcoming disadvantage, fostering personal responsibility, and social responsibility, foster trusting, harmonious and co-operative behavior, acknowledge cultural and community diversity, and foster tolerance, empowering people to participate in decision-making (Baines and Morgan 2004; Sinner et al. 2004). 'Failure to describe these systems in a holistic manner through the synthesis of their different non-reducible and perfectly legitimate perspectives amounts to reductionism. An implication of the above is the fact that not a single sustainability metric at the moment can claim to comprehensively assess sustainability.' (Gasparatos, El-Haram, and Horner 2007). Some authors has notice a shift from a more qualitative perspective that investigate more soft social factors: 'The development and integration process of indicators is hindered further by the shift in the social sustainability discourse from the in-depth analysis of hard themes towards the inclusion of soft themes, as reviewed earlier. As a result, new sustainability indicators are increasingly focused on measuring these emerging themes rather than improving the measurement of more traditional concepts such as equity and fairness. (..) The chronological analysis of social sustainability themes also shows how traditional themes, such as equity, poverty reduction and livelihood, are increasingly been complemented or replaced by more intangible and less measurable concepts such as identity, sense of place and the benefits of social networks'(Colantonio 2009).

The social sustainability has been very often investigated in relation to the urban context and its community aspects. Bramley et al (2006) i.e. focus on the relationship between urban form and social sustainability and propose two main dimensions to the concept, relating to equity of access and the sustainability or quality of community: 'there is a more collective 'sustainability of community' dimension which, although seemingly more nebulous, is also fundamental to the concept. This second dimension is essentially concerned with the continued viability, health and functioning of 'society' itself as a collective entity, generally under the heading of 'community''. They discuss the fact that strategic planning for urban development has paid much attention to provide accessible jobs and affordable housing but other complementary aspects of equity also deserve attention: community participation, community stability and what they call the sense of place.

3 Methodology

This idea of *sense of place* is here considered of primary importance; protecting and supporting as well as learning and giving value to people sense of place is a key approach for the results of this research; the Sustainable Connected Home case study takes into account the sense of place and discusses its significance in the design process. When designing a sustainable home, considering sustainability from multiple perspectives becomes an essential approach for the success of the project. Of course using sustainable architecture is a fundamental part of the design process; in the Sustainable Connected Home the house will be built using sustainable materials and green energy technologies in order to meet the constructive requirements for a green home.

The objective of this research has been to understand how the design of a house could also foster the social aspect of sustainability. For this purpose, qualitative research has been conducted in the area where the sustainable connected home will be built in order to inform the design process.

The method adopted was basically ethnographic: Firstly, a series of interview were conducted in collaboration with a team of ethnographers from the Sorbonne University, CeaQ[2] in Zambana (Italy) from the 8th to the 12th of June 2009; 31 people have been interviewed, 17 woman and 14 men, of the age between 19 and 70 of which 10 in a municipal room and 21 in their house and outside or in the principle bar of the village, a meeting place situated in the town center near the most important buildings of the place (the school, the church, the town hall). For this first phase a qualitative research method with an open and semi structured questionnaire has been used.

Secondly, more in depth interviews were conducted in July 2009 directly in the respondents' houses, were the behaviors that were part of their everyday lives could be discussed in order to elaborate the relation between energy, garbage, water saving and consumption.

This analysis presents and interprets the tendencies appeared during the ethnographical research, considering the condition of the observed context and the theoretical board examined to study the phenomenon. The work has been conducted in accordance to the methods of the participant observation and the visual sociology, integrating the use of the photographic tool. The interviews aimed to map the relation among people and houses, the use of space, with a specific focus on three themes:

- the perception of the sustainability and ecology issues,
- the relation with the house,
- the use of space;

The results here presented question the qualitative research findings from a design point of view trying to:

[2] (Centre d'Etude sur l'Actuel et le Quotidien) directed by Michel Maffesoli at Université Paris Descartes Sorbonne.

- understand how to support and inform the design of a house and in this specific case study the development of the prototype of the Sustainable Connected Home
- investigate the meaning of sustainability when related to the social realm

4 Results

4.1 The Social Meaning of the House in Trentino

The population in Trentino has a widespread attention in behaving in a more sustainable way. Techniques for energy saving as solar panels, thermal coat, double glazing are common. An extensive technical knowledge of these appliances and a diffuse accuracy in conducting everyday practices for saving energy and recycling waste are common. In general people have very technical competences about building materials, energy self-production and management.

Sustainability has not been described as an issue related to large-scale problems as the global warming or the end of natural resources, but in fact has been told as the goal of the everyday life made of small gestures of reverence and respect for the surrounding territory. Sustainability is understood within the everyday life activities, so despite the over-all goal to prevent global warming seems remote and far away, it emerge that design can meet the need of supporting more sustainable everyday behaviors. Those behaviors highlight the importance of designing a house that can support everyday life; the idea of having a *home as personal trainer* involves building a structure that educates its inhabitants and the broader community so as to encourage behavior consistent with sustainability; this notion finds it confirmation in the conducted research.

The ethnography demonstrated as the house plays a major role in the ecology and sustainability discourse: it works as a link between the person and the territory. As a result it seems that a sustainable house should work not only as a passive connection between inhabitants and local reality but it should become an active translator for opening new possibilities of connection to the local community.

According to respondents' answers, the house is the symbol of belonging to their territory; the connection area between the inside and the outside are very important.

Large windows and a balcony are the elements of the house where the relation with the outside is outlined. Respondents report a wish to eliminate barriers within the house the ideal is to have a single house on one level with a door facing the garden where to eat in direct contact with the outside.

The different spaces inside are desired to be full of light: the idea of open space to catch the light from the outside with big large windows and a living room to share with an access outside on the garden is common to the respondents answers.

In the Sustainable Connected Home design we investigate on the relation among the space outside and inside in order to respect and reinforce the local use of space. The notion of *engawa*, the Japanese veranda that links the inside of the building with the outside of the building has been used to foster the social behaviors that allow people to communicate and interact with the community. It is a space belonging to the house but at the same time linked to the outside space that represents the interface between public and private. It fosters the social behaviors that are typical of Italian culture where people chat from window to window or sit on the porch watching outside. The window in particular resulted of primary importance both in the ethnography results and consequently in our design. We investigated how to combine local culture and social values with innovative technologies and sustainable architecture.

5 Windows as Interfaces

The window in a house is the element that relates the inside space with the outside space. It encompasses three design functions related to light, view and spatial articulation. As the contemporary building techniques have given relative autonomy to the building form, these three functions could be made by different elements of the house. That means the window has acquired more freedom in shape and in function; 'whilst in classical architecture the window could be considered a *beautiful object in itself* (which also justified separate analysis of this single element) the beautiful modern window can only be understood in relation to the whole special layout. It has ceased to be an object itself' (Meiss 1990). Taken into account the prior findings of the ethnographic research, the design of the Sustainable Connected Home prototype - that will be build in Trentino (Italy) in summer 2010 - has been designed as an innovative and experimental platform for the discussion about a new role for the window. 'The history of architecture could be written in terms of an ideological and technical struggle between the membrane and the frame, with differing cultures weighing in differently on the balance between solidly opaque and flexibly open, based partly on materials available, but more fundamentally on how definitively inside was to be separated from outside' (Lyndon and Moore 1996).

In the sustainable connected home design the south facade of the house is covered by a dynamic curtain wall with wooden frame and operable triple glazed windows incorporating Electro-chromic and PDLC film. This multifaceted curtain wall allows dynamic management and control of visibility, sunlight penetration and cross-ventilation. The variable configuration of the curtain wall makes possible the dynamic configuration of clear, opaque, open, and closed elements and establishes the currently optimum or the desirable performance.

The state of the Electrochromic glazing and PDLC film of the curtain wall is controlled by a control system that receives input from an implanted network of sensors, as well as from the inhabitants. We call this design Dynamic Window because it allows dynamic management and control of visibility, sunlight penetration and cross ventilation.

With regard to our ethnographic studies on the use of space and windows in the Trentino area, unconventional fenestration practices that are ecologically, socially and culturally sustainable are being explored in this architecture project.

From an architectural point of view the building is designed to perform sustainability under all combinations of environmental conditions. It can dynamically reconfigure its state by taking into account both real-time conditions and long-term goals to optimize its performance. Furthermore, the use of electronically activated variable transmission materials for the design of an interactive, programmable building façade that can exercise environmentally and socially sustainable building behaviors has been explored.

Different applications for this façade have been investigated: automated climate moderation, lighting, view and privacy controllers have been designed in order to foster the aesthetic, social, and cultural implications of the use of the house windows. 'The opening and closing of the windows blinds during different times of the day are important social rituals in different cultures. Windows welcome the new morning, signify the waking up of the inhabitants and communicate their availability to the neighbors. For the dynamic façade, the response to the morning and evening sun can also be exercised by subtle gestures' (Telhan et al. 2010). The importance that windows and balconies have in Trentino culture create a fertile context to experiment the Dynamic Windows technologies both as a platform for testing innovative technologies and as a dimension of research on social sustainable design.

'At stake in every understanding of the window is an interpretation of architecture and of politics, an implicit setting and definition of the terms in which they will be elaborated, practiced, and contested' (Keenan 1993).

The façade is not only the climate moderator, but also the screen that mediates the social dynamics between the inside and outside of the built environment. (..) Thus, conceiving new roles for the building façade is an interesting interaction design challenge when the façade can actively be configured for new relationships between the inside and outside; the environment and the house, the house and its inhabitants as well as the inhabitants among themselves and with their neighbors (Telhan et al. 2010). In (Csikszentmihalyi and Halton 1981) words: 'the house [is seen] primarily as a place where people interact with each other; when the home is seen in positive terms, it is because the interaction is harmonious'. For this reason the Connected Sustainable Home façade allows the user to define its view area designing the window frame cell. Without prescribing a fixed frame as the 'window,' the entire façade can be configured as a series of openings that can admit light and allow the inhabitants themselves to determine how much they would like to reveal themselves to the outside world. Electrically activated chromic can also be configured to dynamically respond to passer-by and allow the façade to follow the presence of a user by a series of embedded sensors. Over the completely transparent façade, a privacy patch in the size of the user can conceal only the moving people from the outside and leave the rest of the house fully open (Telhan et al. 2010).

6 Conclusions

To sum up, this research informs the design from a pragmatically standpoint on different items, the use and distribution of internal spaces, the relation between inside and outside and in particular the use of windows as interfaces for social interactions. Furthermore, this research informs the theoretical approach on social sustainability, in some major directions:

- To include the cultural and social factors in any design process
- To sustain strategies for social interaction and participation
- To works as a *translator* able to create and maintain relations and to foster communication
- To provide instruments for people to understand and address local problems
- To support participation in the creation of a *collective domain*

The local cultural environment people share, change radically the mode they organize the space of their houses; this mode communicate at the same time within the inhabitants and with the outside community. The house is simultaneously a protected and protective inner space to feel sheltered and an outer space working as an interface with the public sphere; those two dimensions are intertwined and complementary. The act of modifying the physical space allows the inhabitants to better understand themselves and to communicate and share their beliefs and what they considered significant in life.

The home space is processed and modified by communication signs narrating about the uniqueness and the identity, the needs and the wishes of the inhabitants. Furthermore, the house conveys values based both on the person singularity – i.e. comfort, protection, privacy or property – and on the person public dimension – i.e. belonging, patriotism, community participation, and politics. The house is more than a physical location, as a result of the interactions with its dwellers it becomes its self a cultural environment: 'The extent to which the physical environment is elaborated with communicative signs that reveal the specific characteristics of the inhabitants is, with language, one of the distinguishing feature of human life. Although we live in physical environments, we create cultural environments within them. We continually personalize and humanize the given environment as a way of both adapting to it and creating order and significance' (Csikszentmihalyi and Halton 1981).

In this framework it becomes obvious how social sustainable design discourse should include the cultural and social factors. The approach to social sustainability in design practice been described in this paper, seeks to push forward the sustainable architecture and building techniques in order to promote and experiment new way of sustaining social behaviors. As McKenzie has stated 'the criteria for inclusion as a 'social sustainability project' are that the project must be innovative, effective, sustainable (in the sense that the resources it requires are renewable), and have potential for replication (in the sense that it can serve as a model for generating projects elsewhere)'. This research adds a further dimension to the existing criteria: not only a project must empower individuals and communities promoting the system enabling capability (Manzini 2006) but also should take into account the socio-cultural dimension of its design, sustaining new strategies for social interaction, participation and communication.

Fostering communication among people and improving the ability of the house space to work as a symbolic environment addressing both the inside users and the outside context is the key concept for accomplish a more social sustainable design. In other words social relation are matters of communication among subject and in becoming a platform for learning, sharing and connecting the house can partake in the moving to a more sustainable society. Social sustainable design works as a *translator* able to create and maintain relations among people and information. Translation means the ability of link technological innovation and local culture to assist and support the individual understanding of our changing reality. When design addresses social sustainability it encourages integration against separation both between people and communities. Social sustainable design allows participation reducing loneliness and separation as a result of its ability in fostering communication to create and maintain links between people who belong to the same community and connect diverse communities. Technologies designed within social sustainability are those who foster the relation between social imaginary and real practice.

Furthermore, social sustainability in design means to support participation in the creation of a *collective domain*; this space is the complex web of habits, values, preferences, and culture of each individual intertwined and co-created with other individuals.

Roger Bastide (1970) said: ‘It is not the group as such that explains to us the communal memory; more precisely it is the structure of the group that gives us the picture of communal memory, that is no longer defined as communal conscience, but rather as a system of interrelations of individual memories. If the other person is necessary in order to remember , it is not because ‘I’ and ‘the other’ are immersed in the same social thought, but because our personal memories are united with memories of other people within a balanced game made up of mutual and complementary images.’

In conclusion is the commitment and participation in this collective domain that consent a community to give birth to creative and innovative solutions to local and global problems.

Acknowledgment. We would like to acknowledge the contributions of the Mobile Experience team to the development of our paper, research and design. This research was conducted within the Green Home Alliance between the Mobile Experience Lab at the Massachusetts Institute of Technology and the Fondazione Bruno Kessler, in Trento, Italy.

References

1. Baines, J., Morgan, B.: Sustainability Appraisal: A Social Perspective. International Institute for Environment and Development, London (2004)
2. Barron, L., Gauntlett, E.: Model of social sustainability. Housing and Sustainable Communities Indicators Project. Western Australian Council of Social Service, Perth (2002)
3. Bastide, R.: Mémoire collective et sociologie du bricolage. L’Année Sociologique 21(3), 65–108 (1970)
4. Bramley, G., Dempsey, N., Power, S., Brown, C.: What is ‘social sustainability’and how do our existing urban forms perform in nurturing it. In: Planning Research Conference, Bartlett School of Planning. University College, London (2006)
5. Colantonio, A.: Social sustainability: a review and critique of traditional versus emerging themes and assessment methods. Loughborough University, Loughborough (2009)

6. Colantonio, A., Lane, G.: Measuring Social Sustainability: Best Practice from Urban Renewal in the EU. EIBURS Working Paper Series (January 2007)
7. Csikszentmihalyi, M., Halton, E.: The Meaning of Things: Domestic Symbols and the Self. Cambridge University Press, Cambridge (October 30, 1981)
8. Elkington, J.: Cannibals with Forks: The Triple Bottom Line of 21st Century Business. New Society Publishers (September 1, 1998)
9. Future, C.: The Brundtland Report. United Nations World Commission (1987)
10. G.V.R.D., The Social Components of Community Sustainability: A Framework. TAC Social Issues Subcommittee, Vanvouver (2004)
11. Gasparatos, A., El-Haram, M., Horner, M.: The argument against a reductionist approach for assessing sustainability. In: International Conference on Whole Life Urban Sustainability and its Assessment, SUE-MoT Conference Proceedings Glasgow, UK, pp. 27–29 (2007)
12. Keenan, T.: Windows: of vulnerability. The Phantom Public Sphere 5. Unversity Minnesota Press (1993)
13. Lilley, D.: Design for sustainable behaviour: strategies and perceptions. Design Studies (2009)
14. Littig, B., Griessler, E.: Social sustainability: a catchword between political pragmatism and social theory. International Journal of Sustainable Development 8(1), 65–79 (2005)
15. Lyndon, D., Moore, C.W.: Chambers for a Memory Palace. The MIT Press, Cambridge Mass (1996)
16. Manzini, E.: Design for sustainability. How to design sustainable solutions. Sustainable Design (2006)
17. New design knowledge. Design Studies 30(1), 4–12 (2009)
18. McKenzie, S.: Social sustainability: towards some definitions. In: Magill. Hawke Research Institute Working Paper Series (2004), `https://www.sapo.org.au/binary/binary141/Social.pdf`
19. von Meiss, P.: Elements of Architecture. Van Nostrand Reinhold International, London (1990)
20. Mitchell, W.J., Casalegno, F.: The Connected Sustainable Home (2008), `http://moble.mit.edu/fbk`
21. Sinner, J., Baines, J., Crengle, H., Salmon, G., Fenemor, A., Tipa, G.: Sustainable Development: A summary of key concepts. Ecologic Research Report 2 (2004)
22. Telhan, O., Casalegno, F., Park, J., Kotsopoulos, S., Yu, C.: Interaction Design with Building Facade, Cambridge, MA (January 25, 2010)

Designing "Healthy" into Green Environment for Taipei City

Ying-Ming Su[1,*], Li-Yu Chen[2], and Annie Chen[3]

[1] Department of Architecture, National Taipei University of Technology,
1, Sec. 3, Zhongxiao E. Rd., Taipei 10608 Taiwan, R.O.C., Taipei, Taiwan
ymsu@ntut.edu.tw
[2] Department of Interior Design, Chung Yuan Christian University, Chung Li, Taiwan
chenly99@gmail.com
[3] Graduate Institute of Commercial Design, Chung Yuan Christian University,
Chung Li, Taiwan
annie928@ms22.hinet.net

Abstract. To achieve the goal of green environment related to an adaptive city of Taipei which is the World Design Capital 2016. We should discuss the effect of wind environment around the buildings at the beginning of design and planning phase of buildings first, for wind environment is the most important factor concerns with greenhouse and heat island effect. This research was based on a method of CFD done by Autodesk Ecotect Analysis software for simulating city building layout, study the two different building massing layout of Shezi Island in Taiwan. Results of simulation showed that the layout characterized by street block type, and therefore affect the residents' health, activities and psychological feelings; while the case of three-sided building layout surrounded by urban of open space, on the other hand, can provide more comfortable, healthy places for rest and outdoor activities.

Keywords: Healthy, Green environment, Wind environment, CFD Analysis, Shezi Island.

1 Introduction

Taipei is the World Design Capital 2016 with the slogan of "Adaptive City". It gives Taipei an opportunity to show how Taipei City to be a sustainable development city with respect to life quality and health, ecological sustainability, smart living and urban regeneration.

With excessive economic growth let the greenhouse effect and urban heat island effect issues become more seriously in recent years that lead to violent global climate change and natural disasters. Therefore, to achieve the goal of sustainable green environment and zero-carbon buildings related to a comfortable, healthy livable city, a new technical method must be used at the beginning of design and planning phase of buildings.

* Corresponding author.

P.L.P. Rau (Ed.): CCD/HCII 2014, LNCS 8528, pp. 331–340, 2014.

The effect of wind environment around the buildings plays an important role in a complex mutualism environment relationship between comfortable, healthy, sustainable and natural ecosystems. To understand the natural mechanism by wind, proper measures must be taken to predict wind environment around the buildings. Open spaces and facilities around buildings must be reviewed for their usages and planned not to displease users from the perspective of wind environment. Additionally, wind environment change by newly constructed buildings must be reviewed in the design and planning stage to prevent negative influence to the existing building in terms of natural ventilation performance, human comfort, psychological feeling and pleasant wind environment for local residents [1-2].

Besides, the growing number of high-rise and high-density buildings due to drastic urbanization is causing a number of issues in urban wind environment, such as the heat island problem, etc. Among these issues, the strong winds that can arise around high-rise buildings cause difficulty for pedestrians, while weak winds owing to the blockage of window by high-rise buildings may stagnate the heat and pollutants, causing discomfort to pedestrians or people resting in the vicinity of the buildings [3-5]. To make comfortable, healthy, sustainable city possible, a building's performance in terms of energy consumption and environmental impact must be analyzed from the first stage of design and planning phase.

2 Adaptive Design Concept of Shezi Island

Shezi Island (Fig.1), located at the intersection of Keelung River and Tanshui River in Taipei, was originally a floodplain. A big urban park is planned to be built in the northern part of it. Meanwhile, a livable, productive, and eco-friendly community both to healthy environment and humanity for Taipei will develop from here, making Shezi Island the green ecological foundation in the city of Taipei. Traditional performance of eco-building performance analysis is based on research papers of questionnaires, observation and interviews and lacks scientific objective evaluation.

This study started from a different point of view of the ecological city, using CFD software as a new technical method to simulate the wind behavior around the building layout [6-11]. This study discussed two design plans of Shezi Island including the wind environmental impact created by different building layout and open space, and other impacts including environmental comfort, activity continuity and comfort level of pedestrian wind system.

In order to improve the quality of healthy environment, residents' requirements on daily working and activity space must be taken into consideration. According to principles of relevant surveys on comfort of open space, factors such as humidity, ventilation, and sunlight exposure are all closely related to wind environment [12-15]. Of all the related factors, building layout is the most important one [16-18].

Hong, Y.A. [19] in his research illustrated that Pedestrian Level Wind usually refers to the wind environment at the height of pedestrians' head that is about 1.5-2 meters above the earth. Therefore human beings are most sensitive to this wind level which makes it the anchor height when researching the flow fields in public spaces. Other factors such as wind characteristic, wind direction, wind velocity, the size of architecture itself, the geometrical shape and neighboring building complex, will also exert an impact on the wind flow around the building, hence, creating an instable turbulence flow field. The annoying Pedestrian Level Wind can directly influence the design of architecture and urban plan in the vicinity. Wind flow has a substantial effect in the comfort of pedestrians, the environmental conditions within public spaces and around building entrance and the activities that might occur there. Wind tunnel tests during the design development process are often critical, particularly where proposed buildings are significantly taller than the neighbor [20].

Case 1 of Shezi Island plan design featured the one-side space of style (linear type) while case 2 highlighted a three-sides space of style (three-sided building layout) and both with 40% building coverage ratio and 60% floor area ratio [21].

This study based on the simulation and analysis of building wind environment of different layout done with the aid of Autodesk Ecotect Analysis CFD software. The experiment location and cases of Shezi Island plan design were showed in Fig.1. In both cases, the urban open space was divided into part A and part B. There were 10 measuring points distributed in Case 1 and 13 points in Case 2. Wind environment and its effect on space continuity, environmental comfort, activity continuity, and access, etc [22-23] were studying on at respective heights of 1.5m and 5m. According to the results of software simulation, further analysis and discussion on the plan design had been carried out.

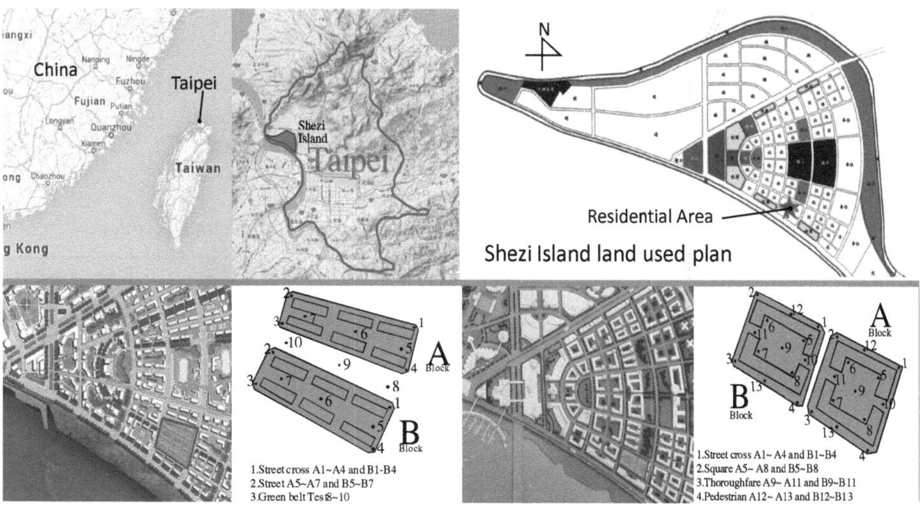

Fig. 1. Location of Shezi Island and two cases of Shezi Island development plan

3 Computational Analysis

This study calculated by the fluid dynamical equations, as suggested by Launder, B.E. and Spalding, D.B. [24], to simulate the incompressible turbulent flow act, under the condition of turbulent flow field.

The selections of simulated area were established on the street block around the base to improve credibility of simulation. In the setting of simulated boundary calculating area, the size of boundary area set by Bouyera, J., Inard, C. and Musy, M. [25] will be the parameter value (Fig.2, 3). For simulation calculation, the method of mean grid setting was adopted to verify the digital simulation.

The climatic condition (Table 1) in the study was provided by Tanshui observation stations from Central Weather Bureau [26]. Statistics of average wind speed, maximum instantaneous wind and wind direction from 2005 to 2011 for the setting of parameters were also collected.

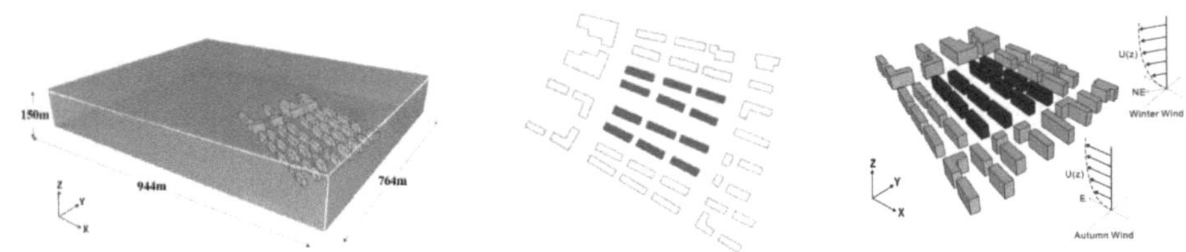

Fig. 2. Parameters setting of simulation model in Case1

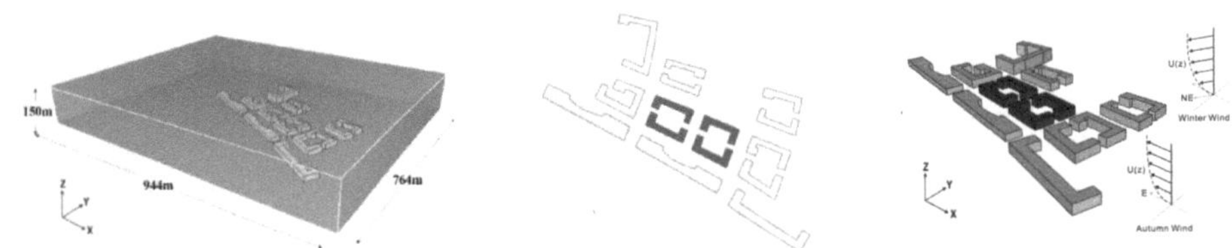

Fig. 3. Parameters setting of simulation model in Case2

Table 1. Tanshui observation stations weather information Velocity :(m/s)

Season	Spring	Summer	Autumn	Winter	The survey period
Average wind speed	0.6	0.5	0.6	0.6	2005-2011
Wind direction	Northeast	Southeast	East	Northeast	
Maximum instantaneous wind (month)	10.7	21	18.8	10.7	2005
	16.1	13	10.7	14.3	2006
	9.8	10.7	27.7	11.2	2007
	13	14.3	10.7	8.9	2008
	12.1	12.1	13.9	8.9	2009
	-	-	8.9	8.5	2010
	7.6	11.6	11.2	13.9	2011
Maximum instantaneous wind (average)	11.6	13.8	14.6	10.9	2005-2011

4 Results and Discussion

4.1 Street Open Space

The results of the CFD simulation was showed in Fig.4, it was clear to see that at the height of 1.5m, the wind flow of the street block went from northeast in winter. As the street block type of layout had formed an area of open space, which was called street canyon, the air flow through both sides of the building and generated a channel effect (Fig.4-e). Since the wind flowed from a wide area to the narrow street, the area of its flowing passage diminished, the wind speed at the end of the side of the building accelerated and formulated an area of high wind speed. In particular, when the wind velocity achieved the utmost, the wind velocity change became more obvious, developed the corner wind at the end of the lower part of the building wall (Fig.4-f).

In Test Point 8 at the windward side, the wind velocity was low due to the block of nearby building in most periods of time (Fig.4-a~b), only with an evident increased when it achieved the maximum instantaneous wind velocity. At the measuring point of Test Point 9, in the middle of the open space between buildings, the air flow was averagely distributed and the change of wind velocity was small. However, in Test Point 10 at the lee side, the building layout caused the air to flow through the side of the building and form a part channel effect at the far end of the open space.

In autumn (Fig.4), the wind came from east into the open space area and developed an evident corner wind, and hence a channel effect with great wind velocity. The whole wind field flowed into the building complex and street canyon from the east, made the wind flow steady along the west fall of the building so that the wind velocity above the pedestrian was low which provided the pedestrian system with activity continuity and space continuity. The channel effect exerted more influence in autumn than in winter with a higher wind velocity. Therefore, it was suggested that the axis of open space in street should avoid windblast to provide proper ventilation facility, creating an environment of comfort.

In case 2, the wind in the flow field at the height of 1.5m in winter came from the northeast (Fig.4-c). Due to the block of building layout, the wind velocity decreased to the speed of less than 1m/s even 0m/s at the foot of the wall in space between the square area in the building and the building walls near both sides of the square that provided comfortable environment for long-term stay and outdoor activities. Outside the west side of the building, where the wind passed by, flow field of swirling air is formed in the back of the building, of which the wind velocity was low and weak. There existed the building awake which meant the ventilation was not good. Therefore, the design plan of the square should consider the activities and matched facilities within the effect of windblast area and their connection with the environment around and the pedestrian system.

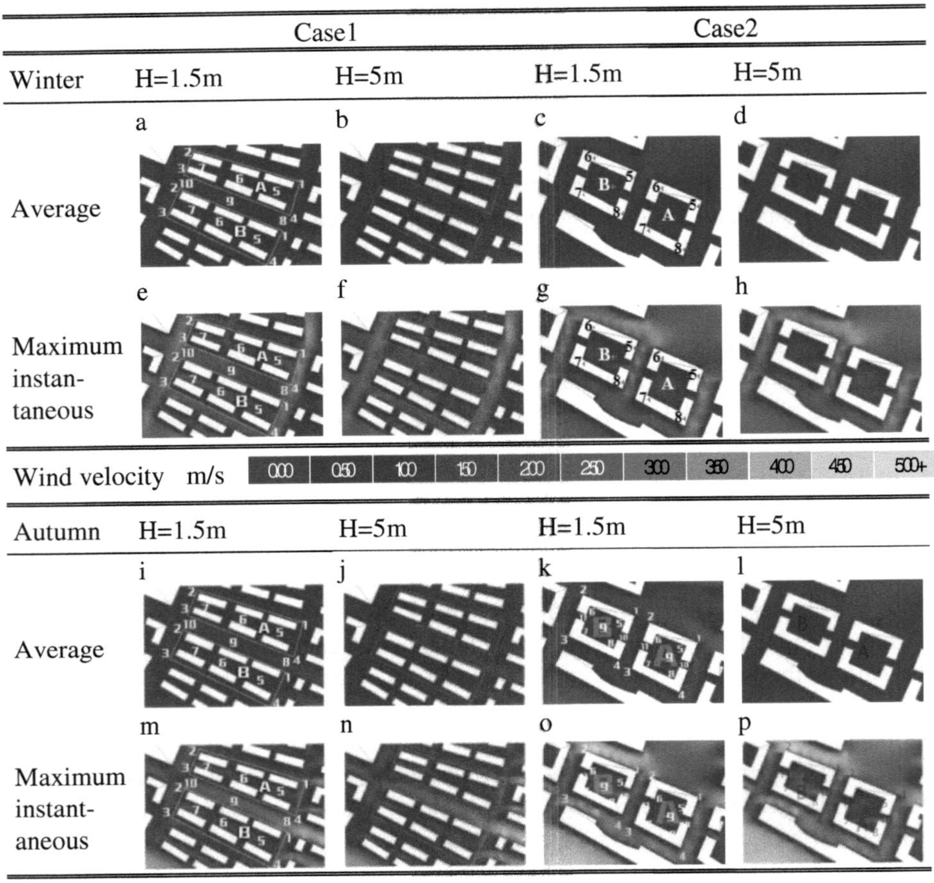

Fig. 4. Diagrams of digital simulation from measuring points in winter and autumn

4.2 The Environmental Comfort of Open Space Area to Street Area

Wind velocity at windward side of open space was high therefore reducing the comfort under the condition of short-term stay both in winter and autumn (Fig.5 a-a', c-c' section). Street of open space was affected by the building layout on each side which could generate a channel effect, higher wind velocity at the side of street, and wind circulations in the middle when wind velocity achieved the maximum in autumn (Fig.5 d-d' section).

In conclusion, the using of space area should take into consideration the environmental comfort while the facade design of the building layout at street side should consider the windblast including plans of trees, plants, and necessary facilities to go with it against the possible windblast.

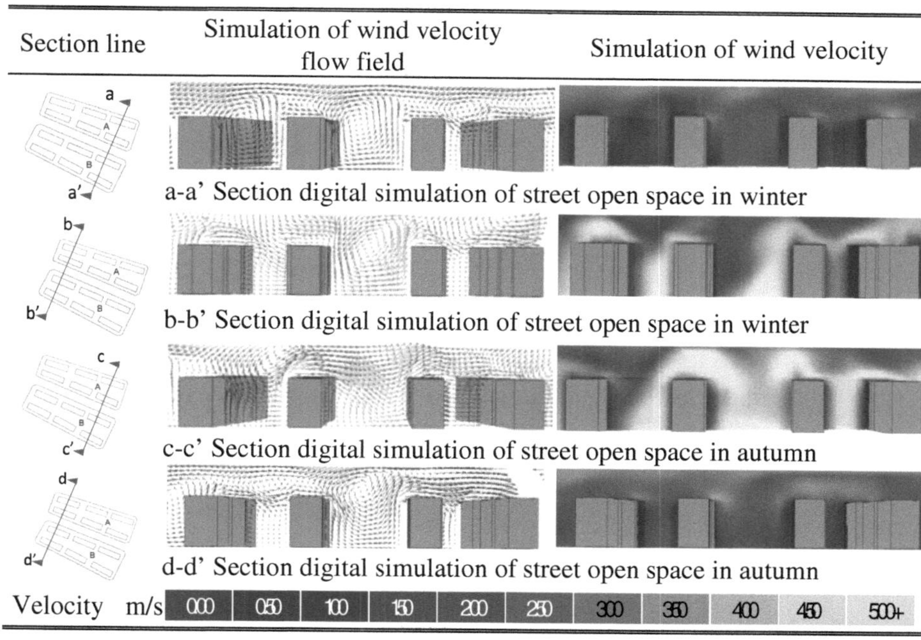

Fig. 5. Diagram of digital simulation of wind velocity in street open space

4.3 The Environmental Comfort of Open Space Area to Square Area

The simulation result of wind environment showed that, in winter, wind flows in from northeast and affected by the windward side and the building layout, wind field created circulations at its entrance. The wind field changed a lot and the wind velocity was high (Fig.6 b-b' section). Rest of the area didn't have such a changing situation of wind field while maintaining a low wind velocity and environmental comfort which was suitable for long-time sitting as relaxation and other relaxing activities (Fig.6 a-a' section). In autumn, at the entrance of open space in square, wind velocity was high and changed a lot because of windward side air flow, corner wind of the building and the entrance of nearby streets or neighborhoods (Fig.6 d-d' section). Rest of the wind field above the pedestrian didn't change much with low wind velocity and enjoyed the environmental comfort.

As a result, design plan for outdoor activities in square open space should consider the wind flow created both at the entrance and in the middle of the square, the windblast and environmental comfort. The architecture design should take into consideration the wind direction, wind velocity and entrance size of the building. As for the building layout, the sides and lee side of the building complex should face the autumn wind while the closure part facing the winter wind so as to block the windblast, meanwhile the comfort of pedestrians was also an important index, so that a comfortable, healthy place for outdoor activities could be built for the residents.

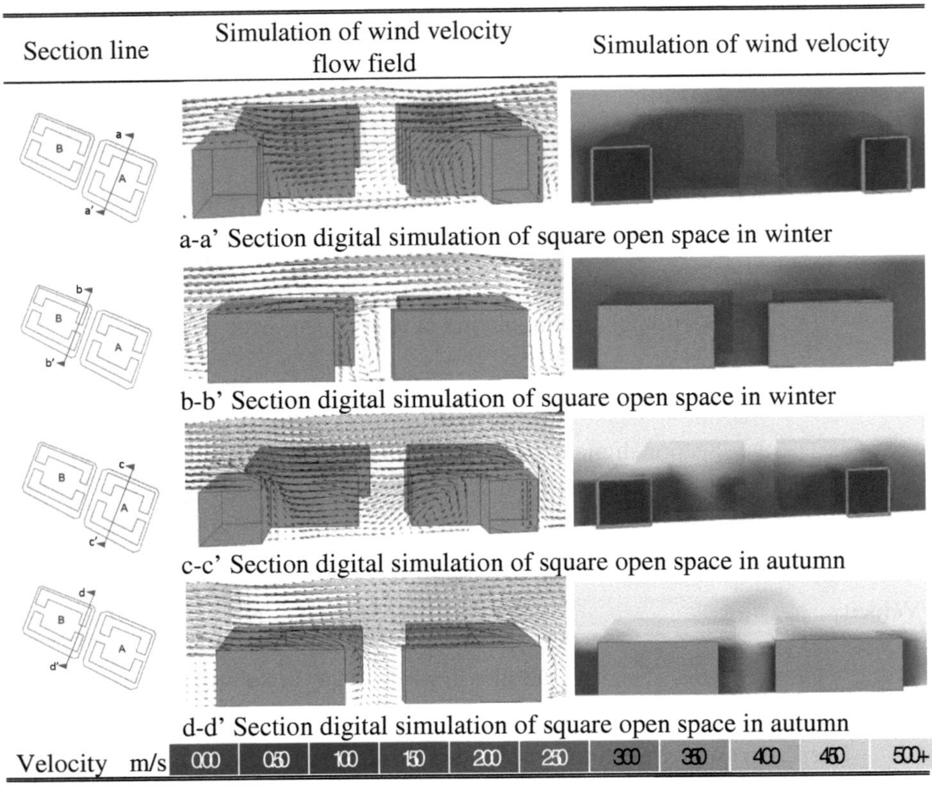

Fig. 6. Diagram of digital simulation of wind velocity in street open space

5 Conclusions

This study showed a new adaptable technology for designing healthy into green environment at the beginning of design and planning phase that we adopted the method of wind simulation and proved that building layouts affected the flow field of open space which was main area for outdoor activities and rest. Wind speed of the monsoon and building layout had an influence on the wind environment of urban open space. Therefore the design of building complex should take into consideration the prevailing wind direction and avoid facing the windward side or an enclosed building compound for the sake of natural ventilation simulation could improve efficacy of advanced evaluation of urban design plan and hence, provided important references to quantifiable projects in the original plan as well as the principles and influence of the design plan. As a result, different urban building layouts and forms of open space had an influence on the usability of the area.

The urban heat island effect was growing significantly related to the growing number of high-rise and high-density buildings. Using CFD simulation in design and planning phase, we could both to consider external and internal airflows, also knew about the behavior and change of the wind environment. It could accurate comparison of different design options quickly. The other purpose of this study was to investigate the incorporation of reality and Ecotect and how they interact in the process. Helps people feel healthy and comfort with graphic presentation in advance of construction, as well as avoided wrong decision and improved the quality of environment for sustainable city. And more efficient materials handling and waste recovery. The results could feedback to the planner and designer to modify the layout of buildings to have a more healthy, comfortable new town and better environment.

Acknowledgement. This paper represents part of the results obtained under the support of the National Science Council, Taiwan, ROC (Contract No. NSC101-2627-E-027-001-MY3).

References

1. Lee, S., Song, D.: Prediction and Evaluation Method of Wind Environment in the Early Design Stage using BIM-based CFD simulation. WCCM/APCOM, J. Materials Science and Engineering 10, 1–10 (2010)
2. Hsieh, C.M., Lin, C.C., Cheng, W.Y.: Comfort Index Establishment of Wind Environment and Evaluation of Improvement Strategy in Urban Residential Areas– A Study of Urban Renewal Plan of Da Lin Public Housing, Tainan. J. Architecture and Planning 11(3), 221–242 (2010)
3. Lee, S., Song, D.: Evaluation of Wind Environment Around the Building in the Early Design Stages Using BIM-Based CFD Simulation. J. Air-Conditioning and Refrigeration 19(4), 263–272 (2011)
4. Bangaleea, M.Z.I., Lin, S.Y., Miaua, J.J.: Wind Driven Natural Ventilation Through Multiple Windows of a Building: A Computational Approach. J. Energy and Buildings 45, 317–325 (2012)
5. Yang, Y.H.: The Effect of Architectural Types on Air Pollutant Dispersion in Urban Wind Field. National Taipei University of Technology, Taipei (2011) (in Chinese)
6. Sapian, A.R.: Validation of the Computational Fluid Dynamics (CFD) Method for Predicting Wind Flow Around a High-Rise Building (HRB) in an Urban Boundary Layer Condition. J. Construction in Developing Countries 14(2), 1–20 (2009)
7. Scargiali, F., Grisafi, F., Busciglio, A., Brucato, A.: Modeling and Simulation of Dense Cloud Dispersion in Urban Areas by Means of Computational Fluid Dynamics. J. Hazardous Materials 197, 285–293 (2011)
8. Labovsky, J., Jelemensky, L'.: Verification of CFD Pollution Dispersion Modeling Based on Experimental Data. J. Loss Prevention in the Process Industries 24, 166–177 (2011)
9. Mochidaa, A., Tominagab, Y., Yoshiec, R.: AIJ Guideline for Practical Applications of CFD to Wind Environment Around Buildings. In: The Fourth International Symposium on Computational Wind Engineering(CWE 2006), Yokohama (2006)
10. Baik, J.J., Park, S.B.: Urban Flow and Dispersion Simulation Using a CFD Model Coupled to a Mesoscale Model. J. American Meteorological Society, 1667–1681 (2009)
11. Tominagaa, Y., Mochidab, A., Yoshiec, R., Kataokad, H., Nozue, T., Yoshikawaf, M., Shirasawac, T.: AIJ Guidelines for Practical Applications of CFD to Pedestrian Wind Environment Around Buildings. J. Wind Engineering and Industrial Aerodynamics 96, 1749–1761 (2008)

12. Chiu, Y.H., Wu, M.F.: Effects of the Wind Environment on Street Characteristics. J. City and Planning 37(4), 501–528 (2010)
13. Wang, W.T.: The Passive Utilization of Venture Effect and Channel Effect on Urban Wind Field. National Taipei University of Technology, Taipei (2010) (in Chinese)
14. Huang, S.W.: Study of the Preference and Satisfaction of Open Space by Senior Population in Taiwan– Case Study of Chang Lung Apartment Building Community. Department of Urban Planning of National Cheng Kung University, Tainan (2010) (in Chinese)
15. Chou, Y.L.: A study of Interior Comfort Improvement in Fluence of Integrate Building Facade with Balcony and PV System Integrated with Fans– Tanshui Area for Example. Department of Architecture of Tamkang University, Taipei (2009) (in Chinese)
16. Carpentieri, M., Robins, A.G., Baldi, S.: Three-Dimensional Mapping of Air Flow at an Urban Canyon Intersection. J. Boundary-Layer Meteorol. 133, 277–296 (2009)
17. Hsu, Y.J.: A Study of Public Open Space System Urban Design Guidelines. Department of Architecture of National Cheng Kung University, Tainan (2002) (in Chinese)
18. Li, W.C.: The Impact of Length to Width Ratio on Wind Environment for Row Houses in Street Canyons– A Case Study of Weather Data in Tainan. J. Architecture Science 75, 135–153 (2011)
19. Hong, Y.A.: A Study on the Ventilation Assessment of Community Environment in Summer. Department of Architecture of National Cheng Kung University, Tainan (2007) (in Chinese)
20. Chou, D.C.: Physical Environment of Architecture. Taipei (1999) (in Chinese)
21. Department of Urban Development, Taipei City Government, `http://www.planning.taipei.gov.tw`
22. Chen, S.C.: A Study on the Life Style Change of Inner Court Community. Department of Urban Planning and Spatial Information of Feng Chia University, Taichung (2002) (in Chinese)
23. Al-Sallal, K.A., Al-Rais, L.: Outdoor Airflow Analysis and Potential for Passive Cooling in the Modern Urban Context of Dubai. J. Renewable Energy. 38, 40–49 (2012)
24. Launder, B.E., Spalding, D.B.: The Numerical Computation of Turbulent Flows. J. Computer Methods in Applied Mechanics and Engineering. 3, 269–289 (1974)
25. Bouyera, J., Inard, C., Musy, M.: Microclimatic Coupling as a Solution to Improve Building Energy Simulation in an Urban Context. J. Energy and Buildings 43, 1549–1559 (2011)
26. Central Weather Bureau Website, `http://www.cwb.gov.tw/V7/index.htm`

Designing "Flourishing" into Green Environment for Taipei City

Ying-Ming Su[1,*], Yu-Chou Wu[2], and Chia-Hui Lin[2]

[1] Department of Architecture, National Taipei University of Technology, Taipei, Taiwan
ymsu@ntut.edu.tw
[2] Graduate Institute of Design, National Taipei University of Technology, Taipei, Taiwan
vk6501@gmail.com, fun_chia@yahoo.com.tw

Abstract. Taipei City became the World Design Capital 2016 with the slogan of "Adaptive City" and "Adaptive Design". When seeking strategies to green environment, this study was adopted a new adaptive approach with semantic differential analysis and questionnaires to show how to design flourishing by conducting a preference cognitive test marked by "morphology" for ecological sustainability, especially in interior space. The analytic results showed that the morphological components of preference ranks from top were: repetition, proportion, gradation. And too complicated or too simple the change of morphological components did both affect viewers' preference; also the presence of morphologies had an emotional effect on the viewers. It should be emphasized on morphological elements and form of aesthetic principles to achieve a balanced proportion of design for indoor vertical greening environment and spatial atmosphere, for the purpose of creating good flourishing visual experience.

Keywords: Image Analysis, Indoor Vertical Greening, Environmental Perception, Morphological Design.

1 Introduction

ICSID (International Council of Societies of Industrial Design) had announced Taipei City the World Design Capital 2016 with the slogan of "Adaptive City" and "Adaptive Design". It gave Taipei an opportunity to show Taipei City of sustainable development with good life quality, health, and ecological sustainability. Because of growing urban population lead to dense building mass layout, reduction of green spaces, destruction to ecological cycle system and acceleration of global warming. Vertical greening came up as a feasible solution to the problem. It didn't take up much space while managing to restore the ecological environment and purify the air through the green plants' self-adjustment ability. More importantly, vertical greening could bring indoor visual pleasure and flourishing space to comfort the physical and psychological perception of indoor viewers. In recent years, there was a rising demand for vertical greening in interior design (e.g., public space, business space,

* Corresponding author.

P.L.P. Rau (Ed.): CCD/HCII 2014, LNCS 8528, pp. 341–350, 2014.

restaurants) in Taiwan as well as its multiple forms, which signified a trend in the future and importance of this study.

In retrospect of past research of vertical greening in Taiwan were focusing on aspects such as building techniques, plant effectiveness [1-3], physical effectiveness of indoor and outdoor vertical greening of buildings [4] and psychological impact of indoor environment on the viewers [5-7]. However, all the researches above hadn't discussed the impact of morphological and shaping preference on indoor vertical greening. This research was adopted a new approach of image preference to study the viewers' attitude towards their visual and psychological feelings. Morphological design could have a direct impact on the basis of users' perception of the contour of the form. Therefore, this research investigated the landscape form and image preference through users' perception. Then designed questionnaires focused on image analysis and semantic differences are given to users to test their preference cognitions marked by "morphology", to study the impact and importance of morphology. The survey results was assessed by Excel and analyzed by statistics software Windows SPSS 18 with the function of One-Way ANOVA. This study concluded the specific form trail and morphological perception of preference and appropriate presence of flourishing images in the interior green environment designed in the aim of providing reference for future design of indoor vertical greening that catered to preference of viewers' from different backgrounds.

2 Study Design

Psychology Dictionary defined image as "a mixture of subjective judgment preferences and attitudes of a wide range of things". Kevin Lynch [8] regarded image as a vast reference structure which could organize activities, beliefs and knowledge, and could play a social role to provide communities with materials of symbol and collective memory to give viewers a sense of emotional security. Kotler [9] put forward that image is an object, which could generate a group of perception, belief and ideas. Gartner [10] proposed that image should include cognitive, affective and cognitive behaviors. Through above it could be concluded that image was an accumulative psychological picture based on personal sensory perception and subjective empirical background. Therefore, landscape image was a product of interaction activities between viewers and environment, and this image could be referred to and studied to help understand and experience the whole environment. To shape the image, we needed a specific basic form which called "morphology", and that's why this research started from a perspective of morphology to study viewers' preference for the design for indoor vertical greening. To do so, we adopted one of the researching methodologies - semantic differential analysis to do a quantitative evaluation of preference degree. The study included three phases: representative morphological screening, defined the measuring gauge of emotional adjective, and questionnaire on perceptual preference as shown in Fig.1.

2.1 Phase I Study: Representative Morphological Screening

The objective of form was always in pursuit of beauty. Aesthetic Principles were people's reflection over natural and man-made beauty concluded after long-term

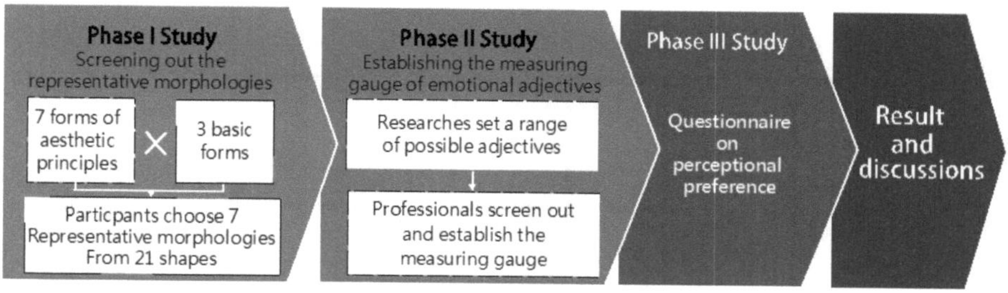

Fig. 1. Research process

organized, systematic research, and served as basis of interpretation or creative aesthetic forms [11]. Altogether 7 aesthetic principles such as Repetition, Eurhythmy, Proportion, Gradation, Contrast, Balance and Unified were studied and found after screening out those of semantic similarity [11-17]. Besides, square, triangle and circle were the basic forms of all morphology [18]. Under the guideline of the two principles above, 21 morphologies in this research on indoor vertical greening were designed as shown in Fig. 2.

For the purpose of the research, the questionnaire was designed in a structured way investigating both professionals with designing background and non-professionals. Professional designers were mainly practitioners in architecture, landscape, interior design, and gardening; while non-professionals were mainly students as Evans and wood [19], Chen and Lin [3] pointed out that the results of evaluation on students were much the same as those on general public.

97% of the 100 questionnaires were valid for further analysis. The socio-demographic characteristics of the participants were carefully monitored. In terms of participants' gender, the male to female ratio was 1:1.37. The age group was between 21-50 years old and half of the participants had professional design background. The research result showed that the participants' preference for the form of aesthetic principles was ranked in the order below: "Repetition", "Proportion", and "Gradation". The statistic result of representative morphological preference for different was shown in Fig. 2.

2.2 Phase II Study: The Measuring Gauge of Emotional Adjective

To understood the preference of viewers for the morphological design for indoor vertical greening, we compiled terms from related references on the methodology of semantic differential analysis and chose "general emotional adjectives" as benchmark measurement with spectrum from extreme negative attitudes to positive attitudes. Also general emotional adjectives used by previously researches on landscape environment were taking into consideration [20-25]. For first preliminary step, we chose 51 adjectives (Table 1) that are easy to understand, frequently used and clear to express emotional response to the morphology. Secondly, another questionnaire was

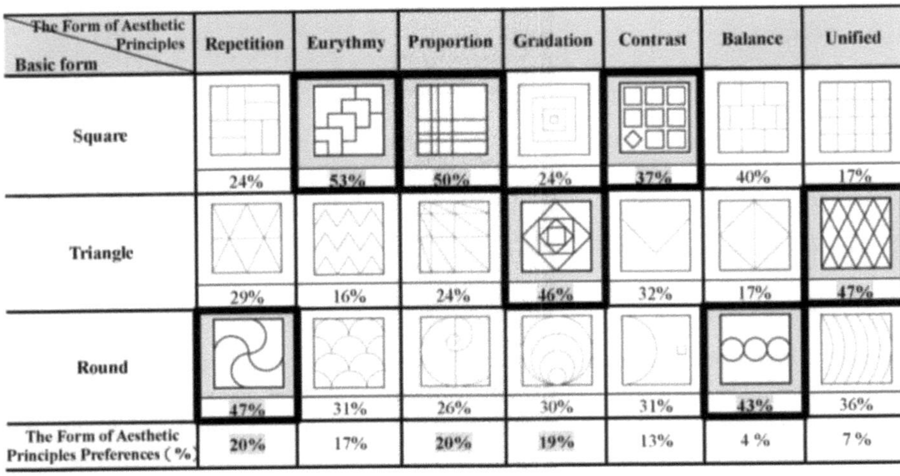

Fig. 2. Morphological design and preference for the seven forms of aesthetic principles

administered to professionals with a design career. The participants of this questionnaire were required to pick out one suitable word that could best describe their preference for the seven representative morphologies (Fig. 2) in Phase I study from the 51 emotional adjectives. The 10 emotional adjectives with highest reference frequency in the result were in bold font as shown in Table 1. 85% of 40 questionnaires are valid for analysis. Participants' socio-demographic characteristics: the male to female ratio was 1. The age group was between 21-50 years old. The non-professional to professional ratio was 1:3.

Table 1. The 51 emotional adjectives screened out in the preliminary step and the 10 emotional adjectives with highest reference frequency (times of reference)

amazing(16)	**mysterious(21)**	anger	cheerful	Fear	melancholy	solemn
attention(20)	**lead(38)**	antipathy	cozy	Gloomy	merry	stimulate
bored(19)	**rigid(35)**	anxiety	dangerous	harmonious	mild	suffering
bother(19)	**tenseness(17)**	aroused	dejection	Inspire	relaxed	tired
calm(23)	**vivid(26)**	atease	desirous	Intimate	relieved	vigilance
control(33)		beautiful	droopy	joy	serene	weary
interest-ing(27)		careful	euphoria	lively	serious	
monotone(22)		chaos	favorite	loneliness	shock	

This research had also matched pairs of words with opposite meanings in the top 10 emotional adjectives screened out in the preliminary step from the measuring gauge of semantic differential analysis. So another 3 adjectives were added to the pairs in underline font as shown in Table 1 and then formed 10 measuring gauge projects.

(Positive)	Very 3	Quite 2	A little 1	Average 0	A little 1	Quite 2	Very 3	(Negative)
lead								obstruct
vivid								rigid
control								loose
interesting								bored
bother								calm
plentiful								monotone
explicable								mysterious
attention								slack
relaxed								tenseness
amazing								commonplace

Fig. 3. Questionnaire and measuring gauge model of semantic differential analysis

Therefore, the final measuring gauge for the preference for indoor vertical greening was shown in Fig.3 to evaluate participants' perceptional preference for different morphologies.

2.3 Phase III Study: Questionnaire on Perceptual Preference

The questionnaire was divided into two parts. The first part was seven simulated diagrams as shown in Fig. 2 by two plants with high landscape preference: silver-net (Fittonia verschaffeltii) and ivy (Hedera helix) [26]. The simulated diagrams on the questionnaire were also arranged according to the principles proposed by Wu [27] on the visual scan sequence of flat images: center, stretching, and direction, etc. In addition, the singlet draft to help participants understand the morphologies was attached as reference. On the right column of each group, ten measuring gauges of adjectives were listed to be ticked by participants as they chose the one that could best describe their emotion and preference for the representative morphologies to examine the relationship between morphological image of indoor vertical greening and the environmental perception. The second part included six questions to investigate participants' background information and familiarity with the environment in order to conduct further analysis on differences between morphological perceptions of indoor vertical greening.

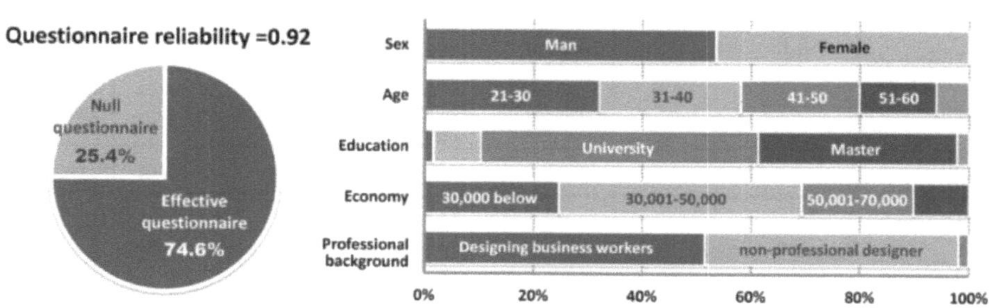

Fig. 4. Feedback of questionnaire of perception preference

Questionnaires on perception preference for morphological design of indoor vertical greening were designed on a judgment sampling method, selecting specific samples and issuing site. The participants of this questionnaire were: 1) professional with design background in architecture, landscape, and interior design, especially gardeners and garden companies. 2) non-professionals mainly regular visitors to flower fairs and interested in plants arrangement. The feedback and analysis of this questionnaire were shown in Fig. 4. Statistic software included Excel and Windows SPSS 18 (One-Way ANOVA function) were used to evaluate participants' preference for morphological design of indoor vertical greening and the differences between participants with different backgrounds.

3 Results and Discussion

3.1 Analysis on Preference for Morphological Designs of Indoor Vertical Greening

In analysis on preference for morphological designs of indoor vertical greening, participants presented seven emotional adjectives towards different morphological representatives as was illustrated in Fig. 5.

Principles and Form	Repetition	Eurhythmy	Proportion	Gradation	Contrast	Balance	Unified
	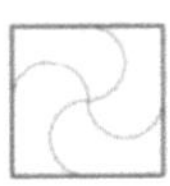	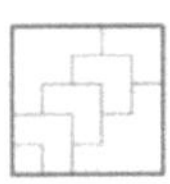	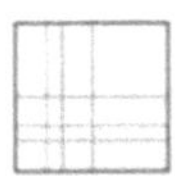	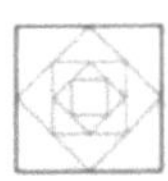	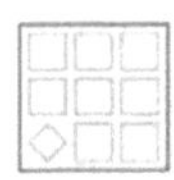	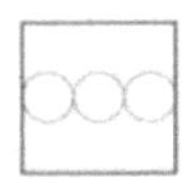	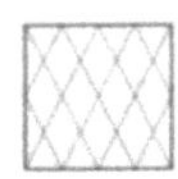
Perceptional Analysis of Morphological Design	Circle: movement, simplicity Repetition: wave, extroverted charm	Square: stability, quantity Eurhythmys: sequence, powerful, reasonable	Square: stability Proportion: relativity, stretching	Square and Triangle: stability & flexibility Gradation: mathematics, changeable, attractive	Square: clarity, certainty Contrast: different arrangement, poor readability	Circle: enclosure, geniality Balance: physics, psychology, poor guidance	Triangle: activity, de-pointing Unified: interconnectedness, vitality
Emotional Adjectives	lead vivid interesting	lead control	Lead vivid control interesting plentiful attention relaxed	lead vivid control interesting plentiful explicable attention	rigid bored calm monotone	rigid bored monotone	lead vivid control interesting plentiful
Preference Reaction	Positive	Positive	Positive	Positive	Negative	Negative	Positive

Fig. 5. Emotional adjectives toward seven representative morphologies

Results showed that the main factor to viewer's morphological perception lay in the constitution of the form of aesthetic principles instead of morphological elements of point, line and surface. Morphologies with high preference should have the features include visual guidance, understandable composition, vitality with movement, and changeable elements in composition, etc. So that they could generate a positive attitude from the viewers characterized by adjectives like vivid, interesting, amazing, control, bother, plentiful and lead. In conclusion, morphological design of indoor vertical greening would have a direct influence on viewers' emotional perception.

3.2 Analysis on Difference in Preference for Morphological Designs of Indoor Vertical Greening between Viewers with Different Background

This research discussed the difference between viewers' perception in three dimensions: morphological design, morphological preference and design perception. Results showed that one factor of background attribute had a decisive influence on the preference for morphological design, especially between those who had and had not accept professional training of design. Besides, among the emotional adjectives described the morphological designs, word pairs with most significant difference appeared to be of positive attitude (Fig. 6), while word pairs without such difference showed neutral attitudes. Emotional description involved words like attractive, active and vital exerted great impact on participant's morphological preference and therefore came a strong positive attitude (Table 2).

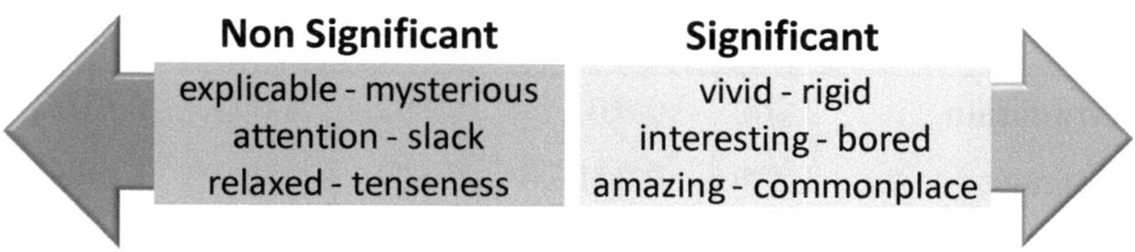

Fig. 6. Emotional adjectives in morphological design

When discussing the morphological preference, the only factor that exerted a difference is "gender". The most significant difference factor was "background" ($P< 0.01$) which meant a huge disparity between professional and non-professional participants' perception. On the other hand, judged by participants' reaction, the difference was most significant between morphological components of "Gradation" and "Balance" (Table 3). The gradation created by staggering of vertical, horizontal lines slashes could generate a sense of change and rhythm while the balance caused by an equalizing arrangement of circles could lead to a stable and simple composition. In the measuring gauge of preference for morphological design, "Gradation" signifies a positive attitude while "Balance" the opposite. This meant that too complicated or too simple a design could both affect participants' choice on differential preference.

Table 2. Result of program on affect of different emotional adjectives

Item Adjective Scale	Principles of Form	Significance Level of Variable
vivid－rigid	Eurythmy	Sex
	Gradation	Education、Professional background
	Contrast	Professional background
	Balance	Economy、Professional background
	Unified	Professional background
interesting－bored	Gradation	Professional background
	Contrast	Professional background
	Balance	Economy、Professional background
	Unified	Professional background
amazing－commonplace	Eurythmy	Economy
	Gradation	Professional background
	Contrast	Professional background
	Balance	Professional background
	Unified	Professional background

Table 3. Significant difference in morphological preference caused by background attributes

Source Adjective Scale	Mean	Std. Deviation	Mean Square	F	Sig.
Gradation	2.700	0.910	0.809	4.695	**0.010**
Balance	3.270	0.841	0.672	9.099	**0.000**
Unified	2.930	0.815	0.630	9.379	**0.000**

312 Valid Samples / *P<.05, P<.01

Results showed that under different conditions, the factor of "working experience" would have the most impact on perception of design. The information participants knew about the research, their preference for the subject, whether they were involved in related careers, and whether they had a stable income were all conditions that had comprehensive judgment for participants to be regard as indication of viewers' familiarity with the environment.

4 Conclusion

Research had yielded four results between the features of morphological images and perception preference. First, the morphological components of preference should have the following features: directional guidance, grouping effect, vitality, distinct morphological components, readability, flexible composition elements. The preference ranks from top were: repetition, proportion, gradation, while "balance" was not a favorable form of aesthetic principles. Second, the morphological perception of preference should have the following features: positive emotions, attractively, and other strong positive emotions connected with sense of vitality, change and direction. Representative description of such preference included: vivid, interesting, amazing, control, bother, plentiful and lead. Third, the presence of morphologies had an emotional effect on the viewers, but the effect mainly lay in the form of aesthetic principles instead of the morphological elements like point, line and surface. Fourth, too complicated or too simple the change of morphological components could both affect participants' choice on differential preference. As a result, it should be emphasized on morphological elements and form of aesthetic principles (point, line, and surface) to achieve a balanced proportion of the impact generated by the presence on viewer's physiological and psychological action.

In addition, according to analysis under other variable condition of the background, we got another few conclusions. First, the gender had a direct effect on preference, in particular the preference on morphological perception. Second, age didn't have significant impact on the research. Third, background attributes mattered a lot. While non-professionals reaction to morphological preference tended to go to extremes, professionals reaction are much the same, which meant professional training and applied experience related to familiarity with the environment would exert a direct influence on the preference for the morphological design of indoor vertical greening.

As was shown in the research, when decorating the internal surface with vertical greening, designers should take into consideration the ethnic background, environmental properties and spatial atmosphere, etc. For example, in a women's department store, the morphological components should pay attention to the rhythm suitable to the atmosphere and round shaping preferred by women; while in a gym for men, it was recommended to apply a composition of horizontal or vertical lines and slashes preferred by men and suitable rhythm. Offices where with high density population weren't suitable for dull or quiet decoration, it was suggested that the plan design cater to viewers preference for morphological presence. In the future promotion of indoor vertical greening, its advantage to indoor environment, spatial atmosphere and perception of viewers should be highlighted, for the purpose of creating good flourishing visual experience.

Acknowledgments. This paper represents part of the results obtained under the support of the National Science Council, Taiwan, R.O.C. (Contract No. NSC101-2627-E-027-001-MY3).

References

1. Chang, K., Chou, P.: Measuring the Influence of the Greening Design of the Building Environment on the Urban Real Estate Market in Taiwan. J. Building and Environment 45(10), 2057–2067 (2010)

2. Cheng, C.Y., Cheung Ken, K.S., Chu, L.M.: Thermal Performance of a Vegetated Cladding System on Facade Walls. J. Building and Environment 45(10), 1779–1787 (2010)
3. Chen, H., Lin, Y.: The Effect of Viewing Sequence on the Landscape Evaluation. J. Chinese Society for Horticultural Science 2(44), 168–178 (1998)
4. Katia, P., Marc, O., Fraaij, A.L.A., Haas, E.M., Rossana, R.: Vertical Greening Systems and the Effect on Air Flow and Temperature on the Building Envelope. J. Building and Environment 46(11), 2287–2294 (2011)
5. Hong, X.: A Study on Restoration Effects of Greening Levels of Plant at Indoor Working Environment. Master's Program of Landscape & Recreation, Feng Chia University, Taichung (2009) (in Chinese)
6. Tina, B., Terry, H., Grete, G.P.: The Psychological Benefits of Indoor Plants: A Critical Review of the Experimental Literature. J. Environmental Psychology 29(4), 422–433 (2009)
7. Ruth, K.R., Katinka, H.E., Debra, R., Gunn, S., Grete, P.: Benefits of Indoor Plants on Attention Capacity in an Office Setting. J. Environmental Psychology 31(1), 99–105 (2011)
8. Kevin, L.: Good City Form. MA MIT Press, Massachusetts (1981)
9. Kotler, P.: Principles of marketing, 2nd edn. Prentice-Hall, Inc., New Jersey (1983)
10. Gartner, W.C.: Image Formation Process. J. Travel & Tourism Marketing 2, 191–216 (1993)
11. Lin, J.: Basic Design. Yi Fong Tang Publishers, Taipei (2005) (in Chinese)
12. Weng, Y.: Form Principle. Cheng Wen Book Co., Ltd., Taipei (1985) (in Chinese)
13. Chen, K.: Basic Form. New Image Publisher, Ltd., Taipei (1991) (in Chinese)
14. Lin, C.: Form and Construct. Visual Communication Cultural Enterprise Co., Ltd., Taipei (2002) (in Chinese)
15. Lin, C.: Form Principle. Chuan Hwa Publishing, Ltd., Taipei (2009) (in Chinese)
16. Wang, W.: Graphic Design Principles. Hsiung-Shih Art Book, Taipei (2004) (in Chinese)
17. Qiu, Y.: Form Principle. Yi Fong Tang Publishers, Taipei (2004) (in Chinese)
18. Lin, C.: Form, Design, Art. Garden City Publisher, Taipei (1999) (in Chinese)
19. Evans, G.W., Wood, K.W.: Assessment of Environmental Aesthetics in Scenic Highway Corridors. J. Environment and Behavior 12(2), 255–273 (1980)
20. Mehrabian, A., Russell, J.A.: Approach to Environmental Psychology. MA MIT Press, Massachusetts (1974)
21. Izard, C.E.: Human Emotion. Springer, New York (1977)
22. Russell, J.A., Pratt, G.: A Description of Affective Quality Attributed to Environment. J. Personality and Social Psychology 38(2), 311–322 (1980)
23. Lai, M.: Influences of Waterscape Patterns and Sounds on Emotional Experiences. Master's Program of Department of Horticulture and Landscape Architecture, National Taiwan University (1994) (in Chinese)
24. Wang, P.: Influence on Emotional Experiences of Luminaries Height and Illuminance on the Park Trail. Master's Program of Department of Horticulture and Landscape Architecture, National Taiwan University (1997) (in Chinese)
25. Liu, Y.: The Role of Emotion between Emotional and Symbolic Expression. J. of SHU-TE University 14(1), 185–125 (2012) (in Chinese)
26. Su, Y.M., Lin, C.H., Chen, Y.J.: A Case Study of Plant Transpiration to Indoor Environment. In: Landscape Forum (2011) (in Chinese)
27. Wu, J.: A case Study of Theoretical Structure of Image Aesthetics in Information Age (1997), `http://www.fotosoft.com.tw/book/papers/library-1-1002.htm` (in Chinese)

How to Promote Patient Safety in Social Media: A Comparison between Messages in Social Media and Newspapers

Na Sun and Pei-Luen Patrick Rau

Institute of Human Factors and Ergonomics, Tsinghua University, Beijing 10084, China
{sun-n10,rpl}@mail.tsinghua.edu.cn

Abstract. The objective of this paper is to evaluate the features of patient-safety related messages in social media and provide suggestions for how to promote patient safety in social media. A hierarchical frame structure especially for patient safety messages was proposed for content analysis. 45 messages from Facebook and 45 reports from newspapers about patient safety were evaluated. The results indicated that messages in social media provided more comprehensive information about patient safety than newspapers. And social media paid more attention on individuals, including doctors, nurses and patients. Furthermore, social media messages provided more positive information than newspapers, such as treatment recommendations and program introductions.

Keywords: patient safety, social media, newspaper, content analysis.

1 Introduction

Patient safety is a new healthcare discipline that emphasizes the absence of preventable harm to patient during the process of health care (WHO). The impact of medical errors has been widely reported and discussed. Institute of Medicine of the National Academies reported that at least 44,000 Americans die each year as a result of medical errors (2000) [1]. More people die in a given year as a result of medical errors than from motor vehicle accidents (43,458), breast cancer (42,297), or AIDS (16,516).

The improvement of patient safety requires the involvement of everyone, because anyone could become a patient sometime and the patients' awareness of patient safety issues is a major step to avoid medical errors. Traditional way to spread patient safety information is via newspapers. The reports in newspapers usually talked about patient safety issues with unexpected accidents or announcements made by organization. For instance, in the March 2010, the UK Medicines and Healthcare products Regulatory Agency (MHRA) released a Medical Device Alert in relation to all silicone gel filled breast implants manufactured by a French company called PIP. After the announcement, a large number of reports about PIP implant failure appeared in many newspapers. Some reports interviewed an unsuccessful implant surgery, and some reports presented the attitude of government and health institutions.

P.L.P. Rau (Ed.): CCD/HCII 2014, LNCS 8528, pp. 351–360, 2014.

Another way to spread patient safety information is via social media. Social media spreads information faster and more flexible than traditional media, especially among young people. Compared with newspapers, social media has less limitation of time-sensitive, so the information can be more comprehensive and cover more topics, such as medical treatment tips and patient-safety related program introduction. Therefore, many patient-safety related organizations have set up their own public homepage on Facebook (the most popular social media), such as National Patient Safety Foundation and Canadian Patient Safety Institute. They use social network to introduce their organization development, to send announcements, and most importantly, to enhance people's awareness of patient safety issues. Social network has become an important way for patient safety education and promotion.

2 Objective

The initial objective of this paper was to find out the difference of patient-safety promotion in social media between China and America. However, this topic did not work out, because there were no public pages on patient safety in the most popular social network websites in China, including Renren.com, Kaixin.com, Weibo.com and T.qq.com. When using patient safety as the key word, only blogs sent by individual returned, and most of the messages had nothing to do with patient safety issues. Even though there were several organizations concentrating on health care promotion in China, none of them built public pages in social media.

Patient-safety promotion in social media is far from satisfactory in China. Similar situation can be observed in other developing countries. Therefore, suggestions on how to use social media to promote patient safety are needed especially for patient safety organizations. The objective of this study is to evaluate the features of patient safety messages in social media, i.e. Facebook, and therefore provide suggestions on patient-safety promotion in social media.

3 Methodology

3.1 Hierarchical Content Analysis

Over the past decades, the study of content analysis methodology has been rapidly expanding. A quantity of approaches has been proposed to measure the frame of content. All the approaches can be divided into five categories [15]. They are hermeneutic approach, linguistic approach, manual holistic approach, computer-assisted approach and deductive approach.

In this study, a mixture of hermeneutic approach and deductive approach was proposed. Firstly, content frames were divided into four dimensions according to previous literature [12]: problem definition, causal interpretation, moral evaluation, and treatment recommendation. Problem definition is the accident or potential risk mentioned in the messages. Causal interpretation identifies the reason that leads to the problem. Moral evaluation describes who should take the responsibility to solve the problem. And treatment recommendation refers to the suggestions provided for patients, physicians, hospitals, or government.

Secondly, a further exploration of key words in each dimension was conducted by hermeneutic approach. A coder read all the sample messages and identifies key words for each dimension. The qualitative assessment of framing depends on careful reading of all messages. For example, after reading a report about spa infection risks, the coder identified the key words as "infection" for problem definition; "lack of regulation for spa service" for causal interpretation; "patient, service-provider & government" for moral evaluation; and "patient involvement" for treatment recommendation. Sometimes a message mentioned less than four dimensions of content frames.

After identify all the key words, the coder started to integrate the key words into systematic variables. The integration followed two principles: first, choose variables that cover as much as problems mentioned in the messages; second, variables are independent with each other, i.e. avoiding overlap among variables. The systematic variables formed the hierarchical frame structure. The hierarchical frame structure served as a codebook for content analysis.

At last, the coder reorganized the sample frame with hierarchical frame structure by adjusting key words into variables in each dimension. The frequency of variables revealed the feature of the sample messages, and therefore indicated the feature of the media. By using sample messages from both newspapers and social media, this paper compared the differences of messages between newspapers and social media and revealed the features of patient safety messages in social media.

3.2 Sampling

There are a number of public pages about patient safety on Facebook. Most of them are set up by non-profit organizations, communities and institutes, whereas some are interest groups, publishers and education groups. The most popular page is National Patient Safety Foundation, with 1,137 "likes" and 31 people "talking about this" in the past 7 days. The second popular page should be Canadian Patient Safety Institute, with 511 "likes" and 9 people "talking about this", followed by the page of Louise H. Batz Patient Safety Foundation with 258 "likes" and 4 "talking about this". The other pages attract relatively less attention, no more than 100 "likes". Thus these three most popular public pages were chosen as the source of sample messages. A total of 45 messages about patient safety were selected from their Facebook pages as the sample messages. Most of these messages contained a link to a new webpage representing a patient-safety related report. Only one message provided no further report but only some tips for patients.

Another set of sample messages were selected from an online database called Library.PressDisplay.com, which provides more than 800 online newspapers from around 70 countries all over the world. In order to avoid too many reports about the same accident, two time periods were chosen as sample time, which are Jan. 5 to Jan. 9 in 2012 and Feb. 18 to Feb. 22 in 2012. At last, 45 reports from different newspapers were selected as the second set of sample messages.

4 Results

4.1 Hierarchical Frame Structure

By integrating all the key words abstracted from sample messages, the hierarchical frame structure was generated, as shown in table 1.

Table 1. Hierarchical Frame Structure

Problem Definition:	
Medication error	Surgery error
Clinical nursing error	Nosocomial infection
Complication	Patient identification
Emergency treatment	Delay
Misdiagnose	Fatigue
Ambulatory care error	Fall
Causal Interpretation:	
Lack of training	Hospital management
Lack of resources	Lack of policy
Professional attitude	Bad facility
Finance	Hospital culture
Lack of knowledge	Cooperation failure
External distraction	
Moral Evaluation:	
Hospital	Government
Service-provider	Patient
Treatment Recommendation:	
Patient involvement	Training
Better medical system	Policy
Hospital culture	More privacy
Medical data releasing	Improving instruction
Technology support	Better cooperation
More researches	

According to the hierarchical frame structure, sample messages were divided into different problems, causes, responsibilities, and recommendations. The following parts explain the comparison results of Facebook and newspapers, which reveal the differences of patient safety messages in social media and in traditional newspapers.

4.2 Types of Sample Messages

Before systematically analyzing the frame of sample messages, a general description was put forward to evaluate what kind of information the messages provide. Four types of typical information were checked, which are statistic fact, practical accident, patient-safety related program or project and recommendation. The evaluation procedure came with questions such as "Is there any statistic fact in the message?" "Does the message mention any program or project to improve patient safety?" Sometimes a piece of message contained more than one type of information. The results are shown in Table 2. The frequency refers to how many messages contain certain information and the percentage represents the percentage of messages that contain certain information.

Table 2. Information Types Analysis of Patient Safety Messages

Info Type	Facebook		PressDisplay	
	Freq.	%	Freq.	%
statistic	22	0.49	22	0.49
recommendation	22	0.49	18	0.40
accident	17	0.38	28	0.62
program	17	0.38	13	0.29

The results indicated that four types of information appear averagely in social media, compared with newspapers. Social media messages contained more program introduction (38%) than newspapers reports (29%), so was the recommendation (49% to 10%). But newspapers reported more accidents (62%) than social media (38%).

This can be easily explained by the difference of newspaper industry and social media. Newspaper companies are aimed at attracting more consumers by providing the most fresh and attractive news. But the public pages on Facebook are all set up by non-profit organization, whose goal is to spread patient safety information. As a result, newspapers preferred the latest accidents reports, and Facebook pages included as many programs and recommendations as accidents. Even though these messages may not be so attractive to readers, they are great progress in patient safety field and worth reading.

4.3 Problem Definition

45 sample messages from social media mentioned 10 problems; while 45 newspaper reports only included 8 problems. This result indicated that messages on Facebook covered more topics than newspapers. The percentage of each problem is shown in table 3. Among social media information, nosocomial infection (26.7%) drew significantly more attention, followed by surgery error (6.7%) and complication (6.7%). As for newspapers, more than half of the messages focused on medication errors (37.8%) and clinical nursing errors (24.4%). This result is partly due to two events during the sample periods. The first one is an unsuccessful breast implant surgery accident, which is classified as medication error and surgery error. The other one is the publication of adverse medical events by Health Quality and Safety Commission, in which medication errors and clinical nursing errors are two common mishaps. As a result, the distribution of problems is unbalanced. Therefore, newspaper topics are relatively concentrated, and depend heavily on practical news of the sample period.

Table 3. Content Frame Analysis: Problem Definition

Problem Definition	Facebook		PressDisplay	
	Freq.	%	Freq.	%
nosocomial infection	12	0.267	7	0.156
surgery error	3	0.067	9	0.200
complication	3	0.067	3	0.067
medication error	2	0.044	17	0.378
clinical nursing error	2	0.044	11	0.244
emergency treatment delay	2	0.044	0	0
misdiagnose	2	0.044	4	0.089
fatigue	2	0.044	0	0
ambulatory care error	1	0.022	0	0
slip and fall	1	0.022	4	0.089
patient identification	0	0	2	0.044

4.4 Causal Interpretation

There were totally 12 interpretations, as shown in Table 4. The most common cause was hospital management failure, followed by lack of medical resources in both media. But none of the accidents in newspapers were caused by hospital culture, which was the third frequent reason on Facebook (8.9%). Facility (2.2%) and finance issues (2.2%) were two interpretations in newspapers, but they were not mentioned on Facebook. Facebook aims at improving the awareness and knowledge of patient safety issues, so it pays more attention on hospital and individuals. That is why 4 of 45 messages on Facebook ascribed problems to hospital culture.

Table 4. Content Frame Analysis: Causal Interpretation

Causal Interpretation	Facebook		PressDisplay	
	Freq.	%	Freq.	%
hospital management failure	11	0.244	7	0.156
lack of resources	5	0.111	5	0.111
hospital culture	4	0.089	0	0
lack of policy	3	0.067	2	0.044
professional attitude	2	0.044	1	0.022
patient knowledge shortage	1	0.022	2	0.044
cooperation failure	1	0.022	1	0.022
lack of training	1	0.022	4	0.089
external distraction	1	0.022	0	0
bad facility	0	0	1	0.022
finance issues	0	0	2	0.044

4.5 Moral Evaluation

Moral evaluation identifies causal agents, which are taking responsibility for the accidents or risks, as in table 5. Hospital was the major causal agents in messages from both media. But patients took higher proportion of moral evaluation in Facebook messages (11.1%) than newspaper reports (4.4%), which means messages on Facebook focused more on individual responsibility regarding patient safety problems. Newspapers paid more attention on government responsibility for patient safety problems (31.1%) than Facebook (15.6%). This result indicated that Facebook focuses on individuals while newspapers focus on macro-environment.

Table 5. Content Frame Analysis: Moral Evaluation

Moral Evaluation	Facebook		PressDisplay	
	Freq.	%	Freq.	%
hospital	27	0.600	25	0.556
service-provider	9	0.200	9	0.200
government	7	0.156	14	0.311
patient	5	0.111	2	0.044

4.6 Treatment Recommendation

Treatment recommendation refers to the suggestions for improving patient safety when accepting medical treatment. Table 6 shows 11 recommendations abstracted from the sample messages. The data revealed that messages from newspapers provided relatively less treatment recommendations than Facebook messages. The major recommendation in Facebook messages was patient involvement (33.3%), following by training (15.6%) and better medical system (15.6%). Three of these treatment recommendations were considered as treatments for individuals: patient involvement, training and better cooperation. 20 of 45 Facebook messages provided treatment recommendation for individuals, but only 10 of 45 newspaper reports provided treatments for individuals.

Table 6. Content Frame Analysis: Treatment Recommendation

Treatment Recommendation	Facebook		PressDisplay	
	Freq.	%	Freq.	%
patient involvement	15	0.333	6	0.133
training	7	0.156	2	0.044
better medical system	7	0.156	6	0.133
policy improvement	4	0.089	2	0.044
better technology	4	0.089	0	0
better cooperation	4	0.089	1	0.022
hospital culture improvement	2	0.044	1	0.022

Table 6. (*continued*)

more privacy	2	0.044	1	0.022
information publicity	1	0.022	3	0.067
Better medical instruction	1	0.022	1	0.022
more researches	1	0.022	2	0.044

5 Conclusion

This study proposed a hierarchical content analysis method to evaluate the feature of patient safety messages in social media, i.e. Facebook. 45 messages from Facebook and 45 reports from newspapers were chosen as sample. The analysis results indicated the following findings.

1. Messages in social media provided more recommendations and program introductions than newspaper reports, while newspaper reports contained more practical accidents. Social media has fewer requirements for timeliness, so social media covers more kinds of information and provide more comprehensive knowledge of patient safety.
2. Facebook messages covered a larger scope of patient-safety related problems and risks. However, the problems in newspaper messages were more concentrated and usually related to recent accidents or policies. As a result, social media is more suitable to promote overall patient safety knowledge even though some of them seldom happens.
3. The most frequent causes were hospital management failure and lack of resources in both media. Hospital culture was a major cause in social media. But newspapers did not include culture issues, and instead newspaper reports talked more about finance and facility issues.
4. Facebook messages emphasized the role of the individual in improving patient safety more frequently than newspaper reports. Newspapers paid more attention on government responsibility than Facebook. Besides, both media indicated that hospital should take the major responsibility of patient safety problems.
5. Facebook messages provided more treatment recommendations than newspaper reports. And a large proportion of treatments were for individuals, including doctors, nurses, paramedic and patients.

6 Discussion

This paper aims to find out the differences of patient-safety related messages in social media and newspapers. The results revealed four features of patient safety messages in social media and provided suggestions on how to design effective messages that are suitable for social media.

Firstly, social media is a perfect platform for non-profit organizations to promote commonweal concept and knowledge, because anyone can send messages in social media for free. What's more, messages in social media can be spread rapidly through social network, and people with the same interest can be associated together by the same message. Organizations should make full use of social media advantages to make the messages more attractive and meaningful. For example, they can provide more colorful pictures and videos on their public pages, which seldom appear in newspapers. In addition, they can set up some activities among users about patient safety topic, such as patient safety knowledge contest, emergency treatment practice and medical environment survey.

Secondly, there are more program introductions and recommendations in social media than in newspapers. Thus positive messages are more appropriate to spread in social media than traditional media. Negative messages are usually astonishing and attract more readers, so traditional media is more likely to report negative information to attract consumers. In contrast, when spreading patient safety information in social media, organizations are aimed at providing comprehensive knowledge to readers, including both negative and positive messages. So there are more positive messages in social media than in newspapers. Besides, users who visit patient safety public pages in social media are concerned with patient safety issues, so the public pages should provide more inspiring and practical information for them. Even though some news is about tragic accident, further improving action or recommendation should be attached. This principle is not only for patient-safety promotion, but also for all the commonweal concept promotion, such as energy conservation, family planning and prevention of child maltreatment.

Another characteristic of social media messages is comprehensiveness. 45 sample messages in social media covered 10 patient safety problems, while 45 sample newspaper reports only mentioned 8 problems. Social media pay less attention on timeliness and readers' interest. Thus social media is a better platform to promote overall knowledge of patient safety. This is also true for other topics, such as non-smoking, healthy diet and animal protection. When spreading knowledge via social media, special attention should be paid on unusual knowledge to open users' minds. For example, National Patient Safety Foundation reported a program on ambulatory patient safety, which is a rare topic in traditional media.

The last characteristic of social media is individually oriented, which means messages in social media concentrate on individual concept and knowledge. For example, social media provides more treatment recommendations for individuals than newspapers. Traditional media usually has the function of public opinion and is able to influence the government, so it focuses more on macro-environment. In contrast, social media mainly aims to increase the awareness and knowledge of individual users, instead of impacting the macro-environment. As a result, more recommendations for patients, doctors and nurses should be provided in social media.

There are some limitations in this study. Firstly, the sample size is small, which partially due to the complexity of hermeneutic content analysis. Secondly, the procedure of content analysis is subjective, so individual differences may impact the results. In further studies, more objective methodology needs to be explored. And the analysis of social media messages should be extended to other topics.

References

1. Kohn, L.T., Corrigan, J.M., Donaldson, M.S.: To Err is Human: Building a Safer Health System. National Academy Press, Washington, DC (2000)
2. Boyd, D.M.: Social network sites: definition, history, and scholarship. Journal of Computer-Mediated Communication 13, 210–230 (2008)
3. Lenhart, A.: Teens and Social Media: An Overview (2009)
4. Kaplan, A.M., Haenlein, M.: Users of the world, unite! The challenges and opportunities of Social Media. Business Horizons 53, 59–68 (2010)
5. Ehara, A.: Are long physician working hours harmful to patient safety. Pediatrics International 50, 175–178 (2008)
6. Ramanujam, R., Abrahamson, K., Anderson, J.G.: Influence of workplace demands on nurses' perception of patient safety. Nursing and Health Sciences 10, 144–150 (2008)
7. Chuang, S., Pan, C., Huang, C.: A system-oriented analysis model to enhance patient safety in healthcare organizations. Systems Engineering 12(3), 218–232 (2009)
8. Wachter, R.M.: The end of the beginning: Patient safety five years after "To Err Is Human". In: Health Affairs, pp. w4.534–w4.545 (2004)
9. Feng, X., Bobay, K., Weiss, M.: Patient safety culture in nursing: a dimensional concept analysis. Journal of Advanced Nursing 63(3), 310–319 (2008)
10. Colla, J.B., Bracken, A.C., Kinney, L.M., Weeks, W.B.: Measuring patient safety climate: a review of surveys. Quality & Safety in Health Care 14, 364–366 (2005)
11. Semetko, H.A., Valkenburg, P.M.: Framing European politics: A content analysis of press and television news. Journal of Communication 50(2), 93–109 (2000)
12. Entman, R.M.: Framing: Toward clarification of a fractured paradigm. Journal of Communication 43(4), 51–58 (1993)
13. Akhavan-Majid, R., Ramaprasas, J.: Framing and ideology: A comparative analysis of U.S. and Chinese newspaper coverage of the Fourth United Nations Conference on Women and the NGO Forum. Mass Communication and Society 1(3-4), 131–152 (1998)
14. Graneheim, U.H., Lundman, B.: Qualitative content analysis in nursing research: concepts, procedures and measures to achieve trustworthiness. Nurse Education Today 24, 105–112 (2004)
15. Matthes, J., Kohring, M.: The content analysis of media frames: Toward improving reliability and validity. Journal of Communication 58, 258–279 (2008)
16. Segvic, I.: The framing of politics: A content analysis of three Croatian newspapers. The International Journal for Communication Studies 67(5), 469–488 (2005)
17. Hsieh, H.F., Shanno, S.E.: Three approaches to qualitative content analysis. Qualitative Health Research 15(9), 1277–1288 (2005)

Design Implications of Digital Social Innovation: A Playful Approach to Analyse Cases Study Dataset

Francesca Valsecchi[1] and Miaosen Gong[2]

[1] Jiangnan University, Wuxi, China
Tongji University, Shanghai
[2] Jiangnan University, Wuxi, China
{f.valsecchi,miaosen.gong}@gmail.com

Abstract. This paper is a preliminary activity of the DESIS Digital Social Innovation Research Cluster, with the purpose to elaborate the cases of the Social Innovation index, from the projects NT100 and digitaleurope.eu, by framing the analysis with the lens of design. We approach the analysis by information visualization methods and data manipulation tools, and in the paper we present process and results of the visualization, and the discussion of the stories we gather through the analysis. We conclude by discussing the lesson learn by this cases study analysis that privileged the heuristics of digital tools to the hermeneutics of more traditional research approaches.

Keywords: Digital Social Innovation, Case study, Information Visualization, Open Data.

1 An Outlook on Digital Social Innovation from Design Perspective

In the recent literature about Social Innovation, specific researches are focussing on the role of digital technologies. We all believe in the peculiar role of Internet as a dominant constant of contemporary human interactions, as well we observe that many of the exciting innovations that enable people to collaboratively address social issues, are being developed online, or within mediated information systems. Yet, the reflective and analytical knowledge about the impact of technologies in cognitive capabilities and model of social engagement, are not deciphered and exploited; *"Yet this technological capacity far outstrips our knowledge of how to use it. We are not entirely sure what any of this is really for"*.[13] Digital Social Innovation is a recent label, that include the challenge of giving a clearer identity to the digital spirit that nurture our way of knowing, and living. The paper addresses the discipline by the framing of relevant literature and mapping knowledge definitions; as a very preliminary step in understand how the disciplinary contribution of design can dialogue, cope, and provide an impact.

P.L.P. Rau (Ed.): CCD/HCII 2014, LNCS 8528, pp. 361–372, 2014.

1.1 The European Input to the Social Innovation Knowledge Base

At the present stage, the more advanced contribution to the studies come from the synergy among European institutions and NGO on soughing best practices for the public impact, and to develop proper funding strategies. In particular, European Commission funded the project to build a living map of organizations that imply a significant use of digital technologies within the framework of social innovation [1]. The preliminary output at the end of 2013 has been an online map at digitalsocial.eu (and related dataset [2]), of significant institutions and organization across Europe; the platform per-se represents an example of early stage social innovation, being a public audit of experiences and actors, giving public access to data and to further implementation, and using mapping as a preliminary knowledge tools.

Another case, the research from the Nominet Trust [3], UK's leading funder of social technology ventures, in collecting 100 cases of digital social innovation as the preliminary index that recognizes the most inspiring applications of digital technology for social good; those selected are again displayed through an online map and an open data-set. Similarly, we would like to name also the Global Innovation Index (GII), published at its sixth edition by Cornell University, INSEAD and the World Intellectual Property Organization (UN). The GII recognizes the key role of innovation as a driver of economic growth and prosperity and acknowledges the need for a broad horizontal vision of innovation that is applicable to both developed and emerging economies, with the inclusion of indicators that go beyond the traditional measures of innovation [4]. In the last report, they conclude that those disruptive innovations that come out of nowhere, are very rare. The vast majority of innovations are in fact incremental changes built on the underpinnings of other knowledge, technologies, or platforms. *"What is important for most innovations to occur is a set of enabling conditions that trigger people and groups with the right knowledge and skills to recognize (even serendipitously) an incremental step that can be taken at that moment in time. Digital technologies, and especially the Internet, are now for the first time in history providing a quantum leap in these enabling conditions on an unprecedented and global scale.*" [4,15].

Europe is fond of positive experiences. A resident project of Lancaster University, Catalyst (mapped on ds.eu), brings together academics and communities to jointly imagine and build the next generation of digital tools for social change, and to explore solutions to major problems in society. Catalyst is a funding based scheme that involve active based research with the citizenship, and through active research pursue to the development of new knowledge that will benefit also the academia. In their words, *"across all these projects lie the common themes of: (1) citizen-led innovation through equal partnerships between the University and its community; (2) digital innovations addressing real problems with real people."* [6,11]

Catalyst explores deep questions about the relationship between digital technology and pressing social problems and it does it by practice, giving tools in the hands of the people and enabling them to the seek of innovation, by failing and learning along a real process, where the social change can be actually experienced. The questions they pose are radical for the notion of interaction design, and for the education we give around it: *"But do modern digital technologies really make it easier for communities to change the world? Or do they lead to problems of access to information, solidifying the status quo in power structures, and illusions of a quick technological fix? And how should we design future digital technologies – technologies with a social conscience built in?"* [11].

These examples demonstrate the demand and the synergy towards more and more researches in the field, and by having them in practices, and connected to the policies and implementation platforms. The research on these topics is *"ongoing, partial, immature, fuzzy"* [13], and experimental, as we add, but also well supported as all these organization have research agenda and corresponding funding for the next two years. At this stage thou, the knowledge we have is in the form of mapping, localization and aggregations of active practitioners.

Making sense out of this mapping is the starting assumption of this paper, gathering the data from the two index and articulating questions about the role of design in this technology paradigm. Being creators of technology we cannot postpone or demand a reflection about its ethos and qualities. Digital technologies inspire three kind of reactions, *"excitement from the super-optimists who believe we are on the verge of a new era of democracy, co-operation and abundance; alarm from pessimists who think we are undermining respect for authority, expertise and discernment; and scepticism from those who cannot see what all the fuss is about because most of what really matters does not come from a microprocessor or smart-phone"* [9, 11]. Sceptic as researchers are, we believe that what "do really matter" is at the core of the our technological concern, because as interaction designers we know it is where the technology will impact, as it is a cognitive device.

1.2 The Reason We Write This Paper (Our Knowledge Contribution)

The premises of this paper are in a recent initiative of the DESIS Network [16], that recently launch a research cluster on DSI, assuming as a prior research question that digital technology are dominant, but critical, for new ways in which people, users and community collaborate and co-create for a wide range of social needs. They represent the organizational tools for very special interconnected communities and individuals, but we still do not have any argument on how far the influence of the media itself can impact messages, actions, and meanings.

Therefore, this paper has the purpose to elaborate the cases from the two projects NT100 and ds.eu, by framing the analysis with the lens of design, whilst taking into account the level of technologies (which is the digital technology we care about, and eventually we could design, affection non cognitive capabilities), and the issue of collaborative communities and their social engagement (how digital technologies are used in practice, how design can leverage on the engagement, interaction, and participation). In those indexes the variety of the cases is *"Inspiring, because these great examples show the massive potential in tech for good. Frustrating, because, bar a couple of exceptions such as Github, Arduino and Patients Like Me, the majority of these initiatives are relatively small scale and sit on the periphery of the mainstream."* [13] Even further researches will be needed to understand what limits, or eventually enables, the disruptive capacity of this innovation to expand on a larger scale; we can learn something from the knowledge we have so far. It emerges, for example, as crucial that digital innovation is community based, and glocal. Social innovation is largely distributed across geographical borders (Fig. 1), coming as well from developing countries; every country share their investment among international (less) and country (more) projects, and we can appreciate the large section defined as global. We can also see also that the innovation in developing country mostly come from self-investment as well as North American ideas are widely spread.

Fig. 1. Alluvional diagram. Relationship between continent of origin of the innovations, and continents where they're active. Colors highlights the comments in the texts.

Social Innovation studies undoubtedly are multidisciplinary, and recently also within design discipline interest arises towards a specific definition of the meaning and role of digital platforms. We believe the multidisciplinary effort will be influential to the scalability asset of those project. By design perspective, we believe that the nature of technology, the structures of interaction and the social qualities represent main challenges for design disciplines, and therefore we proceed in a deeper analysis of the case studies as explained in next paragraphs.

2 Design Concerns

Nowadays, definition of society and societal concerns blends together the physical and the digital contexts in which individuals, people and communities express themselves. Collaborative Services, Social Enterprise, Open Innovation are just some of the definitions already established in literature and innovation practice, which define the boundaries, phenomena that undergo the forms of innovation in which society is involved. Digital applications, often defined as social utilities, have become a staple of our contemporary public networks. Nevertheless, their pervasiveness significantly vary from participative façade (where the interaction is limited to the online publishing and effect in the multiplication of weak and disengaged relationships), to actual social relevant forms of organizations and change (where the digital technology represents the innovation criteria, meaning that technologies are appropriated and used by communities for the generation of specific, shared, incremental social values). This is crucial to designers and practitioner since even we recognize the wild diffusion of digital technologies is growing, we do not necessarily wish for it, whereas as researchers and educators is necessary to inquiry where is the ethos of technology, mostly if it is social: the same way the ethos ground the space of human interactions, it should ground the digital space of interaction inhabited by humans.

2.1 Preliminary Consideration on the Cases

The two index come along with structural characteristics and two different dataset. NT100 is a trustee-compiled list of cases collected with a mixed approach between peer submission and advisory, whilst ds.eu is mainly grass-roots initiatives with multiple contributors. NT100 is a csv files with the 100 entries, and relative categorization. Data are displayed in the web interface [3], where cases are separate entities (Fig. 2.1), labelled with several values (such as the flags (Fig. 2.4), and the technologies involved (2.3), the colours represent instead the societal challenge that the case refers (Fig. 2.2)) and filtered by technology type and categories (Fig. 2.5). There is a major menu by colours in which are identified the societal challenges involved in the different project. This navigation part is somehow limited because disabled colours whilst navigating do not allow to understand relationship across categories. The interface of ds.eu is instead a geo-based mapping of activities (lines) and organizations (dots) (Fig. 3.1), information that are stored in RDF based database. Filtering in the web interface here is more articulated, based on set of keywords (technology focus, organization type, activity type, domain, country) (Fig.3.2), and visually displaying the connections among the organizations on the map (by lines). Each items (organizations or activities) (Fig.3.3) is therefore open in a separate pages where details are categorized as well following the ontology [17, 2].

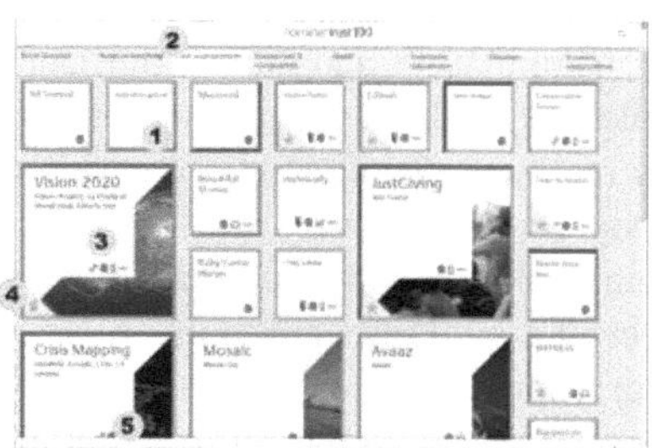

Fig. 2. Web interface of NT100 index

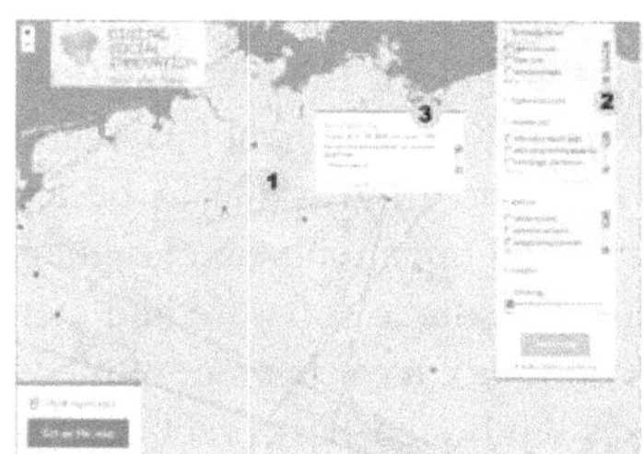

Fig. 3. Web interface of ds.eu project, with a preview on a single items, and the filtering menu

We briefly discuss the ontology: "Organization Type" and "Technology Focus" are the class in which there is correspondence between the filtering keywords and how the items are described in the database. In the class of "activity type" the filtering is limited to the first entries of the class, probably by selecting the threshold of occurrence. "Activity Role" class is not in the filtering, at this is fact very interesting keyword because represent the stakeholder pattern for each case and could say something about the organizational structures behind the successful organizations, and the stakeholder engagement. The concept scheme of "Area of Society" and "Technology Methods" also include much more variety of details not used in the filtering, but these data are not uniform (keyword as well as descriptive sentence are both included in the schema). Technology is clustered differently, but in both system is a keyword of the principal way of displaying (whilst other information are hidden, or in a second relevance). This relevance is a first crucial issue for us. NT100 interface has a filter by technology that can be multiply selected, and in the database three values describe technology "tech_filter" (used in the display) "platform" (that is not used in the visualization, and simply define the basic platform of use mobile, internet, or GIS), and the "technology_type", that include media, models and domains. The ds.eu instead use a semantic in which technology is grouped and clustered by four attributes of openness, whilst the "technology_methods" ontology is disaggregated and disordered. Nevertheless Fig. 4 shows the diagram for the mapping of the new set of merged technology-related category. The logic of having larger cluster, tech domain, and then more detailed items has been maintained. We will discuss in the conclusion part how better improvement of this data analysis can be done.

2.2 Visualizations of the Dataset

According to the dataset, we played with the visualization in order to get sense out of the data. Authors are not familiar with experienced data visualization tools, whilst understanding and appreciating the potential they have to move from data through stories; therefore this is also a preliminary self-training approach, whilst believing the capability manipulation of linked data is a minimum requirements to those want to research in the field of digital social innovation. We focus our attention on the NT100 dataset and using OpenRefine [8] for the data manipulation and Raw from Density Design Lab [7] for the visualization. Very simple queries have been tested out in the SPARQL [9] environment provided by ds.eu, by realizing that due to limited skills we have too short time frame to be able to have significant outputs from this process. These are all open tools and language for data manipulation and visualization, distributed as opensource software and incredibly powerful digital research tools.

Those index have been compiled with the aim of providing an information service of cases study and best practices. As it is, users can access to the information about the single entities, by several degree of depth of the details of the information itself. In our approach instead, the the prior aim is to look at the dataset not from analytical analysis of the cases, but by grouping and clustering for their shared properties. In this case is more important the information we can derive from them, the pattern that all the cases represent or could represent, more than their specific significance.

If we look for example at Fig. 5, where the the *continent_active* value is related with the *social_challenges* of the 100 cases, we can confirm that projects with a global impact are the more numerous, but we also observe the particular weakness of Latin America; whilst both Europe and Asia distribute quite homogeneously their efforts across the social challenges. A particular significant global issue, is "Access to

Knowledge", as well observing that North America has the most investment in "Health". Is nevertheless interesting to observe that the social challenge with less "global" impact is exactly "Health", suggesting probably the culture-based specificity and conditions of each geographical environment. In the same way Europe is particularly poor of investment in "Economic Empowerment", and this is not a surprise given the historical condition in which the countries live, and being known that entrepreneurship is still not a complete mature economical asset yet. We do also notice that Asia as a very narrow impact on "Environment and Sustainability" and this is also a critical point of chronically and global interest.

Fig. 4. (Partial) dendrogram of the merged taxonomies between NT100 and ds.eu dataset, by the values related to technology

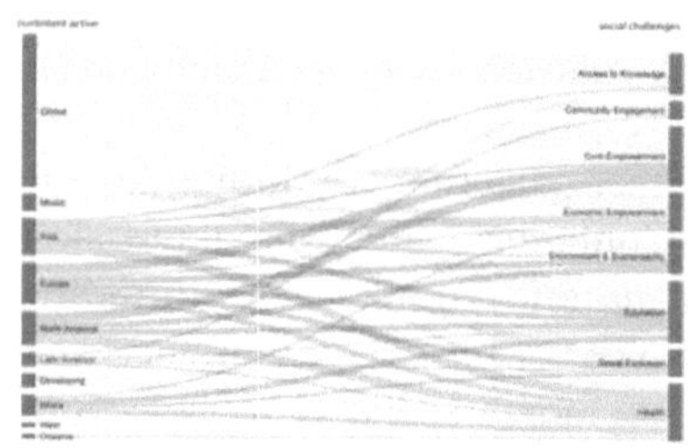

Fig. 5. Alluvional diagram. Overall view of the relationship between continents active and societal challenges. In the next figures the data are the same but differently distributed in the space for a better highlight

In the interface of Fig. 2.4, we mentioned a "flagging" associated to each cases. This is represented by assigning to some of the cases the values of *trailblazer* for those projects that are pioneer in their actions, and *one-to-watch* for those considered particularly promising. Also, in the dataset there is another flag about the development stage of the project. This information is also particularly interesting since we discuss already how much scalability issue will be crucial in the future development of all the social innovation projects.

By Fig. 6 (left) we can observe that among the *trailblazer* a large number is in the "Access to knowledge" challenge, that itself is not that numerous. This could suggest a prominent interest, or need, in that area; as well as for the *one to watch* flag, the more are concentrating in "Environment and Sustainability" where probably the major concerns and intellectual reasoning is concentrated, and where also the involvement of the people through the digital technologies could eventually lead to a real unexpected impact. From the flags and development stages (Fig. 6, right) we can observe something by relating them with the timing of the project. We only know from the database the starting date, but the figure says that pioneer projects are the more recent ones, suggesting that is really in recent times that a certain maturity on technologies has made possible to more robust solution to emerge. On the other side, the *one to watch* are all more mature, suggesting probably that time impact on scalability and stability issues.

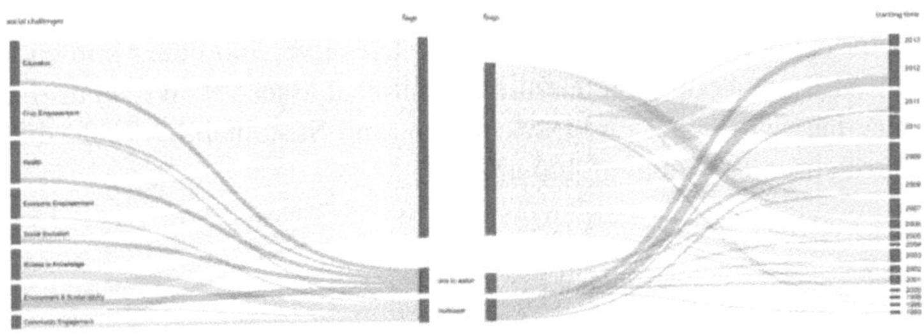

Fig. 6. Left: Alluvional diagram. Distribution of flagged projects along societal challenge. *Right:* Alluvional diagram. Distribution of flagged projects along time.

Others diagram we do not have the space to publish, but will be given online for the Conference time, distribute along the time the different stage of development. Start-up emerge all recent, in the past four years (while projects time span is from early'90s), whilst scaled projects do not get more recent than 2005, and this could refer to more general systemic condition to be suggested.

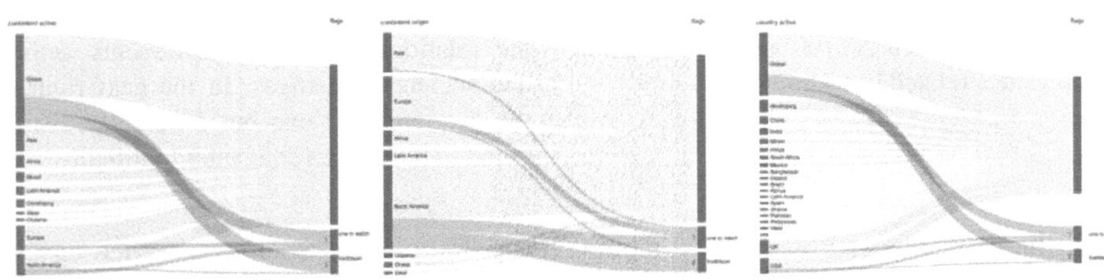

Fig. 7. Alluvional diagram. Continent of origin, and continent/countries active, related with the flags. Note that in the section a,c the visualisation was correct in Raw App, with no overlapping (as it is supposed to be), but it has been manually changed to keep the same labels ordering.

By relating flags with continent of activity, we notice that the both of the flags are indeed assigned to either global, or western countries (EU and USA). This is quite unexpected boundary emerging (Fig.7a). If we view closer from continent of origin point of view (Fig. 7b), and from country view (7c) the boundary is even clearer, with just a contribution from Asia and a clear predominance of USA. Is this saying something about where the innovation come from? And this is definitely a true questions, given the fact that the authors are European and Chinese! In other figures that we do not include, we notice that innovations originated in North America are roughly the half of the start-up, and this is also quite interesting given the global economic scenario, and moreover if related to another figure that shows how almost the half of start-up are connected to "Health" challenge.

2.3 Integration of the Dataset with New Data

We are exploring other queries on the data, like time and geographical distribution, testing mainly if either the Alluvional Diagram or the BubbleChart and Circle Packing would be the best solution. Or by distributing across different continents both flags and development stage in the same view, or flag and social challenges, and verify how Circle Packing is indeed effective.

Being this a first experiment we have been quite free in the manipulation of the data, not only by correcting typos and data incongruity. For example, in the assertion about geographical distribution we cluster in West, Developing, Latin America, according to clear iconic meanings; we grouped the distinction because we were not interesting in specific location, but trends (i.e. Latin America includes Mexico, West is Europe and USA, Developing includes only Africa, Asia (still, there is the big issue if keeping China separate from Asia for its not being anymore developing) and Latin America, etc.). Also, we transform string values in numeric values when more suitable for the visualization format (like flags and development stage). A further activity is instead the real manipulation of the dataset by adding new data. This part is much more aggressive with tools like OpenRefine more than the visualization part. It is actually the phase in which we can create a dataset more suitable for the visualization purpose, and to be interactive with deeper queries.

We start in fact by thinking to merge the two dataset together, and having a larger number of cases to study. Nevertheless, the two formats cannot be directly integrated and time limitations do not allow us to succeed in this part. We, at this stage, have a series of intermediate open process, but not being able to have an outcome yet. As we already referred, Fig. 7 shows the results of the merged technology keywords of the two index. We are doing the next step, clearing and refining the data of ds.eu ontology (that includes several inconsistency, values that represent instead challenges, like "cultural discovery" "co-creation") and merging with the current table to have a several dozens hundreds of technology keywords associates to our cases, instead that 8 like we have now. We are not enough smart (yet) in data refining process to have results yet, but still we believe for the time of the Conference more robust results will be presented. In the NT100, we found three values for defining the social challenge which the project refers, "dom_soc_challenge, a field with unique entry among 8 values, and a "soc_challenge" entry with the same values, but multiple selections, up to five. "soc_challenge" is used to categorize by colour the projects on the web map. Since the association in the database of the different challenges domain are progressive, we believe they could represent a more detailed description, instead that a bunch of unsorted keyword (also because they're only eight, and by a manual random check here and there we kind of evaluate the order of the keyword could make sense).

Moreover, what is the challenge value for the NT100 file, is reasonably mapped with the domain value of ds.eu; for the moment we are still struggling with OpenRefine to find a decent format that could include the mash in a proper way, and we the current output is Fig 8 in which you can see the progressive tagging with the challenges values, and by their proximity relationship, explore possible meanings like how at stage 3 "physical computing" is so connected with "audiovisual". This kind of visualization serves as search and exploration devices, more then extracting well-defined insights like in the previous examples.

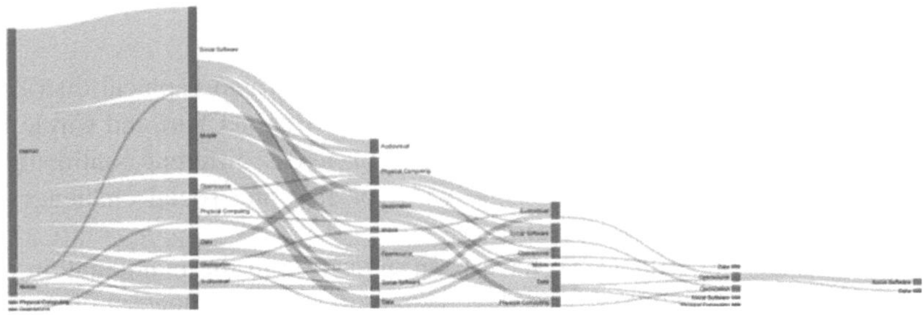

Fig. 8. Alluvional Diagram. Progression of technology-related categorization in NT100 dataset.

There are several others integration of the database that we plan to do and we push to the Conference a deeper discussion. We have quite a clear road-map about this, in the following steps:

- Complete the meshing between "social challenge" and "domain area" in the corresponding database, and adjust the categorization accordingly
- Include in the NT100 database two values derived from the ds.eu dataset, meaning "organization", and "activity type"
- Include in the database a string value that analyse the cases according to the "Attributes of four modes of MCS [14]" as a reference to distinguish the interaction properties of each case
- Dissemination and release of an open data package that includes the visualizations created, and the new dataset generated.

3 Discussion, Limitations and Further Development

In this paper, we acted two kind of methods. Firstly, a reflection about the literature and best practices, whilst giving a scenario about who-is-doing-what in the emerging field of digital social innovation. We clarified the design concerns, that still needs to be developed into a clear agenda. We learn from the literature the power of incremental innovation, that suits with the design expertise on prototype and community engagement, that are by definition resilient and incremental. We therefore proceed to use the data we have so far, from ds.eu and NT100 index, to act a design-based analysis of the cases, not based on analytical hermeneutics, whilst on visual heuristics: by using linked data managing tools, and open-source visualization apps to have an aggregate, transverse view across the dataset.

At the same time, tools, methods and reasoning around open-data is one of the issue within digital social innovation fields, so by practice we were able to draw a clear path on what can be done and what we could do with this data. Taken into account the limitations of the dataset and of our current capabilities, still we believe that the main struggle in this exercise is related to the low semantic features of the data. Both of the index provide detailed description of each case, but they lack on information across them, about qualities, semantic and taxonomies of the vocabulary of digital social innovation. In our case, by playing with the visualization we were able to create stories around the cases, and connections across contents. We believe that this process of data refining-manipulation-visualisation can be powerful to support the population of the DSI vocabulary, and it is particularly coherent with the current activity of DESIS about the qualities of innovation. Moreover it represent a research tool that is supportive of traditional case analysis. The intention of this paper are limited and modest, but we believe useful in giving guidelines for future researches, and grounded on disciplinary capabilities, meaning therefore able to provide a strong disciplinary contribution. And being the limitations of this research mainly in our organizational and capabilities asset, we probably recognize that pushing a movement of more practice, more field-based, more education orientation than learning orientation is necessary in design discipline [12]. As it is meaningless disconnecting the theory of design by the practice of its impact, we cannot talk about digital social innovation without mastering the tools that apparently are making it possible.

By the point of view of the visualization, to learn something about how these innovations look like, we limit the use of Raw to mainly Alluvional diagrams. We have several tests, yet unsatisfactory, with BubbleChart, Circle Packing, Treemap, and Dendrogram, but still the AD, even if limit the correlation among two variables, is quite good with limited size of qualitative variables, and their distribution. In any case at this stage we are much satisfied with the exploratory approach of visualization as a research tools, that not really focus to the qualitative visual accuracy of final visualization itself. The preliminary intent of DESIS Cluster on Digital Social Innovation is being the definition of both analytical and programmatic design directions of the research agenda; the contribution of this paper shape as

- the need of a semantic about digital social innovation that could be translated in an ontology to be used in datased manipulation
- further development and improved accuracy in the visual data analysis
- the implementation on more accurate design-based keyword, and the integration of the current data with design relevant values

As a final recommendation, we reinforce the importance of multidisciplinary contribution in the field of digital social innovation, by implying the two distinct interests of design: a) more and more design is involved in wide social concerns and actions, and the discipline outcomes move to services, strategies, systems, and the blurred edge with other planning/management disciplines: in fact design orients towards public engagement, services for the communities, and sustainable development; b) technology is a designed artefacts, and a mean for designed interactions, that imply the need of methodology, ethos and critical assessment in the way we design the tools for the social interaction. If is true that Digital Social Innovation is related to the way technology is conceived and used, therefore the design of platforms and interaction is responsible of the social impact itself.

Acknowledgement. Density Design Research Lab, Milan Polytechnic and their RAW, kindly given away to the use of everybody, as the spirit of community and opensource inspired. This research has been supported by Ministry of Education Humanities and Social Science Youth Fund (11YJC760018), China, and National Social Science Foundation-Art (12BG055).

References

1. European Digital Social Innovation Project, http://digitalsocial.eu
2. Opendata digitalsocial.eu, http://data.digitalsocial.eu/data
3. Nominet Trust NT100 Digital Social Innovation Index, http://socialtech.org.uk/
4. The Global Innovation Index 2012: Stronger Innovation Linkages for Global Growth, INSEAD, Paris, http://www.globalinnovationindex.org
5. Understanding The Potential in Digital Social Innovation, http://www.nesta.org.uk/blog/understanding-potential-digital-social-innovation
6. Catalyst (Citizens Transforming Society: Tools for Change), UK, http://www.catalystproject.org.uk
7. Raw. The Missed Link between Spreadsheets and Vector Graphics. Software used for the visualisation. Milan Polythecnic, DensityDesign Research Lab, http://raw.densitydesign.org/
8. OpenRefine. A free, opensource, powerful tool for working with messy data. Software used for the data manipulation, http://openrefine.org/
9. SPARQL 1.1 Endpoint, http://data.digitalsocial.eu/sparql
10. Study on Social Innovation in Digital Agenda – SMART 2012/0049
11. Whittle, alii: Beyond Research in the Wild: Citizen-Led Research as a Model for Innovation. In: Digital Economy Digital Futures Conference (2012)
12. Löwgren, J., Reimer, B.: The Computer is a Medium, Not a Tool: Collaborative Media Challenging Interaction Design. Challenges 4, 86–102 (2013), doi:10.3390/challe4010086
13. Leadbeater, C.: Digital Innovation for Social Change. Financial Times (November 8, 2013), http://www.ft.com/cms/s/2/64203e92-4747-11e3-b4d3-00144feabdc0.html
14. Gong, M., Valsecchi, F.: An Interactive and Relational Framework of Mobile Collaborative Services towards Social Innovation. Internal manuscript (2013)
15. Millard, J.: Report on the development of online networking tools (PDF). A deliverable of the project: "The theoretical, empirical and policy foundations for building social innovation in Europe" (TEPSIE), European Commission – 7th Framework Programme, Brussels: European Commission, DG Research (2012)
16. DESIS Network, http://desis-network.org/
17. An Ontology of Terms for Describing Digital Social Innovation Organizations and Activities (Organisation Types / ActivityTypes / Concept Scheme Areas Of Society / Activity Technology Focuses / Activity Technology Methods / Activity Roles), http://data.digitalsocial.eu/def/ontology, http://data.digitalsocial.eu/data/organizations-and-activities

Design Trend Research for Building a Future Physical-Cyber Ecosystem

Hongyan Yan and Yanyan Sun

China Mobile Research Institute, 32 Xuanwumennei West Str., Xicheng Dist., Beijing, China, 100053
{yanhongyan,sunyanyanyj}@chinamobile.com

Abstract. China, now the world's second-largest economy with a massive user crowd, there is a surge growth of mobile internet business, products and users. Every year, numerous of new companies and products are incubated or landed in this market, some of them made huge success, and lots of them failed too.

To those who including companies and individuals invest in this market, they want to find some patterns, design trends, inspiration, and more importantly, to find some leads to the successful future design innovation. They need a better reference and more powerful design cards in hands during the process of creation. However, neither the design trend nor creative ideas are tangible. They are abstract. We all as users can feel mobile products are offering an easier and more and more comfortable user experience to attract users to love using these products. This sensitive cognition is the premise and base of designer's creative learning activity, but it can't be a reliable reference of the next generation of innovation.

Where the design trends are now and where the future design innovations are will be presented in a more tangible way. We need two steps to achieve that.

First of all, we need to find out what design trends are based on the studies of what just happened in mobile product design field. This is about seeing and understanding design trends in a narrow level.

From the most popular mobile platforms like Android, iOS and Widows Phone, top-ranking applications listed as our research object, to the major iteration of applications, with the purpose of summarizing design trends, we built a research model with two study dimensions. The research of the horizontal dimension, which we call it the Combing System, focuses on the design evolution of applications by studying 21 general task-flows and some particular task-flows we defined, as well as the evolution of style guide of platforms themselves. Each task-flow is given a representing color sequence which not only helps us to represent research data in a visualized way, it will be convenient to observe one particular flow from others more clearly in the visualized data map. We can see from our visualized data that which flow the redesign of different type of applications is focused on. The vertical dimension, which we call it Stamping System, focuses on the research of the major iteration of applications. Unlike dyeing different task-flow in the Combing System, we trace every task-flow, so we can observe how the design of each flow changes from the previous form into the latest one by comparing the trace of task-flows of the newest and the previous version of an app together in a visualized data map. More

P.L.P. Rau (Ed.): CCD/HCII 2014, LNCS 8528, pp. 373–381, 2014.

interestingly, this research model can also help us to observe how one platform's style guide including UI and GUI style can affect each other.

Secondly, we relate design trends we summarized with major trends of development of Chinese social context, because isolating design trends research from their social context would be meaningless and pointless. The other reason to put the consideration of Chinese social context in the research system is that it is changing frequently which cause the more complex scenario and user needs.

After relating design trends and social context together, we now need to learn from the process of the creation of classic design by fully understanding offering better user experience design does not only exist in high technology time. We should realize that the reason why classic design became classic design is not only about creating something new successfully, it is about combining different things that already existed to provide a better user experience for the most of the time. Radical design takes years to succeed and most of them failed. Future creation will not all incubated in the rocket high technology labs, we can not just count on that to innovate, most of them will be created by combining different things together to provide a better user experience like how classic design succeeded. We can search for new possible combinations in this bigger picture consists of design trends and their social context, and this also can help us to understand how to build a harmonious physical-cyber ecosystem for both products and users who will use them.

Besides a tangible way that we can tell where the design trends now are and where the future design innovations are in the bigger picture, the physical-cyber ecosystem, we also have some advices for designers: keep searching new possible combinations in the ecosystem to fix problems with better user experience, not just think of yourself as problem solver also the problem seekers. Don't be afraid to put your product in the market once you see a new potential connection. Only these can make us keep creating and innovating.

Keywords: UX, Design, Trend, Research, Innovation.

1 Project Background

Today in China, there is the most rapid growth and development of mobile internet business and products with a largest body of users. Mobile platforms have integrated many important aspect of people's everyday life such as lifestyle, entertainment, social net-work into a portable and personal device. There are many traditional business are attempting to develop products based on mobile platforms: many hospitals are building mobile HIT system in a large scale, and pharmaceutical enterprises are founding their own information management system to help themselves, some of whom might based on a remote area in China, reach out to most advanced drug labs all around the world and cooperate through mobile platforms.

With the purpose of achieving successfully, there is no doubt that we need to design mobile products with positive basic user experience elements. Nonetheless, doing well on basic elements can not assure the success when dealing with the most complex body of users and the rapid changing usage scenario. Besides, Major platforms are offering a better environment to encourage the innovation with more open resources and flexibilities. The situation requires every developer to be more innovative to survive. Innovation can bring more functions and surprises to satisfy the user needs, and it will support the sustainable development of products themselves accordingly.

2 Our Research System

2.1 Overall Introduction

Innovation is an abstract notion, broadly speaking, it can refer to many process. In UX field, innovation reflected in users' feelings and comments. People can sense that mobile products are getting more easy to use and their lives are becoming more convenient because of some new function or a more convenient operation these products provided. However, these feelings, comments and even an emergence and vanishing of concrete functions, can't represent innovation in UX design in a very systematic way. We need to summarize key words of innovation and trend in the design progress thorough research in the recent past, put research result in the background of Chinese social context developing and changing, and by then, we can be indicated from that bigger picture where the ways of near future design innovation are.

With the purpose above, in 2010, we began to build our design research system by studying the evolution of most popular mobile platforms such as Android and iOS. And in 2012, we expanded our research range from platforms only to the most active apps.

Summarizing of the recent past is our first step. We research the newest system version of popular platforms including Android, iOS and WP. Then, we track down and research those top-ranking apps[1], both domestic and international. For example, based on the study of Android 4.0, a system version that is taking more and more system market share of Android, we track down top 5 apps in 11 different download categories.

The research of apps has two dimensions. The horizontal one allows us put all the apps in the same download category together, deconstruct them into separated task flows, only observes and compares the 21 task flows we defined. The vertical one helps us to track down the upgrade of each app by comparing its older version with the newest version.

We can imagine the horizontal research dimension as the Comb, and the vertical one as the Stamp.

2.2 Horizontal Dimension Research Method and Discoveries

Every gap of the comb represents a task-flow. There are basic and particular task flows. We defined 21 basic task flows in the past studies. Though basic task flows are

[1] Ranking Data from App Annie.

defined in our research system, they are universal task flows that every app would have. For instance, basic task flow 1 focus on the registration, login and logout, and basic flow 2 studies information architecture including navigation and search. From the observation of every task flow, we classify features into 5 categories–popular UI, particular UI, popular GUI, particular GUI and function. Comb, the horizontal research dimension, enables us find the design trend of one particular type of apps in the macroscopic level.

Furthermore, we give every basic task flow with 5 color of the same color scheme to represent 5 observation categories–popular UI, particular UI, popular GUI, particular GUI and function. 21 basic task flows have 21 color themes–this is inspired by what bioengineers do to distinct one DNA sequence from others. The horizontal research dimension is all about the deconstruction. In this way we study the overall trend other than specific design details, which will be fully studied in the horizontal research dimension. Any spotted change of design will be marked and become an abstract color block in the visualized information map, and the details of changes will be described in the separated report.

In Fig. 1, the visualized information graph, RED represents tasks like New Features Introducing, ORANGE represents tasks such as sign up, login and logout, BLUE represents information architecture design such as navigation, search and tabs, PURPLE represents tasks related to account settings, TURQUOIS represents tasks connected with system settings, VIOLET represents bookmark related tasks, GREY represents upload and download tasks, and PINK represents particular tasks such as recharges.

Fig. 1. Color themes in the horizontal research dimension studies

With these color themes, we drew the diagram of design change trends of 2013 (2-2). In this image, from left to right, each group of color blocks represents one type of application–Finance, Social Net-working, Lifestyle, Communication, Travel and Local, Video and Media, Audio and Music, Comics, Tools, Reading and shopping.

Now we can see clearly, that developers of different type of application all put the upgrading emphasis on the information architecture design. Especially the design of shopping applications, a more easy to use and hierarchically clear information system, like navigation and searching, is crucial.

Fig. 2. Different types focus on upgrading of different task flows

The horizontal research is not only suitable for summarizing and studying overall features of different task flow design progress, it is an optimal way to observe the platform evolution. We marked elements with strong Android 4.0 features with GREEN in the same visualizing map, and elements with strong iOS styles with BLUE. We got the diagram (2-3) below.

Fig. 3. SNS applications are influenced by Android 4.0 style the most

From where GREEN spots are in image 2-4, we can perceive that features of Android 4.0 impacted the design of UI the most. 16% of UI design upgrading is caused by adopting Android 4.0 controls, and less than 3% features are inspired by iOS UI styles.

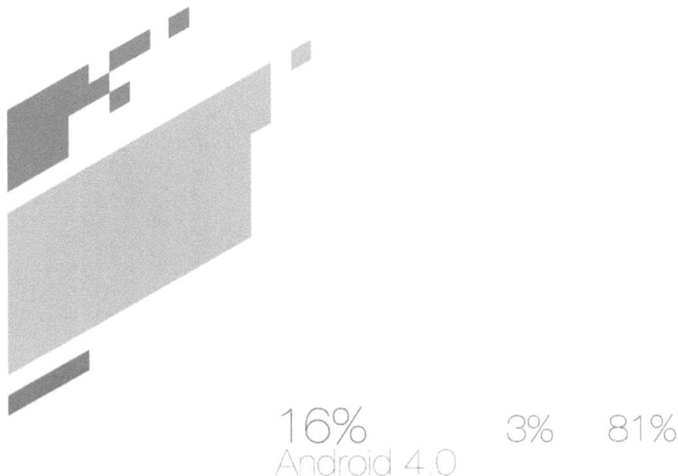

Fig. 4. Android 4.0 features vs. iOS features in research result

Among all the application types, the category of Social Net-working is one type that adopts Android 4.0 features the most. Known from the past, design of social network applications is leading the design progress in many aspects.

And what controls are being adopted most in the design upgrading since Android published its 4.0 version? Seen from the visualized information map, control like Swipe Between Taps is one of them.

Control of Swipe Between Taps is appeared after the Window Phone system was been published, and iOS style, which is influenced by Metro UI apparently, is showing less power to influence Android since iOS 7. Interestingly, what we found is not about which platform is better than the other, it is about they being more universal. This can also reflect the design trend of being seamless when dealing with cross-platform.

2.3 Dimension Research Method and Discoveries

Stamp, the vertical research dimension, allows us overlay two or more "stamp pattern" together to distinguish different features. These differences reflect innovation updates.

We know that whether through log files or user tests, we can trace the path how a user accomplishes one task visually. We trace at least 3 task flows in one version of an application, one or two of them is the core task flow of this app, and the rest are sub-core ones. When overlay the trace of an older version with the one of newest version, we can distinctly perceive the change in the newer version and how the change has been made when compared with the older one.

Stamp, the vertical research dimension, enables us find the more obvious and concrete evidence of innovation in UI, GUI and function throughout application upgrade in the microcosmic level.

Diagram 2-5 below shows an example of how we comparing two different version of the same mobile application. In the newer version, it reduced the steps what a user needs to accomplish its core task flow. And furthermore, it weakened its sub-core function by moving the entrance from the index to a Sub-page. Less operation steps and one strong function, this leads us to the trend of designing Dumb Products. Designing Dumb Products is not conflict with design trends we concluded through the horizontal research, the seamless cross devices and platforms. Dumb products can not exist alone, they have to work with other products in a bigger user-product ecosystem.

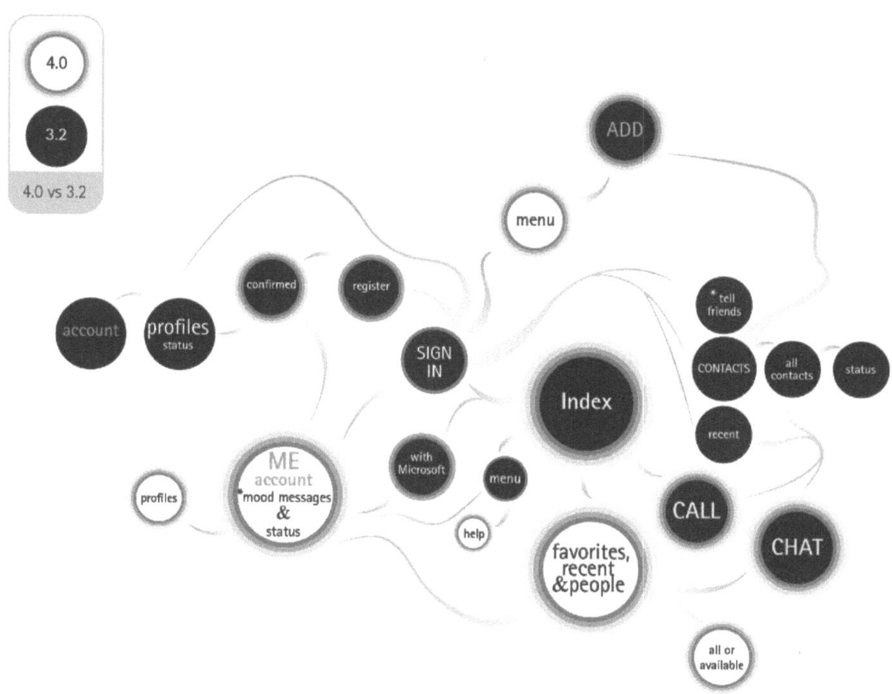

Fig. 5. Task flow paths comparing between the older and the newer version of a study object

3 Research Discoveries, Social Context, and Future Physical-Cyber Ecosystem

3.1 Design Trend and Future Innovation

However scattered information can not be enough to be referred to draw a bigger picture to see where future design innovation goes.

User experience and design innovation does not only exist in mobile-internet era.

When think of innovation, designers should not rely on or put the focus on finding new technologies, instead, look for new connections and tie different things together to create new user experiences. Donald Norman said in a 2013 User Friendly Conference in Shanghai, China, that radical design takes years to succeed, and most of them failed. Learnt from the creation of classic design, it is mostly about establishing new connection between two already existed things to bring users new user experience, it is are not about creating from nothing. For instance, pens and clips exist for years before someone connected the two together to make it become more convenient to use, to pin to your pocket or book.

Nike Fuel Band connected three already existed elements together–the technology supports it, sports wear, and people's awareness of being health, and made a new user experience. And it was just 10 years ago, when talked about Nike, people only described it as a sportswear company not a high tech one.

Today, with all the technologies to support mobile product design ready, all we need, is find more new connections between different things.

3.2 Physical-Cyber Ecosystem Built with Design Trend and Social Context

Our research system helped us conclude trend key words, and we put these key words in the Chinese social context to find possible connections between different things. Though the GDP of China is not ideal but there are surge growths in mobile business and products, like online and mobile shopping, mobile financing, logistics and so on, many big international companies built their research institutes or centers of big data in China including INTEL and EMC. Meanwhile, social conflicts like aging of population, environment, education and medical resource problems are significant. All these are consisting Chinese social context.

We can see lots of potential connections when we put design trend keywords together with social context in illustration 3-1. Also, this illustration is an early model of how the future physical-cyber harmonious ecosystem will look like. We create products by building new connections to create new user experience, and the reverse will also be true that products will offer the right user experience since they are inspired by the ecosystem.

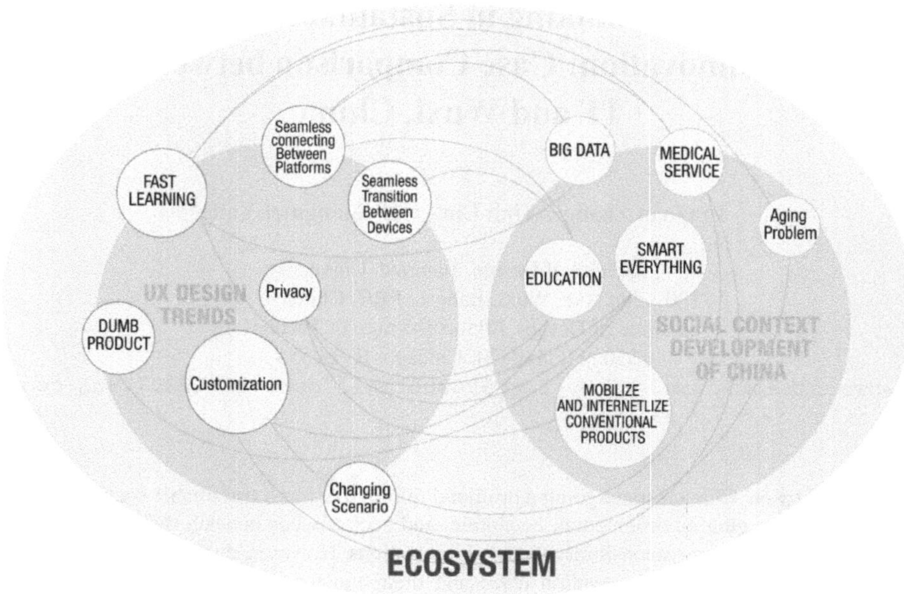

Fig. 6. An an early model of future physical-cyber convergence ecosystem of China

4 Future Research Prospect

Our research project is not on going is a very long time span. If we keep this research project on track for years, and if we put our study in a much longer timeline, we can perceive more evidence showing how design is influenced by social context at that time like popular ideological trend, consumption custom and usage scenario. Observed from history, design trend repeats itself, and reprograms itself under the influence of certain social context. In the future, when some patterns of social context appear, we can predict design tends in some ways accordingly.

With the design trend, and when there are new connections, it may be the best chance to innovate. Reid Hoffman once said in an interview that if you're not embarrassed by the first version of your product, you have launched too tale.

Cross-Culture Thinking in Sustainable Service Design of Social Innovation: Case Comparison between Milan, IT and Wuxi, China

Linghao Zhang[1], Xinli Lin[2], and Guangmei Yang[1]

[1] School of Design, Jiangnan University
1800, Lihu Ave, Wuxi, Jiangsu, PRC. China, 214000
[2] Institute of Design, Illinois Institute of Technology
350 N LaSalle St, Chicago, IL, 60654
wowo.zlh@163.com, kathy_lin1990@hotmail.com, 835193974@qq.com

Abstract. China is undergoing a profound reform to a more sustainable society. The emerging environmental, economic, and social issues beneath this period urge the greater responsibility to social innovations. However, during the global broadcast of social innovation cases and their transformation into appliance, cross-culture elements haven't drawn enough attention. There are rarely any lights shed on the cross-cultural transformation during the exportation of innovation worldwide. Based on the, this paper investigates the evaluation criteria, the broadness of its impact and active participation rate as well as the associated reasons behind from those test and interview to Chinese users about through Chinese user test and interview about two service design cases in Milan and Wuxi, we analyzed related evaluation criteria and other criteria of influence dimensions, participation willingness as well as the causes behind them. So that the designer can, on one hand, learn about the of characteristics of collective cultural cognition of Chinese users and the distinctions between users from west and east; And on the other hand, give suggestions, which is to understand local culture thoroughly and connect users, to lay emphasis on the evaluation of the benefit claim of the proposals and to combine its feasibility, easiness of handling and the design and spread of correlated information.

Keywords: Social Innovation, Service Design, Cross-Culture, Case Study.

1 Introduction

Under the advancement of today's new information technology and mobile Internet, business innovation (including both the technological and business model innovation of products and services) drives both emerging new industries and traditional industries forward; continually increase the fortune of whole society. However, it doesn't turn around the continuing deterioration of relative problems. Therefore, we are facing the challenge of a joint effect of society, culture, policy, market and lifestyle rather than technical problems. A global scale and failed to reverse the direction of development-related issues continued to deteriorate. The challenges we are facing to

P.L.P. Rau (Ed.): CCD/HCII 2014, LNCS 8528, pp. 382–391, 2014.

make a more sustainable world is not only the technological issue but the mutual effect of the society, the culture, the politics, the market and the life style[1]. In other words, we need not only technical solutions, but also comprehensive participation of social innovation to meet the versatility and complexity of environmental and social challenges. China is at the exact moment and social innovation is highlighted and likely to be more responsible for the challenge.

As a concept or social movement first populated in west world, "social innovation" brings the social administrators more opportunities to rearrange the develop direction, as well as an important "window period" for the conception and development of the next generation of public services. For example, in February 2008, President Obama announced the opening of the Office of Social Innovation in White House. Social innovation, defined as "the innovative activities and services that are aimed to meet certain social demands and are mainly developed and spread by social organizations with their primary social oriented goal. " [2] by Young's fund. Here, the "social demands", mostly refers to those vulnerable groups, whose demands haven't been met. One of its important features is the wide involvement of those who are strongly tied to it.

The motivation of individuals to the design and implementation of social innovation is the key element for the success of the whole project. The effectiveness of public service concept relies strictly on the activeness of ultimate users. Individual activity in service design and implementation process of social innovation plays a key role in the success of the project. And it is decisive to effectiveness of public service that whether users will become active participants and cooperators in the end.

Started early in England, Denmark, Italy and Finland, plenty of research methods, tools and success cases related to social innovation are already proposed and examined. For example, the book "100 social innovations in Finland" [3] are of great value, enlightening other nations. However, these successful cases may not fit the slot of those cross-cultural situations, because they are essentially originated from their local culture. In fact, many of the explorations to a more sustainable world are still on socio/technical experimentation of social problems are still in experimental stage. Those personal and cultural values inside these proposals, if not accepted by other cross-cultural societies from real implementation perspective, can affect the scaling-up of entire service mode. Considering the current social and economic situation of China as well as being as a new experimental location for social innovation, its cultural characteristic and diversity should be spotted by designers.

In the following, by comparison of Chinese users' different evaluations on two service design projects of Politecnico di Milano in Italy and Jiangnan University in China, we are trying to analyze the key elements of need, value and cross-culture, which will impact user evaluation.

2 Cross-Culture Theories and Research Methodology

The cultural anthropologist Whistler states that every culture of different regions has its own historical origin. And the diversities in cultural characteristics bring out different types of cultures and cultural regions. Substantially influenced by designated culture, users gains the values, mindsets and behavior patterns with the cultural mark in correspondence with its culture type and cultural region [4]. Therefore, it is undoubted that culture and value will affect users' judgments, evaluation and active participation no matter on product itself or participation in public services. Culture and value are especially important service design for cross-culture regions and Chinese society under fast developing. In fact, it hasn't received enough attention and consideration in academic research and practices.

Among cross-culture research, there are different culture analysis models introduced by various scholars, which combines anthropology, sociology and natural science: some studied cultural differences from language perspective（Mandelbaum，1949；Hoijer, 1994）; some defined cultural differences in social features（Hall，1976）; some defines various manifestations from cultural value perspective （Hofste de, 1980） [5]. According to the "hierarchy of needs" theory of Maslow, it studies the hierarchy and importance of human beings and added the sixth level of "beyond self' latter. Defining behavioral diversity as research topic, Hofstede's theory of cultural value levels studies over 60 national subsidiaries of IBM and concluded Power Distance Index, Uncertainty Avoidance Index, Individualism—Collectivism, Masculinity—Femininity, and the fifth dimension Long-Term—Short-Term Orientation according to the value of Confucianism[6].

Comparatively, the two theories analyze fundamental variables and factors of different cultures and establish clear dimensional structures regarding both values and practices. They both include the structures of users and business cultures themselves, and also deeply dig into the relationship between demands and behaviors in various stages. Based on profound theoretical bases, they made comparative analysis on culture and value related in service design field from more macroscopic views. But the downside is that single theoretical model can hardly determine all the cross-culture factors in service design. So we need to enhance test effectiveness through the combination of quantitative measurement and qualitative interviews.

3 Research Process

3.1 Two Samples for Case Study

Sample1 is a sustainable product service system named ShareRadio—Exchange Your Time. As a design program of TANGO, which was sponsored by EU, ShareRadio mainly aims at social integration and conversation between generations, especially promoting social interpretation between senior citizens and young citizens and boost the development of local social environment. Through time bank established on new service model and Internet radio space, every skilled people can set up their user network in ShareRadio program to offer work hours to gain time credits and use the credits to get services from other people. The Internet radio includes online interview, free subscription, management of offers and demands, community communication and direct checking of credits to make the system more efficient.

Fig. 1. "ShareRadio—Exchange Your Time"

Sample2 is the service design project of used-clothes recycling named "Clothes Bank". In Chinese families, there are many obsolete clothing that fails to find its reusable value. However, they are in urgent need in some rural and mountain and disaster regions. Clothing donation should be a good charity, but there are still some problems, such as lacking of donation information transparency, lacking of long-term durability from donors and charity organizations and secondary treatment. The project provides print service of recycling bins and coupons, an online platform allowing modification design and sell and mobile applications offering delivery information and feedback. In combination of hardware and service, the system provides several new services. Particularly, the activity process counseling online platform and donation information update further improved interaction and information visualization among various people involved.

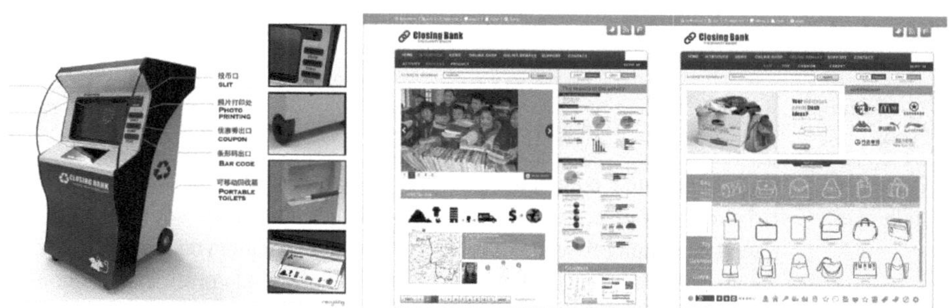

Fig. 2. "Clothes Bank" Used-clothes Recycle Service Design

3.2 Questionnaire Design

Due to multilevel meanings of samples above, the test mainly applies the Method of Semantic Differential (referred as SD Method later). In order to understand young Chinese's cognitive attitude and explore factors behind, we combined social context, social culture and experience and tested the samples with polarized adjectives in our scale chart. Our research group collected evaluation adjectives in three main aspects as follows: first, online analytical reports on relevant cases of social innovation, public services and services design; secondly, academic essays related to the topic mentioned above; thirdly, part of user interviews combined with theory of psychological needs, cross-culture theory, user experience theory and value theory. After we collected 61 pairs of adjectives describing social innovation cases, we selected 15 pairs of adjectives that can more intensively represent interviewers' cognitive situations through user test on more than 20 young users.

The final 15 pairs of adjectives are passive/active, shared/isolated, communicative/conservative, individualism/collectivism, economic interest/social interest, empathetic/unsympathetic, non-profitable/profitable, substantial/spiritual, traditional/modern, positive/negative, motivated/unmotivated and mutually-assistant/assistant, interactive/non-interactive, strong uncertainty avoidance index/weak uncertainty avoidance index, long-term oriented/short-term oriented and willing to join/unwilling to join. Then we divided them into five grades and designed semantic questionnaire for cross-cultural difference in service design in combination of two representative samples mentioned before. Finally, we collected 81 valid data of young users in college aging from 20-30 years old from online questionnaire platform (www.sojump.com) and got specific evaluation about each pair of adjectives from each sample.

3.3 Result Analysis

Through data analysis with online platform and SPSS software, we made cluster analysis, factor analysis, correlation analysis and regression analysis and get analysis results as follows:

First of all, according to the scores that the two samples gained upon each pair of adjectives, we summarized adjectives into three levels of user judgment: consistent, relatively consistent, and inconsistent (Table 1.)

Table 1. Adjectives summary about consistent, relatively consistent, and inconsistent user judgment

Samples / Types	Sample 1	Sample 2
Consistent Judgment	shared/isolated, communicative/conservative, positive/negative, motivated/unmotivated, empathetic/unsympathetic, mutually-assistant/assistant, substantial/spiritual, interactive/ non-interactive, traditional/modern	shared/isolated, positive/negative, individualism/collectivism, empathetic/unsympathetic, non-profitable/profitable, economic interest/social interest, motivated/unmotivated
Relatively Consistent Judgment	individualism/collectivism, passive/active, long-term oriented/short-term oriented	passive/active, long-term oriented/short-term oriented
Inconsistent Judgement	non-profitable/profitable, economic interest/social interest, strong uncertainty avoidance index/weak uncertainty avoidance index	substantial/spiritual, communicative/conservative, interactive/ non-interactive, traditional/modern, mutually-assistant/assistant, strong uncertainty avoidance index/weak uncertainty avoidance index

Based on the chart, we weighted the times that each adjective showed in three categories: twice times of consistent judgment adjectives; original times of relatively consistent adjectives; times of inconsistent judgment adjectives are not counted. Result shows that, shared/isolated (4), empathetic/unsympathetic (4), positive/negative (4), motivated/unmotivated (4), individualism/collectivism (4) get consistent judgment from interviewers while passive/active (1+1) and long-term oriented/short-term oriented (1+1) received relatively consistent judgment. Other adjectives are difficult to be used to judge those cases. On the other hand, various social contents and interviews' social experiences influenced their cognition consistency about above cases.

Through cluster analysis of the evaluations of the adjectives, we can find their correlations with two similarity matrixes (Fig. 3) that: the adjectives close to 1 or -1 can replace each other. Comparing and merging the results of two groups, we basically drew three similar factor dimensions: relationships (positive/negative, interactive/ non-interactive, communicative/ conservative, mutual assistant/assistant, shared/isolated), self-transcendence (empathetic/unsympathetic, long-term oriented/short-term oriented, motivated/unmotivated), personal interests (individualism - collectivism, traditional - modern, substantial - spiritual).

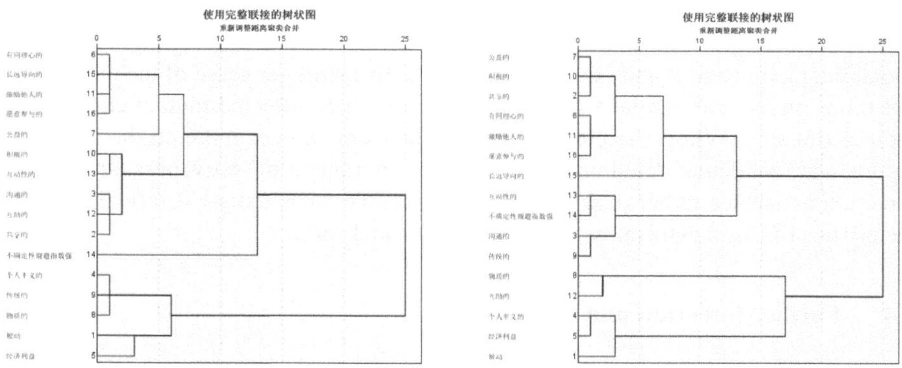

Fig. 3. Cluster Analysis of Evaluations of The Adjectives from Two Samples

In general, from the perspective of participatory willingness of sample 1 and sample 2, Chinese young users prefer to sample 2,the "clothing bank" used clothes recycle service design project. And in both groups, females are more willing to participant than males, as the percentage of females who are willing to join in sample 2 is as high as 72%.

Then to make further correlation analysis, we first conducted scatter spot analysis and find correlation analysis results between each pair of adjective variables and willing-to-participant/ not-willing-to-participant (Table 2.). In data analysis, p value that is less than 0.05 shows that there is a linear correlation between two variables, while less than 0.01 indicates significant correlation, and greater than 0.05 demonstrate no linear correlation.

Table 2. Correlation analysis

Samples / Correlations	Sample1	Sample2
Positive Correlation	shared/isolated, communicative/ conservative, empathetic/unsympathetic, positive/negative, motivated/unmotivated, interactive/ non-interactive, mutual assistant/assistant, long-term oriented/short-term oriented	shared/isolated, empathetic/unsympathetic, non-profitable/profitable, substantial - spiritual positive/negative, motivated/unmotivated, long-term oriented/short-term oriented
Negative Correlation	passive/active, economic interest/social interest, substantial/spiritual, traditional/modern	mutual assistant/assistant, passive/active, individualism/collectivism, economic interest/social interest

Data analysis above shows shared features of two samples that are sharable, empathetic, positive, active, motivated, long-term oriented and social-beneficial. In comparison, users agree to sample 1 "shared broadcast" because it highlights more on social interaction and mutual communications with a stronger sense of technology and not relies on any substantial form. The western project reflected mutual equality and bidireactionality. While Sample 2 "clothing bank" emphasizes more on the non-profit nature and collective relationship, especially in aspect of activeness and single-direction assistance rather than mutual assistance. To some extent, it reflects the characteristics of Confucianism with specific substantial form.

3.4 Further Interview and Analysis

Based on questionnaire, we interviewed five young users (2 males and 3 females) to further understand Chinese youth's unique opinions towards service design for social innovation.

During the interview, several users shows positive attitude to “ShareRadio” service design project with following reasons: First, the service system can promote more natural and harmonious relationships that bring people to the original, pure and mutual-assistance state; Secondly, the new principle behind this service system allows individuals to take advantage of their personal strengths and get recognition and affirmation from others, which undoubtedly satisfy their psychological needs; Thirdly, if such mutual development operates in a healthy way, the society will be in a positive circle, as well as social security issues and so on. However, some interviews thinks the principle is not reasonable enough with a certain compulsiveness (users have to offer services themselves and exchange for other's services) ; In relatively developed Western countries, it's likely to be more acceptable and operate longer. Firstly, People in Italy and other relatively developed western countries with higher social welfare and higher education have stronger social consciousness of serving others. Secondly, there is already practical experience that younger senior citizens serve elder senior citizens in the society.

Many respondents think that Used Goods Donation has high feasibility in Chinese society. Believing that making the best use of everything is materially sustainable, redesign of used goods is recycling. Under the context of relatively large gap in wealth distribution in China, various perceptions toward used goods between people benefit material recycling. Due to the negative impact of Guo Meimei, respondents pay great attention to the feedback of goods donation. They agree to online platform about its transparency in donation and delivery process, rising participator's awareness of self-value. The downside is that redesign and resale of "used goods" need strong need support from mediators with additional consideration about the costs. Those phases will have great influence on sustainable operation of the service system.

4 Design Guidance

Studies above reflect the main concerns of Chinese young users about participating in social service in perspectives of need, value and culture. These concerns accord with economic and social situations in China today. On the other hand, they reflect differences in development stage with western countries. Thus social innovative design for Chinese society must take these factors into consideration and take suggestions with following attentions:

4.1 To Understand Local Context and Existing Resources with Empathy on Users' Economical Interest Claims and Psychological Social Needs

At rapid-development stage, Chinese society share many differences with high-welfare western countries at post-industry stage, even in same issues. Designers should pay attention to their recent general revenue, social healthcare, housing and other economic conditions, personal lifestyle and social resources generated in an upgrading process. In addition, they should concern about users' views towards social events at this stage, such as personal occupation, lack in social trustworthy and no transparency in governmental management etc. Through anthropology research method like observation and interviews, designers need to understand users' thoughts and evaluations with combination of diverse social, economic and environmental characteristics.

4.2 To Pay Attention to Project's Interest Claim Evaluation and Try to Combine Business Innovation with Social Innovation

Recently, Chinese users are advocating social welfare in hope of certain material confirmation from others at the same time. Therefore, during interactive process among stakeholders, we should take into account motivated service sectors to show participators' personal contributions. Concerning sustainable operation of public service, designers need to find appropriate entrepreneurs and bring their resource platform, business strategy and operational experience into social project. Even if the only combination opportunity is certain state of the service process, there is new value for every stakeholder.

4.3 To Pay Attention to the Feasibility and Usability of Public Service Implementation and Take Advantage of Local Development in Culture and Technology

There are various interaction approaches in service design. No matter it is revolutionary innovation or incremental innovation should be combined with user's real life and try to localize foreign projects. As smart mobile terminals, mobile network and applications become increasingly popular among Chinese youth, designers should make use of emerging information technologies. For example, current boom in Wechat will undoubtedly provide greater operation platform to social innovative service design.

4.4 To Pay Attention to the Spread of Service Design Related Information and Influence Participators' Recognition and Participation in New Social Service with "Lean Design"

Same with western users, Chinese users agrees on participatory willingness factors, including: shared, empathetic, active, positive, motivated, long-term oriented and social benefits. With "lean design", sustainable public behavior visualizes service process and management information, making behaviors be better spread, demonstrated and advocated, which helps to stimulate user's enthusiasm and activeness of participation. Take Tendril home energy management systems as an example, by allowing consumers to learn their energy consumption and certain real-time data, it encourages them to make corresponding management plans.

5 Conclusions

As essential stakeholders participating in social innovative service, users' culture and value features are decisive to projects operating effectiveness. Transformation and application of cross-cultural case need deep cultural identity. Based on demand and cross-cultural study, our research collects data from semantic difference test and deep interview of two social innovations projects in Milan and Wuxi. In spite of limitation in study cases and participators, our complete implementation process and verification from beginning to the end give designers an overall understanding of culture cognition features of Chinese user groups, differences between eastern and western users, as well as social and cultural factors behind it. By understanding local context and users, we focus on evaluation of project interest claims and combine feasibility, usability and design broadcast of relevant information to efficiently push forward cross-cultural development of social innovative service projects.

References

1. Miaosen, G.: Design for Chinese Social Innovation——Pilot PSS Design Experiences for Sustainable Lifestyles. Creation and Design 5, 18–23 (2011)
2. Jegou, F., Manzini, E.: Collaborative Services. Social innovation and design for sustainability. Polidesign, Milano (2008)
3. Taipale, I.: 100 Social Innovations from Finland. Common Wealth Co., Ltd. (2012)
4. Liu, L.: Comparison, Measurement and Coordination of Cross-culture Management. Business Age (24), 43–44 (2007)
5. Zhou, J., Li, B.: The Analysis of Cross-Cultural Theory and Product Modeling Design (09), 248 (2009)
6. Hofstede, G.: Culture and Organizations: Software of the mind, p. 255. McGraw-Hill Book Company(UK) Limited, London (1991)

User Adoption and Loyalty of Location Based Social Network Service in China

Yubo Zhang and Pei-Luen Patrick Rau*

Institute of Human Factors and Ergonomics,
Tsinghua University, Beijing, 100084, China
zhangyubo1987@gmail.com,
rpl@mail.tsinghua.edu.cn

Abstract. This study made an investigation of user adoption and loyalty of location based social network service. Regression analysis was conducted to identify the predictors of user adoption measured by intention and frequency according to Innovation Diffusion Theory and the theory of Uses and Gratifications. Personal innovativeness was found to effectively predict future intention. Perceived popularity was found to effectively predict future frequency. Not all five dimensions of perceived innovativeness had equal predicting power to user adoption. Perceived needs proved to effectively predict user adoption measured by both future intention and future frequency. Path analysis showed a structure integrating predictors of e-loyalty together, including trust, satisfaction, flow experience and switching cost. Comparison of continuers, quitters and refusers of LBSNS showed that continuers had higher level of willingness to pursue fashion and behaved more innovative than others. Comparison of three typical LBSNS applications showed a more advantageous position of dedicated LBSNS than SNS and microblog in terms of loyalty.

Keywords: Adoption, loyalty, location-based social network service.

1 Introduction

Location based social network service (LBSNS) is one of the most popular forms of social media. Although there are a big number of adopters of LBSNS, LBSNS did not gain consistent popularity among social media users. Hence, we chose to study the user adoption and its influencing factors of the epidemic check-in behaviors. Besides, there are various ways to check in with mobile phones such as SNS, microblog and dedicated LBSNS. In China, a representative SNS is Renren, which is similar with Facebook. Weibo, which is a translation of microblog in Chinese, is similar with Twitter. Jiepang is a popular dedicated LBSNS which is similar with Foursquare. The three types of LBSNS applications are popular ways to check in. We aimed to study the difference between different ways to check in and what factors influence loyalty of an LBSNS application.

---

* Corresponding author.

P.L.P. Rau (Ed.): CCD/HCII 2014, LNCS 8528, pp. 392–402, 2014.

The burgeoning and declining development process of LBSNS needs to be explained theoretically. So far, studies about user adoption and loyalty of LBSNS are rare. Hence, factors which influence user adoption and loyalty of LBSNS need to be found and the mechanism about how the factors influence user adoption and loyalty of LBSNS needs to be revealed. Besides the theoretical significance, studying user adoption and loyalty of LBSNS also has practical values. The study can provide design implications to improve user experience of existing applications and maintain user stickness.

The objective of this study is twofold. The first one is to find factors which influence user adoption of LBSNS. As a co-product, LBSNS adopters and non-adopters are compared in terms of their personal innovativeness. The second one is to study how factors influence adopters' loyalty of LBSNS. Meanwhile, LBSNS adopters who prefer different applications to check in are compared.

2 Literature Review

In predicting user adoption of new technology or media, previous studies have two theoretical aspects: Innovation Diffusion Theory (IDT) and the theory of Uses and Gratifications (U&G).

IDT was used to explain how personal innovativeness and perceived innovativeness of a new technology influences user adoption [1]. Chang, Lee and Kim [2] used IDT to investigate the relationship between innovativeness and online game adoption and found significantly positive relationship between them. IDT has also been widely used to explain the reason of user adoption such as Facebook [3, 4] and Twitter [5].

There are three constructs in IDT-related studies. The first construct is personal innovativeness. Rogers [6] defined innovativeness as 'the degree to which an individual or other unit of adoption is relatively earlier in adopting an innovation than other members of a social system'. Some studies measured personal innovativeness with perceived behavior control [1], meaning perceived knowledge or ability to use a new technology. Some studies measured personal innovativeness with relative innovativeness [7], which is similar with Rogers' definition of innovativeness. Besides, there were studies measuring innovativeness with fashion and innovative idea [2], meaning users' interest to pursue fashion and innovative idea. The second construct is perceived innovativeness of new technology. Rogers and Shoemaker's five-dimension typology was widely adopted by researchers [8]: relative advantage, compatibility, complexity, trialability and observability. However, there has not been consensus about whether all the five factors consistently predict adoption of social media. Peslak, Ceccucci and Sendall [3] found that four factors except observability were positively correlated with intention to use social network sites while Folorunso, Vincent, Adekoya and Ogunde [4] found that only compatibility and trilability were positively correlated with the attitude of using SNS. The third construct is perceived popularity. It has been proved to positively predict user adoption of online game [2]. In this study, the relationship between the three constructs and user adoption is going to be investigated:

RQ 1: What is the relationship between personal innovativeness and the adoption of LBSNS?

RQ 2: Which of the five dimensions of perceived innovativeness of LBSNS can predict the adoption of LBSNS?

RQ 3: What is the relationship between perceived popularity and the adoption of LBSNS?

As it is indicated in the theory of U&G, users' perceived needs is a primary factor determining and motivating the adoption of media. Previous studies have shown that social media gratifies some unique needs which are different from those gratified by traditional mass media. One study identified six dimensions as gratifications which users obtained from Facebook: pastime, affection, fashion, sharing problems, sociability and social information [9]. Feng once studied user needs gratified by SNS and microblog and found a five-dimension structure including information retrieving, entertainment, self-disclosure, social interactivity and impression management [10]. Lindqvist, Cranshaw, Wiese, Hong and Zimmerman [11] once used the theory of U&G to study why people used Foursquare to share their locations. They summarized the reasons into five dimensions: badges and fun, social connection, place discovery, keeping track of places and game with oneself. Based on the five-dimension model, this study is going to investigate the relationship between perceived needs and the adoption of LBSNS:

RQ 4: What is the relationship between perceived needs and the adoption of LBSNS?

With the development of e-commerce, the concept of loyalty has extended from traditional customer loyalty to electronic customer loyalty (e-loyalty), meaning 'the customer's favorable attitude toward an electronic business, resulting in repeat purchasing behavior' [12]. In studies of SNS, there are two dimensions of e-loyalty: renewal loyalty and referral loyalty. Renewal loyalty indicates users' online stickiness to a certain website and referral loyalty refers to users' intention to recommend a certain brand or product to others. Referral loyalty was proved as a strong signal of loyalty [13].

Trust, satisfaction, flow and switching cost were proved to be significant predictors of e-loyalty. Trust [14-17] and satisfaction [18, 19] have been proved to positively predict e-loyalty of online purchasing. Trust [18] and satisfaction [18, 19] also positively predict e-loyalty of mobile purchasing. Trust was found to positively predict mobile SNS users' e-loyalty [20], and satisfaction was found to mediate trust and loyalty [14, 18]. Flow experience describes people's feelings when they are totally involved in an activity [21]. It was found to positively influence e-loyalty of SNS websites [20, 22]. Previous studies also found that the positive influence of flow experience on e-loyalty was mediated by satisfaction [23, 24]. Since there are multiple choices of LBSNS for users, switching cost from one application to another is an important variable to study. Moderating effect of switching cost on the relationship between perceived value and loyalty [25] was found while in another study significant moderating effect was only found when the level of perceived value was above average [26]. Interestingly, studies about the direct influence of switching cost on e-loyalty did not have consistent findings. Fuentes-Blasco et al. [25] found weak negative relationship between switching cost and customers' loyalty to B2C websites while other studies found positive relationship in the field of mobile device and service [27-29]. Ng and Kwahk [19] found that switching cost did not significantly influence continuance intention of mobile Internet service. Hence, the relationship between switching cost and e-loyalty of LBSNS needs to be studied. Although trust, satisfaction, flow and switching cost have been studied a lot about e-loyalty, there is not a structure integrating all the factors in the context of LBSNS.

RQ 5: What is the structure of trust, satisfaction, flow and switching cost when they are used to predict e-loyalty of LBSNS?

3 Methodology

A questionnaire survey was conducted to study user adoption and loyalty of LBSNS in China. It was released online and with open access to all Internet users. It was then diffused via Renren, Sina Weibo and Jiepang.

The questionnaire was depicted in Chinese. Before specific questions, a paragraph was presented to describe the concept of LBSNS and there were three check-in applications: Renren, Sina Weibo and Jiepang. Each application was introduced with a paragraph and a check-in screenshot on a smart phone.

The questionnaire consisted of four sections. Section 1 was about respondents' demographic information and section 2 was about their experience of social media and LBSNS. Respondents were categorized into three types: those who still check in now are 'continuers'; those who have checked in before but have stopped now are 'quitters'; those who have never checked in are 'refusers'. Continuers had to answer questions in section 3 and 4. Questions in section 3 were about innovativeness and perceived needs to check in. Thereinto, innovativeness was constructed by personal innovativeness, perceived innovativeness and perceived popularity according to Innovation Diffusion Theory. Among variables constructing perceived needs to check in, the majority of them were from items in the factor analysis and interview results by Lindqvist et al. [11], one variable was from Raacke and Bonds-Raacke's study [30] and one variable was came up with via discussion with research colleagues. Questions in section 4 were about factors which were proved to influence loyalty by previous studies. Besides, continuers had to report their preferred application to check in in section 4. This question was for further comparison on loyalty among respondents who preferred to check in with different applications.

4 Results

In total, there were 196 valid respondents from the online survey. Among them, there were 76 (38.8%) continuers, 45 (23.0%) quitters and 75 (38.3%) refusers. The average age was 23.7 (SD=2.63). There were 104 (53.1%) male respondents and 141 (71.9%) respondents who were students.

4.1 Factors Influencing User Adoption of LBSNS

Personal innovativeness, five dimensions of perceived innovativeness, perceived popularity and perceived needs were regressed on two dependent variables measuring user adoption, future intention to adopt LBSNS and future frequency to adopt LBSNS. Stepwise regression was conducted. The entry level was .05 and the removal level was .10. Personal innovativeness was constructed by seven items, the Cronbach's alpha coefficient was .805; perceived needs was constructed by 20 items, the Cronbach's alpha coefficient was .900.

As shown in Table 1, no matter measured by future intention or future frequency, user adoption was significantly positively predicted by perceived needs. Personal innovativeness only significantly predicted future intention. In the five dimensions of perceived innovativeness, compatibility positively predicted future intention and relative advantage positively predicted future frequency. Perceived popularity only positively predicted future frequency. The total variance explained by the two regression model was 45.0% ($F=21.476$, $p<.001$) and 47.8% ($F=23.925$, $p<.001$).

Table 1. Stepwise regression on future intention and frequency to adopt LBSNS

Predictor	*B*	β	*t*	*p*
Future intention to adopt LBSNS				
Compatibility	.414	.460	5.084	<.001
Perceived needs	.374	.276	2.942	.004
Personal innovativeness	.263	.221	2.481	.015
Future frequency to adopt LBSNS				
Perceived needs	.572	.390	4.107	<.001
Perceived popularity	.319	.339	3.821	<.001
Relative advantage	.205	.210	2.264	.027

4.2 Comparison among Three Types of Respondents

Three types of respondents were compared in terms of their perceived behavior control, relative innovativeness, fashion, innovative idea.

As shown in Table 2, continuers and quitters had significantly higher level of relative innovativeness and higher willingness to pursue fashion than refusers. No significant difference was found in terms of perceived behavior control and innovative idea among the three types of respondents.

4.3 Path Analysis of Factors Influencing e-Loyalty of LBSNS

Fig. 1 shows the path analysis of factors influencing e-loyalty of LBSNS. The fitness of this model was $\chi^2=3.531$, GFI=.982, AGFI=.931, RMSEA<.001, which showed that the model had a good fitness.

Under the significant level of <.05, the estimation coefficients of the four factors on e-loyalty were: trust (.361×.405=.146), satisfaction (.405), flow (.163) and switching cost (.207). Satisfaction was a mediator between trust and e-loyalty.

Table 2. One-way ANOVA comparison of personal innovativeness among three types of respondents

Dependent variables	Continuer		Quitter		Refuser				Multiple comparison
	Mean	SD	Mean	SD	Mean	SD	*F*	*p*	
Perceived behavior control	4.45	.67	4.43	.55	4.29	.81	1.046	.353	
Relative innovativeness	3.29	.86	3.16	.93	2.59	.95	11.980	<.001	C>R*** Q>R**
Fashion	3.07	.88	3.03	.96	2.50	1.02	7.828	.001	C>R*** Q>R**
Innovative idea	3.74	.98	3.71	.82	3.81	.97	.204	.816	

Note: (1)**p*<.05, ***p*<.01, ****p*<.001; (2)C=Continuer, Q=Quitter, R=Refuser.

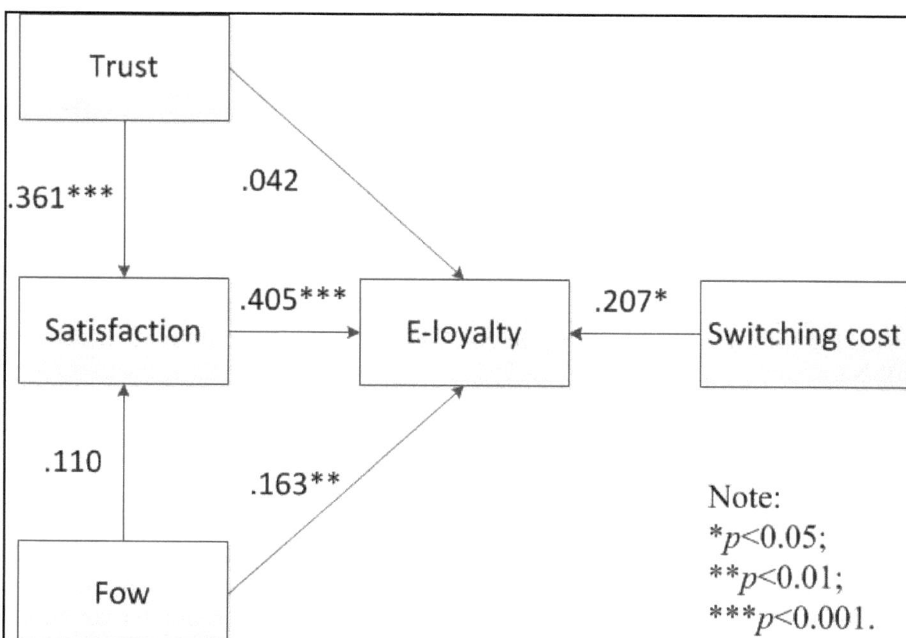

Fig. 1. Path analysis of factors influencing loyalty of LBSNS

4.4 Comparison among Respondents Who Prefer to Check in with Three Different Applications

Among the 76 continuers of LBSNS, there were 23 respondents who preferred to check in with mobile SNS like Renren, 26 respondents who preferred to check in with microblog like Sina Weibo and 23 respondents who preferred to check in with dedicated LBSNS like Jiepang (there were 4 respondents either leaving the question in blank or selecting the option 'others'). Then a comparison was conducted among respondents who preferred to check in with different applications.

As shown in Table 3, there were significant differences in satisfaction and renewal loyalty among respondents who preferred to check in with different applications. Specifically, respondents who preferred to check in with dedicated LBSNS reported higher level of satisfaction than those who preferred to check in with SNS and Microblog, and respondents who preferred to check in with Microblog reported lower level of renewal loyalty than those who preferred to check in with SNS and dedicated LBSNS.

Table 3. One-way ANOVA comparison among respondents who prefer to check in with three different applications

Dependent variables	SNS		Microblog		Dedicated LBSNS		*F*	*p*	Multiple comparison
	Mean	SD	Mean	SD	Mean	SD			
Trust	3.61	.84	3.81	.69	3.91	.51	1.140	.326	
Flow	3.17	.94	2.65	1.09	3.09	.95	1.930	.153	
Satisfaction	3.30	.82	3.38	.70	3.78	.42	3.401	.039	S<D*, M<D*
Switching cost	3.33	.75	3.02	.57	3.28	.69	1.529	.224	
Renewal loyalty	3.61	.66	3.19	.75	3.74	.75	3.885	.025	S>M*, D>M*
Referral loyalty	3.52	.73	3.15	.97	3.70	.76	2.720	.073	

Note: (1)**p*<.05, ***p*<.01, ****p*<.001; (2)S=SNS, M=Microblog, D=Dedicated LBSNS.

5 Discussion

The results showed that when user adoption was measured by future intention, the regression coefficient of personal innovativeness was smaller than that of compatibility which is one of the five dimensions of perceived innovativeness, and when user adoption was measured by future frequency, personal innovativeness did not have a significant predicting role to user adoption. This is consistent with Ostlund's opinion that perceived innovativeness is a better predictor of purchase intention than personal characteristic variables [31]. However, the five dimensions of perceived innovativeness did not have equal predicting roles to user adoption. Compatibility was a better predictor of future intention while relative advantage was a better predictor of future frequency. This result implies that an LBSNS application which complies with users' existing habits or notions has a good chance to gain users' intention to use it. When a user first knows an LBSNS application, if its function model is too far from users' mental model, users may refuse to use it. However, when users have started to use the application, whether or not it has relative advantage over competitive applications is a key factor which influences the continuous adoption.

Besides, perceived popularity was also a significant predictor of future frequency. Like accepting information from family members or friends, the acceptance of LBSNS is influenced by users' social relationship. Schmitz and Fulk [32] support the notion that the social system surrounding an individual can affect the individual's innovation adoption. A person would easily intend to adopt LBSNS if he/she sees family members or friends use it. This phenomenon is described by the construct perceived popularity which turned out to positively predict future frequency. That is, if an individual perceives that LBSNS is popular among friends or the whole society, then the individual will more likely to frequently adopt it in the future.

The theory of U&G proved effective in predicting adoption of LBSNS. Perceived needs was found to significantly predict both future intention and frequency to check in. According to the theory of U&G, needs, uses and gratifications have dynamic reciprocal causality [33]. That is, perceived needs motivate users to use LBSNS and the gratified needs provide feedback for subsequent needs. This is consistent with the result that the coefficient of perceived needs was the largest (.572) when adoption was measured by future frequency to check in.

The structure of trust, satisfaction, flow experience, switching cost and e-loyalty implies that trustworthiness of an LBSNS application does not necessarily predict users' stickness to it. For the design of LBSNS, improving the satisfaction and providing flow experience for users have directer effect on increasing loyalty than improving trustworthiness. This result can set an order of priority if there is trade-off between trustworthiness of information provided by the application and satisfaction or flow experience provided by the application. Satisfaction was an important factor in the aspect of increasing user loyalty of LBSNS not only because of its large estimation coefficient but also because of its mediating role between trust and e-loyalty.

The comparison among three typical check-in applications showed a slightly advantageous position of dedicated LBSNS like Jiepang, whereas in fact Jiepang's development comes across many difficulties. Hence, for applications like Jiepang, their users' loyalty level is high but the problem of their development is that they cannot find a continuous profit model.

6 Conclusion

This study made an investigation of user adoption and loyalty of location based social network service. Regression analysis was conducted to identify the predictors of user adoption measured by intention and frequency. For Innovation Diffusion Theory, personal innovativeness only significantly predicted future intention to check in and not all the five dimensions of perceived innovativeness had equal predicting power to user adoption. The theory of Uses and Gratifications proved to effectively predict user adoption no matter adoption was measured by intention or frequency. Via path analysis, this study found a structure integrating predictors of e-loyalty together, including trust, satisfaction, flow experience and switching cost. Comparison of continuers, quitters and refusers of LBSNS showed that continuers had higher level of willingness to pursue fashion and behaved more innovative than others. Comparison of three typical LBSNS applications showed a more advantageous position of dedicated LBSNS than SNS and Microblog in terms of loyalty.

Future research can be done with empirical studies to validate the findings in the survey or with field observation to acquire real data to study users' check-in behaviors.

Acknowledgement. This study was funded by a National Science Foundation China grant 71188001.

References

1. Ostlund, L.E.: Perceived innovation attributes as predictors of innovativeness. Journal of Consumer Research 1, 23–29 (1974)
2. Chang, B.H., Lee, S.E., Kim, B.S.: Exploring factors affecting the adoption and continuance of online games among college students in South Korea: Integrating uses and gratification and diffusion of innovation approaches. New Media & Society 8, 295–319 (2006)
3. Peslak, A., Ceccucci, W., Sendall, P.: An empirical study of social networking behavior using diffusion of innovation theory. In: Conference on Information Systems Applied Research, Nashville Tennessee, USA (2010)
4. Folorunso, O., Vincent, R.O., Adekoya, A.F., Ogunde, O.: Diffusion of innovation in social networking sites among university students. International Journal of Computer Science and Security 4, 361 (2009)
5. Coursaris, C.K., Yun, Y., Sung, J.: Twitter Users vs. Quitters: A Uses and Gratifications and Diffusion of Innovations approach in understanding the role of mobility in microblogging. In: 2010 Ninth International Conference on Mobile Business and 2010 Ninth Global Mobility Roundtable, pp. 481–486. IEEE (2010)
6. Rogers, E.M.: Diffusion of innovations. Simon and Schuster, New York (1995)
7. Yi, M.Y., Jackson, J.D., Park, J.S., Probst, J.C.: Understanding information technology acceptance by individual professionals: Toward an integrative view. Information & Management 43, 350–363 (2006)
8. Rogers, E.M., Shoemaker, F.F.: Communication of Innovations: A Cross-Cultural Approach. The Free Press, New York (1971)
9. Quan-Haase, A., Young, A.L.: Uses and gratifications of social media: A comparison of Facebook and Instant Messaging. Bulletin of Science, Technology & Society 30, 350–361 (2010)
10. Feng, C.: Research on the Motivation and Behavior Patterns of Social Media Users and Brand Message Content Strategy. Industrial Engineering, vol. Master, p. 224. Tsinghua University, Beijing (2012)

11. Lindqvist, J., Cranshaw, J., Wiese, J., Hong, J., Zimmerman, J.: I'm the mayor of my house: examining why people use foursquare - a social-driven location sharing application. In: Proceedings of the SIGCHI Conference on Human Factors in Computing Systems, pp. 2409–2418. ACM, Vancouver (2011)
12. Anderson, R.E., Srinivasan, S.S.: E - satisfaction and e - loyalty: A contingency framework. Psychology & Marketing 20, 123 - 138 (2003)
13. Gronholdt, L., Martensen, A., Kristensen, K.: The relationship between customer satisfaction and loyalty: cross-industry differences. Total Quality Management 11, 509–514 (2000)
14. Chiou, J.S.: The antecedents of consumers' loyalty toward Internet service providers. Information & Management 41, 685–695 (2004)
15. Cyr, D., Head, M., Ivanov, A.: Perceived interactivity leading to e-loyalty: Development of a model for cognitive–affective user responses. International Journal of Human-Computer Studies 67, 850–869 (2009)
16. Ribbink, D., Van Riel, A.C.R., Liljander, V., Streukens, S.: Comfort your online customer: quality, trust and loyalty on the internet. Managing Service Quality 14, 446–456 (2004)
17. Flavián, C., Guinalíu, M., Gurrea, R.: The role played by perceived usability, satisfaction and consumer trust on website loyalty. Information & Management 43, 1–14 (2006)
18. Lin, H.-H., Wang, Y.-S.: An examination of the determinants of customer loyalty in mobile commerce contexts. Information & Management 43, 271–282 (2006)
19. Ee Hong, N., Kee-Young, K.: Examining the determinants of Mobile Internet service continuance: a customer relationship development perspective. International Journal of Mobile Communications 8, 210–229229 (2010)
20. Zhou, T., Li, H., Liu, Y.: The effect of flow experience on mobile SNS users' loyalty. Industrial Management & Data Systems 110, 930–946 (2010)
21. Csikszentmihalyi, M.E., Csikszentmihalyi, I.S.E.: Optimal experience: Psychological studies of flow in consciousness. Cambridge University Press, Cambridge (1988)
22. Qi, Y., Fu, C.: The Effects of Flow and Attachment on the e-Loyalty of SNS Websites. In: 2011 International Conference on Management and Service Science (MASS), pp. 1–6. IEEE (Year)
23. Hsu, C.-L., Chang, K.-C., Chen, M.-C.: The impact of website quality on customer satisfaction and purchase intention: perceived playfulness and perceived flow as mediators. Information Systems and E-Business Management 10, 549–570 (2012)
24. Hsu, C.-L., Wu, C.-C., Chen, M.-C.: An empirical analysis of the antecedents of e-satisfaction and e-loyalty: focusing on the role of flow and its antecedents. Information Systems and E-Business Management, 1–25 (2012)
25. Fuentes-Blasco, M., Saura, I.G., Berenguer-Contrí, G., Moliner-Velázquez, B.: Measuring the antecedents of e-loyalty and the effect of switching costs on website. The Service Industries Journal 30, 1837–1852 (2010)
26. Yang, Z., Peterson, R.T.: Customer perceived value, satisfaction, and loyalty: The role of switching costs. Psychology & Marketing 21, 799–822 (2004)
27. Aydin, S., Özer, G., Arasil, Ö.: Customer loyalty and the effect of switching costs as a moderator variable: A case in the Turkish mobile phone market. Marketing Intelligence & Planning 23, 89–103 (2005)
28. Deng, Z., Lu, Y., Wei, K.K., Zhang, J.: Understanding customer satisfaction and loyalty: An empirical study of mobile instant messages in China. International Journal of Information Management 30, 289–300 (2010)
29. Min, D., Wan, L.: Switching factors of mobile customers in Korea. Journal of Service Science 1, 105–120 (2009)

30. Raacke, J., Bonds-Raacke, J.: MySpace and Facebook: Applying the uses and gratifications theory to exploring friend-networking sites. CyberPsychology & Behavior 11, 169–174 (2008)
31. Ostlund, L.E.: The role of product perceptions in innovative behavior. In: Fall Conference of American Marketing Association, pp. 259–266 (Year)
32. Schmitz, J., Fulk, J.: Organizational Colleagues, Media Richness, and Electronic Mail A Test of the Social Influence Model of Technology Use. Communication Research 18, 487–523 (1991)
33. Wang, Z., Tchernev, J.M., Solloway, T.: A dynamic longitudinal examination of social media use, needs, and gratifications among college students. Computers in Human Behavior 28, 1829–1839 (2012)

The Study of Interactive Design in Service Systems for Community Self-help Charitable Facilities

Xiaorui Zhou, Zhejun Liu*, and Yangxi Tian

4800 Cao An Road, Tongji University,
Shanghai, China
{03162,wingeddreamer,1235165}@tongji.edu.cn

Abstract. With the birth of ergonomics, interactive design has covered many fields including psychology, physiology, sociology and economics. From a broader perspective, new concepts of interactive design study how to help consumers to use products or services in a more efficient, convenient and pleasant way. In the process of this study of the interactive design in service systems for community self-help charitable facilities, we used a number of different tools including depth interview, questionnaire survey, video logging and so forth to carry out researches on the social experience brought about by the industrial design of interactive products, the emotion cultivation, reconstruction effects of interactive interface, and the methods of arranging and integrating interactive information. We also explored how interactive design helped to raise the additional value and service quality in a systematic service. This article also analyzes deeply on the service design of community self-help charitable facilities, finds out current predicaments and how to get out of them from the perspective of design: making full use of interactive design and its unique properties, innovating in the process of service design, carrying out practical research and finally resulting in the rapid development of charities in communities. The outcome of this article aims to serve as a reference for governmental and social organizations to promote civilian charities in a way benefiting most people. Furthermore, with the in-depth research of interactive design, this article is also expected to propose directions for the studies on service design in the future.

Keywords: Community, Charitable Facility, Service Design, Interactive design.

1 Preface

Interactive design is an important part of service design. In the past, interactive design only focuses on the communication between humans and computers on physiological and psychological levels. With the birth of ergonomics, interactive design has expanded its field to a compound area containing not only physiology and psychology, but also sociology, economics and other principles. Furthermore, its attention has

* Corresponding author.

P.L.P. Rau (Ed.): CCD/HCII 2014, LNCS 8528, pp. 403–414, 2014.

extended from functionality only to all requirements of human beings. The ultimate purpose of interactive design is to better satisfy users' psychological and behavioral needs, to explore methods for an easier, more pleasant and more effective acceptance of the services. Interactive design has unique characteristics, and the mechanism of the interaction between humans and machines has fundamentally changed how people think and communicate. In the past decade, the rapid development of personal portable terminals has brought revolutionary changes to all levels in the society, displaying enormous social and commercial value. This development, however, is still unbalanced. For instance, in a great number of traditional service design fields, the value of interactive design still remains to be better visual effects. From the perspective of interactive design's characteristics, it's highly accordant to the idea of service design that pursues system integration and human oriented innovation. Revolutionary changes will only occur when interactive design and service design are optimally combined.

According to the "2012's Annual Report of Charitable Donations in China" published in September 2013, the total amount of domestic donations, including money and commodities, amount to 13.3 billion USD, while in US, whose GDP is twice China's, this number is 316.2 billion, almost 24 times more. From statistics we may find out that 75% of the total donations came from citizens in US, while only 40% came from organizations other than corporations in China. Besides, the "2013's Annual Report of Charities Transparency in China" shows that only 29.6% charitable organizations got over 60 marks out of 100, and only 30% charitable organizations were qualified as far as transparency was concerned. It's obvious that the lack of charitable habits among citizens and the crisis of public mistrust against charitable organizations are the two primary factors that impede the development of charities in China.

In US, community foundations are the most important components of national charitable foundations. The construction of self-help charitable service systems for communities takes money from and spends it on communities, and makes the concept of public charities less distant. These charitable projects managed by NPO have better transparency and justice, and thus exert a positive impact on the reconstruction of trust and the cultivation of charitable consciousness. The construction of self-help charitable facilities is a systematic service design project. It involves the design of a donation service system, transparent and fair, which not only meets the requirement of community environment and residents' daily donation behavior, but also cultivates residents' charitable habits and self-management concept, leading to more involvement. At present, charitable facilities in communities are still elementary. Self-help donation boxes and used garment donation boxes can be occasionally found in communities as shown in figure 1, but in general they are boring in design, simple in functionality and low in credibility. Most of these facilities do not work as they are expected to, and exist in name only.

Fig. 1. Charitable facilities currently in use

Interactive design may bring revolutionary changes to service design in the following three ways. Firstly, based on a deep understanding of user behavior, interactive design helps users to establish a highly efficient behavior pattern that suits the information society. Secondly, by influencing users' emotions and moods, interactive design affects their altitudes, perceptions and behaviors in a psychological way. Finally, basing on the studies of social and economic rules, interactive design makes full use of information integration to provide a highly efficient platform for people to actualize self-organization and self-management. From the viewpoint of the innovative research of interactive design in service design, this article explores how interactive design may have positive and innovative effects on behavior guidance, emotion cultivation and information reconstruction in a systematic design of community self-help donation facilities.

2 Research Workflow and Methods

The researches for this article involve multiple research methods, analyzing and discovering theoretical and practical values of interactive design in the process of a systematic and innovative research on community self-help charitable services.

- Depth interview: Communicate with community residents in a face-to-face manner in order to confirm the practical values of the research of community based charities, to discover potential problems and their sources, and to conclude research targets and solutions in the end.
- Questionnaire Survey: According to the result from the interviews did in the former step, a survey questionnaire shall be designed. Because this research targets at all communities in China in order to pick a typical research subject for more general adaptability, the community in which our questionnaires are collected was strictly filtered. It was finally decided to be one with even age distribution. Guided by

surveyors, residents at different ages in the community enrolled in the survey, and finally 153 valid copies were collected and used statistically in future researches.

- Video Logging: With video and image logging tools, basic information about the community was recorded in real time. This helped us to know the basic functional regions in communities and the behavioral habits of residents in the community.
- Testers' feedback: Several testers were invited to experience all the periodical outcomes obtained during the design process. Testers' psychological and physical experience was recorded as references for later design improvement.

3 Analysis of the Psychological Model

According to the depth interviews with residents in the community, their motivations of charitable donations were analyzed, as shown in the left part of figure 2. From utilitarianism to the spirit of commonweal, several common psychological motivations of residents' charitable behaviors were listed, where the spirit of commonweal is believed by us to be the ideal target of social development. Residents' charitable donation behaviors may be guided by interactive design, transforming from utilitarianism to the spirit of commonweal which contains more positive energy. In this research, source of each psychological motivation was analyzed, and all the interactive design targets were figured out to realize the positive transformation mentioned above. These design targets might seem separated, however, they are important design elements.

From the viewpoint of consumer psychology, consumer behavior can be divided into 3 stages generally, i.e. perception, emotion and behavior. The use of self-help charitable facilities in a community also follows this rule: users need to know about this self-help donation device, then establish emotional relationship by acquiring more information from this device, and finally turn the emotion into an actual donation behavior. In the analysis of these stages, the most important factors affecting product design on each stage are extracted. For example, on the perception stage, a resident forms initial recognition of the self-help donation device via appropriate advertising and their understanding of the management team's transparency. These factors affect people's initial recognition of the facility directly, and shall contribute significantly to the interactive design.

Based on the targets and directions of interactive design, we may figure out several important design components, e.g. industrial design, placement design, interactive interface design, information architecture design and etc. Donation amount, NPS management and donation methods are several key points of the interactive design for self-help donation facility, which need our special attention. Design targets and directions determine the main structure of the interactive design. In the phase of prototype design, they are very important principles that shall guide the actual design work.

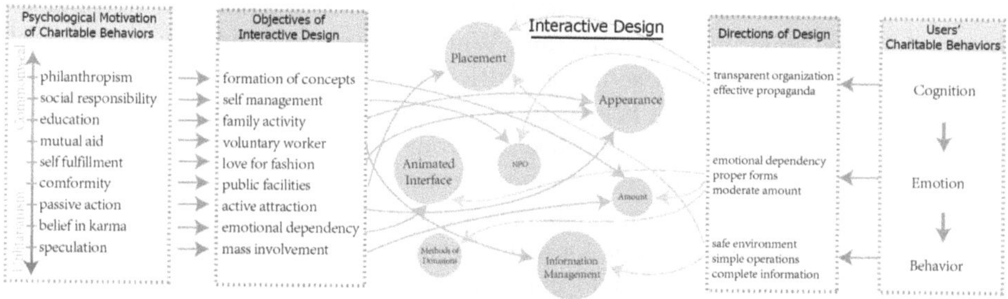

Fig. 2. The relationship among psychological motivation, behavior and interactive design

4 New Concepts of Interactive Design for the Self-help Donation Facility

In the research of interactive design of community self-help charitable facilities, interactive design not only satisfies audience visually, but also creates emotional adherence, cultivates enthusiasm in charities, raises donation behavior ratio and provides effective design patterns for systematic and human oriented services.

4.1 Reconstructing Interactive User Behavior via New Ergonomics

Through analysis on human behavior and its features, we may provide more human oriented physical experience to users through interactive design and thus guide their behaviors in a proper way. In this research, physical experience of a user is the first and foremost factor to consider, where physical experience refers to the idea that a considerate design of a product's placement, appearance and interactive methods offers its user a better, safer and more comfortable physical experience. This better experience will, hopefully, lead to residents' more active and healthy donation behaviors and the actualization of design targets.

- Human oriented interactive industrial design

According to the analysis of the psychological model of charitable behaviors, there are three targets to keep in mind during the interactive design: 1. To meet the requirement of family activities. 2. To satisfy users' flavor of fashion. 3. To actively attract users' attention. In the questionnaire survey, social recognition of charitable behaviors was inspected among residents in the community. 94.77% people are willing to bring children to join daily donation activities held in the community. From the perspective of sociology, community self-help donation facilities can become a very good platform to cultivate charitable habits of the next generation, and thus create profound social influences. Fashionable style is another important stimulation that attracts people and makes them feel that charitable donation is not only a civilized behavior to show their affection, but also a modish behavior to fulfill themselves. Because of this, contours of the machine shall mainly contain simple and stylish lines to suit adults and children at the same time. While we were designing the prototype of the machine, we considered these factors sufficiently. The main shape of the machine was simple and modern. To fit heights of users at different ages, it is best that an interactive screen fill the facade of the machine from top to bottom, but concerning the cost of having a very large screen, it's more cost efficient to have 2 screens. One of them is larger, and the other one is smaller, located at the upper part and lower part separately. The upper larger one is for adults, while the lower smaller one provides a personalized interactive platform to children. To meet different psychological requirements of adults and children, sound sensors are installed in the machine. Children may clap or shout to communicate with virtual characters in the screen, which may hopefully arouse their interests.

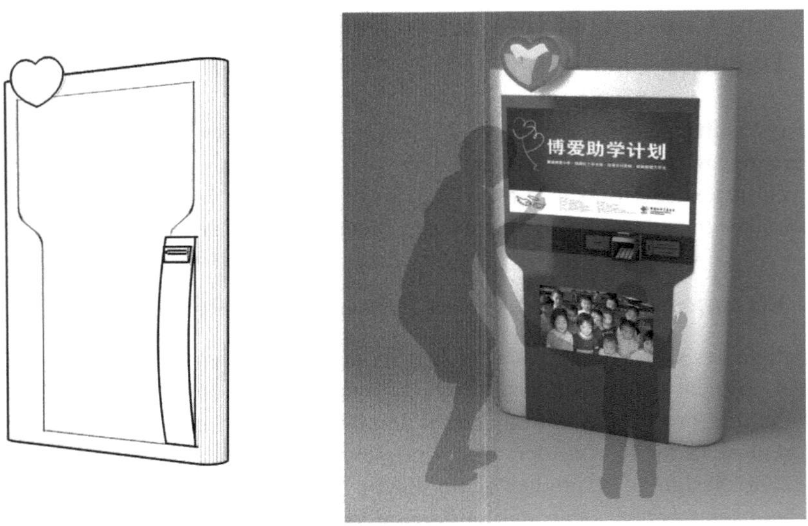

Fig. 3. Industrial design of the donation machine

- Placement of facilities

During the action of donation, convenient access, safe environment and a novel interactive experience can contribute to a participant's donation behavior effectively. Videos were taken to study the active regions and action patterns of residents, and a flow graph was drawn on the basis of resulting data, as shown in figure 4. On weekdays, there were 2 typical types of people streams. One of them was the stream of working people on and off duty mainly during rush hours in the morning and in the afternoon, and their routes began at their buildings and ended at the main entrance of the community, or otherwise. The other typical stream of people were composed of retired elderly people and school age children. They were most active during 3:30 to 5:00 pm, and their main active region was the central garden. From the figure below we concluded that the central garden was the most important gathering region for people in the community, the 2 people streams mentioned above both crossed the central garden. Furthermore, in a typical community central garden usually occupies the community center which is convenient, spacious and safe. In conclusion, central garden is the best location for us to install donation machines. Please note that sensitive areas embodying public authority, e.g. neighborhood committee and property management department, shall be avoided.

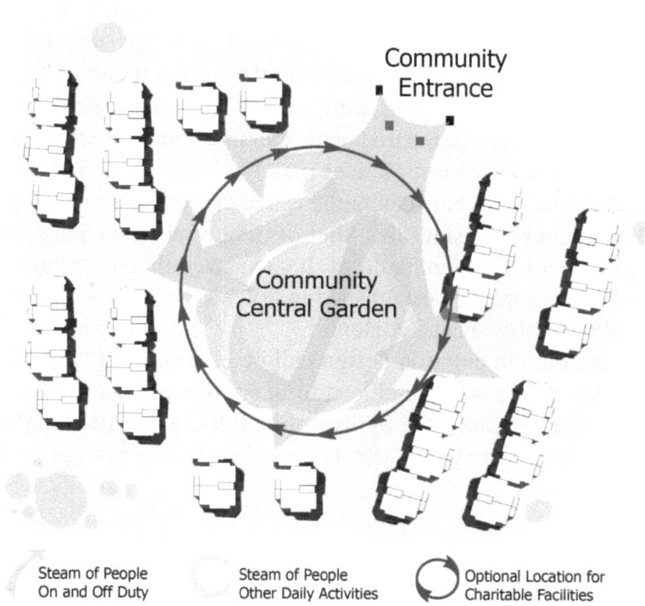

Fig. 4. Placement decision of the self-help charitable donation facilities in a community

4.2 Establishing Emotional Dependency Using Visual Language via Interactive Experience

Mood affects psychological process in many ways, including decision, planning, memory and attention (Berkowitz 2000). Certain moods may be so powerful that they overwhelm all rational thinking. From the perspective of cognitive psychology, mood is an important motivation of cognition, the determinant factor that allows information to enter the brain and build cognition, the switch that filters input information and evokes reasoning. In an article, Beale gave a detailed analysis on virtual mood proxy, and studied how proxy technology and emotional power affect audiences' altitude, perception and behavior in the process of human computer interaction. Therefore, leading users' emotion in a correct direction plays an important role in bringing better cognition, establishing emotional dependency and finally leading to the actual behavior. Interactive design may create a mood atmosphere for users and guide their consumption behaviors. An excellent interactive design may bring audience 2 different types of emotional experience. The first one creates a virtual experience which makes people feel as if he or she is really in a virtual environment. This kind of immersive experience brings a sensory illusion to accomplish the emotional communication. This kind of design usually requires a closed space with projected virtual environment on surrounding space, or the usage of head mounted displays. The other kind establishes a virtual environment psychologically through the development of the content, very similar to what films do to audiences in a short period of time. Interactive design makes use of visual language to create a virtual story telling environment and lets audiences immerge in this environment for a short period of time. What makes it different from a film or video is that an interactive design may use its unique human computer interaction to enhance this emotional relationship. If we prolong the interaction, this relationship is prolonged as well, and its users may develop an emotional dependency on the product. Compared with the first kind of design, the latter one doesn't require expensive hardware. It uses merely virtual visual language to develop a deep emotional relationship between humans and computers, which is more suitable in our case. We'll mainly consider this kind of design when we plan interactions for the community self-help donation facilities. It's expected that an emotional dependency on donation behavior may be established in donors' minds via carefully and scientifically designed interactive visual content.

The target of interaction emotion design call be expressed in "A.C.A", i.e. Attract audiences, Continue their passion and lead to their Actions. On the basis of the 2 dimensional emotion model proposed by Russel in 1991, this article studies deeply the mechanism of emotional proxy and affects a user's altitude, perception and behavior through emotion cultivation.

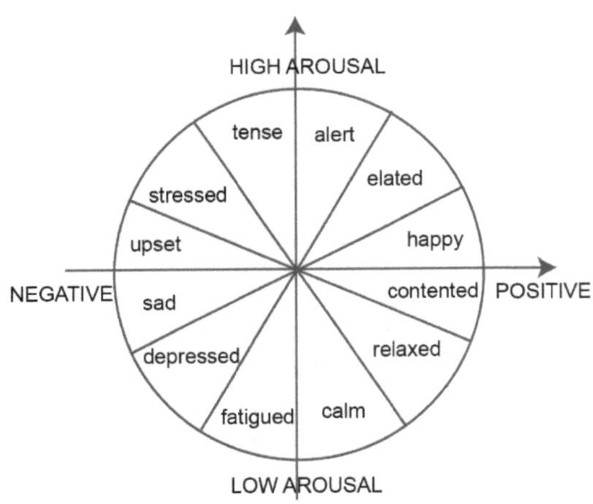

Fig. 5. Russel's 2 dimensional emotion model

- Choosing the donation amount: Mood is a determinant factor of user altitude and behavior, while the amount of donation affects residents' mood directly. A properly designed donation amount is not only an important starting point to encourage donations in a wide range but also an important method to establish emotional relationship between users and the machine. According to the survey result, 69%

people selected 10 RMB or lower for a single donation, suggesting this amount is pleasant and safe for most people, and is also a healthy and sustainable donation amount. This proves the conclusion we drew after reading materials and making interview: small single donations over time is a sustainable and healthy social charitable behavior that may be chosen to encourage nationwide involvement. This concept is also justified by the successful experience from abroad or domestic charitable practices, such as "Yi Foundation". According to the "2012's Annual Report of Charitable Donations in China", although the total amount of donation drops while compared with 2011, non-governmental small donations increased considerably.

- Donation methods: In Russel's emotional model, the more satisfaction one gains, the more positive power is gathered. As for donation behavior, the biggest obstacle is the lack of transparency. To raise transparency and satisfy donors, it's favorable to make donation details and money usages more specific. In our case, donations are divided into 2 categories: continuous foundations and funds for emergent events. Foundations may accumulate without upper limit, and they aim at helping vulnerable and disadvantageous groups in a continuous manner. Funds focus on unexpected accidents. They start at special times and have upper limits set by donation administration committees. Once the upper limit is reached, one donation project ceases automatically.
- Interactive Lights: Interactive design has many means to deliver emotions effectively, including the use of interactive audio and lights. Experiments proved that a physical interaction is more likely to make users feel an actual human computer interaction. When designing the appearance of the donation machine, we added an interactive light shaped like a heart at the top of the machine. In normal times, this heart emits warm and consistent light, sending out positive energy of merciful wishes. While emergent events happen and immediate help is needed, the heart blinks quickly, and blinks to show gratitude when a donation is received. Adding light to a product is not a novel idea, but if used properly in an interactive way, the light may communicate with users and shorten the psychological distance between human and machine. It works especially well to attract distant pedestrians.
- Theme and flow of the interactive animation: It's proven to be an effective method to attract attention that story telling interactive animation is included in the design. It helps to shorten the distance between audience and the product, establishing an intimate emotional relationship. Our questionnaire survey revealed that 90.85% people agreed on this viewpoint. However, not all themed interactive animations can help to obtain the anticipated result. Only the animations with themes fitting the products' basic properties well and customized for specific audience can guarantee success. For example, since the keyword of the product in this article, namely self-help donation machine, is charitable donation, the basic emotional tone shall be friendly and warm. Secondly, different audience directly affect the setting of themes. Target audiences of the donation machine includes everyone in the community, covering all age ranges. As a result, the selection of themes shall take everyone's preference into account, be consistent with universal values and aesthetic perspectives and avoid prominent age bias. Survey results also support our

viewpoint. Among all the options provided in the questionnaire, themes named education game and pet story got 45.75% and 35.59% votes in a single selection question, while the theme named gun game, which has a strong age bias, got less than 1% support.

- Besides, animation based interaction is a very important way to establish an emotional attachment. According to the two dimensional emotion theory introduced by Russel, people gain more positive power when they feel more happiness, fulfillment and relaxation in the course of interacting with animation. In the foundation donation projects, the growth of a panda becomes the primary clue. The x axis is time and the y axis is the growth level of the panda. Time in the animation is correspondent to the time in the real world, and the panda goes through seasons together with us, shortening the emotional distance between people and the machine. The y axis records how little panda grows, gains skills to survive, and begins independent life. Its growth is supported by donations. When a user approaches the machine and makes a donation, the little panda corresponds to thank him or her. When donations have reach a certain amount, the little panda enters a new growth level, suggesting that one's donations help the little panda to grow. This design not only delivers positive energy of mutual beneficial charities, but also encourages donors to care about the growth of the virtual little panda continuously, leading to multiple donations. According to our survey, 59.74% residents will make donations more than once in a month. In other emergent donation projects, the target and concept is expressed in a jigsaw puzzle game. Each donation becomes a piece to fill a heart shape, and when the heart is progressively complete, people get more and more stimulated and are more likely to donate. When the heart is finally complete, the donation mission is accomplished. This vacancy filling visual style encourages residents to strive for a same purpose, enhances cohesion of the community and spreads the idea of transparent, moderate and healthy donation behaviors.

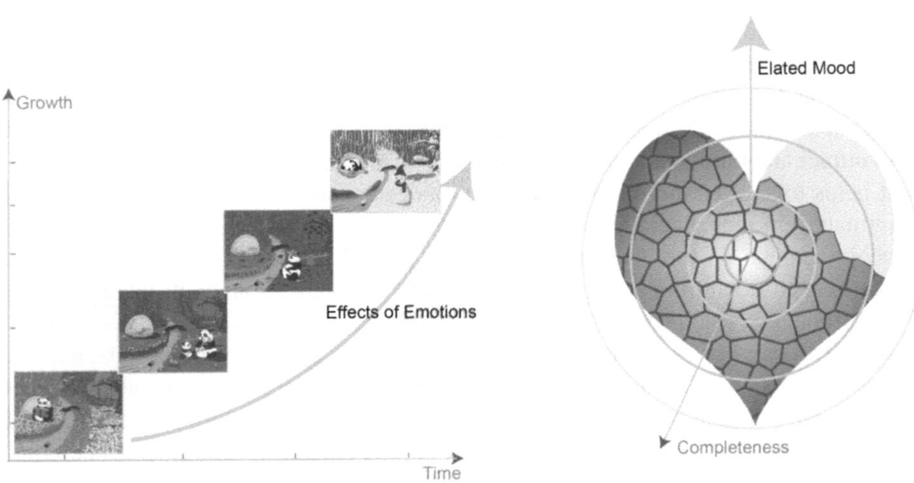

Fig. 6. Design of the interaction animation and the cultivation of user emotion

4.3 The Construction of the Information Reconstruction and Supplement Service System in the Interactive Interface

The scientific organization and delivery of information are two of the most important targets of service design. It is a key point of interactive design to actualize efficient data mining and spreading. In the comments and suggestions section of the survey questionnaire, most feedbacks were concerning the publicizing of information, which suggested transparency is the key to the success of a charitable project. Liu youping, vice director of the "ZhongHua Charitable Donation Information Center" gave his comments on the report about the transparency of charities in China with the following statements: "As for charitable organizations, the public mostly wants to know where the donations go and how they are spent, which are on the contrary done poorly when charitable organizations reveal information to the public." The multimedia property of an interactive interface guarantees that it's a perfect platform for information distribution. How can we use technology properly so as to offer users with the information they need in a convenient way? It is an issue to be solved by designers.

Before feeding data to an interactive interface, it's necessary to analyze information in the first place. Some parts of it might be revealed to users directly, while other parts might need to be processed before revealing. Interactive interfaces cope with information in 2 ways. The first one is a direct display, where the choice of a proper visualization style for convenient and effective communication is the key issue. The second one is data processing, where information are processed for multiple times and data mining is done to achieve more profound effective information. The interactive interface plays an important role in collection and organizing information online. Information is a very important resource to service design, and deep processing of information may raise additional values of the service design remarkably.

In the process of designing the information system for the interactive self-help donation machine, the following steps are followed. Firstly, information are categorized. Some information is suitable to be revealed directly, including members of the administrative committee, workflow of the donation machine, donees' application information, the expenditure of the money and so forth. These kinds of information is visualized in an easy-to-understand way and shown to users directly in the multimedia interface. As for online information collection, users may submit donation applications or give suggestions to the administrative committee by speaking to the voice recorder, and the recorded voices go automatically to the committee via internet. Besides, more information based services might be developed based on the characteristics of the interactive interface. For example, a donee may apply to be a volunteer to provide services to the community and may make appointments using the interface. Potential of an interactive interface is unlimited, which is very meaningful to the continuous expansion and improvement of the service design. By handling information in an appropriate way, many better new services may be developed.

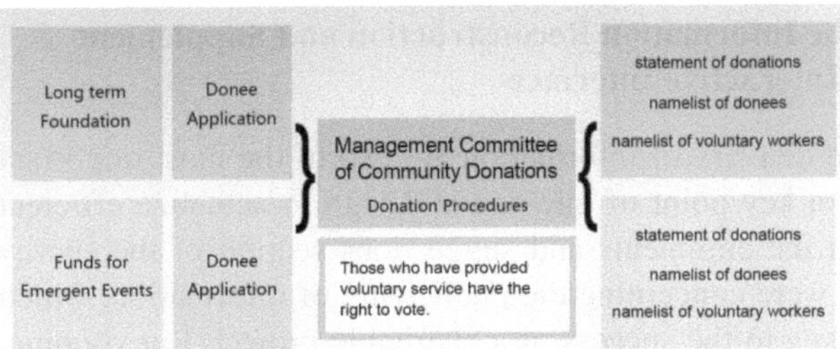

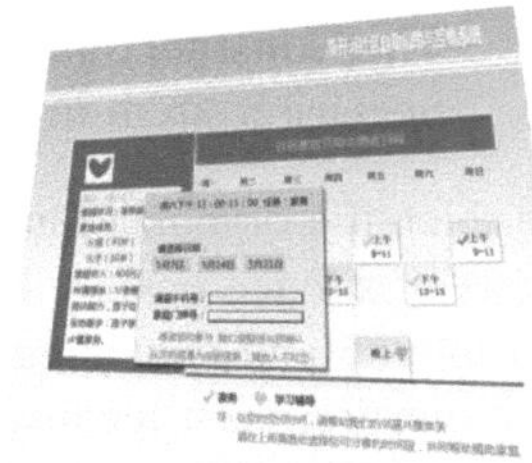

Fig. 7. Management interface for interactive information system and design for additional value

5 Conclusion

Today, interactive design has become the most important tool in product and service design. Better study on interactive design helps to optimize the workflow of service design, to expand its range and augment its value. Based on a practical study on the service design of community self-help charitable facilities, this article did a theoretical study and innovative practice on the values and potential of interactive design in service system design, providing some references for future studies on service design and interactive design. Moreover, how to promote community self-help charitable projects will continue to be an important issue in the development of societies in the future. Paul Brest, the former CEO of Hewlett Foundation, also believed communities play a significant role in charitable activities. With theoretical and practical references for the establishment of more effective charitable projects in communities, we hope that the results from the practical researches in this article will be helpful to governments and non-profitable organizations, promoting the healthy growth of civil charities.

References

1. Zhong Min information center for charitable donations of Chinese Ministry of Civil Affairs, 2012's Annual Report of Charitable Donations in China (2013)
2. Zhong Min information center for charitable donations of Chinese Ministry of Civil Affairs, 2013's Annual Report of Charities Transparency in China (2013)
3. Gan, D.: A special value of community foundations in US, Charities Times (2011)
4. Szameitat, A.J., Rummel, J., Szameltat, D.P., et al.: Behavioral and Emotional Consequences of Brief Delays in Human-computer Interaction. International Journal of Human-Computer Studies 67(7), 561–570 (2009)
5. Shiri, A.: An Examination of Social Tagging Interface Features and Functionalities – An Analytical Comparison. Online Information Review 3(5), 901–919 (2009)
6. Beale, R., Cred, C.: Affective Interaction: How Emotional Agents Affect Users[J]. International Journal of Human-Computer Studies 67(9), 75–76 (2009)
7. Tuch, A.N., Bargas-Avila, J.A., Opwis, K., et al.: Visual Complexity of Websites: Effects on Users' Experience, Physiology, Performance, and Memory. International Journal of Human-computer Studies 67(9), 703–715 (2009)
8. Russel, J.: Culture and the Categorization of Emotions. In: Psychological Bulletin (1991)

Cross-Cultural Issues in E-commerce, Marketing and Branding

Understanding Emerging Markets by Applying Lean UX

Stephanie Chan, Gloria Chen, and Limin Fu

Alibaba.com Inc., 3945 Freedom Circle Suite 600, Santa Clara, California, USA
{stephaniechan,gchen,paulfu}@alibaba-inc.com

Abstract. Emerging markets such as Brazil, Russia, and India are experiencing high growth in various sectors. Businesses and design teams that attempt to break into a market often have limited understanding of the market's ecosystem, and customers' day-to-day environment. This is largely due to low availability of secondary research about emerging countries, the teams' limited local presence, and the teams' limited personal experience with the country of interest. Teams with certain level of resources may partner with third-party local research teams or travel to the country to conduct in-depth ethnographic research. While in-country ethnographic research brings multiple benefits, it can often be time-consuming and costly. In commercial/business environments, where time and resources are limited, gaining an understanding of an emerging market becomes a challenge. In this paper, we'll discuss and propose a process to conduct user research in emerging markets by applying Lean UX principles. The process will be illustrated using a case study, a cross-cultural research comparing U.S. and Russian e-commerce users' attitudes and behaviors.

Keywords: Emerging Markets, Lean UX, User-centered Design.

1 Introduction

In our specific business setup, we have one business unit focused on cross-border trade to support our users from many different countries, especially emerging markets. Our design and research teams are based in the U.S. and China. While we have extensive understanding and experience with U.S. and Chinese users, we have very little understanding of the emerging market users. We started our endeavor with a literature review of cultural values, symbols, and dimensions of those countries. However, as we started to plan the cross-cultural research, we were faced with several key challenges to resolve.

1.1 Understanding a User Base in a Foreign Country

The designers and researchers are not co-located in the same country as the users, and don't have first hand knowledge of the users' culture and behaviors.

Unlike designing experiences for the U.S. and Chinese users, the designers and researchers are not immersed in the daily lives of emerging market users, nor do they

P.L.P. Rau (Ed.): CCD/HCII 2014, LNCS 8528, pp. 417–426, 2014.

understand the languages of those countries, such as Russian, Portuguese, and Spanish. As a result, they do not have first-hand participation in the observation of the users' online and offline shopping behaviors

1.2 User Needs or a Still-evolving E-commerce Industry?

In parallel to literature review, we also conducted peer site review of emerging markets home-grown e-commerce sites, in an effort to understand the users' online shopping habits. We observed many of the common design elements on the sites resemble designs on U.S. e-commerce sites 7-10 years ago (e.g. flat category structure and presentation). In our research, we decided to investigate whether these design elements are driven by user needs, or simply a manifestation of a still evolving e-commerce industry.

1.3 Cannot Fully Follow the RITE Model

In order to deliver designs in a timely manner in a fast-moving e-commerce market, we heavily employ Rapid Iterative Testing and Evaluation (RITE) when conducting research, where we can modify the prototype and test with users after each 2-3 test sessions, near real-time. When conducting research with Russia users, the designers will not be co-located with the users. As a result, they won't be able to observe user feedback real time and make changes to the prototype real time.

1.4 Time Difference

The research team and users are located in the U.S., and other countries, respectively. The time difference makes it challenging to interview users.

1.5 Traveling Costs

Many teams or organizations travel to the country of interest to conduct research. However, it's often costly in time and resources.

1.6 Differences in Interactions with Users, Due to Cultural Differences

Communication styles can be different for different cultures. Our observation revealed that Russian users and U.S. users respond to interviews and interviewers in different ways. For example, female users in Russia may tend to be more agreeable to the interviewer when providing user feedback, rather than offering their true opinions. These differences often stem from cultural differences.

In the Case Study section, we will discuss our research and design process, and how we applied Lean UX principles to resolve the challenges outlined.

2 Literature Review

2.1 Cultural Differences in Terms of Preferences and Satisfaction

With globalization, it is crucial for companies to create flexible and adaptive design according to local markets. But with many companies, the luxury of having teams in those local markets or the opportunity to travel and perform in-depth user study is uncommon. As mentioned by Christiaans and Diehl [1], often times, teams from one culture or context often have to develop products to be used in a completely different culture. Thus, many global companies have begun developing methods and projects to study cross-cultural aspects. In their study, findings demonstrate the existence of cultural differences in terms of preferences and satisfaction of interfaces and websites. Elements found were in regards to content, appearance, structure and navigation with differences in focus on authority, usage of color and abstract, symbolic or realistic images, the extent and depth of used structures, feedback about this structure, tone of voice and focus to individuals or groups of people etc. [1]

2.2 Lean UX Principles

Lean UX references Lean Startup method, which is the extension of Agile principles to include business principles in order to ensure methods for measuring and validating product and market fit [9]. In other words, it is the unification of product development and business aspects, through constant measurement and so-called "learning loops" (Build–Measure–Learn) [2] [3] [4] [8] [12] or according to Laugero, "think-make-check" [8]. Essentially the collaboration between the user research and design team with focus on validating the business objective to ensure there is in fact a market for the product. This is not to be confused with Agile UX, which is the incorporation of UX Design methods to the Agile Software Methodology. Agile UX unites developers, user researchers and designers in the Agile process of product development [12].

Elimination of Waste to Achieve Efficiency. Designing with Lean UX principles refers to searching for ways to provide great customer value with efficiency – in process, time, resource, cost – but without compromising product quality [4] [5] [11] [14]. In the Lean UX world, the key to efficiency is in the elimination or reduction of waste, which are "*activities that consume resources, but serve no useful purpose from the point of view of the customer*" [11]. As noted by Rohner [4] [10] and in the Lean UX manifesto [13], there is no point to use all possible user-centered design methods — rather only apply appropriate methods based on the questions aimed to answer and limitation based on available resources [4].

Design as Hypothesis. Lean UX methods changes the mindset of design from being beauty and perfection [2] [8] to being a hypothesis used for validating the business objective [2] [6] and recognizing it as an educated guess with the expectation of change. As stated by Laugero, spend the time to think and figure out what you need to learn and what you can build to get the right answers [8], not what you build as the answer.

Keeping the Design Process Flexible and Iterative. In the Lean UX world, design is no longer big and upfront with heavy specifications, but rather simplified and iterative to illustrate in the simplest form possible [2] the basic concept understandable by the user as highlighted in the manifesto, "*nimble design over heavy wireframes, comps or specs*" [13]. In other words, designing just enough – the Minimum Viable Product (MVP) – to use as a tool to gather validated information from actual users [4] [8]. Lean UX supports nimble prototypes and encourages the use of rapid prototyping and minimal documentation to allow the design to receive user feedback as early as possible [4].

Team Collaboration. Lean UX principle encourages team collaboration starting from incorporation of the process of design validation with the internal team before proceeding to validation from the user [2]. The removal of heavy documentation also promotes a collaborative environment through the need to review designs in real time with the team [6] instead of design and documentation by oneself and to be reviewed later by the team [13]. However, it must be noted that the act of eliminating or reducing documentation may not be relevant for situations when the team is not co-located [4] [8].

Gather Business Insights verses Usability Testing. As Ramsay [9] describes, Lean UX helps us overturn old approaches to research and measuring quality. Traditionally, research is done before or after the product is made but in the Lean UX model, research is done throughout the product design and delivery process. As Gothelf [6] states, this changes the focus of the usability study to testing for value and viability of an idea to see if it is worth investing in rather than testing for the usability. Such early customer validation minimizes the risk in creating the wrong product [7] [8] [13] in addition to allowing business insights and requirements to emerge, change or be abandoned without wasting resources [4].

In summary, Lean UX principles adopt the following values as outlined in Viviano's Lean UX Manifesto [13]:

- Early customer validation over releasing products with unknown end-user value
- Collaborative design over designing on an island
- Solving user problems over designing the next "cool" feature Measuring KPIs over undefined success metrics
- Applying appropriate tools over following a rigid plan
- Nimble design over heavy wireframes, comps or specs

3 Case Study: Applying Lean UX Principles

With businesses moving global, teams from one culture or context often have to develop products to be used in a completely different culture [1]. In addition, the need to reduce time-to-market and development cost is crucial in emerging markets to remain in the competitive landscape. Faced with these challenges, our designers and user researchers approach the project utilizing Lean UX principles working with Russian users.

3.1 Design Process

The decision to utilize Lean UX principles of business-savvy design, Minimum Viable Product (MVP) and the Build-Measure-Learn cycles was invaluable in finding unique Russian design elements with a simplified design process.

Design Discovery Phase. Tasked with the need to design both within a short timeframe and the lack of same country co-location as the user, the comprehensive nature of traditional information gathering methods was inefficient or relevant. Peer site reviews in its entirety were too time consuming to accomplish. Full-scale competitive analysis were no longer relevant as designers were stripped of the sense of context and understanding to determine if the design elements were driven by user needs, or simply a manifestation of a still evolving e-commerce industry.

The Need for Efficiency. Are there ways to simplify the design gathering process? Determination of the project's bare-bone goals is needed to find the core features that matter most to the user. The determination will help specify whether there are ways to be lean and eliminate the "waste" in the information gathering process. Are there "good to know" information that do not impact the ultimate customer experience? Is reviewing all sections of the e-commerce site crucial in understanding the story or is it a luxury item? Are there specific features or sections of the website that can be focused on to represent the entirety of the site or is significantly impactful to accomplish the goal?

Being Lean and Effective. The elimination of waste was accomplished through the recognition that our efforts can be centralized to one section within an e-commerce website that garners the most interaction, requires the most attention to detail from the user, and holds the most potential in displaying cultural preferences – the search results page within the fashion category.

Challenges of Lack of Co-location. In cases like emerging countries, the polar ranges of design sophistication and maturation in e-commerce websites takes away the ability for designers in a different country to naturally diagnose standard components verses bad design. Moreover, the scarcity of available e-commerce sites and the uncertainty of the user level of technological savviness pose as additional disturbances.

With that in mind, how to discern what factors within peer site reviews that will prove useful?

Focus over Comprehensive. We determined the best approach was to stray from traditionally accumulating a list of features and diagnose its strength and weaknesses. We chose to keep it simple by pinpointing the repeating elements that were different from the U.S. and Russian markets, in an effort to understand Russian users' online shopping habits. The assumption was that the repeating design elements would help us evaluate through user study whether the artifacts were a localized design component driven by user needs and preferences, or simply a manifestation of a still evolving e-commerce industry.

Finding the MVP through Lightweight Prototyping

Hypothesis Formulation. We observed many of the common design elements on the peer sites resemble designs on U.S. e-commerce sites 7-10 years ago: The flat category structure and presentation. Extensive use in saturated color variations combined with greater intensity of movement stimulation through animation, etc. The discoveries were organized into relevant groups to formulate the stories and hypotheses as the basis of the prototype.

Design as the Hypothesis. The design serves as the tool to solve these hypotheses, thus it was designed with the mindset of being flexible, iterative and the least-cost deliverable as possible. It was understood that the design goal is not the delivery of a final product with consideration in the creativity, quality, unification and feasibility of the design to integrate within our own website. The goal is to create a basic concept, the Minimum Viable Product, for users to easily visualize and understand in order to gather more tangible user input. Gather information about the viability of the idea and/or how to build the next step rather than testing the usability of these features.

Internal or External Expertise and Validation. It is crucial to have team members that have experienced the culture and understands local user habits, whether internally or external to the organization. Their presence is key in bridging the design team that is not co-located with the users. Sharing of local experiences and habits during design review sessions or even sparking conversations of everyday life enriches the team with a context into the local experience. Internal colleagues may not have to be designers or researchers, or even within the immediate team or office. The importance of these internal and/or external resources is their roles as reference points and internal validations during design reviews to ensure the avoidance of cultural taboos and confusion from incoherent translations.

Creation of the Prototype. A lightweight clickable prototype was produced to quickly blend the features and functionalities discovered during our peer site reviews. A copy of the category structure, content and refinement options were borrowed from existing Russian websites to be incorporated as features on the prototype. Pictures of Russian models and multiple banner images were also borrowed and combined to create the product images and animated banners. As a result, the prototype composed of screenshots of the existing website with overlays of borrowed static images made clickable to illustrate the key functionalities that needed validation. The informal “copy and paste” nature made the building of the prototype very lightweight, increasing the time efficiency of the design-test cycle.

Build-Measure-Learn Cycle: Modified RITE Model. The Build-Measure-Learn cycle was utilized in order to find the Minimum Viable Product. For that to happen, the initial prototype was constructed with rapid “experimental” iterative prototyping [4] [10] with the user feedback in mind in order to quickly adjust the design and gain the most relevant information. But due to the designers not being co-located with the users, inability to observe user feedback or make changes to the prototype real time became a challenge. The RITE (Rapid Iterative Testing and Evaluation) model and user study schedule had to be modified to accommodate this. Debriefs from local Russian researchers were scheduled after every 2-3 sessions to allow one working day, due to time difference, in between every 2-3 interviews for iterations.

3.2 User Research

Collaboration Between Designers and Local Researchers. Despite the challenge that the designers are not co-located with the users, we strived to find conduits to gain detailed knowledge about the Russian e-commerce users. Partnering with a locally-based researcher who is familiar with the Russian culture and market (in this case a native Russian), the designers were able to gain detailed understanding about Russian users' habits, and iterate the designs to better fit their needs (such as payment habits). Without a local researcher, such detailed yet important habits might not have been uncovered. The partnership between local researchers and designers provided an efficient way for us to design a user-centric experience, rather than designing in a silo.

Leveraging Remote Testing Technology to Increase Efficiency and Effectiveness. Conducting qualitative research often results in various degrees of traveling, whether international or domestic, which can be costly in time and resources. Yet without being at the same location with the users during research sessions, it is often difficult to observe users' interaction with prototypes and follow up with questions real time. To overcome this challenge, in addition to partnering with a local researcher so the U.S. teams were not required to travel, we also employed remote testing technology to conduct the research sessions. Users are able to interact with the prototype via a screen sharing technology. Users logged into each session using their own computer, and were able to view and used the prototype that's running on the researcher's computer. Users were able to carry out all operations, as if the prototype was running on their own computer. Meanwhile, the researcher was able to observe all of the users' actions, and followed up with questions via VOIP or telephone. Leveraging a remote testing tool also allowed us to cover a wide geographic area in a vast country such as Russia, without incurring additional time and costs due to traveling. Technology has truly enabled our process to be Lean.

Applying Interview Techniques to Account for Cultural Differences. Even when applying Lean, it is important to take caution with cultural differences when attempting to understand users in a foreign market. Users from different cultures often exhibit different communication styles and preferences. In the pursuit of efficiency and reduction of waste using Lean, it's tempting to execute research without taking the caution to integrate interview techniques when interacting and eliciting feedback from users of a different culture. Not accounting for cultural differences often compromises the reliability of the research. Hence it's important not to overlook cultural differences even when applying Lean.

4 Conclusion

The application of these Lean UX principles resulted in the ability to complete the project within a short timeframe compared to following the traditional process. The cost efficiency was considerable as the designers and researchers remain in the U.S. without international travel to conduct the study. In addition to the speed and cost effectiveness, resources were significantly saved as the need to produce full-fledge working pages and big upfront designs were not needed. With a simple prototype, the project was successful in validating the hypotheses and differentiating the design elements based on cultural differences verses the dynamics of an emerging e-commerce market.

Following the below guidelines resulted in the success of our project but it is important to consider them as references only. As noted in the Lean UX principles of "applying appropriate tools over following a rigid plan" [13], there are no set processes or formulas to follow, it is important to be flexible and adaptable to the relevancy of each specific project requirements and consider the need in adjustments based on the team skill sets and setup. As in our project, we combined and used only relevant portions of the Lean UX principles.

4.1 Guidelines in Applying Lean UX Principles in Understanding and Designing for Emerging Markets

- Understand the project's bare-bone business goals – what are the core features that will affect the customer?
- Spend the time to figure out the fundamental strategy in forming the hypothesis.
- Rather than designing the final deliverable on assumptions, treat it as the hypothesis to gather user validation and the next steps to build on it.
- Not sure on the savviness of users, it is best to start from the standard across sites rather than spend time guessing and assuming.

- Simplify the design process when possible. Borrow from existing local websites to test the viability for your own website and users.
- Evaluate if there are opportunities to eliminate waste – be able to differentiate what is "good to have" verses the necessity in understanding the user story.
- Strip the design to it's bare minimum only as a tool to help the user visualize the concept and gather feedback on its viability rather than the usability.
- Following the model of Build-Measure-Learn, build in rapid feedback cycle after 2-3 research sessions. It's possible even with time zone differences.
- Iterate designs and test plans as new learnings are obtained from users. Designs and test plans should be living documentation.
- Partner with local researchers that have first-hand understanding of your user base if possible.

4.2 Considerations in Applying Lean UX Principles in Non Co-located Teams

How to Be Lean and Effective. While the elimination of written specifications are impossible in teams that are not co-located, the act of reducing can still be achieved despite the amount of efficiency not matching teams that are. The traditional use of heavy design documentation can be significantly minimized through the combination of simple clickable prototypes supplemented with written specifications for interactions that cannot be visually represented. This integration of prototyping and documentation processes helps notably increase the time and cost efficiency.

Build in Regular Verbal Communication Sessions. Non co-located teams do not enjoy the luxury of synchronous, spontaneous verbal communication as co-located teams do, when applying Lean UX. It's often through verbal communication that teams resolve differences and align their visions. Verbal communication is especially important during periods when intense collaboration is needed, such as during prototype design, and design-test cycle. However, this does not mean that non co-located teams will not be able to apply Lean. During periods of intense collaboration, building in regular time for verbal communication allows team members to clarify hypotheses, design intentions, and users' explicit and implicit feedback. In our experience, even though this may mean scheduling conference calls outside of normal working hours for a period of time, the verbal communication sessions greatly reduced misunderstanding, aligned the team members' visions, and hence shortened the design and research cycles.

Utilizing Time Zone Differences. Often times, non co-located teams are situated in different time zones. This would normally increase the turnaround time due to the increase in back-and-forth communication time. However, the efficiency in time can be obtained if correct combinations of roles and responsibilities can be determined. It is important to be able to separate tasks that require close collaboration verses tasks that can be done independently. Close collaboration tasks such as design and initial prototype construction should be done in co-located teams in order to save in communication cost. While tasks that can be done independently such as copy translations, prototype edits, and locally-based research can be done in teams that are not co-located. This arrangement opens up the opportunity to turn time zone differences into an advantage by allowing for round-the-clock project evolution as seen in our case study.

References

1. Christiaans, H.H.C.M., Diehl, J.C.: Globalization and Cross Cultural Product Design (2006)
2. DiPasquale, G.: Incorporating Lean UX Into Agile (2013), https://speakerdeck.com/aduro/incorporating-lean-ux-into-agile
3. Gasik, V.: Designing for Good User Experience with Lean Principles. The Case of Roomforit.com (2013)
4. Gasik, V., Lamas, D.: Lean Design for Good User Experience (2013)
5. George, M.: Lean Six Sigma for Service (2003)
6. Gothelf, J.: Lean UX: Escaping Product Requirement Hell (2013), http://www.uie.com/brainsparks/2013/06/07/jeff-gothelf-lean-ux-escaping-product-requirement-hell/
7. Gothelf, J.: Lean UX is Not Anti-Deliverable (2012), http://www.neo.com/2012/05/23/lean-ux-is-not-anti-deliverable
8. Laugero, G.: Lean UX is Dead. Long Live Lean UX (2012), http://johnnyholland.org/2012/03/lean-ux-is-dead-long-live-lean-ux/
9. Ramsay, A.: Agile UX vs Lean UX – How They're Different and Why It Matters for UX Designers (2012), http://www.andersramsay.com/2012/04/24/agile-ux-vs-lean-ux/
10. Ries, E.: The Lean Startup: How Today's Entrepreneurs Use Continuous Innovation to Create Radically Successful Businesses. Crown Business, New York (2011)
11. Stauffer, L.A.: Lean Implications for the Design of Products (2006)
12. Treder, M.: Lean UX vs. Agile UX – Is there a difference? (2013), http://blog.uxpin.com/1375/lean-ux-vs-agile-ux-is-there-a-difference/
13. Viviano, A.: The Lean UX Manifesto (2013), http://www.leanuxmanifesto.com/
14. Womack, J., Jones, D.: Lean Thinking (1996)

Co-creative Value for Cultural and Creative Economic Growth – Designing a Cultural Merchandise and Constructing a Marketing Model

Tsen-Yao Chang

Department of Creative Design,
National Yunlin University of Science and Technology, Yunlin County, Taiwan
changty8908@gmail.com

Abstract. With globalization and the advent of technology, consumers are exposed to various cultures through different means; consequently, their self-identity and recognition of their own culture become confused. Designers can develop merchandise by cultural creativity, converting their cultural creation into the core value of the merchandise which will serve as vehicles for conveying cultural messages and generating cultural identity and regional economic value. But, facing the issue of economic production, the development of contemporary cultural merchandise should, apart from creative design, also consider the demands of daily life, before it can further generate productive value as a business. Owing to the present problems in the process of production of cultural merchandise including the contexts of creativity, productivity of fashion trends, and additional functions, the specific basis for the evaluation of designs are often wanting; as a result, designers' works are not echoed to and recognized by consumers, which leads to difficulties in sales. When designers have a commercial concept when they are designing a cultural merchandise, they involve both the design aspect and the commercial value; in this aspect a business model can be a tool offering choices for the core strategies of the business (Shafer, Smith, and Linder, 2005); it is for profit (Afuah, 2004) that designers set and execute business models. This study makes a reference to Osterwalder and Pigneur's (2010) Business Model Canvas, which is comprised of nine elements. These include value proposition, customer segments, distribution channels, customer relationship, revenue streams, key resources, key activities, key partners and cost structure.

With reference made to the said Business Model Canvas, this study contemplated how to establish models for designing cultural merchandise and marketing them. We thus adopted the approach of using an expert focus discussion and gathered information in two stages. Stage one involves two focus group meetings, to which experts with experience in cultural merchandise-related design, business start-up, and marketing, ten of them in all, were invited. The meetings were conducted using semi-structured interviews, encouraging the participating experts to share their practical experiences. The interview transcripts were coded in the scope of commerce and marketing to construct a hub-and-spoke type model for designing and marketing cultural merchandise. Stage two, launched in Northern, Central and Southern Taiwan, respectively, invited

P.L.P. Rau (Ed.): CCD/HCII 2014, LNCS 8528, pp. 427–436, 2014.

experts in the industry, government and academia from these regions, 18 of them in all, to the meetings on the related issues including marketing cultural merchandise. In the phase of data analysis, the recommendations of the participating experts were integrated, and the Business Model Canvas was further referenced in an attempt to establish a model for designing cultural merchandise and to deduce business and marketing models that are consistent with the design of cultural merchandise.

The findings hereof will propose a thinking model for the business operations and marketing of cultural merchandise, in which the key elements interrelate. The mode is intended to encourage the industry or designers to make reference to it when developing their design and implementing subsequent marketing strategies, so as to integrate all aspects such as cultural creativity, creative design, and business economics, in order to jointly generate economic value for the cultural merchandise in the modern market.

Keywords: Co-Creative Value, Cultural Merchandise Design , Business Model Canvas, Business Start-Up, Cultural Industry Business.

1 Research Context and Motivation

With globalization and the advent of technology, consumers are exposed to various cultures through different means which thus creates confusion in terms of their self-identity and recognition of their own culture. Designers can develop merchandise by cultural creativity, converting their cultural creation into the core value of the merchandise which will serve as vehicles for conveying cultural messages and generating cultural identity and regional economic value. Culture has become the critical chance to add value to various fields and to create distinction and uniqueness for marketing, while merchandise provides a media for culture transfer, and an opportunity to create economic value and source of inspiration for designers.

But, facing the issue of economic production, the development of contemporary cultural merchandise should, apart from creative design, also consider the demands of daily life, before it can further generate productive value into a business. Owing to the present problems in the process of cultural merchandise production, such as contexts of creativity, productivity of fashion trends and additional functions, specific basis for evaluation of designs are often wanting; as a result, the designers' works are not echoed to and recognized by consumers, which leads to difficulties in sales. Going back to the consideration of practical marketing and its costs, it often takes a short time for a developed merchandise to appear on the market, easily leading to the gap between abstract concepts and the tangible product; besides, there is a difference between the idea of introducing culture into the merchandise design and designing general merchandise. Therefore, the study hopes to establish a cultural merchandise design dimension model through analyzing the design elements of current cultural merchandise sold in the market and systematically conducting inductive integration, which provides a concept direction for designers, reduces the incorrect use of cultural contexts with the limited development period and increases the feasibility of an opportunity for cultural merchandise design and innovation; and, analyzes the business strategies and ways of overall cultural and creative industry, expecting to conclude a set of rules for an innovative business model for the local industries.

2 Literature Review

2.1 Culture Multiple Value

Lash and Urry (1994) thought there is a reciprocal relationship between culture and economy, and economy can include various commercial behaviors., Culture is manufactured, produced, and presented as different physical merchandise or tourism experience due to economy, while economic activities are added with emotional identification and heterogeneity and recognition brought about by various elements of culture connotation such as stories and emotion. Culture is an indispensable element in our life and spirit. A new design mode should be figured out in this new era to catch up with the trends and be popular among people, using innovative design to find the design balance between globalization and localization of cultural merchandise development. The value of a sustainable culture business should be created and established with innovation as promoted by creative thinking.

In the 21st century, people's lives are much better than that in the previous times. In accordance with psychologist Maslow's Need-Hierarchy Theory proposed in 1953, the spiritual life of security, affiliation, self-esteem as well as self-realization will be pursued after one's physiological needs are achieved. Maslow's theory has been established and spread for a long time; however, in the book Marketing 3.0: From Products to Customers to the Human Spirit, written by Kotler, the father of modern marketing (Kotler, et al., 2010), Zohar's Spiritual Capital: Wealth We Can Live by was cited to reveal that Maslow himself had admitted that the hierarchy theory shall be reversed, namely, self-realization is the basic need. In the past, consumption was thought to be the minimum requirements to maintain life, with thrift, suitability and endurance as principles for public consumption , but there is an increasing pursuit of style as influenced by urbanization, and these styles are no longer considerations depending on function; instead, the single style in a complex modern society cannot satisfy the expectation and requirements of modern consumption any more due to this era shift (Walker, 1990). Some people hold the opinion that there shall be no value judgment on culture, but under the real situation, culture is an important factor whether for commerce or for countries, and it cannot be denied that culture has possessed a strong power and function (Sadashige Aoki, 2010, P37). Thus, the study conceives that cultural merchandise has a characteristic of cultural implication and feasibility of creating value, which are deeply discussed.

2.2 Culture Value in the Design of Merchandise-Cultural Merchandise Design

Values, concepts and vocabularies among different countries can be delivered through cultural merchandise, while excessive dependence on imports can lead to gradual disappearance of the local original culture (Jesse, 2010). The reason for culture generating value lies in the fact that its emotion and story connotation can resonate with the consumers, which conforms to current consumers' purchasing habits and preferences. Danish futurist Dr. Rolf Jensen proposed that consumers seek for a story and emotional experience linkage with the merchandise through purchasing behavior (Jensen, 1999). Chen (2004) pointed out that if the merchandise can render its value through cultural activities, the meaning of the cultural merchandise can thereby be formed. Cultural merchandise plays as the vehicle of deeper emotional communication between the local culture and consumers which can guide the public to further understand the profound connotation of culture and grasp the contained emotional value.

Consumers often consider the invisible psychological satisfaction in addition to the consideration of function and application when purchasing merchandise (Verganti, 2009). Consumers have lost interest in merchandise of mass production (Delaney et al., 2002, P46) and designers intend to convert merchandise into vehicles for culture transfer through design means, which satisfies consumers with emotional, aesthetic and social demands in addition to its functions of use (Moalosi et al., 2007). Thus, the design of cultural merchandise not only focuses on the merchandise itself, but also on the presentation of local culture connotation; the function of local cultural merchandise is not limited to the function of use, but may contain stories, history, local experience, local features and other things behind the place (Chen, 2005). Cultural merchandise can tell the story of a local culture and increase the value of the consumer's connection with the merchandise (Li, 2004). Hence, in terms of the delivery of cultural merchandise, the story and emotion possessed by culture must be followed, and the cultural quality should be adopted to strike a chord to consumers; thus marketing acceptance of cultural merchandise can be increased through design.

2.3 Cultural Industry Business and Development

Among the industry development in various regions, there are many traditional industries which have lasted for many generations and have witnessed the rise and fall of the Taiwan economy. In this era of digital and scientific technology development, how can the traditional industries transform in accordance with the modern consumers' lifestyle and add new marketing appeal? Local cultural industries have profound industrial history and most of them uphold the tradition of producing products with superior quality. With the shift of eras, they are faced with the above consumers' lifestyle transformation, policy, resources and other issues in a large environment; those who cannot conform to the trends will gradually be replaced. These local industries contain a cultural context, and their products represent local advantages; in a time of reconsidering cultural value and experience economy, these traditional local industries implicate infinite opportunities for and feasibilities of recreating economic value.

The creative business model of the local industry shall find out the emotional linkage of industries and places to add design creativity and turn emotion into marketing brand by stories with irreplaceable local flavor, which are creative and have a unique industry charm, which is also an important strategy to reshape the sustainable business of local value. Along with the development of the cultural and creative industry, cultural source can be preserved and infused into consumer's daily life in a timely manner through commercialization and the introduction of digital technology. Local cultural feature is turned into economy through brand creativity, and converts the connotation of local culture into productive value. Creativity is self-identification after being touched, while brand is the vehicle, means or method to realize cultural design creativity. Thus, to put it in a simple way, local brand creativity is to achieve a design taste or lifestyle of local culture through creativity design and brand marketing (Lin, 2005). Local culture has colorful connotations and dimensions, which turns local scenery, folk arts and techniques, traditional industries and history into merchandise with local cultural elements included, bringing culture closer to daily life.

3 Research Method and Phases

The study adopted the approach of qualitative research and expert focus discussion and gathered information in two major phases. Stage one involves two focus group meetings, to which experts with practical experiences in cultural and creative merchandise-related design, business start-up, and marketing, ten of them in all, were invited. The meetings were conducted using semi-structured interviews, leading the participating experts to share their practical experiences. The interview transcripts were coded in the scope of commerce and marketing to construct a hub-and-spoke type model for designing and marketing cultural merchandise. Stage two, launched in Northern, Central and Southern Taiwan, respectively, invited experts in the industry, government and academia from these regions, 18 of them in all, to the meetings on the issues including marketing cultural merchandise. In the phase of data analysis, the recommendations of the participating experts were integrated, and the Business Model Canvas was further referenced in an attempt to establish a model for designing cultural merchandise and to deduce business and marketing models that are consistent with the design of cultural merchandise.

3.1 Expert Focus Group in Stage One

Stage one involves two focus group meetings, to which experts with practical experiences of more than ten years in cultural and creative industry-related fields were invited. The study aims to analyze the design of cultural merchandise. To obtain analysis data of cultural merchandise design, five experts and four experts with practical experiences in cultural and creative industry-related fields were invited, respectively. The first meeting included experts majoring in design and marketing; entrepreneurs in the cultural and creative industry and four experts with practical experiences in design and managing design companies were invited to jointly participate in the second meeting. Through the two meetings, opinions on cultural merchandise design and management were raised by experts with different seniority levels and experiences in the creative and cultural industry, to obtain first-hand information for subsequent qualitative research and analysis. The research copied the contents of the transcripts after the expert focus discussion; by use of the coding method of grounded theory, the main category and sub-categories were clarified to set out and construct a marketing model for cultural merchandise design.

3.2 Expert Focus Group in Stage Two

The expert focus discussion in stage two, launched in Northern, Central and Southern Taiwan, respectively, was intended to deeply understand the feasibility, development and application of Taiwanese local cultural and creative industry. Experts invited were not limited to the industry, but included experts from the academia and the government to discuss the management and development of the local cultural and creative industry.

Six experts each from the industry, academia and government were invited in the focus group of the three sections, respectively, with a total of 18. Two experts from the academia and four experts from the industry were invited to Northern Taiwan; one expert from the government and five experts from the industry were invited to Central Taiwan; one expert each from the academia and from the government and four experts from the industry were invited to Southern Taiwan. Opinions on the cultural and creative industry development status were presented based on their practical experience, which were used for subsequent research and analysis.

4 Research Results and Discussion

The study conceives that marketing and commerce should be considered when designing cultural merchandise, which involves deliberating the subsequent merchandise development opportunities and feasibility, and using the gained profit to extend the life span of the merchandise and creating more productive value and business opportunity. The two-stage study extends from cultural merchandise design and marketing to the business opportunity of the cultural and creative industry, providing designers or those who are interested in running the cultural and creative industry with a guide.

The study in stage one proposed a hub-and-spoke type of thinking model for designing and marketing cultural merchandise (as Figure 1) after coding based on the contents of experts' focus meetings, within which any element can be taken to determine the features of the cultural merchandise that are intended to be developed, and through which whether the existing products possess these marketing elements can be inspected. Taking coming into the market as an example, it is divided into seven major programs, which have to be checked one by one to make sure that they meet the essential requirements before going to the market. This means they have to consider whether technical barriers should be set up, whether capital collection is sufficient, what the size of the economic scale is, whether creative thinking has been included in the merchandise, whether the human aspect of the cultural merchandise should be applied, what the market position is and when the best opportunity for entering the market is, all of which have to be tackled one by one. Whether there is deficiency in the launching plan of the merchandise shall be discovered and enhanced during the course of implementing it; whether there are other aspects for further analysis should also be considered. A referable recyclable design concept for cultural merchandise should be established from the design phase to the product's launch.

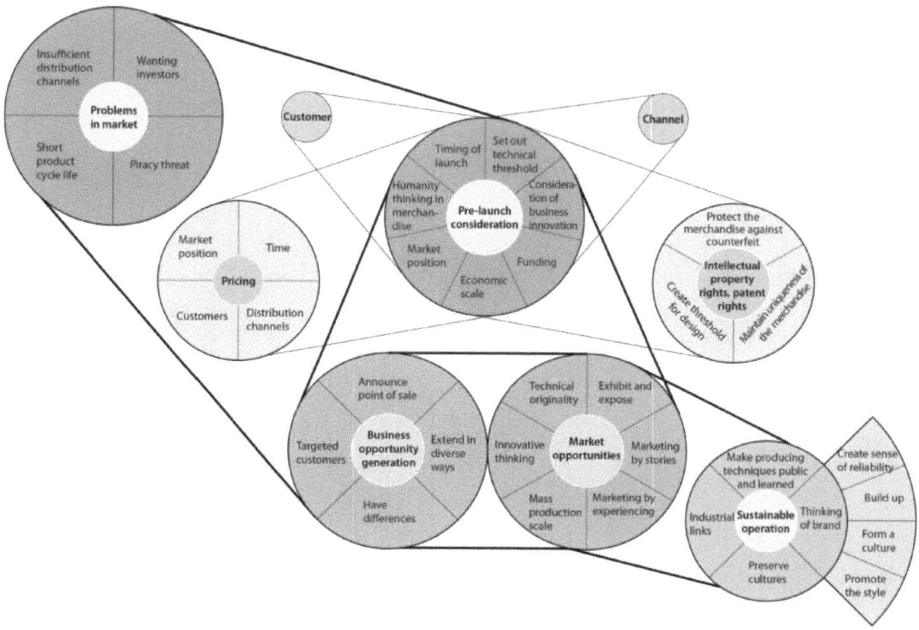

Fig. 1. A cultural merchandise and constructing marketing model

Through this model, the initial stage of design can be shortened with the integrated design thinking way, which makes the concept of cultural merchandise design become more thorough; each element can be considered independently or correlatively, and the influences and choices of other design and marketing should also be taken into consideration when starts from a certain hub-and-spoke in the model, through which the design and development period can be shortened and designers can find new creating opportunities. Personal experiences and ideas can bring different styles to the cultural merchandise and create value through the design.

The study summarizes that the marketing aspect cannot be ignored if creative value of the cultural merchandise shall be achieved. Cultural merchandise has to create commercial value instead of works of arts laid on the shelf. Thus, through grounded theory to code and construct the design strategy and marketing strategy of cultural merchandise, designers are allowed to analyze the commercial aspect of the design and not just consider their work from the perspective of their own profession fields. The cultural merchandise design thinking model has a hub-and-spoke structure, which presents the correlation of different strategies. Designers should think in an integrated way when designing a cultural merchandise so as to construct all design key points of the cultural merchandise completely, and they must think from the angle of brand creation in order to further expand the value of the cultural merchandise,. Thus, through the second stage of the study and by the experience sharing of the experts from the industry, academia and government, the thinking context of cultural merchandise has been extended with brand management as the main axis. With this, the sustainable business cycle of the creative and cultural industry was proposed (Fig. 2).

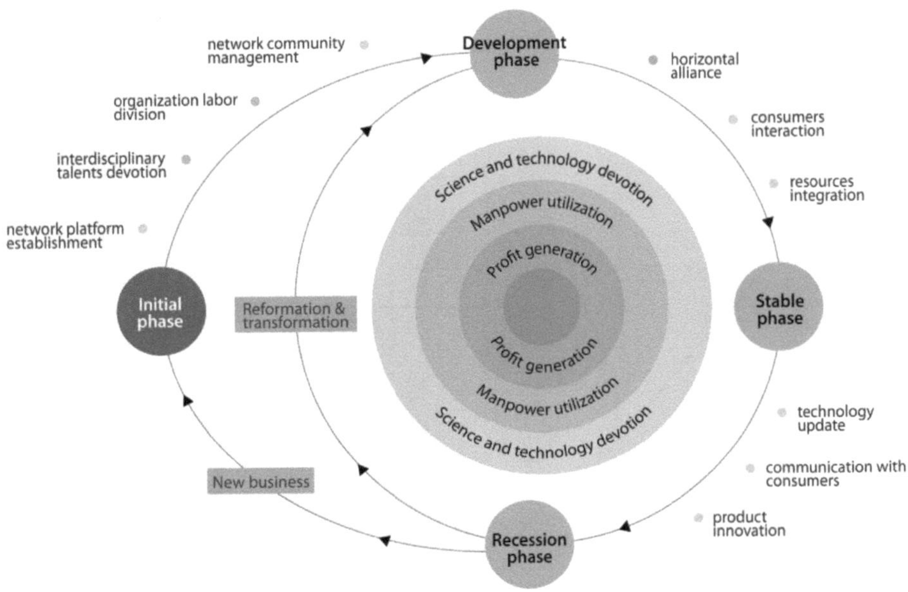

Fig. 2. The sustainable business cycle of the creative and cultural industry

The study proposed three main issues, which include interdisciplinary talents integration, emotional stories and digital technology appreciation, to cut into the business development opportunity of the local cultural and creative industry that are consistent with the coding of the focus discussion. Using emotional connotation as the core, locally featured stories should be dug out to present the product's uniqueness and identity in the global market; as for the combination process of local culture with digital technology, interdisciplinary talents should be introduced to act as bridges for communication to lower time and manpower cost; on the application of digital technology, its aid to the industry shall be understood. Good use of digital technology can reduce business cost and accelerate the advertisement effect of brands; however, what the features and core are shall be clarified first before employing scientific technology to create optimal usage and develop a business model suitable for local cultural and creative industry operation.

Enterprises should keep moving forward even with continued business and must keep itself up to date with the market to achieve the goal of creating a sustainable business by developing and innovating products that are consistent with consumers' preference. The practical aspect of sustainable development is generating profit, with which the business can expand and attract more talents, thereby creating job opportunities. Thus, it is essential whether for operators, designers or interdisciplinary talents acting as a bridge that they shall have commercial concept to construct a business model suitable for brand operation, through which business core strategy and communicative strategy can be selected to obtain profits. .Looking at it from a business cycle, from the initial phase, development phase to its steady phase, the core value shall remain the center of operational strategy in the different phases to maintain the consistency of the enterprise's brand management, and to conduct strategy planning for manpower utilization and scientific technology application. In the business guidelines of the different phases, the demands of various talents and scientific technology are different due to the difference in brand stability. In the initial stage, a future development strategy can be planned according to the overall operation and then the guidelines can be adjusted along with the changes in actual operation status and marketing environment, which allows the enterprises to make use of experience accumulated in the past to develop a new business, or to create a sustainable business cycle by transforming its own capitals when it enters into the recession phase. However, the types and elements of the cultural and creative industry are various. The study proposes an overall thinking direction for the cultural and creative industry business model to provide references for entrepreneurs in such field. In this modern era, they shall ponder over how to use digital technology as a tool, how to adhere to the original purpose of entrepreneurship and how to develop an exclusive sustainable business cycle directed at the creative features of its own brands.

Acknowledgments. The authors gratefully acknowledge the financial support for this research provided by the National Science Council of Taiwan under Grant No. NSC 102-2420-H-224 -004.

References

1. Afuah, A.: Business models a strategic management approach. McGraw-Hill/Irwin, New York (2004)
2. Chen, C.L.: Analyze the Cultural Production and Media Role of the Economic Market-Four Cases as an Example. Shih Hsin University, Taipei (2004)
3. Chen, P.C.: Study On the Cooperative & creative design works for local culture commodities–with a case study of Caotun straw goods straw goods, Yunlin. Unpublished master's thesis, National Yunlin University of Science and Technology (2005)
4. Delaney, M., McFarland, J., Yoon, G.H., Hardy, T.: Global Localization, Innovation – Global Design and Cultural Identity, Summer, pp. 46–49 (2002)
5. Jensen, R.: The dream society: The coming shift from information to imagination. McGraw-Hill, London (1999)
6. Chu-Shore, J.: Homogenization and Specialization Effect of International Trade: Are Cultural Goods Exceptional? World Development 38, 37–47 (2010)
7. Kotler, H.K., Setiawan, I.: Marketing 3.0:From Products to Customers to the Human Spirit. Wiley (2010)
8. Lash, S., Urry, J.: Economies of Signs and Space. Sage, London (1994)

9. Li, Y.F.: The Application to The Symbol of Cultural Commodity –With a Case Study of Cultural Creative Industry in Hu-ban village. Unpublished master's thesis, National Yunlin University of Science and Technology, Yunlin (2004)
10. Lin, R.T.: Cultural creativity added design value. Art Appreciation 1(7), 26–32 (2005)
11. Moalosi, R., Popovic, V., Hickling-Hudson, A.: Product analysis based on Botswana's postcolonial socio-cultural perspective. International Journal of Design 1(2), 35–43 (2007)
12. Osterwalder, A., Pigneur, Y.: Business Model Generation, 1st edn. John Wiley & Sons, Inc., Hoboken (2010) (published simultaneously in Canada)
13. Aoki, S.: Method of Cultural Marketing: The Power of Culture. CommonWealth, Taipei (2010)
14. Shafer, S.M., Smith, H.J., Linder, J.C.: The power of business models. Business Horizons 48(3), 199–207 (2005)
15. Verganti, R.: Design-driven innovation: Changing the rules of competition by radically innovating what things mean. Harvard Business, Boston (2009)
16. Walker, W.A.: Craft and design, design history and the history of design. Pluto, London (1990)

The Study of Service Design with the Perspective of Cross-Cultural Based on the Advertising Events and the Brand Experience

Jianxin Cheng, Hongbo Lai, and Junnan Ye

School of Art Design and Media, ECUST
No.130, Meilong Road, Xuhui District, Shanghai 200237, China
laihongbo2013@163.com

Abstract. With the development and popularization of the new media, both consumers and enterprise awareness and action have changed greatly. The way of information exchanges, interaction and communication between people has also increased a lot. Between people with large data background information, frequent interaction and exchange, consumers do not want to lose in the process of shopping heart more and more be fully released. Therefore, the traditional media (both brand experience and customer communication) is facing more and more challenges. Advertising style is under great change. How contemporary enterprises break the traditional forms of advertising communication, and fulfill the destination of efficient communicate with consumer is one of the hot spot in current academic circle. Through the analyses of the consumption trend changes under the background of new media and communication change, and the discussion of advertising event trend, its connotation and mechanism, and starts from the users' point of view, combined with social media line (O2O) interaction, interactive communication, brand building and customer service design, the study try to help to find something that can increase consumers feeling of achievement and satisfaction, and thus realize the transformation from cognition to action of the customers. Compared with the researches on the typical experience communication service design of Coca Cola, Microsoft brand both at home and abroad, the study found that like other users around the world, Chinese users share the same features: feel boring about the repetition of daily life, willing to escape from their real occupation role, their real role in the family through the fresh experience provided by advertising events. The changes brought by new media including the change of "subject" in the whole advertising communication activities, from the enterprise to the user. The enterprise need to provide customers with the topic, increase customer's participation, regard customers not just as consumers but also as partners, and create profit together. Under this background, this research aimed at how enterprises can enhance the brand communication through events and services design, and pointed out that the new media era enterprise brand experience and communication should value the participation of consumers, from language to truth, from the "flash" to action and accumulation, gradually get the consumers' care and recognition. And in the end, combined with the Shanghai --Yangtze River Delta "industrial design to establish a county (city)" plan, take the four

P.L.P. Rau (Ed.): CCD/HCII 2014, LNCS 8528, pp. 437–448, 2014.

Baoying traditional craft products as an example, the study further elaborated the fulfill of the new way of brand experience and cross cultural communication in the new media era through the advertising event and service design.

Keywords: Advertising Events, Brand Experience, service design, Cross cultural.

1 Raising of Problems

Development of internet, especially development of digital media, has changed the whole media pattern. With popularity of smart terminals, users have gradually shifted from traditional media, such as TV and newspaper, to social media and instant communication tools, such as blog, Wechat, E-business website and comment website, which more and more occupies time and space of consumers. It is obviously everything is changing in the era of digital revolution, i.e., consumers are changing, enterprises are changing and advertising forms are changing. New media development has brough about great change in traditional media. Meanwhile, in the whole process of changing, advertising, especially advertising forms based on traditional media, is confronted with more and more challenges.

Challenge One: diversification of media forms caused by new media, especially mass information caused by rapid development of internet, has brought great impact on traditional advertising and traditional media's capability of capturing mainstream audiences is obviously declining. At present, quantity of Chinese net citizens nearly reaches 600,000,000. As indicated by a survey, many people are relying on internet and internet has commenced to occupy TV prime time. Meanwhile, TV has become an environmental media or an accompanying media. For instance, when TV may be on when family members are chatting, but they are not always watching. TV has become background music or broadcast media. We even find out news on the TV is less than that on the internet.

Challenge Two: advertisement is may be vividly compared to a "love letter" sent by enterprises to consumers. Unde new media background, "love letter" in the traditional advertising from will experience great changes. On the one hand, audiences receive more and more "love letters"; on the other hand, people do not belive "love letters" any more and even take an unkind attitude toward "love letters". Instead, audiences are more willing to belive stories behind enterprises or products and believe comments made by friends. In other words, advertising effect and information value is gradually declining.

It is obvious challenge faced by advertising form of traditional media is fault of informing and communicating function of advertising. First, communication of appeal fails. Second, effect of communication is not good. Under such circumstance, consumers will not take imaged "act". Especially, appearance of new media enables consumers to obtain diversified information and conversion ratio of traditional advertising forms is gradually declining and bottleneck of advertising occurs accordingly. Simple advertising booming of traditional media is more and more ineffective. Enterprises spent a lot money, but failed to obtain favorable brand publicity effect. On the contrast, some brands are continuously becoming social stars in the internet. For instance, Coca Cola, Microsoft and Starbuck are the most active brands in the new media. They need not pay advertising fee. In addition, such brands are discussed and communicated by consumers on the social network and even rank among top keywords in microblog. Why such brands can provide an attribute enabling consumers to actively communicate on the internet? Therefore, it is necessary for enterprises to further analyze how to communicate with consumers under new media background and how to break through adverting communication forms and advertising eventalization trend of traditional media. Research into such problems is of great theoretical value and practical significance.

2 Change in Consumption Trend and Communication under New Media Background

2.1 Change in Consumption Trend under New Media Background

Under the background of new media, the largest effect is change in consumption. Specific analysis is as follows. Change One: internet and new media have brought great change in information. On the one hand, search engines resolve people's problem of searching problems; on the other hand, the era of social media brings about frequent information transmission, interaction and communication among people. Therefore, consumers' intention of refusing to suffer losses in the process of shopping can be fully realized. Each consumer desires to purchase appropriate commodities and actively compare commodities by searching in the internet or communicating with social media tools or consulting comments made by others. For instance, 20% of products on the ranking list of Japanese women cosmetics are sold through internet. Meanwhile, with appearance of reputation websites and comment websites, consumers may comment and mark different brands and restaurants of different cooking styles. Enterprises can not cause customers to take acts and make consumption by simply releasing an advertisement on TV any more. With change in consumption trend, consumers almost can search for information behind all brands or products through internet. Change Two: consumes lay emphasis on selective consumption and are not easily lured by advertising. As for commodities they like, they are willing to spend money and will not blindly belive in top brands, advancement or first class, etc. Meanwhile, life value of most audiences experiences change and they follow consumption trend of pursuing for emotion (Fan Xiucheng, etc, 2003) [1] and psychic gratification. Through interaction and communication with social media, they can experience sense of achievement from discovery of commodities they like instead of blind selection. They take a moderate attitude toward consumption. As for commodities they like, they are not mean and lay emphasis on participation, their own emotion and recognition and hope to obtain pleasure, movement and surprise and even a word or an experience activity that moves themselves. Change Three: under new media background, consumers are gradually returning to the original point and reconsidering, reappraising and redefining. More and more people become fond of traditional and simple products, are willing to jointly participate in consumption or jointly make consumption. They are especially willing to support products or business modes with advanced idea. For instance, on douban network, there is a kind of rice wine from mountainous area of Guizhou, whose original process and products receive recognition and support from many consumers. Meanwhile, consumers also pursue for individualized consumption of commodities on which they can personally make and slightly process and consumption of commodities with social effect, such as products that can save power, energy and protect environment, and support Starbuck's coffee beans passing fair trade certification.

2.2 Change in Communication under the Background of New Media

Meanwhile, communication between enterprises and consumers are experiencing great change, whether in the aspect of communication extent or depth or method. Specific changes as follows:

Change One: communication extent is changing. With popularity of social media, communication of new media tends to be diversified. With appearance of various instance communication tools, such as microblog and wechat, consumers may use powerful terminals to obtain their desired information and service through network available anywhere. Media used to communicate with consumers is not limited to paid TV, broadcast or newspaper. With a large quantity of free communication media, such as we media of enterprises and external social media, enterprises have more right of speech and right of communication.

Change Two: communication depth is experiencing change. Under the background of new media and with consumers paying more attention to participation, experience and having their own judgment, depth of communication between enterprises and consumers are experiencing change and communication is not simple advertising at the era of traditional media. KPI pursued by communication between enterprises and consumes are experiencing change and brand awareness and recognition is not only indicator. Instead, consumers pay more attention to stories behind enterprises or commodities and link between enterprises and consumers becomes more transparent.

Change Three: change in communication method. Under the background of traditional media, consumers are generally passive and long-distant recipients. With popularity of social media, consumers become information communicators from simple information recipients. By virtue of visual communities on social network, consumers may make comments, interact with others and affect other audiences and good information will be rapidly communicated so as to form huge force that can promote and change the society. From unilateral transmission and communication under traditional media to bilateral communication and multilateral communication under the background of new media, change in communication caused by social media is unprecedented. Each person is a consumer as well as a reporter and shifts from a recipient to a communicator and every person participates in exchange and mutual communication. As stated by an advertising slogan of a headhunting company, "each person is a headhunter". Under the background of new media, communication shifts from passive communication to active communication, from unilateral communication to bilateral communication and multi-media interaction.

3 Advertising Eventalization and Brand Experience

A successful brand shall be an organizational system with image, flesh, skeleton and soul. Whether TV advertising of traditional media or event marketing of social media, transmission and communication is intended to create routine and footprint from a product to a brand and establish emotional connection between products and consumers (see Chart 1). We will take advertisings of Nike in recent 20 years for an example. Officially named in 1978, Nike is still a young enterprise. Nike Inc always adopted the method integrating "star and advertising" and finally defeated Adidas, a leading brand in the market. As stated by President of Nike Inc, "we have a magic tool of communicating with "God", i.e., Nike advertisings". Through traditional advertising form, Nike attempts to create a myth of Nike and connect Nike with Jordan, sports and brand religion and make Nike the most influential "totem" in the sports tribe. However, "the success or failure of the affair is all due to the very same reason". Advertising campaign created past brilliance of Nike. With huge advertising expense and low advertising conversion rate, excessive "self" and simple "booming" caused great setback in Nike's development road. As it were, traditional advertising mode has led Nike to an end. With approach of new media economy era, Nike has to reconsider advertising forms of traditional media.

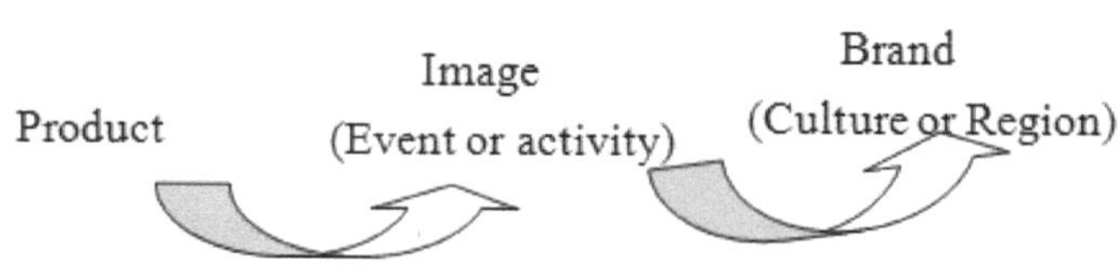

Fig. 1. Progressive Chart of Product Communication Levels

In the era of social media, we should consider how to change advertising, communicate with consumers and realize emotional connection from a product to a brand. With economic growth and the society's gradual departure from shortage and approach to abundance, status and role of consumption is changing accordingly. Change in consumption structure tends to ascend in a staged manner. With increase in income of consumers and gradual decline of proportion of products satisfying basic functional demands in consumption expenditure, customers are not merely satisfied with material consumption of basic existence demands, start to pay attention to change in consumption phycology and gradually pursue for phycological acceptance. In other words, they attach importance to spiritual consumption from product difference and quantifiable functional difference and unquantifiable emotional difference. In-depth communication with consumers by changing brand value into "real" experience realizes transfer from maintenance consumption of existence necessities to experience consumption (See Chart 3). It is obvious that communication between enterprises and consumers shall gradually realize shift from visible product function connection to invisible connection at the level of "relationship", connection at the level of business concept and aggressively approach to inner heart of consumers and obtain their recognition.

How shall we conduct communication design of event marketing so as to realize relationship communication and emotion communication with consumers (See Chart 2). Key to event marketing is to shift from connection at the level of products to connection at the level of relationship below "sea level" and even connection at the level of consumer idea, instead of simple communication of traditional adverting form at the level of products. Meanwhile, an enterprise is an organization in environmental network and the whole network is included into social structure at a larger level (Granovetter, 1985; Uzzi., 1997) [2-3] (see Chart 3). Enterprises or products are in a network of people, things and environment. As for event marketing, enterprises shall conduct communication design by observing change in consumption trend so as to better pay attention to consumers and move consumers in a short-distance. Realization of emotional communication with consumers is not unilateral and simple advertising booming on traditional media. In other words, event marketing is communication design, insight into life or environment and integration of products, people (emotion), things and environment. We may provide information for our transmission and communication design by classifying users and observing their life styles, understanding their life habits and attitude, favorite commodities and use environment and internal mechanism. Event marketing lays emphasis on understanding of consumers' motivation and internal demand for participation in event marketing so as to realize gradual transfer from product communication to relationship communication and idea communication. Surely, it is also the root cause of successful event marketing.

It is obvious that changes brought by social media cause shift of "subject" of the whole advertising communication activity from enterprises to users so as to provide customers with topics, increase customer participation and experience. Enterprises shall deem customers as partners instead of consumers and jointly create value with audiences. Under the background of new media, people is in the midst of mass information and are not satisfied with passive acceptance of advertising information. Instead, consumers are used to erecting an information barrier and actively searching for information they need and sharing such information. Meanwhile, in accordance with behavior model and psychology of people, enterprises (advertisers) shall adopt event marketing so as to cater for preferences and habits of audiences and provide audiences with an option for offline activities. If audiences are attracted and actively participate in marketing event, they will naturally accept information of the activity and information of the brand in subconscious and forward such information in their social media. Under the background of traditional media, consumers are generally passive and short-distance recipients of information. Whether can event marketing shorten distance from consumers and realize integration of idea and media in the ear of internet? Markus Wohlfeil and Susan Whelan (2006) believe marketing event can provide consumers with a platform of experiencing pleasure, excitement, challenge and self realization. The higher consumer participation level is, the higher motivation for participation in marketing event will be[4]. Anne Martensen and Lars Grønholdt (2008) believe high participation level will establish brand preference and consumers will therefore obtain a clearer brand cognition and form their attitude toward brand [5]. Additionally, emotion of consumers at the time of participating in marketing event also will affect their emotion toward brands. Such relationship may be interpreted as value conversion of marketing event or overflow effect. Therefore, cognition of consumers against marketing events will help to create or change brand preference.

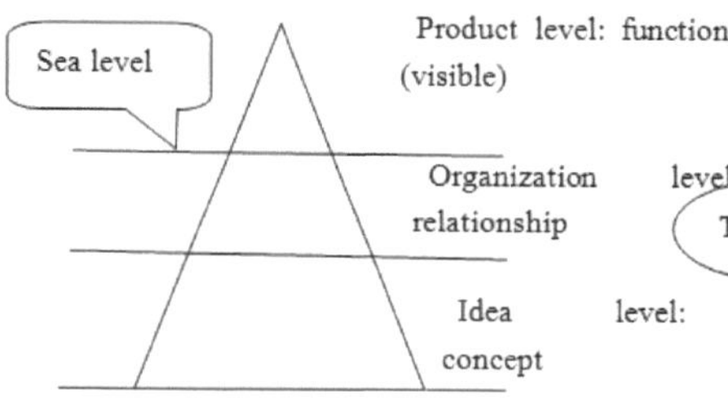

Fig. 2. Iceberg level chart of product transmission

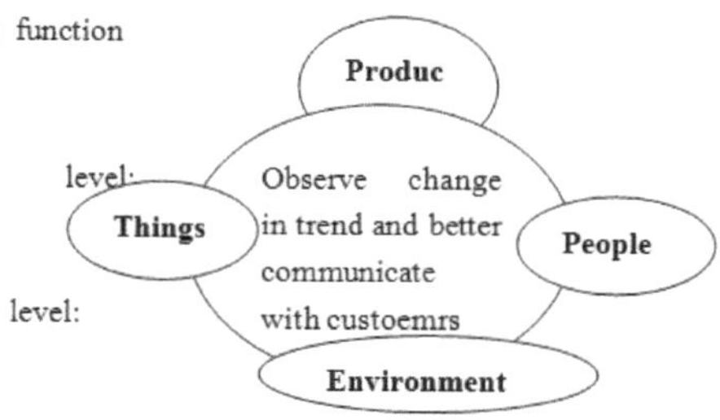

Fig. 3. Communication environment chart of event marketing

4 Cross-Cultural Communication of Service Design-Case Study

Event marketing is also advertising. With small investment and larger effect, event marketing has become another choice of enterprises. Recently, eventalization trend of advertising or event marketing was in full swing, which not only could realize active participation by consumers, but also could realize communication to a larger extent in later online reputation marketing and obtain larger influence. In the following part, we will further interpret application of advertising eventalization in practice.

Case I: "Friendship Vending Machine" of Coca Cola. On the occasion of "Friendship Festival" of Argentina held on July 12, 2010, Coca Cola specially made a "friendship vending machine" with a height of 3.5 meters, twice as high as that of ordinary vending machines. On the top, there is a button ""2*1", indicating you can buy two bottle of cola at the cost of one bottle and share cola with your friend. When the huge vending machine was moved before eyes of the public, it immediately received great attention. If you want to buy cola from this vending machine, your friend shall erect a human ladder so that you can reach the coin slot. So, people stepped to hands of other people, or stepped to or sit on shoulder of other people or several friends together lifted up a person. Through close cooperation among friends, they obtained double cola. The whole site was warmed up by happy laughters and cheerful voices. Some people even took photos. In this case, Coca Cola changed automatic vending machine into an interactive device, which received great attention from and active participation by audiences on the site. In the process of the game, participants can obtain reward through their own efforts or experience happy spirit of Coca Cola brand by completing a small target. Later, through online social media, information was communicated to more audiences not present on the site and finally enhanced the brand and increased sales volume. Coca Cola provided an event marketing platform, which enabled participants to experience excitement in the process of the game and satisfied motivation and demands of consumers so that consumers can spontaneously generate sense of satisfaction. Csikszentmihalyi (1988) also believed in event marketing, people can experience pleasure at a higher level when they spare no effort to break through limit and complete challenge[6].

Case II: Microsoft windows 8 "Slide". Microsoft conducted promotion and publicity activities of windows8 operation system in British market. For the purpose of highlighting features of windows 8, i.e., fast and entertainment, Microsoft erected a large ladder at the stage of a shopping center and immediately attracted a crowd of onlookers at the time of erection. The ladder was printed with such words as "Windows 8" and "fast and funny" and a few advertising elements made people more concentrating on the marketing event. After completion of erection of the slide with bright color, many people, whether children or childish adults, participated in this activity. Their abundant and exciting expressions when they slided down from the slice were recorded in a photo and displayed in a large screen on the site at the same time. Participants may take away photos with them. The simple and easy event paid more attention to bringing pleasure to participants. Brand information was merely visible on the game device and advertising atmosphere was not dense and audiences were not too repulsive. Judging from quantity of onlookers on the site and excitement level of participants, the event itself brought active and positive marketing to audiences on the site. In addition, the video recorded on the site was released to websites and was continuously communicated in a larger extent. With deepening of interaction of social media, information was communicated to more audiences not present on the site and the brand will be finally enhanced. This marketing event of Microsoft merely used a slide, several LED screens and shooting and photo printing equipment. With a few human, physical and financial resources, it very well promoted brand and products and got twofold results with half the effort. The key to success of this marketing event was integration of entertainment mentality of audiences, i.e., audiences'mentality of obtain pleasure from experience.

From foregoing two cases, we can conclude that the era of simple advertising has come to an end and advertising eventalization trend based on social media has begun. More and more enterprises choose to develop activities and events that can be experienced, create a topic or have social significance and events that audiences think good and exciting and are willing to communicate. For may enterprises, cost they can input is generally limited; however, they all expect to have marketing methods with low cost and high effect in addition to conventional advertising input, break through boundary of advertisings and activities and more frequently communicate with consumers with customers and consumers on social media. Zhouyijin ,chen jiahui(2013) think in the context of social media, marketing and concept further analyses, thus to advertising event marketing also has certain promotion[8].Pulizzi&barrett(2009) consider enterprises to adopt useful suggestions from the customers for free through to listen to customer needs, with consumers to create with the common interests of the interdependence and trust [8].Lorenz(2011) consider that event marketing is marketing is a kind of integration includes various channels of online and offline marketing strategy, provide information to customers[9].Liu gang, Xiong lifeng(2013) through dynamic consumer demand response and meet the establishment of enterprise business ecological system and its competitive advantage ,with a case study of Apple Corp. [10]

5 Case: Take "Development of the Country through Design" in Shanghai-Yangze River Delta

In foregoing two cases, we analyzed brand communication and experience from the aspect of demand and users. In this section, we will continuously further analyze experience marketing and brand communication under the background of new media. Within 30 years after reform and opening-up, Chinese economy developed rapidly and realized remarkable growth. Behind rapid economic growth are a series of in-depth problems unbeneficial to sustainable development of the society, such as unbalance of economic structure. Especially, Chinese traditional manufacturing enterprises can not get out the current situation of engaging in production with low added value and transformation pressure is becoming larger and larger. Such enterprises are making endeavors to get out of the difficult situation caused by absence of independent brands and products with independent intellectual property rights.

We will take traditional industries in Shanghai-Yangtze River Delta as an example. For instance, Baoying County, in the north of Jiangsu Province, has four major traditional industries, i.e., crystal, glass, disordered needlework and teaching aids and tools. Technology of such four industries is no bad, but existence status is not good. Owing to absence of connection of modern technology and design, such enterprises are always at the bottom of the industrial chain and merely providing cheap labor force. Therefore, Science and Technology Bureau of Baoying County, Jiangsu Province, Industrial Design Service Center of Shanghai-Yangtze River Delta and East China University of Science and Technology jointly launched service program of "development of the county through design" [11] and invited design experts from

East China University of Science and Technology to conduct industrial planning and product design of four major traditional and characteristic industries of such county, integrate outstanding design from Shanghai with characteristic manufacturing industries of such county so as to realize interaction between creativity industry and manufacturing industry, unblock such steps as design, manufacturing and sales, instill innovation into front line of enterprises, carry out idea of transformation and upgrading in front line of enterprises, change workshop network mode of Baoying's traditional and characteristic industries at the early stage, i.e., store in the front and factory in the back", and accelerate economic transformation and upgrading (see the following chart 4). Under the background of big data, how shall we develop new service through internet and database resources and apply "brand experience" and "service design" to service program of "development of the county through design"? East China University of Science and Technology is one of earliest design institutions that conduct kansei engineering and interactive design research in China. Currently, the university has established a domestically leading virtual reality lab, integrated arts with engineering, conducted product design and evaluation in the whole service life of products, increased user experience and user research in the process of product development so as to provide quantitative sensory evaluation and determination of service design of creativity industry.

Meanwhile, service program of "development of the county through design" in Shanghai-Yangtze River Delta under the background of cloud platform is a very good coordination and cooperation platform. For instance, "51design (51 design network)" established on the basis of the platform for "development of the county through design" can easily connect designers, ideas and enterprises. With unique features, "51design" industrial cloud platform is not only a cloud cluster of designers and ideas, but also a trading and distribution platform of creative products. Online "51design" and offline "slow and happy life hall" flag store interact with each other. Meanwhile, "51design cloud platform" provides a platform for release of tasks and transaction of achievements. Users can select and purchase cultural and creative products they like on the platform just as they use Taobao. This platform not only realizes online transaction of creative products, but also provides a public cloud platform for creation of cultural industry and creates an online cultural creativity community where "everybody is a designer". Meanwhile, development technology of new media is fully used in the process of product design under the program of "development of the county through design". For instance, "automatic tea making machine" adopts QR code technology and "Dafeng" Zhiqing Farm realizes cross-cultural communication and brand transmission through forwarding by VIPs so as to continuously unblock the industrial chain from designer's works to products and commodities, enable designers to continuously understand real demands in the market and design creative products that can satisfy customer demands, really improve life through design and improve life quality of users, such as webpage interactive design and service design of websites.

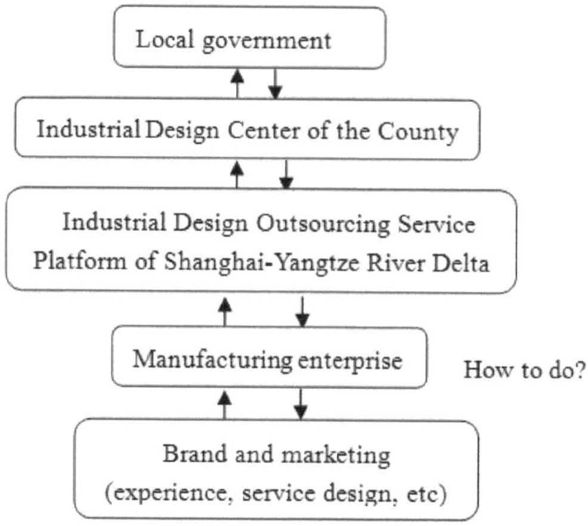

Fig. 4. "Development of the county though design" and brand marketing

6 Conclusion and Suggestion

Through analysis of change in consumption trend and communication under the background of new media, this article discussed connotation and mechanism of advertising eventalization trend and, through two latest cases about event marketing on social media and program of "development of the county through design", interpreted how enterprises shall better communicate with consumers and realize brand transmission through such methods as event marketing and service design. Several conclusions of this article as follows. First, the era when traditional media can make a success relying on advertising has come to an end. Under the background of new media, enterprises must learn how to adapt to change in consumption trend so as to better communicate with consumers. Enterprises shall deem consumers as partners, value passers and driving force of social reform and jointly create value with consumers. Second: at present, more and more enterprises choose to deal with challenges faced by advertising under the background of new media through event marketing. It is not important whether event marketing or advertising eventalization is traditional advertising and the key is that enterprises can obtain right of speech and realize communication with consumers through activities or marketing planning under the background of new media. After all, the purpose of advertising is to solve the problem of communication with consumers instead of simple advertising. This is essential connotation of advertising eventalization. Third: different from advertising that flashes by on the traditional media, event marketing of enterprises under the background of new media pays more attention to participation by consumers. Shifting from words to facts and from "flashing by" to activities and accumulation, event marketing gradually receives care and recognition from audiences.

To sum up, in the era of social media, consumer participation and interaction are becoming more and more. Whether experience marketing, reputation marketing or interactive market, it is one form of advertising. Advertising eventalization trend is becoming more and more obvious. In addition to purchase of products, consumers are willing to participate in events and activities for the purpose of experiencing excitement, challenging or obtaining sense of achievement or merely for fun. Therefore, enterprises (or advertisers) must understand demands that consumers desire to satisfy through participation in marketing event. Change in such consumption trend also brings out change in communication. Event marketing trend is becoming more and more obvious and silently changing advertising forms. For instance, enterprises can obtain resources from internet, realize reputation communication through social media, jointly create value with consumers through participation by users and realize online and offline interaction (O2O).

References

1. Fan, X., Luo, H.: Analysis of service enterprise competitiveness based on customer value. Nankai Business Review, 41–45 (2003) (Chinese)
2. Granovetter, M.: Economic action and social structure: the problem of the embeddedness. American Journal of Sociology 91(3), 418–510 (1985)
3. Uzzi, B.: Social Structure and Competition in Inter-firm Networks: The Paradox of Embeddedness. Administrative Science Quarterly 42(1), 35–67 (1997)
4. Wohlfeil, M., Whelan, S.: Consumer Motivations to Participate in Marketing-Events: The Role of Predispositional Involvement. In: European Advances in Consumer Research, pp. 125–131. Association for Consumer Research, Duluth (2006)
5. Martensen, A., Grønholdt, L.: How events work understanding consumer responses to event marketing[. Innovative Marketing (4), 44–56 (2008)
6. Csikszentmihalyi, M.: The Flow Experience and its Significance For Human Psychology. In: Csikszentmihalyi, M., Csikszentmihalyi, I.S. (eds.) Optimal Experience: Psychological Studies of Flow in Consciousness, pp. 15–35. Cambridge University Press, New York (1988)
7. Zhou, Y., Chen, J.: The era of social media content marketing prospect: preliminary study and research concept. Foreign Economic and Management 35(6), 61–71 (2013) (Chinese)
8. Pulizzi, J., Barrett, N.: Get content get customers:Turn prospects into buyers with content marketing. McGraw-Hill, NewYork (2009)
9. Lorenz, L.: Content marketing-The what,why and how. Hudson Valley Business Journal 22(29), 20 (2011)
10. Liu, L., Xiong, L.: Dynamic consumer demand response: the construction of enterprise boundary selection and business ecosystem. China Industrial Economy, 122–134 (2013) (Chinese)
11. Shanghai hand in hand with small workshops, can become a "model"? 2011.10.24. Liberation Daily, Xumeng, Source (Chinese)

Newsvendor's Response to Demand History*

Wei Geng[1] and Xiaodong Ding[2]

[1] School of Economics and Management,
Southwest Jiaotong University, Chengdu, 610031, China
[2] School of Traffic and Transportation,
Southwest Jiaotong University, Chengdu, 610031, China

Abstract. Mean anchor and chasing demand are two heuristics widely used in literature to explain newsvendor's decision bias. The mean anchor heuristic is an aggregate representation, and static to some extent. In a dynamic setting we significantly control demand chasing behavior and conduct a laboratory experiment. We find that besides the two aforementioned heuristics subject's response to demand history is heterogenous and cannot be neglected.

1 Introduction

In the context of operations management, a conventional newsvendor always faces a decision problem on how much newspaper she should purchase prior to the selling season. If the newsvendor is rational, she is supposed to carefully analyze her purchasing cost and revenue, optimize her profit or utility, and then obtain an optimal order quantity which is determined by a critical fractile and demand distribution simultaneously. The rational assumption is recently challenged by findings in laboratory experiments. Schweitzer and Cachon find that subjects make newsvendor decisions consistently deviating from optimal prediction ([1]). A *pull-to-center effect* is found significant that newsvendor tends to place an order between optimal prediction and mean demand. Schweitzer and Cachon analyze several quite different decision preferences as possible explanations. Some of them are then ruled out after either theoretical or experimental examinations, for instance, risk-averse, risk-seeking, loss-averse preferences, etc. A preference of minimizing ex-post inventory error is left. And a heuristic of anchoring and insufficient adjustment (AIA) is proposed. In the AIA scheme, a decision maker chooses a quantity as an anchor based on available information and her preference, and then adjusts her decision in some direction away from the anchor. Two alternative AIA heuristics are proposed in [1] and frequently investigated thereafter.

One of the two AIA heuristics is the mean anchor heuristic. Applying this heuristic, decision maker always anchors on mean demand and adjusts towards the optimal order quantity. Since both mean demand and optimal order quantity

* This research was supported by National Natural Science Foundation of China (Grant No. 71201134).

P.L.P. Rau (Ed.): CCD/HCII 2014, LNCS 8528, pp. 449–457, 2014.

are determined after the problem parameters are set, this heuristic guarantees a static outcome for decision maker, with a possible noise if random disturbance is considered. Bolton and Katok ([2]), Bostian *et al.* ([3]), and Becker-Peth *et al.* ([4]) develop this heuristic in many aspects.

The other one is the chasing demand heuristic. Applying this heuristic, decision maker consistently anchors on a prior order quantity and adjusts her order quantity in the direction of the previous period's demand. That is, decision maker's order quantity is a convex combination of previous order quantity and previous demand. This heuristic marks dynamic outcomes for decision maker. Lau and Bearden ([5]) revisit and discuss the heuristic.

Let's return to the newsvendor's decision problem at this time. For every single decision, the optimal order quantity is a tradeoff between possible gain and loss when facing a undetermined demand to maximize expected profit or utility. However, the best decision for the newsvendor is to match customer demand, if she possesses enough knowledge of coming demand. An example is that if the newsvendor can place her order after customer demand realizes, she can simply order exactly the same quantity as the demand to hit the highest profit or utility. However in the typical context of the problem, the newsvendor should make decision before demand realization when only knowing demand distribution. It is logical for the newsvendor to turn to put effort on forecasting the coming demand based on available information. Demand history is at the ready. The chasing demand heuristic, which is constructed based on last demand, is actually another representation of exponential smoothing approach well known in the area of forecasting.

In this paper, we consider newsvendor's response on demand history. Historical data may impact decision maker's perceived demand distribution, even though the demand is actually independent on each other. For those new product or seasonal product, such as in fashion industry, this scenario could be observed. We explicitly take demand in further away periods into account besides the last demand. The newsvendor's decision heuristic is generalized from a convex combination of last demand and last decision to a linear function of several variables. Moving average, another forecasting technique, is incorporated into the model.

In the rest of this paper, we first introduce a laboratory experiment in Section 2. Based on the experiment findings, we analyze the performance of aggregate model in Section 3, and develop an individual model to capture the heterogenous nature of population in Section 5. Further discussion and research direction are provided in Section 5.

2 Laboratory Experiment

Laboratory experiment is extensively used in operations management recently. Schweitzer and Cachon develop a fundamental experiment scheme in [1] to investigate newsvendor's decision bias between optimal prediction and actual order quantity. Many scholars replicate the experiment with necessary changes. Here we adopt most of the settings but control decision maker's interaction with prior outcomes.

Subjects in the experiment are asked to solve newsvendor problem to gain credits as many as they can. A subject's reward to participate in the experiment consists of two parts, one is a variable margin depending on total credits gained and the other one is a fixed allowance. The monetary incentive encourages subjects to seriously participate in the experiment.

The subject's task is to place an order of newspaper to satisfy customer demand in the following selling season. Ordering quantity is the only decision. Previous newsvendor experiments usually ask subjects to make decisions repeatedly in consecutive periods. Demand history is hence involved with order history in a complex and twisty way. The chasing demand heuristic is a kind of first order expansion to a certain extent. Here we design 20 instances of newsvendor problem. Each instance is assumed to pick up from a long-run system separately, and has its own demand history on prior 12 periods. In every instance, the newsvendor buys newspaper at a purchasing cost 3 then sells at a higher price 9. No salvage is provided for leftover goods. This is the so-called high profit setting in [1]. Among all the instances, customer demand is assumed to follow a discrete uniform distribution on $[1, 300]$. Subjects are informed the newsvendor parameters except demand history in advance and can check the parameters while they are doing the experiment. Demand history can only be found when a subject is solving corresponding instance.

Table 1. Demand histories in newsvendor instances

Instance	t-12	t-11	t-10	t-9	t-8	t-7	t-6	t-5	t-4	t-3	t-2	t-1	t (Trend)
1	9	292	120	123	51	208	112	109	225	275	59	97	135
2	9	292	120	123	51	208	112	109	225	275	9	97	185
3	170	157	62	35	242	278	127	107	57	269	73	109	145
4	170	157	62	35	242	278	127	107	57	269	23	109	195
5	165	160	255	194	51	276	77	17	23	284	81	118	155
6	165	160	255	194	51	276	77	17	23	284	31	118	205
7	90	182	79	279	49	52	69	273	107	291	89	127	165
8	90	182	79	279	49	52	69	273	107	291	39	127	215
9	123	106	146	149	284	135	58	46	210	258	97	136	175
10	123	106	146	149	284	135	58	46	210	258	47	136	225
11	9	292	120	123	51	208	112	109	225	275	105	145	185
12	9	292	120	123	51	208	112	109	225	275	55	145	235
13	170	157	62	35	242	278	127	107	57	269	113	154	195
14	170	157	62	35	242	278	127	107	57	269	63	154	245
15	165	160	255	194	51	276	77	17	23	284	121	163	205
16	165	160	255	194	51	276	77	17	23	284	71	163	255
17	90	182	79	279	49	52	69	273	107	291	129	172	215
18	90	182	79	279	49	52	69	273	107	291	79	172	265
19	123	106	146	149	284	135	58	46	210	258	137	181	225
20	123	106	146	149	284	135	58	46	210	258	87	181	275

Demand histories in the 20 instances are listed in Table 1. They are in 10 pairs. In each pair, demand in the first 10 periods and the last period are identical respectively, but the demand in the second last period is different. There are plenty of researches providing evidence on the impact of last demand, see in [1] and [5]. Hence we simply let the last demand be identical. In the last column, we show a *trend* value. This value is a kind of forecasting on demand based on last two demands. This forecast is easy to be obtained, maybe only less easy than the naive forecast (to assume coming demand equals to the last one). We do not show the trend value to the subjects through the experiment. Similar design could be found in [6].

As mentioned before, customer demands in all the instances are generated independently from the same random distribution. Optimal decision is actually independent on demand history we designed and given to the subjects but only determined by purchasing cost, price, and demand distribution.

20 graduate students were recruited from Southwest Jiaotong University as subjects. All the subjects came from a graduate program majored in Industrial Engineering, and hence they had sufficient background knowledge on stochastic event and optimization. Brief but adequate introduction to newsvendor problem was given to the subjects both orally and with a printed reminder. A piece of special information was also given as a warning that conventional optimal solution to newsvendor problem is just to maximize expected profit but may not yield the greatest profit against each demand realization.

An additional warm-up session was conducted before the experiment session to help the subjects get familiar with the experiment system and the decision tasks. In the experiment session, the above 20 instances were set to follow a randomized order. Every time a subject placed an order, he or she did not access the corresponding result. Subjects knew their results and rewards only after they had finished all the tasks. Such control on interaction between subjects and their prior performances may eliminate the chasing demand behavior.

Subjects were not requested to finish all the instances, and only 18 subjects completed all their tasks. The results and findings are reported in the next section.

3 Performance of Aggregate Model

The following Figure 1 shows mean order quantities over all 18 subjects for each of the 20 instances. Mean orders falls between mean demand (150) and optimal order quantity (225), i.e., the so-called pull-to-center effect is in evidence in our experiment.

A coming after Lilliefors test on the sample of the 20 mean order quantities indicates that at a reasonable significance level we cannot reject the hypotheses that the mean orders come from a distribution in the normal family ($p = 0.4898$). We can also estimate the distribution parameters with mean 169.1639 and standard deviation 10.5729. The pattern may be observed for decision makers applying mean anchor heuristic. The mean anchor heuristic is usually formulated as

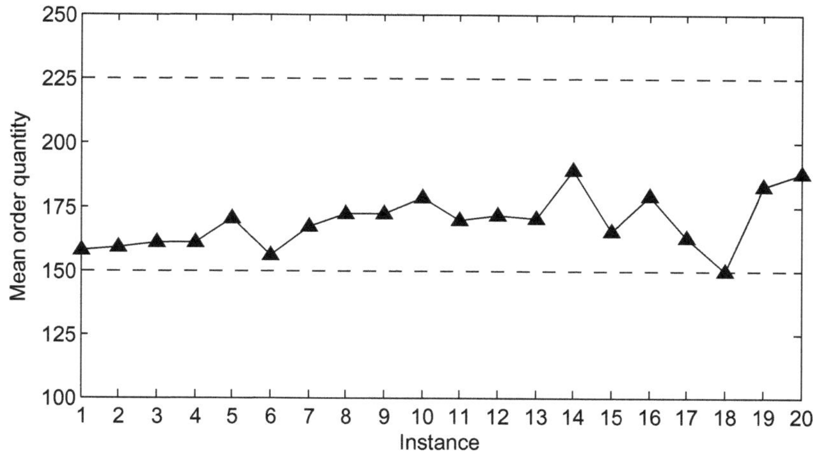

Fig. 1. Mean order for each of the 20 instances

$$q = \alpha q^* + (1 - \alpha)\mu + c + \epsilon \quad (1)$$

where $0 < \alpha < 1$ is a weight parameter, ϵ is a random noise following the standard normal distribution, and q^*, μ, and c are optimal order quantity, mean demand, and constant term, respectively. For a given newsvendor problem, q^* and μ are static. Hence, in multiple-runs newsvendor experiment with stationary purchasing cost, selling price and demand distribution, Equation 1 predicts that the sample of order quantities comes from a normal distribution. However, note that much information vanishes as we calculate mean values. Before we claim that the mean anchor heuristic again is an appropriate candidate to explain the newsvendor's decision bias, we have to conduct some further investigation.

We then test whether every subject's order quantity comes from a normal distribution with mean 169.1639. A $t-$test is performed for every subject, and the results are shown in Table 2. At a 5% significance level, the hypotheses that the subject's order quantities come from the aforementioned normal distribution is rejected for 10 subjects out of the 18.

Table 2. t-test for every subject against the null hypotheses (normal-distributed)

Subjects	1	2	3	4	5	6	7	8	9
t statistic	8.2067	7.0468	-0.3451	7.2554	2.3325	-5.4848	0.4895	-1.9212	0.4737
p value	0.0000	0.0000	0.7338	0.0000	0.0308	0.0000	0.6301	0.0698	0.6411
Subjects	10	11	12	13	14	15	16	17	18
t statistic	2.4063	-6.6661	-1.5966	-0.7482	-3.2972	-4.0418	0.7756	-4.6715	-1.1260
p value	0.0265	0.0000	0.1269	0.4635	0.0038	0.0007	0.4475	0.0002	0.2742

A Lilliefors test is also re-performed on the overall order quantities rather than the mean values. The normal-distributed hypotheses is rejected ($p = 0.0001$). The following histogram exhibits how all the subjects' order quantities distribute. Figure 2 suggests multiple modes in order quantity distribution. One possible reason it that the whole sample consists of several different samples each of which comes from a unimodal distribution.

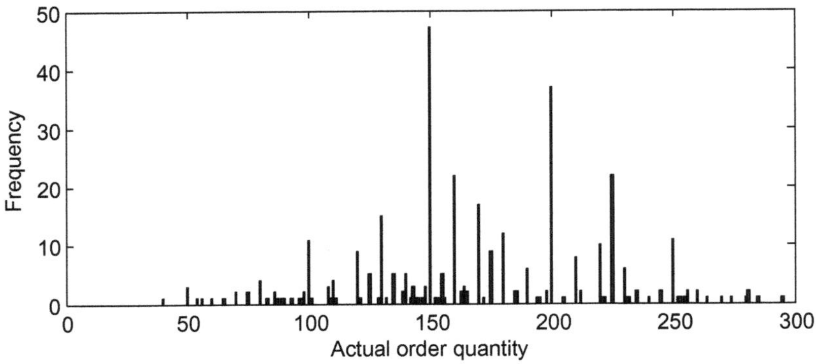

Fig. 2. Histogram on how all the subjects' order quantities distribute

Table 2 and Figure 2 both imply that the population of subjects is of observable heterogeneity nature. An underlying assumption of Equation 1 is homogeny of population. Becker-Peth *et al.* use α_n and c_n to instead α and c in the equation where the subscript n denotes dependence of parameters on different subject. The consequent model based on population heterogeneity is found performed better than aggregate model ([4]). Hence, we build individual model in the next section to capture the heterogeneity.

4 Individual Model

The mean anchor heuristic is an aggregate treatment for the whole subject group's order quantities. After the modification conducted by Becker-Peth *et al.*, the parameters now depend on individuals, and the model treats individual subject separately ([4]). However, for a multiple-run newsvendor system with stationary cost, price and demand distribution, the modified mean anchor heuristic predicts static outcome for every single subject as well. One effort in incorporating dynamic into the model is to consider learning as in [3].

The chasing demand heuristic provides dynamic outcomes. The heuristic is usually formulated as

$$q_t = q_{t-1} + \beta \left(d_{t-1} - q_{t-1}\right) + c + \epsilon \tag{2}$$

where $0 < \beta < 1$ is a weight parameter, ϵ is a random noise following the standard normal distribution, q is ordering quantity, d is demand realization, c is a constant term, and subscript t denotes decision period. Similarly as in [4], if we let parameters β and c depend on subject with additional subscripts n, the modified equation 2 can predict individual's behavior, in a dynamic pattern. In our experiment, the impact of immediate preceding decision (q_{t-1}) has been controlled even if not omitted. Hence we build the following equation to demonstrate newsvendor's response to demand history.

$$q_t = b_{\text{const}} + b_{\text{mean}}\mu_{\text{s}} + b_{\text{last}}d_{t-1} + \epsilon \tag{3}$$

In Equation 3, q_t is newsvendor order quantity in current observed period, μ_{s} is the average value of historical demand, d_{t-1} is demand realization in the last period, ϵ is a random noise following the standard normal distribution, and bs are corresponding coefficients. Equation 3 focuses on newsvendor's response to last demand and mean of historical demand. Another equation focusing on newsvendor's response to last demand and trend value is

$$q_t = b_{\text{const}} + b_{\text{trend}}\bar{d}_t + b_{\text{last}}d_{t-1} + \epsilon \tag{4}$$

where $\bar{d}_t$ is the trend value. Many other similar equations can be developed for various different purposes.

We obtain parameter estimations for Equation 3 through linear regression, and show them in the following Table 3. Only those subjects whose ordering quantities do not come from a normal distribution with mean 169.1639 are taken into consideration this time.

Table 3. Parameter estimation for individual model

Subjects	1	2	3	4	5	6	7	8	9
b_{const}	589.1707	-152.2426		110.9112	143.2809	150.4478			
b_{mean}	-3.1014	2.5748		0.0271	-0.1937	-0.2699			
b_{last}	0.4306	0.1431		0.7172	0.5867	0.2884			
Adjusted R^2	0.2251	-0.0371		0.4029	-0.0284	0.1929			
F statistic	3.7592	0.6601		7.4102	0.7375	3.2698			
p value	0.0445**	0.5295		0.0049***	0.4930	0.0629*			
Subjects	**10**	**11**	**12**	**13**	**14**	**15**	**16**	**17†**	**18**
b_{const}	-105.6061	-363.3647			-281.4275	-6.3006		112.2569	
b_{mean}	1.6466	3.5281			2.9190	1.4293		0.8095	
b_{last}	0.4324	-0.1642			0.1263	-0.4889		-1.1049	
Adjusted R^2	0.0435	-0.0033			0.3607	-0.0414		0.1535	
F statistic	1.4325	0.9689			6.3611	0.6224		2.7227	
p value	0.2661	0.3995			0.0087***	0.5484		0.0942*	

1. * significant at 10% level; ** significant at 5% level; *** significant at 1% level.
2. † Here we estimate parameters for Equation 4 because estimation for Equation 3 is not significant. Hence, we estimate b_{trend} here instead of b_{mean}.

Based on the estimations, we could predict subject's order quantities individually, and compare the aggregate model and the individual model. The following figure illustrates such comparison. The individual model provides dynamic and flexible prediction, and fits actual order quantities better. The aggregate model can only yield static predictions.

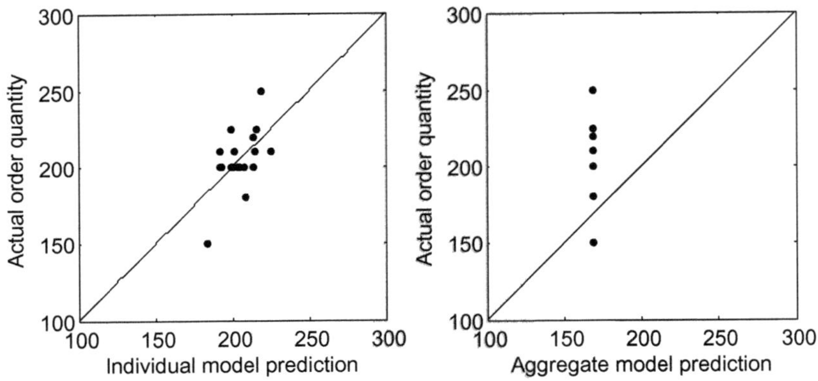

Fig. 3. Comparison between individual model and aggregate model for subject 1

From tables 2 and 3, we could see that the group of subjects consists of dissimilar elements. At least three subgroups could be roughly categorized. The first subgroup consists of subjects 3, 7, 8, 9, 12, 13, 16, 18. The pattern of their order quantities is consistent with prediction of the mean anchor heuristic. The second subgroup consists of subjects 1, 4, 6, 14, 17. Equation 3 (or 4 for subject 17) explains fluctuation of their order quantities at the level ranging from 15.35% to 40.29%. The other subjects form the third subgroup. Their ordering behavior need to be further investigated.

5 Discussion

We conducted a laboratory experiment to examine newsvendor's response to demand history. There are two major contributions of the experiment design. The first is to control the interaction between subjects and their decision processes and performances. Ex-post inventory error is hence invisible for subjects. The second is to manipulate demand history. Subjects make decision for instances rather than consecutive periods. Order history and demand history hence can be separated and controlled.

The two widely used heuristics, mean anchor and chasing demand, are discussed in this paper. The former one is aggregate and static mostly. And the latter one can be individual and dynamic. The linear model (equations 3 and 4) could be treated as a combination of the aforementioned two heuristics. The constant term b_{const} in these equations in a further discussion could be seen as the outcome of mean anchor heuristic. This provides a further research direction.

Based on findings of the experiment, we find that newsvendor's response to demand history is heterogenous. Such heterogeneity needs further investigation. Random coefficients may be incorporated to better describe the ordering behavior. This is another further research direction.

Let's get back to newsvendor's response to demand history. Some ones care little about demand history, and their ordering pattern can be predicted by an aggregate and static model, i.e., the mean anchor heuristic. The other ones are influenced by demand history through different ways. Some are affected by overall demand history, and hence the mean value of realized demand is significant. Some others focus on the recent past, and demands in last few periods make sense. In conclusion, newsvendor's response to demand history is diverse, and need to be carefully considered and treated when managerial suggestions are proposed or decision support system is developed.

References

1. Schweitzer, M.E., Cachon, G.P.: Decision Bias in the Newsvendor Problem with a Known Demand Distribution: Experimental Evidence. Management Science 46(3), 404–420 (2000)
2. Bolton, G.E., Katok, E.: Learning by Doing in the Newsvendor Problem: A Laboratory Investigation of the Role of Experience and Feedback. Manufacturing & Service Operations Management 10(3), 519–538 (2008)
3. Bostian, A.A., Holt, C.A., Smith, A.M.: Newsvendor Pull-to-center Effect: Adaptive Learning in a Laboratory Experiment. Manufacturing & Service Operations Management 10(4), 590–608 (2008)
4. Becker-Peth, M., Katok, E., Thonemann, U.W.: Designing Buyback Contracts for Irrational But Predictable Newsvendors. Management Science 59(8), 1800–1816 (2013)
5. Lau, N., Bearden, J.N.: Newsvendor Demand Chasing Revisited. Management Science 59(5), 1245–1249 (2013)
6. Baucells, M., Weber, M., Welfens, F.: Reference-point formation and updating. Management Science 57(3), 506–519 (2011)

Improving the Predictive Validity of NPS in Customer Satisfaction Surveys

Gang Huang and Huai-lin Wang

User Experience Researcher, Alibaba Group
No. 969, West Wenyi Road, 311121 Hangzhou, China
kaer.hg@tmall.com, kongtuo.whl@tmall.com

Abstract. Though widely used, NPS has been challenged for its doubtful validity in predicting loyalty behaviors and business growth. Its arbitrary assignment of promoters/passives/detractors is one of the factors impacting its predictability. This paper addressed the validity issue by taking into account the scenarios NPS is used: (1) NPS for an organization in developing stage with more of new customers vs. a well established business with more of regular customers; (2) NPS in online survey vs. offline survey. By using the data of an online NPS survey for an online supermarket and tracking the purchase behaviors of all respondents before and after the survey, the authors found that NPS works better for new customers than regular ones in predicting repeat purchase behaviors and changes of purchase volume and value. In addition, in online surveys, a polarized segmentation of promoters/passives/detractors could effectively improve the predictive validity of NPS for new customers.

Keywords: NPS, Customer Satisfaction, Predictive Validity.

1 Background and Research Objectives

1.1 Merits and Criticisms on NPS

The Net Promoter Score (NPS) is one of the simplest customer satisfaction and loyalty measures, which only asks customers on a 0 to 10 rating scale: "How likely is it that you would recommend our company to a friend or colleague?" Based on their responses, customers can be categorized into one of three groups: Promoters (9-10 rating), Passives (7-8 rating), and Detractors (0-6 rating). Subtracting detractors from promoters then draws out the "net promoter" score as an estimate customer loyalty behaviors and business growth.

Thanks for the popularization of Fred Reichheld (2006), NPS has been widely adopted in different industries. It is easy to understand and makes intuitive sense. Compared to traditional customer-satisfaction measures such as American Customer Satisfaction Index (ACSI) model, NPS typically focuses on the measurement of WOM that has gained more and more attention with the popularization of Internet usage and the powerful influence of online WOM for organizations.

P.L.P. Rau (Ed.): CCD/HCII 2014, LNCS 8528, pp. 458–469, 2014.

Despite the merits, NPS has received lots of criticisms that center on its failure to predict loyalty behaviors and business growth and its arbitrary segmentation of promoters/passives/detractors.

Its predictive validity is challenged mainly because this measure is attitudinal rather than behavioral and thus can only reflect present intention than future behavior. Keiningham et al. (2007) found that NPS does not perform better than the ACSI in predicting growth. By examining the robustness of different customer satisfaction and loyalty metrics, Keiningham et al. (2007) also suggested that the NPS alone would not serve as a single predictor of customers' future loyalty behaviors. Instead, multiple indicators performs significantly better.

Regarding its segmentation of three groups, Ken Roberts, CEO of Forethought Research Australia, said this rule-of-thumb score classes is not statically supported and may mask the important changes and potentially mislead management when the organization got a negative NPS whilst this may not be the case. On the other hand, the standard NPS question itself is unipolar (willingness to recommend) but its analysis treats it as bipolar (willingness to detract vs. promote) (blog.verint.com).

Given these criticisms, some researchers have explored different ways to enhance this measure. One of these endeavors is to merge NPS with other loyalty metric and generate a more synthesized measure. For instance, Owyang (2010) has combined NPS with other metrics to create the index of Total Social Customer Value (TSCV). The other part of these efforts focuses on optimizing the 11-point scale given that Reichheld shows flexibility on it. His original work showcases Enterprise Rent-A-Car by using a 5-point scale with 5 as promoters. Schneider, et al. (2007) has also recommended a 7-point bipolar scale for recommendation measuring.

Nevertheless, until now, there is no solid conclusion on either the best scale for NPS or the most effective assignment of promoters/passives/detractors. In addition, the golden rule, if there was, may vary in different survey scenarios which are closely related to business types surveyed, data collection methods used, etc.

1.2 NPS Practice in Online E-Commerce Customer Satisfaction Survey

Facing more and more fierce competition, monitoring customer satisfaction and loyalty is becoming more important for Chinese e-commerce giants. However, when advocating NPS to e-commerce practitioners, two challenges come up:

The first is, the operators in business with well-established e-commerce model and steady sales growth are less likely to accept NPS. The main concern is that their net promoter score may not have major changes over time given that their business is in relatively stable stage. Only those in newly developed e-commerce business pay much attention to NPS and even treat it as a KPI.

The second is that, in the 11-point scale, the point "10" gets much higher ratings than expected. In all the e-commerce customer satisfaction surveys we have done, it counts for around 50% of all responses whilst other ratings are very scattered (see Table 1). Meanwhile, ratings on 0 point are also slightly higher than that of 1, 2, or even 3, though not as obvious as 10 rating. This makes the business operators doubt about the validity of this measure and challenge the design of 11-point scale.

Table 1. 10 ratings in e-commerce NPS surveys

E-commerce business	% of 10 rating in NPS question
A comprehensive B2C site	52%
Large-scale household appliances	61%
Furniture	49%
Milk powder	62%
Online supermarket	47%

Though all these surveys are about different e-commerce businesses, ranging from durables to FMCGs, the common thing is that they were all conducted online via e-mail recruitment and self-administrated web questionnaire. This may be caused the social desirability bias: when respondents fill in the questionnaire online without the presence of interviewers, they may be more likely to give extreme answers if they really think so, without any concern of possible reactions from others.

Bearing these challenges in mind, this paper comes up with the objectives to optimize the design of NPS in online e-commerce customer satisfaction surveys and improve its predictive validity.

2 Key Questions and Hypotheses

With the objectives mentioned above, two questions will be addressed in this paper with respective hypothesis listed below:

Q1. In what kind of e-commerce business scenarios NPS works better in terms of predictive validity?

H1: Our hypothesis is that NPS works better for newly developed business. The first reason is that the likelihood of recommendation fits well with the business objective of growing reputation and enlarging market penetration for this kind of organizations. More importantly, this kind of organizations consists more of new users than regular users. The new users may turn into regular users or lapsed users. Therefore, their responses on NPS may better reflect their future loyalty behaviors. However, for the regular users, their purchase behaviors may not be changed even if they give a very low score in NPS question.

This question is hence turned into a more specific sub-question: does NPS have better predictive validity for new users or regular users? The sub-hypothesis is NPS is more valid in predicting new users retention behaviors than regular users' loyalty.

Q2. What is the better assignment of promoters and detractors when NPS surveys is conducted online?

H2: Our previous experience has led to a hypothesis that the segmentation of promoters/passives/detractors should be more polarized in online surveys, i.e. promoters should be defined with only 10 rating instead of 9-10 rating, while detractors with 0-5 rating or lower instead of 0-6 rating.

3 Research Methodology

To verify our hypothesis, a research-on-research study was conducted by taking an online NPS survey for online supermarket as the showcase.

3.1 Rationale of the Overall Research Design

The core of this research is to test the predictive validity of NPS. Therefore, the purchase behaviors of each respondent in this survey were monitored over 6 months, with 3 months before the survey and 3 moths after. Linking the NPS rating of each respondent with their behavioral changes before the after the survey, we were able to examine the correlations between recommendation intention and purchase behaviors.

To verify the first hypothesis, we tested the predictive validity of NPS for new users and regular users respectively. Each of the testing was not only to compare the behavioral changes between promoters and detractors, but also to do such comparisons between promoters vs. passives, and passives vs. detractors. This is to verify the existence of linear correlation between NPS rating and loyalty behavior. Ideally, promoters should perform better in loyalty behaviors than passives and passives better than detractors.

To verify the second hypothesis, we compared the predictive validity of two segmentations. The first is the standard segmentation advocated by Fred Reichheld as a benchmark. The second is a set of polarized segmentations for comparison. The specific design of the alternative segmentations allows some flexibility for new users and regular users, depending on the actual data got from the survey. This would help us to find out the optimal segmentation in different scenarios.

In addition, to strengthen the second hypothesis, we also looked at the different reasons for recommendation between promoters with 9 and 10 rating. Accordingly, the detraction points were also compared across the detractors with different ratings.

3.2 Choice of the Right Case

To make sure that we can observe the behavioral changes in an acceptable period, the case adopted in this study should be about the organizations with relatively higher purchase frequency. Therefore, we choose one of the leading online supermarkets in China as an example. It sells daily consumption products online, including foods & beverages, personal case and house cleaning products, etc.

3.3 Data Collection

The customer satisfaction survey was conducted online in the last week of August 2013. An email invitation was sent to the current users of this online supermarket with a hyperlink of a web questionnaire. In total, 3,106 valid responses were collected.

The classic NPS question with 11-point scale is adopted in the questionnaire, followed by a set of questions about the reasons to recommend for promoters and the reasons to detract for detractors respectively. Close-end multiple-choice questions were used in this probing session, with a list of attributes generated from qualitative studies as the choices. 30 promotion points and 31 detraction points were covered.

3.4 Sample Coverage

All the respondents surveyed must be customers who had finished at least one purchase order in the past 3 months before the survey, i.e. May – Aug. 2013.

Both the new users and regular users were covered. New users were defined as those who had not bought anything from this site in the 3 months before May, i.e. Feb. - May 2013, whilst the regular users were purchase contributor along the past 6 months including May - Aug. and Feb. - May 2013 (See Table 2 for illustration)[1].

Table 2. Definition of new users and regular users

	Feb. - May. 2013	May. – Aug. 2013	22nd-27th, Aug. 2013
New users	Non-purchasers	Purchasers	Survey period
Regular users	Purchasers	Purchasers	Survey period

3.5 Indicators for Predictive Validity Test

The purchase behaviors we monitored covered repeat purchase, volume changes and value changes, which are closely related to business growth.

- Repeat purchase rate (Repeat rate): the percentage of respondents who have purchase in the subsequent 3 months after the survey (Sep. – Nov. 2013).
- % of respondents with volume increase (Vol. increase)[2]: the percentage of respondents who finished more purchase orders in the subsequent 3 months after the survey (Sep. – Nov. 2013) than that in the 3 months before the survey (May – Aug. 2013).
- % of respondents with value increase (Val. increase): the percentage of respondents who have spend more in this online supermarket in the subsequent 3 months after the survey than that in the 3 months before the survey.

[1] This definition is aligned with business operators. However, we also checked the purchase behaviors 3 months earlier and found that 86% of new users did not purchase anything during Nov. 2012 – Feb. 2013 but only 46% of regular users had no purchase in this period.

[2] The purchase volume may be increased, decreased, or kept same. In this survey, only very few respondents have exactly the same purchase volume between the first and second 3 months, therefore, unless pointed out, usually the test on volume increase is almost equal to that of volume decrease. It is the same case for the indicator of value increase.

4 Research Result

In this survey, respondents with higher ratings in NPS question are more likely to repeat purchase, increase purchase volume and value in the subsequent 3 months. Looking at the 11 points of the scale, 10 and 5, instead of 9 and 6, appear to be the turning points in this curve (see Table 3). This applies to total respondents and new users. However, for the regular users, rating 9 is still an important turning point.

With this respective, the polarized segmentation of promoters/passives/detractors tested in the following sessions were designed as below:

- Total users: Promoters (10 rating), Passives (6-9 rating), Detractors (0-5 rating)
- New users: Promoters (10 rating), Passives (6-9 rating), Detractors (0-5 rating)
- Regular users: Promoters (9-10 rating), Passives (6-8 rating), Detractors (0-5 rating)

Table 3. Behavioral changes across the respondents with different NPS ratings

User group	Indicators	NPS rating							Total
		0-4[3]	5	6	7	8	9	10	
Total users	Repeat rate	55%	58%	64%	67%	67%	71%	76%	70%
	Vol. increase	38%	40%	47%	49%	50%	53%	56%	52%
	Val. increase	37%	43%	50%	53%	53%	55%	59%	54%
New users	Repeat rate	49%	52%	56%	60%	60%	60%	69%	62%
	Vol. increase	32%	39%	44%	45%	46%	45%	51%	46%
	Val. increase	32%	40%	48%	47%	48%	46%	52%	48%
Regular users	Repeat rate	71%	75%	81%	82%	79%	87%	86%	83%
	Vol. increase	52%	43%	53%	58%	58%	65%	64%	61%
	Val. increase	50%	48%	57%	68%	62%	69%	68%	64%

4.1 The Predictive Validity at Total Level

By using the standard segmentation, NPS shows very good predictive validity in general. In the subsequent 3 months after the survey, the tendency of promoters to repeat purchase, increase purchase volume and value are significantly higher than passives, and passives significantly higher than detractors (see Table 4).

Nevertheless, the polarized segmentation was still examined and it turned out to yield perfect prediction for purchase behaviors as well, with its t-test result is slightly more significant than that of standard segmentation (see Table 5).

[3] The 0-4 rating was analyzed as whole due to the small sample size of individual rating.

Table 4. The predictive validity test for total users with standard segmentation

Tests	Indicators	Test groups (standard)		T-test result (2-tailed)		
Test 1		Detractors(0-6)	Passives(7-8)	t	df	Sig.
	Repeat rate	59%	67%	-2.992	1160.0	0.003
	Vol. increase	42%	50%	-3.002	1210.5	0.003
	Val. increase	43%	53%	-3.581	1204.3	0.000
Test 2		Passives(7-8)	Promoters(9-10)	t	df	Sig.
	Repeat rate	67%	75%	-4.164	1617.8	0.000
	Vol. increase	50%	56%	-2.885	1728.6	0.004
	Val. increase	53%	58%	-2.453	1720.9	0.014
Test 3		Detractors(0-6)	Promoters(9-10)	t	df	Sig.
	Repeat rate	59%	75%	-6.798	869.5	0.000
	Vol. increase	42%	56%	-5.856	968.7	0.000
	Val. increase	43%	58%	-6.116	958.4	0.000

Table 5. The predictive validity test for total users with polarized segmentation

Tests	Indicators	Test groups (polarized)		T-test result (2-tailed)		
Test 1		Detractors(0-5)	Passives(6-9)	t	df	Sig.
	Repeat rate	57%	67%	-3.526	604.1	0.000
	Vol. increase	39%	50%	-3.74	642.7	0.000
	Val. increase	40%	53%	-4.464	639.3	0.000
Test 2		Passives(6-9)	Promoters(10)	t	df	Sig.
	Repeat rate	67%	76%	-4.912	2585.3	0.000
	Vol. increase	50%	56%	-3.29	2663.5	0.001
	Val. increase	53%	59%	-2.946	2659.1	0.003
Test 3		Detractors(0-5)	Promoters(10)	t	df	Sig.
	Repeat rate	57%	76%	-6.706	541.8	0.000
	Vol. increase	39%	56%	-6.043	605.7	0.000
	Val. increase	40%	59%	-6.525	1837	0.000

4.2 The Predictive Validity for New Users

Looking at the new users, overall the standard segmentation has yield good predictive validity, but it is better for detractors than promoters. The repeat purchase rate, volume and value increase of detractors are significantly lower than any of the other two groups. However, the volume and value changes between promoters and passives have no major difference though they differ in repeat purchase rate (see Table 6).

It should be noted that the tested volume increase between detractors and passives is not that obvious (sig.=0.046). Meanwhile, the test on volume decrease shows different results: no significant difference between them was found (detractors: 60%, passives: 53%, t=1.94, df=867.7, sig.=0.053).

Table 6. The predictive validity test for new users with standard segmentation

Tests	Indicators	Test groups (standard)		T-test result (2-tailed)		
Test 1		Detractors(0-6)	Passives(7-8)	t	df	Sig.
	Repeat rate	53%	60%	-2.31	849.4	0.021
	Vol. increase	39%	45%	-1.995	870.2	0.046
	Val. increase	40%	47%	-2.184	868.5	0.029
Test 2		Passives(7-8)	Promoters(9-10)	t	df	Sig.
	Repeat rate	60%	68%	-2.97	1114.8	0.003
	Vol. increase	45%	50%	-1.754	1162.7	**0.080**
	Val. increase	47%	52%	-1.585	1159.1	**0.113**
Test 3		Detractors(0-6)	Promoters(9-10)	t	df	Sig.
	Repeat rate	53%	68%	-5.184	695.1	0.000
	Vol. increase	39%	50%	-3.799	753.3	0.000
	Val. increase	40%	52%	-3.852	748.5	0.000

Fortunately, the polarized segmentation shows perfect predictive validity. In the subsequent 3 months, promoters (10 rating) shows significantly higher repeat purchase rate, purchase volume and value increase than passives (6-9 rating), and passives (6-9 rating) higher than detractors (0-5 rating) in all these indicators (see Table 7). This means, the polarized segmentation does improve the validity.

Table 7. The predictive validity test for new users with polarized segmentation

Test	Indicators	Test groups (polarized)		T-test result (2-tailed)		
Test 1		Detractors(0-5)	Passives(6-9)	t	df	Sig.
	Repeat rate	51%	59%	-2.49	461.0	0.013
	Vol. increase	36%	45%	-2.618	482.5	0.009
	Val. increase	37%	47%	-3.003	482.1	0.003
Test 2		Passives(6-9)	Promoters(10)	t	df	Sig.
	Repeat rate	59%	69%	-4.032	1660.6	0.000
	Vol. increase	45%	51%	-2.292	1676.6	0.022
	Val. increase	47%	52%	-2.201	1675.9	0.028
Test 3		Detractors(0-5)	Promoters(10)	t	df	Sig.
	Repeat rate	51%	69%	-5.292	431.8	0.000
	Vol. increase	36%	51%	-4.288	475.0	0.000
	Val. increase	37%	52%	-4.608	472.7	0.000

4.3 The Predictive Validity for Regular Users

Regarding the regular users, however, the predictability of the NPS with standard segmentation seems worse than that of new users. Although the promoters have significant behaviors changes compared with detractors in terms all the three indicators, the difference of promoters vs. passives, and passives vs. detractors are not obvious (see Table 8). For example, even among the detractors, 76% of them repeated purchase in the subsequent 3 months and nearly half of them increased their purchase volume, which has no major difference from the passives. The only difference is that less of detractors increased purchase value than passives, but the absolute rate is still very high (51%). Meanwhile, promoters did not show higher volume and value increase than passives, though they enjoyed higher repeat purchase rate.

Table 8. The predictive validity test for regular users with standard segmentation

Tests	Indicators	Test groups (standard)		T-test result (2-tailed)		
Test 1		Detractors(0-6)	Passives(7-8)	t	df	Sig.
	Repeat rate	76%	80%	-1.048	309.3	**0.295**
	Vol. increase	49%	58%	-1.919	325.0	**0.056**
	Val. increase	51%	64%	-2.589	317.8	0.010
Test 2		Passives(7-8)	Promoters(9-10)	t	df	Sig.
	Repeat rate	80%	86%	-2.184	512.8	0.029
	Vol. increase	58%	64%	-1.863	562.5	**0.063**
	Val. increase	64%	68%	-1.271	562.7	**0.204**
Test 3		Detractors(0-6)	Promoters(9-10)	t	df	Sig.
	Repeat rate	76%	86%	-2.778	213.6	0.006
	Vol. increase	49%	64%	-3.594	235.5	0.000
	Val. increase	51%	68%	-3.849	231.6	0.000

By using the refined segmentation with detractors polarized to the lower ratings of 0-5, the predictability does not change much except the improvement in predicting volume increase for promoters vs. passives (see Table 9).

The implication is, for regular users, their recommendation has little relation with their future purchase behaviors. Detractors, passives, and promoters all enjoy very high repeat purchase rate, volume increase and value increase. It is probably because buying groceries in this online supermarket has become a routine for them and they would not change their purchase channel even if they have some complaints.

Table 9. The predictive validity test for regular users with polarized segmentation

Tests	Indicators	Test groups (polarized)		T-test result (2-tailed)		
Test 1		Detractors(0-5)	Passives(6-8)	t	df	Sig.
	Repeat rate	73%	80%	-1.463	164.7	**0.145**
	Vol. increase	47%	57%	-1.934	463.0	**0.054**
	Val. increase	49%	63%	-2.571	174.0	0.011
Test 2		Passives(6-8)	Promoters(9-10)	t	df	Sig.
	Repeat rate	80%	86%	-2.266	639.7	0.024
	Vol. increase	57%	64%	-2.211	698.6	*0.027*
	Val. increase	63%	68%	-1.676	696.7	**0.094**
Test 3		Detractors(0-5)	Promoters(9-10)	t	df	Sig.
	Repeat rate	73%	86%	-2.827	129.9	0.005
	Vol. increase	47%	64%	-3.423	141.2	0.001
	Val. increase	49%	68%	-3.754	139.4	0.000

4.4 An Optimized Comparison between New Users and Regular Users

The above comparison between new users and regular users may be challenged if these two groups have different profiles. It is true that the new users and regular users are different in some aspects: there are more of females (56%), married people (59%) and elder people (21% aged above 35 y.o.) among regular users, whilst more of young (26% aged 25 y.o. and below) and single (54%) people within the new users.

To avoid the impacts of demographic difference on the test result, weighting on age and gender distributions within each of new users and regular has been done, which yielded similar sample structure in calculation.

Looking at the purchase behavior changes across promoters, passives, and detractors again and compare these changes between new users and regular users, we got the same result as before:

For the new users, the polarized segmentation again improved the predictive validity in all the three behavioral indicators; whilst for the regular users, both the standard and polarized segmentation fails to bring a perfect prediction on future purchase behaviors.

Therefore, even when new users and regular users have similar profiles, NPS still works better for new users than regular users[4].

4.5 The Difference in Promotion and Detraction Points

Given that the polarized segmentation may yield a better predictive validity, especially for new users, the promotion points between respondents with 9 and 10 rating may be different, and the detraction points between respondents with 0-5 and 6 rating may be different. Part of the hypothesis is proved in this research.

For the total respondents, respondents with 9 and 10 ratings have different agreements on 6 out of all the 30 promotion points, which means the strength of this online supermarket are different for promoters rating 9 and 10. However, in the 31 detraction points, only 2 of them have received different agreements between detractors rating 0-5 and 6.

For the new users, there come the similar findings: 5 out of 25 promotion points are different between promoters rating 9 and 10, whilst only 1 out of 20 detraction points differs between detractors rating 0-5 and 6.

For the regular users, however, the case is quite different. Only 1 out of 25 promotion points have different agreements between promotes of 9 and 10 rating. For the detraction points, such comparison is not feasible due to small sample size.

5 Conclusions and Discussions

5.1 Conclusions and Recommendations

In general, the hypothesis addressed at the beginning of this paper are mostly supported:

---

[4] Given the limited length of paper, test result with weighted data is not shown here. Please contact the authors if necessary.

NPS has relatively better predictive validity on subsequent purchase behaviors for new users than regular users. Considering that 63% of the respondents are new users in this study, it is not surprising to see the good predictability of NPS at total level. Therefore, it is recommended that NPS should be more promoted in business at developing stage. If used in the mature business, it is suggested to separate the analysis of new users and regular users whenever sample size allows, which will lead to different marketing implications.

To some extend, it is also proved that, in online surveys, a polarized segmentation of promoters/passives/detractors could make the NPS working better in predicting future loyalty behaviors, especially for new users. However, considering that this result is coming from only one case, we would rather suggest using standard segmentation at the very beginning and being open to alternative segments when necessary. Nevertheless, we do suggest separate the analysis of promotion points between respondents with 9 and 10 rating, and the analysis of detraction points across different the detractors as well. This may help to better understand the strength and weakness of our organization for different customers and thus yield more specific and practical marketing measures.

5.2 Discussions and Suggestions for Future Researches

Although most of the hypothesis has been proved in this case study, there remains some room for further exploration given the limitations of this research.

Firstly, the result of this research is only drawn from a customer satisfaction survey on FMCG e-commerce site. Whether this result is applicable for other categories or other business types is doubtful.

Secondly, this study only tested the predictive validity of purchase behaviors in 3 months right after the survey. However, whether NPS can predict behaviors in a longer period? In predicting behavioral changes of a longer period, will NPS works differently for new users and regular users? Can we suppose that NPS can better predict long-time changes of regular users and short-time changes of new users? All these questions are yet to be explored but can be done by continue tracking the purchase behaviors for a longer time.

Finally, the showcase in this study only contains one wave of survey. Therefore, it is not feasible to monitor the changes of "Net Promoter" score between new users and regular users, as well as its relation to their purchase behaviors. If possible, that will further strengthen the conclusion of this paper.

References

1. Blog of Verint, http://blog.verint.com/net-promoter-score-nps-criticisms-and-best-practices
2. Keiningham, T.L., Cooil, B., Andreassen, T.W., Aksoy, L.: A Longitudinal Examination of Net Promoter and Firm Revenue Growth. Journal of Marketing 71(3), 39–51 (2007)

3. Keiningham, T.L., Cooil, B., Aksoy, L., Andreassen, T.W., Weiner, J.: The Value of Different Customer Satisfaction and Loyalty Metrics in Predicting Customer Retention, Recommendation, and Share-of-wallet. Managing Service Quality 17(4), 361–384 (2007)
4. Owyang, J.: Enhancing Net Promoter Score (NPS) with Total Social Customer Value (TSCV). Web Strategy (June 20, 2010), http://www.web-strategist.com/blog/2010/06/20/enhancing-net-promoter-score-nps-with-total-social-customer-value-tscv/
5. Reichheld, F.F.: The Ultimate Question: Driving Good Profits and True Growth. Harvard Business School Press, Boston (2006)
6. Schneider, D., Berent, M., Thomas, R., Krosnick, J.: Measuring Customer Satisfaction and Loyalty: Improving the "Net-Promoter" Score. Paper Presented at the Annual Conference of the World Association for Public Opinion Research (WAPOR), Berlin, Germany (2007)

Visual Search on E-commerce Category Navigation: A Multi-language Study

Bin Liu, Lijuan Cao, Yumei Tang, and Ming Zhong

Alibaba.com & AliExpress.com, P.R. China
rock.liub@alibaba-inc.com

Abstract. E-commerce websites need effective category navigation especially when they need to be accessible to global users with multi-language backgrounds. An eye tracking laboratory study with English, Chinese, and Russian participants was conducted to investigate search behavior that influenced by different category level and layout design (vertical versus horizontal). The results showed that users employed different search strategies at different levels of categories, and they showed significant differences in search patterns on different layouts. The results also indicated the impact of language on search behavior. These findings provided useful considerations for visual research in category as well as implications for the category design of multi-language e-commerce websites.

Keywords: E-commerce, Category, Multi-language, Eye movements, Visual search.

1 Introduction

The global B2C market has been growing rapidly over the past 10 years. According to a report by Ystats.com, a research company for international market, global business to customer (B2C) e-commerce grows at 20% annually [28]. Emerging markets like China and Russia are leading the growth. In 2012, B2C e-Commerce in Russia has grown by over a quarter. Meanwhile in the third quarter 2013, the Chinese B2C e-commerce market reached 26.66 billion U.S. dollars [27].

However, People using e-commerce websites are frequently faced with the problem of finding products on a category due to inefficient category navigation systems. The major challenge is how to design screen layouts that people can search efficiently. Therefore it is important to understand how users search in the category navigation in order to improve the efficiency and effectiveness of e-commerce websites.

There are plenty of researches on visual search from the perspectives of cognitive psychology and eye movement, and areas cover widely such as search array, perceptual span, eye movement control, and eye movement models. However, visual search behaviors vary a lot depending on the search environment or search array [4,17]. Many of the previous studies were conducted in simulation experiment, or focused on evaluation of designs. Although several studies had shed lights on the visual search on

P.L.P. Rau (Ed.): CCD/HCII 2014, LNCS 8528, pp. 470–481, 2014.

menu [1,14,18], limited researches involve category, a special kind of search array. And there are few researches on multi-language category design. Therefore, visual search is worth further investigation on category in e-commerce website with multi-languages.

This study investigated user's information search behavior when navigating by category items on e-commerce websites within the context of three languages: English, Chinese, and Russian. We started out using eye tracking data to generate search pattern, to gain insight into users' visual search strategy.

2 Related Work

There has been an enormous amount of researches done on visual search, which is one of the major cognitive processing tasks (i.e. reading, visual search, and scene view) that has gained considerable attention over the past decades [4]. Researchers started to use eye tracking technology increasingly in recent years, since the eye movements have been considered as a very important way in understanding cognitive processing in visual search.

The most important factor about visual search is significantly influenced by the characteristics of the search array such as density. Complicated and cluttered array gives rise to more fixations and longer durations [4]. The structure and configuration of the search array can influence the target search efficiency. Other detailed factors such as color, shape, information type (target, distractor) also have effect on fixation position and duration [25]. Apart from array, several studies have tried to investigate the factors associated in eye movement control in visual search [8]. Various visual search models were proposed [7]. The models such as simple search model [15] and guided search model [5] discuss visual search patterns from cognitive and perceptual aspects. Hornof found that people use both random and systematic search strategies [11]. However, these researches were conducted in different visual environment, and there is no universal visual search pattern proposed so far.

2.1 Menu and Category Search

As a type of menu navigation, the category search study was originated from the research on menu, which is regarded as one of the most important visual components and has received increasing attention from researchers. The study of visual search on computer-based menu selection started from forty years ago [3]. Previous theories of menu search focused on the cognitive strategies. Unlike the eye movement pattern in reading narrative text, Aaltonen (1998) found that users read menus in sequential sweeps [1].

Plenty of researches focused on the menus style efficiency. The comparison between vertical menu and dynamic menu was conducted to investigate internal pattern [24]. The efficiency and accuracy study of vertical menus found that users needed less eye fixations, and can complete a search task faster in a vertical menu than in a horizontal menu [2,4]. The comparison of select time in array of digit numbers also indicates that users were quicker in vertical menus than in horizontal menus [26]. Other study about menu details like grouping navigation and group labels showed grouping allows users to access a large number of items with less mouse movement over a few levels [19], and group labels help visual processing [10]. Another eye tracking study found group labels affect users in determining menu reading scan paths [11].

There were other related researches about the manipulate factors which would likely have effect in designing a more reliable visual search experiment [9]. Design elements, including menu item content, the menu items order, the number of items, the items size and spacing, and menu item grouping can influence the menu efficiency. Users adopt diverse mechanisms in interacting with the online environment, and screen usage experience depends largely on the specific task (experiential, goal-directed) intended [12,13]. In addition, the practice effect was also found in target search menu experiment, the more users practice, the quicker they complete the search [15].

In recent years, the research interest on menu has shifted from traditional computer interface to web environment. And the eye tracking research has gradually become popular in investigating how users search on web pages [12]. However, among all the above, limited research involved category menu.

2.2 Linguistic and Semantic Influences on Visual Search

Over the past decades, people are increasingly aware of the various linguistic factors that influence eye fixations. Eye movement patterns like fixation duration and saccade length are directly linked to the difficulties of the text being read. The fixation duration on that word is also determined by the frequency, predictability, meanings, familiarity and semantic relations of the fixated word [17].

Furthermore, there are natural linguistic differences in people's search behavior online. The direction of the language, for example, is shown to influence how people scan and search information [16]. According to Dong and Salvendy (1999), for Chinese menu, Chinese users perform better on vertical layout than horizontal layout. However, when it comes to English menu, the same group of users responded faster when presented with a horizontal layout [6]. Mainland Chinese appear to flexibly adapt their search pattern to the layout of the screen. They used predominantly horizontal searches for row layouts and used vertical searches in column layouts [16]. But that is not applicable in all languages.

3 Hypothesis

Based on previous studies, we expected to find that users' category search behaviors are influenced by their language backgrounds and we held the following hypotheses: H1, Fixation durations are different at different category areas (areas refer to different category levels, target and non-target area for the search task). H2, The visual search strategies employed are influenced by category design. H2a, Users will show different saccade length at different levels of category. H2b, Users will show different saccade direction on vertical and horizontal layout category.

4 Method

In order to study the effects of language and navigation design on user visual search, a 3×2 design was used with the factors category (vertical, horizontal) and language (Chinese, Russian, English). The goal-directed search tasks were designed to uncover eye movement. The dependent variables of this study were eye movement control operationalized by fixation duration and saccade in different area of category menu during task execution, and other dependent variables were visual search strategy measured by calculating the saccade location in particular areas.

4.1 Participants

A total of 31 participants, including 10 native Chinese speakers (5 female, 5 male, M=21.4 years, SD=1.7, range: 19-24), 10 native English speakers (4 female, 6 male, M=20.2 years, range: 19-21), and 11 native Russian speakers (3 female, 8 male, M=20.7 years, range: 19-22) were recruited from Zhejiang university. They had normal or corrected-to-normal vision, and previously had at least one year experience of using e-commerce websites in their own countries. Participants were compensated for their participation.

4.2 Materials

The stimuli for this experiment were the HTML category prototypes to imitate the category menu in real e-commerce environment. A total of 379 category items were presented in the prototype. They were organized by eight top-level categories. Each of them was furthermore divided into four groups, and for each group there were eight to twelve secondary-level category items. Three language versions, that is, English, Chinese and Russian prototypes were created. All items were originally in English with reference to several top e-commerce websites (AliExpress.com, eBay.com, and Amazon.com). The Russian and Chinese versions were translated from the English version without changing its structure or content. The wordings were based on the items used in local e-commerce websites (OZON.ru and Taobao.com), and also double checked by native speakers. The average width of category items of Chinese were ranged from 12 to 96 pixels (M=39.29, SD=14.29), English were ranged from 14 to 171 pixels (M=76.94, SD=35.16), and Russian were ranged from 22 to 191 pixels (M=94.51, SD=40.55).

For each language, we created two designs (horizontal layout and vertical layout) (see Fig. 1). To eliminate the order and memory effects, a program was written to create HTML prototype webpages with randomized item position within the category hierarchy. 16 (tasks per layout) ×2 (layout) ×3 (language) factorial prototypes were generated so that each experimental task was conducted on an exclusive prototypes. The web style of prototypes was based on AliExpress website with a consideration of the menu design guidelines proposed by Mayhew (1992) [21]. Both design layouts shared the same elements style, such as font, line-height, and the width of secondary level category menu. The category items are evenly spaced out. The space between each secondary item in the horizontal layout is 20 pixels.

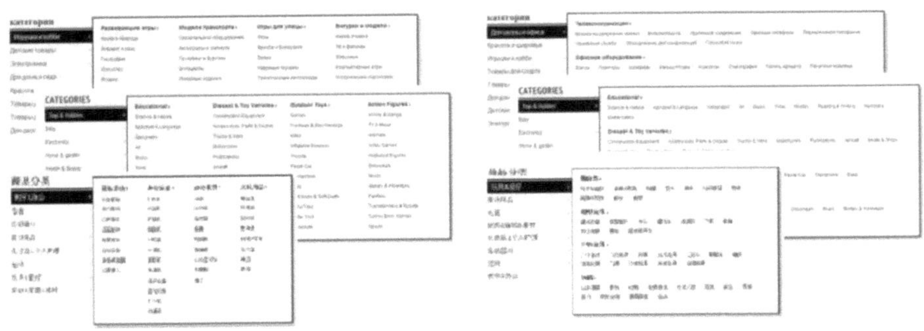

Fig. 1. Samples of horizontal and vertical category designs

4.3 Procedure

After a short introduction about the experiment procedure, participants were briefed with a list of items (such as, basketball, digital camera) they were going to search to prevent misunderstandings caused by semantic reasons. The instructions and prototypes were also in the subjects' native language. They were then asked to perform 32 search tasks with a short break in the middle, during which they need to find and click the best semantically matched target category on the prototype.

4.4 Data Collection and Reduction

Eye-tracking data were recorded by a Tobii T60 eye-tracker with screen resolution of 1280×1024, and were processed with Tobii Studio software. Raw data were exported and processed using MATLAB programs to extract user performance and behavior variables.

In our analysis, the category design was divided into the following areas (see Fig. 2): top-level (A), group titles of secondary-level category (B), non-target secondary-level category (C), target secondary-level category (D), and search target item (E).

All data were aggregated and averaged over all tasks on both the horizontal prototype and the vertical prototype conducted by an individual user. The data we collected focused on the fixation duration, saccade length, and saccade location. A fixation was recorded when a user fixated an area with a radius of 35 pixels for at least 100 ms.

On the top of that, the last fixation before click and the last fixation before the courser moving to the secondary level category were excluded. The reason is that these fixations were accompanied by decision process for navigation and mouse movement and thus were significantly longer than the other fixations during visual search. Saccade length was calculated based on the numbers of items user jumped (how many items between two fixations). For top-level and secondary-level in vertical layout, the saccades in Y coordinate are divided by the item line height. For the secondary level in vertical layout, the saccades in X coordinate are divided by the average category item width. And the saccade directions were measured based on the percentage of saccade from secondary level to the same group, to the other groups, and to the group titles respectively.

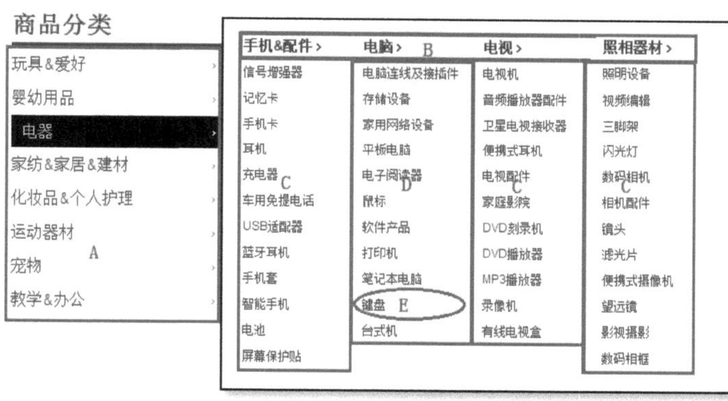

Fig. 2. Sample of area definitions in category design

5 Results

5.1 Fixation Durations

An analysis of repeated measures was conducted to evaluate average duration of fixations with category levels (top level, secondary level) as within-subjects factors and languages as between-subjects factors. This revealed a significant main effect of category level, F (1, 28) = 24.925, p<.001, indicating that the fixation duration on top level were significantly longer than that on the secondary level. There was also a significant main effect of language, F (2, 28) = 7.491, p<.01, indicating that fixation duration were significantly different in language condition. And the levels × language interaction was also significant, F (2, 28) = 6.711, p<.01, indicating that English and Russian users take longer when processing the top level category, while Chinese users didn't show any significant difference. The means and standard deviations for each of the groups are reported in Table 1.

Table 1. Average duration (ms) of fixations on two level categories

	Chinese	English	Russian
Top level category	397(14)	396(14)	340(10)
Secondary level category	384(16)	328(7)	321(10)

An analysis of repeated measures was conducted to evaluate average duration of fixations with searching area (target, non-target) on category, as within-subjects factors, and languages as between-subjects factors. There was a significant main effect of searching area, $F(1, 28) = 34.874$, $p<.001$, and a significant main effect of language $F(2, 28) = 5.474$, $p<.05$, and also a significant interaction $F(2, 28) = 5.223$, $p<0.05$. This indicated that Chinese and English users have longer fixation duration on target category area than in non-target area, while Russian users didn't show any significant difference. The means and standard deviations for each of the groups are reported in Table 2.

Table 2. Average duration (ms) of fixations on target and non-target area

	Chinese	English	Russian
Target category area	399(13)	346(13)	328(13)
Non-target category area	345(12)	310(12)	318(11)

5.2 Saccade Length

A Kruskal-Wallis test was conducted to evaluate differences among the three groups (Chinese, Russian, English) on average saccade length (number of items) on the top level category ($\chi2(2)=19.374$, $p<.001$), on vertical secondary level category ($\chi2(2)=5.737$, $p>.05$), and on horizontal secondary level category ($\chi2(2)=22.229$, $p<.001$) (See Table 3). Follow-up Mann-Whitney tests indicated that Russian users' saccade lengths are shorter than Chinese and English users on the top level category, and the saccade lengths of Chinese users are longer than that of English users and longer than Russian users on the horizontal secondary level category. A Wilcoxon signed-rank test showed that there was a statistically significant different saccade length between top level and secondary level for all languages.

Table 3. Saccade length (measured by the number of menu items)

	Chinese	English	Russian
Top level	1.75 (0.03)	1.90 (0.10)	1.27 (0.07)
Secondary level (Vertical)	2.76 (0.09)	2.77 (0.13)	2.41 (0.12)
Secondary level (Horizontal)	1.62 (0.06)	1.11 (0.05)	0.95 (0.03)

5.3 Saccade Direction

The saccades from secondary level were divided into the following types: to the same category group (A), to the other groups (B), and to the group titles (C) (see Fig. 3). And Fig. 4 shows the percentage of saccade direction of each group respectively.

An analysis of repeated measures was conducted to evaluate average saccade directions (from group to group titles) with layouts (vertical, horizontal) as within-subjects factors, and language (Chinese, English, and Russian) as between-subjects factors. There was a significant main effect of saccade directions, $F(1, 28) = 4.567$, $p<.05$, indicating that there are more saccades from secondary category group to group title in horizontal layout than in vertical layout. However, there was no significant main effect of language ($F(2, 28) = 0.442$, $p=.647$) and interaction between the two factors ($F(2, 28) = 0.297$, $p=.745$).

An analysis of repeated measures was conducted to evaluate average saccade directions (from group to other groups) with layouts (vertical, horizontal) as within-subjects factors, and language (Chinese, English, Russian) as between-subjects factors. There was a significant main effect of saccade directions, $F(1, 28) = 17.120$, $p<.001$, indicating that there are more saccade from secondary category group to other groups in vertical layout than in horizontal layout. However, there was no significant main effect of language ($F(2, 28) = 0.913$, $p=.413$) and interaction between the two factors ($F(2, 28) = 2.125$, $p=.138$).

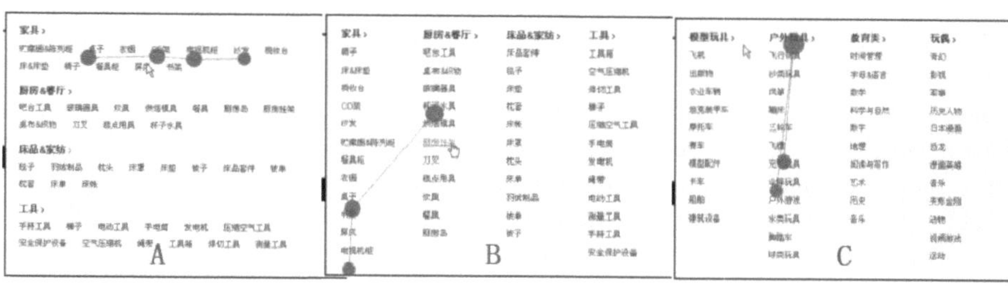

Fig. 3. Samples of the saccade direction on the secondary level category

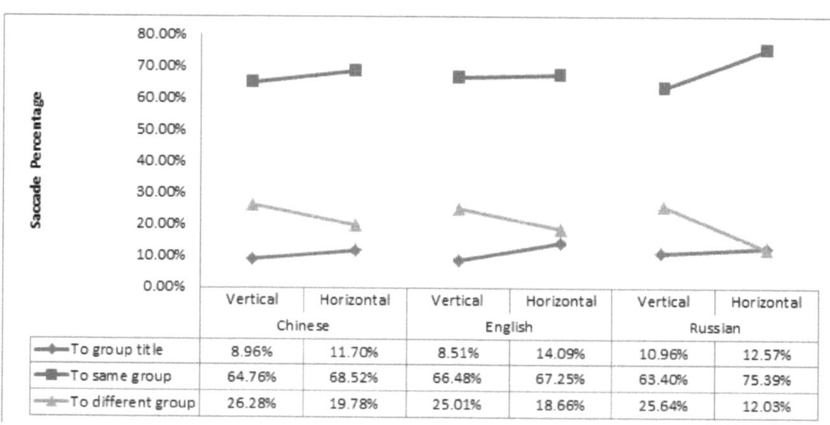

	Chinese		English		Russian	
	Vertical	Horizontal	Vertical	Horizontal	Vertical	Horizontal
To group title	8.96%	11.70%	8.51%	14.09%	10.96%	12.57%
To same group	64.76%	68.52%	66.48%	67.25%	63.40%	75.39%
To different group	26.28%	19.78%	25.01%	18.66%	25.64%	12.03%

Fig. 4. Percentage of saccade direction on secondary level category

6 Discussion

Comparisons on eye fixations between different levels in this study supports that the fixation durations are different at different category areas (H1). Previous research argued that fixation duration is longer on complicated search array [23]. It is contrary to see in this case that fixation durations on the top level items that are less complicated than the secondary category items are longer. Since cognitive processes associated fixated words are important to the fixation duration [4], it is improper to judge fixation duration only based on visual complexity in search. Moreover, there is no measurement of reading difficulty among all category items, which can lead to different fixation duration. From a semantic point of view, the words in the top category are the superordinate terms which are more general and higher in the semantic hierarchy while the secondary category words are the subordinate terms which are more concrete and are lower in the semantic hierarchy. As words higher in the hierarchy have wider scope than those they dominate, it takes longer to comprehend and process, which, in this case, result in longer fixation stay in the top category.

In addition, comparisons between fixation durations in target and non-target areas provided further support to (H1). In the targeted area, all words belong to the same semantic field and carry similar semantic meanings when comparing with words in other groups. The search task requires users to find and select the best semantically matched (either identical match or close approximation) item. Users need to distinguish target from distractors and determine whether it is the desired one or not. Previous studies have pointed out that during searching tasks, users distinguish targets from distractors based on primary features such as shape, size, and orientation [22]. This experiment provided furthermore evidence that the semantic relationship in the array is another fundamental feature for user to distinguish.

H2 states that visual search strategies employed are influenced by category design. This experiment figured out where to look next in category from two main saccade features: direction and extent. The data analysis used number of items as a unit and used saccade location to examine interpretable eye movement patterns. Hornof and Kieras (1997) reported that people process more than one menu item at a time and the average saccade length in vertical direction was 2.21 menu items [11]. Our results demonstrate that the saccade lengths are not fixed. The reason of shorter saccade lengths in the top level category was due to the semantic reason rather than the search array complicity. The higher in semantic hierarchy, the more cognitive workload required and the shorter saccade lengths will be. Furthermore, saccade length varied a lot across different languages. The language influences are especially noticeable on horizontal layout. The reading direction of the Chinese, English, and Russian are congruent, the widths of the words are different. The results indicate that the shorter language word width the more category items covered in one saccade, which may related to the visual search efficiency. Hypothesis (H2a) was confirmed by the findings above.

From the quantitative fixation location data, it is obviously to see that most visual search follow the direction of the category layout within the same group. Most of previous researches focused on the efficiency comparisons of vertical and horizontal layout, however, our study emphasized on the search path. Previous research found that group labels play an important role in facilitating visual processing [13,19], because grouping will introduce another level of search. When titles are presented, an initial search conducted can only examine the group headings to determine whether reading more group items [10]. Our experiment result illustrated how group titles used in searching tasks is largely influenced by the layout. User during visual search rely more on group titles on horizontal layout, while on vertical layout, with better aliment cues, they tend to do direct searches between groups. Thus, we conclude that our data is in accordance with the hypothesis (H2b) that design layout affect users' visual search direction on category navigations.

A limitation of our work was the limited number of participants in our study cannot provide persuasive support for the conclusion associated with the language factor. Another limitation was uncontrolled web elements related to language which can also affect fixations, saccades and regressions such as typographical variables [20]. As far as our prototypes concerned, the participants were novices and their search pattern might be different with experienced users. More research will be needed to validate those differences in the future.

7 Conclusion

This study provides new theoretical and practical insights into the elementary visual search pattern in e-commerce category navigations. The results showed that the semantic scope of the fixated word and semantic relationship in the array have an effect on fixation durations and saccade lengths in visual search. On category design with horizontal layout, the search saccade lengths are highly associated with the language factor which indicated that menu layout is language-sensitive. Different language patterns are observed. Significant differences in search patterns (saccade direction) on different layouts are also found. Insights provided in this study have implications for both fundamental visual search study and improvements in the practical e-commerce category design.

Acknowledgements. We would like to show our sincere gratitude to our colleague Zhao Chen for her valuable reviews and suggestions and the Alibaba International User Research team for their dedicated support and contribution to this paper.

References

1. Aaltonen, A., Hyrskykari, A., Räihä, K.-J.: 101 Spots, or How Do Users Read Menus? In: Proceedings of the SIGCHI Conference on Human Factors in Computing Systems, CHI 1998, vol. 42, pp. 132–139 (1998)
2. Backs, R.W., Walrath, L.C., Hancock, G.A.: Comparison of horizontal and vertical menu formats. In: Proceedings of the Human Factors and Ergonomics Society Annual Meeting, vol. 31, pp. 715–717. SAGE Publications (1987)

3. Card, S.K.: Visual search of computer command menus. Attention and Performance X: Control of Language Processes, pp. 97–108 (1984)
4. Castelhano, M.S., Rayner, K.: Eye movements during reading, visual search, and scene perception: An overview. In: Cognitive and Cultural Influences on Eye Movements, vol. 2175, p. 46 (2009)
5. Cave, K.R., Wolfe, J.M.: Modeling the role of parallel processing in visual search. Cognitive Psychology 22(2), 225–271 (1990)
6. Dong, J., Salvendy, G.: Designing menus for the Chinese population: horizontal or vertical? Behaviour & Information Technology 18(6), 467–471 (1999)
7. Eckstein, M.P.: Visual search: A retrospective. Journal of Vision (2011)
8. Greene, H.H.: The control of fixation duration in visual search. Perception 35(3), 303–315 (2006)
9. Hornof, A.J.: Computational models of the perceptual, cognitive, and motor processes involved in the visual search of pull-down menus and computer screens. Dissertation Abstracts International: Section B: The Sciences and Engineering. ProQuest Information & Learning, US (2000)
10. Hornof, A.J.: Visual search and mouse-pointing in labeled versus unlabeled two-dimensional visual hierarchies. ACM Transactions on Computer-Human Interaction (2001)
11. Hornof, A.J., Kieras, D.E.: Cognitive modeling reveals menu search in both random and systematic. In: Proceedings of the SIGCHI Conference on Human Factors in Computing Systems, CHI 1997, pp. 107–114 (1997)
12. Jacob, R.J.K., Karn, K.S.: Eye tracking in human-computer interaction and usability research: Ready to deliver the promises. Work 2(3), 573–605 (2003)
13. Leuthold, S., Schmutz, P., Bargas-Avila, J.A., Tuch, A.N., Opwis, K.: Vertical versus dynamic menus on the world wide web: Eye tracking study measuring the influence of menu design and task complexity on user performance and subjective preference. Computers in Human Behavior 27(1), 459–472 (2011)
14. MacGregor, J.N., Lee, E.: Menu search: Random or systematic? International Journal of ManMachine Studies 26(5), 627–631 (1987)
15. Neisser, U.: Decision-time without reaction-time: Experiments in visual scanning. The American Journal of Psychology 76(3), 376–385 (1963)
16. Plocher, T.A., Choong, Y.-Y.: Cross-cultural Design for IT Products and Services, vol. 36. CRC Press (2012)
17. Rayner, K.: The Thirty Fifth Sir Frederick Bartlett Lecture: Eye movements and attention in reading, scene perception, and visual search. Quarterly Journal of Experimental Psychology 62(8), 1457–1506 (2009)
18. Shen, M., Tao, R., Liu, Y.: A study on visual search and selection of pull-down menu. Hang Tian Yi Xue Yu Yi Xue Gong Cheng Space Medicine Medical Engineering 16(1), 72–74 (2003)
19. Shneiderman, B., Plaisant, C.: Designing the User Interface: Strategies for Effective Human-Computer Interaction, 4th edn. Pearson Addison Wesley (2004)
20. Slattery, T.J., Rayner, K.: The Influence of Text Legibility on Eye Movements During Reading. Applied Cognitive Psychology 24, 1129–1148 (2010)
21. Smith, S.L., Mosier, J.N.: Guidelines for designing user interface software, Citeseer (1986)
22. Treisman, A.: Features and objects in visual processing. Scientific American 255(5), 114–125 (1986)
23. Vlaskamp, B.N.S., Hooge, I.T.C.: Crowding degrades saccadic search performance. Vision Research 46(3), 417–425 (2006)

24. Ware, C.: Visual thinking: For design. Morgan Kaufmann (2010)
25. Williams, C.C., Henderson, J.M., Zacks, R.T.: Incidental visual memory for targets and distractors in visual search. Perception & Psychophysics 67(5), 816–827 (2005)
26. Woodward, R.M.: Proximity and direction of arrangement in numeric displays. Human Factors: The Journal of the Human Factors and Ergonomics Society 14(4), 337–343 (1972)
27. Xinhuanet. China's B2C e-commerce market booms in Q3 (2014), http://news.xinhuanet.com/english/china/2013-10/29/c_132841948.htm (retrieved February 4, 2014)
28. Ystats. Global B2C E-Commerce Sales & Shares Report (2014), http://ystats.com/en/reports/preview.php?reportId=1040 (retrieved February 4, 2014)

Older Adults' Online Shopping Behavior in China

Caiyue Shen, Lian Zhou, and Shuching Lin

Taobao (China) Software Co., LTD, Xixi Park, 969 Wenyixi Road,
Yuhang District, Hangzhou, Zhejiang, P.R. China
ziyuan.scy@alibaba-inc.com,
{lingluo,shujing.lsj}@taobao.com

Abstract. The purpose of this study was to investigate the online shopping behavior of older adults in China. Participants were members of Taobao, aged 50-65. We observed the following interesting behaviors: For many, tablets or mobile phones are rarely used. "Search" is often used when they shop online. The participants are accustomed to search and rarely know of other webpages that can be browsed. Sometimes, the participants may get lost when multiple webpages are opened; then, they typically close all of the webpages and have to start again from the beginning. Additionally, the participants ask few questions, even if they have some difficulty in browsing a webpage. All of these behaviors can be explained by the attentional cognition of older adults.

Keywords: Older adults in China, Online shopping, Consumer behavior.

1 Introduction

1.1 The Present State of the Chinese Aging Population

With a large population, China has been experiencing its first aging population peak since 2012. By the end of 2012, the aging population in China increased by 8.91 million over 2011, accounting for 14.3% of the total population. The population reached 202 million in 2013, accounting for 14.8% of the total population[1]. The Chinese aging population is expecting an accelerated growth in the 30 years after 2011. By 2030, the portion of the Chinese population that is aged 65 and older will have overtaken that of Japan, accounting for 20.43% of the total population; China will then officially become the nation with the largest percentage of aged population in the world. By 2050, China will enter an advanced stage of aging society[2].

1.2 Lifestyle and Market Potential of Chinese Older Adults

With the increase of aging adults, the physical and mental functions in older adults are changing. Older adults experience mental and physical deterioration with age, including the decline of vision, auditory function, of responsibility, memory loss, and learning ability[3-4]. The life patterns of older adults also change after retirement. Looking for new spiritual sustenance and social responsibility, the empty nesters are trying to take care of their grandchildren because of their tedious lives and the lack of emotional communication.

P.L.P. Rau (Ed.): CCD/HCII 2014, LNCS 8528, pp. 482–488, 2014.

Chinese society is concerned with endowment as China is becoming an aging and well-off society. To cope with this serious situation, the State Council published "The Twelfth Five Year Plan to Develop Chinese Endowment" in September 2011, emphasizing the aim to resolve pensions, medical care, mental health, and the accomplishment and pleasure problems of older adults. Older Chinese adults are demanding more from the market, thus making the aged market in China the largest in the world. It is roughly estimated that the total income of older adults has reached 400 billion in 2011 and will most likely top 1 trillion in 2020[5]. How to guide older adults consumer to spend, especially on online shopping, has become an important trend for the future.

1.3 Chinese Older Adults and Online Shopping

As the population of Chinese netizens increases with the popularity of the internet, so does the population of the older netizens; 6.2% of Chinese citizens were older than 50 by the end of 2012, an increase of 1.4% over that in 2011. The Internet is rapidly becoming popular among older adults (as shown in Figure 1) [6], making this population a major sources of growth in the Chinese netizen population.

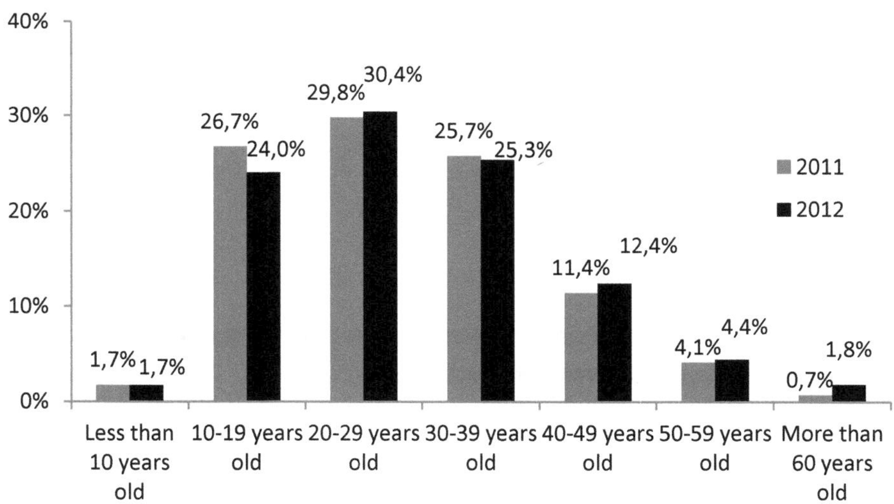

Fig. 1. Age Structure of Chinese netizen (Source: The 31st Statistical Report on Internet Development in China, CNNIC, 2013.1)

Consumers are becoming "older" in the online shopping market. The proportion of consumers over 40 has increased by 4.6% over that in 2011 to a new level of 10.2% in 2012. Comparatively, consumers under 30 are exhibiting a relative decline in their proportion, especially those between 18 and 24, who dropped 7.2% in user ratio (as shown in Figure 2)[7]. Older adults are contributing more than youngsters to on-line shopping.

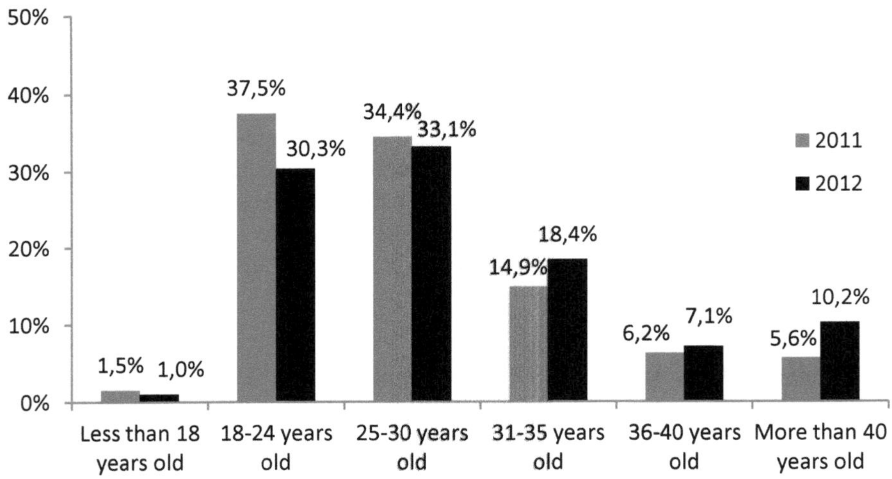

Fig. 2. Age Structure of On-line Shoppers (Source: Studies on Chinese On-line Shopping Market, 2012, CNNIC, 2013.1)

Being the biggest on-line retail service provider in APEC and the most popular on-line shopping platform in China, Taobao has approximately 500 million registered members with a user penetration rate of 88.1%, ranking 1st among various on-line shopping websites in China, 2012[7]. The subjects who were investigated in this paper are mainly older adults who shop on Taobao. By studying their on-line shopping behavior, we have located several difficulties and obstacles for older adults, which will be illustrated in the paper.

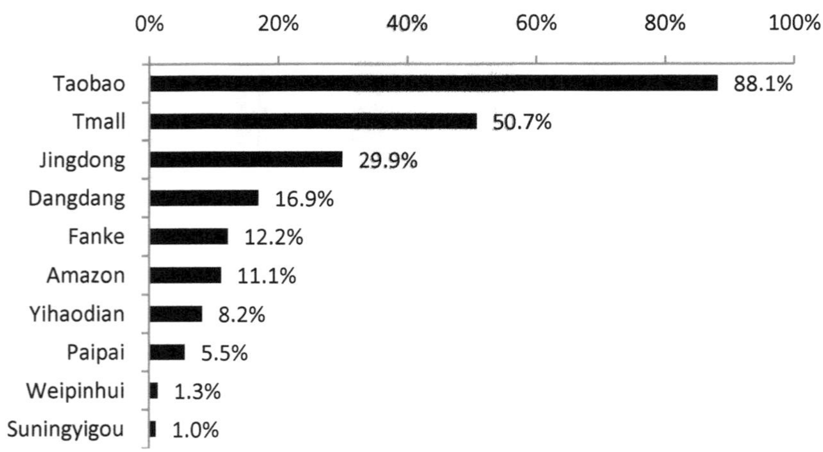

Fig. 3. User Penetration Rate of Major On-line shopping Websites in China (Source: Studies on Chinese On-line Shopping Market, 2012, CNNIC, 2013.1)

1.4 Practical Significance of the Study

Studies of the aged around the world focus mainly on the fields of social security and physical products. However, there is little research on online shopping behaviors in that segment of populations worldwide. This study is important for two main reasons:

First, studies on older adults and their needs are important. It is unclear that how these older adults shop online. By understanding the characteristics of older adults' online shopping features and e-commerce, websites are able to develop a more older-adult-friendly interface.

Second, the study explores the consumer habits and behavior of older adults and their difficulties as well as needs. Expressing more concern for older adults and introducing new lifestyle and concepts of older adults has a practical significance for the development of Chinese ageing industry.

2 Design

This study was conducted to explore older adults' shopping behavior in Taobao, to optimize the existing products, and to build a platform that is suitable for older adults' shopping.

Methods. Household interviews and observation methods were utilized to obtain more real information. The subjects can shop as they usually do, and they may be more comfortable in their house than in our laboratory. Additionally, we can assess the consumer's actual living environment, which is helpful for understanding the values of these elderly consumers. This type of information complements the interview data.

Participants. The major research subjects are older adults who are members of Taobao, the largest e-commercial company in China. Subjects are aged from 50-65 years. Many aspects were considered before choosing the range from 50-65: first, many people retire when they are 50 years old, and they have enough time for entertainment and are relatively wealthy. Second, the major members of Taobao are under the age of 65. They can live on their own and can shop online independently. In our research, subjects were 8 older adults (4 women and 4 men, aged 50-65 years old) who were members of Taobao; all have bought something online in the last 3 months (between 2013.4 and 2013.6). All eight subjects live in Hangzhou.

Procedures. Before the formal interview, we invited the participants into the study by telephone. To obtain some information that is more contextualized, valuable and real, we chose a household interview with their permission. For the household interview, we first chat with them about the first time they learned about the internet and online shopping, and why and how they shop online and so on. Then, the subjects shop online as they usually so that we could obtain more real and accurate information. The entire process was recorded with the subjects' permission. Each household interview lasted 2-3 hours.

Analysis. Qualitative Analysis method

Findings. Based on the observations, several typical behaviors were observed:

Behavior 1. A habitual way of online shopping regarding login-in and browsing the web was observed. Some people are accustomed to login from the homepage, whereas others login from Aliwangwang (a type of instant messaging tool); even if more convenient options were provided, they still chose the path to which they were accustomed. All of older adults people in this study use the search.

Behavior 2. Recommendation information is popular with older adults. The recommendation information may come from children, friends or unofficial platforms such as QQ (an instant messaging tool in China). This trend is opposite to that seen in young people. In our previous research, we found young people do not prefer recommendations, which are considered to be advertisement.

Behavior 3. The subjects easily got lost in Taobao. After they opened numerous webpages, it was not easy for them to go back to the previous page. Then, an interesting behavior emerged: the subjects closed all of the webpages and began browsing again from the start.

Behavior 4. It is difficult to adapt to changing functions. Before our current research, the webpage of Taojinbi (a kind of virtual currency.) was redesigned. However, older people we interviewed did not adapt to the changes and did not know how to navigate the re-designed page.

Behavior 5. The older subjects complained less than young people. An interesting phenomenon is that the older users do more internal attribution when problems arise. This is in contrast to the attitude of young people; based on our previous studies, young consumers complain more about the web site.

Behavior 6. only some goods is bought on the internet. Not all the goods is bought on the internet. They buy some clothes, some socks, foods and so on. Different people have different choices, but these goods that older adults bought on the internet have similar characteristics: Low price, novelty, not easily broken and so on. This behavior in young people is consistent with behavior in older adults.

From our interview with eight subjects, older adults choose online shoping may have several reasons: the direct reason is influenced by family or friends who often shop online, which change attitudes towards online shopping. The important reason is that online shopping has many advantages that are the shortages of the mall. For example, they can do shopping online at any time, can buy cheaper goods, and can enjoy convenient logistics, etc. All the above factors were introduced also by Ziqi Liao & Michael TC (2001) research[8].

Based on the interview, the above behavior can be explained by the following factors:

Factor 1. The lack of effective official propaganda. Over the past few years, Taobao implemented less marketing, and some special shopping channels have had limited exposure, which decreases the chance of older adults online shoppers finding something new.

Factor 2. Little knowledge of Taobao. Older adults adults know that Taobao is a place to shop online, but they do not know the rules and special shopping available at Taobao. They still adopt the original methods of online shopping, which include searching and paying attention to recommendations, amongst others.

Factor 3. The decline of fluid intelligence. With the increasing age of these subjects, the ability to learn new knowledge decreases. It is difficult for older people to learn and to adapt to changes on the internet. The relative lack of attentional resources and the decline of allocation attention have been shown in previous research. According to the theory of limited attention, attention is a finite resource. As age increases, attentional resources decrease[9-11]. When older people shop online at Taobao, they pay more attention to information about goods and pay little attention to other information such as the path and the rules, so that they show habitual ways of shopping and easily get lost.

Factor 4. The perceived risks on online shopping. The perceived risks in the process of trading affect older adults' online shopping, such as they are worried about the quality risk, payment risk and logistics risk[12-13], etc. Thus, older adults may buy particular goods on the internet, and they don't buy valuables goods on the internet, such as iphone, ipad and so on.

Based on the behavior and cognitive characteristics of older people, some suggestions for a platform that is suitable for their shopping habit are as follows:

First, fix the position of the search box and unify the design or the logic of the search box. A good search is better for reducing the cognition load.

Second, optimize the shopping path and maintain the unity of the page design. It is necessary to minimize the chance of getting lost.

Third, establishing a shopping guide website for these older adults, so that their preferences can reduce the cognitive load.

Fourth, improve marketing. Improvement in the marketing is urgently needed and includes the rules, safety awareness, and special shopping webpages, so that the possibility of misunderstanding will be minimized, especially for inexperienced old people, because inappropriate misunderstandings may discourage the enthusiasm of online shoppers, which will not be conducive to the development of the online shopping market in older adults.

In this study, some interesting behavior has been discovered. The research fills a gap which has existed in our online shopping study, and initiates us into the problems of older adults' online shopping in China. However, it is worth thinking deeply about that how we fill the gap between the behavior of older adults and the design of platform suitable for older adults.

In future, older adults' online shopping will be paid more attention, such as the affecting factors will be discussed, which can be discussed in Blanca Hernández

(2011)[14] , but cultural differences maybe exist in different countries. We can study whether there are gender differences or age difference on older adults' behavior, which will be conductive to the establishment of platform. The gender and the age difference have been in our research agenda. In addition, our current research uses older adults who are experienced with computers as our subjects. However, many older adults who are inexperienced with computers desire an online shopping experience but find that using the internet is difficult. Determining how to meet the needs of these people is still a challenge.

References

1. Wu, Y.: China Aging Development Report. Social Sciences Academic Press (2013) (in Chinese)
2. Gao, P.: China's Fiscal Policy Report. China Financial and Economic Publishing Institute (2011) (in Chinese)
3. Ebersole, P., Hess, P., Luggen, A.: Toward Healthy Aging: Human Needs and Nursing Response, St Louis. Mosby, MO (2004)
4. Maylor, E.A., Carter, S.M., Hallett, E.L.: Preserved olfactory cuing of autobiographical memories in old age. The Journals of Gerontology Series B: Psychological Sciences and Social Sciences 57(1), P41–P46 (2002)
5. Cai, C.: Development model and strategy analysis of pension tourist resort. China Tourism News (2011) (in Chinese)
6. China Internet Network Information Center. The 31st Statistical Report on Internet Development in China (2013) (in Chinese)
7. China Internet Network Information Center. The research report on China's online shopping in 2012 (2013) (in Chinese)
8. Liao, Z., Michael, T.C.: Internet-based e-shopping and consumer attitudes: an empirical study. Information & Management 38(5), 299–306 (2001)
9. Kahneman, D.: Attention and Effort. Prentice-Hall (1973)
10. Maylor, E.A., Lavie, N.: The influence of perceptual load on age differences in selective attention. Psychology and Aging 13(4), 563 (1998)
11. Luo, T., Jiao, S.: A Comparison Between Age-related Differences of Attention Allocation and Selective Attention. Psychological Science 27(6), 1307–1309 (2004) (in Chinese)
12. Cases, A.S.: Perceived risk and risk-reduction strategies in Internet shopping. The International Review of Retail, Distribution and Consumer Research 12(4), 375–394 (2002)
13. Crespo, A.H., del Bosque, I.R., de los Salmones Sanchez, M.G.: The influence of perceived risk on Internet shopping behavior: a multidimensional perspective. Journal of Risk Research 12(2), 259–277 (2009)
14. Hernández, B., Jiménez, J., José Martín, M.: Age, gender and income: do they really moderate online shopping behaviour? Online Information Review 35(1), 113–133 (2011)

Behavior Study on Consumer Driven e-Commerce

Yanxia Yang and Grace Deng

TWYWI Consulting, San Jose, CA, USA
marsha_yang@yahoo.com, graceyd2006@gmail.com

Abstract. The growth of internet availability and rise of affordable express parcel delivery services for the general public in China has greatly impacted people's consumer behavior. More and more consumers have joined in on the growing market of online shopping and e-commerce. One group of these consumers prefer searching through various websites, combing through different products and prices, then deciding on what to purchase after comparing and contrasting offers from competing merchants. Another group would rather plan out their purchasing requirements, such as maximum price limit or ideal brand, and let others fulfill their order. Yet others, in order to save both time and effort, decide to join in on group purchasing for group discounts and better package deals. E-commerce users are found in all age groups and among those living in both first class and second tier cities. To serve these various groups of consumers, e-commerce businesses take several forms, ranging from B2C, C2b, and F2C (from factory to consumer). In order to better understand the evolving consumer behavior in China and examine the shopping preference among the different age groups, we designed and conducted an ethnographic study in Shanghai, China to explore the following questions: the various situations in which consumers use different styles of shopping, their specific shopping preferences and concerns, and the various roles that each factor plays in their decision-making process. This paper is a case study that illustrates the different user behaviors across these different age groups of e-commerce consumers.

Keywords: e-commerce, B2C, C2B, F2C, Age group user study, international, consumer behavior.

1 Introduction

With the widespread availability of internet access, online shopping and e-commerce is quickly becoming an important part of daily life in the Chinese economy. According to statistics from iResearch [1], the GMV for the China e-commerce market is estimated steadily grow at an average of 20% per year and reach 21.6 trillion Yuan by 2017, revealing that more and more consumers are choosing to shop and browse online for purchasing products and services. The growth of the e-commerce market is further boosted by the rise of courier and express delivery services, which offers fast shipping and handling services, as well as ensuring a consistent and reliable delivery time for parcels.

P.L.P. Rau (Ed.): CCD/HCII 2014, LNCS 8528, pp. 489–497, 2014.

Furthermore, it has been observed that with the stressful fast-paced lifestyles, especially in urban communities, online shopping has become more popular and convenient amongst young and middle-aged consumers. With less time available to browse and compare products in actual stores, these consumers turn to e-commerce businesses to purchase many of their necessities at a reasonable price, which provide the simplicity of one-stop shopping. In addition, the increasing cost of living, a common phenomenon in first tier cities such as Beijing and Shanghai, and the demand for lower prices have provided further motivation for consumers to join in on group packages and discounts offered by e-commerce vendors.

Our goal in this study is to obtain a better understanding of consumer needs and behaviors in online shopping and e-commerce. This study was conducted in Shanghai, China through a survey of 86 randomly chosen candidates in order to explore the following topics: How will these technological developments and advancements impact the online behavior of consumers? How does online consumer behavior vary across different age groups of users and across different types of e-commerce business models?

2 Background and Hypothesis

The growth of online retail transaction in China had reached 899 billion Yuan by 2011, an increase of 72% [2]. Meanwhile, online shopping users had reached 194 million users. In one year, retail transaction had reached 1300 billion Yuan, increasing nearly 65% by 2012. And by the first quarter of 2013, the total e-commerce transaction in China had reached 2400 billion Yuan, an increase of 45%. On November 11 of 2013, the single day retail transaction on Tao Bao (an e-commerce site) had exceeded 30 billion Yuan, the equivalent of Wal-Mart's sales for half a year in China. The number of e-commerce businesses in China is steadily growing and can be illustrated in the Figure below.

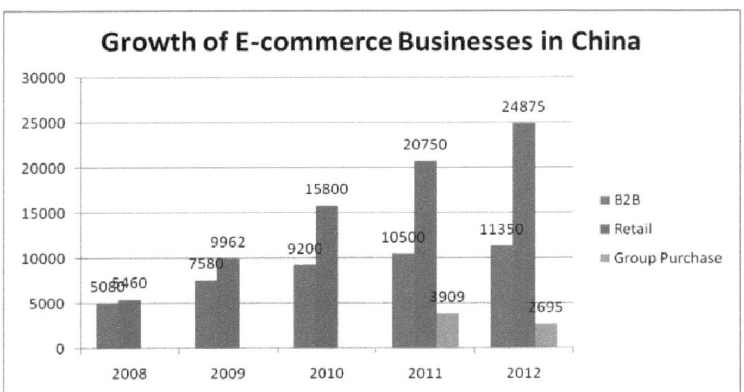

Fig. 1. Growth of E-commerce Businesses in China [2]

As demonstrated by Figure 1, using data provided by China Industry Information (chyxx.com), there is a steady rise in the number of e-commerce businesses in China, ranging from business-to-business, retail, and group purchase business models. Of the three categories, the number of retail e-commerce businesses shows the highest rate of growth, while group purchase businesses have only begun establishing since 2011. The pattern of growth observed, especially in retail, show that not only is there a high consumer demand for online shopping, but that this style of shopping is quickly integrating into the daily lives of many consumers.

Due to the fast growth of e-commerce, many Express Delivery Services (EDS) companies have established and expanded their business, and consumers no longer need to be concerned about the shipping costs and the delivery time. Many young people are more familiar with express delivery services than the actual post offices, due to the convenience that EDS offers by picking up the parcel directly from their home within one hour of a phone call. The order procedure is simple as well: a person merely has to complete an online shipping order or initiate an order by phone, and the parcel will arrive within 2-3 business days to his or her designated destination.

Based on a report from ChinaIRN, the number of daily EDS orders in China reached 25 million, of which 15 million are from e-Commerce [4]. The figure below indicates the growth of EDS.

Fig. 2. 2008-2013 Earnings for Express Delivery Services for Online Retail in China [5]

We expect that along with the rapid growth of e-commerce and express delivery services, the consumer behavior of China's online shoppers is also evolving, and their life style is also changing because of the convenience provided by technology growth [6, 7]. We hypothesize that out of five types of e-Commerce business models, the older age groups from thirty to thirty-nine and forty and above will prefer the traditional business-to-consumer model, while the younger 20s age group will prefer using consumer-to-business model.

3 Methodology

In order to confirm or reject our research hypothesis, a web survey was designed and conducted in Shanghai, China. Included in this survey are a broad range of questions that cover factors such as the various situations in which consumers use different styles of shopping, their specific shopping preferences and concerns, and the various roles that each factor plays in their decision-making process.

The questionnaire was sent to statistical research services for reviewing and proofreading after it was written to ensure that there would be minimal bias in the syntax and diction of the questions. The statistical research services was then responsible for sending the questionnaire to a number of trustworthy websites to be filled out by a fixed number of internet users. By varying the types of websites the questionnaire was sent to, we hoped to ensure that the respondents we surveyed would be from a random and diverse population. When each age group reached over 25 respondents, the survey was closed and removed from the internet, and the resulting data was compiled and analyzed.

We had a total of 86 respondents overall who fully completed the survey. Before a respondent is taken to the survey webpage, we inserted a notice to request that the respondent not fill out the questionnaire if he or she had already completed it through a different website. Therefore, it is safe to assume that each of the responses is valid and not repetitive. In addition, we strived to make sure that the responses were reliable and based on experience to minimize the error of our results by presenting the survey to respondents who were frequent e-commerce users. We assume that the sample population of eighty-six e-commerce users will be a large enough and representative sample. We will also assume that the survey responses are independent of each other because it is unlikely that the response of one consumer will affect that of another consumer.

Table 1. Demographical Breakdown of Respondents by Age

	20~29	30~39	>40
Female	14	17	14
Male	15	14	12
Total	29	31	26

As illustrated by Table 1, there is an approximately equal distribution of respondents across the three different age groups, and slightly more females than males in the 30-40 age group and >40 age group.

Table 2 below summarizes the different categories of business models included in the survey, as well as sample questions for each category that were given to respondents.

Table 2. Sample Survey and Questions Used in Study

Business Model	Questions
Business to Consumer (B2C)	1. I enjoy comparing and contrasting different products and prices over the internet. 2. I enjoy looking through advertisements to find the upcoming sales and best deals. 3. I prefer going to websites such as Tao Bao, etc. to find what I want to buy. 4. I prefer sticking to the websites that sell the types of product that I usually use. 5. I usually go to the same website for the same type of products, such as electronics, books, furniture, etc.
Consumer to Business (C2B)	1. I like getting exactly the product that I asked for. 2. I want to save time by not browsing through all the offers and deals on big e-commerce websites. 3. I enjoy purchasing customized and personalized styles of and additions to products. 4. I dislike looking through advertisements and being bombarded by advertisement pop-ups while surfing through internet. 5. I think that spending time combing through catalogues online is a waste of time. 6. I feel that business should serve my needs.
Factory to Consumer (F2C)	1. I often buy specific brands from the brand's personal website. 2. I expect lower prices from products that sold directly from the brand's website. 3. I have membership for several of my favorite brands in order to earn reward points.
Group Business to Consumer (Group B2C)	1. I enjoy the discounts offered by group purchase deals and packages. 2. I usually look for group discounts before looking at individual retail prices. 3. I use group discounts for services such as dining, traveling, and entertainment.
Group Consumer to Business (Group C2B)	1. I expect vendors to offer lower prices if I purchase as part of a group for the same product. 2. I often organize a group of friends to purchase the same product together and negotiate with the vendor or store. 3. My friends and I purchase the same product together in order to negotiate with the vendor or store. 4. I join groups when paying for services such as traveling, entertainment, and hotels.

4 Findings

The findings of our experiment were based on the eighty-six responses to questions about the five types of business models: business to consumer (B2C), consumer to business (C2B), factory to consumer (F2C), group business to consumer (Group B2C), and group consumer to business (Group C2B).

4.1 The Five e-Commerce Business Models

The business to consumer model represents the typical business model based on transactions between business and consumers [3], and where vendors advertise their products to consumers in the hopes of making a sale. In e-commerce, these businesses often advertise their products through online catalogs and databases, and potential buyers can surf through these lists over the internet before deciding on what to purchase. Examples of the business to consumer model include online banking and investing, food and entertainment, and transportation such as airplane tickets.

The consumer to business model, also called reverse auction, is where the consumer becomes the seller and the merchant or vendor becomes the buyer [3], thus switching places compared to the traditional business to consumer model. Consumers can place a maximum or minimum bound on the price of the product or service that he wants, and different businesses compete with each other to bid for the right to provide the consumer with the specified product or service, usually through offering lower prices than what the consumer is willing to pay. In this model, consumers take the initiative instead of the businesses by specifically listing what their needs.

The factory to consumer model refers to the business model where manufacturers and consumers interact directly, thus eliminating the middleman services such as retail stores. In this model, consumers can directly order products and goods from the manufacturer, and receive generous discounts or deals, especially when purchasing in large quantities. These products, however, are often limited to the specific brands that are produced by the factory.

The group business to consumer model refers to when businesses offer special discounts and package deals for a group of consumers purchasing the same product or for an individual consumer purchasing one product in large quantities. These deals are often posted on websites dedicated to offering group discounts from various vendors. Newly established businesses and lesser known businesses often use these group offers as a method of market promotion and brand name building.

The group consumer to business model is very similar to the group business to consumer model, except that the positions of consumers and businesses are inversed. Consumers that want to buy the same product or service join together to form a group, then jointly negotiate with vendors for a better deal than the current market price. These "similar interest" groups can also simply state what product they want to buy and how much in quantity, and different retailers will compete for the sale transaction by offering lower prices than the group's initially stated price of what they are willing to pay.

4.2 Age Group 20-29

This age group is adventurous and willing to try online shopping on websites from all the business models. They are dedicated to showing off their unique personality and individuality through customized products and gadgets, yet also concerned with saving money through group discounts and purchases. In addition, they believe that businesses should cater to their needs and preferences.

Some statistics:

- 82.7% enjoy purchasing customized and personalized styles of and additions to products
- 68.9% believe that businesses should serve consumers when they specify what they want
- 58.6% enjoy comparing and contrasting different products and prices over the internet.
- 48.3% organize a group of friends to purchase the same product together and negotiate with the vendor or store

4.3 Age Group 30-39

This age group grew up with the rise of the internet age and is the most adept at using online shopping to solve their everyday needs. They use online shopping for almost everything, from products to services, and are happy to browse and search through online catalogs for what they require. They are slightly conservative, staying with the traditional business to consumer model, but are also frequent users of websites that offer group packages and deals, which are often much cheaper than the current market price.

Some statistics:

- 90.3% use group discounts for both products and services such as dining, traveling, and entertainment
- 83.9% enjoy looking through advertisements and catalogs to find the upcoming sales and best deals
- 77.4% prefer to go to websites such as Tao Bao, where a variety of products are offered for sale, rather than a website for a specific type of product (such as furniture or electronics)

4.4 Age Group 40+

This group is perhaps the most traditional compared to the rest. Although they use the internet for work and communication, they do not always choose online shopping and often prefer to go to the actual store to observe the actual product quality and price before purchasing. When shopping online, they mostly stick with business to consumer model websites. Since price is usually a major consideration, they will consider group packages as well, especially for large transactions such as traveling and airplane tickets.

Some statistics:

- 88.5% feel that it is important to compare prices, quality, and reviews of products before purchasing online
- 69.2% prefer sticking to the websites that sell the types of product that they usually use
- 73.1% dislike looking through advertisements and being bombarded by advertisement pop-ups while surfing through internet

5 Conclusion

Through observing the results and statistics, it can be concluded that the age group from twenty to twenty-nine are an ideal target group for consumer driven e-commerce. They are willing to try out all types of e-commerce business models. This analysis is backed by several real life observations. Growing up with the internet integrating with all parts of daily life, they are comfortable with the convenience provided by online shopping and express delivery services. With their fast paced lifestyle and the sea of information provided by the internet, they are unwilling to spend much time browsing and comparing different products and their respective prices. As a result, they prefer consumer driven e-commerce, where they list their requested items or services, and businesses will automatically fulfill these orders within their price limit. Using the services of courier and express delivery, these items can be quickly shipped to the comforts of their home. Finally, they take advantage of social networks [8] to form groups and participate in group discounts and sales offered by vendors.

In comparison, the age group from thirty to thirty-nine is more loyal to the traditional B2C e-commerce model, while the forty and above age group use both internet and physical stores.

In conclusion, the e-commerce market holds vast potential for future growth as the number of online consumers steadily increases. The results of this case study serves to both explore the evolving consumer behavior across different age groups and provide comments on how the various e-commerce business models can be enhanced to better accommodate the needs and preferences of a growing generation of internet shoppers.

References

1. GMV of Chin E-commerce Market Surges to a Landmark 9.9Tn Yuan in 2013, iResearch (January 2014)
2. 2013 Summary of Current and Historical Development of e-commerce in China, China Industry Information chyxx.com (2013)
3. "e-Commerce Models", eServGlobal (2013)
4. 2013 Express Delivery Services Industry Development Analysis, ChinaIRN (2013)
5. China e-Commerce Research Center, 100EC.CN (2013)

6. Phneah, E.: China to Overtake US in e-Commerce in (August 2013)
7. Goddard, P.H., et al.: Five Dimension of User Experience: Balancing business and user experience perspectives to create successful e-commerce sites. Human Factors International
8. Swamynathan, G., et al.: Does social networks improve e-commerce?: A study on Social Marketplaces. In: WOSN 2008, Seattle, Washington, USA (August 18, 2008)

What Chinese Female Online Shoppers Need

A Case Study by Applying the Kano Model in E-Commerce

Zhibo Yin, Lingxiao Zhang, Xinheng Fan, and Wei Li

Taobao (China) Software Co., Ltd.,
Hangzhou, Zhejiang, P.R. China
jianhong@taobao.com

Abstract. Chinese females always become confused by the "more goods, harder choice" principle when they are shopping online without a definite shopping goal. Taobao wants to provide a high quality shopping guide in its women's market to solve this problem. Before the Taobao women's market is established, we should urgently answer the question of which shopping guide functions should be prioritized most highly? In the past, we solved this problem by using the experience of the web-site operator. However, that the website operator plays a decisive role is a very subjective judgment, and the risk cannot be estimated in advance. The Kano model is good at solving the priority problem of functions. Thus, we selected the Kano model for this study. We evaluated 27 shopping guide functions and used them to prioritize the functions of Chinese female consumers' shopping, which provided an important reference basis for the presentation of a new web page and web page design for the Taobao women's market. A total of 19 shopping guide functions have been realized in the Taobao women's market homepage, and each shopping guide function plays a different role. This study fills in the blanks around how the Kano model may be applied in the field of e-commerce.

Keywords: Kano model, e-commerce, Chinese female consumers, shopping online, no definite shopping goals, shopping guide, Taobao women's market.

1 Introduction

Contemporary e-commerce in China has been increasing at a dramatic rate with the rapid development of the internet. In 2013, China's online shopping market reached 1.85 trillion RMB with 42 percent growth, and online shopping captured 7.8% of the total social retail sales market[1]. At the same time, online shopping has become a hot, daily topic for Chinese female consumers. In the Taobao trade platform, for example, more than forty percent of active sellers' business categories are directly related to Chinese female online shoppers, such as women's clothing and skin care. Both from the perspectives of consumer's and merchants' data, the influence of Chinese women in e-commerce is obvious.

P.L.P. Rau (Ed.): CCD/HCII 2014, LNCS 8528, pp. 498–508, 2014.

1.1 Shopping Guide Problems Experienced by Chinese Females When Online Shopping

While dealing with a great deal of merchandise supplied by e-commerce websites, consumers with definite shopping goals can use search functions to find their goods satisfactorily. Usually, however, Chinese women do not have definite goals while shopping online. Hence, many e-commerce companies, such as Mogujie and Meilishuo, seize market share by launching a shopping guide service to promote purchases. However, Chinese females are always puzzled by the "more goods, harder choice" principle when they are shopping online. This puzzle has attracted the attention of e-commerce website managers, who have attempted to solve this problem by providing high quality shopping guides. The Taobao company is no exception, and it has sought to improve the shopping guide experience of Chinese female online shoppers by establishing the Taobao women's market.

The so-called e-commerce shopping guide found on websites helps consumers to complete shopping decision-making processes by providing specific functions (including evoking requirements, collecting information, evaluating information and deciding purchases). Website operators first focus on the conundrum that there are so many shopping guide utilities, which should be used first? Thus, before establishing the Taobao women's market, we should preferentially answer the question about how different shopping guide functions should be prioritized.

In the past, we solved this problem by using the experience of the website operator. However, that manner of solving the problem had two disadvantages. First, that the experience of the website operator plays the decisive role requires a subjective judgment. Second, the risk cannot be estimated in advance, be caused to happen or occur as a consequence. To estimate the risk in advance and to generate more stable, accurate data, we introduced a research model in this study.

1.2 Introduction and Selection of the Kano Model

Many function-need assessment models exist; one of the most famous and widely used is the Kano model (Kano, 1984) [4]. The Kano model is good at solving the priority problem of functions. The outcome of the Kano model is stable and re-useable; thus, we chose the Kano model to research shopping guide functions of the Taobao women's market to solve the business problem. This represents the first time that the Kano model has been used in an e-commerce practical application.

Functional Classification of the Kano Model. According to the algorithm of the Kano model, as shown in table 1, the function of the product can be divided into five categories.

Table 1. Evaluation table for classifying quality attributes using the Kano questionnaire (Kano,1984)

Attribute is fulfilled	Attribute is not fulfilled				
	Satisfied	It should be that way	I am indiffe-rent	I can live with it	Dissatisfied
Satisfied	Q	A	A	A	O
It should be that way	R	I	I	I	M
I am indifferent	R	I	I	I	M
I can live with it	R	I	I	I	M
Dissatisfied	R	R	R	R	Q

Notes: M:must-be, O:one-dimensional, A:attractive, I:indifferent, R:reverse, Q:questionable.

Different categories influence consumer experience to various degrees, and the influences of the qualities in decreasing order is as follows: Must-Be, One-Dimensional, Attractive, Indifferent and Reverse.

According to the one-dimensional quality theory, in situations where an attribute is fulfilled, the customer will tend to feel satisfied. However, when the impact on satisfaction is not proportional, the fulfillment of this attribute will not increase customer satisfaction; instead, non-fulfillment of it will result in dissatisfaction. This represents the Must-Be quality. In situations in which an attribute is not fulfilled, the customer will tend to feel dissatisfied; however, if the impact on dissatisfaction is not proportional, the non-fulfillment of this attribute will not increase customer dissatisfaction. In other words, it will lead to customer satisfaction when fulfilled, but it will not result in customer dissatisfaction when not fulfilled. This is the Attractive quality. In situations in which the quality element results in neither satisfaction nor dissatisfaction, whether fulfilled or not, we have the Indifferent quality. In situations in which the quality element results in dissatisfaction when fulfilled and in satisfaction when not fulfilled, we have the Reverse quality. Fig. 1 illustrates the concept of the non-linear relationship of performance and satisfaction in Kano's two-dimensional quality model. Because the Reverse quality does not represent a legitimate customer need in real world practice, this study focuses on a discussion of the first four qualities: Must-Be, One-Dimensional, Attractive and Indifferent.

The Kano Model's Better–Worse Coefficient Analysis and Functional Sequences. Based on the percentage of the categorizations of functional requirements, and according to the calculation formula of the Kano model's quality, as proposed by Berger (1993) [5], we can obtain the Kano model's Better–Worse coefficient. Better coefficients can be interpreted as satisfaction coefficients; after increases in functions, user satisfaction will rise; the larger the positive value, the more user satisfaction will rise and the more quickly it will rise. The Worse coefficient can be conceptualized as a dissatisfaction coefficient; it shows that, if there is no function or the function is

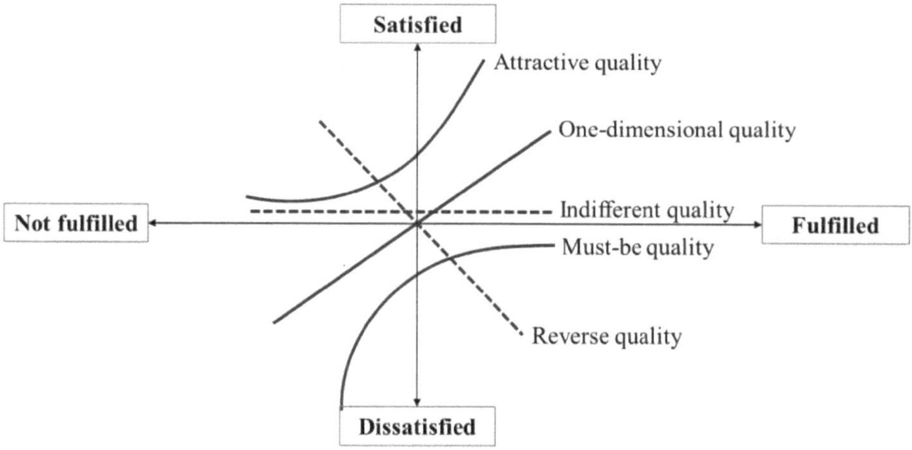

Fig. 1. Kano's two-dimensional quality model (Berger et al., 1993)

eliminated, user satisfaction decreases; the more negative the value, the more user satisfaction declines and the faster it declines. We can combine these two coefficients to obtain the functional sequences. The higher the Better coefficient value, the higher the priority the function has. With the Better coefficient value holding steady, functional sequences increase the worse coefficient value, and the lower Worse coefficient value, the lower priority [5] .

2 Method

2.1 The Questionnaire Design

Function Selection of the Shopping Guide. We used competitive products analysis to determine which functions of shopping guides should be selected. First, considering the status quo of Chinese female online shopping, we chose 19 typical e-commerce websites of four types on which to perform a competitive products analysis, such as Tmall, JD of B2C type, and Mogujie, Meilishuo of Advisory shopping guide website type etc. These selections are shown in Table 2.

Table 2. Names and classification of e-commerce websites of four types

Classification	Detailed names of websites
B2C	Tmall、JD、Amazon、Dangdang、Jumei、Vip、Moonbasa、Glamouar、Suning、Yintai
C2C	TaoBao、Ymatou、Paipai
Brand's official website	Uniqlo、Only
Advisory shopping guide website	Mogujie、Meilishuo、Guang、Xiangqu

Second, we extracted and defined the guide function of the competing products' websites (the non-involvement of the search function, the details shown with merchandise, online payment and other aspects of functional analysis). Considering the similarities and differences between the functions, we extracted 72 specific functions. At the same time, all of the functions were redefined to ensure that each function could be accurately recognized by Chinese women. This extraction produced a challenge insofar as 72 functions far exceeded what has been considered in previous studies investigating the Kano model; meanwhile, we could not obtain valid data.

To solve this problem, we used expert assessment to select the most valuable features of those functions, including two user research experts and two website operator experts. Each expert was weighted equally. The assessment dimensions included the following: 1) the degree of coincidence between shopping guide functions and the Taobao women's market orientation and 2) how the shopping guide function might contribute to the market value. The assessment scores ranged from 1 to 5, with higher scores indicating more qualified representations to the target market and higher contributions to the market value. Ultimately, 27 shopping guide functions' score exceeded 6 points; these were selected to be investigated in the questionnaire. These findings are summarized in Table 3.

Table 3. 27 shopping guide functions and their scores by competitive products analysis

Function	Score	Function	Score
Age guide	7（4，3）	Location guide	6（3，3）
Appearance classification	8（4，4）	Material classification	10（5，5）
Body type guide	8（5，3）	My wardrobe	8（4，4）
Color classification	8（4，4）	My XX home page	6（3，3）
Commodity categories	10（5，5）	New arrivals guide	8（4，4）
Commodity using effects classification	7（3，4）	Public praise recommendation	10（5，5）
Common people try on/trial	10（5，5）	Purpose-specific guide	6（3，3）
Experienced shopper's recommendation	10（5，5）	Seasons classification	6（3，3）
Fashion trends section	8（4，4）	Size assistant tool	10（5，5）
Features recommendation	10（5，5）	Size classification	10（5，5）
Festivals guide	7（4，3）	Style classification	9（5，4）
Friends share/recommendation	8（5，3）	Using occasion guide	9（4，5）
Incentive rebates recommendation	6（3，3）	Workmanship classification	7（4，3）
Match function	10（5，5）		

The Questionnaire Content. The questionnaire included three aspects: 1) the basic consumer shopping situation (e.g., the Taobao Shopping common mode/frequency/ scene); 2) the shopping guide functions (in accordance with the requirements of the Kano questionnaire, users were asked to evaluate how well the site provided this function on a 1 to 5 scale, with options of "Satisfied," "It should be that way," "I am indifferent," "I can live with it," and "Dissatisfied"; and 3) the consumers' basic information (e.g., gender, age, education).

2.2 Questionnaire Administration

From 9:30 on August 26, 2013 to approximately 9:30 on August 27, 2013, we placed the questionnaire on the Taobao homepage, and consumers were invited to click the link to respond to the questionnaire.

2.3 Data Recycling

After 24 hours of data collection, we had collected 26,912 raw data entries. After rigorous data cleaning, we obtained 14,483 valid responses from Chinese women consumers.

2.4 Data Analysis

Functional Requirements Classification. On the basis of this large set of valid data, we classified the functions of a shopping guide according to a data analysis of the Kano model.

Through confirmed functional requirements classification following the Kano model, we proposed a new analysis algorithm.

Upon initiating the research using the Kano model, researchers identify the quality that the largest number of respondents selected as the classification of one function. To classify the results more accurately, some researchers introduce the chi-square test and choose the larger of two quality dimensions for significance testing. If the difference is not significant, according to the M>O>A>I priority order, the quality of the function is classified. If the difference is significant, it is ensured that the sum of the largest proportion of quality as the functional requirements classification.

However, we found that the chi-square test results were affected by the sample size. First, if the sample size was too little, it would have a large error and the results would need to undergo further calculation correction. Second, if the sample size was large enough, the results would be significantly different in theory and would lead to selection of the quality with the largest number of people as the final functional requirements classification.

Focusing on the above problems, we used the sample proportion test(reflecting a condition of small sample size) and the quality convergence figure (a Matlab program that we wrote for a situation representing a largeenough sample size) methods to determine the combined function requirements classification, which successfully reduced the influence of the sample size on the result.

Function Priority Order. First, we assessed according to the functional classification of M>O>A>I priority. For the same classified internal function, we synthesized Better-Worse coefficients and then sorted further. Finally, we obtained the prioritization of all of the functional requirements.

Table 4. Kano model's results

Functional classification	Order	Shopping Guide Function	Better coefficient	Worse coefficient
One-Dimensional quality(10)	1	Common people try on/trial	0.8012	-0.5578
	2	Public praise recommendation	0.7437	-0.4669
	3	Size assistant tool	0.7007	-0.4286
	4	Commodity using effects classification	0.6774	-0.4376
	5	Appearance classification	0.6772	-0.4676
	6	Material classification	0.6681	-0.4524
	7	Seasons classification	0.6650	-0.5206
	8	Size classification	0.6636	-0.5525
	9	Color classification	0.6108	-0.4168
	10	Commodity categories	0.5849	-0.5002
Attractive quality(12)	1	Match function	0.7260	-0.3006
	2	My wardrobe	0.7052	-0.3427
	3	New arrivals guide	0.7036	-0.3339
	4	Style classification	0.6724	-0.3671
	5	Incentive rebates recommendation	0.6573	-0.2890
	6	Using occasion guide	0.6549	-0.3473
	7	Body type guide	0.6471	-0.2867
	8	Festivals guide	0.6388	-0.3122
	9	Purpose-specific guide	0.6376	-0.3030
	10	Features recommendation	0.6278	-0.2683
	11	Fashion trends section	0.6236	-0.3421
	12	Age guide	0.6164	-0.3372
Indifferent quality(5)	1	Experienced shopper's recommendations	0.5317	-0.1735
	2	Location guide	0.5250	-0.2358
	3	Workmanship classification	0.5136	-0.2594
	4	Friends share/recommendation	0.4723	-0.1509
	5	My XX home page	0.4718	-0.1941

3 The Kano Model's Results

The functions' priorities in the Taobao women's market are shown in table 4. From the 27 functions of the shopping guide, 10 functions belonged to the One-Dimensional quality. These functions had the most impact on women's market experiences. If these functions were provided, satisfaction was found to directly improve; if not, satisfaction was found to decrease, and it would be suggested to implement these functions. Furthermore, according to sorting the Better–Worse coefficients, 3 of the 10 One-Dimensional quality functions that fell into the former category were "Common people try on/trial," "Public praise recommendation," and the "Size assistant tool."

12 reflected the Attractive quality: if these functions were provided, it enhanced user satisfaction; if not, it did not affect the user's experience. These functions act as "surprise" functions provided to consumers, and they might be selected according to the actual situation of a business.

5 belonged to the Indifference quality and had no direct effects on customer satisfaction. These might be weighed according to the actual situation of a business.

4 The Application of the Kano Model's Results

In addition to the user researchers, web site operators, product managers, designers, and engineers all participate in the Taobao women's market. The manner in which specific functions on the page are applied is shown in figure 2.

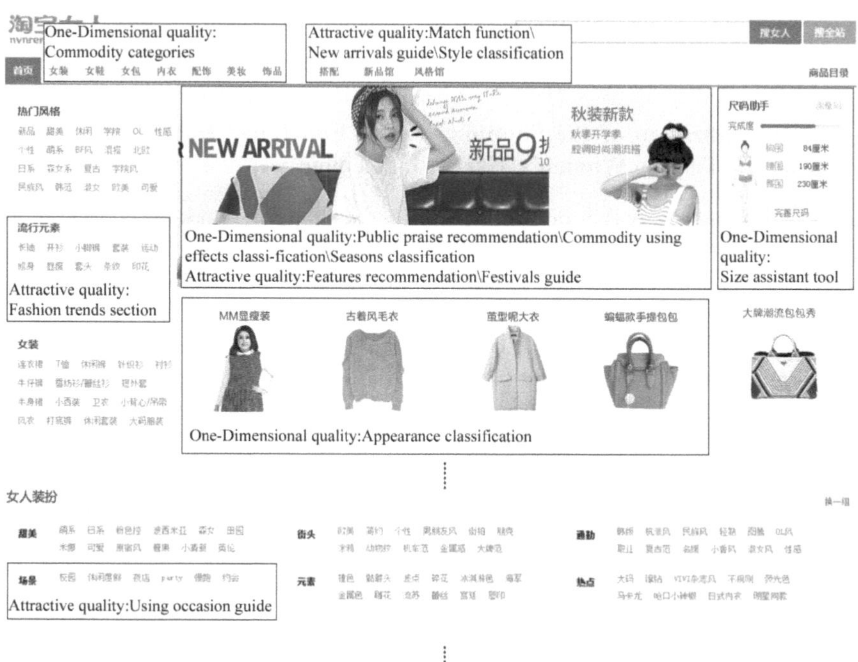

Fig. 2. The realization of shopping guide functions on the Taobao women's market homepage

4.1 The Realization of Shopping Guide Functions' One-Dimensional Quality: 6 on the Taobao Women's Market Homepage and 4 through Relevant Pages

10 shopping guide functions reflecting One-Dimensional quality have been applied on the Taobao women's market to ensure the most fundamental experiences on the page. The "Public praise recommendations", "Size assistant tool", "Commodity using effects classification", "Appearance classification", "Seasons classification" and "Commodity categories" have substantial influences on demand in the early stages of the consumer arousal and are reflected on the homepage of the Taobao women's market. Material, color and size are inherent attributes of commodity, as is the dimension "Common people try on/trial" which consumers think about at a later stage in the shopping guide decision-making process. This reflects the continuous operation of consumers, which is continued through secondary and other pages of the market.

4.2 The Realization of the Shopping Guide Functions' Attractive Quality: 7 on the Taobao Women's Market Homepage

To guide consumers' shopping and to create a characteristic of the Taobao women's market, the market focuses on attractive quality shopping guide functions. There are 7 attractive qualities shown in the Taobao women's market homepage: "Match function", "New arrivals guide", "Style classification", "Using occasion guide", "Festivals guide", "Features recommendation" and "Fashion trends section". As the influence of match on Chinese females increases, "Match function" gradually will become one of the core functions of the Taobao women's market.

4.3 The Realization of the Shopping Guide Functions' Indifference Quality: 2 on the Taobao Women's Market Homepage

The Taobao women's market does not abandon the shopping guide functions' indifference quality. Consumers can see abundant Social Network Site (SNS) information and news to explore SNS's value in the Taobao women's market. Now, "Experienced shopper's recommendation" and "My XX homepage", which reflect the indifference quality, have been realized in the Taobao women's market. Discussion

The applications of this research show that the Kano model can solve the problem of function priority in e-commerce. It can also be applied at present to a new web page and web page design. The results of the Kano model are available in and applicable to the field of e-commerce. In addition to the content presented in the application, the Kano model has further room for development in the field of e-commerce.

4.4 The Extended Application of Research Results

The Results of the Kano Model Help Improve Drainage Efficiency. E-commerce websites often have difficulty in introducing new UV. Through the Kano model, we can obtain the largest function point that affects customer satisfaction. Furthermore, we can focus on these functions to improve drainage efficiency. In Kano model research, larger Better coefficients indicate that user satisfaction can be more greatly promoted. Through the use of the Better coefficient to order functions, we can obtain functions that have the largest influences on consumer satisfaction. For example, when the Taobao women's market, as shown in table 4, is in the process of introducing new UV, it can pay more attention to the "Common people try on/trial", "Public praise recommendation", "Match function", "My wardrobe" and "New arrivals guide."

The Results of the Kano Model Help Realize Personalized Service. In this research, nearly 70% Chinese female customers under 26 years of age regard the Age guide as having an attractive quality; in contrast, nearly 30% Chinese female customers above 27 years old regard the Age guide as having an indifferent quality. Female customers grow with different needs at different stage, so the Taobao women's market should consider personalized services combining user characteristics. To make a bold prediction, we suggest further consideration be based on this study's findings to form specific products' direct applications on corresponding pages and to match customers' needs based on data we obtain to provide the fittest content, thereby boosting the ability to meet the "varied people, varied content"(Precise personalized recommendations and accurate information display) principle.

4.5 The Breakthrough of Study Method of the Kano Model in E-Commerce

In this research, we confronted challenges resulting from particular aspects of e-commerce and then endeavored to make breakthroughs in the following areas.

First, due to our identifying too many shopping guide functions when we first chose function points, valid data could not be collected. We resolved this problem by leveraging expert evaluations, resulting in the identification of the most valuable 27 out of the original 72 function points.

Second, due to a defect of the chi-square test when classifying function points, we combined the sample proportion test and the quality convergence figure (a Matlab program written by ourselves) to confirm the classification of function points, thereby reducing the impact of sample size on results.

Beyond the breakthroughs we have already made, we will conduct more studies to explore the impact of function numbers and customers' experiences, optimizing the Kano model study method's application on the area of e-commerce.

References

1. IResearch. China E-Commerce Research (2014), `http://ec.iresearch.cn/shopping/20140114/224908.shtml`
2. Beatty, S.E., Ferrell, M.E.: Impulse buying: modellig its precursors. Journal of Retailing 74(2), 169–191 (1998)
3. Solomon, M.R., Polegato, R., Zaichkowsky, J.L.: Consumer behavior: buying, having, and being. Pearson Prentice Hall, Upper Saddle River (2009)

4. Chen, L.F.: A novel approach to regression analysis for the classification of quality attributes in the Kano model: an empirical test in the food and beverage industry. Omega 40, 651–659 (2012)
5. Berger, C., Blauth, R., Boger, D., et al.: Kano's methods for understanding customer-defined quality. J. Center for Quality Management Journal 2(4), 3–35 (1993)
6. China Internet Network Information Center (2012), http://www.cnnic.net.cn/hlwfzyj/hlwxzbg/dzswbg/201208/P020120827473850053431.pdf

Responsive Web Design and Its Use by an E-Commerce Website

Yujing Zeng, Jie Gao, and Chunsong Wu

Taobao (China) Software Co., LTD, Xixi Park, Wenyixi Road 969,
Yuhang District, Hangzhou, Zhejiang, P.R. China
qingsui.zyj@taobao.com

Abstract. Responsible architecture design is believed to be the most effective answer to the incompatibility problem of webpages across devices with varying sizes and resolutions. Online shopping behavior is cross-device and continuous; therefore, we believe that it is also important to explore and discuss how to provide a fluent and consistent user experience for the same webpage across various devices (other than simply using the fluid grid technique to maintain cross device compatibility). Inspired by the fluency theory, we assume that the fluency of processing webpages on different devices affects a user's responsive web experience. In this paper, a case study of etao.com was performed to explore how to improve user experience fluency with responsive web design on mobile phones. The study consisted of two experiments: a PC test and a mobile phone test. The PC test was designed to understand the interactions between the users and the information content on etao.com (desktop version), which could facilitate the identification of user preferences and expectations and guide the design layout of the responsive webpage on mobile phones. During the mobile phone test, we examined the responsive webpage, which was designed according to users' preferences and expectations, to determine whether this type of layout could be approved by users. The results showed that users rated the new version of the responsive webpage higher than the traditional responsive page, which was designed by using proportion-based fluid grid technology alone.

Keywords: e-commerce webpages, mobile devices, responsive web, user experience, fluency.

1 Introduction

According to iResearch [1], China now has 420 million mobile users. Moreover, the increased functionality offered by mobile devices provides a significant opportunity for the development of mobile marketing and retailing. In 2012, Chinese online shoppers used their mobile phones and tablets to make 63.17 billion Chinese Yuan (approximately 10 billion US dollars) in purchases last year, an increase of 440.8% over the previous year.

As more and more online shoppers use various devices, such as mobile phones, tablets, and regular PCs, accessing e-commerce websites, how should e-commerce

P.L.P. Rau (Ed.): CCD/HCII 2014, LNCS 8528, pp. 509–519, 2014.

webpage be designed to be compatible with different devices with varying sizes and resolutions? The responsible architectural design (aka, responsive web), suggested by Ethan Marcotte, is believed to be the most effective answer to this incompatibility problem. Based on the responsible architectural design, a responsive webpage should be organized into fluid grids, which should be able to be rearranged by screen size. Thus, responsive webpages are capable of changing their layout and content to adapt to the screen size and resolution of each device.

In China, responsive web design is a relatively new technology. To date, most papers discussing responsive web design have mainly focused on the fluid grid technique, which was required to maintain cross device compatibility. However, we believe that it is also important to explore and discuss how to provide a fluent and consistent user experience for the same webpage across different devices, particularly for e-commerce websites. Data from iResearch [2] showed that 97.7% of mobile shoppers also shopped on PCs. This finding is consistent with our previous unpublished data with Alibaba Group, which also showed that many online shoppers use multi-devices for online shopping. We also found that online shopping is a complex decision-making process. One user's online shopping behavior among multi-device is not independent but relative and even continuous, particularly when he or she is purchasing an expensive or unfamiliar item. This buying process often includes not only a complete one-time shopping process but a process that consists of many choices and operations. For example, online shoppers often use fragmented time, which may include the time lining up, waiting and before going to sleep, to perform product information searches and order status checking on mobile devices.

As online shopping behavior is cross-device and continuous, it is essential to study how to keep the user experience fluent and consistent on responsive webpages on e-commerce websites. However, there is little research on this topic at present. Fortunately, some theories from information processing and cognitive psychology have provided some basic understanding of buyer purchasing behaviors. Previous researchers have shown that ease or fluency of cognitive processing affects the following cognitive decisions. Information processing can be characterized by a variety of parameters that are nonspecific to its content, such as speed and accuracy of processing, which tend to lead to a common experience of processing ease or fluency [3]. For example, fluently processed stimuli have been judged more truthful and less risky [4, 5] because high fluency signals that the stimulus is familiar and, thus, unlikely to be harmful [6].

Inspired by the fluency theory, we believed that the more fluently the responsive webpage on a device is processed, the more this responsive webpage is likely to be evaluated positively. We assume that the fluency of processing webpage on different devices affects the user experience of the responsive webpage, and thus, we attempt to explore how to improve the processing fluency of the responsive web on each device. Previous studies have revealed that if the webpages were designed according to user's expectations or habits, the user's tasks should be simplified. For example, Nielsen's experiments showed that when menu labels were designed to be consistent with user expectation, the probability of searching product success was 80%; however, when the user is unfamiliar with the menu labels, the probability declined to 9% [7].

Researchers have summarized these types of findings and used them as design standards; they have believed that serious usability problems would occur if these design practice were violated. Thus, we further assume that when webpage layouts are consistent with user expectations and habits, the user experience with the responsive web will be evaluated as more fluent and positive. That is to say, when the layout of the responsive webpage is adjusted on different devices, designers should consider not only the completeness of content display, but they should also consider that the content layout should be consistent with user expectations and habits.

In this paper, a case study was conducted to explore how to improve the user experience fluency of the responsive web on e-commerce websites. In particular, we focused on the user experience of mobile phones because mobile phones were widely used by internet users, and the information display was limited on mobile phone screens because of their screen sizes. Therefore, the user experience on mobile phones was more seriously influenced by content layout.

This study investigated etao.com, which is an e-commerce website in China with shopping search, shopping guide and price comparison functions. This website is one of the few e-commerce websites in China that adopts responsive design. In this study, we focused on user behaviors and experiences and not the business objective of etao.com.

2 PC Test

This study consisted of two experiments: A PC test and a mobile phone test. The PC test was designed to understand the interactions between the users and the information content on etao.com (desktop version), which could facilitate the identification of user preferences and expectations and guide the design layout of the responsive webpage on mobile phones. Then, during the mobile phone test, we examined the responsive webpage via a mobile phone, which was designed according to users' preferences and expectations to determine whether this type of layout could be approved by users.

In the PC test, the interaction between users and etao.com was collected by two tasks: an eye-tracking task and an information-sorting task. The purpose of the eye-tracking task (on a desktop computer) was to identify the sections and content of etao.com (desktop version) upon which users commonly fixated. The information-sorting task was designed to determine what information users would like to be presented and how they would like that information presented when they visited etao.com via mobile phones.

2.1 Apparatus and Materials for the PC Test

The computer used for the eye-tracking task was equipped with the Microsoft Windows 7 operation system and a 22-inch LCD monitor with a 1680x1050 screen resolution. The responsive webpage was displayed with highest width on the monitor. Tobii X60 was employed to track and record the user's eye movements.

The information-sorting task cards comprised content components from etao.com (desktop version), including the logo, search box, category navigation, sub-page navigation, and product recommendations (updated in real-time), along with several theme areas, such as free trial, new release, user shopping experience share, and today's topic, as well as several promotion areas, for a total of 20 cards. The theme areas and promotion areas were updated daily.

2.2 PC Test Procedure

This experiment included two tasks, and all participants were asked to independently finish the eye-tracking task and then the information-sorting task.

In the eye-tracking task, the participants were asked to browse etao.com, according to their habits and preferences, on a desktop computer. In this process, the click through operation was limited, meaning that the participant could browse the home page up and down freely but could not click through any components on the webpage to another webpage. The task finished when the browsing time reached one minute or when the participant indicated that he or she had finished browsing. Meanwhile, the eye movement data were recorded for each participant.

In the information-sorting task, the participants were presented information cards represented each section shown on etao.com homepage. They were asked to remove needless sections (i.e., unnecessary when displayed on a mobile phone) based on their needs and preferences. Participants were then also asked to add any information that was not already provided. Finally, they were asked to arrange the information, according to their habits and preferences, in a specific area with a common mobile phone's width and unlimited length.

2.3 PC Test Participants

Based on the frequency that they used etao.com on a PC, all participants were divided into two groups: a novice group and a high-frequency group. Participants in the novice group had seldom or never visited and used etao.com, and participants in high-frequency group had visited or used etao.com more than ten days in the latest month. Twelve participants were tested: six in the novice group and six in the high-frequency group. All participants were asked to finish the eye-tracking test and then to sort the cards.

The participants ranged in age from 20 to 30 years old; they have shopped online for more than three years and have at least three favorite e-commerce websites, and they had all shopped online at least three times in the latest month. In addition, all participants used smartphones and have used their phones to shop online. Two of the participants in the high-frequency group had previously visited etao.com using their smartphones.

2.4 PC Test Results

We divided etao.com (the desktop version used in the eye-tracking task) into 5 AOIs (areas of interest): logo, search box, navigation, products recommendation and themes or promotion, see Figure 1. Both the novice and high-frequency groups' average fixation durations in each AOI were calculated, see Table 1.

The novice group's average fixation durations were greater than that of the high-frequency group in the interest areas of logo, search box and navigation. In addition, in both groups, the fixation duration for the product recommendation area was greater than those in the themes or promotion areas.

The participants in both groups provided a consistent "design" when they were asked to arrange the smart phone page using puzzled components. In the delete/add operation process, the participants did not significantly alter the present information content on the PC webpage. They believed that the display space problem could be solved by using shrinking, scrolling and combining adjustments. As to the layout operation, the logo, search box and navigation cards were placed on the top of the page, which was consistent with the PC layout, except that the navigation was shrunken. Below the top parts of the page, all theme area or promotion area cards were placed together. The products recommendation cards, which included a great deal of product information pushed by many websites, were placed below the theme area or promotion area cards.

Based on the results from the eye-tracking task and information-sorting task, we designed a new version of the responsive webpage for mobile phones. In the new page, the logo, navigation and search box, which are common in shopping sites, were placed at the top, which was consistent with the desktop version. Below the common components were the products recommendations, theme areas and promotion areas. However, these components were placed differently from the layout on the PC page, where product recommendation and themes areas or promotion areas were placed side by side. The page size on mobile phone was limited; therefore, theme or promotion areas were placed below the common components, and then products recommendation was placed below orderly, according to the results of information-sorting task.

Based on the eye-tracking task and the information-sorting task results, we designed a new version of the responsive webpage for mobile phones, see Figure 2. In the new page, the logo, navigation and search box, which are common in shopping sites, were placed at the top, which was consistent with the desktop version. Below the common components were the products recommendations, theme areas and promotion areas. However, these components were placed up and down orderly in this part, which differed from the layout on the PC page, where product recommendation and themes areas or promotion areas were placed side by side. The page size on mobile phone was limited; therefore, theme or promotion areas were placed below the common components, and then products recommendation was placed below orderly, according to the results of information-sorting task. What would the users think about this new version mobile phone page? To find out, we conducted a contrasting test on the mobile phone, which is described in detail below.

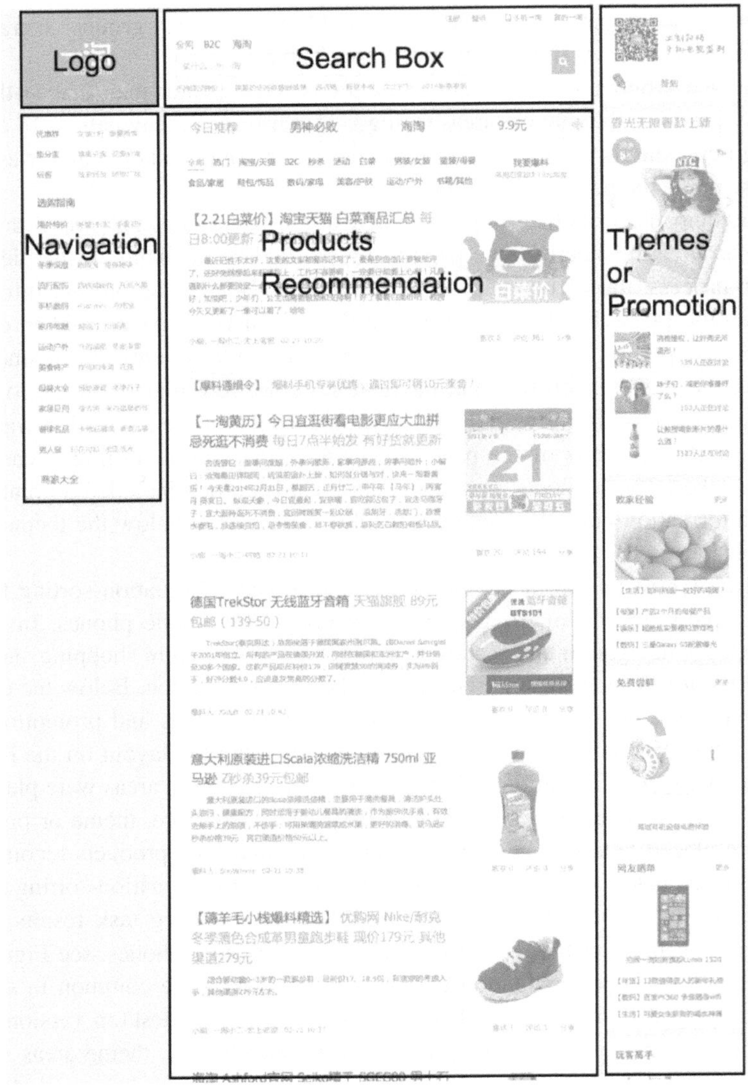

Fig. 1. AOIs on etao.com (desktop version)

Table 1. Fixation duration averages in each AOI in seconds

	Novice group	High-frequency group
Logo	1.78	0.59
Search Box	1.33	0.68
Navigation	2.71	0.96
Products recommendation	14.31	15.77
Themes or promotion	5.54	4.43

Fig. 2. The new version of the responsive webpage for mobile phones

3 Mobile Phone Test

The mobile phone test was designed to determine how users would evaluate the new version of the mobile phone page, which was redesigned according to the results of the PC test (described above). Moreover, we wondered whether it would provide a better experience when user expectations and habits were considered in the responsive webpage design across devices compared with using the proportion-based fluid grids technique alone.

3.1 Materials for Mobile Phone Test

In this experiment, two versions of the responsive page for mobile phones were used: the testing and controlled versions. The testing version was designed considering the completeness of display on mobile phones and according to the users' habits and expectations, as described in the section 2.4. The controlled version was designed only considering the completeness of display on mobile phones using the proportion-based fluid grids technique.

In addition, theme or promotion areas were placed above products recommendation orderly in the testing version. Conversely, theme or promotion areas were placed below products recommendation orderly in the controlled version

3.2 Mobile Phone Test Procedure

In this experiment, we asked the participants to evaluate both the testing version page and the controlled version page on a mobile phone. Participants were shown one version at a time. The presentation sequence of these two version pages was balanced. The participants were asked to browse one version of a page on a mobile phone, according to their habits and preference, until they ended it. The participants were asked to draw what they had browsed based on their impressions. Next, the participants were presented another version page and were asked to evaluate these two versions and to choose which one was better.

3.3 Mobile Phone Test Participants

Six participants in the novice group and six participants in the high-frequency group were tested in a process similar to that of the PC test. None of these participants were involved in the PC test, and they were asked to take this mobile phone test independently.

All participants were 20 to 30 years old and used smart phones. All participants had previously performed mobile purchases but had never visited etao.com via mobile phone.

3.4 Results of The Mobile Phone Test

In the mobile phone test, the participants were asked to draw the webpage layout after they had browsed the first presented page. The results showed that the participants who browsed the testing version webpage drew all components; however, only three of the participants who browsed the controlled version webpage drew all components. The other three participants could not draw the information at the bottom of the traditional page. That is to say, the layout of the testing version page could be easier processed by the participants, and the participants could remember it accurately.

In the evaluation for each version' layout, all the participants preferred theme/promotion areas to be placed above produce recommendations in the mobile phone page.

In addition, all 12 participants chose the testing version webpage as the better one, which indicated that webpages that are designed and adjusted according to users' habits and preferences could more likely be accepted.

4 Discussions

The objective of our study was to examine whether a better experience could be provided when user expectations and habits were considered in the design of responsive webpage across devices compared with using the proportion-based fluid grids technique. We conducted PC test including an eye-tracking task and an information-sorting task to identify the user preferences and expectations that guide the layout design of the responsive webpage on mobile phones. During the mobile phone test, we examined the responsive webpage, which was designed according to users' preferences and expectations, to determine whether this type of layout could be approved by users. The results showed that users evaluated the new version of the responsive webpage higher than the traditional responsive page, which was designed using proportion-based fluid grid technology.

Researchers believed that the search pattern on the web interface was influenced by both display and user expectation. For example, Rensink [8] proposed that the individual could distinguish the specific type of the interface by extracting the abstract sense or the "essence" of the scene, such as webpage, word processing software, and spreadsheet. Our study indicated that the bottom-up influence exerted by display was more significant for novice users. The eye-tracking test results in this study showed that novice users paid more attention on the logo, search box and navigation than high-frequency users. In the e-commerce websites, some components are common, such as the logo, search box and navigation, and even the shopping site sign. We deduced that common components would be some important references or clues to facilitate extracting the "essence" of or to understand the new shopping website quickly.

In addition, previous studies showed that users often have expectations about where the common components could be found in the webpage. When studying individual schema to web pages, Bernard [9] found that most users expected that the navigation menu could be found on the left side of the page. This type of expectation about "something in somewhere" was derived from users past experience Internet use.

Our study indicated that the impact of expectation caused by past experience was cross-platform, which means user experience on PCs affected not only a user's expectation of PC webpages but also affected a user's expectations of webpages on other devices, such as mobile phones. In the information-sorting task, when participants who had never visited etao.com via mobile phone before were asked to "design" the mobile phone webpage, they kept common components, such as the logo, search box and navigation, but they also placed these common components in the places they occupied on the PC webpage. Therefore, we concluded that the common components should be kept continuously when the responsive webpage displayed on different devices. This type of design could facilitate users in extracting the "essence" of a page and in understanding new websites quickly by referring to cross-platform using experiences.

This study also found that users' preferences for special components (i.e., different from common components in e-commerce websites), special content on some e-commerce websites, varied on different devices. There are two types of special information on etao.com: some theme/promotion areas, which are updated daily, and hundreds of product recommendations, which are pushed in real-time. The theme/promotion area is obtained by packing certain information according to certain properties, and the pieces of product recommendations are displayed directly on the page, item-by-item, in time sequence. The eye tracking test results showed that participants paid more attention to product recommendations lists on PCs. The card sorting test results showed that participants would like to place the theme/promotion areas in some obvious parts of a page, a result that was confirmed in the mobile phone test. We propose that this difference is caused by the different user behaviors on PCs and mobile phones. Users often use phones in different places and often in fragmented time; for example, a CNNIC (China Internet Network Information Center) survey showed that 27.2% of mobile phone users often use mobile phone on the road [10]. Therefore, on the mobile phone, themes and promotion areas could be helpful in quickly targeting users who are interested in them compared with a product recommendation list, which requires users to search their interested information one-by-one and was given more attention on the PC. This proposition could not be supported by the data in this study and which needs to be further studied in the future.

We believe that research on responsive web design should study not only how to display information completely on different devices using the fluid grids technique but also pay more attention on how to provide consistent experience to users browsing one page on different devices. Keeping common components of shopping websites consistent and continuous on different devices would help users to understand webpages on new devices quickly based on their past experiences and facilitate the building of uniform brand cognition. However, responsive web design is not a copy edition of webpage on different devices. Because of users' different behaviors on different devices, the differences in webpage display on different devices should be given more attention. This change would help to align the display with a user's behavior characteristics on the related device.

References

1. IResearch China E-Commerce Research, `http://report.iresearch.cn/2018.html`
2. IResearch China E-Commerce Research, `http://report.iresearch.cn/2000.html`
3. Reber, R., Schwarz, N., Winkielman, P.: Processing fluency and aesthetic pleasure: is beauty in the perceiver's processing experience? Personality and Social Psychology Review 8(4), 364–382 (2004)
4. Reber, R., Schwarz, N.: Effects of perceptual fluency on judgments of truth. Consciousness and Cognition 8(3), 338–342 (1999)
5. Song, H., Schwarz, N.: Fluency and the detection of misleading questions: Low processing fluency attenuates the Moses illusion. Social Cognition 26(6), 791–799 (2008)
6. Zajonc, R.B.: Attitudinal effects of mere exposure. Journal of Personality and Social Psychology 9(2p2), 1 (1968)
7. Nielsen, J.: Do interface standards stifle design creativity. Jacob Nielsen's Alertbox (1999)
8. Rensink, R.A.: Seeing, sensing, and scrutinizing. Vision Research 40(10), 1469–1487 (2000)

9. Bernard, M.L.: Developing schemas for the location of common web objects. In: Proceedings of the Human Factors and Ergonomics Society Annual Meeting, vol. 45(15), pp. 1161–1165. SAGE Publications (2001)
10. CNNIC China Mobile Internet Research, http://www.cnnic.cn/hlwfzyj/hlwfzzx/qwfb/201305/W020130514401434509975.pdf

Cross-Cultural Design for Knowledge Sharing and Learning

How Different Cultures Affect Online Communication on Knowledge Sharing between the Thais and Chinese

Pimnapa Atsawintarangkun and Takaya Yuizono

Japan Advanced Institute of Science and Technology
1-1 Asahidai, Nomi, Ishikawa 923-1211, Japan
{pimnapa.a,yuizono}@jaist.ac.jp

Abstract. In today's society, people can share knowledge with others via online communication tools. However, the process of sharing or acquiring knowledge between people from different cultures may involve problems and misunderstandings. To enhance intercultural competences and improve understandings of the cultural variations, this paper investigates how different cultures affect patterns of online knowledge sharing; the study focuses on Thais and Chinese who have a high-context communication style. We set up a laboratory experiment to analyze discourses posted by Thais and Chinese utilizing six categories including declaration, interrogation, exclamation, opinion, acknowledgement, and agreement. The discourse analysis showed that there is a significant difference in the number of interrogation and exclamation discourses. Then, we examined connections between the discourse analysis results and cultural dimensions conducted by Hofstede [6]. A post-questionnaire was provided to investigate participants' attitudes during online knowledge sharing. Our experiment revealed that the main cultural dimensions that influence Thais and Chinese to have the different patterns of online knowledge sharing are individualism, masculinity, and uncertainty avoidance. Moreover, problems with the online communication among people who have a high-context communication style are explained. It can be concluded that the cultural differences and the high-context communication style of the Thai and Chinese can influence the ways knowledge is shared between these groups online.

Keywords: intercultural communication, online communication, knowledge sharing, Thai and Chinese, discourse analysis, cultural dimensions, high-context communication.

1 Introduction

Knowledge sharing is a process of knowledge being exchanged among people. Knowledge can be defined as personalized information related to facts, skills, suggestions, procedures, concepts, interpretations, ideas, observations, and judgments that may or may not be unique, useful or accurate [1].

In the era of globalization, people can use online communication tools such as social media, online forums, and blogs to share knowledge with others. Therefore, user-generated content is becoming a valuable source of knowledge. However, a process to

P.L.P. Rau (Ed.): CCD/HCII 2014, LNCS 8528, pp. 523–533, 2014.

share or acquire knowledge among people who come from different cultures may involve problems such as misunderstanding messages, linguistic problems, and negative feelings. Moreover, we can assume that online knowledge sharing among people who have a high-context style of communication will face problems since the high-context style is often indirect, ambiguous, and uses nonverbal elements.

Previous works have focused on comparing behaviors between "Western" and "Eastern", comparing countries that are on opposite ends of the Hofstede scale and comparing user behaviors between high-context style and low-context style in the online community [3,4,8,9,11,13]. There are few works that investigate how different cultures affect patterns of online knowledge sharing among people who have the high-context communication style.

Thus, this paper aims to enhance understanding of the cultural variations by examining connections between cultural dimensions and online knowledge sharing patterns of users who have the high-context communication style. Thais and Chinese are selected because they have obvious cultural differences and their communication styles are considered to be high-context style [7, 8].

The rest of this paper is organized as follows. In Section 2, some backgrounds and theories are described. Section 3 gives details of the methodology of the study. Our analysis results and discussions are presented in Section 4. Finally, Section 5 gives the conclusions and future directions.

2 Backgrounds and Theories

2.1 Cultural Knowledge

In this work, we focus on the online sharing of cultural knowledge between Chinese and Thais. Cultural knowledge is defined as the state of knowing about behavior, belief, value or practices that people who live in the same society use for living in that society. This type of knowledge can help individuals to become familiar with people from other cultures. It also can reduce miscommunication, conflict, and failure in intercultural communication [10]. To avoid failures in intercultural communication, cultural knowledge of a partner country is required [17]. Thus, two topics in this experiment are related to cultural knowledge of the Thai and Chinese. The first topic asks about metaphorical expressions in their cultures. For example, "Slow as a tortoise" is an expression found in Chinese culture and also recognized in Thai culture. Another example is "Thin as a monkey" in Chinese culture, but in Thai, they say, "Thin as a dry shrimp." The other topic asks about beliefs in daily life such as color and gift giving/taking. For instance, the color white has a negative connotation in China, but white represents pureness in Thailand.

2.2 Cultural Dimensions

Hofstede [6] has developed the most frequently cited model for such cultural measures called national cultural dimensions. This model provides a pragmatic, structured framework for studying culture [15]. First, Hofstede identified four inter-cultural dimensions including power distance, individualism, uncertainty avoidance, and masculinity. After that, Hofstede and Bond added the fifth dimension: long-term orientation. Definitions of five cultural dimensions are as follows:

1. Power distance (PDI): the degree to which members of a society accept and expect that power is distributed unequally in particular society.
2. Individualism (IDV): the degree to which a society reinforces individual or collective achievement and interpersonal relationships.
3. Masculinity (MAS): the degree to which a society is dependent on achievement, assertiveness and competition (masculine characteristics) as opposed to femininity, which reflects how much a society values cooperation, relationships, and caring for others.
4. Uncertainty avoidance (UAI): the extent to which the members of a society feel uncomfortable with uncertainty and ambiguity.
5. Long-term orientation (LTO): the extent to which a society shows a pragmatic, future-oriented perspective rather than a conventional, historical, short-term point of view.

2.3 Communication Styles

Hall [5] has classified styles of communication based on a key factor: "context." It relates to the framework, background, and surrounding situations in which communication or an event happens. Based on Hall's theory, two communication styles were defined as low-context and high-context style. Low-context style, typically Western, is logical, linear, individualistic, and action-oriented. The actions that are characteristic of this style are often verbally explicit and straightforward. High-context style (typically of Eastern cultures) consists of communication with the following characteristics: indirect, formal, ambiguous, and respectful. The following table shows some of the characteristics of low-context style and high-context style.

Table 1. Characteristics of low-context style and high-context style [2]

Low-context style	High-context style
Low use of nonverbal elements: message is carried more by words than by nonverbal means.	High use of nonverbal elements such as voice tone, facial expression, gestures, and eye movement that carry significant parts of conversation.
Verbal message is explicit. Context is less important than words.	Verbal message is implicit; context (situation, people, and nonverbal elements) is more important than words.
Verbal message is direct; one spells things out exactly.	Verbal message is indirect; one talks around the point and embellishes it.
Communication is seen as a way of exchanging information, ideas, and opinions.	Communication is seen as an art form, a way of engaging someone.
Disagreement is depersonalized. One withdraws from conflict with another and gets on with the task. Focus is on rational solutions, not personal ones. One can be explicit about another's bothersome behavior.	Disagreement is personalized. One is sensitive to conflict expressed in another's nonverbal communication. Conflict must be resolved before work can progress or must be avoided because it is personally threatening.

3 Methodology

This study aims to determine what the main cultural dimensions are that influence users from different cultures (both with high-context style) to communicate differently when it comes to online knowledge sharing. In order to investigate connections between the cultural dimensions and knowledge sharing patterns, discussion discourses posted by participants were analyzed.

Participants in the laboratory experiment consisted of twelve Thais (Male = 8, Female = 4) and twelve Chinese (Male = 7, Female = 5) ranging in age from 23 to 36 years (M = 26.92). They were studying at graduate school and all of them can use English fluently (average TOEIC score is 600).

3.1 Experiment Procedure

In this experiment, WordPress [16] (an open source web-based software program that used to build and maintain a website or blog) was provided to collect discussion samples from participants. Then, participants were randomly assigned into four groups

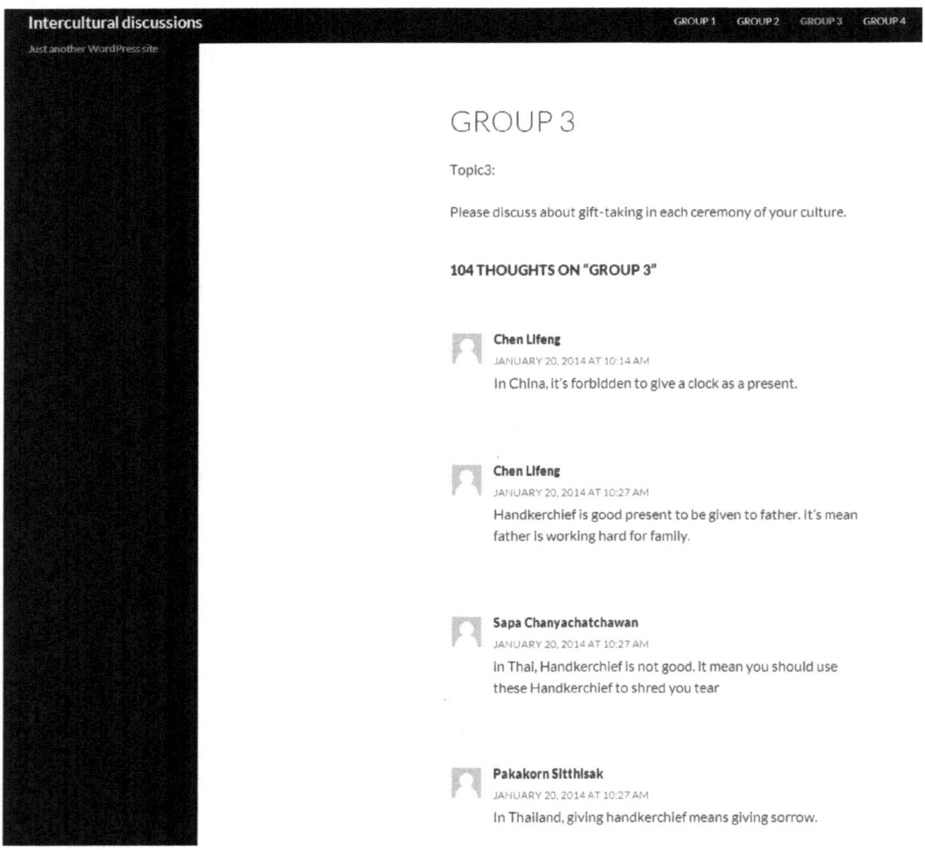

Fig. 1. Interface screen of online knowledge sharing

consisting of three Thais and three Chinese. Each group was given 45 minutes to share and discuss the topics in their own styles. Participants were encouraged to share what they know, ask others to make mutual understandings and compare what are the differences and similarities. They were able to post any types of input such as pictures, emoticons or links, but English had to be the common language in the exchange. At the end, participants had 10 minutes to fill out a questionnaire. The interface screen of online knowledge sharing in this experiment is shown in Figure 1.

3.2 Discourse Analysis

The discourses posted by participants were retrieved from the database and the patterns of those discourses were analyzed by one author. The discourses can be classified into six classes:

1. Declaration: A phrase or a sentence of fact or knowledge that participants had shared in the online knowledge sharing.
   Example: "In China, liquor is just one of the popular presents."

2. Interrogation: A phrase or a sentence of inquiry that asks for a reply.
   Example: "In Thailand, do girls often wear white ornaments?"

3. Exclamation: A phrase or a sentence that expresses strong emotion or feeling and often contains an exclamatory mark.
   Example: "Interesting!", "Oh."

4. Opinion: A phrase or a sentence that shows opinion or comment of audience.
   Example: "I think Thais like white because of their religion.

5. Acknowledgement: A phrase or a sentence that acknowledges or recognizes another person or statement.
   Example: "Yes.", "Thank you"

6. Agreement: A phrase or a sentence that expresses agreement between participants.
   Example: "I agree with you."

Then, we analyzed the connections between cultural dimensions and patterns of online knowledge sharing based on the six classes as mentioned above.

4 Analysis Results and Discussions

4.1 Discourse Analysis Results

For the discourse analysis, the number of discourses in each class and each nationality was counted as shown in Table 1 and Table 2. A percentage of each discourse class in Chinese and Thais was displayed in Table 3. Then, a nonparametric statistic test

(Mann-Whitney U Test) was used for analyzing a significant difference between Chinese and Thais in the number of discourses in the six classes. The statistical result in Table 5 revealed significant difference in two classes including interrogation and exclamation. After that, a post-questionnaire was provided to support our analysis as shown in Table 6 by Mean, Standard Deviation and p-value. It investigates participants' attitudes toward the online knowledge-sharing experience. This questionnaire consists of seven questions, with responses varied on 1 (Very low) – 5 (Very high) Likert scale.

Table 2. Number of discourses from Chinese participants

Class	Chinese participant No.												Total
	1	**2**	**3**	**4**	**5**	**6**	**7**	**8**	**9**	**10**	**11**	**12**	
Declaration	9	4	2	5	9	9	8	14	7	28	33	11	**139**
Interrogation	0	0	0	0	1	3	5	2	1	0	4	1	**17**
Exclamation	0	0	0	0	0	0	1	1	1	0	1	0	**4**
Opinion	2	0	2	1	0	1	1	2	0	0	2	0	**11**
Acknowledgement	1	1	1	0	1	2	0	2	0	1	0	1	**10**
Agreement	2	0	0	0	0	1	2	0	0	0	0	0	**5**
Total	**14**	**5**	**5**	**6**	**11**	**16**	**17**	**21**	**9**	**29**	**40**	**13**	**186**

Table 3. Number of discourses from Thai participants

Class	Thai participant No.												Total
	1	**2**	**3**	**4**	**5**	**6**	**7**	**8**	**9**	**10**	**11**	**12**	
Declaration	9	6	14	5	4	6	16	3	4	13	19	2	**101**
Interrogation	2	1	9	8	3	4	14	6	3	15	4	12	**81**
Exclamation	5	1	2	1	2	1	1	3	0	1	1	4	**22**
Opinion	4	3	4	1	1	0	0	1	2	0	2	2	**20**
Acknowledgement	4	1	5	0	2	2	2	0	0	2	2	0	**20**
Agreement	1	2	3	1	0	1	1	0	0	0	1	0	**10**
Total	**25**	**14**	**37**	**16**	**12**	**14**	**34**	**13**	**9**	**31**	**29**	**20**	**254**

Table 4. A percentage of discourses in Chinese and Thais

Content classes	**Chinese**	**Thai**
Declaration	139 (74.73 %)	101 (39.76 %)
Interrogation	17 (9.14 %)	81 (31.90 %)
Exclamation	4 (2.15 %)	22 (8.66 %)
Opinion	11 (5.91 %)	20 (7.87 %)
Acknowledgement	10 (5.38 %)	20 (7.87 %)
Agreement	5 (2.69 %)	10 (3.94%)
Total	186 (100%)	254 (100%)

Table 5. Mean, Standard Deviation and p-value in each discourse class

Content classes	Chinese	Thai	p-value
Declaration	11.58±9.44	8.42±5.68	n.s
Interrogation	1.42+1.73	6.75±4.81	< 0.01
Exclamation	0.33±0.49	1.83±1.47	< 0.01
Opinion	0.92±0.90	1.67±1.44	n.s
Acknowledgement	0.83±0.72	1.67±1.61	n.s
Agreement	0.42±0.79	0.83±0.94	n.s
Total	15.50+10.43	21.17±9.62	n.s

Table 6. Questionnaire results of participants' attitudes

Question	Chinese	Thais	p-value
Q1. If you know that you and others have different social statuses, ways of your knowledge sharing will be different?	4.17±0.72	3.92±0.79	n.s
Q2. How much do you trust in others' knowledge?	4.00±0.74	4.17±0.39	n.s
Q3. How do you respect for others' knowledge?	4.25±0.87	4.33±0.65	n.s
Q4. Sharing knowledge with others can make your ideas increase more than individual thinking?	4.50±0.67	4.58±0.51	n.s
Q5. Sharing knowledge with others can make your ideas better than individual thinking?	4.33±0.78	4.17±0.72	n.s
Q6. When you share knowledge with others, you expect that you will receive useful knowledge from others?	4.25±0.75	3.83±0.72	n.s
Q7. Would you try to persuade others to agree with your thinking?	4.00±0.85	2.83±1.03	<0.01

4.2 Connections between Cultural Dimensions and Knowledge Sharing Patterns

After analyzing discourses, we investigated how cultural differences influence Chinese and Thais to have the different patterns of online knowledge sharing. The cultural dimensions used in the analysis consist of power distance, individualism, masculinity, uncertainty avoidance, and long-term orientation. The connections between cultural dimensions and the patterns of online knowledge sharing are as follows.

Power Distance

The scores of 80 and 64 as shown in Figure 2 are evidence that China and Thailand are societies in which inequalities are accepted. We cannot find an explicit connection between this dimension and the patterns of online knowledge sharing. This is because the experiment was conducted as an online communication, not face-to-face

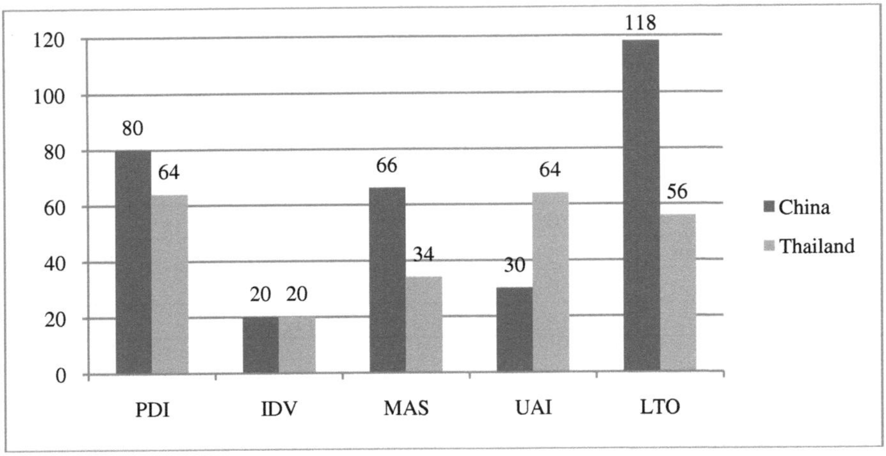

Fig. 2. Cultural Dimensions scores of China and Thailand [14]

communication and our participants did not know information about other participants. They did not have concerns about seniority, hierarchy, or authority when communicating with others online.

However, the result of Q1 from Table 6 reveals that if the participants (both Thai and Chinese) knew that they had different social statuses from one other, their patterns of online knowledge sharing would be different.

Individualism

The score of 20 on this dimension as displayed in Figure 2 shows that both China and Thailand are collectivist cultures that consider the group as the primary element. Communication between people in this culture is indirect. A society with a low score in this dimension has strong group cohesion and the priority of group goals is higher than individual goals. The harmony of the group has to be maintained and open conflicts are avoided. From the discourse analysis, it showed that both Thais and Chinese did not directly dispute others. They often expressed their ideas with opinions to avoid making someone to lose face. Moreover, they often used agreement discourses and acknowledgement discourses to represent their cooperation, modesty, and deference. The results of Q2-Q6 shown in Table 6 can support the connection between this dimension and patterns of online knowledge sharing. It shows that both Chinese and Thais have respect and trust for others in their own group/culture. Furthermore, it can represent a preference for group work.

Masculinity

In Figure 2, China scores 66 on this dimension and it can be considered a society that respects masculinity. The culture values competitiveness, assertiveness, ambition, and power. This society is success oriented and driven which can indicate that Chinese worried about their success in sharing knowledge. From Table 5, the Mann-Whitney U Test showed no significant difference between Chinese and Thais in the declaration. However, the number in the declaration category for Chinese accounted for 74.73 percent of total as displayed in Table 4. This indicated that the Chinese fully use their abilities in contributing their own knowledge. Moreover, the result of Q7 in Table 6 can support this analysis because Chinese tried to persuade others to agree with them to show their conviction.

With a score of 34, Thailand represents a society that values feminine characteristics. People in this society are less assertive and competitive. Moreover, this society shows for a preference for cooperation, modesty, and caring for others. Most of the Chinese expressions in the discussion were declarative sentences, whereas the Thais often used agreement sentences and acknowledgement sentences to represent their cooperation, modesty, and deference.

Uncertainty Avoidance

As shown in Figure 2, Thailand scores an intermediate 64 on this dimension; however, it is also indicating a slight preference for avoiding uncertainty. It means that Thais do not handle unexpected stories or events well. Thai participants felt doubtful during the online discussion because this experiment encouraged exchange of cultural knowledge that is different between each culture.

The statistical analysis using the Mann-Whitney U Test revealed a significant difference between Chinese and Thais ($p<0.01$) in the number in the interrogation and exclamation categories. Thai participants expressed interrogative sentences more than Chinese did in order to reduce doubt and uncertainty during the knowledge-sharing process. Moreover, Thais often expressed exclamatory sentences more than Chinese did because of their amazement and doubtfulness in other expressions.

Compared with Thailand, China has a low score in this dimension (score = 30). It can indicate that Chinese have high tolerance of deviant persons and ideas. The discourse analysis showed that Chinese seldom used interrogative sentences and exclamatory sentences compared to Thais. Moreover, this score suggests that the Chinese participants felt free to share knowledge and used informal language in expressing with others. According to discourse analysis, Chinese used expressions containing abbreviations, slang words, and symbols more than Thais in online exchanges. The number of those words from Chinese participants was twice the number of words from Thais.

Long-Term Orientation

Long-Term Orientation is the fifth dimension of Hofstede that was added after the original four to try to distinguish the difference in thinking between the East and West. For the dimension of long-term orientation, there were no good connections between online knowledge sharing patterns and this dimension because both Thailand and China are in the East.

Besides the cultural characteristics mentioned above, the style of communication can affect online knowledge sharing patterns. Based on Hall's concept of context, both Thais and Chinese have a high-context communication style. In the high-context style, people often use nonverbal elements such as voice tone, facial expression, gestures, and eye movement as parts of communication. Verbal message is indirect and implicit in this style [2]. Words and sentences may be collapsed and shortened. However, online communication requires characteristics of a low-context communication style that is direct and explicit because it is not a face-to-face communication and the nonverbal elements are more effective. Thus, online knowledge sharing between Thais and Chinese might face problems since they use fewer nonverbal elements to express themselves. Another problem is that Thais and Chinese might not be able to interpret symbolic language or abbreviations that are emerging in the present online culture (although they are familiar with indirect message). It leads to misunderstandings and negative feelings in communication. The other problem is that the high-context style is comfortable with a considerable amount of silence. People who are accustomed to utilizing the high-context style tend to leave a lot of space or dead air in conversation.

5 Conclusions and Future Directions

In this study, we explored the connections between cultural dimensions and online knowledge sharing patterns of users who have the high-context communication style. The laboratory experiment was conducted to collect discourses in the process of online knowledge sharing between Thais and Chinese. From the discourse analysis, we discovered that cultural differences can influence the way knowledge is contributed. The major cultural dimensions that influence Thais and Chinese to have the different patterns of online knowledge sharing are individualism, masculinity, and uncertainty avoidance. Our findings help to enhance intercultural communication competencies and improve understanding of the cultural variations. This can be fundamental for designing new tools for intercultural communication. Regarding future directions, we plan to resolve the following limitations.

- The current study focused on only two out of many world cultures and the significance of results might be limited due to the small number of participants.
- Since the study was a laboratory experiment, our participants were studying at graduate school in Japan, which is culturally diverse in some ways, but is relatively homogeneous in terms of age and occupation. Moreover, they have left their countries of origin more than a year ago and have absorbed other cultural characteristics from colleagues. This means they may not represent the larger population of Thais and Chinese. To address this limitation, we plan to extend this study by using a more diverse set of participants.
- Since authors cannot understand both Chinese language and Thai language, English was selected to be the common language in this study. To resolve this limitation, we plan to use native language as the common language and use some techniques of Natural Language Processing to support our study in the future.

References

1. Alavi, M., Leidner, D.E.: Knowledge management systems: Issues, challenges, and benefits. Communication of the Association for Information Systems 1, 1–36 (1999)
2. Context of Cultures: High and Low, http://www2.pacific.edu/sis/culture/pub/Context_Cultures_High_and_Lo.htm
3. Fong, J., Burton, S.: A cross-cultural comparison of electronic word-of-mouth and country-of-origin effects. Journal of Business Research 61(3), 233–242 (2008)
4. Hara, N., Shachaf, P., Hew, K.F.: Cross-cultural analysis of the Wikipedia community. Journal of the American Society for Information Science and Technology 61(10), 2097–2108 (2010)
5. Hall, E.T.: Beyond Culture. Doubleday, New York (1976)
6. Hofstede, G., Hofstede, G.J., Minkov, M.: Cultures and Organizations: Software of the Mind, 3rd edn. McGraw-Hill, USA (2010)
7. Knutson, T.J., Komolsevin, R., Chatiketu, P., Smith, V.R.: A comparison of Thai and US American willingness to communicate. Journal of Intercultural Communication Research 31, 3–12 (2002)
8. Nguyen, T.D., Fussell, S.R.: How did you feel during our conversation? Retrospective analysis of intercultural and same-culture Instant Messaging conversations. In: Proceedings of the 2010 ACM Conference on Computer Supported Cooperative Work, pp. 117–126 (2010)
9. Pfeil, U., Zaphiris, P., Ang, C.S.: Cultural differences in collaborative authoring of Wikipedia. Journal of Computer-Mediated Communication 12(1), 88–113 (2006)
10. Pilhofer, K.: Cultural Knowledge: An Ethical Deconstruction of the Concept as a Foundation for Respect for Cultural Differences from a Post-Colonial and Levinasian Perspective. Master's Thesis, Copenhagen Business School (2010)
11. Setlock, L.D., Fussell, S.R.: What's it worth to you? The costs and affordances of CMC tools to Asian and American users. In: Proceedings of the 2010 ACM Conference on Computer Supported Cooperative Work, pp. 341–350 (2010)
12. Shu, W., Chuang, Y.: Why people share knowledge in virtual communities. Social Behavior and Personality 39(5), 671–690 (2010)
13. Siau, K., Erickson, J., Nah, F.F.H.: Effects of national culture on types of knowledge sharing in virtual communities. IEEE Transactions on Professional Communication 53(3), 278–292 (2010)
14. The Hofstede Centre, http://geert-hofstede.com/index.php
15. Williamson, D.: Forward from a critique of Hofstede's model of national culture. Human Relations 55(11), 1373–1395 (2002)
16. Wordpress.org, http://wordpress.org/
17. Yuizono, T., Li, W., Munemori, J.: Promoting Cultural Learning: Effects of Cultural Knowledge on Text Chats between Japanese and Chinese participants. In: König, A., Dengel, A., Hinkelmann, K., Kise, K., Howlett, R.J., Jain, L.C. (eds.) KES 2011, Part III. LNCS (LNAI), vol. 6883, pp. 167–176. Springer, Heidelberg (2011)

Cultural Difference on the Usage Pattern of Tagging System for Knowledge Sharing

Zhe Chen, Qin Gao, and Yuancheng Yang

Institute of Human Factors & Ergonomics, Industrial Engineering,
Tsinghua University, China
{chenzhe.demi,yangyuancheng}@gmail.com,
gaoqin@tsinghua.edu.cn,

Abstract. Collaborative tagging system in online knowledge sharing system benefits the knowledge management of users. It also inspires us a quantitative way how to investigate the effect of culture on knowledge management as tags reflects the usage pattern of users. In this study, the usage pattern of tag in three types of knowledge management websites (i.e. photo, bookmark and book sharing websites) present the influence of Chinese culture upon knowledge management. A set of indices is used to describe the usage pattern of tags and the results indicate that Chinese users behave differently in all three types of knowledge sharing system.

Keywords: tag, knowledge sharing, Chinese culture.

1 Introduction

Knowledge management has recently gained its prevalence on the web due to collaborative tagging system. Users attach tags to almost any content in the Internet and share these tags to others. A new information categorization method based on tagging is created. This method provides a convenient, fast, personal way for information's retrieval, filtering, and navigation, instead of traditional taxonomy.

The collective tagging system also fosters a quantitative way in the research of knowledge management. Many studies inspired by tagging systems have been conducted. However, few studies considered the effect of culture. This study investigates the cultural effect on tag usage pattern of Chinese user.

Globalization makes communication and co-work between different cultures more common [6]. Cross-culture team is everywhere. So it is necessary to know how culture affects knowledge management activities of user [7]. Collective tagging provides a new perspective to analyze the effect of culture.

2 Literature Review

Sharing of knowledge as knowledge defined as "fluid mix of framed experience, values, contextual information, and expert insight that provides a framework for

P.L.P. Rau (Ed.): CCD/HCII 2014, LNCS 8528, pp. 534–545, 2014.

evaluating and incorporating new experiences and information" [4], are a hot spot in the field of knowledge management. Knowledge sharing on web usually indicates the contribution of knowledge and meanwhile acquirement of others contribution. There are many works at deriving an effective way of knowledge management.

As more and more web 2.0 applications spring up, an online approach for knowledge management and sharing emerges. Collective tagging provides us a new way to organize information, especial categorization. On the contrast of taxonomy, collective tagging of categorization (folksonomy) is considered to be a radical and more effective way of classify contents or documents web [15]. The lack of authority of professional probably leads to chaos of information, rather than form regularities [10].

Tag on the web means an unrestrained descriptor or keyword, added to item, in forms of alphanumeric and symbols, while tagging implicates user's behavior of adding tags. The most distinguishing characteristic of the tag is that it is freely-formed as users use their own terms. Tags are then used for future navigation, filtering and retrieval, which provide a new method of information organization. Tagging for knowledge management becomes prevalent, as the encouragement of Web 2.0 applications. For example, in the del.icio.us (a tagging system), user bookmarked websites with their own descriptors. Thus, users create their personal categorization. Then the stable usage pattern has emerged from collective tagging [5].

Del.icio.us, as a popular website of collective tagging system, is for users to organize their favorite bookmarks online, using description and tag. An empirical research on Del.icio.us indicates that there are stable patterns of tag proportion [5]. Another empirical research on Del.icio.us uses multi-dimensional scaling to analyze tag frequency and co-word pattern of collective tagging [10]. Cameron et al offer us a conceptual model of tagging system, assisting for analysis in depth [13].

As culture has the effect on individual behavior, so it is of little possibility culture has negligible effect on the regularities of users' knowledge sharing activities. Then it is interesting to investigate the effect of culture in the knowledge sharing system [9].

Chinese culture is distinctly different from other cultures. Chinese culture vitiates greatly from other culture and Chinese tend to be more collective than people from western cultures [8]. Chiu [2] presents the differences cognitive styles between Chinese and American, and it refers to that Americans are Inferential-categorical while Chinese are relational-contextual. Chinese are more used to living on a social-relational organization than people from western cultures. Yang [16] describes personality of Chinese as restrained, patient, and self-contained and American as more impulsive, excitable and spontaneous. Moreover, the holistic perspective into objects gives Chinese a wider scope of the world [1]. It is found that Chinese users contribute less than users from other cultures in knowledge sharing websites [3]. Chinese users are likely to show a different pattern on different types of knowledge sharing websites [1].

The objective of this study is to investigate the effect of Chinese culture on knowledge sharing system through the usage pattern of tagging system. The results of this study can be used to improve knowledge sharing the cross-cultural team in global organizations.

3 Method

Marlow et al. state that tag system has three key elements (i.e. Resources, Tag and User) [13]. Then following indices are used to describe the tag usage in tag system as shown in table 1.

Table 1. The indices of usage pattern in tagging system

Abbr.	Meaning of Index
T	Number of Unique tags
UU	Number of Uploading User
UT	Number of tagging user
U	Number of user - user of tag system, including uploading user and tagging user
I	Number of unique item - given to some user share resources without tagging them, some items have no tags attached to them.
NT	Number of tag been used - It record 1 time as a user tag a item using a certain tag.
NU	Number of user tagging - It record 1 time as a certain user tag a item using a tag.
NI	Number of item been tagged - It record 1 time as a user tag a certain item using a tag.
T_U	Number of unique tags for a certain user
I_U1	Number of unique items for a certain user
I_U2	Number of unique tagged items for a certain user
T_I	Number of unique tags for a certain item
U_I1	Number of unique users for a certain item
U_I2	Number of unique tagging users for a certain item
U_T	Number of unique users for a certain tag
I_T	Number of unique items for a certain tag
T_IU	Number of unique tags for a certain item of a certain user
U_TI	Number of unique users for a certain tag of a certain item
I_TU	Number of unique items for a certain tag of a certain user
RU1	Level of repetition that computed as number of unique tags for a certain item of a certain user divided by number of unique items for that user
RU2	Level of repetition that computed as number of unique tags for a certain item of a certain user divided by number of unique tagged items for that user
RI1	Level of repetition that computed as number of unique users for a certain tag of a certain item divided by number of unique users for that item
RI2	Level of repetition that computed as number of unique users for a certain tag of a certain item divided by number of unique tagging users for that item

In the collective knowledge-sharing tagging system, items such as book, websites, photo, and video can be shared with other users. Since both Chinese websites and English websites should have similar tagging systems and users' data can be acquired from webpage, three kinds of knowledge sharing websites are selected for comparison of usage pattern of tag (i.e. photo, website, book sharing websites). Introduction to these websites is in Table 2.

Table 2. Introduction to websites for comparison

Website	Categoriza-tion	Data collection	Url	Function
Yupoo	Photo	From website	www.yupoo.com	Uploading, sharing and tagging photos
Flickr	Photo	From website	www.flickr.com	Uploading, sharing and tagging photos
QQ	Website	From website	shuqian.qq.com	Collecting, sharing and tagging websites
Del.icio.us	Website	From website	www.delicious.com	Collecting, sharing and tagging websites
Douban	Book	API	www.douban.com	Collecting, sharing and tagging books
Shelfari	Book	From website	www.shelfari.com	Collecting, sharing and tagging books

Raw data are observed directly from the knowledge sharing website. Cases are recorded in data collection while one case including information about the id of user, the id of the item, and name of tags. In one case, there are only one user, one item and at most one tag as in some case user doesn't attach tags on the item. In photo sharing websites, cases are recorded from recent uploading photos, the most interesting photos of 7 days and 100 random user's all cases. In book sharing websites, cases are recorded from 1000 random user's cases and their 50 books.[1] In bookmark sharing system, cases are recorded from 100 users. The detailed data collection information is shown in table 3.

Table 3. Data collection

	Method	Date
Recent uploading photo	Refresh the recent page for 80 times as there are 28 photos on one page in Yupoo; Refresh the recent page for 85 times as there are 20 photos on one page in Flickr	2010.05
the most interesting photos of 7 days	Refresh the interesting page for 100 times in both Yupoo and Flickr as there are 9 photos on both of them	2010.05
100 random photo user's all cases	Search the key word "a", "b"... "z" and "0", "1"... "9" to get users name and then randomly chose 100 of them	2010.05
100 random photo hot user's all cases	Search the key word "a", "b"... "z" and "0", "1"... "9" to get users name in the most hot user list and then randomly chose 100 of them	2010.05
1000 random book user's all cases (at most 50 books for each user)[2]	Search the key word "a", "b"... "z" and "0", "1"... "9" to get users name and then randomly chose 1000 of them	2009.05
100 random bookmark user's all cases	Search the key work "a", "b"... "z" and "0", "1"... "9" to get users name and then randomly chose 100 of them	2009.05

[1] Douban's privacy policy allows that at most 50 books for each user can be observed.

[2] There are only two tags for 100 random users of Yupoo, hotest users' cases are recorded for better comparison.

4 Results and Discussion

The table 4-5 shows the descriptive result and t-test results of this study.

Most users share less knowledge (photo, book, and bookmark) and fewer users share most knowledge in knowledge sharing websites. As in figure 1-3, it is shown that both Chinese websites users and English websites users have this usage pattern. The curve for this usage pattern is similar to the curve of inverse function. This curve indicates that most users have fewer shared items, tags. Most items have fewer tags. Fewer users contribute most items and tags in knowledge sharing websites.

Chinese users upload more photos in one time. In the recent photo sharing websites, while collecting similar number of photos, there are fewer sharers in Yupoo than in Flickr. The average number of photos shared by users in Yupoo (12.262) is significant form Flickr (2.508) as the p-value for t-test is 0.000. This result implies that Chinese user tend to sharing more photos in one time possibly through fixed devices as PC. User in Flickr is more willing to share their photo into website right after them taking this photo through mobile devices.

Chinese users are more willing to tag all knowledge they share. In Chinese recent uploading photos, the 7 users who have tags tag all the photos they shared in website recently and are willing using the same tag, but tagging users in Flickr don't tag all the photos they share. This demonstrated in the in value of I_T that Yupoo user is significantly higher than Flickr user because some users tag the entire photos they share in Yupoo. In Flickr, there is no such kind of user and they consider tagging as an optional function. This reflects in the value of R1 and R2. This kind of user will have the same value in R1 and R2. Table 4-5 show that Chinese user have this kind of behavior when they recently upload photos, share interesting photos of 7 days, share book websites and bookmark sharing websites.

In random users' data, more Chinese users have book sharing behavior, but fewer Chinese users have photo and bookmark sharing behavior. This may be demonstrated in value of U and UT. U and UT of Chinese book user is 579 and 276 respectively, compared to 400 and 39 of Shelfari. This indicates a different usage pattern in different knowledge sharing systems. However, sample of book websites is slightly different from other two random users' samples.

Tagging for other users' shared content shows another unique usage pattern of Chinese users. Photo sharing websites have a unique feature, which all knowledge shared in the websites are created and uploaded by the creator himself/herself. So it is an interesting finding that some users tag other users' photos. In recent uploaded photos and random users' photos, users don't tag other users' photos.

The value U_I2 of recent photos and interesting photos photo in Chinese photo sharing websites is 1. In English websites, only photo recently uploaded have 1 in U_I2. This indicates that no other user tag the photo except the user who uploads it in Chinese book sharing websites. Exploring user may not check the recent uploaded photo. Indices of RI1 and RI2 also indicate this kind of usage pattern.

Table 4. The descriptive result and t-test result in photo-sharing websites (Recent, interesting, random user)

		Recent uploaded (photo)				Interesting of 7 days (photo)				100 random users (photo)				
Abbr		Yupoo	Flickr		Test	Yupoo	Flickr		Test	Yupoo	Yupoo *	Flickr		Test
T	n	21	1179			127	582			0	3466	2779		
UU	n	141	685			63	88			7	100	82		
UT	n	7	229			22	87			0	80	40		
U	n	141	685			63	114			7	105	86		
I	n	1729	1718			97	91			613	70844	9296		
NT	Mean	7.381	1.969	t	4.021	1.310	1.130	t	3.390	-	32.040	9.970	t	7.629
	SD	6.160	2.277	p	0.001*	0.587	0.456	p	0.001*	-	145.913	78.562	p	0.000*
NU	Mean	1.099	3.388	t	(3.201)	2.650	5.750	t	(2.806)	0.000	1057.530	322.290	t	1.597
	SD	7.090	10.305	p	0.002*	6.152	8.425	p	0.006*	-	4177.314	1982.014	p	0.112
NI	Mean	0.090	1.351	t	(14.082)	1.720	7.210	t	(5.533)	0.000	1.570	2.980	t	(34.232)
	SD	0.570	3.669	p	0.000*	2.999	9.003	p	0.000*	-	2.666	3.864	p	0.000*
T_U	Mean	0.149	1.942	t	(8.518)	2.140	5.640	t	(3.564)	0.000	40.830	37.140	t	0.196
	SD	0.746	5.257	p	0.000*	4.745	8.308	p	0.000*	-	117.485	142.894	p	0.845
I_U1	Mean	12.262	2.508	t	3.632	1.540	1.000	t	3.485	87.571	674.850	106.900	t	4.735
	SD	31.844	3.663	p	0.000*	1.229	0.000	p	0.001*	-	1066.675	555.637	p	0.000*
I_U2	Mean	7.286	2.115	t	2.225	1.619	1.096	t	1.963	-	418.232	141.375	t	1.808
	SD	6.130	2.718	p	0.067	1.203	0.402	p	0.063	-	908.728	677.871	p	0.074
T_I	Mean	0.090	1.348	t	(14.071)	1.720	7.120	t	(5.474)	0.000	1.570	2.370	t	(20.804)
	SD	0.570	3.663	p	0.000*	2.999	8.949	p	0.000*	-	2.666	3.579	p	0.000*
U_I1	Mean	1.000	1.000	t	-	1.000	1.350	t	(2.043)	0.011	1.000	1.000	t	(0.981)
	SD	0.000	0.000	p	-	0.000	1.642	p	0.044*	-	0.015	0.021	p	0.327
U_I2	Mean	1.000	1.000	t	-	1.000	1.517	t	(2.087)	-	1.000	1.001	t	(1.579)
	SD	0.000	0.000	p	-	0.000	1.918	p	0.041*	-	0.012	0.027	p	0.114

Table 4. *(continued)*

Abbr		Recent uploaded (photo)				Interesting of 7 days (photo)				100 random users (photo)				
		Yupoo	Flickr		Test	Yupoo	Flickr		Test	Yupoo	Yupoo *	Flickr		Test
U_T	Mean	1.000	1.128	t	(7.646)	1.060	1.100	t	(1.316)	-	1.240	1.150	t	5.185
	SD	0.000	0.575	p	0.000*	0.302	0.412	p	0.189	-	0.803	0.525	p	0.000*
I_T	Mean	7.381	1.964	t	4.025	1.310	1.110	t	3.656	-	32.040	7.920	t	8.934
	SD	6.160	2.276	p	0.001*	0.587	0.436	p	0.000*	-	145.913	56.414	p	0.000*
T_IU	Mean	0.717	1.348	t	(6.340)	1.720	5.330	t	(4.599)	0.000	1.570	2.980	t	(34.228)
	SD	2.692	3.663	p	0.000*	2.999	8.027	p	0.000*	-	2.666	3.863	p	0.000*
U_TI	Mean	1.000	1.000	t	-	1.000	1.010	t	(2.844)	-	1.000	1.260	t	(86.719)
	SD	0.000	0.000	p	-	0.000	0.111	p	0.005*	-	0.000	0.444	p	0.000*
I_TU	Mean	7.380	1.740	t	4.193	1.240	1.020	t	5.393	-	25.900	8.680	t	7.384
	SD	6.160	1.797	p	0.000*	0.460	0.171	p	0.000*	-	126.949	73.302	p	0.000*
RU1	Mean	0.911	0.865	t	0.762	0.691	0.975	t	(9.165)	-	0.026	0.237	t	(5.239)
	SD	0.280	0.277	p	0.446	0.356	0.114	p	0.000*	-	0.087	2.276	p	0.000*
RU2	Mean	0.911	0.887	t	0.422	0.691	1.019	t	(10.429)	-	0.041	0.155	t	(11.925)
	SD	0.280	0.259	p	0.673	0.356	0.173	p	0.000*	-	0.158	0.521	p	0.000*
RI1	Mean	1.000	1.000	t	-	1.000	0.905	t	9.877	-	1.000	1.002	t	(5.091)
	SD	0.000	0.000	p	-	0.000	0.245	p	0.000*	-	0.017	0.042	p	0.000*
RI2	Mean	1.000	1.000	t	-	1.000	0.905	t	9.880	-	1.000	1.259	t	(86.682)
	SD	0.000	0.000	p	-	0.000	0.244	p	0.000*	-	0.006	0.444	p	0.000*

Table 5. The descriptive result and t-test result in photo, book, bookmark-sharing websites (Random users)

		100 random users (photo)					1000 random users (book)				100 random users (bookmark)			
abbr		Yupoo	Yupoo (Rec)	Flickr		Test	Douban	Shelfari		Test	QQ	Del.icio.us		Test
T	n	0	3466	2779			2963	291			65	16778		
UU	n	7	100	82			1000	1000			78	79		
UT	n	0	80	40			276	39			31	77		
U	n	7	105	86			579	400			78	79		
I	n	613	70844	9296			7938	5452			3368	52877		
NT	Mean	-	32.040	9.970	t	7.629	3.560	2.529	t	3.297	5.369	8.575	t	(0.577)
	SD	-	145.913	78.562	p	0.000*	10.641	4.163	p	0.001*	9.325	44.797	p	0.564
NU	Mean	0.000	1057.530	322.290	t	1.597	18.219	1.840	t	12.910	4.418	1821.165	t	(5.119)
	SD	-	4177.314	1982.014	p	0.112	27.155	11.597	p	0.000*	15.179	3154.596	p	0.000*
NI	Mean	0.000	1.570	2.980	t	(34.232)	1.329	0.135	t	26.655	0.104	2.721	t	(83.945)
	SD	-	2.666	3.864	p	0.000*	3.889	0.742	p	0.000*	0.306	7.066	p	0.000*
T_U	Mean	0.000	40.830	37.140	t	0.196	9.085	0.895	t	9.762	0.899	391.582	t	(6.095)
	SD	-	117.485	142.894	p	0.845	19.275	4.988	p	0.000*	1.809	569.700	p	0.000*
I_U1	Mean	87.571	674.850	106.900	t	4.735	25.487	20.953	t	3.561	45.410	700.975	t	(5.181)
	SD	-	1066.675	555.637	p	0.000*	20.287	19.085	p	0.000*	50.892	1123.529	p	0.000*
I_U2	Mean	-	418.232	141.375	t	1.808	31.366	43.714	t	(0.731)	11.226	718.143	t	(5.477)
	SD	-	908.728	677.871	p	0.074	19.349	109.142	p	0.469	22.803	1131.985	p	0.000*
T_I	Mean	0.000	1.570	2.370	t	(20.804)	1.321	0.134	t	26.749	0.104	2.719	t	21.481
	SD	-	2.666	3.579	p	0.000*	3.854	0.726	p	0.000*	0.306	7.052	p	0.000*
U_I1	Mean	0.011	1.000	1.000	t	(0.981)	1.859	1.537	t	7.130	1.052	1.047	t	0.889
	SD	-	0.015	0.021	p	0.327	2.685	2.481	p	0.000*	0.333	0.273	p	0.374
U_I2	Mean	-	1.000	1.001	t	(1.579)	1.570	1.056	t	20.635	1.000	1.047	t	(39.686)
	SD	-	0.012	0.027	p	0.114	1.773	0.297	p	0.000*	0.000	0.273	p	0.000*

Table 5. (continued)

abbr		100 random users (photo)					1000 random users (book)				100 random users (bookmark)			
		Yupoo	Yupoo (Rec)	Flickr		Test	Douban	Shelfari		Test	QQ	Del.icio.us		Test
U_T	Mean	-	1.240	1.150	t	5.185	1.775	1.230	t	7.509	1.092	1.844	t	(15.885)
	SD	-	0.803	0.525	p	0.000*	2.956	0.821	p	0.000*	0.341	2.741	p	0.000*
I_T	Mean	-	32.040	7.920	t	8.934	3.538	2.510	t	3.350	5.369	8.568	t	(0.577)
	SD	-	145.913	56.414	p	0.000*	5.431	4.093	p	0.001*	9.325	44.714	p	0.564
T_IU	Mean	0.000	1.570	2.980	t	(34.228)	0.715	0.043	t	31.618	0.099	2.598	t	(84.481)
	SD	-	2.666	3.863	p	0.000*	2.559	0.367	p	0.000*	0.299	6.861	p	0.000*
U_TI	Mean	-	1.000	1.260	t	(86.719)	1.006	1.008	t	(0.582)	1.000	1.001	t	(0.536)
	SD	-	0.000	0.444	p	0.000*	0.085	0.104	p	0.561	0.000	0.030	p	0.592
I_TU	Mean	-	25.900	8.680	t	7.384	2.006	2.056	t	(0.187)	4.915	8.296	t	0.136
	SD	-	126.949	73.302	p	0.000*	5.050	2.788	p	0.852	4.651	16.451	p	0.892
RU1	Mean	-	0.026	0.237	t	(5.239)	0.067	0.059	t	1.396	0.090	0.016	t	3.468
	SD	-	0.087	2.276	p	0.000*	0.143	0.094	p	0.163	0.180	0.146	p	0.001*
RU2	Mean	-	0.041	0.155	t	(11.925)	0.067	0.239	t	(10.008)	0.441	0.016	t	9.767
	SD	-	0.158	0.521	p	0.000*	0.143	0.324	p	0.000*	0.367	0.146	p	0.000*
RI1	Mean	-	1.000	1.002	t	(5.091)	0.551	0.550	t	0.054	0.968	0.947	t	3.114
	SD	-	0.017	0.042	p	0.000*	0.393	0.420	p	0.957	0.129	0.166	p	0.002*
RI2	Mean	-	1.000	1.259	t	(86.682)	0.638	0.855	t	(21.136)	1.000	0.947	t	120.126
	SD	-	0.006	0.444	p	0.000*	0.376	0.258	p	0.000*	0.000	0.167	p	0.000*

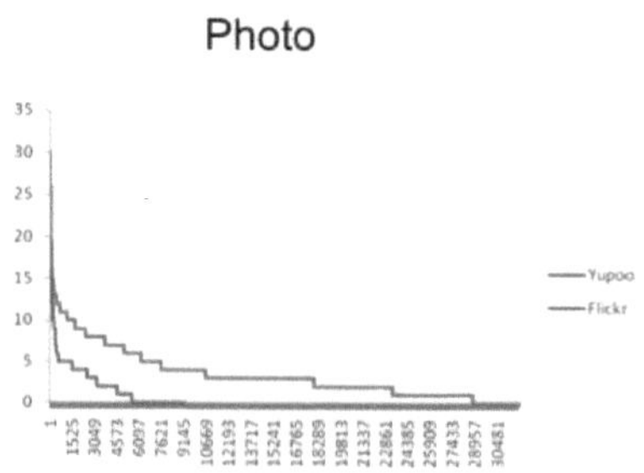

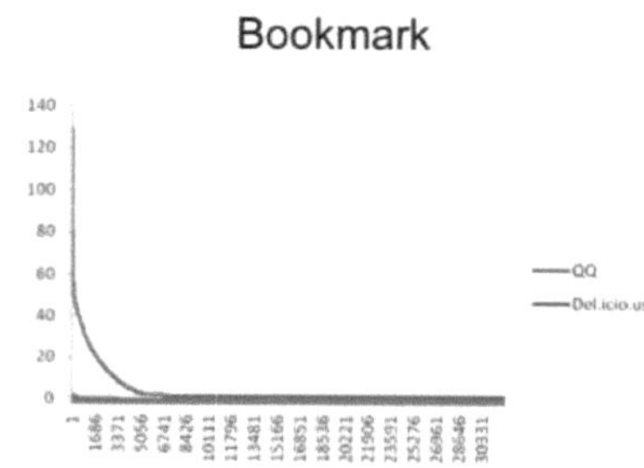

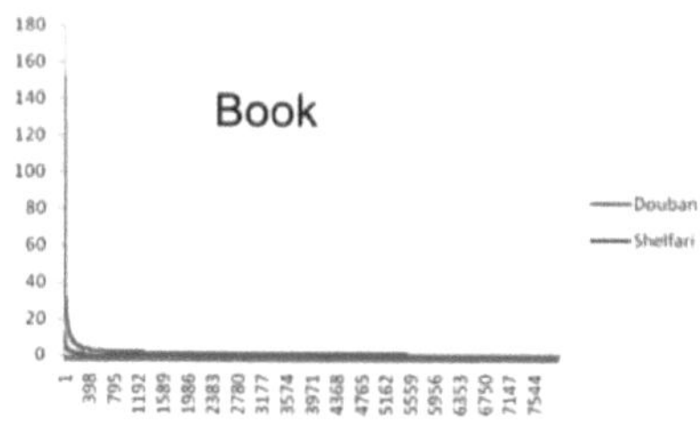

	Yupoo	Flickr		t-test
Mean	1.57	2.37	t	-20.804
Std. dev	2.666	3.579	Sig.	0.000
	QQ	Del.icio.us		t-test
Mean	0.104	2.719	t	21.481
Std. dev	0.306	7.052	Sig.	0.000
	Douban	Shelafri		t-test
Mean	1.321	0.1339	t	26.7486
Std. dev	3.854	0.72615	Sig.	0.000

Fig. 1. Less unique tags for each item in Chinese website (Random user)

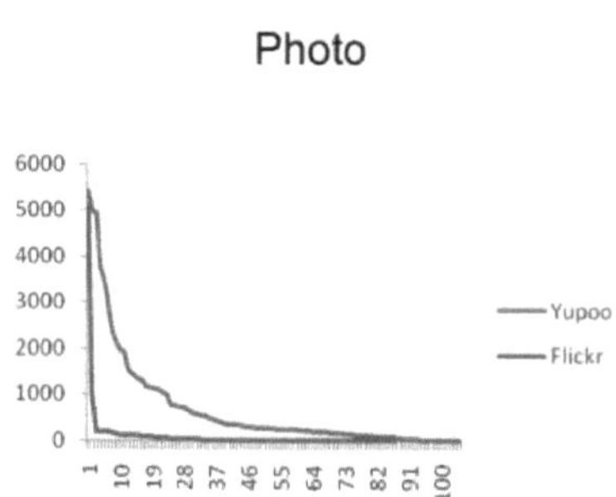

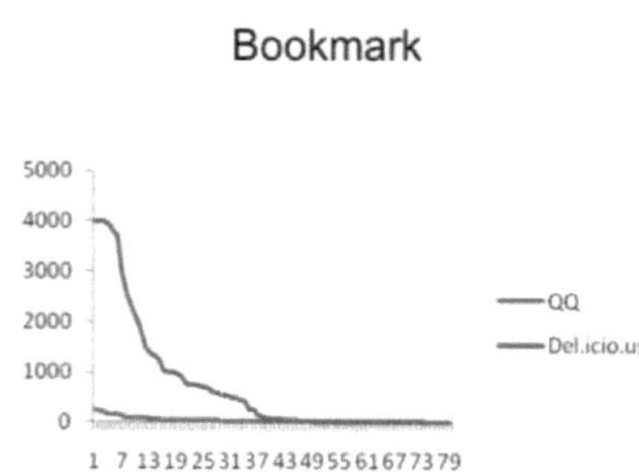

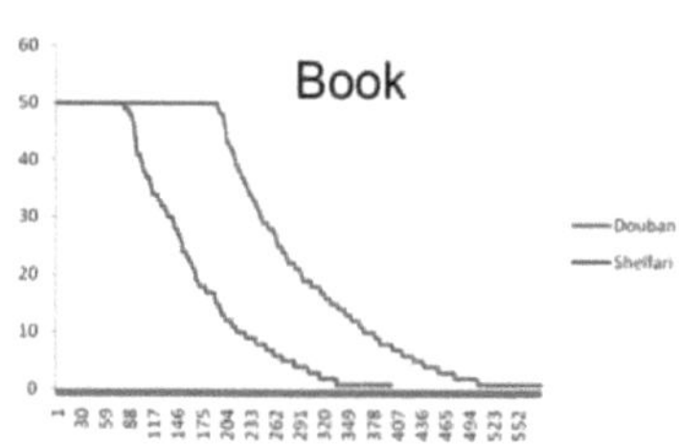

	Yupoo	Flickr		t-test
Mean	674.85	106.9	t	-20.804
Std. dev	1066.68	555.637	Sig.	0.000
	QQ	Del.icio.us		t-test
Mean	45.41	700.975	t	-5.181
Std. dev	50.892	1123.529	Sig.	0.000
	Douban	Shelafri		t-test
Mean	25.487	20.953	t	3.561
Std. dev	20.287	19.085	Sig.	0.000

Fig. 2. More number of unique tags for each Chinese user (Random user)

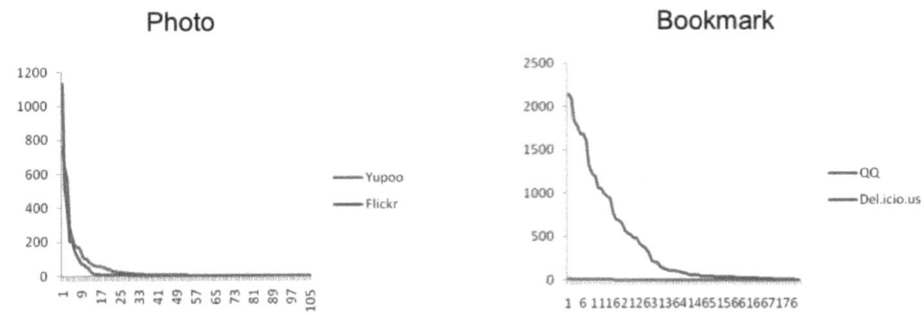

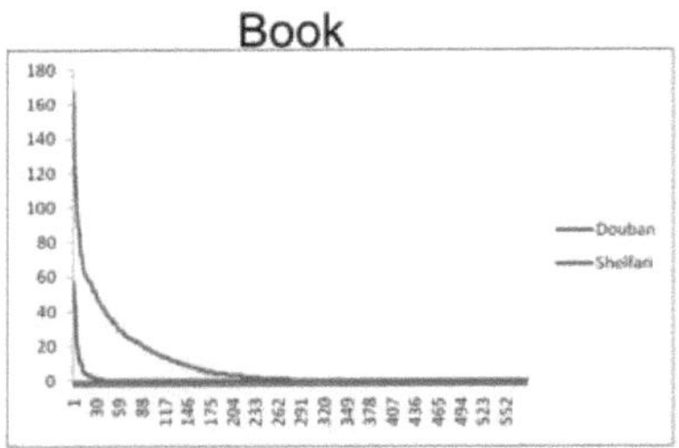

				t-test
	Yupoo	Flickr		t-test
Mean	40.83	37.14	t	0.196
Std. dev	117.485	142.894	Sig.	0.845
	QQ	Del.icio.us		t-test
Mean	0.899	391.582	t	-6.095
Std. dev	1.809	569.700	Sig.	0.000
	Douban	Shelafri		t-test
Mean	9.085	0.895	t	9.762
Std. dev	19.275	4.988	Sig.	0.000

Fig. 3. More number of unique tags for each Chinese user (Random user)

Users use similar tags in photo shared. In recently uploaded photos, Chinese users tend to upload more photos at one time, and they would like to use similar tags for these photos. For example, a user take may photos at Paris and he will upload a lot of photo with tag as Paris on the photo.

Chinese websites users are more willing to share photos, books with tags from his/her history tags and recommendation tag list, but less willing to share bookmarks with tags from his/her history tags and recommendation tag list. This is demonstrated in the value of RU1, RU2, RI1 and RI2.

The result of data analysis demonstrates that most users share less knowledge (photo, book, and bookmark) and fewer users share most knowledge in knowledge sharing websites. Moreover, Chinese culture has effect on the usage pattern in tagging system of knowledge sharing websites; So Chinese users will have a different value in these indices. The reason for this is the restriction of Chinese culture such as modesty. Kurman's research states that this is the main reason that people's low of enhancement [11]. Chinese users tend to use tags from her/his history tags, recommendation tags or tags from other users. Chinese will have a higher value in indices RU1, RU2, RI1 and RI2. These indices can reflect the usage pattern of the situation of a knowledge sharing system with a tagging function. This study is helpful for the cultural difference research in knowledge sharing system, and for managing the cross-culture team.

Further research can be developed in three aspects: 1) to analysis the semantic difference of tag of Chinese users; 2) to conduct a questionnaire and interview to study the reason leading to these differences; 3) to collect data from more types of knowledge sharing websites.

References

1. Bhagat, R.S., Kedia, B.L., Harveston, P.D., Triandis, H.C.: Cultural variations in the cross-border transfer of organizational knowledge: An integrative framework. Academy of Management Review, 204–221 (2002)
2. Chiu, L.H.: A cross-cultural comparison of cognitive styles in Chinese and American children. International Journal of Psychology 7(4), 235–242 (1972)
3. Chow, C.W., Deng, F.J., Ho, J.L.: The openness of knowledge sharing within organizations: a comparative study of the United States and the People's Republic of China. Journal of Management Accounting Research 12, 65 (2000)
4. Davenport, T., Prusak, L., Wills, G., Alani, H., Ashri, R., Crowder, R., et al.: Working knowledge (1998)
5. Golder, S.A., Huberman, B.A.: Usage patterns of collaborative tagging systems. Journal of Information Science 32(2), 198 (2006)
6. Gupta, A.K., Govindarajan, V.: Organizing for knowledge flows within MNCs* 1. International Business Review 3(4), 443–457 (1994)
7. Hambrick, D.C., Davison, S.C., Snell, S.A., Snow, C.C.: When groups consist of multiple nationalities: Towards a new understanding of the implications. Organization Studies 19(2), 181 (1998)
8. Hofstede, G.: Dimensions of national cultures in fifty countries and three regions. Expiscations in Cross-Cultural Psychology, 335–355 (1983)
9. Holden, N.: Knowledge management: raising the spectre of the cross cultural dimension. Knowledge and Process Management 8(3), 155–163 (2001)
10. Kipp, M.E.I., Campbell, D.G.: Patterns and inconsistencies in collaborative tagging systems: An examination of tagging practices. Proceedings of the American Society for Information Science and Technology 43(1), 1–18 (2006)
11. Kurman, J.: Why is Self-Enhancement Low in Certain Collectivist Cultures? Journal of Cross-Cultural Psychology 34(5), 496 (2003)
12. Marlow, C., Naaman, M., Boyd, D., Davis, M.: HT 2006, tagging paper, taxonomy, Flickr, academic article, to read (2006)
13. Marlow, C., Naaman, M., Boyd, D., Davis, M.: HT 2006, tagging paper, taxonomy, Flickr, academic article, to read. Paper Presented at the Proceedings of the Seventeenth Conference on Hypertext and Hypermedia (2006)
14. Nisbett, R.E., Peng, K., Choi, I., Norenzayan, A.: Culture and systems of thought: Holistic versus analytic cognition. Psychological Review 108(2), 291 (2001)
15. Shirky, C.: Ontology is overrated: Categories, links, and tags. Clay Shirky\'s Writings About the Internet (2005)
16. Yang, K.: Chinese personality and its change (1986)

Creating Individualized Learning Paths for Self-regulated Online Learners: An Ontology-Driven Approach

Yu-Liang Chi[1], Tsang-Yao Chen[1], and Wan-Ting Tsai[2]

[1] Dept. of Information Management, Chung Yuan Christian University, 200 Chung-Pei Rd., Chung-Li, Taiwan 32023, R.O.C.
{maxchi,polochen}@cycu.edu.tw

[2] Dept. of Management Information Systems, National Chengchi University, No. 64, Sec. 2, Zhinan Rd., Wenshan District, Taipei City 11605, Taiwan, R.O.C.
lhya623@gmail.com

Abstract. This study extends the ontology-supported modeling of prior studies in learning path personalization to an ontology-driven modeling approach to create a mechanism of online learning path adaptivity. This mechanism is especially applicable for self-regulated learners such as those in flipped learning context. The proposed ontology modeling is based on a conceptualization of education being the function of the triplet of knowledge structure (guide), knowledge content (material), and instruction (teaching). In addition, this study defines cognitive learning as the mapping of the learner's personal knowledge structure to the domain knowledge structure. Furthermore, online learning is viewed as the interaction between the learning management system and the learner. With these conceptualizations, a domain ontology is constructed based on the Common Core State Standards (CCSS) for Mathematics curriculum guide; and a task ontology is constructed to model the problem of learning path adaptivity by including the teaching activity, learning material, and the learner classes. In the case experiment, the Protégé tool is used to construct the ontologies and the semantic rules. The experiment results show that the created mechanism of ontological learning path adaptivity has successfully guided the learner to pre-requisite learning activities and learning objects for remedial learning when current learning activities result in unsatisfactory assessment results.

Keywords: e-Learning, Self-regulated learning, Learning path, Ontology.

1 Introduction

Conventional educational systems deliver learning experiences mainly through classroom instruction and homework assignments, in which instruction is passed from teachers to students. This is no longer the only option when e-learning is becoming more available and viable. In e-learning, learning can happen in between the learning management system (LMS) and the learner without intervention from the teacher.

P.L.P. Rau (Ed.): CCD/HCII 2014, LNCS 8528, pp. 546–555, 2014.

This is especially true in the recent MOOCs phenomenon, and with even greater pedagogical implication in flipped learning, in which classroom teaching and self-regulated learning are "flipped" (Bishop & Verleger, 2013).

Human learning, especially the learning that involves school education, can be seen as the interaction between instruction (typically from the teacher) and learning (of the learner). From the teaching side, education is about "what to teach" and "how to teach" by the curriculum with the materials such as the textbooks, which are what connect teaching to learning. Conceptually, therefore, teaching can be understood to have three dimensions of Guide (the curriculum that guides the teaching), Material (the materials used to teach), and Teach (the action of teaching). The conceptualization of the (G, M, T) triplet is important in e-learning because they are weaved together to interact with the learner. When (G, M, T) is embedded in online learning environment, learning can be the interaction between the LMS and the learner. That is, when the learner is mastery of the concepts and the relations among the concepts, learning is considered successful. In the context of online embedment of (G, M, T), learning object sequencing becomes critical in that personalized adaptive learning could be more effective than conventional one-size-fit-all teaching. This is especially critical in flipped learning when self-regulated learning is facilitated by individualized learning path.

Learning path research is important not only because of learner facilitation, but also because it implies, pedagogically, the existence of a domain knowledge for learner to route through and learn from. Based on the conceptualization of the (G, M, T) triplet, this study aims to create a mechanism of adaptive learning path recommendation. The United States Common Core State Standards (CCSS) for Mathematics (National Governors Association Center for Best Practices, Council of Chief State School Officers, 2010) is formalized as the knowledge domain for modeling and case study. To create adaptive learning paths, a task ontology with flipped learning pedagogy design is constructed. Sematic rules for learning path recommendation are then created to enable knowledge inference and therefore adaptivity mediating between the domain ontology and the knowledge structure of the learner. The domain ontology, task ontology, and sematic rules form the knowledge base with the mechanism of adaptive learning path recommendation.

2 Review of Literature

Major research efforts in learning path personalization and content sequencing have been on LMS-related specifications and learning systems modeling. The technical specifications efforts, represented by SCORM (Sharable Content Object Reference Framework), were led by ADL (Advanced Distributed Learning) initiative, IMS Global Learning Consortium, and the IEEE Learning Technology Standards Committee. SCORM was the de facto standard for LMS and e-learning content interoperability. Other specifications such as Learning Object Metadata (LOM), Learning Design (LD), and Learning Information Profile (LIP) by IMS have also been well received. However, in terms of learning path adaptivity, SCORM enabled platform interoperability from a system-centered view at the cost of learning object sequencing (de Marcos, Pagés, Martinez, & Gutierrez, 2007). As indicated, these learning standards have been important foundations for implementing learning object repository (LOR) in LMS, but are not precise or comprehensive enough for personalizing learning paths (Devedzic, Jovanovic, & Gasevic, 2007).

In contrast to the works in technical specifications, studies in adaptive hypermedia services (AHS) focus on systems modeling. The AHS stream of learning path studies are mainly based on the Dexter reference model (Halasz, Schwartz, Grønbæk, & Trigg, 1994). AHS stresses the flexibility for personalizing content sequencing with major contributions from De Bra (1999), Karampiperis (2006), and Cristea (2003). AHS is ontology-based (Crampes & Ranwez, 2000) and uses modeling of domain, user, and teaching along with pedagogical rules for course adaptation. The modeling approaches allow for flexibility in the design of flows and thus the creation of learner-centered personalized learning paths.

The use of ontological design approaches for learning path adaptivity has attracted attention from researchers due to the recent strive of W3C and semantic web (Cristea & de Mooij, 2003). As indicated, semantic content recommendation in e-learning has the potential of enhancing the efficiency and effectiveness of e-learning (Yu, Nakamura, Jang, Kajita, & Mase, 2007). Many learning path researchers have therefore turned to ontological approach as their research progresses. For example, Karampiperis & Sampson (2006) proposed the use of a competence description ontology for learning object sequencing; Chen (2009) proposed the use of ontology modeling for individual learning path planning; along with others (De Bra, Aroyo, & Chepegin, 2006; Gaeta, Orciuoli, & Ritrovato, 2009), however, the advantages of ontology-driven approach such as concept consistency, classified taxonomy, and computing inference (Chu, Lee, & Tsai, 2011) have not be fully implemented.

3 Design of Knowledge Model

Major research design components of this study includes: (1) a domain ontology for establishing common knowledge concepts and instances using *is-a* relations to express the knowledge categorization structure and to provide a standard terminology set for ontology communication; (2) a task ontology to establish an objective-oriented knowledge framework using *has*-a relations to express the combination of questions; and (3) semantic rules to develop the rules for inferring implicit knowledge.

3.1 Building a Domain Ontology

In this study, CCSS_Math is used as the Guide. Because the knowledge model of an ontology is often represented by conceptual structure, therefore the content of the description-based knowledge model needs to be dissembled and reassembled to obtain its composite concepts, the properties of concepts, and the instances of concepts. Through analysis, the CCSS_Math can be simplified as a regular expression: CCSS.Math.Content.[Grade.Domain.Cluster.Standard]. For example, standard "*CCSS.Math.Content.3.NBT.A.1*" can be dissembled as the following structure:

- Grade: The first symbol uses a digit to denote the grade level of elementary school. For example, '3' represents the third grade.
- Domain: The second symbol uses an abbreviation to denote a subject. For example, "NBT" represents "*Number and Operations in Base Ten*" of mathematics.
- Cluster: The third symbol uses a letter to denote a group of what students should understand and be able to do. For example, "A" denotes the first cluster of "3. NBT." The description of Cluster A is "*Use place value understanding and properties of operations to perform multi-digit arithmetic.*"
- Standard: The forth symbol uses a digit to define a specific item of what students should understand and be able to do. For example, "1" denotes the first standard of "3. NBT.A." Here the standard description is "*Use place value understanding to round whole numbers to the nearest 10 or 100.*"

Domain_CCSS_Math

- Cluster:{has_Description, has_Grade, has_Standards, has_Math_Subject, is_MathDomain }
- Common _Terms
  - Grade_Detail
  - Math_Subject_Detail: { has_Grade, has_Field_Detail }
- Grade_Content: { has_Grade, has_MathDomain }
- MathDomain:{ has_Grade, has_Math_Subject, is_Grade_Contents, has_Cluster }
- Standard:{has_Description, has_Grade, has_Math_Subject, is_Cluster, has_Seqno }

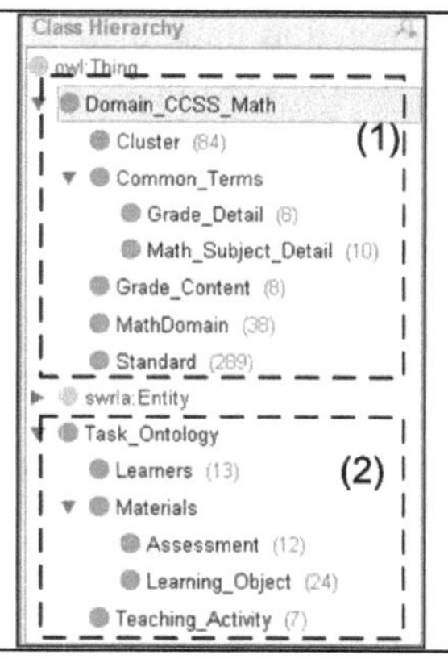

Fig. 1. The conceptual structure, properties, and instances of Domain Ontology

According to the above analysis and dissembling, the structure of CCSS_Math is described as four concepts: `Grade_Content`, `MathDomain`, `Cluster`, and `Standard`. In addition, common terms such as grade year (`Grade`) and content topics (`Math_Subject`) are set as standard terminology of concepts. Under each concept, necessary properties are established to describe the content of the concept. Figure 1 depicts the development results of `Domain_CCSS_Math` (domain ontology). On the left are the concepts and descriptive properties; while on the right is the conceptual structure of the knowledge model edited by Protégé editor: block (1) include the concepts and properties, with the number of instances contained in the concepts. This study established concept instances, including 8 instances under the concept of `Grade_Content`, 38 instances under `MathDomain` (combining grade and mathematic topics), 84 instances under `Cluster`, and 289 instances under `Standard`. In addition, the concept `Math_Subject_Detail` include 10 instances.

3.2 Building a Task Ontology

The objective of the task ontology of this study is to solve the problem of how the learner can use the LMS to precede online learning. To facilitate the conceptual development of the learner, the aforementioned (G, M, T) relationship needs to be completed. Therefore the Task Ontology needs to include the conceptual design of teaching (T) and Material (M). As depicted in block (2) of Fig. 1, three concepts are defined under the task ontology: `Learners`, `Teaching Activity`, and `Material`. Under each concept, necessary properties should be established to describe the content of the concept. Table 1 shows the design of concepts in the task ontology and the corresponding properties. The property is denoted by the following attributes:

1. Name: denotes the name of the property
2. Type: denote the data type and known/unknown attributes. Data type denotes a property as general data or object; while known/unknown denotes a property as asserted or inferred.
3. Range: Denotes the type or scope of the property value. For example, if the Type is denoted as data, then it needs to be further noted as int, string, or float; if the Type is denoted as object, then the acceptable conceptual source needs to be noted.
4. Rule: If the value in Type is denoted as inferred, then the property value needs to be obtained through inference.

Table 1 describes the concepts and the corresponding property design. Due to the fact that the learning is in between the LMS and the learner, the concept of Learners is added. The usages of the properties in the concepts are:

- `Materials`: Providing areas for notification by material producers or assessment developers. Under the sub-concept Assessment, two properties are included: The property that describes name (`has_Assessment_Name`) and the property that denotes cluster (`is_CCSS_Cluster`). Under the sub-concept of Learning object, three properties are included: The property that describes name (`has_LOName`), the property that denotes cluster (`is_CCSS_Cluster`), and the to-be-inferred property of materials with same cluster (`has_Same_LO`);
- `Teaching_Activity`: Providing instructors the arrangement of teaching activities. In the property designs, the first three properties need to be denoted, including the corresponding cluster of each instructional activity (`is_CCSS_Cluster`), the corresponding cluster of the next instructional activity, (`has_Next_Cluster`) and the corresponding cluster of the prerequisite instructional activity (`has_Prerequisite`). These clusters must be connected to the `Domain_CCSS_Math`. Other four properties are to be obtained through inference, including obtaining assessment (`has_Assessment`), obtaining same level learning objects (`has_Available_LO`), obtaining the description of cluster (`has_Cluster_Desc`), and obtaining the description of standards (`has_Standards_Desc`).
- `Learners`: Providing learners with self-regulated learning activities. Among the eight property designs, the first two properties need to be asserted: The learner's (as a person) name property (`has_PName`) and the current Teaching Activity (`has_TActivity`) as assigned by the instructor. Based on the known factual knowledge, the corresponding assessment (`has_Assessment`) and same level

instructional materials (has_Available_LO) properties can be inferred. On the learner assessment results, the fifth property (has_AlreadyKnow) can be obtained. If the value is "*NO*," then the inference for the followed three properties will continue, including has_Pre_TActivity, has_Pre_LO, and has_Pre_Assessment.

Table 1. Detailed design of Task Ontology

Concept		Property			
		Name	Type	Range	Rule
Materials	Assessment	has_Assessment_Name	Data/Asserted	(string)	
		is_CCSS_Cluster	Object/Asserted	Cluster	
	Learning Object	has_LOName	Data/Asserted	(string)	
		is_CCSS_Cluster	Object/Asserted	Cluster	
		has_Same_LO	Object/Inferred	Learning_Object	Rule (1)
Teaching_Activity		is_CCSS_Cluster	Object/Asserted	Cluster	
		has_Prerequisite	Object/Asserted	Cluster	
		has_Next_Cluster	Object/Asserted	Cluster	
		has_Assessment	Object/Inferred	Assessment	Rule (2)
		has_Available_LO	Object/Inferred	Learning_Object	Rule (2)
		has_Cluster_Desc	Data/Inferred	(string)	Rule (3)
		has_Standards_Desc	Data/Inferred	(string)	Rule (4)
Learners		has_PName	Data/Asserted	(string)	
		has_TActivity	Object/Asserted	Teaching_Activity	
		has_Available_LO	Object/Inferred	Learning_Object	Rule (6)
		has_Assessment	Object/Inferred	Assessment	Rule (7)
		has_AlreadyKnow	Data/Asserted	(string)/YES/NO	
		has_Pre_TActivity	Object/Inferred	Teaching_Activity	Rule (8)
		has_Pre_LO	Object/Inferred	Learning_Object	Rule (9)
		has_Pre_Assessment	Object/Inferred	Assessment	Rule (10)

3.3 Developing Inference Rules

Among the properties in the task ontology of Table 1, ten properties are denoted as "Inferred" in the "Type" column and therefore need to develop inference mechanism to obtain the property values. Since properties are used to describe instances, Semantic Web Rule Language (SWRL) therefore can be used to enable inference in the instance layer. The SWRL-based rules are presented in the format of "Premise → Consequence" logic formula. A Premise is usually formed by connecting multiple atoms. According to Chi (2010), the Rule Analysis Form (RAF) can be used to facilitate the development of the rules. RAF simulates the order of problem-solving steps to achieve the purpose of problem-solving through combining the known facts. The rules are first stated in colloquial statement by steps and then listed as ordered formula in a format of {Goal (Problem): Step1; Step2;.. .., Stepn}. Table 2 lists all

SWRL-based rules developed following the RAF procedure. The above deduction steps can be written as"(atom1 ∧... ∧ atomn)→ Consequence." All the rules are edited using the Protégé SWRLTab editor.

Table 2. List of SWRL-based rules

Rule Name	SWRL Rules
Rule-1: Find same learning objects	Learning_Object (?x) ∧ is_CCSS_Cluster (?x, ?a1) ∧ Learning_Object (?y) ∧ is_CCSS_Cluster (?y, ?a1) ∧ differentFrom(?x, ?y) → has_Same_LO(?x, ?y)
Rule-2: Find corresponding assessment	Teaching_Activity(?x) ∧ is_CCSS_Cluster(?x, ?a) ∧ Assessment (?y) ∧ is_CCSS_Cluster(?y, ?a) → has_Assessment(?x, ?y)
Rule-3: Find available learning objects	Teaching_Activity(?x) ∧ is_CCSS_Cluster(?x, ?y) ∧ Learning_Object (?z) ∧ is_CCSS_Cluster(?z, ?y) → has_Available_LO(?x, ?z)
Rule-4: Find cluster's description	Teaching_Activity(?x) ∧ is_CCSS_Cluster(?x, ?y) ∧ Cluster(?y) ∧ has_Description(?y, ?z) →has_Cluster_Desc(?x, ?z)
Rule-5: Find standard's description	Teaching_Activity(?x) ∧ is_CCSS_Cluster(?x, ?y) ∧ Cluster(?y) ∧ has_Standards (?y, ?z) ∧ has_Description(?z, ?a) → has_Standards_Desc (?x, ?a)
Rule-6: Find available LO for learners	Learners(?x) ∧ has_TActivity(?x, ?y) ∧ Teaching_Activity(?y) ∧ has_Available_LO (?y, ?a) → has_Available_LO(?x, ?a)
Rule-7: Find assessment for learners	Learners(?x) ∧ has_TActivity(?x, ?y) ∧ Teaching_Activity(?y) ∧ has_Assessment(?y, ?a) → has_Assessment(?x, ?a)
Rule-8: Find pre-Teaching activity	has_AlreadyKnow(?x, "NO") ∧ has_TActivity(?x, ?y) ∧ has_Prerequisite (?y, ?z) ∧ Teaching_Activity(?a) ∧ is_CCSS_Cluster (?a, ?z) → has_Pre_TActivity(?x, ?a)
Rule-9: Find pre- learning object	has_AlreadyKnow(?x, "NO") ∧ has_Pre_TActivity (?x, ?y) ∧ Teaching_Activity(?y) ∧ has_Available_LO(?y, ?z) → has_Pre_LO(?x, ?z)
Rule-10: Find pre-assessment	has_AlreadyKnow(?x, "NO") ∧ has_Pre_TActivity (?x, ?y) ∧ Teaching_Activity(?y) ∧ has_Assessment(?y, ?z) → has_Pre_Assessment(?x, ?z)

4 Experiment

The aforementioned knowledge model development has completed the conceptual structure of the domain ontology and related instances. The conceptual structure and semantic rules design are also completed. This section is to demonstrate the mechanism of learning path personalization through learning object sequencing. The task is done by applying the concepts of Teaching activity and Learners with the use of inference engine for rule inference to obtain implicit knowledge.

4.1 Teaching Activity

The instructor, instructional designer, or the LMS administrator, with their expertise in instructional activity management, may announce the current curriculum activity as shown in Fig. 2. This show case use "Teaching_Activity1" as an example.

The 3 properties are the corresponding current cluster, the next activity cluster, and the pre-requisite cluster. These annotations are known factual knowledge. As shown in screenshot (1) of Fig. 2, the three property values at individual editor pane are "CCSS.Math.Content.3.OA.A","CCSS.Math.Content.3.OA.B", and "CCSS.Math.Content.2.OA.A", respectively. Other properties of the individual are blank and are marked as corresponding rules Rule-2 through Rule-5 (see Table 2).

Screenshot (2) of Fig. 2 shows the results of running the inference engine. The blank properties in screenshot (1) have obtained property values. For example, the `has_Available_LO` has obtained *"Alphla_3A, Beta_3A, and Delta_3A"*, which are three learning objects of same level. The inference engine used in this study is JESS (Java Expert System Shell), a third party inference tool embedded in Protege platform as a plugin.

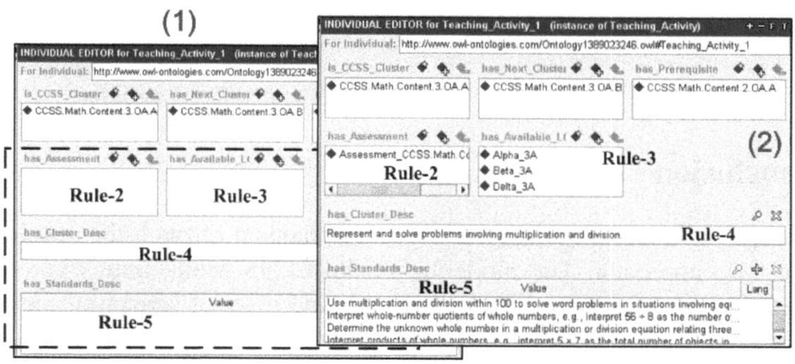

Fig. 2. Results of Teaching Activity after running the inference engine

4.2 Learners

This study is intended to design the self-regulated learning in a flipped learning context. The learner would start the instructor-assigned activity. For example, screenshot (1) of Fig. 3 has Learners_1 as the starting point. The learner and the current learning activity are to be asserted (two properties in the upper part of the individual editor are shown as asserted property values respectively: "Polo Chen" and "Teaching_Activity1"). The other 6 properties are shown blank. For the purpose of elaboration, in Screenshot (1) of Fig. 3, block (1.A) and block (1.B) are marked to explain the two-stage inference:

- In block (1.A), two rules (Rule-6 and Rule-7, see Table 2 for details) are applied to obtain the corresponding learning objects and assessments. After running JESS, the results are shown in Screenshot (2) of Fig. 3.
- In block (1.B), the learner's performance in this teaching activity needs to be shown in `has_AlreadyKnow`. If the results is not satisfactory (shown as *"NO"* in this property), the learner will be routed to the pre-requisite teaching activity. The remained three properties in block (1.B) use the rules Rule-8 to Rule-10 (see Table 2for details). After running JESS, the results are shown in Screenshot (2) of

Fig. 3. In this demonstration, the learner is assigned *"Teaching_Activity_41"* (Rule-8), learning objects *"Alpha_2A, Beta_2A*, and *Delta_2A"* (Rule-9), and *"Assessment_CCSS.Math.Content.OA.A"* (Rule-10)for remedial learning.

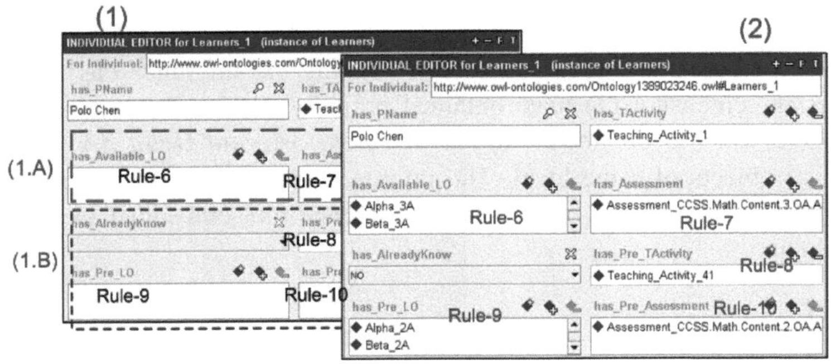

Fig. 3. Results of Learners after running the inference engine

5 Conclusion

This study created a learning path adaptivity mechanism through the ontology-driven knowledge base approach: The modeling of the CCSS Mathematics knowledge domain, a learning path adaptation task ontology, and a set of semantic rules to enable the learning path adaptivity. As the experiment has shown, the ontology-driven knowledge base adaptivity mechanism is able to facilitate learning remediation by specifying a learning path for the learner to return to the needed pre-requisite learning objects and assessment. This mechanism is most suitable for learner's remedial learning in flipped learning context. The value of this study is threefold:

5. The use of ontology-driven approach: Instead of an ontology-supported approach, the ontology-driven design has not only retained the strengths of ontology information systems in terms of concept consistency, classified taxonomy, and computing inference, but also given the advantage of elasticity to knowledge modeling.
6. The teaching-learning reconceptualization: The learning path adaptivity mechanism is enabled through the sematic rules to create causal inferences between the domain ontology and the task ontology, which is based on the conceptualization of education (G, M, T) triplet and the reality that learning could happen in between LMS and learner.
7. Pedagogical embedment: The ontological implementation of learning path adaptivity is practically meaningful for flipped learning. In a time when learning can be the interaction between the LMS and the learner, sound pedagogical considerations are important for further development of learning path research.

Based on the conceptualizations and implementation of this study, future studies in learning path adaptivity may extend from remediation to incorporate more comprehensive pedagogical principles such as the possibility of concurrent learning paths and user profile modeling for better learning path adaptivity.

References

1. Bishop, J.L., Verleger, M.A.: The flipped classroom: A survey of the research. In: 2013 ASEE Annual Conference Proceedings. American Society for Engineering Education, Atlanta (2013)
2. Chen, C.-M.: Ontology-based concept map for planning a personalised learning path. British Journal of Educational Technology 40(6), 1028–1058 (2009)
3. Chi, Y.-L.: Rule-based ontological knowledge base for monitoring partners across supply networks. Expert Systems with Applications 37(2), 1400–1407 (2010)
4. Chu, K.-K., Lee, C.-I., Tsai, R.-S.: Ontology technology to assist learners' navigation in the concept map learning system. Expert Systems with Applications 38(9), 11293–11299 (2011)
5. Crampes, M., Ranwez, S.: Ontology-supported and ontology-driven conceptual navigation on the World Wide Web. In: Proceedings of the Eleventh ACM Conference on Hypertext and Hypermedia, Hypertext 2000, pp. 191–199. ACM Press, San Antonio (2000)
6. Cristea, A.I., Calvi, L.: The three layers of adaptation granularity. In: Brusilovsky, P., Corbett, A.T., de Rosis, F. (eds.) UM 2003. LNCS, vol. 2702, pp. 4–14. Springer, Heidelberg (2003)
7. Cristea, A.I., de Mooij, A.: LAOS: Layered WWW AHS authoring model and their corresponding algebraic operators. In: WWW 2003, The Twelfth International World Wide Web. ACM Press, Budapest (2003)
8. De Bra, P., Aroyo, L., Chepegin, V.: The next big thing: Adaptive Web-based systems. Journal of Digital Information 5(1) (2004), `http://journals.tdl.org/jodi/index.php/jodi/article/view/124/122` (retrieved from)
9. De Bra, P., Houben, G.-J., Wu, H.: AHAM: a Dexter-based reference model for adaptive hypermedia. In: Proceedings of the Tenth ACM Conference on Hypertext and Hypermedia: Returning to Our Diverse Roots, pp. 147–156. ACM Press, Darmstadt (1999)
10. de Marcos, L., Pagés, C., Martinez, J.J., Gutierrez, J.A.: Competency-based learning object sequencing using particle swarms. In: 19th IEEE International Conference on Tools with Artificial Intelligence, ICTAI 2007, vol. 2, pp. 111–116 (2007)
11. Devedzic, V., Jovanovic, J., Gasevic, D.: The pragmatics of current e-learning standards. IEEE Internet Computing 11(3), 19–27 (2007)
12. Gaeta, M., Orciuoli, F., Ritrovato, P.: Advanced ontology management system for personalised e-Learning. Knowledge-Based Systems 22(4), 292–301 (2009)
13. Halasz, F., Schwartz, M., Grønbæk, K., Trigg, R.H.: The Dexter hypertext reference model. Communications of the ACM 37(2), 30–39 (1994)
14. Karampiperis, P., Sampson, D.: Adaptive learning objects sequencing for competence-based learning. In: Proceedings of the Sixth International Conference on Advanced Learning Technologies (ICALT 2006), pp. 136–138. IEEE Computer Society, Kerkrade (2006)
15. National Governors Association Center for Best Practices, Council of Chief State School Officers. Common Core State Standards for Mathematics. National Governors Association Center for Best Practices, Council of Chief State School Officers, Washington (2010)
16. Yu, Z., Nakamura, Y., Jang, S.-I., Kajita, S., Mase, K.: Ontology-based semantic recommendation for context-aware e-learning. In: Indulska, J., Ma, J., Yang, L.T., Ungerer, T., Cao, J. (eds.) UIC 2007. LNCS, vol. 4611, pp. 898–907. Springer, Heidelberg (2007)

Exploring Children's Attitude and Reading Comprehension toward Different Styles of Reading Orientation

Weijane Lin, Hsin-Ying Wu, Pei-Min Wu, Yun Tung, and Hsiu-Ping Yueh

Department of Library and Information Science,
National Taiwan University
Department of Bio-Industry Communication and Development,
National Taiwan University
No. 1., Sec. 4., Roosevelt Rd., Daan Dist.,
Taipei 10617, Taiwan, R.O.C.
vjlin@ntu.edu.tw

Abstract. Library is an institution which aims to provide access to knowledge and information services. For child readers, visual and textual cues including book cover, abstract, and table of contents facilitate them in book selection. However, book browsing could be time- and effort-consuming, and children preferred more intuitive guide. In this study, reading orientation in video form was proposed as solution to provide children with book introduction and help them in book selection process. Elementary school students who start reading Chinese texts independently were recruited as the subjects of this study, and their attitude and performance with different styles of reading orientation were investigated respectively. Preliminarily results showed that for the 24 participants, children who read with the graphical style orientation told more facts and details of the book content, albeit the difference between textual and graphical styles of orientation was not statistically significant. The finding also suggested the presence of graphic might facilitate children's comprehension of the story by coordinating intuitive cues with children's inference. Further investigation is conducted by more structural instrument under larger body of subjects to systematically explore the phenomenon.

Keywords: Reading orientation, graphic and text, children reading.

1 Introduction

Library as an institution striving for providing diverse and organized information resources is responsible for satisfying varied information needs of all levels of patrons. To address its mission, numbers of resources have been organized and cataloged according to classification schemes and cataloging rules in advance of disseminating for public use. For many public libraries, children patrons aged from toddlers, schoolchildren to young adults are major users of the library space and services

P.L.P. Rau (Ed.): CCD/HCII 2014, LNCS 8528, pp. 556–562, 2014.

(Walter, 2003), and they regard library space as familiar and favorable place to access information. According to Eaton's (1991) study, elementary children spent average 12 minutes to complete book locating tasks, which was much slower than the average 6.5 minute of older patrons'. For patrons with limited library literacy as children, library instruction was conducted to enable users with library knowledge to be referenced between bookshelves. There also exist library practices of improved graphical catalog and interface to cope with the difficulties children had when searching in typical keyword OPAC systems (Bilal & Bachir, 2007; Druin et al, 2007; Hutchinson, Druin & Bederson, 2007). However, children patrons actually preferred direct and social search strategies such as going directly to the shelves to find books, or to ask a friend or a librarian for help (Lin, Yueh, Wu, & Fu, 2014).

Previous studies also supported that child patrons tend to browse between the bookshelves and rely on book cover, introductory text on the back cover and table of content as crucial information sources to choose one book from the other (Reuter, 2007; Cunningham, 2011). However, browsing could be time- and effort-demanding for library users in general, and for users of limited library literacy as child patrons in specific. In order to facilitate children in book selection in easier and efficient way, reading orientation is therefore proposed in this study to introduce book content to child readers. Different styles of orientation in terms of interface design are taken into careful consideration in order to facilitate children's comprehension and motivation to reading. Previous studies in educational media supported that different presentation could affect human appraisal and understanding, as Höffler and Leutner (2007) summarized, representational animations was advantageous in instructional purposes compared to static presentation. In this vein, reading orientation is designed in dynamic video form to brief the storyline of a book.

In addition to the state of presentation, the representation media also affected human message processing. For younger children, picture is an attractive element in reading and this element in combination of oral reading from parents help them grasp the meaning of story (Roy-Charland, Saint-Aubin & Evans, 2007). The same study also suggested that younger children tend to depend on graphic information on storybook as they are emergent readers. Meanwhile, as Mayer (2009) addressed, individuals learn better through the combination of words and images than words alone. Studies in cognitive styles and message processing supported that graphic content has its importance on children's reading. However, whether graphic portrayed a positive role on children's reading behavior is still under discussion. Some researchers claimed that graphic might elaborate children's learning on text, as mentioned by previous studies (Carney & Levin, 2002; Glenberg & Langston, 1992); others argued that graphic was distracting in reading since it attracted children's attention and hence imposed extraneous cognitive load (Torcasio & Sweller, 2010). This exploratory study aims to explore children's reading attitude and performance with and without graphical facilitation. Furthermore, as child readers are gradually familiar with text reading and develop literacy to read independently, whether graphical facilitation remained its importance on reading performance is necessarily investigated.

2 Methods

A quasi-experiment was conducted to measure children's reading attitude and performance toward different layouts of reading orientation videos: graphical and horizontal text form (Group 1) and horizontal text layout (Group 2). The experiment design is shown as Figure 1. The awarded illustration book "*I cannot see anything*" was selected as assigned material of reading orientation for the content of the book supported children's reflective thinking (see Figure 2), the illustration book consisted of simple but complete Chinese sentences which were appropriate and recommended by public libraries for elementary school children. Two format orientation videos, as shown in Figure 3, were then designed respectively: one presented both illustrations and text content (Group 1) and the other showed only text in horizontal layout (Group 2). These videos contained a brief introduction to the book and the length of the video was controlled to be equally 1 minute. The videos were installed in iPad and presented in children's reading class in school media center.

Totally 24 school children of the third and forth grade were recruited to participate in this study from an elementary in Taipei City. The third and fourth graders were chosen for their unique features as the emergent independent readers in Chinese reading. The participants were assigned randomly to the two groups. In each group, 7 to 8 participants watched the orientation video of the book together. After completing the orientation, the participant was enquired of their attitude and understanding toward

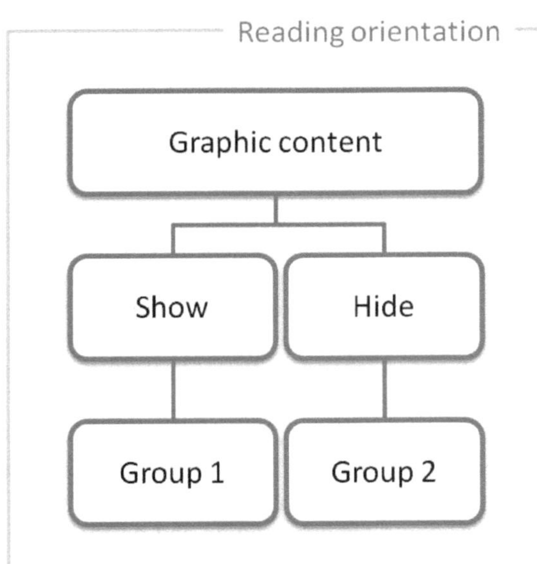

Fig. 1. Experiment design of this study

Fig. 2. The assigned book "I cannot see anything"

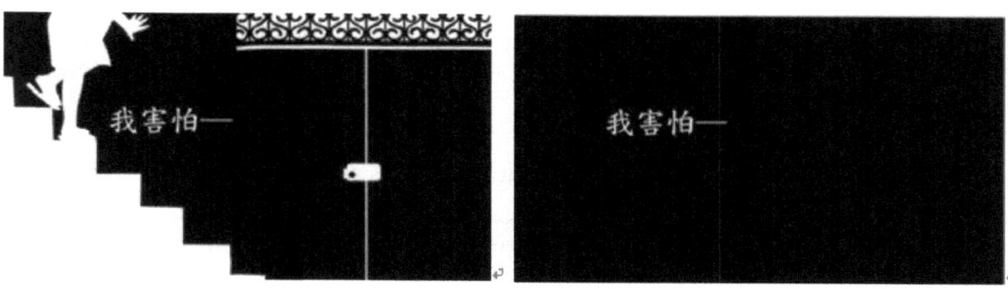

Fig. 3. Two presentations of reading orientation: on the left presented the graphic content (Group 1); on the right presented the non-graphic version (Group 2)

the story presented in the video. Reading attitude was enquired by a two-item 4-Likert scale questionnaire which investigated whether the participants favored the assigned video reading orientation and whether they desired to continuingly read the book after they saw the orientation video; reading comprehension was gathered by a open question required children's writing of what they understood from the video. The preliminary results were analyzed by descriptive statistics and qualitative analysis.

3 Preliminarily Results

The participants in Group 1 and Group 2 were 11 and 13, respectively, and the proportion of each gender was nearly equal, as shown in Table 1.

Table 1. Gender distribution of Group 1 (G1) and Group 2 (G2)

		Graphic content	
		Show(G1)	Hide(G2)
Gender	Boy	5	8
	Girl	6	5

3.1 Children's Attitude toward Reading Orientation

Preliminarily result showed that the two groups of participants who read with graphic content reported similar preference over the reading orientation, as presented in Table 2 and Figure 4. All the 24 participants have never read the assigned illustration book "I cannot see anything" before, and shown their interest to the content.

Among the two groups of participants, the 8 boys and 5 girls in Group 2 showed a slightly higher preference on the reading orientation, and reported higher desire to finish reading the book, albeit the difference was not statistically significant (df=22, t=-.088, p=.931>.05). It could be resulted from a small sample in this study, and also affected by the colors design of the selected reading material. The color scheme of the assigned book "I cannot see anything" was purposefully designed in a black and white monotone to simulate the blind people's perspective. Without the colorful pictures and illustrations, the design might be less attractive to children's attention compared to those with bright and light colors.

Table 2. Reading attitude toward the orientation videos with/without graphic content

	Group 1 Show Graphic Content		Group 2 Hide Graphic Content		*t*
	M	SD	M	SD	
Favorable toward the reading orientation video	2.82	.751	2.85	.801	-.088
Desire to finish reading the book	2.91	1.044	3.08	.954	-.411

Note: **p*<0.05, ***p*<0.01, ****p*<0.001.

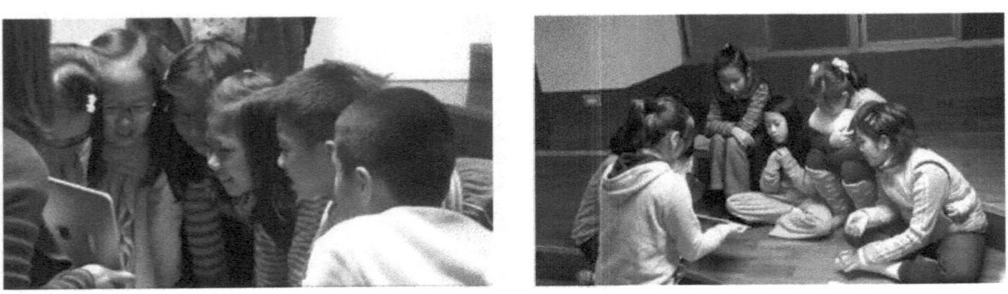

Fig. 4. Children's behavior during the reading orientation

3.2 Children's Reading Comprehension with the Reading Orientation

Further investigation into children's reading comprehension revealed that there was difference existing between these two presentation layouts. Group 1 participants demonstrated much comprehension on the storyline and depicted more details in the story. They described the story with a much completed manner, such as:

> *"There was a person he could not see anything, but he heard some voice and did not know what happened."* (G1S2)

> *"The boy in the video could not see anything. Many people regarded him as an absurd person. Since he could not see anything besides him at home even, he felt very afraid."* (G1S7)

On the other hand, Group 2 participants who watched the orientation video without graphic presentation showed poor understanding toward the storyline. Near half of the children directly reported that:

> *"I totally did not understand what the story was about."*

Only few participants could depict the storyline in the orientation video and provided rather fragmented description such as

> *"There was a person who could not see anything"*. (G2S1; G2S4; G2S6)

Interestingly, Group 1 participants who read with the graphic content tended to describe the story based on the facts in the story, while Group 2 participants who read with the text content only tended to add in their inference when reflected the story. The participants reported their understanding toward the story such as:

> *"The story depicted the pain that a blind person encountered."* (G1S1)

In addition, the judgmental arguments occurred more often in Group 2; for instance, one of the participants mentioned that

> *"The person could not see anything! He's so poor!"* (G2S4)

4 Conclusions and Future Work

In this exploratory study, children's attitude and reading comprehension toward graphic presentation was explored. Preliminarily results showed that for the 24 participants, children who read with the graphical style orientation told more facts and details of the book content, albeit the difference between textual and graphical styles of orientation was not statistically significant. The finding also suggested the presence of graphic might facilitate children's comprehension of the story by coordinating intuitive cues with children's inference. The findings suggested that graphic content might portray an important role in children's reading comprehension. Graphic content provided children with more clues and might help them depict the story in more detailed narration. Further study with improved and structural presentation design will be conducted under larger scale to examine the effect of reading orientation styles on children's reading. Systematic comparison of different forms of textual and graphic content will be also further examined.

References

1. Bilal, D., Bachir, I.: Children's interaction with cross-cultural and multilingual digital libraries. II. Information seeking, success, and affective experience. Information Processing & Management 43(1), 65–80 (2007)
2. Carney, R.N., Levin, J.R.: Pictorial illustrations still improve students' learning from text. Educational Psychology Review 14(1), 5–26 (2002)
3. Cunningham, S.: Children in the physical collection: implications for the digital library. Proceedings of the American Society for Information Science and Technology 48(1), 1–10 (2011)
4. Druin, A., Weeks, A., Massey, S., Bederson, B.B.: Children's interests and concerns when using the international children's digital library: a four-country case study. In: Proceedings of the 7th ACM/IEEE-CS Joint Conference on Digital Libraries, pp. 167–176 (2007)
5. Eaton, G.: Wayfinding in the library: Book searches and route uncertainty. RQ, 519–527 (1991)
6. Glenberg, A.M., Langston, W.E.: Comprehension of illustrated text: pictures help to build mental models. Journal of Memory and Language 31, 129–151 (1992)
7. Hutchinson, H.B., Druin, A., Bederson, B.B.: Supporting elementary - age children's searching and browsing: Design and evaluation using the international children's digital library. Journal of the American Society for Information Science and Technology 58(11), 1618–1630 (2007)
8. Höffler, T., Leutner, D.: Instructional animation versus static pictures: a meta-analysis. Learning and Instruction 17, 722–738 (2007)
9. Lin, W., Yueh, H.-P., Wu, H.Y., Fu, L.C.: Developing a service robot for a children's library: A design - based research approach. Journal of the Association for Information Science and Technology 65(2), 290–301 (2014)
10. Mayer, R.E.: Multimedia learning, 2nd edn. Cambridge University Press, New York (2009)
11. Reuter, K.: Assessing aesthetic relevance: Children's book selection in a digital library. Journal of American Society for Information Science and Technology 58(12), 1745–1763 (2007), doi:10.1002/asi.20657
12. Roy-Charland, A., Saint-Aubin, J., Evans, M.: Eye movements in shared book reading with children from kindergarten to Grade 4. Reading and Writing 20(9), 909–931 (2007)
13. Torcasio, S., Sweller, J.: The use of illustrations when learning to read: A cognitive load theory approach. Applied Cognitive Psychology 24(5), 659–672 (2010)
14. Walter, V.A.: Public library service to children and teens: A research agenda. Library Trends 51(4), 571–589 (2003)

Culture and Student-Faculty Communication in Higher Education: Implications for the Design of Educational Communication Tools

Jun Liu, Pei-Luen Patrick Rau, and Bert Schulz

Institute of Human Factors and Ergonomics, Department of Industrial Engineering, Tsinghua University, Beijing, China, 100084
june.liu.bj@gmail.com, rpl@mail.tsinghua.edu.cn, Bert.Schulz@gmx.net

Abstract. This paper examines the significance of culture and its impact on communication in higher education. The objectives were to compare Chinese and German university students' different patterns of communication with their faculty, and to provide implications for designing educational computer-mediated communication (CMC) tools. The study involved two phases: first, an explorative interview with students and professors from both countries revealing that communication formality is the most significant difference between the two cultures. Second, an online questionnaire evaluating Chinese and German university students' communication formality and uncertainty avoidance in education (N=125) confirmed that German students communicate more formally with faculty than Chinese students, and this difference can be positively predicted by their degree of uncertainty avoidance. Based on these findings, we discussed the implications for designing the CMC tools which can help university faculty to better communicate with their foreign students.

Keywords: Higher education, computer-mediated communication, intercultural communication, communication formality, uncertainty avoidance.

1 Introduction

Internationalization in higher education has created many opportunities for students to learn with faculty from different cultures. From a statistical report (OECD, 2010; see also Coughlan, 2011), 3.43 million students were studying abroad all around the world in 2009. The number continues to rise sharply and may reach approximately to 7 million by the year 2020. As university students acquire international experiences by studying abroad, they develop perceptions of culture and cultural differences, and learn how to act properly in other cultures. Those perceptions and abilities not only impact academic success during their study, but also form an essential foundation for their future culture experience. Therefore, it is important to help international students to develop proper cultural competency, and to form healthy relationships with other people during their university life.

P.L.P. Rau (Ed.): CCD/HCII 2014, LNCS 8528, pp. 563–573, 2014.

One of the most important relationships in university life is that between student and faculty. When they are from different cultures, their cultural conflicts and misunderstandings may become a serious problem in the relationship, and may affect their academic performance directly. Furthermore, the decrease of face-to-face talk and the prevalent of online communication in universities may cause more uncertainty and misunderstandings between faculty and students (Gunawardena, Wilson, & Nolla, 2003). The present study aims to address the problem and explore the student-faculty communication in an intercultural context. Specifically, this paper focuses on German and Chinese students' different perceptions and expectations in their communication with university faculty. This study also highlights the implications for designing cultural adaptive communication tools for students studying abroad and faculty with international students, in order to address their communication problems, to improve their relationship, and to benefit their academic performance.

The rest of the paper consists of four parts. Firstly, the researchers review the literature on Chinese and German cultures and communication in higher education. Secondly, an unstructured interview with Chinese and German university students and faculty is introduced addressing the key differences and challenges in their communication. By analyzing the interview results, communication formality is highlighted as an essential issue. Thirdly, two hypotheses are developed proposing cross-cultural differences in communication formality between students and faculty. A questionnaire study assessing both Chinese and German university students supports the hypotheses. Finally, the implications for higher education communication system design are discussed.

2 Literatures

2.1 Communication in Education

Education is a result of communication. Communication is the medium for education and both aspects are inextricably linked. Lewis (1952) stated that the chief instrument of education is communication, and one of the chief aims of education is to foster communication.

Information technology has brought more computer-mediated communications (CMC) in the education context. E-mail, instant message and social networking sites have enriched the student-faculty communications to a large extent (Gunawardena, et al., 2003; Helvie-Mason, 2011). Three attributes of CMC, time-independence, text based communication, and computer-mediated interaction (Harasim, 1990), influence the ways of communication between students and faculty (Gunawardena, et al., 2003).

Different communication patterns influence the educational system and the education. As Wilson concluded, "the quality of student learning is directly related to the quality of instruction and that professors need to know how students can best learn in their classrooms" (Wilson, 1996). Furthermore, there are many different learning styles and ways to practice these learning styles. Evidence showed "that students taught in their preferred learning styles achieve greater academic success." (Melton, 1990)

In intercultural learning context, communication difference across cultures can cause destructive conflicts between students and faculty. In a study by Adrian-Taylor, Noels, and Tischler (2007), 22% of international graduate students and 34% of faculty supervisors have experienced student-supervisor conflict. And the most important sources of these conflicts were all communication-related: including lack of openness and feedback; unclear expectations; and poor English proficiency. But their study didn't inform how different cultural backgrounds can influence the communication process and how to solve the conflicts in different cultures.

2.2 Cultural Differences in Education

Among the most comprehensive theories of national cultural difference, Hofstede (1986, 1991)'s dimensional theory is widely accepted and adopted in cross-cultural studies. Although it roots from studies in workspace context, the theory is also applied well in educational practice. The following part introduces this four-dimension theory (large vs. small power distance, individualism vs. collectivism, masculinity vs. femininity, and strong vs. weak uncertainty avoidance) and its application in education.

According to Hofstede (1986), the power distance in school and more precisely the teacher-student relationship is comparable with the parent-child relationship. In high power distance situations students show high respect for their teachers with a simultaneous need for dependence. Whatever the teacher says is accepted as he is right and talking back is not appreciated. In contrast, in low power distance situations the student is actively involved in the learning process and the teacher-student relationship is based on a more equal level. "They argue with teachers, express disagreement and criticisms in front of the teacher, and show no particular respect to teachers outside from school" (Hofstede, 1991). As students of low power distance countries reach higher education levels their dependence toward the teacher or academic staff gradually decreases and they tend to channel their study by themselves. High power distance affected students still remain dependent on their teachers.

Hofstede also defines the differences of individualism and collectivism in school. In collectivistic cultures students prefer in-group behavior. They tend not to speak up individually for their group, and instead they take turns presenting results. Students of individualistic oriented cultures tend to speak up for themselves. For the latter, learning means a lifelong progress, in contrast to collectivistic oriented students, who identify learning as a means to reach a certain social status. After reaching higher education such as university, collectivistic students consider the degree they achieved as giving them access to a group of a higher social class. In contrast, the students of individualistic cultures regard their achieved university degree as a symbol of self-respect.

Masculinity and femininity at school can be seen in class behavior. According to Hofstede, students from masculine determined cultures are more competitive toward better appearance and grades. These latter students' specification and educational orientation is strongly determined by career opportunities. On the other hand, in cultures with more feminine-oriented character the students are more modest and their choice of major corresponds to their interests. Teachers can also be differentiated according to the above mentioned cultural dimension patterns. Teachers with masculine-oriented pattern emerge with reputation, while feminine-oriented teachers emerge because of their pedagogical excellence.

Hofstede describes the students from cultures with a high level of uncertainty avoidance as students who prefer precise assignments with detailed information. They expect their teachers, for whom they have a high level of respect, to know the one correct answer and are comfortable with structured learning situations. A student from a culture with a low level of uncertainty avoidance does not like to be restricted by precise assignment. He prefers to grow with creativity, disbelieving that there is only one true answer. He is comfortable with open-ended learning and concerned with intense discussions.

The above presented cultural differences on education are Hofstede's four dimensions, which draw on personal teaching experiences at different Universities. There has also been some practical research on this topic. In a study by Kragh and Bislev (2005), they investigated the correlation of student values and the dimensions of Hofstede through a questionnaire survey covering 31 countries. They compared the students' values of different countries including Germany and China by asking how they evaluated teaching styles in their home countries and exchange counties and their preferences. Their answers were evaluated based on the dimensions of Hofstede, which showed that the most significant correlation between the professor-student relationship and the dimensions of Hofstede was not as expected the power distance, but the uncertainty avoidance and the masculinity/femininity value.

2.3 German and Chinese Cultural Differences in Education

According to Hofstede (1991), German culture is more individualistic, with a higher level of masculinity and a higher level of uncertainty avoidance. Chinese culture has a significant higher level of power distance and a higher level of long term orientation.

There have been several studies on the differences of education in both countries, some concerning the basic idea and transmission of education and others concerning the teacher student relationship. As regards the basic ideas of learning and education, Jarvis, Holford and Griffin (2003) claimed that "westerners believe exploration should precede the development of skill. Chinese educators in contrast believe skills should be developed first (which requires repetitive learning); this provides a basis to be creative with."

The teacher-student relationship differs also in both countries. Recent studies showed that the teacher-student relationship in China is more a personal relationship (Wang, 2006). The relationship is not limited to the classroom and the academic work of that arena. There is a norm that teachers and students should think of each other as members of an extended family. For them, responsibility, authority, and morality (heart) are all part of the relationships (Wang, 2006). This indicates that the teacher-student relationship in China goes beyond the university life. In Germany, however, the student-teacher relationship is more distant. The student-teacher relationship at German Universities is 1 faculty member to 60 students (Jaroch, 2007). Therefore, a familiar relationship as that in China cannot be realizable.

3 Interview

The objective of this study was to single out the communication patterns of students and faculty at institutions of higher education that can be related to their cultural backgrounds. In a first step, an in-depth interview was developed with the objective of collecting spontaneous answers from students and faculty, who actively experienced different cultures in communication processes. The interview was designed to receive personal field reports from individuals who experienced studying or working at Chinese or German institutions of higher education, to evaluate the outcomes on the basis of the previous literature review, and to determine the key cultural differences in student-faculty communication.

3.1 Interview Methodology

For the interviewee sample, it was intended to keep the group size relatively small (n=3) due to the fact that this interview was intended to collect data about personal experiences, field reports, and personal opinions on the most important cultural differences. The intention was not to circumstantiate all the cultural issues, but to underline the most important cultural differences.

The three persons interviewed were a male Chinese and a male German university student, who each had spent one year as an exchange student in the other country. The third person was a male university faculty member, who was responsible for an exchange program between a Chinese and a German university, and had also taught courses for both Chinese and German students. He, therefore, was confronted with students of both nationalities and different cultural communication patterns. All of the participants were from internationally renowned engineering programs.

The participants were interviewed face-to-face. The unstructured interviews had only one priming question at the beginning: "During your education experiences in China and Germany, did you feel any cultural differences in the relationship between faculty and students?" Each interview lasted between 37 and 55 minutes and was recorded for analysis.

3.2 Interview Results

The responses of the interviews showed that the participants experienced significant differences in communication behavior. All three participants shared similar experiences regarding the approach of the student to the professor. The Chinese student explained that students in China can easily address the professor or his assistant whenever they have questions regarding the lectures. In German universities it is expected to make an appointment, which is highly restricted to pre-scheduled office hours of the teaching staff. As a result, German student has to rely more on his or her own competence or on the help of friends.

The participants all agreed on the differences existing in communication formality/informality, which means the level of principle-oriented behavior pattern. In formal communication, people follow pre-determined rules; however in an informal communication, people show less official and more personal behaviors. The Chinese student experienced a high level of formality at German university. Besides making an appointment before meeting, he also gave an example that meeting with German professors required a very well preparation on what to ask. He should never expect a not prepared "flexible" talk with German professors as that with Chinese professors. The German student was also quite surprised about the informality at Chinese university. He felt confused when a Chinese professor talked about informal and personal matters during their meeting.

The professor teaching both Chinese and German students also describes the Germans as well educated with a formal behavior pattern, whereas the Chinese students still lack this type of approach. He said:

"...German students come to the office, knock at the door and wait till I ask them in. Chinese students, especially the undergraduate students just open the door and come in. We are teaching them to behave more formal and to knock at the door, for as if they are finished and they work in a company this will be required. There is now such education in the Chinese scholar system. The Chinese students who have studied abroad have a big advantage because they are aware of these behavior patterns..."

The purpose of the interview was to ask the participants about their experiences regarding the different communication patterns. Surprisingly, all participants mainly focused on the differences in the degree of formality even though the topic was generally explained as "communication between professors and students in a cross-cultural context". These results underline again the significance of formality, which will be the focus of the following survey study.

4 Questionnaire Survey

4.1 Objective and Hypothesis

The interview indicated that there are notable differences in how university students from each culture communicate with their faculty. The most significant difference is that Chinese students approach their faculty less formally than German students and their faculty. We proposed that the difference can be predicted by different level of uncertainty avoidance. Faculty and students with a higher level of uncertainty avoidance have more intension to make an appointment, to prepare for the details, and to stick to decided procedures and norms. In comparison, people with lower level of uncertainty avoidance can allow more flexibility in their behavior and behave more frequently in an informal way. Therefore, German students with a higher level of uncertainty avoidance communicate more formally with the faculty than students with a lower level of uncertainty avoidance. Based on these statements the hypotheses of this study included:

H1: German students communicate more formally with the faculty than Chinese students.

H2: Uncertainty avoidance is a positive predictor of students' degree of communication formality when they communicate with the faculty.

A questionnaire survey was designed to compare the cultural differences on student-faculty communication formality, and to test the hypothesis above.

4.2 Participants and Procedures

Students from China and Germany with the same major and from comparable universities were recruited in the study. After deleting invalid cases, 65 Chinese students from the Department of Industrial Engineering, Tsinghua University, Beijing China and 60 German students from the RWTH Aachen University in Germany were included in the sample. Both universities are internationally renowned, especially for their engineering programs.

The average age of the 65 Chinese participants was 23.16 years. Thirty five of them are male and 30 are female. Concerning their level of education, 27 were undergraduates, 29 were graduates, and 9 were postgraduates at the time of the study. Thirty nine Chinese students have studied in other countries before.

The average age of the German students who participated in this study was 24.97 years. From the total number of 60 German students, 52 are male and 8 are female. Twenty five were undergraduates, 32 were graduates and 3 were postgraduates. Twenty eight of the 60 students have experience studying abroad.

As all the Chinese and German participants have proficient English abilities, it was decided to present the questionnaire in an English version for both nationalities to be comparable. The first version of the questionnaire was tested in a pilot study in prior with two German students and two Chinese students to check if the questions are clearly understandable for non-native English speakers. The pilot study ensured that the terminology was comprehensible and consistent.

The questionnaires were taken online. The students were addressed with an Email explaining briefly the purpose of the study and referring to the link of the online questionnaire.

4.3 Measures

To measure communication formality, we designed 12 questions in a 5-point Likert scale order, ranging from 1-agree to 5-disagree. The students were expected to read these statements and to rate how the individual statement applies to the communication pattern observed at their home university. The statements included both formal aspects and informal aspects of the student-faculty communication, which asked students about their self-reported approach, behavior, and choice of words when communicating with their faculty. The term "formality" stands for the tendency to comply with rules, established forms, or customs, i.e. norms and common attitudes. "Informality", in contrast, stands for a less official, more personal and not so principle-oriented behavior pattern. The items are shown in Table 1. Item 5 to item 8 are reversed statements which should be scored conversely in the analysis. A higher score of the measurement means a higher level of communication formality. The calculated Cronbach's alpha for communication formality scale in this study were 0.62 for Chinese participants and 0.75 for German participants, indicating an acceptable level of reliability.

Table 1. Communication formality scale items

1.	I visit my professor without previous notification.*
2.	My professor always has time to answer my questions.*
3.	When I talk with my professor we also talk about personal matters.*
4.	When I disagree with the professor I disturb him and correct him.*
5.	When talking to my professor I am highly concentrated on my behavior.
6.	I expect my professor to treat me in a formal matter.
7.	I choose my words carefully while talking to the professor.
8.	I am indirect when expressing my ideas to the professor.
9.	I always communicate informally with my professor face to face.*
10.	I always communicate informally with my professor outside of the university.*
11.	I always communicate informally with my professor via E mail.*
12.	I always communicate informally with my professor via telephone.*

*Reversed statements.

Table 2. Uncertainty avoidance scale items

1.	If I get an assignment I prefer a detailed precise description.
2.	If I get an assignment I like to have latitude and be creative.*
3.	If I get an assignment the teaching assistant or professor wants me to be open-minded and find a solution with a different perspective.*
4.	If I go to my professor with a question I am very nervous that I may look foolish, because the question is too simple.
5.	One can be a good professor without having precise answers to my questions.*
6.	I consult my teaching assistant or professor before making a decision regarding your research project or student life in general.
7.	I am nervous when I have to talk with my professor.
8.	I like a structured hierarchy at the university so I know how to address people.
9.	I have fear of saying my opinion to my professor.
10.	My thoughts become confused and jungle when I am talking with my professor.

*Reversed statements.

In measuring uncertainty avoidance, this paper focuses on communication patterns at universities. The statements were based on Hofstede's description of uncertainty avoidance in education (Hofstede, 1986). The present study and the respective questionnaire focused on two characteristics: (1) avoidance of ambiguous situations in the university setting, and (2) avoidance of ambiguous situations while communicating with the faculty.

The first characteristic emphasizes precise assignments and the student's trust in the fact that the professor knows the right answer. The second characteristic included the student behavior when he approaches, addresses, and talks to a professor. In total, there were 10 questions in the measurement. The items were designed in a 5-point Likert scale order, ranging from 1-agree to 5-disagree, with 7 reversed items. A higher score demonstrated higher level of uncertainty avoidance. The calculated Cronbach's alpha for uncertainty avoidance scale in this study were 0.61 for Chinese participants and 0.63 for German participants. All the items are shown in Table 2.

4.4 Results

Hypothesis 1 predicts that German students communicate more formally with the faculty than Chinese students. ANOVA test (Table 3) showed significant cultural difference on communication formality: Germans communicate more formally than Chinese ($F=58.35$, $p<0.001$). Therefore, hypothesis 1 was supported. The cross-cultural difference on uncertainty avoidance was also tested: German students scored higher on uncertainty avoidance than Chinese students, but the difference was not significant ($F=0.822$, $p=0.367$).

Table 3. ANOVA testing results for variables according to culture

Measures	Culture	Mean	*SD*	F	p
Communication formality	Chinese	37.66	5.59	58.35	<0.001*
	German	45.88	6.40		
Uncertainty avoidance	Chinese	27.72	4.67	0.822	0.367
	German	28.52	5.14		

* Result is significant at the 0.05 level (2-tailed).

Hypothesis 2 states that uncertainty avoidance is a positive predictor of students' degree of communication formality when they address their faculty. First, a 2-tailed Pearson correlation analysis showed a significant positive correlation between the two variables (correlation=0.248, $p=0.005$). Second, regression analysis was used to test the hypothesis. The independent variable was uncertainty avoidance and the dependent variable was the degree of formality. As a result, uncertainty avoidance was found to be a significant positive predictor of communication formality ($\beta=0.248$, $t=2.830$, $p=0.005$). Hence, hypothesis 2 was confirmed.

5 Discussion

The objective of this study was to compare Chinese and German university students' different communication patterns with their faculty, and to provide implications for designing intercultural CMC tools. By interviewing Chinese and German students and professors, communication formality was found to be the major cultural difference in their communication pattern. After that, a questionnaire survey confirmed this finding, and further found that the communication formality between faculty and students can be predicted by the different levels of uncertainty avoidance of the students. Therefore, it can be predicted that people with higher uncertainty avoidance are more likely to set roles and adhere to existing norms in social interaction in order to prevent uncertain events. In comparison, people with lower uncertainty avoidance can tolerate more flexible interactions with other people and, therefore, do not value the formal communication as much as high-uncertainty avoidance people.

The findings of this study have implications for designing educational CMC tools to better assist the faculty-student communication in intercultural contexts. First of all, the communication tools should provide choices and options for users in order to provide a flexible environment that will adapt to their cultures (Collis, 1999). For examples, an imbedded calendar and meeting scheduling tool will be very helpful for German professors to emphasize the importance of pre-notification. And for Chinese professors who are used to more flexible communications, displaying the "available" or "busy" status aside the portrait will be more appropriate, and this may encourage the students to start a conversation. Such cases can also be applied to other cultures with different levels of uncertainty avoidance.

Secondly, the communication tools should help the students and professors to get aware of the cultural differences between each other. A Chinese students should understand that informal and personal communications may be strange to their German professors, while German students should notice that Chinese professors welcome instant discussions even through the students have not get a precise idea. One possible way is to display the communicator's preferred communication patterns on the interface using a few tags, such as "precisely", "openly", or "formally". The tags may be manually set by the users or automatically generated from the previous communication behaviors.

Thirdly, the educational CMC tools should be used to supplement rather than to replace the face-to-face communications between students and faculty. From our interview results, face-to-face communication is still the most important media between faculty and students, and it helps to develop cultural expectations for other persons' behavior on CMC. Previous studies also found that face-to-face education is better in terms of cultural fit than computer education (Collis & DeBoer, 1998; Griffiths, Heppell, Millwood, & Mladenova, 1994).

Future studies may compare different CMC tools and designs to better understand the culture issue in educational communication system design. It is also interesting to investigate other cultural variables to predict different communication patterns.

6 Conclusion

With the aim of comparing Chinese and German university students' communication patterns with their faculty, this study conducted interview and survey with students and faculty in both cultures. Both qualitative and quantitative evidence revealed that Chinese and German students had different degrees of communication formality with their faculty. The cultural dimension of uncertainty avoidance can predict such communication differences. The results have practical applications for educational communication tool design, and inspire future studies on cultural adaptive education technologies.

Acknowledgements. This work was supported by the National Science Foundation China [grant numbers 71031005, 71188001].

References

1. Adrian-Taylor, S.R., Noels, K.A., Tischler, K.: Conflict between international graduate students and faculty supervisors: Toward effective conflict prevention and management strategies. Journal of Studies in International Education 11(1), 90–117 (2007)
2. Collis, B.: Designing for differences: Cultural issues in the design of the WWW-based course-support sites. British Journal of Educational Technology 30(3), 201–215 (1999)
3. Collis, B.A., De Boer, W.F.: Rapid prototyping as a faculty-wide activity: An innovative approach to the redesign of courses and instructional methods at the University of Twente. Educational Media International 35(2), 117–121 (1998)
4. Coughlan, S.: Record numbers of international students (2011), http://www.bbc.co.uk/news/business-12671198 (accessed January 11, 2012)
5. Griffiths, D., Heppell, S., Millwood, R., Mladenova, G.: Translating software: What it means and what it costs for small cultures and large cultures. Computers & Education 22(1), 9–17 (1994)
6. Harasim, L.: Online education: An environment for collaborations and intellectual application. In: Harasim, L.M. (ed.) Online Education: Perspectives on a New Environment. Praeger, New York (1990)
7. Helvie-Mason, L.: Facebook,"Friending," and Faculty–Student Communication. Cutting-edge Technologies in Higher Education 3, 61–87 (2011)
8. Hofstede, G.: Cultural differences in teaching and learning. International Journal of Intercultural Relations 10(3), 301–320 (1986)
9. Hofstede, G.: Cultures and organizations. Software of the Mind. McGraw-Hill, London (1991)
10. Jaroch, M.: Exzellenz in der Lehre (2007) (in German), http://bildungsklick.de/pm/51960/exzellenz-in-der-lehre/ (accessed June 20, 2010)
11. Jarvis, P., Holford, J., Griffin, C.: The theory & practice of learning. Taylor & Francis, Sterling (2003)
12. Kragh, S.U., Bislev, S.: Universities and student values across nations. Journal of Intercultural Communication 9, 48–63 (2005)
13. Lewis, M.M.: Communication and education. British Journal of Educational Studies 1(11), 28–32 (1952)
14. Melton, C.D.: Bridging the cultural gap: A study of Chinese students' learning style preferences. RELC Journal 21(1), 29–57 (1990)
15. Gunawardena, C.N., Wilson, P.L., Nolla, A.C.: Culture and online education. In: Moore, M.G., Anderson, W.G. (eds.) Handbook of Distance Education. Lawrence Erlbaum Associates, Mahwah (2003)
16. Organization of Economic Cooperation and Development (OECD). International migration outlook: SOPEMI (2010), http://www.oecd.org/dataoecd/12/9/45612617.pdf (accessed January 11, 2012)
17. Wang, T.: Understanding Chinese culture and learning. The Australian Educational Researcher (2006), http://www.aare.edu.au/06pap/wan06122.pdf (accessed July 8, 2010)
18. Wilson, P.: A Call for closer professor-student relationships: Students at the University of Alaska, Fairbanks, speak out. Anthropology & Education Quarterly 27(3), 432–441 (1996)

The Relations between Interface Design of Digital Game-Based Learning Systems and Flow Experience and Cognitive Load of Learners with Different Levels of Prior Knowledge

Chun-Yi Shen and Hao-Ping Chu

Tamkang University, Taiwan
dannyshen1202@gmail.com, gn00166@hotmail.com

Abstract. Many studies have indicated that game-based learning has become an effective teaching strategy and a teaching tool. In the past decades, empirical studies showed that digital game-based could enhance learners' cognitive, affective and skills as learning objectives. Many studies have shown that learning process in which the flow experience for learning has a significant impact. In addition, researches have also pointed out that the multimedia materials presentation and system interface design would affect the learning of learners carrying out their cognitive load. Researchers indicated that learner's prior knowledge and learning strategies would influence the flow experience, learning outcomes and cognitive load of the learners. According to previous studies, the interface design of learning system would affect learner's learning, motivation, satisfaction, learning efficiency, and quality of interaction and so on. There are many studies have shown the system visibility, cognitive support, efficiency, user control, joyfulness are the important aspects of learning system design. Therefore, the purpose of this study was to explore digital game-based learning systems' visibility, cognitive support, efficiency, user control, and joyfulness for different prior knowledge learners' flow experience and cognitive load. The results show that there are significant differences on flow experience and cognitive load between learners with different prior knowledge. The usability of game-based learning system has significant effect on flow experience but not on cognitive load except joyfulness. Discussion and conclusion are provided in this study.

Keywords: case studies, game-based learning, usability, interface design, flow experience.

1 Research Background

Some scholars have proposed scientific literacy and personal productivity of people and even the country's competitiveness has a close relationship (Jenkins, 1990). However, some scholars have pointed out that the current methods of teaching science and technology in primary and secondary school are mostly the traditional teaching pedagogies (Eisenhart, Finkel, & Marion, 1996). Many studies indicate digital

P.L.P. Rau (Ed.): CCD/HCII 2014, LNCS 8528, pp. 574–584, 2014.

game -based learning has become one of the teaching strategies and tools to effectively enhance the effectiveness of teaching and learning motivation (Liu & Lin, 2009). According to empirical results show the past two decades, digital game-based learning to enhance the learner 's cognitive, affective and skill learning objectives have a significant effect (Kiili, 2005). Henderson, Klemes and Eshet (2000) pointed out that digital game-based learning contain questions to enhance critical thinking, learner information analysis and evaluation. Clark (2004) pointed out that the four elements of teaching game design should contain the background and setting for the game, interactive, rules of the game, the results and evaluation. Prensky (2001) mentioned that in the design of digital game -based learning, should match its design principles in order to design suitable for learners of the game. In summary, digital game -based learning designs, interactive, cognitive factors support, interface design, joyfulness, flexibility and adaptability, ease of use and the challenges and the difficulty is moderate affect learning outcomes.

Many studies have shown that among the learning process flow experience for learning have a significant impact (Pearce, Ainley, & Howard, 2005). Flow experience theory refers to a time when individuals will serve an activity or things. They would concentrate on it and feel happy after the event (Csikszentmihalyi, 1997). The individual's skills and challenges are two important factors in Flow experience (Moneta & Csikszentmihalyi, 1996). People would use different skills in different situations to response the challenges. Therefore, flow experience is personal feelings as a dynamic process (Chen, Wigand, & Nilan, 1999). Some scholars proposed that the flow experience occurs when the computer has the following four main characteristics: interest, focus, curiosity, and user control (Webster, Trevino, & Ryan, 1993). In addition, Winberg and Hedman (2008) mentioned that flow experience should include the following five aspects: enjoyment, concentration, control, exploration, and challenge. In addition, research has also pointed out that the presentation of multimedia materials and system interface design would affect the proliferation of external and cognitive load of learners during the learning time, and excessive cognitive load for learning would have a negative impact (Mayer, & Moreno, 2003). Also, studies have pointed out that the learner's prior knowledge of the learner would influence flow experience, the main factors of cognitive load and learning outcomes (Pace, 2004).

The user interface design generally refers to computer communication symbols when interacting with people used (MacDormana, Whalena, Hoa, & Patela, 2011). A well-designed user interface not only could reduce learning time in the initial period, it could also enhance overall system performance and reduce the probability of system error occurred (Ardito, Costabile, Marsico, & Lanzilotti, 2006). Sim, MacFarlane and Read (2006) found the interface design of digital game-based learning materials will affect the satisfaction of learners. According to previous researches indicated that the interface design or learning system will affect learners learning, motivation, satisfaction, learning efficiency, quality of interaction, and so on. When the interface is difficult to use in the learning system, it would cause poor learning outcomes (Parlangeli, Marchigiani, & Bagnara, 1999).

The interface design of digital game-based learning system is one of the important factors that affect learning (Paas, Tuovinen, & Tabbers, 2003). Many of these studies have shown that the usability of the game-based learning systems could be characterized by cognitive support, efficiency and user control, entertaining, and satisfaction (Liaw, 2008). Therefore, the main purpose of this study was to explore the relationships between system visibility, cognitive support, efficiency, user control, and joyfulness of digital game-based learning system and the learner's flow experience and cognitive load among the learners with different prior knowledge.

2 Methodology

2.1 Research Design

This study contains two independent variables, the learners' prior knowledge and the interface design of the digital game-based learning system. The dependent variables of this study were to flow experience, cognitive load and learning outcome.

2.2 Participants

The participants of this study were 200 college students in Taiwan aged from 18 to 25. They have some digital game-based learning experience and basic concepts of nature and life technology. They were randomly divided into four groups with 50 students in each group. Each group was asked to play one of the four game-based learning systems.

2.3 Digital Game-Based Learning System

Four digital game-based learning system used in this study were Crazy Machines and Crazy Machines 2 HD developed by DTP joyfulness AG company respectively in 2009 and 2011, and Incredible Machines developed by Push Button Labs in 2009, and Casey's Contraptions HD developed by Snappy Touch in 2011. The four games are related to the basic principles of mathematics or physics. The game contains a series of hundreds of checkpoints and dozens of tools. In those games, learners could complete various tasks to learn a lot of hurdles mathematics and physics principles through the use of tools. This study uses the Construction Kit of the four games to create the levels on power of nature and life technology field, such as gravity and electrical and mechanical with the same difficulties.

2.4 Experiment Process

First, learners were asked to fill out pre-test of physics for 10 minutes. Then, the researchers briefly introduced the experiment process and goal of the game for 5 minutes. And, the learners were randomly assigned to play one of the four games for about 40 minutes. After playing, the learners were asked to fill out flow experience scales, digital game-based learning system interface design assessment scale for 25 minutes.

2.5 Data Analysis Methods

The mean and standard deviation for each of the various scales were run. MANOVA was used to analyze the relationships between the interface design (system visibility, cognitive support, efficiency, user control, and joyfulness) and learners' flow experience with different prior knowledge.

3 Results

3.1 Flow Experience by Different Prior Knowledge and Usability

The descriptive statistics of flow experience by prior knowledge and system visibility is shown in Table 1. The learners' reported highest score on flow experience were low prior knowledge with high system visibility (M = 3.66, SD = .21); the learners' reported lowest score on flow experience were low prior knowledge with low system visibility (M = 3.21, SD = .38).

Table 1. Descriptive statistics of flow experience by prior knowledge and system visibility

Variables	Prior Knowledge	System visibility	Mean	SD
Flow Experience	High	High	3.54	.32
		Low	3.22	.44
	Low	High	3.66	.21
		Low	3.21	.38

The results of MANOVA shows that the prior knowledge and system visibility do not have interaction (F = .48, p = .95). Also, there is no significant difference (F = .40, p = .53) on flow experience between different prior knowledge. However, the system with different characterization have significant difference (F = 2.70, p < .01) on flow experience.

Table 2 shows the descriptive statistics of flow experience by prior knowledge and cognitive support. The learners' reported highest score on flow experience were low prior knowledge with high cognitive support (M = 3.53, SD = .32); the learners' reported lowest score on flow experience were low prior knowledge with low cognitive support (M = 3.17, SD = .41).

Table 2. Descriptive statistics of flow experience by prior knowledge and cognitive support

Variables	Prior Knowledge	Cognitive Support	Mean	SD
Flow Experience	High	High	3.43	.42
		Low	3.34	.41
	Low	High	3.53	.32
		Low	3.17	.41

The results of MANOVA shows that the prior knowledge and cognitive support do not have interaction (F = 2.78, p = .10). Also, there is no significant difference (F = .26, p = .63) on flow experience between different prior knowledge. However, the system with different cognitive support have significant difference (F = 7.68, p < .01) on flow experience.

Table 3 shows the descriptive statistics of flow experience by prior knowledge and efficiency. The learners' reported highest score on flow experience were low prior knowledge with high cognitive support (M = 3.62, SD = .22); the learners' reported lowest score on flow experience were low prior knowledge with low cognitive support (M = 3.23, SD = .41).

Table 3. Descriptive statistics of flow experience by prior knowledge and efficiency

Variables	Prior Knowledge	Efficiency	Mean	SD
Flow Experience	High	High	3.40	.41
		Low	3.38	.42
	Low	High	3.62	.22
		Low	3.23	.41

The results of MANOVA shows that the prior knowledge and efficiency have interaction (F = 6.01, p < .05). Also, there is no significant difference (F = .23, p = .63) on flow experience between different prior knowledge. However, the system with different cognitive support have significant difference (F = 7.88, p < .01) on flow experience.

Table 4 shows the descriptive statistics of flow experience by prior knowledge and user control. The learners' reported highest score on flow experience were low prior knowledge with high user control (M = 3.47, SD = .40); the learners' reported lowest score on flow experience were high prior knowledge with low user control (M = 3.30, SD = .36).

Table 4. Descriptive statistics of flow experience by prior knowledge and user control

Variables	Prior Knowledge	User Control	Mean	SD
Flow Experience	High	High	3.44	.44
		Low	3.30	.36
	Low	High	3.47	.40
		Low	3.36	.33

The results of MANOVA shows that the prior knowledge and user control do not have interaction (F = .05, p = .83). Also, there is no significant difference (F = .26, p = .63) on flow experience between different prior knowledge; while there is no significant difference (F = 2.10, p = .15) on flow experience between different user control.

Table 5 shows the descriptive statistics of flow experience by prior knowledge and joyfulness. The learners' reported highest score on flow experience were low prior knowledge with high joyfulness (M = 3.62, SD = .27); the learners' reported lowest score on flow experience were low prior knowledge with low joyfulness (M = 3.27, SD = .39).

Table 5. Descriptive statistics of flow experience by prior knowledge and joyfulness

Variables	Prior Knowledge	Joyfulness	Mean	SD
Flow Experience	High	High	3.61	.25
		Low	3.33	.43
	Low	High	3.62	.27
		Low	3.27	.39

The results of MANOVA shows that the prior knowledge and joyfulness do not have interaction (F = .16, p = .69). Also, there is no significant difference (F = .07, p = .80) on flow experience between different prior knowledge. However, the system with different joyfulness have significant difference (F = 15.06, p < .001) on flow experience.

3.2 Cognitive Load by Different Prior Knowledge and Usability

The descriptive statistics of cognitive load by prior knowledge and system visibility is shown in Table 6. The learners' reported highest score on cognitive load were high prior knowledge with high system visibility (M = 3.89, SD = 2.17); the learners' reported lowest score on cognitive load were low prior knowledge with high system visibility (M = 1.71, SD = .32).

Table 6. Descriptive statistics of cognitive load by prior knowledge and system visibility

Variables	Prior Knowledge	System visibility	Mean	SD
Cognitive Load	High	High	3.89	2.17
		Low	3.51	1.23
	Low	High	1.71	.32
		Low	1.74	.32

The results of MANOVA shows that the prior knowledge and system visibility do not have interaction (F = .66, p = .42). However, the learners with different prior knowledge have significant difference (F = 60.57, p < .001) on cognitive load; while there is no significant difference (F = .47, p = .50) on cognitive load between different system visibility.

Table 7 shows the descriptive statistics of cognitive load by prior knowledge and cognitive support. The learners' reported highest score on flow experience were high prior knowledge with high cognitive support (M = 3.77, SD = 2.14); the learners' reported lowest score on flow experience were low prior knowledge with high cognitive support (M = 1.70, SD = .32).

Table 7. Descriptive statistics of cognitive load by prior knowledge and cognitive support

Variables	Prior Knowledge	Cognitive Support	Mean	SD
Cognitive Load	High	High	3.77	2.14
		Low	3.65	1.31
	Low	High	1.70	.32
		Low	1.79	.32

The results of MANOVA shows that the prior knowledge and cognitive support do not have interaction ($F = .14$, $p = .71$). However, the learners with different prior knowledge have significant difference ($F = 51.21$, $p < .001$) on cognitive load; while there is no significant difference ($F = .003$, $p = .95$) on cognitive load between different cognitive support.

Table 8 shows the descriptive statistics of cognitive load by prior knowledge and efficiency. The learners' reported highest score on flow experience were high prior knowledge with high efficiency ($M = 3.78$, $SD = 1.47$); the learners' reported lowest score on flow experience were low prior knowledge with high efficiency ($M = 1.68$, $SD = .32$).

Table 8. Descriptive statistics of cognitive load by prior knowledge and efficiency

Variables	Prior Knowledge	Efficiency	Mean	SD
Cognitive Load	High	High	3.78	1.47
		Low	3.60	2.16
	Low	High	1.68	.32
		Low	1.77	.31

The results of MANOVA shows that the prior knowledge and efficiency do not have interaction ($F = .27$, $p = .60$). However, the learners with different prior knowledge have significant difference ($F = 93.98$, $p < .001$) on cognitive load; while there is no significant difference ($F = .032$, $p = .86$) on cognitive load between different efficiency.

Table 9 shows the descriptive statistics of cognitive load by prior knowledge and user control. The learners' reported highest score on flow experience were high prior knowledge with low user control ($M = 3.92$, $SD = 2.13$); the learners' reported lowest score on flow experience were low prior knowledge with high user control ($M = 1.65$, $SD = .32$).

Table 9. Descriptive statistics of cognitive load by prior knowledge and user control

Variables	Prior Knowledge	User Control	Mean	SD
Cognitive Load	High	High	3.48	1.28
		Low	3.92	2.13
	Low	High	1.65	.32
		Low	1.80	.31

The results of MANOVA shows that the prior knowledge and user control do not have interaction (F = .36, p = .55). However, the learners with different prior knowledge have significant difference (F = 93.98, $p < .001$) on cognitive load; while there is no significant difference (F =1.37, p = .25) on cognitive load between different user control.

Table 10 shows the descriptive statistics of cognitive load by prior knowledge and joyfulness. The learners' reported highest score on flow experience were high prior knowledge with low joyfulness (M = 4.08, SD = 2.01); the learners' reported lowest score on flow experience were low prior knowledge with high joyfulness (M = 1.70, SD = .30).

Table 10. Descriptive statistics of cognitive load by prior knowledge and joyfulness

Variables	Prior Knowledge	Joyfulness	Mean	SD
Cognitive Load	High	High	2.98	.80
		Low	4.08	2.01
	Low	High	1.70	.30
		Low	1.78	.35

The results of MANOVA shows that the prior knowledge and joyfulness do not have interaction (F = 3.93, p = .05). However, the learners with different prior knowledge have significant difference (F = 47.68, $p < .001$) on cognitive load; while there is significant differences (F =5.18, $p < .05$) on cognitive load between different joyfulness as well.

4 Conclusion

The results of this study indicated that prior knowledge could affect both learners' flow experience and cognitive load in game-based learning. There are significant differences between system visibilities on flow experiences. In another word, when the digital game-based learning system visibility is higher, learners would focus on learning more. This result is consistent with the research by Winberg and Hedman (2008). In addition, cognitive support has significant effect on flow experience. That means adequate cognitive support could help learners to concentrate on the learning materials. Also, efficiency has significant effect on learners' flow experience. The result indicates that when learners do not have to waste their time in navigation or searching, they would focus on learning. Joyfulness has significant effect on flow experience as well. When learners have fun, they are in the state of flow (Csikszentmihalyi, 1997).

Additionally, there are significant differences on cognitive load between different prior knowledge. The learners with higher prior knowledge have higher cognitive load. This result is not consistent with some studies (e.g. Mayer, & Moreno, 2003). The reason might be that the learners with high prior knowledge focus on the tasks more than the learners with low prior knowledge. In another hand, four aspects of usability (system visibility, cognitive support, efficiency, and user control) do not have significant differences on cognitive load. However, there are significant differences on cognitive load between different joyfulness. The game-based learning system with low joyfulness would make learners have higher cognitive load. The learners might feel bored and lack of challenge while playing a game which is not fun at all. The results of this study indicate that the usability of game-based learning system and learners' prior knowledge are two very important elements in game-based learning design. The designers and instructors should notice those two factors. Future studies could compare the learners with different ages in different curriculum.

References

1. Adams, P.C.: Teaching and learning with SimCity 2000. Journal of Geography 97(2), 47–55 (1998)
2. Amory, A.: Building an educational adventure game: Theory, design, and lessons. Journal of Interactive Learning Research 12(2/3), 249–263 (2001)
3. Ardito, C., Costabile, M.F., Marsico, M.D., Lanzilotti, R.: An approach to usability evaluation of e-learning applications. Universal Access in the Information Society 4(3), 270–283 (2006)
4. Barendregt, W., Bekker, M.M., Bouwhuis, D.G., Baauw, E.: Identifying usability and fun problems in a computer game during first use and after some practice. International Journal of Human-Computer Studies 64, 830–846 (2006)
5. Betz, J.A.: Computer games: Increase learning in an interactive multidisciplinary (1995)
6. Environment. Journal of Educational Technology Systems, 24, 195-205
7. Brunken, R., Steinbacher, S., Plass, J.L., Leutner, D.: Assessment of cognitive load in multimedia learning using dual-task methodology. Experimental Psychology 49(2), 109–119 (2002)
8. Clark, C.D.: The principle of game based learning. Paper Presented at the Meeting of NETC/LSC Conference, Crystal city, VA (2004)
9. Chen, H., Wigand, R.T., Nilan, M.: Exploring Web Users' Optimal Flow Experiences. Computers in Human Behavior 15(5), 585–608 (1999)
10. Carlson, R., Chandler, P., Sweller, J.: Learning and understanding science instructional material. Journal of Educational Psychology 95(3), 629–640 (2003)
11. Csikszentmihalyi, M.: Beyond boredom and anxiety. In: Csikszentmihalyi, M. (ed.) Finding Flow: The Psychology of Engagement with Everyday Life. Basic Books. Jossey-Bass Publishers, San Francisco
12. Dix, A., Finlay, J., Abowd, G., Beale, R.: Human-Computer Interaction, 3rd edn. Prentice Hall, Upper Saddle River (2004)
13. Eisenhart, M., Finkel, E., Marion, S.F.: Creating the conditions for scientific literacy: A re-examination. American Educational Research Journal 33(2), 261–295 (1996)
14. Gerjets, P., Scheiter, K.: Goal Configurations and Processing Strategies as Moderators Between Instructional Design and Cognitive Load: Evidence From Hypertext-Based Instruction. Educational Psychologist 38(1), 33–41 (2003)
15. Ghani, J.A., Deshpande, S.P.: Task characteristics and the experience of optimal flow in human-computer interaction. The Journal of Psychology 128(4), 381–391 (1994)

16. Gredler, M.E.: Educational games and simulations: A technology in search of a research paradigm. In: Jonassen, D. (ed.) Handbook of Research for Educational Communications and Technology, pp. 521–540. Macmillan, New York (1996)
17. Henderson, L., Klemes, J., Eshet, Y.: Just playing a game? Educational simulation software and cognitive outcomes. Journal of Educational Computing Research 22(1), 105–129 (2000)
18. Liaw, S.: Investigating students' perceived satisfaction, behavioral intention, and effectiveness of e-learning: A case study of the Blackboard system. Computers & Education 51, 864–873 (2008)
19. Liu, E.Z.-F., Lin, C.-H.: Developing evaluative indicators for educational computer games. British Journal of Educational Technology 40(1), 174–178 (2009)
20. Jenkins, E.: Scientific literacy and school education. School Science Review 71(256), 43–51 (1990)
21. Kiili, K.: Digital game-based learning: Towards an experiential gaming model. Internet & Higher Education 8(1), 13–24 (2005)
22. MacFarlane, S., Sim, G., Horton, M.: Assessing usability and fun in educational software. In: Proceedings of 4th International Conference for Interaction Design and Children (IDC 2005), Boulder, Colo, USA, pp. 103–109 (June 2005)
23. MacDormana, K.F., Whalena, T.J., Hoa, C., Patela, H.: An Improved Usability Measure Based on Novice and Expert Performance. International Journal of Human-Computer Interaction 27(3), 280–302 (2011)
24. Mayer, R.E., Moreno, R.: Nine Ways to Reduce Cognitive Load in Multimedia Learning. Educational Psychologist 38(1), 43–52 (2003)
25. Mayer, R.E., Sims, V.K.: For whom is a picture worth a thousand words? Extensions of a dual-coding theory of multimedia learning. Journal of Educational Psychology 86, 389–401 (1994)
26. Moneta, G.B., Csikszentmihalyi, M.: The effect of perceived challenges and skills on the quality of subjective experience. Journal of Personality 64(2), 275–310 (1996)
27. Norman, D.A.: Human-Centered Design Considered Harmful. Interactions 12(4), 14–19 (2005)
28. Oztekin, A., Kong, Z.J., Uysal, O.: UseLearn: A novel checklist and usability evaluation method for eLearning systems by criticality metric analysis. International Journal of Industrial Ergonomics 40(4), 455–469 (2010)
29. Pace, S.: A grounded theory of the flow experiences of Web users. International Journal of Human-Computer Studies 60(3), 327–363 (2004)
30. Parlangeli, O., Marchigiani, E., Bagnara, S.: Multimedia systems in distance education: effects of usability on learning. Interacting with Computers 12(1), 37–49 (1999)
31. Paas, F., Tuovinen, J.E., Tabbers, H.: Cognitive Load Measurement as a Means to Advance Cognitive Load Theory. Educational Psychologist 38(1), 63–71 (2003)
32. Paas, F., Renkl, A., Sweller, J.: Cognitive Load Theory. Educational Psychologist 38(1), 5–71 (2003)
33. Paas, F., Van Merrienboer, J.: Variability of Worked Examples and Transfer of Geometrical Problemsolvings: A Cognitive-Load Approach. Journal of Educational Psychology 86(1), 122–133 (1994)
34. Pearce, J.M., Ainley, M., Howard, S.: The ebb and flow of online learning. Computers in Human Behavior 21(5), 745–771 (2005)
35. Poon, W., Koo, A.: Mobile learning: the economics perspective. International Journal of Innovation and Learning 7(4), 412–429 (2010)
36. Prensky, M.: Digital Game-Based Learning. McGraw-Hill (2001)

37. Pierotti, D.: Heuristic evaluation: A system checklist (2005), http://www.stcsig.org/usability/topics/articles/he-checklist.html (retrieved on August 4, 2010)
38. Quesenbery, W.: What does usability mean: Looking beyond 'ease of use'. Paper Presented at the the 48th Annual Conference, Society for Technical Communication, Chicago, Illinois, USA (2001)
39. Renkl, A., Atkinson, R.K.: Structuring the Transition From Example Study to Problem Solving in Cognitive Skill Acquisition: A Cognitive Load Perspective. Educational Psychologist 38(1), 15–22 (2003)
40. Shneiderman, B.: Designing the user interface: Strategies for effective human computer-interaction. Addison Wesley Longman, Reading (2002)
41. Sweller, J.: Cognitive Processes and Instruction Procedures. Australian Journal of Education 34(2), 125–130 (1990)
42. Tselios, N., Avouris, N., Dimitracopoulou, A., Daskalaki, S.: Evaluation of Distance-learning Environments: Impact of Usability on Student Performance. International Journal of Educational Telecommunications 7(4), 355–378 (2001)
43. Van Gerven, P.W., Paas, F.G.W.C., Van Merrienboer, J.J.G., Schmidt, H.G.: Cognitive Load Theory and Aging: Effects of Worked Examples on Training Efficiency. Learning and Instruction 12(1), 87–105 (2002)
44. Webster, J., Trevino, L.K., Ryan, L.: The dimensionality and correlates of flow in human-computer interactions. Computers in Human Behavior 9(4), 411–426 (1993)
45. Winberg, T.M., Hedman, L.: Student attitudes toward learning, level of pre-knowledge and instruction type in a computer-simulation: Effects on flow experiences and perceived learning outcomes. Instructional Science 36, 269–287 (2008)
46. Wulf, G., Shea, C.: Principles derived from the study of simple skills do not generalize to complex skill learning. Psychonomic Bulletin & Review 9(2), 185–211 (2002)

Intercultural Design in e-Learning: A Comparison of Three Different Approaches

Vassilia Stefanou

The American College of Greece – Deree College, Athens, Greece
vstefanou@acg.edu

Abstract. This paper attempts to describe and compare three different approaches for accommodating cultural differences in the design of e-learning systems: Collis' [1] ten guidelines for designing online course-support systems; Mercado, Parboteeah, & Zhao's [2] four key issues for designing online courses; and Henderson's [3] multiple cultures model of instructional design for e-learning. These three approaches are contrasted not only to each other, but also to several other related models, theories and frameworks. At the end, the most effective and useful approach appears to be Henderson's theoretical multiple cultures model. The choice of the three approaches was made solely based on their frequent citing in literature, and on the time constraints of this project; a larger research project may use this paper as a starting point, and possibly evaluate more approaches supporting the development of frameworks that acknowledge cultural differences for the design of e-learning systems.

Keywords: cultural differences, e-learning, online learning, intercultural design.

1 Introduction

The purpose of this paper is to compare and contrast some of the currently adopted and used frameworks, theories, and models for acknowledging and accommodating intercultural differences as far as e-learning is concerned. The aim is to identify the commonalities and the differences between these approaches, along with their strengths and weaknesses, in order to assess their suitability, and possibly identify areas for improvement.

This is not a complete review of literature in the area of accommodating cultural differences in e-learning; given the time constraints and the scale of this project, a sampling of what exists is presented here, and the approaches chosen to be compared and contrasted were almost randomly selected from the most-frequent-cited works. A factor that contributed to this selection is that the first (Collis) [1] and the third (Henderson) [3] are related, since Henderson's earlier work served as the basis for Collis' guidelines. Moreover, the second one is based on Hofstede's work, which, according to Williamson [4: p. 1392] "is probably the dominant explanation of behavioral differences between nations", a view which is cited also in quite recent studies such as the one by Cronjé [5]. By no means has the selection of these approaches made them

P.L.P. Rau (Ed.): CCD/HCII 2014, LNCS 8528, pp. 585–596, 2014.

more valuable than others; the work done in this paper can be seen as a starting point for a larger research project that would categorize and compare all available approaches.

2 Definitions

In order to avoid possible misinterpretations of the concepts under investigation, this section attempts to define the meanings of the terms that are used throughout the paper.

2.1 Theories, Models, Frameworks, Guidelines

The development of a framework could be the first step towards formulating a theory, i.e. a speculation; "Theories are formulations of apparent relationships or underlying principles of certain observed phenomena that have been verified to some degree" [6: p. 5]. A model is usually based on a theory, and adapted in a way to address and/or solve a specific issue or problem. As Bélisle [6: p. 5] indicates, "Models are general hypothetical organisations or structures, often based on an analogy, used in analysing or explaining a phenomena and generally conducive to prediction or applied action". Generally speaking, theories and models can be considered as frameworks that aim to explain the interrelationships between the concepts under investigation.

On the other hand, guidelines are more general. The online Cambridge dictionary defines guidelines as "information intended to advise people on how something should be done or what something should be" [7]. Guidelines can be viewed as frameworks for practice; unlike theories and models, guidelines may refer to concepts and issues that are not necessarily related or connected to each other. Nevertheless, guidelines may draw from theories and/or models.

Theories and models have a more explanatory nature, while guidelines a more descriptive one; bringing this discussion to the area of teaching and learning, it can be stated that all three can serve for the development of frameworks that can guide course designers.

2.2 Culture

Different disciplines regard the concept of culture from different viewpoints. From an anthropological perspective, the word culture is associated with the interests of people who belong in a particular society, along with the ways these people behave, while from a sociological perspective culture refers to the people's behaviours and beliefs as these are shaped by the society. [9].

Young [9] maintains that, in the field of Human Computer Interaction, the prevailing definition of culture is the one issued by Hofstede back in 1991. Although old, this definition is embraced by scholars in more recent papers [5], [10]. Moreover, the same definition, slightly refined, also appears in Hofstede's more recent work: "[culture]... is the collective programming of the mind that distinguishes the members of one group or category of people from others" [11: p.6]. In this definition a group refers to "a number of people in contact with each other", whereas "A category consists of people who, without necessarily having any contact, have something in common" [11: p.479]. To illustrate, all students in a Psychology class of a specific college form a group; they know each other, and they communicate with each other. All college students majoring in Psychology can be seen as a category; these students may attend different colleges, and they may not know each other or communicate with each other - they just share a common characteristic. While posting their definition for culture, Hofstede & Hofstede also point out that culture is acquired, rather than inherited. Culture is learned, therefore, it should not be confused either with human nature or with an individual's personality; the former is the common denominator of all humans, while the latter refers to all the unique characteristics of a particular person. It is noteworthy that, although Hofstede & Hofstede [11: p.5] criticize the Western language inaccuracy of considering culture as synonym of "civilization" or "refinement of the mind" arguing that such synonyms have an unacceptably narrow scope, Hofstede's own work on individual differences and cultural dimensions might be seen as being inaccurate; this argument will be further elaborated later in this paper.

Young [9] asserts that the definition listed above is not broad enough to cover the field of Instructional Design; hence, she favors a broader definition, which attempts to embrace the interdisciplinary nature of culture:

...the patterns of behavior and thinking by which members of groups recognize and interact with one another. These patterns are shaped by a group's values, norms, traditions, beliefs, and artifacts. Culture is the manifestation of a group's adaptation to its environment, which includes other cultural groups and as such, is continually changing. Culture is interpreted very broadly here so as to encompass the patterns shaped by ethnicity, religion, socio-economic status, geography, profession, ideology, gender, and lifestyle. Individuals are members of more than one culture, and they embody a subset rather than the totality of cultures identifiable characteristics. [12: p. 7, quoted in [9: p. 8]]

This last definition aligns with the ones adopted by several scholars whose research is related to the acknowledgement of intercultural differences while designing technology enhanced learning (TEL) systems. To illustrate, Watson, Ho, & Raman [13] and Collis [1], in their work about cultural issues in the design of Web-based courses and in the design of group support systems respectively, chose to adopt Watson, Ho, & Raman's definition of culture: "the beliefs, value systems, norms, mores, myths, and structural elements of a given organisation, tribe, or society" [13: p. 45], while Chen et al. [8: p. 220], in their paper about cultural issues in the design of TEL systems define culture "as the beliefs, philosophy, observed traditions, values, perceptions, and patterns of action by individuals and groups"; although Chen et al.'s work may seem outdated, their definition is embraced by several researchers in more recent papers [14-16].

Definitions aside, cultures have dynamic nature; they are not static, they change [8]. As Henderson [3: p. 131] states, culture "...results through a group's continuing adaptation to its changing social, historical, geographic, political, economic, technological, and ideological environment".

One final concept related to intercultural differences whose meaning needs to be clarified is 'internationalization'. Young [9: p. 9] states that "Internationalization is about the inclusion of culture-neutral specific design specifications and the creation of a cross-cultural design". Internationalization is about designing products or systems with features that would be acceptable across different cultures [17].

3 Description and Comparison of the Three Approaches

Learning, regardless of its form, is affected by the different cultural values that characterize learners, and the effectiveness of learning may require a certain degree of adaptation to the particular cultural context. E-learning is not an exception; as Swierczek & Bechter [10: p. 291] point out, "e-learning neither eliminates cultural differences nor is it culture free".

In an attempt to demonstrate the natural progress made through time in the research area of exploring the role of culture in e-learning, the approaches to be described and contrasted will be presented in chronological order. The three main approaches chosen for this purpose are Collis' [1] ten guidelines for designing online course-support systems, Mercado, Parboteeah, & Zhao's [2] four key issues for designing online courses, and Henderson's [3] multiple cultures model of instructional design for e-learning. These three will serve as a basis, and they will be contrasted not only to each other, but also to several other approaches.

3.1 Design Guidelines for Culture-Related Flexibility in WWW-Based Course – Support Sites [1]

Back in 1999, when the use of online resources to support learning was a rather new concept, Betty Collis explored the cultural impact on online course support systems by identifying four levels where culture occurs: societal, personal, organizational, and disciplinary. She developed a set of ten (10) design guidelines for online course-support systems, drawing from the work of several scholars, including Henderson's original "Multiple Cultural Pedagogic Model of interactive multimedia instructional design" [18], which in turn was based on Reeve's fourteen (14) effective dimensions of interactive learning systems [19, cited in [18]].

Collis' ten guidelines for online course support systems are the following [1]:

1. The system should be as flexible and adaptable as possible.
2. Both instructors and students should have a variety of roles, and they should be able to easily exchange and/or modify these roles. This also refers to providing "an eclectic variety of types of learning experiences" (p. 208). An online system should allow both parties involved to adapt it to the learning experience of their choice, such as instructivist or constructivist, group or individual, etc.
3. The system should not be treated as the primary source of content. The instructors and the students should be able to customize the level and type of interactivity aspect. Collis' main arguments were two: one, that people were not constantly connected to the Internet; it seems important to point out the obvious, since this

particular aspect has changed throughout the years, especially with all the smart phones and other portable computing devices that have become available. Her second argument was that people may not particularly enjoy reading from the screen, which, although is still true, it is once more noteworthy mentioning that the situation has improved, and more and more people prefer to read documents on the screens of their e-book readers or tablets.

4. The system should be used as a supplement to the course material, not as a substitute of the teacher. The validity of this guideline can be disputed, given the fact that it was meant for blended courses; pure online courses are a possibility today, and, in some cases it is perfectly possible to have a computer system replacing the teacher; examples include, but are not limited at, Computer and Web Based Training (CBTs and WBTs) systems, or in automatically graded assessments through Learning Management Systems (LMS).
5. The system should provide a variety of learning materials, such as multimedia presentations, instructor notes, web links, student notes, etc. All currently used LMS fully comply with this guideline.
6. The system should have minimal technical requirements. This is still valid today, however, 'minimal' is completely different; to illustrate, the speed of a broadband connection today is incomparable with the speed of an Internet connection back in 1999. The same applies to the speed of processors, memory and storage capacities, etc.
7. The system should have the minimum possible amount of pre-set text and graphics on the screen; it should provide context sensitive help and allow for customized content. Given the degree of customization that characterizes most systems today, one can safely assume that Collis' suggestion for customization has been widely adopted.
8. The methods and the degree of communication and interaction should be customizable. The computer system should act as a transparent intermediary allowing the teacher to communicate with the learner as directly as possible; in Collis's own words, "Design for human–human communication, not human–computer interaction" [1: p. 209].
9. The course organisation should be adaptable and customizable.
10. The system's design should take under consideration the instructors' skills and time availability.

As far as the second guideline is concerned, it can be observed that Collis, quite wisely, neither favors nor condemns a particular learning form over another; instead, she stresses the importance of allowing the student and the teacher to select the learning experience they prefer. This 'eclectic' feature stems from the work of Reeves [19] and Henderson [3], [18]. Collis mentions instructivism and constructivism approaches as examples of the potential choices that can be made. It seems necessary at this point to clarify that these two approaches refer to theories of learning. The constructivist learning theory states that learning occurs as a metacognitive process, as the result of constructing new knowledge and understanding, based mainly on already acquired knowledge and schemata. On the other end lies the instructivist learning theory, sometimes also called 'behaviorist' learning theory because of its roots, which states that learning occurs through replication of knowledge, based on given instructions [3], [6], [18], [20-21].

3.2 Critical Culture-Related Elements to Be Addressed When Designing Online Courses [2]

In 2004, Mercado, Parboteeah, and Zhao identified the following key elements for designing online courses [2: p. 186]:

1. The design and presentation of course materials.
2. The character and form of facilitative information (instruction).
3. Assessment and the nature of assignments.
4. The form and nature of feedback

The three researchers attempted to map these four elements with the following four cultural dimensions, as these were identified by Hofstede [22]:

1. Power distance. The higher the power distance element, the less willing are people to challenge or question their superiors. Consequently, students whose culture has a high power distance regard their instructors as people with ultimate authority and knowledge.
2. Uncertainty avoidance. The higher the uncertainty avoidance, the more structured and familiar options are preferred. Students with high uncertainty avoidance cultural values favor highly structured courses, with predefined step-by-step instructions given to them.
3. Individualism – Collectivism. The more individualistic the culture, the more independent the people, with emphasis on personal liberties. Students with highly individualistic cultural values exhibit good leadership qualities, but they do not favour group work.
4. Masculinity – femininity. The more masculine the culture, the more assertive, competitive, and materialistic the persons. Students with highly masculine cultural values tend to value more personal achievement.

This mapping of Hofstede's [22] cultural dimensions with the four key design elements resulted in the following guidelines [2]:

1. Design / presentation of course materials:

Cultural sensitivity determines the success or failure of web sites. In particular, high power distance can be accommodated by more symmetrical, formal and ordered design. High uncertainty avoidance can be supported by limited choices and fewer data, since users want to be able to predict the behavior of the interface. High individualism would require more operational freedom. More feminine societies place a higher value to esthetics and artistry.

2. Character / form of facilitative information (instructions):

The higher the uncertainty avoidance, the more structured and detailed instructions are recommended, along with more standardized tests.

3. Assessment and the nature of assignments:

Mercado et al. argue that the choice of individual or group assignments can be affected by the four cultural dimensions. In particular, they state that individual assignments are preferred by cultures with high individualism degree, since they tend to become more competitive with group assignments, with high masculinity degree, since competitiveness is higher in these cultures, with low uncertainty avoidance, and finally with high power distance.

4. Form / nature of feedback

Learners with higher power distance cultural values would prefer more formal and critical, definitive and assertive feedback, since the authority of professors is not to be challenged. On the other hand, lower power distance cultures would require more constructive, diplomatic, comprehensive feedback, along with detailed justification, since students with such cultural values have higher expectations from their teachers, and they do not take their instructors' authority for granted.

Mercado et al. [2: p. 187] point out two alternative design approaches, the "culturalization" approach, which advocates for designing multiple different versions of a web site for different target cultures, and the "cultural representation" approach, which prescribes the creation of one single shared version to be used by everyone, regardless of their cultural values. This reference to 'culturalization' vs. 'cultural representation' describes two extremes that can be found in the work of various other scholars. The research work of Eberle & Childress [23] appears to be perfectly aligned with the 'cultural representation' approach; they support the application of the framework of Universal Design for Learning (UDL) in order to accommodate cultural diversity to e-learning. UDL is based on the principles of Universal Design, also known as "inclusive design" and "design for all", which is an architectural concept that suggests that products should be designed in such a way that could be used by all people, to the maximum possible extent, without any customization or adaptation [23]. Universal Design and UDL were developed in order to accommodate users and learners with special needs, but Eberle & Childress suggest that the UDL principles can be applied to online learning as well [23].

Since Mercado et al.'s [2] findings were the results of mapping Hofstede's [22] cultural dimensions with their own key design elements, it is worth mentioning that Mercado et al. chose to overlook Hofstede's fifth cultural dimension, i.e. "Long-Term vs. Short-Term Orientation" (LTO), which advocates that people from cultures with longer-term orientation tend to be more persistent and more future-oriented [25: p. 4). Mercado et al. do refer to the existence of a fifth dimension, but they neither describe it nor justify their rationale for not including it in their mapping with their design elements. This comes as a surprise since the LTO dimension was published in 1991, and the Mercado et al. research in 2004; LTO was already identified by the time the Mercado et al. research took place.

3.3 Multiple Cultures Instructional Design Model for E-Learning and E-Teaching [3]

In the impressive anthology of research in cultural and e-learning issues "Globalized e-Learning Cultural Challenges" edited by Andrea Edmundson, Lyn Henderson presented a refined version of her theoretical multiple cultures model. Adopting Edmundson's [20] views about the inadequacies of "multiculturalism, cultural diversity, and cultural pluralism", Henderson demonstrates the limitations and the weaknesses of the common multicultural and internationalization instructional design models [3: p. 132].

Henderson [3] argues that multicultural and internationalization instructional design models are inadequate mainly because they do not take under consideration all aspects of the various cultural educational contexts, and she proposes this theoretical multiple cultures model as an alternative model.

This alternative approach does not praise the use of a single system for all settings; in her own words, the multiple cultures model is "an alternative way to conceptualize the cultural contextualization of instructional design of e-learning", since it "provides the rationale and strategies for creating and adapting e-learning resources for local, national, and international e-learning contexts" [3: p. 135, 130]. She maintains that the multiple cultures model can overcome the limitations of the traditionally used multicultural and internationalization models, such as stereotyping and tokenism, and that those instructional designs that adopt the multiple cultures model can achieve coherent synergy and coexistence of the various cultural logics and epistemologies (global academic / training/ entrepreneurial cultures, gender / religion / class, dominant and indigenous / ethnic minorities cultures, and workplace cultures). Figure 1 displays the graphical representation of this model.

Henderson's model embraces the integration of three different levels of "cultural players" that are involved in a given teaching and learning situation, the global, national, and minority cultures [3: p. 136]. The shaded area at the center represents the intersection of these cultural players, demonstrating how instructional course designs should allow for the integration of all cultural influences. The bottom part of the diagram points out the eclectic nature of the paradigm; instead of advocating for a single approach, whether a behavioristic, constructivistic, or social constructivistic one, the model enables the adaptation of the learning situation to any of the three approaches according to the learning context.

This eclectic pedagogical paradigm, suggesting that it should be the choice of the instructor to select the learning experience deemed appropriate for the particular learning contexts, is a common element in the methodologies suggested by Collis [1], Henderson [3], [18], and Reeves [19]. However, this feature is not apparent in the guidelines suggested by Mercado et al. [2].

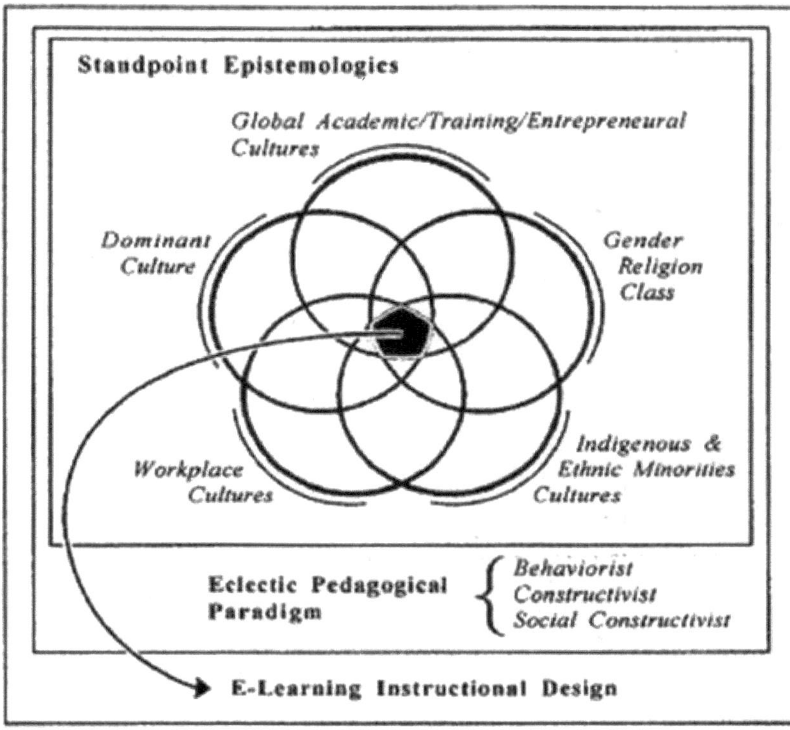

Fig. 1. Multiple cultures theoretical model [3: p. 136]

From the above descriptions of these approaches, one can visualize a continuum with the 'culturalization' design approach at the one end and 'cultural representation' approach at the other. As already explained, the 'culturization' approach promotes the design of different versions of a system to accommodate the different cultures; the methodologies which advocate for this approach include the ones suggested by Collis [1], Henderson [3], [18] and Reeves [19]. At the other extreme, supporting the 'cultural representation' philosophy of universal design, lies the work of several scholars including Aykin [17], Eberle & Childress [23], Steinfeld & Maisel [24], and Young [9]. Mercado et al. [2] do not seem to take a position in this continuum; they merely state the two options as alternative design options. It is noteworthy to state that there are sound arguments for both approaches. However, a more thorough inspection would reveal that Henderson's arguments, which are also reflected in Collis's [1] work, are not actually against universal design. On the contrary, what she actually suggests is that the same model can be used to accommodate different contexts; but this approach should be a highly theoretical one, prescribing strategies that would allow the design of a system that could be adaptable at the users' end.

On another matter, it is notable that one of the main reasons that Henderson [3] condemns the multicultural and internationalization instructional design models is that she maintains that these models rely on unrealistic and deceitful stereotypical assumptions for the learners, such as [3: p. 133-134]:

> (a) the Asian learner is a rote learner and benefits more when a course is structured with step-by-step instructions [...]; (b) students in East-Asia, ex-Soviet Eastern European, and Middle-East Islamic countries do not challenge authority, including that of an author; (c) students from such cultures are individualist competitors due to endemic credentialing; and (d) consequently they are passive and accepting of what is delivered.

A closer inspection on this argument reveals an indirect critique to Hofstede's [22] cultural dimensions. To illustrate, the first example about the Asian learner implies that since Asian culture has a high uncertainty avoidance factor, this allows a designer to predict all Asian learners' behavior. Similar stereotypical assumption can be made for learners from cultures with high power distance (second example), high individualism (third example), and low masculinity. Henderson brings forward the work of numerous scholars as evidence in order to demonstrate that assumptions like the ones described above are in fact incorrect. Other scholars have also explicitly expressed their concern about Hofstede's work; Cronjé [5] lists a wide range of studies that question the validity of Hofstede's work, including the study of Signorini, Wiesemes, & Murphy [26] who point out that in Hofstede has acknowledged that the cultural dimensions that resulted from the results of his research are quite general, since the cultural dimensions are essentially attributes of populations, and not necessarily of specific individuals.

Coming back to comparing the work of Henderson [3] and Mercado et al. [2], it becomes apparent that Henderson's model comes in conflict with Mercado et al.'s guidelines, since the latter are based on Hofstede's work, adopting an oversimplified approach for addressing and interpreting cultural differences.

4 Conclusions

From the three main approaches that were described and contrasted in this paper, the most effective seems to be Henderson's [3]. Collis' [1] guidelines drew on Henderson's earlier work [18], and as it was demonstrated above, some of these guidelines are obsolete and are not applicable any more. Moreover, it is important to state that the value and significance of Mercado et al.'s [2] work should not be undermined; the key elements identified are indeed critical for the design of e-learning systems, although their mapping with Hofstede's cultural dimensions [22] appears to be incomplete and possibly flawed. Consequently, Henderson's [3] theoretical multiple cultures model appears as the most promising.

As it was explained at the beginning of the paper, the choice of the three main models assessed here was made solely based on their frequent citing in literature, and on the time constraints of this project; a larger research project may use this paper as a starting point, and attempt to evaluate more – or even all – such approaches, since there are numerous other models, theories and guidelines supporting the development of frameworks that acknowledge cultural differences for the design of e-learning systems.

References

1. Collis, B.: Designing for differences: cultural issues in the design of WWW-based course-support sites. British Journal of Educational Technology 30(3), 201–215 (1999)
2. Mercado, S., Parboteeah, K.P., Zhao, Y.: On-line course design and delivery: cross-national considerations. Strategic Change 13(4), 183–192 (2004), doi:10.1002/jsc.677
3. Henderson, L.: Theorizing a Multiple Cultures Instructional Design Model for E-Learning and E-Teaching. In: Edmundson, A. (ed.) Globalized e-Learning Cultural Challenges, pp. 130–153. Information Science Publishing - Idea Group Inc. (2007)
4. Williamson, D.: Forward from a Critique of Hofstede's Model of National Culture. Human Relations 55(11), 1373–1395 (2002), doi:10.1177/0018726702551 1006
5. Cronjé, J.C.: Using Hofstede's cultural dimensions to interpret cross-cultural blended teaching and learning. Computers & Education 56(3), 596–603 (2011), doi:10.1016/j.compedu.2010.09.021
6. Bélisle, C.: eLearning and Intercultural Dimensions of Learning Theories and Teaching Models. eLearning Papers 7, 1–18 (2008), `http://elearningpapers.eu/en/article/E-learning-and-intercultural-dimensions-of-learning-theories-and-teaching-models` (retrieved)
7. Cambridge Dictionaries Online (n.d.). Cambridge University Press, `http://dictionary.cambridge.org/dictionary/british/guideline?q=guideline` (retrieved December 9, 2012)
8. Chen, A., Mashhadi, A., Ang, D., Harkrider, N.: Cultural Issues in the Design of Technology-Enhanced Learning Systems. British Journal of Educational Technology 30(3), 217–230 (1999)
9. Young, P.A.: Integrating Culture in the Design of ICTs. British Journal of Educational Technology 39(1), 6–17 (2008), doi:10.1111/j.1467-8535.2007.00699.x
10. Swierczek, F.W., Bechter, C.: Cultural Features of e-Learning. A Euro-Asian Case Study. In: Spector, J.M., Ifenthaler, D., Isaias, P., Sampson, D. (eds.) Learning and Instruction in the Digital Age, pp. 291–308. Springer US, Boston (2010), doi:10.1007/978-1-4419-1551-1_18
11. Hofstede, G., Hofstede, G.J.: Cultures and Organizations: Software for the Mind. McGraw-Hill Publishing (2010), `http://lib.myilibrarycom?ID=296125` (retrieved)
12. Scheel, N.P., Branch, R.C.: The role of conversation and culture in the systematic design of instruction. Educational Technology 33, 7–18 (1993)
13. Watson, R.T., Ho, T.H., Raman, K.S.: Culture: a fourth dimension of group support systems. Communications of the ACM 37(10), 45–55 (1994)
14. Duus, R.: Do virtual learning environments help deliver a consistent learning experience? Exploring the international delivery of UK Marketing degrees. E-Leader Kuala Lumpur (2009), `http://www.g-casa.com/PDF/malaysia/Duus.pdf` (retrieved from)
15. Hartnett, M., Bhattacharya, M., Dron, J.: Diversity in Online Learners: Searching for Differences That Matter. In: Seventh IEEE International Conference on Advanced Learning Technologies, pp. 899–900 (2007)
16. Mcanany, D.: Monkeys on the Screen?: Multicultural Issues in Instructional Message Design. Canadian Journal of Learning and Technology 35(1) (2009), `http://www.cjlt.ca/index.php/cjlt/article/view/512/242` (retrieved)

17. Aykin, N.: Overview: where to start and what to consider. In: Aykin, N. (ed.) Usability and Internationalization of Information Technology, pp. 3–20. Lawrence Erlbaum Associates Publishers, Mahwah (2005)
18. Henderson, L.: Instructional design of interactive multimedia: A cultural critique. Educational Technology Research and Development 44(4), 85–104 (1996), doi:10.1007/BF02299823
19. Reeves, T.: Effective dimensions of interactive learning systems. In: Information Technology for Training and Education Conference (ITTE 1992), pp. 99–113. University of Queensland, St. Lucia (1992)
20. Edmundson, A.: Guidelines for Assessing Cultural Disparity in e-Learning. Turkish Online Journal of Distance Education-TOJDE 4(3), 1–18 (2003), `http://tojde.anadolu.edu.tr/tojde11/articles/edmundson.htm` (Guidelines for Assessing Cultural Disparity in e-Learning)
21. Newhouse, C.P., Trinidad, S., Clarkson, B.: Quality Pedagogy and Effective Learning with Information and Communications Technologies (ICT): a review of the literature. Specialist Educational Services, Perth (2002), `http://www.eddept.wa.edu.au/cmis/eval/downloads/pd/litreview.pdf` (retrieved)
22. Hofstede, G.: Cultural Differences in Teaching and Learning. International Journal of Intercultural Relations 10, 301–320 (1986)
23. Eberle, J.H., Childress, M.D.: Universal Design for Culturally Diverse Online Learning. In: Edmundson, A. (ed.) Globalized e-Learning Cultural Challenges, pp. 239–254. Information Science Publishing - Idea Group Inc., Hershey (2007)
24. Steinfeld, E., Maisel, J.: Universal Design. Wiley (2012), `http://lib.myilibrary.com?ID=361848` (retrieved)
25. Minkov, M., Hofstede, G.: Hofstede's Fifth Dimension: New Evidence From the World Values Survey. Journal of Cross-Cultural Psychology 43(1), 3–14 (2011), doi:10.1177/0022022110388567
26. Signorini, P., Wiesemes, R., Murphy, R.: Developing alternative frameworks for exploring intercultural learning: a critique of Hofstede's cultural difference model. Teaching in Higher Education 14(3), 253–264 (2009), doi:10.1080/13562510902898825

A Cross-Cultural Comparison on Contributors' Motivations to Online Knowledge Sharing: Chinese vs. Germans

Bin Zhu, Qin Gao, and Eike Nohdurft

Department of Industrial Engineering,
Tsinghua University, Beijing 100084, P.R. China
binzhuzb@gmail.com, gaoqin@tsinghua.edu.cn

Abstract. Wikipedia is the most popular online knowledge sharing platform in western countries. However, it is not widely accepted in eastern countries. This indicates that culture plays a key role in determining users' acceptance of online knowledge sharing platforms. The purpose of this study is to investigate the cultural differences between Chinese and Germans in motivations for sharing knowledge, and further examine the impacts of these motives on the actual behavior across two cultures. A questionnaire was developed to explore the motivation factors and actual behavior of contributors. 100 valid responses were received from Chinese and 34 responses from the Germans. The results showed that the motivations were significantly different between Chinese and Germans. The Chinese had more consideration for others and cared more about receiving reward and strengthening the relationship, whereas Germans had more concerns about losing competitiveness. The impact of the motives on the actual behavior was also different between Chinese and Germans.

Keywords: cross-cultural differences, knowledge sharing, Wikipedia.

1 Introduction

Online knowledge sharing platforms are widely used by people from all over the world for acquiring knowledge. Undoubtedly, Wikipedia is one of the most popular platforms. It is in the form of knowledge repository and comprised of millions of topics. Its content is generated and updated by users themselves. Contributors voluntarily invest time and effort to edit and revise the content. To encourage users to contribute more knowledge with high quality, it is necessary to understand why they would like to contribute knowledge to Wikipedia or similar internet encyclopedias.

The knowledge contributors usually come from different regions of the world. Their behavior, values and attitudes are inevitably influenced by the culture in which they grow up [1]. Then, it is very likely that the contributors with distinct cultural backgrounds are driven by different motives. The motivation mechanism designed with western users in mind may not work for eastern users. Shim and Yang's [2] study clearly showed that the cultural differences affect the adoption of Wikipedia in

P.L.P. Rau (Ed.): CCD/HCII 2014, LNCS 8528, pp. 597–605, 2014.

China and Korea. Wikipedia's unsuccessful attempts in eastern counties were attributed to its failure of understanding cultural differences between eastern people and western people. Thus, investigating the cultural differences in the motivations for sharing knowledge is very important for the success of knowledge sharing practice.

In this study, first, we aimed to explore the cultural differences in motivations between Chinese and German contributors. Then, we further examined the impact of the motives on the actual behavior across two cultures. From a theoretical perspective, the results of this study can further uncover the cross-cultural difference in perceptions of online knowledge sharing behaviors. In practical terms, the findings will be beneficial to the cross-cultural design of online knowledge sharing platforms, public or proprietary.

2 Literature Review

2.1 Motivations for Sharing Knowledge

Much of the previous research has identified the motivation factors for contributing knowledge. We conducted a literature review and collected 11 motivational factors that may influence the behavior of contribution. Bock et al. [3] proposed a model to explain why people are willing to share knowledge. Based on the model, we classified the 11 motives into three groups: individual motives, social-psychological motives and sociological motives. Contributors usually have the concern of whether contributing knowledge can bring individual benefit or any cost. Four individual factors were examined in this study: getting reward, challenges of work, having fun, and fear of losing competitiveness. Contributors are also motivated by social-psychological factors. Four social-psychological motives were identified: strengthening relationship with others, gaining recognition, fear of misleading, and fear of losing face. Sociological factors are from the perspective of organization or community. Social norm and rules belong to this group, which contain three factors: reciprocity, altruism, and sense of community. Table 1 gives the detailed explanation for each factor.

Table 1. Summary of motivation factors collected from literature

Group	Motivation Factors
Individual	Getting reward: refers to that contributors can obtain extrinsic rewards for knowledge sharing, e.g. bonus points, medals [4].
	Challenges of work: refers to the challenge of sharing knowledge, which can promote contributors' sense of achievement [5].
	Having fun: refers to that contributors believe sharing knowledge is an interesting activity [6].
	Losing competitiveness: refers to that contributors are afraid of losing individual competitiveness after sharing their own knowledge with others [7].

Table 1. *(continued)*

Social-psychological	Strengthening relationship: refers to that contributors expect to strengthen relationship with other users through knowledge sharing [4].
	Gaining recognition: refers to that contributors hope to get the acceptance and compliments from other people for their contributions [8].
	Fear of misleading: refers to that contributors are fear of misleading readers due to the poor quality or irrelevance of his/her contribution [9].
	Fear of losing face: refers to that contributors are afraid of losing face, because the shared knowledge is wrong or inadequate [10].
Sociological	Reciprocity: refers to that contributors believe the knowledge users should give knowledge back to the platform [11].
	Altruism: refers to that contributors think that giving knowledge is more appreciated than acquiring knowledge [8].
	Sense of community: refers to that contributors have the feeling of being as a part of a group [12].

2.2 Cultural Influence on Knowledge Sharing

So far, a few studies have explored the relationship between national culture and knowledge sharing behavior in Wikipedia communities [13, 14]. Using content analysis method, they found that culture plays a role in contributors' behavior patterns. Pfeil et al. [13] showed that contributors' co-editing behavior is significantly correlated with their cultural background. The *Power Distance Index* (one of Hofstede's culture dimensions) [15] is negatively correlated with the percentage of *delete link* behavior (r = -0.72). The percentage of *add information* has a negative correlation with the *Individualism Index* (r = -0.98), and a positive correlation with *Masculinity Index* (r = 0.99). Hara et al. [14] examined typical behaviors across different cultures and as a result, they found that eastern Wikipedias have significantly more courteous messages than western Wikipedias. However, whether the contributors from different cultures have the same motivations are not examined by these studies.

People's behavior is driven by their motivations, which are the purpose and psychological cause of an action [16]. The knowledge sharing behaviors have been shown to be different between cultures. Thus, it is very likely that the motivations for sharing knowledge are also different between cultures. Moreover, Markus and Kitayama [17] indicated that the western people, who are dominated by independent self-construal, involve more internal and individually rooted motives – to enhance one's self-esteem, the motive to achieve or self-actualize. On the contrary, most of eastern people view self as interdependent, and they express more social motives or the motives that have the other as referent.

3 Methodology

Based on the literature review, a questionnaire was developed to investigate the motives and actual behavior of contributors. The questionnaire consisted of two parts. The first part contained demographic information and the information about the user's experience with computer/internet and frequency of knowledge contribution. The frequency of knowledge contribution was measured with a five-point Likert's scale, from "never" to "always". The second part was about the motivational factors for knowledge contribution. The items were adapted from previous studies, and the validity has been checked by researchers. There were 28 items in total, which covered the above 11 motivational factors. Besides, we designed two pairs of reverse questions to check the response consistency. Participants were asked to indicate the agreement level with each statement using a five-point Likert's scale, anchored from "strongly disagree" to "strongly agree". The English version questionnaire was first developed. Then two native Chinese speakers and two native German speakers were invited to translate it into Chinese version and German version respectively.

The questionnaire was administrated on the internet. The Chinese participants were recruited from Baidu Baike, and German participants were from German version Wikipedia. Because Chinese version Wikipedia is not widely used in China [2], we selected the biggest Chinese online encyclopedia – Baidu Baike as the substitute. Only the users who had the records of sharing knowledge were eligible for our survey. An invitation message was randomly sent to the eligible users to ask them to participate in the survey. Respondents took part in the survey voluntarily, and finished the questionnaire through internet.

As a result, we collected 100 valid questionnaires from Chinese people, and 34 valid questionnaires from German people. The responses which did not pass the consistency check had already been excluded.

4 Results and Discussion

4.1 Demographic Information

Among the Chinese respondents, 82% were male and 18% were female. The mean age of Chinese participants was 24.3 (SD = 7.17) years. Of German respondents, 91.2% were male and 8.8% were female, and the mean age was 37.5 (SD = 10.71) years. 61% of Chinese respondents were students, whereas 85.3% of German respondents were salary workers. The result shows that the core users of Baidu Baike are young students, but for German Wikipedia, the main contributors are young and middle – aged working people.

German participants used computer (Mean = 20.8 years, SD = 6.39) and internet (Mean = 12.8 years, SD = 3.21) longer than Chinese participants (Mean = 9.1 years, SD = 4.05; Mean = 7.4 years, SD = 2.78). This is because Germany had more advanced infrastructure than China in the past 20 years. However, Chinese participants spent longer time per week on the internet than German participants. For Chinese, the mean hours per week on the internet was 31.1 hours (SD = 22.83), and for Germans it was 25.7 hours (SD = 1.08). There was no significant difference in the frequency of sharing knowledge between Chinese (Mean = 3.1, SD = 1.07) and Germans (Mean = 2.9, SD = 1.08). Both of them shared knowledge sometimes.

4.2 Factor Analysis

In order to identify the underlying factor structure for the 11 motives, we conducted an exploratory factor analysis. Due to its larger sample size and better data adequacy, the Chinese data set was used to conduct the analysis. The Kaiser-Meyer-Olkin (KMO) value was 0.701 and the Bartlett's Test of Sphericity was significant ($p < 0.001$). This result indicated that the sample was appropriate for factor analysis [18]. The factors were extracted through principal component analysis with varimax rotation method. The following criteria were used to determine the number of factors: (1) only the factors whose eigenvalues were greater than 1.0 were retained [19]; (2) only the factors before the "elbow" point in the scree plot were retained [20]. If an item's factor loading was below 0.45 for all factors, or its cross-loading was less than 0.4, this item was removed for further analysis [18, 21]

A 7-factor structure was derived, as shown in Table 2. The seven factors accounted for 68.60% of the total variance. The overall internal consistency was 0.761 for Chinese and 0.751 for the Germans. Factor 1, which was labeled as *strengthening relationship with others*, describes the purpose of strengthening or expanding relationship network through knowledge sharing. Factor 2, termed as *gaining recognition*, is the motive of seeking others' acceptance of him/her. Factor 3, labeled as *reciprocity*, refers to the value of helping each other. Factor 4, named *fear of losing competitiveness*, refers to the concern of losing personal competitiveness due to sharing knowledge. Factor 5, labeled as *getting reward*, refers to the motive of receiving extrinsic reward. Factor 6, termed as *consideration for others*, refers to the consideration for readers when contributing knowledge. Factor 7, named *having fun*, refers to the purpose of seeking pleasure from knowledge sharing.

Table 2. Results of factor analysis

Factor	Item	Loading
Strengthening relationship with others	Strengthen relationship	0.85
	Expand relationship network	0.80
	Increase the understanding between users	0.79
Gaining recognition	Other's opinion with my knowledge is important.	0.83
	Other's comments to me are important.	0.78
	I would like to receive compliments.	0.78
Reciprocity	I should help others because others help me.	0.70
	Others would always help me if I need help.	0.69
	After the acquisition, I will give knowledge back.	0.62
	I have a positive feeling towards Wikipedia, because it brings helps to me.	0.53

Table 2. *(continued)*

Fear of losing competitiveness	I'm afraid I may lose outstanding position.	0.88
	I'm afraid the value of knowledge gets lost.	0.86
	I'm afraid others plagiarize my knowledge.	0.67
Getting reward	I should receive reward for contribution.	0.74
	I expect my work to be valued.	0.69
	I'm motivated by getting more status points.	0.53
Consideration for others	I will consider whether my contribution may mislead others.	0.85
	I agree to "giving is better than acquiring".	0.52
Having fun	I share knowledge in order to kill time.	0.86
	I'm more interested in a fun topic.	0.59

4.3 T-Test

Based on the result of factor analysis, the score of each factor was computed and compared between Chinese and Germans. Two independent samples t-test was conducted to test the significance of difference.

The results are shown in Table 3. Significant differences were found on the factors of *strengthening relationship with others*, *fear of losing competitiveness*, *getting reward*, and *consideration for others*. Among these four factors, Germans rated higher than Chinese only on *fear of losing competitiveness*. This indicates that German contributors (Mean = 4.67) were more concerned about losing competitiveness than Chinese contributors, although this concern was also important for Chinese contributors (Mean = 4.04). On the other three factors, the assessment of Chinese was significantly higher than Germans. In particular, Chinese contributors considered a lot for readers (Mean = 4.37), but German contributors have little consideration for others (Mean = 2.06). As well, *strengthening relationship with others* and *getting reward for contribution* were more important for Chinese people.

As expected, Chinese and Germans do have different motives for sharing knowledge. Chinese people focus more on social-psychological factors and extrinsic reward, whereas Germans pay more attention to personal development. This result is consistent with Markus and Kitayama's theory [17], which claims that eastern people are motivated more by social motives and western people motivated more by individually rooted motives.

4.4 Multiple Regression Analysis

A stepwise regression analysis was conducted to further investigate the impact of the seven factors on the actual behavior and the pertinent cultural differences. The results are shown in Table 4. Only the factors with significant impacts on the actual behavior are presented in the table. For Chinese people, only the factor of *strengthening relationship with others* had significant influence on the actual behavior, and 15.3% of

Table 3. T-test results

Factors	Chinese (N=100)		German (N=34)			
	Mean	SD	Mean	SD	*t*	*p*-value
Strengthening relationship	3.58	0.88	2.84	1.02	4.03	<.001***
Gaining recognition	3.28	0.94	2.93	0.82	1.91	0.06
Reciprocity	4.05	0.58	3.96	0.73	0.76	0.45
Losing competitiveness	4.04	0.73	4.67	0.76	-4.30	<.001***
Getting reward	3.73	0.75	2.47	0.95	7.91	<.001***
Consideration for others	4.37	0.85	2.06	0.95	13.30	<.001***
Having fun	2.92	0.93	2.74	0.93	0.97	0.33

*** p < .001.

Table 4. Regression of actual behavior

	Chinese (N = 100)			German (N= 34)		
	β	*t*	*p*-value	β	*t*	*p*-value
Strengthening relationship	0.40	4.35	<.001***			
Gaining recognition				0.46	2.93	0.006**

** p < .01, *** p < .001.

variance ($F_{(1, 98)}$=18.94, p<0.001) was explained by this factor. In contrast, the actual behavior of German people was significantly influenced by the factor of *gaining recognition*, which explained 18.7% of variance ($F_{(1, 32)}$=8.58, p=0.006).

The results indicate that the factors that influence the actual contribution frequency are different for Chinese and Germans: whereas German users pursue to establish acknowledgement and recognition of ones own in the community, Chinese users consider knowledge sharing a way to further develop and strengthen their social relationships with others. This result is also supported by previous cross-cultural findings: being recognized by a lot of readers is a drive for German Wikipedia contributors [22], whereas Chinese contributors' intention for knowledge sharing is significantly influenced by relationship orientation [10].

5 Conclusion

This study investigated the influence of culture on the motives for sharing knowledge. The results showed that Chinese and Germans had different motivations for sharing knowledge. Chinese are motivated to contribute more by strengthening relationship with others, whereas Germans are motivated by gaining recognition from others. During sharing knowledge, Chinese have more consideration for others and care more about receiving reward and strengthening relationship. In contrast, Germans have more concerns about losing competitiveness caused by contributing knowledge.

The study has demonstrated the role of culture on the knowledge sharing practice. The results provide some implications for cross-cultural design of online knowledge sharing platforms. For Chinese users, the channels used for social connection should be enhanced. Even in the virtual world, Chinese people still prefer to recognize more people. Moreover, designing an attractive rewarding system is a useful means for encouraging Chinese users to contribute more. Chinese users are enthusiastic about promoting their status and obtaining more privileges in the virtual environment. For Germans, the service provider should encourage users to provide their opinions after they acquire knowledge. Other people's opinions can be an acceptance of contributors or a supplement to contributors' knowledge base.

There are two limitations with the study. First, the sample size of Germans is small. All of the participants in the study were invited by sending messages on Wikipedia, which set several rules to protect their contributors. As a result, we could not send many invitation messages to contributors. Otherwise, the message would be blocked as spams. Second, several questions in the questionnaire were not applicable to this study, because these items were developed in the context of organization. More items should be designed according to the context of this study.

References

1. Boyd, R., Richerson, P.J.: Culture and cooperation. In: Hinde, R.A., Groebel, J. (eds.) Cooperation and Prosocial Behaviour. Cambridge University Press, Cambridge (1991)
2. Shim, J.P., Yang, J.: Why is Wikipedia not more widely accepted in Korea and China? Factors affecting knowledge-sharing adoption. Decision Line 40(2), 12–15 (2009)
3. Bock, G.-W., Zmud, R.W., Kim, Y.-G., Lee, J.-N.: Behavioral intention formation in knowledge sharing: Examining the roles of extrinsic motivators, social-psychological forces, and organizational climate. MIS Quarterly 29(1), 87–111 (2005)
4. Wu, S.: Exploring knowledge sharing behavior of IS personnel with theory of planned behavior (Master thesis). National Sun Yat-sen University, Taiwan (2003)
5. Hendriks, P.: Why share knowledge? The influence of ICT on the motivation for knowledge sharing. Knowledge and Process Management 6(2), 91–100 (1999)
6. Jin, X.-L., Lee, M.K.O., Cheung, C.M.K.: Predicting continuance in online communities: model development and empirical test. Behaviour & Information Technology 29(4), 383–394 (2010)
7. Alexandre, A., Maurer, M., Li, W., Wentling, T., Stuedemann, R.: Cultural influences on knowledge sharing through online communities of practice. Journal of Knowledge Management 10(1), 94–107 (2006)

8. Oreg, S., Nov, O.: Exploring motivations for contributing to open source initiatives: The roles of contribution context and personal values. Computers in Human Behavior 24(5), 2055–2073 (2008)
9. Ardichvili, A., Page, V., Wentling, T.: Motivation and barriers to participation in virtual knowledge-sharing communities of practice. Journal of Knowledge Management 7(1), 64–77 (2003)
10. Huang, Q., Davison, R.M., Gu, J.: Impact of personal and cultural factors on knowledge sharing in China. Asia Pacific Journal of Management 25(3), 451–471 (2008)
11. Chiu, C.-M., Hsu, M.-H., Wang, E.T.G.: Understanding knowledge sharing in virtual communities: An integration of social capital and social cognitive theories. Decision Support Systems 42(3), 1872–1888 (2006)
12. Hars, A., Ou, S.: Working for free? Motivations of participating in open source projects. Paper Presented at the 34th Annual Hawaii International Conference on System Sciences, USA, Hawaii, January 3-6, pp. 1–9 (2001)
13. Pfeil, U., Zaphiris, P., Ang, C.S.: Cultural differences in collaborative authoring of Wikipedia. Journal of Computer-Mediated Communication 12(1), 88–113 (2006)
14. Hara, N., Shachaf, P., Hew, K.F.: Cross-cultural analysis of the Wikipedia community. Journal of the American Society for Information Science and Technology 61(10), 2097–2108 (2010)
15. Hofstede, G.: Culture's Consequences: International Differences in Work-related Values. SAGE Publications, Beverly Hills (1980)
16. Schacter, D.L., Daniel, T.G., Daniel, M.W.: Psychology. Worth Publishers (2010)
17. Markus, H.R., Kitayama, S.: Culture and the self: Implications for cognition, emotion, and motivation. Psychological Review 98(2), 224–253 (1991)
18. Comrey, A.L., Lee, H.B.: A First Course in Factor Analysis. Lawrence Erlbaum, Hillsdale (1992)
19. Kaiser, H.F.: The application of electronic computers to factor analysis. Educational and Psychological Measurement 20(1), 141–151 (1960)
20. Cattell, R.B.: The scree test for the number of factors. Multivariate Behavioral Research 1(2), 245–276 (1966)
21. Ferguson, E., Cox, T.: Exploratory factor analysis: A users' guide. International Journal of Selection and Assessment 1(2), 84–94 (1993)
22. Jørgensen, R.F.: Making sense of the German Wikipedia community. MedieKultur. Journal of Media and Communication Research 28(53), 101–117 (2012)

Cross-Cultural Design
for the Smart City

Building the Co-design and Making Platform to Support Participatory Research and Development for Smart City

Zhiyong Fu and Xu Lin

Department of Information Art and Design,
Tsinghua University, Beijing, China
fuzhiyong@tsinghua.edu.cn, linxu8891@gmail.com

Abstract. This paper focuses in particular on the participatory innovation model in the context of smart city in China. Based on the practices from design thinking, living lab and maker space, we integrated the action researches and participatory practices in our smart city R&D projects. The integrated co-design process will facilitate the interdisciplinary professionals, open communities and citizens to involve in the smart city design. This paper present our co-design framework, which combines the exploration of the territory, integration of stakeholders' resource and issues, ideation of co-created experimentations, implementation of solution, products and service, and evaluation of conclusion & outcomes into a holistic process. The case study on crowd sourcing environmental solution project that applied the co-design model of development and participatory evaluation was launched as pilot in Beijing. These will be the helpful reference and support for the co-design practice in the city of China.

Keywords: Co-design, Smart City, Open Platform, Living Lab, Makerspace.

1 Introduction

In this paper, we will focus in particular on the potential model and framework of participatory design and practice in context of smart city. The core concept of co-design is to involve the citizens in the whole planning, design and evaluation process, and provide the suggestion and solutions based on their real urban experience. The mission of this research is to explore the new model and platform for designer, engineer and citizen to participate in the smart city innovation. Currently, smart city planning and design in China is mainly driven by the government and big companies, we want to give another option, which could integrate the citizen science, digital anthropology and ground theory to establish new participatory design process and framework.

1.1 International Movement of Smart City

The initial prototype of the city is formed by aggregation of population and commodity exchange. A real sense of the city is to make citizens living well with

P.L.P. Rau (Ed.): CCD/HCII 2014, LNCS 8528, pp. 609–620, 2014.

support of urban infrastructure and energy, food, water, transportation, recreation and finance system etc. Cities built on culture of the region, lifestyle and daily activities of residents, while traditional urban design and planning tend to be top-down, lacking of attention to the actual needs of the local lifestyle and behavior. The intervention of new ICT technology, change the built environment to a sensible, interactive and transferred place, which can support human activities in all levels, and make the city's physical space and intangible networks merge together to form a very complex ecosystem.

In its current state, smart city are envisioned as wired and ICT-driven cities, which will provide better urban life [1], innovative services [2], new business opportunities [3], efficient governance and sustainable environment development [4]. More and more cities began to consider civic participation, and regard the smart citizen as a new direction of smart city. Currently, governments around the world are taking actions to cooperate with their citizens in design and construction process of smart city, based on their specific situations and objects. Social media is widely used as a way to get citizens involved, and participatory sensing, which is empowered by the development of ICT, is also a significant approach for collecting data from citizens. Some government municipalities also launch urban sensing applications, such as the NYC 311 service [5]. New York City held its annual city hackathon 2013, the theme is called "Reinvent Green", aimed to help build digital tools and applications to support New York in leading greener lives [6].

1.2 Smart City Development in China

In China, the smart city evolution is mainly driven by rapid urbanization. It is reported that about 250 million citizens will move from rural areas to cities by 2020. China's Ministry of Housing has selected about 200 pilot cities [3]. At present, Governments are the major drivers of the smart city efforts, but only about a dozen Chinese cities have completed operable smart city plans this year, although close to 400 local governments pledged to carry out the strategy[7].

The development of smart city is facing higher challenges, including the rising of participation awareness in all aspects of political, social, management and economy affair. Particularly in the promoting of social technology, society tends to be more open-minded as the main development model. So the design of smart city must to accept and integrate the bottom-up model to involve the citizen participation.

Development of Chinese smart cities still lacks the successful cases. The smart city's construction requires a long-term or short-term planning, and should consider the various and transformable needs of citizens. Smart City is not only the concern of urban life, but also to bring new business, employment and industrial opportunities. Government needs to disclose more data in order to meet the needs of innovative public service, and to build up the dialogue channels to support the citizen participation in all aspects.

2 Related Researches

There are a few practical models related with collaborative design and co-creation, such as living lab and maker space, which become the new driving force for urban related innovation. Based on these practices and researches, we could raise our framework and process for co-design in the context of smart city.

2.1 Co-Design

Co-design can be broadly defined as the creativity of designers and people not trained in design working together in the design development process [8]. While it is not only about interacting and cooperating constructively with customers, but also with people with technical backgrounds and with other stakeholders [9]. The power of co-design is that it can prevent many of the communication problems that occur in traditional development teams when the work is organized sequentially or in parallel, but not simultaneously [10].

Co-design shares the tools and methods with human-centered design, participatory design and service design, including typical methods like brainstorming, mind mapping, mood boarding and role-playing. The tools are used to help improve the collaboration between different stakeholders involved in the co-creation process.

With the trend of smart city development, big data is no longer only controlled by top- down systems, but also generated and processed through a bottom-up structure integrated with the crowd and the Internet of Things [11]. And the traditional top-down design approaches can hardly reach design goals or meet citizens' real-life needs, according to the increasingly complex and integrated relationships between technologies and human experiences. There is a need to involve citizens in the decision-making for smart city and take bottom-up processes for sensing the dynamics of cities based on citizens' participation [5].

Co-design, which can help involve the crowd and leverage citizen participation for a citizen-centric smart city, describes the process of bringing stakeholders into the service design process and could be seen as part of a broader shift towards citizens and professional staff working together to co-produce services in municipalities [12].

The word 'co-design' in smart city project can be explained as the activity where the users of the planned new system actively collaborate in defining what the system should do (problem definition), the development process and acceptance of the results [12].

A typical form of collaboration with citizens under smart city context is the research on citizen science, in which the data is usually collected in a crowdsourcing way, such as Project Noah [13], a biodiversity observation project, encouraging people with diverse background to upload data of their observation.

2.2 Living Lab

Living Labs are citizen-driven open innovation ecosystems in real-life settings in which innovation is fully integrated in the co-creative co-design processes for new technologies, products, services, and societal infrastructures [14]. The key principles of Living Labs are continuity, openness, realism, empowerment of user, and spontaneity. Living Labs involve end-users or potential end-users as the innovation co-creators and valuators, and carry out the researches in the real-world's usage scenarios. Living labs apply the new and existing ICT technology to facilitate new ways of cooperating and co-creating innovations among the partners and stakeholders. Standards and methods are emerged as the best practice within the Living Labs environment and the partners make collective contribution with their specific wealth of knowledge and expertise [15].

Although the specific processes of living labs differ with the focus and themes, the main processes of living labs research mainly go through four phases [16][17]:

- **Identification or Co-conception:** stakeholders (users, creative communities, political and economic stakeholders, technology partners and related experts etc.) will be involved to co-identify the local issues and potential solutions through a scoping-ideation-elicitation process. Co-design methods will be used to help stakeholders express opinions and demonstrate concepts and ideas.
- **Implementation:** iterative processes including engineering, exploration and development will be deployed under the collaboration between stakeholders, and prototypes at different levels of completeness will be built for testing.
- **Experimentation:** prototypes and trials will be tested and revised through an exploring process. Activities, such as workshops and open day events, will also be held to help conduct the exploration. Research methods like interviews, shadowing and diary keeping will be used for data collection.
- **Evaluation:** hi-fi prototypes or final outcomes will be launched for testing and user study, using methods from design research and anthropology research. Evaluation reports, roadmaps, solutions or suggestions will be raised from the outcomes.

Differing from tradition research, the Living Lab approaches carry out research in the real world settings, involving multiple stakeholders and varies interaction patterns; allow users to take an active role as co-innovators and facilitate dynamics of collective action; involve multi-disciplinary research teams actively in the research settings; and take joint collaboration to create a desired outcome [18]. When it comes in particular to smart city design contexts, the methods and processes may change and develop with the increasing impact of the bottom-up power from the citizens, and with the support of the development of new ICT technology and varies types of social media.

2.3 Maker Movement and Maker Space

Hackerspaces are community-operated physical places, where people can meet and work on their projects. A German space known as c-base was one of the first independent hackerspaces that opened in 1995. Then similar spaces in the United States were found, such as NYC Resistor (2007), HacDC (2007), and Noisebridge (2008), etc. These spaces provide electronic product, programming and physical prototyping, include classes and access to tools. Makerspaces is an extension of hackerspace, which become the publicly-accessible places to design and create [19]. Makerspaces represented the democratization of design, engineering, fabrication and education. Maker space are beginning to produce notable products like the Pebble Watch, MakerBot and Square, etc. [20].

Currently in Beijing, Shanghai, Shenzhen and other cities of China had established the makerspaces. Maker used to be the civilian population and grass-roots inventors, but encouraged by national promoting policies of creative industries in China, maker became the most attractive representatives of the creative groups. HCI researchers have increasingly turned to processes and reflective modes of making, the community-operated workspaces, and co-working model in startup team. Support by anthropological research methods. Those maker studies focused on exploration of social backgrounds and capability development, and the mechanism of social interactions and modes [21]. In a quantitative study of an interview of nine hackers, they personalized the IKEA products and shared them in online community, then discussed the relationship among information technology, self-customized culture and HCI, as well as today's creative action [22].]Maker has become a cultural phenomenon, and innovation for those related activities, such as building space design and writing the code to have the help [23].

The fragmentation of knowledge and the popularity of mobile Internet make the access to knowledge become increasingly easy, and it begins to challenge the traditional. More and more methods are introduced into classroom of universities [24]. Innovative media or DIY productions, whether curricular and extra-curricular, are considered as indispensable part of education [25]. Because citizens are facing environmental, resource, political and economic challenges in city, the Maker Movement become the important driver to address and solve these challenges. In San Francisco, Gray Area Foundation For The Arts (GAFFTA) hosted Summer of Smart, a hackathons focusing on smart city. Participants could contribute, develop and vote on ideas, and one of app called Smart Muni, was chosen to become part of the city's infrastructure. The other projects like Code for America, Code for Australia help the citizens involve in designing and making the smart city [26]. Maker movement and Maker Space didn't contribute the design methodologies and process yet, but it is a very important participatory platform and implementation model for the smart city practices. The maker space consists of community network, toolkits, project database, learning lab, training and support [27].

3 Co-Design Process and Case Studies

We formed Design Beijing Lab in 2011 as collaboration between Tsinghua University, Parsons The New School for Design in New York, and the lab functions as a platform for research, planning, design and experimentation in smart city. Multi-disciplinary teams conduct analysis of urban activity in both the physical and the virtual realms and the patterns of citizen interaction, providing valuable data for the identification of key trends and opportunities for new urban technologies. As a result, the platform will be enabled to better adapt and improve, creating solutions for the public's future wellbeing and quality of urban life.

3.1 Co-Design Process

The basis of Design Beijing Lab incorporates the design methods drawing from the intersection of several disciplines including urban planning, service design and industrial design, etc. This convergence is critical to defining a new integrated practice that investigates the operation of cities from a broader systems perspective while recognizing the perception, motivations and actions of the individual citizen. The scope of smart city practice has led to the emergence of a promising new field, design for smart citizen, offering practical applications for everyday urban life.

We define this platform as a self-generating environment in which students, faculty and participating sponsoring companies work together to create customized, on-demand tools to facilitate the research, design and prototyping of a range of specialized products for new urban lifestyles. The objective of the lab is two-fold: experiment with new co-working tools and methods, and products development that use the latest in advanced collaboration, on-demand manufacturing, user-generated content and crowd-source funding to create useful, high-quality, commercially viable new product solutions.

Table 1. Framework of Co-design Process

Steps	Description	Main Methods
Exploration	Top design with sustainable and people-centered vision; Positioning the R&D territory in the macro-micro level. • Define the means of Smart City. • Analysis stakeholder group. • Co-create a specific Smart City vision. • Establish credible decision-making process.	Road map Territory Mapping Interview Workshop
Integration	Participatory Research with big/open data; Deep research for the real challenges of the city. • Draw on the available resources and expertise. • Structure the approach to a Smart City. • Establish the policy framework. • Populate a roadmap that can deliver the vision.	Storytelling Scenario User journey Frame opportunities Business plan
Ideation	Form the team through open activities and generate first prototype; Co-design with smart citizen based on lean startup model • Identify the target user groups and do user study. • Analyze the data and build user models. • Identify specific contexts for different models. • Concept generation.	Brainstorming Role play Focus group Workshop
Implementation	Frame new service ecosystem with Physical/ Virtual ICT. • Refine design contexts and solutions. • Put the financing in place. • Run pilot project.	Rapid prototype Iterative design Crowd development
Evaluation	Evaluation and testing with public; Summarize research approaches and solutions for future research. • Analyze the data for refining the user models and reframing the contexts. • Enable communities and engage with informality. • Make a self-sustaining process for citizen.	Tracking Learning Usability Testing Guide / Report

Research teams will be comprised of a combination of designers, technologists, branding, manufacturing and business experts working from diverse contexts in both academic and commercial environments to enable real product development opportunities to emerge from this collaborative framework. Integral to the R&D focus of the lab, will be the development of co-working technologies to enable teams to optimize communications and collaboration across industry, language, cultural, and geographic borders. Rick Robinson, an executive architect at IBM, gave the frameworks to create and achieve a smarter city vision through seven steps [28], which is a good reference to develop our process. Based on the main concept of design thinking and living lab methodologies, we developed the co-design process, seen in Table 1, as the practical methodology of smart city and conducted a few research projects. The design process and methods help the team to establish the holistic design perspective, and also very useful for them to observe and collaborate with different stakeholder groups.

3.2 The Framework for Open Platform

Integrating the maker space and living lab, we constructed the Design Beijing Lab as a platform for the re-combination of multi-disciplinarians resource, including the maker, designer, engineer and entrepreneur. Through participatory workshop or focus group, citizens and other stakeholders' requirements and need will be explored and identified. Taken the designer from colleague or company as main facilitator, the team will carry out the field survey and action research in the real scenario of the city.

Through the co-design workshop and focus group, teams will interact with participants to find opportunities for innovation in a broader perspective; developing viable smart city visions and proposals by the way of conceptualizing and prototyping. Many participatory pathways, like open day party, maker-a-thon are used to facilitate the development of concepts and prototype. The integrated framework will become the basis for the participatory practice of smart city, as seen in Figure 1.

In the ideation phase, DBL will help to combine internal and external, technical and commercial resources, like the open technology party, open source communities, adopting lean startup and design thinking approach to develop rapid prototypes and exploring the possibilities in commercialization and marketization. Through 2 days weekend workshop and make-a-thon/ hack-a-thon, participants will work as group to deal with selected topics of smart city or intelligent product development. After the workshop, few successful teams will continue to develop and refine their prototype in the support of Design Beijing Lab's 3 months incubation program.

An official website, Microblog and WeChat public page were developed to create the online community and ecosystem to facilitate the public participation, which made this platform as the combination of online community and offline practice. A number of high-quality project results are produced in the process from ideation to incubation after maker workshop and 3 months incubation. Collaborated with the entrepreneurs, angel investors and venture capital investors, we created the business opportunities for the start up team involved into the further productization process.

During the Beijing Design Week 2013, we introduced 14 projects to attend the Smart City 2013 —International Design Exhibition at China Millennium Monument Museum of Digital Arts. Focus on presenting demo's and pilots of innovative product and system applied to the smart city, the projects covered most of smart city areas, such as mobility application, public service, co-working, urban farming, health Kiosk, etc., which present our vision about the smart city movement by investigating co-design's role and contribution potential [29].

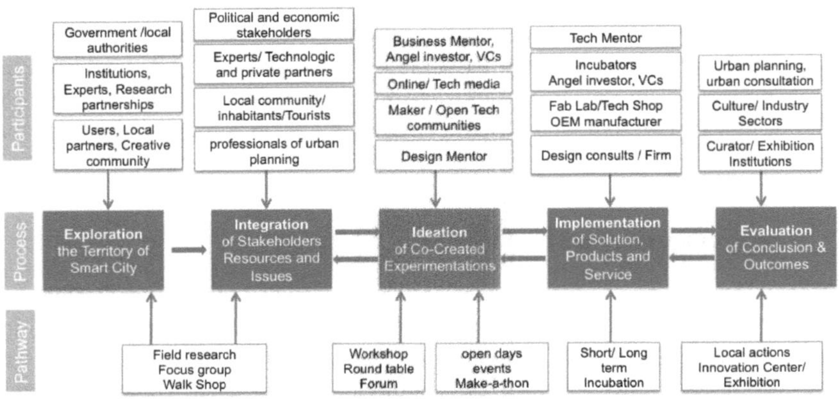

Fig. 1. Practical Framework for Co-Design Platform

3.3 Co-Design Project

The PiMi Air project, as seen in Figure 2, is one of joint projects implemented by interdisciplinary teams, focusing on one of the most concerned environment problems in China, air quality. PiMi Air is a personal air quality monitor, measuring the temperature, humidity and PM2.5 of indoor environment. The mobile application and cloud service provided by PiMi Air system can help user to read and share the real-time data from the device, and explore the macro data of the whole platform online through the crowd scouring model.

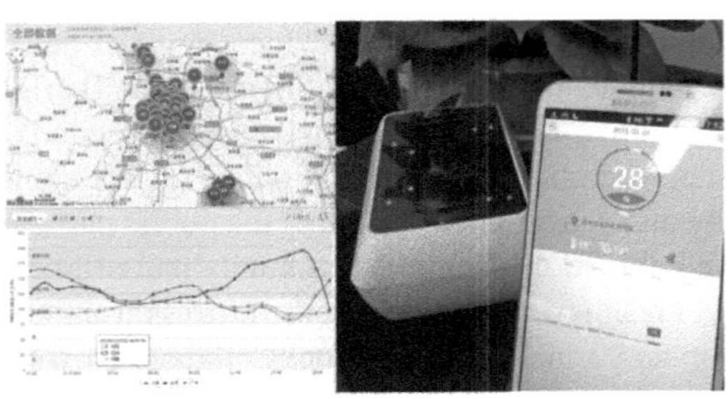

Fig. 2. PIMI Air Project as a Co-design Example

In this collaborated project, we adopted our co-design process to develop PiMi. During the **exploration** phase, we organized open forum with the laboratory at electronic engineer department to gain general vision of the air quality monitoring service in smart environment, including customized data sensing and recording, convenient data sharing, and reliable analysis for future decision-making. A video sketch was made to express our vision and the relationship between potential stakeholders in this service.

For **integration**, research on end-users and other potential stakeholders was deployed. Open data of city air quality was considered as a part of the initial database, and the information of chips and sensors for prototyping and implementation was also collected.

Then we formed an interdisciplinary team for **ideation** through workshops, involving end-users into our co-design process. Interview, focus group and other design methods were used to understand users' needs and concerns on air quality, while personas and scenarios were created to illustrate our findings and possible solutions, which finally focused on monitoring indoor air quality for working places and users' homes. Toolkits like lean canvas were also adopted to help explore business opportunities in our service during the ideation process.

To **implement** the prototypes and final products, we detailed the functions of application and online service, considering user needs for long term data analysis and platform data exploration. We also tried different solutions for the development of the device. The first batch of products was sent to users for testing and data collection at the end of this process.

For the final **evaluation**, we not only collected data sensed by devices, but also communicated with participated citizens directly on social platforms, like Sina Weibo. The problems reported and suggestions given by participants reflected potential user needs and contributed to our iteration of the products, and the constant conversation between participants and our team helped keep them interested in the project and engaged in sensing and sharing the data. After a period of observation, we also found competition mechanisms, such as ranking, can be taken in the system to encourage participants to be more active in participation.

4 Discussions and Future Works

In this research, we want to explore the potential model to support the citizen-driven design in the city of China. An open platform, which integrated the interdisciplinary team, design thinking and engineering practice, will be an essential support for smart city development.

We present a combined framework to apply the bottom-up research and design in smart city innovation since there is no mature public participation model in China. There are still long way for co-design with citizens in the real smart city projects, but we show the potential benefit to improve the quality of public service and fast the product development through getting involved in the maker and open communities.

The maker movement and startup team are playing an increasingly important role in technology and design innovation in China. The supported theories of maker movement are usually come from participatory design, citizen science and collective intelligence. Acting as the early-phase mode of startup, maker and open communities become one of dominant forces in driving innovation. When we hosted the make-a-thon or open party, the related IT companies and the investors gave actively supports. Creative industry promotion sector of government paid lots of attention to our pilot projects and invite our team to join the preparation of National Smart City Innovation Center.

Based on the online community and offline practice, the open platform not only allows participants to more deeply immerse in the whole process of smart city related product design and service planning, but also builds the empathetic connections among stakeholders both on social networking and co-working circle, which strive to establish a long-acting cooperation.

Although we launched many successful small-scale projects, but there are still lacks of the pilots to unfold the role of co-design in the early stage of smart city planning. And a long-term mechanism to involve the stakeholders, professionals and citizen is big challenges as well. Further more, we need to make a deeper understanding about how to refine the evaluation techniques, and provide better participatory mechanism for the citizens to contribute their viewpoints and test the smarter service and solutions.

5 Conclusions

This paper explored the academic and practical perspective of combining the open and participatory model through organic integration of designer, maker, technology community, investor and media. To design and plan for smart cities, participatory platforms that incubate, promote and evaluate the intelligence and wisdom from a diverse set of stakeholders play an indispensable role. Participatory platforms work as frameworks that allow different participants to explore the territory, integrate stakeholders and issues, share their ideas, co-create experimentations, and work towards collaborative solutions to resolve problems or evaluate the outcomes.

Among the research on empowering the collective intelligence of citizens through co-design approaches, we shape and inspire interdisciplinary teams to generate the rapid prototype and integrate multiply resources through the weekend workshops and make-a-thon, as well as long-term program offered by our open platform.

An participatory platform can also help the smart city planner, designer and manager to better understand the planning and renovation of the existing urban system, improve the quality of urban life, and develop new integrated application and service to enhance the social engagement and participation through open and collaborative approaches.

Acknowledgements. The design researches and prototypes in this paper involve the results of Design Beijing Lab. Many thanks for Mr. Christopher Kirwan to co-conduct the projects with me, and for the related students including Qinghua Guo,Yin Li, Linglong Li, Yixin Zheng, Shuang Zhao, Zhicong Lu, Zhan Su and Yamei Ou, I express my sincere thanks to their works.

References

1. Yigitcanlar, T.: Urban management revolution: intelligent management systems for ubiquitous cities, In: The International Symposium on Land, Transport and Marine Technology (2008)
2. Naphade, M., Banavar, G., Harrison, C., Paraszczak, J., Morris, R.: Smarter Cities and Their Innovation Challenges. Computer 44, 32–39 (2011)
3. Caragliu, A., Del Bo, C., Nijkamp, P.: Smart cities in Europe. Journal of Urban Technology 18, 65–82 (2011)
4. Gibson, W.: Life in the Meta City. Scientific American 305, 88–89 (2011)
5. Salem, M., Schonowski, J., Küpper, A.: Citizen-centric Smart Cities: M-Technology for realizing Smart Participatory Urban Sensing in E-Government. Information Technology & Computer Science 12(1), 82–92 (2013)
6. Reinvent Green Hackathon, `http://www.nyc.gov/html/digital/html/opengov/reinventgreen.shtml`
7. China and Europe ride the smart wave, `http://europe.chinadaily.com.cn/epaper/2013-12/20/content_17186394.htm`
8. Govt backing essential to success of 'smart cities', `http://europe.chinadaily.com.cn/business/2013-12/27/content_17200951.htm`
9. Sanders, E.B.-N., Stappers, P.J.: Co-creation and the new landscapes of design. International Journal of CoCreation in Design and the Arts 4(1), 5–18 (2008)
10. Steen, M., Kuiper-Hoyng, L., de Boer, J., Visser, F.S.: Co-design: Practices, Challenges and Lessons Learned. In: 10th International Conference on Human Computer Interaction with Mobile Devices and Services, pp. 561–562. ACM Press, New York (2008)
11. Townsend, A.M.: Smart Cities: Big Data, Civic Hackers, and the Quest for a New Utopia. W. W. Norton & Company, New York (2013)
12. Cruickshank, P., Deakin, M.: Co-design in Smart Cities. Technical Report, SmartCities Project of Institute for Informatics and Digital Innovation, Edinburgh Napier University (2011)
13. Project Noah, `http://www.projectnoah.org`
14. ENoLL-PPP-Scoping-Paper, `http://enoll-ppp-scoping-paper.wikispaces.com/Living+Labs`
15. Bergvall-Kareborn, B., Stahlbröst, A.: Living Lab: an open and citizen-centric approach for innovation. International Journal of Innovation and Regional Development 1(4), 356–370 (2009)
16. City of the Future Living Lab, `http://www.eservices4life.org/cityofthefuturelab/what-we-do/`

17. Membership Application ENOLL 6TH WAVE: Smart City Living Lab, http://www.openlivinglabs.eu/sites/enoll.org/files/021_ENoLL6W_FR_SmartCityLL_POUR_ENVOI.pdf
18. Higgins, A., Klein, S.: Introduction to the Living Lab Approach. In: Tan, Y., Bjorn-Andersen, N., Klein, S., Rukanova, B. (eds.) Accelerating Global Supply Chains with IT-Innovation: ITAIDE tools and methods, pp. 31–36. Springer, Berlin (2011)
19. Make Magazine. Is it a Hackerspace, Makerspace, TechShop, or FabLab?
20. http://makezine.com/2013/05/22/the-difference-between-hackerspaces-makerspaces-techshops-and-fablabs/
21. Maker Space, http://makerspace.com/
22. Lindtner, S.: Li, David, 2012. Created in China. The Makings of China's Hackerspace Community. In: Interactions, XIX.6, p. 18 (November, December 2012)
23. Rosner, D., Bean, J.: Learning from IKEA Hacking: I'm Not One to Decoupage a Tabletop and Call It a Day. In: Creative Thought and Self-Improvement, CHI 2009, pp. 419–422. ACM, New York (2009)
24. Kafai, Y.B., Peppler, K.A.: Youth, Technology, and DIY: Developing Participatory Competencies in Creative Media Production. Review of Research in Education 35, 89–119 (2011)
25. Harrop, P.: Open Sourcery: When Hacker Culture Informs the Design Studio. Journal of Architectural Education 69(1), 69–72 (2007)
26. Kafai, Y.B., Peppler, K.A.: Youth, Technology, and DIY: Developing Participatory Competencies in Creative Media Production. Review of Research in Education 35(1), 89–119 (2011)
27. Future Now, The IFTF Blog. Maker Cities, http://www.iftf.org/future-now/article-detail/maker-cities2/
28. Makerspace Playbook, http://makerspace.com/maker-news/makerspace-playbook
29. Rick Robinson's Blog, http://theurbantechnologist.com/
30. Smart City, — International Design Exhibition (2013), http://www.modachina.org/en/page/activity-534.html

Designing "Qualia" into Night Market for Taipei City

Yu-Di Huang, Yi-Tsu Peng, Chun-Wen Fang, and Jun-Liang Chen

Graduate School of Creative Industry Design,
National Taiwan University of Arts, Taipei, Taiwan
{artistted,fcwabc}@hotmail.com,
{freeimage5361,yitsupeng}@gmail.com

Abstract. This research focuses on night market, emphasizing both the eating style and users eating emotion. It investigates the user's need for Taiwan tradition food as a replacement place for regular restaurant. The study presents a process, based on user requirements, for developing guidelines for night market Qualia design targeted at community, and contributes to our understanding of community's eating preferences and the effects of this new style on eating environment. Fore factors affecting night market qualia design are identified and discussed; these guidelines can be categorized into tree principles of design dimensions. Some ideas for night market qualia design are verification, and finally, a new design dimensions based on Taipei city style is proposed. Future research could apply the principles to other groups of night market users based on the concept of design dimensions.

Keywords: Qualia, Night market, Design dimensions, Taipei City.

1 Introduction the Night Market in Taipei

Taiwan is ranked 20 one of the world's most densely populated areas. U.S. Cable News Network (CNN) just enumerated ten better things in Taiwan than other places, where the first thing throughout is the night market in Taiwan [1]. Night Market is the main market for trading done at night; it may sell food, clothing, groceries and even amusement. Night Market is often important tourist attractions in tropical and subtropical countries; it is an important representative of the common people living culture in Taiwan, Hong Kong and Southeast Asia [2]. In this research, the **Chien-Cheng Circle** (Chinese: 建成圓環; pinyin: *Jiànchéng Yuánhuán*) or **Taipei Circle** will be the target of investigate sample, it was once a bustling food market and a city landmark in the Datong district of Taipei. It existed 96 years from its opening during the Japanese colonial era [6].

2 Purpose of Investigation

In recent years, the urban renewal plan makes people of each region in Taiwan sparked mixed reactions. This research want to know is it because of this design event

P.L.P. Rau (Ed.): CCD/HCII 2014, LNCS 8528, pp. 621–629, 2014.

such will trigger different emotions and reactions that specific changes people in Taiwan have different night market consumer behavior. According to field investigation, Taipei Circle was a very flourish traditional night market before 2006, because it's meager firefighting equipment, after urban renewal such a crowd gustatory landmarks turned into popularity less glass ruin even it has the modernization glossy appearance. Thence, Taipei Circle is a clear sampling, but in this study, the research and analysis will focus on attributes of consumer behavior between urban renewal using questionnaire. Based on timeline recording approach, it described all images, evolution, and development related to Qualia and night market in Taiwan as shown in Fig. 1.

Fig. 1. Images, evolution, and development related to Qualia and night market in Taiwan

Table 1. Questionnaire Design and sample1

Part 1 No.	What is your level of understanding related to the environment of Taipei Cycle	Not very understand	Not understand	Common	Understand	Very understand
1.	I understand Taipei Cycle for overall overview					
2.	I understand Taipei Cycle for urban landscape					
3.	I understand Taipei Cycle for economic development					
4.	I understand Taipei Cycle for sales policy					
5.	I understand Taipei Cycle for historical background					
6.	I understand Taipei Cycle for environmental characteristics					
7.	I understand Taipei Cycle for specific practices (such as festivals)					
8.	I understand Taipei Cycle for food Culture					
9.	I understand Taipei Cycle for design style					
10.	I understand Taipei Cycle for an event					

Table 2. Basic information and sample2

Gender	○Male ○Female
Age	○Under 15 years old ○16~20 years old ○21~25 years old ○26~30 years old ○31~35 years old ○36~40 years old ○41~45 years old ○46~50 years old ○Above 51 years old
Education	○Under High school ○Colleges ○Above Graduate school
Monthly family income (NT dollar)	○Under 49,999 NT ○50,000~99,999 NT ○100,000~149,999 NT ○150,000~199,999 NT ○Above 200,000 NT
Personal monthly expend (NT dollar)	○Under 4,999 NT ○5,000~9,999 NT ○10,000~14,999 NT ○15,000~19,999 NT ○20,000以上
Profession	○Academia ○Industry ○Commerce ○Service Industries ○others

Table 3. Population and sample

B1 fx I understand Taipei Cycle for overall overview

	A	B	C	D	E	F	G	H	I	J	K	L	M	N	O	P	Q	R	S	T	U	V	W	X	Y
1	時間戳記	i ew	'2.我	3.我	4.我	5.我	6.我	7.我	8.我	9.我	10.	二1.	2.我	3.我	4.我	5.我	6.我	7.我	8.我	9.我	10.	三1.	2.我	3.我	4.我
2		101	102	103	104	105	106	107	108	109	110	201	202	203	204	205	206	207	208	209	210	301	302	303	304
3	12/24/2013 5:18:08	3	3	2	2	3	4	3	3	4	3	4	3	2	4	4	3	4	4	4	3	1	2	3	4
4	12/24/2013 5:40:51	3	3	3	2	3	4	3	4	4	3	4	4	4	3	3	3	4	4	4	4	3	2	2	4
5	12/24/2013 5:40:53	2	3	2	2	2	3	3	4	4	3	4	3	3	4	4	3	4	4	4	4	3	2	3	3
6	12/24/2013 5:44:05	4	3	3	3	3	4	3	4	4	3	4	3	4	4	4	3	4	4	3	3	4	4	3	5
7	12/24/2013 5:49:20	1	3	3	2	2	4	3	3	4	1	5	4	3	5	5	2	4	3	4	4	1	1	5	5
8	12/24/2013 5:54:49	4	4	4	3	4	4	4	4	3	4	5	4	3	4	4	4	4	5	4	4	4	2	2	3
9	12/24/2013 21:59:14	5	4	5	5	5	5	5	5	5	5	3	3	3	4	3	3	3	3	4	3	2	4	4	5
10	12/25/2013 9:54:04	3	2	3	2	3	4	3	4	4	3	4	3	4	3	4	2	4	4	4	4	4	3	3	4
11	12/25/2013 9:57:37	2	2	2	2	3	3	2	3	3	2	3	3	3	3	3	3	3	3	3	2	2	3	3	3
12	12/25/2013 9:59:02	3	4	3	3	4	4	4	4	4	2	4	4	4	4	4	3	5	5	5	4	2	4	4	4
13	12/25/2013 10:59:35	3	2	3	2	4	4	3	4	4	2	4	4	3	4	2	2	4	4	3	3	3	2	4	4
14	12/25/2013 11:35:40	3	3	4	2	3	4	3	4	4	4	4	4	3	4	3	3	4	4	4	4	2	3	3	4
15	12/25/2013 11:49:39	4	3	3	2	4	4	2	3	4	4	4	3	4	4	4	3	3	4	4	3	3	3	1	3
16	12/25/2013 13:21:25	4	4	4	4	3	4	4	4	4	3	4	4	4	4	4	3	4	4	4	3	2	3	4	5
17	12/25/2013 13:29:34	3	3	2	2	3	3	2	3	3	2	4	4	4	4	3	1	4	4	3	3	2	3	3	4
18	12/25/2013 13:46:50	3	3	3	3	3	3	3	3	3	3	4	4	4	4	4	3	4	4	4	3	3	3	4	3
19	12/25/2013 14:19:19	2	2	3	2	2	3	2	3	3	2	3	2	2	3	3	3	3	3	3	3	1	5	5	5
20	12/25/2013 14:21:16	3	3	3	2	2	4	4	4	4	1	5	4	5	4	3	2	4	5	4	4	2	4	4	4
21	12/25/2013 14:54:42	3	3	3	3	3	3	3	4	3	3	4	3	4	4	3	3	3	4	4	3	2	4	3	4
22	12/25/2013 16:06:17	3	4	4	3	3	4	4	5	5	4	5	4	4	5	3	3	5	5	5	5	2	3	3	3
23	12/25/2013 20:55:59	3	4	3	3	4	4	3	4	4	3	3	3	3	3	3	3	3	3	3	3	2	4	4	5
24	12/26/2013 10:40:06	3	4	4	3	3	4	3	4	4	2	4	4	3	4	3	3	3	4	4	3	2	3	3	4
25	12/30/2013 16:32:20	3	3	3	2	3	3	3	4	4	2	5	3	4	5	4	2	4	4	4	3	2	4	4	5
26	1/1/2014 17:20:18	3	3	3	2	4	4	3	4	4	1	4	4	4	4	4	1	3	4	4	3	2	4	4	4
27	1/5/2014 23:54:19	4	4	3	3	3	4	4	4	4	3	4	4	4	5	4	3	3	4	4	3	3	2	2	3
28	1/5/2014 23:59:26	3	3	2	1	2	3	2	3	4	2	2	2	2	4	1	1	3	4	3	2	3	2	2	4
29	1/6/2014 0:05:01	3	3	3	3	3	3	3	4	4	3	5	4	4	4	3	3	4	4	4	4	3	3	3	3
30	1/12/2014 13:22:29	4	4	4	4	4	4	4	5	5	3	5	5	5	5	5	3	4	5	4	5	2	4	5	5
31	1/12/2014 13:29:59	3	3	3	3	2	2	2	3	4	2	4	4	3	3	3	2	2	2	3	2	1	5	5	5
32	1/12/2014 13:30:41	3	3	2	2	2	3	3	3	3	3	3	3	3	3	3	3	3	3	3	3	3	3	3	3
33	1/12/2014 13:31:39	3	4	3	2	3	3	3	3	3	2	2	2	2	3	2	2	2	3	2	3	2	2	2	2
34	1/12/2014 13:31:57	3	3	2	3	3	3	3	3	3	3	3	3	3	3	3	3	3	3	3	3	3	3	3	3
35	1/12/2014 13:32:02	3	3	3	2	4	3	3	3	2	2	5	5	2	3	5	3	3	4	4	3	3	2	3	3
36	1/12/2014 13:32:35	3	3	3	3	3	3	3	3	3	3	4	3	3	3	3	3	3	3	3	3	3	5	5	5
37	1/12/2014 13:33:06	3	3	4	3	3	3	4	4	4	2	3	3	3	3	4	2	3	3	4	3	2	3	3	4
38	1/12/2014 13:33:10	3	3	3	3	3	3	3	3	3	3	3	3	3	3	3	3	3	3	4	5	3	3	3	3
39	1/12/2014 13:33:12	3	3	3	2	3	4	3	3	4	3	4	3	4	4	2	3	3	3	4	3	2	4	4	5
40	1/12/2014 13:33:45	1	3	3	3	2	4	4	5	5	2	3	3	3	4	3	3	5	4	4	4	1	1	1	5
41	1/12/2014 13:34:12	4	4	3	2	3	3	4	4	4	3	3	4	4	3	3	4	4	4	3	3	4	4	3	4
42	1/12/2014 13:34:29	3	3	3	3	4	4	2	4	4	4	4	4	4	5	4	4	4	4	3	4	3	3	3	4
43	1/12/2014 13:36:09	3	3	4	3	4	4	4	4	4	3	4	5	4	5	5	3	4	4	5	4	3	1	1	3
44	1/12/2014 13:36:36	3	2	4	3	3	3	5	4	4	3	4	4	5	3	5	3	3	5	4	2	3	1	3	5
45	1/12/2014 13:36:41	3	3	2	2	4	4	4	4	4	3	5	5	3	4	5	4	4	4	5	4	2	3	2	4
46	1/12/2014 13:36:51	3	3	3	3	4	4	4	4	4	3	3	3	3	3	3	3	3	3	3	3	3	3	2	5
47	1/12/2014 13:39:30	1	1	3	3	3	3	3	3	3	3	1	1	3	4	5	3	2	1	1	2	2	3	1	5
48	1/12/2014 13:40:23	4	4	4	3	4	3	3	4	4	4	4	4	4	4	4	3	4	4	4	4	4	4	3	4
49	1/12/2014 13:41:30	3	3	4	3	3	3	3	4	4	3	3	3	3	3	3	2	3	3	3	3	1	3	3	4

工作表1

編輯

3 Designing "Qualia" into Night Market

3.1 Designing "Qualia"

Emotional feeling when stimulated by stimulus in the environment. Qualia the meaning of life; It is a kind of emotional satisfaction; It is a moving experience; It is felt with the heart of a romantic touches and the deepest emotions of consumers heart [7]. Thus, with the building and displays change in the way, snacks in Taipei Circle also transformed into two levels, first into commodities from food (livelihood sense) (consumer sense), and then into the atmosphere from the commodity (the symbolic meaning), so Taipei Circle has been completely reborn, food court replace the original meaning. Food converted from making sense of practical value to mean "display the atmosphere". The room quality is increase, but the traditional social connect is far away lose.

Fig. 2. Before urban renewal
From http://47go.org.tw/article/845

After urban renewal

3.2 Subjects within the Factor

Table 4. T test Single sample statistics

	Number	Mean	Standard deviation	Standard error of the mean
I understand Taipei Cycle for overall overview	**75**	**2.9733**	**.73472**	**.08484**

Table 5. One-sample test

I understand Taipei Cycle for overall overview	Test value = 3					
	T	DOF	Significant (two-tailed)	Mean difference	95% confidence interval of the difference: Lower bound	95% confidence interval of the difference: Upper bound
	-.314	**74**	**.754**	**-.02667**	**-.1957**	**.1424**

3.3 Frequency Distribution Table

Table 6. Frequency distribution table

		Number	Percentage	Valid Percent	Cumulative Percentage
Valid	**2.00**	**5**	**18.5**	**18.5**	**18.5**
	3.00	**17**	**63.0**	**63.0**	**81.5**
	4.00	**5**	**18.5**	**18.5**	**100.0**
	Total	**27**	**100.0**	**100.0**	

I understand Taipei Cycle for overall overview:

4 Case Study Analysis

In early 2014, after the questionnaire is completed, there will be the subjects of each data processing and statistics; in this case using SPSS17.0 statistical software for data processing and analysis. The statistical methods used include:

1. (Descriptive Statistics) statistics measure the number of testing persons, ages and education level, in order to understand around the ring urban renewal period's consumers behavior to the night market perception of both qualia sense of the best combination sequence, the mean (M) and standard deviation (SD).
2. Quantity dependent samples repetition two-factor analysis of variance (Two-way ANOVA): To distinguish the degree preferences of night market, in order to understand before and after the Taipei cycle urban renewal period, consumers whether are significant differences on image qualia of night market.
3. post-mortem analysis: A simple main effect test and LSD method dependent samples post hoc comparisons, in order to understand before and after Taipei cycle urban renewal period, consumers whether are differences on quality exists of night market, was it significant?
4. The average number of paired samples tests (T-test): Questionnaire results are compared to each other for whether are differences and locate the way to present the night market qualia is significantly different before and after Taipei cycle urban renewal period.

4.1 Research Method and Discussion

In this experiment, 76 tester both acceptance testing by four groups (10 questions, 10 questions, 7 questions, 11 questions) questionnaire experimental treatment, therefore, every subjects were repeated observations under 38 experimental conditions, resulting 4 groups have relevant between significant differences under different conditions; Thus, the sense of the different samples tested qualia assessment mused from the same group of people, this called Repeated Measure Design; And because those two independent variables are all dependent repetition number samples, so execute a two-factor of variance dependent samples analysis (Two-way ANOVA), to test

"Taipei cycle around the urban renewal" and "consumer behavior" these two independent variables whether are the existence of interaction. If there is an interaction that means the main effect of a variable depends on the level of other independent variables, there must be execute simple main effects test and post multiple comparisons to determine which groups of consumer behavior tested samples are significantly different.

4.2 Two-Way ANOVA Analysis

Factorial Analysis of variance is researcher while using two or more independent variables Xa 、 Xb..... For a certain impact on dependent variable is involved in mean differences test [4]. Multi-factor analysis of variance usual divided into Two-Way analysis of variance and Three-Way analysis of variance, More than three-factor analysis of variance test rarely appear on the general research. At the same time, it based on design consider, the independent variables may be an independent sample design or dependent sample design. It has led to multiple factors design completely independent, totally dependent, mix design, such as different forms: information simplifying and abstract.

Three independent variables are understand, normal and not understand of Taipei Cycle night market that are degree of common horizontal axis, make one of them individual line, after swap is still considered. In this investigate design, the dependent variable is qualia rating around the urban renewal period of Taipei Cycle and consumer behavior is fixed factor.

In additional options, it is better select the narrative analysis of the statistics, homogeneity test, the effect size of the appraised value and the ability to observe the test, after comparing the three levels of self-selected variables into the list then select the appropriate method such as LSD post hoc comparisons, Turkey and Scheffe method. Through above discussion, Factor loading values for each subject after the shaft must be up to 0.5 above as selection criteria.

5 Result and Discussion

5.1 Fuzzy Logic Describes Night Market

Fuzzy theory is developed on the basis of mathematics professor L.A.Zadeh in the University of California at Berkeley's Department of Electrical Engineering was founded in 1965 on the theory of fuzzy sets, including fuzzy set theory, fuzzy logic, fuzzy reasoning and fuzzy control content and other aspects of contents [10]. Therefore, it called fuzzy concept refers to the extension of the concept of uncertainty such is it not clear extension, it is ambiguous. For example, "night market is fun" of this concept, it is clear that we connotation, but its extension, that is what market within fun, it is difficult to say clearly, because "fun" and "not fun" between does not have a defined boundary, which is a vague concept. Thus, Taipei Circle should within feeling; it is not easy distinguish right from wrong, because "feeling" and "no feeling" between does not have a clear demarcation line. And this is the reason which made Taipei Circle decay. The design dimension is not clear at once.

Table 7. Achievements of designing "Qualia" into night market for Taipei City

Comparison differences of Taipei Circle after urban renewal plan		
Items of comparison	Traditional scene	New virtual scene
Space Demands	*Space separate*	*Space connected together, Not easy to find position, entrance and surround*
Space visual effects	*Real photo panorama presented, but only 2D plane effect*	*meticulous 3-dimensional detail, but inevitably the actual gap*
Range of presents	*From any angle of any object or any object in any corner of the scene can easy move*	*360-degree glasses from the inside and out, and scene is bright and have air condition*
Scenes interaction	*Easy sneak into the space, walk and interact with objects and around*	*first-person orbital rotation on Left and right or up and down, the designated space narrow*
Production costs	*Production process is easy and fast*	*Production process is difficult and time-consuming long*
Use threshold	*Lower requirements of hardware and less fire equipment*	*Requirements of hardware and full of fire equipment*
Extending the application	*Unlimited*	*limited*

These are all attributes which can be further improved in the future. It is clearly, architecture is the main point, only architect's design concept of the building. After the completion built of hardware then placed "Software Elements" into it, What a pity, these software elements are food with emotion come from people who use their hands made, but even more tragic is the original link to social relationships between people, as the social context are excluded, only Architecture is the subject, the rest are not thing. That's the reason why Taipei Circle waned.

5.2 The Relevance between Taipei Circle Urban Renewal and Consumer Behavior

Table 8.

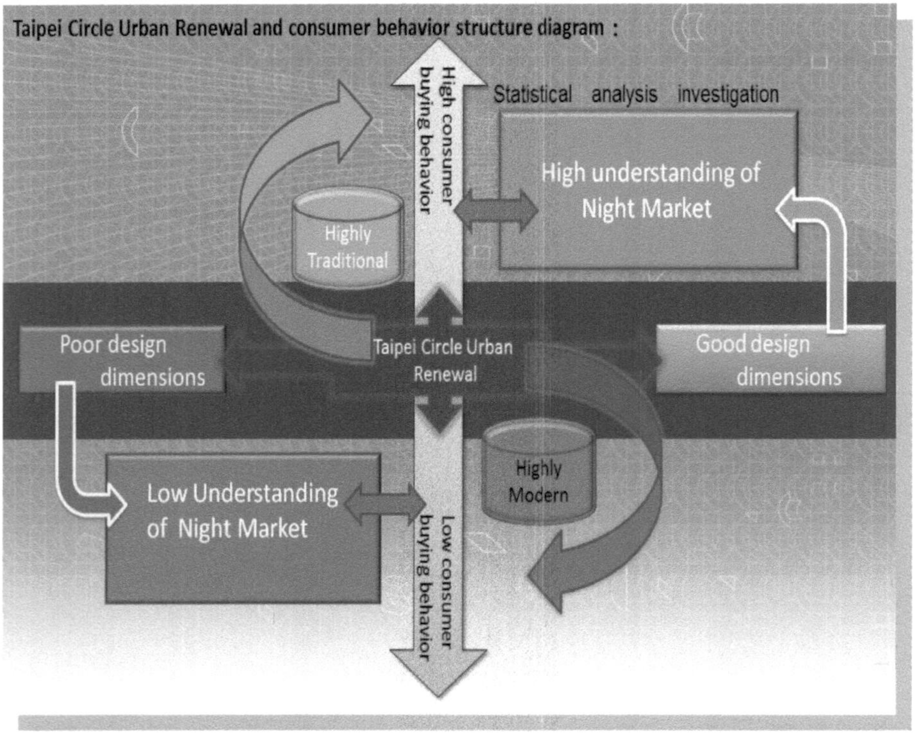

6 Conclusion

From the above analysis can be learned: This ANCOVA analysis three standards average of each 1-2,3,4-5, three standards average after adjusting are 1.6667,3,4.0769, those are approach significantly standards. It showed whether understanding of night market or not, their consumer behavior has a significant difference ($F(2,538) = 14.907$, $p < 0.122$), because interaction effect level not significant, which means that linear relationship between common variables and dependent variables of each group are consistent, The main effect of the test should be carried out simply to discuss under what circumstances, the degree of understanding will increase or decrease, it also shows the degree of understanding has to reach large certain extent which will affect consumer buying behavior. Analysis can be learned by another: This independent samples two-way ANOVA whether two main effects or interaction effects all reached significant standards. It Shows whether the impact of Taipei Circle urban renewal, the degree of understanding of night market was no significant difference ($F(3,61) = 13.182$, $p = 0.05$), Taipei Circle Urban renewal also has an impact as expected in consumer buying behavior differences (F(0,544)=4.773, p=0.000), Furthermore, the understanding of night market and the urban renewal plan of Taipei Circle will all interaction and affect consumer behavior(F(2,538)=7.04, p=1.000).Since the interaction effect was significant, the main effect will lost analysis value, but it should be run simple main effects test to discuss under what circumstances, the consumer buying behavior will increase or decrease.

In addition, recommended this design dimensions as project templates to the county and city Department of Cultural Affairs, apply for build the local famous night market and also for cultural digital archives extension, monuments promotion, digital archives, protection of its tangible benefits. It can be a reference for the government to develop a new urban renewal category and development more positive educational urban renewal plans.

References

1. Yam News: Night Market (2014), http://n.yam.com/liontravel/travel/20140116/20140116057064.html
2. Wikipedia: Night Market Night Market (2014), http://zh.wikipedia.org/
3. Pixnet (2012), http://chiuyi800405.pixnet.net/blog/post/91041560
4. Qiu, H.T.: Quantitative research and statistical analysis. Wunanbooks (2010)
5. Wikipedia: Qualia design (2014), http://en.wikipedia.org/wiki/%E7%B4%A2%E5%B0%BC
6. Wikipedia: Taipei circle (2013), http://en.wikipedia.org/wiki/Chien-Cheng_Circle
7. Norman, D.A.: Emotional design: Why we love (or hate) everyday things. Basic Books, New York (2004)
8. Lin, R. T.: Syu - Wun Hua Chuang Yi Chan Ye De Ben Jhih Yu Yan Jiou. Journal of Design 16(4), i–iv (2011) (in Chinese, phonetic translation)
9. Yen, H.Y., Lin, R.: A study of value-added from Qualia to business model of cultural and creative industries. Journal of National Taiwan University of Arts 91, 127–152 (2012) (in Chinese, semantic translation)
10. Wikipedia: Fuzzy logic (2013), http://en.wikipedia.org/wiki/Fuzzy_logic
11. Peng, Y.T.: The demand of neighborhood park for women in Taichung city, Tunghai University (1995)
12. Burgstahler, S.: Universal Design: Process, Principles, and Applications, University of Washington (2012)
13. College of Design: The Center for Universal Design, North Caloraindo University (2008)

Building Trust in Hospitality and Culture Exchange Travel Sites: Lessons from Heuristic Evaluation of CouchSurfing

Yu-Hsiu Hung, Lian-Fan Wu, and Chia-Chun Chen

Department of Industrial Design, National Cheng Kung University, Tainan, Taiwan
{idhfhung,P36013018,p36011040}@mail.ncku.edu.tw

Abstract. Travel is gaining popularity among people and around the world. The number of people relying on social networking resources and hospitality/culture exchange travel websites is also increasing. However, there have been voices criticizing hospitality/culture exchange websites for deception, violations of privacy, and lack of dispute resolution process, etc. To address this problem and to glean design insight, our study performed Heuristic Evaluation (with six subject matter experts) on the features and interfaces of CouchSurfing (one of the most popular hospitality exchange websites). The purpose was to understand if current features and interfaces of hospitality travel websites support trust-building among users. Results of the study showed barriers in differing stages of the trust-building process. Results also revealed that the establishment of trust was challenged by the current graphic design, the structure design, as well as the social cue design of CouchSurfing. Design recommendations were made from this study for hospitality/culture exchange travel websites.

Keywords: Trust, Hospitality Exchange, Travel, and CouchSurfing.

1 Introduction

More and more people are arranging their itineraries with travel-related websites rather than guidebooks or the assistance of travel agencies. According to the world travel market global trends report, the rate for planning trips over the Internet is expected to exceed 8% [9]. The flourishing of social networking sites also enabled the phenomenon of hospitality exchange, allowing travelers to stay at strangers' places for free [15]. The tenet of hospitality exchange is different than the conventional social norm; it is a concept where strangers are welcomed into the privacy of homes [14]. Hospitality exchange websites (e.g., BeWelcome, HomeExchang.com and CouchSurfing) bring travelers in touch with people in the place they visit. They provide a platform for people to help each other when they are traveling. However, deceptions and security issues came up recently in the online traveler communities, which challenged the positive impressions/experiences people already had with these websites. Research showed that trust is more crucial in the online situations than in the offline circumstances [7] [16]. Tan discussed the definition of online trust from the users of

P.L.P. Rau (Ed.): CCD/HCII 2014, LNCS 8528, pp. 630–642, 2014.

CouchSurfing. He fund that trust defined by the users not only included physical safety, but also included building an open-minded community [15]. In addition, some scholars also put forward that friends who have known each other for a long time will be easier to be believed than friends who have known each other for a short time in CouchSurfing [3]. The hospitality exchange website, CouchSurfing, has the largest number of registered members [5] [18]. Furthermore, it is important to build trust of CouchSurfing.org between each other [15]. And we hope to increase the trust of users by identifying website-trust design factors as well as providing website-trust design reference through the assessment methods. The targets of our research are as follows: (a.) to explore the trust standard of users concerning the web; (b.) to learn about the users' trust degree on the free accommodation system based on mutual-aid memberships in CouchSurfing; (c.) to explore the mechanism of trust design of the site by the standard of security trust defined by researchers; (d.) to give advice and applications according to the trust-building among the website members. The result of this research may offer references on the improvement of trust-building issues to accommodation exchange websites and help to construct the sense of mutual trust among the site users.

2 Literature Review

2.1 Trust

Currently, a number of academics did many studies and discussions on what is trust in many fields. Anderson believes that trust is a belief that people who believe their peers will not make adverse or unpredictability behavior to themselves [2]. Coleman thinks trust can be considered a subset of risk, which requires individuals to take risks when you trust someone [4]. And some researchers think trust is an interaction between the trustor (someone who put trust in another person) and the trustee (someone who assumes the trust from the trustee) in which the trustor will achieve their promise based on the expectation of trustee's behavior [10]. Therefore, it can be concluded that trust is a kind of belief in trustor's mind based on the behavior of trustee, and any trust involves an element of risk. Some scholars have tried to find out the characteristics of trust to summarize the definition of trust. Doney thinks that there are three qualities in the trust: vulnerability, uncertainty and risk. These three points interact to affect the generation of trust. Doney and Cannon consider that the trust-building process is divided into five steps according to the process of buyers and sellers to build mutual trust [6] (Table 1).

2.2 Online Trust

With the development of Internet, many researchers have explored the website of trust in the past few years. And most researchers agree that online trust is established in the process of trust-building in the real world. Aljazzaf considers that trust is important on the Internet, and summarized 16 principles of online trust establishment based on the trust-building theories [1] (Table 2). In addition, Wang proposed a framework of trust-inducing features from the perspective of interface design in 2005 [17]. The components of the framework are shown as follows:

Graphic Design (refers to the graphical design factors on the web site that normally gives consumers a first impression.)

Structure Design (defines the overall organization and accessibility of displayed information on the web site.)

Content Design (refers to the informational components that can be included on the web site, either textual or graphical.)

Social Cue Design (relates to embedding social cues, such as face-to-face interaction and social presence, into web interface via different communication media.)

Table 1. Trust-building processes (adapted from Doney and Cannon, 1997)

Process	Explanation
Calculative	Trustor calculates the costs or rewards of a target acting in an untrustworthy manner.
Prediction	Trustor develops confidence that target's behavior can be predicted.
Capability	Trustor assesses the target's ability to fulfill its promises.
Intentionality	Trustor evaluates the target's motivations.
Transference	Trustor draws on "proof sources," from which trust is transferred to the target.

Table 2. The principles of online trust (adapted from Aljazzaf, Perry, and Capretz, 2010)

The principles of online trust	
Trust and risk	First party information
Trust development phases	Third party ratings
Dynamic nature of trust	Trust approaches
Trust and identity	The distinction between trust and quality of service
Categories of trust semantics	Security and privacy
Trust relationship properties	Provider's trustworthiness
Global and local rate	Trustor's preferences
Trust is based on information	Trust classes

3 Methodology

3.1 Evaluation Framework

In order to make a more comprehensive and appropriate heuristic evaluation on the hospitality exchange website, we integrate the process of trust-building, the principles of online trust and the framework of trust-inducing features to form a new framework. Some online trust principles such as trust semantics, provider's trustworthiness and the distinction are abandoned by us in the new estimate framework for they are usually used to estimate trust-building between websites as well as their services and users rather than trust-building in the interaction among users. Besides, we combine the principles cf trust classes and trust approaches in the framework of trust-building process because the assessment range of the three principles widely contains the framework of trust-building process. What's more, the principle of third party ratings is combined into the transference process of trust-building for it is one of the evaluation parts of transference process. Table 3 shows the evaluation form of online trust principles. The framework of trust-inducing features, used in the evaluation website, assists us tc promote credence among users. Based on the online trust principles, we gave up part of the framework of content design in the new evaluation framework.

Table 3. The evaluation form of online trust principles

Principles	Explanation
Information	To evaluate whether the website has the information about building the trust between parties or not, e.g. mutual friends, friends recommend, and real-time updates, etc.
First party information	The entrusted one has the means to provide information or not, e.g. complete personal information, the fields to fill security and privacy in, presented in an easy-to-understand way, to help the other party and to trust the entrusted one.
Trust development phases	Building trust: To assess whether the website helps every user develop his evaluation or not. Stabilizing trust: To evaluate whether the website could stabilize the long-term trust between parties or not through user interaction, observation and recommendation, etc. The fading trust: To evaluate whether the website could pass messages about failing evaluation and help users to rebuild their trust and reputation or not.
Trust relationship	To assess whether the website could be directed to different trust relationships (e.g. fans and fans, individuals and individuals.) to change their trust needs (e.g. limiting specific users to browse accommodations info or restrictions on posting) contra different conditions or not.
Dynamic nature of trust	To evaluate whether the website could increase or stabilize the degree of trust of the users themselves, and could change the degree of trust of the others or not, e.g. introducing, recommending and evaluating others, etc.
Global and local	To evaluate whether the website provides the evaluation of the overall (e.g. all users) and the portion (e.g. the fans in personal fans group), has a trusted third party (such as the website) to help establish the evaluation, generates individual's way of evaluating different communities and could be linked to the evaluation of overall and portion or not.
Identity	To evaluate whether the website has a good authentication or not, e.g. User Name, Password, Digital Identification and Authentication and Identity Label.
Security and privacy	To evaluate whether the website has reliable security and privacy settings or not, including making sure on the safety of the users life and property, the complete exchanging accommodation process and not disclose user information, etc.
Risk	To evaluate whether the website could reduce the risk of users' interaction or not, including providing incentives, penalties, insurance mechanisms, and remedies of the offense to users.

3.2 Participants

In this study, in order to discover the problems of strange users in the trust-building process on CouchSurfing.org, we choose six postgraduates whose major is Industrial Design from NCKU to be our estimators according to the description of outstanding estimators by heuristic evaluation [11], [12]. All of them are well experienced in the interface web design and aware of the usability knowledge. Before starting, we would prepare assessment criteria for estimators in advance. And our observer will record the evaluation process of the evaluators.

3.3 Targeted Website: CouchSurfing.org

CouchSurfing.org is a reciprocal tourism website with more than six million users that offers users exchangeable hospitality and social websiteing services. It provides users a platform to "surf" on couches by staying as a guest at a host's home, host travelers etc. After registering, everyone can use the various features for free. The main features of CouchSurfing include finding a host, inviting guests, participating in activities, joining the community, commenting, member certification and guaranteeing [5], [18].

Table 4. The evaluation form of online trust-inducing features

Item	Features
Graphic Design	Use of dynamic, 3D, and big size picture.
	Symmetric use of moderate pastel color of low brightness and cool tone.
	Use of well-chosen and good-shot photos.
Structure Design	Implementation of easy to use navigation, e.g., simplicity, consistency.
	No inaccessible information, e.g., no broken links and missing pictures.
	Inclusion of navigation reinforcement, e.g., guides, tutorials, instructions.
	Application of web page design techniques, e.g., white space, margin, and visual density.
Social Cue Design	Inclusion of representative photo or video.
	Inclusion of synchronous communication tools, e.g., instant messaging, video telephony.

3.4 Procedure

We chose evaluators according to the standard above and used the heuristic evaluation to evaluate the data of trust situation that are built by "CouchSurfing." The evaluators were asked to freely operate the interfaces and then evaluated the website based on the provided evaluation forms. There were three focuses of the evaluation:

- Firstly, experts need to analyze whether the ways, used to build trust between users, offered by CouchSurfing website really helpful. Then, they should rate the website services based on principles of the trust-building process.
- Secondly, the experts need to assess whether the services provided by the website are in accordance with the online trust principles when the user communicates with others. A detailed rating from the experts is required during this assessment.
- At last, the experts need to assess whether the website delivers some features of trust-inducing, which help users build trust easily. Also, they should rate the whole framework of trust-inducing features on CouchSurfing.org.

Through the heuristic evaluation, we got the trust problems of CouchSurfing.org among the users of the website, and we checked the problem that users think they are appeared during the users making it one by one. Then, according to disadvantage that the users think, we will offer the suggestion for the website and make it better.

4 Result and Discussion

It is important to enhance user's willingness of hospitality exchange tourism through improving trust-building among the strange users. The aim of research is to create a new trust-building evaluation framework, to reduce the barriers of trust-building among the users, and to help more people who are willing to select the hospitality exchange tourism. Heuristic evaluation was chosen for the study methods, because it can quickly and easily find out the usability issues on the web [8], [11]. Based on the results, we have found out that there are still many issues in online trust-building. We have summarized those problems and recommendations, and showed those data into three parts.

4.1 The Evaluation of Trust-Building Process

In the first stage of evaluation, we discovered that CouchSurfing failed to deliver good service of trust-building during the whole process of encouraging trust between users. According to trust-building problem and rating (the full mark is 5, 1 stand for minimum score, 5 stand for maximum score.) that experts think, it is difficult to meet the needs of users about online trust-building except capability and transference process. And most of issuers was found in the process of calculation (Mean=2.5, SD=0.55) and prediction (Mean=2.33, SD=0.82). It may be a result of the lack of good behavioral norms and no way to confirm the authenticity of the users' information on CouchSurfing.org. Through testing, evaluators have suggested that it is vital to show more trustworthy information to users who want to communicate with others. Thus video features have been proposed to help users understand each other easily, as is shown in Table 5.

4.2 The Evaluation of Online Trust Principles

Based on our estimation of online trust principles, we summarized some similar problems or recommendations, and have found 13 problems and 17 pieces of advice. Experts discovered that the most serious problems of online trust-building are concentrated on several principles, such as information (Mean=2.67, SD=0.82), trustee's information (Mean=2.33, SD=0.82) and risks (Mean=2.33, SD=0.52). The possible reasons are that the website does not have a good mechanism to encourage users to upload personal information and there is insufficient dangerous warning to the users during their communication. So, they feel that the enhancement of the comment system, the feature of member certification, web alert of risk, etc. are required (Table 6).

In the final evaluation stage, we have found out certain inadequacies in terms of graphic design, structure design and social cue design (Table 7). For graphic design of CouchSurfing.org, the evaluators have considered that the evaluation principles of use of dynamic, 3D, and big size picture (Mean=2.67, SD=0.52) and the color and hue (Mean=2.67, SD=0.82) of website decreases the possibility of trust establishment among users. Some problems also exist in the structural design within the principles of implementation of easy to use navigation (Mean=2.33, SD=0.52) and use of navigation reinforcement (Mean=2.67, SD=0.82), such as poor usability of web and lack of adequate navigation. In addition, a lack of adequate communication media (Mean=2.67, SD=0.82) affects online trust-building in the social cue design as well. We have summarized the main recommendations, and proposed a number of ideas which includes improving the interactivity and dynamics of pictures, reducing usage complexity, and diversifying communication media.

Table 5. The evaluation form of trust-building process

Process	Problems	Recommendation	Mean (SD)
Calculative	• No clear reward and punishment to encourage users build trust.	• Deliver rewards to the hosts with a good reputation, like member integral. • Punishment for malicious users, such as closing the account.	2.5 (0.55)
Prediction	• Difficult to confirm the authenticity of the users' data.	• To add more certification, addresses certification, academic qualifications, etc. • Regularly publish the good/poor credibility users.	2.33 (0.82)
Capability	• Difficult to assess user's ability to perform promises because of lack info.	• Increase the protocol functions for discussing more details of hospitality exchange tourism. • Encourage to upload the hospitality exchange data.	3.00 (0)
Intentionality	• Difficult to detect whether other users have bad intentions.	• Help to users distinguishing the liar's motivation through regularly publishing their chats in some interfaces.	2.67 (0.52)
Transference	• Difficult to provide the trusted third party advice in the comment system.	• The pictures of hospitality exchange experience are encouraged to join in the comment system. • Add the function of friends' advices which could recommend the trustworthy users. • To recommend some users who have higher credibility and your friends when you search the hosts of targeted cities.	3.33 (0.82)

Table 6. The evaluation form of trust-building process

Principles	Problems	Recommendation	Mean (SD)
Information	• The arrangement of info is unreasonable on the website. • Users can't see if their friends are using this web.	• The beginners might need some info that they are familiar with, e.g. some people who are related to oneself according to the destination could be recommended.	2.67 (0.82)

Table 6. (*continued*)

First party information	• The personal information of trustee is too simple.	• The recommendation function should be improved, which may include the suggestion level for users, such as 1 is very weak and 5 is very strong. • The website asks users to fill out their addresses and then certificate in the personal info page. • The website should also provide the users privacy settings to protect their personal info.	2.33 (0.82)
Trust development phases	• Users don't know how to rebuild trust afterwards in case they lost trust via this website.	• Should have an official team to help users to rebuild trust.	3.83 (0.41)
Trust relationship	• Not found Related functions of trust relationship	• Adding a function of fans group could be taken into consideration, which will make the website more vividly.	3.33 (0.82)
Dynamic nature of trust	• Users don't know how to increase their own level of trust by other users.	• It's suggested to refine the levels of users' trust, such as separating host and guest rating scales • "Proposed" function could be added in user recommendation, which allows users recommend some users to others.	3.67 (0.82)
Global and local	• Just provides the function of giving general comment instead of detailed comment.	• Improve the function of mutual-comment, such as increasing the@ function, and showing more useful info on personal info page.	3.33 (0.41)
Identity	• Errors occurred when using Facebook account to login. • Applying for an account without requiring identity authentication is too simple.	• Reduce the possibility of occurrence of login errors. • Users need to be encouraged to do the authentication of identification.	3 (0.63)
Security and privacy	• There is a risk of leaking out privacy if the users want to use Facebook account to log in.	• Prevent data leakage in terms of private info, other ways (e.g. private message) should be used to communicate accommodation details. • Add the function of mobile-phone certification • Allows users to set personal info to be public or confidential.	3 (0.63)
Risk	• Few tips on interaction risk for the users. • The identity authentication function is poor, which leads to frauds. • There is no mechanism to protect personal data from being messily filled.	• Add the function of Blacklist for users, and regularly publish the Blacklist on the website. • More pages should show the info of interaction risk on the website. • Only those who have more than fifty friends can successfully login though CouchSurfing.org when they want to use Facebook account to log in.	2.33 (0.52)

Table 7. The problems and recommendations of online trust-inducing features

Dimensions	Principles	Problems	Recommendations	Mean (SD)
Graphic Design	Use of dynamic, 3D, and big size picture	• The picture is too small, words are too much and the title is unclear. • The picture lacks dynamic.	• Encourage users make more use of high quality pictures. • More interaction between users and pictures on website.	2.67 (0.52)
	Symmetric use of moderate pastel color of low brightness and cool tone	• The dominant hue of this homepage is bright orange, and there are strong color contrasts on CouchSurfing.org. • The website tends to warm tones.	• To adjust the dominant hue of website based on the principles of graphic design, such as light blue.	2.67 (0.82)
	Use of well-chosen and good-shot photos	• Most users just upload several photos, because the picture lacks interaction. • No mechanism to encourage users to upload high-quality photos. • Most users do not upload the photos of home.	• Encourage users to upload high-resolution photos of person and family. • Encourage guests to take and upload the photos with hosts, and link to the host's info page.	3 (0.63)
Structure Design	Implementation of easy to use navigation	• Overall, the user is not easy to find the info one needs because of the visual effects of interface design are complex. • Hard to find the function of group on the website. • Only text comments and the rate of success to live. • Need to spend much time finding some useful comments, and comments are easy to be operational.	• To re-arrange the whole info on the website. • It needs to be arranged in the order of the info of richness and credibility in the comments list. • Strengthen the evaluation and transparent evaluation in this regard. • Suggested to do better on district web consulting area, and guide the user to find out the info easily.	2.33 (0.52)
	No inaccessible information	• Several meaningless pictures in some pages.	• None.	3.83 (0.75)
	Inclusion of navigation reinforcement.	• Interface design is not easy to use for novice, register and finds other parts of the suffer process with navigation are not.	• Increase more navigation. • Make a demonstration to introduce how to find sofa process using website.	2.67 (0.82)
	Application of web page design techniques.	• The website of info presented visually is confusing, so users can't find the info they need.	• None.	3 (0.62)

Table 7. (*continued*)

Social Cue Design	Inclusion of representa-tive photo or video.	• The graphic on behalf of the other info is too little.	• Encourage users to upload some videos or photos to introduce themselves.	3.17 (0.75)
	Inclusion of synchron-ous communica tion tools.	• Just find the function of leaving messages.	• To provide many types of communication functions, such as video telephony.	2.67 (0.82)

We summarized the users' interfaces of CouchSurfing.org based on those trust establishment problems and recommendations among the users which the experts have founded through heuristic evaluation. We suggest to redesign the login page, personal page, profile page and searching page of CouchSurfing in order to increase possibility of online trust among the unfamiliar users:

- **The web login page:** In the login page, we will change the original bright orange into light blue due to the suggestions of graphic design. And we add the new sign in Twitter or Google account, which will attract more users who used to login with social network accounts as well as helping users of CouchSurfing find reliable information easily. Besides, it reduces the failure possibility if users use social website login.
- **The personal page:** On the CouchSurfing personal page, available interactive photo wall will take place of unavailable photo that can view information of other user in the photo wall, and surf their personal information page by a click. Moreover, the photo wall in personal page will refresh regularly so that different users' portraits are shown up. Our design could improve the interactivity and dynamics of photo wall.
- **The profile page:** In order to increase the online trust for other users, we will improve the album function that shows three pieces of small-size personal pictures on the right hand side of the location of big size photo, and encourages the users to upload family photos, and the photos which were taken with other hosts or guests in the profile page. Besides, the big-sized pictures of album in profile page will also refresh frequently so that different photos will be shown up, as is shown in Figure 1.
- **The searching page:** In order to enhance the user trust in others, two more features are included in the searching page. One is host recommendations and the other is the member certification in search of host list. In the recommendation feature, the searching system will automatically recommend several people with higher credit or the friends of the user of the travel places where user chooses. The icon of identity authentication will be displayed in the hosts' information of search list. If the users authenticate their identity, and then it can influence users click the host of search list and affect the user to build the network trust in the first sight, as is shown in Figure 2.

Fig. 1. The Profile Page of CouchSurfing Redesign

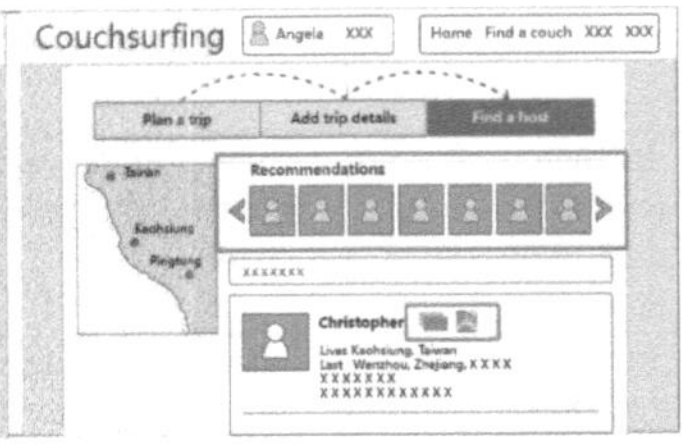

Fig. 2. The Searching Page of CouchSurfing Redesign

Tan think users who want to establish mutual sense of trust on the CouchSurfing should build a kind of open-minded atmosphere in it, which is related to reinforce more and more reliable information of our recommendations on the website [15]. In addition, Overgoor consider the trust behaviors of CouchSurfing that between users further rely on every reliable behavior of trustees [13]. Increasing video communication function and reinforcing prediction process, so as to it is easier to judge trust behaviors are whether reliable, which it is consistent with our suggestion. Besides the problem of trust-building among the users on the CouchSurfing, some limitations occurred in this study are: 1. We only considered trust-building among CouchSurfing users other than issues like brand positioning and cost. So part of our result may be not suitable for practical application; 2. We find it difficult to find some experts who have rich experience in usability testing to take part in our experiment due to practical limitations. Six evaluators are found in industrial design students to do this. Although they have web design experience and some usability knowledge, it's their first time to participate in heuristic evaluation. And they came up with a few difficulties in the process of heuristic evaluation because of lack of experience. To sum up, we find that there are many trust-building problems in the process of trust-building and trust-inducing features of CouchSurfing. These problems would affect the trust-building for both hosts and suffers. Based on the process of trust-building and trust-inducing features, the construction of the trust-building evaluation is built to improve the trust building problem of the users on CouchSurfing.org. In this way, more and more uses would be willing to join hospitality exchange tourism.

5 Conclusion

The purpose of this study aims to create a framework which combines the framework of trust-building process, trust-inducing features and the principles of online trust. Based on this model, we summarized the shortcomings of trust-building on the hospitality exchange web (CouchSurfing) via the heuristic evaluation, and have found the section of web design is not perfect. We found that more or less some deficiencies are existed in 5 processes of trust-building. And most of problems are concentrated in the process of calculative, prediction and intentionality among whole trust-building process. It leads to the problem which is hard to verify users' personal information and comment authenticities without favorable reward and punishment mechanism. Furthermore, it also is hardier to assess trustees' real intention on account of lack detailed information. Thus we recommend CouchSurfing.org to improve the norm of reward and punishment and add more verification process to help build trust among users. On the assessment section of online trust principles, a number of problems were found in the principles of information, first party information and risk. Arrangements of page information are too disorder and have no detail comment. Too simple trustees' information and lack identity authentication are the primary difficulties that encountered in the process of establishing network trust. So we believe it could facilitate the trust-building process among users by encouraging them to upload more information and popping up sufficient risk warnings in some interfaces on the website. In the assessment of the framework of trust-inducing features, color and hue of website is excessively warm, pictures on website lack of interactivity and dynamic, interface visual is too complicated, short of appropriate navigation functions and diversified communication media have an impact on establishing sense of trust between users. So we suggest the website to have a more proper layout design and hue mixing in order to provide a better visual experience. And it needs to improve its pictorial interactivity and dynamics, as well as add the video function to increase users' mutual trust. At last but not least, we are surprised to find that there are many trust-building problems on the CouchSurfing (as a most population hospitality exchange web). Therefore, we can conclude that it's more similar than other hospitality exchange webs. So we believe that this framework could apply the evaluation of trust-building to others, and could help users build trust easily. It could affect more travelers to join on the hospitality exchange tourism, and experience humanistic culture of travel.

References

1. Aljazzaf, Z.M., Perry, M., Capretz, M.A.: Online trust: Definition and principles. In: 2010 Fifth International Multi-Conference on Computing in the Global Information Technology (ICCGI), pp. 163–168. IEEE, Valencia (2010)
2. Anderson, J.C., Narus, J.A.: A model of distributor firm and manufacturer firm working partnerships. The Journal of Marketing 42–58 (1990)
3. Bialski, P., Batorski, D.: Trust Networks: Analyzing the Structure and Function of Trust. In: International Network of Social Network Analysis SUNBELT Conference, Corfu (2007)
4. Coleman, J.: Characterization of Escherichia coli cells deficient in 1-acyl-sn-glycerol-3-phosphate acyltransferase activity. Journal of Biological Chemistry 265, 17215–17221 (1990)
5. CouchSurfing, http://www.CouchSurfing.org/about
6. Doney, P.M., Cannon, J.P.: An examination of the nature of trust in buyer-seller relationships. The Journal of Marketing 35–51 (1997)
7. Harris, L.C., Goode, M.M.: The four levels of loyalty and the pivotal role of trust: a study of online service dynamics. Journal of Retailing 80, 139–158 (2004)

8. Hvannberg, E.T., Law, E.L.C., Lérusdóttir, M.K.: Heuristic evaluation: Comparing ways of finding and reporting usability problems. Interacting with Computers 19, 225–240 (2007)
9. International, E.: World Travel Market Global Trends Report. Travel Report (2013)
10. Madhok, A.: Opportunism and trust in joint venture relationships: an exploratory study and a model. Scandinavian Journal of Management 11, 57–74 (1995)
11. Nielsen, J.: Usability engineering. Morgan Kaufmann, San Francisco (1994)
12. Nielsen, J., Molich, R.: Heuristic evaluation of user interfaces. In: Proceedings of the SIGCHI Conference on Human Factors in Computing Systems, pp. 249–256. ACM, Seattle (1990)
13. Overgoor, J., Wulczyn, E., Potts, C.: Trust Propagation with Mixed-Effects Models. In: ICWSM, Dublin (2012)
14. Rosen, D., Lafontaine, P.R., Hendrickson, B.: CouchSurfing: Belonging and trust in a globally cooperative online social network. New Media & Society 13, 981–998 (2011)
15. Tan, J.-E.: The leap of faith from online to offline: An exploratory study of couchsurfing.org. In: Acquisti, A., Smith, S.W., Sadeghi, A.-R. (eds.) TRUST 2010. LNCS, vol. 6101, pp. 367–380. Springer, Heidelberg (2010)
16. Verbiest, N., Cornelis, C., Victor, P., Herrera, V.E.: Trust and distrust aggregation enhanced with path length incorporation. Fuzzy Sets and Systems 202, 61–74 (2012)
17. Wang, Y.D., Emurian, H.H.: An overview of online trust: Concepts, elements, and implications. Computers in Human Behavior 21, 105–25 (2005) Wikipedia, http://en.wikipedia.org/wiki/CouchSurfing

From Adaptive Design to Adaptive City-Design in Motion for Taipei City

Rungtai Lin[1], Ching-Chiuan Yen[2], and Robert Chen[3]

[1] Graduate School of Creative Industry Design, National Taiwan University of Arts, New Taipei City, Taiwan
rtlin@mail.ntua.edu.tw
[2] Division of Industrial Design, National University of Singapore, Singapore
chingchiuan@gmail.com
[3] School of Design, Faculty of Art, Design and Humnities, De Montfort University, UK
rchen1@dmu.ac.uk

Abstract. Taipei has officially become the World Design Capital 2016 with the slogan of "Adaptive City". Taiwan economic development is a fusion of Dechnology (Design-Technology) and Humart (Humanity-Art) which is also a process of design evolution showing an "Adaptive Design" in Taiwan design development. Therefore, this study proposes a design conceptual approach not only for Taipei to meet the requirements of WDC 2016, but also for Taiwan to establish a design strategy for the future. Hence, the purpose of this paper is to provide designers, companies, organizations as well as Taipei City with an approach for applying design thinking and with an idea for how to direct their efforts to meet the requirements of a new proposed design strategy.

Keywords: Taiwan design development, localization, globalization, glocalization, design strategy, cross-cultural.

1 Introduction

The World Design Capital (WDC) is a city promotion project proposed by the International Council of Societies of Industrial Design (ICSID, http://www.icsid.org/) that celebrates the merits of design, and leads a major step for the global design community. WDC is a biannual honor to a city across the globe to show its commitment to using design as a social, cultural and economic development tool. The WDC project seeks to maximize opportunities arising from multidisciplinary design collaboration through the WDC. ICSID seeks to promote several purposes of the WDC program such as promoting global understanding of design as an economic development tool. In 2005, ICSID officially named the city of Torino (Italy) as the first city to hold the WDC title and appointed it as the pilot city for the WDC project. In recognition of this crucial role, Torino with the design goal of "Flexibility" plays on an international level. Torino renewed its image from an industrial city to a WDC based in large part on "Design Thinking" which is a combination of innovation and creativity (Brown, 2009).

P.L.P. Rau (Ed.): CCD/HCII 2014, LNCS 8528, pp. 643–649, 2014.

During the closing ceremony of the 2007 ICSID Congress in San Francisco, ICSID announced the appointment of the City of Seoul (South Korea) as the WDC title holder for 2010. With the designation of WDC 2010, Seoul is making efforts to transform itself into becoming a city in which its citizens are at the heart of every consideration. The vision of Seoul is to create an attractive and desirable city: "Design for All". The appointment of WDC 2012 was conferred to the City of Helsinki (Finland) in November 2009 during the ICSID World Design Congress in Singapore. In Helsinki, design is the enabler of building an open city, the booster of its social, economic and cultural development. The slogan of Helsinki as WDC is "Embedding Design in Life". The concept of 'Embedded Design' has tied design to innovation and has enabled desirable solutions that have addressed the needs of its inhabitants. The city of Cape Town (South Africa) was appointed as WDC 2014 at the 2011 IDA Congress in Taipei. It is a growing and vibrant city where design has for decades been a significant factor in its desire to build an open city. The theme for WDC 2014 is "Live Design. Transform Life". The city plans to develop and promote a program of events to run throughout 2014 focusing on using design as a tool that will help to transform the city.

Taipei has officially become WDC 2016 on November 19 following a vote by the ICSID and Taipei will be the fifth city to receive this accolade. The World Design Capital in 2016 has given Taipei the opportunity to show Taipei City to be a city of sustainable development with respect to life quality and health, ecological sustainability, smart living and urban regeneration. The slogan of Taipei City for WDC 2016 is "Adaptive City – Design in Motion: By the People, For the People. "Adaptive City" is a process showing the evolution of Taipei city's development. Moreover, Taipei will face the challenges of redefining itself by understanding the past, dealing with the present and facing the future through design thinking (http://www.taipeidesign.org.tw/).

The WDC seeks to promote global understanding of design as an economic development tool. On the other hand, Taiwan economic development is a fusion of Dechnology (Design-Technology) and Humart (Humanity-Art) which could be represented as a process from OEM to ODM to OBM. The three stages reflect the tendency of Taiwan design development, from "use" to "user", from "function" to "feeling", and from "hi-tech" to "hi-touch" (Lin & Chen, 2012; Lin & Lin, 2010; Lin, 2009). This is also a process of design evolution showing an "Adaptive Design" in Taiwan design development. Therefore, based on the Taiwan experience, the purpose of this paper is to merge the concept of Dechnology and Humart into design thinking in order to investigate the Taiwan design development (Lin, 2012). This study also explores other implications through the Dechnology and Humart perspectives for design strategy. The study results provide an approach for looking back at how Taiwan design development crosses over Dechnology and Humart as well as illustrating the interwoven experience of local design and global market in Taiwan's economy, industry and design development. This study then proposes an approach for establishing design strategy for how to direct these efforts in designing Taipei City as a WDC to meet the requirements of design in motion.

2 From Adaptive Design to Adaptive City

Taiwan's companies have seen a recent shift from technological innovation to cultural product design based on discovering new opportunities in the global marketplace. Companies are now more focused on adapting new technologies and combining them in ways that create new experiences and value for customers. With the process of Taiwan design development, most companies gradually realized that the keys to product innovation are not only aspects of market and technology but also local design. Thus, Taiwan's economic development was identified as progressing from OEM to ODM to OBM and was represented as a smile curve (IDB, 2012; Lin & Chen, 2012; Lin & Lin, 2010; MOEA, 2012; Lin, 2009).

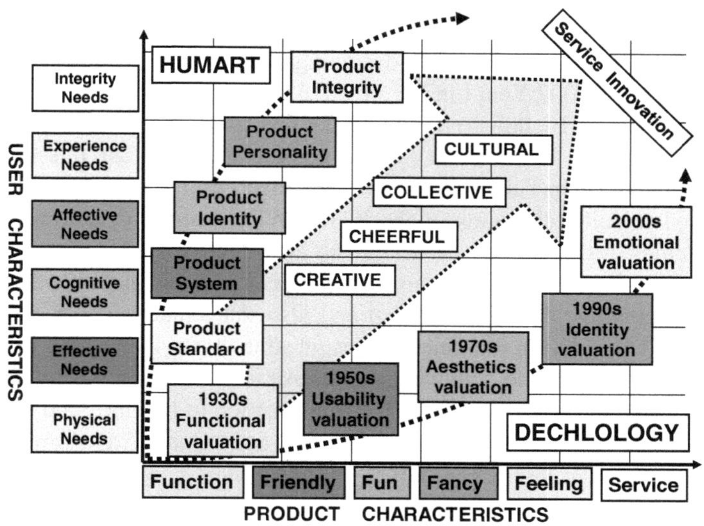

Fig. 1. Adaptive Design for Taiwan Design Development

Taiwan economic development is a fusion of Dechnology and Humart Art which is a process of design evolution showing an adaptive design in Taiwan design development (Lin, 2012). Hence, the Adaptive Design of Taiwan design development could support Taipei as a WDC with the core value of Adaptive City. In the OEM era, the "function" of the product will come first when designing a product. Then in the ODM era, what the "use" should be in the "function" will come next. Thus, the function focuses on the specification for the manufacturer, and the use concerns about usability for the users. Finally, the designer will seek the "Hi-Tech" to produce the product. In the OBM era, user-centered approach plays an important role in the product design. The question of who are the users always comes first while designing a product. Then, how to design "Feeling" into products becomes an important issue. Finally, designers will consider "Hi-Touch" beyond "Hi-Tech". The change of Taiwan design development, from "function" to "feeling", from "use" to "user", and from "hi-tech" to "hi-touch" are shown in Figure 1 (Lin & Chen, 2012; Lin & Lin, 2010; Lin, 2009).

3 Design in Motion for Taipei City

In today's competitive market, "Design Thinking" serves as a competitive advantage allowing companies to dominate particular market segments. With respect to corporate design strategy, design thinking is the key not only to extending market share, but also to increasing commercial gains. Tim Brown (2009) in the book entitled "Changed by Design" stated how design thinking transformed organizations and inspired innovation. For designers, design thinking develops through three stages from "inspiration" to "ideation" to "implementation" while functioning within a framework of three intersecting constraints of "feasibility", "viability", and "desirability", all of which require the three characteristics of "insight", "observation", and "empathy". For organizations, companies need a "user-centered" design strategy to explore the relationships between not only product and service, but also producer and consumer. In addition, innovation should focus on designing for the user's emotional experience (Desmet & Hekkert, 2007;Yen, Lin & Lin, 2013; Yen &Lin, 2012).

To host WDC in 2016, how to design Taipei City as an "adaptive city" becomes an important issue. Based on Taiwan's experience of adaptive design, this study is using "design thinking" to help Taipei City become an adaptive city. A glocal design strategy was proposed to fulfill the aims of the ICSID WDC program, such as recognizing innovative cities for their use of design as an effective tool for social, cultural, environmental and economic development in order to promote global understanding of design as an economic development tool and also share innovative design programs and strategies. Thus, design thinking is a design strategy for identifying the problems, developing the solutions and achieving the innovation. Based on design thinking, the framework combines "from use to user", "from function to feeling", and "from hi-tech to hi-touch" with "Environment", "Authenticity" and "Qualia" as shown in figure 2 (Yen, Lin & Lin, 2013; Yen & Lin, 2012).

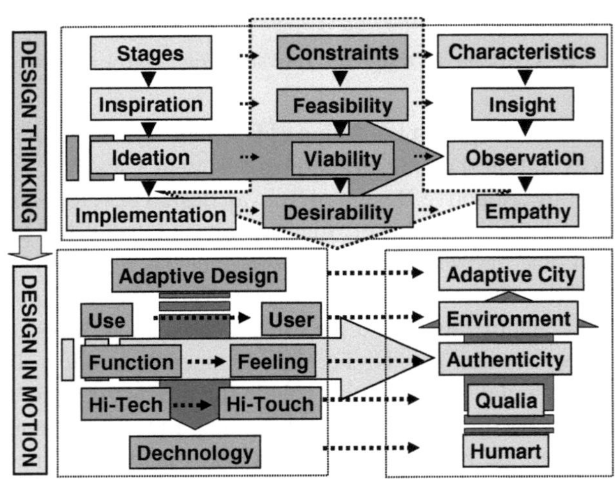

Fig. 2. The framework from "Adaptive Design" to "Adaptive City"

For the process from use to user to environment, environment is a core mission of Taipei. environment is an important issue of Taipei to become a WDC 2016. That means localization within a specific area, the life style of the residents is taken for granted as a habitual and cultural activity. Localization is a way of designing and marketing the product to the inhabitants of Taipei City. Localization integrates the product into both the life style and the local culture of the intended region. To be successful in localization, designers must pay particular attention to the technical specifications, sub-culture, and life style of the consumers, and to the nature of the product itself. There are numerous factors to consider for successful localization which must take the needs of the environment into account (Yen, Lin & Lin, 2013; Yen & Lin, 2012).

For the process from function to feeling to authenticity (Gilmore & Pine II, 2007), authenticity is the core value of the user's emotional experience which refers to the increasingly global relationships of residents, culture, and economic activity. Authenticity is a part of Globalization accompanying and allegedly contributing to economic growth. It means the process of crossing time and space limits by the social life, and the generation of interactive links by local cultural features through media propagation. In the globalization process, different societies, cultures, systems and individuals in the world fuse and leads to products which enrich regional, ethnic, etc., characteristics. Due to the fusion of cultures of similar nature, the consumer can become familiarized with a more diversified and wider local culture. (Chen & Jaw, 2009; Lee, 2011; Leong & Clark, 2003; Lin, 2011; Lin, 2009).

For the process from Hi-Tech to Hi-Touch to Qualia (Lin, 2011; Gilmore & Pine II, 2007), basically, qualia are things that we cannot easily describe to one another or that we might each perceive slightly differently based on a variety of reasons. Hi-touch refers to experiential properties of perceptions, feelings, and sensations. Qualia and the similarly "glocal" are properties of "Hi-tech" and "Hi-touch" such as, divisibility, comparability, connectivity, and satisfiability. The term "glocal" then refers to the individual, group, division, unit, organization, and community which are willing and able to "think globally and act locally." The portmanteau "glocalization" combines the influences of economic globalization and design localization. From the design point of view, glocalization is the trend of qualia in expressing a difference from similarity in local design under the concept of globalization and localization (Yen, Lin & lin, 2013; Yen & Lin, 2012).

4 Summary

The slogan of Taipei City for WDC 2016 is "Adaptive City – Design in Motion: By the People, For the People". "Adaptive City" is a process showing the evolution of Taipei city development. Moreover, Taipei will face the challenges of redefining itself by understanding the past, dealing with the present and facing the future through design thinking. The World Design Capital in 2016 has given Taipei the opportunity to show Taipei City to be a city of sustainable development with respect to life quality and health, ecological sustainability, smart living and urban regeneration. (http://www.taipeidesign.org.tw/).

Based on the previous studies and Taiwan experience, this paper studied the relationships between Dechnology and Humart which were merged into design thinking to explore Taiwan design development. Firstly, this paper explored Taiwan design development and identified the three stages of OEM, ODM and OBM for illustrating how to transform "local culture" into "global market" through a process of design evolution showing an "Adaptive Design" in Taiwan design development. Next, a conceptual frame work was used to study the tendency of Taiwan design development, from "use" to "user", from "function" to "feeling", and from "hi-tech" to "hi-touch". Finally, This paper proposed a design in motion approach not only for Taipei to meet the requirements of "Adaptive City" for WDC 2016, but also for Taiwan to adopt this design development for the future. Hence, this paper provides designers, companies, organizations and even Taipei City with an approach for applying design thinking in order to direct their efforts to meet the requirements of the design strategy. In order to achieve design in motion for Taipei City, we need to study how to link "Adaptive Design" to "Adaptive City"; then the results can be transformed into design strategy. In order to transfer "Adaptive Design" to "Adaptive City", this study establishes a conceptual framework to provide companies, organizations, and designers with a valuable reference for using design thinking to build a design strategy. The preceding discussion mentioned several researchable adaptive city questions. Others are summarized below in no particular order.

1. Designing "Taipei City" as a World Design Capital
2. Designing "Cloud Computing" into Taipei City
3. Designing "Fashion" into Uniform of Public Cleaner Team for Taipei City
4. Designing "Friendly" into Public Transportation for Taipei City
5. Designing "Female Prospect" into Public Space for Taipei City
6. Designing "Innovation" into Eslite Group for Taipei City
7. Designing "Qualia" into night market for Taipei City.
8. Designing "Culture and Humanity" into Taipei City
9. Designing "Friendly" into Public Park for Taipei City
10. Designing "Healthy" into Green Environment for Taipei City
11. Designing "flourishing" into Green Interior for Taipei City

These papers will be presented in a special session entitled " From Adaptive Design to Adaptive City" in HCI 2014 which is an attempt to provide an platform for looking back at how Taiwan design development crosses over Dechnology and Humarts as well as illustrating the interwoven experience of Adaptive Design and Adaptive City in Taiwan's economy, industry and design development. Furthermore, while cross-cultural factors become important issues for product design in the global economy, the intersection of service innovation design and culture becomes a key issue making both local design and the global market worthy of further in-depth study (Chen & Jaw, 2009; Ko, Lin & Lin, 2009; Hsu, Chang & Lin, 2013; Hsu, Lin & Lin, 2011).

References

1. Brown, T.: Change by design: How design thinking transforms organizations and inspirs innovation. Harper Collins Publisher, New York (2009)
2. Chen, C.L., Jaw, Y.L.: Building global dynamic capabilities through innovation: A case study of Taiwan's cultural organizations. Journal of Engineering and Technology Management 26(4), 247–263 (2009)
3. Desmet, P.M.A., Hekkert, P.: Framework of product experience. International Journal of Design 1(1), 57–66 (2007)
4. Gobe, M.: Emotional branding: The new paradigm for connecting brands to people. Allworth Press Pages, New York (2010)
5. Heskett, J.: Creating economic value by design. International Journal of Design 3(1), 71–84 (2008)
6. Hsu, C.H., Chang, S.H., Lin, R.: A design strategy for turning local culture into global market products. International Journal of Affective Engineering 12(2), 275–283 (2013)
7. Hsu, C.-H., Lin, C.-L., Lin, R.: A study of framework and process development for cultural product design. In: Rau, P.L.P. (ed.) IDGD 2011. LNCS, vol. 6775, pp. 55–64. Springer, Heidelberg (2011)
8. IDB. 2012 Annual report of Taiwan's cultural & creative industries. Taipei: Industrial Development Bureau (IDB) of Ministry of Economic Affairs (2012)
9. Ko, Y.-Y., Lin, P.-H., Lin, R.: A Study of Service Innovation Design in Cultural and Creative Industry. In: Aykin, N. (ed.) IDGD 2009. LNCS, vol. 5623, pp. 376–385. Springer, Heidelberg (2009)
10. Lee, K.: Looking Back, to Look Forward: Using Traditional Cultural Examples to Explain Contemporary Ideas in Technology Education. Journal of Technology Education 22(2), 42–52 (2011)
11. Leong, D., Clark, H.: Culture -based knowledge towards new design thinking and practice - A dialogue. Design Issues 19(3), 48–58 (2003)
12. Lin, R.: From Dechnology to Humart in Taiwan Design Development. Research Project Supported by Taiwan National Science Council (2012)
13. Lin, R.: Designing friendship into modern products. In: Toller, J.C. (ed.) Friendships: Types, Cultural, Psychological and Social, pp. 1–24. Nova Science Publishers, New York (2009)
14. Lin, R., Chen, C.T.: A Discourse on the Construction of a Service Innovation Model:Focus on the Cultural and Creative Industry Park. In: Ifinedo, P. (ed.) E-BUSINESS – Application and Global Acceptance, pp. 119–136. InTech, Croatia (2012)
15. Lin, R., Lin, C.L.: From digital archive to e-business: A case study of turning "art" to "e-business". In: Proceedings of 2010 International Conference on E-Business, pp. 1–8. Springer, Berlin (2010)
16. MOEA, Taiwan annual report: Cultural and creative industries. Ministry of Economic Affairs, Taiwan, Republic of China (2012)
17. Gilmore, J.H., Pine II, B.J.: Authenticity: what consumers really want. Harvard Business School Press, Boston (2007)
18. Yen, H.-Y., Lin, C., Lin, R.: A Study of Applying Qualia to Business Model of Creative Industries. In: Rau, P.L.P. (ed.) HCII 2013 and CCD 2013, Part I. LNCS, vol. 8023, pp. 148–156. Springer, Heidelberg (2013)
19. Yen, H.Y., Lin, R.: A Study of Value-added from Qualia to Business Model of Cultural and Creative Industries. Journal of National Taiwan University of Arts 91, 127–152 (2012) (in Chinese, semantic translation)

Designing "Innovation" into Eslite Group for Taipei City

Mei-Ting Lin[1], Po-Hsien Lin[2], and Jun-Liang Chen[2]

[1] Department of Commercial Design, Hsing Wu University, Taiwan
gua_gua@mail2000.com.tw
[2] Graduate School of Creative Industry Design, National Taiwan University of Art, Taiwan
t0131@ntua.edu.tw
freeimage5361@gmail.com

Abstract. After holding 2011 Design at the Edges in Taipei, the global design thinking and styles have entered into Taiwan; design have improved the standards of industries, creative thinking, design capabilities, talents training and living environment, changed multiple levels in Taiwan society, and the design atmosphere in the cities thus enhanced both the people and the knowledge. Therefore to manage the city by design and to improve the people's quality are important factors how Taipei City won the bid to hold 2016 World Design Capital on November 19th, 2013. This study attempted to understand how Eslite Group contributes and influences the city through document analysis of relevant published documents, and realized that the development of Eslite Group may be divided into three stages. First stage is "chain bookstore brand competition period"; second stage, "publication platform development period"; and third stage, "ambience development period". Through the three stages, Eslite Group developed the initial business philosophy: culture, art, creativity and life. First off, it provides consumers with good shopping services and the comfortable spaces for free reading; next, it provides online digital platform and publish design publications, virtually improved the consumers' aesthetics quality; in recent years, it incorporates new stores with local aesthetics, both the indoor and outdoor spaces provide consumers with great ambience and experiences. Over the past 24 years, Eslite Group 's services have invisibly improved the people's quality and taste; a "bookstore", although a commercial space, is also a carrier of culture and knowledge as well as an important symbol of the people's taste of life, which is able to influence the life styles and knowledge development. Eslite Group has successfully improved the people's taste and influenced the development and design value of the city.

Keywords: Innovation, Taipei City, Eslite Group.

1 Introduction

A desirable city is where economy, society, culture and environment develop coordinately, which provides good living environment, satisfies material and spiritual needs in life, and where suitable for human to work, live and reside. Speaking of

P.L.P. Rau (Ed.): CCD/HCII 2014, LNCS 8528, pp. 650–659, 2014.

"globalization" and "glocalization", Taipei is the center of Taiwan's knowledge circle, the publishing center of "Traditional Chinese", and the city of many colleges and universities which produced great talents and works. If we say the "local specialties" or "local attractions" are Taipei 101, Shilin Nightmarket, National Palace Museum, Chiang Kai-shek Memorial Hall or the Presidential Office completed in the Japanese era, what continuously improve the city's quality and culture is nothing else but Eslite Bookstore [11]. Eslite Bookstore has created many First in Taiwan over the past 24 years: the first 24-hour bookstore, the first Asia's Best bookstore, the first bookstore that contacts with local readers with diverse store types, and the first company of the cultural and creative service category listed in the "Top 100 Taiwanese Brands" by the MOEA. In order to discuss whether the group has provided critical influences for Taipei City to earn the bid of 2016 World Design Capital, this study analyzed and compiled the past documents related to Eslite Group through document analysis methods, and discuss how it influenced the development of the city and how it improved the quality and culture of the city.

2 The Development of Design and Bookstore

The development of global economic trends follow the design, thus the terms of aesthetic economy and creative economy were created. As Taipei was officially approved for 2016 World Design in November 2013, "Adaptive City" is the central focus of Taipei City Government on the city development, striving to shape Taipei City with unique city design while performing the researches and application of "Design Evolution and City Upgrade" in the physical urban spaces and virtual information spaces in the digital era of intellectual environment. In the past decade, the City Government has continued to strengthen the basic infrastructure required for the development of the design industry, including the establishment of industrial parks, creative tribes, industrial counseling services, cultural and creative design exhibitions and forum activities and so on, with which Taipei has gradually developed into a city full of features and quality. For the people, the development of culture and the elevation of art are the factors to improve the taste of life, however, the most direct factors come from different directions; following the influences of education, the development of bookstores is also critical. Bookstores may improve the urban quality and culture while providing knowledge.

2.1 Design Development in Taiwan

"Culture" is a lifestyle, design is a taste of life, and "creativity" is a kind of recognition through sensations [1]. Today, the nation, cities, industries and the people are facing the impact of "economic globalization", thus, how to incorporate culture into crative design and form urman characteristics by "design localization" to confront the challenge of "market globalization" are the inital issues when we develop future cultural and creative industry and improve the city competitiveness by design [2].

In the past, the development of Taiwan design was influenced by many aspects including policies, education, technology, society and foreign design thinking. Before 1961, Taiwan has gone through the Japanese era and the entering of national government, the products focused more on the functionality and were mostly for daily uses, practicality was the highest basic principles, and the industries were of OEM stage. Between 1961 to 1981, the industries and economy of Taiwan started to take off, with the support of China Productivity Center, Ministry of Economic Affairs and the Ministry of Education, Professor Koike Shinji (pioneer of Japanese industry) and Oochi Hiroshi gave speeches in Taiwan, injected new concepts of industrial design into domestic industries and deeply influenced the presentation of design style back then. With all kinds of effort, Taiwan earned a place in the international economy as one of the "Four Asian Tigers"; with the rapid changes of the entire economic environment, the industries were in great need of designers, thus facilitated the establishment of design education. From 1981 to 1991, the government has realized the importance of design for the national competitiveness, therefore Industrial Development Bureau, Ministry of Economic, planned and pushed the three five-year projects in order to transform design industry: the first five-year project from 1989 to 1994 focused on the industrial transformation, which triggered the trend of commercial design; commercial design and visual design were then gradually separated from fine art and became independent professional fields; design and industrial development had entered the stage of ODM in this ten years. The second five-year project took place from 1995 to 1999, focused on fully improving the product design capabilities. Together with the rise of digital media and internet, the thinking of new media art was introduced to design, personalized and fashion digital design had become the mainstream. The third five-year project started from 1999 and ended in 2004, together with the popular thoughts of "design leads competitiveness", design differentiation and design endemism has promoted the cultural and creative industry. Also in 2002, the government promoted the "Challenge 2008—National Development Plan", which was to realize "Global vision, Taiwan realization" with "people-oriented sustainable development" and "global connection, local actions" as strategies. It is obvious that "People + Culture + Feelings + Sustainability + Creativity=Design" had become the most important nature of Taiwanese design, and the industries had also officially entered the OBM stage [4].

2.2 Development of Chain Bookstores in Taiwan

The development of large bookstores in Taiwan started with the establishment of "Senseio Bookstore" in 1960; it started the first transformation trend of Taiwan bookstores for the cultural industry, and was also the first chain bookstore that incorporated POS logistics system (Fig. 1). In 1980s, "Kinstone Cultural Square" appeared and brought the bookstore industry the first revolution from traditional to modern operations (Fig. 2); in 1990s, "Eslite Bookstore" led the second revolution of bookstore industry, while other bookstores focused on adding more branches, it made its name by the artistic book selection and spatial ambience (Fig. 3). Since the establishment in 1989, "Eslite Bookstore" has opened 40 branches in Taiwan and has become the symbol of Taiwan bookstores; 19 of the 40 bookstores are located in Taipei City, and the bookstores contact with local readers with different spatial design and operational content which fully represent the local customs and culture of each town. With the influence of economic development, the theories of experiential marketing and experiential economic times emphasize that the consumer market wants more experiential cultural production in addition to the traditional industrial production. As for the selection process at the consumers, besides the rational function-oriented choices, the irrational shopping demand has become another focus [10]. Currently, Eslite ranks number one for the brand memory among Taiwan chain bookstores, followed by Kingstone. One of the major reasons is that Eslite Group established the first 24-hour bookstore on Dunhua South Road, Taipei, in 1999; in addition to the year-round services, it also provides the existence value of the people and the spaces as you may meet college professors, urban yuppies, movie stars, famous writers and people from different fields. Eslite Group is very influential to this city, as it was elected by the "Time" magazine in 2004 as the "Asia's Best Bookstore", and listed in the "Top 100 Taiwanese Brands" of the cultural and creative service category by the MOEA.

Fig. 1. Senseio Bookstore Source: http://blog.udn.com/jason080/2423389

Fig. 2. Kingstone Flagship Store at Zhonghe Yuanhuan Source: http://www.flickr.com/photos/verybooks/5660352985/

Fig. 3. Eslite Bookstore Source: http://mbainlife.blogspot.tw/2011/05/blog-post_05.html

3 Research and Analysis Related to Eslite Group

Since 1989, Eslite has continued to adjust its brand positioning and business practices with the new ideas and the market changes. With the continued correction of marketing trends, activity design, spatial furnishings and brand positioning, Eslite has become a well-known successful brand and a major research subject. Previous studies about Eslite Group include brand positioning, business strategies, marketing strategies, activity design analysis and experience analysis on consumer point of view, from which we can understand how Eslite Bookstore continued to improve the quality and culture of the city within the past 25 years.

By searching "Eslite" as the title keyword on National Dissertations and Theses Website, we found 52 related researches about Eslite from 1997 to 2012; the research topics and results of each period are analyzed as follows.

3.1 Research and Analysis of Relevant Papers of Each Period

Here is the abstract analysis of the 52 papers, arranged by years:

2012—10 papers published. 7 of the 10 papers mentioned the ambience designed by Eslite, which improves the emotion and satisfaction of the consumers; 1 suggested that the innovative services and interface upgrade may generate positive critics of the consumers; 1 suggested that the consumers show more loyalty when the book publishing industry perform its social responsibilities; and 1 discussed how the brand culture and product awareness influence consumers' choices of bookstores.

2011—1 paper published. The thesis is named "Marketing models of Taiwanese galleries for contemporary art—with Big Future Gallery, InSian Gallery and Eslite Gallery as examples"; as it is a topic research about three different galleries, it was not able to provide sufficient information about Eslite Bookstore.

2010—5 papers published. 2 of the 5 papers mentioned that Eslite Group provides more services to the consumers by multiple platforms, which improved the value and services and also set the differences from other bookstores; 1 discussed how Eslite outsourced art and culture activities to bring people closer to the brand and indirectly enhanced the brand awareness; 1 discussed about enterprise successors with Eslite as an example because it incorporated femininity by female succession; and the last one is about consumers' preference value for Eslite, where the spatial design and ambience improved the consumer preference for the bookstore, and created the impression of "enrich oneself", "utopia", "aesthetic appreciation", "life application", "sense of belonging", "careful management", "relaxation" and "comfort".

2009—4 papers published. 2 of the papers researched the positive influences of store at-mosphere, emotional experience and store image; 1 analyzed how Facebook promotes the store image and activities to the consumers; 1 discussed how Eslite Bookstore influenced the urban fable, which is highly connective with this study, however, this paper merely analyzed the coexistence of contemporary Eslite and the city and focus less on the transformation and services of Eslite in different periods and how it influenced the urban development.

2008—6 papers published. 1 analyzed Esliste's plane advertisements and suggested that the advertising semantics improve the emotional brand connection and significance construction; 1 analyzed how the art and cultural activities help to influence the consumer experience and produce economic benefits; 1 studied the new bookstore services—how Eslite targets the customers on top of the pyramid and intellectual elite, combines literature and art, promotes the in-store spaces and outdoor gardens, and presents special brand uniqueness helps to improve the brand awareness; 1 analyzed Eslite's market positioning—in addition to the cultural innovation, Eslite Group also adopted the "dynamic" market positioning strategy to keep upgrading the brand effectively; 1 discussed how successful Eslite incorporates branches into local features within different era and urban lifestyle, with Taichung Eslite Bookstore as the analysis sample; and 1 discussed how Eslite differentiate its compound spaces and other bookstores and successfully attracts consumers.

2007—7 papers published. 3 of the 7 papers researched the experiential marketing —the spaces designed by Eslite provides consumers opportunities to freely experience the products, which attracts consumers to stay in the stores for a longer period of time, thus successfully promotes the consuming willingness, improves the brand recognition and shortens the distance with consumers; 1 discussed the core competence of businesses—with its core competences of learning by doing, information integration and innovation, Eslite Group succeeded to elevate the competitiveness of the bookstore; 1 discussed how the mall value and strategies bring brand awareness and how Eslite Group identified and established its market positioning through opportunities; 1 compared the online information and services of Eslite Bookstore and Cave Bookstore; and 1 discussed contemporary plane media, and researched the cultural significances generated from book reviews.

2006—2 papers published. 1 analyzed the Eslite's 《Eslite Reading》 and 《 Eslite Reader》 magazines, by which Eslite successfully shaped its brand culture, taste, and lifestyle; 1 analyzed how the store ambience, consumer emotion and experiential value influence behavioral intention, and suggested that the consumers are only looking for tangible goods or intangible services but also a unique and intoxicating experiential feeling.

2005—5 papers published. 1 discussed Eslite's 《 Eslite Reader》 magazine and how Eslite Group improve the bookstore brand and visual image by the plane plane propaganda publications; 1 was about the key success factors of the chain bookstore (Eslite Group) including customer service, logistics systems, branch intensity, complete range of books and products, and the construction of information system; 1 discussed how the train bookstore IMC application influences the customer loyalty—Eslite enhances its customer loyalty through integrated marketing; 1 discussed and analyzed the factors of retention willingness and turnover intention through employees of Eslite Bookstore—this is not discussed in this study because it is not a suitable sample; the last one was an analysis about eBooks Online Bookstore but was mistakenly input as Eslite, thus it is also not discussed in the analysis sample of this study.

2004—2 papers published. 1 discussed the influences of Eslite's 《 Eslite Reader》 magazine via book reviews; another one discussed the organizational culture of Eslite Group that shaped the image and future of the bookstore, and analyzed the ideas of the founder, the leadership of the bookstore manager, locations, customer resources, consuming habits and the spatial design.

2003—2 papers published. The two papers were mainly discussing "experiential marketing" through cross-sample analysis of Kingstone, Eslite and PageOne, and the analysis results emphasized the professional niche of the bookstores and the differences of the brands in marketing capabilities.

2002—3 papers published。1 discussed the crowd and spatial interpretation of Eslite bookstores in the metropolitan areas in Taiwan—the spatial design, minority and elite style, together with its marketing methods, Eslite Group has not only attracted consumers but also urged scholars into researching this brand—it also suggested that Eslite Group's title of "Cultural Landmark" is leading the society towards refinement; 1 discussed the phenomenon of industrial chain stores and their strategies, respectively studied Eslite Group and Kingstone as research samples; and 1 discussed the chain bookstore positioning and satisfaction, also with Eslite Group and Kingstone as research samples.

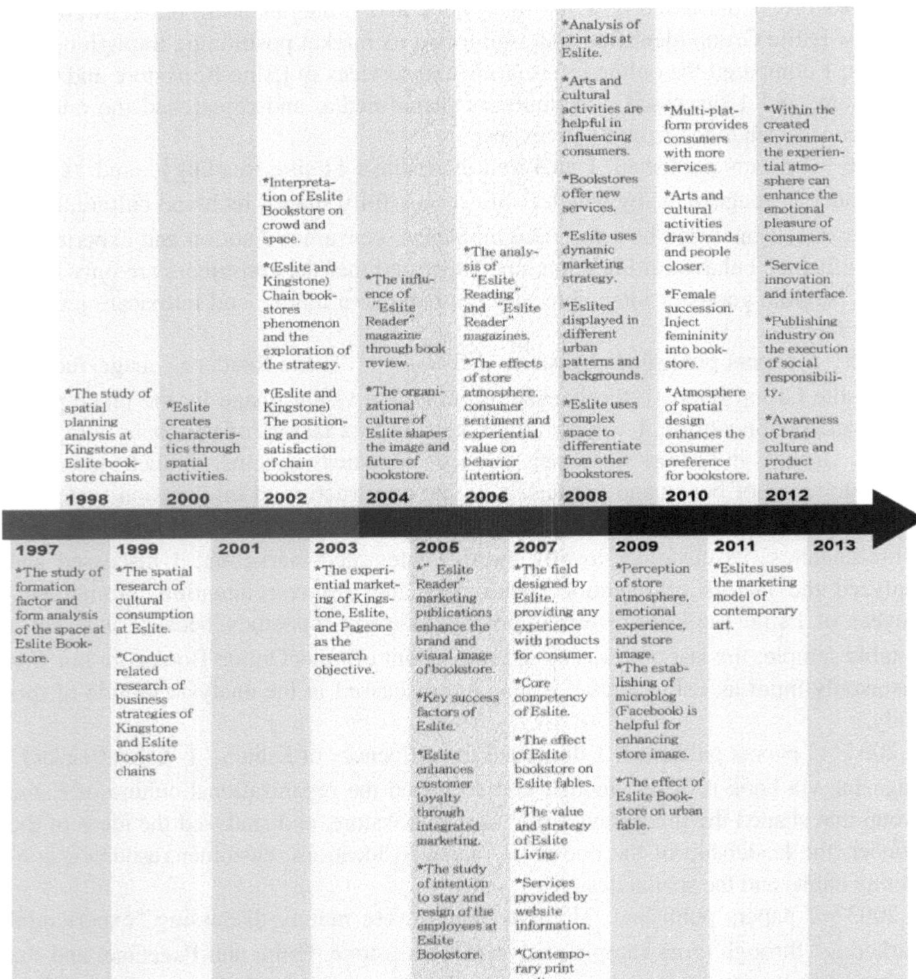

Fig. 4. Published issues with "Eslite" as the topic in each year (organized for the study)

2000 – 1 paper published. The paper named "Read Eslite: the Spatial Cultural Style of the Eslite Bookstore in Globalization" analyzed the brand through different atmospheric features of the spatial activities.

1999 – 2 papers published. 1 is a spatial research on the cultural consumption and 1 is related to the business strategies of Kingstone and Eslite. 1998 – 1 paper published. The paper investigated the spatial planning of chain bookstores by analyzing Kingstone and Eslite . 1997 – 1 paper published. The paper analyzed and researched the formation factors and forms of Eslite Bookstore spaces. The thesis development in each period is shown in Fig. 4.

3.2 Summary

"Build a corner suitable for reading" is the primitive mind set forth by Ruixian Chen, Eslite's designer, for creating Eslite bookstores in every corner around the country. Under such a premise, Chen holds on to two principles - "simplicity" and "blanking", and infuses the traditional Chinese gardening spirit - "landscape reflection", by consciously inducing the outside landscape into the limited indoor space, so as to magnify the visual depth and width, and shape up Eslite's distinguished humane, cultural sense of quality [12]. Chen uses interior design to build the bookstore into a reading and living museum, so that bookstore shopping is no longer merely an act of purchase; instead, it has become a cultural, elegant living attitude. The results of past researches reveal that the stylish images and spacical atmospheres shaped up by Eslite are the key elements soliciting consumers[5], [6]. Eslite's annual revenue of NT$9.8 billion tells the colossal number of visitors every year. This consumer trend will certainly raise the citizens' aesthetic quality in daily life. Through the remarkable designs, Eslite has successfully created a humane and aesthetic ambience that manifests the value of design.

After an inductive analysis of the above research papers published in various times, it is interesting to note that not until 8 years after Eslite was established in 1989 was there a researcher who initiated the study of Eslite in 1997. Obviously, Eslite had showed its branding muscle by then. There were 52 papers about Eslite published between 1997 and 2012, which can be divided into three stages. The first stage is from 1997 to 2003, defined as the "chain bookstore brand competition period", and two of the most competitive bookstores - Kingstone and Eslite - are taken for cross analysis, with focuses on the bookstore space design and business strategy. The second stage is from 2004 to 2008, defined as the "publication platform development period", and the "Reading" magazine and "Love Reading" magazine are taken as the study objects to analyze the digital service platform provided by Eslite. By way of publication of magazines, Eslite has created its brand image and boosted its visibility. The major research topics in this period are about analyses of the magazines, Eslite marketing strategy of space experiencing, as well as the influence of multiple platforms provision on consumer behaviors. The third stage is from 2009 to 2012, defined as the "ambient atmosphere development period", with focuses on the creation of bookstore atmosphere that influences the emotions in the bookstore, and the major research topics cover the store atmospheres, sensational experiencing, innovative services, etc.

From the above three stages of Eslite studies, we can take an insight into Eslite's business operations and strategies in various periods of time in the past 24 years. In the very beginning, Eslite broke away from the traditional way of running a bookstore by presenting consumers open bookshelves with well organized and categorized book display. It adapts its strategies to the market demands by offering various services. Mr. Qingyou Wu, the founder of Eslite, has taken the ideas of humanity, culture, innovation and living as the core business principles, and set forth distinguished marketing products in various periods of time. For the image, Eslite publishes "Reading" and "Love Reading" magazines that combines literature and aesthetics to meet the consumers and provide information about literature related events; for the service, it provides random queries of books, shopping mechanism, and digital online shopping platform, not only offering books but also music products, living goods as well as cultural innovation products; for the space, it presents a clean and neat display, a space design infused into the local environment, a cozy and comfortable reading ambience, and even an extension to the outdoor space linkage, as well as the underground shopping street of the its own brand. "Eslite" has become a symbol of cultural innovation branding, and distinguished itself as the far largest bookstore in Taiwan. In 2012, there are 10 research papers about Eslite, the largest quantity ever. As a result, for academic researches, "Eslite" is always easily taken as a study object. The influence Eslite has made on the public in the past 24 years can hardly be ignored.

4 Conclusions

Various studies have revealed that Eslite not only provides book queries and purchases, but also constantly stretches into the consumer fields of food, clothing, living, transport, education and entertainment, quietly implanting its services and images into the consumers' minds. Eslite bookstore is a commercial space and a carrier of culture and knowledge as well. It is significantly different from traditional bookstores in the space design, events, displays and services. Eslite's philosophy is to promote reading, stimulate innovation, root culture, and raise spirit. It constantly takes in local features and exerts international visions for cultural development, and builds its exquisite and diversified quality into an influential brand that symbolizes culture and innovation. It builds Eslite bookstores, Eslite galleries, Eslite Internet business, Eslite logistics, and Eslite living that includes catering and traveling and related supplies, clothing, and living goods. Eslite manifests diversified services that integrate culture and reading, innovative display and sales, music and movies, as well as greenery and culture enriched hotels.

In November 2013, the City of Taipei was qualified as a "Year 2016 Design City of the World". As an Expedient City, Taipei means a city of economic, social, cultural and environmental development in a harmonious coordination, offering a good living environment that satisfies the material and spiritual demands of everyday living, and is appropriate for human work, living and inhabitance. "Eslite" is an important branding of Taipei in the past 24 years, which has provided the city and the citizens with various innovations for growth, including the free book reading, music search, gift shopping, and even a venue for holiday hangouts and lovers dating, all of which have unwittingly infused humanity, art and innovation into the city and the life of its people. This research has used the literature analysis method with the doctoral dissertations and master's theses published in the past to explore Eslite's development history and observe how it has influenced the quality of the city and its citizens. The result has concluded that Eslite has different business strategies in the aforementioned three stages, with each one having appropriate services or publications specifically suitable for that period of time, leading the citizens to the growth of knowledge. Its design of bookstore environment is local culture oriented to offer a comfortable knowledge acquisition environment for the locals, and indirectly bringing more elegant life styles to the people, helping the city to develop, and appreciating the value of city design.

References

1. Lin, R.: Cultural and Innovative Product Design: A Discourse Set Out from Sensational Technology, Humane Design, and Cultural Innovation. Humanities and Social Sciences Newsletter 11(1), 32–42 (2009)
2. Lin, R., Wang, M.: The Status Quo and Visions of Taiwan Design Industry. Art Journal 4(1), 49–69 (2009)
3. Lin, M.-T. : Analysis of Taiwan Design Transformation, A Perspective From the Styles of Industrial Design Magazines; Art Journal, Issue 93 9(2), 153–184 (2013)
4. Jiang, W.: Reading Eslite: The Space and Cultural Patterns of Eslite Bookstore in the Globalization; Master's Thesis, Institute of Building and Planning, National Taiwan University (2000)
5. Tseng, K.: Customer Value in Eslite Bookstore; Master's Thesis, Crafts and Design Department, National Taiwan University of Arts (2010)
6. Chu, C.: The Study on Corporate Images of Chain Bookstores: A Case of the Visual Images of Publications and Spaces of Eslite Bookstore; Master's Thesis, Department of Visual Communication, Kunshan University (2005)
7. Chan, N.: A Study of Impact on Store Atmosphere to Customer Emotions, Customer Satisfaction, and Behavioral Intention: A Case Study of Eslite Xinyi Store; Master's Thesis, Department of International Business, Tamkung University (2012)
8. Ching, S.: The configuration of design and behavior in bookstore space: A case study of two Eslite bookstore; Master's Thesis, Institute of Interior Design, Chung Yuan Christian University (2012)
9. Liao, W.: Construct Model of Brand Equity on Eslite Bookstore; Master's Thesis, Department of Culture and Creative Industries, National Taipei University of Education (2012)
10. Torng, Y.: The Application on Experiential Marketing - The Case Study of Eslitebooks; Master's Thesis, Institute of Management Science, Tamkang University (2007)
11. Wang, H.: No Eslite, No Taipei City; NPF Commentary, National Policy Foundation; No.100-176 (2011)
12. World Design Capital, electronic book

Designing "Friendly" into Public Bicycle for Taipei City

Yuhsuan Lin[1] and Yen-Yu Kang[2]

[1] National Taiwan University of Arts, Taiwan
yulin-sophie@hotmail.com
[2] National Kaohsiung Normal University, Taiwan
yenyu@nknu.edu.tw

Abstract. The purpose of this study is to define problems of YouBike's design, and then, to provide designers with public bicycle design advice. Firstly, an observation was carried out to discover the general process among YouBike users. Secondly, case studies were conducted. Time and period were recorded following each correspondent's activities, including withdrawing YouBike, returning YouBike, confirming the transaction fee. Research findings include: (1) Attaching magnetic on the bike's locking plate to reduce the occurrence of error.(2) Changing the color of the lights contrasting colors to enhance the degrees in visual recognition.

Keywords: Universal Design, YouBike.

1 Introduction

To solve environmental pollution and energy consumption, reducing the number of private vehicles has become an important purposes in recent years. Therefore, Taipei City Government has promoted a policy which concerned of Taipei City public bicycle renting system to encourage people ride bicycles as short distance modes of transport. The policy contains the building process of bike paths and bike rental service. In order to achieving this goal and improving the urban traffic congestion, Taipei City Government cooperated with Giant to research the public bicycle rental system. This service referred to as the "YouBike" and started to operate in 2009. The most impressed part of this system is that we could rent bicycle at A place yet return it at B place. Owing to this advantage, people are willing to use "YouBike." Thus, the number of service sites has grown from 11 to 120. In future, more than 162 service sites will be established in 2014.The purpose of this study is to define problems of people using "YouBike" rental system. The researchers focus on the convenience of rental procedure and record the behaviors. To provide designers a better way and advice on how to adaptive the operate processes of "YouBike." This study chooses the "YouBike" services as a case study and experiment. Focusing on the usage situation and user experience of the inexperienced users. To clarify as much usage situation as possible, the experiment scope include top three service sites of number of users.

P.L.P. Rau (Ed.): CCD/HCII 2014, LNCS 8528, pp. 660–667, 2014.

The research will be guided most generally by Universal Design model. The core spirit of Universal Design comes from the caring on disadvantaged minority. It combines the concept of Friendly Design and free access for the disabled, considering every kind of demands in a variety of degrees. The seven principles of Universal Design are as follows: 1.Equitable Use 2.Flexibility in Use 3.Simple and Intuitive Use 4.Perceptible Information 5.Tolerance for Error 6.Low Physical Effort 7.Size and Space for Approach and Use. In this paper, we discuss about the different user experiences and demands on "YouBike" which is in accordance with Universal Design's core spirit. On the basis of this, we can have a foundation to construct experiment design and measurement.

Taipei City Government Department of Transportation to promote the bicycle as a short shuttle ride public transport carriers , for " Taipei build public bicycle renting system operation and management ," hopes to turn the building bike paths and bike rental service, encourage people to make short public bicycle transport, reducing the number of private vehicles held in order to improve the urban traffic congestion, environmental pollution and energy consumption purposes. Taipei City Government to cooperate with Taiwan Giant this service plan , referred to as the " YouBike smile bicycle ." A land lease which , B to the car service has become one of the main promotion services. "Universal design" for disadvantaged groups of people from the care , combined with a friendly design, barrier-free space, and a wide range of design concept, consider the differences between the different ethnic groups and demand of the fair use doctrine . For users who " YouBike Smile Bike " is concerned, the car rental service experience and behavior of these two is the most commonly used and the experience. Universal design is not just for people with disabilities raised . Seven principles of universal design , which contains as : equitable use , flexibility of use, simple and intuitive to use, easy perception of information, allow errors, reduce their burden on the appropriate use of size and space. 2009 began working to build a " YouBike Smile Bike " from the original 11 sites so far in 2013 has grown to 120 renters service points, 162 more are expected to establish a Service Station in 2014 . In recent years, the design principle of " user centric" increasing attention . To human - centered, how to use and experience the mode of " YouBike Smile Bike " more perfect , for research to explore the topic.

2 Literature Review

2.1 YouBike

Taipei public bike rental system is a public bicycle rental system in Taipei, Taiwan , the Taipei City Government Department of Transportation commissioned the BOT model huge Giant Machinery Co., Ltd. to build and operations and to " YouBike Smile Bike " as the brand name of the external service (the sign labeled U bike), the second seat for the whole station to enable the public bike rental system , using unmanned self-service . As early as March 11, 2009 demonstration began operations , initially set only 11 stations and 500 bikes in the surrounding Xinyi District . On August 31, 2012 began trial operation , the system on November 30, 2012 officially opened. After the official opening , YouBike has issued a total of 130,000 membership cards , the cumulative number of leases over 100 million times . As of October 2013 , YouBike a total of 120 districts in Taipei lease site (Taipei City Government Department of Transportation , 2013) . Taipei City Government 's Department of Transportation partners Giant companies, use the following procedure for YouBike (2013) [1] :

YouBike 24- hour unattended self-service , each site has an automatic service machines (kiosk), users can take advantage of the service machine to apply for membership , pay and rental bicycles . Leasing model is divided into two kinds of members and non-members , the membership application can be completed in YouBike website , automated service machine , or two service centers. After the bike racks are leased stations are installed EASYCARD sensing device , members can directly travel card holders registered post to each parking sensors pick up the car cards , non-members shall be paid through automatic service machines after the election the car (you can use a money payment cards, credit cards or chips Chunghwa Telecom mobile phone numbers) , and within 90 seconds to remove the bike bicycle column .

2.2 KIOSK

KIOSK originally referred to the absence of the newsstand, after Japan JR Railway Bureau will set up in each station convenience stores or convenience kiosk on the platform are called KIOSK. Today, digital signage, touch kiosks, navigation system, enabling consumers to obtain useful guidance, effective transmission of advertising or selling information stations are called KIOSK. YouBike automatic service machines without commissioner staffing for automated service systems. Therefore, YouBike automatic service machines called "KIOSK." Users can take advantage of KIOSK application to join, pay and rental bicycles[2].

3 Methods

3.1 Subjects

YouBike user to students the most. Respondents in this study using population-based YouBike students, divided into "first time users" and "proficient user" groups. Each group selected four, a total of eight experiments.

3.2 Location

The experiment was set up in place of the Taipei MRT, MRT Exit 5 of the mansion YouBike experimental locations. The experiment location near the main entrance of National Taiwan University.

3.3 The Process of YouBike

By using flow multiplied observation, we can understand the facilities to carry out this activity when passengers will encounter and understand the mode of operation, and to understand the operation of the passenger problem often encountered through these steps.

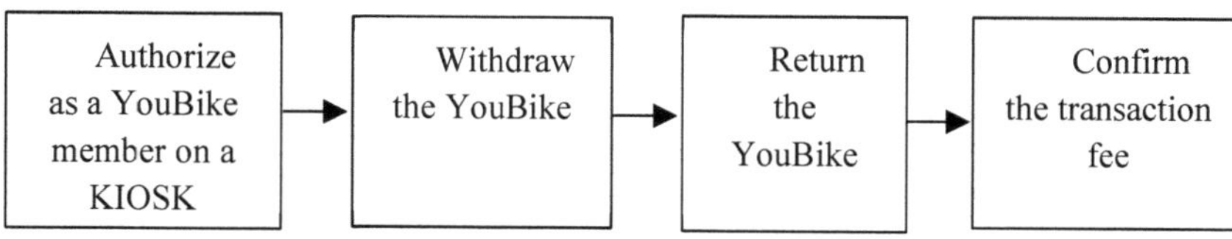

Fig. 1. Remark 1 Novice's YouBike using procedure

Fig. 2. Remark 2 Expert's YouBike using procedure

Through the flowchart, you can learn to use two different ethnic groups have different processes used when using YouBike. Differences in first-time users must first Kiosk after registration, in order to use. In addition to using the Kiosk machines, there is no difference between the two subsequent steps. For each of the steps of the flow diagram of the sorting table 1

Table 1. The using process of YouBike

Process	Step	Action
A. Withdraw YouBike	A1	select a bike
	A2	swipe Easy Card to rent a bike
	A3	confirm the indicator green light starts flashing
	A4	pull the bike from the dock
B. Return YouBike	B1	select an unoccupied dock
	B2	confirm dock with a blue indicator light on the dock panel
	B3	insert the bike's locking plate into the dock's locking spot
C. Confirm the transaction amount	C1	swipe Easy Card on the dock panel to pay
	C2	wait the panel shows remaining balance for the rental
	C3	confirm the blue indicator turns green, to complete the return process

3.4 Case Study

YouBike subjects using step schedule, where S1, S2, S3, S4 for the first time user, S5, S6, S7, S8 is proficient users.

Table 2. Time recorder of users

subject / step	S1	S2	S3	S4	S5	S6	S7	S8
B1	00'23	00'47	01'01	00'37	00'12	00'10	00'10	00'09
B2	00'03	00'03	00'02	00'03	00'02	00'01	00'01	00'01
B3	00'04	00'06	00'04	00'05	00'02	00'02	00'01	00'02
B4	00'06	00'06	00'07	00'08	00'02	00'01	00'02	00'02
C1	00'32	00'20	00'09	00'17	00'05	00'03	00'05	00'04
C2	00'04	00'03	00'03	00'05	00'01	00'01	00'01	00'00
C3	00'07	00'06	00'08	00'07	00'02	00'03	00'02	00'02
D1	00'45	01'23	00'38	00'59	00'23	00'13	00'09	00'09
D2	00'04	00'04	00'05	00'05	00'03	00'04	00'02	00'02
D3	00'04	00'04	00'03	00'04	00'01	00'01	00'01	00'00

Table 2 that by the time required to eight users at YouBike each step, the novice users and expert users record time compared to that between the action first-time users, and proficient users differences are significant, as shown in Table 3.

In each step of the process, in order to "pull back the bicycle", "bike pushed forward into the latch," "confirm Parking column panel display is green," three of the significant t values were less than .001, less than the rest. 05 is greater than .001

4 Results and Discussion

4.1 YouBike Operating Time Difference

The results showed that the initial use YouBike user in operating time , more than the average are proficient users. T values between the two positive presentation . Which " pull back bicycle ", " bike pushed forward into the latch ," " confirm Parking column

Table 3. The difference between expert and novice in using YouBike

process	step	Subject's type	Number of subject	M	SD	t values
A. Withdraw YouBike	A1. select a bike dock	Novice Expert	4 4	42 10.2	16.04 1.25	** 3.94
	A2. swipe Easy Card to rent a bike	Novice Expert	4 4	2.75 1.75	0.50 0.50	** 4.24
	A3. confirm the indicator green light starts flashing	Novice Expert	4 4	4.75 1.75	0.95 0.50	** 5.55
	A4. pull the bike from the	Novice Expert	4 4	6.75 1.75	0.95 0.50	*** 9.25
B. Return YouBike	B1. select an unoccupied dock	Novice Expert	4 4	19.5 4.25	9.53 0.95	** 3.18
	B2. confirm dock with a blue indicator light on the dock panel	Novice Expert	4 4	3.75 0.75	0.95 0.50	** 4.52
	B3. insert the bike's locking plate into the dock's locking spot	Novice Expert	4 4	7.00 2.25	0.81 0.50	*** 9.92
C. Confirm transaction amount	C1. swipe Easy Card on the dock panel to pay	Novice Expert	4 4	56.25 13.50	19.85 6.60	** 3.18
	C2. wait the panel shows remaining balance for the rental	Novice Expert	4 4	4.50 2.75	0.57 0.95	** 3.13
	C3. confirm the blue indicator turns green, to complete the return process	Novice Expert	4 4	3.75 0.75	0.50 0.50	*** 8.48

panel display is green ," three of t values have significant differences . Where " bikes pulled back " and " push the bike forward latch " two are fixed YouBike body of related tabs . Latch design is right to left sloping design of the hole , at the time of the body and push forward , to be pushed into the first body to improve . The first time a user during operation of these two movements , pushing the body is horizontal , and therefore likely to fail or produce situations difficult to operate generation. "Confirm Parking column panel display is green " and associated parking pillar panel . Will first display panel design in blue light after stopping , on behalf of the debit line success will make green. Initial user undetermined chargeback is successful, and if there is subsequent steps need to operate , and therefore significantly after the green light so that it stays in the column before stopping . This step can be learned at the proficient user of the record , when after receiving the green light flashes , then left before stopping column . In terms of s8 of the record , " confirmed Parking column panel display is green " operation this action has not been time consuming . According to the size of t values, p values ranged from 0.5 to 0.05 between steps are arranged as follows : pick up the car waiting for the green light flashes and emits short beeps > confirmation parking light blue column > EASYCARD column panel sensors placed in parking area > Bicycle select select parking spaces = EASYCARD column placed in the column panel parking sensor area > wait panel displays debit balances with the times .

Significant differences in the operation of action, " confirmed Parking column panel display is green ", " pick up the car waiting for the green light flashes and emits short beeps ", " confirmation parking light blue column " with LED display related. " Pull back the bicycle ", " bike pushed forward into the latch ", " bicycle select ',' select column parking space " this action with four columns relating to the use of parking .

4.2 Design Friendly into YouBike

When expert and novice use YouBike from the comparison between the time required for each action. Through this, if we want to make YouBike become more friendly or convenient for everyone, there are some conclusion as follow:

1. Improve dock's design : According to the study, novices spend more time pulling or pushing bike into dock than experts. Due to novices don't familiar with the special angle of bike's locking plate. The design of dock should be improved. Attaching magnetic on the bike's locking plate to reduce the occurrence of error.
2. Change panel's flashing light's colors: The different flashing lights on the panel represent different meaning. We can set the interpretative signs, so that novice can understand through narrative text. Also in the flash of recognition, it is recommended to change the color of the lights contrasting colors to enhance both degrees in visual recognition.

5 Future Works Suggestion

In this study, the degree of YouBike a friendly discussion compile the findings and give recommendations based on the above analysis, the following description may provide direction for future researchers can develop:

(1) YouBike for first-time users are interested in, the reason mostly "fresh", "fashion", "leading", "elegant", "participation." This research is YouBike main user groups - the student group interviews as the main target, but other ethnic groups are also frequently used for YouBike gradually rising trend. Therefore, future studies can then discuss other different age and identity of the Discussion on YouBike friendliness make YouBike design more in line with the needs of all kinds of ethnic groups.

(2) This study provides the first user YouBike less likely to use design, follow-up studies can be compared against unfriendly designs, improved after the experimental tests. Through experimental purposes, in order to learn the most common bike-friendly design patterns.

References

1. Taipei City Government Department of Transportation (2012), http://www.dot.taipei.gov.tw/
2. David, W.: Analysis: Kiosk Uptime, Revenue. Airport Business, 9–11 (2006)

A Design of Smart Travel Based on City User Experience

Ping Liu and Young Hwan Pan

[1] Department of Media Creative Design, Communication University of China
No. 1 Ding fu zhuang East Street, Chaoyang District, Beijing, 100024, P.R. China
pingshui2001@hotmail.com
[2] Interaction Design Lab, Graduate School of Techno Design, Kookmin University
861-1, Jeongneung-dong, Seongbuk-gu, Seoul,136-702, Korea
peterpan@kookmin.ac.kr

Abstract. Tourism as a typical service industry, which is directly related to the level of quality of service the long-term development of tourism. Perfect service system and high-quality service quality can not only affect the number of tourists and tourism revenue, such as the dominant value, better able to improve the city's reputation and resident people's quality of life. This paper is designed for the study of smart travel of city, first the status of the Nanjing tourism conducted a comprehensive investigation to the theory of service design and user experience as the core, in order to improve tourism services in Nanjing system, through scientific and systematic survey methods(heuristic evaluation, expert interviews , shadow tracking, fixed-point observation, etc.) and advanced and effective analytical methods (affinity diagram , customer behavior maps, etc.), to explore Nanjing Tourism service system inadequate for the service provided by the foreigners . We found foreign tourist pain points and analyzed them and ultimately derived directional insights for improvement.

Keywords: City User Experience, Smart Travel, User Research, Service Design.

1 Introduction

Income growth and technological development is changing the behavior of the travel. Diverse forms of travel are available, and a lot of technological supports are possible before traveling, during, and after. Tourism is travel for recreational, leisure, or business goals, usually of a limited duration. The World Tourism Organizations defines tourists as people "traveling to and staying in places outside their usual environment for not more than one consecutive year for leisure, business and other purposes."[1] Smart travel doesn't only focus on the role of technology. It also focuses on the role of user sides. Travel providers have to service effectively, efficiently, and emotionally to the traveler. Travelers interact with travel providers and travel resources (Fig. 1).

Travel resources are nature, cultural sites, facilities, exhibition center, and industry sites. Travel providers are government agencies, enterprises, and organizations. Travel resources and travel providers' services don't only used by travelers, also used by resident people, so called citizen. So if we design travel resources and services, we

P.L.P. Rau (Ed.): CCD/HCII 2014, LNCS 8528, pp. 668–675, 2014.

have to consider travelers and resident people at the same time. In our research users include travelers and resident people. City includes travel resources and travel providers. Model of user city interaction (UCI) is shown Figure 2.

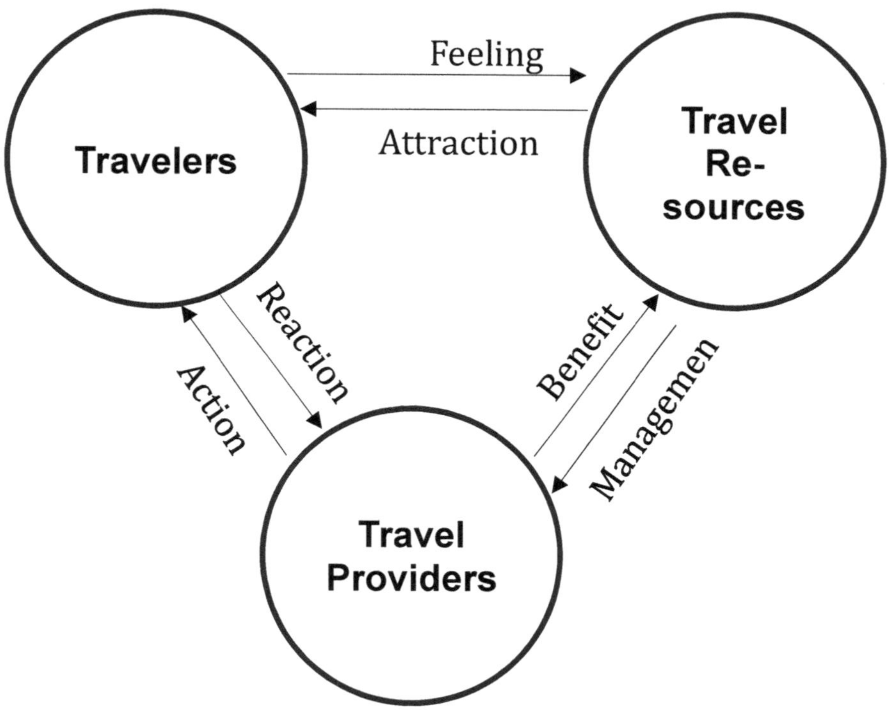

Fig. 1. Traveler's interaction model with travel resources and travel providers

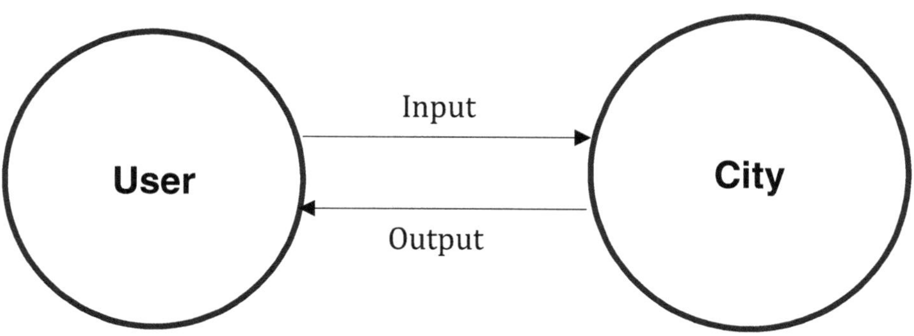

Fig. 2. User-city interaction model

2 Design Characteristics of Smart Travel

Smart travel means travelers travel more efficiently and effectively, and satisfactorily. Travel providers are government agencies, companies, and individual. They provide a variety of services at many levels. So it is not easy to evaluate quality of service in system view or city view. User side evaluation is more acceptable. The following are characteristics of smart travel.

- Total user experience design

  ISO 9241-210 defines user experience as "a person's perceptions and responses that result from the use or anticipated use of a product, system or service"[2]. Total means we have to consider the experience from beginning to end. We have not only to consider the experience of a specific time. The value of total experience is not just sum of experience of touch points. First experience and last experience more impact to the user. Best or worst experience highly impact to the user. Before traveling, travelers get the information about destination and reserve transportations, accommodations, facilities. During traveling, travelers experience about accommodation, food, transportation, sightseeing, shopping and entertainment. After traveling, travelers share the experience of the travels and buy local products with internet.

- Effective use of technology

  Intelligent cities refer to physical environments in which information and communication technologies and sensor systems disappear as they become embedded into physical objects and the surroundings in which we live, travel, and work [3]. A lot of technology is used in city infrastructure for helping traveling. There are two kinds of technology. One is based on back side system and the other is based on front side system. Back side system is infrastructure on the city. Front side system is touched by users. Traveler's accessibility and connectivity to the internet and network is most critical point in front side system.

- Sustainable Service Design

  Sustainable design is the philosophy of designing physical objects, the built environment, services to comply with the principles of social, economic, and ecological sustainability [4]. Business sustainability and environmental sustainability are necessary conditions for sustaining travel services. If there is no business sustainability, it is difficult to sustain travel services. Service system design and operation design have to be well designed. Environmental sustainability is important in a world where resources are scarce. Designers have to design systematically to keep natural resources and to reduce individual's ecological footprint.

3 Design Activities for Smart Travel

Understanding, design, and launching are basic activities in design processes of smart travel. Understanding stage, users, providers, and travel resources should be well defined. User includes citizen as well as traveler. Providers include government agencies, companies and non-profit organizations. Travel resources are historical

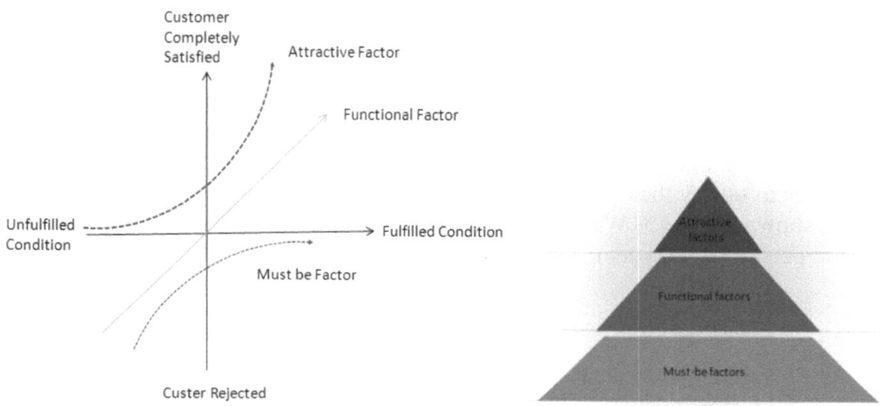

Fig. 3. Attractive, functional, and must-be elements in Kano model

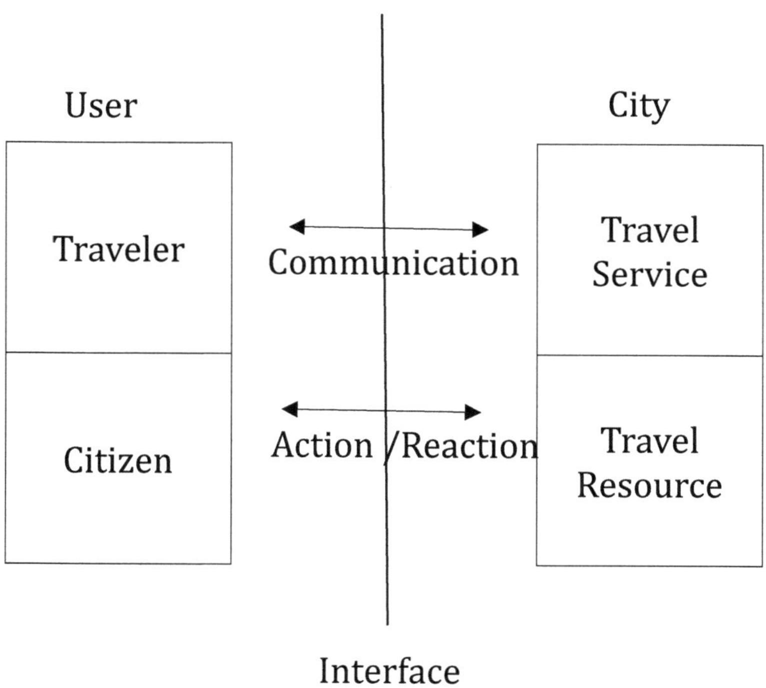

Fig. 4. Interaction model between user and city

something, relaxation something, and living resources. Designers have to understand these resources are attractive, functional, and must-be factors based on Kano model [5]. Figure 3 show the three categories in travel resources.

In design stage, service blueprint, service architecture, and service interaction have to be designed. Communication strategies also have to be planned (Figure 4)

In launch stage, we have to evaluate the service system and also plan the operation

4 Case Study: Nanjing Culture City

Nanjing is the capital of Jiangsu province in China and has a prominent place in Chinese history and culture, having been the capital of China on six dynasties. Cultural tourism has been defined as the movement of persons to cultural attractions away from their normal place of residence, with the intention to gather new information and experiences to satisfy their cultural needs [6]. In this study we define the users by four types as shown Figure 5. We focused on foreigners (A, C types) but also considered domestic people (B, D types).

	Foreigner	Domestic People
Residents	A type	B type
Non-Residents	C type	D type

Fig. 5. 4 types of users for Nanjing research

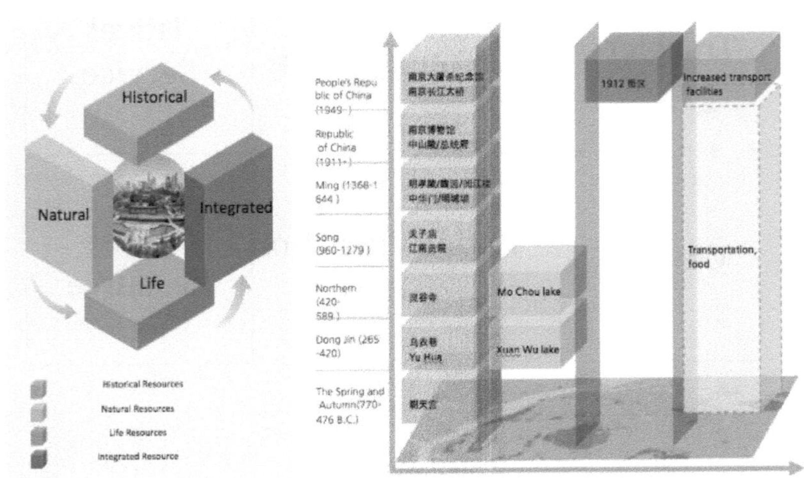

Fig. 6. A spatial and time framework in Nanjing

Nanjing has rich historical resources. In order to understanding the resources, designers use time and space framework. Nanjing was investigated the historical places with mapping the spatial information. (Figure 6)

Service providers include government agencies, companies, and non-profit organizations. Three entities and relations for smart travel are shown figure 7. Users have 6 categories of tasks about food, accommodation, sightseeing, shopping, and entertainment between users and travel resources.

Fig. 7. Relations between three travel entities

In order to improve travel services in Nanjing through qualitative and systematic research methods (heuristic evaluation, expert interview, shadow tracking, fixed-point observation, etc.) and advanced and effective analytical methods (affinity diagram , customer behavior maps, etc.) are researched (Figure 8)

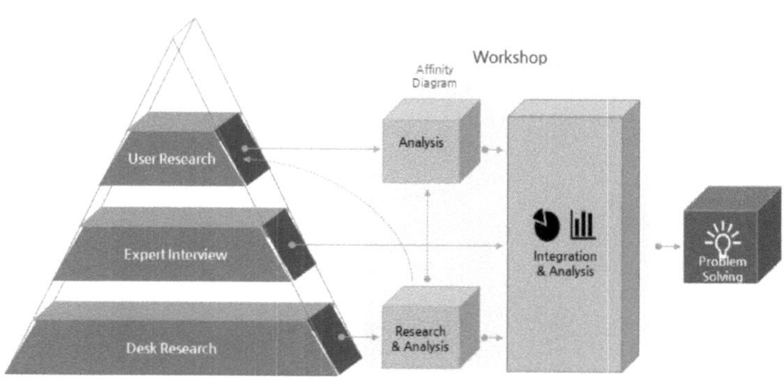

Fig. 8. A research map for Nanjing travel improvement

User study is considered their total lifecycle; before travel, during, and after. (Figure 9) Before traveling travelers focus get the information and reserve transportation and accommodation. During traveling travelers are doing 6 categories of tasks. Travelers showed different behavior between independent and associated travel.

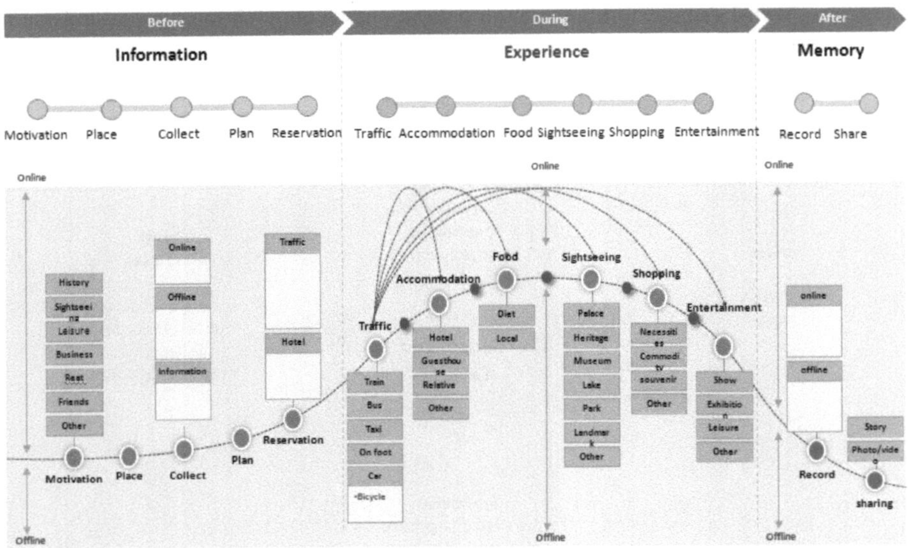

Fig. 9. User's activities in travel lifecycle

After analyzing the user data, expert opinions, and desk research data, we found strength and weakness in Nanjing travel services. We had creative, design and critique workshops to improve travel service system in Nanjing. We suggested solutions based on attractive factor and must-be factors.(Figure 10) We suggested many experience based solutions for attractive resources. We also designed detail scenarios and user experience.

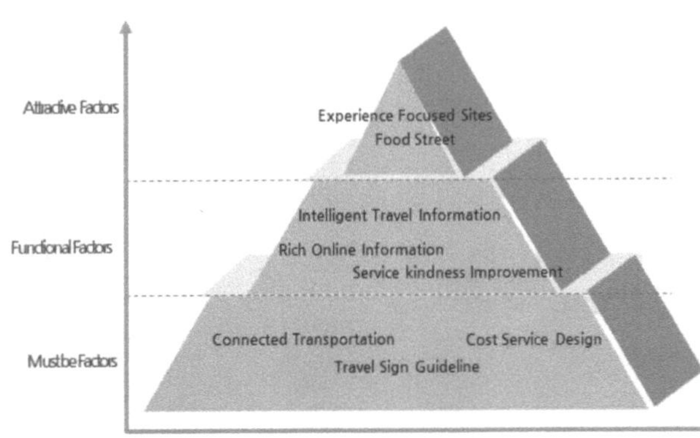

Fig. 10. Solution directions in Nanjing travel

5 Conclusion

Users, Providers, and Resources have to understand at the same time in design of smart travel. Smart travel based on considering total user experience design, using proper technology, targeting sustainable situation. We researched a rich culture city, Nanjing. Before traveling, travelers get the information about destination and reserve transportations, accommodations, facilities. During traveling, travelers experience about accommodation, food, transportation, sightseeing, shopping and entertainment. After traveling, travelers share the experience of the travels and buy local products with internet. We found a lot of insights to improvement travel service system in Nanjing.

References

1. WTO, UNWTO technical manual: Collection of Tourism Expenditure Statistics. World Tourism Organization, p. 10. (1995)
2. ISO FDIS 9241-210:2009. Ergonomics of human system interaction - Part 210: Human-centered design for interactive systems (formerly known as 13407). International Organization for Standardization (1996)
3. Steventon, A., Wright, S. (eds.): Intelligent spaces: The application of pervasive ICT. Springer, London (2006)
4. McLennan, J.F.: The Philosophy of Sustainable Design (2004)
5. Noriaki, K., Seraku, N., Takahashi, F., Tsuji, S.: Attractive quality and must-be quality. Journal of the Japanese Society for Quality Control 14(2), 39–48 (1984)
6. Richards, G.: Cultural Tourism in Europe. CABI, Wallingford (1996)

Design for the Public Usage of Rural Surplus Space (PURSS): The Case Study of DEISGN Harvests*

Yongqi Lou[1,2] and Dongjin Song[1]

[1] College of Design and Innovation, Tongji University
[2] Institute of Environment for Sustainable Development, IESD, Tongji University
{Lou.yongqi,susan.sdj}@gmail.com

Abstract. One of the consequences of the regional urbanization in the Yangtze River Delta is that the mass transferring of surplus labor power from the rural area to the urban area, which resulted directly in a large amount of surplus space in the locality. A possible solution to this problem could be transforming the rural surplus space for public use (PURSS) through redesigning the system in a creative way. DESIGN Harvests, a pilot design-driven innovation and entrepreneurship project, is one of the first systemic attempts from China's design society. Based on the analysis of the needs and insights on PURSS, the paper explores the strategies, patterns and product service system design of PURSS, which provides a new scenario of reusing the spare and scattered resources in the countryside. The service based rather than construction based solution conforms to the principle of sustainability as a social process towards the restorative economy.

Keywords: Rural, Surplus Space, Public Usage, Product Service System Design, DESIGN Harvests.

1 Introduction

Since 1992, the regional urbanization in the Yangtze River Delta has exhibited an accelerated process. One of the consequences is that the mass transferring of surplus labor power from the rural area to the urban area resulted directly in a large amount of surplus space in the locality; meanwhile, although most of the villages have built their public spaces such as community centers, culture centers and elder activity centers, the actual use of these spaces are not very much. Rural public life in the Yangtze River Delta, active in history, has now become stagnant, which is one of the factors inhibiting the sustainable development of the rural area.

One possible solution to this problem could be transforming the surplus space for public use through redesigning the system, functions, spaces, services and business in a creative way. By this means, the surplus spaces could become a unique resource that

---

* DESIGN Harvests, a pilot project on Chongming Island launched by Tongji University and Studio TAO, aims to find bottom-up sustainable solutions that integrates urban and rural resources and opportunities based on design thinking.Here we use capitalised DESIGN to differentiate from the traditional artefact-based design.

P.L.P. Rau (Ed.): CCD/HCII 2014, LNCS 8528, pp. 676–687, 2014.

can be used to activate the urban-rural interaction and exchange, to encourage entrepreneurship based on rural resources, and to improve rural social and economic life. Connecting rural surplus space to potential social, economic and cultural needs from both urban and rural areas can not only activate the surplus space, but also promote diversity in rural social and economic life due to the incoming talents and capital. The reconstruction of diversity will bring new resources and motivate energy in the rural area, especially in fostering the formation of the local innovation community. Furthermore, it is a great opportunity for "Design" and "Innovation" to play crucial roles in the reconstruction process. Meantime, it also provides new solutions to Fei Xiaotong's (Fei, X. 1986) observation of the Social Erosion phenomenon.

The "user insights tool (UIT)" developed by Vijay Kumar and Patrick Whitney from IIT are adopted by this research (see Kumar, 2012). There are three issues regarding PURSS: Supply (the amount of rural surplus space), Demand (needs analysis for the rural surplus space) and the Solution (the possibility and feasibility of the transformation of the rural surplus space for public use). Based on the field research conducted in Xianqiao Village, we first collected the basic data and information in terms of the amount, forms and characteristics of the surplus spaces and stakeholders there, and then we analysed the needs and insights on the reuse of these spaces. During this process, great effort was made to dig out the true needs. At the same time, we developed strategies through data analysis, system mapping, etc. Combining needs and insights in a matrix helped us develop several reuse patterns. Filtered based on the criteria of values and effectiveness, these patterns eventually generated the final solution. Each solution can be developed through the Product Service System Design.

2 Background Research

2.1 Types of Surplus Spaces

In terms of surplus space, there are two types: the objective (physical) surplus and the subjective (mental) surplus. The former concerns spaces which have seldom been used by the owners in their daily life; the latter denotes spaces that the owner identifies as surplus and is willing to provide for other functions or uses under appropriate conditions. According to our research, there is a close relationship between the input-output ratio and the identification of whether the space is subjective surplus or not. As far as occupation is concerned, two forms of surplus space exist in the village: one totally surplus and the other partly surplus, which is the major form. In terms of function, however, these spaces are mainly spaces in families, in public and agricultural areas.

Role/ Needs	School children	University Students	Working adults	Retired Elderly
Use Needs	natural/rural knowledge, social experience	knowledge, social contact, social practice, entrepreneurship	food safety issues, physical and mental health, rural entrepreneurship, child rearing	health, sense of belonging, convalescence, vacation

From the perspective of space supply and function, several common characteristics can be identified. These are as follows:

Small in Size: most of the spaces belong to the rural families; the houses are typically of brick masonry structure and the rooms are always small with many partitions; the bay width is normally less than 4 meters;

Overlapped with Residential Functions: when the original owners provide their family space for public use, mixed use of the space and multi-functionality continue. It is difficult to avoid disturbance in daily life caused by tenants. Thus redesign of the internal traffic flow is one of the key issues;

Scattered Spaces: available spaces are always dispersed within the community. Therefore, to correspond to different PURSS situations and to connect the individual spaces into a network should become the primary strategy.

There are three forms of rural houses in terms of their relationships with external traffic flow: punctuate, linear, and clustered, which respectively means scattered houses, houses built along the road, and a group of houses clustered around a common space with a path connecting to the main road. According to our research, the layout of the houses always has a close relationship with the social structure.

2.2 Stakeholder Analysis

The main stakeholders of the PURSS include :

- Local space providers
- Local service providers
- The local community
- External communities
- Consumers from the city
- Investors from the city
- Government
- NGOs
- Operators of the PURSS related business

While the operators of the PURSS are the "bridge" and "actor" of the urban-rural exchange, the consumers from the city are the key issues. People from the city are not only the customers of rural resources, but also the producers of the interaction between the rural and urban area. Some needs, such as setting up businesses, is at the same time also a production resource.

The consumer-needs research aimed at urban residents consists of two parts: first, the categorization of the urban residents' needs; second, the existing resources and potential possibilities of the countryside, which can fulfill or cultivate the needs coming from the city. Based on the case studies and the consumer-needs research workshops conducted by TEKTAO and IDEO Shanghai office in 2009, we found the target groups could be divided into four categories according to age and social roles: schoolchildren, university/college students, working adults and retired elderly. Our study show that the needs from the city mainly focus on five areas: learning, leisure, elderly care, food, and entrepreneurship. The table below displays city people's needs based on these four categories:

Based on the needs research on different topics, we further identified the challenges and opportunities of the urban-rural interaction. This part of work helped us form a comprehensive understanding of urban-rural needs; on the other hand, it also provided a basis to define the target user groups. To conclude our investigation of urban/rural relationships and needs research, several findings are summarized:

- the needs covers all ages, but those of working adults are the most prominent;
- the needs of different target groups are notably different and thematically clustered;
- the interest in countryside and the rural ways of living increases with age;
- the middle class in the city, with higher education background and relatively more wealth, is the most important target group;
- the ways of participation mainly include consumption, experience, and entrepreneurship;
- the existing ways of PURSS solution cannot meet the demands of urban residents;
- the intensity of needs and the interest in the PURSS solution are two main aspects which direct our further action.

3 Insights: Challenges and Strategy

3.1 Challenges

From the consumer's perspective, the main challenges to the PURSS can be described as follows:

Accessibility: accessibility including distance, time, and means of transport is one of the key challenges of motivating city people to go to the countryside. Especially in case of short stays, the easier the destination is to access, the more people want to go there. As for longer stays, say more than 3 days, the impacts of accessibility weaken. To people who rely on public transport, the biggest concern is the "last kilometer"—the distance between the destination and the nearest station.

Information: it is clear that the needs are out there, but at present the relevant information and service are always difficult to get. This is another kind of accessibility. In most cases, consumers are accustomed to being pushed by the service providers rather than searching such kind of services proactively. This situation is somewhat similar with that of insurance buyers in China.

Trust: trust is a bottleneck in connecting the needs and possible PURSS solutions. People are not so inclined to believe advertisements as before. The trust issue arises if the needed information is missing. Increasing transparency with adequate information is an effective solution.

Cost: Our research indicates that people are sensitive to cost, no matter whether their incomes are high or not. But they are sensitive in different ways. The low-income group is more concerned with direct benefits. If the cost is visibly cheaper, this group of people are more willing to accept countryside living or services. In contrast, the high-income group is more concerned with the quality, especially the experience, of such living and services.

Viewed from the local perspective, the main challenges are:

Scale: the domestic spaces available are always very small, and they are scattered in different places. This greatly limits the possibilities of using the space for other purposes;

Know-How: the local community members generally lack necessary know-how on how to provide high quality service or to run a creative PURSS-related business;.

Capital: local capital and resources are generally too limited to scale up and create PURSS businesses in a systemic way;.

3.2 Strategies

To rise to these challenges, the DESIGN Harvests team set up several strategies, which can be described as follows:

Community-Supported: In view of various aspects, ranging from social impacts through operating costs to ecological footprint, the PURSS should adopt a community-supported strategy. That is to say, these aspects should be characterized by features of being in the community; belonging to the community, with the community (community-participant management), and by the community (to continuously achieve benefit). This strategy could optimize the resource allocation as well as help all related stakeholders get the benefits (Seyfang & Smith, 2007). The term "community" used here refers to both the local community and the community of the specific stakeholders such as the consumer, creative community, and so on.

Entrepreneurship-Driven: There are two types of PURSS-related business models: one is the extension of the traditional business model, and the other is entrepreneurship-based. It is evident that the traditional economy has seen the opportunities in rural business and generally extended into the rural market. To date many large enterprises like Bright Food Group, for instance, have already enlarged their rural business in Chongming Island. At the same time, small economic bodies, starting from individual entrepreneurship, are also emerging. The entrepreneurs are mainly young people, intellectuals and local leaders with passion and ideas. As reported by lots of China's mainstream media, a great number of young people have formed the NEET group who do not want to go to work; 40% of the jobless in Shanghai are the youth. Most people regard it as a huge social problem nationwide. However, if we can consider this situation from a different point of view, these young people are huge societal resources. They are not those who accept any job without thinking. If their passion and motivation can be inspired, and if the environment is suitable, they might become the main force for positive social change, for example, as rural entrepreneurs. Both premises require us to investigate human needs and combine creativity, business, and technology to provide new innovative solutions.

Ubiquitous Information: The digital way of living has opened up new opportunities to bridge urban-rural resources and needs. Based on the internet and the internet of things, the ubiquitous ways of sharing, communication, learning, and materials circulation are reshaping many aspects of our daily life as well as social-economic relationships, both online and offline. In the meanwhile, ICT provides us with many new possibilities of democratic and innovative collaboration. For example, dispersed knowledge, information, goods and data could be connected, shared and exchanged on a commonly-shared open digital platform. The traditional game rule, defined by the location, capital, and brand, is facing great challenges. A brand new small-and-interconnected social-economic system is on its way.

Collective Use of Space: There are at least two situations in space use. Some functions make few demands on space, normally the space of a single house being enough. Such kind of reuse could be implemented immediately. Agritainment is a typical example of this situation. Other functions with greater space requirements need to employ a decentralized layout, integrating services and functions into a whole. For instance, one large-scale rural hostel or an elderly care center with 50 beds might need to integrate several houses and even other types of spaces together. Such collective solutions could create a new meaning of "size"—"big" can be achieved through connecting "small" together.

Adaption to Changes: As the result of public use of rural surplus space, urban-rural population exchange will be stimulated. Such kind of exchange will bring higher quality services, more job opportunities, better education, and development opportunities into the countryside. Apart from its advantages with regard to the natural environment and life pace, the rural areas can attract more urban residents to come, and enable more entrepreneurs from both the locality and the outside. Then, the diversity of both the social-economic situation and the members of the rural community will get enhanced. A multi-class society in the rural community will be formed, which will in turn introduce new demands and resources for rural development. One of the possibilities is that, when more immigrants move into the village, they enrich the role, function, and image of a community center to satisfy their needs.

4 From Pattern to PSSD

4.1 Pattern

Based on the background research including data collection and analysis, the needs and insights were elicited. Combining Needs and Insights in a matrix helps us to develop four PURSS patterns, which can be described as follows:

(A) Independent Unit: This pattern mainly refers to the initiatives of turning the individual rural surplus spaces to some specific functions, such as leisure or summer house, elderly care house, and hostel for vacation and short-term stay. Agritainment is an example of this. This pattern relies little on the community. However, if the nearby community could offer the needed services, the relationship between such independent units and the surrounding communities are likely to become very active.

(B) Dependent Unit: This pattern is normally the commercially-functioning PURSS, with strong dependence on external resources. In other words, these spaces are mainly service- and commerce-based. Successful realization and operation of such spaces depends on the activities of the urban-rural interaction. Their functions include catering, leisure, workshops, performances, and other services. The operators of these businesses can come from local as well as from outside of the village.

(C) Small and Interconnected Combo: Once the rural surplus spaces are opened to the rest of the world, the new incoming labor force, materials, capitals, and social relationships bring in the new energy to rural development and transformation. As mentioned above, although the amount of the surplus rural space is quite huge, the spaces tend to be scattered all over the villages and, normally, each is relatively small. How to connect this fragmented resource to a larger system by networking social, economic, information and logistical aspects, and through interacting with the local community, are crucial to realizing the fundamental changes. Moreover, the nodes connected by the network could generate new orders and produce a systemic impact.

As a result, a series of 'small and interconnected' combos (a combination of spaces, activities and businesses) could be developed in the scenarios of such a rural-urban interaction. These combos could form entities with the common identity and functionalities despite their different locations in the village. The corresponding functions include community-supported agriculture, community-supported hospitality, community-supported leisure, and community-supported elderly care.

(D) Hot Spots with a Centralizing Function: These are the public places playing the role of hubs: collecting and providing information on services and public activities in the villages and beyond. Within the current scenario, one possible key strategy is to enable the current public spaces, including community centers, to function as "hot spots". It could be the community center, service center, education center, and so on. Apart from the connection of the spaces and functions, these spaces also play a crucial role in social governance. These "hot spots" may have different characteristics during the process of the urban-rural interaction. For instance, the functions and image of the community center were quite monotonous in the past because of the singular structure of the rural community. Nevertheless, with urban residents and entrepreneurs coming, community centers will raise new requests for their own functions and forms, the changes in which will further push the transition of these centers' roles in villages.

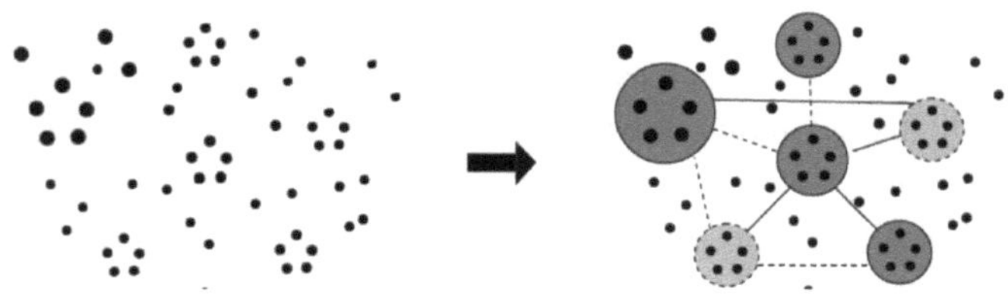

Fig. 1. A series of 'small and interconnected' combos could be developed with the identity and functionalities

4.2 Value and Criteria

The PURSS is the reuse and restructuring of fragmented resources that were previously neglected. According to the social economic changes of today, especially the features of being "small, local, open and connected"(see the SLOC Scenario - Manzini, 2010), such kind of initiatives can have a collective effect on social changes through a process of social innovation. It also offers a new definition of the region, scale, quality of life, and possible ways of social change. Some ethical criteria for various transitions are summarized below.

Restorative Sustainability (See: Thackara, 2011): The public use of the rural surplus space will provide urban-rural interaction with a platform of resource exchange. In the flow of the exchange of urban and rural resources, numerous changes are inevitably brought into the original orders in the locality. Among these changes, frictions and conflicts are unavoidable. Seen from another perspective, however, these changes and the energy behind them also signal the new social and economic opportunities of rural development, and they offer a possible new urban-rural scenario apart from urbanization (Lou, 2010). It has been generally acknowledged that the current world economy and the dominant ways of living cannot lead to a sustainable future. The possibility of change is a mixed blessing: while it is a great asset, it could also make things even worse. How to design new ways of urban-rural interaction to enable restorative sustainable changes will become one of the biggest challenges, for instance, how to minimize ecological footprints during the urban-rural exchange.

Benefit-all: One of the main objectives is to secure participation, the interests of and benefits to most stakeholders (including rural residents, urban citizens, the entrepreneurs, the local community, governments, and enterprises). This means that an interconnected economic and social eco-system should be established. The creative community and cooperative network could create and enable a new system of interest and the related business and services based on the energy of social changes.

Duplicability: Addressing the identified common problem in rural surplus spaces, the design solution of the PURSS must be duplicable. The duplicability here is twofold: 1) it can produce a series of design solutions that can apply to various situations, and can be duplicated at the level of technology and operation; 2) it can go beyond the traditional mode of design-implementation-operation process. The traditional boundaries between clients, designers, and operators can be blurred and redefined. The task can become a bottom-up social innovation process, rather than a professional-driven issue. Here, the role of designers is mainly as mediator and the strategic planner. In this case, business design and entrepreneurship are the first priority.

4.3 The Product and Service System Design of PURSS

Based on the former analysis, we created several personas for concept development of the PURSS. In each case, in-depth interviews were adopted to test if the preconception of the persona was accurate and representative. These Personas are the future actors and the eventual users of the PURSS artifacts and services scenarios that we developed.

Each PURSS concept can be further developed, through the "Product service system design (PSSD)," into a holistic solution. In the village, several projects, supporting one another, can be connected to form an interactive system. The DESIGN Harvests team has developed a couple of PSSDs on the PURSS, which cover a collection of activities such as hospitality, community-supported agriculture, community supported eco-tourism, and knowledge exchange. The design of the "Touch Points" is extremely important, as it is about the interface between the user and the project. The DESIGN Harvests team started to implement this prototype project in Xianqiao village in 2010.

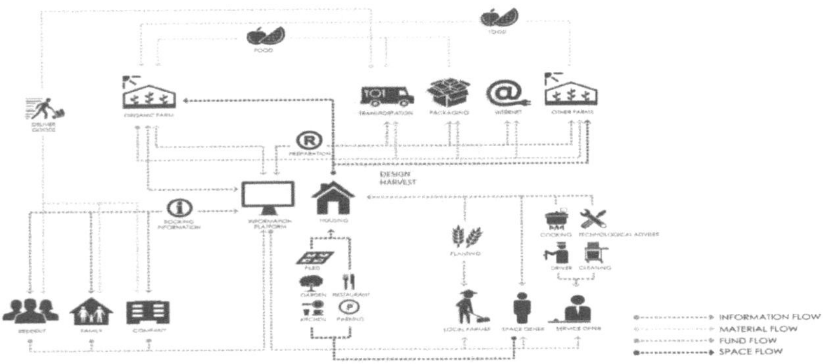

Fig. 2. A system map of Product Service System Design of the community supported eco-tourism

5 Designing the Touch Points in Xianqiao Innovation Hub

Innovation Hub is a multifunctional network, which integrates public service platform, entrepreneurship supporting center, knowledge and social communication center, and community center. This platform can support the entrepreneurs both from local and outside to use and integrate the urban-rural social, economic, and cultural resources; foster urban-rural cooperation and the complementary network by means of a series of closely-connected projects; and further adjust the society in an acupunctural but systemic way (Lou, 2010).

The first attempt of the DESIGN Harvests team is: a vacant warehouse in the village was renovated as the first innovation hub, which combines many necessary functions together. However, the process, due to several reasons, failed to continue. Therefore, based on the concept of SLOC (Small, Local, Open and Connected, see Manzini, 2010), the team decided to deconstruct the space, function, and service of the innovation hub into a networked solution, namely shifting from pattern (D) to (C). Put another way, the necessary functions are realized by virtue of connecting rural surplus space in different locations together. We selected and designed some experimental touch points in Xianqiao Village. They are depicted below.

5.1 DESIGN Harvests Greenhouse

Our research indicates that one of the key motivations for the urban residents' village visits is the attraction of rural experiences. Apart from the space for hospitality, eating, and outdoors activities, a multifunctional social space with an appropriate scale is vital. Such kind of space is very difficult to find in the villages since the space of the farmers' houses is generally not big enough.

The DESIGN Harvests team found that the greenhouse commonly used in villages could serve as a special kind of space resource. It is large, open and flexible, so the problem of lacking large indoor open space in rural areas is resolved. Since 2012, the DESIGN Harvests team has successfully transformed one greenhouse to an open space with the multifunction of planting, education, exhibition, catering, communication, and event venue. These, working together, allow the greenhouse to become a platform to support the activities of in-depth rural experiences. The team has already organized many activities there, including the team-building, happy weekend, design workshops, rural knowledge safari for kids, and so on.

Fig. 3. DESIGN Harvests Greenhouse and the activities

5.2 DESIGN Harvests "Tian Geng" Farmhouse

With the help of the local community, the DESIGN Harvests team renovated a vacant house with four rooms at the east end of Xianqiao Village, and named it "Tian Geng," which means "lane in the field." "Tian Geng" is a multifunctional space that provides the tourists and workers with accommodation, catering, public life, and communication. During the initial phase, the DESIGN Harvests team launched a two-week workshop in collaboration with Tongji University, Jiangnan University, Universitat Politecnica de Valencia, Escuela de Arte Superior de Diseno de Valencia, Politecnico di Milano, and Queensland University of Technology. The students were divided into several groups that worked respectively on systems of kitchen, bathroom, lighting, information, and landscape. Within the ten days, the students not only proposed contextualized concepts, but also partly implemented their concepts. In November 2012, the designers from TEKTAO finalized the design and implementation.

Simultaneously, several PSSDs were developed for "Tian Geng." Of course, these services can only be realized through the connection and interaction with other platforms such as DESIGN Harvests Greenhouse, DESIGN Harvests field, and other existing resources and activities in the village. In addition to business feasibility, one of the goals is to enable the urban residents to stay longer to minimize their daily footprint.

As the project unfolded, the DESIGN Harvests team also attracted several young designers to participate in the reformation of another vacant residential house, making it a holiday hostel. Moreover, a handcraft workshop and a knowledge exchange center have already been put on the agenda.

Fig. 4. DESIGN Harvests "Tian Geng" Farmhouse

5.3 DESIGN Harvests' Digital Platform

Based on the principle of Collaborative Services, we redesigned the DESIGN Harvests digital platform. In the first step, it was converted into an interactive website. In addition to the function of information broadcasting, it conveys the relevant philosophies, strategies and outcomes of the DESIGN Harvest Project and also functions as a business platform for its products and services. Also, we intended to integrate the resources of different stakeholders to form a social-economic ecosystem. This website serves not only as the social network for the stakeholders, but also as a platform to support entrepreneurship.

In terms of technology, it is the combination of the mainstream social media including Weibo and other B2C and B2B platforms such as Alipay, for example. It is our hope that this platform will be able to bear the peculiar characteristics of anti-competition and inclusiveness of the collaborative production (Cooper, 2005; Baek, 2010). In this network, these implicit bonds can facilitate the spreading of social innovation. In the long run, it not only serves the DESIGN Harvests project but will also be able to move itself closer towards becoming an open social innovation platform.

6 Conclusions

The public use of rural surplus space is the reuse of the spare and scattered resources. It goes in concert with the social and economic transformation from extensive modes to elaborate ones. The new socioeconomic model and sustainable ways of living require a new definition of quality of life. It will be the subversion of the prevailing resource-oriented, productive, consumptive, and top-down quality that is characterized by high speed, large quantity, and great efficiency. The sustainable development gives rise to the appreciation of an alternative quality of life, characterized by slow speed, high quality, integration, bottom-up, and service-orientation, and it provides the new understanding of the values of fragmented resources. In the context of sustainability, when the alternative quality becomes the solution to the crises caused by the currently-prevailing quality, a large-scale socioeconomic reform will inevitably happen. It is time that the design discipline and designers refocused and rethought the resources in our daily life, which were intentionally neglected in the past. It is designers' duty to use design and innovation to adjust and improve the social and economic circumstances and to foster active social change in sustainable, inclusive and creative ways. It provides a new meaning and fields for today's social design (Papanek, 1985; Margolin 2002). The PURSS project is exactly an example of this way of thinking.

Acknowledgement. The project has been supported by National Natural Science Foundation of China, No.50908162, and Mistra Urban Futures in Sweden, ISBN 978-91-980696-0-0.

References

1. Baek, J.S.: A socio-technical framework for collaborative services, PhD thesis, Politecnico di Milano (2010)
2. Cooper, M.: The Economics of Collaborative Production in the Spectrum Commons, pp. 379–400. IEEE (2005)
3. Kumar, V.: 101 Design Methods: A Structured Approach for Driving Innovation in Your Organization. John Wiley & Sons, New Jersey (2012)
4. Lou, Y.: Enabling Society: New Design Processes in China: The Case of Chongming. The Journal of Design Strategies 4(1), 23–28 (2010a)
5. Lou, Y.: DESIGN Harvests. An Acupunctural Design Approach Towards Sustainability, Design & Creativity 2010(4) (2010b)
6. Margolin, V., Margolin, S.: A "Social Model" of Design: Issues of Practice and Research. Design Issues 18, 24–30 (2002)
7. Manzini, E.: Design, Visions, Proposals and Tools.In: Changing the Change Conference: Turin (2008)
8. Manzini, E.: SLOC, The Emerging Scenario of Small, Local, Open and Connected. In: Harding, S. (ed.) Grow Small Think Beautiful, Edinburgh, Floris, pp. 216–231 (2010)
9. Papanek, V.: Design for the Real World; Human Ecology and Social Change, 2nd edn., Chicago, pp. 63–68 (1985)
10. Seyfang, G., Smith, A.: Grassroots Innovations for Sustainable Development: Towards a New Research and Policy Agenda. Environmental Politics 16(4), 584–603, p. 585 (2007)
11. Thackara, J.: Design for a new restorative economy, Cumulus Working papers Shanghai. Aalto University School of Art and Design Press, Helsinki (2011)

Designing Cloud Computing into Taipei City: A Pilot Study of the Service Design from Taipei Cloud

Jui-Ping Ma[1], Stanley Wei[2], and Rungtai Lin[3]

[1] Department of General Education,
National Taipei College of Business, Taipei City, Taiwan
rupm08@gmail.com
[2] Oneness International Group Limited, Shanghai, China
Stanely.wei@onenessint.com
[3]Graduate School of Creative Industry Design,
National Taiwan University of Arts, New Taipei City, Taiwan
rtlin@mail.ntua.edu.tw

Abstract. For offering holistic service quality, in 2013, the Taipei City Hall promote "Taipei Cloud" service for citizen to enhance web services based on convenient, free, and public Wi-Fi hotspots all over the city. This pilot experiment explores on user experience and perception of "Taipei Cloud" service from subjects' usage by participant-observation to know whether "Taipei Cloud" service can match subjects' demand in their daily life. Six subjects use "Taipei Cloud" service randomly to obtain their cloud computing data record by their smart mobile phone APP during their own trips. Then, time-geography theory is applied to be evaluated subjects' usage. The finding are shown that: (1). there is no direct correlation between time and spatial facts through subjects' usage on citizen cloud service; (2).Until now, in subjects' opinion, to share or contact others should be a function added in citizen cloud; (3).To compare subjects' usage of citizen cloud, "command" is more popular than other online actions.; (4).In holistic user experiences, subjects usually prefer higher interaction with cloud computing service.

Keywords: Taipei Cloud, Location-Based Service, Time-Geographic.

1 Introduction

Recently, due to full-fledged technology of IT, the mobile value-added application is increasing to be the hottest topic. The cloud computing is vital to success of value-added application. Moreover, the cloud computing technology can affect directly the preference, effects, and experience of users in the area of mobile value-added application. In 2013, Taipei City Hall begins to promote "Taipei Cloud" service, not only for citizen to offer convenient, multifaceted web platform, but also for conducting better public quality. Especially, "Taipei Cloud" service is constructed at the base of "TPE Free"; it is official, convenient, and free Wi-Fi service, spread in all over Taipei city just like many traffic stations, libraries, and official units have been set hotspots.

P.L.P. Rau (Ed.): CCD/HCII 2014, LNCS 8528, pp. 688–695, 2014.

This study chooses the "Taipei Cloud" service as a case study and experiment. The purpose of this paper aims at exploring on the different user experience by mobile devices through "Taipei Cloud". To focus on the usage situation and user experience of the commuters and travelers, move outdoor with specific distance traffic-demand. The researchers engage in participant-observation to focus and record the behaviors of six subjects on using "Taipei Cloud" service in their own trips. After experiment is finished, the researchers conduct draw down the space-time prism figures. The study do questionnaire interview of participants. They are asked individually to describe and explain the user experience of "Taipei Cloud" service they feel. Finally, the researchers integrate all result to conclude the study.

The research will be guided most generally by literatures of time-geographic theory combined. The models of the space-time prism from time-geographic theory will offer principle of experiment design and measurement. Moreover, the study adopts service design process based on service thinking as applied approach.

2 Literature Review

This section firstly reviews related literatures of time-geography and its space-time prism concept, methodology; then, introduces the features of the service design process that will be applied to arrange this experiment design.

2.1 Time-Geography Concept and Space-Time Prism

The time-geography concept is proposed initially by Hägerstrand [3] for regional scientists as a research approach. According to Hägerstrand [3], time geography theory is placed emphasis on individuals' movements in space-time path as well as how individuals, groups, and institutions route activities through space–time of daily life that defined by the availability of these two interrelated resources. Taking time and space as two elements to be a shared social arena or stage, people can interact with other individuals, agencies, and institutions [4-5]. However, the time–space interactions are naturally limited and constrained and extremely dependent on the daily geographies of people [5-6].

As above mentioned, a concept of time-geography theory so-called "space-time prism" proposed by Hägerstrand [3] has been developed to estimate the some locations of people's daily life. In space-time prism, the fixed venue and the actors involved in the formation of two locations prism on a continuous timeline constitutes a trip arranged by travel plan the day's activities.

Moreover, every place crosses its time point to form a space-time path [9]. Typically, the space-time prism concept has been used to explore on activity patterns in a theoretical sense and the effect of constraints, such as work hours and family activities [1]. Recently, the applications of space-time prism have focused on examining to the people from numerous segments what extent activity patterns can be accommodated [7-8, 10-11]. The space-time prism and space-time path are shown by Figure 1.

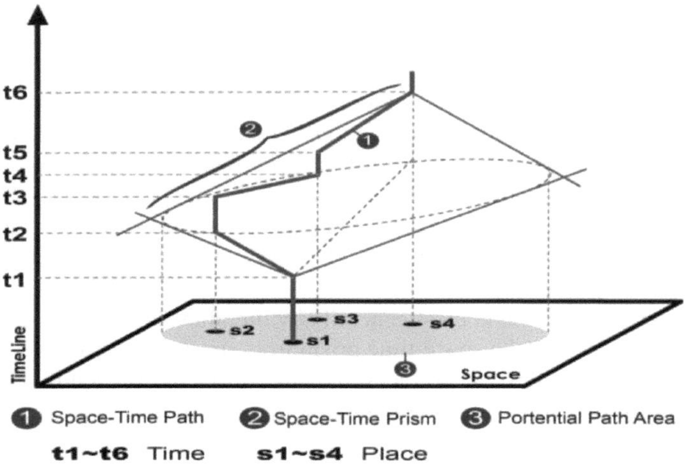

Fig. 1. Space-Time Prism Model

2.2 Service Design Process

Even if every designer requires a little diverse design approach and different design background also own their methods of working, whereas the value of co-creation emphasized in a service design project, hence, to care common novices there is a general model for all participants to use. The Design Council UK [2] has developed the "double diamond design process" model to divide into four distinct phases: Discover, Define, Develop and Deliver named the 4D method. In this model: 1. Discover: the first quarter of the 4D method, designers gather inspiration and insights, identifying user needs and developing initial ideas; 2. Define: within this step, designers try to make sense of all the possibilities identified in the Discover phase; 3. Develop: from this process of trial and error, designers construct some solutions, prototyped, tested. It also helps designers to improve and refine their ideas. 4. Deliver: the resulting product or service is completed and launched by all participants.

The 4d method leads how the design process forwards from one point where thinking and any possibility is as broad as possible to situations what they are consciously narrowed down and focused on distinct objectives. The double diamond design process is shown by Figure 2.

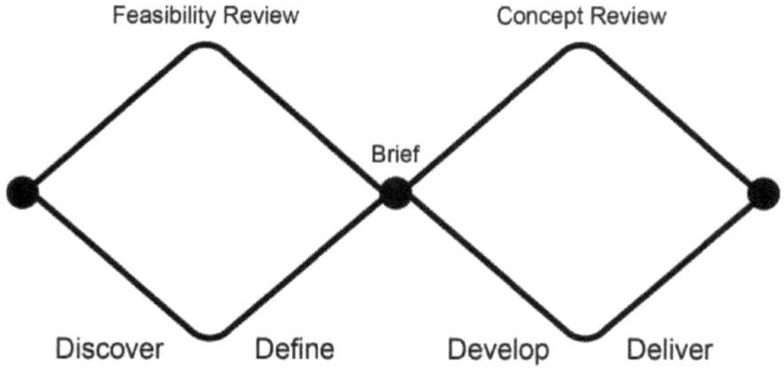

Fig. 2. The Double Diamond Design Process (Design Council, 2005)

3 Research Design

This section represents the research design that adopted in this pilot study. The main research method is experiment. The mobile devices are adopted in experiment to record space-time data of citizen cloud going with space-time prism model from time-geography theory.

3.1 Research Flowchart

The study is separated four steps to explore the usage of "Taipei Cloud" service and subjects' user experience. The research flowchart refers to 4D method developed by design council UK. We modify the 4D method as well as integrate cloud computing and time geography method into the research flowchart, shown by Figure 3.

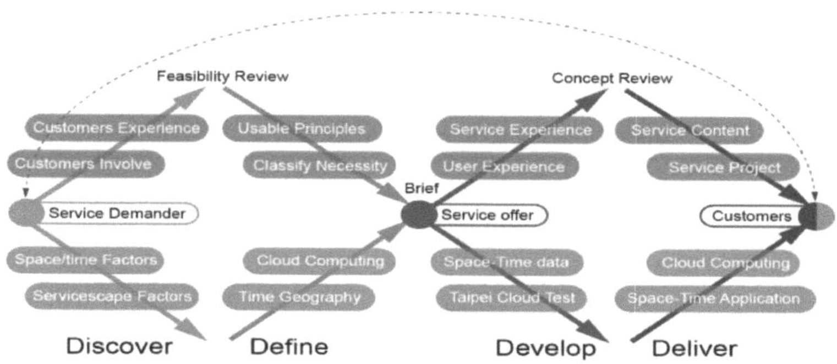

Fig. 3. Research Flowchart

3.2 Estimative Material and Subjects

The web platform named "Taipei Cloud" service contains 5 group-networking services: 1. Citizen cloud service; 2. Enterprise cloud service; 3. Education cloud service; 4. Health cloud service; 5. Opening data cloud service. Although the "Taipei Cloud" service platforms are established by different organizations, through monitor of government, some of them are not online yet like Enterprise cloud and Health cloud.

Therefore, to consider the holistic, essential, and functional constraining of cloud computing, the study selects Citizens' cloud service to be our estimate materials. For handling experiment smoothly and avoid the visual interference, we separate four teacups to put in independent boxes and cover top only retain front transparent for taking pictures. The citizen cloud service includes any contents of information, data that citizens should need and obtain, at the same time, it offers all registered web citizen to own 5GB web space to store, upload, and download data.

The study chooses subjects with the different carrier randomly as possible through social network websites. Six subjects volunteered to take part in the experiment. The age ranged from 19 to 24 years. All subjects are chose randomly from a social network website. Caused by experimental necessity, all subjects are asked to confirm that they have a mobile device with cloud computing app ready to run in 3G internet environment. The information of six subjects is listed by Table 1.

Table 1. The Information List of Subject Teams

No.	Age	Gender	Code Name
1	22	Male	M122
2	23	Female	F223
3	19	Male	M319
4	21	Female	F421
5	23	Male	M523
6	24	Female	F624
Total	F:22.6 (mean)	F:3	6
	M:21.3(mean)	M:3	

3.3 Experimental Procedure and Method

Before beginning of experiment, all subjects must own mobile device with 3G/Wi Fi function (like smart phone, tablet etc.). Then, researchers tell the subjects the aim, rules and explain that there is no time limited, just feel free to record their own using state of citizen cloud during their journey by their mobile device. This procedure is adopted individually from any place where subjects move to another one. When the subjects interact with citizen cloud service, the time and places of operation are recorded.

Finally, all contents of data are generalized to analyze. The relationship among one-day mobile application, subjects' behaviors by Facebook's "check in places", Google map "search" can assist our study to explain the usage of subjects in citizen cloud service. The experiment procedure of "Taipei Cloud" service is shown by Figure 4.

4-1 Link to Taipei Cloud 4-2 Login Citizen Cloud 4-3 Upload / Download Data 4-4 Generalize web log Files

Fig. 4. Experiment Procedure

4 Result

4.1 Spatial-Temporal Behavior

The space-time path made by all subjects and the usable behavior of citizen cloud can be shown by Figure 5. By Figure 5, the behavior of six subjects on citizen cloud is spread on the space-time paths. The more common behavior on all paths is "command" and "search". On other hand, the behavior of fewer times is "download".

From Figure 5, the study classifies the total time and contents on usage of citizen cloud are shown by Table 2.

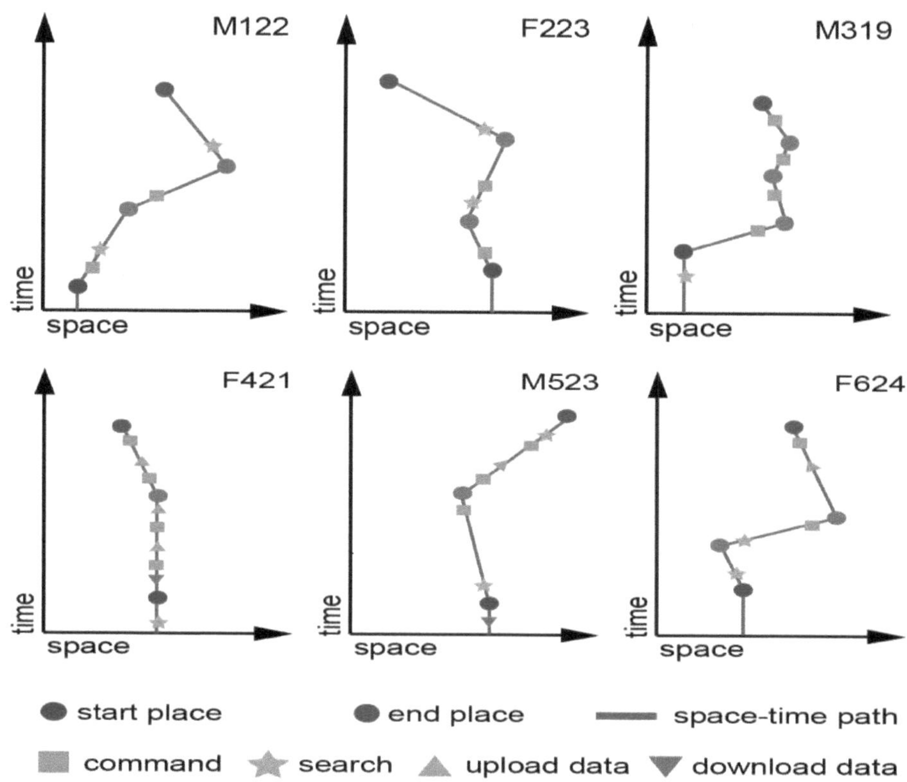

Fig. 5. The Subjects' Behavior of Citizen Cloud on Space-Time Path

By Table 2, it takes 272 minutes totally from six subjects on citizen cloud and the much time is devoted to "command" than other actions.

Table 2. The Information List of Subject Teams(unit: minutes)

subject.	■ command	★ search	▲ upload data	▼ download data	Total
M122	14	22	0	0	36
F223	19	26	0	0	45
M319	37	10	0	0	47
F421	34	12	11	6	63
M523	32	8	4	4	48
F624	14	16	3	0	33
Total	150	94	18	10	272/6=45.3

5 Conclusion

Although this pilot study we adopt small samples in test experiment, the findings are shown as followed:

1. In this pilot study, there is no direct correlation between time and spatial facts through subjects' usage on citizen cloud service.
2. According to the subjects' commands, the speed of internet result in directly different preference of usage during their journey.
3. When subjects login their own account into Taipei Cloud services, there are some intruption to bother them.
4. Even if users can only share or contact others by citizen cloud, the subjects still would like generate contents through cloud computing.
5. In holistic user experiences, subjects usually prefer higher interaction with cloud computing service, such as social networking, search engine with electric map service.

By the theory of time-geographic, this study tracks contents of spatial-temporal behavior for the people (commuters and travelers), middle dependent on moving around Taipei city. In addition, to classify the patterns on usages of mobile devices and types of activity place, the study can realize the characteristics demand on cloud computing and spatial-temporal behavior of interaction with citizen cloud on different places.

References

1. Burns, L.D.: Transportation, Temporal and Spatial Components of Accessibility. Lexington Books, Lexington (1979)
2. Design Council, The Design Process (2005)
3. `http://www.designcouncil.org.uk/designprocess` (accessed: October 10, 2013)
4. Hägerstrand, T.: What about people in regional science? Regional Science Association 24(1), 7–24 (1970)

5. Hägerstrand, T.: Survival and arena: on the life-history of individuals in relation to their geographical environment. In: Carlstein, T., Parkes, D., Thrift, N. (eds.) Timing Space and Spacing Time: Human Activity and Time-geography, vol. 2, pp. 122–145. Edward Arnold, London (1978)
6. Hägerstrand, T.: Escapes from the cage of routines: observations of human paths, projects and personal scripts. In: Long, J., Hecock, R. (eds.) Leisure, Tourism and Social Change. Dunfermline College of Physical Education, pp. 7–19 (1984a)
7. Hägerstrand, T.: Presence and absence: a look at conceptual choices and bodily necessities. Regional Studies 18(5), 373–379 (1984b)
8. Jones, P.M., Dix, M.C., Clarke, M.I., Heggie, I.G.: Understanding Travel Behavior. Gower, Aldershot (1983)
9. Kwan, M.-P.: Gender and individual access to opportunities: A study of space-time measures. The Professional Geographer 51(2), 210–227 (1999)
10. Miller, H., Shaw, S.L.: Georgraphic Inforation Systems for Transportation: Principles and Applications. Oxford University Press, New York (2001)
11. Miller, R.: Household activity patterns in nineteenth-century suburbs: A time-geographic exploration. Annals of the Association of American Geographers 72(3), 355–371 (1982)
12. Ritsema van Eck, J., Burghouwt, G., Dijst, M.: Lifestyles, spatial configurations and quality of life in daily travel: An explorative simulation study. Journal of Transport Geography 13(2), 123–134 (2005)

When China Encounters Smart TV: Exploring Factors Influencing the User Adoption in China

Yuming Tao, Jing Chang, and Pei-Luen Patrick Rau

Department of Industrial Engineering, Tsinghua University, Beijing 100084, P.R. China
{taoym08,changj12}@mails.tsinghua.edu.cn,
rpl@tsinghua.edu.cn

Abstract. Smart TVs, providing users with the access to abundant number of Internet video contents as well as other 'smart' functionalities, are gradually becoming more and more popular within Chinese households. Chinese internet companies and TV manufactures has been actively developing two forms of smart TV, namely embedded smart TVs and smart set-top boxes. The objective of the study is to explore the factors that affect user adoption of both the embedded smart TV and the set-top box and comprehensively analyze the difference in user adoption of the two smart TV forms. We carried out an online survey and collected 245 valid responses. With the help of exploratory factor analysis and hierarchical multiple regression analysis, we built a smart TV user adoption model based on TAM with 6 antecedent factors. The model helps to explain the difference between user adoption of embedded smart TV and smart set-top box and also figured out that perceived usefulness on video functionality is the priority concerns for developing both embedded smart TV and smart set-top box.

Keywords: Smart TV, Set-top box, Technology Acceptance Model.

1 Introduction

As an information and entertainment medium that has traditionally occupied the largest share of leisure time [1], TV has the greatest potential after mobile phone to bring about a revolution to the internet industry. Smart TVs enable users to have infinite access to Internet videos and applications in living room, making it easier for people to share Internet contents together with their families and friends. Smart TV differentiates itself from a traditional TV by integrating an OS platform, which grants a smart TV with all its smart functionalities.

A smart TV can come into two forms: an embedded smart TV set or a traditional TV branched with a smart set-top box. Even though the two forms of smart TVs are similar in terms of their functionalities as well as their user experiences, installation of the two forms are quite different to Chinese users. Installing a smart TV means the replacement of previous TV set, and the price to be paid can go from several thousands to tens of thousands RMB. In comparison, installing a set-top box is a much cheaper alternative, and the prices go between 200 - 500 RMB in general cases.

P.L.P. Rau (Ed.): CCD/HCII 2014, LNCS 8528, pp. 696–706, 2014.

According to a research by Liu et al., the cost is amongst the most important factors that influence the user acceptance of mobile entertainment of Chinese rural users. [2] In their study, Liu further attributed this phenomenon to the social-economic structure in China. So far, no studies of this kind were carried out in the case of smart TV. We expected the intention to adopt the two forms of smart TV will be also very different to Chinese users particularly in the less developed area, and we meant to explore it in this study.

Smart TVs has witnessed considerable growth in China since 2012. The Chinese big internet companies, including Baidu, Alibaba, Huawei and Xiaomi, has all launched their own embedded smart TV products or smart set-top boxes in recent two years. The TV manufactures were also actively taking part in this newly emerged market. Some expected that the era of Smart TVs would come at a much faster rate following the success of the smartphone. There are also prediction that smart TVs would become a hub at home by connecting computers and telephones in homes and automating electricity, home security and other entertainment systems [3].

While smart TV nowadays provide various kinds of so called 'smart' functionalities to its users, for example, online video streaming, TV gaming, online shopping & hotel booking, website browsing, etc., no one is sure of what kind of functionalities lead Chinese consumers to adopt this device. Yet, besides these seemingly 'powerful' functionalities provided by smart TVs, Chinese consumers seem to adopt smart TVs for other reasons, for example, the feeling of self-esteem as the early adopters of the device 'in fashion', or be persuaded by friends and relatives. It's still unknown which are the main factors that influence Chinese users' adoption of the forms of smart TV respectively, and how to accordingly optimize the current smart TV products to make it more concurrent amongst its peers.

The objective of our research is to explore the factors that influence the user adoption of smart TV in China, including the personal factors (user demographic characteristics, past experiences with smart devices, user innovativeness, etc.), social factors (social influence, etc) and product property factors (perceived product quality, relative advantage, etc.). We aimed to build up a comprehensive user adoption model for both embedded smart TV and smart set-top box. The results will help to explain the following questions which have bothered the industry for many years.

1. What kind of people is most likely to adopt embedded smart TV and smart set-top box?
2. What are the most important property factors that influence the adoption of embedded smart TV and smart set-top box?
3. How the intention of adoption is affected by social factors like social influence?

The study provides both theoretical and industrial contributions. Theoretically, it is the first comprehensive smart TV user adoption model that distinguishes the differences between embedded smart TV and smart set-top box, particularly under the social-economic situation in China. For the industry, it helps to figure out the potential smart TV adopters. It also helps to gain insights on how to optimize the current TV products and how to exert external influences over the potential user to accelerate the process of adoption.

2 Theoretical Foundation and Research Framework

2.1 Technology Adoption Theories

Technology acceptance or technology adoption theories has been studied for tens of years, and there're two theoretical model has been most widely used: the technology acceptance model (TAM) [4] and the innovation diffusion theory (IDT) [5].

TAM was initially developed to predict user acceptance of computers. According to Davis [4], user acceptance is fundamentally determined by two specific variables, perceived usefulness and perceived ease of use. Perceived usefulness is defined as "the degree to which a person believes that using a particular system would enhance his or her job performance". Perceived ease of use, in contrast, refers to "the degree to which a person believes that using a particular system would be free of effort." This model is a convergence of Self-efficacy theory [6], Cost-benefit paradigm [7], and Tornatzky and Klein's [8] findings about the adoption of innovations.

Another important model for an innovation's user acceptance is the innovation diffusion theory (IDT) [5]. According to Roger, diffusion is the process by which an innovation that is communicated through certain channels over time among the members of a social system. A new innovation is always adopted firstly by some early adopters, and then spreads through some social channels. According to the innovation diffusion theory, there are five other elements that affect the adoption rate of an innovation, namely the relative advantage, compatibility, complexity, trialability and observability.

2.2 Research Framework

In our study, we tried to extend the TAM model. Perceived usefulness (PU) and perceived ease of use (PEOU) were expected to be directed related to intention to use (ITOU), and we aimed to explore the antecedents that will influence PU and PEOU. Based on the previous theories and research, we concluded 5 candidate factors that will affect PU and PEOU, namely compatibility (COM), relative advantage (RA), innovativeness (INV), product quality (PQ) [9]. Although, after interviewing several experts in the smart TV industry, we come up with two other factors: past experiences with other smart devices and willingness to share TV contents with families.

Past experience with other smart devices (PE) was expected to have two-fold effect on the intention to adopt smart TV. On the one hand, subjects which have satisfying experiences in using smart phones or smart tablets were expected to have better understanding of the smart functionalities that smart TV provides, thus have a higher PU and PEOU. However, on the other hand, if the subject has satisfying past experience with smart phones or smart tablets, he/she might find smart TV redundant in terms of functionality, because most the 'smart' functionalities that smart TV provide, has already been realized on smart phones and smart tablets. Thus, PE could also have negative impact on PU and PEOU.

Willingness to share TV contents with families (SH) was regarded as another factor that will influence the intention to adopt smart TV. Different from other personal devices like PC and smart phone, TV is better suited for multi-user situation. A higher willingness to share TV contents with families may result in higher PU.

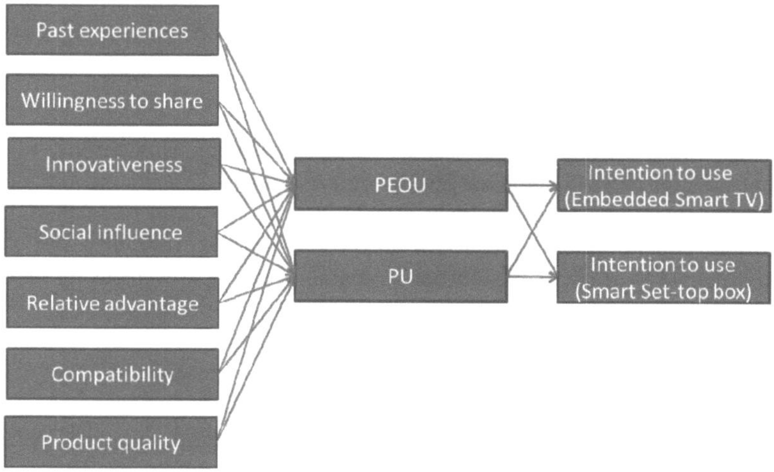

Fig. 1. Research framework for smart TV user adoption

3 Survey Study

Based on the research framework proposed previously, we developed the questionnaire for our survey. The questionnaire consisted 3 parts. The first part is constituted of the questions on personal profile, including gender, age, education level, household size and if the subject is currently using an embedded smart TV or smart set-top box. The second part is constituted of the questions on subject's usage of PC and smart phone. The third part is constituted of a total of 48 7-likert scale items for the 9 antecedent factors of intention to use in the framework. The subjects' intention to use embedded smart and smart set-top box was asked at the end of the survey.

The items for the 6 factors namely innovativeness [10, 11], social influence [12], relative advantage [5, 13, 14], compatibility [2, 5], product quality [2, 5]. For the 2 factors, perceived usefulness (PU) and perceived ease of use (PEOU), we further divided them into several sub-dimensions in regards to different functionalities a TV provide. The different functionalities considered in our research are: online video on demand, online live streaming, TV games, TV shopping, TV online browsing. For the two factors past experiences and willingness to share, we constructed the items under the guidance of several experts of human computer interaction as there're no previous literatures discussing these factors.

An online survey was conducted on the professional questionnaire website Sojump (www.sojump.com) from December 24, 2012 to January 2, 2013. We posted the hyperlink through BBS, social network, email in order to spread the survey to across China. In order to prevent duplicate submits each unique IP address was authorized to summit the response once.

A total of 245 valid responses (45.7% effective rate) were collected for this study. The invalid samples were filtered out based on the completion time (less than 300 seconds) and the consistency of the responses over two pairs of contrary questions.

4 Results Analysis

4.1 Sample Profile

Table 1 shows the general profile as well as the demographic characteristics of sample respondents. Of all the 245 subjects, 56.3% were male and 43.7% were female. Most of the respondents were aged less than 40 (77.2%) and a majority of them had received college education. Only 48.6% of all the respondents were currently using an embedded smart TV or smart set-top box and among them 76 were using an embedded smart TV.

Table 1. Demographic profiles of sample respondents

	Category	Frequency	Percentage
Gender	Male	138	56.3%
	Female	107	43.7%
Age	≤ 29	130	53.1%
	30 – 39	59	24.1%
	40 – 49	48	19.6%
	≥ 50	8	3.3%
Educational Level	High School or below	52	21.2%
	College	131	53.5%
	Master or higher	62	25.3%
Occupation	Student	66	26.9%
	Specialist	44	18.0%
	Teacher	26	10.6%
	Technician	18	7.4%
	Executive	16	6.5%
	Sales	9	3.7%
	Others	66	26.9%
Household size	1	24	9.8%
	2	24	9.8%
	3	123	50.2%
	4	53	21.6%
	≥ 5	21	8.6%
Current Usage of Smart TV	Traditional TV user	126	51.4%
	Embedded smart TV user	76	31.0%
	Smart set-top box user	43	17.6%

4.2 Group Compare

In order to find out what kind of people have a higher intention to use smart TV, we compared the average Intention to use (ITOU) between different groups.

While comparing between three groups of subjects: embedded smart TV users, smart set-top box users and traditional TV users, their intentions to adopt an embedded smart TV in the future were significantly different (one way ANOVA, $F=10.067$, $p<0.001$). Smart TV users have the highest intention to use, while smart box users go after. As well smart box users are more likely to buy a smart TV in the future than the regular TV users. ($t = 2.212$, $p = 0.028 < 0.05$ two tailed).

4.3 Exploratory Factor Analysis

We used a screening process to perform an exploratory factor analysis over the total of 48 likert-scale question items of the survey. Factors with loadings greater than 0.80 were retreated, with the following rules followed in the screening process.

- The cumulative sum of squared variance should be as large as possible. [15]
- Variables with loading smaller than 0.50 on all common factors should be deleted; Variables with loading larger than 0.50 on two or more factors should be deleted. [16]
- If a factor contains only one variable, the factor should be merged with other factors or be deleted. [17]
- The extracted model should be simple and easy to explain from a professional point of view. [15]

With the help of EFA and after the rotation of varimax, instead of retreating 9 constructs as expected, we had retreated 10 constructs from 27 items and the other 21 items were deleted.

The items for PU were however divided into two sub-factors after EFA: one factor is related to perceived usefulness of video functionality (PU-V), and the other for the perceived usefulness of non-video 'smart' functionalities (PU-NV). This was unexpected when constructing the survey but it showed that the subjects distinguish the video functionality from other 'smart' functionalities. By comparing the means of PU-V and PU-NV, the mean of PU-V is significantly higher than that of PU-NV (Paired t-test, $t = 8.979$, $p < 0.001$), showing that video functionalities is perceived more useful than the others.

The 10 factors had explained a total of 72.50% variances. The KMO were 0.757 and the Bartletts' Tests have significances less than 0.001, which demonstrated that the method of factor analysis was appropriate. The Cronbach's alpha value for all the construct are above 0.60, which was considered appropriate for exploratory research. [16]

4.4 Predicting Perceived Ease of Use

We performed a hierarchical multiple regression analysis to test how PEOU are affected by SI, PQ, SH, PE, RA, INV and COM. Also the demographic characteristics including the current usage of smart TV as well as the age group of the user was also taken into analysis. The results are shown in the table below.

Table 2. Hierarchical regression analysis predicting PEOU

Predictor	Incremental (adjusted) R^2	Standardized Coefficients (β)[1]	Sig.[1]
PQ	**0.054**	**0.211**	**0.001 ****
SH	**0.148**	**-0.450**	**<0.001 *****
PE	**0.042**	**0.230**	**<0.001 *****
INV	0.001	-0.071	0.254
RA	-0.003	0.034	0.622
COM	-0.003	0.013	0.840
SI	-0.003	-0.014	0.838
Age	0.005	-0.096	0.099
Current Usage of Smart TV	-0.002	-0.023	0.694
Total	**0.239**		

* $p < 0.05$; ** $p < 0.01$; *** $p<0.001$.

It shows that willingness to share the TV contents with the family (SH) is a very strong predictor for perceived ease of use (contributing 14.8% to the total variance). Product quality (PQ) and past experience with other smart devices (PE) are two other strong predictors (contributing a total of 9.6% to the variance). Demographic characteristics had no significant impact over user's perceived ease of use.

PE and PQ Have Significant Positive Impact on the PEOU. A higher PE reflects that the subject is quite familiar with the operations on smart devices, which leads to a higher PEOU. Better product quality also leads to a higher PEOU, which is coherent with our assumptions and the results of other researchers.

SH Have Significant Negative Impact on the PEOU. This is contrary to our previous assumption, and a probable reason is that a certain mediator exists between SH and PEOU but not yet discovered in this study. Smart TVs today may not be easy enough to use, thus those who want to share video contents with families may seek for alternatives other than smart TV and finally find that PEOU of smart TV is relatively lower compared to its alternatives.

4.5 Predicting Perceived Usefulness

We also performed a hierarchical multiple regression analysis on PU-V and PU-NV, the results are shown in tables below. Age and current usage of smart TV were combined into one hierarchical level.

Table 3. Hierarchical regression analysis predicting PU-V

Predictor	Incremental (adjusted) R^2	Standardized Coefficients (β)[1]	Sig.[1]
PQ	0.042	-0.039	0.501
SH	**0.149**	**0.170**	**0.012 ***
PE	**0.033**	**0.133**	**0.024 ***
INV	0.000	-0.011	0.850
RA	**0.090**	**0.293**	**<0.001 *****
COM	-0.003	-0.052	0.377
SI	**0.048**	**0.273**	**<0.001 *****
PEOU	-0.002	-0.006	0.921
Age		0.064	0.923
Current Usage of Smart TV	-0.002	0.005	0.234
Total	**0.355**		

* $p < 0.05$; ** $p < 0.01$; *** $p<0.001$.

The result in Table 3 shows that willingness to share (SH), relative advantage (RA), social influence (SI) and past experience with other smart devices (PE) are the strong predictors of the perceived usefulness of video functionality (PU-V) and they explained a total of 35.5% adjusted variance. **SH, RA, SI and PE have positive impact on PU-V and SH contributed to the largest total variance among them.**

Table 4. Hierarchical regression analysis predicting PU-NV

Predictor	Incremental (adjusted) R^2	Standardized Coefficients (β)[1]	Sig.[1]
PQ	0.000	0.047	0.491
SH	0.032	-0.018	0.819
PE	-0.004	-0.010	0.888
INV	**0.03**	**0.163**	**0.016 ***
RA	**0.026**	**0.190**	**0.011 ***
COM	-0.003	0.024	0.728
SI	-0.002	0.055	0.444
PEOU	**0.026**	**0.195**	**0.006 ****
Age		0.002	0.971
Current Usage of Smart TV	-0.002	0.080	0.205
Total	**0.103**		

* $p < 0.05$; ** $p < 0.01$; *** $p<0.001$.

The result in Table 4 shows that innovativeness (INV), relative advantage (RA) and perceived ease of use (PEOU) are the strong predictors of the perceived usefulness of non-video functionalities (PU-NV), but they explained a mere 10.3% of total variance. INV, PEOU and RA have significant positive impact on PU-NV. The non-video functionalities of smart TV is still in early stage and those with higher innovativeness will most likely try these functionalities and PEOU and RA is still a bottle neck.

4.6 Predicting the Intention to Use

Finally, we performed a hierarchical regression analysis, and tried to predict user's intention to adopt an embedded smart TV or smart set-top box by PEOU, PU-V and PU-NV. The results shows that PU-NV, PEOU, PU-V are all strong predictors for intention to use embedded smart TV, while PU-V is the only predictor for intention to use a smart set-top box. And by combining with the previous results, we built up the following smart TV user adoption model. The construct "compatibility" is not a strong predictor for none of PU-NV, PEOU and PU-V, and is eliminated from the model.

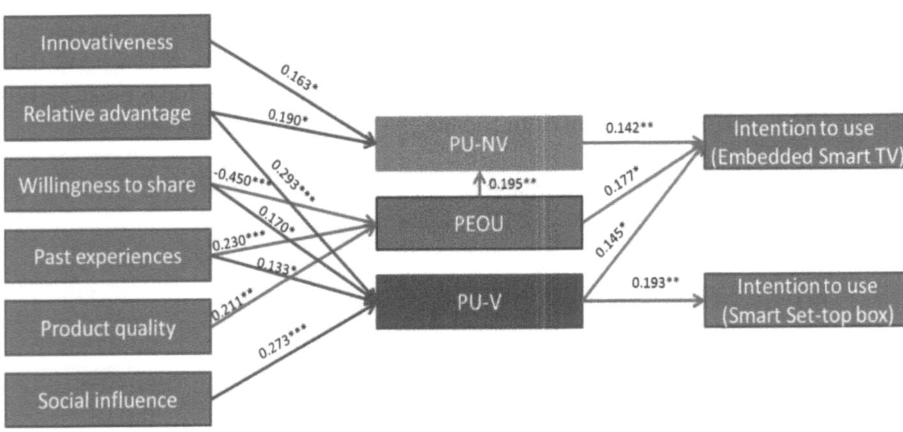

Fig. 2. Smart TV User Adoption Model

5 Conclusion and Discussion

In this research, we adapted the TAM model to explore the factors that impact Chinese users' intention to adopt two forms of smart TV: embedded smart TV and smart set-top box and how the adoptions of the two are different from each other. The construct of perceived usefulness was spitted into two in our model: perceived usefulness of video functionalities and perceived usefulness of non-video functionalities. Six factors were distinguished as the antecedents to perceived ease of use and the two perceived usefulness constructs. Based on the model we achieved, the following conclusions were drawn.

Firstly, video functionality is more important than the other smart functionalities for smart TVs. The exploratory factor analysis divided the survey items for the construct "perceived usefulness" into two groups: one group related to video functionality, and the other group related to non-video functionalities and this led us to split perceived usefulness into two: perceived usefulness for video functionality and perceived usefulness for non-vide functionality. The mean of the former is significantly higher than the later. For Chinese TV manufactures, the first priory in developing a smart TV is to provide users with abundant online video contents to make their product useful to consumers. Other functionalities like TV games and TV shopping are not as important as online video in driving the consumers to make the purchase decision.

Secondly, even though smart set-top boxes are similar with embedded smart TV in terms of functionalities, the factors that impact the attention to adopt them are different. Embedded smart TVs are much higher in price than set-top box, so both the video functionality and the other smart functionalities are important. Besides, an embedded smart TV should be fully optimized to facilitate its usage. In comparison, users' expectation for smart set-top box is much lower. Only the usefulness of video functionality is a big concern. This finding instructs the TV manufactures to differentiate their embedded TV products and the smart box products. The latter should focus themselves on online video, while the former should be positioned to a relatively high end market and make themselves worth the price.

Thirdly, antecedent factors for perceived usefulness on video functionality and non-video functionalities are different. Those with satisfying experiences in using smart phones and smart tablets and a high willingness to share video contents together with families will most likely find the video functionality useful, while those who are highly innovative are most likely to find other smart functionalities useful. Social influence will affect users' opinion on usefulness of smart TV video, but not smart TV games, smart TV shopping etc. According to the innovation diffusion theory, the smart TV video and other functionalities are in different stage of diffusion. Smart TV video is gradually being accepted by the early adopter or even early majority in China, while other smart functionalities are still in the earliest stage of diffusion, thus only those highly innovative users are likely to try.

Finally, users with experience on smart phone and smart tablets are more likely to find smart TV useful and easy to use. The smart device users are potential target consumers of smart TVs. This finding is intuitive for both designing and marketing of smart TV products. For designer of smart TV, the product should be designed compatible with the habits of smart phone or smart tablets consumers. As well, internet channel, particularly the mobile internet is an ideal place to promote smart TV products, because the mobile internet user group coincides with that of the smart TVs.

There're also several limitations to the study. Firstly, we used the hierarchical regression analysis to build the model, but the total variances explained by the regression are quite low, this resulted in a lower reliability of the results and other factors that can better predict the user adoption might have been omitted. The current model still has large space for improvement. Secondly, the survey questionnaire is quite long and it spread online, the quality of the responses could not be fully guaranteed (with only 45.7% of effective rate) even though we've taken measures of precautions. A better design of the survey and more precautious selection of the subjects may lead to more convincing results.

References

1. Zillmann, D.: The coming of media entertainment. In: Zillmann, D., Vorderer, P. (eds.) Media Entertainment: The Psychology of Its Appeal, pp. 1–20. Erlbaum, Mahwah, NJ (2000)
2. Liu, J., Liu, Y., Rau, P.L.P., Li, H., Wang, X., Li, D.: How socio-economic structure influences rural users' acceptance of mobile entertainment. In: Proceedings of the SIGCHI Conference on Human Factors in Computing Systems, pp. 2203–2212. ACM (April 2010)
3. Cabrer, M.R., Redondo, R.P.D., Vilas, A.F., Pazos Arias, J.J., Duque, J.G.: Controlling the smart home from TV. IEEE Transactions on Consumer Electronics 52(2), 421–429 (2006)
4. Davis, F.D.: Perceived Usefulness, Perceived Ease of Use, and User Acceptance of Information Technology. MIS Quarterly 13(3), 319–339 (1989)
5. Everett, R.: Diffusion of innovations, vol. 5, pp. 11–27. The Free Press, New York (1995)
6. Bandura, A.: Self-Efficacy Mechanismin Human Agency. American Psychologist 37(2), 122–147 (1982)
7. Beach, L.R., Mitchell, T.R.: A Contingency Model for the Selection of Decision Strategies. Academy of Management Review 3(3), 439–449 (1978)
8. Tornatzky, L. G., Klein, K.J.: Innovation Characteristics and Innovation Adoption - Implementation: A Meta-Analysis of Findings. IEEE Transactions on Engineering Management 29(1), 28–45 (1982)
9. Venkatesh, V., Davis, F.D.: A theoretical extension of the technology acceptance model: four longitudinal field studies. Management Science 46(2), 186–204 (2000)
10. Park, C., Jun, J.K.: A cross-cultural comparison of Internet buying behavior: Effects of Internet usage, perceived risks, and innovativeness. International Marketing Review 20(5), 534–553 (2003)
11. Garcia, R., Calantone, R.: A critical look at technological innovation typology and innovativeness terminology: a literature review. Journal of Product Innovation Management 19(2), 110–132 (2002)
12. Lu, J., Yao, J.E., Yu, C.S.: Personal innovativeness, social influences and adoption of wireless Internet services via mobile technology. The Journal of Strategic Information Systems 14(3), 245–268 (2005)
13. De Ruyter, K., Wetzels, M., Kleijnen, M.: Customer adoption of e-service: an experimental study. International Journal of Service Industry Management 12(2), 184–207 (2001)
14. Shin, D.H., Hwang, Y., Choo, H.: Smart TV: are they really smart in interacting with people? Understanding the interactivity of Korean Smart TV. Behaviour & Information Technology 32(2), 156–172 (2013)
15. Smith, B., Caputi, P., Rawstorne, P.: The development of a measure of subjective computer experience. Computers in Human Behavior 23(1), 127–145 (2007)
16. Hair, J.F., et al.: Multivariate data analysis: with readings. Macmillan (1995)
17. Stiggelbout, A.M., Molewijk, A.C., Otten, W., Timmermans, D.R.M., Van Bockel, J.H., Kievit, J.: Ideals of patient autonomy in clinical decision making: a study on the development of a scale to assess patients' and physicians' views. Journal of Medical Ethics 30(3), 268–274 (2004)

Cross-Cultural Design for Creativity

Designing "Taipei City" as a World Design Capital

Jun-Liang Chen[1,3], Yu-Ju Lin[2,3], Stanley Wei[4], and Yen-Yu Kang[5]

[1] Freeimage Design, Taipei 10555, Taiwan
freeimage5361@gmail.com
[2] Department of Visual Communication Design,
Taipei College of Maritime Technology
Taipei 25172, Taiwan
naralin@mail.tcmt.edu.tw
[3] Graduate School of Creative Industry Design,
National Taiwan University of Arts
Ban Ciao City, Taipei 22058, Taiwan
[4] Oneness International Group Limited, Hong Kong
stanley.wei@onenessint.com
[5] Graduate School of Industrial Design, National Kaohsiung Normal University
Kaohsiung 80201, Taiwan
yen@nknu.edu.tw

Abstract. This paper focuses on the Taipei City as the World Design Capital Planning, through curatorial concepts into urban governance, the completion of substantial city transformation, the implementation of bid idea, especially the establishment of a "Public Policy by Design" and "Public participation in the design" two-track operation mechanisms platform. The study presents a process, based on the International Council of Societies of Industrial Design (ICSID) requirements, for developing guidelines for bid spindle philosophy: "Adaptive City", and contributes to improve Taiwan's visibility, and the effects of while promoting related design, tourism industry development. Factors affecting content Application design are identified and discussed; these guidelines can be categorized into three principles of design. Some ideas for Tenders Book design are developed, and finally, made by Jun-Liang Chen the use craft techniques to new design based on "dragon-scale binding" is proposed. Future research could apply the design to other groups of City Curatorial Concept Design. How to design into public policy, designed to carry through the city's social reform movement.

Keywords: World Design Capital, Curatorial Design, Craft Techniques.

1 Introduction

The International Council of Societies of Industrial Design (ICSID) initiated the World Design Capital (WDC) program globally, with the goal of encouraging people to solve the problems that exist in modern cities by design, fulfilling the vision of city

P.L.P. Rau (Ed.): CCD/HCII 2014, LNCS 8528, pp. 709–720, 2014.

development. By applying to become the next WDC, Taipei committed to becoming a city with a design vision under its program "Design Taipei." Becoming a World Design Capital is not merely a matter of developing a vision of Taipei as a design city, but of inviting the world to witness Taipei's progress [1]. The "Adaptive City—Design in Motion" exhibition was intended to make the story of Taipei city visible to the world. The city of Taipei has been established for 130 years. The landscape of the city has changed over time, and Taipei has been transformed from a simple town into the prosperous, glimmering capital of Taiwan. Amid this transformation, Taipei's courage in creatively seeking breakthroughs, its will to promote quality of life, and its determination to explore a sustainable future, have remained unchanged. Taipei is one of the most prominent famous, young, rapidly developing Asian metropolises. Within these short130 years, Taipei has emerged to become a highly prosperous city. Over time, changes in Taipei have reflected its spirit of modernity, unrestricted vitality and constant transformation. On November 19, 2013, the ICSID announced Taipei City as the fifth WDC.

This study would like to emphasize the importance of considering relationship between bid book creation and the selection committee in applying to host urban curatorial activities. Bid books must be written, fabricated, and expressed in a way that transcends limited regulations and formats, and creates new design concepts that belong to the experience economy; this is a superior example of the recent trend where bid books have to confer emotions in an era driven by curators. Therefore, cities must put forth all their efforts and create surprises when applying to become WDCs. The ICSID profoundly experienced Taipei's innovative energy when opening the bid book, which was bound in dragon-scale binding. From the perspective of urban curation, this study determined the approaches by which Taipei acquired recognition from the selection committee regarding the design process, resulting in its obtaining the honor of hosting this international activity.

2 Literature Review

2.1 World Design Capital: Promoting Urban Creativity

The WDC is a global activity that was initiated by the ICSID, and the selection process is conducted every two years. The designated city is selected from numerous candidate cities by the selection committee, and is named as a WDC. Torino, Italy was designated a WDC in 2008; Seoul, South Korea in 2010; Helsinki, Finland in 2012; and Cape Town, South Africa in 2014. The ICSID selected these cities to become WDCs not only because they are conducive environments for their respective design industries, but because design thinking in these places is applied to crucial urban development problems to yield admirable solutions. Every WDC employs innovative and creative methods in pursuing visions of urban development.

Increasing numbers of people live in cities; this rapid population growth has facilitated increasingly dramatic changes to the urban environment. City residents responsible for urban planning, design, and management are responsible for facilitating smooth urban transitions during such changes. WDC candidate cities must satisfy the following selection criteria: (A) Highlight the importance of promoting design through cooperation with the ICSID. (B) Express the practical correlation between design and the quality of life in a city. (C) Ensure the mobilization and participation of a majority of citizens. (D) Promote communication between designers and other social communities. (E)Fulfill international standards promoted by the ICSID, and incorporate those standards in the WDC bid book. Thus, in addition to the creation of a compelling bid book, city characteristics and overall policy planning must satisfy the aforementioned criteria. Bid books must exhibit enhanced characteristic and unique features that cannot be predicted by other international competitors.

2.2 World Design Capital Taipei 2016 — Adaptive City

Taipei is the political, cultural, business, entertainment, and broadcasting capital of Taiwan. In Taipei, service industry workers constitute more than 80% of the population, and the city's GDP wasUS$48,400 in 2009. More than 50% of the population has received higher education; this has produced many active and innovative creative professionals. In Taipei, one out of every 10 workers is involved in the cultural and creative industries. In 2010, Taipei companies involved in the cultural and creative industries reached 15,561, constituting more than 30% of the industry in all of Taiwan, and producing a total output of NT$413 billion. Recently, Taipei has become devoted to developing all kinds of cultural establishments and investments. With the establishment of art galleries, museums, galleries, theaters, art centers, and cultural and creative parks, Taipei is a young city full of creativity and energy [2]. As modern cities confront novel urbanization problems and global challenges, the insufficiency of old governance thinking regarding public policy has become clear. Further cross-disciplinary communication is required in the future to allow innovative solutions to be adjusted, evolved, and gradually developed. Taipei's bid for WDC 2016 is actually a social reform movement. Being an advanced city is not only about architectural appearance; citizen participation is crucial [3]. The process of engaging public policy is crucial to expressing national creative strength through design concepts.

2.3 Viewing Globalization and Glocalization from a City

As competition has become globalized, "global market and local design" has become a trend in creative design. In Taiwan, the focus of economic development has shifted from original equipment manufacturers (OEMs), which create products based on technology and concerns about function and use, to an era dominated by original design manufacturers (ODMs), who are engaged in questions about design. For ODMs, design is crucial and feelings and users are the major concern. The era that succeeds ODMs is dominated by original brand manufacturers (OBMs), in which hi-touch becomes the core value of the design process, and requires support from the arts and humanities. Only a few countries in the world completely progressed from OEM, to ODM, to OBM [4]. This is a process of design evolution, and reflects the progression of Taiwanese economic development from technology to humart. The core values of humart are aesthetics, economics, culture, and creativity. Taipei was formally designated the WDC 2016, and the adaptive city is its working vision. The success of WDC can be expressed in design concepts. (A) The design concept "from usage to user" was converted to establish urban perceptive environments. (B) The design concept "from function to feeling" was converted to provide urban authenticity. (C) The design concept "from high technology to high perception" was converted to the design of city qualia. Adaptive design was adopted to conceptualize Taipei's status as an emerging city. Regarding the locus of design development, Taiwan expresses the core values of design technology that are eventually fused in art and the humanities. Thus, modern designers must combine perceptual technology and humanization design in building a humanized product and service environment that possesses qualia creativity [6].

2.4 Building Humanity, Design, and Technology in the City

From the perspective of design development, leaps in technological progress have facilitated a revolution in design and form [6]. Thus, technology is surely the root of design. Design developments since the beginning of the20thcentury can be divided into five stages, which all feature words with the letter F. The five stages are described as follows: (A) Design for function in the 1930s; (B) Design for user-friendliness in the 1950s; (C) Design for fun in the 1970s; (D) Design for fancy in the 1990s; (E) Design for feeling in the 21stcentury. In the world of the 21st century digital technology, human-centered design is increasingly essential, and designs that focus on feelings and affect have become the mainstream in design: in other words, form follows feeling [7]. With this alteration in design trends, the previous design procedure triangle of design, market, and manufacture was transformed into a three-in-one concept: user, designer, and manufacturer. This change in trends implies a shift from technology to designing and developing culture. The previous concept of design, market, and manufacturing was structured on the basis of technology. The present concept of designer, user, and manufacturer is structured on the foundation of culture. The difference between these two concepts is that the present concept is additionally concerned with humanity (Fig 1). From the perspective of design practice undertaken by this study, the bid book is not only a product of manufacturing but an article of designers and users. In the communication and transmission process, the delegator (client), designer (work design), and recipient (organizer) operate in different cognitive modes; the resulting designed works are endowed with divergent meanings. Therefore, cognitive modes differently affect the transmission of messages and the expression of meaning [8].

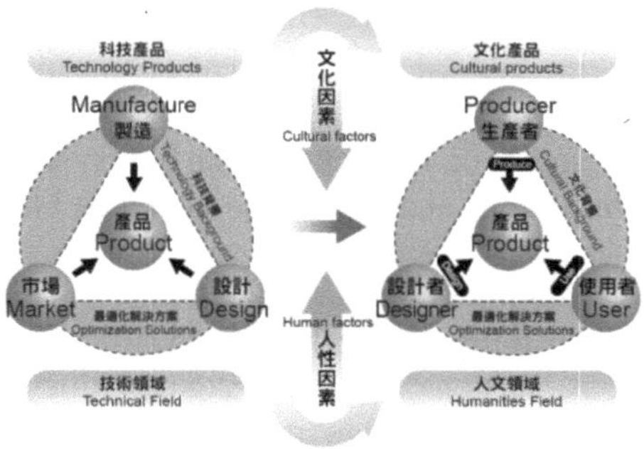

Fig. 1. The relationship between culture Design and Technology Humanities (Lin, 2005)

3 Research Methods

The Taipei City Government established a working group for executing the bid for WDC 2016, which was a focus in municipal policy. Under the premise of maintaining and strengthening the characteristics of Taipei city, the working group conducted case studies and current situation investigations. The goal was to stimulate city design power and induce the energy for advancement. Discussions between citizens, community residents, experts, and enterprise representatives were held, in which design thinking was taken as the focus; historical memory, major current achievements, and primary problems were considered the foundation of these discussions. These discussions established the main discourse of the urban development vision and suggested 10–15 possible urban development concerns and highlights, the feasibilities of which were also evaluated. The mandatory bid book is crucial to the application process. The bid book is the medium through which the ICSID clearly understands city. However, bid books are usually presented in the format of a standard official document; they lack unique cultural characteristics, thus hindering in-depth understanding and recognition of the selection committee. During the bid book design process, strategies were implemented to present the highlights of the city of Taipei. Cultural characteristics enrich people's experiences. However, government documents that are rich in cultural characteristics are rarely realized. This study was conducted in two stages. In the first stage, we summarized the relevant literature, developed the cultural properties of the bid book, and provided possible references for the design with the expectation of guiding applicants of urban curatorial activities. In the second stage, the bid book design for WDC 2016 was practically created. The effectiveness of applying design in bid books is provided as a reference for subsequent curatorial activity applicants.

4 Research Results and Discussion

4.1 Taipei Bids for the WDC-The Design and Development of the Dragon-Scale Binding Bid Book

The theme of the adaptive city, expressing the characteristics of Taipei and global design trends, was proposed in Taipei's bid for the WDC. The appeal of "WDC legacy and Taipei model" was presented in the brilliant contents. To design the bid book, Jun-Liang Chen, the general manager of Free Image Design, designed a five-volume book with five theme covers, 23 charts, 47 bid questions, and 342 photographs, to depict the evolution of Taipei City. The bid book exhibited Taipei's unique history, proximity to mountains and water, and abundant blend of culture. The book emphasized that the citizens of Taipei have come to understand themselves through the process of urban evolution and internationalization: they are able to transform historical experiences into future possibilities, and difficulties into opportunities. In the five-volume bid book, sections on basic design facilities, the design industry, urban planning, talent cultivation, design policy, and promoting participation were included according to the requirements of urban revitalization. The dragon-scale binding book binding method was adopted in the international bid book. The binding was inspired by the profundity of Chinese culture and precision of its craft techniques.

4.2 Content and Information Transmission and Design Considerations

The bid for WDC 2016 initiated a series of transformative urban actions, and promoted urban progress. The project activities involved in bidding for WDC 2016 aimed to enable more citizens to grasp, feel, and enjoy design, to gradually fulfill the concept of human-centered design, and induce citizens to participate in advancing Taipei. Generally, bid books are square in shape, and easily appear restricted and cliché. Therefore, the content of the Taipei bid book was designed to make the ICSID fully aware of the city's complete preparation for hosting the WDC 2016. In the design of the bid book's content, the ubiquity of design in Taipei City and its close connection with citizens' lives was emphasized. All the contents mentioned in the bid book were from the city of Taipei. The contents were easy to understand, and the objects and services Taipei offers were easily expressed. The core of the design proposal was the continuous uplifting of Taipei, user orientation, and design energy adapted to local conditions. The designer proposed that the culture and manufacturing of the bid book should allow the ICSID to fully perceive Taipei City's texture and creativity. Thus, touch is a type of fashion of feelings and a new economic mode that echoes the inner needs of modern people [9]. To reduce the complications caused by

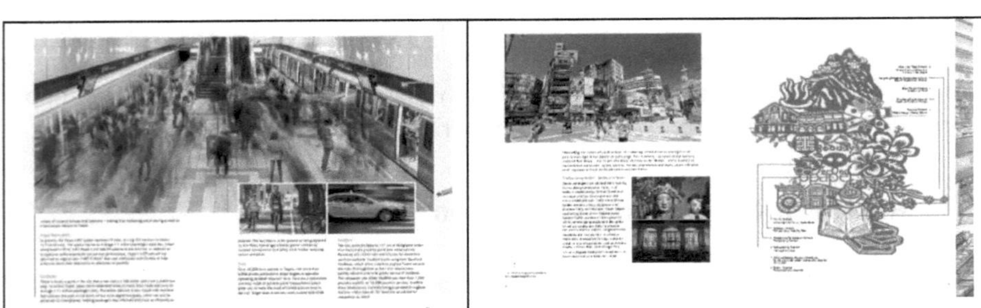

Fig. 2. The bid book Content info for Taipei's bid for WDC 2016

the diversity in content of the 47 bid questions, the focused design improvements were as follows: (A) Divide the bid book into multiple volumes present various topics; (B) Transform the texts into images to transmit the humanistic expressions and emotional vocabulary of the city, as shown in Fig. 2.

4.3 The Principal Considerations of the Bid Book Design

Regarding the interactions between the bid book format and the emotional affect, the designer should serve as a satisfactory communication bridge between the client/design work/organizer during the whole design process. Preferences and optimization capability considerations influenced the bid book design during the design process. Jun-Liang Chen is an expert in finding design inspirations in traditions. However his designs are neither retro nor regressive, but refined. In the design of the WDC 2016 bid book, three design principles were considered.

1. Natural Refinement: Life experiences are superior design inspirations. Design is a type of social force, and an excellent designer can propose contemporary perspectives. Environmental protection was the driving reason behind the selection of dragon-scale binding. The designer aimed to elicit resonance among the selection committee with the emotion of treasuring things. Design is a process of seeking resonance, as shown in Fig. 3.

2. The Display of Craft Value: Locally produced Moso bamboo and black jade were applied in packaging the bid book. Craft masters built the delicate cabinet box packaging and the packaging of the bid box was delicate and full of qualia. Jade flakes were delicately embedded on the cover of the square bamboo box. In the box was a five-volume dragon-scale binding bid book; a small embedded box on the side contained a USB flash drive that contained the bid video. From its internal structure to its appearance, the whole dragon-scale binding bid book was likened to the scales of the auspicious Chinese creature, the dragon. The dragon scales were glued in a tiered fashion layer by layer. The expended scroll transformed into a complete figure, where every page was a surprise, as shown in Fig. 4.

3. Advocacy of Cultural Characteristics: On the covers of the 5-volume dragon-scale binding bid book were Yangtze Tong's calligraphy, the collections of the National Palace Museum, Jimmy Liao's works, Ray Chen interior design drawings of the Eslite Bookstore, and a shanghais painting that depicted an overview of Taipei, as shown in Figs. 5–9. The contents of the five covers are described as follows.

(1) Yangtze Tong's calligraphy. The first bid book cover featured calligraphy of the renowned Taiwanese calligrapher, Yangtze Tong. She wrote 16 Chinese characters, which read: "As from the knife and the file, as from the chisel and the polisher! Pure as gold or as tin, soft and rich as a sceptre of jade! " The words were adopted from the ancient book Classic of Poetry, and their meaning was that an adaptive spirit requires continuous polishing, reflecting, and uplifting. Because Yangtze Tong's calligraphy

exceeds the points and lines of traditional calligraphy, her calligraphy is more similar to an ink wash painting, and is rich in poetic meaning. Her work also implied that Taipei not only inherits 5,000 years of Chinese traditional culture, but actively faces coming challenges through the spirit of continuous design creativity.

(2) The collections of the National Palace Museum. The second bid book cover depicted five specially selected artifacts from the National Palace Museum collections as compared to modern Taiwanese industrial design works. This cover implied that the Chinese cultural heritage exhibits the adaptive design spirit of Taiwan.

(3) Jimmy Liao's works. The third bid book cover featured the work of one of the most influential illustrators in Taipei, Jimmy Liao. In the 2010 Taipei International Flora Exposition, Jimmy Liao used abundant fantasy to paint the wall of the Pavilion of Dreams, with giant flowers lively decorating the city and expressed the vigorous vitality of Taipei citizens.

(4) Ray Chen's interior design drawings of the Eslite Bookstore. The fourth bid book cover displayed the interior design drawings of the Eslite Bookstore by the famous interior designer Ray Chen, in showing the image crossed by lines in a collage manner. Ray Chen constructed a special design style that implied the interdisciplinarity and diversity of Taipei design.

(5) Shanshui painting of Taipei. The landscape overview presented on the fifth bid book cover was the most original and natural appearance of the city. The painting is also the most precious property of the city. Taipei is a better and continuously adapting city, because of design.

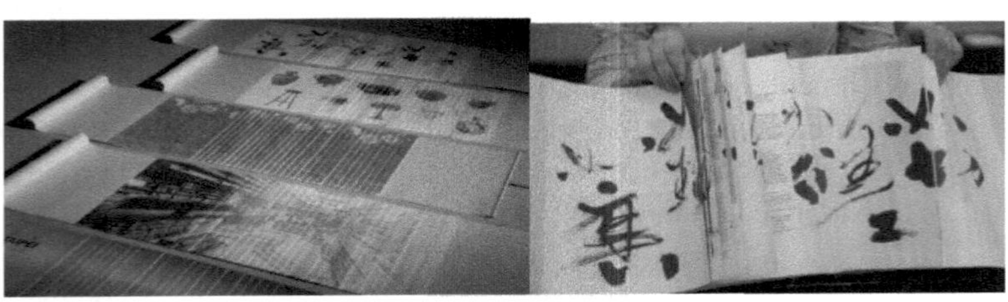

Fig. 3. The concept of environmental protection—the dragon-scale binding bid book of Taipei's bidding for the WDC 2016

Fig. 4. The dragon-scale binding bid book box for Taipei's bid for WDC 2016

Fig. 5. First bid book cover Yangtze Tong's calligraphy

Fig. 6. Second bid book cover collections of the National Palace Museum

Fig. 7. Third bid book cover Jimmy Liao's works

Fig. 8. Fourth bid book cover—Interior design drawings of the Eslite Bookstore

Fig. 9. Fifth bid book cover Shanshui painting of Taipei

4.4 Considerations in the Book Binding Design

The invention of dragon-scale binding was adapted to alterations in social and cultural needs. In addition, the dragon-scale binding constituted a creative reform of an improvement on the inconvenience of scroll binding. An illustration of dragon-scale binding is provided in Fig. 10. The binding technique of dragon-scale binding was lost at least a thousand years ago. This type of book binding faintly reveals elegant spiritual beauty, and cultural and historical connotations. With the advances in technology, a number amount of modern technologies have been applied to fulfill the needs of the modern industrialized era. The dragon-scale binding bid book of the WDC 2016 applied ancestral creative design to attract the ICSID's attentions and make a favorable impression. Thus, this all but lost book binding technique reappeared in the official document of the bid book, and anew image of dragon-scale binding, surpassing tradition, was adopted in bid book. The design was based on the traditional inspiration that Jun-Liang Chen discovered, namely, the concept of dragon-scale binding. Consequently, a 5-volume bid book bound with dragon-scale binding was designed, as shown in Fig. 11.

Fig. 10. Books bound with the traditional Chinese book binding method, dragon-scale binding

Jun-Liang Chen, the designer, mentioned that before this bid book, dragon scale bound ancient books were extremely rare. Throughout the whole world, only one book remained in the National Palace Museum. Jun-Liang Chen studied book binding in graduate school and was familiar with 13 types of ancient Chinese book binding, including wooden slips, thread-bound, palm leaf, and accordion binding. Thus he found the reappearance of the long-neglected dragon-scale binding gorgeous. The rationale for the existence of dragon-scale binding was given a thousand years ago, during the Tang dynasty: the pages fell out of the thread-binding books too easily. The ancient people then glued the fell-out pages on a scroll, forming a repaired book. Dragon-scale binding resulted from treasuring things, which is a practice of environmental protection.

The bid book was presented in the unique form of dragon-scale binding, which was inherited from the ancient book collection of traditional culture and creative design. The shape of the dragon-scale binding book is similar to the scales of the auspicious Chinese creature, the dragon, whose scales are stacked layer by layer and extended orderly. Turning every single page, inch by inch, brings a surprise. Every scale is a single page, but is also independent; the cascading pages thus resulted in a complete picture. The scales also signified that city cultural experiences that were lively, story-related, special, or touched people were created by every design aspect, energy, and dimension of Taipei. The design procedure of the bid book is summarized and presented in Fig. 12.

Fig. 11. Bid book volumes of the dragon-scale binding design

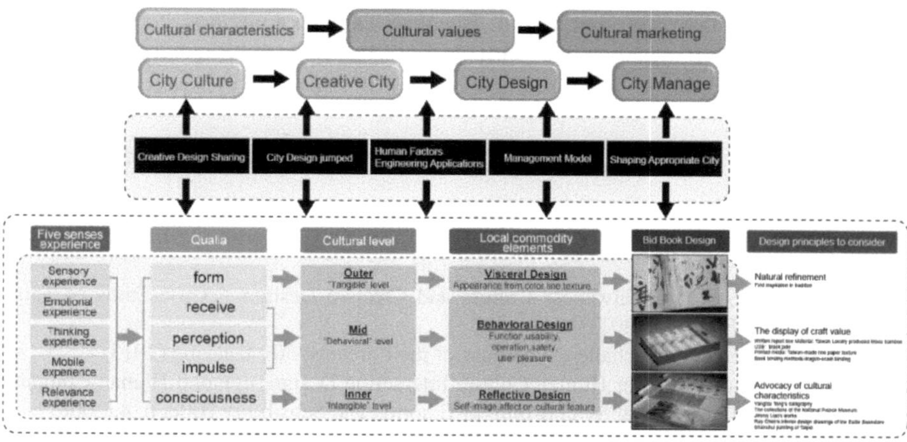

Fig. 12. Bid book design procedure

5 Conclusion

Design is a superior tool for solving social problems and realizing life visions. Design is for people; therefore, design works must be interesting and full of novel experiences. Life forms culture, culture affects design, and design alters life. Design is crucial in enhancing national competitiveness and is also a consensus that can be applied in expanding the international market. Design reflects technology, politics, and cultures of every era, and the meaning of design changes over time. In the future, design will play a more inclusive and integrated role, transcend the boundary of design and non-design, penetrate every domain, and become a new international language. The 2011 International Design Alliance Congress Taipei adopted the theme of "design at the edges" to convey the interactions between design and other domains. During the bidding process for WDC 2016, governmental, industrial, and private resources were integrated. The goal was not only to introduce top-down public policy and initiate the new project of urban refurbishment, but also to stir up the whole city through bottom-up citizen participation, and fill the city with the vision and energy for continuous transformation.

From the beginning of bidding for WDC 2016, Taipei managed to establish a city brand and increase city competence through design, reflecting both the characteristics of living culture and culturalized industry. In the global trend toward aesthetic and experiential economies, the added value of design is employed in building in-depth consumer experiences, developing consumer experiential values, and thereby creating value beneficial to deeply rooted cultural values. The cultural and creative industries have become a novel economic force in the 21st century. Only cultural creativity can increase national competitiveness, and imperceptibly increase cultural content and creative aesthetics. The bidding also implied the expectation of raising national cultural and creative soft power through national efforts, and making cultural and creative industries the driving force of the next wave of economic growth. Modern urban governance must have a design vision. Because Taipei knows how to apply design thinking, people will observe that with design, Taipei is driving city progression, creating urban governance, and building a city worth expecting progress from.

References

1. Affairs, TCDOC. Design Taipei Adaptive City. Taipei City Department of Cultural Affairs, Taipei (2013)
2. Kua, C.W.: A Study of Taiwanese Culture and Creative Design: A Case Study of Taipei City's Cultural Elements (2011)
3. Wang, W.L.: Taipei great challenge because of their dreams. 30 Magazine (2013)
4. Lin, R.T.: A Framework for Human-Culture Interaction Design –Beyond Human-Computer Interaction. In: International Symposium for Emotion and Sensibility 2008, p. 8 (2008)
5. Lin, R.T.: Designing "Emotion" into modern Products. In: International Symposium for Emotion and Sensibility 2008, p. 11 (2008)
6. Lin, R.T.: Sensibility Field. Moving Experience. Qualia Commodity - To build the World Design Capital in Taipei. Taipei Economic Quarterly (7), 14–21 (2011)
7. Feng, Z.: The development and improvement of modern industrial system. Hainan Teachers College 10(37), 104–108 (1997)
8. Lin, R.T.: Combination of technology and human cultural and creative. Journal of Scientific Development (396), 68–75 (2005)
9. Huang, A.: Designers feel is to pass the palm of temperature. Commonwealth Magazine (2011)

Designing 'Culture and Heritage' into the C1D1 District of Taipei City

Lihrong Chiou[1], Kung-Ling Chang[1], Yu-Chi He[1], and Richard H. Lee[2]

[1] National Taiwan University of Arts,
Taipei, Taiwan
{lihrong,kling}@ntua.edu.tw,
he.chi415@gmail.com
[2] C.Y. LEE & PARTNERS Architects / Planners, Taipei, Taiwan
richardlee@mail.cylee.com

Abstract. This paper focuses on the development of C1D1 District of Taipei City, emphasizing its cultural perspective and oriental spirit. With the concept of the creative city, this study explores the cultural and industrial heritage of the Western District. To lead the C1D1 District to turn into a new core of Taipei City designated as the World Design Capital 2016, the concepts of Oriental Cloud Platform, City's Living Room, 3D Catalog, and Cultural and Industrial Link are proposed as development guidelines.

Keywords: Culture and Heritage, Oriental Spirit, Creative City, Cultural Link.

1 Introduction

For the development of the Taipei Station and its surrounding area, the C1D1 District was designated as high-rise building block in 2011. Located on the main gate and core area of Taipei City, the C1D1 District was planned to develop shopping malls, offices for international headquarters, international hotels, and cultural and leisure facilities. The development of Taipei City originated from the Western District along the Danshui River. The Western District thus accumulated abundant cultural and industrial heritage within the areas of North Gate, Dadaocheng, Ximending, Chongcing Bookstore Street, Wholesale Industrial Zone, etc. With the passage of time, the Western District today comprises rich and multi-faceted cultural contents that interact to create a unique tapestry. The threads of this tapestry are political, cultural, transporting, and economic, which are sometimes in conflict, sometimes harmonious, and still sometimes chaotic.

During recent decades 'the Creative City' has turn into a clarion call for productive and imaginative action in urban development (Landry, 2008; 2012). The creative city became the new hot theme among urban policymakers, planners and economists. Various creative cities around the world reflect different inspirations for development in this regard (Andersson, Andrsson, and Mellander, 2013). The development of the creative city in advanced countries has been focusing on the characterized local culture and rich historical heritage. The re-organization and practice of the city has

P.L.P. Rau (Ed.): CCD/HCII 2014, LNCS 8528, pp. 721–730, 2014.

regarded culture as the first priority and main consideration. Utilizing creative manpower and organization to deal with broad perspectives of cultural issues, a creative city environment and atmosphere is therefore possibly formulated, and developed as a center of creativity. Researchers assert that even although the 'cultural economy' and 'creative industry' are normally conflated perspectives and distinct segments of contemporary city economies, they actually may be connected to make great contribution to a city's character, attractiveness and competitiveness through thinking, planning and acting in addressing urban issues creatively (Cooke and Zazzeretti, 2007).

The main challenge of the development of the C1D1 District lies in how to reconnect the existing cultural and industrial heritages with the new creation. With the concepts of the creative city, this study explores the cultural and industrial heritage of the Western District and its surrounding areas. To create a new composition and structure, which contains rich cultural experiences and convenient living functions, the concepts including Oriental Cloud Platform, City's Living Room, 3D Catalog, and Cultural and Industrial Link are proposed.

1.1 The Great Future of Taipei City

An innovative design has proven to be a fundamental approach to reach the goal of rendering cities more livable, aesthetic, attractive, and competitive. The World Design Capital designation is held biennially to celebrate and present the success of cities that have applied design as a tool to improve general city life. Through showcasing a designated city and its design approaches of enhancing economic growth, innovation, quality of life and social interaction, an international network is created for sharing innovative design programs and strategies between developed countries and emerging economies.

In November 2013 Taipei City was announced as World Design Capital 2016 with the core concept of 'Adaptive City'. Taipei City will be the fifth Design Capital following Torino in Italy, Seoul in Korea, Helsinki in Finland, and Cape Town in South Africa. The theme 'Adaptive City – Design in Motion insists that Taipei City should become a city that applies design thinking to urban development with limited resources, and to continue to demonstrate innovative vitality. The theme also contains the core spirit of being people-oriented that aims to enable Taipei City to be a city of sustainable development with respect to life quality and health, ecological sustainability, smart living and urban regeneration (Wu, 2013). Reflecting the theme of Adaptive City and utilizing the approaches of reconnecting and representing culture and humanity, the development of the C1D1 District shows a significant and distinct opportunity to turn the Western District into a new city center of cultural, technological and industries innovation.

1.2 The C1D1 District as the New Core of Taipei City

The C1D1 District is located on the main Gate to Taipei City, as well as in the central part of the Western District, which was the origin of Taipei City (Fig. 1). This area has accumulated the most abundant historical and cultural heritage of Taipei. However, as the focus of city development transferred to the Eastern District, the Western District has declined for 30 years. For the development of the Taipei Station and its surrounding area, the C1D1 District was designated as high-rise building block in 2011. It was planned to develop shopping malls, offices for international headquarters, international hotels, as well as other cultural and leisure facilities. The main challenge of the development of the C1D1 District lies in how to reconnect the existing cultural and industrial heritages with the new creation to recall the memories of the Western District, and to lead the C1D1 District to turn into a new core of Taipei City.

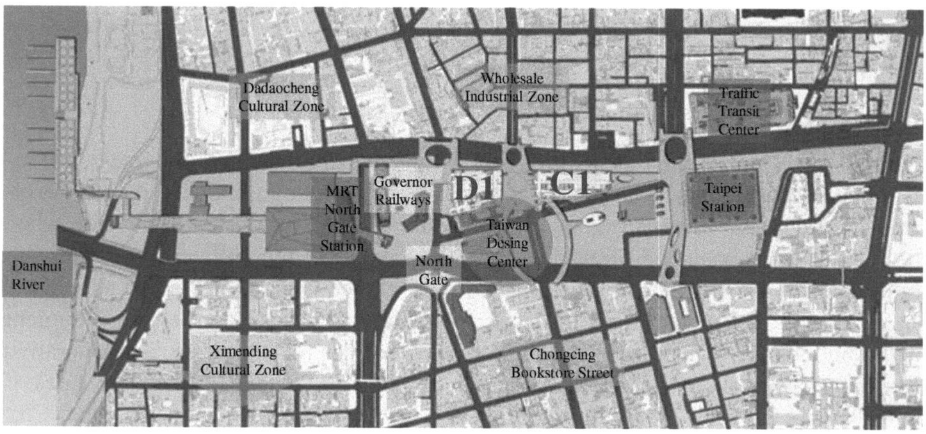

Fig. 1. The C1D1 District and its surrounding area

2 Exploring Heritage for City Innovation

2.1 Heritage and Memories from a City

The term 'heritage' contains many complex implications. It originally was applied to the aspect of the preservation of monuments and historical buildings. In the cultural arena, heritage is used in describing material forms such as monuments, historical or architectural remains and objects on display in museums; or immaterial forms such a philosophy, traditions and art in their manifestations, the celebration of great events or personalities in history, distinct ways of life, and education as expressed through literature and folklore (Herbert, 1989: 10-11, Nuryanti, 1996: 251, Zepple and Hall, 1992). Heritage is a mode of cultural production in the present that has resource to the past, as well as a specific way interpreting and utilizing bygone times that link individuals to a larger collective (Kirshenblatt-Gimblett, 1998: 7). In this sense heritage is what we select in the present for contemporary purposes and it helps define the meanings of culture.

Through heritage of a place, people's memories are aroused and mediated presentations that utilize a variety of media including tangible or intangible cultural forms.

As peoples' memories are organized around objects and particular spaces, through the process of perceiving and remembering, people perceive the world they live in, shape their comprehension and knowledge about the world and transfer to the following generations. The collective memory theory by Halbwachs (1992) provides insight into how people create expressions of collective meanings when encounter with particular objects through common experiences. As collective memories plays as the basis for all memories, people's reconstruction of the past must launch from the shared content of collective memory (Crane, 2006: 104). These notions illustrate the close interrelations between heritage, collective meanings and memories of a city. Therefore before carrying out the development project for the C1D1 District, it is crucial to explore the heritage and culture of the Western District in order to develop creative guidelines for the project.

2.2 Cultural and Industrial Heritage of the Western District

Taipei City as one of the oldest cities in Taiwan has experienced and witnessed flourishing and prosperous development. Since three centuries ago, Taipei City has developed from a rural to an international metropolis. Taipei City started to develop when the Qing Empire occupied Taiwan in 1709. In the end of the 19th century, following traditional Chinese urban format, Taipei City developed with a north-south axis in the square shape. Taipei City encompassed four key categories of urban development including temples for god worship, schools and colleges for education, administrative offices for political control, and street and industrial areas extended from five gates of the city (Fig. 2). From 1895 until 1945, Taiwan was occupied by Japan. Taipei City thus experienced another stage of modern development under the attempt of Japanese colonization (Fig. 3).

Fig. 2. Taipei City in the Qing Dynasty

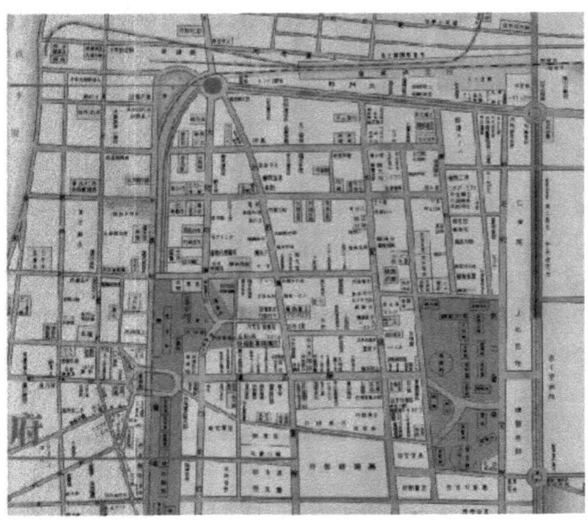

Fig. 3. Taipei City during 1895 and 1945

During the period of Japanese colonization in the Western District Japanese government constructed a large number of classic western-style buildings including the Office of the President and other administrative offices, theaters, hospitals, bank and post office, etc. These became the most important cultural and industrial heritage of the Western District, such as the Taiwan Governor Railways Buildings and the Taipei Post Office (Fig. 4), the North Gate (Fig. 5), Dadaocheng, etc. The facades of these buildings and the human-scale open spaces created classic and historical atmosphere of the Western District and formed a unique image of the core area of Taipei City.

In 1945, Taiwan was taken over by China, when the Qing Dynasty was overthrown and the Republic of China was established. From the 40s to the 60s, the Western District played the role as the Central Business District (CBD) of Taipei City. As the most bustling and flourishing area of the Western District, the Ximending was the first pedestrian precinct in Taipei City (Fig. 6). Chongcing Bookstore Street was an important showcase for Taiwan's publishing industry (Fig. 7). The bookstores also fulfilled the needs for people's cultural lives and leisure activities. The Wholesale Industrial Zone playing as a wholesale distribution center of Taipei City also presents a unique type of industrial heritage (Fig. 8).

Fig. 4. Taipei Post Office

Fig. 5. The North Gate

Fig. 6. Ximending in the 1950s

Fig. 7. Chongcing Bookstore Street

Fig. 8. Wholesale Industrial Zone

2.3 Loss of Memories of the Western District

From the 70s, the CBD of Taipei City transferred from the Western district to the Eastern District due to the establishment of the new Taipei City Hall, 101Tower, and several Cultural and Creative Industrial Parks. Even though the Western District still played an important role with respect to traffic function, its prosperity declined owing to the absence of an appropriate and effective development plan. During the past decades Western District lost the image inspired from cultural and industrial heritage due to two main reasons. On the one hand the development of subway and underground shopping malls led people to travel around Western District through moving from one functional point to the other by capturing traffic signal and modern commercial information without sensing the image and characteristics of the place. On the other hand certain historical architecture and open space were turned down for urban renewal. As a result people gradually lost the memories of the Western District.

3 Concepts for Developing the C1D1 District

From the perspectives of global competition, the most powerful competitive strength of an international city comes from its unique value of historical and cultural resources driven from land use and people's living content. In this sense, the living memory, cultural, and industrial heritage altogether formulate the unique cultural authenticity and identity of a city. These are the most crucial and significant conditions for becoming a great city. To reconnect cultural and industrial heritage with the development of the C1D1 District, four concepts are proposed as follows.

3.1 Oriental Cloud Platform

Chinese culture as one of the oldest cultures in the world plays a significant role among oriental cultures including Chinese culture, Japanese culture, Indian culture, and other cultures of Asian countries. The most significant philosophy and connotations of oriental culture are integration, multiplication, complexity, harmony and interweaving. As we try to apply these implications on urban planning, it is crucial to integrate and locate physical construction with virtual space implying humanity and cultural meanings. In oriental architecture, intermediary space such as entrance, lobby, porch, corridor and yard all play the role as space intermediate to harmoniously connect variant practical structures and functional spaces. Based on this oriental space philosophy, architecture is integrated into environment and nature with harmony, coherence and flexibility. Cloud as a mega natural body with Oriental cultural significations implies future anticipation and imagination. The Oriental Cloud Platform as the core concept for the development of the C1D1 District aims to integrate variant architecture, traffic zones and open space, and to fulfill multiple urban functions through an intermediary space.

3.2 City's Living Room

The raid tempo of contemporary city life makes it crucial to provide a space for people to calm down from tense city lives for contemplation. With the idea of regarding a city as a house, providing a living room for a city would be very crucial for people to interact and communicate within this public open space with the practical functions of transportation, shopping, and with cultural functions. Based on the concept of Oriental Cloud Platform, the concept of City's Living Room is a practical architectural approach to create a mega public space that allows citizens and international tourists to interact, communicate, and to be fulfilled with commercial functions by shopping spaces and facilities and with cultural facilities such as museums, theaters and other leisure facilities (Fig. 9, Fig. 10).

Fig. 9. The image of City's Living Room

Fig. 10. The open space of the C1D1

3.3 3D Catalog

With the consideration that the C1D1 District is located on the main Gate to the Taipei Station, the 3D Catalog is created to present a complete list of cultural, industrial, artistic, technological and living aesthetic content of the Western District and Taipei City. The practical forms of the 3D Catalog include exhibition in the public open spaces, digital signage, and characterized architectural elements, etc. More than providing road signs, travel guide or city introduction, the 3D Catalog introduces the abundant cultural and industrial content of Taipei City through multiple forms. Particularly when being settled in the C1D1 District as the main gate to Taipei City, the 3D Catalog becomes a powerful instrument to reinforce international tourists' image of Taipei City. This will be an efficient approach to create the brand of Taipei City.

3.4 Cultural Link and Industrial Link

In order to connect the heritage of the Western District with the new creation of the C1D1 District, the concept of cultural link and industrial link is proposed (Fig. 11). Focusing on the Taiwan Governor Railways Buildings and the Taipei Post Office, the North Gate, the Dadaocheng Cultural Zone, and the Ximending Cultural Zone, the cultural link is based on the development of the Museum Cluster of the North Gate. In the west end of the Museum Cluster of the North Gate, the Cultural Corridor is created to connect with the Dadaocheng Cultural Zone (Fig. 12). Within the Museum Cluster of the North Gate, the Fashion and Digital Exhibition Hall is developed to connect with Ximending Cultural Zone and representing its cultural characteristic (Fig. 13). On the other hand, the industrial link is based on the development of the Taiwan Design Center. In the Center, the Cultural and Creative Industry Bookstore is created for gathering multiple shops on Chongcing Street. Moreover, the Museum of Crafts and Cultural Creative Industry is developed to facilitate the social and professional education on cultural and creative industries. The Cultural and Creative Workshop is developed as the incubators for assisting creative designers and business.

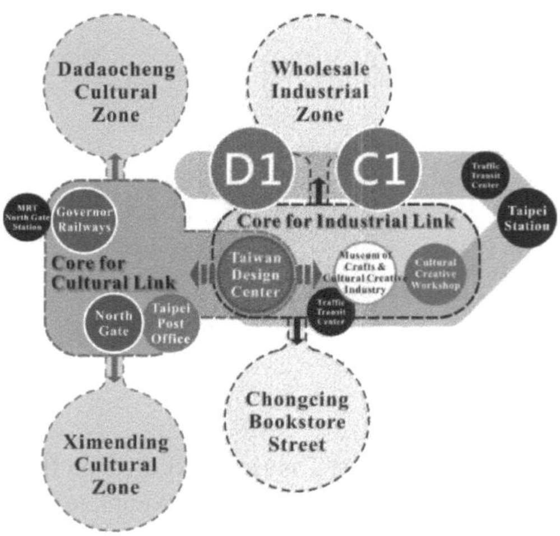

Fig. 11. Diagram of Cultural Link and Industrial Link

Fig. 12. The Cultural Corridor

Fig. 13. The Fashion and Digital Exhibition Hall

4 Conclusion

Creative design with culture and heritage has proven to be fundamental approach to reach the goal of rendering cities more livable, aesthetic, attractive, and competitive. Characterized local culture and rich historical heritage have been regarded as the first priority and main consideration for city innovation. These notions reflect the close interrelations between heritage, collective meanings and memories of a city. The main challenge of the development of the C1D1 District of Taipei City thus lies in how to reconnect the existing cultural and industrial heritages with the new creation via integrating urban space, place characteristics, cultural atmosphere and industrial potential. To respond to challenge successfully, it is crucial to re-explore the heritage and culture of the Western District with contemporary perspectives. The 'Oriental Spirit' is inspired from the re-examining and re-thinking the contemporary implications of the heritage of the Western District. Based on this core theme, the concept of Oriental Cloud Platform, City's Living Room, 3D Catalog, and Cultural Link and Industrial Link are proposed. These unique and innovative concepts provide guidelines for the D1D1 District to develop into a new core of the Taipei City

References

1. Andersson, D.E., Andrsson, A.E., Mellander, C.: Handbook of Creative Cities. Edward Elgar Pub., Cheltonham (2013)
2. Cooke, P., Zazzeretti, L. (eds.): Creative Cities, Cultural Clusters and Local Economic Development. Edward Elgar Pub., Cheltonham (2007)
3. Crane, S.A.: The conundrum of ephemerality: time, memory, and museums. In: Macdonald, S. (ed.) A Companion to Museum Studies. Blackwell, Oxford (2006)
4. Halbwachs, M.: On Collective Memory. In: Coser, L.A. (ed. and trans.). University of Chicago Press, Chicago (1992)
5. Herbert, D.T.: Leisure trends and the heritage market. In: Herbert, D.T., Prentice, R.C., Thomas, C.J. (eds.) Heritage Sites: Strategies for Marketing and Development. Avebury, Aldershot (1989)

6. Kirshenblatt-Gimblett, B.: Destination Culture: Tourism, Museums, and Heritage. University of California Press, Berkeley (1998)
7. Landry, C.: The Creative City: A Toolkit for Urban Innovators, 2nd edn. Routledge, London (2008)
8. Landry, C.: The Origins & Futures of the Creative City. Comedia, UK (2012)
9. Nuryanti, W.: 'Heritage and postmodern tourism'. Annals of Tourism Research 23(2), 249–260 (1996)
10. Wu, I.: City of Taipei announced as World Design Capital 2016 (2013), `http://www.taipeidesign.org.tw/en/about.aspx?type=2` (accessed November 22, 2013)
11. Zeppel, H., Hall, C.M.: Review: art and heritage tourism. In: Weiler, B., Hall, C.M. (eds.) Special-Interest Tourism. Belhaven Press, London (1992)

Analysis of Application of Digital Archives to Value-Added Design in Cultural Creative Products

Chi-Hsien Hsu[1], Robert Chen[2], and Rungtai Lin[3]

[1] Department of Product and Media Design, Fo Guang University
Yilan County 26247, Taiwan
[2] Faculty of Art, Design and Humanities, De Montfort University
Leicester LE1 9BH, United Kingdom
[3] Graduate School of Creative Industry Design, National Taiwan University of Arts
New Taipei City 22058, Taiwan
assah16@gmail.com, RChen1@dmu.ac.uk, rtlin@ntua.edu.tw

Abstract. With the development of technology, we see more and more possibilities in the methods of conservation and application for traditional culture. Currently, the content in the data base of digital archives information in Taiwan is quite extensive and versatile. It is necessary to study future applications to add to its value. The purpose of this study explored the issue and procedure of value-added design on the basis of digital archives transformed into cultural creative. The research includes two phases. In the first phase, we had interviews with experts exploring the current application issues of digital archives in the design fields. By this way, we created the transforming model by collecting theories and principles of design and combining the experts' opinions. In the second phase, we carried out the design and application to review the possibility of digitally archived cultural instruments as applied to the design.

Keywords: Digital Archives, Cultural Creative Products.

1 Introduction

With changing customers' demands and perceptions, the consumer market advances in an era of experience and aesthetic economics. The distinctness of local culture and the structure of innovation-knowledge become the national core competency. Advanced countries already show their competitive edge which is based on technology and with designs and innovations that have added value through culture and aesthetics. Hence, activities and products related to the culture are gradually being deemed as a profitable commodity, which causes the culture to be commercialized and industrialized [1]. The phenomenon offers an opportunity of the development of cultural and creative industries. The UNESCO [2] being convinced that cultural products have both economic and cultural value, and through cultural embodiment and heritage, become a vehicle for cultural identity, value and meaning.

From the perspective of cultural and creative application, the design of cultural creative products must not only satisfy consumer needs but more importantly, through

P.L.P. Rau (Ed.): CCD/HCII 2014, LNCS 8528, pp. 731–742, 2014.

the product form, transmit cultural heritage and manifest culturally distinctive aesthetics. Since the latter half of the 20th century, content-based cultural and creative industries have become a highly value-added market because of unique regional cultures and diverse creativity applications. As cultural and creative industry is the trend of economic development of many countries, the distinctive native cultural features and prosperous digital archives information of cultural instruments in Taiwan are of great value.

Conventional cultural documents are often limited by factors such as difficulties in preservation and sharing. However, with the development of technology, we see more and more possibilities in the methods of conservation and application for traditional culture. Digital archives are becoming more developed and common. Current digital archives in Taiwan are increasingly abundant and diverse, and their application and value-added have become noteworthy. This study examined value-added designs resulting from the transformation of digital archives into cultural creative.

2 Digital Archives and Cultural Creative Design

Industries are the driving force behind the development of cultural creativity, and added cultural value can result in innovative value in goods or services. The innovation and application of information technology and the internet have created a new industry in digital content. The Taiwan e-Learning and Digital Archives Program (2008-2012) established the Union Catalog of E-Learning and Digital Archives Program platform to showcase digital media such as digitalized images and audio-video files in the fields of humanities and nature thereby also establishing a rich database of information. Moreover, through international information system that crosses disciplines and organizations, the preservation and innovation of cultural assets and academic research and teaching application can be pursued [3].

2.1 Taiwan e-Learning and Digital Archives Program

Innovations and applications of information technologies and the internet facilitate the emergence of the digital content industry. With the continuous promotion of the "Taiwan e-Learning and Digital Archives Program" (2008-2012), Taiwan, in addition to the digital preservation and innovation of important cultural assets, advances open learning resources and equal learning opportunities, and with the integration of information technology and humanities, promotes industrial and economic development [3] (Figure 1). Through the transformation of information technology and the establishment of digital archives, as well as through reorganization and innovation, the basis of industrial development was built. Since applications of digital archive materials have become more diverse, a variety of business models have gradually been developed. And in order to integrate the content of digital archives into industry, education and the humanistic and social development, the "Taiwan e-Learning and Digital Archives Commercial Application Competition" was started in 2006, the purpose of the contest is the promotion of value-added applications of digital archives, highlighting the value of Taiwan's diverse and rich digital archives that invigorate Taiwan's cultural creative design capabilities and create business opportunities.

Fig. 1. Digital Taiwan - Culture & Nature [4]

2.2 The Application of Digital Archives

The development of digital technology has affected everyday life and changed conventional learning and research methods. From conceptualization to implementation, digital archives or digital museums have developed rapidly with advances in information technology. Many information technology significant terms have appeared, such as electronic museum, virtual museum and web museum, indicating that museums and archives are digitizing. Without time and space limitations, such digital archives are available to readers globally. Furthermore, cooperation with schools and community cultural organizations results in value-added information in the digital archives thereby achieving creative learning through their use [5]. Through restructuring and innovation, digital archives established by information technology and storage have become the foundation for developing digital content industries.

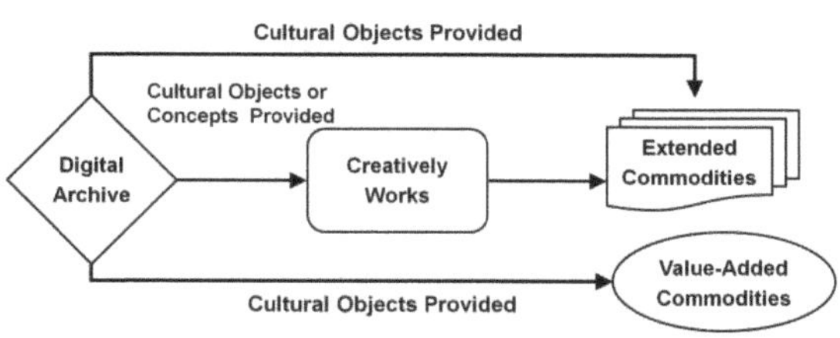

Fig. 2. The application of digital archives in digital content industry [6]

With increasing diversified applications of digital archives materials, a variety of business models have also emerged. Therefore, the use of digital archives and creative designs of the traditional cultural characteristics are turned into cultural creative products, which provide the source of creative design. Hsiang, Chen, Chen and Kuo [7] divided commercial models of digital archive application industries into five categories, namely (1)value-added digital content industry; (2)integrative products; (3)value-added cultural creative products and cultural innovation industry; (4)added content service for digital products; and (5)digital software technology and service. However, Hsiang, Chen, Cheng and Wei [8] also pointed out that digital archives cannot be completely and directly adopted, but through the application of cultural characteristics, story themes, anecdotal allusions and even the inspirations of the artist, value-added goods are produced (see Figure 2). For designers, a touchable product is designed with innovation by scratching elements of cultural characteristic.

2.3 Design Theories Relevant to Cultural Creative Products

Thanks to the improvement of technology, it is easier to implement innovation. In the future industrial design should concern aesthetics of humanity. Norman [9] also suggested that a successful design should consider the suitability, practicability and aesthetics of the product in which emotion is the most important factor. The design concept for emotion can be accomplished by the aesthetic value of the product. As a result, the intention of the design gradually focuses on humanity with consideration of the consumers' feelings when they use the product.

Designers often cleverly create innovative designs in some sort of logical thinking, and understanding the relationship between seemingly unrelated things. However, in order to run a business constantly, designers and producers rely not on sudden inspirations but on well-organized systems of creativity [10]. Tam, Au, and Taylor [11] have concluded that Planning and Collecting, Conceptualizing Ideas, Synthesizing Ideas and Evaluation are four common stages in the design process of Hong Kong fashion designers. Tim Brown [12], the CEO of IDEO, has ever mentioned the design thinking process is better thought of as a system of overlapping spaces rather than a sequence of orderly steps and there are three spaces to keep in mind: inspiration, ideation, and implementation. In summary, the four phases of inspiration, ideation, synthesizing idea and implementation can be the core concept of product design as the designer wants to do a cultural creative design. Furthermore, Stage-Gate System, designed by Cooper [13], is one of the tools of management during the process of new product development. Hung [14] added the phase of "transformation of cultural creative concepts" to the Stage-Gate System. They improved the development process applicable to cultural creative design. In this phase, cultural elements and innovation concepts should be reviewed, reselected and reconstituted. It declares the review of cultural creative concept should be the checkpoint in the development process of cultural creative product.

A good understanding of the cultural attributes will benefit articulating the context between the culture and product design and therefore accelerate concept development. Based on the cultural creative product design framework and process of Hsu, Lin, & Lin [15], the cultural creative product is designed using scenario and semantics approaches. And according to literature review and expert opinions, design guidelines are developed based on the research of consumers' needs, cultural content and design theories. Finally a ten step practical design process divided into four phases was provided to design a cultural creative product. The four phases are: identification (telling a situation), investigation (setting an objective), interaction (writing an analysis), and implementation (designing a product).

3 Research Method

The research includes two phases. In the first phase, we had interviews with experts exploring the current application issues of design fields after the digital archives in Taiwan was online. By this way, we created the transforming model by collecting theories and principles of design and combining the experts' opinions. In the second phase, we carried out the design and application to review the possibility of digitally archived cultural instruments as applied to the design.

This exploration is to build up the model of the transformation of cultural creative design integrating consumers' expectations and design behavior through the previous studies [11-14], the amendment of Hsu, Lin, & Lin's [15] steps six to ten of the design procedure of cultural creative products, the explorations in regards to cultural creative products derived from the ceramic pot and poetry [16-18], and Norman's (2004) three levels of emotional design: visceral, behavioral and reflective level. Having analyzed and synthesized a literature review, we constructed a model for transferring cultural elements into product design. The five design implementation steps are: (A) analyzing the culture; (B) connecting the relationships; (C) developing the concept; (D) examining the context; (E) completing the design. Steps A, B and C refer to the processes which reciprocally connect the cultural elements and the product. Steps D and E address the rationality and embodiment of the product and maturity of the transformation of the cultural elements.

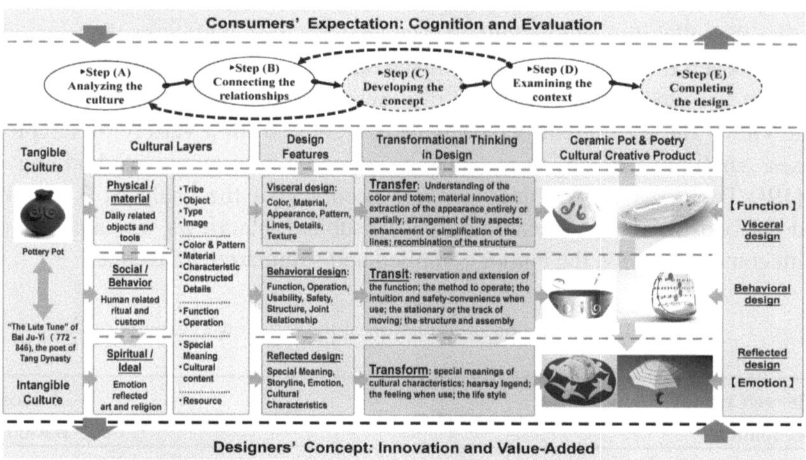

Fig. 3. The transformation model for cultural creative product design

When we design a cultural creative product, we must analyze its property first in order to discover the reasonable connection between cultural elements and the product in each culture. During the design procedure much uncertainty exists which is hard to control by designers. The "design features" and "transformation of design consideration" in Figure 3 help us not only to understand and explore the cultural elements but also to consider the application scope of a cultural creative product.

We will be able to design a product in which there's cultural transformation of application and product design with cultural elements instead of merely copying the appearance of relics or totem. This model is a reference for designers which can lead logically to an adequate design transformation and expose the cultural elements properly no matter whether the design is transformed from a tangible or intangible culture.

4 Expert Interviews and Data Analysis

Based on the study prupose and the exploring results of the references, we gradually formulated interview questions and adopted semi-structured in-depth interiew. Formal interviews were conducted in the inviewee's laboratory or studio. Prior to the interview, the purpose of the interview was explained again and the interviewees were provided with interview question information on paper. The interviewer is to explain and clarify the meaning of the questions one by one to ensure that the respondents gained a clear understanding of the interview questions (Table 1). During the actual interview, after the interviewee replied, the interviewer is to continue to ask for more details regarding the responses. The interview is to use a digital voice recorder and camera to completely record the whole interview process.

For the content of the recorded interview content, a third person is to objectively compile them verbatim, and the content is subsequently re-compiled by the author. Due to the different interview subjects, interview time varies from 30 minutes to an hour. For the reliability and validity of data analysis, this study uses the triangulation method approach to ensure the quality of the data analysis. Triangulation method is a method that uses more than one point of view to observe the goal to obtain a more accurate view. These different perspectives can come from a variety of samples and databases, multiple investigators, and a variety of research methodology and theory[19]. To increase the objectivity and accuracy of the analysis, 3 researchers worked on focusing on the research purposes, subject interviews, and analysis of the verbatim content. Finally, the author compiled and summarized the data.

Table 1. Background introduction of the intervewed experts

Interviewee/Current Occupation	Field of Expertise	Years of Experience	Education Background
A/ Professor	Craft product design, wood craft, aesthetics, art theory and education	25 years of design education and research	PhD
B/ Assistant Professor	Product design and development, pleasure product design and research, model semantic research , toy design	20 years of design practice, education and research.	PhD
C/ Company Director	Craft design, cultural product design	8 years of design practice	Master
D/ Company Director	Product design, graphic design, creative design	10 years of design practice	Master

The 4 interviees of the study all had contact with or purchased cultural creative products. They also instructed students and used digital archive sites to conduct cultural creative product design. The intervewees shared their views on how what roles the Taiwan Digital Archives website in the cultural creative product design applications. Their interview opinions were compiled as follows:

1. Network information is currently well-developed; a lot of digital archives and digital data storage websites are available, and relevant information can easily be found. These sites also allow cultural resources to be not limited to a few people, so these sites are beneficial to the popularization of cultural knowledge (interviewee A, C).
2. Do not be one-sidedly impressed with cultural elements. Do not engage in design immediately after seeing the cultural elements of the image and picture or after hearing some stated opinions. The Digital Archives picture is taken from a photographer's point of view. Even if you can gather a wide range of angles with many different types of pictures, its effect for inspiration of design is still very limited (interviewee A, C).
3. Some digital archives are built adequately but some information is a little too complicated. Otherwise, only pictures are available without much explanation. When designing, the problem that designers usually encounter is that they cannot only use the data of the digital archives as a source of inspiration. The designers would like to know more content such as the background information, the history, and the uses of the antiques. Designers need to search in depth and summarize the data, actually come into contact with the antiques or personally experience the ceremony process. I believe they would have many more mature design ideas (interviewee A, C, D).
4. If the time for design is urgent, then designers can rapidly search for the data from the Digital Archives Web or Internet. These sites can temporarily help. However, the usefulness depends on the adequacy of the database (interviewee A).
5. In this Internet era, the amount of information is more than enough, but finding a way to interpret the information is crucial. Most current digital archives put a lot of pictures and information on the site. However, follow-up organization and compiling is required. Through analysis and integration of information, information can be effectively transformed and applied so they can become useful knowledge. Many fields have been engaging in discussion. However, in the application of design, the issues are not that clear (interviewee B, D).
6. Digital Archives websites seem to use the same method to compile artifacts. However, not all artifacts are suitable for organization in the same way. For example, we can hang up clothes to organize them but we cannot do the same thing for sneakers and furniture. Digital Archives should have different classifications according to the different types of artifacts, or have different arrangements and presentations on the web (interviewee D).
7. For promoting the use of the Archives, Taiwan Digital Archives website seems to require more work. When searching for information in general, most people directly search for the site from the search engine on the default homepage such as

Google or Yahoo. People only enter the site when there is a link to the Digital Archives Web site or when they think that the site may have required data. In addition, people often encounter problems when using keywords to search on the digital archives websites and not finding them (interviewee D).

8. Regardless of digital archive website or pictures and data of other network resources, issues on citation of design or copyright disputes require solutions. For some design projects, if the direct explanation is a quote from an artifact, they may have to pay licensing fees or face the issue of subsequent payment. Most companies or designers will want to dodge this issue, the use of cultural elements can only be limited for inspiration or partial usage (interviewee C).

5 Design Practices by Digital Archives

Currently, many design ideas arise gradually in the design field compared to the appearance of functional-orientation decades ago. The thought of design trend is not only in the consideration of product's function and manufacture, but also the focus on cultural heritage and connection, creation of lifestyle, experience of life-taste and the realization of life values. As we are in a period of the prosperous development of cultural and creative industry, the consumer market values the product which contains cultural and aesthetic characteristics.

Through the transformation model for cultural creative product design (Figure 3), the designer endeavors to design experience. As described below, in the actual design, the designer applies Transformational Thinking in Design to the cultural information from digital archives platforms to design different levels of cultural creations and explore the application of value-added designs.

5.1 The Taiwan's Endangered Species Application of the Cultural Creative Product

Designers show great interests for carpentry. They were fascinated after they are exposed to foreign famous wooden toy brand works. For example, the Japanese brand Take-g toy adopted splicing techniques of different colors of woods and showed excellent role characteristics. The Danish brand Kay Bojese provided traditional toys played by Danish children with new life and new fun. As a result, in the process of becoming exposed to cultural creative products, designers also became interested and were inspired to produce wooden playing objects that represented Taiwanese style and features. This design exemplifies was awarded honorable mention in the 2011 Creative Toy Design Competition of Maxim Enterprise. The design process are as follows (see Figure 4):

1. Analyzing the culture: Taiwan designers start thinking about what cultural features can be made into wooden objects. Their initial thoughts included gods, animals, and children toys. However, as the acceptance of animal imagery is more popular, animals were chosen as the sources of ideas. Designers first thought about Formosan Black Bear and Black-faced Spoonbill, and browsed the internet at related digital archives for text information and picture data.

2. Connecting the relationships: for animal appearance, some characteristics include the white v shape formed by white hairs on the chest of Formosan Black Bear; Formosan Sika Deer are named for their white plum-like spots on their back; and Formosan rock-monkeys have obvious large reddish brown sports between their two bottoms. Designers want to make functional wooden playing toys, so they focus on the outer features and actions of the animals. They try to think of ideas that can link the characteristics with the product function.
3. Developing the concept: the special features found on the body of animals are transformed to functional office wooden playing objects that allow office workers to enjoy their time at work. The objects used a variety of wooden materials and they were used to make collages of special designs. People can also touch the different wood grains and fulfill their psychological needs of owning a small pet.
4. Examining the context: the designers discuss whether the outer features or actions of the animal can match the set function of the wooden playing object. The designers also want to produce a style similar to the Japanese brand Take-g toy's. However, the production technical capacity is technically insufficient at the moment, and this would be the future working goal.
5. Completing the design: the primary materials of the finished products are rosewood and cedar. Formosan Black Bear playing object can use its strong body and wave its arms to meet the function of lifting objects or placing glasses. Formosan Sika Deer playing objects can use its unique deer antlers as a place to put pens and hang accessories, and the deer head can be used to place post-it notes. Formosan rock-monkey playing objects' long arms can be used for hanging small items, and its mouth is designed with a magnet inside, which can clamp memo pads.

Fig. 4. "Taiwan's endangered species" office playing objects, design by Lin, S. E. (2011)

5.2 The Poetry Application of the Cultural Creative Product

The character is the most important tool to record the history and culture. The Chinese character presents not only the heritage and development of the culture but also the symbol of the traditional esthetics. Literary works as rhymes derived from Chinese character, such as classical poetry, tune, are very touching and worthwhile exploring. Sometimes the wording of Chinese poetry describes concrete articles but other times the feeling hiding behind the articles or circumstances. As a result, the reference information for design will be rich with good understanding of the poetic rhymes. This design was honored by being nominated for the 2012 Taiwan e-Learning and

Digital Archives Application Competition. The design process are as follows (see Figure 5):

1. Analyzing the culture: Chinese literature is full of literati's insights, ideas, and feelings regarding the world. These feelings and thoughts produce many poetic writings that were passed down for many generations. Designers obtained inspiration from the more familiar and common poetic writings, and selected Song dynasty's poet Su, Shih's poetic writings from *Recalling the Old Days at Mianchi*. They tried to feel the atmosphere of the words to design their ideas: "To what can we liken human life? Perhaps to a flying bird's footprints on snow and mud."
2. Connecting the relationships: the meaning of the words is that birds resting on the snow ground and occasionally leave their claw prints. The timing may be a slight instant and the birds immediately fly far away. The designers want to link the idea that the flying birds taking a rest on the snow ground to leave slight claw print marks shortly and then flying away with the action of using a stapler to staple papers.
3. Developing the concept: the mood of the flying birds stepping on the snow mud is integrated with the operation of the stapler. The action of briefly stapling the mark on paper is like that of the flying birds leaving footprints when stepping on snow mud. The appearance of the stapler is the shape of a flying bird. However, the style of the birds was abstract and simplified. The designers made sketches of the design drawing.
4. Examining the context: the designers discuss whether the bird's head should be facing forward or backward and the shape of the wings. These features can affect having the feelings of a flying bird stepping on snow mud and then flying away when the stapler staples the paper in that instant. Also, the features should make the stapler easy to grip and use.
5. Completing the design: the final design decision is a product that integrates the colors of black, gray and white. The colors intend to convey the cultural beauty of Chinese water ink painting. After users finish stapling papers, the stapled marks would be in the shape of the claw. This incorporation of poetry into stationery products allow the products to carry a story-like east literati thinking and feelings.

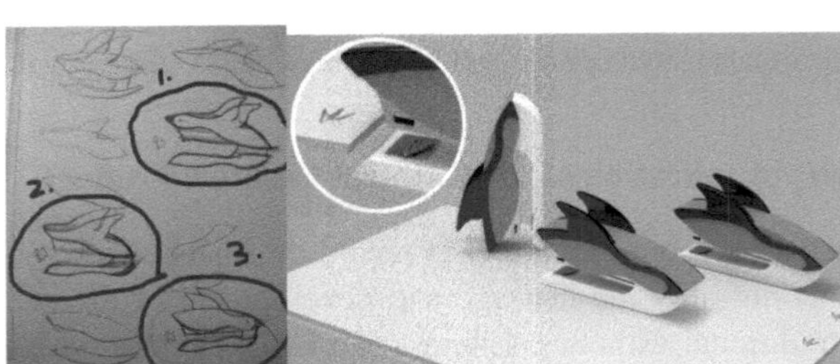

Fig. 5. "A flying bird stepping on snow mud" stapler, design by Lu, Y. (2012)

6 Conclusions and Recommendations

Globalization brings people convenience in life but their localized culture drives people to look for a prosperous quality in their life and mind-set. In cultural creative product design and application, development and innovation are critical for creating products that not only pass on cultural assets and demonstrate cultural aesthetics, but are also practical in daily life so that consumers can once again realize the beauty of traditional culture. Digital Archives websites are conducive to the popularization of cultural knowledge. However, the sites may also lead to controversies related to ownership of intellectual property rights. Currently, the completeness of the various types of digital archive data is different, and the web page presentation effect also differs. When engaging in design, digital archives website is conducive to quick access regarding cultural information and pictures. However, to know more about the background, history, and uses of the artifacts, continuous in-depth search, analysis, and compilation of the cultural context are required. Having an actual access to the artifact in person would be more helpful in inspiring design ideas.

The transformation of digital archives into cultural innovations has become a practice in value-added designs and creations so that through analyzing and exploring product presentation, designers can bring out the cultural significance in their product designs and applications. However, during the process, designers often encounter difficulties in obtaining cultural information, and hence establishing digital archives for cultural relics can help fulfill such needs. Through the design practices based on the transformation model for cultural creative product design, we participated in various competition and had good performance. We expect this innovative learning with digital archives will help to improve the teaching and cultural creative product design. The results of this study can be used as future reference for designers in their value-added application of digital archives and designing cultural creative products or products in other domains.

The unique ethnic cultures in Taiwan and rich diversity of digital cultural archives are not only of historical significance but are also important assets in the development of cultural and creative industries and therefore their creative applications are worthy of further exploration. More in-depth studies on creative design can be conducted to facilitate more unique depth and substance in the development of Taiwan industries.

References

1. Kuo, W.F.: Global Vision of Cultural Policy, 2nd edn., Taipei. Psychological (2009) (in Chinese)
2. UNESCO: Convention on the Protection and Promotion of the Diversity of Cultural Expressions (2005), http://unesdoc.unesco.org/images/0014/001429/142919e.pdf
3. National Science Council: Taiwan e-Learning and Digital Archives Program (2008), http://teldap.tw/en/index.html
4. Digital Taiwan - Culture & Nature (2011), http://culture.teldap.tw/culture/

5. Lin, R., Siao, M.T., Fan, C.H.: Creative Learning Model for Digital Archives - A Case Study of Taiwan Aboriginal Garment. In: 2006 Digital Archives into Teaching Conference, pp. 302–313. National Taiwan University, Taipei (2006) (in Chinese)
6. Hsiang, J., Chen, H.H., Cheng, D.F.: The Forecasting of Digital Archives' Application in Industry. In: 2002 Ministry of Economic Affairs, Department of Industrial Technology, Non-technical Areas of Technology Development Program for Academia Conference, pp. 435–447. Department of Industrial Technology, Ministry of Economic Affairs, Taipei (2002) (in Chinese)
7. Hsiang, J., Chen, H.H., Chen, C.C., Kuo, C.Y.: An Investigation of Business Models for the Cultural Digital Archives Industry. Bulletin of the Library Association of China 75, 63–74 (2005) (in Chinese)
8. Hsiang, J., Chen, H.H., Cheng, D.F., Wei, Y.H.: On the Application of Digital Archives. Journal of Library and Information Studies 2(1), 1–17 (2004) (in Chinese)
9. Norman, D.A.: Emotional Design: Why We Love (or Hate) Everyday Things. Basic, New York (2004)
10. Cheng, C.S.: Good originality, but also need to better management. Suncolor Culture Publishing, Taipei (2007)
11. Tam, A.I., Au, J.S., Taylor, G.: A Theoretic Framework of Factors Influencing Fashion Design in Hong Kong. The Design Journal 11(2), 183–202 (2008)
12. Brown, T.: Design Thinking. Harvard Business Review, 1–10 (June 2008)
13. Cooper, R.G.: Stage-gate Systems: A New Tool for Managing New Products. Business Horizons 33(3), 44–54 (1990)
14. Hung, W.Y.: Management of Originality. In: Summary of Cultural and Creative Industries, 2nd edn., pp. 378–395. Wu-Nan Culture Enterprise, Taipei (2008)
15. Hsu, C.H., Lin, C.L., Lin, R.: A Study of Framework and Process Development for Cultural Product Design. In: Rau, P.L.P. (ed.) IDGD 2011. LNCS, vol. 6775, pp. 55–64. Springer, Heidelberg (2011)
16. Lin, R.: Transforming Taiwan Aboriginal Cultural Features into Modern Product Design: A Case Study of a Cross-Cultural Product Design Model. International Journal of Design 1(2), 45–53 (2007)
17. Hsu, C.H., Yeh, M.L., Lin, P.H., Lin, R.: Representing Traditional Culture - Poetry Applying Elements on Product Design. In: Vink, P. (ed.) Advances in Social and Organizational Factors, pp. 757–766. Taylor and Francis, London (2012)
18. Hsu, C.H., Lin, P.H., Lin, R.: Analysis of Digital Archives Applied to Value-Added Design in Cultural Products. In: 3rd International Service Innovation Design Conference, pp. 279–287. National Cheng Kung University, Tainan (2012)
19. Patton, M.Q.: Qualitative Research & Evaluation Methods, 3rd edn. SAGE Publications, New York (2001)

Cultural Creativity in Design Exhibition – A Case Study of Emotional Effects Experienced by the Audience

Yu-Ju Lin[1,2], Jui-Ping Ma[2], and Jun-Liang Chen[2]

[1] Department of Visual Communication Design,
Taipei College of Maritime Technology
Taipei 25172, Taiwan
[1,2] Graduate School of Creative Industry Design,
National Taiwan University of Arts
Ban Ciao City, Taipei 22058, Taiwan
naralin@mail.tcmt.edu.tw,
{rupm08,freeimage5361}@gmail.com

Abstract. From the past few years, the public and the private sectors have been encouraging the development of culture and creative industries. Many departments of design and visual communication have their graduate exhibitions focused on the concept of culture and creativity. Among them, "Lost Memories" was awarded with the Golden Prize in the annual design exhibition for the new generation. The exhibition was held in Culture and Creative Expo organized by Taipei City Government and received many resonances. This study attempts to use the exhibited images from "Lost Memories" as the sample and via literature review, content analysis, survey-questionnaire and statistical analysis, the images and the corresponding and related theories will be induced and integrated for the subject analysis, which will eventually present an analytical framework of "exhibition content-audience experience." This will explore the contribution of the curator towards the cultural exhibition and provide a further reference for future studies. As a result, it is discovered that the emotional effects experienced by the audience can produce a consistent effect after the book is published by the curator after the exhibition. Between the curator and the audience, the spirit has lasted through the content of the exhibited images. The content of the exhibited images in the cultural exhibition include the concepts of "touching", "adhere to the spirit," "realistic," for which the curator expects the audience to appreciate and to value the traditional craftsmen of the images. A positive influence was achieved. In terms of "liking the overall images and recording of the images in the exhibition", there is a positive effect over "this exhibition has made me experience the insistent spirit of craftsmen in the local industries." This empirical study discovered that the emotional effects experienced by the audience have certainly a significant impact for the situational interpretations of the cultural themes.

Keywords: Cultural and Creative, Design Exhibition, Audience Experience, Emotional Effects.

P.L.P. Rau (Ed.): CCD/HCII 2014, LNCS 8528, pp. 743–752, 2014.

1 Introduction

Taiwan has gradually become more industrialized. This change to the industrial structure has caused the rapid demise of various local and uniquely Taiwanese industries that relied primarily on selling traditional handicrafts. Local industries gave rise to creative cultural industries and, thus, the preservation of local industries has become a crucial process in the strengthening of creative cultural industries and the unification of national identity. In response to this trend, college-level design students have become increasingly focused on learning and implementing the information provided in cultural creativity courses. Taiwanese government has continually promoted the transformation of local industries into local creative cultural industries in an attempt to create an image of a "Cultural Taiwan" and a "Creative Taiwan."The forefathers of Taiwan created handmade traditional handicrafts that are rich in character and regionally diverse. The creation of these crafts, however, largely depended upon master tradesmen who verbally and physically passed on their skills to the next generation. Without successors, these crafts are lost to history with the death of each master.

Because of global trends in the 1980s, Taiwan began applying original equipment manufacturer (OEM)-based production patterns, which are a manufacturing process based on quantity and low cost. This shift threatened the survival of numerous local industries that featured handicrafts or manual labor. In the 1990s, governments worldwide began promoting cultural and creative industries. To meet economic needs and international standards, the Taiwan government also began proposing policies and raising concerns that stressed the preservation of Taiwan's local cultural and creative industries. This international atmosphere of valuing the development of cultural and creative industries has led to increased regulations and supportive measures aimed at preserving traditional handicrafts industries that are nearly extinguished. Taiwan considers the continuation and preservation of local industries that employ handicraft or manual labor as the primary skill or technique as a crucial topic in the sustainable development of cultural- and creative-oriented industrialization. We examined the observation experiences, cultural cognition, and attitudes toward the curated exhibit Lost Memories among Taipei-area students majoring in design-related fields.

2 Literature Review

2.1 Experience

Experience is obtained from the interaction between the mentality of a person with a certain event. During the process of gaining experience, the senses, feelings, mentality, and behavior of a person constantly interact with the surrounding environment. People feel emotions and gain empirical knowledge from these interactions, thus creating personal experiences. Pine II and Gilmore (1999) proposed a construct for consumer experience: (a) consumer participation—divided into active and passive participants; (b) the correlation between consumer status and environmental status—divided into absorption and immersion [1]. These two major dimensions form four types of experiences: (a)aesthetically pleasing experiences that compel consumers to enter a space, sit down, and fully appreciate the surroundings; (b) an escape from reality that allows consumers to become immersed in specific activities; (c)educational experiences that require active participation from the consumers similar to the level of participation involved in escape-from-reality experiences; (d)similar to aesthetics, entertainment is a passive experience. When customers are happy, they are not required to be active, but are merely responsive to the experience.

2.2 Knowledge and Attitude

Cognition refers to the understanding of human behavior and the analysis of mental processes and memory structure. Therefore, cognition is the knowledge and opinions that people have and form following internal information processing that analyzes the stimulations resulting from the messages conveyed by external events and objects. Cognition is a process where people attach meaning to the environment, organize and interpret objects and events, and obtain information by using the senses [2]. Cultural awareness is a psychological process where humans, through the use of their senses, create various spiritual and material activities for a particular survival mode or lifestyle and subsequently develop recognition and understanding [3]. Therefore, regarding the exhibition, the attitude of the audience must be understood. The message conveyed through the contents of the exhibition illicit a certain response from the audience. Through the rationalization and emotional recognition processes undertaken by the audience, an attitude toward the viewing is evoked. Specifically, the cognition aspect refers to the understanding and evaluation of the audience regarding the content of the viewing experience, and the emotional aspect signifies the degree to which the audience enjoyed the viewing experience.

2.3 Cultural Exhibition and Curatorial

Cultural demonstrations, such as craft exhibitions, often involve the collective demonstration and display of craft objects or non-art objects. The purpose of these demonstrations is orientated toward knowledge building and the collection of research. Burcaw stated that a display is where objects are arranged in a designated fashion with explanatory details to achieve the purpose of communicating with the viewer through a public exhibition [4]. Therefore, display is an art form and interpretation outcome, where objective display skills are used to enable the communication between the audience and the implications and charm of ancient artifacts. The exhibitor must have professional and technical knowledge regarding the designation of a theme, the presentation method of an exhibition, media promotion and application, and marketing strategies [5]. Cultural exhibitions are an ongoing process. During the process of cultural participation, people internalize particular cultural objectives and values. Subsequently, the cultural similarities between individual people are emphasized, and a sense of belonging to a certain cultural group is instilled. Regarding the curatorial tasks of creating a modern exhibition, how an exhibitor should present an exhibition has become the most critical topic in the discussion of cultural curatorial activities.

2.4 Emotional Effects

Emotions are the positive and negative attitudes produced by internal changes and external manifestations towards objective things or events. There are several reasons for causing the emotions. When people get in touch with external things, several responding behaviors are produced. These responsive behaviors are commonly named as emotions and feelings. Reviewing the study of Maslow (1943), Jordan (1999) proposed the hierarchy of needs theory, classifying the product characteristics that people require into three hierarchies: functionality, ease-of-use, and pleasure [6]. Norman (2004) contended that in addition to functionality, emotion was a key element of products; Based on the classic ABC (Antecedent, Behavior, Consequences) model employed in psychology, Norman classified emotional designs into three hierarchies: instinct (the pattern and texture of the product appearance), behavior (product functionality), and reflection (individual feelings and opinions). Norman explained that emotion is critical in everyday decision-making. Furthermore, hierarchical design principles increasingly influence the design and service industries, which are gradually emphasizing customization and integration; thus, emotional designs are the key to future industrial development [7]. Lin (2007) expanded this framework, incorporating the perspectives of Norman to classify the elements needed to design cultural and creative products into three levels that affect consumers: the extrinsic (e.g., color, texture, shape, and ornamentation), the middle or behavioral (e.g., function, workability, and usability), and intrinsic or psychological (e.g., story, emotion, and cultural content) levels [8]. Fig.1. shows a comparison of Maslow's hierarchy of needs and Jordan's hierarchy of user needs; we also considered the product design factors proposed by Norman and Lin. As times change, people's needs are also changing with the changing of time. Apart from the functions of products, they also need emotional manifestations. The content of the exhibition follows the same reasoning. Not only the technique and the theme are considered, but also the spiritual or emotional interactions with the viewers.

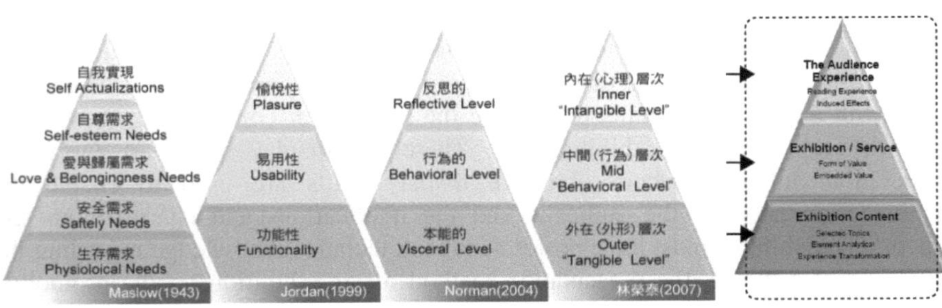

Fig. 1. Referential chart of the hierarchical theory applied on the exhibition model

2.5 "Lost Memories" Curatorial Content Analysis

The study exhibition was presented using the following four displays: (a) a large monochromatic visual display; (b) craft work; (c) a postcard tower; and (d) a DM design depicting all one hundred crafts. The large visual display was presented using a grayscale color scheme to allow the images to be free from the interference of color. The images presented in the exhibits were established as the focal point to reflect the utmost concentration shown on the faces of the craftsmen. This exhibition emphasizes the connection between people and life and allows viewers to consider profoundly the relationship between cultural value and heritage. The emotionally touching aspect of Taiwanese culture was observed from a humanitarian perspective. By using photographic exhibits and displaying the tools used by craftsmen, real-life scenarios that had disappeared were recreated. These exhibits represented the lifestyles of people working in various industries and professions—elegance of the one hundred crafts. The postcard tower that was constructed encouraged visitors to comment on the exhibition and to directly relay their messages to the traditional master craftsmen by sending a postcard as a sign of support. A master of each trade was filmed and interviewed to produce a DM of the hundred craftsmen. Through the application of aesthetics and imagery, their stories were conveyed using simple graphics and short texts. In addition to visual efficacy, these recordings served to preserve an image of Taiwan that is emotionally touching.

Fig. 2. Exhibition Space (Source: Freeimage Design Studio)

3 Research Methods

3.1 Curatorial Content Planning and Study Sample

This study was based on the "Lost Memories" exhibition and supplemented by a book jointly written by four graduates of Furen University titled, the search for the one hundred crafts – the story of four youngsters and 100 street masters. The exhibition contents primarily comprise the creations of100 local craftsmen and were divided into five categories: (a) Good taste: traditional local food and the relationship between food and people, events, time, place, and objects. (b) Refined and useful objects: artifacts related to the production of a livelihood – this category comprises all types of production tools. (c) Art and culture: artifacts created to facilitate the cultivation of the mind, to be used during leisure time, and for personal collections. (d) Traditional customs and rituals: artifacts created for the purposes of practicing etiquette or cultural customs, and crafts that were used to decorate architecture. (e) Smart living: tools or artifacts created to assist with eating and drinking, to wear as clothes, to construct shelter, and for transport. Five industries that are significantly in decline are selected, and 20 samples are chosen for the questionnaire design. Students of the department of design and visual communication are sampled. Through questionnaire survey, this study is able to understand the emotional effect experienced by the audience after they visited the cultural exhibition of the traditional art-crafts, in particular to their attention, valuation, and the impact of the image content, so it is able to construct the emotional elements for the images in the cultural exhibition.

This study adopts Likert five-point scale for the questionnaire as to represent the degree of supportiveness to the question or item. The five-point is the following: 1. strongly disagree; 2. Disagree; 3. No comments; 4. Agree; 5. strongly agree. The questionnaires were used to explore and analyze how the work and image arrangements in the curated exhibit, Lost Memories, affected participants based on two aspects: cognition of the viewing experience, attitudes toward the viewing experience, and the degree to which the viewing experience shaped cultural identification. Participants were asked items that were categorized into two categories: (a) the viewing process (items began with "After seeing these photographs, I feel..."), (b) participant overall feelings toward the exhibition (items began with "After seeing these images, I think this exhibition is...").

Table 1. The study sample- Shokunin photos

3.2 The Analytical Model of "Exhibition Content-Audience Experience"

This study has integrated the aforementioned the "exhibition mode of communication" and "hierarchical model reference" and established an analytical model of "exhibition content-audience experience." This model is able to filter the emotional feelings of the audience towards the content of the cultural exhibition and to find out the connection between the curators's transmitted messages. By Exhibition mode of communication, two main activities are proceeded via the communication team – the conveyed message of the exhibition content between the curator and the audience as well as the audience absorption of the messages. Through a series of learning and feelings by the audience in the exhibition, the audience emotional effects are established by understanding the interaction of the implicit and explicit values in the cultural exhibition. This study proposes the analytical model of "exhibition content-audience experience" which is as shown in Fig.3.

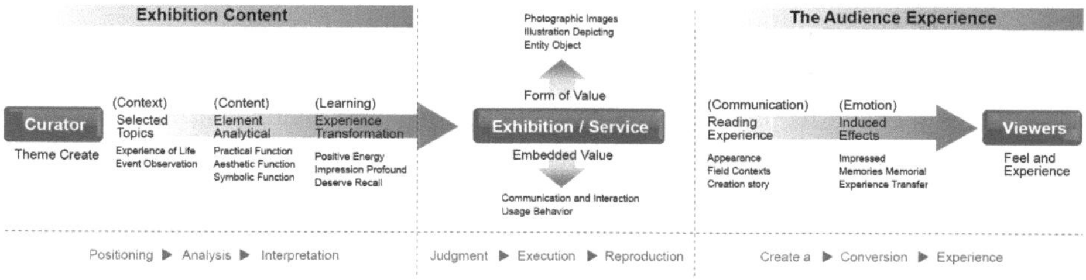

Fig. 3. "Exhibition Content-Audience Experience" analytical framework

What the audience experiences is the conveyed message of the exhibition/service transmitted by the curator, so the audience can have an intensified memory and feelings as well as understanding the connotations behind the images. If the interpersonal connections will be created by story creations, then the stories shall be of much significance, so the audience can feel the deepest emotions of the images; by creating an immersive feeling for the audience, a new sensational experience can be offered.

4 Research Results and Discussion

4.1 Questionnaire Survey

The students majoring in design-related fields were chosen as participants for the following reasons:

- Analysis of the works from this exhibit showed that most of the industries were located in Southern Taiwan and are novel to students from Northern Taiwan;
- The four exhibit curators were Taipei students majoring in design-related fields. Undertaking a curated exhibit of relatively unfamiliar regional crafts that are disappearing from the viewpoint of Northern Taiwanese students could help exhibition attendees in the greater Taipei area to accept and understand the importance of this topic.

These two points were related to the beliefs the curators expressed and the experiences of the exhibit attendees. The focus of this study was to explore whether student cognition and perceptions of the viewing experience that the exhibit was designed to evoke could enhance the cultural identification of students with design-related backgrounds. The initial questionnaires were designed to obtain basic demographic data and were distributed randomly. Students who met the study criterion of having been enrolled in courses in the creative or performance arts fields were provided with a follow-up questionnaire. These were distributed to 180 students.

Overall, 32 questionnaires were incomplete or otherwise deemed unusable and analysis was conducted on the remaining 148 questionnaires. The results were obtained from 69 male and 79 female participants.

4.2 Statistical Results

As to the explore the impact of the degree of emotional effects of the audience towards the local craftsmen, in particular their appreciation and valuation of the eight exhibited image content, the study has designed eight independent variables of different dimensions. These include the feeling of touching, the transmitted feeling of the insistent spirit of the craftsmen, content focus, realistic, vitality, value, attractiveness and connotation of traditional culture of the images. The degree of emotional effects of the audience towards the content of the exhibition is the dependent variable. Through multiple regression analysis, the description of the result of the 20 photos is shown later (Table 2.)

Table 2. Multiple regression analysis summary tables with 8 evaluation items to predict the feeling of "I will appreciate and value the craftsmen of the local industries in the photo"

Dependent variables	Predictor variables	B	r	β	t
I will appreciate and value the craftsmen of the local industries in the photo.	The photo is touching.	.345	.905***	.592	1.751
	The photo has transmitted the insistent spirit of the craftsmen.	.350	.923***	.483	1.201
	The content of the photo is much focused.	-.255	.851***	-.354	-1.177
	The photo is very realis-tic.	.333	.790***	.325	1.436
	The photo contains its vitality.	-.242	.848***	-.308	-1.101
	The photo is valuable.	.179	.890***	.289	1.035
	The photo is attractive.	-.068	.883***	-.108	-.340
	The photo connotes the traditional culture.	.058	.786***	.098	.491
	R=.956	R^2=.915		F=14.750***	

***p<.001.

From the correlation between the independent variables and the content of the image content of the exhibition, the correlation coefficients of the degree of emotional effects between the eight dimensions and the image content are .905, .923, .790, .890 and .786 respectively. All of them are positively correlated with certain significance. The F value of the overall regression model is 14.750, achieving a significant standard (p<.001). This means that the scores of 5 dimensions can be the reference for the prediction of the degree of emotional effects. In the regression formula, the importance of the dependent variable depends on the standardized number of coefficient having "the picture is touching" as the first one followed by "the picture has transmitted the insistent spirit of the craftsmen" and lastly "the picture connotes the traditional culture." Among them, "the picture is touching" has achieved a significant standard ($\beta = .592$, $p < .001$). in terms of the nature of the image content, this exhibition inclines to be "Viewing / Realistic." For the students of design and visual communication department, the dimensions of touching pictures, the transmission of the insistent spirit and picture realisticness are greater than the dimensions of picture focus, vitality and attractiveness in terms of the overall degree of emotional effects. Thus, audience would further appreciate and value the local craftsmen of the industries.

When exploring the four overall images of the exhibition, in terms of the degree of emotional effects (liking the overall images and recordings of the exhibition) for the students of design and visual communication department students of the region of Taipei, the study has felt the spirit of insistency, benevolence, love, caring and pricelessness, which are designed as the independent variables. The degree of emotional effects of the audience towards the image content of the exhibition is the dependent variables. The results from the multiple regression analysis of the following ten pictures are described as follow (Table 3).

Table 3. Multiple regression analysis summary table using 4 assessment items to predict the degree of "I like the overall images and recordings of the exhibition"

Dependent variables	Predictor variable	B	r	β	t
I like the overall images and recordings of the exhibition.	This exhibition makes me feel the insistent spirit of the local craftsmen of the industries.	.473	.000***	.422	5.119
	This exhibition makes me feel love.	.260	.004**	.264	2.900
	This exhibition makes me feel caring and pricelessness.	.120	.186	.128	1.329
	This exhibition makes me feel benevolence.	-.042	.677	-.036	-.418
	R=.657	R2=.432		F= 27.135 ***	

***$p < .001$.

From the correlation of the independent variables and the degree of emotional effects of the audience towards the overall images and recordings of the exhibition, the correlation coefficients of the four dimensions with the degree of emotional effects of the audience towards the overall exhibition are .000, .004 and .186 respectively, showing positive and significant correlations. The F value of the overall regression model is 27.135, achieving a significant standards ($p > .001$). This means that the scores of the three dimensions can be used as the reference for the prediction of emotional effects towards the exhibition. In terms of the regression formula, the importance of the dependent variables depends on the number sequence of the standardized regression coefficient, having “this exhibition makes me feel the insistent spirit of the local craftsmen of the industries” as the first one followed by “this exhibition makes me feel love” and lastly, “this exhibition makes me feel caring and pricelessness.” Among them, the dimension of “this exhibition makes me feel the insistent spirit of the local craftsmen of the industries” has achieved a significant standard of (β=.422, $p<.001$). In terms of the nature of the overall exhibition, the exhibition is well-planned allowing the students of design and visual communication department to feel the insistent spirit of the local craftsmen of the industries.

5 Conclusion

After the transition of Taiwan towards an industrial country, changes have also produced over the societal and the business models, so traditional industries could not meet the market’s demands and would eventually disappear. For the young learners of the latest generations, there are industries that they have not heard neither been in touch resulting in their cognitive distancing. Through the exhibition design and planning as well as book publishing after the exhibition, the experience of the audience from the content can be extended as to create a resonance with them. From the resulted data, students from the design and visual communication departments from Taipei region have experienced the feeling of “the picture is touching”, “the pictures has transmitted the insistent spirit of the craftsmen” and “the picture is realistic,” and feelings to appreciate and value local craftsmen of the industries are produced. In terms of the connoted value of the overall impression of the exhibition, the audience would like the pictures and recordings of the exhibition and achieved the emotional cognition of feeling “the insistent spirit of the craftsmen.” Looking to the future, it is possible to use cultural traditional artistry when designing exhibition to trigger emotional sympathy and to root the local consciousness.

References

1. Pine II, B.J., Gilmore, J.H.: Welcome to the Experience Economy. Harvard Business Review 4, 97–105 (1998)
2. Rao, J.W.: Field Theory of knowledge: perception, thinking and educational integration theory. Wuana, Taipei (1994)
3. Su, M.L.: The Design added-value Model for Aborgines’ Culture Merchandise- Amis Crafts as examples. National Cheng Kung University, Tainan (2005)
4. Burcaw, G.E.: Introduction to Museum Work. The American Association for State and Local History, Nashville (1987)
5. Lin, C.R.: Study of The Internatonal Crafts Curating Praticality—Taking “Nature. Stride” Exhibition for Example. National Taipei University of Education, Taipei (2007)
6. Jordan, P.W.: Pleasure with products: Human factors for body, mind and soul. In: Green, W.S., Jordan, P.W. (eds.) Human Factors in Product Design: Current Practice and Future Trends. Taylor & Francis, London (1999)
7. Norman, D.A.: Emotional Design: Why We Love (or Hate) Everyday Things. Basic Books, New York (2004)
8. Lin, R.T.: Transforming Taiwan aboriginal cultural features into modern product design: A casestudy of a cross-cultural product design model. International Journal of Design 1(2), 45–33 (2007)

A Study of Applying Sakizaya Tribe's Palamal (The Fire God Ritual) into Cultural Creative Products Design

Po-Hsien Lin[1], Jao-Hsun Tseng[2], and Pei-Chen Lin[1]

[1] Graduate School of Creative Industry Design,
National Taiwan University of Arts
Daguan Rd., Banqiao Dist., New Taipei City 22058, Taiwan
t0131@ntua.edu.tw
[2] Department of Dance, National Taiwan University of Arts
Daguan Rd., Banqiao Dist., New Taipei City 22058, Taiwan
t0190@ntua.edu.tw

Abstract. The Palamal is a memorial ceremony during which the Sakiazya people to worship their ancestors. This study is based on searching for possibilities in applying the Sakiazya Palamal to the creative culture industry as the main research issue, emphasizing the integration of interdisciplinary fields. Besides conferring the dance gestures, ritual clothing and decorations for the Sakiazya Palamal, research for product design development will also be held in coordination with the Sakiazya performance promotion. As for the research methodology, collecting literature data and onsite interview will be used for this project; through the investigation of the Sakiazya cultural tradition and the understanding of ceremony rituals and worship utensils, this study intends to present the rich and vivid culture with a new look, the combination of traditional elements with modern creative ideas will transform our cultural essence into commercial culture products and artistic performance. The transformation process must be treated with respect, thus, we must understand the taboo and the deeper meaning of the culture to prevent conflicts due to cultural differences.

Keywords: Sakizaya, Palamal (the Fire God Ritual), culture creative industry.

1 Introduction

The Sakizaya tribe was the subject of this study. The Sakizaya were officially recognized as the 13th Taiwanese aboriginal tribe in 2007. In 1878, the government of the Qing Dynasty advanced into Eastern Taiwan in the name of developing Taiwan. This advance resulted in a famous conflict between the Qing government and the Sakizaya people, who are native to the Daguhuwan Lake, Hualien County. This conflict, historically known as the Kaliawan Incident, caused an extreme sacrifice among the Sakizaya people. Fearing reprisals following the event, the survivors fled their homes, concealed their identities, and hid themselves among the Amis tribe. During the colonial period, the Japanese classified the aboriginals and categorized the Sakizayas as Amis. Subsequently, the name, Sakizaya, became nonexistence in the official

P.L.P. Rau (Ed.): CCD/HCII 2014, LNCS 8528, pp. 753–765, 2014.

literature [5, 12]. Through the present, the Sakizaya have suffered substantial losses in their identity, bloodline, and language. Cultural reconstruction is extremely difficult. The Sakizaya tribe has wandered for more than a hundred years, during which its culture has integrated with and been affected by the Amis tribe. However, after the Sakizaya people have gained official recognition following the name rectification campaign, what faces them now is series of difficult challenges.

2 Research Purpose

In *The Invention of Tradition*, Hobsbawm indicated that "traditions which appear or claim to be old are often quite recent in origin and sometimes invented" [3]. In this study, the remnants of the culture of the Sakizaya tribe were used as elements for cultural and creative design, to develop products featuring Sakizaya tribal characteristics. Through a literature review, interviews with Sakizaya elders and tribal members, and participation in the Sakizaya tribe's festival activities (i.e. the Palamal Ceremony [the Fire God Ritual] and the Sakur Tribal Harvest Festival), characteristic cultural elements were extracted and applied to derive creative cultural product designs. Subsequently, this study endeavored to understand the evaluations and response of the tribal people and consumers toward these designs, thereby promoting Sakizaya cultural characteristics.

3 Literature Review

3.1 Culture and Society of the Sakizaya Tribe

Chun-Nan Chen is a member of the Sakizaya tribe. In his PhD thesis, *Study of Sakizaya Culture and Official Recognition*, the social culture, name rectification process, and current predicaments that the tribe is encountering were extensively described [1]. The Sakizaya referred to God as Dito; this figure corresponded to the Amis' figure of Kawas. Like the Amis and other aboriginals, the Sakizaya believe that all things possess spiritual essence and that supernatural powers exist everywhere. Additionally, they believe that Dito includes ancestral spirits. The Sakur believe that when people die, their spirits pass through the valleys of Malon Mountain, drifting toward the east, into the ocean. During the Sakur tribe's harvest festival, sacrificial offerings are placed in the direction of Malon Mountain; the chief priest reads prayers toward Malon Mountain, facing the ocean. The houses of the Sakizaya all face the direction in which sunrise occurs; the Sakizaya view the east as sacred and irreplaceable. To enhance tribal sentiments and cohere tribal identity, since 2006, the Sakizaya have held Palamal ceremonies annually to commemorate the people who sacrificed themselves in 1878 during the Kaliawan Incident. During the occurrence of the name rectification process, the Palamal ceremony became the representative ritual of the Sakizaya tribe.

Social Structure. Originally, the Sakizaya followed a system by which heredity was matrilineal, and men were married into their wives' families. However, after 1930, with the increasing trend of typical matrimony, the matrilineal system began to collapse. Similar to the Amis, the Sakizaya tribe was also divided according to age. Young age-based hierarchy groups provide labor and military protection for the tribe, and engaged in major organizations of public affairs. Between settlements, the Sakizaya used common age-based hierarchy names, whereas the Amis used different age group names in different settlements.

The Palamal Ceremony (The Fire God Ritual). Since 2006, the Sakizaya tribe has held the Palamal ceremony annually. The Palamal ceremony is viewed as the most major and representative traditional ceremony, and is held in memoriam of the Sakizaya tribal hero Komod Pazik and his wife Icep' Kanasaw [1].

Fig. 1. The Palamal Ceremony (Retrieved from Taiwan's Aboriginal Culture History and Language Dictionary)

In 1878, the Sakizaya tribe experienced a conflict with the Qing army, and eventually resisted the Qing army in conjunction with the Kavalan tribe, resulting in the Kaleawan Incident. After the conflict, the chief couple was executed by the Qing army through the process of "slow slicing (*Lingchi*)". The remaining members of the tribe fled their homes and hid themselves among the Amis, to avoid being massacred by the Qing army. One hundred years later, these ancestors who had sacrificed themselves to defend the homes and lives of their fellow tribe members had yet to be enshrined. During the process of regaining recognition, the Sakizaya decided to enshrine Komod Pazik and Icep' Kanasaw as the god and goddess of fire, and through the Palamal ceremony, commemorate all tribal people who had sacrificed their lives [2].

3.2 Theory and Practice of Cultural Creative Design

Norman presents in his book "Emotional Design" three levels of emotional design-visceral, behavioral and reflective. The visceral level involves direct feelings when in touch with a product, including shape, style, tactile impression, material and weight. The behavioral level is non-conscious, including the pleasure after exercise, or the delight after a shower. The reflective level presents conscious behaviors such as the pop culture or style and tastes [11]. Leong and Clark suggest a brief framework for investigating cultural product design, dividing it into three space structures as the external concrete tactile level, middle behavioral level and the inner invisible spiritual level [7]. Hsu, Lin and Chu expand the three levels, offer more detailed explication, and provide a cultural creative design model which could further facilitate comparison, application and thinking for design (Figure 2) [4, 8]. This theoretical framework could serve as the focal points when investigating individual stages for cultural product design.

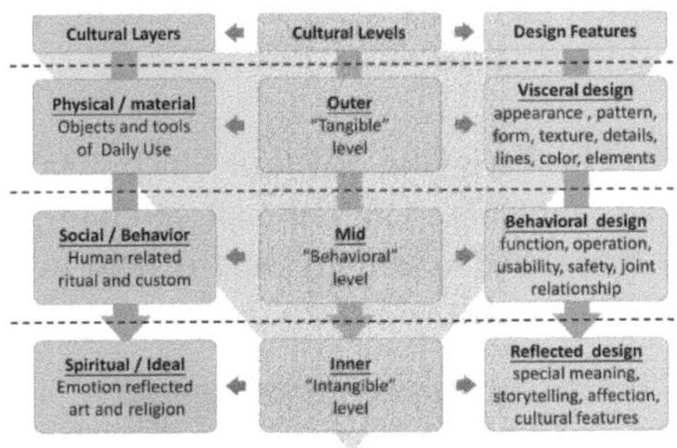

Fig. 2. Three Layers of Cultural Creative Design Model (Hsu, Lin, & Chu, 2004)

Starting the 80s, design scholars has been devoted in research of product semantics. Krippendorff and Butter claimed that conventional semantics stress the interrelationship among sigh, referent and though, emphasizing linguistic expression; product semantics, on the other hand, looks at a product as a symbol system, investigates the symbolic qualities of a product from the perspectives of its operation and application and employs the knowledge for product design [10]. They suggested that, from product semantics, the success of product design relies not only on the physical and biological functions of the product but also its psychological functions and its links with the social and cultural context.

4 Analysis of Design Cases

4.1 Design Case A: Eraser

Design Concept. In the Kuofu neighborhood of Hualien, festivals are held at the Sakizaya ceremonial square, where eight boulders representative of admonitions for Sakizaya people were erected. The first four boulders represent God's duties: making the wind blow, the rain drizzle, the earth grow, and the fire roast; the last four represents the principles of living: work hard, love God, love oneself, and love others. Erasers were designed to mimic the appearance of the boulders, representing the ability to correct small mistakes. Based on Figure 2, the external appearance of the white boulder represents the outer, tangible cultural level, and the symbol of the boulder represents the admonitions of the tribe and belongs to the inner ideal cultural level.

4.2 Design Case B: Pulong Fruit Platter

During major Sakizaya ceremonies, sacrificial offerings are surrounded by miscanthus posts, called pulongs in the Sakizaya language. The pulongs prevent evil spirits from entering the space where sacrificial offerings are presented to the ancestral spirits. Other spirits and ghosts are prohibited from entering. The fruit platter is designed to create the image of the pulongs. Fruit forks are designed according to the appearance of the miscanthus posts, and can be erected around the fruit platter. When the fruits are placed at the center of the plate, a certain sacrificial offering image is created, representing the pulongs protecting the fruits, preventing evil spirits from consuming them.

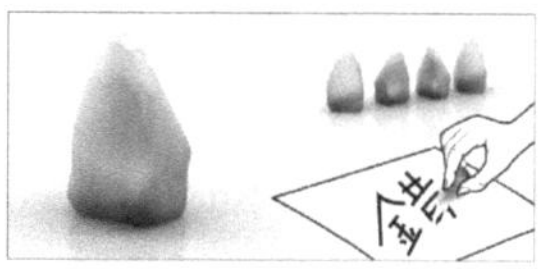

Fig. 3. Array of boulders describing God's duties

Fig. 4. 3D schematic of admonition eraser

Fig. 5. Miscanthus posts

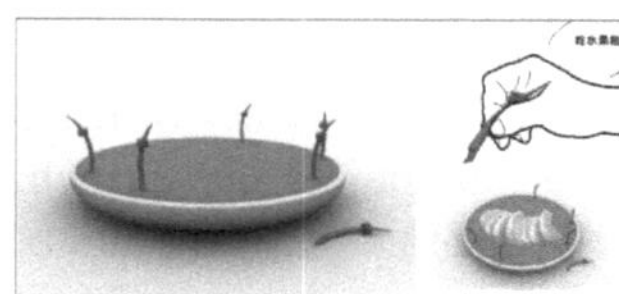

Fig. 6. Schematic 3D diagram of pulong fruit plater

According to Figure 2, the appearance of the green miscanthus posts is associated with the tangible cultural level; insertion of the miscanthus posts by users represents the behavioral level; and the imagery of protecting the offerings from outer evil spirits represents the inner ideal level.

4.3 Design Case C: Bamboo (Bitonay) Fence Keychain

The building of bitonay fences was the most essential and special custom involved in the age hierarchy ritual of the Sakizaya tribe; interviews with tribal elders confirmed that the building of bitonay fences was a well-established tradition. During the Kaleawan Incident, the Qings were reportedly in an inferior position to the Sakizaya, and could not break through the more than 50 bitonay fences despite repeated attacks during their invasion. The age advancement ritual (Langat) was held every 8 years in the past, and thus the bitony fences may have had a history of more than 400 years. Regrettably, the Qing army burnt the fences, forcing the Sakizaya out of their homes [14]. The fence building was not only critical in the age advancement ritual, but also implicated the protection of Sakizaya homes. In the present day, keys are essential tools for entering one's home. Thus, the bitonay fence can be designed to form a keychain that can be used to store keys and symbolize a device that protects one's home.

The fence represents the tangible cultural level; the Langat ritual is a custom for celebrating the advancement of age, which represents the behavioral level; and the bitonay fences represent protecting the homes and aging of tribal people, which is associated with the inner ideal cultural level.

Fig. 7. Guarding *Pass* (Source: Chan, 2007)

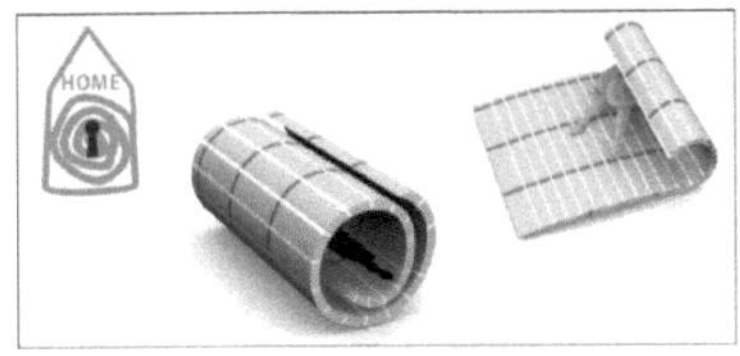

Fig. 8. 3D schematic of Bitonay Fence Keychain

4.4 Design Case D: The Triangle Stone Double Bolster Pillow

Sakizaya apparel is often decorated with triangles, the concept of which originated from the legend of the triangle stone mark. According to legend, God carved a wall of chastity for Damo and Namoh on the side of the mountain; this carving appears as a triangular mark when viewed from the Kuofu neighborhood. The green pillow represents the mountain, and the white triangle represents God's mark described in the legend. In the design of the double bolster pillow, the undying affection between man and woman is represented. The triangular totem embroidered on the pillow protrudes slightly. After waking, the sleeper's cheek is imprinted with the triangular mark.

Fig. 9. The triangle stone mark on the Shapotang mountain

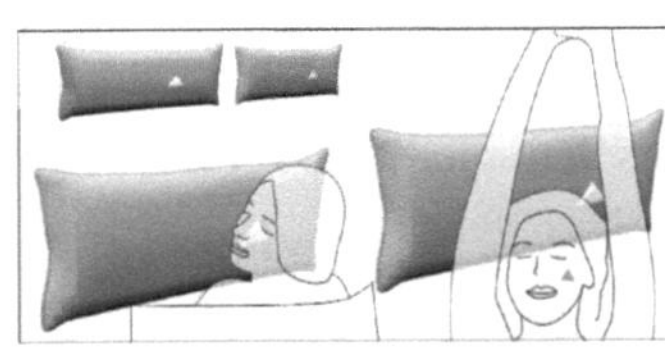

Fig. 10. 3D schematic of the triangle stone double bolster pillow

According to Figure 2, the white triangular stone mark represents the tangible cultural level, and a couple's sacrificial and dedicated spirit represents the inner ideal cultural level.

4.5 Design Case E: The Totem Dishware

Each of the boulders located in the Sakizaya ceremonial square features a totem. As shown in Fig. 11, the curves on each of the four corners represent God's duties: the blowing of the wind (upper left), the roasting of fire (lower left), the drizzling of the rain (upper right), and the growing of the earth (lower right), which create the cycle of universe and denotes God's duties. God fulfills his duty to allow the people to be fed. Dishware engraved with totems representing God's operation was designed, to thank God for providing the people with food today. The Sakizaya tribal totem represents the tangible cultural level, and the implication of the totem represents the inner ideal cultural level.

Fig. 11. Totem on the boulder

Fig. 12. A 3D schematic of the totem dishware

4.6 Design Case F: The Tables of Earth, Wind, and Fire

This design also applied the boulder totems to the design of a table set. The transparent material in the center symbolized the water, wind, fire, and earth, which were each represented by blue, transparent, red, and brown, respectively. The tabletops were paired with a white surface, incorporating the natural landscape into the furniture design.

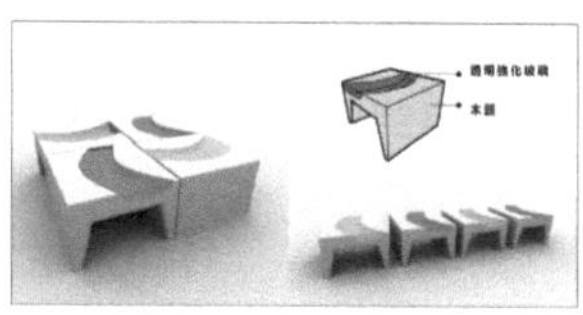

Fig. 13. 3D schematic of the tables of earth, wind, water, and fire

The Sakizaya tribal totem is associated with the tangible cultural level, and the implication of the totem is the inner ideal cultural level.

4.7 Design Case G: The Slingshot Chair

According to literature, the Sakizaya were often harassed by the Taroko in the past. To protect their tribe, Sakizaya warriors shot tree nuts with slingshots, stopping the enemy beyond 100 yards. A chair designed based on the concept of the slingshot can increase interaction between people. A person pulls the slingshot while another sits on the chair, simultaneously receiving a massage and feeling euphoric. The slingshot is no longer used as a weapon of human onslaught, but is adopted in the chair design to symbolize the relegation of past rivalries.

The appearance of the slingshot chair is the tangible cultural level; the action of pulling the slingshot is the behavioral cultural level; and attacking the enemy and protecting fellow tribal members is the inner ideal cultural level, which was transformed into a symbol of reconciliation with other tribes in this study.

Fig. 14. Aboriginal slingshot

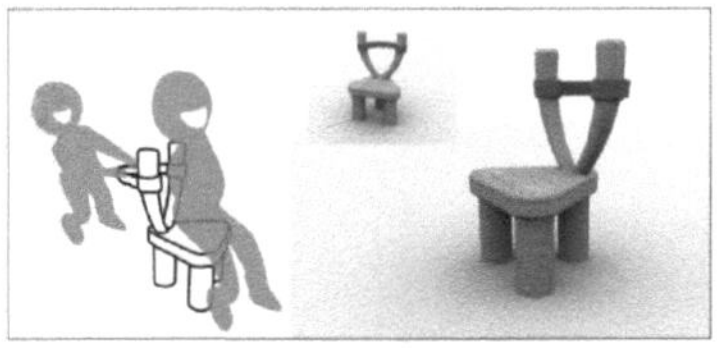

Fig. 15. 3D schematic of slingshot chair

5 Research Methodology

5.1 Research Process

In this study, the history and culture of the Sakizaya tribe were used as a foundation to apply extracted cultural elements to the design of innovative cultural products. Through a literature review, interviews with Sakizaya members (i.e., elders, a clothing designer, and the chief), and participation in the Sakizaya harvest festival and the Palamal ceremony, an in-depth understanding of tribal culture and stories was obtained. Subsequently, innovative cultural products were designed incorporating Sakizaya cultural elements. Finally, a design case evaluation survey was conducted.

5.2 Research Instrument

The survey was divided into four sections. The first section involved collecting demographic information. The second section comprised an evaluation survey of design cognitions. The third section involved requesting participants to rank their three favorite design cases. The fourth section involved assessing the properties of the design cases by using adjectival vocabularies. The second and fourth sections of the survey are described in detail as follows. Lee proposed a cross-cultural design research framework, to investigate cultural variables, design characteristics, and the relationship between function, aesthetics, and symbols [6]. The survey content of the second part of this study was divided into four dimensions—design sense, functionality, the application of cultural elements, and overall preference. Using a 5-point Likert scale, the participants were asked to assess the design cases. In assessing the properties of the design cases by using adjectives, the data obtained were analyzed using the multidimensional scaling (MDS). MDS is used to classify observational values, and is a data analysis method for determining whether a potential structure exists in the data [13]. In this study, eight sets of semantic vocabularies that describe the design styles were selected by experts to construct a 5-point scale semantic analytic survey. The results were analyzed by using MDS. The eight sets of semantic vocabularies were as follows: "austere-cool," "elegant-gorgeous," "ornamental-practical," "abstract-figurative," "serious-humorous," "fashionable-traditional," "complex-simple," and "refined-rough."

6 Research Results and Data Analysis

6.1 Design Evaluation and Discussion

A total of 166 surveys were completed in this study. The study participants were Taiwanese and their academic backgrounds were divided into three categories: product-design-related, design-related, and nondesign-related. Finally, seven design cases were sent to the tribal members through the mail, and the relationship between the responses of the participants and tribal member was determined. The key results and findings were classified and sorted as follows.

Cognitive Difference between Study Participants and Tribal Members. The 166 participants were asked to rank the three designs they preferred, where the most preferred design was assigned a score of 3, followed by 2 and 1, and no scores were given for the remaining items. After tabulating the scores, the slingshot chair, totem dishware, and totem table set were ranked respectively from first to third.

Table 1. The rankings of study participants' and tribal members' favorite products

Ranking	1	2	3
Tribal Members		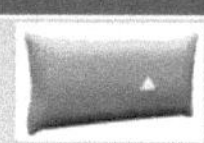	
Study Participants			

The seven design works were presented to the tribal members (Chief De-Yung Huang and Tribal Elder Huang, Chin-Wen), and Chief Huang was satisfied with and intrigued by the design products; his three personal favorites, in descending order, were the bitonay keychain, the triangle stone double bolster pillow, and the boulder eraser. Clearly, product rankings were substantially different between tribal members and the study participants.

ANOVA Analysis of the Preference of the Design Works. The analysis of variance (ANOVA) results indicated that academic background significantly affected how people evaluated each design case dimension (Table 1). Participants with design-related and nondesign-related academic backgrounds appreciated the products more than did participants with product-design-related knowledge. We speculated that participants with product-design-related academic backgrounds used stricter product design evaluation standards compared with those possessing design-related and non-design-related backgrounds.

6.2 MDS Analysis of the Design Cases

The seven design works and eight sets of adjectival vocabularies were analyzed by using MDS. SPSS software was used to compute the two crucial correspondence indices of the two-dimensional (2D) spatial plot; the Kruskal's stress and the determination coefficient (RSQ) were 0.08497 and 0.98545, respectively. The former was less than 0.01, whereas the latter approached 1, indicating that the spatial relationships between the seven products and eight sets of attributes could be appropriately represented in 2D. The stress index indicated that the 2D plot and the original data exhibited satisfactory fit; the RSQ indicated that the 2D plot was capable of explaining 98.55% of the variance in the seven products and eight-set attributes [9]. A 2D plot was formulated following MDS analysis, and factor analysis was conducted on the eight sets of adjectival vocabularies selected by the participants. The preliminary 2D distribution plot of the seven design works was divisible into three major groups, which also happened to include the high and low scoring groups. The first group (high score) comprised the totem dishware, totem table set, and pulong fruit platter; the second group (high score) consisted of the slingshot chair; and the third group (low score) comprised the triangle stone double bolster pillow, bitonay keychain, and the boulder eraser.

Table 2. ANOVA for overall assessment by the influence of academic background

Product	Factor	Source of Variance	SS	DF	MS	F	Scheffe
A. Eraser	application of cultural elements	Between groups	13.493	2	6.747	9.763***	2>1
		Within group	112.642	163	0.691		
		Total	126.136	165			
B. Pulong Fruit Platter	design sense	Between groups	5.781	2	2.891	3.901*	2>1
		Within group	120.766	163	0.741		
		Total	126.547	165			
C. Bamboo (Bitonay) Fence Keychain	design sense	Between groups	6.678	2	3.339	4.573*	2>1
		Within group	118.998	163	0.73		
		Total	125.675	165			
D. The Triangle Stone Double Bolster Pillow	application of cultural elements	Between groups	6.863	2	3.431	4.052*	2>1
		Within group	138.024	163	0.847		
		Total	144.887	165			
E. Totem Dishware	application of cultural elements	Between groups	5.546	2	2.773	4.841**	2>1 2>3
		Within group	93.36	163	0.573		
		Total	98.906	165			
F. Tables of Earth, Wind, Water, and Fire	design sense	Between groups	5.981	2	2.991	5.002**	3>1
		Within group	97.456	163	0.598		
		Total	103.437	165			
G. Slingshot Chair	design sense	Between groups	8.623	2	4.311	7.013***	3>1 2>1
		Within group	100.205	163	0.615		
		Total	108.828	165			
G. Slingshot Chair	functionality	Between groups	10.768	2	5.384	10.918***	3>1 2>1
		Within group	80.385	163	0.493		
		Total	91.154	165			
G. Slingshot Chair	overall preference	Between groups	6.915	2	3.458	4.065*	3>1
		Within group	138.628	163	0.85		
		Total	145.543	165			

*P <0.05 **p <0.01 ***P <0.001

1: product-design related 2: other design fields 3: non-design fields

A multiple regression equation was used to further compute the included angles on the plot between each property, to plot the cognitive spatial distribution diagram of the seven design works and 16 attributes. The totem dishware, totem table set, and the pulong fruit platter of the first group (high score) were determined by the participants to be "cool," "practical," "fashionable," and "refined"; the slingshot chair of the second group (high score) achieved the highest score and was determined to be "humorous" and "gorgeous"; the triangle stone double bolster pillow, bitonay fence keychain, and the boulder eraser of the third group were determined to be "rough," "traditional," and "ornamental."

7 Conclusion and Recommendations

7.1 Conclusion

Cognitive Difference of Participants with Different Backgrounds. The ANOVA results revealed that participants with design-related and nondesign-related academic backgrounds had a greater appreciation of the design cases in all of the dimensions. We speculated that participants with product-design-related academic backgrounds used a stricter product design evaluation standard. However, participants with design-related and nondesign-related academic backgrounds both had a greater appreciation of the design cases compared with those with product-design-related backgrounds. The cognitive differences between tribal members and the study participants were clearly distinct. This distinction necessitates further investigation. We speculate that because of differences in identity, the general public may not understand the cultural characteristics associated with the Sakizaya tribe. By contrast, Chief Huang and Elder Huang, being tribal members themselves, truly understood the importance of their culture, and thus selected designs that symbolized the legends of the fence and triangle stone mark. Moreover, aboriginals live in nature and favor design styles that are strongly associated with their culture; thus, they have a preference for rough and simple designs. By contrast, the general public is deeply infused with the culture of high refinement, showed a preference for more refined products. Various social groups inevitably exhibit differences in social cultural cognition, leading to cognitive discrepancies; therefore, developing a method by which these discrepancies can be mitigated is worthy of further investigation.

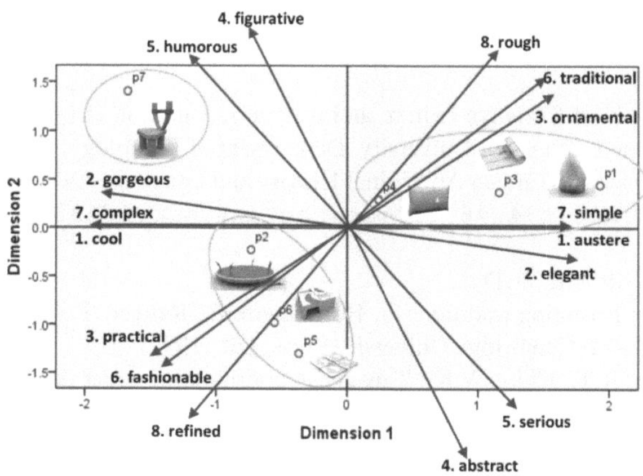

Fig. 16. Cognitive space distribution of the seven design works and 16 attributes

Comparison of Design Attributes and Participant Opinions. By using MDS semantic differential analysis, the seven product designs in this study were divided into three major groups, which were also classified into high and low scoring groups. The totem dishware, totem table set, and pulong fruit platter of the first group (high score) were determined by participants to be "cool," "practical," "fashionable," and "refined"; the slingshot chair of the second group (high score) was determined to be "humorous" and "gorgeous." These two groups were the high scoring groups, indicating that the public preferred the imagery of these products. The triangle stone double bolster pillow, bitonay fence keychain, and boulder eraser of the third group were determined by participants to be "rough," "traditional," and "ornamental." This group was the low scoring group, which suggested that the public lest preferred these products.

7.2 Further Research and Recommendations

Expansion and Extension of Basic Participant Data. Considering the scarce population and scattered settlements of Sakizaya tribes in Hualien, studying the Sakizaya was relatively difficult. Thus, the participants in this study were the general public, and design cases were shared with participants through telephone interviews and other means of communication. The results showed that product preferences between the Sakizaya tribe and the study participants differed. Future surveys of the Sakizaya (or other aboriginals) are warranted.

Derivation of Interdisciplinary Research. This study typically adopted the appearance of the cultural elements to develop and design products; however, we assert that the historical events of the Sakizaya are the source to dramatically representing the Sakizaya tribe. Future researchers are recommended to apply stories with emotional connotations to drama performances or, despite the challenges entailed, to developing innovative cultural products.

References

1. Chen, J.N.: Study of Sakizaya culture and official recognition (Unpublished doctoral dissertation). National Chengchi University, Department of Ethnology, Taipei (2009)
2. Cultural Dictionary of Taiwan Aboriginal History and Language (2007), `http://210.240.134.48/citing_content.asp?id=3367&keyword=%` (retrieved)
3. A4%F5%AF%AB%B2%BD
4. Hobsbawm, E.: Inventing tradition. In: Hobsbawm, E., Ranger, T. (eds.) The Invention of Tradition, pp. 1–14. Cambridge University Press, UK (1992)
5. Hsu, C.H., Lin, R.T., Chiu, W.K.: Taiwanese aboriginal product design. International Innovation Design Symposium Thesis, 157–164 (2004)
6. Information Gateway of Taiwan Aboriginal Culture (2013), `http://www.sight-native.taipei.gov.tw/mp.asp?mp=cb01` (retrieved)

7. Lee, K.P.: Design methods for a cross-cultural collaborative design project. In: Redmond, J., Durling, D., de Bono, A. (eds.) Proceedings of Design Research Society International Conference –Futureground (Paper No.135). Monash University, Melbourne (2004)
8. Leong, B.D., Clark, H.: Culture-based knowledge towards new design thinking and practice—A dialogue. Design Issues 19(3), 48–58 (2003)
9. Lin, R.T.: Transforming Taiwan aboriginal cultural features into modern product design: A case study of cross-cultural product design model. International Journal of Design 1(2), 45–53 (2007)
10. Lin, Z.Y.: Multivariate analysis. Best-Wise Publishing Co., Ltd., Taipei (2007)
11. Krippendorff, K., Butter, R.: Product semantics: Exploring the symbolic qualities of form. Innovation, pp. 4–9 (Spring 1984)
12. Norman, D.A.: The design of everyday things. Basic Books, New York (2002)
13. Pan, C.C., Shi, Z.F.: The battle of Kaliawan. College of Indigenous Studies at National Dong Hwa University Press, Hualien County (2010)
14. Wang, B.J.: Multivariate analysis. Cultural Enterprises of Higher Education Ltd., Taipei (2004)
15. Zhan, S.J.: Old literatures, new findings: Interpreting historical documents of Taiwanese aborigines. Cultural Enterprises of Ri Chuang Ltd., Taipei (2007)

The Sino-Italian Collaborative Design Platform: Designing and Developing an Innovative Product Service System

Wei Liu and Yongqi Lou

Tongji University, China
{liuwei.dk,lou.yongqi}@gmail.com

Abstract. This research aims to explore how to bring the richness of collaborative design into the (formal) context of the offices and colleagues. This research went through five stages to design product service systems: 1) product service system analysis, 2) collaborative design, 3) Research on computer supported cooperative work (CSCW) model, 4) User experience research, and 5) Product service system design. Recommendations are given to design and develop interactive collaborative design platforms in the work context. Researchers and designers who are interested in designing and developing rapidly evolving and experiential ICT systems would benefit from learning this research.

Keywords: Product service system, collaborative design, user experience, information technologies.

1 Introduction

Social innovation requires collaboration between individuals. Collaboration requires individuals working together in a coordinated fashion, towards a common goal. Accomplishing the goal is the primary purpose for bringing the team together. Collaborative platform helps facilitate action-oriented teams working together over geographic distances by providing tools that aid communication, collaboration and the process of problem solving. Additionally, collaborative platform may support project management functions, such as task assignments, time-managing deadlines and shared calendars. The artefacts, the tangible evidence of the problem solving process and the final outcome of the collaborative effort, require documentation and may involve archiving project plans, deadlines and deliverables. This would create a more sustainable working and living environments, which is in line with the theme of this session: Future urban sustainability and social innovation. In this research, by integrating international design resources and the most advanced information technologies (e.g., cloud computing), we aim to achieve a real-time, remote, collaborative and digital product service system from a 'human-centered' perspective. This product service system is called the Sino-Italian collaborative design platform, which includes a set of technological toolkit, intellectual property databases, an easy-to-use cross-border digital prototype and a collaborative design network. This platform connects

P.L.P. Rau (Ed.): CCD/HCII 2014, LNCS 8528, pp. 766–774, 2014.

professional design laboratories geographically spread around the world, and supports co-design through seamless digital and physical computer supported cooperative work (CSCW) collaborations. Researchers and designers who are interested in designing and developing rapidly evolving and experiential ICT systems would benefit from learning this research.

2 Related Work

In the work context, Keller [8] designed cabinet that helps designers collect and organize their visual material for inspiration. The design makes interaction with digital material more physical by dragging digital images on a table as if they are real objects. It offers a fluent way to add physical material to the digital collection by digitizing and projecting any objects placed on the table. This type of study was followed by several other recent projects in the domain of computer supported collaborative work (CSCW), such as designing an intelligent robot worker that transports goods and samples in semi-public hospital context [11] and designing a shape-changing communication device that facilitates expressive 'knocking' communications between two office workers [16]. Another example is the intelligent reading lamp, which aims to demonstrate ethics and esthetics in products and systems [21]. By moving the hand over the lamp, a 'living light' can be directed onto an object such as a book. This interaction design can fit into both the home and work contexts.

3 Research Objectives

Our research objective has been to explore how to bring the richness of collaborative design that people currently experience in the experimental context into the (formal) context of their offices and colleagues. This is an interesting challenge that presents itself to developers, designers and researchers.

4 Approach

From the beginning and throughout the whole research, digital and physical prototypes that are rich in aesthetic, expressive and experiential quality will be built and tested in real contexts. In the first phases of the project emphasis lies in the exploration of new ways of interacting and new technologies, while later on in the project the focus shifts to applying these new techniques within the domain of collaborative design platform. To ensure a high flow of thoughts, ideas and knowledge, a research through design approach is taken, in which the generation of knowledge and the development of applications go hand in hand. Research through design is used as a form of research to contribute to a design activity [1], [21]. It is recognized as a form of action research, defined as systematic investigation through practical action calculated to devise or test new information, ideas, forms or procedures and to produce communicable knowledge [1], [9]. Action research is an iterative process involving researchers and practitioners acting together in a particular cycle of activities [2], [20]. The research through design approach is highly iterative, integrating theory and practice from different fields into working experiential prototypes. These prototypes can be experienced as working artefacts and can be used as research means to demonstrate and explore these theories [14]. Designing and building working prototypes that are rich in experiential quality therefore plays a key role in this approach. The reflection on the action (of designing and building) creates new knowledge. The designing act of creating prototypes is in itself a potential generator of knowledge [6], [17], leading to new design insights and refinement of research issues.

Our research went through the following 5 stages: 1) Product service system analysis: analyzing the characteristics of collaborative products service systems, understanding their information architecture, comparing the advantages and disadvantages of existing systems, referencing these systems for the our design and development. 2) Collaborative design: comparing creative design approach (e.g., brainstorming and exchanging ideas with co-workers through inspirational channels) and other design approaches (e.g., engineering design). 3) Research on computer supported cooperative work (CSCW) model: researching on possible technical solutions of realizing creative collaboration and looking for a new computer supported cooperative work model. 4) User experience research: understanding user behaviors and demands on collaborative product service systems. 5) Product service system design: designing specific use cases, user stories and user interface, developing the whole product service system, e.g., user interface and cloud solutions.

4.1 Product Service System Analysis

Products are no longer just products, services not only services. This type of thinking requires new design and development structures, moving people out of their traditional compartments, meeting the needs of an often diverse and evolving group of end-users [3]. Product service systems are designed in highly dynamic network environments, mixing people and parties, models, interests and goals. The design of PSS requires an integrated effort to create the product, the related service and the underlying business model in one comprehensive proposition. For many companies and creative professionals this a relatively new way of working, requiring a more strategic way of thinking. By creating tools and methods, the projects will enable designers to strategically contribute to product service system development. From a conceptual point of view, product service system design requires the creation of experiential value for users. This is a complex process, as the design effort of the sum is greater than that of the individual parts. The user experience research line will look for knowledge, methods and tools to allow the designer to more effectively design these experiences. The intelligence incorporated in functions as an extension to both the product and service components. This may significantly influence the design, testing and prototyping of product-service combinations. The intelligence research line will focus on the optimal application of smart, enabling technology by developing new knowledge, tools and methodologies.

4.2 Collaborative Design

Collaborative design is a generic term, which combines the understanding of the way people design in groups with the enabling technologies of computer networking, and associated hardware, software, services and techniques [4]. Essentially, collaborative design goes beyond building technology itself and looks at how people work within groups and organizations and the impacts of technology on those processes. 'Collaborative' means we have to creatively solve problems and engage in design project activities, management and coordination in both public and private organizations. Techniques for generating and communicating good ideas are needed, both independently and as part of a team. 'Design' means we need a deep understanding of the process of design. We have to understand, advocate and facilitate good design. We have to obtain an understanding of the range and purpose of several design disciplines, strong communication skills and knowledge about the sustainability and economic impact of design thinking.

4.3 Research on CSCW

CSCW is a design-oriented academic field that is interdisciplinary in nature and brings together economists, organizational theorists, educators, social psychologists, sociologists, anthropologists and computer scientists, among others [5]. The expertise of researchers in various and combined disciplines help researchers identify venues for possible development. It is an identifiable research field focused on understanding characteristics of interdependent group work with the objective of designing adequate computer-based technology to support such cooperative work [12].

Collaborative design has a great extent of mixing between social scientists and technologists as developers work together to overcome both technical non-technical problems within the same user spaces [13]. For example, many professionals working with collaborative design are computer scientists who have realized that social factors play an important role in the development of collaborative design systems. On the opposite side, many innovation designers and social scientists who understand the increasing role of technology in our social world become 'technologists' who work in research labs to develop cooperative systems [19]. Over the years, researchers have identified a number of core dimensions of collaborative work, including:

- Awareness: individuals designing together need to be able to gain shared knowledge about each other's activities [5].
- Articulation: cooperating individuals to partition design into units, divide it amongst themselves and, after the work is performed, reintegrate it [12].
- Appropriation: how an individual or group adapts a technology to their own particular situation; the technology may be appropriated in a manner completely unintended by the designers [7], [19].

4.4 User Experience Research

User experience was considered as an important dimension in designing and developing this product service system. User scenarios in using software and hardware were fully considered and compared in the design and development process. Literature research paid specific attention to ergonomic platform, handheld terminals, input and output devices and operating experience. Analysis of creative collaboration helped to summarize the characteristics of user experience of existing systems. Design and development took care of software interface, logical relationships, user interactions, interface visual experience and user testing at different stages of software development.

12 interviews with 12 office workers have taken place at 12 companies, with the number of office workers varying from 10 to 1000 employees. They were young entrepreneurs, wholesalers and office managers. We used basic interviewing technique [9], [10], [15] in the form of face-to-face conversation between researcher and participants. The interview made use of generative toolkit [18]. See Fig. 1 for an impression. Each interview included six steps as described below:

1. Start with an observation of the work context.
2. Ask the participants to work on the toolkit, i.e., select a number of pictures, which express their behaviors and interactions in life and work the best.
3. Participants use the words and the selected pictures to make collages in order to illustrate their personal experiences.
4. Collect stories, trigger discussion and gain reflection from their experiences.
5. Cluster the collages in order to find categories of interaction qualities.
6. Round up discussion and reflection. Audio recordings were taken for the interviews, which

Audio recordings were taken for the interviews, which then later were turned into transcripts. Photographs were also taken during the interviews. In addition, during the interviews, field notes were taken by the researcher to capture informal conversations and contextual observations.

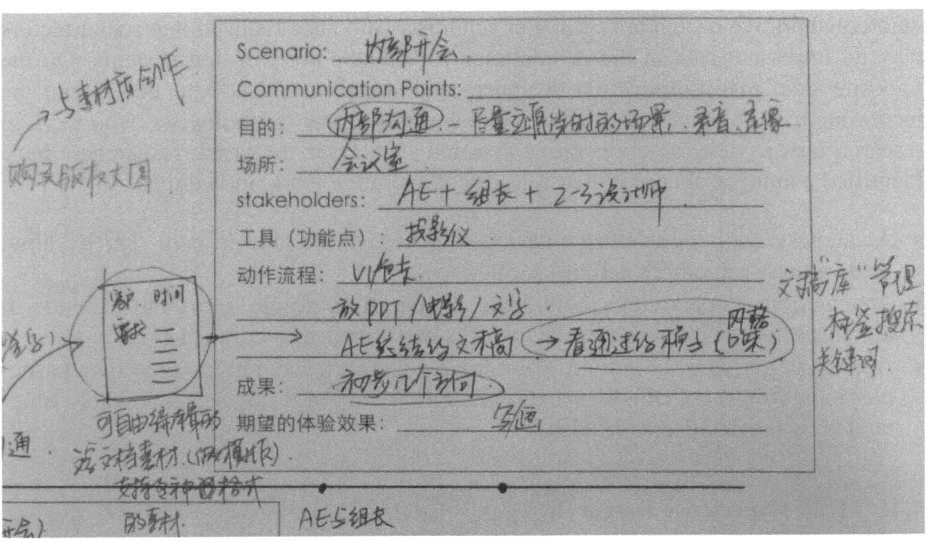

Fig. 1. Example of the filled toolkit

Qualitative analysis started with all the data (transcripts, collages, field notes and visual materials) gathered in the interviews, followed by communicating the 'selected and distilled insights' [17]. First, each researcher individually read the transcript, marking possibly relevant quotes. Secondly, the researchers consolidated the selection by turning about 80 quotes into explicit interpretations in the format of a statement card. Key part of the format was the interpretation (paraphrase), in which the researchers made explicit in their own words what the quote is saying. Third, the researchers clustered these statement cards into manageable groups, which were labeled and described. Finally, the words and pictures from the collages were also clustered together with the statement cards to help describe the interpretations and convey insights.

4.5 Product Service System Design

From the perspective of experience and service to the major stakeholder in-depth product analysis, rendering the overall economic trend graph and cooperation from key areas, key activities, core resources, the promotion of economic operators and other design subsystems. Positioning of the main attributes of specific platforms: design tools, creative showcase, the owners issued a platform for design projects, entrepreneurs seeking venture platform, shared resource platform, global network manufacturing alliance. High low-end platform defines different forms. Consider intertwined stakeholder and design procedures, and specifically designed to select a representative scenario as in the late part of the project implementation.

Platform overall system architecture design and software interface design was performed. On the basis of the first part of the research on the needs and status of the building, products, clothing, media, creative design five typical areas of in-depth analysis. Depending on the stage of the design ideas of user needs further categorized,

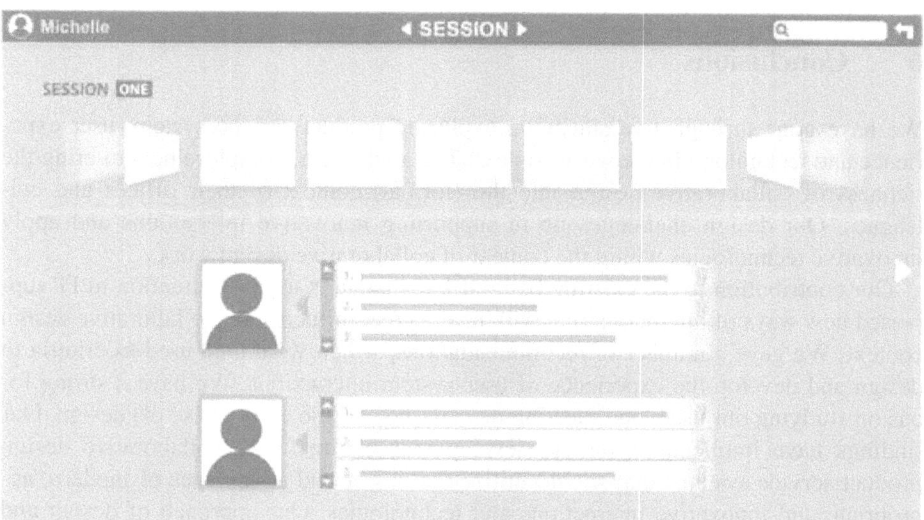

Fig. 2. Example of the user interface design

and each corresponds to the specific needs of the platform elements were conceived and finishing. Based on the above-depth study on the overall system architecture platform preliminary build. In the software interface has also made the concept, structure and interaction design with features to support the design and creative process. Platform and operating environment of space design and related components of product design was also performed. Domestic and foreign high-tech office space and products for the study, combined with the overall system architecture of the platform design of the physical space in the form of interface platform and the platform for the overall planning and design. See Fig. 2 for an impression of the user interface design.

5 Recommendations

Based on the results of our research approach, we identified a number of key design recommendations, which are given to design and develop interactive collaborative design platforms in the work context. These recommendations are as follows:

- Support typical user behaviors and meet their expectations
- Optimize styles of interaction
- Match context of use and design tasks
- Adopt iterative design and evaluation process
- Move from product to service system and platform
- Enable cross-platform seamless connection
- Reach ease-of-use and joy-of-use level
- Establish collaborative and multi-tasking user experience
- Apply and innovate modern technologies
- Promote rapid prototyping

6 Conclusions

We have gone through five stages on exploring product service system, user experience and technology in the work context. The goals were to explore how to bring the richness of collaborative design into the (formal) context of their offices and colleagues. Our design challenges lie in supporting innovative interactions and apply innovative technologies within the context of collaborative design work.

Our contribution to the existing body of knowledge is to draw attention to IT supported new ways of interacting that will have a great influence on collaborative design context. We gave a number of recommendations, which were then used as criteria to design and develop the experience of user-system interactions. We have a strong focus on studying our users and meeting their wishes in (the early phase of) design. Our findings have implications on the development of the future collaborative design product service systems that should utilize the power and advantages of modern, appropriate and innovative interactions and technologies. Our approach of design and development can also be used in the development of other services and/or tools for conceptualization.

7 Future Work

In the future, we envision going further by completing developing the collaborative design platform prototype in which the design recommendations are implemented. The prototype will also get evaluated based on how it functionally works, how its user interactions fit into the work context and how it can benefit future collaborative design work.

References

1. Archer, B.: The nature of research. Journal of Codesign (2), 6–13 (1995)
2. Avison, D.E., Lau, F., Myers, M.D., Nielsen, P.A.: Action research. Communications of ACM 42(1), 94–97 (1999)
3. CRISP Platform (2014), `http://www.crispplatform.nl/projects/pss-101`
4. Crowley, T., Milazzo, P., Baker, E., Forsdick, H., Tomlinson, R.: MMConf: an infrastructure for building shared multimedia applications. In: Proceedings of the 1990 ACM Conference on Computer-Supported Cooperative Work, pp. 329–342. ACM Press, New York (1990)
5. Greenberg, S., Marwood, D.: Real time groupware as a distributed system: concurrency control and its effect on the interface. In: Proceedings of the 1994 ACM Conference on Computer Supported Cooperative Work, pp. 207–217. ACM Press, New York (1994)
6. Hoeben, A., Stappers, P.J.: Taking clues from the world outside: Navigating interactive panoramas. Journal of Personal and Ubiquitous Computing 10(2-3), 122–127 (2006)
7. Hughes, J.A., Randall, D., Shapiro, D.: Faltering from ethnography to design. In: Proceedings of the 1992 ACM Conference on Computer-Supported Cooperative Work, pp. 115–122. ACM Press, New York (1992)
8. Keller, A.I.: For inspiration only, designer interaction with informal collections of visual material. Doctoral dissertation. Delft University of Technology, Delft (2005)
9. Koskinen, I., Zimmerman, J., Binder, T., Redström, J., Wensveen, S.: Design research through practice, 1st edn. Morgan Kaufmann (2011)
10. Kumar, R.: Research methodology: A step-by-step guide for beginners, 2nd edn. Sage Publications, Thousand Oaks (2005)
11. Ljungblad, S., Kotrbova, J., Jacobsson, M., Cramer, H., Niechwiadowicz, K.: Hospital robot at work: Something alien or an intelligent colleague? In: Proceedings of the ACM 2012 Conference on Computer Supported Cooperative Work (CSCW). ACM Press, New York (2012)
12. Nardi, B.A., Whittaker, S., Bradner, E.: Interaction and outeraction: instant messaging in action. In: Proceedings of the 2000 ACM Conference on Computer Supported Cooperative Work, pp. 79–88. ACM Press, New York (2000)
13. Neuwirth, C.M., Kaufer, D.S., Chandhok, R., Morris, J.H.: Issues in the design of computer support for co-authoring and commenting. In: Proceedings of the 1990 ACM Conference on Computer-Supported Cooperative Work, pp. 183–195. ACM Press, New York (1990)
14. Norman, D.A.: Emotion and design: Attractive things work better. Interactions 9(4), 36–42 (2002)

15. Rasmussen, M.K., Lehoux, N., Ocnarescu, I., Krogh, P.G.: I'll knock you when I'm ready...: Reflecting on media richness beyond bandwidth and imitation. In: Proceedings of the ACM 2012 Conference on Designing Interactive Systems (DIS), pp. 106–115 (2012)
16. Paton, M.: Qualitative research and evaluation methods (, 3rd edn. Sage Publications, Thousand Oaks (2002)
17. Sanders, L., Stappers, P.J.: Convivial toolbox: Generative research for the front end of design, pp. 224–225. BIS Publishers (2013)
18. Sleeswijk Visser, F., Stappers, P.J., van der Lugt, R., Sanders, E.B.-N.: Contextmapping: Experiences from Practice. Journal of Codesign 1(2), 119–149 (2005)
19. Tang, J.C., Isaacs, E.A., Rua, M.: Supporting distributed groups with a Montage of lightweight interactions. In: Proceedings of the 1994 ACM Conference on Computer Supported Cooperative Work, pp. 23–34. ACM Press, New York (1994)
20. Whyte, W.: Advancing scientific knowledge through participatory action research. Sociological Forum 4(3), 367–385 (1989)
21. Zimmerman, J., Forlizzi, J., Evenson, S.: Research through design as a method for interaction design research in HCI. In: Proceedings of the SIGCHI Conference on Human Factors in Computing Systems. ACM Press, New York (2007)

Cultural Creativity in Design Strategy: A Case Study of User's Preference of a Bird-Shaped Teapot

Chi-Chang Lu[1] and Po-Hsien Lin[2]

[1] Crafts and Design Department, National Taiwan University of Art
Ban Ciao City, Taipei 22058, Taiwan
t0134@ntua.edu.tw
[2] Graduate School of Creative Industry Design, National Taiwan University of Arts
Ban Ciao City, Taipei 22058, Taiwan
t0131@ntua.edu.tw

Abstract. The bionic design has become an important creative tool in the time of "perceptual consumption". Although the systematized concept and method for bionic design matured late as 1960s, but in essence it is an important method for creating artifacts in prehistoric era. The pottery Gui-tripod is just the masterpiece of bionic design pottery in Chinese Neolithic. Moreover, it represented the worship of sun - the spiritual power that ancient people relied on, and relating totems. In this article, the author wants to create a bird-shaped teapot transferred from the Pottery Gui-tripod. Besides the traditional Eastern charm, how can it have the style - the Modern fashion is the preoccupation. The research results show: shape extracted through Cezanne's "Cylinder, Sphere and Cone" theory not only be able to achieve the goal of fashion, but also conducive to the implementation of computer-aided design tools.

Keywords: Bionic design, Product design, teapot, Pottery Gui-tripod, Cezanne, fashion.

1 Introduction

The bionic design has become an important creative tool in the time of "perceptual consumption". Although the systematized concept and method for bionic design matured late as 1960s, but in essence it is an important method to create artifacts in prehistoric era.

There was bird-totem belief distributed widely and had a far-influence in prehistoric China. Therefore, bird-shaped pottery was very common and had a long span of years of evolutionary history in Neolithic China. From the modeling point of view, whether figurative or abstract, simple or complex, are successfully demonstrated the dynamic feature of bird. Among them, the Gui-tripod was a very unique and attractive pottery and eventually developed into Bronze Age ritual vessels, such as Jue-tripod, Jia-tripod and He-tripod.

The author had ever to conduct a comprehensive study for pottery Gui-tripod and write a book: The secret of Bronze Jue-tripod and Jia-tripod: from prehistoric Pottery

P.L.P. Rau (Ed.): CCD/HCII 2014, LNCS 8528, pp. 775–785, 2014.

Gui-tripod to the origin and dating Problem of the Xia and Shang Culture (Lu, 2007). This book reveals the important position in Chinese history and craft history of Pottery Gui-tripod series objects (Pottery Gui-tripod, Bronze Jue-tripod, Bronze Jia-tripod, Bronze He-tripod).

Whether from historical and cultural significance, or outstanding performance in the plastic arts, Pottery Gui-tripod enough to be one of the most objects of the representative in the history of China. Therefore, the author in a bird-shaped Teapot project design, Pottery Gui-tripod as a reference for the basis of shape, trying to develop a teapot with excellent functionality, and can present the qualities of modern fashion styling.

2 Research Purpose

This bird-shaped teapot design case is targeted to both of the important tourism resources – birds and the distinctive culture of tea in Taiwan. The regional flag of Tea culture and bird resources, guided the bird-shaped teapot idea. This study adopted the shape of Pottery Gui-tripod, the author most familiar to design a teapot with practical functionality and integration of traditional charm and modern fashion aesthetic. Its purpose and expected results are as follows:

a. possess the shapes characteristic elements of Pottery Gui-tripod and traditional oriental flavor.
b. possess contemporary characteristics with both the style of abstractionism and minimalism.
c. in addition to the image of the performance, but also have a utility function.

3 Literature Review

3.1 The "Function" and "Aesthetic" with Pottery Gui-Tripod

The Usage of the Pottery Gui-tripod is generally considered to boil water or warm wine. In addition to simulate the shape of a bird, the Pottery Gui-tripod also has a very superior design function.

The shape of the Pottery Gui-tripod was very unique in prehistoric artifacts. It not only extracted the abstract forms of the birds, but also very prominent on the dynamic performance of the simulated creatures. Its perfect combination of practical function and bionic form is also outstanding from the perspective of the present.

3.2 Abstract, Minimalist – Modern Fashionable Style

Abstract trend of Modern Art began with Cezanne and developed into cubism and abstract art. They followed rationalism and used geometric shapes and minimalist color to extract the performance of objects. These features were just in tune with the requirements of mass production and considered to be the best choice for machine production. Modernism design is born on this basis and became the most stable, most influential style in the First half of the 20th century.

Although Modernism design had been criticized by Post-modernism and leaving the design style to become more diverse. However, the trend that the shape and decoration of abstract and simplify is already taking shape, not possible to go back to the old ways of the traditional complicated fine decorative.

3.3 Cezanne's "Cylinder, Sphere and Cone"

Cezanne's famous quote: "treating nature by means of the cylinder, the sphere, the cone." (traitez la nature par le cylindre, la sphere, le cone) It is often cited as the Declaration of Western art began to move toward the abstract structure. However, scholars have different views that why is the implication of the famous words. "Made merely to introduce the one on perspective "(Reff, 1977:47) "This meant that he wanted to capture those features of nature that one regular and constant, independent of chance arrangement." (Tartakiewicz, 1980:284)"He presumably meant that he should always keep these basic solid shapes in mind when organizing his pictures." (Gombrich, 1995:574) Regardless of the original intention of Cezanne, art history gave the honorific title of "father of modern art" to him. This is definitely his "treating nature by means of the cylinder, the sphere, the cone", that is the influence of modern art. Cubist painter claimed: "who understand Cezanne will come to understand Cubism" (Osborne, 1979).

4 Practice of the Works

4.1 Consideration of the Work Function

Teapot is generally with body, mouth, spout, handle, lid five basic elements. Pottery Gui-tripod is a practical Stemware in prehistoric period, also with the basic elements of body, mouth, spout, handle, and some with the lid. Therefore, capture the shape of Pottery Gui-tripod transformed into a teapot is a convenient application.

4.2 Consideration of the Work Form

Pottery Gui-tripod is the ancient Chinese works, shape style tend to Oriental traditional organic form. In order to give this teapot with Modern Fashionable Style, try the father of modern art - Cezanne's theory to construct the basis for the development of design. Therefore, extract the Pottery Gui-tripod as a combination of the sphere, cylinder to get in line with contemporary fashionable abstract, minimalist style. Geometry is also conducive to the operation of 3D computer software to complete the design of the product.

In addition to emphasizing the modern minimalist style, freehand traditional Oriental plastic arts - "Wonder from the Similarity and Dissimilarity" should always take into account. Pottery Gui-tripod's shape originally had this trait, but also be designed in accordance with this principle as a return of the other possible additional features, such as bird's eye and crest.

Fig. 1. Computer-aided design and ceramic finished product

4.3 Practice of Cases: Computer-Aided Design

Use stereoscopic 3D modeling software - Rhino to construct the teapot body. For detailed decorative accessories will be constructed by the reverse engineering of 3D scanning technology. Then, obtain a solid model with CNC machining. Finally, finish the product through the ceramic molding process (Figure 1).

5 The Evaluation of the Feature of Fashion

5.1 Development of Questionnaire

The creation of fashion feature is the goal of this design case. For this issue, the author proposed final design results as a sample. A questionnaire survey was conducted to evaluate its degree of user's Preference. In addition, through this study observed users' preferences for cultural and creative product design.

Table 1. The bird-shaped teapot samples

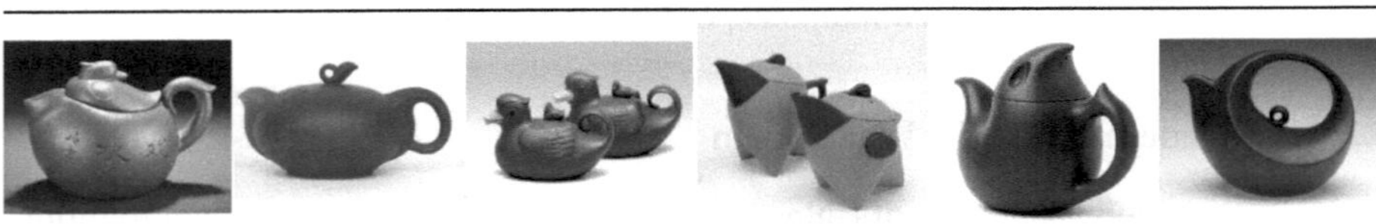

1	2	3	4	5	6

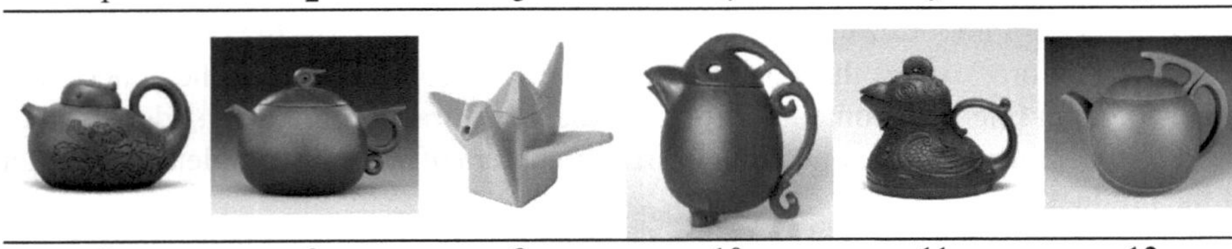

7	8	9	10	11	12

1. Stimulus samples: Bird-shaped teapot selected the China and Taiwan products through the Internet. The selection criteria was hoped to cover in the shape of most types. Finally, select a total of 12 products as a sample of the questionnaire, including the author's design case (Table 1). Many of these pieces are contemporary

"Yixing pot" well-known works of important writers, with a very high level of design and production. Due to the shape is the main focus of the study, the product photo is rendered to grayscale performance to avoid interference with the color section.

2. Dimensions and related attributes: Research topic is for the bird-shaped teapot. Teapot's performance is mainly in the "visual perception" and "utility function". Thus, use "visual perception", "utility function", "thematic" as three dimensions. After the initial test and remove the poor reliability items, obtained 9 bipolar adjectives and 3 questions related to attributes of three dimensions (Table 2).
3. Preference evaluations: In addition to 15 attributes, there is an overall performance evaluation including three indicators: "attractiveness of people put it down", "sophisticated ideas of design sense", and "classic of modern craft". And for personal preference, add a favorite product options.

Table 2. Three dimensions and their related attributes

Dimension	Attribute
Visual perception	(1) Vanguard vs. classical, (2) innovative vs. ordinary, (3) smart vs. stable, (4) harmonious vs. contrast, (5) minimalist vs. complicated, (6) pure vs. decorative, (7) comfortable-leisurely vs. stiff-serious, (8) something-more-to-say vs. plodding.
Utility function	(9) Functional vs. appreciate, (10) durable vs. fragile, (11) easy-to-use vs. bad-to-use, (12) easy-to-clean vs. bad-to-clean.
Thematic	(13) Bird's shape express good, (14) can fully convey the dynamic sense of animals, (15) will affect my preference.

Participants were asked to evaluate each stimulus sample with the fifteen attributes and three overall evaluations based on a five-point Likert scale, and to choose only one for the favorite from nine samples. A total 144 undergraduate and graduate students served as the subjects. Subjects include basic information: (1) gender, (2) age, (3) learning background, (4) the use of teapots experience, as shown in Table 3.

Table 3. The subjects in the experiment

Group	Gender		Age		Learning background		Tea-experience	
	Female	101	Under17	0	Product design	55	Often	9
	Male	43	18～30	117	Other design	41	Sometimes	52
			31～50	25	Art	23	Rarely	83
			Anove51	0	Other	25		
Total		144		144		144		144

5.2 Analysis of the Reliability and Validity

1. Factor analysis: Through factor analysis, reliability analysis and Cronbachα coefficient after the inspection, the attributes No.6, 12, 15 was discarded. The other attributes were also divided into four groups after conducting an exploratory factor analysis (Table 4).

2. Validity analysis: to analysis the validity of four dimensions and 12 attributes as follows: (1) Perception: 5 attributes of eigenvalue (3.314) were found to explain 66.278% of the total variance, and factor loadings started from .743 to .895. (2) Form: 2 attributes of eigenvalue (1.514) were found to explain 75.708% of the total variance, and factor loadings for each question are .870. (3) Function: 3 attributes of eigenvalue (2.627) were found to explain 87.574% of the total variance, and factor loadings started from .931 to .938. (4) Thematic: 2 attributes of eigenvalue (1.183) were found to explain 94.155% of the total variance, and factor loadings for each question are .970. Overall, exploratory factor analysis identified the four dimensions and 12 attributes with eigenvalue which greater than 1, and the factor loadings of each topic was greater than 0.7. The above data shows this scale has well construct validity.
3. Item analysis: The internal correlation between the research dimension and the total scale are .842, .856, .717, .665. All of the items are reach the level of significance of $P < .001$.
4. Reliability analysis: The alpha value of all dimensions are .872, .679, .929, .938, respectively. Whole scale is .880. These data reflected well reliability for this questionnaire.

Table 4. Dimensions and related attribute

Dimension	Attribute
Perception	(1) Vanguard vs. classical, (2) innovative vs. ordinary, (3) smart vs. stable, (7) comfortable-leisurely vs. stiff-serious, (8) something-more-to-say vs. plodding.
Form	(4) Harmonious vs. contrast, (5) minimalist vs. complicated,
Function	(9) Functional vs. appreciate, (10) durable vs. fragile, (11) easy-to-use vs. bad-to-use.
Thematic	(13) Bird's shape express good, (14) can fully convey the dynamic sense of animals.

5.3 Different Subjects in Data Analysis for the Evaluation of the Overall Feeling

T test and ANOVA analysis were executed for three overall evaluation: "attractiveness of people put it down", "sophisticated ideas of design sense", and "Classic of modern craft". The author's design case No.4 shows significant difference only in the learning background (Table 5). For the learning background, art-related groups seem to appreciate this piece.

5.4 Analysis of the Preference for Stimulus Samples

Through "chi-square test" and "correspondence analysis" shows the "preference" (most favorite product) is no significant difference for any backgrounds.

Table 5. ANOVA for impact Assessment of learning background dimension

Overall feeling	Source of variation	SS	df	MS	F	Scheffe
Attractiveness	Between Groups	10.328	3	3.443	5.322**	1<3
	Within Groups	90.561	140	.647		3>4
	Total	100.889	143			
Design sense	Between Groups	6.590	3	2.197	3.798*	1<3
	Within Groups	80.966	140	.578		
	Total	87.556	143			

*P<.05 **P<.01

Note: product design related background(1), other design related background(2), art related background(3), other background(4).

Subjects on 12 stimulus samples of preference data are shown in Table 6. The No.6 ranked first, the number of choice ratio up to 52.1%. No.4 - the author designed is also selected by 16.7% of the subjects, ranked second. The other 10 samples is relatively much lower, the ratio of choice are between 6.3-0.7%. The table also lists the three overall evaluation score and order as a reference, also shows the prominence of the No.6 and No.4 sample.

Table 6. User's preference and overall evaluation scores and ranking

No	Image	preference		attractiveness		design sense		Classic	
		Percentage	Ranking	Mean	Ranking	Mean	Ranking	Mean	Ranking
1		6.3	3	3.37	6	3.73	3	3.45	7
2		2.1	9	3.26	8	3.57	7	3.43	8
3		0.7	11	3.07	11	3.36	10	3.07	11
4		16.7	2	3.73	2	4.06	2	3.92	2
5		2.8	8	3.33	7	3.64	5	3.48	5
6		52.1	1	4.46	1	4.35	1	4.25	1
7		0.7	11	2.91	12	3.04	12	3.05	12
8	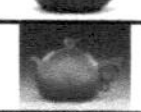	2.1	9	3.08	10	3.26	11	3.19	10
9	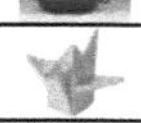	3.5	7	3.48	3	3.64	5	3.47	6
10	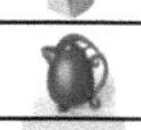	4.2	5	3.47	4	3.65	4	3.61	3
11		4.2	5	3.22	9	3.47	9	3.4	9
12	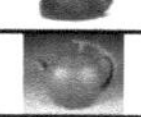	4.9	4	3.45	5	3.55	8	3.55	4

5.5 Explore the Relationship between the Evaluation and Various Dimension

Multiple regression analysis results are shown in Table 7. Four dependent variables in multivariate regression analysis of F values all are significant (P<.001). These explain the four dimensions can be used as a basis for predicting three overall evaluate. In the regression equation, β values related to the ability to predict the impact; but the results show that the prediction of the four dependent variables, only the "perception" and "thematic" dimensions have reached a significant level (P<.001). Besides, only "function" in "attractiveness of people put it down" reached a significant level (P<.01).

Table 7. The multiple regression for four dimensions and overall evaluation

Dependent	Independent variable	B	SE	β	t
Attractiveness	perception	.361	.100	.275	3.601***
	Form	-.116	.109	-.078	-1.066
	Function	.185	.070	.187	2.662**
	Thematic	.479	.076	.450	6.259***
		R=.683	Rsq=.467	F=30.435***	
Design sense	perception	.491	.080	.409	6.144***
	Form	-.001	.087	.001	.010
	Function	-.003	.056	-.037	-.597
	Thematic	.482	.061	.496	7.909***
		R=.771	Rsq=.594	F=50.844***	
Classic	perception	.517	.084	.418	6.156***
	Form	-.064	.091	-.046	-.697
	Function	-.021	.058	-.022	-.353
	Thematic	.492	.064	.491	7.678***
		R=.760	Rsq=.578	F=47.534***	

*P<.05 **P<.01 ***P<.001

Since the two dimensions of "form" and "thematic" bigger impact on the overall Evaluate, so try use all attributes of this two dimensions for the multiple regression analysis (Table 8). Data show that "innovative vs. ordinary", "something-more-to-say vs. plodding", "bird's shape express good" three indicators for the overall Evaluate is particularly important.

Table 8. The multiple regression for seven attributes and the average of overall evaluation

Dependent variable	Independent variable	B	SE	β	t
Average of overall evaluation	vanguard vs. classical	-.162	.080	-.170	-2.031*
	innovative vs. ordinary	.230	.087	.256	2.653**
	smart vs. stable	.080	.068	.087	1.173
	comfortable-leisurely vs. stiff-serious	.041	.066	.044	.621
	something-more-to-say vs. plodding	.258	.074	.272	3.496**
	bird's shape express good	.271	.100	.295	2.715**
	dynamic sense of animals	.169	.097	.192	1.745
	R=.819	Rsq=.671	F=39.659***		

*P<.05 **P<.01

5.6 Multidimensional Scaling

In order to understand the correlation between each stimulus samples and all attributes, multidimensional scaling (MDS) was used.

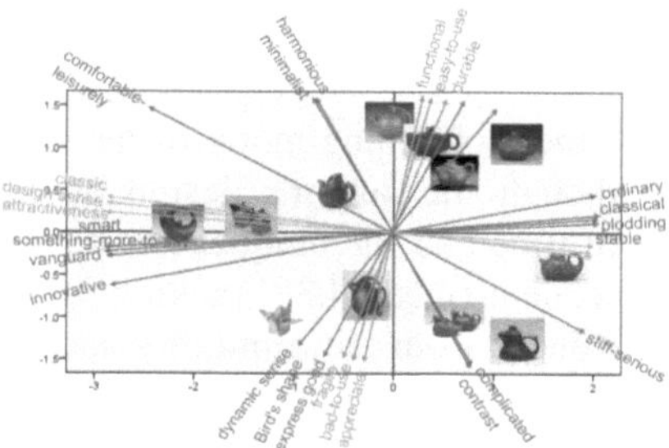

Fig. 2. The cognitive map of the 12 samples with all attributes

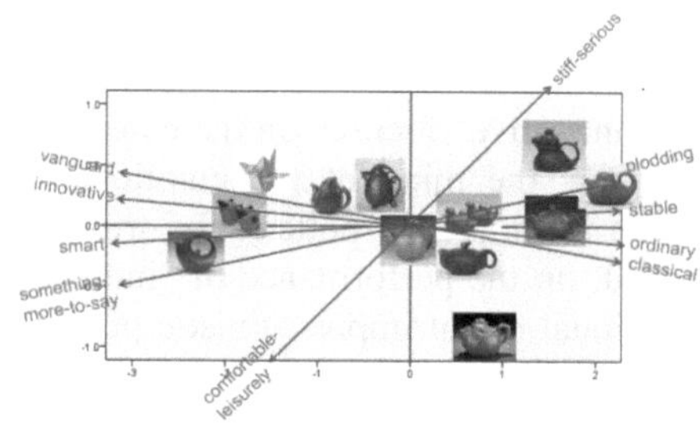

Fig. 3. The cognitive map of the 12 samples with 5 attributes of perception

First analysis all dimensions of the questionnaire, Kruskal's Stress =.09745, RSQ=.95673. It shows the two dimensions sufficient to describe the spatial relationship of the 12 samples with 15 attributes. The visual perceptual space shows: three indicators of "overall evaluate" and four indicators of "perception" just distributed near the x-axis. It shows that the "overall evaluate" and "perception" are the most relevant. Reference to the results of multiple regression analysis, can be considered the extent of recognition in "perception" sufficient to affect the results of its "overall Evaluate".

Second, to analysis the "perception" dimension, Kruskal's Stress =.01533, RSQ=.99902. The visual perceptual space shows: "vanguard", "innovative", "smart", and "something-more-to-say" all are close to the upper and lower sides of the x-axis symmetrically. In addition, the top four works are distributed in the quadrant II and III, and the top two just in the farthest distance from the origin. This illustrates the "vanguard", "innovative", "smart", and "something-more-to-say" as the most able to meet the tastes of contemporary users.

6 Discussion and Conclusion

6.1 "Perception" Is Greater Influence on the Level of User's Preferences

The results of questionnaire analysis shows: "emotional design" has become the focus of attention in the "perceptual consumption" era. Considered the "multiple regression analysis" and "multidimensional scaling" data, abstract and multiple "perception" dimension on the "overall evaluation" has the greatest impact. Among them, the "innovative" and " something-more-to-say" are the most decisive attributes.

Schimmack & Derryberry (2005) examined the attentional interference arising from emotional pictures, and found that the most arousing pictures produce the strongest interference. Not just pictures, the "innovative" styling products also have a higher degree of arousal. Post-modern design is distinguished by its unconventional form that denies the modernism.

"Something-more-to-say" means to arouse the imagination under appearance, and thus deeply enter the mind of the emotional level. Ancient Chinese Art emphasizes on "poetic" performance, such as: "there's an end to the words, but not to their message". In the field of contemporary design, "poetic design" shall also become the focus of designers' attention.

"Innovative" focuses on the external form, and the "something-more-to-say" deeply enters the mind of the emotional level. Although the author's design projects derive from ancient pottery Gui-tripod, the gap of time and the uniqueness of three-legged, on the performance of "innovative" is excellent (mean 4.38, ranking 3). The traditional orient impressionistic performance: "wonder from the Similarity and Dissimilarity"- that the author pursued also gets high evaluation in the indicator of "something-more-to-say" (mean 3.97, ranking 2).

"Bionic design" can make people think, and thus conducive to get the "perception" effect of "something-more-to-say". Analysis of multiple regression shows that the degree of fit "Thematic" for "overall evaluation" a high degree of correlation.

6.2 "Form" and "Function" Do Not Have a Direct Impact on User's Preferences

"Multiple regression analysis" and "multidimensional scaling" data also show that "form" and "function" dimensions do not have a direct impact on user's preferences.

Post-modern design style tends to have diverse performance. Questionnaire analysis shows "form" dimension such as "harmonious vs. contrast", "minimalist vs. complicated" are not absolutely critical. The top two samples of all ratings, No.6 gets the first place in "harmonious" but No.4 only gets the eleventh. A great gap is between the two samples. As for the "concise" indicator, one is at the rating third, the other is at sixth.

"Abstract" and "minimalist" had been considered to be a modern fashionable style in this case of a bird-shaped teapot. But the "abstract vs. concrete" indicator was removed due to poor reliability measure in the trial test. As for the "minimalist" attribute, the ones that have higher scores in "minimalist" also have slightly better performances, but it is not an absolute indicator of fashion. For example the No.11 is the most "complicated" and "Contrast" sample, and is not very good in three overall evaluation score. But there are some subjects who chose it as their favorite work (4.2%, ranking 5), which is far better than the most simple one, No.2 (2.1%, ranking 9). From the comprehensive observation, it seems that the minimalist and full of symbolic meaning can cause the most emotional resonance for consumer. Such works are more able to perceive the "something-more-to-say" effect.

About "function" dimension, it is hard for those who do not have a lot of tea experience to judge by only pictures. For example, I had considered about No.4 while designing, and it was admitted by tea experts. Yet it is quite different from the traditional teapot generally fall the scores on the middle degree. Nevertheless, the scores confirm that "function" dimension does not directly affect the user's preference. Evaluation of the top two, the No.6 and the No.4 sample, their "function" dimensions fall between the sixth to the eighth, and the No.4 is higher than No.6 sample.

6.3 The Feasibility of the Cezanne's Theory in Product Design Applications

Based on the analysis of the questionnaire, the bird-shaped teapot designed by Cezanne's theory can be considered successful. From the experience of the practice process, the author analyzes the reasons that lead it to success:

a. Cezanne's theory is the pioneer that guides the modern Western art to the abstract structure. It not only leads the trend of modern art, but also affects the design industry. Although being criticized by the "post-modernism", it still leads the design style to more diverse. However, the shape and decoration of abstract and simplify trend still dominate the development of the fashionable design route. Therefore the products which are designed in Cezanne's theory approach the trend of contemporary style easily.
b. While 3D computer construct being used as the main mean, Cone, sphere, cylinder to implementation of the design is a very efficient way.
c. Geometry is the mainstream of traditional Western styling. It gives people simple and certainly feeling, however it is also lack of stimulus. The organic form is a traditional orient aesthetic taste which presents a natural and hazy mood. How can we apply more organic form to the geometry shape had been considered in this case.

The success of this case display Cezanne's theory as a model of modern design is a practicable method and worth continuous exploring. It based on modern art theory, and accordance with the fashionable style of abstract and minimalist. Moreover it also meets the trend of technological development in the design and production process to achieve the goal of the pursuit of efficiency and cost savings.

Acknowledgment. This study was partly sponsored with a grant, NSC99-2622-H-144-002 -CC3, from the National Science Council, Taiwan.

References

1. Gombrich, E.H.: The Story of Art, 16th edn. Prentice-Hall, Englewood Cliffs (1995)
2. Lu, C.C.: The secret of Bronze Jue-tripod and Jia-tripod: from prehistoric Pottery Gui-tripod to the origin and dating Problem of the Xia and Shang Culture. Zhejiang University Press, Hangzhou (2007)
3. Osborne, H.: Abstraction and Artifice in Twentieth-Century Art. Clarendon Press, Oxford (1979)
4. Reff, T.: Painting and Theory in The Final Decade. In: Cézanne: The Late Work (exh. cat.). Museum of Modern Art, NY (1977)
5. Rewald, J.: Cézanne, A Biography. Harry N. Abrams, NY (1986)
6. Schimmack, U., Derryberry, D.: Attentional interference effects of emo-tional pictures: threat, negativity, or arousal? Emotion 5(1), 55–66 (2005)
7. Tatarkiewicz, W.: A History of Six Ideas. Polish Scientific Publishers, Warszawa (1980)

The GamiMedia Model: Gamifying Content Culture

Mizuki Sakamoto and Tatsuo Nakajima

Department of Computer Science and Engineering, Waseda University, Japan
{mizuki,tatsuo}@dcl.cs.waseda.ac.jp

Abstract. In Japan, gamified media has recently become popular. Among Japanese youth, one manifestation of this trend is the expansion of original media content to create fanfic content. This process changes passive consumers into active agents with the ability to advance society. However, no model currently exists for discussing and analyzing this phenomenon in contemporary Japanese anime, comics, and games—media whose fictionality penetrates the real world. In this paper, we develop the *GamiMedia* model to addresses this need. Because the model explicitly accommodates transmedia storytelling concepts, it can be used to explain how the fictional stories in Japanese media content are extended into the real world. The model presented in the paper may aid the design of a *digital-physical hybrid world* that could improve our lifestyles.

Keywords: game analysis, digital-physical hybrid design, culture-based design.

1 Introduction

The "*Cool Japan*" [20] concept was coined in 2002 to describe Japan's emergent cultural power. Japanese anime, comics, and games have become recognizable symbols of the "*Cool Japan*" trend. The Japanese government planned to expand Japan's economy by exporting this cultural content abroad. It was proposed that Cultural power in "*Cool Japan*" could be used to enhance digital hybrid artifacts [8, 11, 16, 17]. Studies showed that such an approach enables passive users to become active agents with the power to advance society. Specifically, as shown in [12, 14, 15], incorporating fictionality into the real world may offer a way to alter human attitudes and behaviors to achieve better lifestyles. However, no model is currently available for discussing and analyzing this phenomenon in contemporary Japanese anime, comics, and games—media whose fictionality penetrates the real world. Such a model should explicitly represent the meaning of objects in the content and identify Japan's unique cultural concepts.

In Japan, gamified media has recently become popular. Among Japanese youth, one manifestation of this trend is the expansion of original content to create fanfic content. This content is published on social networking sites. The collective, community development of this content has contributed to the emergent cultural phenomenon that is the essence of "*Cool Japan*". Existing models, including *Robin Hunicke*'s *Mechanics-Dynamics-Aesthetics* (MDA) framework [5] and *Jesper Juul*'s *Half-Real* model [6] are not suitable for analyzing the meaning of this cultural content and therefore have difficulty explaining the cultural gamification phenomenon.

P.L.P. Rau (Ed.): CCD/HCII 2014, LNCS 8528, pp. 786–797, 2014.

In this paper, the *GamiMedia* model is developed to address these problems. Because the model explicitly accommodates transmedia storytelling, it can be used to explain how the fictional stories found in Japanese media content are extended into the real world. After presenting an overview of the *GamiMedia* model in Section 2, we use the model to analyze four popular Japanese games in Section 3. These case studies demonstrate how Japanese media content penetrates the real world. In Section 4, we discuss the cultural implications of the model when it is used to design media content. In particular, we describe the development of fictional stories that can be integrated into the real world. We also suggest that incorporating universal ideological messages may make the content more acceptable to a variety of cultures. Section 5 concludes the paper.

2 The GamiMedia Model

In the *GamiMedia* model, each *GamiMedia* component contains at least one of the following three elements: Dynamics[1],Visuals, and Narrative. In our model, the Aesthetic dimension of the MDA model is divided into the Visuals and Narrative dimensions. In addition, a *GamiMedia* component is linked to another *GamiMedia* component when the meaning of that *GamiMedia* component is explained by the other *GamiMedia* component. This model enables us to determine how the meaning is constructed in the game.

In this section, we provide an overview of the *GamiMedia* model by analyzing Jason Rohrer's Passage,[2] which was released in 2007. The game lasts exactly five minutes and takes human life as its theme. An analysis of Passage shows that a player understands the meaning of the game by relying on metaphors represented by visual objects and by observing the interactions among these visual objects during the game. Because the metaphors are not culture-specific, most players can easily understand the meaning of the game.

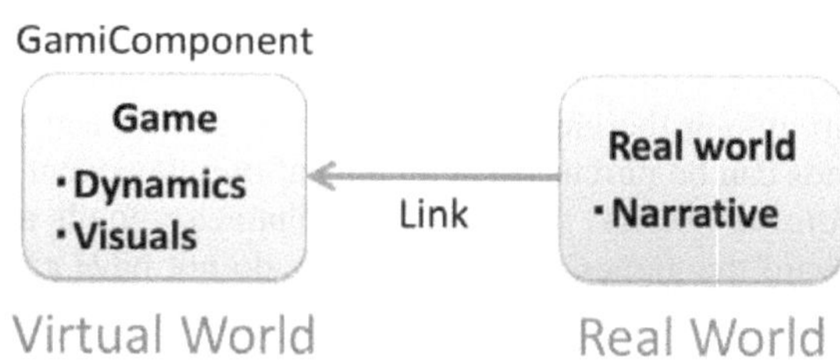

Fig. 1. GamiMedia Model of *Passage*

Passage represents an individual's life. The game's *visuals*, including treasure chests and obstacles, and the character's aging process indicate the main character's gender. However, meaning is communicated through more than *visuals*. The *dynamics* also

---

[1] Our definition of dynamics is similar to the concept of procedural rhetoric [2].
[2] `http://hcsoftware.sourceforge.net/passage/`

help players understand the concept of the game. For example, "*The game has a time limit,*" "*A male leading character couples with a female character when he approaches her,*" and "*The score increases when the character touches the treasure chests*" also communicate meaning to the player. The second *dynamic* represents "*marriage*"; the third represents "*earning money*". There are also obstacles near some of the treasure chests, making it difficult to collect the treasures. This represents the principle that people must work hard and overcome difficulties to receive rewards in life. Treasure chests and obstacles in the game are metaphors for the rewards and trials, respectively. The role of the *visuals* is to provide simulated objects or metaphors, and the role of the *dynamics* is to give them meaning. *Passage* does not provide any textual messages, but the players understand the essence of human life while playing the game because of their experience in the real world. Therefore, as Fig. 1 shows, the meaning of the *narrative* is defined outside of the game, and there is a *link* between the game and real world experience.

3 Case Studies

In this section, we analyze four games using the *GamiMedia* model: Nintendo's *Animal Crossing*,[3] Namco's "*Tales of*" series,[4] Nintendo's *Pokémon*,[5] and Broccoli's *Uta no Prince-sama*.[6] The analyses focus on the games' transmedia storytelling, exploring how the original game is expanded into other media, such as novels, anime, social media, and festival events. The approach can also explain the phenomena of Japanese fanfic and gamification and offers guidelines for exporting such cultural phenomena to foreign countries.

3.1 Story-Centered Game: "Tales of" Series

The "*Tales of*" series produced by Namco includes the *Tales of Phantasia*, *Tales of Destiny, Tales of the Abyss*, and others. Each game is a story-based role-playing game whose stories therefore play a prominent role. In the "*Tales of*" series, the stories exist exclusively in the game world. The stories are clearly presented through a series of messages that help players interpret the *visuals* and understand the characteristics of and the relationship among the characters in each game. To add value to the game, some character goods can be purchased at an annual two-day event called the *Tales of Festival*. In the "*Tales of*" series, the purpose of character goods and events is to increase empathy toward the games' characters; they do not have a direct effect on the games' content. Novels, anime, and smart phone applications based on the games have been produced. The game components used in each media element differ, as shown in Fig. 2. The novels contain only *narratives*, and the anime, though omitting the *dynamics* present in the original games, retain their *visuals* and the *narrative* arcs. If these media add meaning to the original games, they qualify as examples of transmedia storytelling.

[3] http://en.wikipedia.org/wiki/Animal_Crossing
[4] http://en.wikipedia.org/wiki/Tales_(series)
[5] http://en.wikipedia.org/wiki/Pok%C3%A9mon
[6] http://en.wikipedia.org/wiki/Uta_no_Prince-sama

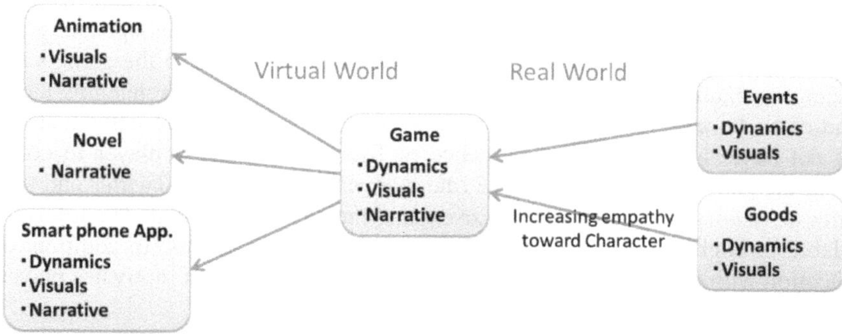

Fig. 2. GamiMedia Model of the "Tales of" series

3.2 Real Simulation Game: Animal Crossing

Animal Crossing is a community game published by Nintendo. This game simulates aspects of human life. However, all of the game characters, except for the player, are animals. In the game, a player can communicate with the animals, collect items such as furniture and clothes, arrange his/her own house and village, and participate in several seasonal events. Each event is strongly associated with actual human activities. The game simulates the *dynamics* of the real world, but they are represented in different forms through attractive *visuals*. *Twitter* and *Miiverse*[7] offer players information about the seasonal events. The *Animal Crossing* character's certified account tweets information about events in the game and the distribution of rare furniture. The character's tweet is consistent with the game character's personality, which maintains a sense of reality.[8] *Miiverse* is a service that allows players communicate with other players across the globe. It is accessible via *Wii U* and *Nintendo 3DS*. *Miiverse* hosts a community for each *Wii U* and *Nintendo 3DS* game, including one for the *Animal Crossing* community. Through the *Miiverse* community, players can send and share

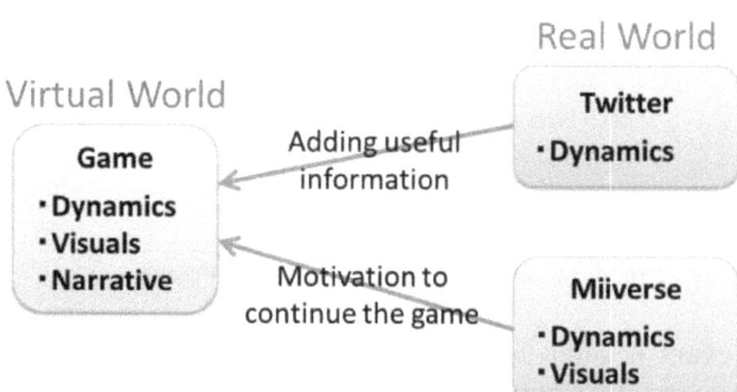

Fig. 3. GamiMedia Model of Animal Crossing

---

7 `https://miiverse.nintendo.net/`

8 In [12, 14], we discuss how reality is maintained when the real world and the fictional world are integrated.

impressions, questions, and information about *Animal Crossing* via text message or by drawing pictures. They can interact with others by sending a message and pressing the *"Yeah"* button. In some cases, these interactions contribute to the game's development. For example, players can visit other players' villages by exchanging a unique friend code. In another player's village, it is possible to obtain rare items that he/she does not have. In addition, the existence of friends motivates a player to continue playing the game. As shown in Fig. 3, the *dynamics* produced by *Twitter* and the *dynamics* or *visuals* provided by *Miiverse* expand the game's potential. The information available through *Twitter* reminds the players about game events. In addition, communication with other players can enhance the game's events and motivates players to continue to play *Animal Crossing*.

3.3 Transmedia Game 1: Uta no Prince-sama

The important elements of *Uta no Prince-sama* are Love and Music. The main female character enjoys falling love with boy singers, who are typically called *Prince*; her bond with her favorite *Prince* is deepened through music. A player chooses her favorite *Prince* from 11 main boy singer characters. *Uta no Prince-sama* offers an immersive experience for female players. The game is expanded by collecting goods and attending festival events. Each boy singer's goods are for sale, and a player can purchase her favorite *Prince*'s goods. The goods are designed to appeal to a typical female and include key holders, accessories, dolls, and fragrances. Some goods are fictionally promoted as being *"produced by Prince,"* and a player can purchase the goods with a message card from *Prince*. In addition, festival events are staged whose concepts correspond to the themes of Love and Music.

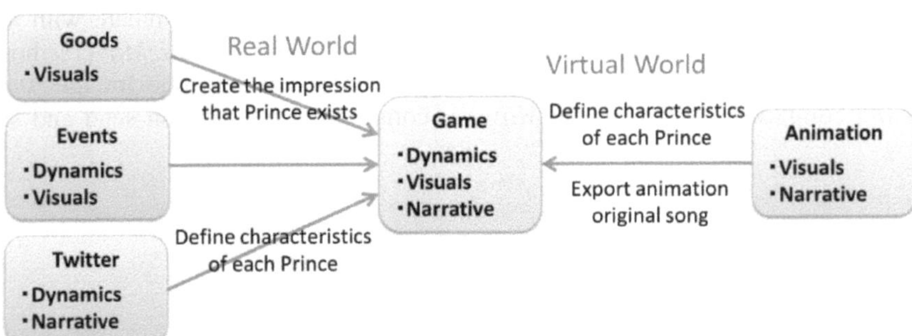

Fig. 4. GamiMedia Model of Uta no Prince-sama

The festival event is often held in a popular dating spot, such as an amusement park or karaoke room. This creates the sense that the participant is dating her *Prince* not only in the game's world but also in the real world and increases her empathetic feelings toward *Prince*. The anime and conversations hosted on *Twitter* offer additional stories that differ from the game's story. In addition, the boy singers perform original songs in the anime that can be imported into the game. In *Animal Crossing*, only one character tweets information about the game on *Twitter*. In *Uta no*

Prince-sama, each of the 11 boy singers have their own certified accounts and communicate with each other via *Twitter*. Through these interactions and the anime series, the players learn more about each singer and their relationships with each other. Because boy singing groups are popular in Japan, many females believe in the realistic nature of their *Prince*. It is difficult to date a real singer, but it is possible to date *Prince* in the game. The fulfillment of this desire is used to engage females in the game. The *dynamics*, *visuals*, and *narrative* are deployed well in each medium to create the *Uta no Prince-sama* world, making it another good example of transmedia storytelling. Fig. 4 shows how the multiple media channels can be organized using the *GamiMedia* model. The virtual world, including the game and the anime, reveal the characteristics of each *Prince*. The sense of each *Prince*'s existence is produced by goods, events, and *Twitter* conversations in the real world, all of which contribute to the player's love of her favorite *Prince*.

3.4 Transmedia Game 2: Pokémon

The basic concepts of *Pokémon* are the battle and the collection of *Pokémon* throughout the game story. Some players value the battle while other players value collecting and amassing *Pokémon*. *Pokémon* is an open game, which means that enjoyment can be felt even after completing the game. The *Pokémon world* contains multiple media channels through which the details of the world are defined using a transmedia storytelling concept, including *Pokémon*-related comics, animated cartoons, movies, card games, festival events, amusement parks, and character goods. Each medium is synergized with the game. Movies and festival events often provide players the opportunity to collect rare *Pokémon*. Several legendary *Pokémon* cannot be collected by only playing the game and must be collected at the *Pokémon* movie or festival events. The movies and events are therefore considered part of the game. Like the original video game, card games and amusement parks also have the *agency property* [15].

In the arcade game *Pokémon Tretta*, whose concept is also to battle and collect *Pokémon*, tangible toys, paper cards also called *Pokémon Tretta*, are collected. Because of the cards' tangibility, a player feels like he/she "*is a Pokémon trainer*" in both the real and game worlds.

Animated cartoons and character goods immerse the player in the game's world. The *Pokémon* cartoon has been broadcasted at the same time and the same day every week for more than 15 years in Japan. In addition, *Pokémon Center*, a character goods shop, has stores located throughout Japan. *Pokémon Center* has attracted many visitors seeking to immerse themselves in the *Pokémon* world outside of the game world. The regularly broadcasted cartoons and a variety of goods improve *Pokémon*'s integration into the real world. Each *Pokémon*'s detailed characteristics are defined in the cartoon's story, not in the game. The collaboration among the media channels increases the sense of reality and imbeds the *Pokémon* story in the real world. Fig. 5 shows how the multiple media channels can be understood using the *GamiMedia* model. In *Pokémon*, collaboration among many *GamiMedia* components and links immerses players in the *Pokémon* world. In these ways, the *narrative* of the virtual *Pokémon* world, whose leading character is the player himself/herself, enters the real world.

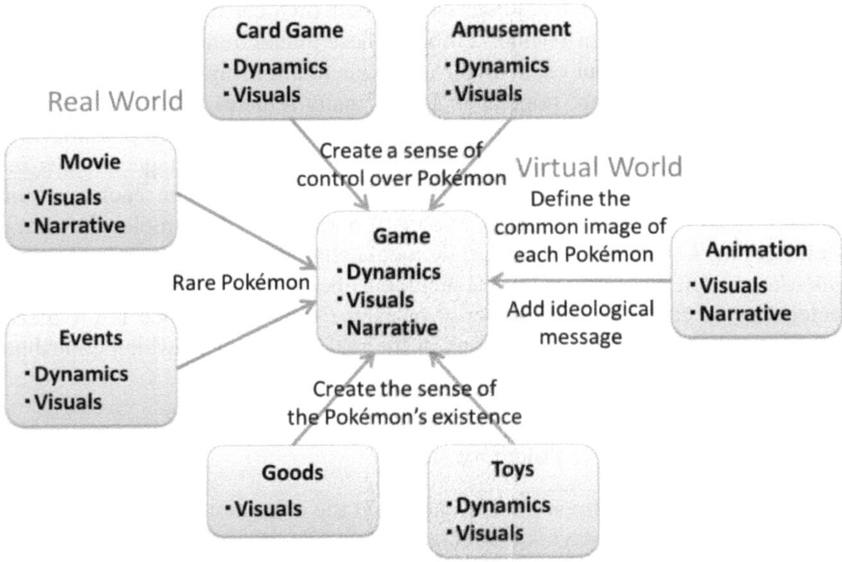

Fig. 5. GamiMedia Model of Pokémon

4 Cultural Implication

The design of media content such as anime and games is strongly associated with the culture in which it is produced. As shown in [15], the *GamiMedia* model can be used to embody fictional stories in the real world. If the fictionality does not match the players' culture, the player does not perceive the fiction as realistic. In this section, we discuss the cultural implications of the model when it is used to design media content.

4.1 Culture-Based Design

Tokimeki Memorial is a dating simulation game developed by Konami and the first game in the *Tokimeki Memorial* series.[9] Because the game's content depends on an understanding of Japanese culture, its American version, *Brooktown High*,[10] was significantly modified to suit American culture. For example, the typical social relationships among Japanese and American high school students are significantly different. Because social interaction is a fundamental theme of the game, changing the theme requires a complete re-implementation of the game. It is therefore difficult to modify *Tokimeki Memorial* for other cultures. On the other hand, when popular Japanese anime are exported to other countries, it is typical to change the characters' names. Some of the goods typical in Japan are also changed to become more appealing in other countries. This translation process is not difficult if the characters and goods are easily replaced by other characters and goods. The *GamiMedia* model can

[9] http://www.konami.jp/gs/game/Girls_Side/
[10] http://www.ign.com/games/brooktown-high/psp-826688

show whether the translation will be easy or not because it explicitly specifies these characters and goods and defines their meanings.

One way to create media content that will appeal to people of different cultures is to adopt the cultural events or goods of those countries. If the content reflects the events and goods of the players' cultures, their empathy toward the game will increase.

For example, in *Animal Crossing*, players can participate in various seasonal events. In mid-August, players can participate in "*Obon*," during which the player acquires symbolic objects, such as "*Cucumber Horse*" and "*Eggplant Cow*." "*Obon*" is an important Japanese holiday, and these objects are cultural metaphors. If players understand the cultural background of "*Obon*," their interest in the game will increase. Because *Animal Crossing* contains various seasonal events from different counties, the possibility that players from different counties will be satisfied by the game is high.

Using transmedia storytelling is an advantageous approach because a variety of media can be used to provide details about other cultures' events or goods. The potential for using games to teach about other cultures is notable. Many social problems arise from misunderstanding other cultures' religions. Games could address this problem by teaching players about the traditions and beliefs of other cultures. Furthermore, the *GamiMedia* model allows *GamiMedia* components to be replaced by other components that are familiar to another culture or to integrate stories that explain the meaning of elements in the components. This characteristic has the potential to improve the treatment of cultural content.

Japanese anime studios have recently begun to adopt 3D computer graphics (3DCG) for economic reasons. When an animated production is based on a game, the game's 3D character models can be used to create the animation. Recent releases such as *009 Re:Cyborg*[11] and *Arpeggio of Blue Steel*[12] used 3DCG in almost every scene. All of the objects and backgrounds, including battleships, buildings, and special effects, were also represented by 3D models. This approach facilitates the modification of characters and goods to reflect the cultures of different audiences.

The *GamiMedia* model is a useful tool for analyzing the consistency of the content represented in different media while maintaining its connection to reality. The design patterns presented in [12, 14] provide guidelines for creating attractive media content for different cultures. In addition, transmedia strategies increase the possibility of embodying this media content in the real world and altering attitudes and behaviors [13, 15]. In the following subsections, we discuss two methods for creating media content that can be changed to reflect the player's culture.

4.2 Transmedia Storytelling Design

Transmedia storytelling is an effective tool for integrating a fictional story into the real world [3, 7]. When using transmedia storytelling, media content is fragmented into multiple media and distributed in several locations. If an anime series and a game are designed for transmedia storytelling, they are easily incorporated into the real

[11] `http://009.re-cyb.org/`

[12] `http://aokihagane.wikia.com/wiki/Aoki_Hagane_no_Arpeggio_Wiki`

world because the fragmented media content can appear anywhere at any time through the use of nearly ubiquitous projectors and displays [15]. In this subsection, we present two examples of how narratives originally appearing in Japanese anime can easily be expanded through transmedia storytelling and incorporated into the real world.

The first example is the *Fate* series,[13] a *Type-Moon* media collective. The main elements include battles called *Holy Grail Wars* in which *Masters*, typically accomplished magi, summon *Servants* and *Heroic Spirits* as they battle each other. The last remaining pair claims the *Holy Grail*. The series began with the visual novel *Fate/stay night* and has developed many spinoffs under the "*Fate*" name. For instance, *Fate Zero* is a popular spinoff and prequel of *Fate/stay night*. A new spinoff can be easily created, even in a different cultural context, because the battles (battle royale) in which the characters destroy each other until only one remains is typical of role playing games, and the *Servants* in the series include famous heroes from world literature, such as *King Arthur* and *Gilgamesh*. A new story can also use new heroes and heroines that are popular in any culture as long as it maintains the atmosphere of the *Fate* series. Therefore, defining a basic battle style makes it possible to create a variety of stories that share similar qualities. Analysis shows that any fan community can create a new story in the *Fate* series independently. By embedding the story in their own cultural context, players feel that the story becomes more realistic.

The second example is *AKB0048*,[14] a story based on *AKB48*, a singing group popular in Japan[15] and other Asian countries. *AKB0048* is a fictional singing group that resists the existing government system. Each singer uses an *AKB48*'s singer's name, and her basic personality is inherited from the original singer. Fans in Asian countries enjoy the story because they are familiar with the *AKB48* singers. The storyline easily accommodates new stories through the creation of new characters who inherit the basic personality traits of the original singers. Therefore, it appears to be effective to create characters who inherit qualities from well-known people. The story is temporally asynchronous with current events and is therefore not suitable for integration into the real world. However, the strong connections between the current culture and the culture depicted in the futuristic story lend a sense of reality to the fiction.

The *GamiMedia* model describes how the new story can maintain the qualities of the original story by extracting the stories' common structures.

4.3 Designs with Ideological Messages

Currently, virtual characters are ubiquitous in daily life. Famous *Disney* characters such as *Mickey Mouse* and *Donald Duck* can provoke empathetic feelings regardless of the setting, and *Hello Kitty* and *Pokémon* are now found all over the world [1]. In cartoons and games, each virtual character has its own personality and story, which can be used to convey special information and messages. If people are familiar with the fictional narrative behind a cartoon or game, the action or interactions of the

---

[13] `http://typemoon.wikia.com/wiki/Fate_series`
[14] `http://akb0048.wikia.com/wiki/AKB0048_Wiki`
[15] `http://www.akb48.co.jp/`

story's characters will easily recall the story elements without additional cues. Daily life is becoming increasingly complex, and our ability to manage significant information is crucial. In modern society, there are many social problems that need to be solved urgently, but it is difficult to convey important ideological messages succinctly [9, 13].

Ideological messages are often deployed in literature and movies to increase the tension of the stories and maintain their reality or consistency [19]. The interpretation of these ideological messages is usually universal. Thus, once incorporated into stories, these messages can be easily understood across cultures. In this subsection, we describe two examples of the use of universal ideological messages in stories. These examples are from recent Japanese animated television series, indicating that imbedding ideological messages in this media form is common in Japan.

The first example is *Arpeggio of Blue Steel.* In this television series, a humanoid life form that pilots the submarine *I-401* acquires a human mind and begins to make decisions through her ego instead of following others' orders. The story tells a typical story of the growth of a young person learning to face the demands of the real world. Other humanoids also encounter mental conflicts as they become conscious of their egos. The ideological message is the importance of accepting other people; we begin in isolation, like the humanoids, but as we accept others, we grow to be able to meet the challenges of the real world. Because the message is familiar to most cultures, a story based on this message can be easily understood in any cultural context.

The second example is *Gatchaman Crowds*,[16] a 2013 television anime series based on the 1972 anime series *Science Ninja Team Gatchaman*. The *Gatchaman* are warriors who fight in special reinforced suits that manifest their unique spiritual powers. The ideological message of the series is to indicate the role of a hero in an age in which social media affects citizens and politics may soon become controlled from the bottom up. In such a society, it is difficult to identify the antagonist. Because of this uncertainty, a hero cannot solve a problem or identify the evil that he needs to fight by himself. This message is also universal.

However, ideological messages can become diluted when the original story is combined with other stories. For example, *Arpeggio of Blue Steel* is currently being used in a game called *Kantai Collection*,[17] a popular online game in Japan. The game borrows its characters and part of its storyline from *Arpeggio of Blue Steel*. Similarly, *Gatchaman Crowds* is set in *Tachikawa*, a city in the Tokyo Metropolis. The real *Tachikawa* plans to host many attractions related to the series. It is more difficult to communicate the ideological message through *Kantai Collection* or during events in *Tachikawa* because understanding the message is not the purpose of the game or the events, which are meant simply to entertain. Future studies should examine how to effectively incorporate ideological messages into transmedia storytelling [11, 17]. The *GamiMedia* model represents the first step toward discussing the integration of these ideological messages into the real world through transmedia storytelling.

---

[16] http://gatchaman.wikia.com/wiki/Gatchaman_Crowds

[17] http://en.wikipedia.org/wiki/Kantai_Collection

5 Conclusion and Future Directions

Games are half real and half fiction [6], and integrating the fiction into the real world increases engagement and motivation. The *GamiMedia* model demonstrates how fiction can be seamlessly integrated into our daily lives. However, we need to investigate how the relationship between fiction and reality should be controlled. A magic circle concept [18] could provide a model for controlling the boundary between fiction and reality on a case-by-case basis, allowing appropriate feedback to be offered to a user about his/her treatment of his/her fictional situation.

We are enhancing the *GamiMedia* model in the following two directions. First, the model is being modified to consider individual personality traits when designing transmedia content. As indicated in [10], one's preference depends on one's personality. To attract more users, media content should appeal to multiple types of personalities. The value-based design framework [8, 16] aids the design of such media content. By using participatory design within the framework, it is possible to create media content with broad appeal.

Second, the model is being used to formulate a critical design methodology for media [4]. Designing media content containing ideological messages is usually highly experimental. The critical design approach provides a basic foundation for creating more ideological content for addressing serious social problems.

References

1. Allison, A.: Millennial Monsters: Japanese Toys and the Global Imagination. University of California Press (2006)
2. Bogost, I.: Persuasive Games: The Expressive Power of Video Games. MIT Press (2007)
3. Dena, C.: Transmedia Practice: Theorising the Practice of Expressing a Fictional World across Distinct Media and Environments, Dissertation Thesis, University Sydney (2009)
4. Dunne, A., Raby, F.: Speculative Everything: Design, Fiction, and Social Dreaming. The MIT Press (2013)
5. Hunicke, R., Leblanc, M., Zubek, R.: MDA: A Formal Approach to Game Design and Game Research. In: Proceedings of the Challenges in Game AI Workshop, Nineteenth National Conference on Artificial Intelligence
6. Juul, J.: Half-Real: Video Games between Real Rules and Fictional Worlds. MIT Press (2005)
7. Ruppel, M.N.: Visualizing Transmedia Network: Links, Paths and Peripheries, Dissertation Thesis, University of Maryland (2012)
8. Sakamoto, M., Nakajima, T., Alexandrova, T.: Digital-Physical Hybrid Design: Harmonizing the Real World and the Virtual World. In: Proceedings of the 7th International Conference on the Design & Semantics of Form & Movement (2012)
9. Sakamoto, M., Nakajima, T.: Micro-Crowdfunding: Achieving a Sustainable Society through Economic and Social Incentives in Micro-Level Crowdfunding. In: Proceedings of International Conference on Mobile and Ubiquitous Multimedia (2013)
10. Sakamoto, M., Alexandrova, T., Nakajima, T.: Analyzing the Effects of Virtualizing and Augmenting Trading Card Game based on the Player's Personality. In: Proceedings of The Sixth International Conference on Advances in Computer-Human Interactions (2013)

11. Sakamoto, M., Alexandrova, T., Nakajima, T.: Augmenting Remote Trading Card Play with Virtual Characters used in Animation and Game Stories - Towards Persuasive and Ambient Transmedia Storytelling. In: Proceedings of the 6th International Conference on Advances in Computer-Human Interactions (2013)
12. Sakamoto, M., Nakajima, T., Akioka, S.: Designing enhanced daily digital artifacts based on the analysis of product promotions using fictional animation stories. In: Yoshida, T., Kou, G., Skowron, A., Cao, J., Hacid, H., Zhong, N. (eds.) AMT 2013. LNCS, vol. 8210, pp. 266–277. Springer, Heidelberg (2013)
13. Sakamoto, M., Nakajima, T.: Gamifying Social Media to Encourage Social Activities with Digital-Physical Hybrid Role-Playing. In: Meiselwitz, G. (ed.) SCSM/HCII 2014. LNCS, vol. 8531, pp. 581–591. Springer, Heidelberg (2014)
14. Sakamoto, M., Nakajima, T.: A Better Integration of Fictional Stories into the Real World for Gamifying Intelligent Daily Life. In: Proceedings of the First International Symposium on Simulation and Serious Games (2014)
15. Sakamoto, M., Nakajima, T., Akioka, S.: A Methodology for Gamifying Smart Cities: Navigating Human Behavior and Attitude. In: Streitz, N. (ed.) DAPI 2014. LNCS, vol. 8530, pp. 593–604. Springer, Heidelberg (2014)
16. Sakamoto, M., Alexandrova, T., Nakajima, T.: Designing Values for Digital-Physical Hybrid Artifacts, Waseda University Distributed Computing Laboratory Research Report 2014-2 (2014)
17. Sakamoto, M., Alexandrova, T., Nakajima, T.: Introducing Virtuality for Enhancing Game-related Physical Artifacts. International Journal of Smart Home 8(2), 137–152 (2014)
18. Salen, K., Zimmerman, E.: Rules of Play: Game Design Fundamentals. The MIT Press (2003)
19. Okada, T.: Yuigon. Chikuma Publisher (2010) (in Japanese)
20. Is Japan Cool?, `https://www.ana-cooljapan.com/`

Applying the Time and Space Forms of Poetry to Creative Design

Mo-Li Yeh[1], Ming-shean Wang[2], and Pey-Chwen Lin[3]

[1] Design College, Hsing Wu University
Linkou, Taipei 24452, Taiwan
[2] Digital and Design Department, Mingdao University
Peetow, Changhua 52345, Taiwan
[3] New Media Art, National Taiwan University of Art
Ban Ciao City, Taipei 22058, Taiwan
1101moli@gmail.com

Abstract. In recent years, countries worldwide have actively employed culture-inspired creativity to add value to designs. Poetry is a means by which poets express profound and subtle emotions and thoughts using refined words. Classical and renowned poems that have survived for thousands of years are undoubtedly excellently refined masterpieces. We established a series of operable steps for converting abstract creative poetry concepts into concrete poetry designs to enhance the enriched literary connotations of designs and improve the values of the affective and aesthetic experience of poetry. Based on the spiritual characteristics of classical Chinese poetry and theories related to time and space, this study references literature regarding the feasibility of applying cultural creativity to designs and summarizes 4 forms of poetry, namely, time/space reflection, time/space separation, time/space sympathy, and time/space integration. When designing actual cases, we considered the method by which a logical inference procedure can be developed and the concrete steps for reasonably converting poetry into design. Subsequently, this study describes the extraction and control of critical meanings from the context and themes of traditional poetry to analyze structural forms and content of time and space. The converted poetry design cases were then integrated to construct a creative design application model for the time and space forms of poetry. Integrating traditional poetry culture with modern designs provides the current cultural and creative industry with a feasible design model. Furthermore, creative design revitalizes traditional poetry, which enables the value of poetry to be fully developed and realized in cultural and creative applications.

Keywords: poetry, time and space, cultural creativity, creative design.

1 Introduction

Various countries have attempted to leverage their cultural characteristics to enhance the implied value of creative design and promote a culturally oriented aesthetic economy. According to Lin (2007), culture is a lifestyle; design is a taste; creativity is a

P.L.P. Rau (Ed.): CCD/HCII 2014, LNCS 8528, pp. 798–807, 2014.

type of recognition achieved through affection; and industry is a medium, approach, or method that can be used to realize creativity in cultural design. The essence of creative cultural design is extracting cultural elements, converting cultural symbols, and endowing designs with novel aesthetic implications. Most cultural product designs currently available in Taiwan are derived from tangible cultural assets such as historical sites and buildings, natural scenery, cultural landscapes, and utensils; however, few creative ideas have originated from intangible cultural assets. Poetry is a root of traditional culture, providing an explicit form of communication and implicit representation and connotations that can be used to inspire creative cultural design. Thus, the intangible cultural elements of poetry can be extracted and referenced to conceptualize creative cultural design. We explored converting the time and space forms of classical poetry and the feasibility of applying these forms to modern design. This application should benefit cultural preservation, enhancing the meaning and profoundness of overall creative cultural design.

2 Relationship between Poetry and Design

2.1 Poetry: Design Thinking of Cultural Creativity

Li (1996) defined culture as "products created by people through common activities; culture includes the tools used by people, the codes and systems on which social life is based, art products that enrich people's spiritual life, and people's mental activities during creative processes." Chinese history and culture spans 5,000 years, and the culture of classical poetry that has accumulated for generations is an invaluable and intangible cultural asset. The German philosopher Cassirer (1944) stated that culture is the externalization and objectification of human beings and the actualization and concretization of symbolic activities. In addition, all human cultural forms are symbolic forms. Influenced by this theory, Langer (1953), an American philosopher, argued, "Art is the creation of forms symbolic of human feeling." This argument profoundly influenced modern aesthetic theories. Poetry culture comprises the artistic expressions of concrete text symbols that poets use to express psychological and emotional dimensions. In his book *Abstraction and Empathy*, the German philosopher Worringer (2007) indicated that humans derive happiness from art primarily because people can extract individual objects and events of the external world from all contingency and caprice; thus, abstract forms are used to eternalize the extracted objects. Regarding the creation of poetry, Zhu (1988) asserted that depression originates from discontentment with the finiteness or limitations of life and that imagination and fantasies represent the pursuit of the infinite. In addition, he claimed that "poetry consists of implicit and explicit meanings. Implicit meanings focus on the principles and reasons of objects, whereas explicit meanings emphasize the appearance. Poetry is only complete when it contains both implicit and explicit meanings." Put simply, poetry is the process of using finite language to seek infinite imagination and create poetic images that stand the test of logical thinking. Rapaille (2006) reasoned that effective commodities must be able to activate the cultural codes relevant to consumers. Thus, the classical poetry culture that has been transmitted through the generations can be employed to interpret the implicit forms of poetic emotion. These interpretations can be converted to poetic products that feature cultural creativity, satisfying the desires and demands of contemporary people, who experience internal emptiness, and enhancing the meaning and depths of creative cultural design. The inner cultivation of poets often affects the level of artistic conception and emotions delivered through their works. In the *Shanjingju Hualun* (*Shanjingju Critiques of Paintings*), the Qing Dynasty artist Fang Xun stated that "the magic of brushes and ink lies in the magic of the painters' ideas. Therefore, ancient painters take up brushes to paint only after they have developed ideas." He also stated that "painters must first conceptualize ideas to position their works. Surprising ideas result in interesting paintings; advanced ideas yield thought-provoking paintings; pioneering ideas create forward-looking paintings; profound ideas constitute deep paintings; nostalgic ideas form reminiscent paintings; ordinary ideas give birth to mediocre paintings; and vulgar ideas generate inferior paintings." These comments enforce the viewpoint that the depth of poetic emotions and ideas determines the elegance of the ideologies underlying poetic works. Famous poems that have survived thousands of years are typically works that have undergone constant revisions. Consequently, poetry can be used to enhance the literary connotations of designs, endowing them with poetic conceptions and aesthetic experiences.

2.2 Significance of the Time and Space Design in Poetry

In his book *Chinese Poetics: Design*, Huang (1976) adopted the perspective of modern aesthetics and established an objective aesthetic system in abstract poetic art, implementing interdisciplinary integration. Specifically, art psychology and the relations among various art forms (e.g., plastic arts) were emphasized to develop the theoretical core of poetics. This facilitated exploring the artistic qualities of classical Chinese poetry, allowing the thoughtfulness in these poems to be acknowledged and understood. Li (2007) argued that "the conceptualization of poems is the most creative and crucial stage in creating poetry. An excellent poem is typically based on excellent ideas, which are essentially creative imagination. This imagination is an expression of creative association." Li (2007) further asserted that "time and space have mystical and undeniable bonds with human beings, who are integral components of the universe. Time and space are also eternally linked to poetry, which is a wonderful art form that never withers. Only in the contexts of time and space can poetry blossom, radiate fragrance, and glow with its unique hues." In his sonnets, Shakespeare expressed his ideas as a poet and author, regarding the transience of time and the eternity of poetry. Huang (1976) offered a poetic definition of poetry: "The sayings that poetry is an audible landscape and painting in time, or that poetry is visible music and painted time are both reasonable because poetry is an art interwoven in time and space. Rather than static, poetry is extensive and variable through time and space." Therefore, time and space design in poetry is vital when examining Chinese poetry because the contents of poems are primarily based on time, space, emotion, and reason. These complex elements connect and transcend time and space, becoming alternately evident or absent during the natural transition of time and space. The magical and seamless immersion between human beings and time and space, and the connection between emotions and philosophies cannot be uprooted from the contexts of time and space. Instead, the interactions of concrete temporal and spatial images are essential for visualizing these relationships. Therefore, time and space design is the most vital link in Chinese poetry. In summary, time and space has been explored by domestic and international philosophers and scientists in ancient and modern times; it is a vital aesthetic theme expressed by domestic and international poets in ancient and contemporary times.

2.3 Applying the Time and Space Forms of Poetry to Design

The time and space forms of art works are objectified and concretized expressions of the artists' aesthetic awareness of time and space realized using artistic approaches. Time and space are two basic forms through which artistic images sustain and express themselves (Li, 2007). Xie He was a scholar in the Southern Qi period who proposed the idea of six principles in the *Guhua Pinlu* (*A Critique of Ancient Paintings*). Specifically, the concept of operating position essentially refers to the temporal and spatial structures of works. The composition principles used in contemporary painting theories are derived from the classical concept of operating position, and spatial combination is a critical aesthetic principle for determining the formal beauty in contemporary paintings. In his book *Aesthetics: Pursuits of Torment*, Xia Fang defined formal beauty as the natural attributes (e.g., color, form, and sound) that constitute the material appearance of objects, combined with the aesthetic characteristics generated using artistic rules (e.g., symmetry, balance, proportion, and repetition). This definition is consistent with those stated in numerous design principles. In addition, the temporal and spatial structures of poetry vary substantially and constantly, resembling changes in clouds that spread across an autumn sky. Consequently, these structures cannot be regulated using fixed models. Analyses of structural forms vary depending on the perspective adopted. In his book, Huang (1976) conducted a detailed analysis of temporal and spatial art in poetry. In the current study, we adopted the poetry classification that Huang proposed for time and space design, using his examples to explain particular poems; thus, the correlations between these principles and those of art design were identified. Chou (2002) examined the mental processes that artists experience during creation, stating the following: "As stated by Chen (1991), 'the forms of article composition vary depending on the operating approaches designed by the authors.' However, when authors outline their works, they are inevitably and subconsciously affected or dominated by common human principles. Consequently, the completed works, if compared to trees, share fundamental and common trunks despite differing branches." Aesthetic feelings, which are special and complex psychological phenomena, share similar qualities when observed in regularly diverse aesthetic subjects. This similarity is particularly evident when appreciating formal beauty." Only by exploring and understanding the affections and aesthetics that poets intend to convey and identifying the principles governing these phenomena can we comprehend the aesthetic effects of time and space design in poetry. Applying these techniques to design can manifest the value of poetry in cultural creativity.

3 Transforming the Time and Space Forms of Poetry into Design

In this section, we referenced the time and space forms of poetry developed by Huang (1976) and Li (2007), adopting the following categories: time/space reflection, time/space separation, time/space sympathy, and time/space integration. We analyzed actual design cases to investigate the process of logical deduction and the specific steps used to logically transform poetry to design. The results are detailed in the following subsections (Yeh, 2014).

3.1 Time/Space Reflection

"Amid complex temporal and spatial relationships, temporal changes may exist in poems that contain only spatial descriptions in the literal texts, because temporal changes are implied in the spatial variations. Similarly, spatial changes may exist in poems that contain only temporal descriptions in the literal texts, because spatial changes are implied in the temporal variations. This conversion between explicit and implicit ideas is called time/space reflection." Huang (1976) This can be divided into two approaches: expressing time through spatial variations and expressing space through temporal variations. *A Message*, a poem by Zhang Bi provides an example of time/space reflection: "I go in a dream to the house of Xie; through a zigzag porch with arching rails; to a court where the spring moon lights forever; phantom flowers and a single figure." Analyzing the temporal and spatial structures of the poem shows that the words describe only spaces. However, the spatial transitions from "the house of Xie" to "porch" and "court" indicate the differing times progressing through and waking from a dream. Thus, the actual temporal and spatial transitions are expressed. A corresponding composition design should reflect the transition between the explicit and implicit elements and the form relation in reflection. The visual context of the design should be based on the meanings of crucial words such as "a zigzag porch with arching rails" and "flowers," and color and composition should be designed accordingly. The overall design should focus on realizing the conversion, contrast, symmetry, and reflection between explicit and implicit meanings (Fig. 1).

Fig. 1. A case of time/space reflection

Fig. 2. A case of time/space separation

3.2 Time/Space Separation

"In a poem, time and space coexist as mutual hosts and guests." Time/space separation refers to the alternate expressions (at the verse or couplet level) of time and space that are separated from, yet reflected in each other. In *jueju* and *lushi*, two categories of classical Chinese poems, spatial scenes are often used to express vigor, whereas temporal virtual images are used to represent harmony and subtlety. The separation of and contrast between time and space can connect the virtual and physical environment and dynamic and static situations, complementing both types of scenes. In his poem *The Tai Town*, Wei Zhuang wrote, "The grass by the river grows evenly in the fine rain; Six dynasties are like a dream and birds cry in vain. Nothing is more heartless than the willows of Tai Town; Still veiling the ten-mile-dike just like a misty gown." Analyzing the temporal and spatial structures and patterns of the poem shows that the first verse is a spatial description, the second is a temporal description, and the third and fourth verses return to spatial descriptions. This alternation indicates explicit and contrasting arrangements of time and space. Converting the visual compositions to design requires using structured paragraphs. Based on keywords, such as "fine rain," designers can use ripple shapes to represent the incessant rain. Additional keywords, such as "dream" and "mist" can be used as the basis for the visual design and soft and dreamy materials and colors can be employed. The overall design should focus on recreating the circular and gradually changing relations implied in the poem (Fig. 2).

3.3 Time/Space Sympathy

"Sometimes, time and space blend and intertwine in poetry or act as interchangeable exterior and interior elements. The interactions between temporal and spatial elements are dynamic and flexible. Differentiating between time and space is difficult in particular poems. The blending of time and space often creates an impression of lingering emotions, and this type of intricate illusion is called time/space sympathy." In his poem *An Autumn Night,* Du Mu wrote, "A candle flame flickers against a dull painted screen on a cool autumn night; she holds a small silk fan to flap away dashing fireflies. Above her hang celestial bodies as frigid as deep water; she sat there watching Altair of Aquila and Vega of Lyra pining for each other in the sky." Analyzing the spatial and temporal structures and patterns of the poem shows that although all four verses appear to focus on spatial scenes, the theme of "an autumn night" is implied throughout the verses. Specifically, in the first verse, "candle flame" and "flicker" introduce the concept of an autumn night; in the third verse, an autumn night is implied in "as frigid as deep water;" and the "Altair of Aquila and Vega of Lyra" in the fourth verse again contain references to an autumn night. Therefore, the spatial and temporal elements in this poem blend, serving as simultaneous explicit and implicit meanings in temporal and spatial dimensions; thus, converting the visual elements to design requires expressing complex, illusive, and chaotic, yet orderly dynamics. The converted visual design should be based on keywords such as "a small silk fan" and "painting screen" to express the dynamics of materials. Furthermore, the overall design should focus on expressing the relations among the interchangeable explicit and implicit meanings and balanced proportions (Fig. 3).

Fig. 3. A case of time/Space sympathy

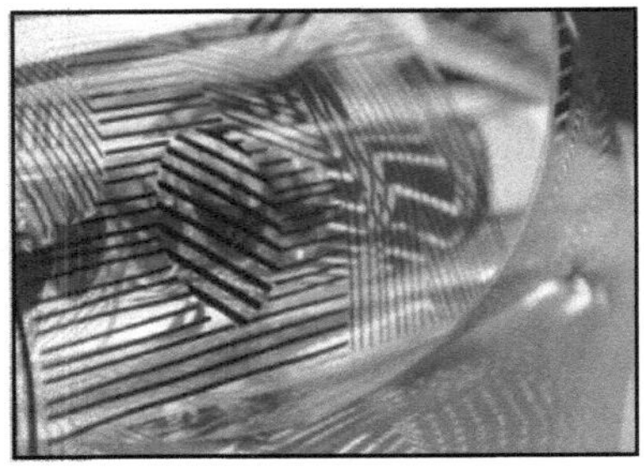

Fig. 4. A case of time/space integration

3.4 Time/Space Integration

"Time and space are continuous in the real world; however, they can be divided and overlapped in a poem. Past, present, and future spaces can be reorganized using a new order. This reorganization is called time/space integration." In *An Ascent*, Du Fu, a Tang poet, wrote, "All over such a vast expanse, the rustling leaves off branches dance. The Yangtze River rises yon, and passes raging on and on. Apart from home so far and long, with autumn, myriad sorrows throng. With illness all my life to fight, I now alone ascend this height." Analyzing the spatial and temporal structures and patterns of the poem shows that the first two verses describe the external scenery the poet saw during a climb, and the following two verses were intended to express the internal self-pity and sorrow the poet experienced during the climb. In this poem, Du Fu created multiple overlapping and continuous artistic conceptions. The poetic ambience created by this overlap and integration is unmatchable by ordinary poems. Thus, converting the visual compositions to design requires reorganizing diverse elements. The conversion to a visual design should be based on keywords such as "off branches" and "the Yangtze River" to express the dynamics of these features. The overall design should focus on expressing the relations among the overlapping, interacting, circulating, and harmonious movements (Fig. 4).

4 A Model for Transforming the Time and Space Forms of Poetry to Design

After conducting case analyses of the four aforementioned types of designs, we examined the following steps for transformation: identifying the origin and background of a poem, analyzing the theme of a poem, exploring the meaningful structure of a poem, converting the time and space forms of a poem to design, determining the expressional properties of the design, and finally completing a design based on the time and space forms of a poem (Table1). The proposed model for converting the time and space forms of poetry to design is detailed in the following sections.

4.1 Identifying the Origin and Background of a Poem

The background and theme of a poem affects the directions of content development and design conversion. This background can be understood by examining external cultural and environmental elements, such as the formation of thoughts, changes in literary materials, effects of religious factors, appreciation of regional scenery, expansion of poetic skills, and the psychology of the poet, and internal individual factors such as family traditions, habits, and inspirations from previous scholars (Lee, 2003). The essence depicted in poems and subjective emotions and ideas of poets are reflected by the following: the pride and ideals hidden in the subconscious, frustrations resulting from obstacles and being unappreciated, sarcastic criticisms regarding absurd political or religious superstitions, concerns regarding national destiny and emperors, the interactions and conflicts between the ideals of pursuing benefits to the family and country versus achieving inner tranquility, the spiritual freedom and liberation that poets pursue in old age, and the dedication to achieving Zen Buddhist states (Liu, 2007). We suggest that the backgrounds and creative motivations of poems are derived from the spiritual awareness, life philosophy, and realizations of the poet. These aspects can be converted to creative design concepts during the brainstorming stage of the creative process and employed to facilitate designing emotional communications.

4.2 Selecting the Themes of Poems

It is possible to examine the connotations of the temporal and spatial design, visual context representation, and dynamic temporal and spatial variations in poems. Appropriate poetic contents can be selected based on the anticipated categories and properties of the design. Furthermore, the signifier of reality should be considered.

4.3 Analyzing the Temporal and Spatial Structures and Patterns of Poems

Appropriate connotations and implications can be selected from poems after analyzing the composition; this encompasses the external verbal presentations and hidden moral contents of poems. The structures and patterns can be analyzed to explore the sequential levels and structural composition of the poetic conceptions. Visual contexts are examined to determine the presented elements of movement, color, material, and shape. Based on these properties, we divided poems into four time/space categories: reflection, separation, sympathy, and integration.

4.4 Converting the Time and Space Forms of Poetry to Design

The artistic conceptions and keywords of poems are converted to various elements, such as shapes, materials, and colors, in actual designs. Specifically, poems featuring time/space reflection focus on expressing the relations among interchangeable exterior and interior positions, contrast, symmetry, and reflection. Poems featuring time/space separation are characterized by well-structured paragraphs and circular and evolving relationships. Poems featuring time/space sympathy are often intended to express integrated explicit and implicit meanings, complex illusions, chaos with implicit order, and balanced and harmonious proportions. Poems featuring time/space integration emphasize diverse reorganization, movement, and harmony.

4.5 Cases of Poetry-Inspired Design

These cases show the proposed model for converting the time and space forms of poetry to design; we designed this model after examining several design cases, and it should serve as a reference during the execution stages in creative cultural design.

5 Conclusion

Li (2007) stated: "Amid the infinity of time and the boundlessness of the universe, thoughts enable people to transcend thousands of years and visions enable people to travel thousands of miles. Poets can roam through the eternity of time and space." Poems represent endless life, and "emotions live on to eternity. An emotion represents imagery, and imagery represents a spiritual realm. In other words, emotions are derived from the scene observed and vice versa" (Zhu, 2003). People are motivated by the sentiments caused by deaths, births, separation, the frustrations of long-distance relationships, and the sorrow resulting from the awareness of the finiteness of human life; thus, people actively seek the elements of timelessness that poets and scholars have described in their writings throughout human history. Dialogs conducted across time and space enable adapting classical Chinese poetry to contemporary and novel images. In this study, we developed a model for converting the time and space forms of poetry to design. Specifically, the emotional demands underlying contemporary design and the beauty of poetry were used as the approaches to creating designs. We also explored the feasibility of applying the cultural connotations of classical poetry to contemporary design.

In recent years, the Taiwanese government has dedicated itself to promoting cultural and creative industries, primarily focusing on industrial applications that involve converting traditional cultural relics into creative designs; however, Chinese cultural relics are diverse, exhibiting distinctive characteristics. Analyzing the connotations and formal changes in the classical poetry culture indicates that the dimensions of poetry differ substantially. In addition, the narratives in poems vary immensely. When analyzing the structural implications of poems, such as color, visual images, temporal and spatial artistic conceptions, and aesthetic expressions, it is worthwhile to discuss methods of converting these forms to designs that apply cultural creativity. This study involved converting poetic elements to designs to allow people to experience and appreciate the ancient beauty of language, enabling traditional culture to regain its vigor.

References

1. Cassirer, E.: An essay on man: An introduction to a philosophy of human culture. Yale University Press, London (1962); (Original work published in 1944)
2. Chou, H.P.: The Aesthetics of the Temporal and Spatial Design in Classical Poetry. Wen Chin Publishing Co., Ltd., Taipei (2002)
3. Chen, M.M.: A Collection of Essays on Chinese Teaching. The World of Chinese Language and Literature, Taipei (1991)
4. Xun, F.: Shanjingju Hualun. Yee Wen Publishing Company, Taipei (1971)
5. Huang, Y.W.: Chinese Poetics: Design. Chuliu Publisher, Taipei (1976)
6. Langer, S.K.: Feeling and form: A theory of art developed from philosophy in a new key. Charles Scribner's Sons, NY (1953)
7. Lee, B.R.: The Aesthetics of Du Fu's Poems Inscribed on Paintings. Unpublished Master's Thesis. Master's Program, Department of Chinese, National Taiwan Normal University, Taipei (2003)
8. Liu, M.C.: Explore the Aesthetics Hidden in the Scenery Poems of Xie Lingyun. Unpublished Master's Thesis. Graduate Program, Department of Chinese Literature, National Cheng Kung University, Tainan (2007)
9. Lin, R.-T.: Transforming Taiwan Aboriginal Cultural Features into Modern Product Design: A Case Study of a Cross-cultural Product Design Model. International Journal of Design 1(2), 45–53 (2007)
10. Li, Y.L.: Aesthetics of Poetry. Tung Da Publishing, Taipei (2007)
11. Li, Y.Y.: Culture and Self-Cultivation. Youth Culture Publishing Company, Taipei (1996)
12. Rapaille, C.: The Culture Code. Broadway Books, New York (2006)
13. Worringer, W.: Abstraction and empathy: A contribution to the psychology of style. Ivan R. Dee, Publisher, Chicago (2007)
14. Yeh, M.L.: Application of Poetry in Creative Design. Unpublished doctoral dissertation, National Taiwan University of Arts, Taipei (2014)
15. Zhu, G.Q.: Psychology of Arts. Jin Feng Publishing, Taipei (1988)
16. Zhu, G.Q.: On Beauty. Morning Star Publishing Company, Taipei (2003)

Author Index

MIX
Papier aus verantwortungsvollen Quellen
Paper from responsible sources
FSC® C105338

If you have any concerns about our products,
you can contact us on
ProductSafety@springernature.com

In case Publisher is established outside the EU,
the EU authorized representative is:
Springer Nature Customer Service Center GmbH
Europaplatz 3, 69115 Heidelberg, Germany

Printed by Libri Plureos GmbH
in Hamburg, Germany